The THOMSON READER
CONVERSATIONS *in* CONTEXT

Robert P. Yagelski

State University of New York at Albany

with Amy Crouse-Powers

State University of New York at Oneonta

THOMSON

WADSWORTH

Australia ▪ *Brazil* ▪ *Canada* ▪ *Mexico* ▪ *Singapore* ▪ *Spain* ▪ *United Kingdom* ▪ *United States*

The Thomson Reader: Conversations in Context
Robert P. Yagelski

Publisher: *Michael Rosenberg*
Senior Acquisitions Editor: *Dickson Musslewhite*
Associate Development Editor: *Marita Sermolins*
Editorial Assistant: *Jonelle Lonergan*
Technology Project Manager: *Tim Smith*
Managing Marketing Manager: *Mandee Eckersley*
Marketing Assistant: *Dawn Giovanello*
Associate Marketing Communications Manager:
   Patrick Rooney
Senior Project Manager, Editorial Production:
   Lianne Ames
Senior Art Director: *Bruce Bond*
Senior Print Buyer: *Mary Beth Hennebury*
Senior Permissions Editor: *Isabel Alves*

Text Permissions Editor: *Roberta Broyer*
Production Service: *Matrix Productions*
Text Designer: *Anne Carter*
Photo Manager: *Sheri Blaney*
Photo Researcher: *Marcy Lunetta*
Cover Designer: *Bruce Bond*
Cover Printer: *Phoenix Color Corp.*
Compositor: *Graphic World*
Printer: *Quebecor World*
Cover Photos: *Royalty free images from Hemera Photo
   Objects; Getty Images; Corbis; Index Stock Imagery;
   SuperStock; owned images from The Thomson Corporation/
   Heinle Image Resource Bank. All images are copyrighted.*

Printed in the United States of America
2 3 4 5 6 7 09 08 07

Library of Congress Control Number: 2005923281

ISBN-13: 978-1-4130-0998-9
ISBN-10: 1-4130-0998-0
Thomson Higher Education
25 Thomson Place
Boston, MA 02210-1202
USA

For more information about our products, contact
us at:
Thomson Learning Academic Resource Center
1-800-423-0563

For permission to use material from this text or
product, submit a request online at
http://www.thomsonrights.com
Any additional questions about permissions can be
submitted by e-mail to **thomsonrights@thomson.com**

CONTENTS

PART 2 THEMES FOR WRITING AND INQUIRY

Comp21

image, 1960s College Classroom
image, Embossed Book Cover Illustration
image, Protests against School Segregation
text, Edmund Burke, from *Beauty and the Sublime*
text, Mike Rose, I Just Wanna Be Average
text, Jonathan Swift, A Modest Proposal
text, Brett Aronowitz, Can You Write Computerese?
video, From *Salvation* by Langston Hughes
video, IQ and Race
video, Caught Cheating

7. RELATIONSHIPS   221

Comp21

8. COMMUNICATION   295

Comp21

image, Adolf Hitler Addressing a Crowd
image, Antiwar Protestors, 1967
image, Civil Rights March on Washington
image, Vote Here Sign beside American Flag
text, Samuel Adams, On American Independence
text, Thomas Jefferson, Declaration of Independence
text, Niccolo Machiavelli, from *The Prince*
text, Adam Smith, The Division of Labour
text, Bill Berkeley, Is America An Empire?
video, Homeland Security at Any Cost

10. SPACES   493

Comp21

image, Ceiling Paintings in the Strahov Library
image, A Chinese Garden
image, Fence over Hill
image, New York City Street Scene
text, Joan Didion, from *Los Angeles Notebook*
text, Ralph Waldo Emerson, Nature
text, How to Share the Earth
text, Maya Lin, Between Art and Architecture
video, Suburban Sprawl

11. RESOURCES   571

Comp21

image, The Colosseum
image, First Successful Powered Wright Brothers Flight
image, Ford Motor Company Assembly Line
image, Suffragist Marching, 1912
text, John F. Kennedy, Inaugural Speech
text, Erik L. Goldman, *Roe v. Wade* at 30 Years
text, Samuel P. Huntington, The Hispanic Challenge
text, Richard Lowry, Profiles in Cowardice
text, Women's Lives and Post-Abortion Syndrome, 30 Years Later:
    A Long, Cold Journey to the Truth
video, For Better or Worse

RHETORICAL CONTENTS

ANALYSIS

ARGUMENT AND PERSUASION

CAUSE-EFFECT

DESCRIPTION

NARRATIVE

AUTOBIOGRAPHY

HUMOR

SATIRE

PREFACE TO INSTRUCTORS

Composition instructors know that helping student writers learn to read carefully and critically is a crucial part of helping them learn to write effectively. *The Thomson Reader* can help composition instructors meet that challenge. Based on three fundamental principles that have emerged from research and theory in the field of composition in recent decades, *The Thomson Reader* can help students learn that

- *Writing and reading always occur in context.* To write well is to be able to recognize, assess, and manage rhetorical situations effectively. To read effectively, especially the increasingly sophisticated texts that college students are asked to read today, requires readers to place texts in context and to understand how the meaning of a text is always related to context.

- *The meaning of a text can be understood as part of ongoing conversations about important issues, questions, and ideas.* Writers and readers do not encounter texts in a vacuum. Texts are responses to other texts, and in that sense, they are part of the world of discourse—the larger conversations about life that are always happening. Because the meaning of words and texts is a function of how they are used—that is, because meaning emerges in discourse—effective writing and reading require students to be aware of the ways in which discourse shapes the meaning of texts.

- *Writing is a form of inquiry.* Writing is more than a basic skill; it is also a mode of intellectual engagement—a powerful way to explore ideas and information. Writing is a way to make sense of our lives and to deepen our understanding of the world around us.

Enhancing the Way You Teach

Because writing is a matter of context, conversations, and inquiry, *The Thomson Reader* offers students opportunities to read and write in ways that focus on context, conversations, and inquiry. But it also offers instructors opportunities to supplement their course with trusted methods by providing

- recognizable and flexible themes instructors are familiar with;

- a mix of classic authors, such as George Orwell and Annie Dillard, and modern readings on interesting topics, such as economic considerations of vegetarianism and how language informs rap music, to incite students' interests;

- marginalia designed to train students to be versatile, inquisitive readers by building on the discussions held every day in the classroom;

- writing activities calling for a variety of captivating papers and projects, including research topics, personal narratives, and technology-based documents.

With broad themes and thematic clusters that can be adapted to any instructor's preferences, *The Thomson Reader* can be a flexible tool for composition teachers using any course structure and pedagogical style, enabling instructors to enhance their courses without having to change them wholesale.

In addition, *The Thomson Reader* is based on the idea that writing itself is a technology. Today's students are more familiar with technology than any previous generation, and this book incorporates into its pedagogical apparatus and its supplementary resources *Comp21: Composition in the 21st Century* CD-ROM and InfoTrac® College Edition—important new technologies that are shaping the way we communicate. In this sense, *The Thomson Reader* can help students gain an understanding of how new and emerging technologies are influencing how we write and read. It can also give students valuable experience in using technologies they are familiar with to create their own texts and help them appreciate the complex relationship between text and image in an increasingly multimedia world.

Informed by the belief that writing effectively and reading critically are essential, *The Thomson Reader* also helps students learn to navigate the complexities of contemporary life as citizens, consumers, and professionals. By helping students develop their skills and knowledge, *The Thomson Reader* strives to prepare students for writing in a changing world. The book's features have been designed to give students relevant practice in writing and reading a variety of texts in a variety of contexts so that they can develop an awareness of how writing shapes their world. It rests on the hope that students will use writing to participate in the important conversations of their time.

Attempting to incorporate all these important elements into one course can be overwhelming, but *The Thomson Reader* integrates the familiar with the new so that instructors can effectively help students produce smart, thoughtful, and critical writing.

Where Do Themes Come From? An Innovative Approach to Content

Most composition readers include similar themes that reflect important issues or questions in contemporary life. That's because the themes themselves are longstanding, enduring issues every person faces. But *The Thomson Reader* is unique among thematic readers in the way it focuses students' attention on the very idea of *themes*, inviting students to consider the following questions: Where do these themes come from? What do they reveal about how we understand the world? How do they influence the way we write and read? By encouraging students to address these questions, *The Thomson Reader* helps students understand how all acts of writing and reading are part of broader conversations about important issues in their lives, conversations that shape how they understand their world. In this way, *The Thomson Reader* helps students experience writing as engagement with the world.

Accordingly, Part Two of *The Thomson Reader* (Chapters 5–12) presents reading selections that address familiar, timely, and important issues. But the organization of these chapters into *clusters*, or subthemes, highlights the contextual nature of writing and reading and helps students see how individual texts fit into ongoing conversations that shape their understanding of those texts. Each of the eight thematic chapters is divided into three clusters of three to four readings to provide a subtheme to the larger theme, reinforcing to students how broader conversations can be carried on in the form of distinct but related conversations about more specific questions. For instance, the chapter on change includes a cluster of readings on scientific and technological progress, a second cluster on changes in contemporary lifestyle, and a third cluster on where change has taken us. All these clusters relate to the larger chapter theme of change, yet each represents a distinct discourse or conversation about an important social issue that reflects some kind of important change.

The Thomson Reader's eighty-four readings represent fresh variations on eight traditional themes: Identity, Understanding, Relationships, Communication, Power, Spaces, Resources, and Change. Each of these main themes is presented in the form of innovative clusters that reflect ongoing conversations about important issues. For example, instead of a separate chapter on *education*, a theme that regularly appears in composition readers, *The Thomson Reader* presents readings related to education in a cluster about Understanding; additional readings related to education appear in the chapters on Relationships, Communication, and Power. In this way, students are asked to think about how educational issues are part of other important ongoing conversations about such matters as relationships or power and how those conversations shape our understanding of education. Readings are presented in thought-provoking ways that encourage students (and teachers) to look at these themes anew and examine how the themes themselves reflect and influence the way we understand our world. Instead of simply providing readings on important themes that students can write about, *The Thomson Reader* encourages students' inquiry into the themes themselves to gain deeper insight into those themes and to examine *how the very acts of writing and reading help construct those themes.* Flexible for instructors, who can select individual readings on specific topics, assign entire clusters, or create their own clusters, the themes and clusters of *The Thomson Reader* provide students with a groundwork for critically examining larger issues and encouraging them to enter conversations that are important to them.

To further expand the readings, *Comp21: Composition in the 21st Century* CD-ROM, a supplementary CD-ROM that accompanies *The Thomson Reader*, offers an additional thematic cluster that includes readings, images, audio clips, and video clips for each of the eight chapter themes so that students can see how critical reading and writing go beyond the standard essay. A Media Library offers a wide variety of text, images, audio clips, and video clips students can choose from to explore their own topics for their writing; using Wadsworth's unique Explicator technology, which guides students to analyze texts and media critically, students can create useful notes for their work to enhance their inquiry into their chosen topics. *Comp21* is accompanied with a passcode, which allows students access to InfoTrac College Edition, the online library, right from their desktops. In addition to the wealth of essays, visuals, audio clips, and video clips included on *Comp21*, InfoTrac College Edition provides full-length articles from thousands of newspapers, magazines, and scholarly journals.

The reading selections also reflect the many different discourse forms and genres that students are likely to encounter today: traditional essays, sophisticated academic analyses, editorials from various print and online sources, excerpts from books, and texts from a variety of periodicals, including newspapers, political and cultural journals, trade publications, and popular magazines. This variety helps students appreciate the many different textual forms through which writers and readers explore the important issues of the day and engage age-old questions about how we live together. In addition, these readings provide students with models of the different textual forms that they themselves may be asked to write in the classroom, the workplace, and elsewhere.

The Importance of Context

Instructors can sometimes find it difficult to devote class time to helping students recognize and understand the context of an essay, but since good writing depends on understanding the context of any piece of writing, students become more informed and effective writers when they appreciate the role of context in their writing. *The Thomson Reader* can help instructors solve this dilemma. It includes innovative features that provide a new and effective way to help students appreciate the crucial role of *context* in writing. Every reading is accompanied by *marginalia* designed to place each reading in rhetorical context and encourage students' inquiry into the importance of the various kinds of contexts that affect writing.

These innovative marginalia make *The Thomson Reader* distinctive among currently available composition readers. They advance the book's purpose of highlighting the contextual nature of writing and supporting students' inquiry into the ideas presented in each reading and into writing itself. In other words, they enable students to learn to read in more sophisticated ways by helping them place each reading in context and by calling students' attention to the ways in which each reading can be seen as part of ongoing conversations about important issues and questions. They also foster students' awareness of their own ways of reading. Five kinds of marginalia boxes accompany the readings in *The Thomson Reader*:

- *Contexts* call students' attention to the rhetorical context of the reading, focusing on important historical, cultural, and related background information that is essential for understanding the reading selection. The material in these boxes encourages students to examine how contextual factors influence both the writing and reading of the text.

- *Conversations* examine how the reading selection at hand can be understood as part of ongoing conversations about relevant issues, problems, or "themes"; these marginalia also make connections between the reading in question and other readings in the book.

- *Glosses*, akin to traditional footnotes, provide explanations or definitions of key concepts or terms; they also provide historical and biographical information about events, people, and text mentioned in the reading selection.

- *Strategies* direct students' attention to how the writer uses certain words and phrases, adopts particular styles, or employs certain forms that address the rhetorical context and reflect the relevant discourses that might influence the writer's strategic choices.

- *Visual Connections* incorporate various kinds of images into the students' inquiry of the reading selection; these marginalia help students see how visual elements are equally a part of the discourses that shape the way we read and write.

These marginalia function not only as sources of information and ideas about the reading selection but also as supplements to the questions and writing activities at the end of the reading selection. They help sustain the book's focus on how ideas and information are not only conveyed in writing but are also constructed *through* writing. The marginalia therefore reinforce the main ideas about writing that lie at the center of the book. Striving to point out to students things they should be aware of in any given reading, the marginalia do not reveal everything about the context but rather prompt the student to think more closely about the issue at hand. In addition, they provide instructors with readily available materials that can easily be incorporated into their lessons.

Inquiring about the Conversations

By fostering student inquiry into writing through features such as the marginalia, *The Thomson Reader* encourages students to ask questions about texts that will help them understand that *what* we write and read about isn't arbitrary but emerges from the ways in which we talk about ourselves, our actions, and our beliefs. Such inquiry can help students gain insight into how language shapes what we know and do; it can deepen students' understanding of how writing and reading influence what we "see" in the world. And it provides substantive motivation and justification for learning to write effectively.

The Thomson Reader combines conventional pedagogical elements, such as carefully constructed questions and varied writing activities for each reading, with the innovative marginalia that explore context and encourage careful inquiry into each reading. In addition to engaging introductory headnotes that help place each reading in context, each reading selection includes three kinds of pedagogical features:

- *Understanding the Text* questions help students recognize and understand the writer's ideas and goals, enabling them to better understand the text and consider similar strategies in their own writing.

- *Exploring the Issues* questions highlight important issues and ideas that actively engage students in pursuing the ideas and arguments presented in the reading, as well as encouraging students to examine their own ideas and opinions about the larger chapter theme or cluster topic.

- *Entering the Conversations* exercises provide varied writing activities related to the reading itself and the chapter theme that include conventional assignments, such as personal narratives and formal research papers, as well as inquiry-based projects that encourage the use of InfoTrac, and more innovative projects, such as creating a brochure, Web site, or PowerPoint presentation that incorporates text and images to explore a personal experience or important question related to the chapter theme. Using visuals with carefully selected questions gives students the opportunity to work with a medium that is familiar to them, yet teaches them how to critically evaluate the images in relation to the larger conversation at hand.

To encourage students to generate their own ideas about the chapter themes and to extend the conversations they have been participating in, *The Thomson Reader* also includes *Creating Themes* writing activities at the end of each chapter. From rearranging the given clusters, to examining relevant films, to selecting images to create visual essays, students can participate in the conversation in a variety of ways through text, film, and media.

The pedagogical features of *The Thomson Reader* are presented in an innovative and attractive design that makes them accessible to students and artfully combines text and image. In this sense, *The Thomson Reader* both reflects and models recent developments in writing and communication as multimedia technologies become increasingly common.

Supporting Students' Writing

The first four chapters of *The Thomson Reader* lay the foundation for the book by introducing students to the principles that have been described, including the central ideas of context and discourse. These chapters are designed to help students gain insight into the contextual nature of all writing, to train students how to "read" and choose images for their writing, to offer advice for writing in a variety of rhetorical situations, and to guide students' research on the topics they write about. Of special note is the attention devoted to visual rhetoric throughout this reader but especially in Chapter 2.

By giving students guidance in defining context, how to recognize discourse, and turning a larger theme into a thesis, *The Thomson Reader* helps students overcome common writing difficulties at the same time that it highlights the way each "theme" in the book grows out of one or more discourses—discourses with which students may be unfamiliar. As composition instructors well know, students often struggle to write effectively when they are writing about unfamiliar topics or when they write in unfamiliar forms or genres. Recent theoretical work in Composition Studies has helped us understand that such difficulties result not only from students' lack of knowledge about specific topics but also from their lack of experience with—and understanding of—the discourses within which they are being asked to write. *The Thomson Reader* is a tool for instructors to help their students overcome this struggle.

The Thomson Reader also helps students learn to appreciate and negotiate the changing relationship between text and image in a world that is being reshaped by new technologies and media. Chapter 2: "Understanding Media as Contexts for Writing" gives students practice in "reading" images in terms of context and discourse, in using new technologies for communication, and in incorporating visual elements into their documents in a variety of media. With nearly twenty visual examples in Chapter 2 alone, students begin to see the importance of the visual in writing.

A brief research guide, Chapter 4: "Engaging in Research and Inquiry," gives students advice for conducting research, finding and using evidence effectively, and appropriately documenting sources with MLA format, including fifteen sample MLA entries. At the same time, this chapter reinforces the idea that all writing is a form of inquiry.

Other Ancillary Materials

The Thomson Reader gives considerable support to instructors through these ancillary materials:

- **Instructor's Manual.** Containing useful synopses of every reading and suggested class activities and discussion topics, the Instructor's Manual also includes in-depth treatment of the context of the reading, providing ideas for incorporating the marginalia into discussions and for engaging students in the larger conversations about the chapter themes.

- **Companion Web site.** This site provides students with interactive exercises on the fundamentals of writing, including grammar, mechanics, and punctuation. A student paper library provides sample papers with accompanying editing and revising activities.

Acknowledgments

A textbook is really an extensive collaboration involving many people, and I am grateful to everyone at Thomson Wadsworth who contributed to *The Thomson Reader* in some way, including the terrific people who helped design and produce this book, whose professionalism and support helped keep the project moving and who contributed so much to the quality of the final product. I am especially grateful to Marita Sermolins, the development editor for this book, whose patience, insight, diligence, and good humor enabled us to overcome many obstacles and challenges without compromising the project. I am also deeply indebted to Dickson Musslewhite, whose insight led to the concept for this book and whose support for me and for the project was not only essential but also extremely gratifying. Thanks, too, to Michael Rosenberg, whose confidence in my work helped energize my own confidence to pursue the project. Lianne Ames and Merrill Peterson ushered the book through the production process, and I am thankful for their hard work to create the book you hold in your hands. I also wish to thank Amy Crouse-Powers, researcher *par excellence,* whose savvy research and ability to work fast enriched this book and whose sympathetic ear was always available when the pressure of meeting deadlines was most intense. Roberta Broyer and Marcy Lunetta undertook the difficult task of securing text and visual permissions with ease.

I would also like to thank the following colleagues, as well as those who wished to remain anonymous, who gave their encouragement and constructive criticism as this book was being developed:

Jesse Airaudi, *Baylor University*
Andrea Beaudin, *Southern Connecticut State University*
Rebecca Boggs, *Yale University*
Monica Bosson, *City College of San Francisco*
Mona M. Choucair, *Baylor University*
Sandra Coffey, *Columbus State University*
Linda Daigle, *Houston Community College*
Julie Eckerle, *SUNY–Brockport*
Anthony Farrow, *St. Bonaventure University*
Ruth A. Gerik, *University of Texas at Arlington*
Bonnie Gunzenhauser, *Roosevelt University*
William Trent Hamlin, *University of Kentucky*
Brenda Hardin, *Western New England College*
Amanda Hiber, *University of Detroit–Mercy*
Sandra Jamieson, *Drew University*
Trish Jenkins, *University of Alaska, Anchorage*
Brian Johnson, *Southern Connecticut State University*
Kathryn Kuhlman, *Truman State University*
Sylvia Skaggs McTague, *Fairleigh Dickinson University*
Connie Mietlicki, *Governors State University*
Roxanne Mountford, *University of Arizona*
Linda Norris, *Indiana University of Pennsylvania*
J-Son Ong, *Long Beach City College*
Sean Prentiss, *University of Idaho*
Anna Priddy, *Louisiana State University*
Teresa Reed, *Jacksonville State University*
David Rollison, *College of Marin*
David Ross, *Houston Community College*
Iris Rozencwajg, *Houston Community College–Central*
Renee H. Shea, *Bowie State University*
Cathleen Snyder, *California State University Sacramento*
Dawn Terrick, *Missouri Western State College*
Erin Webster-Garrett, *Radford University*
Crystal Woods, *Columbus State University*
Joseph Zeppetello, *Marist College*

Carol Forman-Pemberton, my codirector at the Capital District Writing Project, deserves special thanks for her genuine support and patience as I completed the project, even when she had many pressures of her own to deal with. Thanks, too, to my students over the years, especially the students in the English teacher education program at the State University of New York at Albany, who taught me so much about writing and gave me the motivation to learn more. I also wish to thank my sons, Adam and Aaron, who are always willing to listen to my rants and whose own rants convey insights that deepen my thinking and writing. And most important, I wish to thank Cheryl, my wife, whose selfless love, support, and confidence always sustain me, whose smile lights even the most difficult day of writing, and whose impact on this book—and on all my writing—is profound.

INTRODUCTION TO STUDENTS

The first thing you need to know about writing is that it matters.

If you're reading this book for a college composition course, then you are living proof that writing matters. In most colleges and universities, composition courses are the only courses required of *all* students, regardless of their majors. Obviously, the people who set college graduation requirements believe that writing matters.

So do state lawmakers. In most states, high school students are required to take four years of English to receive a high school diploma. Other than social studies, English is the only subject that most states require students to study for four years. Perhaps that's because lawmakers believe that writing and reading are the most important skills for students to develop. Doing well in school is largely a matter of writing and reading well. That's especially true in college, where you are asked to read and write increasingly sophisticated texts.

The second thing you need to know about writing is that it matters. It matters more than you probably think. Here are a few ways in which writing matters:

- *Writing is a powerful means of communicating ideas and information.* The book you are holding in your hands is proof of that. Any book is. Just think for a moment about how effectively writing can convey complicated ideas or information—through books, newspapers, Web pages, and all sorts of other documents and media. Writing makes those ideas available to readers in other places and at other times. It's really a remarkable thing. You are reading this book, which contains so many ideas, many months after I have written these words.

- *Writing is a powerful tool for learning.* It is no coincidence that schools and colleges require students to learn how to write well because writing and reading are central to academic learning. When you write, you use your mind in ways that differ from listening or talking or watching. You engage in an important kind of thinking that can result in greater learning about any subject. Researchers have spent countless hours studying how writing facilitates learning, but if you've spent any time writing, and if you've paid attention, you already know that writing is a unique learning tool.

- *Writing is a powerful means of self-expression.* There are few ways to express your ideas that are as effective as writing. An essay, a poem, a personal letter, a letter to a newspaper editor, a story, a memo, a report, an e-mail message—all these can be ways for a writer to make a statement, share a feeling, express a political opinion, explain a point of view, stake a claim, provide information, explore an idea, or issue a challenge. Writing can be a way to present yourself to others, to convey a sense of who you are. Writing allows writers to do these things more effectively and more widely than other common means of communication. You can shout your opinion about a political issue to a group of people on a street corner, but a carefully written letter to a newspaper editor has the potential to reach a much wider audience, and with greater impact.

- *Writing is a social activity.* When you write, you are connecting with others. In that sense, writing is always social, even if you're doing it in a small isolated cabin by some pond in the forest, far away from the nearest town. Even if you're only writing for your teacher, you are engaging in a social act that inherently connects you and your teacher. And when you follow rules for writing certain kinds of texts—like job letters or science reports or editorial essays—you are using forms of writing that have been developed over many years by many different people. When you write about a philosophical question for your philosophy class, you are using ideas that have been around for thousands of years, and you are engaging in a conversation about philosophy that has been going on for just as long. In all these ways, writing is a deeply social activity.

- *Writing is a political act.* Obviously, writing about a controversial political issue can be seen as a political act. But any time you write anything that is important to you and is likely to be read by someone else, you are engaging in a potentially political act that can have consequences for you and for others. Writing can be a means to challenge power or resist oppression. That's why slave owners in the American South before the Civil War made it a crime to teach Blacks to read and write. Writing was a way for slaves to exchange ideas that might provoke them to resist White domination; it was a way for slaves to oppose slavery without necessarily taking up arms. Why do governments regulate and control publications and media? For the same reasons that slave owners made it illegal for slaves to read and write. Why do high school principals sometimes censor student newspapers? Ditto. Because of the potential political power of writing.

- *Writing is a way to participate in the world around you.* Whether you are writing a job application, a letter to the editor of your local newspaper, a message on a blog, or an essay for one of your classes, you are engaging with the world around you. Writing is not just a solitary intellectual activity; because of the power of writing to affect others, writing is also an *act*—a way to participate in important activities. As many of the readings in this book will illustrate, writing can make things happen. It can change the world—in big, dramatic ways as well as in small but no less important ways.

So writing matters. And it matters more today than ever because the world you are living in is so profoundly shaped by writing.

This book is intended to help you write and read more effectively in a complicated and changing world. It is designed to help you gain insight into the most important aspects of writing and to help you learn to manage many different kinds of writing tasks. I hope it will also help you gain a deeper appreciation for the power of writing and the ways it matters in your life.

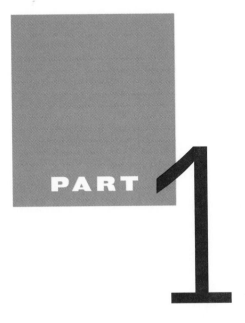

PART 1

Writing *in* Context

What Is "Good" Writing?

WHEN I WAS IN COLLEGE, I BEGAN WRITING ARTICLES FOR NEWSPAPERS AND MAGAZINES. ONE DAY, I STOPPED AT MY LOCAL GAS STATION, AND THE OWNER, WHOM MY FAMILY HAD KNOWN FOR YEARS, MENTIONED THAT HE HAD READ AN ARTICLE OF MINE IN A MAGAZINE TO WHICH HE SUBSCRIBED. HE ASKED ME SOME QUESTIONS ABOUT THE PIECE, AND WE CHATTED FOR A WHILE. IT WAS FUN FOR ME TO TALK ABOUT A PIECE OF WRITING I HAD DONE MONTHS EARLIER WITH A GUY WHO USUALLY discussed car problems with me. As I was leaving, he said, "You're a good writer." I was proud to hear that, but I was also surprised. It was the first time anyone had said that about writing I had done outside school. The only feedback I had previously received on my writing was from teachers, who usually pointed out problems and gave grades. But the gas station owner read my article because he was interested in the topic, not because he wanted to evaluate the writing. It was the first time I had the experience of connecting with a reader for reasons other than grading.

At the time, I assumed that if I was a good writer in school, then I must also be a good writer outside school. I assumed that good writing is good writing, no matter what the circumstances. Was I right? I don't think so. Here's why.

Writing Depends on Context

You probably do much more writing and reading in a day than you realize: reading the morning paper, sending a text message, checking your e-mail, writing a letter to your school's financial aid department, paging through a recent issue of a newsmagazine in the dentist's office, filling out a job application. All these are common but important literate activities that require a certain level of skill and knowledge. Yet in many ways, they are not the same kind of writing and reading expected in school. What counts as good writing in a text message or a letter to your financial aid officer obviously may differ from what counts as good writing in school. That's because good writing is always related to the context of the writing. There's really no such thing as good writing in general. Writing can only be judged good in a particular situation. What makes a letter to your financial aid officer effective will not necessarily be the same as what will earn you an A on a research report in your biology class. By the same token, writing that earns an A in your biology class may earn you a lower grade in a history class. Of course, some aspects of good writing will apply no matter what the context (I'll address some of those aspects in Chapter 3). But those aspects—which include things like correct grammar, proper form, and coherent paragraphs—do not by themselves make writing good. It's much more complicated than that.

Rhetorical triangle

Good Writing Fits the Rhetorical Situation

What is good writing, then? How can we know when we've produced a good piece of writing? The short answer is that good writing is an appropriate response to a given situation. Writing is good when it fits the context. This means that good writers examine the writing situation, or what theorists call the *rhetorical situation,* and try to address it effectively. Writing is good because it somehow connects with readers in a given rhetorical situation. It is good if it communicates something meaningful to those readers in that situation. The gas station owner liked my magazine article in part because that article spoke to his interests and met his expectations for an article in that magazine at that point in time. This book includes many reading selections that might be considered good writing in terms of the writing style or the ideas conveyed by the writer. But mostly, the selections in this book are examples of writing that is effective within specific rhetorical situations. And to understand what makes that writing good requires that you understand something about those rhetorical situations.

Effective Writers Take Audience into Account

Of course, no piece of writing is always good. Readers are just as complicated as writers, and they can respond very differently to the same piece of writing. The gas station owner liked my article, but his mechanic might have considered it boring. You probably have disagreed with a classmate about whether a piece of writing is good or not. Maybe your best friend doesn't like your favorite book. Scholars debate the quality of Shakespeare's writing. And you certainly have had teachers who prefer a certain kind of writing that other teachers disliked. Does that mean that good writing is completely subjective? No. But it does mean that the question of what is good writing is complicated and that readers are always part of the equation. Writers must take that complexity into account, which is part of what makes writing so challenging—and so interesting. The fact is that to write well is always a challenge. But you probably already know that from your own experience. Here's something else you need to know: to write well is a challenge that everyone can meet.

In my experience as both a professional writer and a teacher of writing, I have learned that the easiest part of learning to write well is learning the basic rules of writing. It may be boring to learn some of the rules of grammar or to run a spelling check on the draft of an essay, but those aspects of writing are really not very difficult. What's challenging is learning how to assess the rhetorical situation for your writing and to respond effectively to the context within which you're writing. The most effective writers are those who understand the importance of context in writing. You will learn a lot about how to write well by reading this book and by doing the work required in your composition course, but if nothing else, I hope you will come to appreciate this crucial role of context. And the first step is to examine what context in writing is.

Defining Context in Writing

The Jungle by Upton Sinclair is one of those books that people say changed the world. It's one of my favorite examples of the power—and the complexity—of writing. And it can help us better understand the role of context in writing. There are two useful ways to think about context: (1) as a conversation among readers and writers and (2) as the right moment for writing. The story of *The Jungle* can help us understand both.

The Jungle was published in 1906, but this wrenching story about the travails of a Lithuanian immigrant named Jurgis Rudkus in Chicago's meat-packing plants at the turn of the twentieth century still moves readers today. You might have been asked to read *The Jungle* for a high school English class and discuss its powerful themes of family, responsibility, power, fate, love, and justice. But *The Jungle* is much more than a moving story that explores important literary themes. When it was first published, it helped create a national uproar that led to the passage of food safety laws that continue to protect Americans a century later. Its **descriptions** of the horrible conditions inside meat-packing plants and the poor treatment of workers in those plants outraged many readers. Initially, many publishers refused to publish the novel, which first appeared in serial installments in a socialist newspaper called *Appeal to Reason*. But the demand for the novel was so great that one publisher decided to print it—although only after verifying the novel's descriptions of the Chicago meat-packing plants. The meat-packing industry tried to discredit Sinclair and his novel. But eventually, congressional hearings revealed that Sinclair's harrowing depiction of working in the meat-packing plants was accurate, and Congress subsequently passed the law establishing the Food and Drug Administration (FDA) to oversee the food industry. In effect, Sinclair's novel moved an entire nation to address serious health and safety issues related to the food industry.

Context as Conversation

How did one novel have such a big impact on a whole nation? You might answer that question by saying that *The Jungle* was just good writing. But that wouldn't really explain the novel's impact. To do that, we have to look a little more closely at the circumstances surrounding the novel and the era in which it was written. The novel fueled a national debate about how food was processed in the United States at the beginning of the twentieth century. But

---

POWERFUL DESCRIPTION

Here's a sample of the kind of description in Sinclair's novel that provoked such a public outcry in 1906. In this passage, Jonas (the uncle of Jurgis's wife) is describing to his family what he experienced in the meat-packing plants:

> Jonas had told them how the meat that was taken out of the pickle would often be found sour, and how they would rub it up with soda to take away the smell, and sell it to be eaten on free-lunch counters; also of all the miracles of chemistry which they performed, giving to any sort of meat, fresh or salted, whole or chopped, any color and any flavor and any odor they chose. In the pickling of hams they had an ingenious apparatus, by which they saved time and increased the capacity of the plant—a machine consisting of a hollow needle attached to a pump; by plunging this needle into the meat and working with his foot a man could fill a ham with pickle in a few seconds. And yet, in spite of this, there would be hams found spoiled, some of them with an odor so bad that a man could hardly bear to be in a room with them. To pump into these the packers had a second and much stronger pickle which destroyed the odor—a process known to the workers as "giving them thirty per cent." Also, after the hams had been smoked, there would be found some that had gone to the bad. Formerly these had been sold as "Number Three Grade," but later on some ingenious person hit upon a new device, and now they would extract the bone, about which the bad part generally lay, and insert in the hole a white-hot iron. After this invention there was no longer Number One, Two, and Three Grade—there was only Number One Grade.

Because of the growth of food processing in the United States at the time, such descriptions caused great concern among American consumers. But the novel contains even more disturbing descriptions about how food was processed and how workers were mistreated. The impact of such writing is partly a function of the context: These descriptions were so disturbing to many readers at the time because increasing numbers of Americans were eating processed food.

Sinclair did not create the problems he described in his book, nor was he the first person to write about them. In a sense, when Upton Sinclair wrote *The Jungle,* he was joining a conversation about these issues that was already going on. And the power of his book was partly a matter of how it fit into that conversation.

Here's what I mean. First of all, when Upton Sinclair's novel appeared, the U.S. Congress was already debating a bill that would regulate the food industry. Many Americans were concerned about the safety of food produced by the rapidly growing food processing industry. But the big food producers didn't want regulations, and they helped stall the bill in Congress. The descriptions of the terrible conditions in the meat-packing plants in *The Jungle* helped energize a national debate that was already occurring and put pressure on Congress to pass the bill. People began talking and writing about Sinclair's novel as part of that debate. If that debate had not been happening, *The Jungle* might not have received the attention it did, and it might not have affected so many readers as deeply as it did, no matter how engaging its story. In other words, Sinclair was writing about something people cared about, something they were already talking and thinking and reading about. He was joining a conversation that mattered to him and to his readers. If we think about context in this way, we can see that *context includes more than just a topic that interests readers at a given point in time; it also includes what people are saying and thinking in general about that topic at that time.*

> **MORE THAN ONE CONVERSATION**
>
> When writers write about a topic of interest and importance, they are often joining several "conversations" at once. Sinclair was actually joining several related conversations, as I'll discuss a little later. It's important to understand that the contexts of writing can be complicated, and often, writers may be focusing attention on one conversation while they are actually part of several. How readers respond, then, will be partly a result of which conversations they believe they are taking part in.

Although it is rare for a book or article to have the wide impact that Sinclair's novel had, the basic elements of this example apply to all writing. When you write an essay for an English class, you are responding to a specific rhetorical situation (usually a response to a question or writing prompt), much as Sinclair did. Your audience will be much smaller than his was, and your purpose may be very different, but you are still writing for an audience (even if that audience is only your teacher or your classmates) and you still have a purpose (even if your immediate purpose is only to earn a good grade). How effective your essay is depends in large part on how well you respond to the elements of that rhetorical situation. How good your essay is depends on how well it fits the context. And the same is true of any writing you do.

It is helpful to think of your writing as part of a conversation. When you write an essay for a course, you are taking part in ongoing conversations about your topic that influence what you write and how your readers will respond. If you write an essay about prison rehabilitation programs for your sociology class, you are really joining conversations about that issue that have been going on within sociology as well as within the society at large for many years. What you learn about your topic and how you understand the issues you are writing about will be influenced by those conversations. Like Sinclair, you have to address your topic in a way that fits those ongoing conversations.

The Right Timing: Understanding Historical Context

So the impact of *The Jungle* can be explained in part by understanding the context as an ongoing conversation about food safety in the United States at that time. But there's more to the story. The descriptions in Sinclair's novel of the living and working conditions in the food industry appalled many readers at a time when Americans were already worried about the larger problems of immigration and the effects of industrialization. **The early years of the twentieth century** were marked by the rapid growth of industry as well as a wave of immigration that was profoundly changing American society. Some Americans wanted to limit immigration. Others, like Sinclair himself, were deeply concerned about the treatment of immigrants and the exploitation of workers by American industry. So *The Jungle* was not only part of the national debate about food safety; it was also part of other important conversations about immigration, industrialization, and the protection of workers.

These conversations mattered to Sinclair as a writer. He hoped his novel would help Americans see how workers were exploited by American industry. He believed that the problems in the meat-packing plants depicted in his novel were really the fault of the American capitalist system. As a socialist, he believed sweeping economic and political reforms were needed to protect Americans from what he saw as the evils of capitalism. As I noted earlier, his novel was first published in a socialist newspaper, and Sinclair hoped that his story would convert many readers to his view that capitalism was bad for American workers. In writing *The Jungle,* he was participating in the national debates at the time about the American political and economic system and about individual worker's rights. In fact, **these debates had really been going on among philosophers and political thinkers for centuries.** Famous philosophers like Plato and Karl Marx wrote about these same basic issues, and their ideas influenced writers like Sinclair. Ultimately, Sinclair hoped that his writing would help sway American opinion about industrialization and capitalism. So he was actually disappointed that the public reaction to his book focused on the food industry. He was hoping for a workers' revolution, not for the formation of the FDA. Amazingly, despite the great impact of his novel, Sinclair felt he had failed in his primary goal: to convince Americans to resist the rise of industrial capitalism.

Why did readers react so strongly to *The Jungle*'s descriptions of the food processing plants but largely ignore the novel's message about capitalism? We can explain this "failure" if we think about context as including the historical moment. While American readers at that time were ready for a story about the food processing industry, they were not as ready for a critique of capitalism. The national debate about food safety made it an issue that readers knew about and were concerned about. Those debates shaped readers' reaction to *The Jungle* more directly than the ongoing debates about workers' rights and capitalism. At that moment in time, more readers were more in tune with food safety as a problem than with industrialization or capitalism as impor-

---

USING HISTORICAL CONTEXT

Notice how I'm giving important background information here to help you understand the historical context within which Sinclair was writing. Readers need to appreciate the historical context just as much as writers do. Usually, we don't think about historical context when we're writing because we're writing in the present. But when we examine a text like *The Jungle,* we can more easily see how important historical context can be. Without your realizing it, historical context influences your writing. For example, you will sometimes write about topics that are controversial right now—topics that interest readers today but perhaps not in a week or a year. In other words, historical context influences your choice of subject matter for your writing. In addition, beliefs and attitudes may be related to historical context. For instance, if you write about gender today, you will be writing to readers whose attitudes about gender are probably different from the attitudes of readers twenty or thirty years ago, and your own attitudes about gender will likely reflect the times. In these and other ways, historical context is an integral part of all the writing and reading we do.

ONGOING CONVERSATIONS

This is another important point about context: The conversations that writers are joining are usually conversations with long histories. When Sinclair wrote about workers' rights, he was drawing on ideas that had been debated for many years—ideas about the nature of government, about civil society, about individual rights, and related matters. The specific issues may have changed over time, but the fundamental questions did not. Many of the essays in this book are part of important conversations that have been going on for many centuries.

Food as culture / Possible short writing assignment

CULTURE AS CONTEXT

Another important component of context is culture, and food is a good example of how issues and ideas can be shaped by culture. Think of the significance of food in important religious and cultural rituals: the Jewish rules for kosher food, the meatless meals during the Catholic celebration of Lent, the fasting among Muslims during Ramadan. Think also of the cultural meaning of certain foods: a hot dog at a Fourth of July picnic or the lamb slaughtered for an important event such as a wedding in many Arab nations. These examples help us see that our attitudes about things like food are deeply shaped by the culture we live in. Inevitably, then, culture shapes our writing and reading, too. For Sinclair, part of the challenge was that capitalism was widely accepted in American culture, so it may be that American readers were less likely to respond to his criticisms of capitalism than to his descriptions of the food processing plants.

tant issues. As a result, Sinclair's novel was read by more people as part of **the conversation about food safety** and not as a critique of capitalism, as he had hoped. Thus, Sinclair was able to connect with his audience in one sense but not in another. Like all writers, Sinclair could write in a way that was appropriate for the context, but he could not control readers' reactions. As a writer, he could understand and respond to the rhetorical situation, but no writer can manage all the complexities of that situation.

Does that mean Sinclair's novel was not good writing? You'll have to answer that for yourself. But I hope you'll see that there is no easy "yes" or "no" answer to that question. Any useful answer to the question must take into account the complexity of context. To be effective in any writing task, a writer must examine that context and try to respond to it appropriately. Your challenge in doing so may not be as great as Sinclair's, but it is fundamentally the same kind of challenge. And it is the kind of challenge that makes writing so meaningful and worthwhile.

Context and Reading

Everything in this chapter about the importance of context for writers also applies to readers. When you read a text, you read it in a specific context. That context includes:

- when and why you are reading the text (for a class assignment, for your own pleasure or knowledge, for your job)

- your background (your age, gender, ethnic or racial identity, and so on)

- your beliefs and values (religious, ethical, and so on)

- your experiences (with the topic as well as with texts like the one you're reading)

- your knowledge (about the topic and related matters)

All these factors influence how you read that text. For example, imagine reading a newspaper editorial about a controversial issue that you have strong feelings about. Your response to that editorial is likely to be shaped not only by your own opinion, but also by many of the factors I just mentioned. Now think about a textbook in an introductory sociology course. When you read that textbook, you are probably reading it as someone who is not an expert in sociology, and that will influence how you read it. So part of your challenge as a reader is to place that text in the larger context of the field of sociology.

Now back to *The Jungle*. Think about the different ways you can read that one text:

- as a story about immigrants

- as a critique of American capitalism

- as a literary work that explores certain themes

- as a historical artifact that had an important role in the formation of the FDA

- as a reflection of ideas and conditions at a certain point in American history
- as an example of the power of writing
- as an example of the importance of context in writing

What you know about *The Jungle* and the context in which it was written affects how you read it. When and why you read the book will also affect how you read it. Similarly, your own background and your identity shape how you read it. Context matters—for writers *and* readers.

Discourse and Why It Is Important

If you think about writing as a matter of participating in ongoing conversations about important or interesting issues, you are more likely to pay attention to some of the complex elements of context that I have been describing; as a result, you are more likely to write effectively in the various rhetorical situations you encounter. But this idea of writing as conversation can also help us see that writing is not just a matter of discussing relevant topics or questions that are part of ongoing conversations; it is also a matter of understanding how language is used in those conversations. It is a matter of what theorists call *discourse*. In other words, the ongoing conversations that writers participate in often involve different ways of using language that affect what they write and how readers understand what they write. Let me explain with an example.

Early in 2005, a controversy erupted in the small town of Glens Falls in upstate New York. A year earlier, a local artist had been commissioned by the school district to paint a mural that covered the entire wall of an elementary school's main hallway. The

Details from a school mural by Esmond Lyons in Glen Falls, NY.

© Esmond Lyons, 2004.

artist decided his mural should depict the region around Glens Falls, and he asked the students for their ideas about what he should include in the mural.

One of the suggestions he received was to include an image of a man who stood every day in the town square holding a sign that said, "Support Our Troops." The man, who claimed to be encouraging people to support the U.S. soldiers fighting in Iraq at the time, became a kind of local celebrity. For more than two years after the war in Iraq began, he stood with his sign on the town square every day. Anyone living in Glens Falls would know about him, so the students felt he should be depicted in the mural. The artist agreed, and he painted a tiny image of the man in one section of the mural. However, on the mural, the artist painted the man's sign to read "Blessed Are the Peace Makers Who Make Peace" instead of "Support Our Troops" (see photo on p. 9). After the mural was finished, some town residents and members of the school board complained about the artist's representation of the man's sign. They argued that the artist's change to the man's sign amounted to a political statement against the war in Iraq, which they believed was inappropriate for a school mural. To understand why they interpreted the change in that way, we have to examine what the two phrases—"Support Our Troops" and "Blessed Are the Peace Makers Who Make Peace"—might mean in this context.

Words Acquire Meaning within Discourses

At first glance, these phrases seem straightforward. To "Support Our Troops" obviously means offering some kind of support for them; that support might include verbal expressions of support, encouragement, or perhaps sending them letters or packages. Similarly, "Blessed Are the Peace Makers Who Make Peace" seems to be an obvious statement of praise for people who work for peace. But of course, these two phrases have additional meanings depending on how and when they are used and who uses them. In other words, what these phrases mean depends on their *use in context*. In 2005, "Support Our Troops" was generally understood to be a statement of support not only for the troops themselves but also for the war in Iraq and the policies of the American government; by contrast, "Blessed Are the Peace Makers Who Make Peace" in reference to the war was understood to be a statement against the war and U.S. government policies. These meanings resulted from the way these phrases were used at that historical moment. Moreover, if the artist had painted "Blessed Are the Peace Makers Who Make Peace" somewhere else on his mural, it would not likely have been interpreted as an antiwar statement. But putting it on the sign of the man who was well known as a supporter of the war effort gave it meaning as an antiwar statement.

The point is that context influences the meaning of words. Both writers and readers rely on context for those meanings. Those two phrases—"Support Our Troops" and "Blessed Are the Peace Makers Who Make Peace"—were part of ongoing national conversations

CONTEXT AND IMAGES

Context doesn't affect only words but images, too. Consider the yellow ribbon with the phrase "Support Our Troops" that became a common sight in the United States after the invasion of Iraq in 2003. That image symbolized support for U.S. policies in Iraq and came to represent a certain political viewpoint. Its meaning was shaped by the contexts in which it was used and by the historical circumstances. It's also worth noting that the yellow ribbon came from a popular song from the 1970s, "Tie a Yellow Ribbon 'round the Old Oak Tree," in which a woman is waiting for her lover to return home after a long absence. In this case, several different discourses are "blended" to give the yellow ribbon its symbolic meaning.

Support Our Troops

about U.S. foreign policy and about the war in Iraq. How those phrases are used in such conversations gives them certain meanings or significance. The phrase "Support Our Troops" came to mean support for U.S. government policies in Iraq in part because it tended to be used that way in the public conversations about the war; it also tended to be used by those who supported the war effort and not by those who opposed it. So the significance of that phrase arises from the way it is used at a specific point in time.

Scholars use the term *discourse* to describe this process of meaning arising from the way language is used in various situations by various groups of people. We can think of the phrases "Support Our Troops" and "Blessed Are the Peace Makers Who Make Peace" as part of the political discourse surrounding American foreign policy in the early part of the twenty-first century. But there are many kinds of discourse. There are specialized discourses in professional fields like medical science or engineering. There are discourses related to certain ideas, such as capitalism, socialism, environmentalism, or globalization. There are religious discourses and discourses related to specific cultures. And there are discourses related to academic fields, like sociology or anthropology. Each of these discourses has its own practices and conventions for us-

other examples?

ing language, and the language used within these discourses reflects certain ideas, values, and beliefs. At the same time, certain words and phrases acquire specific and sometimes special meanings within these discourses. So in the political discourse in the United States in 2005, "Support Our Troops" tended to convey a viewpoint about the war in Iraq, and it also reflected certain beliefs about the U.S. role in the world and about the use of the military to accomplish certain goals.

These various discourses are not entirely separate from each other, of course. **Different discourses can overlap,** and they can influence each other, too. So, for example, discussions about educational issues among education scholars can influence public discussions about education among politicians and private citizens. But the idea of discourse helps us identify special uses of language to see how the meanings of words and phrases are related to the way they are used by certain groups of people in certain situations.

OVERLAPPING DISCOURSES

A good example of the way discourses can overlap and influence each other is the ongoing debates about copyright for digital materials, especially music. As digital technologies developed in the late 1990s, music lovers began to share digital music files over the Internet through web sites like Napster. Music companies believe that this file sharing violates copyright laws and is therefore illegal; they argue that people who share such files should pay for them. Music lovers who use file-sharing services argue that they are just sharing music privately and should not have to pay to do so. These public debates about copyright violations that might be involved in file sharing are related to intense discussions within the legal profession and among academics interested in intellectual property. In fact, the term *intellectual property*, which was once a specialized legal term usually seen only in academic journals and books, has recently become a common term in public discussions about file sharing. The changing use of this term by different groups illustrates how specialized discourses—in this case, professional and academic discourses about copyright—can influence broader discourses about issues like music, and vice versa.

Writers Are Always "within" Discourse

What does all this have to do with you as you sit down to write an essay for your history or psychology class? Well, in writing such an essay, you are not only participating in ongoing conversations about history or psychology, but your understanding of the ideas and issues you're writing about is influenced by the discourses of those academic fields. What you say in your essay about a topic in psychology, for example, will be determined in part by the discourse of psychology. That discourse includes the important issues that define the field of psychology, the views and values of those in the field, and the

---

JARGON

We tend to think of jargon as a negative thing, but actually, jargon can serve useful purposes. Sometimes special words or phrases are needed to refer to ideas or developments that are difficult to capture with more common words. One example is *discourse*. Some people might protest the use of this term, which sounds academic and may confuse many readers. Why not use a more common term like *language*? In some ways, the term *language* can convey some of what is meant by *discourse*, but it doesn't quite capture the complexity of the idea of discourse as it has come to be understood by scholars. So this kind of jargon is actually an efficient and easy way for scholars to convey their ideas to one another. As a college student, you will be introduced to specialized terms like *discourse* within the different academic disciplines you will study. Each discipline has specialized terms that might seem like so much jargon but which actually help people in those fields communicate effectively with each other.

significance of certain ideas or words within the field. When you write that psychology paper, you are—whether you realize it or not—part of that discourse. And to write that paper effectively means that you can "enter the discourse" of psychology effectively. To write well in a specific field about a specific topic requires that you have some sense of the important ideas in that field; it also requires that you understand the language of that field to some extent. In psychology, for example, you would probably need to know what terms like the *unconscious* or *ego* mean because they are important ideas in that field. And what those terms mean in psychology is not necessarily what they mean in other contexts. If you use the term *ego* in a discussion with psychology majors, they will likely assume that you are referring to a part of the human subconscious that famed psychologist Sigmund Freud identified. If you use the term in casual conversation with some friends, they are likely to assume that you're referring to a personal trait (for example, someone's "big ego").

Throughout this book, I refer to the idea of participating in conversations about various issues. Participating in these conversations is also a matter of entering the discourses that shape those conversations. As you gain experience as a writer and reader, you will also be learning about various discourses. Your ability to write well and to read effectively depends in large part on your knowledge of these discourses. Even the matter of *what* you write about is shaped by discourse. The important questions, ideas, and problems in a given academic field or in the society at large are determined in part by the discourses we are subject to. So having a sense of how discourses work is part of becoming a more sophisticated and effective writer and reader.

Where Do Themes Come From?

Like many other composition textbooks, this one is organized around topics or *themes*. If you look at the Contents, you'll see that each chapter from 5 through 12 has a main theme: understanding, communication, relationships, and so on. And within each chapter are clusters of readings that reflect other themes related to the main theme of the chapter. These themes should be familiar to you. They are not only common themes in writing classes, but they also reflect important issues in society in general. And it's worth asking where these themes come from.

That question may seem silly. You might wonder what difference it makes to ask why education, for example, or identity is considered an important issue to read and write about. Most composition textbooks include readings devoted to these themes, and it would be difficult to find a teacher or a student who would argue that these themes are not important. But examining how these specific themes have come to be considered important can help us better understand the key point of this chapter: that writing is best understood in context. If we look at how and why certain issues seem important to most readers and writers while other issues do not, we can gain a better sense of how the writing and reading we do is part of an ongoing process that affects how we understand the world around us. Let me explain what I mean.

Pick up almost any U.S. newspaper and you'll find the same main sections: news, editorials and opinion, sports, and business/money. There are usually sections devoted to arts or lifestyle as well, and many newspapers include a section on travel. Most also include classified ads and comics. These sections—which are really themes—have become so commonplace in modern news media that you probably think of them as natural. Even local television news includes versions of these themes: national news, local news, sports, and weather. But in a sense, these sections divide the world into categories, and they convey implicit messages about what's important. So it's worth wondering why most newspapers have the same main sections. Is it because we all see the world in more or less the same way, and newspapers simply describe the world around us (as many journalists claim)? Or do the sections of a newspaper reflect a certain view of the world, which emphasizes a certain way of thinking about the world and therefore shapes our sense of the world and how we view it? I think it's a little bit of both—and more.

THE WORLD OF THE NEWSPAPER

USA Today, the largest circulation newspaper in the United States, includes the main sections seen at the upper left in this image: News, Travel, Money, Sports, Life, Tech, and Weather. Consider what these categories suggest about the world around us. Where do these sections—or themes—come from?

USA Today Home Page

© USA Today, Inc., 2005

Think about the fact that most newspapers have a business section and a sports section, implying that these activities—business and sports—are important and that readers should pay attention to them. The very existence of these sections, no matter what stories they contain, conveys messages about the value of these activities. It tells us that business matters, for example. The business section directs our attention toward certain events, activities, ideas, and issues that are somehow classified as "business." The same is true of the other sections of the newspaper. But it's also worth thinking about what might be left out of these common sections of a newspaper. For example, why isn't there a section devoted to, say, environmental issues? Or one devoted to communication? Why is there a business section but not a labor section?

You might answer that these issues—the environment, communication, or labor—are included in the other main sections of the newspaper. For instance, a story about an environmental problem in a local river might be included in the local news section, or a story about toxic waste at a local factory might be included in the business section. That may be true. But what if such stories were included in a separate section called The Environment? How would that change the way we read those stories? Would a story on toxic waste at a local factory have a different meaning if it were included in a section on the environment as opposed to the section on business? What difference would that make? For one thing, any story appearing in the business section is implicitly defined as a business issue. The focus of the story would therefore not necessarily be on environmental protection or conservation but on the implications of the toxic waste for business and perhaps for the economy in general. In a sense, a value judgment is being made simply by placing the story in the business section: The environment is being defined in economic terms, and business is perhaps given greater value than environmental protection. On the other hand, placing that story in a section on the environment might suggest that the focus of attention is the environment itself rather than the activities of business or the economy; it would convey a message that the environment matters. Would that affect how readers understood the issue? Such questions help us see that how we categorize the world reflects our values and beliefs; it reflects what we think is important. So *themes are not just groups of topics or subjects; themes reflect our understanding of the world.*

The same principle applies to this book. When I began to compile the Contents, I started with main themes that seemed important for a first-year writing course: education, politics, identity, and so on. And I looked for essays and articles that fit those themes. But as I reviewed individual reading selections and tried to decide which themes they fit best, I began to realize that I might be influencing what those selections mean to a reader. For example, if I took an essay like E. B. White's famous "Once More to the Lake" and put it in a chapter about relationships, it would imply that the focus of White's essay is on relationships of some kind. Maybe that *is* the focus of his essay. But it's also an essay about an important place, so it could fit nicely into Chapter 10: Spaces. If I had included a chapter on memory, it could have fit there, too, since the essay is based on White's childhood memories. Or I might have included it in a chapter on growing up. If so, then you might be inclined to read it as a story about growing up and getting older.

There are three important points to keep in mind here. First, any piece of writing can be about a number of things; it can have many themes. E. B. White's essay is so often reprinted in textbooks like this precisely because it explores several complex themes that engage many different readers. The second point is that what a piece of writing means will depend on context. In this case, readers may see a certain meaning in White's essay just because it is placed in a chapter on spaces or relationships. Students may read it a certain way because of how their teacher presents it to them. Understanding an essay is therefore partly a matter of paying attention to the context in which you are reading it as well as trying to understand the context within which it was written. Third, a reader's experience and viewpoint can also affect what an essay means. Different readers may see different meanings in the same text depending on who they are and how they view the subject of the essay at that time.

This book is designed to help you explore the contexts of writing and reading in just these ways. I have organized the book into themes and subthemes in a way that I hope will call your attention to how context affects the meaning we make as writers and readers. The book is organized into these themes and subthemes to help you appreciate how your sense of the world is influenced by such themes and by the way writers and readers explore them. Throughout this book, you will be asked questions that will focus your attention on how an essay or an article fits into a context and how its messages may be related to that context. These questions will focus your attention on how ideas and viewpoints develop over time as a result of the way writers and readers use language to examine and understand the world around them. Being aware of these messages is part of being a critical and sophisticated reader. It is also essential for being an effective writer.

So what does it mean to be a good writer? Part of the answer to that question, as I discovered when I began writing for different audiences, like the gas station owner in my hometown, is that good writers understand the importance of context. Your success as a writer, in school as well as outside the classroom, is partly a matter of your ability to recognize that context and make the choices in your writing that best fit that context. This book can help you learn to do that.

FIRST BEGAN TO APPRECIATE THE IMPORTANCE OF IMAGES IN THE EARLY 1980S WHEN I WAS A NEW TEACHER OF WRITING. ONE OF THE BOOKS ASSIGNED TO THE FIRST-YEAR COMPOSITION CLASS I WAS TEACHING INCLUDED A PROVOCATIVE ESSAY CALLED "THE BOSTON PHOTOGRAPHS" BY WRITER AND FILMMAKER NORA EPHRON. THE ESSAY WAS ABOUT A SERIES OF DRAMATIC PHOTOGRAPHS TAKEN AT THE SCENE OF A FIRE AT A HIGH-RISE APARTMENT BUILDING IN BOSTON IN 1975. AS THE PHOTOGRAPHER WATCHED the firefighters trying to rescue residents stranded on the upper floors of the building, he noticed a young woman and her small child standing on the fire escape with a fireman who was reaching desperately for a rescue ladder. Suddenly, as the photographer was snapping pictures of the scene, the fire escape gave way, and the woman and her child plunged many stories to the street below. The woman was killed, but her child, who landed on top of her, survived.

The next day, three photographs showing the horrifying scene were published in newspapers around the world, sparking a controversy that raged for weeks. Many people were upset that the photos were published, arguing that they were not only unnecessary, since a

fire at the apartment building in Boston would normally not have been news anywhere else, but also that the photos sensationalized the event and violated the woman's privacy at the moment of her death. Arguments criticizing or supporting the decision to publish the photos appeared in the editorial pages of many newspapers around the United States.

I asked the students in my composition course to take up the controversy. Their assignment was to decide whether to publish the photographs and then to write a brief statement explaining their de-

Stanley Forman, *The Boston Photographs*, 1975

© Stanley J. Forman, Pulitzer Prize, Spot News, 1976.

© Stanley J. Forman, Pulitzer Prize, Spot News, 1976.

cision. The discussion in class that day was lively and intense, and there was no consensus about whether the newspaper editors were right to publish the photographs. Some students argued that the photos were published just to sell newspapers. Others argued that the photos merely documented a tragic event. Some students asked whether the story about the fire would have been different without the photos. Others pointed out that newspapers in other states and countries would not even have published a story about a fire in Boston without those dramatic photos. A few students argued that the photos were an intrusion on an intimate, private moment for the woman who died, and some asked whether the controversy would have been any different if the woman had survived. Whatever their opinion about the decision, *all* the students agreed that the riveting photos had a profound impact on anyone who saw them.

That discussion highlighted for me the impact that images can have on us. Those photographs affected readers in ways that the written text of the news articles did not. Even though the articles about the fire described the scene and informed readers that the woman died, somehow seeing the images of the woman and her child falling seemed to have greater power than writing alone. Why?

There is no easy way to answer that question. But as a writer and a reader, you should appreciate not only the power of images to convey feelings, ideas, and information but also *how* images do so. We live in a multimedia world in which we are bombarded with images of all kinds—in television commercials, in magazine and newspaper advertisements, on billboards, on flyers and posters, on clothing, and on the Internet. Increasingly, as new technologies evolve, images are not only more common

[1]Gunther Kress, "'English' at the Crossroads: Rethinking Curricula of Communication in the Context of the Turn to the Visual." In Gail E. Hawisher and Cynthia L. Selfe (Eds.), *Passions, Pedagogies, and 21st Century Technologies* (Logan: Utah State University Press, 1999), pp. 66–88.

IMAGES AS INFORMATION

A few years ago, a scholar named Gunther Kress pointed out that "the visual is becoming more prominent in the landscape of public communication."[1] Kress argued that images and text can convey information differently, and new technologies enable writers to take advantage of the power of both image and text more effectively than ever before. He used the example of a textbook to make his point. Textbooks today, like the one you're reading now, make use of images in different ways from textbooks thirty or forty years ago, which usually included a few illustrations to supplement the text. Today, according to Kress, images are used to convey important information rather than simply to illustrate.

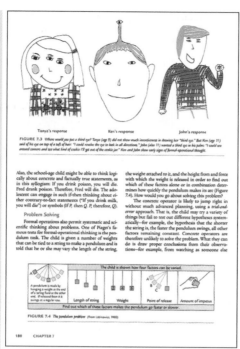

A Contemporary Textbook. From *Psycholinguistics,* 2nd Edition by Dan I. Slobin. Copyright © 1979, 1974 by Scott, Foresman and Company. Reprinted by permission of Addison Wesley Longman, Inc.

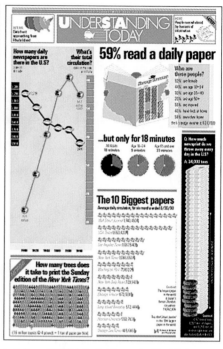

Imitation of *USA Today* front page by Nigel Holmes, from *Understanding USA* by Richard Saul Wurman.

in communication but also more important. In addition, with these new technologies, writers can more easily combine images with text to help make their messages more effective. These capabilities mean that writers can create documents in which images and text work together to convey complex messages and ideas. In short, new technologies create new contexts for writing that enable writers to take advantage of text, image, and even sound in ways they could not do previously.

Keep in mind that when we examine images in communication, we're really examining another component of *context.* The technological media we use for communication are not just tools but are also an integral part of the context of writing. If you are using the Internet to communicate a message, that technological context can influence your decisions as a writer. Learning to incorporate images into your writing and becoming familiar with new technologies for communication are part of the process of learning to write in context and to assess different rhetorical situations.

What all this means for writers is that they have more sophisticated tools to accomplish their purposes in writing and more opportunities to reach audiences through different media. It also means that both writers and readers face new challenges as they communicate with one another in various media. They have to develop a better understanding of how these media work—how a medium can influence a message, how it can place limitations on a writer. They also have to understand how images convey messages and how the visual can be an important part of a writing task. That's what this chapter is about. It will help you understand the importance of the visual in communication today, and it will give you some ideas for using visual elements in your own writing tasks in different media.

"Reading" Images

When we view an image, we are not only making sense of the visual elements of that image, but we are also looking for messages that the image might convey. In other words, we can "read" images for what they say to us. And learning to read images is part of being an informed reader and writer. Reading images involves three main considerations:

- Context
- Background Knowledge
- Perspective

Images in Context

The most important thing to understand about the impact of an image is that its meaning is related to context. For example, consider this photograph by Subhankar Banerjee. Most people wouldn't need to know much about the photograph to appreciate the beauty of the wilderness scene it shows. You might have a calendar on your desk with photographs like this for each month of the year. Obviously, how you react to this photograph is influenced by your feelings about the outdoors, wilderness, or natural beauty and perhaps by your prior life experiences.

© Subhankar Banerjee, courtesy of Gerald Peters Gallery, Santa Fe/New York

Subhankar Banerjee, Arctic National Wildlife Refuge

But how might the meaning of this photograph change if you knew that it was taken in the Arctic National Wildlife Refuge (ANWR) in Alaska in 2002 and that ANWR has been the subject of controversy because of various bills before the U.S. Congress that would allow oil drilling there? How would that influence the way you read this photo? Would its message about wilderness be different if you did not know about those controversies? Consider that in 2004 Senator Barbara Boxer from California used this and similar photographs during a debate in the U.S. Senate about oil drilling in ANWR. For Boxer, these images refuted a statement made by Gale A. Norton, who was secretary of the interior, that the refuge is "a flat white nothingness." In the context of those debates about developing energy resources in wilderness areas, these photographs were not just depictions of natural beauty; they also acquired a certain political significance.

The point is that we read an image within a specific context that can significantly influence what that image might mean. Obviously, we can discuss the technical merits of Subhankar Banerjee's photograph, such as how he positions the elements in the scene—the water, the vegetation in the foreground, the distant mountains, and the clouds—to convey certain messages about wilderness. We might discuss the color or lighting of the scene in the same way. A photographer or an artist uses such elements to convey what he or she sees in the scene. This use of various visual elements is sometimes called *composition*. But the political significance of that photograph does not come from the composition of the photograph itself; rather, it comes from the context within which it is seen. To understand images and how they convey their messages, therefore, we always need to take context into account—just as we do when we are reading a text. In Chapters 5 through 12, you will be asked to think about the messages conveyed by various images. Answering those questions will often require you to consider context in the same way we have done here with Banerjee's photograph.

Context, of course, includes *time*, or *historical context* (see page 6 in Chapter 1). For example, here's an airline advertisement that appeared in the 1970s, when attitudes about women in American culture were very different. At that time, this image of a smiling, well-dressed woman serving passengers would have been considered a positive one by most readers. But what messages about women might be read in this image today? Your answer to that question is influenced by current attitudes or beliefs regarding gender roles—attitudes or beliefs that may be different from the 1970s. It is in this sense that the historical moment influences what an image might mean to viewers.

Delta is an air line run by professionals. Like Christa Beck, Stewardess. Christa is attractive, considerate, courteous, kind, orderly, personable, poised, polite and truly dedicated. And her service goes far beyond the call of duty.

Those aren't our words. Those words are from letters we've received about Christa. Written by Delta passengers. And we've got 4,000 Christas. Delta is ready when you are.

© Delta Airlines, Inc.

Delta Advertisement from the 1970s.

This photograph also illustrates an important point made earlier: that images and text can work together to convey powerful messages differently than the image or text alone could convey. In this case, the text below the paragraph is intended to shape the message of the photograph. The second paragraph of the text emphasizes qualities that many Americans at that time might have associated with women *(attractive, considerate, orderly, courteous, poised)*, and in conjunction with that text the photo, which shows a woman helping a young child, suggests motherhood. Without that paragraph, the photograph would still convey certain messages about women and specifically about flight attendants, but the text in the ad "frames" those messages so that viewers are more likely to read the image as the airline intended. Of course, context comes into play here again. Today, the words used to describe the stewardess—*attractive, orderly, poised*—might carry negative connotations when applied to women that those words might not have carried for most readers in the 1970s. So readers today might read this advertisement very differently, and no doubt many would find this ad offensive. This example thus helps us see not only the importance of historical context in how we read images but also the ways in which attitudes and values can change over time, which also affects the meaning of an image.

> **QUESTIONS TO ASK YOURSELF ABOUT READING IMAGES IN CONTEXT**
>
> - How is this image being used?
> - Where does it appear? Is it part of an article, a series of images, an advertisement, or something else? What purpose does it have in that article, series, and so on?
> - Does any text or caption accompany the image? If so, how does that text affect the messages the image might convey?
> - What purposes is this image being used for?
> - Who created this image? Who is presenting or using it?
> - When was the image made? When was it presented to an audience?
> - Who is its intended audience?

The Role of Background Knowledge

Very often, the messages you see in an image are shaped by your relevant background knowledge. Here's a simple example. The impact of the photograph below depends in large part on your knowing that the man is President George W. Bush and that the background shows Mount Rushmore, the famous national monument in South Dakota

© AP Photo/Ken Lambert

President George W. Bush at Mount Rushmore

where the faces of four U.S. presidents—George Washington, Thomas Jefferson, Theodore Roosevelt, and Abraham Lincoln—are carved into a mountainside. Because Mount Rushmore is widely associated with patriotism, viewers of this photo who are familiar with Mount Rushmore are likely to read a patriotic message. Without that background knowledge, however, the patriotic message may be lost on a viewer who might see this photo as simply showing a man speaking in front of a large sculpture.

Here's a slightly more complicated example. Do you get the joke in the comic strip above, from 2005? If not, it may be because you need background knowledge that you don't have. To appreciate the humor, you have to be familiar with current events of the time—specifically, the Iraq war and the public debates about the war at the time, especially the criticisms of the Bush administration's lack of a "mission goal" in that war. But to fully appreciate the humor, you also have to be familiar with Herman Melville's classic novel *Moby Dick*. The main character, a nineteenth century sea captain named Ahab, is killed in his fanatical pursuit of a white whale named Moby Dick by becoming entangled in the harpoon lines. The cartoonist is relying on readers' familiarity with the story of Ahab and Moby Dick. Only if you know that story and are also familiar with the debate about mission goals in Iraq will the humor and message of this comic strip be clear to you. Without that knowledge, what this comic strip means to you may be different from what the artist intended.

So background knowledge can incorporate a variety of elements:

- general knowledge about a subject
- familiarity with current events
- familiarity with public discussions about current events
- cultural knowledge (in the form of literature or art)
- historical knowledge

Perspective

How you read an image is also influenced by your own viewpoint or perspective. Your values, beliefs, and opinions about the subject matter will shape the way you react to an image. Let's return to the photograph of President Bush, for example (page 21). Obviously, your opinion of the President would affect your reaction to this photograph. In addition, your political viewpoint will influence your reaction. Someone with a conservative viewpoint is likely to read this photo differently from a liberal. A Bush supporter is more likely to read a straightforward and positive patriotic message in this photo than someone who voted against Bush. Even if these two people see more or less the same message in the photograph (that is, a patriotic message about George W. Bush), their political viewpoints will affect how they interpret and react to that message. The Bush opponent is more likely to reject the photo's patriotic message, for instance, or he or she might read the message as an ironic one. (We could do the same sort of analysis of the comic strip on page 22.) If you use images in your writing, keep in mind that readers may respond very differently to those images. Anticipating those responses is part of analyzing your audience (see page 38 in Chapter 3).

Putting It All Together: Reading Complex Images

Photographers, artists, and designers use these principles of context, background knowledge, and perspective to try to reach their intended audiences and convey their messages effectively. Understanding these principles can help you read images more critically and carefully. And it can make you aware of how your own response to an image is perhaps more complicated than it might seem. Let's look at one more example, a poster (top right) from a consumer and environmental advocacy group called Adbusters. What messages do you read in this poster?

The text on the poster sends an obvious message about curbing consumption. But there may be other, less obvious messages as well. The poster recalls the famous military recruiting advertisements during World War II such as the one shown here (bottom right). Those advertisements were thought to convey a sense of patriotic duty, suggesting that citizenship included self-sacrifice for one's country. The poster about curbing consumption relies on your familiarity with those World War II recruiting advertisements and their patriotic

messages. But in this case, there is a twist: You are not being recruited for military service but for opposition to consumer culture. In making this twist, the poster suggests that reducing the consumption of consumer goods is patriotic, an idea that might strike many Americans as counterintuitive because it is widely believed that economic consumption is good for America.

In this case, then, a seemingly simple message—curb your consumption—is more complex and relies on a complicated set of associations and background knowledge for its impact. Moreover, a viewer's response to this poster may not be a straightforward matter of that viewer's political viewpoint. In other words, patriotism is often associated with a conservative political viewpoint, but in this case, it is associated with a more progressive argument against consumerism. So even conservative viewers who consider themselves very patriotic may have a more complicated reaction to the image. To appreciate this complexity, consider your own reaction to this poster. Do you find its message appealing or valid? Why or why not? How you answer those questions might enable you to understand better why the image has the impact on you that it does. Throughout this book, you will be asked similar questions about different images and texts. Understanding your own reactions to images and texts is an important part of understanding how messages are communicated through them.

The examples in this section also help us understand that although there are many different kinds of images—in this case, a photograph, a comic strip, or poster—these basic principles about context, background knowledge, and perspective usually apply to any kind of image.

Using Images in Your Writing

As a writer today, you have the advantage of powerful, accessible, and easy-to-use technologies that were unavailable to writers even five or ten years ago. Word processing programs enable writers to incorporate images into documents very easily and to control document layout and design. Used in conjunction with color printers, these word processing programs enable writers to create professional-looking documents of all kinds: flyers, posters, brochures, and reports with tables, graphs, and other images. Other programs like PowerPoint®, which enable users to create slide shows, are now routinely used in schools and businesses. Desktop publishing programs allow users to create documents with very sophisticated visual elements. In addition, the Internet has become a rich venue for publishing that allows you to take advantage of visual elements and even sound to convey your messages effectively to a variety of audiences.

These technological tools create new media—and new contexts—for your writing, which can extend beyond the text itself. Although many such tools are accessible and relatively easy to use, they require you to consider various issues—such as color, layout, and composition—that writers have traditionally not had to worry about. With these new possibilities, then, come new challenges for both writers and readers.

Deciding to Use Images

In deciding whether to incorporate images into an assignment, the first step is to ask whether images would enable you to convey your message to your audience more effectively than text alone. Sometimes adding an image just to illustrate your text may not make your writing more effective. However, in some cases, an image can enhance the impact of your writing. *The Boston Photographs* on pages 16 and 17 surely enhanced Nora Ephron's essay by allowing her readers to experience the power of those photos directly. If you're writing about, say, a controversy over a proposal to build a new big-box retail store in your town, including well-composed photographs of the stream or meadow on the proposed building site can help you make a more effective argument against the proposal, especially if your audience includes people who share your environmental concerns. So your decision to incorporate photographs should always take your audience and your purpose into account.

Beach Up Close

If you decide that images will make your writing more effective, select them carefully. In the previous example of an argument against a proposed big-box retail store, a poorly done photograph of the proposed site won't do much to enhance your argu-

Beach Far Away

ment, but a carefully composed photo that might evoke a reader's sense of the site's beauty will likely have a more appropriate effect on your readers. Or let's say you live in a coastal town that is considering allowing more development on a natural public beach. Which of the photographs on this page might work better if you wished to write an essay opposing such development? Which would work better if you were in favor of the development? Your answer to those questions depends on your audience, the message you want to convey to that audience, the specific points you want to make about the proposed development, and **your own sense of responsibility as a writer.** If you wished to emphasize the natural beauty of the location, the first photograph would make sense. If you believe that the development would be consistent with what is already there, then the

THE ETHICS OF USING IMAGES

The decision to use an image in a document is not just a technical or strategic decision; it is also an ethical one. In this case, although both photographs on page 25 may have been taken at the same beach, neither shows the whole scene. Which photo you select and how you use it in your document can affect the messages you convey about the scene. Selecting the first photograph, for instance, may convey the beauty of the beach but it may also be misleading, because it seems to show no development at all along the beach. The second photo might suggest a housing development where one does not really exist. As a writer in this instance, you would have to decide how best to use one or both of these photographs to accomplish your purpose without misleading your audience or misrepresenting the circumstances surrounding the issue. It is important to think about your rhetorical decisions as ethical decisions. As a writer you should always consider the ethical implications of your decisions. In such cases, it's a good idea to ask yourself not only whether the image will make your document more effective but also whether it is the right thing to do.

second photograph would help you convey your point by showing that some homes already exist at that site.

Selecting Images

The considerations discussed in the previous section apply to *any* kind of image you decide to use—not only photographs but sketches, paintings, cartoons, graphs, or logos as well. Sometimes deciding which kind of image to use is important. In some cases, a graph or chart is an obvious choice. For example, the graph below is from a report by the testing company ACT about the readiness of high school graduates for college-level academic work. The graph shows the percentage of high school graduates who meet the criteria for readiness for college-level math based on the math courses they took in high school. Presenting this information in the form of a graph effectively conveys the differences between students who took few math courses in high school and students who took more math, including more advanced courses. This same information could easily be presented in the text itself, but it might have more impact on a reader in the form of a graph. Obviously, a photograph or other kind of image would not work as well in this case. Given the audience and purpose of the ACT report, using a graph makes sense.

Sometimes deciding which kind of image to use isn't so clear cut. For example, let's say you were writing a research paper examining the social, economic, and environmental effects of the automobile on U.S. society. Both of the images on page 27 convey messages about such effects, but which would be most appropriate for your paper?

In answering that question, you would, as always, consider your purpose and audience. But in deciding between these two images, you would also want to consider the different impact a photograph and a poster might have on readers. The photograph depicts a real scene, whereas the poster makes a comment through a color sketch. Readers might see the photograph as more "objective" and real;

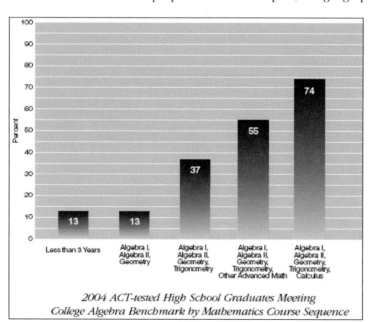

2004 ACT-tested High School Graduates Meeting College Algebra Benchmark by Mathematics Course Sequence

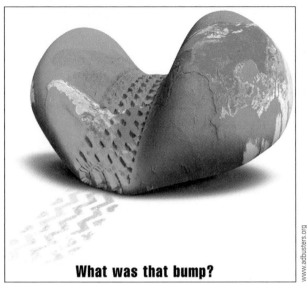

What was that bump?

Run Over Earth Advertisement.

www.adbusters.org

Rearview Mirror with Traffic

© Clarita/Morguefile.com

the photograph might thus be a more effective choice if you wanted to take a balanced view of the subject. In this case, the type of image—not just what the image depicts—is an important consideration.

Considering Layout and Design

If you are using photographs, charts, graphs, or other visual elements in your assignment, you'll need to think about how to incorporate those elements effectively into your document. In many cases, you may simply be able to insert a photograph or chart into the text of your paper (which is easy to do with most word processing programs). Documents with more sophisticated formats, such as brochures, flyers, web pages, or PowerPoint presentations, require you to think more carefully about layout and design. Here are a few simple principles to keep in mind:

- *Design should be appropriate to your purpose.* Flashy images, unconventional fonts, or an unusual page layout would probably not be appropriate for a research paper for your sociology class. By contrast, if you are building a web site devoted to, say, progressive music, you might consider a more unconventional design to convey a sense of the unconventional nature of the music. The point is to design your document so that it meets your purposes for your intended audience. An inappropriate design will undermine your document's ability to convey your message effectively.

- *Less is more.* Too many visual elements in a report or essay may overwhelm your reader and weaken the impact of the images. Select only those images that you think will enhance your text. Also, remember that a crowded page or screen can

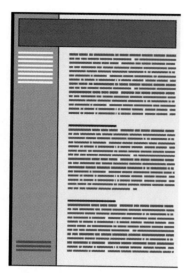

Contrast Design Example

A WORD ABOUT POWERPOINT

Today, it is common for teachers to allow or assign students to use programs like PowerPoint for in-class presentations and projects. If you have the opportunity to use PowerPoint, you can apply the principles discussed in this chapter to your presentation. One advantage of programs like PowerPoint is that they provide ready-made templates for you to use that follow the advice about symmetry, layout, and color given in this chapter. If you are making a presentation with PowerPoint, keep in mind that your slides should supplement your talk. It is ineffective to simply read what is on a slide. It is much more effective to use the images and words on your slides to supplement what you are saying (or reading). For example, if you are making a presentation about suburban sprawl in a geography class, you might show a slide with a chart that indicates the increase in sprawl in the past few decades and the loss of open space as a result. While your audience views that chart, you can be talking about some of the consequences of that growth (rather than simply reading the chart to the audience). In this way, PowerPoint can enhance your presentation rather than *become* the presentation.

be hard to read. Graphic designers understand the value of "white space"—that is, leaving blank areas around graphics and text to make it easier for readers to make sense of what's on the page. Try not to put too many elements on a single page. Select elements that fit together or are intended to convey similar messages. The idea is to make it easier for your readers to understand the ideas and information on the page.

- *Symmetry and balance can enhance your design.* Good designers strive for a page or screen that is visually balanced. Often, the elements on a page are arranged in a pattern that directs a reader's eyes first to the most important material and then to the less important material. These patterns tend to make it easier for readers to get the message. For example, the front page of a newspaper is usually divided into three or four main columns; text and graphics are positioned within or across these columns in a basic rectangular pattern. (When we read a print text in English, our eyes move from left to right and top to bottom. Accordingly, designers will often lay out a page to take advantage of this "natural" movement of a reader's eyes.) Other common patterns include *radial* design, in which several elements are arranged around a main image or graphic, and *collage,* in which a number of different images and graphics along with blocks of text overlap on the page. Whatever pattern you use, the main principle to remember is that it should help readers or viewers understand your message and find the information you are trying to convey.

- *Use contrast.* On a well-designed page of a print document or a web site, contrasting elements are arranged in a visually appealing and efficient way. For example, the blue box shown here at the top of the page can be used for a main heading or title, while the lighter box on the left side might be used to highlight key points or references (or links on a web site). Both boxes contrast nicely with the main text, which is placed in a white box. This contrast makes the various kinds of information on the page easier for a reader to access.

For detailed advice about designing documents, consult a handbook or a more specialized guide for the medium you're working with. But keep in mind that the design of your document will have a lot to do with how effectively it conveys your messages or information to your intended audience.

Using Color

For most assignments, you may not have to deal with color, but many documents can be enhanced through the careful use of color. This is especially true of web pages. Here are a few general guidelines for using color:

- *Use color only if it will enhance your document.* Using colored fonts or graphics in a biology lab report or a history paper may look nice but will likely contribute little to the effectiveness of the paper. On the other hand, a web page without any color is likely to be unappealing and ineffective in addressing your intended audience. Use color only if it is appropriate or necessary.

- *Choose colors carefully.* Colors can be very effective in creating a certain mood or "feel" to a document, but poorly selected or inappropriate colors will probably make your document less effective. Consider audience and purpose when selecting colors. Bright yellow lettering on a red background is probably a poor choice for a brochure about a church retreat or a food service for senior citizens, for example. In general, professional graphic artists suggest using subtle colors for the majority of a document, reserving brighter colors for emphasizing specific elements or ideas.

- *Use colors according to a pattern or scheme.* Some colors work well together, whereas others clash. In well-designed documents, you'll notice that a few colors are used throughout the document, perhaps in various shades. Too many different colors create visual confusion. And using colors that clash may give your document an unappealing look. For example, putting bright red and bright green may create a very noticeable look, but your document will also be "loud" in a way that may not appeal to your readers.

CONSIDERING OTHER MEDIA FOR WRITING

Many different media are available to writers today. In addition to traditional print media, such as newspapers, magazines, and books, and the established media of television and radio, the Internet and other electronic technologies such as text messaging provide a wide array of outlets for communication that did not exist even a decade ago. Through television, film, the Internet, and print media, you are exposed to countless messages every day, and making sense of those messages is an important part of making your way in the world, both inside and outside the classroom. The principles discussed in this chapter for reading images and for designing documents apply in general to many of these different media. For example, interpreting the way a television commercial tries to convey its message is similar to reading a photograph, as discussed earlier (see page 19). Learning to interpret messages critically in a variety of media is part of being an informed reader and can also help you become a more effective writer.

World War II Concentration Camp

© Michael St. Maurshell/Corbis

It's important to keep in mind that black-and-white images can be just as effective as color images, and in some cases, they can be more appropriate. Consider this photograph of the World War II Nazi concentration camp at Auschwitz. The use of a black-and-white format for this photograph helps convey the terrible sense of loss and emptiness that we associate with that place; in this case, black and white may be more appropriate to the subject than color.

Combining Text and Image

Using visual elements in your writing isn't just a matter of inserting an image into a document or creating an appealing page layout. To communicate effectively means combining visual elements with your text in ways that take advantage of the power of both writing and images. You can often convey messages visually without using words, and your words can have greater impact when combined with carefully selected images or when presented visually in certain ways. Here's an example of a writer's effective use of the visual in combination with his words to make a point. The "essay" on page 31 appeared on the editorial page of the *New York Times*. Like other essays that appear in the editorial section of a newspaper, this one makes an argument—in this case, about some of the implications and risks of our common uses of computers. The writer, Evan Eisenberg, could have made his argument in a conventional essay, but he chose to use a visual format to make his point. He relies on his audience's familiarity with computers and particularly with the kinds of error messages that often appear in "dialogue boxes" on the computer screen. And he combines his text with the visual elements to convey his point. In evaluating the effectiveness of this essay, consider the following questions:

- What specific point or criticism do you think Eisenberg is making in this editorial essay?

- In what ways do the visual elements—the computer screen "look" of the essay and the dialogue box graphics—contribute to his argument?

- What specific messages or information are conveyed by the visual elements in this essay?

- In what ways does the text rely on the visual elements for its meaning? (In other words, would the text in the dialogue boxes be understandable without the visual elements?)

- How might Eisenberg's argument be different if he had not included the visual elements?

This example illustrates a writer's careful use of the visual in combination with his text. Each component of this essay—the visual and the textual—conveys important information and contributes to Eisenberg's main point.

As a reader, you can learn to become more aware of how the visual and the textual can be used in combination to convey messages. That awareness makes you a more informed, sophisticated, and careful reader. As a writer, that awareness can help you take advantage of the power of both images and text.

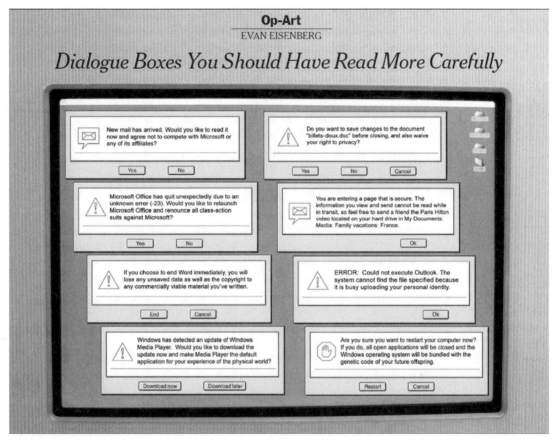

"Dialogue Boxes You Should Have Read More Carefully," by Evan Eisenberg. *New York Times,* Sept. 30, 2004.

DURING THE 1980S, I WAS A FACULTY ADVISER TO A STUDENT CHAPTER OF AMNESTY INTERNATIONAL, A WELL-KNOWN HUMAN RIGHTS ORGANIZATION. AMONG THE MOST IMPORTANT ACTIVITIES WE ENGAGED IN WERE LETTER-WRITING CAMPAIGNS ON BEHALF OF POLITICAL PRISONERS AROUND THE WORLD. HERE'S HOW IT WORKED. WHENEVER AMNESTY INTERNATIONAL LEARNED ABOUT A PERSON BEING IMPRISONED ILLEGALLY OR TORTURED FOR POLITICAL REASONS anywhere in the world, it would alert its members by sending brief newsletters called "Action Alerts" by mail. These Action Alerts described the imprisoned person, explained the circumstances, and provided information about the government offices or officials to whom we were being asked to write; they also included suggestions for writing effective letters to those officials. When our chapter received an Action Alert, we'd meet to discuss the situation, talk about strategies we could use in our letters, share drafts, and help each other with revisions. At the end of the meeting, we would have a dozen or so letters to send off on behalf of the imprisoned person.

Amnesty International had learned that publicizing cases of illegal imprisonment or torture was one of the most effective ways to help prisoners. It also knew that if a government received hundreds or thousands of letters about such a case, it was usually more likely to reconsider its actions against the prisoner in question. Often, such letter-writing campaigns resulted in a trial for the prisoner or even in the prisoner's release; sometimes they saved a prisoner's life.

My students learned important lessons about writing by participating in those letter-writing campaigns, which is why I'm sharing this story with you. They learned that writing is a powerful medium for communicating ideas and information. Letters were an effective way to express our concerns about troubling government actions and to convey to people in power that others around the world were aware of what was happening. This was real writing that had real consequences. It was a way for the students to enter important conversations that mattered to people all over the world—and especially to the political prisoners on whose behalf we were writing. But in joining those conversations about specific cases of political prisoners, my students were also taking part in larger conversations about human rights, about government policies, and about individual responsibility. As I noted in Chapter 1, writing is really a matter of joining conversations about issues that matter in our lives, whether you are writing a letter to a government official about a political prisoner, an entry on a blog about an en-

CHANGING TECHNOLOGIES FOR WRITING AND COMMUNICATION

Keep in mind that these letter-writing campaigns were happening before the Internet became such an important medium for communication. Today, such campaigns are managed through web sites maintained by organizations like Amnesty International, and the process is not only much faster but also more effective because of the power of the Internet to communicate instantly to millions of people all over the world. In the 1980s, we did not have access to the Internet, so we wrote letters. The idea was for member chapters of Amnesty International to send as many letters as possible and to publicize—through writing—the situation so that the prisoner might receive justice. Some of the readings in this book discuss the impact of the Internet on writers and writing (see Deborah Tannen's essay in Chapter 12).

vironmental policy, a letter to the editor of a newspaper about a local land-use controversy, or an essay for your economics course. We write because we need to be part of these conversations that affect our lives. And writing well means entering these conversations in effective and knowledgeable ways. My students were learning these lessons in ways that perhaps they didn't always think about when they were writing their school assignments.

They were also learning some important lessons about *how* to write effectively—lessons that you will learn as you engage in the writing assignments in your composition course:

- *Writers write for specific rhetorical situations.* As I explained in Chapter 1, all writing is done in context, and to be effective, writers must write in ways that fit the context. By writing letters as part of the Amnesty International campaigns, my students were learning how to take context into account—assessing the rhetorical situation, learning about their audience, and writing letters that addressed their audience under those special circumstances. Good writing means being able to assess the rhetorical situation effectively and respond to it appropriately.

- *Purpose guides a writer's decisions.* Whether you are writing a letter that you hope will help free an illegally held prisoner or a report for your economics course or an essay in your composition class, you are writing for a specific purpose. That purpose should shape the choices you make as you draft and revise your text.

- *Form fits purpose.* You have probably learned in school how to write book reports, business letters, science reports, research papers, and various kinds of essays, such as narratives or arguments. The reason for learning to write in these different forms is to be able to use them for specific purposes in appropriate situations. When you write a business letter to apply for a job, the reader expects your letter to follow a certain format. A science report also follows a certain format that has become a standard way for scientists to communicate the results of their research to each other. My students were writing a certain kind of persuasive letter to convince a government official to act in a certain way. All these forms serve specific purposes. Good writers learn to write in different forms and use those forms appropriately for a variety of purposes.

- *Writing is a process.* All writers move through a process from the time they conceive an idea to the finished text. In the letter-writing campaigns, my students were given topics to write about, but they still had to go through the various steps of the writing process, including generating ideas for their letters, organizing and developing their ideas in their drafts, getting help from other readers to improve their drafts, and revising and editing the letters before sending them to their intended audience. You move through these same steps for any writing you do. To write well is partly a matter of learning to manage that process effectively.

- *Writers adopt a style that is appropriate for the context.* The specific choices writers make about their writing style are guided by their sense of what is appropriate for the specific situation. My students had to adopt a relatively formal writing style for their letters, and sometimes they had to use special words depending on the government or country they were writing to. An informal writing style

[handwritten margin notes: Context + Audience Awareness; Purpose; Specific forms for specific purposes; PROCESS!; Appropriate style]

would not have been effective in those situations. Writing style is a tool writers use to achieve their purposes in specific situations. A personal essay for your composition course calls for a different style of writing than a lab report for your biology class or a letter to your financial aid officer. To write effectively means adapting your writing style to the context, no matter what kind of writing you're engaged in.

- *Effective writers use technology appropriately.* Today, writers have at their disposal all kinds of powerful technologies, including computers with sophisticated word processing programs, the Internet, and various kinds of multimedia tools. My students were using technologies available to them at the time: typewriters, word processors, and basic pen and paper. You will have to make choices about which technologies make sense for you, not only for writing your drafts but also for doing research and sharing your writing with readers. Part of the challenge of writing well today is learning to use these new and powerful technologies effectively.

The rest of this chapter provides a brief overview of these important aspects of writing. It offers some basic advice to help you complete whatever writing tasks you are engaged in; it will also help you read more carefully because it can give you insight into the challenges facing the writers whose essays appear in Chapters 5 through 12 of this book.

Theme into Thesis

It may sound obvious, but the writer's first job is to decide what to write about. As you probably know from your own experience, finding a topic is not always easy. In many cases, you may be provided with a topic, such as in a course assignment that specifies a topic or in the letter-writing campaigns I described earlier. But even when you are given a topic, what you say about that topic is up to you. A big part of your task is to determine what main idea or point you will make about your topic. That main idea or point is your *thesis*. For any writing activity, whether or not your topic is provided, you must develop a thesis.

Developing your thesis may be a little easier if you keep in mind that when you're writing, you're participating in a conversation about an important issue or *theme*. Many of the exercises in Chapters 5 through 12 offer specific suggestions for writing activities that will help you identify a thesis for your essay. But the principle guiding these activities applies to *any* writing situation: Your thesis grows out of your effort to enter a conversation about an important issue in a specific rhetorical situation. In other words, your thesis is your contribution to the conversation about the issue you're writing about.

What does that mean in practical terms? Well, let's say your composition instructor asks you to write an essay about an important experience you had as a teenager. That's a pretty open-ended assignment (which is not uncommon in composition courses), so part of the challenge is to consider *why* you might want to write about such an experience (aside from having to complete the assignment to earn a good grade for the course). If you think about the assignment as part of an ongoing conversation about adolescence and the challenges of being a teenager, then your purpose becomes easier to identify; you want to add something to those conversations. For example, many parents, educators, and others have concerns about how teens often feel overly sensitive about their physical appearance, which can lead to common problems like low self-esteem or more serious problems like eating disorders or the use of substances like steroids. The popular media are full of stories about these issues. Maybe you played a sport in high school and felt pressure to use steroids or other substances to enhance your physique and performance. In deciding to write about your experience, you would be identifying a specific topic that is part of these ongoing conversations about a theme (problems in adolescence) that matters to many people in our society. So as you decide just how to approach writing about your experience, you would want to consider how your specific experience might add to these conversations. Your *thesis* would be your contribution to those conversations about the *theme* of the challenges of being a teen; it is the statement you are making about that theme. Accordingly, you would want to tell your story in a way that focuses attention on how the pressure to look a certain way or to perform athletically at a high level affects teenagers.

Developing your thesis is really a matter of exploring your topic in a way that meets the needs of the rhetorical situation. In writing about the pressures on teen athletes, for example, you would want to consider what your experience might reveal about those pressures. Let's say you were on a track-and-field team on which some of the other players used steroids and encouraged their teammates to do so. You might ask yourself a series of questions to identify important events or issues related to your experience:

- What exactly was the nature of your experience on that team? What pressures did you feel? How did steroids come into play?

- What happened to athletes who took steroids? What happened to those who didn't? What reasons did athletes have for taking steroids or refusing to do so?

- What role did the coaches or parents play in the situation?

- Were there any key moments in your experience, such as someone getting hurt or getting caught with steroids? What led up to those moments? What resulted from them?

- What did you learn about athletics from this experience? What did you learn about teenagers? What did you learn about yourself?

In trying to answer such questions, you would not only generate material for your essay, but you would also begin to formulate the main point you wish to make about that experience. As you explore the experience and its consequences, you are working toward the statement you want to make about it—the main idea or point you wish to convey to your readers about that experience. That is, you're working toward your thesis.

Keep in mind that your thesis need not be a one-sentence statement of your main point, but sometimes it can be helpful to make such a statement. In our example, it might look like this:

> Teenagers are often unprepared to deal with the pressures that are created by the high value that our society places on success in athletics.

Or maybe like this:

Teens cheat in sports by taking steroids because of their need to succeed in a highly competitive environment.

WRITING AS INQUIRY

If your thesis changes as you develop your essay, it's an example of what writing teachers mean when they talk about "writing as inquiry": By writing about a topic, you are engaging in a substantive intellectual inquiry into the topic that can result in your gaining new insights into that topic. (See Chapter 1 for more on this topic.)

Such a statement might capture what you want to say about your experience, and it can be a good idea to try to write it out to help you identify your thesis and to keep it in mind as you develop your essay. But this issue of steroid use among teen athletes is very complicated, and one sentence might not quite do justice to that complexity. Boiling your experience down to one sentence may not enable you to capture the complexity of the experience and the issues it raises. If that's the case, it can be helpful to write a brief paragraph that essentially summarizes your thesis. A few sentences are all you need. The point is to identify what you want to say about your experience.

It's important to note that **your thesis can change** as you develop your essay. In fact, if you carefully explore your topic, it is likely that you will learn more about the issues and perhaps gain insight into your experience that you didn't have previously. Your opinion or perspective may change as a result of writing about the experience. For example, in writing about experiences with steroid use on your high school track-and-field team, you may have started out blaming your teammates who took steroids, especially if they caused problems for you or other team members. But as you explore your experience and develop your thesis, you may come to the realization that those students were responding to the same pressure all teens can feel and therefore had understandable reasons for deciding to take steroids. You may still believe they were wrong, but you may now appreciate the difficulties they faced and the complexities of the situation in a way that perhaps you had not done previously. As a result, you may find your thesis changing slightly as you develop your essay. That's good. It means that you are learning and developing a more complicated and sophisticated viewpoint about the issue.

Because your essay is your contribution to the ongoing conversations about an important issue—in this case, the issue of steroid use among teens—it makes sense to consider what others are saying and writing about the issue as you develop your thesis. In this way, reading what has been written about your topic is part of the process of developing your thesis. (Chapter 4 describes how research can be an integral part of *any* writing task, not just research papers.) And considering what your audience knows and believes is also part of the process. In other words, as you develop your thesis, you are considering how to present that thesis effectively to your audience. Doing so may change your own viewpoint. So part of developing your thesis involves assessing the rhetorical situation.

QUESTIONS TO ASK YOURSELF AS YOU DEVELOP YOUR THESIS

- What general question, issue, or problem am I exploring in this essay?
- What is the current status of this question, issue, or problem? What is being said (or written) about it?
- What are my general beliefs or opinions about this question, issue, or problem?
- What do I know about it? What do I want to know about it?
- What experiences have I had that might be related to this question, issue, or problem?
- What specific concerns do I have about it?
- Who might share my concerns?
- What do I have to say about the question, issue, or problem?

Assessing the Rhetorical Situation

Assessing a rhetorical situation is both straightforward and complex. (See Chapter 1 for an explanation of *rhetorical situation*.) The basic elements of any rhetorical situation—*writer, subject,* and *audience*—are usually pretty obvious, but the closer you look at those elements, the more complicated they can become. Effective writing depends on the extent to which you can assess those elements appropriately and fit your writing to the situation.

For example, your composition teacher may ask you to write a persuasive essay about a current issue on your campus—let's say, a proposal to restrict alcohol sales at all athletic events. Here's a look at the rhetorical situation for this assignment:

- *Audience.* Your audience might include members of your campus community as well as local residents and officials, who might have concerns about the sale of alcohol at sporting events, and fans who attend those events. The first step is to try to identify that audience and consider their connection to the controversy. What's at stake for them in this situation? What do they know and think about it?

- *Subject.* Your subject may seem obvious—in this case, you're writing about the proposed policy regarding alcohol sales at sporting events. But as you develop your thesis, it's important to look more carefully at that subject. How did the controversy about alcohol sales at sporting events arise in the first place? Were there incidents that led to concerns about alcohol sales at sporting events on your campus? If so, what happened? Did members of the community question campus policies? Is this a recent issue or one that has been of concern for some time? Just what would the new policy do? Who would be affected by it and how? Such questions help you explore the subject you're writing about and may lead you to a different perspective on that subject than the one you started with.

- *Writer.* Looking at the issue and the circumstances surrounding it leads to questions about your own interest in or connection to the issue. Why does this issue concern you? Are you a sports fan who regularly attends games on your campus? Have you had any experiences that are relevant to the current controversy? How would the new policy affect you? Do you have something to say about it? In short, consider your purposes or motivation for writing about the issue as well as your experiences with or connection to it.

As you explore these elements of the rhetorical situation, you may find that the immediate rhetorical situation (writing about a proposed campus policy to a local audience) may actually be broader than it seems. Alcohol consumption by young people, especially on college campuses, is a national issue that has been addressed not only by officials on college campuses around the country but also by state and federal officials as well as by organizations like SADD (Students Against Drunk Driving). The behavior of fans at sporting events also concerns Americans in general. So in writing about your campus's proposed policy regarding alcohol consumption at sporting events, you're actually writing about larger issues that concern a much broader audience. And in joining the debate in your community about alcohol consumption at sporting events, you are also joining the ongoing conversations in American society about youth, sports, alcohol, and related social issues. So it makes sense to take into account what has been

---

QUESTIONS TO ASK YOURSELF WHEN ASSESSING RHETORICAL CONTEXT

- *Audience:* Who is my audience? What connection to the topic does my audience have?
- *Subject:* What is the issue? What are the circumstances surrounding the issue? Why is this issue important or interesting to me and to my audience?
- *Writer:* What is my interest in this issue? What connection do I have to the issue? What contribution to the conversations or debates about this issue can I make?

---

said in those conversations—the local ones in your community as well as the larger ones in society in general. That's part of the process of assessing the rhetorical situation.

The more carefully you explore these elements of the rhetorical situation, the more likely you are to identify important questions, concerns, and viewpoints relevant to your topic. You can therefore make more informed decisions about what to include in your essay, what to leave out, how to present your position as well as the positions of others involved in the issue, and what style or voice to use to best convey your point, or thesis, to your intended audience.

As I noted earlier, part of the challenge a writer faces with any writing task is identifying a thesis within a larger theme. In this case, the theme includes the uses of alcohol in American society as well as the role of sporting events as social activities. Your thesis will be the point you wish to make about those themes in the context of your campus's proposed policy change. Making that point effectively in your essay will be determined in large part by how well you assess the rhetorical context.

Knowing Your Audience

Identifying your audience is only the first step in deciding how to address that audience effectively. Knowing something about your audience and anticipating what your audience knows and believes are also crucial components of assessing the rhetorical situation. Let's return to the example of writing an essay about a proposed change in the policy regarding alcohol consumption at athletic events on your campus.

Let's say you intend your essay for your campus newspaper. In that case, you would have a pretty good idea about your audience, since it would be a relatively local audience composed of students and faculty on your campus community and perhaps some members of the surrounding community. Even such a specific audience could be very diverse, and you could never really know exactly who your readers might be, what they know, and how they might feel about the issue. But you could safely assume a great deal about what they might know about the local situation. For example, they would probably be familiar with the proposed policy change and with any incidents that might have led to it. They would also be familiar with some of the viewpoints people have expressed about the situation in the local media. In writing for such an audience, then, you would probably not need to include a great deal of background information about the situation. A reference to the policy change would be enough.

Writers always make assumptions about what their intended audience might know about their topic. But sometimes it can be tricky to anticipate what your audience knows. For instance, if you wanted to write a letter to the editor of a much larger publication—say, *USA Today* or a sports-related web site like ESPN.com—about the issue of alcohol consumption at college athletic events, you could not assume that readers of such a publication would be familiar with the situation on your campus. You would have to decide how much background information to include for these readers. Even with such a large audience, though, you could make some assumptions about what they know. Readers of *USA Today* would likely be familiar with the general problem of alcohol abuse on college campuses because it is a much-discussed problem in national media. They might also know about well-publicized incidents involving alcohol abuse at college sporting events, particularly if those incidents took place at colleges with high-profile sports teams. So as a writer, you might refer to such incidents as a way to set the stage for your own thesis, and you wouldn't necessarily need to fill in much background information.

The point is that you always have to try to anticipate what your audience might know about your topic, even when that audience is large and diverse. And you also should have a sense of what their expectations might be. For example, readers of *USA Today* would not expect a very formal writing style in a brief editorial essay or letter to the editor. On the other hand, your sociology instructor might expect a more formal academic style for an assignment on the same topic. In short, as you examine your audience, you must consider that audience in the context of the rhetorical situation as a whole.

Keep in mind, too, that your sense of audience can be shaped by a variety of complicated factors having to do with the identities of your readers—things like race, gender, religion, sexual orientation, ethnicity, age, income, and so on. For example, if your primary audience is composed of students in your composition class, which includes several international students, you would want to be aware of how they might respond to a reference to Americans as "we." Referring to Americans in that way might alienate your international classmates, and you would want to be careful about such references in your writing.

How you address your audience in a piece of writing— whether that writing is a formal academic essay, a biology report, a post on your favorite blog, or a letter to the editor of a local newspaper—will help determine how effective your writing will be for the specific rhetorical situation you're in. Making your best guess about your audience will probably mean that you will have a better chance of achieving your purpose in that rhetorical situation. Your sense of your audience will guide the specific choices you make as you write—choices about information to include or leave out, about writing style, and about specific words or phrases to use or avoid.

SHADES OF MEANING

Words are not neutral; they often have shades of meaning that go beyond the literal dictionary definition (see the section *Discourse and Why It Is Important* on page 9 in Chapter 1). Some words and phrases will send powerful messages to certain audiences, and as a writer, you need to take those messages into account. For example, in the heated debates about abortion, *pro-choice* and *pro-abortion* technically mean the same thing: They generally refer to people who support legal abortion. But these two phrases carry very different messages depending on the context and the audience. For some people who oppose abortion, *pro-choice* can be considered a misleading term. For people who consider themselves pro-choice, the term *pro-abortion* can seem misleading. These differences are a result of how these terms are used in ongoing conversations about controversial issues. Writers should be aware of these complexities when they are choosing words and refining their writing style.

QUESTIONS TO ASK YOURSELF WHEN ANALYZING AUDIENCE

- Do I have a specific audience in mind for this particular writing task? If so, who is that audience?
- What do I know about my audience that is relevant to my topic? Is there anything about my audience that I should find out before finishing this writing task?
- What can I assume my audience knows about that topic? What background information about my topic should I provide for them?
- What beliefs or opinions will my audience likely have regarding my topic? Do I need to take these beliefs or opinions into account in my writing?
- What is my connection to my audience, if any? Does that connection matter for my writing task? If so, how? What might my audience know about me? Does it matter whether or not they know me?
- What interest in my topic does my audience have?
- What ideas or language might be especially controversial for my audience? Should I avoid these ideas or language in my writing?
- How do I want my audience to react to my writing?

Managing the Writing Process

The great American writer Ernest Hemingway was once asked in an interview about the famous last chapter of his novel *A Farewell to Arms,* which has been the subject of a great deal of discussion among literary critics over the years. Hemingway told the interviewer that he rewrote the chapter thirty-eight times. When asked why, Hemingway replied that he had to get the words right.

I like to tell that story to students to emphasize the role of revision in effective writing. It's unlikely that you will find yourself having to revise something three dozen times, as Hemingway did, but that story can teach us that even the greatest writers must work through the process of writing carefully and assiduously. Part of being an effective writer is learning how to manage that process efficiently. The most important thing to remember is that there is no formula for engaging in the writing process. Writing is not a step-by-step, paint-by-number activity. It's much messier than that. And part of the challenge is accepting some messiness and uncertainty in writing.

Most writing involves some version of three main activities: generating, gathering, and organizing ideas and/or information; writing the draft; and revising and editing. Often, these three activities are called *prewriting, drafting,* and *rewriting.* Whatever they're called, keep in mind that at some point in any writing task, you'll have to come up with ideas and collect information, organize those ideas and information in a draft, and rewrite that draft so it is effective and correct. The specific activities you do for each of these parts of the writing process will vary depending on many factors, including the assignment, how much time you have, how familiar you are with your topic, and your past experiences as a writer.

The biggest mistake student writers make is trying to do all these activities at once. Many students wait until the last minute and then try to complete their assignment in a single draft, essentially collapsing all these activities—prewriting, drafting, and revising—into one writing session. The result is usually a less effective text and a tedious and unenjoyable writing experience. You have probably done this; most students have (I did when I was a student!). But it's rarely a good idea because writing well requires more kinds of thinking than most people can do at once. (Multitasking may be a trend these days, but it doesn't necessarily help writers write well.) Writers can do a better job if they complete the writing task in parts. Spending some time generating ideas or collecting information can mean that writing the first draft will be a little easier than if you try to think of ideas at the same time that you're actually writing the essay. Similarly, writing a rough draft without worrying about things like spelling and grammar will usually enable you to concentrate on making your point rather than stopping to correct errors or look up a word in the dictionary. You can go back later to fix spelling or punctuation errors—*after* you've done the hard work of organizing your ideas into a coherent, readable draft. Managing your writing process in this way usually means allowing yourself sufficient time to complete these various activities and to revise

---

WRITING UNDER PRESSURE

Sometimes you have a tight deadline, so you have to complete a writing assignment at the last minute. But some students rationalize their procrastination by claiming that they do their best work under pressure. I don't buy it. Students who say this usually wait until the last minute to begin their writing, which leaves little time to engage in all the activities described in this chapter. Inevitably, they have to cut corners—perhaps gathering insufficient information on their topic, rushing their draft, revising quickly or not at all, or even plagiarizing, which is more tempting when the pressure is on. Don't kid yourself like this. Starting your writing assignments a little earlier can make your task easier because it enables you to break the task up into sections rather than trying to do it all at once. And it usually means that you will produce better writing.

your draft before your deadline. The trick is to learn what works best for you. It's always better to start sooner so that you have sufficient time for the most challenging parts of a writing task.

Learning through Writing

Learning to manage your own writing process is not a matter of just identifying the steps you should take as you complete an assignment; writing is also a form of inquiry—a means of exploring your ideas and learning new concepts or information. When you write carefully about a topic, you come to know that topic better; you might also come to learn more about yourself and the world around you in the process. That's one reason students are asked to write reports and papers not just in English or composition courses but in all disciplines.

It is important to keep this idea of writing as inquiry in mind as you complete your writing assignments so you don't think that once you come up with your thesis, all you have to do is put it down on paper. Often, students will tell me, "I know what I want to say, but I just can't find the words." Well, that's not quite true. Rarely is an idea for an essay or a report completely worked out in your mind before you begin writing. In fact, our own ideas are often not entirely clear to us; they get worked out in our heads as we write about those ideas. In addition, ideas can change as a result of the act of writing because through writing we are learning more about a topic than we knew when we started working on it. So once you identify your thesis, consider it a tentative thesis, one that may change as you explore your topic further. In the end, your finished paper is not just an expression of your thesis; it is also a reflection of your process of inquiry and what you have learned through writing.

Thinking of writing as a process of inquiry also means that you may have to do research at any point in the process. (Research techniques are discussed in detail in Chapter 4.) Often, especially when writing research papers, students proceed with the idea that they must first collect as much information about their topic as they can before they start writing. Then they write their papers based on that information. But the act of writing your draft may reveal gaps in your information, or it may raise questions about your topic that you cannot answer without further research. If that happens, it's a sign that you're learning as you write, and you have to explore your topic further. You may have to stop writing your draft and go back to gather more information or change your plan for organizing your paper. The same thing can happen with any kind of writing: a personal essay, a letter to an editor, a science report, or a poem or story.

Revising Is Not Editing

When you revise a piece of writing, you are doing more than correcting spelling or punctuation errors or tinkering with sentences. Genuine revising is a crucial part of exploring your topic, developing your thesis, and working out your ideas fully; it is an integral part of addressing your audience effectively. I first learned this lesson about revising when I wrote one of my first magazine articles while I was in college.

Like many students, I wrote a lot of my course assignments in one draft but I still earned good grades for most assignments (see *Writing under Pressure* on page 40). So when I started writing for magazines, I thought I knew what I was doing. For one

EDITING STRATEGIES

The most important thing to keep in mind when editing a paper is to avoid looking for minor errors until after you have done the harder work of revising. Once you've revised your draft sufficiently, you can attend to surface matters, such as spelling, punctuation errors, and similar problems. There are many different ways to do this kind of editing, or "proofreading." One very effective strategy is to develop a list or log of the kinds of errors you tend to make; once you've completed your draft, read through it several times, each time trying to find the specific errors on your list. For example, if you know that you tend to confuse *effect* and *affect,* read through your draft to look for those words and check to see whether you've used them correctly. The trick is to become aware of the particular errors you tend to make and to concentrate on those, rather than just reading through your draft looking for *anything* that might be wrong.

USING LANGUAGE EFFECTIVELY

Following the rules of correct writing is part of the process of communicating effectively through writing, but it isn't the whole process or even the most important part. In fact, a writer can communicate effectively using "incorrect" language as long as that language is appropriate to the context in which he or she is writing. Think about hip-hop music, for example. The lyrics of hip-hop songs often use nonstandard or incorrect English, yet some of those songs communicate powerful messages to listeners. That doesn't mean that you should use incorrect or nonstandard language in your own writing whenever you want, but it does mean that effective writing involves much more than using correct language; it requires using the *right* language for the situation. You wouldn't necessarily want to use the language of a hip-hop song in a job application letter, for example. So to write effectively means adapting your writing to the context in which you are writing. Without an adequate understanding of context, a writer's knowledge of the basic rules of writing and his or her skill with words will only go so far. You can write a perfectly correct and carefully organized essay that might have nothing important to say to a reader. At the same time, learning the basic rules and conventions of writing enables you to meet the challenges of most any writing situation.

assignment, the magazine editor asked me to write about the challenges of providing good health care in rural areas, which was then a topic of national concern. So I did my research, wrote the article, and sent it to the editor by my deadline. I had essentially written the article in one draft from start to finish, and then I did some editing for minor errors and awkward sentences. I assumed the article was finished and the next step was to see it in print (and receive my check!).

A few weeks later, however, an envelope arrived from the editor. It contained five single-spaced pages of questions, comments, and suggestions for revising my article. There were no errors in my article—no misspellings or punctuation errors—nor were there problems with my writing style. I had made sure of that. Instead, the editor's letter posed many questions that he assumed readers of his magazine would ask—questions that I had not answered sufficiently in my article. He made many comments about sections that worked well and sections that didn't. And he offered numerous detailed suggestions for revisions—large and small—to improve the article. In effect, the editor was telling me to revise extensively if I wanted to have my article published in his magazine (and if I wanted to get paid for my work). Never had a teacher read my writing so carefully, and never had a teacher asked me to revise so extensively.

At first, I was stunned. Did this mean I was a poor writer? Well, no. As I reread the editor's letter and considered his various questions, comments, and suggestions, I began to see that I had indeed neglected to address many important issues in my article. I could see that I did not consider what readers of the magazine might need to know. I had obviously left out important information, which meant I had to do additional research. I had also included some unnecessary information that I could eliminate. In short, I was rethinking my article in ways that took my audience and purpose more fully into account. And as I began revising the manuscript, I was doing so with my readers in mind. I used the editor's questions and comments and suggestions as a guide for revising, but I also made revisions that he didn't suggest. I was really *rewriting* my article. And the result was not only a better article for that situation but also a better experience for me as a writer because I learned a great deal more about my subject as well as about the act of writing.

The most important lesson I learned was that revising is not just the editing you do after you finish writing a draft; revising is an integral part of the process of writing because it is through revising that you can really begin to see where your writing is going. If you want to learn to write well in various rhetorical situations—outside school as well as in school—then you will eventually have to learn how to revise effectively. And the best way to do that is by taking your writing seriously and engaging in your own writing process genuinely and honestly. If you do that, you will find yourself returning to your drafts, as Hemingway did, to make them better. And eventually, they *will* become better.

QUESTIONS TO ASK YOURSELF WHEN REVISING

There are no hard-and-fast rules for revising, but you can make the process a little easier if you break it up into several steps. The basic idea is to start with the big issues and work toward the smaller ones. I like to think of the process as having three main parts: revising for meaning, revising for strategy, and revising for style.

Revising for Meaning. After you've completed your rough draft, read through to see whether you've addressed your topic sufficiently.

- Have I included everything I intended to include in this essay or paper?
- Is anything missing? If so, what?
- Have I included anything that is unnecessary or irrelevant? Can I leave anything out without weakening my draft?
- Is my thesis clear? Is anything confusing about my main ideas?
- Do I maintain my focus throughout the text? Do I drift off my main idea anywhere in the draft?

Revising for Strategy. Once you are satisfied that you have addressed the big questions, you can begin to narrow your focus to address matters of structure and strategy. At this stage, concern yourself with whether your paper is written in a way that makes your point clear and conveys your ideas effectively to your readers.

- Is the paper organized in a way that will make sense to my intended audience? Do I move effectively from one main point to the next? Are any parts of the paper out of place? If so, where might they work better?
- Do I make clear transitions from one main section to the next?
- Does the introduction set up my paper effectively? Does it provide a good sense of what the paper will be about?
- Does the conclusion wrap up my main ideas effectively? Does it emphasize the ideas or the point I want to leave my readers with?
- Have I addressed my audience in ways that make sense for my topic and thesis? Have I taken my audience's perspective sufficiently into account (what they might know, what they might need to know, and so on)? (See *Knowing Your Audience* on page 38.)

Revising for Style. Now you can focus on your prose. At this point, you want to work with sentences, rhythm, word choice, and the rules of standard written English. You want to bring your voice out effectively and appropriately for the rhetorical situation. Move through your draft sentence by sentence and try to craft each sentence so that it is as effective as possible.

- Are there any confusing passages? If so, how can I rewrite specific sentences to make these passages clearer?
- Is my voice strong and consistent throughout the paper? Are there sections where my voice seems less effective?
- Can any sentences be improved by restructuring them or eliminating words or phrases that aren't essential?
- Can I improve any passages with more appropriate word choice?

In your composition class, you may be asked to share drafts of your writing with classmates so that you can get feedback on how to improve your draft. Sharing your drafts before they are finished is one of the most effective ways to improve your writing, and it is also a good way to develop your revision skills. If you are not asked to share your drafts in your composition class, consider finding a friend or family member who might offer useful feedback on your drafts. Or visit the writing center on your campus, where you can get feedback from trained writing tutors.

Using Technology

Today, most student writers have access to computers with sophisticated word processing programs that can make many aspects of the writing process easier. A program like Microsoft Word makes it easy to save drafts. You can also track your changes using special features of such programs so that you can see what revisions you've made; other features enable you to have a classmate or friend make suggestions or comments without changing your main text. You can also use spelling check or grammar check features to help with editing. It is a good idea to become familiar with these many capabilities of word processing programs to make your writing process more efficient. Try them out and use what works best for you. In addition, e-mail is an easy and effective way to share writing and exchange comments about drafts in progress. Many composition instructors now use e-mail or web-based programs such as WebCT so that students can easily share drafts of their writing. These technologies can help you make your writing process more efficient.

A WORD ABOUT SPELLING CHECKERS AND GRAMMAR CHECKERS

Many students like to run the spelling and grammar checking features that are included with most word processing programs. These features can find misspelled words and suggest corrections; they can also find many kinds of punctuation and grammar errors. But be careful when you use these features. They do not always find all the errors or problems in your drafts, and sometimes they suggest corrections that may actually create new errors. If you do use these features, make sure you review the suggestions for correcting errors before you make any changes to your draft. And be especially careful with the thesaurus feature on your word processing program. Very often, the thesaurus will suggest a word that is inappropriate for the context.

We live in a technology-rich world that offers an amazing variety of tools for writers that go well beyond word processing. For writers, the Internet offers a wealth of information for research (which I'll discuss in Chapter 4) and also provides access to audiences that were unavailable to most writers in the past. You may already have experience with blogs and other web-based forums where you can share your writing and communicate with different audiences through writing. Or perhaps you maintain your own web site where you publish your writing. The Internet provides unparalleled opportunities for writers to find and connect with audiences and to participate in the many ongoing conversations about important matters in our lives. It is likely that your composition instructor will encourage (or even require) you to explore these opportunities. Many of the exercises in this book will also encourage you to venture online to engage in various kinds of writing. If you do, keep in mind that writing in these new media enables you to enter conversations that are reshaping our world today.

These new technologies are also changing the way we combine text with images and sound. Even the most basic word processing programs enable you to incorporate different kinds of images, including photographs, icons, graphs, and charts, into your writing. Creating a web page often involves using images as well as color and design in conjunction with your writing. These issues are discussed in Chapter 2, but it is important to remember that for some kinds of writing tasks, you do not need to limit yourself to text alone. The nature of the task and the rhetorical situation will help you determine whether you can or should use images, graphics, or other kinds of media to achieve your purpose and address your audience effectively.

Chapter 4 Engaging in Research and Inquiry

Writing as Inquiry

THE FAMOUS ESSAYIST E.B. WHITE IS SAID TO HAVE MADE THE FOLLOWING STATEMENT ABOUT WRITING:

HOW DO I KNOW WHAT I THINK UNTIL I SEE WHAT I SAY?

WHAT WHITE MEANT IS THAT A WRITER CAN NEVER BE COMPLETELY SURE OF HIS OR HER VIEWPOINT OR THESIS UNTIL THE WRITING ITSELF IS FINISHED. THAT'S BECAUSE WRITING IS NOT JUST A MATTER OF PUTTING YOUR THOUGHTS OR IDEAS DOWN ON PAPER; IT IS ALSO A MEANS OF EXPLORING those thoughts or ideas, a way to inquire into a topic. I'd like you to think of research in this same way: Research is part of the process of learning about something through writing. It is a process of "knowing what you think" by "seeing what you say," as E.B. White puts it.

A few years ago, a student of mine named Kristen decided to write an argument in favor of becoming a vegetarian. She intended her argument for a general audience, such as the readers of a widely circulated publication like *USA Today*. She wanted to persuade her readers that becoming a vegetarian is a good idea because a vegetarian diet is healthier than a diet that includes meat. As she looked into the issue, however, she began to see that it was more complicated than she first thought. Her research into the health benefits of a vegetarian diet revealed that it is possible to have a healthy diet that includes meat and that there are actually some health risks to a vegetarian diet. That led her to examine arguments *against* becoming a vegetarian, and she began to explore other points of view, which deepened her understanding of the issue. She also began to encounter environmental arguments for becoming a vegetarian that she hadn't previously considered. She learned, for example, that raising beef cattle, chickens, and hogs on a large scale causes serious environmental damage. As a result, Kristen began to develop an ethical argument for becoming a vegetarian that she considered more powerful than her original argument based on health benefits. Her basic opinion about becoming a vegetarian did not change—she was still in favor of it—but her argument shifted from a focus on individual health benefits to larger social, environmental, and ethical concerns. As a result of her writing about becoming a vegetarian, she gained a better understanding of the issue—and I think she wrote a more effective paper, too.

Many of the assignments in this book ask you to engage in inquiry about a topic to understand it better, just as Kristen did. When Kristen examined opposing viewpoints that her readers might have, she was exploring her topic with her audience and her purpose in mind, and they shaped her exploration. By writing a more informed argument, she was able to participate more effectively in our society's larger conversations about diet and health and social responsibility. Ultimately, that's an important part of your goal whenever you write—to communicate effectively and knowledgeably about a given topic.

Conducting Research

As I just noted, researching your topic is a process of inquiry through which you not only gather information and develop ideas about your topic but also gain a greater understanding of it. This is why I think it's a mistake to approach your research as a separate activity from your writing. Conducting research is an integral part of the writing process.

Here are a few main principles to help you understand this process of researching a topic:

- *Conducting research is not a linear process.* It may be possible in some cases to gather all the information you need before you actually begin writing a draft of your paper, but if you are genuinely engaged with your topic, it is more likely that as you start writing your draft, you will find you need to do more research. As you revise a draft for the second or third time, you might discover that you need some information that you don't have, so you need to go back to the library or the Internet to find that information. When Kristen was trying to write about the health benefits of vegetarianism, she discovered that there were also health risks. That discovery meant that she had to find out more about those risks. Later, as she tried to develop her argument in favor of vegetarianism, she began to see an ethical and environmental argument rather than simply a health-related argument. Again, she had to do more research to gain a better understanding of the ethical and environmental issues. In short, research can lead to more research. It's all part of the process of exploring your topic for your intended audience.

- *Research depends on the nature of the writing assignment.* Although it's probably true that you don't need to do formal research for every writing assignment, it's also true that you may need to do research for assignments that are not, strictly speaking, research papers. For example, if you're writing a letter to the editor of your school newspaper about a local controversy, you may have to do some research to gather information about that controversy. Similarly, you may be asked to write a paper for a psychology class on an experience you had with, say, a school guidance counselor; that assignment may require you to find information about school guidance counselors. Putting together a web page for a student organization you belong to may require you to examine the web sites of similar organizations. So almost any writing activity may require you to look for information or consult sources.

  Obviously, some kinds of writing require specialized kinds of research. A report for your chemistry class may require you to consult certain scientific journals. Your sociology instructor may ask you to use only certain kinds of academic books or articles for a paper on government drug policies, whereas your communications instructor may ask you to examine sources from the popular press for an assignment on the news coverage of political campaigns. In each case, the nature of the assignment makes certain kinds of sources useful or necessary and other sources inappropriate. It's your job as a writer to determine what kinds of sources you need to explore for your assignment. So doing research doesn't mean just going to the Internet and doing a Google search or checking your library's listings for your topic; it means identifying the *kinds* of sources that are most appropriate and relevant to your assignment.

- *An open mind can mean greater learning.* If you begin your research with the idea that you already know exactly what kinds of information you need, you may miss an opportunity to explore your topic fully and therefore to understand it better. For example, let's say you are writing a paper for a criminology class about reasons for the rising prison population in the United States. After making some notes about your topic and reading some sections of your course textbook, you have compiled a list of the kinds of information you need for your paper, including statistical data about the prison population, information about changes in state laws that have led to higher incarceration rates, and information about different incarceration rates for different racial groups. So you set off looking for sources with that kind of information. After finding the information, you write your paper, focusing on just those reasons that are discussed in the sources you have found. But let's say that one of your sources mentions the fact that most new prisons are being built in rural areas. When you were developing your list of information that you had to find, you hadn't thought about the matter of *where* prisons are being built. So that wasn't on your list, and you didn't include it in your paper. But if you then went back to look for additional sources that relate specifically to this matter of where prisons are being built, you might find that there is another important reason for the increasing prison population in the United States that has to do with the economics of the criminal justice system. Exploring that issue might enhance your understanding of your topic—and lead to a better paper.

The point is that even if you begin your research with a good idea of the kinds of information or sources you need to find, keep yourself open to the possibility that there are other kinds of sources or information that you haven't thought about. Keeping an open mind about your research will likely mean that you'll learn more about your topic and therefore be more likely to write an effective paper.

> **CURIOSITY IN RESEARCH**
>
> Curiosity is another important component of the research process. Research—and writing in general—is a way to satisfy your curiosity about questions or issues or ideas that are important or interesting to you. Research should be a process of allowing your curiosity to guide you. Follow your questions and hunches. Look to see what's around the next corner, even if that direction doesn't seem to be the one you're going in. A course assignment is likely to be much more enjoyable if you allow yourself to be curious about your topic. Not knowing exactly what you will learn is part of what makes research—and writing—interesting and worthwhile.

Tools for Your Inquiry

You are fortunate to live at a time when the tools available to writers for their research are much more powerful and extensive than what was available even a few years ago. In addition to traditional sources like books, newspapers, and journals available through your library, the Internet is a vast resource that provides ready access to an astonishing variety of information. Moreover, traditional print sources, such as newspaper and magazine articles and even books, are increasingly available in digital form, either on CD-ROMs or online. I can remember spending hours in the library as an undergraduate student laboriously paging through indexes like *The Reader's Guide to*

WHAT COUNTS AS A SOURCE?

The short answer is "almost anything." The right sources for a writing assignment depend on the nature of that assignment. If you're writing about the effects of government policies on farming in your state, then it would make sense to talk to an expert in your state agriculture department or your local agriculture extension service in addition to consulting more conventional sources, such as journal articles or books about farm policy. For a PowerPoint presentation on hip-hop culture for your sociology class, you might visit hip-hop web sites or talk to local musicians. For an assignment in his history course, my son visited the Saratoga Battlefield National Monument in upstate New York to speak to the museum curator there about that famous Revolutionary War battle. The point is that you should seek relevant information and ideas wherever they might be. The library or the Internet may not always be the best places to find sources for your assignment. Be curious and creative as you research your topic.

Periodical Literature to find sources that looked useful, checking the card catalog, and then plodding through the library stacks to find those articles or books on the shelves. Usually, the library didn't have all the sources I needed for my paper, and often, a list of twenty potential sources would result in only four or five articles or books that I could actually find. If those articles or books weren't exactly what I needed, then I'd have to go back to *The Reader's Guide* to try to find more sources.

Today, you can log onto the Internet, go to the web site for your school's library, and find hundreds and even thousands of sources in online indexes like *The Reader's Guide* or more specialized databases for various subjects. Once you find relevant sources in an index or database, you can often read the full article online—without ever getting up from your desk. You can also check to see if your library has any of the books you need before you actually go to the library to check them out. These many online resources can be a gold mine for a writer.

The variety and extensive nature of these resources also mean greater challenges for writers in determining which sources are credible and useful. The rest of this chapter offers some general advice to help you identify, assess, and cite sources for your writing. In the following section, we'll examine some of the tools you can use for your research. Later, we'll discuss how to cite your sources.

The Library and the Internet

Many of the resources that were once available only through your library are now available on the Internet. Today, most college and university libraries offer access to the library's holdings, many indexes, databases, and other kinds of resources and research services through their web sites. So "going to the library" to do research might mean logging onto the Internet and using your library's web site to search for sources. But there remain important differences between using your library and using the Internet for research:

- A university or college library will usually provide access to specialized indexes and databases that are not always available on the web.

- Libraries carefully evaluate the resources they provide, which is not always true of resources available on the Internet.

- Libraries provide access to books, various reference guides, and newspaper, magazine, or journal articles that are not always available on the Internet.

So it's still a good idea to begin your research at your library or on your library's web site.

Using Indexes and Databases

An *index* is basically a listing of published books and articles; a *database* is the same thing, although it may contain more information than an index. For many assignments that require research, you may need to consult one of the many different indexes or databases to find sources. When you use an index or database, you are looking for information about books and articles that might be relevant to your topic. A listing in an index or database will usually provide the title of the book or article; the author (if available); the journal, magazine, or other publication in which the article appeared; the publisher; the date of publication; and the length of the article. Using this information, you can decide whether the article or book is likely to be useful in your research. If the title sounds relevant to your topic, if the article is from a reputable source or written by a well-known author in the field, or if the article was written during a relevant time period for your topic, then you might consider reading the selection. At that point, you would go to your library (or the Internet) to find that article or book.

A visit to your library's web site will reveal that there are dozens of indexes and databases available to you. Obviously, the first step is to decide which ones to search. Since searching a database for information can be time-consuming, this step is important. You don't want to spend time searching through a database only to discover that it does not list the kinds of sources you need for your project. If you're not sure what a database contains, ask your librarian.

The basic task of searching an index or database is straightforward: You look for titles of articles or books that seem relevant to your topic. Most databases have similar basic search functions. For example, below is the keyword search screen for InfoTrac.

KINDS OF INDEXES AND DATABASES

There are two basic kinds of indexes and databases: general and specialized. General indexes are just that: very general listings of sources on a broad range of topics. *The Reader's Guide to Periodical Literature* is one of the oldest and best-known general indexes; it includes listings of articles published in many popular and commercial magazines, journals, and newspapers. InfoTrac College Edition is a newer general index that offers listings similar to *The Reader's Guide* but includes many contemporary digital as well as academic sources. For many academic writing assignments, you might need to consult a specialized index or database, which contains listings of publications related to a specific academic discipline, such as psychology, sociology, or medicine. *Psychological Abstracts*, for example, contains listings of articles from professional and academic journals in psychology; similarly, the *MLA International Bibliography* includes sources for the study of literature and literary theory. Such specialized indexes and databases are useful in finding materials that would not usually appear in popular newspaper or magazine articles.

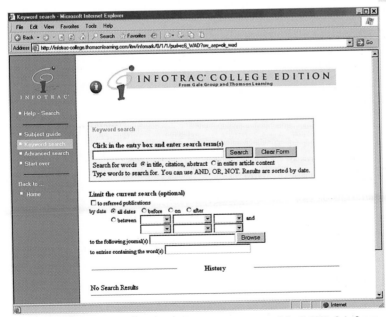

InfoTrac Screen Shot. From INFOTRAC ONEFILE PLUS by Thomson Gale, © 2005, Gale Group. Reprinted by permission of the Gale Group.

This screen allows you to search the InfoTrac database using a keyword. Suppose you're writing a report on alternative energy. You can begin by using *alternative energy* as your keyword. You might also try searching for related terms, such as *solar power, wind power, sustainable energy,* or *renewable energy.* Notice the blue bar on the left side of the screen, which has several options for other kinds of searches that will allow you to search by subject, journal type, and similar factors. You may have to try these different search functions to see which ones will yield the most useful results for your topic.

Your database search will yield a list of articles, and you will have to select which articles might be useful for your paper. Review the list to see whether it is worth finding the article itself. If your library has access to that article, you can go to the article directly.

Databases such as InfoTrac College Edition can be extremely useful in finding information and materials you need for your project. But using these databases can also be time-consuming. Often, there is no substitute for just spending time searching a database for what you need, so be sure to leave yourself sufficient time for your research.

Searching the Internet

The Internet is becoming an increasingly important resource for research. That's not surprising because the Internet contains an unimaginable amount of information and is growing rapidly. But searching the Internet is different in two important ways from searching materials in your library or on your library's web site:

1. The Internet is not organized into neat databases and indexes such as those in your library. To find relevant materials on the Internet requires different strategies than you would use when searching for materials in your library. The most common method of searching the Internet is to use a *search engine,* such as Google. Search engines work more or less like an index or database you might find at your library, but they generally do not limit their searches to specific kinds of materials, such as academic journals or newspapers, as indexes or databases do. Instead, a typical search with a search engine will turn up many different kinds of materials—and usually far more material than you could possibly sort through for your research.

2. Because the Internet is largely unregulated and anyone with access to it can put up a web site, materials on the Internet cannot be considered as trustworthy as the materials you might find at your library. Whereas your librarians evaluate materials before including them in the library's collections, no one is required to evaluate materials before they are posted to the web. So it is important to evaluate the credibility of materials you find on the web.

A search engine is a program that searches the Internet according to specific criteria and then indexes what it finds. Google (http://www.google.com) is one of the better known search engines. (Google also has an excellent scholarly search engine at http://scholar.google.com that provides access to scholarly sources on the web.) Other popular search engines include http://www.ask.com and http://www.yahoo.com. Search engines use different criteria for finding materials on the Internet, so it is good practice to use more than one when doing Internet research.

Like more formal indexes or databases, Internet search engines allow you to search by keyword, and many of them allow you to refine your searches. Let's say you are writing an essay about an emergency you had with your dog, and you wanted to find more information about emergency medical care for animals. You might begin your search with terms like *veterinary medicine* or *animal care.* Such terms by themselves are likely to turn up many thousands of web sites. When I was writing this chapter in 2005, for example, a search for *veterinary medicine* turned up almost 6 million sites! So you want to be as specific as possible. You might include *all* of these search terms as keywords: *veterinary medicine, emergency,* and *animal care.* That search turned up 27,000 sites in 2005. But even that's too many sites for you to visit and evaluate, so it's a good idea to narrow your search even further by being more specific. You might focus on pets or dogs, for instance. Or you might focus only on animal care in the United States or on a specific kind of situation, such as *dog sprayed by a skunk.* The more specific your search terms, the better your results are likely to be.

In addition to search engines, you can also use online encyclopedias, such as Wikipedia.com, Answers.com, or Britannica.com. The web sites of many organizations also contain resource pages with links to specific kinds of information.

> **AN IMPORTANT SEARCH TRICK**
>
> Here is a strategy for using search engines more efficiently. If you place your search terms in quotation marks, the search engine will look for exactly those words in that order. For example, if you search for *veterinary medicine,* your search will turn up sites with both those words as well as sites that have either one word or the other; however, placing that term in quotation marks (*"veterinary medicine"*) will yield only sites with the term *veterinary medicine.* Using quotation marks in this way can help you narrow your search and find more relevant web sites.

Discuss Wikipedia

Evaluating Internet Resources

Once you find relevant materials on the Internet, you need to determine whether they are credible or trustworthy, which can sometimes be tricky. Because anyone can put up a web site, and because there is no official review process for web sites, it's important to be cautious when deciding whether to use material from a web site, even if that material looks reliable. Here are some guidelines for evaluating Internet sources.

- *Who sponsors the web site?* Obviously, a university web site, the site of a respected news organization like the *New York Times* or CNN, a government web site, or the site of a well-known organization like the Red Cross or the American Heart Association is likely to contain reliable and trustworthy information. Such sites make it easy to determine who the sponsor is. But often, it isn't clear who sponsors a site, and in these cases, you should try to determine the sponsor before deciding whether to use the information. You can do this in several ways:

  - Check the Internet address, or URL, which can provide information about the site's sponsor.

  - Read the "About" page, which many web sites include and which often contains information about the site's sponsor.

  - Check the bottom of the home page, which often has copyright information about the site.

    If you cannot determine who sponsors the site, it is probably best not to use the information you find there.

- *What is the purpose of the site?* In the case of a recognizable web site, such as *USA Today* or a university web site, the purpose is usually very clear. But for less familiar sites, it's a good idea to try to get a sense of the site's purpose. Is it an informational site—for example, the site of a consumer advocacy group intended to provide consumers with information about certain kinds of products? Is its purpose to sell a product? Often, by exploring the site for a few moments, you can determine the site's general purpose, which can help you decide whether the information on the site is trustworthy.

- *Who is the author?* If you find an article or some other kind of document on a web site, look for the name of the author. Sometimes information about the author is included with the article (usually at the end), but if not, you can search the Internet to find out more about that author. Many articles and pages on web sites list no author; however, that isn't necessarily a problem because many organizations include material on their web sites that is produced by staff members, who are not always listed as authors. But if there is no author and you already have questions about the web site, you probably should be skeptical about using material from that site.

- *Is the web site current?* The web sites of news organizations, universities, and other reliable organizations are usually updated regularly, often daily. But many web sites are rarely, if ever, updated. That can be a problem if the information you find on that site relates to a topic of current interest. For example, if you are writing about problems in education in the United States, you should be wary of a web site that criticizes "recent" education reform efforts that occurred in the early 1990s. Check the bottom of the home page of a web site for a date. Most reliable web sites list the date when they were last updated. If there is no such date, don't assume the information on the site is current.

READING INTERNET ADDRESSES

The address of a web site is referred to as a URL (Uniform Resource Locator). You can often learn a lot from the address itself. The suffix of a URL conveys important information: *.com* means the web site is a commercial or business site; *.edu* means the site is an educational institution (university web sites end in *.edu,* for example); *.org* means the site is sponsored by a nongovernmental organization; *.gov* means it's a government web site. A site with an *.edu* suffix is likely to be relatively trustworthy because it is probably sponsored by a university or college. A *.org* site may also be trustworthy, but organizations sometimes have interests and agendas that might make you skeptical about the information included on the site. For example, a site for a political action committee might reflect a very conservative or liberal political viewpoint, which may affect the kind of information the site contains. A site for an environmental group is likely to favor information that supports its perspective. A *.com* site may mean that the site is a moneymaking venture, so information on the site may reflect the business's efforts to sell its products. Keep these things in mind when you're visiting web sites for your research.

- *Is there evidence of bias?* Sometimes it's easy to determine that a web site reflects a certain point of view. But often, bias is subtle. For example, White supremacist organizations have sponsored web sites about Martin Luther King, Jr. that seem credible at first glance. But a closer look reveals that these sites are intended to look like an objective resource about King's life while concealing their real purpose: to raise questions about King and his work and to convey misinformation about him. Even if a site seems credible, always check for signs of bias, especially if you are unfamiliar with the organization or person sponsoring the site.

- *Is the information on the web site accurate?* Even if a web site passes these other tests and seems trustworthy, you should still be cautious about trusting the information you find there if you know little about the site or its sponsors. It's a good idea to check the accuracy of the site by corroborating its information elsewhere. For example, if you're writing a paper about the Civil Rights Movement and you find a web site that contains historical information, check a few of the facts on that site by referring to a history book or similar reference

Cross-check w/ othe Sour ce

book or by visiting a web site that you know is trustworthy. You might, for instance, check the dates listed for Martin Luther King, Jr.'s life or information about the passage of the Voting Rights Act. Checking a few facts in this way can help you determine whether you can trust other information on the site.

INTERNET HOAXES

Hoaxes have become common on the Internet, but they're not always easy to identify.

Northeastern U.S. Power Outage Fake Image
This photograph (top right) began circulating on the Internet shortly after the power outage in the northeastern United States in August 2003 and was said to have been taken from a satellite during the power outage, but it was actually a hoax. Here The actual satellite photos are below.

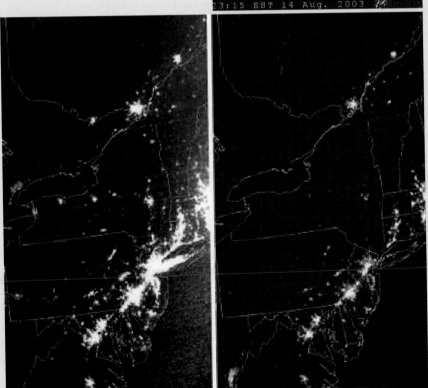

The lesson is clear: Be cautious about using information and materials you find on the Internet.

Other Source Material

Many of the exercises and assignments in this book ask you to write about topics that require you to look beyond the library and the Internet in your research. For example, an essay about a controversy surrounding a new big-box retail store proposed for your town may require you to talk to local officials and residents to get information and hear various points of view. The library or Internet might provide relevant information about similar controversies in other towns, but they may not have information about the specific situation in your town. For an assignment like this, your library or the Internet may not provide the information or material you need. You might need to interview people from the town or look at town records such as the minutes of town council meetings. It might also be a good idea to get information from organizations involved in the controversy (for example, an organization like the Sierra Club, which has opposed certain kinds of development). It's worth considering these three kinds of sources for writing assignments that you might not be able to complete using traditional sources.

Interviews

Interviewing is an art that can take many years to master, but here are a few guidelines to keep in mind if you do any interviewing:

- Carefully prepare your questions in advance. Create a list of the most important questions you want to ask. Try to keep your questions brief.

- Do your homework. Try to learn something about the person you're interviewing and about your topic so that you don't waste time asking about information you should already know.

- Allow the person to do most of the talking. The biggest mistake inexperienced interviewers make is talking too much.

- Take notes or use a tape recorder. If you use a tape recorder, be sure to ask the person for permission to do so.

- Check your information. Before leaving the interview, be sure to check important facts with the person and also check the spelling of important names you might use in your writing.

Public Records and Documents

For many writing assignments, the best information may be located in town, state, or federal documents. Often, these documents can only be found in a town, state, or federal building and may not be available on the Internet. If you need to examine such materials for your research, check with the appropriate office about how you can access the materials. Find out whether you can make photocopies of the documents, which can save time. For state or federal documents, this process can be time-consuming, so plan ahead.

Materials from Organizations

Let's say you are creating a web site about the loss of wetlands in your region and its effects on local wildlife populations. For such an assignment, it would be a good idea to search your library or the Internet for information about wetland loss in general. But for your local situation, there may be better sources, such as the local or state chapter of the Audubon Society or a similar environmental organization. Often, these organizations have publications, such as flyers or pamphlets, that they distribute to the public. They may also have reports about issues that concern them. Such documents may not be available in libraries or on the Internet, and the only way to get them may be through the organization itself. Usually, a phone call or e-mail is the best first step to find out what resources the organization has and how you can access them.

Citing Sources

If you use any kind of source for a writing assignment, you must cite that source. Citing a source means two things: (1) letting readers know that a quotation, an idea, or information in your text came from that source and (2) including information about that source in a bibliography or works cited page. There are different ways of citing sources, but one of the most common for most college writing assignments is MLA (Modern Language Association). Generally, MLA is used in the humanities (e.g., history, philosophy, English).

The following section includes some guidelines for citing common kinds of sources. (For complete guidelines, consult the *MLA Handbook for Writers of Research Papers*). Whichever style you use, keep in mind that the primary purposes of citing your sources properly are (1) to credit and document the source of your information and (2) to enable readers to find the source.

Parenthetical (In-Text) Citations Using MLA Style

A parenthetical citation tells a reader that you have cited a source. For example, let's say you're writing an essay about the popularity of mountain climbing, and you want to discuss some of the history of American mountaineering. You want to include in your essay the fact that there were five unsuccessful American attempts to climb K2, the world's second highest mountain, before the successful 1978 expedition—something you learned about on page 6 of a book called *The Last Step: The American Ascent of K2* by Rick Ridgeway. How would you use a parenthetical citation to cite your source?

- *Using In-Text MLA Parenthetical Citation Format.* Here's what a sentence citing information from Ridgeway's book might look like in your essay:

  ```
  Before the Americans finally climbed K2 in 1978, five previ-
  ous expeditions had failed to reach that mountain's elusive
  summit (Ridgeway 6).
  ```

- Notice that the parenthetical citation contains only the author's last name and the page reference with no punctuation between them. (Also notice that the parentheses are placed *inside* the final period of the sentence.) If you mention Ridgeway's name in your sentence, then you only have to include the page reference in parentheses:

  ```
  As famed mountaineer Rick Ridgeway explains in The Last
  Step: The American Ascent of K2, American climbers failed
  to reach K2's elusive summit in five previous attempts be-
  fore the successful American expedition in 1978 (6).
  ```

- This information tells a reader that you found this information on page 6 of Ridgeway's book. If the reader wants more information about that book, he or she will find it in your bibliography or works cited page. (Format for bibliographic or works cited entries is discussed in the next section.)

Here are some additional guidelines for parenthetical citations using MLA style:

- *In general, include the least amount of necessary information in parentheses.* If you can, include the author's name or the title of the work in your sentence, and place only the page reference in parentheses.

- *If the work you're citing has no listed author, include the title in parentheses.* Let's say you have a document called "Helping the Homeless" from the organization Habitat for Humanity. If you were using information from page 2 of that document, your parenthetical citation would look like this: ("Helping the Homeless" 2).

Compiling a Bibliography or Works Cited Page

If you cite a source in your paper, you should include a bibliography or works cited page. For example, let's return to our example of citing information from Rick Ridgeway's book in a paper about the popularity of mountaineering. Here's what the entry in your bibliography would look like in MLA style:

Ridgeway, Rick. <u>The Last Step: The American Ascent of K2</u>. Seattle: The

  Mountaineers, 1980.

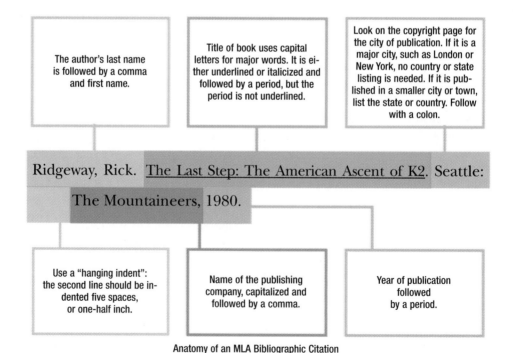

Anatomy of an MLA Bibliographic Citation

The basic information you need for a citation in a bibliography or works cited page is similar. When doing your research, therefore, be sure to record this information so that it is available when you begin compiling your bibliography. Also remember that your bibliography should be in alphabetical order regardless of which style you're using.

In the following sections, examples are provided for common kinds of sources in MLA format.

Sample MLA Citations
Printed Resources

1. **Book with One Author**

   Gibaldi, Joseph. <u>MLA Handbook for Writers of Research Projects</u>. 5th ed.

   New York: The Modern Language Association, 1999.

2. **Book with a Corporate Author**

   American Allergy Association. <u>Allergies in Children</u>. New York: Random

   House, 1998.

   Use this type of entry when the book wasn't written by an individual but was produced by an organization. In this case, the name of the organization is placed where the author's name would go.

3. **Book with Multiple Authors**

   Lowi, Theodore J., Benjamin Ginsberg, and Steve Jackson. <u>Analyzing</u>

   <u>American Government: American Government, Freedom and Power</u>.

   3rd ed. New York: Norton, 1994.

   If there are more than three authors, include only the first author's name and add *et al.*: Jones, Robert, et al.

4. **Article, Essay, or Story from an Anthology or Collection**

   Jackson, Shirley. "The Lottery." <u>The Norton Anthology of Literature by</u>

   <u>Women</u>. Ed. Sandra M. Gubar. New York: Norton, 1985. 1872–1880.

5. **Article from an Encyclopedia**

   Franklin, Mark N. "Voting Behavior." The <u>Encyclopedia of Democracy</u>.

   1995 ed. 782-783.

6. Magazine Article

Wallace, David Foster. "Host." <u>The Atlantic Monthly</u>. April 2005: 51–77.

7. Journal Article

Warner, Megan B., et al. "The Longitudinal Relationship of Personality

Traits and Disorders." <u>Journal of Abnormal Psychology</u> 113 (2004):

217–227.

The number that follows the title of journal is the volume number; the number in parentheses is the date of publication. The last numbers are the page numbers.

8. Newspaper Article

Gladstone, Valerie. "Shiva Meets Martha Graham, at a Very High Speed."

<u>New York Times</u> 10 Aug. 2003, New England ed., sec. 2: 3.

9. Personal Interview

Powers, Jonathan. Personal interview. 23 Feb. 1989.

Web or Other Computer Resources

1. Article, Essay, or Story from an Online Database

Edmondson, Elie A. "Martin Amis Writes Postmodern Man." <u>Critique</u> 42

(2001): 145. <u>Expanded Academic ASAP</u>. Gale Group Databases. SUNY

Oneonta Lib., Oneonta, NY. 13 Nov. 2003

<http://infotrac.galegroup.com>.

When you use a reference from an online database, you not only include the date of the publication but also the date you retrieved the source. Note that in MLA style, you also provide the name of the library from which you retrieved the information.

2. Entry in an Online Encyclopedia.

"Angelfish." <u>Microsoft Encarta Encyclopedia Online</u>. 2005. Microsoft Corp.

24 Jan. 2005 <http://encarta.msn.com/encyclopedia_761555978/

Angelfish.html>.

Notice that there is no author, so the title of the article is placed first.

3. **Newspaper Article from an Online Service or Database**

> Louv, Richard. "Reseeding Environmentalism." <u>The Oregonian</u> 27 Mar.
>
> 2005, sunrise edition, commentary forum: E01. <u>LexisNexis</u>. SUNY
>
> Oneonta Lib., Oneonta, NY. 9 Apr. 2005
>
> <http://www.lexis-nexis.com/universe>.

4. **Unsigned Article on a Web Site**

> "Aboard the Underground Railroad: A National Register Travel Itinerary."
>
> > National Park Service: Our Shared History African American Heritage.
> >
> > US Park Service. 12 Apr. 2005 <http://www.cr.nps.gov/nr/travel/
> >
> > underground/>.

Notice that in this example MLA style requires including the sponsor of the web site (in this case, the U.S. Park Service).

5. **Signed Personal Web Site**

> Nathanson, Betty. <u>Dejavu Standard Poodles</u>. 2 Feb. 2005 <http://
>
> community-2.webtv.net/bnathanson/dejavustandard/>.

6. **Personal E-mail**

> Stonebraker, Gabriel. Personal e-mail. 16 June 2005.

PART 2

Themes *for* Writing *and* Inquiring

HESE TWO HEADLINES APPEARED ON *THE NEW YORK TIMES* WEB SITE ON THE SAME DAY IN 2004:

"HISPANICS RESIST RACIAL GROUPING BY CENSUS"
"IDENTITY THEFT IS EPIDEMIC: CAN IT BE STOPPED?"

"Hispanics Resist Racial Grouping by Census" reported on a woman named Kathia Mendez, who was raised in the Dominican Republic, where she was known as an Indian, a term often used in that country to refer to people of mixed race who do not have indigenous roots. In the United States, however, Mendez is more likely considered Black or Hispanic. But when she filled out the U.S. Census Bureau's questionnaire, she checked the box for Some Other Race. "I'm not black and I'm not white; we don't define ourselves that way," she told the reporter.

> But when she filled out the U.S. Census Bureau's questionnaire, she checked the box for Some Other Race. "I'm not black and I'm not white; we don't define ourselves that way," she told the reporter.

Kathia Mendez is a good example of someone who doesn't seem to fall into the categories we use to describe racial or ethnic identity, and her situation helps reveal the complexities of such categories. Is she Hispanic because she is from a country where Spanish is spoken? Is she Black because of her skin color? Is she Indian because of her ethnic heritage? Is she Dominican because of where she was born? Is she American because she has been a resident of the United States for nine years? And would she be an "American" if she had remained in the Dominican Republic, which is also in the Americas? Such questions indicate how difficult it can be to pin down one's identity.

Reading about Mendez, I couldn't help thinking about a former student of mine named Donna who was born and raised in New York City but whose parents had immigrated to the United States from Haiti before she was born. In school, Donna was often described as African American, the term that many people prefer to Black. But Donna told me that her parents rejected the term African American. They considered themselves Black Americans, not African Americans, because they were from a Caribbean country, not from Africa. So they are Black, American, and Haitian, but not African American. Like Mendez, Donna helps us see that identity is a much more complicated matter than we might think, especially when we so casually use terms like African American or Hispanic. As these situations suggest, racial identity also has something to do with where we are born and where we live as well as with how we look and how we speak. Sorting out all these characteristics isn't always easy.

Stories like Mendez's also raise the question of why we even need such categories. Why is it important to describe someone as Black or White, Asian or Latina, European or Native American? And what are the consequences of being categorized in these ways? As the readings in this chapter reveal, how we categorize one another does matter—often in very obvious ways, such as when certain groups of people are denied the rights available to other groups, as has been the case with Black Americans, Native Americans, Asian Americans, women, and other groups in the United States for much of its history. And consider that many people like Kathia Mendez, who have been categorized as Hispanic, have been opposed to a U.S. government proposal to eliminate the category of Some Other Race from the U.S. Census. These people argue that none of the other categories used by the Census Bureau accurately describes who they are. This is not just a matter of words because the decision by the Census Bureau about this category will directly affect the lives of millions of Americans by influencing government decisions about issues like education funding and various kinds of government benefits. Identity matters.

But identity is about more than race and ethnicity. It's also about gender, sexual orientation, age, social class, and national origin. It's about religious background and belief: We can be Muslim, Christian, Hindu, Jewish, Buddhist, atheist. It can be about political ideology: conservative, liberal, socialist, libertarian, anarchist. It's about the roles we play in our families and communities: mother, daughter, father, son, uncle, neighbor. It's also about the activities we take part in that help define who we are: student, teacher, writer, doctor, climber, athlete, activist, social worker, carpenter. And it can also be about the choices we make as consumers, including financial and business transactions that are increasingly shaped by new technologies that make it possible to steal someone's identity.

The very idea of identity theft seems odd. After all, your identity is yours. It's unique, isn't it? How can someone steal your identity? According to the *New York Times* article mentioned earlier, "Identity Theft Is Epidemic: Can It Be Stopped?", in our consumer-oriented society identity is often a matter of numbers: your Social Security number, bank account numbers, driver's license number, credit card account numbers. These numbers are, in a sense, who you are when it comes to things like buying a car, getting a loan, renting an apartment, or saving money from your paycheck in a bank account. They are your identity. And they can be stolen and used by someone else. This kind of theft has become a multibillion dollar problem in recent years as more and more important financial transactions are conducted through electronic means, including the Internet. It's another reminder not only that our identities are important but also that they are shaped by a variety of complex factors, including technology.

This chapter explores the complexity of identity. Each of the three clusters looks at identity from a different angle. The first cluster asks you to think about the many different ways we define ourselves, offering three different perspectives on what it means to claim an identity for yourself. The second cluster shifts the focus to how others define us and what the consequences of those definitions might be. And the third cluster explores the idea that each of us can have more than one identity.

I hope all of the clusters prompt you to think about how we use common categories, such as race, class, gender, ethnicity, sexual preference, and nationality, to define ourselves and each other. In a sense, in creating this chapter, I simply rearranged categories of identity that we already use. But of course, I couldn't really avoid

> After all, your identity is yours. It's unique, isn't it? How can someone steal your identity?

those categories because they have become so deeply ingrained in our thinking about ourselves and each other. They have become powerful lenses through which we see and understand each other. And that's part of the point of this chapter: to help you look more closely at the categories we so often use without often thinking about what they really mean. I also wanted to organize this chapter in a way that might call your attention to how artificial yet powerful our ways of defining each other can be. Most important, what I hope you'll see in this chapter are the interesting ways in which writers work within and against these categories to help us understand ourselves. As you read through the selections in this chapter, pay attention to how writing itself enables these authors to define themselves—and consider how your own writing and reading define you.

CREATING OUR SELVES

HAVE YOU EVER HEARD SOMEONE TALKING ABOUT HOW SHE "FOUND HERSELF"? OR PERHAPS YOU'VE HEARD SOMEONE DESCRIBING A TIME IN HIS LIFE WHEN HE DIDN'T KNOW WHO HE WAS. IT'S A RELATIVELY COMMON WAY OF TALKING ABOUT HOW PEOPLE CAN COME TO A

new understanding of themselves. for a long time, though, i was puzzled by such talk. how could you not know who you are? how do you find yourself? Where were you before you found yourself? The question of who you are seemed simple, even silly, to me. You are who you are. Aren't you?

Well, yes and no. Think about it like this: Are you the same person at school as you are at home or at work or with a group of your closest friends? Do you just act differently in each of these settings? Or are you somehow a different person in each of these settings? My guess is that your answer to these questions is something like, well, yes and no. You probably have a sense of yourself that stays pretty much the same no matter where you are or what you're doing. But I'd bet that if you spoke to the different people you interact with in different settings—your coworkers, your family members, your classmates, your neighbors—you might be surprised to find out that these different people think somewhat differently about "who you are." In some ways, you are always you. But your identity is not necessarily constant. It can relate to the different roles you have in your life (such as daughter or son, student, professional, friend) and the different contexts in which you live your life (work, home, school, community). And in each of these situations, you have some control over who you are. In other words, to some extent, you can "create" your self.

If this all sounds too abstract or fuzzy, the reading selections in this cluster may help to make it more concrete. For example, Sojourner Truth, a Black American activist for women's rights in the nineteenth century, poses a seemingly straightforward question in her famous speech: "Ain't I a Woman?" As you'll see, the answer to this question is not as simple as it seems. Of course, she's a woman. But what exactly did that mean when women were not allowed to vote, when they were not allowed to own property in many re-

gions, when they were seen as inferior to men? In asking that question, Sojourner Truth begins to create a new way of defining what it means to be a woman. She creates a new kind of female self, one that challenges the conventional way of understanding who a woman is. In the same way, the other authors in this cluster call our attention to how we define ourselves. They challenge us to reexamine our familiar ways of thinking about identity—about what it means to be a Native American or a rural dweller or a woman or whomever. They help us see that we can indeed create ourselves, but we don't do so in isolation and we don't have complete control over our identities.

There is both power and risk in this ability to create ourselves. Some aspects of our identities may seem out of our control, such as our sex. But how we define sex or gender and what those definitions mean to others can make all the difference, as Sojourner Truth encourages us to see in her speech. Yes, she is a woman, but she wants to define that identity in a certain kind of way, despite the fact that others may define it differently. Thus, the effort to create a self is always a kind of struggle between how we as individuals understand our identities and how others do. As you read the selections in this cluster, consider how these authors deal with that struggle.

Consider, too, how the very act of writing is an act of creating a self. N. Scott Momaday may be Kiowa, for example, because he was born with that racial and ethnic identity, but he also creates a certain kind of self as a Kiowa in writing his essay about Rainy Mountain. Through the act of writing, he claims a certain way of understanding who he is as a Kiowa. And the same is true of the other authors. Each uses writing as a way to imagine their identities and to present themselves to us. I hope they help you see that you engage in the same act of self-creation whenever you write.

In 1851, the following address was delivered by a former slave named Sojourner Truth (1797–1883) to the Women's Rights Convention in Akron, Ohio. By that time, Truth was a famous abolitionist and activist for women's rights. The previous year, a book by Oliver Gilbert titled The Narrative of Sojourner Truth, *based on Gilbert's interviews with Truth, was published, and it brought national attention to Truth. It told the story of a domestic servant*

Ain't I A Woman?

named Isabella who in 1843 changed her name, left her work and her home, and journeyed through the country preaching about God's salvation. Over time, she began to speak out forcefully about women's voting rights, the abolition of slavery, and social justice. Along with her fame came controversy, and accounts of her 1851 speech in Ohio suggest that some of the convention's organizers did not want her to speak, fearing that her presence would negatively influence public opinion about their efforts to gain the right to vote for women. But Truth did speak, and Frances Gage, one of the convention leaders, recorded Truth's words. The speech has become a classic American expression of women's rights. And it has helped make Sojourner Truth a symbol of the struggle for equality and justice.

But controversy remains. There is some question about the accuracy of Gage's text. Truth did not read or write, so there was no "official" version of her speech. And some newspaper accounts at the time contradict Gage's text. But it is Gage's text that has become the accepted version of Truth's speech, and it is worth thinking about why. In other words, what is it about this version of Sojourner Truth's speech that seems to touch people even today? What does (continued)

SOJOURNER TRUTH

Well, children, where there is so much racket there must be something out of kilter. I think that 'twixt the negroes of the South and the women at the North, all talking about rights, the white men will be in a fix pretty soon. But what's all this here talking about?

That man over there says that women need to be helped into carriages, and lifted over ditches, and to have the best place everywhere. Nobody ever helps me into carriages, or over mud-puddles, or gives me any best place! And ain't I a woman? Look at me! Look at my arm! I have ploughed and planted, and gathered into barns, and no man could head me! And ain't I a woman? I could work as much and eat as much as a man—when I could get it—and bear the lash as well! And ain't I a woman? I have borne thirteen children, and seen most all sold off to slavery, and when I cried out with my mother's grief, none but Jesus heard me! And ain't I a woman?

Then they talk about **this thing in the head;** what's this they call it? [member of audience whispers, "intellect"] That's it, honey. What's that got to do with women's rights or negroes' rights? If my cup won't hold but a pint, and yours holds a quart, wouldn't you be mean not to let me have my little half measure full?

SOJOURNER TRUTH, "AIN'T I A WOMAN?" (1851).

(continued) *this speech say about what it means to be a woman? What does it say about the importance of claiming the right to define "woman" in a certain way—or claiming the right to define any kind of identity? And does it matter that this version of the speech may not be exactly what Sojourner Truth said in 1851?* ◩

STRATEGIES: THIS "THING" AN INTELLECT
In this part of her speech (par. 3), Sojourner Truth seems to forget the word for *intellect*. It's possible that she may have genuinely forgotten the word for "this thing in the head." It may also be that this is just the way Frances Gage, the person who wrote down the speech, re-membered it. But it's also possible that Truth may have feigned not knowing the word *intellect*. If that were true, what might her purpose have been? What point might she have been making by pretend-ing to forget the word for intellect?

CONVERSATIONS: WOMEN'S RIGHTS
When she gave this now-famous speech in 1851, Sojourner Truth was actively engaged in a national movement to help women gain the right to vote in the United States. It might surprise you that the struggle for women's voting rights continued for nearly sev-enty years after Truth's speech until 1920, when the U.S. Congress passed the Nineteenth Amendment, extending the right to vote to all women. But that didn't end the movement for women's rights. It continued through the twentieth century and gained momentum in the 1970s and 1980s, when activists were proposing the Equal Rights Amendment to the U.S. Constitution, which would extend women's rights beyond voting into other areas of law, including employment and taxation. Perhaps it isn't surprising that Sojourner Truth has once again become a revered figure for women's rights. Her famous 1851 speech has become part of the ongoing conversations about women's rights and social justice today. Consider what this speech, delivered when it was illegal for women to vote, might contribute to that conversation.

Then that little man in black there, he says women can't have as much rights as men, 'cause Christ wasn't a woman! Where did your Christ come from? Where did your Christ come from? From God and a woman! Man had nothing to do with Him.

If the first woman God ever made was strong enough to turn the world upside down all alone, these women together ought to be able to turn it back, and get it right side up again! And now they is asking to do it, the men better let them.

Obliged to you for hearing me, and now old Sojourner ain't got nothing more to say.

UNDERSTANDING THE TEXT

1. What is Sojourner Truth's definition of *woman,* based on her words in this speech?

2. What main arguments does Truth make in favor of women's rights? Do you find these arguments convincing? Why or why not?

3. What evidence does Truth offer to support her view of women? What do you think her evidence suggests about her beliefs and values?

EXPLORING THE ISSUES

1. This speech was originally delivered at a women's rights convention in 1851. In what ways did Sojourner Truth address her speech to that specific audience? How effectively do you think she addressed that audience? Why do you think her words still have an impact on readers today?

2. In her speech, Truth used common language to make a point about a very complex issue—namely, how women were understood in a White, male-dominated society. In what ways do you think her use of common language influences her message? Do you find this kind of language effective in this case? Why or why not?

3. Sojourner Truth makes an argument in favor of women's rights. Evaluate her argument. How effectively do you think she makes her case in this very brief speech? How persuasively does she support her case? Do you think her main points are still valid today? Explain.

ENTERING THE CONVERSATIONS

1. Drawing on Sojourner Truth's speech and any other relevant text, write an essay in which you define *woman.*

2. Rewrite Truth's speech for a contemporary audience.

Suffragettes Picketing outside Jail, 1917

Suffragettes during March for the Vote, 1912

INFOTRAC

3. Using InfoTrac College Edition and any other relevant sources, explore the history of the women's rights movement in the United States. Find out more about the movement to gain voting rights for women in the late nineteenth and early twentieth centuries, and look into the more recent women's movements in the late twentieth century. What were the key events of these movements? What obstacles did they face? What were the main arguments made on behalf of women's rights? Then write a report in which you discuss what you learned in your research. Alternatively, create a web site based on your research.

4. These photographs were taken in 1912 and 1917, a few years before the Nineteenth Amendment was passed, which gave women in the United States the legal right to vote. Examine what these photographs might reveal about the women's rights movement in the early twentieth century. What ideas do you think these photographs communicate? What do the photos emphasize? What's missing? What do the photos suggest about the *suffragettes,* the term used to describe the women who fought for women's rights? Write an essay in which you analyze the messages in these photographs.

Where you are born can be a big part of your identity. I remember the first time I began to realize this. I grew up near the Pocono Mountains of northeastern Pennsylvania and then lived for several years in northern New England before moving to Ohio. During my first winter in Ohio, I felt a subtle homesickness that I assumed was just a result of missing my family and friends. But the feeling became intense one day when I was looking at photographs from Vermont. I

THE Way TO *Rainy* Mountain

kept coming back to one photograph of a very ordinary scene of an empty, snow-covered farm field on a low hillside. The photo had been taken in Vermont, but the scene could have been almost anywhere in the northeastern United States. It suddenly occurred to me that what was so powerful about the photograph was that it showed the typical landscape I had lived in for so many years. I had become so accustomed to that landscape that I almost didn't notice it—until I left. And I missed it almost in the same way I missed family and friends. That landscape is in some ways a part of who I am.

In the following essay, N. Scott Momaday (b. 1934) writes about that same kind of connection to a place. But perhaps in some ways, Momaday, a Native American, describes a deeper connection to the land than I could understand. He describes the central importance of place not only to his own identity as an individual but to the identity of his people as a whole. Whereas my ancestors left their native Poland to immigrate to the United States, Momaday's ancestors, like so many other Native Americans, were forced from their homeland and had to abandon the land they identified with as well as their lifestyle. In that (continued)

N. SCOTT MOMADAY

A single knoll rises out of the plain in Oklahoma, north and west of the Wichita range. For my people, the Kiowas, it is an old landmark, and they gave it the name Rainy Mountain. The hardest weather in the world is there. Winter brings blizzards, hot tornadic winds arise in the spring, and in summer the prairie is an anvil's edge. The grass turns brittle and brown, and it cracks beneath your feet. There are green belts along the rivers and creeks, linear groves of hickory and pecan, willow and witch hazel. At a distance in July or August the steaming foliage seems almost to writhe in fire. Great green and yellow grasshoppers are everywhere in the tall grass, popping up like corn to sting the flesh, and tortoises crawl about on the red earth, going nowhere in the plenty of time. Loneliness is an aspect of the land. All things in the plain are isolate; there is no confusion of objects in the eye, but *one* hill or *one* tree or *one* man. To look upon that landscape in the early morning, with the sun at your back, is to lose the sense of proportion. Your imagination comes to life, and this, you think, is where Creation was begun.

I returned to Rainy Mountain in July. My grandmother had died in

N. SCOTT MOMADAY, "THE WAY TO RAINY MOUNTAIN" FROM *THE REPORTER* (1967). REPRINTED BY PERMISSION OF UNIVERSITY OF NEW MEXICO PRESS.

(continued) *regard, their very identity was threatened. As you read, consider the role that* place *plays in Momaday's sense of himself as a person and especially as a Native American. It might help to think about your own sense of connection to a specific place—your birthplace, for example— as you read Momaday's description of Rainy Mountain.*

Born to a Kiowa father and a mother who was part Cherokee, N. Scott Momaday is the author of several books of poetry, a Pulitzer Prize–winning novel, and a collection of Kiowa legends called The Way to Rainy Mountain *(1969), in which the following essay first appeared.* ▼

STRATEGIES: DESCRIBING A PLACE
Notice the physical details Momaday uses in the opening paragraph to convey a sense of the region in Oklahoma where Rainy Mountain is located. Notice, too, that he uses the second person (you) near the end of the paragraph. Consider how that strategy helps him convey a sense of what it is like to be at Rainy Mountain. If you have ever been to the high plains of western Oklahoma or similar places, such as western Nebraska or eastern Colorado, you might consider whether Momaday's description matches your own sense of those places. If you haven't been to such places, how effectively does Momaday's description help you understand what it might be like to be at Rainy Mountain? Also think about how Momaday uses the descriptions in this essay to communicate his ideas about place and about who he is.

the spring, and I wanted to be at her grave. She had lived to be very old and at last infirm. Her only living daughter was with her when she died, and I was told that in death her face was that of a child.

I like to think of her as a child. When she was born, the Kiowas were living the last great moment of their history. For more than a hundred years they had controlled the open range from the Smoky Hill River to the Red, from the headwaters of the Canadian to the fork of the Arkansas and Cimarron. In alliance with the Comanches, they had ruled the whole of the Southern Plains. War was their sacred business, and they were the finest horsemen the world has ever known. But warfare for the Kiowas was pre-eminently a matter of disposition rather than of survival, and they never understood the grim, unrelenting advance of the U.S. Cavalry. When at last, divided and ill provisioned, they were driven onto the Staked Plains in the cold of autumn, they fell into panic. In Palo Duro Canyon they abandoned their crucial stores to pillage and had nothing then but their lives. In order to save themselves, they surrendered to the soldiers at Fort Sill and were imprisoned in the old stone corral that now stands as a military museum. My grandmother was spared the humiliation of those high gray walls by eight or ten years, but she must have known from birth the affliction of defeat, the dark brooding of old warriors.

Her name was Aho, and she belonged to the last culture to evolve in North America. Her forebears came down from the high country in western Montana nearly three centuries ago. They were a mountain people, a mysterious tribe of hunters whose language has never been classified in any major group. In the late seventeenth century they began a long migration to the south and east. It was a journey toward the dawn, and it led to a golden age. Along the way the Kiowas were befriended by the Crows, who gave them the culture and religion of the Plains. They acquired horses, and their ancient nomadic spirit was suddenly free of the ground. They acquired Tai-me, the sacred sun-dance doll, from that moment the object and symbol of their worship, and so shared in the divinity of the sun. Not least, they acquired the sense of destiny, therefore courage and pride. When they entered upon the Southern Plains they had been transformed. No longer were they slaves to the simple necessity of survival; they were a lordly and dangerous society of fighters and thieves, hunters and priests of the sun. According to their origin myth, they entered the world through a hollow log. From one point of view, their migration was the fruit of an old prophecy, for indeed they emerged from a sunless world.

Though my grandmother lived out her long life in the shadow of Rainy Mountain, the immense landscape of the continental interior lay like memory in her blood. She could tell of the Crows, whom she had never seen, and of the Black Hills, where she had never been. I wanted to see in reality what she had seen more perfectly in the mind's eye, and drove fifteen hundred miles to begin my pilgrimage.

Yellowstone, it seemed to me, was the top of the world, a region of deep lakes and dark timber, canyons and waterfalls. But, beautiful as it is, one might have the sense of confinement there. The skyline in all directions is close at hand, the high wall of the woods and the deep cleavages of shade. There is a perfect freedom in the mountains, but it belongs to the eagle and the elk, the badger and the bear. The Kiowas reckoned their stature by the distance they could see, and they were bent and blind in the wilderness.

Descending eastward, the highland meadows are a stairway to the plain. In July the inland slope of the Rockies is luxuriant with flax and buckwheat, stonecrop and larkspur. The earth unfolds and the limit of the land recedes. Clusters of trees, the animals grazing far in the distance, cause the vision to reach away and wonder to build upon the mind. The sun follows a longer course in the day, and the sky is immense beyond all comparison. The great billowing clouds that sail upon it are shadows that move upon the grain like water, dividing light. Farther down, in the land of the Crows and the Blackfeet, the plain is yellow. Sweet clover takes hold of the hills and bends upon itself to cover and seal the soil. There the Kiowas paused on their way; they had to come to the place where they must change their lives. The sun is at home on the plains. Precisely there does it have the certain character of a god. When the Kiowas came to the land of the Crows, they could see the dark lees of the hills at dawn across the Bighorn River, the profusion of light on the grain shelves, the oldest deity ranging after the solstices. Not yet would they veer southward to the cauldron of the land that lay below; they must wean their blood from the northern winter and hold the mountains a while longer in their view. They bore Tai-me in procession to the seat.

A dark mist lay over the Black Hills, and the land was like iron. At the top of a ridge I caught sight of **Devil's Tower** upthrust against the gray sky as if in the birth of time the core of the earth had broken through its crust and the motion of the world was begun.

CONTEXT: DEVIL'S TOWER

This distinctive landmark in eastern Wyoming became the first U.S. national monument in 1906. It has long been considered a special place by Native Americans, and the Kiowa legend about its origins that Momaday relates in this paragraph conveys a sense of that importance. But it is also a tourist destination as well as a world-famous rock-climbing area. In the past few decades, there has been some controversy when Native American tribes have asked the U.S. Park Service to close Devil's Tower to climbers during religious rituals that some tribes hold there in June. Although Momaday wrote this essay many years before this controversy emerged, his depiction of Devil's Tower helps give us a sense of why conflict exists over what happens there. For many Native Americans, it is a sacred place; for many rock climbers, it is a world-class recreational destination. Who should determine which uses of Devil's Tower take precedence? And what might such a controversy suggest about the different ways that people relate to the land?

© Raymond Gehman/Corbis

Devil's Tower

There are things in nature that engender an awful quiet in the heart of man; Devil's Tower is one of them. Two centuries ago, because of their need to explain it, the Kiowas made a legend at the base of the rock. My grandmother said:

> "Eight children were there at play, seven sisters and their brother. Suddenly the boy was struck dumb; he trembled and began to run upon his hands and feet. His fingers became claws, and his body was covered with fur. There was a bear where the boy had been. The sisters were terrified; they ran, and the bear after them. They came to the stump of a great tree, and the tree spoke to them. It bade them climb upon it, and as they did so, it began to rise into the air. The bear came to kill them, but they were just beyond its reach. It reared against the tree and scored the bark all around with its claws. The seven sisters were borne into the sky, and they became the stars of the Big Dipper."

From that moment, and so long as the legend lives, the Kiowas have kinsmen in the night sky. Whatever they were in the mountains, they could be no more. However tenuous their well-being, however much they had suffered and would suffer again, they had found a way out of the wilderness.

My grandmother had a reverence for the sun, a holy regard that now is all but gone   10
out of mankind. There was a wariness in her, and an ancient awe. She was a Christian in her later years, but she had come a long way about, and she never forgot her birthright. As a child she had been to **the sun dances;** she had taken part in that annual rite, and by it she had learned the restoration of her people in the presence of Tai-me. She was about seven when the last Kiowa sun dance was held in 1887 on the Washita River above Rainy Mountain Creek. The buffalo were gone. In order to consummate the ancient sacrifice—to impale the head of a buffalo bull upon the Tai-me tree—a delegation of old men journeyed into Texas, there to beg and barter for an animal from the Goodnight herd. She was ten when the Kiowas came together for the last time as a living sun-dance culture. They could find no buffalo; they had to hang an old hide from the sacred tree. Before the dance could begin, a company of soldiers rode out from Fort Sill under orders to disperse the tribe. Forbidden without cause the essential act of their faith, having seen the wild herds slaughtered and left to rot upon the ground, the Kiowas backed away forever from the tree. That was July 20, 1890, at the great bend of the Washita. My grandmother was there. Without bitterness, and for as long as she lived, she bore a vision of deicide.

GLOSS: THE SUN DANCE
Usually performed during the summer solstice, the sun dance was an important religious ritual of self-sacrifice and renewal among many of the Native American tribes of the Plains, including the Kiowas. During the ceremony, men seeking to cleanse themselves spiritually for the good of the tribe would fast, dance, pray, and have their chests or backs pierced in a way that resulted in their being suspended by their flesh to attain a trancelike state of purity. When the U.S. Army took control of Native American lands during the nineteenth century, it often banned the ritual.

Now that I can have her only in memory, I see my grandmother in the several postures that were peculiar to her: standing at the wood stove on a winter morning and turning meat in a great iron skillet; sitting at the south window, bent above her beadwork, and afterwards, when her vision failed, looking down for a long time into the fold of her hands; going out upon a cane, very slowly as she did when the weight of age came upon her; praying. I remember her most often at prayer. She made long, rambling prayers out of suffering and hope, having seen many things. I was never sure that I had the right to hear, so exclusive were they of all mere custom and company. The last time I saw her she prayed standing by the side of her bed at night,

STRATEGIES: DESCRIPTION AND THEME
Paragraph 12 is a good example of how a
writer can use description to do more
than just provide readers with an image
of a place or a thing. In this paragraph,
Momaday shifts abruptly from his memories of his grandmother in the previous
paragraphs to a description of houses on
the plains. But this description seems
different from descriptions earlier in the
essay of the various places Momaday
has visited, such as Yellowstone or the
Black Hills. Is it different? If so, in what
way? What idea or point do you think
Momaday is trying to convey through this
description?

naked to the waist, the light of a kerosene lamp moving upon her dark skin. Her long black hair, always drawn and braided in the day, lay upon her shoulders and against her breasts like a shawl. I do not speak Kiowa, and I never understood her prayers, but there was something inherently sad in the sound, some merest hesitation upon the syllables of sorrow. She began in a high and descending pitch, exhausting her breath to silence; then again and again—and always the same intensity of effort, of something that is, and is not, like urgency in the human voice. Transported so in the dancing light among the shadows of her room, she seemed beyond the reach of time. But that was illusion; I think I knew then that I should not see her again.

Houses are like sentinels in the plain, old keepers of the weather watch. There, in a very little while, wood takes on the appearance of great age. All colors wear soon away in the wind and rain, and then the wood is burned gray and the grain appears and the nails turn red with rust. The window panes are black and opaque; you imagine there is nothing within, and indeed there are many ghosts, bones given up to the land. They stand here and there against the sky, and you approach them for a longer time than you expect. They belong in the distance; it is their domain.

Once there was a lot of sound in my grandmother's house, a lot of coming and going, feasting and talk. The summers there were full of excitement and reunion. The Kiowas are a summer people; they abide the cold and keep to themselves, but when the season turns and the land becomes warm and vital they cannot hold still; an old love of going returns upon them. The aged visitors who came to my grandmother's house when I was a child were made of lean and leather, and they bore themselves upright. They wore great black hats and bright ample shirts that shook in the wind. They rubbed fat upon their hair and wound their braids with strips of colored cloth. Some of them painted their faces and carried the scars of old and cherished enmities. They were an old council of warlords, come to remind and be reminded of who they were. Their wives and daughters served them well. The women might indulge themselves; gossip was at once the mark and compensation of their servitude. They made loud and elaborate talk among themselves, full of jest and gesture, fright and false alarm. They went abroad in fringed and flowered shawls, bright beadwork and German silver. They were at home in the kitchen, and they prepared meals that were banquets.

There were frequent prayer meetings, and nocturnal feasts. When I was a child I played with my cousins outside, where the lamplight fell upon the ground and the singing of the old people rose up around us and carried away into the darkness. There were a lot of good things to eat, a lot of laughter and surprise. And afterwards, when the quiet returned, I lay down with my grandmother and could hear the frogs away by the river and feel the motion of the air.

15   Now there is a funereal silence in the rooms, the endless wake of some final word. The walls have closed in upon my grandmother's house. When I returned to it in mourning, I saw for the first time in my life how small it was. It was late at night, and there was a white moon, nearly full. I sat for a long time on the stone steps by the kitchen door. From there I could see out across the land; I could see the long row of trees by the creek, the low light upon the rolling plains, and the stars of the Big

Dipper. Once I looked at the moon and caught sight of a strange thing. A cricket had perched upon the handrail, only a few inches away. My line of vision was such that the creature filled the moon like a fossil. It had gone there, I thought, to live and die, for there, of all places, was its small definition made whole and eternal. A warm wind rose up and purled like the longing within me.

The next morning, I awoke at dawn and went out on the dirt road to Rainy Mountain. It was already hot, and the grasshoppers began to fill the air. Still, it was early in the morning, and birds sang out of the shadows. The long yellow grass on the mountain shone in the bright light, and a scissortail hied above the land. There, where it ought to be, at the end of a long and legendary way, was my grandmother's grave. She had at last succeeded to that holy ground. Here and there on the dark stones were ancestral names. Looking back once, I saw the mountain and came away.

VISUAL CONNECTIONS: BEING AN INDIAN
In many ways, Momaday's essay is about what it means to be an Indian. Consider what this advertisement from the American Indian College Fund says about being an Indian. In what ways do you think the ad relies on stereotypes of Indians to convey its point? Also consider whether the view of Indians suggested by this advertisement is similar to or different from Momaday's view.

American Indian College Fund Advertisement

UNDERSTANDING THE TEXT

1. Momaday writes that he returned to Rainy Mountain when his grandmother died. What significance does he see in his grandmother's life? What does he mean when he writes that "the immense landscape of the continental interior lay like memory in her blood"? What "pilgrimage" does his grandmother's death prompt Momaday to make? Why is this pilgrimage important to him?

2. What do we learn about the history of the Kiowa people in this essay? Why is this history important to Momaday? What purpose do you think it serves in this essay and in helping Momaday convey a sense of his identity?

3. At the conclusion of this essay, Momaday has returned to his grandmother's house near Rainy Mountain. Why do you think he focuses on that specific place? What importance does that house have for him? What connection does he see between that house and the larger landscape of the Plains where his people once lived? What do you think that connection might suggest about his sense of himself as a Native American?

EXPLORING THE ISSUES

1. Periodically in this essay, Momaday includes information about the history of the Kiowas as well as other Native American tribes. What sense of the Kiowas as a people does he convey through this information? What are the Kiowas like based on Momaday's descriptions of them? In what ways are their characteristics related to the land where they live? What point do you think Momaday is making about the importance of the land in our sense of identity?

2. What event or events does Momaday use to organize his essay? Why do you think he organizes the essay in this way? How effectively do you think this way of organizing the essay helps him convey his ideas?

3. In many ways, Momaday's essay is not only about a sense of place but also about a sense of time. How does Momaday use time in this essay? What role does the past play in his understanding of himself? What is the relationship between the past and the present for him? Do you think the sense of time that he conveys is universal, or does it apply only to Native Americans? Explain.

4. Compare the descriptions in the first and last paragraphs of this essay. In what ways do you think they are similar? In what ways are they different? What do you think Momaday means when he writes in the very last sentence of this essay that he "saw the mountain and came away"? What main point do you think he wishes to convey with that final sentence?

ENTERING THE CONVERSATIONS

1. Write an essay in which you describe a place that is important to you. Like Momaday, try to convey a sense of that importance through your descriptions of that place, and include any historical or background information that you think your readers will need to help them understand the importance of that place.

2. Write an essay for an audience of your classmates about an important memory you have of a family member or of your family in general.

3. In a group of classmates, share the essays you wrote for Question 2. Discuss the significance of the memories that each of you has written about. What might these essays suggest about the importance of memory to our sense of self?

4. Using the Internet and relevant sources at your library, find photographs or other illustrations that you think would be appropriate for Momaday's essay. Select these images so that they not only illustrate the landscape that Momaday describes but also communicate what you believe are his main points about the importance of the land and the connections between the land and one's identity. Then use the images you have selected to make a photo essay or a web site. In other words, try to create a visual version of Momaday's words. Alternatively, create a visual document representing a place that is important to your identity.

INFOTRAC

5. Using InfoTrac College Edition, the Internet, and any other relevant sources, examine a controversy over the use of a specific place, such as Devil's Tower (see *Context: Devil's Tower* on page 72). In recent years, as development has occurred in many places that were once considered wilderness, such controversies have become increasingly common. If possible, focus on such a controversy in the region where you live. Try to find out what the focus of the controversy is and how it has developed over time. Try to understand the arguments of all sides in the controversy. Then write a report based on your research. In your report, provide sufficient background and present the main arguments in the controversy. Draw conclusions about the importance of place on the basis of what you have learned about this controversy.

This essay offers a twist on the old saying *that you are what you eat. Award-winning fiction writer Bobbie Ann Mason (b. 1940) recalls growing up in rural Kentucky in the 1950s, and she focuses our attention on the food that her family ate. For Mason, her family's diet was a reflection of their rural identity. And that diet was not just about nutrition and health. It was also about social status, and it was central to Mason's sense of herself. But as she tells us in this*

Being Country

passage, she wasn't entirely happy about it. In sharing these memories, Mason addresses old questions about the relationship between our identities and the places where we live, but she also reminds us that our attitudes toward place are complicated by prevailing ideas about social class and geographical regions. For example, as a young girl, Mason felt that being "country" meant being backward and somehow having less status than people from the nearby town with its "centers of pleasure," including places to shop and eat and be entertained. Those places seemed more glamorous to Mason than her country life. It's worth thinking about whether that difference between city and country might have changed since Mason's childhood in the 1950s. Do the city and the country still represent what they once did? Do they still matter in our identities as they seem to have mattered to Mason when she was young?

Bobbie Ann Mason has enjoyed much acclaim for her fiction, especially for her collection of short stories Shiloh and Other Stories *(1983) and her novel* In Country *(1984). The following essay originally appeared in* Clear Springs: A Memoir *(1999).* ▼

BOBBIE ANN MASON

One day Mama and Granny were shelling beans and talking about the proper method of drying apples. I was nearly eleven and still entirely absorbed with the March girls in *Little Women*. Drying apples was not in my dreams. Beth's death was weighing darkly on me at that moment, and I threw a little tantrum—what Mama called a hissy fit.

"Can't y'all talk about anything but food?" I screamed.

There was a shocked silence. "Well, what else is there?" Granny asked.

Granny didn't question a woman's duties, but I did. I didn't want to be hulling beans in a hot kitchen when I was fifty years old. I wanted to *be* somebody, maybe an airline stewardess. Also, I had been listening to the radio. I had notions.

Our lives were haunted by the fear of crop failure. We ate as if we didn't know where our next meal might come from. All my life I have had a recurrent food dream: I face a buffet or cafeteria line, laden with beautiful foods. I spend the entire dream choosing the foods I

The Simple Life, with Paris Hilton and Nicole Ritchie

CONVERSATIONS: THE CITY AND THE COUNTRY
Reading this passage, I couldn't help thinking of the old fable about the city mouse and the country mouse. In that fable, a mouse from the city and a mouse from the country visit each other's homes and each learns to appreciate his home. The fable may tell us something about the longstanding tensions between city life and country life in Western culture. For most of its history, the United States was largely a rural nation. According to the U.S. Census Bureau, before 1920, most of the population lived in rural areas. In 1990, however, more than 75 percent of Americans were city dwellers. Not everyone agrees that these changes represent progress, and many scholars, artists, and critics have examined the relative benefits and drawbacks to a nation defined by cities rather than by a more rural existence. Examine how Mason presents this contrast between the city and the country. In what ways does Mason's depiction of each depend on stereotypes about the city and the country? How does Mason challenge those stereotypes? Consider, too, how the stereotypes might be part of the larger conversations in our society about city and country. For example, in 2003, a new television series called *The Simple Life* focused on two wealthy women from the city who take up a rural lifestyle. How might this image from that show draw on, challenge, or reinforce stereotypes about city and country? Or consider the two photographs on the facing page by Peter Menzel, who traveled the world photographing people with all their possessions. What do these two photographs suggest about city and rural life?

want. My anticipation is deliciously agonizing. I always wake up just as I've made my selections but before I get to eat.

Working with food was fraught with anxiety and desperation. In truth, no one in memory had missed a meal—except Peyton Washam on the banks of Panther Creek wistfully regarding his seed corn. But the rumble of poor Peyton's belly must have survived to trouble our dreams. We were at the mercy of nature, and it wasn't to be trusted. My mother watched the skies at evening for a portent of the morrow. A cloud that went over and then turned around and came back was an especially bad sign. Our livelihood—even our lives—depended on forces outside our control.

I think this dependence on nature was at the core of my rebellion. I hated the constant sense of helplessness before vast forces, the continuous threat of failure. Farmers didn't take initiative, I began to see; they reacted to whatever presented itself. I especially hated women's part in the dependence.

My mother allowed me to get spoiled. She never even tried to teach me to cook. "You didn't want to learn," she says now. "You were a lady of leisure, and you didn't want to help. You had your nose in a book."

I believed progress meant freedom from the field and the range. That meant moving to town, I thought.

10   Because we lived on the edge of Mayfield, I was acutely conscious of being country. I felt inferior to people in town because we grew our food and made our clothes, while they bought whatever they needed. Although we were self-sufficient and resourceful and held clear title to our land, we lived in a state of psychological poverty. As I grew older, this acute sense of separation from town affected me more deeply. I began to sense that the fine life in town—celebrated in magazines, on radio, in

CONVERSATIONS: THE CITY AND THE COUNTRY continued

Caven Family, American Canyon, California

Regzen Family, Ulaanbaatar, Mongolia

movies—was denied us. Of course we weren't poor at all. Poor people had too many kids, and they weren't landowners; they rented decrepit little houses with plank floors and trash in the yard. "Poor people are wormy and eat wild onions," Mama said. We weren't poor, but we were country.

We had three wardrobes—everyday clothes, school clothes, and Sunday clothes. We didn't wear our school clothes at home, but we could wear them to town. When we got home from church, we had to change back into everyday clothes before we ate Mama's big Sunday dinner.

"Don't eat in your good clothes!" Mama always cried. "You'll spill something on them."

Mama always preferred outdoor life, but she was a natural cook. At harvest time, after she'd come in from the garden and put out a wash, she would whip out a noontime dinner for the men in the field—my father and grandfather and maybe some neighbors and a couple of hired hands: fried chicken with milk gravy, ham, mashed potatoes, lima beans, field peas, corn, slaw, sliced tomatoes, fried apples, biscuits, and peach pie. This was not considered a banquet, only plain hearty food, fuel for work. All the ingredients except the flour, sugar, and salt came from our farm—the chickens, the hogs, the milk and butter, the Irish potatoes, the beans, peas, corn, cabbage, apples, peaches. Nothing was processed, except by Mama. She was always butchering and plucking and planting and hoeing and shredding and slicing and creaming (scraping cobs for the creamed corn) and pressure-cooking and canning and freezing and thawing and mixing and shaping and baking and frying.

CONTEXT: FOOD
Notice Mason's descriptions of hamburgers in pagaraph 15: She writes that hamburgers bought in town were "better." In
this passage, Mason is describing a scene
from her childhood in the 1950s, but she
wrote this memoir in the 1990s. Attitudes
about food—about what is healthy and
desirable in a diet—have changed consid-
erably in that time and so has the nature
of the American diet. With these changes
in mind, consider how Mason describes
"better" food here. Do you think she is
trying to re-create her attitudes from the
1950s? Or might she have some other
purpose in mind? How does the changing
context regarding attitudes toward food
affect the way you read this passage?

We would eat our pie right on the same plate as our turnip greens
so as not to mess up another dish. The peach cobbler oozed all over
the turnip-green juice and the pork grease. "It all goes to the same
place," Mama said. It was boarding-house reach, no "Pass the peas,
please." Conversation detracted from the sensuous pleasure of filling
yourself. A meal required meat and vegetables and dessert. The bev-
erages were milk and iced tea ("ice-tea"). We never used napkins or ate
tossed salad. Our salads were Jell-O and slaw. We ate "poke salet" and
wilted lettuce. Mama picked tender, young pokeweed in the woods in
the spring, before it turned poison, and cooked it a good long time to
get the bitterness out. We liked it with vinegar and minced boiled eggs.
Wilted lettuce was tender new lettuce, shredded, with sliced radishes
and green onions, and blasted with hot bacon grease to blanch the
rawness. "Too many fresh vegetables in summer gives people the
scours," Daddy said.

15   Food was better in town, we thought. It wasn't plain and everyday. The
centers of pleasure were there—the hamburger and barbecue places, the
movie shows, all the places to buy things. Woolworth's, with the pneumatic tubes overhead rushing money along a metallic mole tunnel up to a balcony; Lochridge &
Ridgway, with an engraved sign on the third-story cornice: STOVES, APPLIANCES, PLOWS. On
the mezzanine at that store, I bought my first phonograph records, brittle 78s of big-
band music—Woody Herman and Glenn Miller, and Glen Gray and his Casa Loma
Orchestra playing "No Name Jive." A circuit of the courthouse square took you past the
grand furniture stores, the two dime stores, the shoe stores, the men's stores, the ladies'
stores, the banks, the drugstores. You'd walk past the poolroom and an exhaust fan
would blow the intoxicating smell of hamburgers in your face. Before she bought a
freezer, Mama stored meat in a rented food locker in town, near the ice company. She
stored the butchered calf there, and she fetched hunks of him each week to fry. But
hamburgers in town were better. They were greasier, and they came in waxed-paper
packages.

At the corner drugstore, on the square, Mama and Janice and I sat at filigreed
wrought-iron tables on a black-and-white mosaic tile floor, eating peppermint ice
cream. It was very cold in there, under the ceiling fans. The ice cream was served el-
egantly, in paper cones sunk into black plastic holders. We were uptown.

The A&P grocery, a block away, reeked of the rich aroma of ground coffee. Daddy
couldn't stand the smell of coffee, but Mama loved it. Daddy retched and scoffed in
his exaggerated fashion. "I can't stand that smell!" Granny perked coffee, and
Granddaddy told me it would turn a child black. I hated coffee. I wouldn't touch it
till I was thirty. We savored store-bought food—coconuts, pineapples, and Vienna
sausages and potted meat in little cans that opened with keys. We rarely went to the
uptown A&P. We usually traded at a small mom-and-pop grocery, where the propri-
etors slapped the hands of black children who touched the candy case. I wondered
if they were black from coffee. . . .

UNDERSTANDING THE TEXT

1. In paragraph 7, Mason writes, "I think this dependence on nature was at the core of my rebellion." What specifically does she mean by "dependence on nature" in this passage? Why does she rebel against this? What might this rebellion suggest about Mason's sense of herself as a rural person?

2. Mason devotes much of this brief essay to descriptions of and references to food. Why do you think she does so? What importance does food have in her sense of identity? Why was the source of her food so important?

3. What was special about the town, according to Mason? What do you think Mason intended the town to represent, as she describes it in this essay? Do you think cities and towns still represent the same things to most people today? Explain.

EXPLORING THE ISSUES

1. At one point in her essay, Mason writes that she and her family lived in a state of "psychological poverty," though she also tells us that her family was not poor. Where did her feeling of being poor come from? What might this psychological poverty suggest about how people develop a sense of identity in American society?

2. Mason writes that her mother insisted that her family was not poor; they were "country." What do you think is the difference between being poor and being country, based on Mason's descriptions? What might this essay suggest about American attitudes toward social class? How does this distinction between poor and country fit in with your own sense of social class?

3. Mason's prose has been described by some critics as straightforward and down-to-earth. Do you

agree with that description? Why or why not? Cite specific passages from her essay to support your answer.

4. Mason wrote this essay in the late 1990s, about forty years after the experiences she describes in it. She describes her feelings about "being country" as a young girl. What do you think is Mason's attitude about being country today, based on this essay? Do you think she wishes to present her experiences as a rural dweller in a positive way? Explain, citing specific passages from the essay to support your answer.

ENTERING THE CONVERSATIONS

1. Write an essay based on memories of your own childhood. In your essay, try to focus on a particular aspect of your upbringing and how the place where you were raised might have influenced your sense of your own identity.

2. Visit several web sites devoted to country life and analyze them in terms of the image they present of rural life and the assumptions they seem to make about living in the country. Try to get a sense of the audience they are trying to reach. Then write a report on the basis of your analysis.

3. Write a contemporary version of the old fable of the city mouse and the country mouse. (See *Conversations: The City and the Country* on page 78.)

 INFOTRAC

4. Using InfoTrac College Edition and any other relevant resources, examine the changes that have occurred in the United States regarding the relationship between rural and urban life. As a starting point for thinking about this topic, look at *Conversations: The City and the*

Country on page 78. Try to find out how life has changed in American cities and in rural areas in the past decades, and identify the major challenges facing urban and rural dwellers today. Then write a report on the basis of your research.

5. On the basis of your research for Question 4, write a letter to your senator or state representative (or some other appropriate political representative) in which you express your concerns about important issues facing urban or rural dwellers in your region of the country.

6. Write a letter to the editor of your local newspaper or another publication you think is appropriate in which you discuss what it means to be from the city or from the country today.

DEFINING EACH OTHER

I N THE PAST FEW DECADES, THE TERM *THE OTHER* HAS BECOME AN INCREASINGLY COMMON ONE IN DISCUS-SIONS ABOUT DIFFERENCE, DIVERSITY, PREJUDICE, AND RACISM. IT IS EVEN SOMETIMES USED AS AN ODD-SOUNDING VERB: YOU CAN BE "OTHERED"—THAT IS, YOU CAN BE

categorized as "other" than something, which usually means less than or inferior to that something. Most often, people belonging to minority groups or nonmainstream cultures are "othered" in this way, but the idea can apply to any person or group treated in a way that reflects prejudice or bias. All of us have probably been in circumstances in which we have been The Other, but it's clear that some groups have long been categorized as Other in systematic ways that are damaging and disturbing.

> Most often, people belonging to minority groups or nonmainstream cultures are "othered" in this way, but the idea can apply to any person or group treated in a way that reflects prejudice or bias.

It's worth thinking about what this idea of The Other says about how we respond to each other's identities. In discussions of injustices based on such things as race, gender, ethnicity, religion, and culture, this term has acquired a particular kind of meaning. It suggests something more than prejudice. To have prejudice is to dislike or have negative feelings about someone or something; conversely, we can have a prejudice in favor of something—for example, a sports fan can be prejudiced toward a favorite team. But to consider someone as an Other is to place that person in a category that is separate from ourselves and, importantly, somehow inferior to ourselves. It is to consider that person's

identity undesirable in some way. It is to define another in ways that the person would never define himself or herself. And it is to do all these things in subtle ways that might not be apparent. The ways in which we define The Other can be less visible than, say, racism, which is often much more obvious and recognizable. We can, for instance, assume someone is less than we are without seeming to treat that person in an openly disparaging or racist way. So this idea of The Other serves the useful purpose of describing a specific way of categorizing people on the basis of prejudices or biases about certain identities.

If the idea of The Other seems vague to you, the three essays in this cluster may help you get a better handle on it. Each writer addresses a slightly different way in which the category of The Other can emerge in our interactions with each other. Some of these categories are more obvious than others. For example, Gregory Jay writes about race, though his focus is not on so-called "minority" races but on how Whiteness becomes the category by which other races are measured. In a sense, he examines how various races are implicitly "othered" by the assumed dominance of Whiteness as a racial category. Similarly, Maxine Hong Kingston and Dagoberto Gilb describe racial categories—Asian and Hispanic—that are often defined as The Other. But they also help us see less obvious ways in which people are defined as Other—for example, as immigrants or women. All these essays thus give us concrete ways of seeing The Other. They call our attention to how we constantly categorize people in ways that emphasize difference, and they may also help us gain insight into the consequences of this "othering."

"My aunt haunts me," Maxine Hong Kingston (b. 1940) *writes at the end of the following essay. Yet Kingston does not even know her aunt's name, nor has she ever met her aunt. She only knows bits and pieces of the story her mother has told her about her aunt, whose very existence her family has tried to forget. Kingston's essay offers a vivid and compelling picture of how our identities can be shaped by those around us, especially members of our families and our*

No Name Woman

communities, and by the traditions and history of our culture. Kingston's aunt was a Chinese woman and as such was expected to be a certain kind of person who acted in certain accepted ways. But her actions prompted her family and neighbors to give her other identities: adulterer, betrayer, suicide. Her story is a stark reminder that we don't necessarily control our identities. And if you think that the story Kingston tells about her aunt is extreme, a closer look at what it means to be a woman or a man in our society today will reveal that, like Kingston's aunt, we are all subject to expectations and beliefs that shape who we are and who we can be.

Kingston's essay is also about the stories we tell each other and ourselves about who we are. As Kingston writes about her aunt, she is also telling a story about herself as a Chinese American woman. And as you'll see, it isn't an easy story to tell. It makes me wonder about our need to try to define ourselves even as we are being defined by others. If you've ever felt that you have been unfairly labeled by other people as something that you believe you are not—a nerd or a jock or worse—then you might begin to get a sense of Kingston's need to understand her aunt's story and how it might affect her own sense of self.   (continued)

MAXINE HONG KINGSTON

"Y**ou must not tell anyone,"** my mother said, "what I am about to tell you. In China your father had a sister who killed herself. She jumped into the family well. We say that your father has all brothers because it is as if she had never been born.

"In 1924 just a few days after our village celebrated seventeen hurry-up weddings—to make sure that every young man who went 'out on the road' would responsibly come home—your father and his brothers and your grandfather and his brothers and your aunt's new husband sailed for America, the Gold Mountain. It was your grandfather's last trip. Those lucky enough to get contracts waved good-bye from the decks. They fed and guarded the stowaways and helped them off in Cuba, New York, Bali, Hawaii. 'We'll meet in California next year,' they said. All of them sent money home.

"I remember looking at your aunt one day when she and I were dressing; I had not noticed before that she had such a protruding melon of a stomach. But I did not think, 'She's pregnant,' until she began to look like other pregnant women, her shirt pulling and the (continued) *Maxine Hong Kingston is a widely acclaimed author of many articles, essays, and books, including* Tripmaster Monkey: His Fake Book *(1989),* The Fifth Book of Peace *(2003), and the award-winning* The Woman Warrior: Memoirs of a Girlhood among Ghosts *(1976), in which the following excerpt first appeared.* ▼

STRATEGIES: TELLING STORIES
Kingston has been both praised and criticized for the way she uses fictional techniques in telling stories about her life and her family. Some critics have charged that her writing is not really autobiographical because she incorporates fictional elements into her narratives. Others have hailed her innovative blending of fiction and nonfiction. As you read this essay about her aunt, consider how Kingston's narrative style and the techniques she uses for telling her story might influence your reaction to that story.

white tops of her black pants showing. She could not have been pregnant, you see, because her husband had been gone for years. No one said anything. We did not discuss it. In early summer she was ready to have the child, long after the time when it could have been possible.

"The village had also been counting. On the night the baby was to be born the villagers raided our house. Some were crying. Like a great saw, teeth strung with lights, files of people walked zigzag across our land, tearing the rice. Their lanterns doubled in the disturbed black water, which drained away through the broken bunds. As the villagers closed in, we could see that some of them, probably men and women we knew well, wore white masks. The people with long hair hung it over their faces. Women with short hair made it stand up on end. Some had tied white bands around their foreheads, arms, and legs.

5   "At first they threw mud and rocks at the house. Then they threw eggs and began slaughtering our stock. We could hear the animals scream their deaths—the roosters, the pigs, a last great roar from the ox. Familiar wild heads flared in our night windows; the villagers encircled us. Some of the faces stopped to peer at us, their eyes rushing like searchlights. The hands flattened against the panes, framed heads, and left red prints.

"The villagers broke in the front and the back doors at the same time, even though we had not locked the doors against them. Their knives dripped with the blood of our animals. They smeared blood on the doors and walls. One woman swung a chicken, whose throat she had slit, splattering blood in red arcs about her. We stood together in the middle of our house, in the family hall with the pictures and tables of the ancestors around us, and looked straight ahead.

"At that time the house had only two wings. When the men came back, we would build two more to enclose our courtyard and a third one to begin a second courtyard. The villagers pushed through both wings, even your grandparents' rooms, to find your aunt's, which was also mine until the men returned. From this room a new wing for one of the younger families would grow. They ripped up her clothes and shoes and broke her combs, grinding them underfoot. They tore her work from the loom. They scattered the cooking fire and rolled the new weaving in it. We could hear them in the kitchen breaking our bowls and banging the pots. They overturned the great waist-high earthenware jugs; duck eggs, pickled fruits, vegetables burst out and mixed in acrid torrents. The old woman from the next field swept a broom through the air and loosed the spirits-of-the-broom over our heads. 'Pig.' 'Ghost.' 'Pig,' they sobbed and scolded while they ruined our house.

"When they left, they took sugar and oranges to bless themselves. They cut pieces from the dead animals. Some of them took bowls that were not broken and clothes that were not torn. Afterward we swept up the rice and sewed it back up into sacks. But the smells from the spilled preserves lasted. Your aunt gave birth in the pigsty that night. The next morning when I went up for the water, I found her and the baby plugging up the family well.

"Don't let your father know that I told you. He denies her. Now that you have started to menstruate, what happened to her could happen to you. Don't humiliate us. You wouldn't like to be forgotten as if you had never been born. The villagers are watchful."

Whenever she had to warn us about life, my mother told stories that ran like this one, a story to grow up on. She tested our strength to establish realities. Those in the emigrant generations who could not reassert brute survival died young and far from home. Those of us in the first American generations have had to figure out how the invisible world the emigrants built around our childhoods fit in solid America.

The emigrants confused the gods by diverting their curses, misleading them with crooked streets and false names. They must try to confuse their offspring as well, who, I suppose, threaten them in similar ways—always trying to get things straight, always trying to name the unspeakable. The Chinese I know hide their names; sojourners take new names when their lives change and guard their real names with silence.

Chinese-Americans, when you try to understand what things in you are Chinese, how do you separate what is peculiar to childhood, to poverty, insanities, one family, your mother who marked your growing with stories, from what is Chinese? What is Chinese tradition and what is the movies?

If I want to learn what clothes my aunt wore, whether flashy or ordinary, I would have to begin, "Remember Father's drowned-in-the-well sister?" I cannot ask that. My mother has told me once and for all the useful parts. She will add nothing unless powered by Necessity, a riverbank that guides her life. She plants vegetable gardens rather than lawns; she carries the odd-shaped tomatoes home from the fields and eats food left for the gods.

Whenever we did frivolous things, we used up energy; we flew high kites. We children came up off the ground over the melting cones our parents brought home from work and the American movie on New Year's Day—*Oh, You Beautiful Doll* with Betty Grable one year, and *She Wore a Yellow Ribbon* with John Wayne another year. After the one carnival ride each, we paid in guilt; our tired father counted his change on the dark walk home.

Adultery is extravagance. Could people who hatch their own chicks and eat the embryos and the heads for delicacies and boil the feet in vinegar for party food, leaving only the gravel, eating even the gizzard lining—could such people engender a prodigal aunt? To be a woman, to have a daughter in starvation time was a waste enough. My aunt could not have been the lone romantic who gave up everything for sex. Women in the old China did not choose. Some man had commanded her to lie with him and be his secret evil. I wonder whether he masked himself when he joined the raid on her family.

Perhaps she encountered him in the fields or on the mountain where the daughters-in-law collected fuel. Or perhaps he first noticed her in the marketplace. He was not a stranger because the village housed no strangers. She had to have dealings with him other than sex. Perhaps he worked an adjoining field, or he sold her the cloth for the dress she sewed and wore. His demand must have surprised, then terrified her. She obeyed him; she always did as she was told.

When the family found a young man in the next village to be her husband, she stood tractably beside the best rooster, his proxy, and promised before they met that she would be his forever. She was lucky that he was her age and she would be the first wife, an advantage secure now. The night she first saw him, he had sex with her. Then he left for America. She had almost forgotten what he looked like. When she tried to envision him, she only saw the black and white face in the group photograph the men had taken before leaving.

The other man was not, after all, much different from her husband. They both gave orders: she followed. "If you tell your family, I'll beat you. I'll kill you. Be here again next week." No one talked sex, ever. And she might have separated the rapes from the rest of living if only she did not have to buy her oil from him or gather wood in the same forest. I want her fear to have lasted just as long as rape lasted so that the fear could have been contained. No drawn-out fear. But women at sex hazarded birth and hence lifetimes. The fear did not stop but permeated everywhere. She told the man, "I think I'm pregnant." He organized the raid against her.

On nights when my mother and father talked about their life back home, sometimes they mentioned an "outcast table" whose business they still seemed to be settling, their voices tight. In a commensal tradition, where food is precious, the powerful older people made wrongdoers eat alone. Instead of letting them start separate new lives like the Japanese, who could become samurais and geishas, the Chinese family, faces averted but eyes glowering sideways, hung on to the offenders and fed them leftovers. My aunt must have lived in the same house as my parents and eaten at an outcast table. My mother spoke about the raid as if she had seen it, when she and my aunt, a daughter-in-law to a different household, should not have been living together at all. Daughters-in-law lived with their husbands' parents, not their own; a synonym for marriage in Chinese is "taking a daughter-in-law." Her husband's parents could have sold her, mortgaged her, stoned her. But they sent her back to her own mother and father, a mysterious act hinting at disgraces not told me. Perhaps they had thrown her out to deflect the avengers.

20 She was the only daughter; her four brothers went with her father, husband, and uncles "out on the road" and for some years became western men. When the goods were divided among the family, three of the brothers took land, and the youngest, my father, chose an education. After my grandparents gave their daughter away to her husband's family, they had dispensed all the adventure and all the property. They expected her alone to keep the traditional ways, which her brothers, now among the barbarians, could fumble without detection. The heavy, deep-rooted women were to maintain the past against the flood, safe for returning. But the rare urge west had fixed upon our family, and so my aunt crossed boundaries not delineated in space.

The work of preservation demands that the feelings playing about in one's guts not be turned into action. Just watch their passing like cherry blossoms. But perhaps my aunt, my forerunner, caught in a slow life, let dreams grow and fade and after some months or years went toward what persisted. Fear at the enormities of the forbidden kept her desires delicate, wire and bone. She looked at a man because she liked the way the hair was tucked behind his ears, or she liked the question-mark line of a long torso curving at the shoulder and straight at the hip. For warm eyes or a soft voice or a slow walk—that's all—a few hairs, a line, a brightness, a sound, a pace, she gave up family.

She offered us up for a charm that vanished with tiredness, a pigtail that didn't toss when the wind died. Why, the wrong lighting could erase the dearest thing about him.

It could very well have been, however, that my aunt did not take subtle enjoyment of her friend, but, a wild woman, kept rollicking company. Imagining her free with sex doesn't fit, though. I don't know any women like that, or men either. Unless I see her life branching into mine, she gives me no ancestral help.

To sustain her being in love, she often worked at herself in the mirror, guessing at the colors and shapes that would interest him, changing them frequently in order to hit on the right combination. She wanted him to look back.

On a farm near the sea, a woman who tended her appearance reaped a reputation for eccentricity. All the married women blunt-cut their hair in flaps about their ears or pulled it back in tight buns. No nonsense. Neither style blew easily into heart-catching tangles. And at their weddings they displayed themselves in their long hair for the last time. "It brushed the backs of my knees," my mother tells me. "It was braided, and even so, it brushed the backs of my knees."

At the mirror my aunt combed individuality into her bob. A bun could have been contrived to escape into black streamers blowing in the wind or in quiet wisps about her face, but only the older women in our picture album wear buns. She brushed her hair back from her forehead, tucking the flaps behind her ears. She looped a piece of thread, knotted into a circle between her index fingers and thumbs, and ran the double strand across her forehead. When she closed her fingers as if she were making a pair of shadow geese bite, the string twisted together catching the little hairs. Then she pulled the thread away from her skin, ripping the hairs out neatly, her eyes watering from the needles of pain. Opening her fingers, she cleaned the thread, then rolled it along her hairline and the tops of her eyebrows. My mother did the same to me and my sisters and herself. I used to believe that the expression **"caught by the short hairs"** meant a captive held with a depilatory string. It especially hurt at the temples, but my mother said we were lucky we didn't have to have our **feet bound** when we were seven. Sisters used to sit on their beds and cry together, she said, as their mothers or their slave removed the bandages for a few minutes each night and let the blood gush back into their veins. I hope that the man my aunt loved appreciated a smooth brow, that he wasn't just a tits-and-ass man.

25

CONTEXT: FEMALE BEAUTY

In paragraph 25, Kingston provides a vivid description of two traditional practices among Chinese women to create a certain physical appearance considered beautiful. The first is the removal of some hair along the forehead and temples; the other is the binding of feet, which was done because small feet were considered desirable. Although these practices may seem odd or even extreme to people outside Chinese culture, every culture—including contemporary American culture—has its own peculiar practices related to certain beliefs about physical beauty. Consider, for example, the practice of waxing, by which hair is removed from certain parts of the body. This practice has become increasingly common in the United States in recent years, and both men and women will pay hefty sums to have their bodies waxed, which is not always a pleasant experience.

Once my aunt found a freckle on her chin, at a spot that the almanac said predestined her for unhappiness. She dug it out with a hot needle and washed the wound with peroxide.

More attention to her looks than these pullings of hairs and pickings at spots would have caused gossip among the villagers. They owned work clothes and good clothes, and they wore good clothes for feasting the new seasons. But since a woman combing her hair hexes beginnings, my aunt rarely found an occasion to look her best. Women looked like great sea snails—the corded wood, babies, and laundry they carried were the whorls on their backs. The Chinese did not admire a bent back;

goddesses and warriors stood straight. Still there must have been a marvelous freeing of beauty when a worker laid down her burden and stretched and arched.

Such commonplace loveliness, however, was not enough for my aunt. She dreamed of a lover for the fifteen days of New Year's, the time for families to exchange visits, money, and food. She plied her secret comb. And sure enough she cursed the year, the family, the village, and herself.

Even as her hair lured her imminent lover, many other men looked at her. Uncles, cousins, nephews, brothers would have looked, too, had they been home between journeys. Perhaps they had already been restraining their curiosity, and they left, fearful that their glances, like a field of nesting birds, might be startled and caught. Poverty hurt, and that was their first reason for leaving. But another, final reason for leaving the crowded house was the never-said.

30 She may have been unusually beloved, the precious only daughter, spoiled and mirror-gazing because of the affection the family lavished on her. When her husband left, they welcomed the chance to take her back from the in-laws; she could live like the little daughter for just a while longer. There are stories that my grandfather was different from other people, "crazy ever since the little Jap bayoneted him in the head." He used to put his naked penis on the dinner table, laughing. And one day he brought home a baby girl, wrapped up inside his brown western-style greatcoat. He had traded one of his sons, probably my father, the youngest, for her. My grandmother made him trade back. When he finally got a daughter of his own, he doted on her. They must have all loved her, except perhaps my father, the only brother who never went back to China, having once been traded for a girl.

Brothers and sisters, newly men and women, had to efface their sexual color and present plain miens. Disturbing hair and eyes, a smile like no other, threatened the ideal of five generations living under one roof. To focus blurs, people shouted face to face and yelled from room to room. The immigrants I know have loud voices, unmodulated to American tones even after years away from the village where they called their friendships out across the fields. I have not been able to stop my mother's screams in public libraries or over telephones. Walking erect (knees straight, toes pointed forward, not pigeon-toed, which is Chinese-feminine) and speaking in an inaudible voice, I have tried to turn myself American-feminine. Chinese communication was loud, public. Only sick people had to whisper. But at the dinner table, where the family members came nearest one another, no one could talk, not the outcasts nor any eaters. Every word that falls from the mouth is a coin lost. Silently they gave and accepted food with both hands. A preoccupied child who took his bowl with one hand got a sideways glare. A complete moment of total attention is due everyone alike. Children and lovers have no singularity here, but my aunt used a secret voice, a separate attentiveness.

She kept the man's name to herself throughout her labor and dying; she did not accuse him that he be punished with her. To save her inseminator's name she gave silent birth.

He may have been somebody in her own household, but intercourse with a man outside the family would have been no less abhorrent. All the village were kinsmen, and the titles shouted in loud country voices never let kinship be forgotten. Any man within visiting distance would have been neutralized as a lover—"brother," "younger brother," "older brother"—115 relationship titles. Parents researched birth charts probably not so much to assure good fortune as to circumvent incest in a population that has but one hundred surnames. Everybody has eight million relatives. How useless then sexual mannerisms, how dangerous.

As if it came from an atavism deeper than fear, I used to add "brother" silently to boys' names. It hexed the boys, who would or would not ask me to dance, and made them less scary and as familiar and deserving of benevolence as girls.

But, of course, I hexed myself also—no dates. I should have stood up, both arms   35
waving, and shouted out across libraries, "Hey, you! Love me back." I had no idea, though, how to make attraction selective, how to control its direction and magnitude. If I made myself American-pretty so that the five or six Chinese boys in the class fell in love with me, everyone else—the Caucasian, Negro, and Japanese boys—would too. Sisterliness, dignified and honorable, made much more sense.

Attraction eludes control so stubbornly that whole societies designed to organize relationships among people cannot keep order, not even when they bind people to one another from childhood and raise them together. Among the very poor and the wealthy, brothers married their adopted sisters, like doves. Our family allowed some romance, paying adult brides' prices and providing dowries so that their sons and daughters could marry strangers. Marriage promises to turn strangers into friendly relatives—a nation of siblings.

In the village structure, spirits shimmered among the live creatures, balanced and held in equilibrium by time and land. But one human being flaring up into violence could open up a black hole, a maelstrom that pulled in the sky. The frightened villagers, who depended on one another to maintain the real, went to my aunt to show her a personal, physical representation of the break she made in the "roundness." Misallying couples snapped off the future, which was to be embodied in true offspring. The villagers punished her for acting as if she could have a private life, secret and apart from them.

If my aunt had betrayed the family at a time of large grain yields and peace, when many boys were born, and wings were being built on many houses, perhaps she might have escaped such severe punishment. But the men—hungry, greedy, tired of planting in dry soil, cuckolded—had been forced to leave the village in order to send food-money home. There were ghost plagues, bandit plagues, wars with the Japanese, floods. My Chinese brother and sister had died of an unknown sickness. Adultery, perhaps only a mistake during good times, became a crime when the village needed food.

The round moon cakes and round doorways, the round tables of graduated size that fit one roundness inside another, round windows and rice bowls—these talismans had lost their power to warn this family of the law: a family must be whole, faithfully keeping the descent line by having sons to feed the old and the dead who in turn look after the family. The villagers came to show my aunt and lover-in-hiding a broken house. The villagers were speeding up the circling of events because she was too shortsighted to see that her infidelity had already harmed the village, that waves of consequences would return unpredictably, sometimes in disguise, as now, to hurt her. This roundness had to be made coin-sized so that she would see its circumference: punish her at the birth of her baby. Awaken her to the inexorable. People who refused fatalism because they could invent small resources insisted on culpability. Deny accidents and wrest fault from the stars.

40   After the villagers left, their lanterns now scattering in various directions toward home, the family broke their silence and cursed her. "Aiaa, we're going to die. Death is coming. Death is coming. Look what you've done. You've killed us. Ghost! Dead Ghost! Ghost! You've never been born." She ran out into the fields, far enough from the house so that she could no longer hear their voices, and pressed herself against the earth, her own land no more. When she felt the birth coming, she thought that she had been hurt. Her body seized together. "They've hurt me too much," she thought. "This is gall, and it will kill me." With forehead and knees against the earth, her body convulsed and then relaxed. She turned on her back, lay on the ground. The black well of sky and stars went out and out forever; her body and her complexity seemed to disappear. She was one of the stars, a bright dot in blackness, without home, without a companion, in eternal cold and silence. An agoraphobia rose in her, speeding higher and higher, bigger and bigger; she would not be able to contain it; there would be no end to fear.

Flayed, unprotected against space, she felt pain return, focusing her body. This pain chilled her—a cold, steady kind of surface pain. Inside, spasmodically, the other pain, the pain of the child, heated her. For hours she lay on the ground, alternately body and space. Sometimes a vision of normal comfort obliterated reality: she saw the family in the evening gambling at the dinner table, the young people massaging their elders' backs. She saw them congratulating one another, high joy on the mornings the rice shoots came up. When these pictures burst, the stars drew yet further apart. Black space opened.

She got to her feet to fight better and remembered that old-fashioned women gave birth in their pigsties to fool the jealous, pain-dealing gods, who do not snatch piglets. Before the next spasms could stop her, she ran to the pigsty, each step a rushing out into emptiness. She climbed over the fence and knelt in the dirt. It was good to have a fence enclosing her, a tribal person alone.

Laboring, this woman who had carried her child as a foreign growth that sickened her every day, expelled it at last. She reached down to touch the hot, wet, moving mass, surely smaller than anything human, and could feel that it was human after all—fingers, toes, nails, nose. She pulled it up on to her belly, and it lay curled there, butt in the air, feet precisely tucked one under the other. She opened her loose shirt and buttoned the child inside. After resting, it squirmed and thrashed and she pushed it up to her breast. It turned its head this way and that until it found her nipple. There, it made little snuffling noises. She clenched her teeth at its preciousness, lovely as a young calf, a piglet, a little dog.

She may have gone to the pigsty as a last act of responsibility: she would protect this child as she had protected its father. It would look after her soul, leaving supplies on her grave. But how would this tiny child without family find her grave when there would be no marker for her anywhere, neither in the earth nor the family hall? No one would give her a family hall name. She had taken the child with her into the wastes. At its birth the two of them had felt the same raw pain of separation, a wound that only the family pressing tight could close. A child with no descent line would not soften her life but only trail after her, ghostlike, begging her to give it purpose. At dawn the villagers on their way to the fields would stand around the fence and look.

Full of milk, the little ghost slept. When it awoke, she hardened her breasts against   45
the milk that crying loosens. Toward morning she picked up the baby and walked to
the well.

Carrying the baby to the well shows loving. Otherwise abandon it. Turn its face into
the mud. Mothers who love their children take them along. It was probably a girl;
there is some hope of forgiveness for boys.

*   *   *

"Don't tell anyone you had an aunt. Your father does not want to hear her name.
She has never been born." I have believed that sex was unspeakable and words so
strong and fathers so frail that "aunt" would do my father mysterious harm. I have
thought that my family, having settled among immigrants who had also been their
neighbors in the ancestral land, needed to clean their name, and a wrong word
would incite the kinspeople even here. But there is more to this silence: they want
me to participate in her punishment. And I have.

In the twenty years since I heard this story I have not asked for details nor said my
aunt's name; I do not know it. People who comfort the dead can also chase after
them to hurt them further—a reverse ancestor worship. The real punishment was
not the raid swiftly inflicted by the villagers, but the family's deliberately forgetting
her. Her betrayal so maddened them, they saw to it that she would suffer forever,
even after death. Always hungry, always needing, she would have to beg food from
other ghosts, snatch and steal it from those whose living descendants
give them gifts. She would have to fight the ghosts massed at crossroads for the buns a few thoughtful citizens leave to decoy her away
from village and home so that the ancestral spirits could feast unha-
rassed. At peace, they could act like gods, not ghosts, their descent
lines providing them with paper suits and dresses, spirit money, paper
houses, paper automobiles, chicken, meat, and rice into eternity—
essences delivered up in smoke and flames, steam and incense rising
from each rice bowl. In an attempt to make the Chinese care for people outside the family, **Chairman Mao** encourages us now to give our
paper replicas to the spirits of outstanding soldiers and workers, no
matter whose ancestors they may be. My aunt remains forever hungry.
Goods are not distributed evenly among the dead.

GLOSS: CHAIRMAN MAO
Mao Zedong was the Communist leader of
China from 1949 to 1976. In his efforts to
consolidate Communist control over
China, Mao instituted a variety of policies
intended to change longstanding Chinese
cultural traditions. In this paragraph,
Kingston is referring to one such policy by
which the Chinese Communist government promoted the honoring of outstanding citizens who devoted themselves to
the state, rather than honoring one's ancestors, which is an ancient tradition in
China.

My aunt haunts me—her ghost drawn to me because now, after
fifty years of neglect, I alone devote pages of paper to her, though not origamied
into houses and clothes. I do not think she always means me well. I am telling on
her, and she was a spite suicide, drowning herself in the drinking water. The
Chinese are always very frightened of the drowned one, whose weeping ghost, wet
hair hanging and skin bloated, waits silently by the water to pull down a substitute.

UNDERSTANDING THE TEXT

1. In the beginning of this essay, Kingston describes in detail the villagers' raid on her family's home in China in the 1920s. Why does Kingston's mother tell her this story? What importance does the story have for Kingston's mother? Does it have the same importance for Kingston? Explain.

2. In many ways, this essay focuses on family and cultural traditions and the desire to preserve them. It also explores some of the consequences of preserving those traditions. In paragraph 21, Kingston writes, "The work of preservation demands that the feelings playing about in one's guts not be turned into action." What does Kingston mean by that statement? What does the statement indicate about an individual's responsibility in Chinese culture? What might it suggest about the connections between an individual's identity and his or her family and cultural traditions?

3. In paragraph 29, Kingston writes that one reason the uncles, cousins, nephews, and brothers in her family left their home in China was "the never-said." Elsewhere in the essay, she tells us that her mother warned her not to mention her aunt, the "no name woman," who died without speaking the name of the man who had fathered her baby. Kingston refers to other secrets and silences in her family's history. What is the importance of these secrets and silences? What do they reveal about the cultural traditions with which Kingston's family grew up?

4. What effect did her family's cultural traditions regarding relationships between men and women and regarding sexuality have on Kingston as a young girl? What might these effects suggest about how individuals develop an identity?

EXPLORING THE ISSUES

1. In a sense, this essay is about how the ability to bear children affects women's sense of identity. This aspect of being a woman is what ultimately led to Kingston's aunt's death. Yet bearing children is also considered miraculous and wonderful. What do you think Kingston is saying about how cultures treat this special part of a woman's identity? What might this essay suggest about the way women are defined within communities or cultures?

2. How would you describe Kingston's narrative voice in this essay? In what ways do you think her voice helps convey her own views about her family's history and traditions? Cite specific passages to support your answer.

3. What aspects of a woman's identity as described in this essay do you think are unique to Chinese culture? How do the attitudes toward women that Kingston describes compare to attitudes toward women in your own culture?

4. In telling the story of her aunt, Kingston offers several different scenarios to explain what happened and why. This is one example of the blending of fiction and nonfiction techniques for which Kingston is well known as a writer. Examine the effectiveness of this technique in this essay. To what extent do you think it enhances or weakens Kingston's effort to convey her ideas? Do you think the essay would have been as effective if she had not used this kind of technique and simply explained that no one is really sure just what happened to her aunt?

ENTERING THE CONVERSATIONS

1. Write an essay in which you tell some of your own family history as a way to explore your identity. Focus your essay on a specific event, ex-perience, or person that you consider important in your family life and describe it in a way that will help readers understand its significance to you and your family.

2. Create a web site or photo essay based on the essay you wrote for Question 1.

 INFOTRAC

3. Using InfoTrac College Edition, your library, and any other relevant resources, try to find out about family traditions in a culture other than your own. If possible, visit the office for international students on your campus to gather information about that culture or to talk to someone you might know from another culture. Write a report in which you describe some of the most important traditions related to family life in the culture you have studied. Compare those traditions to the traditions in your own culture. Try to draw conclusions about important similarities and differences in these traditions and what they might suggest about the role of family in various cultures.

4. Popular television shows often focus on families. *The Bill Cosby Show, Malcolm in the Middle, Roseanne,* and even the animated series *The Simpsons* are some of the many successful television sitcoms that focus on families or family life. Select several such shows and examine the ways in which they present these families. What do these shows reveal about families and family identity? What attitudes or beliefs about families do these shows convey? Most important, what do these shows suggest about how our families influence our own sense of identity? Write an essay in which you address these questions. In your essay analyze of what these shows reveal about the connection between our identities and our families.

Dagoberto Gilb (b. 1950) has focused much of his writing on his Chicano identity. One critic noted that what he found most impressive about Gilb's essays is "his measured indignation at the inability of white America to grasp Chicano beliefs or culture." I was struck by that comment not only because it so nicely describes the distinctive quality of Gilb's writing, but also because it says something interesting about how people understand others from backgrounds that differ

You Know Him BY His Labors, BUT Not His Face

from their own. In a sense, Gilb's writing is an effort to define his Chicano identity and to resist the ways in which mainstream America defines that identity. That is not a straightforward task because for many people, Chicano is associated with other kinds of identities, such as immigrant or migrant worker, that can be thought of as negative— as "Other" (a term discussed in the introduction to this cluster on page 82). In the following essay, as in much of his writing, Gilb challenges such attitudes. Here, he asks his readers to go beyond the surface, to consider the humanity that can be hidden behind labels like "immigrant." As you read this thoughtful and unusual essay, you might consider whether Gilb is challenging your own attitudes about people who may be different from you.

Dagoberto Gilb is the author of Gritos: Essays (2003), which was a finalist for the Nation Book Critics Circle Award, as well as three other books of fiction. The following essay was first published in the Los Angeles Times in 2004. ▼

DAGOBERTO GILB

The one who left wasn't the only one sleeping on a stained twin mattress under a carpet remnant in the room near the stench of sewage, wasn't the only one making shadows from a single light bulb dangling by a wire, who laughed at that old snoring dog, who liked to praise that dinner of beans and rice and chiles, not the only one who shared a torn love seat to watch a fuzzy TV with so many brothers drinking beer and soda and sisters getting married and having babies, that crowd of aunts, uncles, cousins, nephews and nieces, not the only one with unfaded scars and bad teeth, not the only one who complained about that so-loud radio always somewhere, not the only one who could pick out the best used retread tires.

He wasn't the only one loving a mother who wore that same housedress and apron, warming tortillas in the morning and early evening, who was still a beautiful woman.

He was the one who left and he will never stop loving her either. He had to leave behind a wife. The one who left had to leave behind his children. It was as though where he was going was a distant uncle's place, a man not blood, on his father's side, or it was the ex-husband of his godmother.

Somebody close to somebody else, somebody known but who is not in the family. That rich man has a successful construction business, or is a landowner, or he is just from "the States." He is the one many have seen drinking, laughing, talking loud in his language. He wouldn't live in even the nicest house in Mexico.

5   In "the States," there is work that pays and that is what the one who left needs and wants and he knows how to work, he is not afraid of any work, of earning. He is the one who left and he met good people, and bad people, and it was always dirty and mean, the same clothes no matter where or when or what. And that rich man does have lots of work. The one who left sweeps the sawdust and scrubs the cement and masonry tools and coils the hoses.

He stoops low for the cinder blocks and he lifts a beam that has to be set high. He pushes the wheelbarrow and pounds spikes with a flattened waffle-face metal hammer and he pulls out pins with its claws. He hauls the trash scraps and he digs the plumbing trench.

He always says yes and he means yes. He is a **cheap wage,** and he is quiet because he is far from home, as paperless as birth, and he not only acts grateful, he is grateful, because there is always worse at home.

The one who left is nobody special, and he knows it himself.

There are so many others just like him, hungry, even hungrier once they've been paid. His only home is work and job. His only trust, his only confidence, is the work, the job.

10   The one who left lives near streets in the States that were the first and are now the last. He shops at markets where others who left go.

He does not go to banks, but of course he wants to. He does not have a driver's license, but of course he wants one. He does not have a phone, but of course he wants one. He wants his family to be with him.

He learned early to live like a shadow watching a single light bulb and now he moves with almost a natural invisibility, carefully crossing into the light of night, not really seen when he's working in the sun.

He is someone who left his mother to get work.

He left his wife to find work.

15   He left his children to get work.

His citizenship is not in Mexico or in "the States" but is at a job.

He is not a part-time citizen, a temporary citizen.

He is loyal to work, and he is a patriot of its country.

He does not want to leave it in three years, or in six years. Like everyone else, he wants to become wealthy in his country.

UNDERSTANDING THE TEXT

1. Who is "the one who left" that Gilb describes in the opening paragraph? What is noteworthy about him, if anything? Why does Gilb describe him as "nobody special" later in the essay (par. 8)?

2. Who is the "somebody close to somebody else" that Gilb describes in the fourth paragraph? In what ways is he different from the people described elsewhere in this essay? Why are these differences important?

3. What is the significance of work to the people described in this essay? Why does Gilb write that the "person who left" is "loyal to work, and he is a patriot of its country"? What does this suggest about immigrant workers?

EXPLORING THE ISSUES

1. Examine Gilb's decision not to identify the people in this essay in more specific terms. What effect do you think this decision has on Gilb's essay? What effect did it have on you as a reader? Do you think the essay would have been more or less effective if Gilb had identified specific people in specific locations? Explain.

2. Notice how Gilb ends this essay: "Like everyone else, he wants to become wealthy in his country." Why do you think he ends with this line? What point do you think he is making? What might this line suggest about the similarities and differences between the immigrant worker described in this essay and the people in the United States that he works for? Do you agree with Gilb that "everyone else" wants to become wealthy? Why or why not?

3. What do you think this essay suggests about the United States and about Americans? What do you think it suggests about Mexico? Do you think Gilb is criticizing one or both of these countries? Explain, citing specific passages from the essay to support your answer.

ENTERING THE CONVERSATIONS

1. Write an essay in which you express your views about immigration. Be sure to support your position appropriately. (You may wish to do some research about immigration for this assignment, as described in Question 4.)

2. In a group of classmates, share the essays you wrote for Question 1. What main arguments do you and your classmates present regarding immigration? What do these arguments suggest about how you define *American* and *immigrant*? In what ways might Gilb's essay influence your position on immigration or the positions of your classmates?

3. Try to find a friend or family member who is an immigrant or whose ancestors immigrated to the United States. Or visit the office for international students on your campus to meet someone from another country who might be willing to talk to you about his or her experiences. Interview this person and try to get a sense of what it has been like to come to the United States from somewhere else. Or get a sense of how the fact that their parents or grandparents were immigrants has affected their sense of who they are. Then write an essay on the basis of this interview in which you explore the identity of *immigrant*. If you are yourself an immigrant, write an essay about your experiences in coming to the United States.

INFOTRAC

4. Search InfoTrac College Edition, the World Wide Web, and other relevant resources for information and viewpoints regarding immigration in the United States. (Currently, many advocacy groups both for and against greater restrictions on immigration to the United States maintain web sites, so be aware that much information about immigration on the web is presented from these viewpoints.) Try to identify the main arguments for and against greater or fewer restrictions on immigration, and focus specifically on illegal immigrant workers and their role in these arguments. Then write a report on the basis of your research. In your report, provide an overview of these debates about immigration, and try to draw conclusions about how attitudes toward people of certain races, ethnicity, cultural backgrounds, religious beliefs, and national origin seem to influence the ongoing debates about immigration.

5. On the basis of your research for Question 4, write a letter to the editor of your local newspaper or another appropriate publication in which you express your views about immigration.

For many people, race is the most powerful aspect of identity. Certainly, it is among the most complex and controversial ways that we define ourselves and each other. The history of relations among races, not just in the United States but around the world, is an often sobering story of conflict, discrimination, and violence. In the United States, the legacy of slavery seems to influence any discussion of race, and very often, discussions of race relations and racial identity focus on

Who Invented *White* People?

what it means to be Black in America. But in the past decade or so, a number of scholars and social critics have argued that when it comes to addressing the complexities and problems associated with race, we should be focusing attention not exclusively on Blacks or Latinos or Native Americans or people of color; rather, we should be looking at Whiteness. One of those scholars is Gregory Jay (b. 1952), a professor of English at the University of Wisconsin at Milwaukee. Like many other scholars interested in understanding race, Jay believes that the way we tend to discuss issues related to race makes Whiteness invisible. Whenever we discuss race, we discuss people of color but not Whiteness itself. And that's a problem, he believes, because it assumes that Whiteness is the standard by which other races are understood. In other words, according to Jay, when we examine how various racial categories are understood, we also have to look at Whiteness as a racial category; to avoid examining Whiteness as a racial category is to give it special status. In this way, how we discuss race both conveys and reinforces certain messages about the status of various racial categories.

In his provocative essay, which was originally delivered as a speech on (continued)

GREGORY JAY

"What is it for? What parts do the invention and development of whiteness play in the construction of what is loosely described as 'American'?"
—Toni Morrison, *Playing in the Dark: Whiteness and the Literary Imagination*

This week we celebrate Martin Luther King, Jr. day. What should our celebration focus on, and how can we best continue the work that he began? For most of us, Dr. King represents the modern Civil Rights Movement. That Movement was a struggle against the legal and social practices of racial discrimination—against everything from separate drinking fountains, white and colored public bathrooms, and segregated schools and lunch counters to the more subtle, everyday prejudices of ignorance and injustice that are common in America. The Civil Rights Act of 1965 is among Dr. King's greatest legacies, transforming the face of America more decisively than al-

GREGORY JAY, "WHO INVENTED WHITE PEOPLE" FROM SPEECH GIVEN BY GREGORY JAY, HTTP://WWW.UWM.EDU/%7EGJAY/WHITENESS/WHITENESSTALK.HTMREPRINTED BY PERMISSION.

(continued) *Martin Luther King, Jr. Day in 1998, Jay explores how the racial category of White emerged from historical and cultural developments. He argues that only by understanding "where White people came from" can we hope to address longstanding conflicts and injustices associated with race. It is a challenging task, one that reminds us that there are profound consequences to how we define others.* ◪

CONTEXT: MARTIN LUTHER KING, JR. DAY
Jay uses Martin Luther King, Jr. Day as the occasion for his examination of whiteness. Although there seems to be an obvious connection between a holiday that celebrates the famous civil rights leader and a discussion of race, the matter is more complex than it might seem. Martin Luther King, Jr. Day has been a U.S. national holiday since 1986, but it remained controversial for a number of years. Some states resisted declaring the holiday, notably Arizona, which did not approve the holiday until 1992; New Hampshire, which changed its "Civil Rights Day" to "Martin Luther King, Day" in 1999; and Utah, which changed "Human Rights Day" to "Martin Luther King, Jr. Day" in 2000. Consider how Jay relies on the complex historical background to this holiday in making his argument. Consider as well how the historical context might influence the way readers might respond to Jay's argument.

most any other legislation since the Civil War. Dr. King gave his life for the fight against injustice, and as we survey the changes in the thirty years since then we must say that his was a great and glorious victory.

Yet the promised land still eludes us. Once the crude legal structures of discrimination were torn down, Americans faced the fact that changing the laws did not change the feelings and beliefs of individuals, black or white. Beyond the abstract words of law and legislation, real people continued to carry with them the history of racism, whether as victims of its horrors or as beneficiaries of its privileges. To this day, racial discrimination remains pervasive in America. The old-boy networks at major corporations ensure the continuation of white male dominance. Banks regularly discriminate against minorities in business and housing loans. Homeowners and apartment owners refuse to sell or rent across color lines, partly because of the threats and violence that still occur when they do. Parents express discomfort or outright rage when children love or marry across the lines of race. Government subsidizes white suburban life with everything from freeway construction and business tax exemptions to mortgage write-offs while starving urban neighborhoods and cutting welfare programs. Ivy league schools give preference to the children of alumni and wealthy donors for admission, which, given the fact that the alumni and donors are overwhelmingly white, means that white applicants have an artificially easy time getting into the best colleges, and thus into the best jobs. It is hard to have many alumni of color, after all, when in the past colleges refused to enroll people of African or Asian or Hispanic descent, and placed strict quotas on Jews as well. Most of us could pluck similar examples out of the newspaper every day. This is not the legacy that Dr. King envisioned when he stood on the mountain top and saw his dream.

What keeps racism alive in America? I don't pretend to be the one to know the answer to this question. It's a question, however, that every one of us needs to ask. We need to ask it not only of ourselves, looking into our hearts, but to ask it of each other—to ask our friends, our family, our coworkers, and our church members. But in talking about race, what, exactly, should we talk about? I want to propose today that we talk about whiteness. Too often in America, we talk about race as if it were only something that people of color have, or only something we need to talk about when we talk about African Americans or Asian Americans or American Indians or Latino Americans. One thing that has changed radically since the death of Dr. King is that most white people do not want to call themselves white people, or see themselves in racial terms. From the days of the founding fathers until the Civil Rights movement, "white" was a common term in the law as well as society. Federal, state, and local officials regularly passed laws containing the word "white," defining everything from slavery and citizenship to where people could sit on a bus. Today, the movement against racism has had the unexpected effect of letting whiteness off the hook. Over and over we hear people say that "race shouldn't matter," that we should, or even do, have a "color blind society." What has happened, I think, is that we have instead created a blindness to whiteness, or been blinded by whiteness itself. As the title of Cornel West's best selling book insists, *Race Matters,* and to that I would add that whiteness still matters the most.

The trouble, then, with the Dr. Martin Luther King, Jr. holiday, with Black History Month, and such token expressions of concern is that they once more ghettoize the question of race. Worse, they tend to make race a black matter, something that we only discuss when we talk about African Americans, as if they were the only ones with a race. By distracting our glance, such tokenism once more blinds us to the race that is all around us, to what Herman Melville, in *Moby Dick,* called "the whiteness of the whale." The great white whale of racism is a white invention. It was white people who invented the idea of race in the first place, and it is white people who have become obsessed and consumed by it until, like Captain Ahab, they have become entangled so deeply in pursuing its nature that they self-destruct in the process. As the Nobel prize winning black author Toni Morrison has argued, in her wonderful book titled *Playing in the Dark: Whiteness and the Literary Imagination,* Melville and the other great writers of the American tradition tell the story of whiteness over and over. White identity defines itself against the backdrop of an African or colored presence: Ishmael and Queequeg in *Moby Dick,* Huck and Jim in *Huckleberry Finn,* right on up through Bill Cosby and what's-his-name on *I Spy* or any number of black-white buddy films in Hollywood. Ironically, white Americans can only define themselves by comparison to that which they are not, and so whiteness depends on blackness for its very definition.

5   Where did white people come from, anyway? Who invented whiteness? Scholars of race generally agree that the modern meaning of whiteness emerges in the centuries of European colonialism and imperialism that followed the Renaissance. Now granted, human begins have always clustered themselves in groups—families, clans, tribes, ethnic populations, nation states, etc.—and these groups have regularly been the source of discrimination and violence. At times it seems that an "us versus them" mentality starts on every playground and extends into every neighborhood, society, and government. Since human beings appear to require a sense of identity, and since identity is constructed by defining whom and what you are different from, it may be that the politics of difference will never be erased from human affairs.

That said, why did something called "racial" difference become so important in people's sense of their identity? Before the age of exploration, group differences were largely based on language, religion, and geography. The word "race" referred rather loosely to a population group that shared a language, customs, social behaviors, and other cultural characteristics—as in the French race or the Russian race or the Spanish race (differences we might now call "ethnic" rather than "racial"). As European adventurers, traders, and colonists accelerated their activities in Africa and Asia and the Americas, there emerged the need to create a single large distinction for differentiating between the colonizers and the colonized, or the slave traders and the enslaved. At first, religious distinctions maintained their preeminence, as the Africans and American Indians were dubbed pagans, heathens, barbarians, or savages—that is, as creatures without the benefits of Christian civilization or, perhaps, even as creatures without souls. Efforts to Christianize the Indians and the Africans, however, were never separate from efforts to steal their lands or exploit their labor. To justify such practices, Europeans needed a difference greater than religion, for religious justification melted away once the Indian or African converted.

Now the European had always reacted a bit hysterically to the differences of skin color and facial structure between themselves and the populations encountered in Africa, Asia, and the Americas (see, for example, Shakespeare's dramatization of racial conflict in *Othello* and *The Tempest*). Beginning in the 1500s, Europeans began to develop what became known as "scientific racism," the attempt to construct a biological rather than cultural definition of race. Biological races were said to predict and determine the cultural traits of peoples, so that cultural differences could be "explained" on a "scientific" basis. Scientific racism divided the world's populations into a few large species or groups. By the nineteenth century, race scientists settled on the term "Caucasians," first used as a synonym for Europeans in 1807, probably because the term's association with the Near East and Greece suited white people's desire to see themselves as having originated in the Golden Age of Classical Civilization. Caucasian usually appeared in a list of "major" race groups including also Mongolian (people of Asian descent), Ethiopian (people of African descent), and American Indian.

The fantasy of a "white race" with historical origins in Classical Civilization white-washed the complexion of Greece and Rome (whose people were a mixture of Mediterranean, Semitic, and African populations each bringing unique cultural traditions to the table). Postulating a direct biological descent from this Classical fantasy to the present helped justify contemporary racist practices. White plantation owners in the American South, for example, built their plantations according to Neo-Classical architecture (as did the architects of our nation's capitol), so that the slave master's mansion would recall the Parthenon of Ancient Greece, suggesting a racial continuity between the Classical forefathers and the slave owners. In the construction of whiteness, it was regularly said that slavery and democracy were not a contradiction, since the ancient Greeks had themselves been slave owners and regularly persecuted races considered "barbarians." What was good enough for the original whites, it was thought, was good enough for the people of Virginia and South Carolina and Mississippi (an argument that was not widely contested by white Americans in the North).

Whiteness, then, emerged as what we now call a "pan-ethnic" category, as a way of merging a variety of European ethnic populations into a single "race," especially so as to distinguish them from people with whom they had very particular legal and political relations— Africans, Asians, American Indians—that were not equal to their

VISUAL CONNECTIONS: WHAT IS RACE?
As Jay indicates in paragraph 6, scholars have argued for many years about how to define race. Many have tried to find a scientific basis for the apparent differences in skin color and facial features that we associate with race. Consider this image from a project called *Human Race Machine* by artist Nancy Burson, which shows the same face in several different racial categories. What does this image communicate about race?

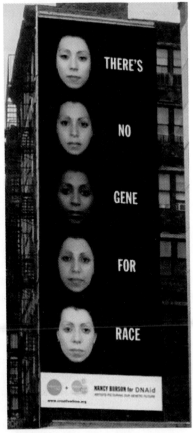

© Nancy Burson

The Human Race Machine, Nancy Burson, 2000

relations with one another as whites. But what of America as the great "melting pot"? When we read our history, we come to see that the "melting pot" never included certain darker ingredients, and never produced a substance that was anything but white. Take, for example, that first and most famous essay on the question "What is an American?" In 1781, an immigrant Frenchman turned New York farmer named Hector St. Jean de Crèvecoeur published his book *Letters from an American Farmer.* Here are some lines from its most quoted pages:

> . . . whence came all these people? They are a mixture of English, Scotch, Irish, French, Dutch, Germans, and Swedes. From this promiscuous breed, that race now called Americans have arisen. What, then, is the American, this new man? He is neither an European nor the descendant of an European; hence that strange mixture of blood, which you will find in no other country. I could point out to you a family whose grandfather was an Englishman, whose wife was Dutch, whose son married a French woman, and whose present four sons have now four wives of different nations. *He* is an American, who, leaving behind him all his ancient prejudices and manners, receives new ones from the new mode of life he has embraced, the new government he obeys, and the new rank he holds. . . . The Americans were once scattered all over Europe; here they are incorporated into one of the finest systems of populations which has ever appeared.

10   No longer a European, the American represents a new race made from the stock of various European nations. No mention is made of Africans or Indians, perhaps because this new American race does indeed receive new prejudices from the new mode of life it has embraced. Crèvecoeur candidly describes the process by which the American race originated as a white race; or rather, the way in which the descendants of Europeans constructed a myth of themselves as a white race with special claim on the answer to the question "What is an American?" An American was a white man. Just as importantly, America was that place where the downtrodden classes of Europe could throw off the oppression of aristocrats and attain not only fraternal equality among themselves, but superiority over those who were not of the new white race. When the Constitution of the United States was written, it thus specifically enshrined slavery into law and denied citizenship to enslaved Africans. When the Naturalization Act of 1789 was made law, it stipulated that only "whites" were eligible for naturalization as citizens (a clause persistently contested by people of Chinese and Japanese ancestry for the next 150 years).

In a fascinating, provocative book called *How the Irish Became White,* Noel Ignatiev describes this process of Europeans becoming white in the case of the Irish immigrants of the nineteenth century. Ireland was a colony devastated by English imperialism, and by a racial stereotyping of the Irish as backward, primitive, savage, and barbarian (in no small measure because of their Catholicism). When the Irish set foot in America, they were still subject to much of the racial prejudice and discrimination they had suffered at home at the hands of the British. Irish immigrants to America occupied a position only just above that of the blacks, alongside whom they often labored on the docks or railroads. For the Irish, becoming white would offer many advantages, not least of which would be the elimination of their major competitors for jobs. The Irish began to organize the exclusion of Northern free blacks from shipyard or factory employment, and continued this discrimination in later generations when the Irish dominated the police and firemen's unions in most cities. The Irish formed a key ingredient in the pro-slavery coalition that sat at the core of the Democratic Party in America before the Civil War, and which was brought to full power by the Indian killer and Southern patriot Andrew Jackson. White working class men, many of them Irish, opposed the abolition of slavery because of the threat they believed free blacks would pose to their economic prosperity, just as they opposed the extension of slavery into the new territories because of the threat slavery would pose to the creation of high wage jobs in the West. The hostility between the Irish and the blacks that lives on until today has its roots in this early history of how the Irish became white, and of how various Irish-dominated institutions in urban America—especially police and fire departments and labor unions—prospered through racial discrimination.

Whiteness, of course, is a delusion—as the insane Captain Ahab of *Moby Dick* demonstrates. Scientists today agree that there is no such thing as "race," at least when analyzed in terms of genetics or behavioral variation. Every human population is a mongrel population, full of people descended from various places and with widely differing physical qualities. Racial purity is the most absurd delusion, since intermarriage and miscegenation have been far more the norm than the exception throughout human ethnic history. "Race," then, is what academics like to call a "socially constructed" reality. Race is a reality in the sense that people experience it as real and base much of their behavior on it. Race, however, is only real because certain social institutions and practices make it real. Race is real in the same way that a building or a religion or a political ideology is real, as each is the result of human effort, not a prescription from nature or God. Thus the concept of race can have little or no foundation, yet it can still be the force that makes or breaks someone's life, or the life of a people or a nation.

For white people, race functions as a large ensemble of practices and rules that give white people all sorts of small and large advantages in life. Whiteness is the source of many privileges, which is one reason people have trouble giving it up. It is important to stress that to criticize whiteness is not necessarily to engage in a massive orchestration of guilt. Guilt is often a distracting and mistaken emotion, especially when it comes to race. White people are fond of pointing out that as individuals they have never practiced discrimination, or that their ancestors never owned slaves. White people tend to cast the question of race in terms of guilt in part because of the American ideology of individualism, by which I mean our tendency to want to believe that individuals determine their own destinies and responsibilities. In this sense it is un-American to insist that white

CONVERSATIONS: THE IRISH IN AMERICA

In paragraph 11, Jay discusses the history of the Irish people and how they have been viewed both in Europe and in the United States. The status of the Irish has long been a matter of cultural and political controversy and conflict, complicated by longstanding religious tensions between Catholics and Protestants. These controversies continue to be the focus of attention today. The film *Gangs of New York* (2002) portrays some of the history of the Irish in New York. It's worth considering what a film like this one might suggest about the struggles of a people to define itself and to resist being defined in certain ways. It's also worth thinking about how popular films like this one contribute to ongoing discussions about specific racial or ethnic groups. In this essay, Jay is arguing in part that how we discuss race makes a difference. Since popular films are a medium by which these discussions take place, we might consider how they influence such discussions.

STRATEGIES: USING EXAMPLES TO ILLUSTRATE A POINT

In paragraphs 12 and 13, Jay is discussing complex theoretical ideas related to what he calls the "social construction" of reality. (If you're interested in exploring these ideas further, you can consult the work of Pierre Bourdieu and Peter Berger, two important theorists who have written about social construction theory.) Here, Jay provides several general but concrete examples of how his own racial "whiteness" might affect his daily life. Consider how effectively these brief examples help you understand his larger abstract point about the privileges of the racial category of whiteness.

CONVERSATIONS: THE ABOLITION OF WHITENESS
Jay's reference in this paragraph to the work of David
Roediger is one example of how scholars and critics use
each other's work to continue discussions of issues like
race. Roediger is a well-known historian and author of
Towards the Abolition of Whiteness (1994). Jay's reference to Roediger's work helps him make his point in this
paragraph. What else might this reference accomplish?

Americans benefit every day from their whiteness, whether
or not they intend to do so. But that is the reality. Guilt,
then, has nothing to do with whiteness in this sense of benefiting from structural racism and built-in privileges. I may
not intend anything racial when I apply for a loan, or walk
into a store, or hail a cab, or ask for a job—but in every circumstance my whiteness will play a role in the outcome,
however "liberal" or "anti-racist" I imagine myself to be.
White men have enormous economic advantages because
of the disadvantages faced by women and minorities, no matter what any individual
white men may intend. If discrimination means that fewer qualified applicants compete with you for the job, you benefit. You do not have to be a racist to benefit from
being white. You just have to look the part.

The privileges of whiteness are the not-so-secret dirty truth about race relations in
America. Three decades after Dr. King, we should be able to see that our blindness
to whiteness has crippled us in our walk toward equality and justice and freedom. As
the national conversation on race continues, let us resolve to make whiteness an issue, and not just on this holiday or during Black History Month. When we talk about
race in America, we should be talking about the invention of whiteness, and about
what David Roediger calls the "abolition of whiteness." From this perspective, the
end of racism will not come when America grants equal rights to minorities. Racism
will end only with the abolition of whiteness, when the white whale that has been the
source of so many delusions is finally left to disappear beneath the sea of time forever.

UNDERSTANDING THE TEXT

1. In what ways have people become blind to whiteness, according to Jay? What are the consequences of this blindness? Do you agree with him? Why or why not?

2. Explain Jay's statement that "ironically, white Americans can only define themselves by comparison to that which they are not, and so whiteness depends on blackness for its very definition." What is ironic about this situation? What are the implications of this idea in Jay's view?

3. According to Jay, where did the racial category of whiteness come from? What evidence does he offer to support his analysis of the emergence of white as a racial category? How persuasive do you find this evidence?

4. What are the privileges of whiteness, according to Jay? How does our blindness to whiteness affect these privileges? Do you think Jay is right about the privileges of whiteness? Explain. You might draw on your own experience or the experiences of people you know to support your answer.

EXPLORING THE ISSUES

1. Throughout this essay, Jay refers to and quotes from various scholars and other authors who have written about race. Examine these references. Who are the authors Jay refers to? What kind of credibility or expertise do they have? How effectively do you think Jay uses these references to support his arguments? What might the specific references Jay uses suggest about the audience Jay imagined for this essay?

2. In paragraph 5, Jay writes, "Since human beings appear to require a sense of identity, and since identity is constructed by defining whom and what you are different from, it may be that the politics of difference will never be erased from human affairs." Do you think Jay is right? Explain, drawing on other readings in this chapter to support your answer. If Jay is right that we will always define ourselves as different from others, what might this mean for our efforts to eliminate some of the terrible effects of racism and racial conflict?

3. Writing about race can be a difficult task, especially because it is such a sensitive issue for many people and because it remains among the most charged and controversial issues in American culture. Certainly, Jay must have known that by making his argument about whiteness he risked angering many readers. What evidence do you see that Jay tried to be sensitive to readers of certain backgrounds or beliefs? Do you think he wrote this essay in a way that is intended to provoke certain readers? Explain, citing specific passages from his essay to support your answer.

4. How do you describe Jay's voice in this essay? In what ways do you think his voice contributes to or detracts from his argument? Provide examples from his essay to support your answer.

ENTERING THE CONVERSATIONS

1. Write an essay in which you discuss how your racial identity has affected your life. In your essay, define your race as you understand it and draw on your experiences to describe how it has impacted your life and your relationships to others.

2. In a group of classmates, share the essays you wrote for Question 1. Identify similarities and differences in the way race seems to have been a factor in your lives. Try to draw conclusions about the way we use race to define one another.

3. Write an essay for your local newspaper expressing your thoughts on the occasion of Martin Luther King, Jr. Day.

4. At one point in his essay, Jay writes, "Since human beings appear to require a sense of identity, and since identity is constructed by defining whom and what you are different from, it may be that the politics of difference will never be erased from human affairs." Write an essay in which you respond to this point. What are the consequences of this point of view? What does it mean in terms of our collective efforts to combat racism and solve racial conflict? To what extent do you think Jay is right? Try to address such questions in your essay.

DIVERSE SELVES, MULTIPLE IDENTITIES

EVERY FOUR YEARS DURING THE U.S. PRESIDEN-TIAL ELECTION, WE HEAR A LOT ABOUT "THE AMERICAN PEOPLE." I OFTEN WONDER WHAT THAT PHRASE MEANS. WHO EXACTLY ARE *THE AMERICAN PEOPLE*, ANYWAY? POLITICIANS LIKE TO USE THE PHRASE AS IF WE ARE all essentially the same, as if the differences among us are irrelevant. But hearing someone say "the American people" always reminds me of how diverse the people of the United States really are.

Try this little experiment: Make a list of people you know, such as your close friends, family members, coworkers, people in clubs or organizations you belong to, or neighbors— anyone you see regularly. Then, next to each name, write down a description of who that person is. Include any important details about that person. Chances are that even on a short list, you'll have many different kinds of people. For example, on my list would be people who are White, Black, Asian, and Hispanic; people from several different parts of the United States and a few from other countries; people who are Catholic, Jewish, Buddhist, and Protestant; people of many different ages and people who do many different things for a living; and people with different political views. Many of the people I am thinking of fall into several of these categories at the same time. For example, one of my coworkers is a bilingual Catholic, Hispanic woman from the northeastern United States. One of my students is also a bilingual Catholic woman, but her mother is from Spain whereas her father is an Irish American. The more I think about the people I know, the more diverse they seem to become.

The readings in this cluster call attention to that kind of diversity. They explore different racial, ethnic, and cultural identities. And they reveal that none of us has a single identity; rather, each of us has many identities related to important aspects of our lives, such as race, national origin, gender, ethnicity, age, and so much else. In many ways, I find this to be the most fascinating aspect of the whole idea of *identity:* the multiplicity of identities that a single person can have and the many different ways that those identities can affect a person's life. My race might be the most impor-tant aspect of my identity in some contexts, but in other situations, my age or gender or perhaps the fact that I am a father or a teacher may be more important. That's part of the richness and the challenge of living in a diverse society. We can be many things to many people.

But although this kind of diversity is often celebrated, the multiple identities we each have can often complicate our lives in less desirable ways. The writers whose essays appear in this cluster explore that complexity and the challenges it can bring to individuals who sometimes struggle with different identities. My hope is that these readings not

> That's part of the richness and the challenge of living in a diverse society. We can be many things to many people.

only help you appreciate this complexity in others but also enable you to see it in yourself.

I also hope these readings call your attention to the many issues that relate to *identity*. For example, the essays in this cluster address such issues as immigration and assimilation, culture, national identity, multiculturalism, and racism. To some extent, *identity* is a term that helps us make sense of age-old questions about who we are. But it is also a term that can divert our attention from other ways of seeing the world and other people around us. Imagine, for example, if we strictly adhered to the Zen Buddhist ideal of "erasing the self." What if we stopped focusing on identity as an issue? How would that change the way we understand and interact with each other?

What if you woke up one morning and discovered that you were a different race? If
that sounds far-fetched, you'll want to read
the following essay by Erin Aubry Kaplan
(b. 1961), which first appeared in LA
Weekly in 2003. Kaplan, a journalist, tells
the story of Wayne Joseph, who lived his life
believing that he was a Black man until he
took a DNA test when he was fifty-one years
old. (A DNA test identifies a person's genetic
makeup, which can be matched with people

Black Like I Thought I Was

of similar racial backgrounds.) That test indicated that Joseph actually had no Black
blood in him. He is Indo-European and
Native American, but not Black. Under-
standably, the results of the DNA test
shocked Joseph, and it left him deeply uncertain about his own identity. After living his
entire life as a Black person, he was now
faced with the knowledge that he was not
Black. How could he suddenly give up a
part of his identity that was so central to his
life and his way of understanding himself?

If Wayne Joseph's experience raised hard
questions for him, it raises similarly hard
questions for all of us. As Joseph asks at the
end of this essay, "The question ultimately
is, are you who you say you are, or are you
who you are genetically?" What makes someone Black or White or Asian or any other
race? Is Joseph Black because he was raised
as a Black person? Is he Black because for
his entire life other people accepted him as a
Black person? And does race overshadow
other important aspects of his—or anyone's—
identity? Such questions highlight the complexity of race as an identity. But we might
also ask why race matters so much in the
first place. Isn't Joseph the same person now
that he was before his DNA test? Keep that
question in mind as you read about his remarkable experience. ▼

ERIN AUBRY KAPLAN

Wayne Joseph is a 51-year-old high school principal in
Chino whose family emigrated from the segregated parishes of
Louisiana to central Los Angeles in the 1950s, as did mine. Like me, he
is of Creole stock and is therefore on the lighter end of the black color
spectrum, a common enough circumstance in the South that predates
the multicultural movement by centuries. And like most other black
folk, Joseph grew up with an unequivocal sense of his heritage and of
himself; he tends toward black advocacy and has published thoughtful
opinion pieces on racial issues in magazines like *Newsweek*. When
Joseph decided on a whim to take a new ethnic DNA test he saw described on a *60 Minutes* segment last year, it was only to indulge a casual
curiosity about the exact percentage of black blood; virtually all black
Americans are mixed with something, he knew, but he figured it would
be interesting to make himself a guinea pig for this new testing process,
which is offered by a Florida-based company called DNA Print Gen-
omics Inc. The experience would at least be fodder for another essay
for *Newsweek*. He got his kit in the mail, swabbed his mouth per the instructions and sent off the DNA samples for analysis.

ERIN AUBRY KAPLAN, "BLACK LIKE I THOUGHT I WAS" *LA WEEKLY*, OCTOBER 3, 2003
HTTP://WWW.LAWEEKLY.COM/. REPRINTED BY PERMISSION.

GLOSS: MISCEGENATION
Miscegenation is the mixing of races through marriage and/or sexual relations. The term has long been used to refer to the mixing of Blacks and Whites in the United States.

Now, I have always believed that what is now widely considered one of slavery's worst legacies—the Southern "one-drop" rule that indicted anyone with black blood as a nigger and cleaved American society into black and white with a single stroke—was also slavery's only upside. Of course I deplore the motive behind the law, which was rooted not only in white paranoia about **miscegenation,** but in a more practical need to maintain social order by keeping privilege and property in the hands of whites. But by forcing blacks of all complexions and blood percentages into the same boat, the law ironically laid a foundation of black unity that remains in place today. It's a foundation that allows us to talk abstractly about a "black community" as concretely as we talk about a black community in Harlem or Chicago or South-Central (a liberty that's often abused or lazily applied in modern discussions of race). And it gives the lightest-skinned among us the assurance of identity that everybody needs in order to feel grounded and psychologically whole—even whites, whose **public non-ethnicity is really ethnicity writ so large** and influential it needs no name. Being black may still not be the most advantageous thing in the world, but being nothing or being neutral—the rallying cry of modern-day multiculturalists—has never made any emotional or real-world sense. Color marks you, but your membership in black society also gives you an indestructible house to live in and a bed to rest on. I can't imagine growing up any other way.

CONNECTIONS: WHITENESS
Kaplan states that the "public non-ethnicity" of White people is "really ethnicity writ so large and influential it needs no name." Compare this statement to Gregory Jay's idea that whiteness is "invisible" (see page 96).

Wayne Joseph can't, either. But when the results of his DNA test came back, he found himself staggered by the idea that though he still qualified as a person of color, it was not the color he was raised to think he was, one with a distinct culture and definitive place in the American struggle for social equality that he'd taken for granted. Here was the unexpected and rather unwelcome truth: Joseph was 57 percent Indo-European, 39 percent Native American, 4 percent East Asian—and zero percent African. After a lifetime of assuming blackness, he was now being told that he lacked even a single drop of black blood to qualify.

"My son was flabbergasted by the results," says Joseph. "He said, 'Dad, you mean for 50 years you've been passing for black?'" Joseph admits that, strictly speaking, he has. But he's not sure if he can or wants to do anything about that at this point. For all the lingering effects of institutional racism, he's been perfectly content being a black man; it has shaped his worldview and the course of his life in ways that cannot, and probably should not, be altered. Yet Joseph struggles to balance the intellectual dishonesty of saying he's black with the unimpeachable honesty of a lifelong experience of *being* black. "What do I do with this information?" he says, sounding more than a little exasperated. "It was like finding out you're adopted. I don't want to be disingenuous with myself. But I can't conceive of living any other way. It's a question of what's logical and what's visceral."

5   Race, of course, has always been a far more visceral matter than a logical one. We now know that there is no such thing as race, that humans are biologically one species; we know that an African is likely to have more in common genetically with a European thousands of miles away than with a neighboring African. Yet this knowledge has not deterred the racism many Europeans continue to harbor toward Africans, nor the wariness Africans harbor toward Europeans. Such feelings may

never be deterred. And despite all the loud assertions to the contrary, race is still America's bane, and its fascination; Philip Roth's widely acclaimed last novel set in the 1990s, *The Human Stain,* features a **Faustian protagonist** whose great moral failing is that he's a black man who's been passing most of his life for white (the book was made into a movie in 2003).

GLOSS: FAUSTIAN PROTAGONIST
Dr. Faustus is a famed character in a German legend who makes a deal with the Devil in return for power. The term *Faustian bargain* is used to refer to morally or ethically questionable deals in which someone gains something by selling out in some way. A Faustian protagonist is someone who makes such a deal.

Joseph recognizes this, and while he argues for a more rational and less emotional view of race for the sake of equity, he also recognizes that rationality is not the same thing as fact. As much as he might want to, he can't simply refute his black past and declare himself white or Native American. He can acknowledge the truth but can't quite apply it, which makes it pretty much useless to other, older members of his family. An aunt whom he told about the test results only said that she wasn't surprised. "When I told my mother about the test, she said to me, 'I'm too old and too tired to be anything else,'" recalls Joseph. "It makes no difference to her. It's an easy issue."

After recovering from the initial shock, Joseph began questioning his mother about their lineage. He discovered that, unbeknownst to him, his grandparents had made a conscious decision back in Louisiana to *not* be white, claiming they didn't want to side with a people who were known oppressors. Joseph says there was another, more practical consideration: Some men in the family routinely courted black women, and they didn't want the very public hassle such a pairing entailed in the South, which included everything from dirty looks to the ignominy of a couple having to separate on buses and streetcars and in restaurants per the Jim Crow laws. I know that the laws also pointedly separated mothers from sons, uncles from nephews, simply because one happened to be lighter than the other or have straighter hair. Determinations of race were entirely subjective and imposed from without, and the one-drop rule was enforced to such divisive and schizophrenic effects that Joseph's family—and mine—fled Louisiana for the presumably less boundary-obsessed West. But we didn't flee ourselves, and didn't expect to; we simply set up a new home in Los Angeles. The South was wrong about its policies but it was right about our color. It had to be.

Joseph remains tortured by the possibility that maybe nobody is right. The essay he thought the DNA test experience would prompt became a book that he's already 150 pages into. He doesn't seem to know how it'll end. He's in a kind of limbo that he doesn't want and that I frankly wouldn't wish on anyone; when I wonder aloud about taking the $600 DNA test myself, Joseph flatly advises against it. "You don't want to know," he says. "It's like a genie coming out of a bottle. You can't put it back in." He has more empathy for the colorblind crowd than he had before, but isn't inclined to believe that the Ward Connerlys and other professed racial conservatives of the world have the best interests of colored people at heart. "I see their point, but race *does* matter, especially with things like medical research and other social trends," he says of **Connerly's Proposition**

CONTEXT: CONNERLY'S PROPOSITION 54
In 2003, Californians defeated Proposition 54, the Racial Privacy Initiative, a state ballot initiative that would have made it illegal for the government to collect any information regarding the race of individual citizens. Ward Connerly, a regent of the University of California, was a leader in the effort to pass Proposition 54. He argued that ignoring race altogether would benefit Blacks and other minorities. Consider how Wayne Joseph's experience might influence someone's view of an initiative like Proposition 54 and the idea of "color blindness." What is the significance of his experience in view of Proposition 54?

54, the much-derided state measure that seeks to outlaw the collection of ethnic data that will be voted on in the recall election next Tuesday. "Problems like that can't just go away." For the moment, Joseph is compelled to try to judge individually what he knows has always been judged broadly, to reconcile two famously opposed viewpoints of race not for the sake of political argument—he has made those—but for his own peace of mind. He's wrestling with a riddle that will likely outlive him, though he doesn't worry that it will be passed on to the next generation—his ex-wife is black, enough to give his children the firm ethnic identity he had and that he embraced for most of his life. "The question ultimately is, are you who you say you are, or are you who you are genetically?" he muses. The logical—and visceral—answer is that it's not black and white.

UNDERSTANDING THE TEXT

1. Why does Wayne Joseph struggle with the question of whether to tell people that he is Black or not? What do you think his struggle with this question suggests about him? What does it suggest about race as an aspect of our identity? Do you think he should continue to identify himself as Black? Why or why not?

2. How did Joseph's family come to be identified as Black? Why is this part of their history important? What might it suggest about how race is defined and treated in American society?

3. What does Kaplan mean when she writes at the end of paragraph 7 that "the South was wrong about its policies but it was right about our color. It had to be." Do you think she's right? Explain.

EXPLORING THE ISSUES

1. In paragraph 7, Kaplan tells some of the history of Wayne Joseph's family and of her own family. Why do you think she includes this reference to her own background in an article that is about Joseph? What advantages and disadvantages do you see to Kaplan including this information about herself? How does this knowledge about Kaplan affect the way you read this article?

2. Kaplan writes in paragraph 2 that being Black gives someone "an indestructible house to live in and a bed to rest on." Examine her use of metaphor to make this point. What does this metaphor of a house suggest about racial identity? Do you find the metaphor effective in this case? Explain.

3. Near the end of her article, Kaplan refers to Proposition 54 (see *Context: Connerly's Proposition 54* on page 107). Examine how this context might affect the way readers react to Kaplan's article. Given that Proposition 54 would have effectively outlawed official records of a person's race, does Proposition 54 affect the significance of Wayne Joseph's experiences in any way?

ENTERING THE CONVERSATIONS

1. Write an essay in which you discuss whether Wayne Joseph should continue to identify himself as a Black man, even after DNA testing shows that he is not. In your essay, support your position on Joseph's decision and discuss your view of the role of race in our identities and the importance of racial identity in contemporary society.

2. In a group of classmates, share the essays you wrote for Question 1. Try to identify the main arguments in support of Joseph's decision to continue identifying himself as a Black man and the arguments against that decision. Debate these positions with your group members, and try to draw conclusions about the way race is used as a category in contemporary society.

INFOTRAC

3. In this essay, Kaplan criticizes a movement that has come to be called *multiculturalism,* which is a general view that celebrates diversity and promotes racial, ethnic, and cultural tolerance. She writes that "being nothing or being neutral— the rallying cry of modern-day multiculturalists—has never made any emotional or real-world sense." Using InfoTrac College Edition and any other appropriate resources, find out about multiculturalism. What is this movement? How did it get started? What are the main views and goals of people that Kaplan calls "multiculturalists"? What impact has it had on American society? Try to address such questions in your research. You might consider speaking to someone on your campus who has expertise in these issues (for example, a professor who specializes in cultural studies or African American studies). Write a report providing a description of multiculturalism and its impact on American society. Draw your own conclusions about whether or not Kaplan is right in her criticisms of multiculturalism.

4. Write an essay for an audience of your classmates in which you tell the story of an incident or experience in which your racial identity was somehow important.

5. Create a web site, PowerPoint presentation, or other kind of document that conveys your sense of racial identity.

I grew up in a family whose Polish traditions *were kept alive by my grandmother and a few other relatives of her generation. My great grandparents were immigrants who came to the United States from Poland at the turn of the twentieth century, and as far as my grandmother was concerned, Polish was the way we should describe ourselves. In fact, in the small Pennsylvania town where I grew up, people often described themselves as Polish, Lithuanian, Ukrainian, Czech, or*

Crossing THE Border WITHOUT Losing Your Past

some other eastern European nationality, even though they were all born and raised in the United States. For my father's generation, however, being Polish wasn't necessarily something to be celebrated, partly because of the prejudice against eastern European immigrants that was held by people of other nationalities in that part of Pennsylvania during the first half of the twentieth century. My father liked to say that we weren't Polish; we were Americans. And over the years, our Polish identity seems to have faded.

Writer Oscar Casares (b. 1964) also has a family history that includes immigration to the United States. But his Mexican identity remains a central part of who he is. Indeed, although he and his parents were born and continue to live in the United States, Casares refuses to use the label Mexican American. He prefers Mexican to describe himself. As I read this essay, I wondered why Casares' family has held onto its immigrant roots, while my family—and the other families where I grew up—have not. Does it have to do with time?   (continued)

OSCAR CASARES

Along with it being diez y seis de septiembre, **Mexican** Independence Day, today is my father's 89th birthday. Everardo Issasi Casares was born in 1914, a little more than a hundred years after Miguel Hidalgo y Costilla rang the church bells of Dolores, summoning his parishioners to rise up against the Spaniards.

This connection has always been important in my family. Though my father was born in the United States, he considers himself a Mexicano. To him, ancestry is what determines your identity. If you have Mexican blood, you are Mexican, whether you were born in Mexico City or New York City. This is not to say he denies his American citizenship—he votes, pays taxes and served in the Army. But his identity is tied to the past. His family came from Mexico, so like them he is Mexicano, punto, end of discussion.

In my hometown, Brownsville, Tex., almost everyone I know is *(continued) It has been 100 years since my ancestors immigrated to the United States, whereas Casares' ancestors were more recent arrivals. Is it skin color? All my ancestors were White, whereas Casares and his family are not. Is it language? My family gave up the Polish language long before I was born, but Spanish continues to be spoken in the region of the United States where Casares and his family live. I'm not sure what the answer is, but my family history and Casares' reflect some of the complexities of the identities that we claim for ourselves and that others assign to us. Chances are that your own identity is just as complex.*

Oscar Casares is a fiction writer whose collection of stories, Brownsville: Stories, *was published in 2003. This essay first appeared in the* New York Times *in 2003.* ◪

STRATEGIES: LANGUAGES

In the opening paragraph, Casares includes a brief Spanish phrase, "diez y seis de septiembre," without translating it into English. Writers sometimes include quotations in other languages in this way if they wish to preserve the quotation's original language. But here, Casares is not quoting from a text in another language; rather, he is using Spanish for this phrase (which means "September 16," the date in 1810 when Father Hidalgo, a Catholic priest, began a rebellion in the town of Dolores against the Spanish rulers in Mexico). Consider why Casares would include a Spanish phrase without translation in an essay written in English and published in an English-language newspaper, the *New York Times,* many of whose readers do not understand Spanish. What might he be trying to suggest by doing so? What do you think he is revealing about his attitudes toward his readers?

Mexicano: neighbors, teachers, principals, dropouts, doctors, lawyers, drug dealers, priests. Rich and poor, short and tall, fat and skinny, dark- and light-skinned. Every year our Mexican heritage is celebrated in a four-day festival called Charro Days. Men grow beards; mothers draw moustaches on their little boys and dress their little girls like Mexican peasants; the brave compete in a jalapeño-eating contest. But the celebration also commemorates the connection between two neighboring countries, opening with an exchange of gritos (traditional cowboy calls you might hear in a Mexican movie) between a representative from Matamoros, Mexico, standing on one side of the International Bridge and a Brownsville representative standing on the other.

Like many Americans whose families came to this country from somewhere else, many children of Mexican immigrants struggle with their identity, as our push to fully assimilate is met with an even greater pull to remain anchored to our family's country of origin. This is especially true when that country is less than a quarter of a mile away—the width of the Rio Grande—from the new one. We learn both cultures as effortlessly as we do two languages. We learn quickly that we can exist simultaneously in both worlds, and that our home exists neither here nor there but in the migration between these two forces.

But for Mexican-Americans and other immigrants from Spanish-speaking countries who have been lumped into categories like Latino or Hispanic, this struggle has become even more pronounced over the last few years as we have grown into the largest minority group in the United States. Our culture has been both embraced and exploited by advertisers, politicians and the media. And as we move, individually, from our small communities, where our identity is clear, we enter a world that wants to assign us a label of its choosing.

When I left Brownsville in 1985 to start school at the University of Texas at Austin one of the first things I was asked was, "What are you?" "I'm Mexican," I told the guy, who was thrown off by my height and light skin. "Really, what part of Mexico are you from?" he asked, which led me to explain I was really from Brownsville, but my parents were Mexican. "Really, what part of Mexico?" Here again I had to admit they weren't really born in Mexico and neither were my grandparents or great-grandparents. "Oh," he said, "you're Mexican-American, is what you are."

Mexican-American. I imagined a 300-mile-long hyphen that connected Brownsville to Austin, a bridge between my old and new world. Not that I hadn't seen this word combination, Mexican-American, on school applications, but I couldn't remember the words being spoken to me directly. In Brownsville, I always thought of myself as being equally Mexican and American.

CONVERSATIONS: ETHNIC LABELS

Throughout his essay, Casares devotes much attention to the different terms that can be used to identify himself: Mexican, Mexican-American, Latino, and Hispanic. In this paragraph, he discusses some of the reasons he does not prefer the term Hispanic to refer to himself, and he explains some of the connotations of that term. In explaining why he rejects this term, Casares is taking part in a much larger set of conversations about racial and ethnic identity that have been going on in American society for many years. He reminds us that certain terms may mean different things to different people and that the meanings of terms can evolve. Just as the term Negro, which was once an accepted term for Blacks, came to be seen as a negative label, Hispanic has taken on negative meanings when it is used to refer to people who come from Spanish-speaking countries. As a person of Mexican descent, Casares is obviously aware of the complexity of these terms. As a writer, he must be aware of the different meanings, both positive and negative, that these terms might have for different readers. (The readings in Chapter 8, *The Politics of Language,* may help you further explore the ways in which words can acquire various political meanings.)

When I graduated that label was again redefined. One of my first job interviews was at an advertising agency, where I was taken on a tour: the media department, the creative department, the account-service department, the Hispanic department. This last department specialized in marketing products to Spanish-speaking consumers. In the group were men and women from Mexico, Puerto Rico and California, but together they were Hispanic. I was hired to work in another department, but suddenly, everyone was referring to me as Hispanic.

Hispanic? Where was the Mexican in me? Where was the hyphen? I didn't want to be Hispanic. The word reminded me of those Mexican-Americans who preferred to say their families came from Spain, which they felt somehow increased their social status. Just hearing the word Hispanic reminded me, too, of people who used the word Spanish to refer to Mexicans. "The Spanish like to get wild at their fiestas," they would say, or "You Spanish people sure do have a lot of babies."

10   In this same way, the word Hispanic seemed to want to be more user friendly, especially when someone didn't want to say the M word: Mexican. Except it did slip out occasionally. I remember standing in my supervisor's office as he described calling the police after he saw a car full of "Mexicans" drive through his suburban neighborhood.

STRATEGIES: FIGURATIVE LANGUAGE

This paragraph includes a wonderful example of a writer skillfully using figurative language to help convey several ideas. Casares opens the paragraph with an explanation of the negative meanings of the word Mexican, including "criminal." A few sentences later, he uses the metaphor of a knife to help convey how he feels when he thinks about someone calling him a "Mexican." But notice how Casares subtly creates an image of a criminal, perhaps a mugger, pulling a knife suddenly on a victim. And he twists the expected meaning of this image so that he, the Mexican, becomes the victim, and the hypothetical person calling him "Mexican" becomes the criminal wielding the knife. Consider how Casares manipulates this metaphor and relies on prejudices against Mexicans to convey several messages in this passage.

Away from the border, **the word Mexican** had come to mean dirty, shiftless, drunken, lustful, criminal. I still cringe whenever I think someone might say the word. But usually it happens unexpectedly, as though the person has pulled a knife on me. I feel the sharp words up against my gut. Because of my appearance, people often say things in front of me they wouldn't say if they knew my real ethnicity—not Hispanic, Latino or even Mexican-American. I am, like my father, Mexican, and on this day of independence, I say this with particular pride.

UNDERSTANDING THE TEXT

1. Why is it important for Casares to identify himself as Mexican rather than as Mexican American or Hispanic? What differences does he see among these ways of defining his ethnic or racial identity? Do you think these differences are important? Explain.

2. Given that neither Casares nor his parents were born in Mexico, what is the role of their family history in how Casares identifies himself as Mexican? Do you agree with him that this history is as important to his identity as his American citizenship? Why or why not?

3. In paragraph 5, Casares writes that immigrants from Spanish-speaking countries "have been lumped into categories like Latino or Hispanic." Who has done this lumping? Why? What might this lumping suggest about how racial or ethnic labels are used?

EXPLORING THE ISSUES

1. In the opening paragraph, Casares refers to Mexican Independence Day, which celebrates Mexico's independence from Spain. Later, Casares discusses why he dislikes the term Hispanic as a way to refer to himself. What connection does Casares make between this history of Mexico and the term Hispanic? Why is this connection important to him? What does it suggest about race, ethnicity, and national origin as aspects of our identities?

2. Casares discusses several different labels for his identity (such as Mexican-American, Latino, Hispanic) and how the meanings of those labels can change or be redefined. What do you think the changing meanings of these labels suggests about how we describe our own identities and the identities of others?

3. Casares draws heavily on his own experiences as a person of Mexican descent in the United States to support his points and to explain his views. Evaluate his use of these experiences. How effectively do you think he uses them to make his points and convey his ideas?

ENTERING THE CONVERSATIONS

1. Write an essay in which you describe your own ethnic or racial identity.

2. Select a term that is used to identify people of a particular race, ethnicity, or nationality and write an essay in which you research the meanings and uses of that term. In your essay, provide some history of that term and how it has been used. Try to identify the meanings it has for different people. Draw conclusions about the use of such labels when referring to one's identity. (You may have to do some research for this assignment depending on the term you choose.)

3. Create a web site or photo essay depicting your identity or identities.

4. In a group of classmates, share the projects you created for Question 3. What do these projects indicate about how each of you understands his or her identity? What conclusions can you draw about the many different identities we can have?

5. Search the Internet for web sites devoted to people identified with a particular racial or ethnic group (or some other kind of group). Select several of these web sites, taking care to be sure that they are credible and analyze them for the way they present the identity of the people they represent. Write a report of your analysis in which you describe the web sites you reviewed and discuss what these sites might suggest about the racial or ethnic identity of the people the sites claim to represent.

6. In recent decades, discussions of immigration in the United States have focused on people of Hispanic descent, in part because of the large numbers of people from Mexico who cross illegally into the United States. Photos like the one below have become common in newspapers, in magazines, and on web sites. Using this photo and others that you find in print or online sources depicting immigrants, write an essay in which you analyze the way immigrants are portrayed in the media today.

© Paul Fusco/Magnum Photos

USA-Mexico Border Wall: Aliens prepare to cross over, under, or through the 10 foot high steel wall, 1993.

As I was writing this book, I happened to have a conversation with a former student of mine who had been living in Sweden for the past several years. He was born and raised in the United States, but he and his wife, who is Swedish, had decided to raise their family in Sweden because they consider it a safer, more tolerant society than the United States today. My former student believes this is the right choice for his family, but it was not an easy decision for him be-

American Dreamer

cause he considers himself an American, not a European or a Swede.

I was thinking about him as I read the following essay by Bharati Mukherjee (b. 1940), an immigrant from India who is a naturalized U.S. citizen and who unequivocally describes herself as an American. Mukherjee has strong views on what it means to be American—and on the issue of identity in general. For her, to be an American has less to do with one's culture or race than it does with the ideals that are reflected in the U.S. Constitution. In her view, America is as much an idea as it is a place. I think my former student would agree with her, yet his understanding of the idea of America has led him to a different conclusion about what it means to be an American. I don't know whether Mukherjee's essay would change his mind. It may change yours.

Bharati Mukherjee is an acclaimed writer whose books include The Middleman and Other Stories *(1988) and* Jasmine *(1999). This essay appeared in* Mother Jones *magazine in 1997.* ▼

BHARATI MUKHERJEE

The United States exists as a sovereign nation. "America," in contrast, exists as a myth of democracy and equal opportunity to live by, or as an ideal goal to reach.

I am a naturalized U.S. citizen, which means that, unlike native-born citizens, I had to prove to the U.S. government that I merited citizenship. What I didn't have to disclose was that I desired "America," which to me is the stage for the drama of self-transformation.

I was born in Calcutta and first came to the United States—to Iowa City, to be precise—on a summer evening in 1961. I flew into a small airport surrounded by cornfields and pastures, ready to carry out the two commands my father had written out for me the night before I left Calcutta: Spend two years studying creative writing at the Iowa Writers' Workshop, then come back home and marry the bridegroom he selected for me from our caste and class.

In traditional Hindu families like ours, men provided and women were provided for. My father was a patriarch and I a pliant daughter. The neighborhood I'd grown up in was homogeneously Hindu,

Bengali-speaking, and middle-class. I didn't expect myself to ever disobey or disappoint my father by setting my own goals and taking charge of my future.

When I landed in Iowa 35 years ago, I found myself in a society in which almost everyone was Christian, white, and moderately well-off. In the women's dormitory I lived in my first year, apart from six international graduate students (all of us were from Asia and considered "exotic"), the only non-Christian was Jewish, and the only nonwhite an African-American from Georgia. I didn't anticipate then, that over the next 35 years, the Iowa population would become so diverse that it would have 6,931 children from non-English-speaking homes registered as students in its schools, nor that Iowans would be in the grip of a cultural crisis in which resentment against immigrants, particularly refugees from Vietnam, Sudan, and Bosnia, as well as unskilled Spanish-speaking workers, would become politicized enough to cause the Immigration and Naturalization Service to open an "enforcement" office in Cedar Rapids in October for the tracking and deporting of undocumented aliens.

In Calcutta in the '50s, I heard no talk of "identity crisis"—communal or individual. The concept itself—of a person not knowing who he or she is—was unimaginable in our hierarchical, classification-obsessed society. One's identity was fixed, derived from religion, caste, patrimony, and mother tongue. A Hindu Indian's last name announced his or her forefathers' caste and place of origin. A Mukherjee could *only* be a Brahmin from Bengal. Hindu tradition forbade intercaste, interlanguage, interethnic marriages. Bengali tradition even discouraged emigration: To remove oneself from Bengal was to dilute true culture.

Until the age of 8, I lived in a house crowded with 40 or 50 relatives. My identity was viscerally connected with ancestral soil and genealogy. I was who I was because I was Dr. Sudhir Lal Mukherjee's daughter, because I was a Hindu Brahmin, because I was Bengali-speaking, and because my *desh*—the Bengali word for homeland—was an East Bengal village called Faridpur.

The University of Iowa classroom was my first experience of coeducation. And after not too long, I fell in love with a fellow student named Clark Blaise, an American of Canadian origin, and impulsively married him during a lunch break in a lawyer's office above a coffee shop.

That act cut me off forever from the rules and ways of upper-middle-class life in Bengal, and hurled me into a New World life of scary improvisations and heady explorations. Until my lunch-break wedding, I had seen myself as an Indian foreign student who intended to return to India to live. The five-minute ceremony in the lawyer's office suddenly changed me into a transient with conflicting loyalties to two very different cultures.

The first 10 years into marriage, years spent mostly in my husband's native Canada, I thought of myself as an expatriate Bengali permanently stranded in North America because of destiny or desire. My first novel, *The Tiger's Daughter,* embodies the loneliness I felt but could not acknowledge, even to myself, as I negotiated the no man's land between the country of my past and the continent of my present. Shaped by memory, textured with nostalgia for a class and culture I had abandoned, this novel quite naturally became an expression of the expatriate consciousness.

It took me a decade of painful introspection to put nostalgia in perspective and to make the transition from expatriate to immigrant. After a 14-year stay in Canada, I

CONVERSATIONS: MULTICULTURALISM
Since the 1980s, the idea of multiculturalism has become an influential way of thinking about diversity and differences related to race, ethnicity, culture, gender, and other important aspects of identity. But in recent years, many observers have criticized the idea of multiculturalism, which seems to promote tolerance and celebrate diversity, on the grounds that it actually reinforces problematic attitudes about race, ethnicity, culture, and so on. Here, especially in paragraph 22, Mukherjee weighs in on this important conversation, offering her own criticism of multiculturalism. You might compare Mukherjee's position on multiculturalism to Erin Aubry Kaplan's discussion of it in her essay (par. 2 on page 106).

forced my husband and our two sons to relocate to the United States. But the transition from foreign student to U.S. citizen, from detached onlooker to committed immigrant, has not been easy.

The years in Canada were particularly harsh. Canada is a country that officially, and proudly, resists cultural fusion. For all its rhetoric about a cultural "mosaic," Canada refuses to renovate its national self-image to include its changing complexion. It is a New World country with Old World concepts of a fixed, exclusivist national identity. Canadian official rhetoric designated me as one of the "visible minority" who, even though I spoke the Canadian languages of English and French, was straining "the absorptive capacity" of Canada. Canadians of color were routinely treated as "not real" Canadians. One example: In 1985 a terrorist bomb, planted in an Air-India jet on Canadian soil, blew up after leaving Montreal, killing 329 passengers, most of whom were Canadians of Indian origin. The prime minister of Canada at the time, Brian Mulroney, phoned the prime minister of India to offer Canada's condolences for India's loss.

Those years of race-related harassments in Canada politicized me and deepened my love of the ideals embedded in the American Bill of Rights. I don't forget that the architects of the Constitution and the Bill of Rights were white males and slaveholders. But through their declaration, they provided us with the enthusiasm for human rights, and the initial framework from which other empowerments could be conceived and enfranchised communities expanded.

15   I am a naturalized U.S. citizen and I take my American citizenship very seriously. I am not an economic refugee, nor am I a seeker of political asylum. I am a voluntary immigrant. I became a citizen by choice, not by simple accident of birth.

CONTEXT: ANTI-IMMIGRATION SENTIMENTS
In this paragraph, Mukherjee describes the increasing opposition in the United States to immigration and the violence associated with the prejudice and bigotry that sometimes accompanies anti-immigration movements. Mukherjee wrote this essay in 1997, when concerns about immigration—both legal and illegal—were high among many Americans. Some states, notably California, considered legislation to limit immigration or to make it more difficult for illegal immigrants to receive social services in the United States. Consider whether the situation regarding immigration in the United States has changed much since Mukherjee wrote this essay. Are her concerns about anti-immigration sentiments still valid? How might developments since 1997 affect the way we read her essay today? She writes in the following paragraph that "it is imperative that we come to some agreement about who 'we' are, and what our goals are for the nation, now that our community includes people of many races, ethnicities, languages, and religions." Is that statement still valid today?

Yet these days, questions such as who is an American and what is American culture are being posed with belligerence, and being answered with violence. Scapegoating of immigrants has once again become the politicians' easy remedy for all that ails the nation. Hate speeches fill auditoriums for demagogues willing to profit from stirring up racial animosity. An April Gallup poll indicated that half of Americans would like to bar almost all legal immigration for the next five years.

The United States, like every sovereign nation, has a right to formulate its immigration policies. But in this decade of continual, large-scale diasporas, it is imperative that we come to some agreement about who "we" are, and what our goals are for the nation, now that our community includes people of many races, ethnicities, languages, and religions.

The debate about American culture and American identity has to date been monopolized largely by Eurocentrists and ethnocentrists whose rhetoric has been flamboyantly divisive, pitting a phantom "us" against a demonized "them."

All countries view themselves by their ideals. Indians idealize the cultural continuum, the inherent value system of India, and are properly incensed when foreigners see nothing but poverty, intolerance, strife, and injustice. Americans see themselves as the embodiments of liberty, openness, and individualism, even as the world judges them for drugs, crime, violence, bigotry, militarism, and homelessness. I was in Singapore in 1994 when the American teenager **Michael Fay** was sentenced to caning for having spray-painted some cars. While I saw Fay's actions as those of an individual, and his sentence as too harsh, the overwhelming local sentiment was that vandalism was an "American" crime, and that flogging Fay would deter Singapore youths from becoming "Americanized."

Conversely, in 1994, in Tavares, Florida, the Lake County School Board announced its policy (since overturned) requiring middle school teachers to instruct their students that American culture, by which the board meant European-American culture, is inherently "superior to other foreign or historic cultures." The policy's misguided implication was that culture in the United States has not been affected by the American Indian, African-American, Latin-American, and Asian-American segments of the population. The sinister implication was that our national identity is so fragile that it can absorb diverse and immigrant cultures only by recontextualizing them as deficient.

Our nation is unique in human history in that the founding idea of "America" was in opposition to the tenet that a nation is a collection of like-looking, like-speaking, like-worshiping people. The primary criterion for nationhood in Europe is homogeneity of culture, race, and religion—which has contributed to blood-soaked balkanization in the former Yugoslavia and the former Soviet Union.

America's pioneering European ancestors gave up the easy homogeneity of their native countries for a new version of utopia. Now, in the 1990s, we have the exciting chance to follow that tradition and assist in the making of a new American culture that differs from both the enforced assimilation of a "melting pot" and the Canadian model of a multicultural "mosaic."

The multicultural mosaic implies a contiguity of fixed, self-sufficient, utterly distinct cultures.

VISUAL CONNECTIONS: THE AMERICAN MELTING POT
In this paragraph, Mukherjee refers to the common metaphors of the melting pot and the mosaic to describe the diversity of American society. Consider how these images draw on those same metaphors. What do they communicate about American culture? About diversity?

© Christine Thresh, 2001

We the People Quilt, 2002.

GLOSS: MICHAEL FAY'S CANING
Michael Fay was the son of an American living and working in Singapore in 1994 when he was arrested for vandalism. The legal punishment for such a crime in Singapore was caning—that is, being flogged on the buttocks with a wooden cane. His sentence provoked an outcry among many Americans who viewed it as barbaric. But as Mukherjee notes, people in Singapore supported it.

© Chien-Chi Chang/Magnum Photos

Kindergarten Graduation in Chinatown, New York City, 1996.

GLOSSES
CULTURAL BALKANIZATION
The term *balkanization* has been used since World War I to describe the breaking up of a nation into several smaller, hostile states or regions, as occurred after World War I on the Balkan Peninsula, a region that includes Greece, Bulgaria, Albania, and the former Yugoslavia (which now includes Croatia, Serbia, and Bosnia). Here, Mukherjee expands the use of the term to refer to cultural identity rather than nation-states.

DIASPORAS
Diaspora originally referred to the dispersing of the Jewish people after the Babylonian exile. It is now often used, as Mukherjee uses it here, to refer to the scattering of any people with a common origin or cultural background.

Multiculturalism, as it has been practiced in the United States in the past 10 years, implies the existence of a central culture, ringed by peripheral cultures. The fallout of official multiculturalism is the establishment of one culture as the norm and the rest as aberrations. At the same time, the multiculturalist emphasis on race- and ethnicity-based group identity leads to a lack of respect for individual differences within each group, and to vilification of those individuals who place the good of the nation above the interests of their particular racial or ethnic communities.

We must be alert to the dangers of an "us" vs. "them" mentality. In California, this mentality is manifesting itself as increased violence between minority, ethnic communities. The attack on Korean-American merchants in South Central Los Angeles in the wake of the Rodney King beating trial is only one recent example of the tragic side effects of this mentality. On the national level, the politicization of ethnic identities has encouraged the scapegoating of legal immigrants, who are blamed for economic and social problems brought about by flawed domestic and foreign policies.

We need to discourage the retention of cultural memory if the aim of that retention is cultural **balkanization.** We must think of American culture and nationhood as a constantly re-forming, transmogrifying "we."

25   In this age of **diasporas,** one's biological identity may not be one's only identity. Erosions and accretions come with the act of emigration. The experience of cutting myself off from a biological homeland and settling in an adopted homeland that is not always welcoming to its dark-complexioned citizens has tested me as a person, and made me the writer I am today.

I choose to describe myself on my own terms, as an American, rather than as an Asian-American. Why is it that hyphenation is imposed only on nonwhite Americans? Rejecting hyphenation is my refusal to categorize the cultural landscape into a center and its peripheries; it is to demand that the American nation deliver the promises of its dream and its Constitution to all its citizens equally.

My rejection of hyphenation has been misrepresented as race treachery by some India-born academics on U.S. campuses who have appointed themselves guardians of the "purity" of ethnic cultures. Many of them, though they reside permanently in the United States and participate in its economy, consistently denounce American ideals and institutions. They direct their rage at me because, by becoming a U.S. citizen and exercising my voting rights, I have invested in the present and not the past; because I have committed myself to help shape the future of my adopted homeland; and because I celebrate racial and cultural mongrelization.

What excites me is that as a nation we have not only the chance to retain those values we treasure from our original cultures but also the chance to acknowledge that the outer forms of those values are likely to change. Among Indian immigrants, I see a great deal of guilt about the inability to hang on to what they commonly term "pure culture." Parents express rage or despair at their U.S.-born children's forgetting of, or indifference to, some aspects of Indian culture. Of those parents I would ask: What is it we have lost if our children are acculturating into the culture in which we are living? Is it so terrible that our children are discovering or are inventing home-lands for themselves?

Some first-generation Indo-Americans, embittered by racism and by unofficial "glass ceilings," construct a phantom identity, more-Indian-than-Indians-in-India, as a defense against marginalization. I ask: Why don't you get actively involved in fight-ing discrimination? Make your voice heard. Choose the forum most appropriate for you. If you are a citizen, let your vote count. Reinvest your energy and resources into revitalizing your city's disadvantaged residents and neighborhoods. Know your con-stitutional rights, and when they are violated, use the agencies of redress the Constitution makes available to you. Expect change, and when it comes, deal with it!

As a writer, my literary agenda begins by acknowledging that America has trans-formed me. It does not end until I show that I (along with the hundreds of thousands of immigrants like me) am minute by minute transforming America. The transfor-mation is a two-way process: It affects both the individual and the national-cultural identity.

Others who write stories of migration often talk of arrival at a new place as a loss, the loss of communal memory and the erosion of an original culture. I want to talk of arrival as gain.

30

UNDERSTANDING THE TEXT

1. What does Mukherjee mean when she writes that America is "the stage for the drama of self-transformation"? Why is this self-transformation important to her?

2. What differences does Mukherjee see between how identity is understood in her native India and how it is understood in the United States? Why are these differences important to her?

3. Why does Mukherjee believe it is necessary for Americans to come to some agreement about who they are, about what "America" is? Do you agree with her? Why or why not? What might your answer to that question suggest about your own views regarding what it means to be an American?

4. What is distinctive about America, according to Mukherjee? Do you think most Americans would agree with her? Do you? Explain.

EXPLORING THE ISSUES

1. Mukherjee presents her experiences in this essay. What kinds of experiences does she describe? What do these experiences suggest about her as a person? What might

they suggest about the nature of identity? How effectively do you think she uses her experiences in this essay?

2. In paragraph 7, Mukherjee states that her "identity was viscerally connected with ancestral soil and genealogy." In the essay by Erin Aubry Kaplan on page 105 in this cluster, Wayne Joseph uses the same term—visceral—in discussing his identity (par. 4 and par. 8 in Kaplan's essay). Look up the meaning of this term and evaluate how Mukherjee (and Joseph) use it in this context. What does this term suggest about identity?

3. At several points, Mukherjee challenges and criticizes other immigrants, including those from her native India, for their complaints about losing their cultural identity. What effect do you think these criticisms have on the essay as a whole? How did they affect your sense of Mukherjee as the author of this essay?

4. This essay was published in *Mother Jones,* a magazine that covers political and cultural issues from a progressive perspective. Based on this essay, what assumptions do you think Mukherjee made about her audience? In what ways does she

seem to address readers of *Mother Jones*? Does knowing something about *Mother Jones* change the way you read this essay? Explain, citing specific passages to support your answers.

ENTERING THE CONVERSATIONS

1. Write an essay in which you define cultural identity. You may wish to consult sources to help you understand the idea of culture and the ways in which it is understood by various scholars and critics.

2. Write an essay for an audience of your classmates in which you define what it means to be an American.

3. Rewrite the essay you wrote for Question 3 as an op-ed (opinion) piece for your local newspaper or some other publication that reaches an audience outside your school.

4. The images below were published during the 2004 U.S. presidential election. Consider what they communicate about American cultural identity. Drawing on these photos and others you can find that reflect your ideas about American identity, create a photo essay or website that defines American identity as you understand it.

"Don't judge a book by its cover." How often have you heard that old saying? More important, how often have you violated that rule? How often have you judged others on the basis of their appearance? Usually, we think of judging others in that way as a bad thing. But writer Ranjani Nellore (b. 1967) isn't so sure about that. In the following essay, she reminds us that the way we look may say a lot about who we are. Nellore describes her upbringing as a Hindu girl in her na-

THE Girl WITH THE *Red* Dot

tive India and she tells us about her youthful rebellion against the rigid dress codes for Hindu women. I'm sure many of us can remember dressing—or not dressing—in ways that would upset our parents or grandparents, as Nellore did. But through her experiences as an immigrant to the United States, Nellore comes to understand the significance of the Hindu dress codes and other cultural traditions related to appearance, and she begins to see the complex relationship between these traditions and her cultural, ethnic, and religious identities. In sharing her story with us, Nellore raises interesting questions about how we present our identities to others and how we make sense of our own identities. She demonstrates that "identity is an elusive concept, neither static nor dynamic," as she puts it. She herself has struggled with her sense of identity, and in this regard, I suspect her essay will speak to many readers, no matter what their cultural or ethnic backgrounds.

Ranjani Nellore, who now lives in India, has written for the Pacific News Service and India Currents. This essay was published at Alternet.org, an online news service, in 2004. ▼

RANJANI NELLORE

"**Y**ou look like a Christian girl," my grandmother would sometimes say if she happened to see me leave for school. Like other girls in my class, I wore my blue uniform with its three round, white, plastic buttons and a shield-shaped badge to school. My hair would be tightly braided into two stiff stalks tied up with white ribbons with a satin trim. Some of my friends who went to other schools would occasionally wear a *bindi* or bangles, while I displayed a curiously blank forehead and arms at all times because I went to a convent school. My mother chose to send me to an all-girls school run by gentle nuns in this then sleepy suburb of Bombay. She hoped that I would turn into a polite and polished young woman, much like an admired childhood friend of hers.

I don't know if my convent school education turned me into the person my mother had envisioned, but I certainly knew that I stood out among my peers, the good little Hindu girls in the Bombay of the 70s. First, I had a good command of the English language; second, I turned into an outspoken tomboy, much to the consternation of my

RANJANI NELLORE, "THE GIRL WITH THE RED DOT" FROM ALTERNET.ORG, MAY 12, 2004. REPRINTED BY PERMISSION.

GLOSSES
BINDI
A *bindi,* or holy dot, is worn by Hindu women on their foreheads. Usually red, the bindi is often applied as makeup with vermillion, a fine powered substance. It was traditionally a sign of marriage but more recently has become a popular decoration worn by unmarried Hindu women and by women of other religions as well.

BOMBAY
Bombay, one of India's largest cities, is now known as Mumbai.

mother. While my brothers recited Sanskrit *shlokas* (prayers) at assembly, I knew the Lord's Prayer by heart. On a daily basis, I did not miss wearing the *bindi.* In fact, it was one less item to keep track of in the hectic morning routine. While I secretly rejoiced at the knowledge that my bare forehead caused grief to my grandmother—with whom I had a tumultuous relationship—I secretly harbored the feminine wish to sport jewelry or flowers in my hair.

By calling me "Christian," my grandmother was not being disrespectful towards Christians, but merely commenting about my lack of conformity to the traditional ways of dressing. In a country where you don't generally see racial differences, my appearance and choice of accessories were my identity. As a traditional woman and a widow herself, my grandmother acutely missed the trappings and the attendant respect granted to married woman in Indian society; the prominent *bindi,* the twinkling string of black and gold beads around her neck, the glass bangles that clinked musically as she completed her household chores.

I was free of the rigid dress code once I graduated from school but the college years are just a blurred memory. The days passed in a haze of classes, labs and exams, weighed down by the stress of doing well, a burden familiar to children of all middle class families whose only inheritance is a good education. The thought of how much my clothes, *bindis* and bangles contributed to my identity did not seem important enough to register in my overloaded teenage brain.

5   Fate brought me a husband who lived in America and that is how I found myself in graduate school one day; a newly-wed with colorful glass bangles, an embroidered cotton *salwar kameez* and Nike sneakers. There were several other Indians in the department and it did not strike me as odd that I was the only one who showed up for the 8 A.M. classes mostly in jeans, sometimes in a *kurta* but always with a *bindi.* I sensed that I stood out but I was comfortable with my appearance and so was everyone who saw me. With all the other Indian faces on campus, I was easy to identify as the "girl with the red dot." I got the usual questions about the significance of the dot. More often, I was asked about the material that it was made of, whether it was a tattoo or some permanent marking. Most questions were asked in good faith, with genuine curiosity just as I asked my African-American colleagues about the procedure used for straightening their curly hair.

Given my fiery relationship with my grandmother, and my rebellious nature, I wonder what made me define my identity in such an obvious manner so far away from home. Was it because I had left behind everything and everyone that was familiar and chose to cling to tradition as a way of connecting with the past? Was it in deference to my grandmother who passed away the same month that I boarded my plane to the US? Was it to please my new husband with my Indianness?

Identity is an elusive concept, neither static nor dynamic. The dictionary defines it as "exact likeness in nature or qualities." A large part of our identity is inherited, whether it is language or lineage that stays with us in our body, in our manners, in our attitudes. It is this sameness that makes us feel that we belong, whether it is with our family (you look just like your mother) or the larger community (your accent is so distinct). This is why Indians make friends selectively with other Indians, celebrate

Indian festivals and give Indian names to their children. Is identity a static object then, rooted in the past, in the familiar, in a sense of belonging to a group?

But don't we also grow through life trying to develop a separate identity, something that defines us uniquely? No wonder then that identity is also defined as **"the condition of being oneself** (or itself) and not another." As children grow up and away from the parents, each step, each milestone is an effort to forge a separate personality, a distinct self. For immigrants who move to a country that is very different from their place of origin, trying to fit in by dressing like the locals, by picking up nuances of speech, of gestures is another attempt at blending in with the majority, to demonstrate a willingness to change. Is identity dynamic then? Like water, you take the shape of the container.

These points of view still do not address my original question of what made me decide to dress the way I did. Perhaps I wanted to look different, to make a bold, visual statement "Here, I am Indian, make what you will out of it." I stood apart in America by doing precisely what makes me merge with the millions in India. The fact that I am offered the freedom to do so, to dress as I please, is something that I took for granted. My choice of clothes was less of an indication of my cultural identity but more of an expression of my individual personality. It was my innate rebellious core that made me pick this path. Identity need not always be in the context of community. It is, after all, an assertion of individual choice over societal norms and expectations. Perhaps, identity is more like Jell-O than water; it can take any shape but maintains an inherent strength.

As one who has lived in America, my identity may irrevocably be linked to my   10
Indianness but my metaphors can certainly be American!

CONVERSATIONS: BE YOURSELF

In paragraph 8, Nellore discusses her view that each person ultimately tries to create a "distinct self." This idea of a unique self is a very American idea. It is in many ways at the heart of the emphasis on individualism that seems to characterize American culture. Often, other cultures, particularly Asian cultures, are contrasted with American culture because those cultures seem to value the community over the individual. Here, though, Nellore, a native of India, seems to express an idea about the individual that is consistent with the way Americans tend to think of it. It is worth considering how the idea of a unique self compares across different cultures and how Nellore might be drawing on differences and similarities in the way people of different cultures understand individual identity.

UNDERSTANDING THE TEXT

1. What various identities does Nellore describe for herself in this essay? In what ways do these identities relate to or conflict with each other? What might Nellore's experience with these various identities suggest about the ways in which we understand our selves?

2. What is the significance of the *bindi*, or red dot, to Nellore? How does its significance to her change over time? What might that change suggest about one's ethnic or cultural identity?

3. How does Nellore define identity in this essay? What contradictions does she see in how we understand identity. Do you agree with her definition? Why or why not?

EXPLORING THE ISSUES

1. In the opening paragraph, Nellore writes that her grandmother told her that she looked "like a Christian girl" because of the way she was dressed and how she wore her hair. This brief anecdote raises the issue of the connection between physical appearance and cultural, religious, or ethnic identity. Often, when we think of physical appearance and identity, we think of skin color. But here the suggestion is that the way you dress and groom yourself can also reflect aspects of your ethnicity, culture, or religion. What do you think Nellore hopes to suggest about these connections between physical appearance and other aspects of identity? How important are these connections in the way we understand our identities?

2. Nellore writes that it was her "innate rebellious core" that prompted her to dress as she did and to declare her Indian identity by wearing a bindi. She also states that one's identity is to some extent inherited, even though our culture shapes our identity. In some ways, she seems to be taking part in the age-old debate about nature versus nurture. In other words, how much of who we are is determined biologically—by our genes, for example—and how much is a result of social and cultural influences, such as the way we are raised, the culture of the region we grow up in, or the religion we may be born into? Where does Nellore stand in this debate? Do you agree with her? Why or why not? To what extent do you think her essay makes a persuasive case for her position?

3. Many people find it difficult to discuss racial, ethnic, cultural, or other such differences. In paragraph 5, Nellore describes some of the conversations she had with Americans about her Indian culture, and she tells us that she sometimes asked other people about aspects of their racial or ethnic identity. She does not seem hesitant or reluctant about such conversations. Do you think Nellore may be making an implicit point here about how people of different backgrounds can relate to one another? Explain.

ENTERING THE CONVERSATIONS

1. Write an essay in which you discuss the sources of your own identity. How much of who you are is a result of your upbringing, your racial or ethnic background, your cultural or religious traditions, or similar influences? How much is a result of your genetic or biological makeup? Try to address these questions in your essay, drawing on your own experiences and on Nellore's essay or any other relevant essays in this cluster.

2. In a group of classmates, share the essays you wrote for Question 1. Try to identify how much agreement there is among your classmates about the sources of one's identity.

 INFOTRAC

3. On the basis of Questions 1 and 2, write an essay in which you address the question: Does it matter whether our identities are biologically determined or determined by social and cultural influences? Use InfoTrac College Edition and any other appropriate sources to find information and various viewpoints about this question. Write this essay for a specific audience, such as readers of your local newspaper or some other publication that you read regularly.

4. Create a photo essay, PowerPoint presentation, or web site in which you present your own sense of identity.

5. Write an essay examining the connections among physical appearance, including fashion as well as cultural dress traditions, and one's identity. In your essay, draw on your own experiences, Nellore's essay, and any other relevant sources to help support your points about these connections. Try to draw conclusions about the importance of appearance when it comes to identity. Consider including photographs or other images in your essay to help illustrate or support your point.

CREATING THEMES: Extending the Conversations

WITH TEXT

1. Drawing on several of the essays in this chapter, define *identity* and discuss its importance in our lives. Try to identify the various aspects of identity that you consider important, referring where appropriate to the essays in this chapter.

2. Several of the writers in this chapter, including Erin Aubry Kaplan and Bharati Mukherjee, directly address the issue of multiculturalism in their essays. Several other writers, such as Ranjani Nellore and Oscar Casares, implicitly discuss the diversity of American society. Drawing on several of the essays in this chapter, write an essay in which you present your own view of multiculturalism in contemporary American society. (For this essay, you may wish to do some research on multiculturalism as a movement or an idea.)

3. Many writers in this chapter describe changes or transformations in the way they understand themselves and describe their identities. Let's assume this chapter was not called "Identity" but was called something like "Transformations." Select several of the essays in the chapter (or from other chapters) in which the authors describe some kind of important change or transformation in their sense of identity, and write an essay about these transformations. Try to examine these transformations so that you can draw conclusions about our identities and about how we can change over time.

4. Reorganize the clusters in this chapter to create new ones that you think best reflect your views about identity; then write a brief introduction to the chapter that justifies your reorganization.

5. Identify an issue—a problem or controversy or question—that emerges for you from one or more of the readings in this chapter. For example, several of the essays in this chapter discuss immigration. Identify such an issue that is important to you and, drawing on the relevant essays, discuss the issue and why it is significant. Present your own view of the issue and draw conclusions about the way the essays you have selected address that issue.

6. Write a dialogue involving Erin Aubry Kaplan, Oscar Casares, Bharati Mukherjee, or some other combination of writers whose essays appear in this chapter about what it means to be an American. Alternatively, select several authors from this chapter and write a dialogue in which they address an issue or problem that emerges from their essays.

7. Several of the essays in this chapter describe places that are important to the author (for example, Bobbie Ann Mason, N. Scott Momaday). Other essays discuss places as important in some way (for example, Maxine Hong Kingston, Dagoberto Gilb). Write an essay in which you discuss the importance of place in identity. Draw on any authors in this chapter that seem appropriate to help support your points about place and identity.

WITH MEDIA

1. Watch television commercials for a week or so, trying to vary your viewing habits so that you are seeing commercials that air during many different kinds of shows (such as sporting events, prime-time sitcoms, weekend news shows). Try to identify commercials that seem to have something to do with being an American. Select several such commercials and write an analysis of the way they seem to present the identity of an American.

2. Do the same kind of assignment described in Question 1 for another aspect of identity, such as race, gender, ethnicity, or culture.

3. In recent years, a number of new drugs have appeared on the market to treat male sexual dysfunction—for example, Viagra and Cialis. These drugs have been the focus of extensive advertising campaigns on television, radio, the Internet, and in print media. Examine some advertisements for these drugs in terms of what they might suggest about male and female identities. Write an essay in which you analyze such advertisements, drawing conclusions about the messages they seem to convey about being a man or a woman.

4. Automobile advertising—on television and in print—is one of the most extensive segments of the advertising market. Often, advertisements for cars or trucks imply an image of a certain kind of driver or person. Select several such advertisements and analyze them for the kind of person or identity they seem to be targeting. Then write an essay on the basis of your analysis.

5. On the basis of your research for Question 4 and working with a group of classmates, create an advertisement for a car or truck that depicts a certain kind of identity. Consider creating a web site or use the desktop publishing capabilities of your word processing program to create a print advertisement. (You might review Chapter 2 of this book for advice on using images and visual elements in your ads.)

6. Select several popular songs and analyze them for what they suggest about identity.

CREATING THEMES: Extending the Conversations

WITH FILM

1. The idea of identity is often explored in popular films. In *The Truman Show* (1998), for example, the main character has been raised in a completely contrived environment and his life has been the focus of a popular television reality show, without his knowing it. As he begins to suspect that his life has been constructed for him, he rebels and tries to find a way out of his television show existence. The film asks us to consider what our "true" identity is. Using this film or any others you select, write an essay examining how the film (or films) depicts a person's identity and what the film (or films) suggests about identity in general.

2. Many popular films tell the story of someone whose identity changes in some way, either by personal choice or because of forces beyond an individual's control. In *American Beauty* (1999), for instance, the main character is a successful family man living in an American suburb who decides that his life is meaningless and sets about changing himself in several ways, which creates conflict with his wife, his coworkers, and others in his life. Select several such films that portray someone whose identity seems to change in important ways and write an essay in which you discuss how the films depict these changes. Draw conclusions about what these films might say about identity.

Bettmann/Corbis

MY DOG, SUMMIT, A TWELVE-YEAR-OLD GOLDEN RETRIEVER, IS LYING ON THE FLOOR NEAR MY DESK. SHE'S SNOOZING AT THE MOMENT, AS SHE OFTEN DOES WHEN I'M WRITING IN THE MORNING, BUT SOMETIMES I THINK SHE UNDERSTANDS WHAT I'M DOING. SHE SEEMS TO KNOW THAT EVERY MORNING AFTER I'VE FINISHED BREAKFAST

and poured a second cup of coffee, I'll sit down at my desk. So she follows me from the kitchen into my study and settles into a comfortable position near my desk. After an hour or two, she'll get up and look at me, as if to say, "Are you finished yet?" If I go into the kitchen for another cup of coffee, she won't move, though. She seems to know that I'm not yet finished writing. But if it's around noon, she'll follow me, expecting me to let her outside. And after I let her back in, she'll lie down in her customary spot near the kitchen table as I eat lunch. Sometimes, she'll pick up her head and stare at me with what seems to be a knowing expression on her face. And I can't help but wonder, "What is she thinking?"

> In other words, our daily lives are shaped so profoundly by our own thoughts, which seem to rush through our minds in a constant stream.

It may seem silly to wonder about what a dog might be thinking or even whether a dog *can* think. But we do. If you've spent any time with a dog or a cat or maybe a larger animal like a horse, you've probably asked yourself the same question. But why would we even bother to ask such a question? Maybe it's because of our own experience as thinkers. In other words, our daily lives are shaped so profoundly by our own thoughts, which seem to rush through our minds in a constant stream. Thoughts are always coming and going. And that constant stream of thought is an important part of how we experience the world around us and, more important

still, how we experience ourselves in the world. It's only natural to wonder if animals like Summit, with whom we develop close bonds, might also *think* in some way.

Of course, philosophers, psychologists, and other theorists have been thinking about thinking for a long time. "I think; therefore I am," René Descartes, the influential eighteenth century philosopher, famously declared. What Descartes was saying is that the capacity to understand ourselves as beings in the world is what makes us human; in a sense, it's our intellect that gives us our very existence, for without this capacity to think in this way, we would not be aware of ourselves as we are. We'd be more like my dog, Summit, who certainly can learn and maybe can even *know*, but who is not aware of herself as a being in the way we humans are.

If you think about thinking like this for a while, soon you'll start wondering about related matters, like learning and knowing and education. Are these all the same thing? Philosophers and psychologists say no. They see important differences among these most basic cognitive activities. *Learning* something isn't the same thing as *knowing* something. And learning is not necessarily the same thing as *education;* in other words, you don't need formal education to learn something, and you know a great many things that you learned outside school. And of course, there's also the matter of *understanding.* What exactly does it mean to understand something? Is that the same thing as knowing? If not, what does learning or education have to do with understanding?

Now, I wasn't really thinking about all this when I first began to put together this chapter. Instead, I was trying to come up with a theme that would be a good category for some of the essays in this chapter about education. For instance, the essay by Paulo Freire called "The Banking Concept of Education" is one that I really wanted to include, because it raises some important issues about education that I believe students should think about. But when you read Freire's essay (which is a very challenging piece of writing), you'll quickly see that it's not just about formal education. It's also about knowing and learning more broadly. His critique of formal education is based on certain ideas about knowing and learning—and yes, understanding—that he believes make us truly human. So to place his essay in a chapter about education makes sense, but it doesn't quite do justice to the complexity and the depth of his ideas.

The same is true of an essay like Maya Angelou's. This famous excerpt from her autobiography, *I Know Why the Caged Bird Sings,* describes her eighth-grade graduation ceremony at a racially segregated school in the American South in 1930s. If you read it carefully, you realize that Angelou isn't just writing about the ritual of graduating from school or even about formal education in general. She's also describing an epiphany: a new and profound insight into who she was as a young Black girl. She's describing how she came to a different understanding about herself in society. So the category of education seemed too limited to classify this essay, too.

What Angelou and Freire and the other authors in this chapter are really writing about is how we understand ourselves and the world around us and how we come to that understanding. But they do so in the context of many different yet related conversations. The first cluster, for example, includes essays in which the writers describe personal journeys that lead to new ways of understanding themselves. You might say that these essays are part of a neverending process of learning that we all experience. The focus of the second cluster, "Schooling," is obvious, but I hope the essays in this cluster complicate and challenge your ideas about formal education. These essays are about formal education in some way, but they push us to think differently about what happens in schools and what we should expect from education. The third cluster, "Knowing and Believing," shifts attention to the connection between what we think we know and what we be-

> *Learning* something isn't the same thing as *knowing* something. And learning is not necessarily the same thing as *education.*

lieve. I might have called this cluster "Faith" or "Spirituality," and you might consider whether such a title for the cluster would have changed the way you read these essays, which examine how we as human beings understand who we are and how we make sense of our place in the world around us.

All three clusters are intended to get you to think in new ways about thinking. And I hope the readings in this chapter also help you appreciate the power of writing in our neverending efforts to understand ourselves and our world.

LEARNING

N 1995, POP SINGER ALANIS MORISSETTE RELEASED A SONG TITLED "YOU LEARN." HERE'S A PORTION OF THE LYRICS TO THAT SONG:

I recommend biting off more than you
    can chew to anyone
I certainly do
I recommend sticking your foot in your
    mouth at any time
Feel free
Throw it down (the caution blocks you
    from the wind)
Hold it up (to the rays)
You wait and see when the smoke clears
You live you learn
You love you learn
You cry you learn
You lose you learn
You bleed you learn
You scream you learn

In a sense, Morissette's song is one kind of answer to the question: What does it mean to learn? In her song, she suggests that we are learning all the time just by living. She suggests, too, that learning isn't always easy or obvious. In fact, we may learn most from our most difficult experiences.

Morissette's song repeats an insight that philosophers and psychologists have long known: We learn through experience. In fact, some philosophies and theories, such as the "pragmatist" philosophy of John Dewey and William James, are based on the idea that experience is central to all learning. This may seem commonsensical, but scholars have long tried to understand just how we do learn by experience.

The essays in this cluster might be considered part of that longstanding effort to examine how we learn from experience. They provide four angles on Morissette's song, for each essay describes a challenging or unusual circumstance that led to some important learning on the part of the writer. Take Helen Keller's essay. You probably already know a little about Keller, who at a very early age lost her sight and hearing. Imagine being unable to see or hear and therefore unable to

ALANIS MORISSETTE, "YOU LEARN" FROM *JAGGED LITTLE PILL.*

speak (Keller lost her sight and hearing before she learned to speak). Without sight or hearing, how can you learn about yourself or the world around you? Keller's essay gives us part of an answer: She had the sense of touch, which enabled her to develop a crude sense of herself as a being among a few other beings in her life. She knew certain things by their touch, but she had no way to understand them aside from how they felt. Now imagine the dramatic change that occurred when she began to acquire language—the ability to name those things that she touched, the ability to communicate with others through words. That ability fundamentally changed the way she understood herself. Keller's essay is thus a stunning look at what it means to learn.

It's also a good story, and it reminds us that we often make sense of our experiences by telling stories. And if we learn by telling stories to each other, then we also learn through writing. By writing about their experiences, writers can gain insight into those experiences. Writing itself is learning.

The essays by Richard Wright, Annie Dillard, and Susan Sawyer are as compelling as Keller's, though in different ways. Each of these writers explores a different kind of experience that led to a new way of thinking, a new understanding of something. Sometimes the learning described in these essays is subtle, such as when Dillard gains insight into how to live by paying attention to a weasel that she observed near her home. Sometimes the learning leads to a reexamination of what was previously thought. That's what Susan Sawyer reveals in her essay, "On Being Proved Wrong." And sometimes the learning is dramatic, as was the case for Richard Wright, who had to fight racism to pursue a kind of learning that many of us take for granted.

But you don't need to have that kind of dramatic experience to learn. As Morissette's song suggests, learning happens. You just have to pay attention. I hope these essays help you do so.

I suspect that most of us take sight and hearing and speech for granted. I almost never think about how essential these senses are to my experience of the world and my understanding of myself as a human being. Helen Keller (1880–1968) did not have the luxury of taking sight, hearing, and speech for granted. Keller lost her sight and hearing to a disease when she was not yet two years old. As she relates in the following excerpt from her autobiography, The Story of My

THE Day Language Came INTO My Life

Life (1903), she lived as a young child in a fog of "tangible white darkness." That changed when she was almost seven years old. It was then that a remarkable woman named Anne Sullivan became Keller's teacher and brought language into Keller's life.

On one level, this essay is about the power of language and its capacity to shape the way we experience the world and ourselves in it. Sullivan taught Keller how to name objects that Keller knew only by touch. In doing so, Sullivan fundamentally changed Keller's sense of the world around her. She gave Keller a way to understand that world that she did not have before. On another level, this essay is about how Keller came to know herself as something more than a being with basic needs. With Sullivan's patient help, Keller learned new and more complex ways to think about herself and about her relationships to others. In a sense, her essay is about the power of learning and the crucial role of others in our learning.

Keller's autobiography made her famous, but she is not known as a great writer. In many ways, her writing is as concrete and straightforward as the tangible world was to her before Anne Sullivan became her teacher. But Keller nevertheless tells a (continued)

HELEN KELLER

The most important day I remember in all my life is the one on which my teacher, Anne Mansfield Sullivan, came to me. I am filled with wonder when I consider the immeasurable contrasts between the two lives which it connects. It was the third of March, 1887, three months before I was seven years old.

On the afternoon of that eventful day, I stood on the porch, dumb, expectant. I guessed vaguely from my mother's signs and from the hurrying to and fro in the house that something unusual was about to happen, so I went to the door and waited on the steps. The afternoon sun penetrated the mass of honeysuckle that covered the porch, and fell on my upturned face. My fingers lingered almost unconsciously on the familiar leaves and blossoms which had just come forth to greet the sweet southern spring. I did not know what the future held of marvel or surprise for me. Anger and bitterness had preyed upon me continually for weeks and a deep languor had succeeded this passionate struggle.

Have you ever been at sea in a dense fog, when it seemed as if a tangible white darkness shut you in, and the great ship, tense and (continued) *powerful story of how lan-guage transformed her world from one of touch to a richer, more complex landscape shaped by words and ideas. Consider as you read the extent to which Keller's straightfor-ward writing style fits her story and how it might invite us as readers into that story.* ◪

STRATEGIES: DESCRIBING HER WORLD
Notice Keller's descriptive language in paragraph 2 (and elsewhere in this es-say). Keller is referring to a time in her life when all she knew was the sense of touch and could not see or hear. How well do these physical descriptions help con-vey a sense of the world as she knew it?

CONTEXT: THE PERKINS INSTITUTION
The Perkins Institution in Watertown, Massachusetts, was opened in South Boston in 1832 as the New England Asylum for the Blind. It was moved in 1912, and from 1877 to 1955 it was known as the Perkins Institution and Massachusetts School for the Blind. It was the first chartered school for blind children in the United States.

anxious, groped her way toward the shore with plummet and sound-ing-line, and you waited with beating heart for something to happen? I was like that ship before my education began, only I was without compass or sounding-line, and had no way of knowing how near the harbour was. "Light! Give me light!" was the wordless cry of my soul, and the light of love shone on me in that very hour.

I felt approaching footsteps. I stretched out my hand as I supposed to my mother. Some one took it, and I was caught up and held close in the arms of her who had come to reveal all things to me, and, more than all things else, to love me.

The morning after my teacher came she led me into her room and gave me a doll. The little blind children at **the Perkins Institution** had sent it and Laura Bridgman had dressed it; but I did not know this un-til afterward. When I had played with it a little while, Miss Sullivan slowly spelled into my hand the word "d-o-l-l." I was at once interested in this finger play and tried to imitate it. When I finally succeeded in making the letters correctly I was flushed with childish pleasure and pride. Running downstairs to my mother I held up my hand and made the letters for doll. I did not know that I was spelling a word or even that words existed; I was simply making my fingers go in monkey-like imitation. In the days that followed I learned to spell in this uncomprehending way a great many words, among them *pin, hat, cup* and a few verbs like *sit, stand* and *walk.* But my teacher had been with me several weeks before I understood that everything has a name.

One day, while I was playing with my new doll, Miss Sullivan put my big rag doll into my lap also, spelled "d-o-l-l" and tried to make me un-derstand that "d-o-l-l" applied to both. Earlier in the day we had had a tussle over the words "m-u-g" and "w-a-t-e-r." Miss Sullivan had tried to impress it upon me that "m-u-g" is *mug* and that "w-a-t-e-r" is *water,* but I persisted in confounding the two. In despair she had dropped the subject for the time, only to renew it at the first opportunity. I be-came impatient at her repeated attempts and, seizing the new doll, I dashed it upon the floor. I was keenly delighted when I felt the frag-ments of the broken doll at my feet. Neither sorrow nor regret fol-lowed my passionate outburst. I had not loved the doll. In the still, dark world in which I lived there was no strong sentiment or tender-ness. I felt my teacher sweep the fragments to one side of the hearth, and I had a sense of satisfaction that the cause of my discomfort was removed. She brought me my hat, and I knew I was going out into the warm sunshine. This thought, if a wordless sensation may be called a thought, made me hop and skip with pleasure.

We walked down the path to the well-house, attracted by the fra-grance of the honeysuckle with which it was covered. Some one was drawing water and my teacher placed my hand under the spout. As the cool stream gushed over one hand she spelled into the other the word *water,* first slowly, then rapidly. I stood still, my whole attention fixed upon the motions of her fingers. Suddenly I felt a misty consciousness as of something forgotten—a thrill of returning thought; and somehow the mystery of language was revealed to me. I knew then that "w-a-t-e-r" meant the wonderful cool something that was flowing over my hand. That living word awakened my soul, gave it light, hope, joy, set it free! There were barriers still, it is true, but barriers that could in time be swept away.

I left the well-house eager to learn. Everything had a name, and each name gave birth to a new thought. As we returned to the house every object which I touched seemed to quiver with life. That was because I saw everything with the strange, new sight that had come to me. On entering the door I remembered the doll I had broken. I felt my way to the hearth and picked up the pieces. I tried vainly to put them together. Then my eyes filled with tears; for I realized what I had done, and for the first time I felt repentance and sorrow.

I learned a great many new words that day. I do not remember what they all were; but I do know that *mother, father, sister, teacher* were among them—words that were to make the world blossom for me, "like Aaron's rod, with flowers." It would have been difficult to find a happier child than I was as I lay in my crib at the close of that eventful day and lived over the joys it had brought me, and for the first time longed for a new day to come.

CONVERSATIONS
WHO WAS HELEN KELLER?

Sometimes a well-known figure becomes a symbol. That has certainly been true of Helen Keller. Her life has often been presented as the story of a heroine who overcame severe physical disabilities to live a full and productive life. Told in this way, her life symbolizes self-reliance. But scholar Ruth Hubbard has argued that this common version of Helen Keller's story ignores the important fact that she was a well-known activist for social justice and a famous advocate for the poor and disenfranchised. Hubbard also notes that Keller was often criticized for her activism, even as she was praised for her work on behalf of the hearing impaired. Such disagreements about a famous life such as Keller's raise questions about how we make sense of our lives through stories.

DISABILITIES

Today, people with disabilities live in a very different world than Keller knew. They not only have access to sophisticated medical care and technology that can minimize the effects of many disabilities, but they also have legal protections that did not exist at the time Keller published her autobiography in 1903. In 1990, for example, the U.S. Congress passed the Americans with Disabilities Act (ADA) to protect people with disabilities from discrimination. The ADA and similar developments reflect changing attitudes about people with disabilities. And those changing attitudes are reflected in language. For example, whereas people without hearing were once referred to as "deaf," they are now more commonly described as "hearing-impaired". Such changes suggest that we as a society have come to understand disabilities differently. But these changes did not happen by themselves. They resulted from persistent and often difficult struggles on the part of advocates for people with disabilities. In a sense, these struggles were an effort to change how people understood each other. Consider, for example, how this photograph reflects such changes. In 1975, the first wheelchair racer completed the famed Boston Marathon. Today, most marathons not only have a separate wheelchair division, but also have a visually impaired/blind division and a mobility-impaired division. What might this photo say about people with disabilities?

New York City Marathon Wheelchair Race Participants, 2003.

UNDERSTANDING THE TEXT

1. How would you summarize the change that occurred in Keller's life after Anne Sullivan became her teacher? What did Keller learn about herself? About the world around her?

2. What are the "barriers" that Keller refers to in paragraph 7? What does she mean when she says that these barriers "could in time be swept away"? What does this statement reveal about Keller and about the kind of changes she was experiencing at that time in her life?

3. *Strategies: Describing Her World* (p. 132) calls attention to Keller's descriptive language. Examine Keller's descriptions in paragraph 2 and other descriptive passages in her essay. What does Keller tend to emphasize in these descriptions? How might these descriptions contribute to the overall effect of her story? How effective do you find these descriptions?

EXPLORING THE ISSUES

1. What kind of person do you think Keller was, based on this brief excerpt from her autobiography? What does Keller reveal about herself in this excerpt? What questions about her does this excerpt raise for you? Cite specific passages to support your answer.

2. Keller's story has often been described as one of triumph over adversity, an example of individual determination and success. Based on this excerpt, how accurate do you think such a description of this story is? In what ways might such a tale of triumph be problematic when it comes to addressing issues related

to disabilities? In what ways might Keller's story about overcoming her disabilities hide or minimize important issues related to disabilities?

3. Look carefully at the passages that describe how Keller learned specific words and ideas. What might these passages suggest about the connections between language and thought? What do they suggest about the role of language in our lives?

ENTERING THE CONVERSATIONS

1. Write an essay describing an experience that you or someone you know had in which you faced great adversity or hardship. Tell the story of that experience in a way that conveys a sense of the difficulties you faced and what you learned about yourself. Write your essay for an audience of your classmates or for a different audience that you think would be interested in your story.

2. In a group of classmates, share the essays you wrote for Question 2. What similarities or differences do you see in the experiences your classmates wrote about and in the way they told their stories? What do these stories suggest about the authors? What might they suggest about our culture and how we understand hardship and individual responsibilities?

INFOTRAC

3. Using InfoTrac College Edition, the Internet, and other appropriate resources, try to find out how Keller's autobiography, *The Story of My Life,* has been received over the

years. If possible, find early reviews of the book as well as discussions of the book in other contexts (such as in debates about disabilities). Then write an essay discussing the significance of Keller's book. What kinds of reactions did people have to her story? What importance did people see in her story? What might the reactions of her book's readers tell us about our ways of understanding ourselves or about people with disabilities? In your essay, describe the various reactions to Keller's book and discuss what they might say about how her story has been understood by different readers. Try to draw conclusions about how an experience or event can have different meanings to different readers.

4. Examine your school's (or your workplace's) policy on disabilities. What specific issues does the policy address? What specific measures does it provide to protect people with disabilities? What does it convey about our attitudes regarding disabilities? What does it suggest about how your school (or employer) understands disabilities? Do you think this policy is adequate? Is it fair? Do you think any changes should be made to the policy? Now write a letter to the person at your school (or employer) who is responsible for overseeing this policy. In your letter, discuss the policy on disabilities and identify any problems you see with the policy. Propose appropriate changes to address those problems. Alternatively, working with a group of classmates, create a web site devoted to disability issues at your school or workplace. In creating your site, consider your audience and the messages you want to convey to them.

When I was in the seventh grade, I bought a paperback copy of Battle Cry, *a novel by Leon Uris about the experiences of a group of young American marines fighting in the Pacific theater during World War II. I enjoyed reading military history and fiction, and I often read novels like* Battle Cry. *In school one day, during a study period, my teacher noticed me reading and asked about the book. She borrowed it from me, returning it at the end of the day. As she gave it back*

THE Library Card

to me, she asked, "Do you think you can handle this?" At the time, I assumed she was referring to the graphic descriptions of violence and sex in the book. But as I look back on that incident, I see that she was monitoring my reading. If she considered the book inappropriate for me, she may have contacted my parents. It's possible that the school might have tried to prevent me from reading the book.

I thought of that incident as I read the following excerpt from Richard Wright's autobiography, Black Boy *(1945). In this compelling passage, Wright describes his efforts to obtain books from a library at a time when it was risky for Blacks to do so. His story is about the impact of racism on the lives of Black Americans, which affected even what and how they read. But it is also about the impact that reading can have on a person. Wright explores the effects of his reading on his sense of who he was as a Black man, and he describes how his reading helped him learn some difficult lessons. In many ways, his reading—as well as the writing he eventually did—changed him dramatically; it helped him gain a new understanding of himself. And it represented a challenge to the Whites who controlled the southern communities like the* (continued)

RICHARD WRIGHT

One morning I arrived early at work and went into the bank lobby where the Negro porter was mopping. I stood at a counter and picked up the Memphis *Commercial Appeal* and began my free reading of the press. I came finally to the editorial page and saw an article dealing with one **H. L. Mencken.** I knew by hearsay that he was the editor of the *American Mercury,* but aside from that I knew nothing about him. The article was a furious denunciation of Mencken, concluding with one, hot, short sentence: Mencken is a fool.

I wondered what on earth this Mencken had done to call down upon him the scorn of the South. The only people I had ever heard denounced in the South were Negroes, and this man was not a Negro. Then what ideas did Mencken hold that made a newspaper like the *Commercial Appeal* castigate him publicly? Undoubtedly he must be advocating ideas that the South did not like. Were there, then, people other than Negroes who criticized the South? I knew that during the Civil War the South had hated northern whites, but I had not encountered such hate during my life. Knowing no more of Mencken (continued) *one where Wright grew up. In this regard, Wright's passage helps us understand why there have always been attempts to control what people read and write. It also helps us see why people will resist efforts to control their reading and writing.*

Richard Wright (1908–1960) is considered one of the foremost American writers of the twentieth century. In addition to his autobiography, Black Boy, *he was author of a number of collections of stories, works of nonfiction, and novels, including* Native Son *(1940) and* Uncle Tom's Children *(1938). He was a passionate voice for the victims of oppression and a controversial figure in part because of his sympathies for the Communist Party.* ▼

GLOSS: H. L. MENCKEN
Henry Louis Mencken (1880–1956), who is mentioned in the first paragraph, was one of the best-known writers and political observers of his time. A prolific author of newspaper columns as well as poetry and books of social commentary, he was known for his sharp wit and often biting criticisms of public figures and human nature. In paragraph 61, Wright offers his own description of Mencken's writing.

than I did at that moment, I felt a vague sympathy for him. Had not the South, which had assigned me the role of a non-man, cast at him its hardest words?

Now, how could I find out about this Mencken? There was a huge library near the riverfront, but I knew that Negroes were not allowed to patronize its shelves any more than they were the parks and playgrounds of the city. I had gone into the library several times to get books for the white men on the job. Which of them would now help me to get books? And how could I read them without causing concern to the white men with whom I worked? I had so far been successful in hiding my thoughts and feelings from them, but I knew that I would create hostility if I went about the business of reading in a clumsy way.

I weighed the personalities of the men on the job. There was Don, a Jew; but I distrusted him. His position was not much better than mine and I knew that he was uneasy and insecure; he had always treated me in an offhand, bantering way that barely concealed his contempt. I was afraid to ask him to help me get books; his frantic desire to demonstrate a racial solidarity with the whites against Negroes might make him betray me.

5   Then how about the boss? No, he was a Baptist and I had the suspicion that he would not be quite able to comprehend why a black boy would want to read Mencken. There were other white men on the job whose attitudes showed clearly that they were Kluxers or sympathizers, and they were out of the question.

There remained only one man whose attitude did not fit into an anti-Negro category, for I had heard the white men refer to him as a "Pope lover." He was an Irish Catholic and was hated by the white southerners. I knew that he read books, because I had got him volumes from the library several times. Since he, too, was an object of hatred, I felt that he might refuse me but would hardly betray me. I hesitated, weighing and balancing the imponderable realities.

One morning I paused before the Catholic fellow's desk.

"I want to ask you a favor," I whispered to him.

"What is it?"

10   "I want to read. I can't get books from the library. I wonder if you'd let me use your card?"

He looked at me suspiciously.

"My card is full most of the time," he said.

"I see," I said and waited, posing my question silently.

"You're not trying to get me into trouble, are you, boy?" He asked, staring at me.

15   "Oh, no sir."

"What book do you want?"

"A book by H. L. Mencken."

"Which one?"

"I don't know. Has he written more than one?"

"He has written several."   20

"I didn't know that."

"What makes you want to read Mencken?"

"Oh, I just saw his name in the newspaper," I said.

"It's good of you to want to read," he said. "But you ought to read the right things."

I said nothing. Would he want to supervise my reading?   25

"Let me think," he said. "I'll figure out something."

I turned from him and he called me back. He stared at me quizzically.

"Richard, don't mention this to the other white men," he said.

"I understand," I said. "I won't say a word."

A few days later he called me to him.   30

"I've got a card in my wife's name," he said. "Here's mine."

"Thank you, sir."

"Do you think you can manage it?"

"I'll manage fine," I said.

"If they suspect you, you'll get in trouble," he said.   35

"I'll write the same kind of notes to the library that you wrote when you sent me for books," I told him. "I'll sign your name."

He laughed.

"Go ahead. Let me see what you get," he said.

That afternoon I addressed myself to forging a note. Now, what were the names of books written by H. L. Mencken? I did not know any of them. I finally wrote what I thought would be a foolproof note: *Dear Madam: Will you please let this nigger boy*—I used the word "nigger" to make the librarian feel that I could not possibly be the author of the note—*have some books by H. L. Mencken?* I forged the white man's name.

I entered the library as I had always done when on errands for whites, but I felt that I would somehow slip up and betray myself. I doffed my hat, stood a respectful distance from the desk, looked as unbookish as possible, and waited for the white patrons to be taken care of. When the desk was clear of people, I still waited. The white librarian looked at me.

"What do you want, boy?"

As though I did not possess the power of speech, I stepped forward and simply handed her the forged note, not parting my lips.

"What books by Mencken does he want?" she asked.

"I don't know, ma'am," I said, avoiding her eyes.

"Who gave you this card?"   45

"Mr. Falk," I said.

"Where is he?"

"He's at work, at the M—— Optical Company," I said. "I've been in here for him before."

"I remember," the woman said. "But he never wrote notes like this."

Oh, God, she's suspicious. Perhaps she would not let me have the books? If she had   50
turned her back at that moment, I would have ducked out the door and never gone back. Then I thought of a bold idea.

CONVERSATIONS: RACIAL SLURS
Wright tells us that when he forged the note to the librarian, he used the word "nigger." Notice how that racially charged word, which we consider a slur, carries several meanings in this scene. What are those meanings? Consider what that word might have meant in 1945, when Wright's book was published, compared to today. Consider, too, how Wright uses the word as a tool in this context. What might this scene reveal about the way political and historical context influences the meaning of words?

"You can call him up, ma'am," I said, my heart pounding.

"You're not using these books, are you?" she asked pointedly.

"Oh, no, ma'am. I can't read."

"I don't know what he wants by Mencken," she said under her breath.

55   I knew now that I had won; she was thinking of other things and the race question had gone out of her mind. She went to the shelves. Once or twice she looked over her shoulder at me, as though she was still doubtful. Finally she came forward with two books in her hand.

"I'm sending him two books," she said. "But tell Mr. Falk to come in next time, or send me the names of the books he wants. I don't know what he wants to read."

I said nothing. She stamped the card and handed me the books. Not daring to glance at them, I went out of the library, fearing that the woman would call me back for further questioning. A block away from the library I opened one of the books and read a title: *A Book of Prefaces*. I was nearing my nineteenth birthday and I did not know how to pronounce the word "preface." I thumbed the pages and saw strange words and strange names. I shook my head, disappointed. I looked at the other book; it was called *Prejudices*. I knew what that word meant; I had heard it all my life. And right off I was on guard against Mencken's books. Why would a man want to call a book *Prejudices*? The word was so stained with all my memories of racial hate that I could not conceive of anybody using it for a title. Perhaps I had made a mistake about Mencken? A man who had prejudices must be wrong.

When I showed the books to Mr. Falk, he looked at me and frowned.

"That librarian might telephone you," I warned him.

60   "That's all right," he said. "But when you're through reading those books, I want you to tell me what you get out of them."

That night in my rented room, while letting the hot water run over my can of pork and beans in the sink, I opened *A Book of Prefaces* and began to read. I was jarred and shocked by the style, the clear, clean, sweeping sentences. Why did he write like that? And how did one write like that? I pictured the man as a raging demon, slashing with his pen, consumed with hate, denouncing everything American, extolling everything European or German, laughing at the weaknesses of people, mocking God, authority. What was this? I stood up, trying to realize what reality lay behind the meaning of the words . . . Yes, this man was fighting, fighting with words. He was using words as a weapon, using them as one would use a club. Could words be weapons? Well, yes, for here they were. Then, maybe, perhaps, I could use them as a weapon? No. It frightened me. I read on and what amazed me was not what he said, but how on earth anybody had the courage to say it.

STRATEGIES: DETAILS
Notice the details in the first sentence of paragraph 61. Writers often use details not only to describe a scene or event but also to convey messages about that scene or event. What messages do these details convey?

Occasionally I glanced up to reassure myself that I was alone in the room. Who were these men about whom Mencken was talking so passionately? Who was Anatole France? Joseph Conrad? Sinclair Lewis, Sherwood Anderson, Dostoevski, George Moore, Gustave Flaubert, Maupassant, Tolstoy, Frank Harris, Mark Twain, Thomas Hardy, Arnold Bennett, Stephen Crane, Zola, Norris, Gorky, Bergson, Ibsen, Balzac, Bernard Shaw, Dumas, Poe, Thomas Mann, O. Henry, Dreiser, H. G. Wells, Gogol, T. S. Eliot, Gide, Baudelaire, Edgar Lee Masters, Stendhal, Turgenev, Huneker, Nietzsche, and scores of others? Were these men real? Did they exist or had they existed? And how did one pronounce their names?

I ran across many words whose meanings I did not know, and I either looked them up in a dictionary or, before I had a chance to do that, encountered the word in a context that made its meaning clear. But what strange world was this? I concluded the book with the conviction that I had somehow overlooked something terribly important in life. I had once tried to write, had once reveled in feeling, had let my crude imagination roam, but the impulse to dream had been slowly beaten out of me by experience. Now it surged up again and I hungered for books, new ways of looking and seeing. It was not a matter of believing or disbelieving what I read, but of feeling something new, of being affected by something that made the look of the world different.

As dawn broke I ate my pork and beans, feeling dopey, sleepy. I went to work, but the mood of the book would not die; it lingered, coloring everything I saw, heard, did. I now felt that I knew what the white men were feeling. Merely because I had read a book that had spoken of how they lived and thought, I identified myself with that book. I felt vaguely guilty. Would I, filled with bookish notions, act in a manner that would make the whites dislike me?

I forged more notes and my trips to the library became frequent. Reading grew   65
into a passion. My first serious novel was Sinclair Lewis's *Main Street*. It made me see my boss, Mr. Gerald, and identify him as an American type. I would smile when I saw him lugging his golf bags into the office. I had always felt a vast distance separating me from the boss, and now I felt closer to him, though still distant. I felt now that I knew him, that I could feel the very limits of his narrow life. And this had happened because I had read a novel about a mythical man called George F. Babbitt.

The plots and stories in the novels did not interest me so much as the point of view revealed. I gave myself over to each novel without reserve, without trying to criticize it; it was enough for me to see and feel something different. And for me, everything was something different. Reading was like a drug, a dope. The novels created moods in which I lived for days. But I could not conquer my sense of guilt, my feeling that the white men around me knew that I was changing, that I had begun to regard them differently.

Whenever I brought a book to the job, I wrapped it in newspaper—a habit that was to persist for years in other cities and under other circumstances. But some of the white men pried into my packages when I was absent and they questioned me.

"Boy, what are you reading those books for?"

"Oh, I don't know, sir."

"That's deep stuff you're reading, boy."   70

"I'm just killing time, sir."

"You'll addle your brains if you don't watch out."

I read **Dreiser's Jennie Gerhardt and Sister Carrie** and they revived in me a vivid sense of my mother's suffering; I was overwhelmed. I grew silent, wondering about the life around me. It would have been impossible for me to have told anyone what I derived from these novels, for it was nothing less than a sense of life itself. All my life had shaped me for the realism, the naturalism of the modern novel, and I could not read enough of them.

CONVERSATIONS: FAMOUS NOVELS

Wright refers to two novels by Theodore Dreiser, one of the best-known American novelists in the first half of the twentieth century. Dreiser's novels, especially *Sister Carrie* and *An American Tragedy*, are considered sharp criticisms of American capitalism. Wright himself came to sympathize with the anticapitalist views of the Communist Party. In a sense, Wright's reading helped shape his political and social views—as well as his own novels. His descriptions of the novels he read can be seen as an example of how fiction can be part of the broader discussions of social and political issues that are carried on in our society through the political process and the press.

Steeped in new moods and ideas, I bought a ream of paper and tried to write; but nothing would come, or what did come was flat beyond telling. I discovered that more than desire and feeling were necessary to write and I dropped the idea. Yet I still wondered how it was possible to know people sufficiently to write about them? Could I ever learn about life and people? To me, with my vast ignorance, my Jim Crow station in life, it seemed a task impossible of achievement. I now knew what being a Negro meant. I could endure the hunger and I had learned to live with hate. But to feel that there were feelings denied me, that the very breath of life itself was beyond my reach, that more than anything else hurt, wounded me. I had a new hunger.

75   In buoying me up, reading also cast me down, made me see what was possible, what I had missed. My tension returned, new, terrible, bitter, surging, almost too great to be contained. I no longer *felt* that the world about me was hostile, killing; I *knew* it. A million times I asked myself what I could do to save myself, and there were no answers. I seemed forever condemned, ringed by walls.

I did not discuss my reading with Mr. Falk, who had lent me his library card; it would have meant talking about myself and that would have been too painful. I smiled each day, fighting desperately to maintain my old behavior, to keep my disposition seemingly sunny. But some of the white men discerned that I had begun to brood.

"Wake up there, boy!" Mr. Olin said one day.

"Sir!" I answered for the lack of a better word.

"You act like you've stolen something," he said.

80   I laughed in the way I knew he expected me to laugh, but I resolved to be more conscious of myself, to watch my every act, to guard and hide the new knowledge that was dawning within me.

If I went north, would it be possible for me to build a new life then? But how could a man build a life upon vague, unformed yearnings? I wanted to write and I did not even know the English language. I bought English grammars and found them dull. I felt that I was getting a better sense of the language from novels than from grammars. I read hard, discarding a writer as soon as I felt that I had grasped his point of view. At night the printed page stood before my eyes in sleep.

Mrs. Moss, my landlady, asked me one Sunday morning:

"Son, what is this you keep on reading?"

"Oh, nothing. Just novels."

"What you get out of 'em?"

85   "I'm just killing time," I said.

"I hope you know your own mind," she said in a tone which implied that she doubted if I had a mind.

I knew of no Negroes who read the books I liked and I wondered if any Negroes ever thought of them. I knew that there were Negro doctors, lawyers, newspapermen, but I never saw any of them. When I read a Negro newspaper I never caught the faintest echo of my preoccupation in its pages. I felt trapped and occasionally, for a few days, I would stop reading. But a vague hunger would come over me for books, books that opened up new avenues of feeling and seeing, and again I would forge another note to the white librarian. Again I would read and wonder as only the naïve and unlettered can read and wonder, feeling that I carried a secret, criminal burden about with me each day.

That winter my mother and brother came and we set up housekeeping, buying furniture on the installment plan, being cheated and yet knowing no way to avoid it. I began to eat warm food and to my surprise found that regular meals enabled me to read faster. I may have lived through many illnesses and survived them, never suspecting that I was ill. My brother obtained a job and we began to save toward the trip north, plotting our time, setting tentative dates for departure. I told none of the white men on the job that I was planning to go north; I knew that the moment they felt I was thinking of the North they would change toward me. It would have made them feel that I did not like the life I was living, and because my life was completely conditioned by what they said or did, it would have been tantamount to challenging them.

I could calculate my chances for life in the South as a Negro fairly clearly now.   90

I could fight the southern whites by organizing with other Negroes, as my grandfather had done. But I knew that I could never win that way; there were many whites and there were but few blacks. They were strong and we were weak. Outright black rebellion could never win. If I fought openly I would die and I did not want to die. News of lynchings were frequent.

I could submit and live the life of a genial slave, but that was impossible. All of my life had shaped me to live by my own feelings, and thoughts. I could make up to **Bess** and marry her and inherit the house. But that, too, would be the life of a slave; if I did that, I would crush to death something within me, and I would hate myself as much as I knew the whites already hated those who had submitted. Neither could I ever willingly present myself to be kicked, as Shorty had done. I would rather have died than do that.

I could drain off my restlessness by fighting with **Shorty and Harrison.** I had seen many Negroes solve the problem of being black by transferring their hatred of themselves to others with a black skin and fighting them. I would have to be cold to do that, and I was not cold and I could never be.

I could, of course, forget what I had read, thrust the whites out of my mind, forget them; and find release from anxiety and longing in sex and alcohol. But the memory of how my father had conducted himself made that course repugnant. If I did not want others to violate my life, how could I voluntarily violate it myself?

GLOSS: BESS, SHORTY, AND HARRISON
Bess was a woman with whom Wright was in love and whom he describes elsewhere in his autobiography, *Black Boy,* from which this passage is excerpted. Shorty and Harrison are friends of his who are also described elsewhere in *Black Boy.*

I had no hope whatever of being a professional man. Not only had I been so con-   95
ditioned that I did not desire it, but the fulfillment of such an ambition was beyond my capabilities. Well-to-do Negroes lived in a world that was almost as alien to me as the world inhabited by whites.

What, then, was there? I held my life in my mind, in my consciousness each day, feeling at times that I would stumble and drop it, spill it forever. My reading had created a vast sense of distance between me and the world in which I lived and tried to make a living, and that sense of distance was increasing each day. My days and nights were one long, quiet, continuously contained dream of terror, tension, and anxiety. I wondered how long I could bear it.

UNDERSTANDING THE TEXT

1. What prompted Wright to try to obtain books from the library? What might this episode reveal about Wright as a person?

2. What is Wright's reaction to the books he reads by H. L. Mencken (par. 61–63)? Why do you think he focuses attention on Mencken's writing? What does Wright mean when he writes that reading Mencken's book convinced him that he "had somehow overlooked something terribly important" in his life? What was it that he had overlooked?

3. Why does Wright say that "reading was like a drug, a dope" for him? What does this simile suggest about reading? Do you think this is an appropriate simile to describe the effects of reading on him? Why or why not?

4. What dilemma does reading lead to for Wright? What does he realize as a result of confronting this dilemma? How does he resolve it? What does his dilemma suggest about the circumstances within which Blacks lived in the American South?

EXPLORING THE ISSUES

1. In a sense, this excerpt from Wright's autobiography is a description of the effect of reading on one person. Examine the sections in this passage (par. 63–65 or par. 73, for example) where Wright describes how he was affected by the specific books he read. What were the effects of these books on him? How did they change his thinking? Were there similarities in the way the different books he read affected him? Explain.

2. Imagine if you were prevented from having access to books, newspapers, the Internet, or other sources of information you use regularly. What impact might that have on your life? What might Wright's difficulties obtaining books tell us about reading and writing and their roles in our society?

ENTERING THE CONVERSATIONS

1. In paragraph 63, Wright tells us that after reading H. L. Mencken's book, he "hungered for books, new ways of looking and seeing." Write an essay about a time you experienced new ways of looking and seeing as a result of reading a book or having a profound experience.

2. Given Wright's descriptions about the power that Whites had over Blacks during the time he was growing up, I might have put this essay in Chapter 9 on Power. Using Wright's essay and any of the essays in Chapter 9 that seem appropriate, write an essay in which you discuss the relationship between power and learning. In what ways did the power dynamics between Whites and Blacks affect Wright's learning? What do his experiences tell us about how such dynamics can hinder learning or result in certain kinds of learning?

INFOTRAC

3. Throughout history, there have been many attempts to control what people read and even whether they can read. Today, we continue to see efforts to control reading and writing—from attempts by totalitarian governments to ban certain kinds of books to efforts by individuals and groups in the United States to prohibit schools from assigning certain books to students. Using InfoTrac College Edition and other appropriate resources, examine previous and current efforts to control writing and reading. Try to find examples of attempts to ban certain kinds of reading materials, and examine those examples to understand the reasons for them. Write a report in which you describe such efforts to control reading and writing. Describe these situations and explain the views of the people involved. Draw conclusions about reading and writing on the basis of the examples you discuss.

4. This painting by Jacob Lawrence (1917–2000), an African American artist interested in the struggles of freedom during the Civil Rights Movement, depicts a scene entitled *The Library* (1960). Write an essay in which you analyze the messages this painting communicates about libraries and reading.

Jacob Lawrence, *The Library*, 1960

I have seen a weasel in the wild only once in my life, while I was sitting on the shore of a remote lake in the Adirondack Mountains in New York. The weasel appeared suddenly on a brush pile near the shore. Like Dillard, I found that brief encounter exhilarating. It was an unexpected moment of wonder when I was close to a wild creature that I had previously seen only in photographs—an opportunity to experience the wild more intimately than most of us usually do. But for

Living LIKE Weasels

Dillard, the chance encounter with a weasel takes on much greater meaning. It prompts her to reflect on her life in a profound way and to raise questions about the choices she has made about how to live. These seem to be weighty issues to ponder as a result of a brief glimpse of a wild creature. But perhaps that's part of what makes Dillard such a respected and popular writer. If you read carefully, you'll see that her vivid descriptions are more than descriptions; they are part of her efforts to explore complex ideas with seemingly simple prose. With careful choices of words, Dillard directs our attention to seemingly obvious things in which she sees great significance. Just as Dillard's observations of her surroundings can reveal surprises and insights, paying careful attention to her words can reward you with surprises and insights as well. Her essay reminds us that learning can happen unexpectedly and in the most mundane circumstances.

Annie Dillard (b. 1945) is the author of a number of books, including the award-winning Pilgrim at Tinker Creek (1974) and Teaching a Stone to Talk (1982), in which the following essay was first published. ▼

ANNIE DILLARD

A weasel is wild. Who knows what he thinks? He sleeps in his underground den, his tail draped over his nose. Sometimes he lives in his den for two days without leaving. Outside, he stalks rabbits, mice, muskrats, and birds, killing more bodies than he can eat warm, and often dragging the carcasses home. Obedient to instinct, he bites his prey at the neck, either splitting the jugular vein at the throat or crunching the brain at the base of the skull, and he does not let go. One naturalist refused to kill a weasel who was socketed into his hand deeply as a rattlesnake. The man could in no way pry the tiny weasel off, and he had to walk half a mile to water, the weasel dangling from his palm, and soak him off like a stubborn label.

And once, says Ernest Thompson Seton—once, a man shot an eagle out of the sky. He examined the eagle and found the dry skull of a weasel fixed by the jaws to his throat. The supposition is that the eagle had pounced on the weasel and the weasel swiveled and bit as instinct taught him, tooth to neck, and nearly won. I would like to have seen that eagle from the air a few weeks or months before he was shot: was the whole weasel still attached to his feathered throat, a fur pendant? Or did the eagle eat what he could reach, gutting the living weasel with his talons before his breast, bending his beak, cleaning the beautiful airborne bones?

*   *   *

I have been reading about weasels because I saw one last week. I startled a weasel who startled me, and we exchanged a long glance.

Twenty minutes from my house, through the woods by the quarry and across the highway, is Hollins Pond, a remarkable piece of shallowness, where I like to go at sunset and sit on a tree trunk. Hollins Pond is also called Murray's Pond; it covers two acres of bottomland near Tinker Creek with six inches of water and six thousand lily pads. In winter, brown-and-white steers stand in the middle of it, merely dampening their hooves; from the distant shore they look like miracle itself, complete with miracle's nonchalance. Now, in summer, the steers are gone. The water lilies have blossomed and spread to a green horizontal plane that is terra firma to plodding blackbirds, and tremulous ceiling to black leeches, crayfish, and carp.

5   This is, mind you, suburbia. It is a five-minute walk in three directions to rows of houses, though none is visible here. There's a 55 mph highway at one end of the pond, and a nesting pair of wood ducks at the other. Under every bush is a muskrat hole or a beer can. The far end is an alternating series of fields and woods, fields and woods, threaded everywhere with motorcycle tracks—in whose bare clay wild turtles lay eggs.

So. I had crossed the highway, stepped over two low barbed-wire fences, and traced the motorcycle path in all gratitude through the wild rose and poison ivy of the pond's shoreline up into high grassy fields. Then I cut down through the woods to the mossy fallen tree where I sit. This tree is excellent. It makes a dry, upholstered bench at the upper, marshy end of the pond, a plush jetty raised from the thorny shore between a shallow blue body of water and a deep blue body of sky.

The sun had just set. I was relaxed on the tree trunk, ensconced in the lap of lichen, watching the lily pads at my feet tremble and part dreamily over the thrusting path of a carp. A yellow bird appeared to my right and flew behind me. It caught my eye; I swiveled around— and the next instant, inexplicably, I was looking down at a weasel, who was looking up at me.

*   *   *

Weasel! I'd never seen one wild before. He was ten inches long, thin as a curve, a muscled ribbon, brown as fruitwood, soft-furred, alert. His face was fierce, small and pointed as a lizard's; he would have made a good arrowhead. There was just a dot of chin, maybe two brown hairs' worth, and then the pure white fur began that spread down his underside. He had two black eyes I didn't see, any more than you see a window.

The weasel was stunned into stillness as he was emerging from beneath an enormous shaggy wild rose bush four feet away. I was stunned into stillness twisted backward on the tree trunk. Our eyes locked, and someone threw away the key.

Our look was as if two lovers, or deadly enemies, met unexpectedly on an overgrown path when each had been thinking of something else: a clearing blow to the gut. It was also a bright blow to the brain, or a sudden beating of brains, with all the charge and intimate grate of rubbed balloons. It emptied our lungs. It felled the forest, moved the fields, and drained the pond; the world dismantled and tumbled into that black hole of eyes. If you and I looked at each other that way, our skulls would split and drop to our shoulders. But we don't. We keep our skulls. So.

He disappeared. This was only last week, and already I don't remember what shattered the enchantment. I think I blinked, I think I retrieved my brain from the weasel's brain, and tried to memorize what I was seeing, and the weasel felt the yank of separation, the careening splashdown into real life and the urgent current of instinct. He vanished under the wild rose. I waited motionless, my mind suddenly full of data and my spirit with pleadings, but he didn't return.

Please do not tell me about "approach-avoidance conflicts." I tell you I've been in that weasel's brain for sixty seconds, and he was in mine. Brains are private places, muttering through unique and secret tapes—but the weasel and I both plugged into another tape simultaneously, for a sweet and shocking time. Can I help it if it was a blank?

What goes on in his brain the rest of the time? What does a weasel think about? He won't say. His journal is tracks in clay, a spray of feathers, mouse blood and bone: uncollected, unconnected, loose-leaf, and blown.

*   *   *

I would like to learn, or remember, how to live. I come to Hollins Pond not so much **to learn how to live** as, frankly, to forget about it. That is, I don't think I can learn from a wild animal how to live in particular—shall I suck warm blood, hold my tail high, walk with my footprints precisely over the prints of my hands?—but I might learn something of mindlessness, something of the purity of living in the physical senses and the dignity of living without bias or motive. The weasel lives in necessity and we live in choice, hating necessity and dying at the last ignobly in its talons. I would like to live as I should, as the weasel lives as he should. And I suspect that for me the way is like the weasel's: open to time and death painlessly, noticing everything, remembering nothing, choosing the given with a fierce and pointed will.

I missed my chance. I should have gone for the throat. I should have lunged for that streak of white under the weasel's chin and held on, held on through mud and into the wild rose, held on for a dearer life. We could live under the wild rose wild as weasels, mute and uncomprehending. I could very calmly go wild. I could live two days in the den, curled, leaning on mouse fur, sniffing bird bones, blinking, licking, breathing musk, my hair tangled in the roots of grasses. Down is a good place to go, where the mind is single. Down is out, out of your ever-loving mind and back to your

10

15

CONVERSATIONS: LEARNING TO LIVE
In his classic book, *Walden,* Henry David Thoreau (1817–1862) explains his reasons for living alone in a small cabin in the forest this way: "I went into the woods because I wished to live deliberately, to front only the essential facts of life, and see if I could not learn what it had to teach, and not, when I came to die, discover that I had not lived." I wondered if Dillard had this passage in mind when she wrote, "I would like to learn, or remember, how to live" (par. 14). If so, she would be joining a longstanding conversation in Western culture about our relationship to the land.

careless senses. I remember muteness as a prolonged and giddy fast, where every moment is a feast of utterance received. Time and events are merely poured, unremarked, and ingested directly, like blood pulsed into my gut through a jugular vein. Could two live that way? Could two live under the wild rose, and explore by the pond, so that the smooth mind of each is as everywhere present to the other, and as received and as unchallenged, as falling snow?

We could, you know. We can live any way we want. People take vows of poverty, chastity, and obedience—even of silence—by choice. The thing is to stalk your calling in a certain skilled and supple way, to locate the most tender and live spot and plug into that pulse. This is yielding, not fighting. A weasel doesn't "attack" anything; a weasel lives as he's meant to, yielding at every moment to the perfect freedom of single necessity.

I think it would be well, and proper, and obedient, and pure, to grasp your one necessity and not let it go, to dangle from it limp wherever it takes you. Then even death, where you're going no matter how you live, cannot you part. Seize it and let it seize you up aloft even, till your eyes burn out and drop; let your musky flesh fall off in shreds, and let your very bones unhinge and scatter, loosened over fields, over fields and woods, lightly, thoughtless, from any height at all, from as high as eagles.

UNDERSTANDING THE TEXT

1. How does Dillard encounter the weasel? Why is this encounter unusual or remarkable to her? What was it about this encounter that made such an impression on Dillard?

2. What do you think Dillard learns about herself in thinking about her encounter with the weasel?

3. What does Dillard believe she can learn from an animal like a weasel? Why does she believe that she missed her chance to live like a weasel? What does this reveal about her and her views about modern living?

EXPLORING THE ISSUES

1. Dillard begins this essay with a description of weasels. What does this description suggest about weasels? Why do you think Dillard begins in this way? What ideas are introduced in this beginning that will become important in her essay?

2. In paragraph 10, Dillard describes in detail the look she exchanged with the weasel. Examine this description for what it seems to suggest about the weasel and about Dillard. Look especially at the figures of speech she uses in her description (for example, she describes the encounter as if "two lovers, or deadly enemies, met unexpectedly"). What do you think she is trying to convey through such figures of speech and through her choice of details?

3. Assess Dillard's use of metaphor in this essay—not only the specific metaphors she uses to describe scenes she has witnessed but also the metaphor of living like a weasel. What ideas does that metaphor allow Dillard to convey? How effectively do you think that metaphor conveys her ideas?

4. How would you describe the tone of this essay? In additional to her detailed descriptions of her surroundings and her encounter with the weasel, Dillard also includes thoughts about how she lives her life and raises questions about how she should do so. What impact do these thoughts and questions have on the essay? How did you react to them? What might your reaction suggest about you as a reader?

ENTERING THE CONVERSATIONS

1. In an essay intended for your classmates, describe an encounter you had with wildlife or something else that struck you as special in some way. Write your essay in a way that might convey an idea or insight you gained from that encounter. Try also to convey a sense of what you learned about yourself.

2. Writers have long examined the idea that we humans can learn a great deal from nature. Dillard's essay can be seen as an example of such learning. Drawing on her essay and on any other essays that seem appropriate, write an essay in which you discuss how these writers understand nature and how and what they learn from their encounters with the natural world. (For this assignment, you might consider using the following essays: Scott Russell Sanders, "Stillness" (page 522); Wallace Stegner, "The Sense of Place" (page 544); Karen Piper, "Remembering Water" (page 558); or Brenda Peterson, "Growing Up Game" (page 575).

INFOTRAC

3. Many educators argue that environmental education should be a required part of the school curriculum. One justification they offer for this requirement is that through environmental education students not only can learn more about preserving the environment but they can also learn about themselves, as Dillard did in this essay. Using InfoTrac College Edition and any other relevant resources, find out what environmental education is and how its proponents justify it. Try to find examples of schools and colleges where environmental education is a part of the curriculum. If possible, interview people in your own school who are involved in environmental education. Then, on the basis of your research, write a proposal in which your make a case for or against an environmental education curriculum at your school. (If your school already has such a curriculum, you can make a proposal for changing it in ways that you believe would improve it.) In your proposal, draw on your research to support your specific recommendations. Draw also on Dillard's essay and others like it.

How often have you heard someone say that *we all learn from our mistakes? We tend to take this idea for granted. And often, we acknowledge that learning from our mistakes can be unpleasant, humbling, even painful—partly because it's not always easy to admit we're wrong. In the following essay, pediatrician Susan Sawyer (b. 1960) offers a twist to the idea of learning from mistakes: In the situation she describes involving one of her patients, she was quite happy to be*

ON Being Proved Wrong

wrong. Sawyer tells the story of her encounter with a teenage girl whom Sawyer suspected of suffering from anorexia nervosa, a serious eating disorder that can cause severe health problems and sometimes even death. She bases her suspicions on her experience with young people suffering from the disease, and she devises a treatment plan accordingly. But her patient resists, and that creates a dilemma for Sawyer. In describing this dilemma, Sawyer invites us to consider how we base our decisions on our knowledge, our experience, and our best judgments. But even then, we are not always sure. In this regard, Sawyer's essay is really about some of the complexities of learning.

Sawyer's essay is also about the complexities of a disease—anorexia nervosa—that has received a great deal of attention in the popular press and the entertainment media in recent years. You might consider how your knowledge of this disease influences your reading of Sawyer's essay—and how her essay might in turn influence your understanding of this disease.

Susan Sawyer is the director of the Centre for Adolescent Health at the Royal Children's Hospital and Professor of Adolescent Health at the University of Melbourne, Australia. Her essay first appeared in 2002 in Meanjin, *an Australian literary magazine.* ▼

SUSAN SAWYER

It is Tuesday afternoon. I call out the name of the teenage girl whom I'd agreed to see outside my usual times. The clinic waiting list is weeks long but she needed urgent assessment. She is all too easily identifiable in the waiting room. I feel relieved, as she hadn't wanted to come. She walks slowly into my consulting room after demanding her mother stay put outside. She confirms she doesn't want to be here, telling me she doesn't have any health problems, that she's only here because her mother made her come. She tells me she's doing much better now, eating really well. She doesn't believe she's underweight and hopes to lose more. I choose not to respond yet. I know that logical explanations will not get me far.

She has fine facial features, dominated by dark, luminous eyes. They seem sad and confused, or are they angry eyes? Her pale skin looks tired. She pulls obsessively at her hair, which is dull and lank. Despite my experience, I am astounded at her physical appearance and try not to stare. She is grossly emaciated, severely physically malnourished. This girl is so obviously unwell. How have her parents explained her weight loss? What attempts have they made to get help? What was her **GP** thinking? What was the school's response?

SAWYER, SUSAN. "ON BEING PROVED WRONG." FROM *MEANJIN* (DEC. 2002). VOL 61, NO. 4, 2002. REPRINTED BY PERMISSION OF THE AUTHOR.

Through an interpreter, her mother confirms that she has lost at least 10 **kilograms** in the past three months, although neither mother nor daughter is certain of her earlier weight. They agree on 42 kilograms. Her current weight is way off the growth charts by which we define normality. My physical examination confirms first impressions: 31 kilograms—a dangerously low weight.

It is a warm day but she wears many layers of clothing. She objects to my request to remove them, but I quietly insist. Ever so slowly, the layers get removed. Again, I am shocked by how wasted she is when fully exposed in her underwear. Her pulse rate is dramatically slow at forty beats per minute and her blood pressure can't be recorded by the blood pressure cuff, measurable only by palpation. My examination reveals no physical explanation for her dramatic weight loss: no evidence of thyroid disease, no malignant masses, no features of organ failure. I will perform a few tests but the diagnosis seems fairly straightforward: another young girl with anorexia nervosa.

I talk quietly with mother and daughter about why I think the girl has anorexia nervosa and needs to be admitted to hospital. Through the interpreter, this takes longer than usual, but I had put the time aside. The severity of the girl's condition makes the focus on the physical the only option for today. There will be time ahead of us to explore what has led her to this point.

The mother sits passively, without questioning. It is the daughter who becomes distressed and tells me that she couldn't possibly be admitted to hospital. She reiterates that she is not sick enough, that she is eating better than before, and she also tells me that she couldn't cope with being separated from her family. She pleads with me to allow her to stay home. I explore her expectations and any previous experience of hospitalisation, but her distress doesn't seem focused on any particulars. I reassure her and her mother that we manage many young people with anorexia at the Centre for Adolescent Health and that while most young people don't want to come to hospital they generally don't find the adolescent ward at the Royal Children's Hospital so bad. I say that hospitalisation might last about two weeks.

The girl's distress does not settle, it gets worse. The interpreter tells me that the mother has just reassured her daughter that she won't have to go to hospital if she doesn't want to. He steals me a quick glance of concern. He is clearly worried. I nod to him, sharing his concern. Wordlessly, though, I try to reassure him that we will work it out. The emotional context of anorexia nervosa is not new territory for me.

Hearing of the mother's ambivalence about hospitalisation, I refocus my attention and explore her concerns. She cannot understand why her daughter refuses to eat or what else might be wrong. It is clear that neither she nor her daughter was expecting what I have told them. I emphasise to them the risk of sudden death from cardiac arrhythmia when weight loss is as severe as this. I try not to use this information threateningly but feel it needs to be said. Perhaps I am just trying to make myself feel less of an ogre. Railroading the hospital admission is one option and I feel more comfortable that her mother could now be persuaded. But is it truly necessary today? I consider what I might be prepared to compromise on. The risk of sudden death is real if weight loss continues, but she has had severe weight loss for the past three months. Another day or two should be safe.

GLOSSES

GP

GP is short for general practitioner, a term for family doctor.

KILOGRAMS

A kilogram, which is a standard unit for measuring weight in Europe and throughout much of the world, is about 2.2 pounds.

5

CONTEXT: ANOREXIA NERVOSA

Anorexia nervosa is a recognized medical and psychological condition in which the patient goes to extreme lengths to lose weight. Often, patients believe they are fat even when their body weight is abnormally low. Anorexia nervosa patients typically have 85 percent or less of normal body weight for their age and gender and often suffer from a variety of health problems as a result of the disorder, as Sawyer indicates in this essay. Girls are much more commonly afflicted with the disease than boys. Much attention to this disease in the popular media in the past decade or so has made more people aware of it, but the media have also called attention to some of our cultural beliefs about physical appearance. For example, consider what these images of a fashion model and teenage celebrities, the Olsen twins—Mary-Kate (on the right) has reportedly suffered from anorexia nervosa—suggest about physical beauty.

Barcelona Fashion Week, 2004.   Mary-Kate and Ashley Olsen, 2004.

As an alternative, I suggest that I will agree to her going home today if she agrees to seeing me in three days' time. On Friday, if she can demonstrate she has improved, it would be safe to stay home until she is seen in clinic the following week. However, if her physical assessment were unchanged, and certainly if it were any worse, she would then need to be admitted. I choose not to inform either of them that should her clinical state be worse on review and the mother refuses to allow hospital admission, there are legal options available to me that would ensure her daughter obtained the required medical care. I have no doubt I would invoke this if the girl were to deteriorate further.

10   I feel relieved when the compromise is agreed to. I provide clear instructions about a meal plan between now and Friday. Three meals a day: normal meals like the rest

of the family, no "low fat" products. Three snacks a day: high-energy snacks, not the piece of apple or air-filled rice crackers she has been eating. Because she is so unwell, there is to be no school and she must stay within the house. I feel like I am demanding the impossible, as I know how few girls with such severely disordered eating can achieve this. I tell her that I very much hope she can prove me wrong, but in my heart of hearts I sense I am simply buying time.

I call her GP, who sounds greatly relieved. I quietly explore with him why he hadn't sought specialist help earlier, and he tells me that she had refused to allow him to examine her, let alone weigh her. Yet his "eyeball" assessment had been sufficient for him to lose sleep over her. Perhaps the real reason lay in his explanation that he hadn't known where to get help.

I make detailed notes in her hospital file about what has led me to the diagnosis of an eating disorder. I describe the various features of anorexia nervosa. I record the abnormal physical features, her altered body image, the features of depression and anxiety. I ponder an apparent paradox: that while her physical and mental health is severely disturbed, her history of disturbed eating is very short. I consider the unknowns: the features within herself, her family, and her social circles (friends, school) that might have led to this sudden descent into disordered eating. Do we have a case of depression here, and is the disordered eating a symptom of that? Is it true anorexia nervosa? What might this difference be? Given that the treatment is the same, does it matter?

As I make my notes, I feel my own anxiety rise about allowing her to go home. What if she dies from an acute cardiac arrhythmia? Have I allowed my medical judgment to be compromised? Would my colleagues have made the same decision? I have to remind myself why I have allowed her to go home.

First thing the next day, I check her blood tests. Normal. I race off to our team meeting, grabbing a coffee and a muffin on the way. The euphemistically named Healthy Eating Clinic meets weekly, generally over food. Our team consists of multidisciplinary staff at the Centre for Adolescent Health and the Royal Children's Hospital: physicians, dieticians, mental health professionals, nurses, and others. We generally have a few students on placement and I remind them about the confidentiality of our discussions of patients. We provide updates about the ups and downs of the long-term patients, our "frequent flyers." "Remember Jane? She's doing really well. Wants to do psychology!" We grin. Nutrition and psychology seem standard career choices for young women with anorexia. "Margaret will need admitting again soon." We sigh about the apparent lack of progress, the lack of treatment alternatives. Primarily, however, our team meeting is where we build a shared understanding about how we work therapeutically with patients and their families. It is where secondary consultation is provided, and where we support each other in managing this complex work. I know my junior staff understand that I need their support as much as they need mine.

Six years ago, I had no experience of eating disorders. In retrospect it seems a [15] pretty bold move to have started the Healthy Eating Clinic. Our idea back then was

> **CONVERSATIONS: PROFESSIONAL JUDGMENT**
> In paragraph 13, Sawyer admits to having doubts about her compromise with her patient, and at one point, she asks, "Would my colleagues have made the same decision?" This question suggests how our individual judgments are often made in the context of a group or community of which we are a part. In this case, Sawyer is part of a professional community of physicians and other health-care professionals at her hospital as well as the larger medical community. You might consider how Sawyer, by writing this essay for a general audience, is participating in conversations with other communities who might be concerned about eating disorders.

STRATEGIES: BACKGROUND INFORMATION
Notice the kinds of facts and information about anorexia nervosa and related eating disorders that Sawyer includes in paragraphs 15 and 16. Consider how this information provides context for her story of this patient. Would her story be less effective if this passage were excluded from the essay?

CONVERSATIONS: SOLVING MEDICAL PROBLEMS
Sawyer's discussion in paragraph 16 is an excellent example of how individual writers participate in larger, ongoing conversations about specific issues of interest to them—and how those conversations influence their writing. Here, Sawyer offers several explanations for the growing number of young patients with eating disorders. She did not develop these explanations by herself; instead, she is summarizing what the medical community believes about the increase in these disorders among young people. And by sharing her story, Sawyer is part of the medical community's efforts to understand and deal with the increasing incidence of the disease.

that we wanted to "provide a clinical focus for teenagers with emerging eating disorders." The impact of anorexia on individuals and families is immense. Mortality is about 5–10 percent of all cases presenting in adolescence, varying with the duration of the disorder and the length of follow-up treatment. It is not uncommon that, once established, anorexia nervosa lasts for five to ten years. And while over half of all adolescents with anorexia nervosa are predicted to recover, a significant proportion continue to suffer from relapses or maintain some milder features of anorexia or bulimia. Given this impact, and the difficulty for young people in gaining access to services, our goal was to focus on early intervention that might prevent the development of more severe symptoms.

It is ironic that the lack of multidisciplinary facilities for adolescents with eating disorders in Victoria has meant we are perceived as running a specialist service. We deal increasingly with severely disturbed people presenting at increasingly young ages. One explanation is that eating disorders are becoming more common in our community. It is estimated that 0.1–0.5 percent of adolescent females have anorexia nervosa, but that up to 5 percent of young women have some features of disordered eating. Another explanation is that health professionals have become better at identifying the signs of eating disorders in young people and are referring them to us earlier. However, the clandestine aspects of a disorder, whether it is anorexia or bulimia, continue to make early identification difficult. The more likely explanation for our increasing numbers is our growing reputation. At the end of our weekly meeting spent discussing a group of very disturbed patients, I wonder how well this reputation is deserved.

I mention yesterday's new outpatient. One of my colleagues asks what it would take for her not to be admitted. I explain that my decision will be based primarily on her pulse rate. "But what increase would you be satisfied with?" someone else pushes. I'd be happy with a four-beat-per-minute increase in three days. To be honest, I'd be satisfied with any increase. The challenge is whether it could be maintained. No one disagrees. Like me, they know she'll be admitted on Friday. I invite them to criticise me for allowing her to go home yesterday. They agree my decision was reasonable—but brave. I feel reassured.

I review my new patient as planned on Friday. Initially, I saw her alone again, and she told me that she was eating well. But they all say that. As anticipated, her weight and blood pressure were unchanged over the three days. However, I was surprised that her pulse rate was significantly better. Fifty-two beats per minute! Her mother confirmed that she was eating well, with no evidence of bingeing or purging. I found it hard to credit such a change, but there was little doubt about the improvement. I cancelled the bed that I'd ended up booking for that day.

I arrange to review her the following Tuesday. Crunch time. Occasionally patients with eating disorders can improve their eating for a short period when faced with significant consequences, but it is less common for them to sustain this improvement. She walks into the consulting room with her mother, smiles at me shyly, and tells me how much better she feels. Her resting pulse rate is sixty beats per minute and she has gained 1.2 kilograms.

By the following week she has gained another kilogram and grins at me openly. 20
Her mother is almost chirpy today. It is school holidays but the girl is starting to spend time with her friends. She is convinced that she is on the path to recovery. I am the one needing reassurance. This pattern feels too good to be true. This is not usual for anorexia nervosa, although we've all seen it. She more openly discusses school concerns and her belief that it was these issues that led to depression last year and that, somehow, she lost her appetite with it. How easy it seems to lose one's way! We talk of her anxiety about school starting again next week. I encourage her simply to take one step at a time.

I had been absolutely certain that she would be admitted to hospital within the week. Given how unwell she was at presentation, I was sure we'd be here for the long haul. It feels good to be proved wrong. With anorexia, it would be nice if it happened more often.

UNDERSTANDING THE TEXT

1. What do we learn from the description Sawyer gives of her patient in the early paragraphs of this essay? Why is this information important?

2. What challenges does Sawyer face in trying to treat this particular patient? Why are these challenges important to Sawyer's overall point in this essay?

3. What compromise does Sawyer reach with her patient? Why is this compromise necessary? What do you think it tells us about both Sawyer and her patient? Why does it subsequently cause Sawyer such anxiety? What might that anxiety reveal about Sawyer as a physician?

4. In paragraph 15, Sawyer discusses some of the characteristics of anorexia nervosa. Why is this information important in Sawyer's treatment of her patient? What do you think this passage reveals about Sawyer as a physician and as a person?

5. Why is Sawyer happy to be wrong about this patient? What do you think this reveals about Sawyer? Do you think her being happy to be wrong suggests anything about medicine as a profession? Explain.

EXPLORING THE ISSUES

1. Consider how Sawyer's response to her patient is influenced by her previous experiences with eating disorder patients. Sawyer herself admits that she did not really believe her patient when the patient first told Sawyer that she was eating more (par. 18). Why? What specifically causes Sawyer to begin to re-examine her view of this patient? What does this situation suggest about how people make decisions? What does it suggest about how we learn?

2. This essay was originally published in a literary magazine. Knowing that and knowing that Sawyer is a physician, what kind of audience do you think she imagined for her essay? In what ways do you think she tries to address this audience? Cite specific passages to support your answer.

3. In paragraph 14, Sawyer describes the team meeting of health-care professionals at her clinic. What does this description emphasize about this meeting? What do the specific details that Sawyer includes in this description reveal about the team members? In what ways do you think this passage affects your sense of Sawyer as a physician and as a person?

4. How would you describe Sawyer's voice in this essay? Cite specific phrases or sentences to illustrate your answer. Do you think her voice is appropriate for the subject matter of this essay? Explain.

ENTERING THE CONVERSATIONS

1. Write an essay in which you tell the story of a time when you were wrong. Tell your story in a way that will help your readers understand what you learned from that experience.

INFOTRAC

2. Anorexia nervosa, bulimia, and related eating disorders have become big news in the United States and many other nations in the past decade or two. Using InfoTrac College Edition and other relevant resources, find out more about these eating disorders: what they are, how they affect different populations, why they seem to have increased in recent years. Then write a report based on your research.

3. On the basis of your research for Question 2, create a pamphlet or flyer intended for teenagers explaining eating disorders and offering them advice about such disorders.

4. Review several print, Internet, or television advertisements for popular products in which beautiful women are depicted. Examine these adds for what the images they use seem to suggest about physical appearance, especially regarding weight. Then write an essay in which you discuss how physical appearance is depicted in popular advertising. What do the images used in advertising suggest about how women and men should appear? How do they communicate their messages? Try to draw conclusions about how such ads influence our ways of understanding physical appearance and especially our weight. Alternatively, create a web site for the same purpose.

SCHOOLING

MOST AMERICANS SHARE THE EXPERIENCE OF GO-
ING TO SCHOOL. APPROXIMATELY 96 PER-
CENT OF SCHOOL-AGE CHILDREN (UP TO
ABOUT THE AGE OF SIXTEEN) ATTEND SCHOOL, AND STATES
HAVE VARIOUS LAWS THAT MANDATE SCHOOL ATTENDANCE.

That means just about everyone you know has been to school. And the experience of school is remarkably similar, whether you're in a small rural town like Pinedale, Wyoming, or a huge city like Los Angeles. There are obvious differences between these situations, but the basic elements of schooling are the same for everyone: the courses, the curriculum, the way classrooms look, the way the school day is structured, and of course, the tests, the homework, the rules, the extracurricular activities, and the ceremonies like school assemblies and graduation. I'm guessing that nothing in this list sounds unfamiliar to you. And I find that pretty remarkable: Despite the great focus on diversity in our culture in recent decades and despite the great value that Americans place on individuality, if you look at schools, what you see is sameness.

At least, that's what I see. But there's more to schooling than meets the eye, and that's what this cluster of readings is all about. These essays go beyond "readin', writin', and 'rithmetic." They examine some of the complicated learning that occurs in school that is not always obvious and not always intended. These writers prompt us to look more closely at what we are learning in school, and they help us see that we learn much more in school than the material we study for tests. And what we learn in schools may not always be positive or beneficial.

Maya Angelou's description of her eighth-grade graduation, for example, is not a typical essay of celebration and hope, as you might expect in an essay about a graduation. For Angelou, graduating from a segregated school in the American South was a hard lesson in some of the realities of being Black in the United States. In some ways, that lesson contradicted the lessons she had learned in her classes. And because of that contradiction, Angelou's essay asks us to rethink some of our most basic beliefs about what education is for and who benefits from it. Like Angelou, famed education theorist Paulo Freire prompts us to rethink our beliefs about education. But his purpose is somewhat more pointed: He offers a harsh critique of formal education and of the way he believes it indoctrinates students into becoming passive learners. In Freire's view, formal education serves the primary purpose of maintaining an unfair and unjust status quo. Essayist Richard Rodriguez writes about how education can shape the way we think about ourselves, and in some ways, his autobiographical essay offers a concrete example of Freire's theories about education. He asks us to consider the consequences of schooling and wonders whether its opportunities require some students to pay too dearly. Likewise, celebrated poet and activist Adrienne Rich challenges our usual ways of thinking about how schooling provides opportunities for students. She addresses the way women have been treated unequally in schools and calls on women to resist that treatment.

The longer I have been involved in education, the more complicated schooling seems to get and the less convinced I am that everything we ask students to do in school is worth their time or effort. (Indeed, you may feel that much of what I ask you to do in this book is useless!) I have been teaching for more than two decades, and like the authors in this cluster, I have learned that the most important learning that happens in schools often has little to do with the formal curriculum or those standardized tests that we all sweat through. These authors invite us to examine what some theorists have called "the hidden curriculum" of schools and to question what happens in schools. I'm guessing that you have done some of that questioning already. I hope these essays prompt you to continue such questioning.

Sizer's "what High School Is"

When we think of graduation, we tend to think of celebration, recognition, and a sense of possibility. We think about the future. And the hopefulness we associate with graduation is a reflection of our belief in the benefits of an education and the idea that it creates opportunities for those who are willing to work hard. Certainly, that's how Maya Angelou (b. 1928) was thinking about her eighth-grade graduation in the excitement leading up to the ceremony. But

Graduation

that ceremony didn't live up to her expectations. Instead, it forced her to face some of the disturbing realities of growing up as a Black person in the segregated American South in the 1930s. The future for Black graduates wasn't the same future of possibility and opportunity that was open to Whites in her small town of Stamps, Arkansas—or for that matter, in any other American town. Her graduation story is thus a reminder that some of our beliefs about schooling may not necessarily conform to the realities we face. And it suggests that the never-ending conversations in our society about education may encourage beliefs about schooling that are problematic and misleading. Angelou's essay asks: Does success in school really lead to opportunity? The answer to that question, if we pay attention to Angelou, is, "It depends." The question for you is, "On what?"

As you'll see, Angelou manages to retrieve hope from what seems to be an almost hopeless situation, and her ability to find that hope may be one reason that this excerpt from her autobiography, I Know Why the Caged Bird Sings (1970), is so widely read and so often reprinted. In a sense, Angelou's story is a classic American tale of success, and ironically it   (continued)

MAYA ANGELOU

The children in Stamps trembled visibly with anticipation. Some adults were exited too, but to be certain the whole young population had come down with graduation epidemic. Large classes were graduating from both the grammar school and the high school. Even those who were years removed from their own day of glorious release were anxious to help with preparations as a kind of dry run. The junior students who were moving into the vacating classes' chairs were tradition-bound to show their talents for leadership and management. They strutted through the school and around the campus exerting pressure on the lower grades. Their authority was so new that occasionally if they pressed a little too hard it had to be overlooked. After all, next term was coming, and it never hurt a sixth grader to have a play sister in the eighth grade, or a tenth-year student to be able to call a twelfth grader Bubba. So all was endured in a spirit of shared understanding. But the graduating classes themselves were the nobility. Like travelers with exotic destinations on their minds, the graduates were remarkably forgetful. They came to school without their books, or tablets or even pencils. Volunteers fell over them-

(continued) *makes it easy to overlook the fact that her race is perhaps the biggest reason that she had to struggle to attain that success. But how can you read this story without feeling uneasy about how American schools encouraged racism? And if you're paying attention, you'll notice that we're having the same conversations about schools and race today—more than sixty years after Angelou's eighth-grade graduation and more than thirty years after she published this account of it. What might that say about schooling and learning?* ◪

selves to secure replacements for the missing equipment. When accepted, the willing workers might or might not be thanked, and it was of no importance to the pregraduation rites. Even teachers were respectful of the now quiet and aging seniors, and tended to speak to them, if not as equals, as beings only slightly lower than themselves. After tests were returned and grades given, the student body, which acted like an extended family, knew who did well, who excelled, and what piteous ones had failed.

Unlike the white high school, Lafayette County Training School distinguished itself by having neither lawn, nor hedges, nor tennis court, nor climbing ivy. Its two buildings (main classrooms, the grade school and home economics) were set on a dirt hill with no fence to limit either its boundaries or those of bordering farms. There was a large expanse to the left of the school which was used alternately as a baseball diamond or basketball court. Rusty hoops on swaying poles represented the permanent recreational equipment, although bats and balls could be borrowed from the P.E. teacher if the borrower was qualified and if the diamond wasn't occupied.

Over this rocky area relieved by a few shady tall persimmon trees the graduating class walked. The girls often held hands and no longer bothered to speak to the lower students. There was a sadness about them, as if this old world was not their home and they were bound for higher ground. The boys, on the other hand, had become more friendly, more outgoing. A decided change from the closed attitude they projected while studying for finals. Now they seemed not ready to give up the old school, the familiar paths and classrooms. Only a small percentage would be continuing on to college—one of the South's A & M (agricultural and mechanical) schools, which trained Negro youths to be carpenters, farmers, handymen, masons, maids, cooks and baby nurses. Their future rode heavily on their shoulders, and blinded them to the collective joy that had pervaded the lives of the boys and girls in the grammar school graduating class.

Parents who could afford it had ordered new shoes and readymade clothes for themselves from Sears and Roebuck or Montgomery Ward. They also engaged the best seamstresses to make the floating graduating dresses and to cut down secondhand pants which would be pressed to a military slickness for the important event.

Oh, it was important, all right. Whitefolks would attend the ceremony, and two or three would speak of God and home, and the Southern way of life, and Mrs. Parsons, the principal's wife, would play the graduation march while the lower-grade graduates paraded down the aisles and took their seats below the platform. The high school seniors would wait in empty classrooms to make their dramatic entrance.

*   *   *

In the Store I was the person of the moment. The birthday girl. The center. Bailey had graduated the year before, although to do so he had had to forfeit all pleasures to make up for his time lost in Baton Rouge.

My class was wearing butter-yellow piqué dresses, and Momma launched out on mine. She smocked the yoke into tiny crisscrossing puckers, then shirred the rest of the bodice. Her dark fingers ducked in and out of the lemony cloth as she embroidered raised daisies around the hem. Before she considered herself finished she had added a crocheted cuff on the puff sleeves, and a pointy crocheted collar.

I was going to be lovely. A walking model of all the various styles of fine hand sewing and it didn't worry me that I was only twelve years old and merely graduating from the eighth grade. Besides, many teachers in Arkansas Negro schools had only that diploma and were licensed to impart wisdom.

The days had become longer and more noticeable. The faded beige of former times had been replaced with strong and sure colors. I began to see my classmates' clothes, their skin tones, and the dust that waved off pussy willows. Clouds that lazed across the sky were objects of great concern to me. Their shiftier shapes might have held a message that in my new happiness and with a little bit of time I'd soon decipher. During that period I looked at the arch of heaven so religiously my neck kept a steady ache. I had taken to smiling more often, and my jaws hurt from the unaccustomed activity. Between the two physical sore spots, I suppose I could have been uncomfortable, but that was not the case. As a member of the winning team (the graduating class of 1940) I had outdistanced unpleasant sensations by miles. I was headed for the freedom of open fields.

10   Youth and social approval allied themselves with me and we trammeled memories of slights and insults. The wind of our swift passage remodeled my features. Lost tears were pounded to mud and then to dust. Years of withdrawal were brushed aside and left behind, as hanging ropes of parasitic moss.

My work alone had awarded me a top place and I was going to be one of the first called in the graduating ceremonies. On the classroom blackboard, as well as on the bulletin board in the auditorium, there were blue stars and white stars and red stars. No absences, no tardinesses, and my academic work was among the best of the year. I could say the preamble to the Constitution even faster than Bailey. We timed ourselves often: "We the people of the United States in order to form a more perfect union . . ." I had memorized the Presidents of the Untied States from Washington to Roosevelt in chronological as well as alphabetical order.

My hair pleased me too. Gradually the black mass had lengthened and thickened, so that it kept at last to its braided pattern, and I didn't have to yank my scalp off when I tried to comb it.

Louise and I had rehearsed the exercises until we tired out ourselves. Henry Reed was class valedictorian. He was a small, very black boy with hooded eyes, a long, broad nose and an oddly shaped head. I had admired him for years because each term he and I vied for the best grades in our class. Most often he bested me, but instead of being disappointed I was pleased that we shared top places between us. Like many Southern Black children, he lived with is grandmother, who was as strict as Momma and as kind as she knew how to be. He was courteous, respectful and soft-spoken to elders, but on the playground he chose to play the roughest games. I admired him.

Anyone, I reckoned, sufficiently afraid or sufficiently dull could be polite. But to be able to operate at a top level with both adults and children was admirable.

His valedictory speech was entitled **"To Be or Not to Be."** The rigid tenth-grade teacher had helped him write it. He'd been working on the dramatic stresses for months.

15   The weeks until graduation were filled with heady activities. A group of small children were to be presented in a play about buttercups and daisies and bunny rabbits. They could be heard throughout the building practicing their hops and their little songs that sounded like silver bells. The older girls (nongraduates, of course) were assigned the task of making refreshments for the night's festivities. A tangy scent of ginger, cinnamon, nutmeg and chocolate wafted around the home economics building as the budding cooks made samples for themselves and their teachers.

In every corner of the workshop, axes and saws split fresh timber as the woodshop boys made sets and stage scenery. Only the graduates were left out of the general bustle. We were free to sit in the library at the back of the building or look in quite detachedly, naturally, on the measures being taken for our event.

Even the minister preached on graduation the Sunday before. His subject was, "Let your light so shine that men will see your good works and praise your Father, Who is in Heaven." Although the sermon was purported to be addressed to us, he used the occasion to speak to backsliders, gamblers and general ne'er-do-wells. But since he had called our names at the beginning of the service we were mollified.

Among Negroes the tradition was to give presents to children going only from one grade to another. How much more important this was when the person was graduating at the top of the class. Uncle Willie and Momma had sent away for a Mickey Mouse watch like Bailey's. Louise gave me four embroidered handkerchiefs. (I gave her crocheted doilies.) Mrs. Sneed, the minister's wife, made me an undershirt to wear for graduation, and nearly every customer gave me a nickel or maybe even a dime with the instruction "Keep on moving to higher ground," or some such encouragement.

Amazingly the great day finally dawned and I was out of bed before I knew it. I threw open the back door to see it more clearly, but Momma said, "Sister, come away from that door and put your robe on."

20   I hoped the memory of that morning would never leave me. Sunlight was itself young, and the day had none of the insistence maturity would bring it in a few hours. In my robe and barefoot in the backyard, under cover of going to see about my new beans, I gave myself up to the gentle warmth and thanked God that no matter what evil I had done in my life He had allowed me to live to see this day. Somewhere in my fatalism I had expected to die, accidentally, and never have the chance to walk up the stairs in the auditorium and gracefully receive my hard-earned diploma. Out of God's merciful bosom I had won reprieve.

Bailey came out in his robe and gave me a box wrapped in Christmas paper. He said he had saved his money for months to pay for it. It felt like a box of chocolates, but I knew Bailey wouldn't save money to buy candy when we had all we could want under our noses.

He was as proud of the gift as I. It was a soft-leather-bound copy of a collection of poems by Edgar Allan Poe, or, as Bailey and I called him, "Eap." I turned to "Annabel

---

CONTEXT: "TO BE OR NOT TO BE"
I'm sure you recognized this line, perhaps the most famous line from Shakespeare's play, *Hamlet.* It has become part of Western culture. In selecting that line for the title of his valedictory speech, Henry is calling attention to certain ideas that we associate with that famous play. Consider what those ideas are and how Angelou uses them later in her essay. You might also think about what this reference means to you as a reader—and whether or not that meaning matches what Angelou seems to intend.

Lee" and we walked up and down the garden rows, the cool dirt between our toes, reciting the beautifully sad lines.

Momma made a Sunday breakfast although it was only Friday. After we finished the blessing, I opened my eyes to find the watch on my plate. It was a dream of a day. Everything went smoothly and to my credit, I didn't have to be reminded or scolded for anything. Near evening I was too jittery to attend to chores, so Bailey volunteered to do all before his bath.

Days before, we had made a sign for the Store, and as we turned out the lights Momma hung the cardboard over the doorknob. It read clearly: CLOSED. GRADUATION.

25 My dress fitted perfectly and everyone said that I looked like a sunbeam in it. On the hill, going toward the school, Bailey walked behind with Uncle Willie, who muttered, "Go on, Ju." He wanted him to walk ahead with us because it embarrassed him to have to walk so slowly. Bailey said he'd let the ladies walk together, and the men would bring up the rear. We all laughed, nicely.

Little children dashed by out of the dark like fireflies. Their crepe-paper dresses and butterfly wings were not made for running and we heard more than one rip, dryly, and the regretful "uh uh" that followed.

The school blazed without gaiety. The windows seemed cold and unfriendly from the lower hill. A sense of ill-fated timing crept over me, and if Momma hadn't reached for my hand I would have drifted back to Bailey and Uncle Willie, and possibly beyond. She made a few slow jokes about my feet getting cold, and tugged me along to the now-strange building.

Around the front steps, assurance came back. There were my fellow "greats," the graduating class. Hair brushed back, legs oiled, new dresses and pressed pleats, fresh pocket handkerchiefs and little handbags, all homesewn. Oh, we were up to snuff, all right. I joined my comrades and didn't even see my family go in to find seats in the crowded auditorium.

The school band struck up a march and all classes filed in as had been rehearsed. We stood in front of our seats, as assigned, and on a signal from the choir director, we sat. No sooner had this been accomplished than the band started to play the national anthem. We rose again and sang the song, after which we recited the pledge of allegiance. We remained standing for a brief minute before the choir director and the principal signaled to us, rather desperately I thought, to take our seats. The command was so unusual that our carefully rehearsed and smooth-running machine was thrown off. For a full minute we fumbled for our chairs and bumped into each other awkwardly. Habits change or solidify under pressure, so in our state of nervous tension we had been ready to follow our usual assembly pattern: the American national anthem, then the pledge of allegiance, then the song every Black person I knew called the Negro national Anthem. All done in the same key, with the same passion and most often standing on the same foot.

30 Finding my seat at last, I was overcome with a presentiment of worse things to come. Something unrehearsed, unplanned, was going to happen, and we were going to be made to look bad. I distinctly remember being explicit in the choice of pronoun. It was "we," the graduating class, the unit, that concerned me then.

The principal welcomed "parents and friends" and asked the Baptist minister to lead us in prayer. His invocation was brief and punchy, and for a second I thought we were getting on the high road to right action. When the principal came back to the dais, however, his voice had changed. Sounds always affected me profoundly and the principal's voice was one of my favorites. During assembly it melted and lowed weakly into the audience. It had not been in my plan to listen to him, but my curiosity was piqued and I straightened up to give him my attention.

He was talking about **Booker T. Washington,** our "late great leader," who said we can be as close as the fingers on the hand, etc. . . . Then he said a few vague things about friendship and the friendship of kindly people to those less fortunate than themselves. With that his voice nearly faded, thin, away. Like a river diminishing to a stream and then to a trickle. But he cleared his throat and said, "Our speaker tonight, who is also our friend, came from Texarkana to deliver the commencement address, but due to the irregularity of the train schedule, he's going to, as they say, 'speak and run.'" He said that we understood and wanted the man to know that we were most grateful for the time he was able to give us and then something about how we were willing always to adjust to another's program, and without more ado— "I give you Mr. Edward Donleavy."

Not one but two white men came through the door off-stage. The shorter one walked to the speaker's platform, and the tall one moved to the center seat and sat down. But that was our principal's seat, and already occupied. The dislodged gentleman bounced around for a long breath or two before the Baptist minister gave him his chair, then with more dignity than the situation deserved, the minister walked off the stage.

Donleavy looked at the audience once (on reflection, I'm sure that he wanted only to reassure himself that we were really there), adjusted his glasses and began to read from a sheaf of papers.

He was glad "to be here and to see the work going on just as it was in the other schools."

At the first "Amen" from the audience I willed the offender to immediate death by choking on the word. But Amens and Yes, sir's began to fall around the room like rain through a ragged umbrella.

He told us of the wonderful changes we children in Stamps had in store. The Central School (naturally, the white school was Central) had already been granted improvements that would be in use in the fall. A well-known artist was coming from Little Rock to teach art to them. They were going to have the newest microscopes and chemistry equipment for their laboratory. Mr. Donleavy didn't leave us long in the dark over who made these improvements available to Central High. Nor were we to be ignored in the general betterment scheme he had in mind.

He said that he had pointed out to people at a very high level that one of the first-line football tacklers at Arkansas Agricultural and Mechanical College had graduated from good old Lafayette County Training School. Here fewer Amen's were heard. Those few that did break through lay dully in the air with the heaviness of habit.

He went on to praise us. He went on to say how he had bragged that "one of the best basketball players at Fisk sank his first ball right here at Lafayette County Training School."

CONTEXT: BOOKER T. WASHINGTON
A famous Black educator who helped establish the Tuskegee Institute in 1881, Washington is often invoked as an inspiration for the way he overcame hardship to find great success. He came to be known as "The Great Accommodator" for his view that Blacks should strive to improve their economic and personal prospects rather than struggle for equal rights with Whites. Such views made Washington controversial among many Blacks because he was seen as giving in to White prejudice and dominance. Many believed that true equality could never be achieved through the kind of approach Washington advocated. How might that knowledge of Washington affect the way readers react to this passage? And consider how Henry was participating in a certain kind of conversation about race relations by referring to Washington in his speech. In other words, what does Henry's reference to Booker T. Washington really mean in the context of his graduation speech?

35

CONVERSATIONS: RACE, SPORTS, AND INTELLIGENCE
In paragraph 37, Angelou describes the graduation speech given by the White superintendent, Donleavy, to the Black audience at the Lafayette County Training School. In his speech, Donleavy makes a clear distinction between the opportunities waiting for Black graduates, which are mostly in athletics, and the opportunities available to Whites, which include just about every other kind of career. Does this speech sound familiar? It reminds me of more recent controversies that have been sparked by comments about race and intelligence. In 1987, for example, Al Campanis, a former baseball star and a successful executive with the Los Angeles Dodgers, suggested in a television interview that the reason there weren't more Black managers, coaches, and team owners in professional baseball is that Blacks may not have the necessary intelligence to do such jobs. More recently, in 2004, former star football player Paul Horning argued in an interview that the college he attended, Notre Dame, which has a reputation for high academic standards, should "loosen up" those standards to attract better Black athletes, suggesting that good Black athletes are incapable of meeting high academic standards. Although the comment provoked immediate criticism and condemnation, it's worth noting that it's not too different from the attitude reflected in the comments of Superintendent Donleavy at Angelou's graduation more than sixty years earlier. Think about how these attitudes shape our conversations about race and equal rights and how they might shape the meaning of Angelou's story.

The white kids were going to have a chance to become Galileos and Madame Curies and Edisons and Gauguins, and our boys (the girls weren't even in on it) would try to be Jesse Owenses and Joe Louises.

Owens and the Brown Bomber were great heroes in our world, but what school official in the white-goddom of Little Rock had the right to decide that those two men must be our only heroes? Who decided that for Henry Reed to become a scientist he had to work like George Washington Carver, as a bootblack, to buy a lousy microscope? Bailey was obviously always going to be too small to be an athlete, so which concrete angel glued to what country seat had decided that if my brother wanted to become a lawyer he had to first pay penance for his skin by picking cotton and hoeing corn and studying correspondence books at night for twenty years?

The man's dead words fell like bricks around the auditorium and too many settled in my belly. Constrained by hard-learned manners I couldn't look behind me, but to my left and right the proud graduating class of 1940 had dropped their heads. Every girl in my row had found something new to do with her handkerchief. Some folded the tiny squares into love knots, some into triangles, but most were wadding them, then pressing them flat on their yellow laps.

On the dais, the ancient tragedy was being replayed. Professor Parsons sat, a sculptor's reject, rigid. His large, heavy body seemed devoid of will or willingness, and his eyes said he was no longer with us. The other teachers examined the flag (which was draped stage right) or their notes, or the windows which opened on our now-famous playing diamond.

Graduation, the hush-hush magic time of frills and gifts and congratulations and diplomas, was finished for me before my name was called. The accomplishment was nothing. The meticulous maps, drawn in three colors of ink, learning and spelling decasyllabic words, memorizing the whole of *The Rape of Lucrece*—it was for nothing. Donleavy had exposed us.

45   We were maids and farmers, handymen and washerwomen, and anything higher that we aspired to was farcical and presumptuous.

Then I wished that Gabriel Prosser and Nat Turner had killed all whitefolks in their beds and that Abraham Lincoln had been assassinated before the signing of the Emancipation Proclamation, and that Harriet Tubman had been killed by that blow on her head and Christopher Columbus had drowned in the *Santa Maria*.

It was awful to be a Negro and have no control over my life. It was brutal to be young and already trained to sit quietly and listen to charges brought against my color with no chance of defense. We should all be dead. I thought I should like to see us all dead, one on top of the other. A pyramid of flesh with the whitefolks on the bottom, as the broad base, then the Indians with their silly tomahawks and teepees and wigwams and treaties, the Negroes with their mops and recipes and cotton sacks and spirituals sticking out of their mouths. The Dutch children should all stumble in their wooden shoes and break their necks. The French should choke to death on the Louisiana Purchase (1803) while silkworms ate all the Chinese with their stupid pigtails. As a species, we were an abomination. All of us.

Donleavy was running for election, and assured our parents that if he won we could count on having the only colored paved playing field in that part of Arkansas. Also—he never looked up to acknowledge the grunts of acceptance—also, we were bound to get some new equipment for the home economics building and the workshop.

He finished, and since there was no need to give any more than the most perfunctory thank-you's, he nodded to the men on the stage, and the tall white man who was never introduced joined him at the door. They left with the attitude that now they were off to something really important. (The graduation ceremonies at Lafayette County Training School had been a mere preliminary.)

The ugliness they left was palpable. An uninvited guest who wouldn't leave. The choir was summoned and sang a modern arrangement of "Onward, Christian Soldiers," with new words pertaining to graduates seeking their place in the world. But it didn't work. Elouise, the daughter of the Baptist minister, recited "Invictus," and I could have cried at the impertinence of "I am the master of my fate, I am the captain of my soul." 50

My name had lost its ring of familiarity and I had to be nudged to go and receive my diploma. All my preparations had fled. I neither marched up to the stage like a conquering Amazon, nor did I look in the audience for Bailey's nod of approval. Marguerite Johnson, I heard the name again, my honors were read, there were noises in the audience of appreciation, and I took my place on the stage as rehearsed.

I thought about colors I hated: ecru, puce, lavender, beige and black.

There was shuffling and rustling around me, then Henry Reed was giving his valedictory address, "To Be or Not to Be." Hadn't he heard the whitefolks? We couldn't *be,* so the question was a waste of time. Henry's voice came out clear and strong. I feared to look at him. Hadn't he got the message? There was no "nobler in the mind" for Negroes because the world didn't think we had minds, and they let us know it. "Outrageous fortune"? Now, that was a joke. When the ceremony was over I had to tell Henry Reed some things. That is, if I still cared. Not "rub," Henry, "erase." "Ah, there's the erase." Us.

Henry had been a good student in elocution. His voice rose on tides of promise and fell on waves of warnings. The English teacher had helped him to create a sermon winging through Hamlet's soliloquy. To be a man, a doer, a builder, a leader, or to be a tool, an unfunny joke, a crusher of funky toadstools. I marveled that Henry could go through with the speech as if we had a choice.

I had been listening and silently rebutting each sentence with my eyes closed; then there was a hush, which in an audience warns that something unplanned is happening. I looked up and saw Henry Reed, the conservative, the proper, the A student, turn his back to the audience and turn to us (the proud graduating class of 1940) and sing, nearly speaking, 55

"Lift ev'ry voice and sing
Till earth and heaven ring
Ring with the harmonies of Liberty . . ."

It was the poem written by James Weldon Johnson. It was the music composed by J. Rosamond Johnson. It was the Negro national anthem. Out of habit we were singing it.

Our mothers and fathers stood in the dark hall and joined the hymn of encouragement. A kindergarten teacher led the small children onto the stage and the buttercups and daisies and bunny rabbits marked time and tried to follow:

"Stony the road we trod
Bitter the chastening rod
Felt in the days when hope, unborn, had died.
Yet with a steady beat
Have not our weary feet
Come to the place for which our fathers sighed?"

Each child I knew had learned that song with his ABC's and along with "Jesus Loves Me This I Know." But I personally had never heard it before. Never heard the words, despite the thousands of times I had sung them. Never thought they had anything to do with me.

On the other hand, the words of Patrick Henry had made such an impression on me that I had been able to stretch myself tall and trembling and say, "I know not what course others may take, but as for me, give me liberty or give me death."

And now I heard, really for the first time:

"We have come over a way that with tears
has been watered,
We have come, treading our path through
the blood of the slaughtered."

While echoes of the song shivered in the air, Henry Reed bowed his head, said "Thank you," and returned to his place in the line. The tears that slipped down many faces were not wiped away in shame.

We were on top again. As always, again. We survived. The depths had been icy and dark, but now a bright sun spoke to our souls. I was no longer simply a member of the proud graduating class of 1940; I was a proud member of the wonderful, beautiful Negro race.

Oh, Black known and unknown poets, how often have your auctioned pains sustained us? Who will compute the lonely nights made less lonely by your songs, or the empty pots made less tragic by your tales?

If we were a people much given to revealing secrets, we might raise monuments and sacrifice to the memories of our poets, but slavery cured us of that weakness. It may be enough, however, to have it said that we survive in exact relationship to the dedication of our poets (include preachers, musicians and blues singers).

CONVERSATIONS: SONGS, POETRY, AND HOPE

In paragraph 55 and the following paragraphs, Angelou describes a stirring scene in which her classmate began singing a song that Angelou refers to as "the Negro national anthem." She includes excerpts from the song itself, which was based on a poem by James Weldon Johnson. It is common for speakers at graduations to quote from well-known songs or poems. In that sense, Angelou describes a rather typical graduation scene. But this particular song adds a twist to that typical scene because of the song's association with the Black struggle for equal rights. Thus, Henry's singing the song is part of the American ritual of graduation at the same time that it challenges that ritual. Consider how different that song would sound to a Black person compared to a White person, especially in Arkansas in the 1930s or 1940s. How does it sound today? Consider, too, how Angelou's description of that compelling moment at her graduation seems both timeless and specific.

UNDERSTANDING THE TEXT

1. Why, specifically, was Angelou so excited about her upcoming graduation from eighth grade? In what way is this excitement central to the story that Angelou tells?

2. Why does Angelou state that graduation "was finished for me before my name was called. The accomplishment was nothing"? What led her to that conclusion?

3. Why is the Negro National Anthem important to this story? What do you think is the significance of Henry's decision to begin singing the song at that point in the ceremony? How does the song influence the way you read the final paragraphs of Angelou's story?

EXPLORING THE ISSUES

1. Angelou devotes the first half of this essay to a description of the events leading up to the graduation ceremony. How effective do you think this description is? What role does it play in the narrative of the graduation itself? What expectations does it set up for the rest of the essay?

2. In paragraphs 44–47, Angelou refers to several famous literary works, important historical figures, and events. Why does she do so?

What effect do these specific references have? What do you think Angelou meant them to convey? How might they relate to her overall theme in this essay?

3. In some ways, this essay is about the beliefs that Americans have about schooling. What are those beliefs? In what ways do you think Angelou shares those beliefs? In what ways do you think she challenges them?

ENTERING THE CONVERSATIONS

1. Write an essay for an audience of your classmates in which you tell the story of your high school graduation (or your graduation from another school or program). Try to tell the story in a way that develops or emphasizes important ideas that you want to convey about the experience to your readers.

2. Imagine that you have been invited to give the address at the graduation ceremony at your old high school. Write that address.

3. In a group of classmates, compare your addresses written for Question 2. What similarities or differences can you identify in these graduation speeches? What do the speeches convey about education? Consider differences in the learning

situations that each classmate came from—an urban or rural school, a school with a very diverse student population, a wealthy suburban school, and so on. Now, based on your discussion, write a brief analysis of graduation speeches in which you discuss the main features of that very specialized genre and discuss the purposes that these speeches serve in American culture.

4. Consider the below images and how they depict education. The photograph on the left shows Black students being prevented by National Guard troops from entering high school in Little Rock, Arkansas, a famous standoff that led to a nationwide controversy about segregation in American schools. The other two images are from the Web site of Arkansas State University, available on the Internet in 2004. What values do the images communicate regarding schooling? Find images online or in print media that you think reflect the state of education in the U.S. today when it comes to race. Write an essay discussing the messages those images communicate and draw your own conclusions about the current state of education in the U.S., discussing what you believe are the basic values regarding education in the U.S.

Will Counts: A White Student Passes Through an Arkansas National Guard Line as Elizabeth Eckford is Turned Away, 1957. From *The Arkansas Democrat*.

Unless you're an educator (and even if you *are an educator*), *you may never have heard of Paulo Freire (1921–1997). Yet he is one of the most influential education theorists of the twentieth century. In professional discussions about formal education, Freire's has been as important a voice as anyone's. At the center of his theories of education is the notion that schooling should be about becoming "fully human," which means understanding that reality is not fixed but is a*

THE *Banking* Concept OF Education

process in which individual human beings participate. In other words, we don't simply live in the world as it is; we create it. Being fully human is knowing that we have the capacity to change the world through our active participation. But conventional schooling, according to Freire, teaches students to be passive components of the status quo and in doing so it "dehumanizes" them. This conventional approach to schooling, which Freire calls the "banking concept of education," thus helps maintain the status quo, with all its inequalities and injustices.

Now, if this seems abstract to you, consider that Freire was jailed in his native Brazil in the 1960s for the "subversive" act of developing literacy programs for rural peasants. He was subsequently exiled by the military dictatorship that ruled Brazil at the time, but his ideas about "liberatory" education began to influence other educators. The publication of his now-famous book Pedagogy of the Oppressed, *which appeared in English in 1970 and in which the following essay first appeared, brought his ideas to a worldwide audience. By the time he returned to Brazil in the 1980s as an internationally prominent voice for education reform, Brazil was once again under civilian rule, and he became* (continued)

PAULO FREIRE

A careful analysis of the teacher-student relationship at any level, inside or outside the school, reveals its fundamentally *narrative* character. This relationship involves a narrating Subject (the teacher) and patient, listening objects (the students). The contents, whether values or empirical dimensions of reality, tend in the process of being narrated to become lifeless and petrified. Education is suffering from narration sickness.

The teacher talks about reality as if it were motionless, static, compartmentalized, and predictable. Or else he expounds on a topic completely alien to the existential experience of the students. His task is to "fill" the students with the contents of his narration—contents which are detached from reality, disconnected from the totality that engendered them and could give them significance. Words are emptied of their concreteness and become a hollow, alienated, and alienating verbosity.

The outstanding characteristic of this narrative education, then, is the sonority of words, not their transforming power. "Four times four is sixteen; the capital of Pará is Belém." The student records, memo-

(continued) *minister of education for the city of São Paulo. He remained in Brazil and continued to push for education reform until his death.*

The first time I read the following essay, I was a recent college graduate. I was excited by Freire's critique of conventional education, but I don't think I fully understood his complicated ideas. Maybe that's because Freire's essay is less about schooling and more fundamentally about how we understand ourselves as beings in the world. In that sense, it is really a philosophical text that addresses age-old questions: Who are we? How do we know the world? What is our relationship to the world? What is reality? Don't be put off by some of the difficulties of Freire's essay. His ideas are sometimes hard to understand, and his writing can be challenging as well. So you may need to work through his essay carefully. But I think you'll find that it's worth the effort. As you read, ask yourself whether Freire's ideas, which grew out of his experiences in South America, are valid for American schools. That's a question that many educators— those who agree with Freire and those who don't—have asked. In trying to answer it, you will be joining one of the most vigorous conversations about education that continues today, so many years after Freire first presented his ideas in this essay. ▼

rizes, and repeats these phrases without perceiving what four times four really means, or realizing the true significance of "capital" in the affirmation "the capital of Pará is Belém," that is, what Belém means for Pará and what Pará means for Brazil.

Narration (with the teacher as narrator) leads the students to memorize mechanically the narrated content. Worse yet, it turns them into "containers," into "receptacles" to be "filled" by the teacher. The more completely she fills the receptacles, the better a teacher she is. The more meekly the receptacles permit themselves to be filled, the better students they are.

Education thus becomes an act of depositing, in which the students are the depositories and the teacher is the depositor. Instead of communicating, the teacher issues communiqués and makes deposits which the students patiently receive, memorize, and repeat. This is the "banking" concept of education, in which the scope of action allowed to the students extends only as far as receiving, filing, and storing the deposits. They do, it is true, have the opportunity to become collectors or cataloguers of the things they store. But in the last analysis, it is the people themselves who are filed away through the lack of creativity, transformation, and knowledge in this (at best) misguided system. For apart from inquiry, apart from the praxis, individuals cannot be truly human. Knowledge emerges only through invention and re-invention, through the restless, impatient, continuing, hopeful inquiry human beings pursue in the world, with the world, and with each other.

In the banking concept of education, knowledge is a gift bestowed by those who consider themselves knowledgeable upon those whom they consider to know nothing. Projecting an absolute ignorance onto others, a characteristic of the ideology of oppression, negates education and knowledge as processes of inquiry. The teacher presents himself to his students as their necessary opposite; by considering their ignorance absolute, he justifies his own existence. The students, alienated like the slave in the Hegelian dialectic, accept their ignorance as justifying the teacher's existence—but, unlike the slave, they never discover that they educate the teacher.

The *raison d'être* of libertarian education, on the other hand, lies in its drive towards reconciliation. Education must begin with the solution of the teacher-student contradiction, by reconciling the poles of the contradiction so that both are simultaneously teachers *and* students.

This solution is not (nor can it be) found in the banking concept. On the contrary, banking education maintains and even stimulates the contradiction through the following attitudes and practices, which mirror oppressive society as a whole:

a. the teacher teaches and the students are taught;

   b. the teacher knows everything and the students know nothing;

   c. the teacher thinks and the students are thought about;

   d. the teacher talks and the students listen—meekly;

   e. the teacher disciplines and the students are disciplined;

   f. the teacher chooses and enforces his choice, and the students comply;

   g. the teacher acts and the students have the illusion of acting through the action of the teacher;

   h. the teacher chooses the program content, and the students (who were not consulted) adapt to it;

   i. the teacher confuses the authority of knowledge with his or her own professional authority, which she and he sets in opposition to the freedom of the students;

   j. the teacher is the Subject of the learning process, while the pupils are mere objects.

It is not surprising that the banking concept of education regards men as adaptable, manageable beings. The more students work at storing the deposits entrusted to them, the less they develop the critical consciousness which would result from their intervention in the world as transformers of that world. The more completely they accept the passive role imposed on them, the more they tend simply to adapt to the world as it is and to the fragmented view of reality deposited in them.

CONVERSATIONS: THE PROBLEMS WITH SCHOOLS
Freire's list of "the attitudes and practices" of conventional education might serve as a list of the top ten things wrong with schools. In a sense, this is a summary of Freire's basic criticisms of formal schooling. His criticisms have influenced many well-known educational theorists, including Henri Giroux, Peter McLaren, and bell hooks. (Essays by bell hooks appear on page 244 and page 480 in this book.) If those names don't ring any bells for you, it's probably because you haven't read the kind of educational theory that they write. Their articles and books—and the articles and books of their critics—amount to a lively but specialized conversation about education among academics and theorists. It's worth asking whether that conversation is different from the larger public conversations about education reform that are always occurring in the popular media and in political campaigns. We always seem to be hearing about crises in our schools and about various government programs to improve education. For example, in 2001, President George W. Bush signed into law a sweeping education reform bill that has come to be known as No Child Left Behind. But what supporters of that law say is wrong with schools seems very different from Freire's list. Why? If Freire is such an internationally known and influential education theorist and reformer, why do his ideas seem to have been left out of the public discussions about education reform efforts such as No Child Left Behind? What might that tell us about how different ideas reach different audiences at different times?

The capability of banking education to minimize or annul the students' creative power and to stimulate their credulity serves the interests of the oppressors, who care neither to have the world revealed nor to see it transformed. The oppressors use their "humanitarianism" to preserve a profitable situation. Thus they react almost instinctively against any experiment in education which stimulates the critical faculties and is not content with a partial view of reality but always seeks out the ties which link one point to another and one problem to another.

Indeed, the interests of the oppressors lie in "changing the consciousness of the oppressed, not the situation which oppresses them";[1] for the more the oppressed can be led to adapt to that situation, the more easily they can be dominated. To achieve this end, the oppressors use the banking concept of education in conjunction with a paternalistic social action apparatus, within which the oppressed receive the euphemistic title of "welfare recipients." They are treated as individual cases, as marginal persons who deviate from the general configuration of a "good, organized, and just" society. The oppressed are regarded as the pathology of the healthy society, which must therefore adjust these "incompetent and lazy" folk to its own patterns by changing their mentality. These marginals need to be "integrated," "incorporated" into the healthy society that they have "forsaken."

The truth is, however, that the oppressed are not "marginals," are not people living "outside" society. They have always been "inside"—inside the structure which made them "beings for others." The solution is not to "integrate" them into the structure of oppression, but to transform that structure so that they can become "beings for themselves." Such transformation, of course, would undermine the oppressors' purposes; hence their utilization of the banking concept of education to avoid the threat of student *conscientização*.°

The banking approach to adult education, for example, will never propose to students that they critically consider reality. It will deal instead with such vital questions as whether Roger gave green grass to the goat, and insist upon the importance of learning that, on the contrary, *Roger gave green grass to the rabbit*. The "humanism" of the banking approach masks the effort to turn women and men into automatons—the very negation of their ontological vocation to be more fully human.

Those who use the banking approach, knowingly or unknowingly (for there are innumerable well-intentioned bank-clerk teachers who do not realize that they are serving only to dehumanize), fail to perceive that the deposits themselves contain contradictions about reality. But, sooner or later, these contradictions may lead formerly passive students to turn against their

This photograph depicts a typical college classroom. Consider how this scene might help illustrate some of Freire's criticisms of what he calls the "banking concept of education." What does it reveal about schooling?

Cartoons are often used to critique public education. Consider whether the criticism of schooling made by Mike Keefe's cartoon coincides with Freire's critique of formal schooling. Consider, too, whether the medium of a cartoon can convey such criticisms as effectively as a conventional academic essay.

°**conscientização** According to Freire's translator, "The term *conscientização* refers to learning to perceive social, political, and economic contradictions, and to take action against the oppressive elements of reality."

domestication and the attempt to domesticate reality. They may discover through existential experience that their present way of life is irreconcilable with their vocation to become fully human. They may perceive through their relations with reality that reality is really a *process,* undergoing constant transformation. If men and women are searchers and their ontological vocation is humanization, sooner or later they may perceive the contradiction in which banking education seeks to maintain them, and then engage themselves in the struggle for their liberation.

15   But the humanist, revolutionary educator cannot wait for this possibility to materialize. From the outset, her efforts must coincide with those of the students to engage in critical thinking and the quest for mutual humanization. His efforts must be imbued with a profound trust in people and their creative power. To achieve this, they must be partners of the students in their relations with them.

The banking concept does not admit to such partnership—and necessarily so. To resolve the teacher-student contradiction, to exchange the role of depositor, prescriber, domesticator, for the role of student among students would be to undermine the power of oppression and serve the cause of liberation.

Implicit in the banking concept is the assumption of a **dichotomy between human beings and the world:** a person is merely *in* the world, not *with* the world or with others; the individual is spectator, not re-creator. In this view, the person is not a conscious being (*corpo consciente);* he or she is rather the possessor of *a* consciousness: an empty "mind" passively open to the reception of deposits of reality from the world outside. For example, my desk, my books, my coffee cup, all the objects before me—as bits of the world which surrounds me—would be "inside" me, exactly as I am inside my study right now. This view makes no distinction between being accessible to consciousness and entering consciousness. The distinction, however, is essential: the objects which surround me are simply accessible to my consciousness, not located within it. I am aware of them, but they are not inside me.

It follows logically from the banking notion of consciousness that the educator's role is to regulate the way the world "enters into" the students. The teacher's task is to organize a process which already occurs spontaneously, to "fill" the students by making deposits of information which he or she considers to constitute true knowledge.[2] And since people "receive" the world as passive entities, education should make them more passive still, and adapt them to the world. The educated individual is the adapted person, because she or he is better "fit" for the world. Translated into practice, this concept is well suited to the purposes of the oppressors, whose tranquility rests on how well people fit the world the oppressors have created, and how little they question it.

The more completely the majority adapt to the purposes which the dominant minority prescribe for them (thereby depriving them of the right to their own purposes), the more easily the minority can continue to prescribe. The theory and practice of banking education serve this end quite efficiently. Verbalistic lessons, reading

---

CONVERSATIONS: THE NATURE OF REALITY
In paragraph 17, when Freire refers to a "dichotomy between man and the world," he is participating in an age-old philosophical conversation about the nature of reality and how (or if) we can come to know that reality. This conversation has been occurring at least since the time of the ancient Greek philosophers and has preoccupied some of the world's greatest philosophical minds ever since. To anyone who has studied philosophy, Freire's discussion of "consciousness" may sound familiar. If his discussion seems abstract to you, it may help to keep in mind that what Freire calls the "banking concept of education" is based on the assumption that knowledge exists separately from the knower. In other words, reality is "out there," separate from us, and we can know it only through careful observation—for example, through science. We can only describe what is real; we can't create or change it. Although this may sound abstract, it's actually the idea on which modern science—and modern education—is based. And part of what Freire is trying to do in this essay is to challenge this way of thinking about knowledge. For Freire, believing that reality is "objective," as modern science asks us to do, makes it possible for all kinds of injustices to seem "natural" or "inevitable." But understanding reality as something we can change means that we can eliminate those injustices. You might think about it in this way: This is where philosophy meets real life.

requirements,[3] the methods for evaluating "knowledge," the distance between the teacher and the taught, the criteria for promotion: everything in this ready-to-wear approach serves to obviate thinking.

The bank-clerk educator does not realize that there is no true security in his hy-   20 pertrophied role, that one must seek to live *with* others in solidarity. One cannot impose oneself, nor even merely co-exist with one's students. Solidarity requires true communication, and the concept by which such an educator is guided fears and proscribes communication.

Yet only through communication can human life hold meaning. The teacher's thinking is authenticated only by the authenticity of the students' thinking. The teacher cannot think for her students, nor can she impose her thought on them. Authentic thinking, thinking that is concerned about *reality,* does not take place in ivory tower isolation, but only in communication. If it is true that thought has meaning only when generated by action upon the world, the subordination of students to teachers becomes impossible.

Because banking education begins with a false understanding of men and women as objects, it cannot promote the development of what Fromm calls "biophily," but instead produces its opposite: "necrophily."

> While life is characterized by growth in a structured, functional manner, the necrophilous person loves all that does not grow, all that is mechanical. The necrophilous person is driven by the desire to transform the organic into the inorganic, to approach life mechanically, as if all living persons were things. . . . Memory, rather than experience; having, rather than being, is what counts. The necrophilous person can relate to an object—a flower or a person—only if he possesses it; hence a threat to his possession is a threat to himself; if he loses possession he loses contact with the world. . . . He loves control, and in the act of controlling he kills life.[4]

Oppression—overwhelming control—is necrophilic; it is nourished by love of death, not life. The banking concept of education, which serves the interests of oppression, is also necrophilic. Based on a mechanistic, static, naturalistic, spatialized view of consciousness, it transforms students into receiving objects. It attempts to control thinking and action, leads women and men to adjust to the world, and inhibits their creative power.

When their efforts to act responsibly are frustrated, when they find themselves unable to use their faculties, people suffer. "This suffering due to impotence is rooted in the very fact that the human equilibrium has been disturbed."[5] But the inability to act which causes people's anguish also causes them to reject their impotence, by attempting

> . . . to restore [their] capacity to act. But can [they], and how? One way is to submit to and identify with a person or group having power. By this symbolic participation in another person's life, [men have] the illusion of acting, when in reality [they] only submit to and become part of those who act.[6]

Populist manifestations perhaps best exemplify this type of behavior by the op-   25 pressed, who, by identifying with charismatic leaders, come to feel that they themselves are active and effective. The rebellion they express as they emerge in the historical process is motivated by that desire to act effectively. The dominant elites

Standardized testing

consider the remedy to be more domination and repression, carried out in the name of freedom, order, and social peace (that is, the peace of the elites). Thus they can condemn—logically, from their point of view—"the violence of a strike by workers and [can] call upon the state in the same breath to use violence in putting down the strike."[7]

Education as the exercise of domination stimulates the credulity of students, with the ideological intent (often not perceived by educators) of indoctrinating them to adapt to the world of oppression. This accusation is not made in the naïve hope that the dominant elites will thereby simply abandon the practice. Its objective is to call the attention of true humanists to the fact that they cannot use banking educational methods in the pursuit of liberation, for they would only negate that very pursuit. Nor may a revolutionary society inherit these methods from an oppressor society. The revolutionary society which practices banking education is either misguided or mistrusting of people. In either event, it is threatened by the specter of reaction.

Unfortunately, those who espouse the cause of liberation are themselves surrounded and influenced by the climate which generates the banking concept, and often do not perceive its true significance or its dehumanizing power. Paradoxically, then, they utilize this same instrument of alienation in what they consider an effort to liberate. Indeed, some "revolutionaries" brand as "innocents," "dreamers," or even "reactionaries" those who would challenge this educational practice. But one does not liberate people by alienating them. Authentic liberation—the process of humanization—is not another deposit to be made in men. Liberation is a praxis: the action and reflection of men and women upon their world in order to transform it. Those truly committed to the cause of liberation can accept neither the mechanistic concept of consciousness as an empty vessel to be filled, nor the use of banking methods of domination (propaganda, slogans—deposits) in the name of liberation.

Those truly committed to liberation must reject the banking concept in its entirety, adopting instead a concept of women and men as conscious beings, and consciousness as consciousness intent upon the world. They must abandon the educational goal of deposit-making and replace it with the posing of the problems of human beings in their relations with the world. "Problem-posing" education, responding to the essence of consciousness—*intentionality*—rejects communiqués and embodies communications. It epitomizes the special characteristic of consciousness: being *conscious of*, not only as intent on objects but as turned in upon itself in a Jasperian "split"—consciousness as consciousness *of* consciousness.

Liberating education consists in acts of cognition, not transferrals of information. It is a learning situation in which the cognizable object (far from being the end of the cognitive act) intermediates the cognitive actors—teacher on the one hand and students on the other. Accordingly, the practice of problem-posing education entails at the outset that the teacher-student contradiction be resolved. Dialogical relations—indispensable to the capacity of cognitive actors to cooperate in perceiving the same cognizable object—are otherwise impossible.

Indeed, problem-posing education, which breaks with the vertical patterns characteristic of banking education, can fulfill its function as the practice of freedom only if it can overcome the above contradiction. Through dialogue, the teacher-of-the-students and the students-of-the-teacher cease to exist and a new term emerges:

teacher-student with students-teachers. The teacher is no longer merely the-one-who-teaches, but one who is himself taught in dialogue with the students, who in turn while being taught also teach. They become jointly responsible for a process in which all grow. In this process, arguments based on "authority" are no longer valid; in order to function, authority must be *on the side of* freedom, not *against* it. Here, no one teaches another, nor is anyone self-taught. People teach each other, mediated by the world, by the cognizable objects which in banking education are "owned" by the teacher.

The banking concept (with its tendency to dichotomize everything) distinguishes two stages in the action of the educator. During the first, he cognizes a cognizable object while he prepares his lessons in his study or his laboratory; during the second, he expounds to his students about that object. The students are not called upon to know, but to memorize the contents narrated by the teacher. Nor do the students practice any act of cognition, since the object towards which that act should be directed is the property of the teacher rather than a medium evoking the critical reflection of both teacher and students. Hence in the name of the "preservation of culture and knowledge" we have a system which achieves neither true knowledge nor true culture.

The problem-posing method does not dichotomize the activity of the teacher-student: she is not "cognitive" at one point and "narrative" at another. She is always "cognitive," whether preparing a project or engaging in dialogue with the students. He does not regard cognizable objects as his private property, but as the object of reflection by himself and the students. In this way, the problem-posing educator constantly re-forms his reflections in the reflection of the students. The students—no longer docile listeners—are now critical co-investigators in dialogue with the teacher. The teacher presents the material to the students for their consideration, and reconsiders her earlier considerations as the students express their own. The role of the problem-posing educator is to create, together with the students, the conditions under which knowledge at the level of the *doxa* is superseded by true knowledge, at the level of the *logos*.

Whereas banking education anesthetizes and inhibits creative power, problem-posing education involves a constant unveiling of reality. The former attempts to maintain the *submersion* of consciousness; the latter strives for the *emergence* of consciousness and *critical intervention* in reality.

Students, as they are increasingly posed with problems relating to themselves in the world and with the world, will feel increasingly challenged and obliged to respond to that challenge. Because they apprehend the challenge as interrelated to other problems within a total context, not as a theoretical question, the resulting comprehension tends to be increasingly critical and thus constantly less alienated. Their response to the challenge evokes new challenges, followed by new understandings; and gradually the students come to regard themselves as committed.

Education as the practice of freedom—as opposed to education as the practice of domination—denies that man is abstract, isolated, independent, and unattached to the world; it also denies that the world exists as a reality apart from people. Authentic reflection considers neither abstract man nor the world without people, but people in their relations with the world. In these relations consciousness and world are simultaneous: consciousness neither precedes the world nor follows it.

35

CONTEXT: CHILE IN THE 1960
In paragraph 36, Freire refers to his literacy work with peasants in Chile in the 1960s. At the time, Chile was experiencing political tensions, which worsened after socialist leader Salvadore Allende was elected president in 1970. In 1973, Allende was killed in a coup led by Chile's military. Subsequently, the military leader who took control of the nation, Augusto Pinochet, declared martial law. Many people believed that Allende's overthrow was orchestrated in a plot that involved the U.S. CIA. In the years that followed, many Allende supporters and others who criticized or opposed the government were persecuted; thousands disappeared or were executed in what the Chilean government claimed was an effort to protect the nation from communist subversion. How might this context have shaped Freire's ideas about education and freedom? And how might this context lead some of Freire's critics to complain that his education theories are too political?

La conscience et le monde sont dormés d'un même coup: extérieur par essence à la conscience, le monde est, par essence relatif à elle.[8]

In one of our culture circles in Chile, the group was discussing (based on a codification) the anthropological concept of culture. In the midst of the discussion, a peasant who by banking standards was completely ignorant said: "Now I see that without man there is no world." When the educator responded: "Let's say, for the sake of argument, that all the men on earth were to die, but that the earth itself remained, together with trees, birds, animals, rivers, seas, the stars . . . wouldn't all this be a world?" "Oh no," the peasant replied emphatically. "There would be no one to say: 'This is a world.'"

The peasant wished to express the idea that there would be lacking the consciousness of the world which necessarily implies the world of consciousness. *I* cannot exist without a *non-I*. In turn, the *not-I* depends on that existence. The world which brings consciousness into existence becomes the world *of* that consciousness. Hence, the previously cited affirmation of Sartre: "*La conscience et le monde sont dormés d'un même coup.*"

As women and men, simultaneously reflecting on themselves and on the world, increase the scope of their perception, they begin to direct their observations towards previously inconspicuous phenomena:

In perception properly so-called, as an explicit awareness [*Gewahren*], I am turned towards the object, to the paper, for instance. I apprehend it as being this here and now. The apprehension is a singling out, every object having a background in experience. Around and about the paper lie books, pencils, ink-well, and so forth, and these in a certain sense are also "perceived," perceptually there, in the "field of intuition"; but whilst I was turned towards the paper there was no turning in their direction, nor any apprehending of them, not even in a secondary sense. They appeared and yet were not singled out, were not posited on their own account. Every perception of a thing has such a zone of background intuitions or background awareness, if "intuiting" already includes the state of being turned towards, and this also is a "conscious experience," or more briefly a "consciousness of" all indeed that in point of fact lies in the co-perceived objective background.[9]

STRATEGIES: TALKING PHILOSOPHY
In paragraph 37, Freire includes a long quotation from well-known twentieth century German philosopher Edmund Husserl. Elsewhere, Freire includes quotations from other famous philosophers, including Jean-Paul Sartre, Reinhold Niebuhr, and Erich Fromm. What does Freire accomplish with these quotations and references? What do these quotations suggest about Freire's sense of his audience? Who might be familiar with such philosophers? What do these references reveal about Freire's sense of his purpose in writing this essay?

That which had existed objectively but had not been perceived in its deeper implications (if indeed it was perceived at all) begins to "stand out," assuming the character of a problem and therefore of challenge. Thus, men and women begin to single out elements from their "background awarenesses" and to reflect upon them. These elements are now objects of their consideration, and, as such, objects of their action and cognition.

In problem-posing education, people develop their power to perceive critically *the way they exist* in the world *with which* and *in which* they find themselves; they come to see the world not as a static reality, but as a reality in process, in transformation. Although the dialectical relations of women and men with the world exist independently of how these relations are perceived (or whether or not they are perceived at all), it is also true that the form of action they adopt is to a large extent a function of how they perceive themselves in the world. Hence, the teacher-student and the students-teachers reflect simultaneously on themselves and the world without dichotomizing this reflection from action, and thus establish an authentic form of thought and action.

Once again, the two educational concepts and practices under analysis come into conflict. Banking education (for obvious reasons) attempts, by mythicizing reality, to conceal certain facts which explain the way human beings exist in the world; problem-posing education sets itself the task of demythologizing. Banking education resists dialogue; problem-posing education regards dialogue as indispensable to the act of cognition which unveils reality. Banking education treats students as objects of assistance; problem-posing education makes them critical thinkers. Banking education inhibits creativity and domesticates (although it cannot completely destroy) the *intentionality* of consciousness by isolating consciousness from the world, thereby denying people their ontological and historical vocation of becoming more fully human. Problem-posing education bases itself on creativity and stimulates true reflection and action upon reality; thereby responding to the vocation of persons as beings who are authentic only when engaged in inquiry and creative transformation. In sum: banking theory and practice, as immobilizing and fixating forces, fail to acknowledge men and women as historical beings; problem-posing theory and practice take the people's historicity as their starting point.

Problem-posing education affirms men and women as beings in the process of *becoming*—as unfinished, uncompleted beings in and with a likewise unfinished reality. Indeed, in contrast to other animals who are unfinished, but not historical, people know themselves to be unfinished; they are aware of their incompletion. In this incompletion and this awareness lie the very roots of education as an exclusively human manifestation. The unfinished character of human beings and the transformational character of reality necessitate that education be an ongoing activity.

Education is thus constantly remade in the praxis. In order to *be*, it must *become*. Its "duration" (in the Bergsonian meaning of the word) is found in the interplay of the opposites *permanence* and *change*. The banking method emphasizes permanence and becomes reactionary; problem-posing education—which accepts neither a "well-behaved" present nor a predetermined future—roots itself in the dynamic present and becomes revolutionary.

Problem-posing education is revolutionary futurity. Hence, it is prophetic (and, as such, hopeful). Hence, it corresponds to the historical nature of humankind. Hence, it affirms women and men as beings who transcend themselves, who move forward and look ahead, for whom immobility represents a fatal threat, for whom looking at the past must only be a means of understanding more clearly what and who they are so that they can more wisely build the future. Hence, it identifies with the movement which engages people as beings aware of their incompletion—an historical movement which has its point of departure, its Subjects and its objective.

The point of departure of the movement lies in the people themselves. But since people do not exist apart from the world, apart from reality, the movement must begin with the human-world relationship. Accordingly, the point of departure must always be with men and women in the "here and now," which constitutes the situation within which they are submerged, from which they emerge, and in which they intervene. Only by starting from this situation—which determines their perception of it—can they begin to move. To do this authentically they must perceive their state not as fated and unalterable, but merely as limiting—and therefore challenging.

45   Whereas the banking method directly or indirectly reinforces men's fatalistic perception of their situation, the problem-posing method presents this very situation to them as a problem. As the situation becomes the object of their cognition, the naïve or magical perception which produced their fatalism gives way to perception which is able to perceive itself even as it perceives reality, and can thus be critically objective about that reality.

A deepened consciousness of their situation leads people to apprehend that situation as an historical reality susceptible of transformation. Resignation gives way to the drive for transformation and inquiry, over which men feel themselves to be in control. If people, as historical beings necessarily engaged with other people in a movement of inquiry, did not control that movement, it would be (and is) a violation of their humanity. Any situation in which some individuals prevent others from engaging in the process of inquiry is one of violence. The means used are not important; to alienate human beings from their own decision-making is to change them into objects.

This movement of inquiry must be directed towards humanization—the people's historical vocation. The pursuit of full humanity, however, cannot be carried out in isolation or individualism, but only in fellowship and solidarity; therefore it cannot unfold in the antagonistic relations between oppressors and oppressed. No one can be authentically human while he prevents others from being so. Attempting *to be more* human, individualistically, leads to *having more*, egotistically, a form of dehumanization. Not that it is not fundamental *to have* in order *to be* human. Precisely because it *is* necessary, some men's *having* must not be allowed to constitute an obstacle to others' *having*, must not consolidate the power of the former to crush the latter.

Problem-posing education, as a humanist and liberating praxis, posits as fundamental that the people subjected to domination must fight for their emancipation. To that end, it enables teachers and students to become Subjects of the educational process by overcoming authoritarianism and an alienating intellectualism; it also enables people to overcome their false perception of reality. The world—no longer something to be described with deceptive words—becomes the object of that transforming action by men and women which results in their humanization.

Problem-posing education does not and cannot serve the interests of the oppressor. No oppressive order could permit the oppressed to begin to question: Why? While only a revolutionary society can carry out this education in systematic terms, the revolutionary leaders need not take full power before they can employ the method. In the revolutionary process, the leaders cannot utilize the banking method as an interim measure, justified on grounds of expediency, with the intention of *later* behaving in a genuinely revolutionary fashion. They must be revolutionary—that is to say, dialogical—from the outset.

NOTES

[1]Simone de Beauvoir, *La pensée de droite, aujourd'hui* (Paris); ST, *El pensamiento politico de la derecha* (Buenos Aires, 1963), p. 34.

[2]This concept corresponds to what Sartre calls the "digestive" or "nutritive" concept of education, in which knowledge is "fed" by the teacher to the students to "fill them out." See Jean-Paul Sartre, "Une idée fundamentale de la phénomenologie de Husserl: L'intentionalité," *Situations* I (Paris, 1947).

[3]For example, some professors specify in their reading lists that a book should be read from pages 10 to 15—and do this to "help" their students!

[4]Eric Fromm, *The Heart of Man* (New York, 1966), p. 41.

[5]Ibid., p. 31.

[6]Ibid.

[7]Reinhold Niebuhr, *Moral Man and Immoral Society* (New York, 1960), p. 130.

[8]Sartre, op. cit., p. 32. [The passage is obscure but could be read as "Consciousness and the world are given at one and the same time: the exterior world as it enters consciousness is relative to our ways of seeing and understanding that world."—Editors' note]

[9]Edmund Husserl, *Ideas—General Introduction to Pure Phenomenology* (London, 1969), pp. 105–06.

UNDERSTANDING THE TEXT

1. Summarize the "banking concept of education," as Freire understands it. What are the main features of this kind of education?

2. What is the "teacher-student contradiction," according to Freire? Why is it important for his criticism of conventional schooling? Do you agree with him? Why or why not?

3. In what ways is education "the exercise of domination," as Freire sees it?

4. What is "liberating education," or "problem-posing education," according to Freire? How is this kind of education different from the banking concept of education that Freire criticizes? Do you think problem-posing education, as Freire describes it, would solve the problems he sees with conventional education? Explain.

5. What does Freire mean when he says that problem-posing education should foster a "critical intervention in reality"? In what sense can students "intervene" in reality, as Freire sees it? Why is this intervention so important to him?

6. Why does Freire's problem-posing approach to education describe people as "beings in the process of becoming"? What exactly does that mean? Why is that important in his approach to education?

EXPLORING THE ISSUES

1. What does Freire mean when he describes students as "oppressed" and teachers as "oppressors"? Using Freire's ideas, explain how you as a student might be described as oppressed within formal schooling. Cite specific passages from his essay to support your answer.

2. Review Freire's list of the ten "attitudes and practices" of conventional education listed in paragraph 8. Does this list sound at all familiar to you? Do you think it accurately describes schools you have attended? Explain.

3. In paragraph 41, Freire discusses *permanence* and *change*. He claims that conventional education, which he describes as the "banking model of education," emphasizes permanence, whereas his problem-posing approach to education is based on the possibility of change. Based on your own experiences as a student and your own knowledge of education, do you think Freire is right on this point? Why or why not? Refer to your own experiences as well as to specific passages from Freire's essay to support your answer.

4. What would Freire's problem-posing method of education mean for American schools? What exactly do you think it would look like if it were applied to American schools? What specific changes would it lead to? Do you think it would work? Why or why not?

5. Freire's educational theories and proposed reforms have been criticized as too political. Based on this essay, do you think those criticisms are justified? Explain.

6. Why do you think Freire's ideas about education have been so influential? What appeal do you see in his theories? What might the appeal of his ideas in Western nations like the United States suggest to you about the problems facing the educational systems in those nations?

ENTERING THE CONVERSATIONS

1. Write a conventional essay in which you explain Freire's ideas about education. In your essay, summarize his criticisms of what he calls the "banking concept of education" and describe his "problem-posing" method. Explain his basic ideas regarding knowledge and reality and how those ideas figure into his criticisms of conventional education. Draw your own conclusions about the effectiveness of his proposed method of education.

2. Rewrite the essay you wrote for Question 1 for a general audience, such as readers of a publication like *USA Today* or the readers of your local newspaper.

3. Using Freire's ideas about education, write an analysis of your own school (you can choose to analyze your high school or your college). In your essay, summarize what you believe are the most important of Freire's ideas. Then apply those ideas to your own experiences in your school. In what ways might Freire's ideas help explain your experiences? What do his ideas reveal about the school you attended? On the basis of your critique, draw conclusions about any changes that you believe should be made to your school.

4. In a group of classmates, compare the essays you wrote for Question 3. In what ways do your essays describe similar or different problems in the schools you attended? On the basis of your discussion, try to draw conclusions about the usefulness of Freire's ideas about education or about problems you see with his ideas.

INFOTRAC

5. Using InfoTrac College Edition, the Internet, your library, and any other relevant sources, try to determine whether Freire's ideas have been applied to schools in the United States or elsewhere. Examine how those schools have used Freire's ideas. Try to find reviews or criticisms of Freire's work that might help you gain a better understanding of some of the benefits or drawbacks of using his ideas about education in an American school setting. Then write a report for your classmates in which you describe these efforts and evaluate their effectiveness.

6. Using appropriate technology and working with several classmates, create a video or photo collage that illustrates Freire's criticisms of the banking concept of education. Alternatively, create a web site with the same purpose.

In the following essay, Richard Rodriguez (b. 1944) writes that "education requires radical self-reformation." In a sense, Hunger of Memory (1981), the autobiography in which this essay first appeared, is Rodriguez's explanation of that statement. And his explanation is a sobering one. He shares his experiences as the son of Mexican immigrants who becomes a successful student in American schools, pursuing his education all the way to doctoral studies in English literature. Such academic success is usually celebrated, but Rodriguez writes movingly of the profound personal costs of his success. In doing so, Rodriguez joins a longstanding and often intense set of conversations about schooling in America. Those conversations have in recent decades often focused on the rigid and even oppressive nature of formal education in the United States. Many scholars have argued that schools reflect a narrow set of values that exclude students like Rodriguez, who come from diverse backgrounds. But Rodriguez complicates the issue by describing how a "non-mainstream" student like himself could achieve success in schools.

When it was first published, Hunger of Memory received much attention—and criticism—and it eventually became an important part of national discussions about bilingual education in the United States. Since then, Rodriguez's voice has continued to be heard in discussions about education. He has worked for the Pacific News Service in San Francisco and has appeared as an essayist on PBS's The News Hour with Jim Lehrer. He has also written essays for newspapers and magazines and has authored several other books, including Days of Obligation: An Argument with My Mexican Father (1993), which was nominated for the Pulitzer Prize in nonfiction. ◪

THE Achievement OF Desire

RICHARD RODRIGUEZ

I stand in the ghetto classroom—"the guest speaker"—attempting to lecture on the mystery of the sounds of our words to rows of diffident students. "Don't you hear it? Listen! The music of our words. 'Sumer is icumen in. . . .' And songs on the car radio. We need Aretha Franklin's voice to fill plain words with music—her life." In the face of their empty stares, I try to create an enthusiasm. But the girls in the back row turn to watch some boy passing outside. There are flutters of smiles, waves. And someone's mouth elongates heavy, silent words through the barrier of glass. Silent words—the lips straining to shape each voiceless syllable: "Meet meee late errr." By the door, the instructor smiles at me, apparently hoping that I will be able to spark some enthusiasm in the class. But only one student seems to be listening. A girl, maybe fourteen. In this gray room her eyes shine with ambition. She keeps nodding and nodding at all that I say; she even takes notes. And each time I ask a question, she jerks up and down in her desk like a marionette, while her hand waves over the bowed heads of her classmates. It is myself (as a boy) I see as she faces me now (a man in my thirties).

The boy who first entered a classroom barely able to speak English, twenty years later concluded his studies in the stately quiet of the reading room in the British Museum. Thus with one sentence I can summarize my academic career. It will be harder to summarize what sort of life connects the boy to the man.

With every award, each graduation from one level of education to the next, people I'd meet would congratulate me. Their refrain always the same: "Your parents must be very proud." Sometimes then they'd ask me how I managed it—my "success." (How?) After a while, I had several quick answers to give in reply. I'd admit, for one thing, that I went to an excellent grammar school. (My earliest teachers, the nuns, made my success their ambition.) And my brother and both my sisters were very good students. (They often brought home the shiny school trophies I came to want.) And my mother and father always encouraged me. (At every graduation they were behind the stunning flash of the camera when I turned to look at the crowd.)

CONTEXT: BILINGUAL EDUCATION
Rodriguez's first language was Spanish, but he writes here that he was proud to be losing his Spanish accent. He tells us that he tried to emulate his teachers, who of course spoke English. The elementary school classrooms he attended were really "English-only" classrooms, in which Spanish-speaking students were required to do their work in English. In part because of the difficulties faced by such students, many schools throughout the country implemented bilingual education programs, in which students could be taught in both English and their first language. Proponents of these programs argued that students would learn the content of the curriculum better if they studied in their first language, and eventually, they would be able to learn in English, too. They also argued that bilingual approaches indicated that schools valued the students' home cultures. Critics of these programs argued that bilingual education placed students like Rodriguez at a disadvantage because it treated them differently from "mainstream" students and delayed their learning of English. After his book *Hunger of Memory* was published, Rodriguez became an outspoken opponent of bilingual education. Consider how his criticisms of bilingual education relate to his experiences as a student.

As important as these factors were, however, they account inadequately for my academic advance. Nor do they suggest what an odd success I managed. For although I was a very good student, I was also a very bad student. I was a "scholarship boy," a certain kind of scholarship boy. Always successful, I was always unconfident. Exhilarated by my progress. Sad. I became the prized student—anxious and eager to learn. Too eager, too anxious—an imitative and unoriginal pupil. My brother and two sisters enjoyed the advantages I did, and they grew to be as successful as I, but none of them ever seemed so anxious about their schooling. A second-grade student, I was the one who came home and corrected the "simple" grammatical mistakes of our parents. ("Two negatives make a positive.") Proudly I announced—to my family's startled silence—that a teacher had said I was losing all trace of a Spanish accent. I was oddly annoyed when I was unable to get parental help with a homework assignment. The night my father tried to help me with an arithmetic exercise, he kept reading the instructions, each time more deliberately, until I pried the textbook out of his hands, saying, "I'll try to figure it out some more by myself."

5   When I reached the third grade, I outgrew such behavior. I became more tactful, careful to keep separate the two very different worlds of my day. But then, with ever-increasing intensity, I devoted myself to my studies. I became bookish, puzzling to all my family. Ambition set me apart. When my brother saw me struggling home with stacks of library books, he would laugh, shouting: "Hey, Four Eyes!" My father opened a closet one day and was startled to find me inside, reading a novel. My mother would find me reading when I was supposed to be asleep or helping around the house or playing outside. In a voice angry or worried or just curious, she'd ask: "What do you see in your books?" It became the family's joke. When I was called and wouldn't reply, someone would say I must be hiding under my bed with a book.

(How did I manage my success?)

What I am about to say to you has taken me more than twenty years to admit: *A primary reason for my success in the classroom was that I couldn't forget that schooling was changing me and separating me from the life I enjoyed before becoming a student.* That simple realization! For years I never spoke to anyone about it. Never mentioned a thing to my family or my teachers or classmates. From a very early age, I understood enough, just enough about my classroom experiences to keep what I knew repressed, hidden beneath layers of embarrassment. Not until my last months as a graduate student, nearly thirty years old, was it possible for me to think much about the reasons for my academic success. Only then. At the end of my schooling, I needed to determine how far I had moved from my past. The adult finally confronted, and now must publicly say, what the child shuddered from knowing and could never admit to himself or to those many faces that smiled at his every success. ("Your parents must be very proud. . . .")

I

At the end, in the British Museum (too distracted to finish my dissertation) for weeks I read, speed-read, books by modern educational theorists, only to find infrequent and slight mention of students like me. (Much more is written about the more typical case, the lower-class student who barely is helped by his schooling.) Then one day, leafing through Richard Hoggart's *The Uses of Literacy,* I found, in his description of the scholarship boy, myself. For the first time I realized that there were other students like me, and so I was able to frame the meaning of my academic success, its consequent price—the loss.

Hoggart's description is distinguished, at least initially, by deep understanding. What he grasps very well is that the scholarship boy must move between environments, his home and the classroom, which are at cultural extremes, opposed. With his family, the boy has the intense pleasure of intimacy, the family's consolation in feeling public alienation. Lavish emotions texture home life. *Then,* at school, the instruction bids him to trust lonely reason primarily. Immediate needs set the pace of his parents' lives. From his mother and father the boy learns to trust spontaneity and nonrational ways of knowing. *Then,* at school, there is mental calm. Teachers emphasize the value of a reflectiveness that opens a space between thinking and immediate action.

Years of schooling must pass before the boy will be able to sketch the cultural differences in his day as abstractly as this. But he senses those differences early. Perhaps as early as the night he brings home an assignment from school and finds the house too noisy for study.

> He has to be more and more alone, if he is going to "get on." He will have, probably unconsciously, to oppose the ethos of the hearth, the intense gregariousness of the working-class family group. Since everything centers upon the living-room, there is unlikely to be a room of his own; the bedrooms are cold and inhospitable, and to warm them or the front room, if there is one, would not only be expensive, but would require an imaginative leap—out of the tradition—which most families are not capable

CONVERSATIONS: HOGGART'S SCHOLARSHIP BOY
Notice how Rodriguez uses Richard Hoggart's book *The Uses of Literacy* in this passage and elsewhere in this essay. In a way, Rodriguez is engaging in a conversation about literacy and education that Hoggart was also engaging in. Rodriguez relies heavily on Hoggart's ideas in his discussion of his own experiences as a "scholarship boy," a term he borrows from Hoggart. Consider how this use of Hoggart's ideas and even his phrases helps Rodriguez make his points.

10

STRATEGIES: SUMMARY
Rodriguez devotes much attention to summarizing and highlighting the ideas of Richard Hoggart, as expressed in Hoggart's book *The Uses of Literacy.* Examine Rodriguez's summaries of Hoggart's ideas and consider how the summaries help him make sense of his own experiences as a young student. This is a good example of how a writer can use a summary strategically to accomplish his or her purpose in an essay.

of making. There is a corner of the living-room table. On the other side Mother is ironing, the wireless is on, someone is singing a snatch of song or Father says intermittently whatever comes into his head. The boy has to cut himself off mentally, so as to do his homework, as well as he can.[1]

The next day, the lesson is as apparent at school. There are even rows of desks. Discussion is ordered. The boy must rehearse his thoughts and raise his hand before speaking out in a loud voice to an audience of classmates. And there is time enough, and silence, to think about ideas (big ideas) never considered at home by his parents.

Not for the working-class child alone is adjustment to the classroom difficult. Good schooling requires that any student alter early childhood habits. But the working-class child is usually least prepared for the change. And, unlike many middle-class children, he goes home and sees in his parents a way of life not only different but starkly opposed to that of the classroom. (He enters the house and hears his parents talking in ways his teachers discourage.)

Without extraordinary determination and the great assistance of others—at home and at school—there is little chance for success. Typically most working-class children are barely changed by the classroom. The exception succeeds. The relative few become scholarship students. Of these, Richard Hoggart estimates, most manage a fairly graceful transition. Somehow they learn to live in the two very different worlds of their day. There are some others, however, those Hoggart pejoratively terms "scholarship boys," for whom success comes with special anxiety. Scholarship boy: good student, troubled son. The child is "moderately endowed," intellectually mediocre, Hoggart supposes—though it may be more pertinent to note the special qualities of temperament in the child. High-strung child. Brooding. Sensitive. Haunted by the knowledge that one *chooses* to become a student. (Education is not an inevitable or natural step in growing up.) Here is a child who cannot forget that his academic success distances him from a life he loved, even from his own memory of himself.

GLOSS: FORMS
"Forms" is a British term that refers to school grades. "Upper forms" would be equivalent to American high school grades 9–12.

Initially, he wavers, balances allegiance. ("The boy is himself [until he reaches, say, the upper **forms**] very much of *both* the worlds of home and school. He is enormously obedient to the dictates of the world of school, but emotionally still strongly wants to continue as part of the family circle.") Gradually, necessarily, the balance is lost. The boy needs to spend more and more time studying, each night enclosing himself in the silence permitted and required by intense concentration. He takes his first step toward academic success, away from his family.

15   From the very first days, through the years following, it will be with his parents—the figures of lost authority, the persons toward whom he feels deepest love—that the change will be most powerfully measured. A separation will unravel between them. Advancing in his studies, the boy notices that his mother and father have not changed as much as he. Rather, when he sees them, they often remind him of the person he once was and the life he earlier shared with them. He realizes what some Romantics also know when they praise the working class for the capacity for human closeness, qualities of passion and spontaneity, that the rest of us experience in like measure only in the earliest part of our youth. For the Romantic, this doesn't make

working-class life childish. Working-class life challenges precisely because it is an *adult* way of life.

The scholarship boy reaches a different conclusion. He cannot afford to admire his parents. (How could he and still pursue such a contrary life?) He permits himself embarrassment at their lack of education. And to evade nostalgia for the life he has lost, he concentrates on the benefits education will bestow upon him. He becomes especially ambitious. Without the support of old certainties and consolations, almost mechanically, he assumes the procedures and doctrines of the classroom. The kind of allegiance the young student might have given his mother and father only days earlier, he transfers to the teacher, the new figure of authority. "[The scholarship boy] tends to make a father-figure of his form-master," Hoggart observes.

But Hoggart's calm prose only makes me recall the urgency with which I came to idolize my grammar school teachers. I began by imitating their accents, using their diction, trusting their every direction. The very first facts they dispensed, I grasped with awe. Any book they told me to read, I read—then waited for them to tell me which books I enjoyed. Their every casual opinion I came to adopt and to trumpet when I returned home. I stayed after school "to help"—to get my teacher's undivided attention. It was the nun's encouragement that mattered most to me. (She understood exactly what—my parents never seemed to appraise so well—all my achievements entailed.) Memory gently caressed each word of praise bestowed in the classroom so that compliments teachers paid me years ago come quickly to mind even today.

The enthusiasm I felt in second-grade classes I flaunted before both my parents. The docile, obedient student came home a shrill and precocious son who insisted on correcting and teaching his parents with the remark: "My teacher told us. . . ."

I intended to hurt my mother and father. I was still angry at them for having encouraged me toward classroom English. But gradually this anger was exhausted, replaced by guilt as school grew more and more attractive to me. I grew increasingly successful, a talkative student. My hand was raised in the classroom; I yearned to answer any question. At home, life was less noisy than it had been. (I spoke to classmates and teachers more often each day than to family members.) Quiet at home, I sat with my papers for hours each night. I never forgot that schooling had irretrievably changed my family's life. That knowledge, however, did not weaken ambition. Instead, it strengthened resolve. Those times I remembered the loss of my past with regret, I quickly reminded myself of all the things my teachers could give me. (They could make me an educated man.) I tightened my grip on pencil and books. I evaded nostalgia. Tried hard to forget. But one does not forget by trying to forget. One only remembers. I remembered too well that education had changed my family's life. I would not have become a scholarship boy had I not so often remembered.

Once she was sure that her children knew English, my mother would tell us, "You should keep up your Spanish." Voices playfully groaned in response. "*¡Pochos!*" my mother would tease. I listened silently.   20

After a while, I grew more calm at home. I developed tact. A fourth-grade student, I was no longer the show-off in front of my parents. I became a conventionally dutiful son, politely affectionate, cheerful enough, even—for reasons beyond choosing—my father's favorite. And much about my family life was easy then, comfortable, happy in the rhythm of our living together: hearing my father getting ready for work; eating the breakfast my mother had made me; looking up from a novel to hear my brother or one of my sisters playing with friends in the backyard; in winter, coming upon the house all lighted up after dark.

But withheld from my mother and father was any mention of what most mattered to me: the extraordinary experience of first-learning. Late afternoon: in the midst of preparing dinner, my mother would come up behind me while I was trying to read. Her head just over mine, her breath warmly scented with food. "What are you reading?" Or, "Tell me all about your new courses." I would barely respond, "Just the usual things, nothing special." (A half smile, then silence. Her head moving back in the silence. Silence! Instead of the flood of intimate sounds that had once flowed smoothly between us, there was this silence.) After dinner, I would rush to a bedroom with papers and books. As often as possible, I resisted parental pleas to "save lights" by coming to the kitchen to work. I kept so much, so often, to myself. Sad. Enthusiastic. Troubled by the excitement of coming upon new ideas. Eager. Fascinated by the promising texture of a brand-new book. I hoarded the pleasures of learning. Alone for hours. Enthralled. Nervous. I rarely looked away from my books—or back on my memories. Nights when relatives visited and the front rooms were warmed by Spanish sounds, I slipped quietly out of the house.

It mattered that education was changing me. It never ceased to matter. My brother and sisters would giggle at our mother's mispronounced words. They'd correct her gently. My mother laughed girlishly one night, trying not to pronounce *sheep* as *ship*. From a distance I listened sullenly. From that distance, pretending not to notice on another occasion, I saw my father looking at the title pages of my library books. That was the scene on my mind when I walked home with a fourth-grade companion and heard him say that his parents read to him every night. (A strange-sounding book— *Winnie the Pooh*.) Immediately, I wanted to know, "What is it like?" My companion, however, thought I wanted to know about the plot of the book. Another day, my mother surprised me by asking for a "nice" book to read. "Something not too hard you think I might like." Carefully I chose one, Willa Cather's *My Antonia*. But when, several weeks later, I happened to see it next to her bed unread except for the first few pages, I was furious and suddenly wanted to cry. I grabbed up the book and took it back to my room and placed it in its place, alphabetically on my shelf.

*　*　*

"Your parents must be very proud of you." People began to say that to me about the time I was in sixth grade. To answer affirmatively, I'd smile. Shyly I'd smile, never betraying my sense of the irony: I was not proud of my mother and father. I was embarrassed by their lack of education. It was not that I ever thought they were stupid, though stupidly I took for granted their enormous native intelligence. Simply, what mattered to me was that they were not like my teachers.

25　　But, "Why didn't you tell us about the award?" my mother demanded, her frown weakened by pride. At the grammar school ceremony several weeks after, her eyes were brighter than the trophy I'd won. Pushing back the hair from my forehead, she whispered that I had "shown" the *gringos*. A few minutes later, I heard my father speak to my teacher and felt ashamed of his labored, accented words. Then guilty for the shame. I felt such contrary feelings. (There is no simple road-map through the heart of the scholarship boy.) My teacher was so soft-spoken and her words were edged sharp and clean. I admired her until it seemed to me that she spoke too carefully. Sensing that she was condescending to them, I became nervous. Resentful. Protective. I tried to move my parents away. "You both must be very proud of Richard," the nun said. They responded quickly. (They were proud.) "We are proud of all our children." Then this afterthought: "They sure didn't get their brains from us." They all laughed. I smiled.

*   *   *

Tightening the irony into a knot was the knowledge that my parents were always behind me. They made success possible. They evened the path. They sent their children to parochial schools because the nuns "teach better." They paid a tuition they couldn't afford. They spoke English to us.

For their children my parents wanted chances they never had—an easier way. It saddened my mother to learn that some relatives forced their children to start working right after high school. To *her* children she would say, "Get all the education you can." In schooling she recognized the key to job advancement. And with the remark she remembered her past.

As a girl new to America my mother had been awarded a high school diploma by teachers too careless or busy to notice that she hardly spoke English. On her own, she determined to learn how to type. That skill got her jobs typing envelopes in letter shops, and it encouraged in her an optimism about the possibility of advancement. (Each morning when her sisters put on uniforms, she chose a bright-colored dress.) The years of young womanhood passed, and her typing speed increased. She also became an excellent speller of words she mispronounced. "And I've never been to college," she'd say, smiling, when her children asked her to spell words they were too lazy to look up in a dictionary.

Typing, however, was dead-end work. Finally frustrating. When her youngest child started high school, my mother got a full-time office job once again. (Her paycheck combined with my father's to make us—in fact—what we had already become in our imagination of ourselves—middle class.) She worked then for the (California) state government in numbered civil service positions secured by examinations. The old ambition of her youth was rekindled. During the lunch hour, she consulted bulletin boards for announcements of openings. One day she saw mention of something called an "anti-poverty agency." A typing job. A glamorous job, part of the governor's staff. "A knowledge of Spanish required." Without hesitation she applied and became nervous only when the job was suddenly hers.

"Everyone comes to work all dressed up," she reported at night. And didn't need   30
to say more than that her co-workers wouldn't let her answer the phones. She was only a typist, after all, albeit a very fast typist. And an excellent speller. One morning there was a letter to be sent to a Washington cabinet officer. On the dictating tape, a voice referred to urban guerrillas. My mother typed (the wrong word, correctly): "gorillas." The mistake horrified the anti-poverty bureaucrats who shortly after arranged

to have her returned to her previous position. She would go no further. So she willed her ambition to her children. "Get all the education you can; with an education you can do anything." (With a good education *she* could have done anything.)

When I was in high school, I admitted to my mother that I planned to become a teacher someday. That seemed to please her. But I never tried to explain that it was not the occupation of teaching I yearned for as much as it was something more elusive: I wanted to *be* like my teachers, to possess their knowledge, to assume their authority, their confidence, even to assume a teacher's persona.

In contrast to my mother, my father never verbally encouraged his children's academic success. Nor did he often praise us. My mother had to remind him to "say something" to one of his children who scored some academic success. But whereas my mother saw in education the opportunity for job advancement, my father recognized that education provided an even more startling possibility: it could enable a person to escape from a life of mere labor.

In Mexico, orphaned when he was eight, my father left school to work as an "apprentice" for an uncle. Twelve years later, he left Mexico in frustration and arrived in America. He had great expectations then of becoming an engineer. ("Work for my hands and my head.") He knew a Catholic priest who promised to get him money enough to study full time for a high school diploma. But the promises came to nothing. Instead there was a dark succession of warehouse, cannery, and factory jobs. After work he went to night school along with my mother. A year, two passed. Nothing much changed, except that fatigue worked its way into the bone; then everything changed. He didn't talk anymore of becoming an engineer. He stayed outside on the steps of the school while my mother went inside to learn typing and shorthand.

By the time I was born, my father worked at "clean" jobs. For a time he was a janitor at a fancy department store. ("Easy work; the machines do it all.") Later he became a dental technician. ("Simple.") But by then he was pessimistic about the ultimate meaning of work and the possibility of ever escaping its claims. In some of my earliest memories of him, my father already seems aged by fatigue. (He has never really grown old like my mother.) From boyhood to manhood, I have remembered him in a single image: seated, asleep on the sofa, his head thrown back in a hideous corpselike grin, the evening newspaper spread out before him. "But look at all you've accomplished," his best friend said to him once. My father said nothing. Only smiled.

35   It was my father who laughed when I claimed to be tired by reading and writing. It was he who teased me for having soft hands. (He seemed to sense that some great achievement of leisure was implied by my papers and books.) It was my father who became angry while watching on television some woman at the Miss America contest tell the announcer that she was going to college. ("Majoring in fine arts.") "College!" he snarled. He despised the trivialization of higher education, the inflated grades and cheapened diplomas, the half education that so often passed as mass education in my generation.

It was my father again who wondered why I didn't display my awards on the wall of my bedroom. He said he liked to go to doctors' offices and see their certificates and degrees on the wall. ("Nice.") My citations from school got left in closets at home. The gleaming figure astride one of my trophies was broken, wingless, after hitting the ground. My medals were placed in a jar of loose change. And when I lost my high school diploma, my father found it as it was about to be thrown out with the trash. Without telling me, he put it away with his own things for safekeeping.

*   *   *

These memories slammed together at the instant of hearing that refrain familiar to all scholarship students: "Your parents must be proud. . . ." Yes, my parents were proud. I knew it. But my parents regarded my progress with more than mere pride. They endured my early precocious behavior—but with what private anger and humiliation? As their children got older and would come home to challenge ideas both of them held, they argued before submitting to the force of logic or superior factual evidence with the disclaimer, "It's what we were taught in our time to believe." These discussions ended abruptly, though my mother remembered them on other occasions when she complained that our "big ideas" were going to our heads. More acute was her complaint that the family wasn't close anymore, like some others she knew. Why weren't we close, "more in the Mexican style"? Everyone is so private, she added. And she mimicked the yes and no answers she got in reply to her questions. Why didn't we talk more? (My father never asked.) I never said.

I was the first in my family who asked to leave home when it came time to go to college. I had been admitted to Stanford, one hundred miles away. My departure would only make physically apparent the separation that had occurred long before. But it was going too far. In the months preceding my leaving, I heard the question my mother never asked except indirectly. In the hot kitchen, tired at the end of her workday, she demanded to know, "Why aren't the colleges here in Sacramento good enough for you? They are for your brother and sister." In the middle of a car ride, not turning to face me, she wondered, "Why do you need to go so far away?" Late at night, ironing, she said with disgust, "Why do you have to put us through this big expense? You know your scholarship will never cover it all." But when September came there was a rush to get everything ready. In a bedroom that last night I packed the big brown valise, and my mother sat nearby sewing initials onto the clothes I would take. And she said no more about my leaving.

Months later, two weeks of Christmas vacation: the first hours home were the hardest. ("What's new?") My parents and I sat in the kitchen for a conversation. (But, lacking the same words to develop our sentences and to shape our interests, what was there to say? What could I tell them of the term paper I had just finished on the "universality of Shakespeare's appeal"?) I mentioned only small, obvious things: my dormitory life; weekend trips I had taken; random events. They responded with news of their own. (One was almost grateful for a family crisis about which there was much to discuss.) We tried to make our conversation seem like more than an interview.

II

From an early age I knew that my mother and father could read and write both   40
Spanish and English. I had observed my father making his way through what, I now suppose, must have been income tax forms. On other occasions I waited apprehensively while my mother read onion-paper letters airmailed from Mexico with news of

a relative's illness or death. For both my parents, however, reading was something done out of necessity and as quickly as possible. Never did I see either of them read an entire book. Nor did I see them read for pleasure. Their reading consisted of work manuals, prayer books, newspaper, recipes.

Richard Hoggart imagines how, at home,

> . . . [the scholarship boy] sees strewn around, and reads regularly himself, magazines which are never mentioned at school, which seem not to belong to the world to which the school introduces him; at school he hears about and reads books never mentioned at home. When he brings those books into the house they do not take their place with other books which the family are reading, for often there are none or almost none; his books look, rather, like strange tools.

In our house each school year would begin with my mother's careful instruction: "Don't write in your books so we can sell them at the end of the year." The remark was echoed in public by my teachers, but only in part: "Boys and girls, don't write in your books. You must learn to treat them with great care and respect."

OPEN THE DOORS OF YOUR MIND WITH BOOKS, read the red and white poster over the nun's desk in early September. It soon was apparent to me that reading was the classroom's central activity. Each course had its own book. And the information gathered from a book was unquestioned. READ TO LEARN, the sign on the wall advised in December. I privately wondered: What was the connection between reading and learning? Did one learn something only by reading it? Was an idea only an idea if it could be written down? In June, CONSIDER BOOKS YOUR BEST FRIENDS. Friends? Reading was, at best, only a chore. I needed to look up whole paragraphs of words in a dictionary: Lines of type were dizzying, the eye having to move slowly across the page, then down, and across. . . . The sentences of the first books I read were coolly impersonal. Toned hard. What most bothered me, however, was the isolation reading required. To console myself for the loneliness I'd feel when I read, I tried reading in a very soft voice. Until: "Who is doing all that talking to his neighbor?" Shortly after, remedial reading classes were arranged for me with a very old nun.

At the end of each school day, for nearly six months, I would meet with her in the tiny room that served as the school's library but was actually only a storeroom for used textbooks and a vast collection of *National Geographics*. Everything about our sessions pleased me: the smallness of the room; the noise of the janitor's broom hitting the edge of the long hallway outside the door; the green of the sun, lighting the wall; and the old woman's face blurred white with a beard. Most of the time we took turns. I began with my elementary text. Sentences of astonishing simplicity seemed to me lifeless and drab: "The boys ran from the rain . . . She wanted to sing . . . The kite rose in the blue." Then the old nun would read from her favorite books, usually biographies of early American presidents. Playfully she ran through complex sentences, calling the words alive with her voice, making it seem that the author somehow was speaking directly to me. I smiled just to listen to her. I sat there and sensed for the very first time some possibility of fellowship between a reader and a writer, a communication, never *intimate* like that I heard spoken words at home convey, but one nonetheless *personal*.

One day the nun concluded a session by asking me why I was so reluctant to read by myself. I tried to explain; said something about the way written words made me feel all alone—almost, I wanted to add but didn't, as when I spoke to myself in a room just emptied of furniture. She studied my face as I spoke; she seemed to be watching more than listening. In an uneventful voice she replied that I had nothing to fear. Didn't I realize that reading would open up whole new worlds? A book could open doors for me. It could introduce me to people and show me places I never imagined exited. She gestured toward the bookshelves. (Bare-breasted African women danced, and the shiny hubcaps of automobiles on the back covers of the *Geographic* gleamed in my mind.) I listened with respect. But her words were not very influential. I was thinking then of another consequence of literacy, one I was too shy to admit but nonetheless trusted. Books were going to make me "educated." *That* confidence enabled me, several months later, to overcome my fear of the silence.

In fourth grade I embarked upon a grandiose reading program. "Give me the names of important books," I would say to startled teachers. They soon found out that I had in mind "adult books." I ignored their suggestion of anything I suspected was written for children. (Not until I was in college, as a result, did I read *Huckleberry Finn* or *Alice's Adventures in Wonderland.*) Instead, I read *The Scarlet Letter* and Franklin's *Autobiography.* And whatever I read I read for extra credit. Each time I finished a book, I reported the achievement to a teacher and basked in the praise my effort earned. Despite my best efforts, however, there seemed to be more and more books I needed to read. At the library I would literally tremble as I came upon whole shelves of books I hadn't read. So I read and I read and I read: *Great Expectations;* all the short stories of Kipling; *The Babe Ruth Story;* the entire first volume of the *Encyclopedia Britannica* (A–ANSTEY); the *Iliad; Moby Dick; Gone with the Wind; The Good Earth; Ramona; Forever Amber; The Lives of the Saints; Crime and Punishment; The Pearl. . . .* Librarians who initially frowned when I checked out the maximum ten books at a time started saving books they thought I might like. Teachers would say to the rest of the class, "I only wish the rest of you took reading as seriously as Richard obviously does."

But at home I would hear my mother wondering, "What do you see in your books?" (Was reading a hobby like her knitting? Was so much reading even healthy for a boy? Was it the sign of "brains"? Or was it just a convenient excuse for not helping about the house on Saturday mornings?) Always, "What do you see . . . ?"

What *did* I see in my books? I had the idea that they were crucial for my academic success, though I couldn't have said exactly how or why. In the sixth grade I simply concluded that what gave a book its value was some major idea or theme it contained. If that core essence could be mined and memorized, I would become learned like my teachers. I decided to record in a notebook the themes of the books that I read. After reading *Robinson Crusoe,* I wrote that its theme was "the value of learning to live by oneself." When I completed *Wuthering Heights,* I noted the danger of "letting emotions get out of control." Rereading these brief moralistic appraisals usually left me disheartened. I couldn't believe that they were really the source of reading's value. But for many more years, they constituted the only means I had of describing to myself the educational value of books.

In spite of my earnestness, I found reading a pleasurable activity. I came to enjoy the lonely good company of books. Early on weekday mornings, I'd read in my bed. I'd feel a mysterious comfort then, reading in the dawn quiet—the blue-gray silence interrupted by the occasional churning of the refrigerator motor a few rooms away or the more distant sounds of a city bus beginning its run. On weekends I'd go to the public library to read, surrounded by old men and women. Or, if the weather was fine, I would take my books to the park and read in the shade of a tree. A warm summer evening was my favorite reading time. Neighbors would leave for vacation and I would water their lawns. I would sit through the twilight on the front porches or in backyards, reading to the cool, whirling sounds of the sprinklers.

I also had favorite writers. But often those writers I enjoyed most I was least able to value. When I read William Saroyan's *The Human Comedy,* I was immediately pleased by the narrator's warmth and the charm of his story. But as quickly I became suspicious. A book so enjoyable to read couldn't be very "important." Another summer I determined to read all the novels of Dickens. Reading his fat novels, I loved the feeling I got—after the first hundred pages—of being at home in a fictional world where I knew the names of the characters and cared about what was going to happen to them. And it bothered me that I was forced away at the conclusion, when the fiction closed tight, like a fortune-teller's fist—the futures of all the major characters neatly resolved. I never knew how to take such feelings seriously, however. Nor did I suspect that these experiences could be part of a novel's meaning. Still, there were pleasures to sustain me after I'd finish my books. Carrying a volume back to the library, I would be pleased by its weight. I'd run my fingers along the edge of the pages and marvel at the breadth of my achievement. Around my room, growing stacks of paperback books reenforced my assurance.

50   I entered high school having read hundreds of books. My habit of reading made me a confident speaker and writer of English. Reading also enabled me to sense something of the shape, the major concerns, of Western thought. (I was able to say something about Dante and Descartes and Engels and James Baldwin in my high school term papers.) In these various ways, books brought me academic success as I hoped that they would. But I was not a good reader. Merely bookish, I lacked a point of view when I read. Rather, I read in order to acquire a point of view. I vacuumed books for epigrams, scraps of information, ideas, themes—anything to fill the hollow within me and make me feel educated. When one of my teachers suggested to his drowsy tenth-grade English class that a person could not have a "complicated idea" until he had read at least two thousand books, I heard the remark without detecting either its irony or its very complicated truth. I merely determined to compile a list of all the books I had ever read. Harsh with myself, I included only once a title I might have read several times. (How, after all, could one read a book more than once?) And I included only those books over a hundred pages in length. (Could anything shorter be a book?)

There was yet another high school list I compiled. One day I came across a newspaper article about the retirement of an English professor at a nearby state college. The article was accompanied by a list of the "hundred most important books of Western Civilization." "More than anything else in my life," the professor told the reporter with finality, "these books have made me all that I am." That was the kind of remark I couldn't ignore. I clipped out the list and kept it for the several months it took me to read all of the titles. Most books, of course, I barely understood. While reading Plato's *Republic,* for instance, I needed to keep looking at the book jacket comments to remind myself what the text was about. Nevertheless, with the special patience and superstition of a scholarship boy, I looked at every word of the text. And by the time I reached the last word, relieved, I convinced myself that I had read *The Republic.* In a ceremony of great pride, I solemnly crossed Plato off my list.

III

The scholarship boy pleases most when he is young—the working-class child struggling for academic success. To his teachers, he offers great satisfaction; his success is their proudest achievement. Many other persons offer to help him. A businessman learns the boy's story and promises to underwrite part of the cost of his college education. A woman leaves him her entire library of several hundred books when she moves. His progress is featured in a newspaper article. Many people seem happy for him. They marvel. "How did you manage so fast?" From all sides, there is lavish praise and encouragement.

In his grammar school classroom, however, the boy already makes students around him uneasy. They scorn his desire to succeed. They scorn him for constantly wanting the teacher's attention and praise. "Kiss Ass," they call him when his hand swings up in response to every question he hears. Later, when he makes it to college, no one will mock him aloud. But he detects annoyance on the faces of some students and even some teachers who watch him. It puzzles him often. In college, then in graduate school, he behaves much as he always has. If anything is different about him it is that he dares to anticipate the successful conclusion of his studies. At last he feels that he belongs in the classroom, and this is exactly the source of the dissatisfaction he causes. To many persons around him, he appears too much the academic. There may be some things about him that recall his beginnings—his shabby clothes; his persistent poverty; or his dark skin (in those cases when it symbolizes his parents' disadvantaged condition)—but they only make clear how far he has moved from his past. He has used education to remake himself.

It bothers his fellow academics to face this. They will not say why exactly. (They sneer.) But their expectations become obvious when they are disappointed. They expect—they want—a student less changed by his schooling. If the scholarship boy, from a past so distant from the classroom, could remain in some basic way unchanged, he would be able to prove that it is possible for anyone to become educated without basically changing from the person one was.

Here is no fabulous hero, no idealized scholar-worker. The scholarship boy does not straddle, cannot reconcile, the two great opposing cultures of his life. His success is unromantic and plain. He sits in the classroom and offers those sitting beside him no calming reassurance about their own lives. He sits in the seminar room—a man with brown skin, the son of working-class Mexican immigrant parents. (Addressing the professor at the head of the table, his voice catches with nervousness.) There is no trace of his parents' in his speech. Instead he approximates the accents of teachers and classmates. Coming from *him* those sounds seem suddenly odd. Odd too is the effect produced when *he* uses academic jargon—bubbles at the tip of his tongue:

"*Topos* . . . negative capability . . . vegetation imagery in Shakespearean comedy." He lifts an opinion from Coleridge, takes something else from Frye or Empson or Leavis. He even repeats exactly his professor's earlier comment. All his ideas are clearly borrowed. He seems to have no thought of his own. He chatters while his listeners smile—their look one of disdain.

When he is older and thus when so little of the person he was survives, the scholarship boy makes only too apparent his profound lack of *self*-confidence. This is the conventional assessment that even Richard Hoggart repeats:

> [The scholarship boy] tends to over-stress the importance of examinations, of the piling-up of knowledge and of received opinions. He discovers a technique of apparent learning, of the acquiring of facts rather than of the handling and use of facts. He learns how to receive a purely literate education, one using only a small part of the personality and challenging only a limited area of his being. He begins to see life as a ladder, as permanent examination with some praise and some further exhortation at each stage. He becomes an expert imbiber and doler-out; his competence will vary, but will rarely be accompanied by genuine enthusiasms. He rarely feels the reality of knowledge, of other men's thoughts and imaginings, on his own pulses. . . . He has something of the blinkered pony about him.

But this is criticism more accurate than fair. The scholarship boy is a very bad student. He is the great mimic; a collector of thoughts, not a thinker; the very last person in class who ever feels obliged to have an opinion of his own. In large part, however, the reason he is such a bad student is because he realizes more often and more acutely than most other students—than Hoggart himself—that education requires radical self-reformation. As a very young boy, regarding his parents, as he struggles with an early homework assignment, he knows this too well. That is why he lacks self-assurance. He does not forget that the classroom is responsible for remaking him. He relies on his teacher, depends on all that he hears in the classroom and reads in his books. He becomes in every obvious way the worst student, a dummy mouthing the opinions of others. But he would not be so bad—nor would he become so successful, a *scholarship* boy—if he did not accurately perceive that the best synonym for primary "education" is "imitation."

Those who would take seriously the boy's success—and his failure—would be forced to realize how great is the change any academic undergoes, how far one must move from one's past. It is easiest to ignore such considerations. So little is said about the scholarship boy in pages and pages of educational literature. Nothing is said of the silence that comes to separate the boy from his parents. Instead, one hears proposals for increasing the self-esteem of students and encouraging early intellectual independence. Paragraphs glitter with a constellation of terms like *creativity* and *originality*. (Ignored altogether is the function of imitation in a student's life.) **Radical educationalists** meanwhile complain that ghetto schools

CONVERSATIONS: RADICAL EDUCATIONALISTS
In discussing the effects of his experiences in school, Rodriguez mentions "radical educationalists" who argue that "ghetto schools 'oppress' students by trying to mold them." Here, Rodriguez directly joins a lively debate about education reform that has been going on in the United States since public schooling came to be widespread during the nineteenth century. In particular, Rodriguez is referring to more recent discussions among scholars and theorists who believe that schooling in the United States reflects White middle-class values and compromises students, like Rodriguez, who come from different backgrounds. The writings of Paulo Freire, whose essay appears earlier in this cluster, have been influential in these professional discussions about education. Consider how Rodriguez's story carries certain kinds of meaning when it is read in the context of those discussions.

"oppress" students by trying to mold them, stifling native characteristics. The truer critique would be just the reverse: not that schools change ghetto students too much, but that while they might promote the occasional scholarship student, they change most students barely at all.

From the story of the scholarship boy there is no specific pedagogy to glean. There is, however, a much larger lesson. His story makes clear that education is a long, unglamorous, even demeaning process—*a nurturing never natural to the person one was before one entered a classroom.* At once different from most other students, the scholarship boy is also the archetypal "good student." He exaggerates the difficulty of being a student, but his exaggeration reveals a general predicament. Others are changed by their schooling as much as he. They too must re-form themselves. They must develop the skill of memory long before they become truly critical thinkers. And when they read Plato for the first several times, it will be with awe more than deep comprehension.

The impact of schooling on the scholarship boy is only more apparent to the boy himself and to others. Finally, although he may be laughable—a blinkered pony—the boy will not let his critics forget their own change. He ends up too much like them. When he speaks, they hear themselves echoed. In his pedantry, they trace their own. His ambitions are theirs. If his failure were singular, they might readily pity him. But he is more troubling than that. They would not scorn him if this were not so.

IV

Like me, Hoggart's imagined scholarship boy spends most of his years in the classroom afraid to long for his past. Only at the very end of his schooling does the boy-man become nostalgic. In this sudden change of heart, Richard Hoggart notes: 60

> He longs for the membership he lost, "he pines for some Nameless Eden where he never was." The nostalgia is the stronger and the more ambiguous because he is really "in quest of his own absconded self yet scared to find it." He both wants to go back and yet thinks he has gone beyond his class, feels himself weighted with knowledge of his own and their situation, which hereafter forbids him the simpler pleasures of his father and mother.

According to Hoggart, the scholarship boy grows nostalgic because he remains the uncertain scholar, bright enough to have moved from his past, yet unable to feel easy, a part of a community of academics.

This analysis, however, only partially suggests what happened to me in my last year as a graduate student. When I traveled to London to write a dissertation on English Renaissance literature, I was finally confident of membership in a "community of scholars." But the pleasure that confidence gave me faded rapidly. After only two or three months in the reading room of the British Museum, it became clear that I had joined a lonely community. Around me each day were dour faces eclipsed by large piles of books. There were the regulars, like the old couple who arrived every morning, each holding a loop of the shopping bag which contained all their notes. And there was the historian who chattered madly to herself. ("Oh dear! Oh! Now, what's this? What? Oh, my!") There were also the faces of young men and women worn by long study. And everywhere eyes turned away the moment our glance accidentally met. Some persons I sat beside day after day, yet we passed silently at the end of the day, strangers. Still, we were united by a common respect for the written word and for scholarship. We did form a union, though one in which we remained distant from one another.

More profound and unsettling was the bond I recognized with those writers whose books I consulted. Whenever I opened a text that hadn't been used for years, I realized that my special interests and skills united me to a mere handful of academics. We formed an exclusive—eccentric!—society, separated from others who would never care or be able to share our concerns. (The pages I turned were stiff like layers of dead skin.) I began to wonder: Who, beside my dissertation director and a few faculty members, would ever read what I wrote? And: Was my dissertation much more than an act of social withdrawal? These questions went unanswered in the silence of the Museum reading room. They remained to trouble me after I'd leave the library each afternoon and feel myself shy—unsteady, speaking simple sentences at the grocer's or the butcher's on my way back to my bed-sitter.

Meanwhile my file cards accumulated. A professional, I knew exactly how to search a book for pertinent information. I could quickly assess and summarize the usability of the many books I consulted. But whenever I started to write, I knew too much (and not enough) to be able to write anything but sentences that were overly cautious, timid, strained brittle under the heavy weight of footnotes and qualifications. I seemed unable to dare a passionate statement. I felt drawn by professionalism to the edge of sterility, capable of no more than pedantic, lifeless, unassailable prose.

Then nostalgia began.

65   After years spent unwilling to admit its attractions, I gestured nostalgically toward the past. I yearned for that time when I had not been so alone. I became impatient with books. I wanted experience more immediate. I feared the library's silence. I silently scorned the gray, timid faces around me. I grew to hate the growing pages of my dissertation on genre and Renaissance literature. (In my mind I heard relatives laughing as they tried to make sense of its title.) I wanted something—I couldn't say exactly what. I told myself that I wanted a more passionate life. And a life less thoughtful. And above all, I wanted to be less alone. One day I heard some Spanish academics whispering back and forth to each other, and their sounds seemed ghostly voices recalling my life. Yearning became preoccupation then. Boyhood memories beckoned, flooded my mind. (Laughing intimate voices. Bounding up the front steps of the porch. A sudden embrace inside the door.)

For weeks after, I turned to books by educational experts. I needed to learn how far I had moved from my past—to determine how fast I would be able to recover something of it once again. But I found little. Only a chapter in a book by Richard Hoggart. . . . I left the reading room and the circle of faces.

*   *   *

I came home. After the year in England, I spent three summer months living with my mother and father, relieved by how easy it was to be home. It no longer seemed very important to me that we had little to say. I felt easy sitting and eating and walking with them. I watched them, nevertheless, looking for evidence of those elastic, sturdy strands that bind generations in a web of inheritance. I thought as I watched my mother one night: Of course a friend had been right when she told me that I gestured and laughed just like my mother. Another time I saw for myself: my father's eyes were much like my own, constantly watchful.

But after the early relief, this return, came suspicion, nagging until I realized that I had not neatly sidestepped the impact of schooling. My desire to do so was precisely the measure of how much I remained an academic. *Negatively* (for that is how this idea first occurred to me): my need to think so much and so abstractly about my parents and our relationship was in itself an indication of my long education. My father and mother did not pass their thinking about the cultural meanings of their experience. It was I who described their daily lives with airy ideas. And yet, *positively:* the ability to consider experience so abstractly allowed me to shape into desire what would otherwise have remained indefinite, meaningless longing in the British Museum. If, because of my schooling, I had grown culturally separated from my parents, my education finally had given me ways of speaking and caring about that fact.

My best teachers in college and graduate school, years before, had tried to prepare me for this conclusion, I think, when they discussed texts of aristocratic pastoral literature. Faithfully, I wrote down all that they said. I memorized it: "The praise of the unlettered by the highly educated is one of the primary themes of 'elitist' literature." But, "the importance of the praise given the unsolitary, richly passionate and spontaneous life is that it simultaneously reflects the value of a reflective life." I heard it all. But there was no way for any of it to mean very much to me. I was a scholarship boy at the time, busily laddering my way up the rungs of education. To pass an examination, I copied down exactly what my teachers told me. It would require many more years of schooling (an inevitable miseducation) in which I came to trust the silence of reading and the habit of abstracting from immediate experience—moving away from a life of closeness and immediacy I remembered with my parents, growing older—before I turned unafraid to desire the past, and thereby achieved what had eluded me for so long—the end of education.

NOTES

[1]All quotations in this essay are from Richard Hoggart, *The Uses of Literacy* (London: Chatto and Windus, 1957), chapter 10. [Author's note]

UNDERSTANDING THE TEXT

1. Why does Rodriguez say that his family's support for him and the encouragement of his grammar school teachers do not adequately explain his academic success? How does he explain his success?

2. In paragraph 7, Rodriguez states that success in school separated him from his life at home. He offers several anecdotes that reveal how his relationship with his family changed as he became more successful in school. In what ways did that relationship change? Why did it change, in his view? How does he feel about these changes? Do you agree with him? Why or why not?

3. What is the primary effect of schooling on the student, especially the working-class student, according to Rodriguez? Do you think he is right? Explain.

4. Who is the "scholarship boy"? What distinguishes this kind of student? Why is this idea of the scholarship boy so important to Rodriguez?

5. What was the role of reading in Rodriguez's life as a young student? How is his reading different from his parents' reading? Why does he describe himself as "not a good reader" but "bookish"?

6. Why does Rodriguez eventually quit school before completing his doctoral program? What does this decision suggest about Rodriguez as a person? About his values?

EXPLORING THE ISSUES

1. In the opening two paragraphs of this essay, Rodriguez describes a scene in which he is speaking to a classroom full of teenage students, one of whom reminds him of himself twenty years earlier. He "summarizes" his academic career in a single sentence (par. 2) and then writes, "It will be harder to summarize what sort of life connects the boy to the man." Examine how these two paragraphs introduce this essay. What tone does Rodriguez set in his introduction? What expectations does he create for you as a reader? What does he reveal about himself as a person? How might the sense you get of him in these two paragraphs influence the way you read the rest of the essay?

2. Rodriguez describes his life at home and his life at school as two separate worlds. How does he characterize these separate worlds? What are the main features of each, in his view? Why does he believe that success and comfort in one requires losing the other? Do you agree with him? Why or why not? What do Rodriguez's experiences suggest about schooling?

3. Rodriguez devotes much attention to describing his parents and telling his readers about their experiences and lives. What do we learn about his mother and father? What details does Rodriguez provide about them? What do his descriptions of his parents contribute to this essay? How do they help Rodriguez make his main points?

4. In some ways, this essay is a conventional autobiography, in which Rodriguez tells the story of his experiences as a student more or less in chronological order. But he doesn't strictly follow a timeline of his life, and he often includes commentary about his experiences from his perspective many years after the events he is describing happened. Examine how Rodriguez tells his story and look in particular at how he organizes his essay. What does he emphasize? What do you think he leaves out? How effectively does he narrate his experiences to make his point?

ENTERING THE CONVERSATIONS

1. Write an essay in which you tell the story of your own experience as a student—your own educational autobiography. Try to tell your story in a way that emphasizes what you believe was most important about your experience, and use your experience to make a point—in the way Rodriguez uses his experiences to make a point about education.

2. In a group of classmates, share the essays you wrote for Question 1. What kinds of experiences in schools did you and your classmates focus on in your essays? What similarities and differences can you identify among these experiences? What conclusions can you draw about schooling from these experiences?

3. On the basis of your discussions in Question 2, write an essay for an audience of your classmates in which you offer your own view of schooling. In your essay, identify what you see as the problems and the benefits of schooling, as you experienced it, and propose changes in schools that you believe should be made. Draw on Rodriguez's essay, your classmates' essays, and any other relevant texts to help you make your points. Alternatively, write your essay as an editorial page essay for your local newspaper.

4. Interview a student whose first language is not English but who has attended American schools. (If you don't know someone like this, you might contact the office in your school that supports international students.) Try to get a sense of that person's experience as a student in English-speaking schools. Write an essay on the basis of your interview, presenting this person's experience and drawing your own conclusions on the basis of that experience. (If you are a student whose first language is not English, write your essay based on your own experience.)

5. Rodriguez writes in his essay that "education requires radical self-reformation." Explain what he means and respond to his statement.

A few years ago, I had the good fortune to be *at a writing awards dinner at which Adrienne Rich (b. 1929) was the keynote speaker. The event was a typical banquet in which student writers were celebrated for award-winning essays. Faculty members and parents were there, and the atmosphere was polite and celebratory. When Rich spoke, she also celebrated the winning writers, congratulating them on their accomplishments and encouraging them to*

Taking Women Students Seriously

continue writing. But she went on to say that writing wasn't about winning awards. It was about making change. "Write as if your life depended upon it," she told her audience, with great conviction in her voice.

Adrienne Rich has always written as if her life depends upon it. For Rich, writing is a way to fight for justice and to raise her voice in support of those she believes have been victimized. She is not only an internationally acclaimed poet, with sixteen books of poetry to her credit; she is also one of the most vocal and respected proponents of feminism in education and in society generally. The following essay, which was first delivered as a talk to a gathering of women academics in 1978, has become a well-known critique of the treatment of women in education. It reflects some of the power of Rich's voice that has made her the influential thinker and writer that she is. As you read, consider whether her arguments about gender in education have the same force today as they did in 1978.

In addition to poetry, for which she has won numerous awards, Adrienne Rich has written several books of essays, has won a MacArthur Foundation "genius" grant, and has taught writing at many colleges and universities, including Rutgers University and Stanford University. ▼

ADRIENNE RICH

I see my function here today as one of trying to create a context, delineate a background, against which we might talk about women as students and students as women. I would like to speak for a while about this background, and then I hope that we can have, not so much a question period, as a raising of concerns, a sharing of questions for which we as yet may have no answers, an opening of conversations which will go on and on.

When I went to teach at Douglass, a women's college, it was with a particular background which I would like briefly to describe to you. I had graduated from an all-girls' school in the 1940s, where the head and the majority of the faculty were independent, unmarried women. One or two held doctorates, but had been forced by the Depression (and by the fact that they were women) to take secondary school teaching jobs. These women cared a great deal about the life of the mind, and they gave a great deal of time and energy—beyond any limit of teaching hours—to those of us who showed special intellectual interest or ability. We were taken to libraries, art museums, lectures at neighboring colleges, set to work on extra research projects, given extra French or Latin reading. Although we sometimes felt "pushed" by them, we held those women in a kind of respect which even then we dimly perceived was not generally accorded to women in the world at large. They were vital individuals, defined not by their relationships but by their personalities; and although under the pressure of the culture we were all certain we wanted to get married, their lives did not appear empty or dreary to us. In a kind of cognitive dissonance, we knew they were "old maids" and therefore supposed to be bitter and lonely; yet we saw them vigorously involved with life. But despite their existence as alternate models of women, the *content* of the education they gave us in no way prepared us to survive as women in a world organized by and for men.

From that school, I went on to Radcliffe, congratulating myself that now I would have great men as my teachers. From 1947 to 1951, when I graduated, I never saw a single woman on a lecture platform, or in front of a class, except when a woman graduate student gave a paper on a special topic. The "great men" talked of other "great men," of the nature of Man, the history of Mankind, the future of Man; and never again was I to experience, from a teacher, the kind of prodding, the insistence that my best could be even better, that I had known in high school. Women students were simply not taken very seriously. Harvard's message to women was an elite mystification: we were, of course, part of Mankind; we were special, achieving women, or we would not have been there; but of course our real goal was to marry—if possible, a Harvard graduate.

CONTEXT: OPEN ADMISSIONS

Open admissions policies, which began at the City University of New York (CUNY) system in 1969, changed the criteria for students seeking admission to college, guaranteeing that students who graduated from accredited high schools would be admitted to CUNY. Many other colleges and universities followed CUNY's lead in implementing open admissions policies. These controversial policies enabled many students to attend college who previously would have been denied admission. Many educators believe that open admissions policies have made college more accessible to Americans; critics have argued that the policies have watered down the college curriculum and diminished the value of a college degree. In recent years, many colleges and universities, including CUNY, have eliminated open admissions policies. Consider what Rich's references to the SEEK program and to open admissions suggest about her own views about such programs and about higher education in general.

In the late sixties, I began teaching at the City College of New York—a crowded, public, urban, multiracial institution as far removed from Harvard as possible. I went there to teach writing in the SEEK Program,° which predated **Open Admissions** and which was then a kind of model for programs designed to open up higher education to poor, black, and Third World students. Although during the next few years we were to see the original concept of SEEK diluted, then violently attacked and betrayed, it was for a short time an extraordinary and intense teaching and learning environment. The characteristics of this environment were a deep commitment on the part of teachers to the minds of their students; a constant, active effort to create or discover the conditions for learning, and to educate ourselves to meet the needs of the new college population; a philosophical attitude based on open discussion of racism, oppression, and the politics of literature and language; and a belief that learning in the classroom could not be isolated from the student's experience as a member of an urban minority group in white America. Here are some of the kinds of questions we, as teachers of writing, found ourselves asking:

(1) What has been the student's experience of education in the inadequate, often abusively racist public school system, which rewards passivity and treats a ques-

---

°An acronym for "Search for Education, Elevation, and Knowledge."

tioning attitude or independent mind as a behavior problem? What has been her or his experience in a society that consistently undermines the selfhood of the poor and the nonwhite? How can such a student gain that sense of self which is necessary for active participation in education? What does all this mean for us as teachers?

(2) How do we go about teaching a canon of literature which has consistently excluded or depreciated nonwhite experience?

(3) How can we connect the process of learning to write well with the student's own reality, and not simply teach her/him how to write acceptable lies in standard English?

When I went to teach at Douglass College in 1976, and in teaching women's writing workshops elsewhere, I came to perceive stunning parallels to the questions I had first encountered in teaching the so-called disadvantaged students at City. But in this instance, and against the specific background of the women's movement, the questions framed themselves like this:

(1) What has been the student's experience of education in schools which reward female passivity, indoctrinate girls and boys in stereotypic sex roles, and do not take the female mind seriously? How does a woman gain a sense of her *self* in a system—in this case, patriarchal capitalism—which devalues work done by women, denies the importance and uniqueness of female experience, and is physically violent toward women? What does this mean for a woman teacher?

(2) How do we, as women, teach women students a canon of literature which has consistently excluded or depreciated female experience, and which often expresses hostility to women and validates violence against us?

(3) How can we teach women to move beyond the desire for male approval and getting "good grades" and seek and write their own truths that the culture has distorted or made taboo? (For women, of course, language itself is exclusive: I want to say more about this further on.)

In teaching women, we have two choices: to lend our weight to the forces that indoctrinate women to passivity, self-depreciation, and a sense of powerlessness, in which case the issue of "taking women students seriously" is a moot one; or to consider what we have to work against, as well as with, in ourselves, in our students, in the content of the curriculum, in the structure of the institution, in the society at large. And this means, first of all, taking ourselves seriously: Recognizing that central responsibility of a woman to herself, without which we remain always **the Other,** the defined, the object, the victim; believing that there is a unique quality of validation, affirmation, challenge, support, that one woman can offer another. Believing in the value and significance of women's experience, traditions, perceptions. Thinking of ourselves seriously, not as one of the boys, not as neuters, or androgynes, but as *women.*

CONVERSATIONS: THE OTHER
In this paragraph, Rich argues that women must be taken seriously or they risk remaining "always the Other, the defined, the object, the victim." This term, the Other, has become a common one in academic discussions of cultural diversity. It refers to the ways in which nonmainstream groups, as defined by race, ethnicity, class, or as in this case, gender, can be understood and treated as something other than normal. An entire body of academic research and cultural criticism has developed around this idea. To use the term "the Other" is to refer implicitly to that research and criticism. Adrienne Rich is one of the scholars who have helped make this term part of our ongoing discussions about diversity and difference. (To read more about this idea of "the Other," see the introduction to Cluster 2, Defining Each Other, of Chapter 5 on page 82.)

Suppose we were to ask ourselves, simply: What does a woman need to know? Does she not, as a self-conscious, self-defining human being, need a knowledge of her own history, her much-politicized biology, an awareness of the creative work of women of the past, the skills and crafts and techniques and powers exercised by women in different times and cultures, a knowledge of women's rebellions and organized movements against our oppression and how they have been routed or diminished? Without such knowledge women live and have lived without context, vulnerable to the projections of male fantasy, male prescriptions for us, estranged from our own experience because our education has not reflected or echoed it. I would suggest that not biology, but ignorance of our selves, has been the key to our powerlessness.

But the university curriculum, the high-school curriculum, do not provide this kind of knowledge for women, the knowledge of Womankind, whose experience has been so profoundly different from that of Mankind. Only in the precariously budgeted, much-condescended-to area of women's studies is such knowledge available to women students. Only there can they learn about the lives and work of women other than the few select women who are included in the "mainstream" texts, usually misrepresented even when they do appear. Some students, at some institutions, manage to take a majority of courses in women's studies, but the message from on high is that this is self-indulgence, soft-core education: the "real" learning is the study of Mankind.

CONVERSATIONS: SEXIST GRAMMAR
When Rich accuses journalists and academics of using sexist grammar, as she does in this paragraph, she is joining a debate about grammar rules and conventions that was raging among educators and activists in the 1970s and 1980s. The debate sometimes focused on the use of *he* as a generic pronoun to refer to "anyone" or "one." Here's an example: "Anyone can climb a mountain if he has the desire and the will." Traditionally, this use of *he* was considered proper. But activists like Rich protested such "correct" uses of pronouns, arguing that they reinforce the idea that women are less important than men and that "the male is the norm," as Rich writes. Today, it is often considered inappropriate to use the male pronoun *he* in this way. Instead, writers employ what is now called nonsexist language, as in this example: "Anyone can climb a mountain if he or she has the desire and the will." Often, writers will simply rewrite sentences to avoid the indefinite pronoun altogether: "Anyone with the desire and will can climb a mountain." This debate about the pronoun *he* is a good example of how language rules and conventions often reflect certain values that are controversial or problematic.

If there is any misleading concept, it is that of "coeducation": that because women and men are sitting in the same classrooms, hearing the same lectures, reading the same books, performing the same laboratory experiments, they are receiving an equal education. They are not, first because the content of education itself validates men even as it invalidates women. Its very message is that men have been the shapers and thinkers of the world, and that this is only natural. The bias of higher education, including the so-called sciences, is white and male, racist and sexist; and this bias is expressed in both subtle and blatant ways. I have mentioned already the exclusiveness of grammar itself: "The student should test himself on the above questions"; "The poet is representative. He stands among partial men for the complete man." Despite a few half-hearted departures from custom, what the linguist Wendy Martyna has named "He-Man" grammar prevails throughout the culture. The efforts of feminists to reveal the profound ontological implications of **sexist grammar** are routinely ridiculed by academicians and journalists, including the professedly liberal *Times* columnist, Tom Wicker, and the professed humanist, Jacques Barzun. Sexist grammar burns into the brains of little girls and young women a message that the male is the norm, the standard, the central figure beside which we are the deviants, the marginal, the dependent variables. It lays the foundation for androcentric thinking, and leaves men safe in their solipsistic tunnel-vision.

Women and men do not receive an equal education because outside the classroom [10] women are perceived not as sovereign beings but as prey. The growing incidence of rape on and off the campus may or may not be fed by the proliferations of pornographic magazines and X-rated films available to young males in fraternities and student unions; but it is certainly occurring in a context of wide-spread images of sexual violence against women, on billboards and in so-called high art. More subtle, more daily than rape is the verbal abuse experienced by the woman student on many campuses—Rutgers for example—where, traversing a street lined with fraternity houses, she must run a gauntlet of male commentary and verbal assault. The undermining of self, of a woman's sense of her right to occupy space and walk freely in the world, is deeply relevant to education. The capacity to think independently, to take intellectual risks, to assert ourselves mentally, is inseparable from our physical way of being in the world, our feelings of personal integrity. If it is dangerous for me to walk home late of an evening from the library, *because I am a woman and can be raped,* how self-possessed, how exuberant can I feel as I sit working in that library? How much of my working energy is drained by the subliminal knowledge that, as a woman, I test my physical right to exist each time I go out alone? Of this knowledge, Susan Griffin has written:

> . . . more than rape itself, the fear of rape permeates our lives. And what does one do from day to day, with *this* experience, which says, without words and directly to the heart, *your existence, your experience, may end at any moment.* Your experience may end, and the best defense against this is not to be, to deny being in the body, as a self, to . . . avert your gaze, make yourself, as a presence in the world, less felt.°

Finally, rape of the mind. Women students are more and more often now reporting sexual overtures by male professors—one part of our overall growing consciousness of sexual harassment in the workplace. At Yale a legal suit has been brought against the university by a group of women demanding an explicit policy against sexual advances toward female students by male professors. Most young women experience a profound mixture of humiliation and intellectual self-doubt over seductive gestures by men who have the power to award grades, open doors to grants and graduate school, or extend special knowledge and training. Even if turned aside, such gestures constitute mental rape, destructive to a woman's ego. They are acts of domination, as despicable as the molestation of the daughter by the father.

But long before entering college the woman student has experienced her alien identity in a world which misnames her, turns her to its own uses, denying her the resources she needs to become self-affirming, self-defined. The nuclear family teaches her that relationships are more important than selfhood or work; that "whether the phone rings for you, and how often," having the right clothes, doing the dishes, take precedence over study or solitude; that too much intelligence or intensity may make her unmarriageable; that marriage and children—service to others—are, finally, the points on which her life will be judged a success or a failure. In high school, the polarization between feminine attractiveness and independent intelligence comes to an absolute. Meanwhile, the culture resounds with messages. During Solar Energy Week

°From Griffin's *Rape: The Power of Consciousness* (New York, 1979).

in New York I saw young women wearing "ecology" T-shirts with the legend: CLEAN, CHEAP AND AVAILABLE; a reminder of the 1960s antiwar button which read: CHICKS SAY YES TO MEN WHO SAY NO. Department store windows feature female mannequins in chains, pinned to the wall with legs spread, smiling in positions of torture. Feminists are depicted in the media as "shrill," "strident," "puritanical," or "humorless," and the lesbian choice—the choice of the woman-identified woman—as pathological or sinister. The young woman sitting in the philosophy classroom, the political science lecture, is already gripped by tensions between her nascent sense of self-worth, and the battering force of messages like these.

Look at a classroom: look at the many kinds of women's faces, postures, expressions. Listen to the women's voices. Listen to the silences, the unasked questions, the blanks. Listen to the small, soft voices, often courageously trying to speak up, voices of women taught early that tones of confidence, challenge, anger, or assertiveness, are strident and unfeminine. Listen to the voices of the women and the voices of the men; observe the space men allow themselves, physically and verbally, the male assumption that people will listen, even when the majority of the group is female. Look at the faces of the silent, and of those who speak. Listen to a woman groping for language in which to express what is on her mind, sensing that the terms of academic discourse are not her language, trying to cut down her thought to the dimensions of a discourse not intended for her *(for it is not fitting that a woman speak in public)*; or reading her paper aloud at breakneck speed, throwing her words away, deprecating her own work by a reflex prejudgment: *I do not deserve to take up time and space.*

As women teachers, we can either deny the importance of this context in which women students think, write, read, study, project their own futures; or try to work with it. We can either teach passively, accepting these conditions, or actively, helping our students identify and resist them.

15   One important thing we can do is *discuss* the context. And this need not happen only in a women's studies course; it can happen anywhere. We can refuse to accept passive, obedient learning and insist upon critical thinking. We can become harder on our women students, giving them the kinds of "cultural prodding" that men receive, but on different terms and in a different style. Most young women need to have their intellectual lives, their work, legitimized against the claims of family, relationships, the old message that a woman is always available for service to others. We need to keep our standards very high, not to accept a woman's preconceived sense of her limitations; we need to be hard to please, while supportive of risk-taking, because self-respect often comes only when exacting standards have been met. At a time when adult literacy is generally low, we need to demand more, not less, of women, both for the sake of their futures as thinking beings, and because historically women have always had to be better than men to do half as well. A romantic sloppiness, an inspired lack of rigor, a self-indulgent incoherence, are symptoms of female self-depreciation. We should help our women students to look very critically at such symptoms, and to understand where they are rooted.

Nor does this mean we should be training women students to "think like men." Men in general think badly: in disjuncture from their personal lives, claiming objectivity where the most irrational passions seethe, losing, as Virginia Woolf observed, their senses in the pursuit of professionalism. It is not easy to think like a woman in a man's world, in the world of the professions; yet the capacity to do that is a strength which we can try to help our students develop. To think like a woman in a man's world means thinking critically, refusing to accept the givens, making connections between facts and ideas which men have left unconnected. It means remembering that every mind resides in a body; remaining accountable to the female bodies in which we live; constantly retesting given hypotheses against lived experience. It means a constant critique of language, for as Wittgenstein (no feminist) observed, "The limits of my language are the limits of my world." And it means that most difficult thing of all: listening and watching in art and literature, in the social sciences, in all the descriptions we are given of the world, for the silences, the

VISUAL CONNECTIONS: BREAKING SILENCES
These two images might be considered current examples of women breaking their silences, as Rich urges them to do in this paragraph. Consider how these images might convey Rich's message about women. Consider, too, that these images appeared in 2004, whereas Rich made her call for women to fight discrimination in 1978.

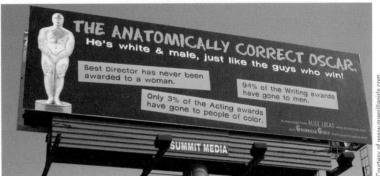

absences, the nameless, the unspoken, the encoded—for there we will find the true knowledge of women. And in breaking those silences, naming our selves, uncovering the hidden, making ourselves present, we begin to define a reality which resonates to *us,* which affirms *our* being, which allows the woman teacher and the woman student alike to take ourselves, and each other, seriously: meaning, to begin taking charge of our lives.

UNDERSTANDING THE TEXT

1. What kinds of experiences did Rich have in school, as both a student and a teacher? What did these experiences teach her about education?

2. What does Rich mean when she insists that women must think of themselves *as women*? Why is this important to her? What are the consequences of failing to do so, in her view?

3. What are Rich's main criticisms of education as it relates to women? Do you agree with her? Why or why not?

4. What connection does Rich see between the physical abuse of women and the way women are treated in classrooms? Do you think this connection is valid? Why or why not? Is Rich's criticism valid today? Explain.

5. What solutions does Rich offer to the problems she describes in this article? Do you think these solutions have been tried in the twenty-five years since Rich first wrote this essay? Can they achieve Rich's goals? Explain.

EXPLORING THE ISSUES

1. Rich devotes the first several paragraphs of her essay to an overview of her own education as a young woman. What purpose does this overview serve in this essay? How does it help set up Rich's main argument? How did it influence your sense of Rich as the writer of this essay? Does it give her greater (or less) credibility, in your view? Explain.

2. Examine the questions Rich lists in paragraphs 4–5, which she tells us were posed to students at City College of New York and later at Douglass College. What do these questions indicate about the purposes of education as Rich and her

colleagues understood them? Do you think these are appropriate questions to pose to students? Why or why not? What might your answer to that question suggest about your own views regarding schooling? In answering these questions, you might compare Rich's views to those of other writers in this book whose essays are about education in some way, including Paulo Freire (page 166) and Min Zhan Lu (page 343).

3. What kinds of evidence does Rich offer to support her claims about the treatment of women in education? Evaluate her evidence. How valid do you find it? How persuasively do you think she supports her positions?

4. This essay is adapted from a talk that Rich gave to women academics in 1978. Assess how Rich addresses this audience. What does she assume about her audience? In what ways does she define her audience as special or different? How effectively do you think she speaks to this audience in this essay? Do you think her essay would be as effective for a different audience? Explain, citing specific passages from the essay to support your answer.

ENTERING THE CONVERSATIONS

1. Write an essay in which you discuss your own experiences in schools in terms of gender. How has your gender affected your schooling, in your view? What kinds of opportunities, obstacles, or challenges have you had as a result of being a man or a woman in school? In your essay, try to draw conclusions about the role of gender in schooling. If appropriate, refer to Rich's essay or to any other relevant essay in this book.

2. In a group of classmates, share the essays you wrote for Question 1. What similarities and differences can you identify among the views of your classmates regarding gender in

education? What conclusions can be drawn from the experiences of your classmates about the role of gender in education?

3. Organize a classroom forum in which you debate the validity of Rich's argument about women in education. Agree to a format (for example, each participant can speak for three minutes followed by questions from other participants). Try to identify the main issues regarding gender in education that emerge from the forum. Alternatively, write an essay responding to Rich's viewpoint about women in education.

INFOTRAC

4. Using InfoTrac College Edition and any other appropriate resources, examine the role of gender in education today. Narrow the focus of your research to a specific issue involving gender, such as the experiences of women in certain academic fields (such as physics or philosophy), the position of women in school administration, or women's athletics. Explore that specific issue, trying to determine the current state of the issue regarding gender and identifying changes in the status of women in recent decades. Then write a report on the basis of your research.

5. Many popular films have depicted women in education—for example, *Mona Lisa Smile* (2003), *Legally Blonde* (2001), and *Educating Rita* (1983). Focusing on one or more such films, write an essay in which you discuss how women in education are portrayed in film (and other popular media). What attitudes regarding women in education are conveyed in these films? What conclusions can you draw about what these films might say about the status of women in American society?

KNOWING AND BELIEVING

I N 1999, WELL-KNOWN SCHOLARS GEORGE LAKOFF AND MARK JOHNSON PUBLISHED A BOOK CALLED *PHILOSOPHY IN THE FLESH*, IN WHICH THEY WROTE,

Living a human life is a philosophical endeavor. Every thought we have, every decision we make, and every act we perform is based upon philosophical assumptions so numerous we couldn't possibly list them all. We go around armed with a host of presuppositions about what is real, what counts as knowledge, how the mind works, who we are, and how we should act. Such questions, which arise out of our daily concerns, form the basic subject matter of philosophy.

That quotation is as good a definition of philosophy as I've ever encountered, and it conveys very well why philosophy has been an important area of human inquiry for thousands of years. What Lakoff and Johnson state so well in this passage is that we seem to have a basic need to understand who we are and what we do. And philosophy, that age-old subject that is so often poked fun at for being impractical, is the result of that need.

But a closer look at this passage reveals that it might also serve as a description of religion, which is also based on some of those same questions about what is real, who we are, and how we should act. So is science. Although we tend to think of philosophy, religion, and science as different kinds of endeavors, in a very basic way they are all based on fundamental *beliefs*. It is those beliefs that enable us to make sense of the world around us and our place in that world. And those beliefs help determine what we know about the world.

The essays in this cluster all examine this connection between knowing and believing. At least that's how I see them. When Thomas Moore, a former Catholic monk, writes about water as both a physical and spiritual thing, he is exploring the connection between what we know and what we believe. These essays reveal that knowing and believing are intimately related to each other.

This may all seem very abstract and, well, philosophical. But as these authors try to help us see, what we *think* we know and what we believe shape our day-to-day decisions about how we live. As Lakoff and Johnson suggest in the passage I quoted, we base everything we do on our assumptions about the world—that is, on what we believe to be true. And if these issues were not important, we wouldn't still be talking and writing and arguing and wondering about them after so many centuries of religious, philosophical, and scientific inquiry.

> You don't have to look far for evidence of the fact that what we believe and what we think we know are deadly serious matters.

As you read the essays in this cluster, you might keep in mind that they address issues that lead to some of the most intense and even deadly disagreements and conflicts among human beings. You don't have to look far for evidence of the fact that what we believe and what we think we know are deadly serious matters. As I am writing these words, the world is witnessing countless armed conflicts that have their origins in disagreements about basic beliefs—sometimes religious beliefs, sometimes cultural or political beliefs. I hope these essays can help you gain some insight into these hard questions. And I hope they help you think in useful ways about your own beliefs and how they shape your world.

Thomas Moore (b. 1940) has written widely *about deepening our spiritual life. The following brief and deceptively simple essay gives you a glimpse of how Moore thinks about spiritual life. In this essay, which was first published in 2003 in* Resurgence, *a British magazine devoted to issues of spirituality and community, Moore explores a seemingly straightforward topic: water. But as you quickly discover, from Moore's point of view, there is more to water than meets the*

Satisfying THE Thirst OF THE Soul AND THE Needs OF THE Body

THOMAS MOORE

eye. For him, water is both spiritual and physical. In exploring this dual nature of water, Moore is also exploring the connection between what we know through experience (the physical) and what we believe (the spiritual). His essay examines how knowing and believing are intimately related and perhaps not as distinct from each other as we usually think. His essay also brings together several different conversations: about spirituality, about the environment, about living with pain and joy, about family. As you read, pay attention to how he joins these various conversations using the topic of water.

A teacher, psychologist, and former Catholic monk, Thomas Moore is a popular speaker on matters of spirituality and the author of many books, including Care of the Soul *(1992) and* Original Self *(2003).* ▼

I grew up in the Great Lakes region of America, surrounded by lakes large and small, and by many rivers and ponds. My father taught plumbing all his life and was fascinated by every aspect of water. He loved to teach city children how water arrived in their homes in great quantities, fresh and clean. But I also had problems with water. When I was four years old, every Sunday my grandfather would take me in a boat, fishing. One day, for some reason he stood up in the boat and it capsized. I couldn't swim. He hauled me up onto the overturned bottom of the boat and saved my life. He drowned.

I love water, and fear it. It was years before I learned how to swim, and even now in water I am always close to panic. But I love to look at water. One of the most idyllic days of my life was spent at **Henley-**

THOMAS MOORE, "ETERNAL WATER: SATISFYING THE THIRST OF THE SOUL AND THE NEEDS OF THE BODY" FROM *RESURGENCE,* NO. 217 (MARCH/APRIL 2003) REPRINTED WITH PERMISSION FROM RESURGENCE MAGAZINE. WWW.RESURGENCE.ORG.

on-Thames. My wife was pregnant with our daughter, and we walked the riverbank watching passing punts and small boats. When I taught at the University of Windsor in Canada, I would spend many an afternoon sitting on the banks of the wide Detroit River, watching the lake freighters go by. I can meditate best alongside a body of water, and I can appreciate **Siddhartha,** in Herman Hesse's novel, finding himself, at the end of a long search, in a flowing river.

This is all to say that water has a central role in my emotional life. It's a spiritual thing primarily, and only secondarily physical. **Alchemists** made a distinction between material water and the water they named Aqua Permanens—Eternal Water. This is the fluidity of life and the stream of consciousness, flowing time and surging emotions. I learned from both James Hillman and Ivan Illich to distinguish between H_2O and the "waters of imagination." I learned from religion that a person can be fundamentally transformed by baptismal water.

I don't want to choose between the water I see in a river and the symbolic substance I find at church. They are distinct, and yet the same. We need the one in order to enjoy the other. We need fresh, beautiful, unobstructed rivers, lakes and oceans, and we need the imagination to perceive their beauty and their spiritual significance. We need to protect our waters for several reasons: to save species, to protect our health, to stay alive. But we also need water for our souls. Just as **Narcissus** came to life at a pond in the woods, we need to look at water and be restored by it. All water is baptismal water. Every time we look into its mysterious surfaces and depths, we become a new person. And any day that goes by when we are not renewed is not a good day.

Not becoming a dried-up husk of a person requires a fluid disposition—an ability to be a mermaid, a merman, a melusine. As Aldous Huxley used to say, "you need to be amphibious." Where does one find this transformation? Alongside a river, ocean-side, beneath a waterfall, in the rain. There is a mysterious linkage between physical water and the Piscean, moist, tidal soul. For those who have the eye to see, all water is eternal, and so it is essential that we protect, preserve and give access to our waters.

In the town where I live, a beautiful small river flows. A painting in the town hall shows how, in the nineteenth century, life in the town huddled around the river. Today it is impossible to get within yards of this little waterway, and the stores on the main street hide the river and don't allow any visual or physical access. It is like shutting off your heart and trying to live without its pulse and flow. The town has a natural, spiritual treasure that would

VISUAL CONNECTIONS: HENLEY-ON-THAMES
This photograph depicts a scene on the Thames River near Henley, England, similar to the scene Moore describes in paragraph 2. In many ways, this is a very familiar water scene. Consider how Moore relies on his readers' familiarity with such scenes in making his point in this paragraph.

Thames River near Henley, England

CONNECTIONS: SIDDHARTHA
The main character in the novel of the same name by German writer Herman Hesse, Siddhartha is based on the historical figure of Siddhartha Gautama, better known as the Buddha, who lived in India in the sixth century. At the end of Hesse's novel, after a long and often risky journey to find truth, Siddhartha finds peace on the banks of a river.

GLOSSES

ALCHEMISTS (par. 3)
Alchemy usually refers to the medieval science of chemistry, which was based on an understanding of water and other substances that differs from modern science.

NARCISSUS
In Greek mythology, Narcissus (par. 4) was a handsome youth who refused all offers of love, including that of a god, who punished him by having him fall in love with his own image, reflected in a pool of water. Think about how Moore uses the story of Narcissus to make his point about water in paragraph 4.

help humanise its citizens and prevent many problems. But the modern eye simply doesn't see the river. It looks but doesn't know that it is there.

I wish my father could begin his career all over again and teach the world to love this precious substance, this Eternal Water that satisfies the thirst of the soul as well as the needs of the body.

UNDERSTANDING THE TEXT

1. In what sense is water a "spiritual thing" in Moore's life? Why is it important, in his view, to have both a spiritual and physical sense of water?

2. What does Moore mean when he writes that "all water is baptismal water"? What does this statement reveal about his own beliefs and values?

3. Why does Moore state "the modern eye simply doesn't see the river"? Why is this inability to see a problem important, according to Moore? Do you agree? Why or why not?

EXPLORING THE ISSUES

1. The first paragraph of this essay ends with a very short but stunning sentence, which refers to Moore's grandfather: "He drowned." Although Moore tells us in the next paragraph that he still fears water, he never mentions his grandfather again in this essay. Why? Why do you think Moore shares this terrible anecdote at the beginning of the story and then says nothing more about it? What does this anecdote convey? How does it help set up Moore's discussion of water and his main point in this essay?

2. What do you think was Moore's purpose in writing this essay? Do you think he is interested only in conveying his ideas about water? Does he have a larger message to convey? Explain, citing specific passages to support your answer.

3. Moore makes a number of references to historical figures, to literature, to science, and to religion in this essay. What do you think these references suggest about the audience Moore was writing for? Are you part of that audience? Explain.

ENTERING THE CONVERSATIONS

1. In this essay, Moore tells us that he has learned about water from science, from philosophy, and from religion. In doing so, he implies a connection among these three ways of knowing. Using Moore's essay as a starting point, write an essay in which you discuss what you see as the relationship among science, philosophy, and religion. How does each contribute to your understanding of the world? Do they complement one another? Or do they compete with one another? Try to address such questions in your essay.

2. Write an essay for an audience of your classmates in which you describe an experience that somehow affected your beliefs about yourself and the world around you. Write about your experience in a way that shows how it helped shape your spiritual life.

3. Water may be the subject of more paintings than any other thing. If possible, visit a local art gallery (there may be one on your campus) and view some paintings that depict water scenes. (If you can't visit a gallery, find images of paintings in your library or on the Internet. There are also several images of waterfalls on page 216 in this book.) Then write an essay discussing what these paintings suggest about the way humans think about water.

I can remember as a young child asking my grandmother, who was a very religious person, questions about religious matters that puzzled me. Often, her response was, "You just have to have faith." I'm sure many people have heard such a comment. It seems natural to question some of the things we are taught to believe as children, and it is not unusual for people to experience great doubt about what they have been taught as they get older and learn more about themselves and

Salvation

the world. In the following essay, Langston Hughes (1902–1967) writes about that kind of doubt. But for Hughes, the religious doubt he experienced was dramatic and frightening. He writes of a time in his church when he was asked to declare his faith publicly as a Christian. It was an agonizing moment for Hughes, who was just twelve years old at the time, for he was not sure what he was supposed to be feeling. He was unable to wholeheartedly embrace the faith that everyone else in the church seemed to embrace. And the consequences of that inability were profound.

In a sense, this brief excerpt from Hughes's autobiography, The Big Sea (1940), is about the public and private aspects of religious faith. It seems likely that Hughes would not have experienced this wrenching moment if he had not been among believers in church, who set certain expectations regarding faith and salvation. His story asks us to think about the relationship between religion as a social institution, with its doctrines that shape what we believe, and our individual faith. To what extent is our faith our own? To what extent is it a function of social convention and upbringing? These are not easy questions, and Hughes's essay may prompt you to wrestle with them.   (continued)

LANGSTON HUGHES

I **was saved from sin when I was going on thirteen. But not** really saved. It happened like this. There was a big revival at my Auntie Reed's church. Every night for weeks there had been much preaching, singing, praying, and shouting, and some very hardened sinners had been brought to Christ, and the membership of the church had grown by leaps and bounds. Then just before the revival ended, they held a special meeting for children, "to bring the young lambs to the fold." My aunt spoke of it for days ahead. That night I was escorted to the front row and placed on the mourners' bench with all the other young sinners, who had not yet been brought to Jesus.

My aunt told me that when you were saved you saw a light, and something happened to you inside! And Jesus came into your life! And God was with you from then on! She said you could see and hear and feel Jesus in your soul. I believed her. I had heard a great many old people say the same thing and it seemed to me they ought to know. So I sat there calmly in the hot, crowded church, waiting for Jesus to come to me.

(continued) *Hughes was a prolific poet, essayist, fiction writer, and playwright who is considered one of the key figures in the great American literary movement of the 1920s called the Harlem Renaissance. The experience described in the following essay took place in Missouri, where Hughes was born.* ▼

CONTEXT: REVIVAL MEETINGS

The meeting that Hughes attended at his Auntie Reed's church was part of a much larger movement in the late nineteenth and early twentieth centuries in the United States that some historians call the Second Great Awakening. This movement was characterized by an increase in religious activity in response to concerns about the immoral state of society. An important component of this movement was "revival meetings," such as the one Hughes describes in this essay, which were often organized by traveling preachers and sometimes attracted thousands of people for several days of preaching and worship.

The preacher preached a wonderful rhythmical sermon, all moans and shouts and lonely cries and dire pictures of hell, and then he sang a song about the ninety and nine safe in the fold, but one little lamb was left out in the cold. Then he said: "Won't you come? Won't you come to Jesus? Young lambs, won't you come?" And he held out his arms to all us young sinners there on the mourners' bench. And the little girls cried. And some of them jumped up and went to Jesus right away. But most of us just sat there.

A great many old people came and knelt around us and prayed, old women with jet-black faces and braided hair, old men with work-gnarled hands. And the church sang a song about the lower lights are burning, some poor sinners to be saved. And the whole building rocked with prayer and song.

Still I kept waiting to *see* Jesus.   5

Finally all the young people had gone to the altar and were saved, but one boy and me. He was a rounder's son named Westley. Westley and I were surrounded by sisters and deacons praying. It was very hot in the church, and getting late now. Finally Westley said to me in a whisper: "God damn! I'm tired o' sitting here. Let's get up and be saved." So he got up and was saved.

Then I was left all alone on the mourners' bench. My aunt came and knelt at my knees and cried, while prayers and song swirled all around me in the little church. The whole congregation prayed for me alone, in a mighty wail of moans and voices. And I kept waiting serenely for Jesus, waiting, waiting—but he didn't come. I wanted to see him, but nothing happened to me. Nothing! I wanted something to happen to me, but nothing happened.

I heard the songs and the minister saying: "Why don't you come? My dear child, why don't you come to Jesus? Jesus is waiting for you. He wants you. Why don't you come? Sister Reed, what is this child's name?"

"Langston," my aunt sobbed.

"Langston, why don't you come? Why don't you come and be   10
saved? Oh, Lamb of God! Why don't you come?"

Now it was really getting late. I began to be ashamed of myself, holding everything up so long. I began to wonder what God thought about Westley, who certainly hadn't seen Jesus either, but who was now sitting proudly on the platform, swinging his knickerbockered legs and grinning down at me, surrounded by deacons and old women on their knees praying. God had not struck Westley dead for taking his name in vain or for lying in the temple. So I decided that maybe to save further trouble, I'd better lie, too, and say that Jesus had come, and get up and be saved.

So I got up.

Suddenly the whole room broke into a sea of shouting, as they saw me rise. Waves of rejoicing swept the place. Women leaped in the air.

CONNECTIONS: RELIGION AND FILM

Many films have been made about religion and religious themes, and a few have focused on the character of the traveling preacher and the kind of revival meeting described in this essay. One such film was *Leap of Faith* (1992), which starred Steve Martin as Jonas Nightingale, a con artist who used high-tech gimmicks to convince people at his revival meetings that they were "saved" and to encourage them to contribute cash to his traveling church. Martin's character is part of a longstanding tradition in stories and film that pokes fun at religious revivals and calls into question the faith of people caught up in such movements. But Hughes's essay presents this revival meeting in a very serious way. It's worth thinking about what his essay might contribute to the ongoing conversations in American culture about the role of religion and faith in our lives.

My aunt threw her arms around me. The minister took me by the hand and led me to the platform.

When things quieted down, in a hushed silence, punctuated by a few ecstatic "Amens," all the new young lambs were blessed in the name of God. Then joyous singing filled the room.

That night, for the first time in my life but one for I was a big boy twelve years old—I cried. I cried, in bed alone, and couldn't stop. I buried my head under the quilts, but my aunt heard me. She woke up and told my uncle I was crying because the Holy Ghost had come into my life, and because I had seen Jesus. But I was really crying because I couldn't bear to tell her that I had lied, that I had deceived everybody in the church, that I hadn't seen Jesus, and that now I didn't believe there was a Jesus anymore, since he didn't come to help me.

UNDERSTANDING THE TEXT

1. What expectations does Hughes have about the revival meeting that he was attending with his aunt? Where did these expectations come from? What might they suggest about religious faith and religious events like the meeting at his aunt's church?

2. What prevents Hughes from going up to the preacher during the revival meeting? What do you think Hughes's hesitation reveals about him as a person?

3. What role does Westley play in this experience? In what ways do you think Westley helps Hughes convey his perspective on faith and religion?

EXPLORING THE ISSUES

1. What main ideas about religion and faith do you think Hughes is trying to convey in this essay? Do you agree with him? Why or why not?

2. In this essay, Hughes describes an experience that happens during a relatively short time—a few hours at most. Examine how he conveys a sense of time. What moments during the experience does he emphasize? How does he describe those moments? How does his manipulation of time in this essay help him convey his ideas about faith?

3. How would you describe Hughes's voice in this essay? He is describing an experience he had when he was twelve years old, but he wrote this passage when he was nearly forty. Do you think he tries to capture the voice of a twelve-year-old boy? Explain, citing specific passages to support your answer.

ENTERING THE CONVERSATIONS

1. Write an essay in which you describe your own understanding of faith. In your essay, define faith as you understand it, drawing on your own experiences and on Hughes's essay (or any other relevant essay or book) to support your explanation.

2. In a group of classmates, share your essays from Question 1. How does each of you define faith? What similarities and differences can you identify among your respective ideas about faith? What questions about faith might be raised by the essays that each of you wrote?

3. Write an essay in which you describe an important experience you have had involving your faith or religion.

4. Interview several people you know about their views regarding religion and faith. Try to determine whether they see any distinction between religion and faith. Then write a report for your classmates about what you learned through your interviews.

5. Create a visual document (such as a web site or photo essay) that reflects your view of faith.

6. In recent years, several popular television shows have focused on issues of faith. Shows like *Touched by an Angel,* for example, assume a certain kind of understanding of faith and spirituality. Select one or more such shows and examine how they present faith, spirituality, or religion. Then write an essay in which you discuss these shows and what they seem to suggest about faith in contemporary culture.

Many people think of Zen Buddhism as a religion, but in fact, Zen is nontheistic; that is,
Zen teachings do not include a belief in a
Supreme Being or in any deities. Although
other Buddhist sects (such as Tibetan
Buddhism) do believe in a God or gods and
many Zen Buddhists share that belief, Zen itself does not require such a belief. However,
Zen does hold a number of fundamental beliefs about the world and about the place of
humans in the world. Some of those beliefs are

Waterfall

evident in the following essay by the eminent
Zen teacher Shunryu Suzuki (1904–1971).
In this brief essay, Suzuki uses the metaphor of
the waterfall to explore the basic Buddhist idea
of oneness, or the unity of all life. Although
this idea might seem simple, it is very different
from the way most Western religions understand the human self in relation to the world.
Perhaps that's why reading Zen texts, such as
Suzuki's essay, can be so challenging to many
readers from the United States and other
Western cultures. Or maybe it's because Zen
teachers do not teach directly; rather, they try to
point students in a direction that might lead
to the students' enlightenment, which the student must attain on his or her own. All true
learning, Zen teachers believe, is a process of
self-discovery. A teacher doesn't teach; a
teacher guides the student on the path to true
learning. Zen writings often try to guide in the
same way. As you read Suzuki's essay, try to be
aware of how he is guiding you to an understanding of oneness and the path to truth.
Consider what his essay suggests about a Zen
view of knowing and believing.

Suzuki, a world-renowned Zen master,
came from Japan to the United States in 1959
to establish the first Zen training center in the
West. His book, Zen Mind, Beginner's
Mind (1970), from which the following essay
is taken, continues to be one of the world's
best-selling books on Zen practice. ▼

SHUNRYU SUZUKI

If you go to Japan and visit Eiheiji monastery, just before you
enter you will see a small bridge called Hanshaku-kyo, which means
"half-dipper bridge." Whenever **Dogen**-zenji dipped water from the
river, he used only half a dipperful, returning the rest to the river
again, without throwing it away. That is why we call the bridge
Hanshaku-kyo, "Half-Dipper Bridge." At Eiheiji when we wash our
face, we fill the basin to just seventy percent of its capacity. And after
we wash, we empty the water towards, rather than away from, our body.
This expresses respect for the water. This kind of practice is not based
on any idea of being economical. It may be difficult to understand why
Dogen returned half of the water he dipped to the river. This kind of
practice is beyond our thinking. When we feel the beauty of the river,
when we are one with the water, we intuitively do it in Dogen's way. It
is our true nature to do so. But if your true nature is covered by ideas
of economy or efficiency, Dogen's way makes no sense.

I went to Yosemite National Park, and I saw some huge waterfalls.
The highest one there is 1,340 feet high, and from it the water comes
down like a curtain thrown from the top of the mountain. It does not
seem to come down swiftly, as you might expect; it seems to come

down very slowly because of the distance. And the water does not come down as one stream, but is separated into many tiny streams. From a distance it looks like a curtain. And I thought it must be a very difficult experience for each drop of water to come down from the top of such a high mountain. It takes time, you know, a long time, for the water finally to reach the bottom of the waterfall. And it seems to me that our human life may be like this. We have many difficult experiences in our life. But at the same time, I thought, the water was not originally separated, but was one whole river. Only when it is separated does it have some difficulty in falling. It is as if the water does not have any feeling when it is one whole river. Only when separated into many drops can it begin to have or to express some feeling. When we see one whole river we do not feel the living activity of the water, but when we dip a part of the water into a dipper, we experience some feeling of the water, and we also feel the value of the person who uses the water. Feeling ourselves and the water in this way, we cannot use it in just a material way. It is a living thing.

Before we were born we had no feeling; we were one with the universe. This is called "mind-only," or "essence of mind," or "big mind." After we are separated by birth from this oneness, as the water falling from the waterfall is separated by the wind and rocks, then we have feeling. You have difficulty because you have feeling. You attach to the feeling you have without knowing just how this kind of feeling is created. When you do not realize that you are one with the river, or one with the universe, you have fear. Whether it is separated into drops or not, water is water. Our life and death are the same thing. When we realize this fact, we have no fear of death anymore, and we have no actual difficulty in our life.

When the water returns to its original oneness with the river, it no longer has any individual feeling to it; it resumes its own nature, and finds composure. How very glad the water must be to come back to the original river! If this is so, what feeling will we have when we die? I think we are like the water in the dipper. We will have composure then, perfect composure. It may be too perfect for us, just now, because we are so much attached to our own feeling, to our individual existence. From us, just now, we have some fear of death, but after we resume our true original nature, there is **Nirvana.** That is why we say, "To attain Nirvana is to pass away." "To pass away" is not a very adequate expression. Perhaps "to pass on," or "to go on," or "to join" would be better. Will you try to find some better expression for death? When you find it, you will have quite a new interpretation of your life. It will be like my experience when I saw the water in the big waterfall. Imagine! It was 1,340 feet high!

We say, "Everything comes out of emptiness." One whole river or one whole mind is emptiness. When we reach this understanding we find the true meaning of our life. When we reach this understanding we can see the beauty of human life. Before we realize this fact, everything that we see is just delusion. Sometimes we overestimate the beauty; sometimes we underestimate or ignore the beauty because our small mind is not in accord with reality.

CONNECTIONS: WATER

Compare Suzuki's description of water in the opening paragraph to the discussion of water in Thomas Moore's essay on page 206. Both writers discuss water in spiritual terms. Are there other similarities in the way they use water in their essays? What might the descriptions of water in these two essays—one by an American writer, the other by a Japanese Zen teacher—suggest about the way water is understood in different cultures?

GLOSSES
DOGEN
A renowned thirteenth century Japanese philosopher, Dogen-zenji helped establish the Soto sect of Zen Buddhism in Japan. He is widely considered to be among the greatest thinkers in Japanese history. His teachings form the basis of several schools of Zen Buddhism throughout the world today.

NIRVANA
Nirvana refers to a state of enlightenment in which one is free of desires and attachments.

ZAZEN
In Zen Buddhism, *zazen* refers to the practice of sitting meditation, which is a central component of Zen spiritual practice. As Suzuki suggests in paragraph 6, Zen practitioners believe that zazen is a way to experience the feeling of emptiness and enlightenment that Suzuki mentions in the previous paragraph.

VISUAL CONNECTIONS: WATERFALLS

The waterfall is a common subject in traditional Japanese painting, as seen in these two examples. The one on the left was painted by Katsushika Hokusai sometime around 1830. The one on the right is by Ando Hiroshige (1797–1858). Consider how Suzuki relies on the image of the waterfall in his essay. In what ways might these images reflect the idea of a waterfall as he describes it? You might also consider what larger messages these two images seem to convey.

Katsushika Hokusai, *Kirifuri Waterfall, Mount Kurokami, Shimotsuke Province*

Ando Hiroshige, *Fuji from the Mountains of Izu*

To talk about it this way is quite easy, but to have the actual feeling is not so easy. But by your practice of **zazen** you can cultivate this feeling. When you can sit with your whole body and mind, and with the oneness of your mind and body under the control of the universal mind, you can easily attain this kind of right understanding. Your everyday life will be renewed without being attached to an old erroneous interpretation of life. When you realize this fact, you will discover how meaningless your old interpretation was, and how much useless effort you had been making. You will find the true meaning of life, and even though you have difficulty falling upright from the top of the waterfall to the bottom of the mountain, you will enjoy your life.

UNDERSTANDING THE TEXT

1. What is "mind-only," "essence of mind," or "big mind" as Suzuki explains these terms? Why are these concepts important, in his view? What role do they play in helping Suzuki make his main point?

2. What does Suzuki mean when he refers to "original oneness"?

3. What is the true meaning of life, as Suzuki understands it? How does his view of the meaning of life correspond to—or contrast with—your own?

EXPLORING THE ISSUES

1. Suzuki uses the waterfall as a metaphor for human life. What point does he make with this metaphor? How effectively do you think this metaphor conveys his point?

2. In paragraph 3, Suzuki describes the classic Buddhist view of the origins of human life. Consider how this view compares to your own. What similarities and differences do you see between Suzuki's beliefs about the origins of human life and your own? How do your beliefs influence the way you respond to this passage—and to this essay?

3. In the final paragraph, Suzuki writes that to talk about the true meaning of life is easy, but "to have the actual feeling is not so easy."

Here, he is referring to a belief in Zen Buddhism that there is a limit to what words and language can teach, especially when it comes to seeking truth. Zen emphasizes the experience of truth, which is attained through regular, disciplined spiritual practice. Consider how Suzuki's writing is a reflection of the traditional Zen suspicion of language. Do you think his writing style is consistent with the Zen belief in the importance of experience rather than thought or language? Explain.

ENTERING THE CONVERSATIONS

1. Write an essay in which you compare Suzuki's ideas about enlightenment to your own religious or spiritual beliefs.

2. Suzuki uses the metaphor of the waterfall to convey the Zen Buddhist idea of oneness. Write an essay in which you use a metaphor to convey a fundamental belief that you hold.

3. Write an essay in which you discuss the kind of spiritual understanding that Suzuki describes in this essay in comparison to the ways in which other writers in this cluster (or in this chapter) seem to describe what it means to understand. What similarities and differences can you identify between Suzuki's view of the self, the world, and enlightenment and the views expressed by the other writers you

have selected? Try to draw conclusions about the relationship of these views to each other, and discuss what you think are the consequences of the similarities and differences you have found among them.

INFOTRAC

4. Ecumenism is a movement to foster cooperation among different religions. It is based on the belief that all religions share fundamental views and worship the same God. Yet, we don't have to look hard to see terrible and often bloody conflicts between people with opposing religious views. Using InfoTrac College Edition, your library, and any other appropriate resources, examine one such conflict that grows out of religious differences. For example, you might choose the conflict in Northern Ireland between Protestants and Catholics or the conflict between Israelis and Arabs in the Middle East. Try to find out the history of that conflict and identify the main points of conflict among the involved parties. Then write a report in which you describe what you have learned about that conflict. Try to draw conclusions about the role of religious belief in contemporary politics. Alternatively, focus your research on ecumenism as an international movement.

CREATING THEMES: Extending the Conversations

WITH TEXT

1. Drawing on the readings in this chapter, write an essay in which you discuss the differences between knowing and believing.

2. The title of the third cluster in this chapter is *Knowing and Believing,* which names the theme that I see in these readings. But these essays are about other themes—some directly related to the ideas of knowing and believing, some not. Identify an important idea or theme that you see in the readings in this cluster. Then write an essay in which you explore that idea or theme, drawing on the readings in this cluster where appropriate. Alternatively, select an important theme that you see in this chapter and write an essay for an audience of your classmates in which you draw on several readings in the chapter to discuss that theme.

3. How we learn has been a subject of investigation by philosophers, psychologists, and educators for centuries. Various theories of learning exist in different fields. For example, in the field of educational psychology, well-known scholar Howard Gardner has developed a theory of multiple intelligences to explain how we learn. His theories have influenced many educators, who have tried to change schooling according to Gardner's ideas. Using InfoTrac College Edition, the Internet, and any other appropriate resources, find out what you can about other influential theories of learning. Then write a report about one of those theories, such as Gardner's theory of multiple intelligences. In your report, draw on your own experience and the experiences of authors whose essays are in the second cluster to evaluate the theory. Alternatively, on the basis of your own experience, the essays in that cluster, and any other relevant

resources, write an essay in which you discuss your own ideas about learning and offer advice to individuals or groups about how to enhance learning.

4. By grouping the essays in this chapter into three clusters, I have given them certain kinds of meaning and significance. I have implicitly defined *understanding* (the title of the chapter) as somehow related to the titles of the three clusters: *learning, schooling,* and *knowing and believing.* In doing so, I have highlighted several ongoing conversations that I think are important—for instance, conversations in our society about schooling or about faith or philosophical conversations about knowledge. But these essays can be seen as part of many other conversations as well. For example, we might see the essays by Helen Keller, Richard Wright, Maya Angelou, and Richard Rodriguez as narratives about individuals who have overcome great personal hardships because of their race or physical abilities. If we grouped those essays together, we could see them as part of the ongoing conversations in our culture about individual initiative and responsibility. You might read them as examples of how American culture emphasizes the individual's capacity to define himself or herself. They are also stories about identity, and in that sense, I might have placed them in Chapter 5. The point is that in each case, you would be reading the same personal narratives, but what those narratives mean would be slightly different. I have suggested that they are all about understanding ourselves in some way, but exactly what they tell us about understanding ourselves depends a lot on how you categorize them—on how you understand the conversations that each essay is part of. With that in mind, identify what you see as a compelling theme

that runs through the readings in this chapter. Select four (or more) essays that explore that theme in some way, and write an essay in which you discuss that theme, drawing on those four (or more) essays. Write your essay in a way that participates in a conversation about that theme. In other words, write it for an audience who would have an interest in that theme.

5. Select several authors in this chapter and write a dialogue in which they explore the relationship between knowing and believing.

6. Drawing on several essays in this chapter for your ideas, write an essay for your local newspaper or another appropriate publication with a general audience in which you discuss the changes that should be made to schools so they foster what you believe to be true learning and understanding of the world.

WITH MEDIA

1. Select an important theme that you see in the readings in this chapter and create a PowerPoint presentation in which you explore that theme, drawing on any relevant essays in the chapter.

2. Every university and most schools now have web sites, many of which are very sophisticated and extensive. Select several school or university web sites and examine the way they present their school or university. What kinds of images do they present? What information do they include? How do they address visitors to the website? How do they seem to assume that visitors will use these sites? What general impressions are conveyed about the specific school or university and about education in general? Then write a report of your investigation, describing the web sites you reviewed and presenting your conclu-

CREATING THEMES: Extending the Conversations

sions about what these sites reveal about their schools and about education. Alternatively, create a web site on the basis of your investigation. Construct your web site as a resource for students, parents, and others who may wish to learn about schools or universities through the Internet. On your web site, provide tips for such an audience about how to view school or university web sites. Or create a new web site for your school or university based on the results of your investigation.

3. In the introduction to Cluster 1 of this chapter, I included some of the lyrics from Alanis Morissette's song "You Learn." Select several songs that you think convey important insights about learning, understanding, or spirituality, and write an essay in which you discuss these themes as they are explored in these songs. Alternatively, write your own song about what it means to learn or understand something.

4. Select several popular television shows in which science seems to play an important role. For example, the popular program *CSI* depicts the work of criminal investigators who use scientific methods to solve crimes. The popular *The X Files* included a character (Scully) who was a physician and who believed in science as a means of answering questions and solving problems. Examine such shows for what they seem to suggest about science. Then write a review essay in which you discuss what you have learned from your analysis. Draw conclusions about how science is por-

trayed in the media as a way of knowing the world.

WITH FILM

1. Many films and television shows have spiritual themes that explore our beliefs about God, the afterlife, and spirituality in general. Among such recent films are *Michael*, about an angel living on Earth, and *Bruce Almighty*, a comedy in which a man is temporarily given God's powers. Some recent television shows have explored similar themes—for example, *Touched by an Angel*. Unlike the film *The Passion of the Christ*, these films are not based directly on Bible stories or explicit religious doctrines. Yet, they do explore themes associated with established religions, most commonly Christianity. Select one or more such films and examine the way they explore themes of spirituality. What ideas about spirituality do they seem to convey? What religious beliefs do they reflect? Write an analysis of the films you have selected in which you try to answer such questions. Draw conclusions about what these films might suggest about our cultural attitudes regarding knowing and believing.

2. Many popular films tell stories of people who have experienced some kind of change or important kind of learning in their lives. The classic film by Orson Welles, *Citizen Kane*, for example, tells the story of a wealthy publisher who learns some difficult lessons as he pursues his quest for power and influence. Similarly, the main characters in the more recent film version of the pop-

ular fantasy trilogy *The Lord of the Rings* experience great trials that ultimately change them. Select one or several films that you believe tell the story of an important learning experience, and write an essay in which you discuss what the main character (or characters) learned and how that learning happened. In your essay, draw conclusions about what it means to learn. Consider writing your essay as a review essay that might appear in a popular magazine or on a web site devoted to film.

3. Many films depict schools, including many classic films, such as *To Sir with Love* or *The Paper Chase*. Other well-known films that deal directly with schooling in some way include *Animal House*, *The Dead Poets' Society*, *The Breakfast Club*, *Stand and Deliver*, and *Dangerous Minds*. Although these films are very different, they all include familiar images of schools and they all portray teachers, students, and conventional school activities in ways that are familiar to most Americans. Choose one or more such films and examine what they seem to suggest about school and about learning. Then write an essay in which you present your analysis, drawing conclusions about what these films reveal about American attitudes and values regarding schooling and education.

4. Write a script of a film or play that tells the story of an important kind of learning or spiritual transformation.

Chapter 7 Relationships

© Paul Kaye: Cordaiy Photo Library Ltd./Corbis

AT THE END OF HIS CLASSIC FILM *ANNIE HALL* (1973), WOODY ALLEN, SPEAKING AS THE CHARACTER ALVIE SINGER, TELLS AN OLD JOKE ABOUT A MAN WHO GOES TO THE DOCTOR, COMPLAINING THAT HIS BROTHER THINKS HE'S A CHICKEN. WHEN THE DOCTOR ASKS WHETHER THE MAN HAS HAD HIS BROTHER HOSPITALIZED, THE MAN REPLIES, "I WOULD, BUT

we need the eggs." Allen then explains that relationships are just like that: They're crazy and illogical, but we all need them.

When I began putting together the chapters of this book, it seemed obvious that I should include a chapter on relationships, for what could be more important or fundamental to human life than relationships? As Woody Allen says, we all need the eggs. And as his film *Annie Hall* makes clear, relationships are extremely complicated, often difficult, and sometimes painful. No wonder writers have been writing about relationships forever. Think of any great novel or story, and relationships are likely to be at the center of it. That's because our lives are so

> **Entire sections of bookstores are devoted to relationships of all kinds: romantic, parental, family, professional.**

deeply defined and shaped by our relationships. This is indeed rich ground for writers to till.

My guess is that when you hear someone use the term *relationships,* you assume that they mean relationships between people. Most of the time, you're probably right. As I've already noted, there is nothing more central to our lives than our relationships with other people. Entire sections of bookstores are devoted to relationships of all kinds: romantic, parental, family, professional. And entire professions are devoted to them as well; for example, much of psychology focuses on relationships between individuals and groups. Most of us will devote a great deal of time and energy in our lives to developing and maintaining our relationships with others, and most of us will spend some time dealing

with the damage that can be done in a relationship.

But the term *relationships* doesn't necessarily refer exclusively to people. We can have a relationship with a pet, a place (our hometown or college campus), an activity (a sport like football or swimming), an organization (the military or a political party), or a thing (a car or motorcycle). We might even have a relationship to a time or era, like the 1960s. As humans, we *relate to* so many things. And the complexity of our many relationships is perhaps a big reason we so often write about them. We want—and need—to understand relationships because they are so much a part of being human. We want to examine the complexities and wonders and challenges of relationships.

The reading selections in this chapter reflect some of the complexities as well as the challenges of relationships. The truth is that almost any of the readings in this book could be placed in this chapter because all of them are about some kind of relationship. And it's a pretty good bet that the writers whose essays are included in this chapter didn't start out with the goal of writing about relationships. Instead, they had some experience, person, event, or problem that they wanted to explain or explore. So what's the point of having a chapter with such a broad theme? That's a question I'd like you to think about as you read through the selections in this chapter.

I'd argue that placing readings in this chapter affects how you understand them and therefore helps shape what they mean to you. For example, the first essay in the chapter, "Attila the Honey I'm Home," by Kristin van Ogtrop, is about a modern woman's efforts to have both a career and a family. In that sense, it might fit nicely under the theme of "Work" or "Lifestyle" or "Women." It might even fit into Chapter 11 on Change. But placing it in a chapter about relationships gives it a certain significance and perhaps suggests how you should read it. And it's worth asking whether van Ogtrop intended it to be read as an essay about relationships—rather than as an essay about work or family or lifestyle or women. The point is that essays like van Ogtrop's address rich and complicated issues that are really part of many different ongoing conversations that we, as members of a society, are always having. And what her essay, or any essay, "means" is determined in part by what conversation it fits into and how it fits into that conversation.

Each of the three clusters in this chapter offers a slightly different way to think about relationships. The first focuses on love, which is perhaps the most profound expression of a relationship. I wanted to find essays that might get you thinking about the many different ways that we understand love and the many different kinds of love we can experience in our lives. The second cluster, Complicating Relationships, includes readings that examine ways we can encounter various kinds of obstacles in relationships, and it raises questions about how relationships are affected by beliefs, values, traditions, and even laws. The third cluster asks you to rethink your understanding of relationships

in general. These three essays pose questions about some of our most basic values regarding relationships among people and even our relationship to the natural world. What is a wife? A husband? What is love? And what about relationships that happen because of certain traditions or activities—such as schooling? How should we understand relationships between teachers and students and among students? These are some of the tricky questions that the writers in the third cluster pose.

> **As humans, we *relate to* so many things.**

In reading these essays, you are joining a complex conversation that humans have long been having. When you watch a film like Woody Allen's *Annie Hall* or listen to a love song or read a newspaper editorial about same-sex marriage, you are participating in that conversation about how we relate to one another. The significance of the readings in this chapter will be determined in part by how you have been participating in that conversation. Pay attention to how you read—and pay attention to how these writers have joined that conversation.

EXPLORING LOVE

T IS POSSIBLE THAT MORE HAS BEEN WRITTEN ABOUT LOVE THAN ABOUT ANY OTHER TOPIC. IT HAS BEEN THE SUBJECT OF COUNTLESS STORIES, PLAYS, POEMS, SONGS, AND FILMS, AND IT SEEMS AT TIMES TO CONSUME US. BUT FOR ALL THE ATTENTION WE GIVE IT, LOVE REMAINS AS MYSTERIOUS AND HARD TO DEFINE AS EVER. MAYBE THAT'S WHY so many writers have turned their attention to it. Or maybe it's because love is as important as anything else we can experience in our lives.

The four essays in this cluster offer four very different perspectives on love. I selected them because I wanted to try to highlight how complex and multifaceted love can be. We can experience many different kinds of love, so it seems important to pay attention to what we might call the diversity of love. But I also wanted to find essays that help us see that when we write or talk about love, we are drawing from a huge well of cultural traditions and stories that help us

> **Because the idea of someone being lovesick is part of our culture.**

make sense of this crazy thing called love. Writers rely on that cultural well to convey their ideas about love. For example, Richard Selzer's tongue-in-cheek essay, "Love Sick," assumes that readers have some familiarity with the common image of someone who is experiencing intense romantic love. If you have had such an experience, you'll understand exactly what Selzer means, and you'll appreciate his medical metaphor. But even if you have never been so deeply in love, even if you've never experienced "lovesickness" yourself, you will still understand Selzer's point and his use of the medical metaphor. Why? Because the idea of someone being lovesick is part of our culture. We know it from our experiences with cultural texts, including songs, films, and stories. It is not something that Selzer invented

but something he borrowed from that larger cultural tradition that he assumes his readers share. Without that shared tradition, Selzer's essay might not be as effective—or humorous—in conveying his point about romantic love.

The other essays in this cluster also rely on a shared cultural background, though what that background is differs slightly for each essay. The essay by bell hooks, for instance, draws on both Western and Eastern cultural traditions in examining what we mean by love in a larger sense—not romantic love, but the kind of love described by religious thinkers and philosophers. In this case, she assumes her readers will have a sense of what that kind of love is, even if they are unfamiliar with the Buddhist tradition that she refers to in her dialogue with Buddhist teacher Thich Nhat Hanh. In a similar way, Mark Doty assumes that readers will understand something about the deep commitment that two people can make to one another in a relationship, such as in a marriage, but in this case, he describes that kind of love as it existed in an unconventional relationship between two people of the same sex. The force of his essay is partly a result of cultural values regarding such relationships.

As a reader, you may often be unaware of how much background knowledge you bring to a piece of writing. And you may not realize that your reaction to an essay may reflect your culture as much as your individual experiences or preferences. But I hope these essays help you become more sensitive to how much knowledge and experience you draw on as a reader and how deeply that knowledge and experience can shape the way you read. I hope, too, that these essays give you some insight into this wonderful and complicated thing called love.

At first glance, this essay by a successful *magazine editor is about what it takes to be a career woman and mother in the United States today. Kristin van Ogtrop (b. 1964) writes vividly about balancing the roles of wife, mother, and successful professional. But in describing her hectic struggles to balance her many responsibilities, van Ogtrop is also implicitly describing the challenges of certain kinds of love: for family, for spouse, for career, and for self. Van Ogtrop's love for*

Attila THE Honey I'm Home

her family is reflected in her constant efforts to meet her family's needs and in her feelings of guilt that perhaps she doesn't always do so. In complaining about her husband, for example, she admits to feeling that she is perhaps not the wife she could be. In this sense, she is describing some of the challenges spouses face in trying to maintain a marriage. Van Ogtrop also raises questions— questions that she herself has trouble answering—about the nature of these kinds of love and perhaps about the costs of love, too.

The images van Ogtrop shares from her life are familiar ones in our society's ongoing discussions about what is often called the "balancing act"—that is, the effort of men and especially women to balance career and family and marriage. As you read, you might consider why these images are familiar. Is it partly because women's magazines like the one van Ogtrop edits often include articles about this balancing act and therefore help shape our perceptions and expectations about things like career and family and marriage—and love?

Kristin van Ogtrop has been an editor at a number of magazines, including Glamour, Vogue, *and* Travel & Leisure, *and has written for many others, including* Seventeen *and* Outside. *She* (continued)

KRISTIN VAN OGTROP

It's a typical night:

I arrive home from work, after first stopping to pick up my two boys from my friend Gabrielle's house, where my nanny has left them on a play date. It's seven thirty. No one has had a bath. Foolishly, I have promised that we will make milk shakes. The boys have eaten dinner. I haven't. My husband is at a basketball game and won't be home until ten.

Owen, who is six, tosses a bouquet of flowers—a gift from Gabrielle's garden—onto the grass as we get out of the car. Three-year-old Hugo sees the moon. I mention that the sun is out, too; he runs from one end of the front walk to the other, trying to find it, getting closer to the street with each lap.

Owen says he wants the milk shake *now*.

I unlock the front door and step in. George the cat meows and rubs against my legs, begging to be fed.

I walk back outside to pick up the flowers, the wet towel (swimming lessons), and my own two bags from work (contents: three unread

KRISTIN VAN OGTROP, *"ATTILA THE HONEY I'M HOME."* FROM *THE BITCH IN THE HOUSE* (2002) BY CATHI HANAUER. REPRINTED BY PERMISSION OF THE AUTHOR.

(continued) *is currently managing editor of* Real Simple *magazine. This essay appeared in* The Bitch in the House: 26 Women Tell the Truth about Sex, Solitude, Work, Motherhood, and Marriage, *edited by Cathi Hanauer (2002).* ▼

STRATEGIES: FIRST-PERSON DESCRIPTION
In these opening paragraphs and throughout her essay, van Ogtrop describes scenes from her daily life. Consider what these various scenes tell us about who van Ogtrop is and the kind of life she leads. What specific details does she choose to share with her readers? Why do you think she shares these details?

newspapers, two magazines, a birthday party invitation for Owen, a present for the party, and a folder of work that, ever the optimist, I'm hoping to do tonight).

Back into the house with flowers, towel, bags. As I put my keys in the bowl next to the front door (small attempt at order), I knock over a framed picture beside it. The glass in the frame shatters.

Hugo calls, insistent, for me to come back outside.

Owen hovers behind me, barefoot. He wants to know why, when you combine chocolate and vanilla, does the ice cream turn brown instead of white?

I maneuver Owen around the broken glass and ask him to get the Dustbuster as I begin to pick up the shards. He disappears into the kitchen for what seems like ten minutes. I glance out for Hugo, whose voice is fainter but *definitely* still audible. George stands on his hind legs, clawing holes in the screen.

10   Owen reappears with the Dustbuster, revving the motor. He wants to know exactly how long until we make the milk shake, and are we sure we even have chocolate ice cream?

I am talking in my Mr. Rogers voice as my desperation rises. Any minute now my head is going to blast off my body, burst through the screen door, and buzz around my little town, eventually losing steam before landing with a thud somewhere near the train station, where it will be run over by one of my smiling neighbors being picked up by what I imagine are calm spouses who will drive them calmly home to houses calm and collected where the children are already bathed and ready for bed.

As for me, it's time to start yelling.

                              *   *   *

The next day:

I get up at 5:30 to leave the house at 6:00, to be driven to the TV studio for hair and makeup at 6:45, to go on the air, live, at 7:40. I'm the executive editor of an enormously popular women's magazine and am appearing as an "expert" on a local morning show to discuss "what your wallet says about you." I have a hairstylist I've never met and he makes the back of my head look ridiculous, like a ski jump. At 7:25 the segment producer hands me the anchor's script; it contains five questions that weren't part of yesterday's pre-interview. I make up answers that sound informed-clever-peppy enough for morning TV with two minutes to spare. Total airtime: ninety seconds.

By the time I get to the office at 8:30 I have six voice mail messages (boss, nanny, human resources manager, unhappy writer, underling editor wanting guidance, my mother), twenty-seven e-mails, and, on my chair, a 4,000-word article I need to edit by the end of the day. I run to the cafeteria to get something to eat, then call boss and nanny and answer most of the e-mails before my 9:30 meeting.

At 10:45 two fact-checkers come into my office to describe the problems of a recent 15 story, which kept them at work until 4:00 A.M. the night before. Are fact-checkers or editor to blame? Editor, I decide, and call her in. She is flustered and defensive, and starts to cry. My tissue box is empty, so I hand her a napkin. We talk (well, I talk; she nods) about the fact that she's made similar mistakes in the past, and perhaps this isn't the job for her. After she leaves I call the human resources manager to discuss the problematic editor, a looming legal problem, and staff salaries.

I have lunch at my desk and a second cup of coffee while I edit the piece, until two editors visit to complain about coworkers. A third tells me she is overloaded. A fourth confesses her marital problems and starts to cry; now I'm out of napkins, too. I give her the number of a counseling service and suggest she use it. Someone calls to ask about the presentation I'm giving tomorrow; I haven't even begun to think about it, which probably should worry me but somehow doesn't.

I finish the edit and drop it in my out box. Before leaving the office at 5:30 I pick up all the paper that blankets my desk and divide it into four discrete piles for the morning. I very well might forget to look through the piles and something will get overlooked, but when I return to work, the neat stacks will make me feel organized and calm. And at work, I usually am.

Here are a few things people have said about me at the office:

- "You're unflappable."
- "Are you ever in a bad mood?"
- "You command respect as soon as you walk into a room."
- "Your straightforward, no-nonsense style gets things done."
- "You're good at finessing situations so people don't boil over."

Here are things people—OK, the members of my family—have said about me at home:

- "Mommy is always grumpy."
- "Why are you so tense?"
- "You just need to relax."
- "You don't need to yell!"
- "You're too mean to live in this house and I want you to go back to work for the rest of your life!"

That last one is my favorite. It's also the saddest, because it captures such a painful 20 truth: too often I'm a better mother at work than I am at home. Of course, at work, no one shouts at me for five minutes straight in what parents universally refer to as an "outside voice." No one charges into my office, hands outstretched, to smear peanut butter all over my skirt or Vaseline all over my favorite needlepoint rug. At work, when someone is demanding something of me, I can say, "I'll call you back" or "Let's talk about that in the next meeting." When people don't listen to me, they do so after they've left my office, not right in front of me. Yet even if shouting and random acts of destruction were to become the norm at work, I probably would not respond with the angry tantrums that punctuate so many nights at home. We have our own form of chaos in the office, after all. I work with creative people—temperamental, flaky, "difficult"—but my job is to be the eye of the storm.

So why this angel-in-the-office, horror-at-home division? Shouldn't the skills that serve me so well at work help me at the end of the day? My friend Chrissie, heroic stay-at-home mother of four, has one explanation: My behavior simply reproduces, in the adult world, the perfect-at-school/demon-at-home phenomenon that is acted out daily among children throughout America. I am on my best behavior at work, just as Owen is on his best behavior at school, but at home we have to ask him seven times to put on his shoes and by the seventh time it's no longer a request but a shouted, boot-camp command. And I am on my worst behavior at home because that's where I can "unwind" after spending eight (or ten, or fourteen) hours at the office keeping my cool.

CONVERSATIONS: THE "BALANCING ACT"
Throughout this essay, van Ogtrop includes vivid descriptions of her hectic days as a mother and a career woman. If these scenes are familiar to you, it may be because popular media often depict such scenes as typical in modern American life, especially for women. For example, the kinds of women's magazines that van Ogtrop herself edits publish articles about how women can balance their roles as mothers, wives, and professionals. In this paragraph, van Ogtrop refers to Arlie Hochschild's book *Time Bind: When Work Becomes Home and Home Becomes Work* (1997), one of many such books published in the 1980s and 1990s as increasing numbers of women pursued careers. Books like Hochschild's are part of an ongoing discussion about the implications of these changes in American society and the challenges they present not only to women but also to the society as a whole. Consider how van Ogtrop's essay fits into that larger discussion and how van Ogtrop herself seems to be participating in it.

Arlie Russell Hochschild has other ideas about this apparently widespread condition. In her 1997 book *Time Bind: When Work Becomes Home and Home Becomes Work*, she writes, "In this new model of family and work life, a tired parent flees a world of unresolved quarrels and unwashed laundry for the reliable orderliness, harmony, and managed cheer of work." At the office, I do manage, in all senses of the word. I am paid to be bossy—a trait that, for better and worse, has always been a predominant part of my personality. But at home, that bossiness yields unpleasant dividends, both from two boys who are now officially Grade A backtalkers and from a husband who frequently lets me know he's not someone I need to supervise. Still, the impulse isn't likely to go away, as long as I remain the only one in our household who knows where the library books/soccer cleats/car keys have gone—and what to

do with them. At home I am wife, mother, baby-sitting and housekeeping manager, cook, social secretary, gardener, tutor, chauffeur, interior decorator, general contractor, and laundress. That many roles is exhausting, especially at those times when my mind is still in work mode. The other night I said to Hugo, "Do you want to put on your pj's in Owen's office?" It's a messy juggling act, and when a ball drops, I'm never laughing.

Last Friday I picked up the cheery note that Owen's kindergarten teacher, Ms. Stenstrom, sends at the end of every week. "We had an exciting morning!" it began. "We finished our touch unit by guessing what was in all the bags—thanks for sending in SUCH mysterious objects!" I had forgotten that Owen was supposed to have taken something interesting to touch in a brown paper bag to school that day. Standing alone in the kitchen, I started to cry. I read the note again, feeling miserable for Owen, miserable for me, miserable for lovely, infinitely patient Ms. Stenstrom. Then I climbed the stairs, cornered Dean, and cried some more. Is that appropriate? To cry for an hour and then have a long, tedious, completely unproductive discussion with an equally sleep-deprived husband about All The Things We're Doing Wrong? How did I turn into this?

* * *

Start with my mother, end with my father. In 1976, when I was twelve, fully two-thirds of all American households that consisted of married couples with children had one parent staying home full-time, according to the U.S. Census Bureau. My mother was one of those parents. With her tuna cashew casserole recipe, I won the 4-H Ready Foods Contest at the Delaware State Fair when I was in fourth grade. From my mother I learned that when you assemble a place setting, the knife should be one thumb-knuckle distance from the edge of the table; when you arrange flowers in a vase, the largest blooms should be at the bottom; when you hem a skirt, you should turn the ends of the fabric under twice. From my mother I also learned that grades are important, that feelings are neither right nor wrong, and that I am capable of just about anything I make up my mind to do.

College, graduate school, first jobs (art gallery, film production company); they all   25
happened without much planning. Along the way I met Dean, and for a few years

---

VISUAL CONNECTIONS: THE CHANGING ROLES OF AMERICAN WOMEN
In this and the following paragraphs, van Ogtrop describes some of her duties as a mother and wife, comparing herself to her father and mother and their roles as husband and wife. Obviously, the roles of women have changed since van Ogtrop's childhood. Examine what these two images might say about those changes. The first image is from an advertisement from 1963. The second is an ad from early 2000. What messages do they convey about who women are? What do they say about the expectations for women in American society?

Bell Telephone System Advertisement, circa. 1963

Secret Antiperspirant Advertisement, 2004

nothing else mattered. Then, when I was twenty-seven, I landed at *Vogue*—and suddenly found myself living on a planet where I spoke the native tongue. Dean left graduate school and got a magazine job, too. Of course, while he and I were fetching coffee and confirming the spelling of proper names (standard duties for editor wanna-bes, for a salary dangerously close to minimum wage), our closest friends were finishing law school and business school and accepting $100,000 jobs and getting pregnant and buying houses. I despaired: we would never have children! never buy a house! never pay off my student loan!

But I got promoted. I got pregnant. By the time Owen was a year old, the charms of our romantic brownstone floor-through in Brooklyn were obliterated by overflowing closets and a litter box in the living room. For the sake of matrimonial harmony Dean allowed himself to be talked into the suburbs (hello! nearly the happiest day in my life!). Our once-minuscule salaries got bigger, our once-mansionlike house eventually felt smaller, but we're still here; our choice has stuck.

I left *Vogue* and had job after job, and as I moved from one magazine to another, this thought formed on the border of my consciousness. It got less peripheral, gradually bigger, until it was large and clear as day: in spite of years of training, I had not become my mother. I was my father, with ovaries. I have his square shoulders and his ease with strangers; I also have his extraordinarily short fuse. Like my father, I am polite to people in the workplace because I am trying to charm them, to win them over—and to be fair, to do the right thing. At work I give people the benefit of the doubt. At home there is no such thing. At home I—like my father—blame first, ask questions later. My mother is the soul of patience. My mother is nothing like this.

I can still arrange flowers and set a table, but I can't remember how my mother disciplined without raising her voice. Where my kids are concerned, I am volatile but deeply sentimental, like my father. I keep locks of their hair, a drawer full of their drawings. And when they're asleep, I kneel beside their beds in atonement for my sins, press my nose to their sweaty blond heads, and ask forgiveness for my take-no-prisoners parenting style.

I work because I have to financially, and because I love to. Like my dad, I get enormous personal satisfaction from career success. But the smoothness with which my career flows makes life at home even harder to manage. Like me, my father is missing the microchip that processes chaos. When his three daughters were small, he would come home from work (by six, in time for family dinner) and pour himself a drink before he'd even taken off his tie. The drink was not a reward for a hard day's work, but a buttress for what he'd face over the next four hours. On a recent visit to our house, while attempting to work an ice maker that had been broken for four months, he announced, "If I lived in this house, I'd have to drink all day long." Ice makers, you see, don't stay broken for four months in his house. My father has a wife.

*   *   *

30   Ah, a wife. Sometimes when describing the work my nanny does to women of another generation who find my life perplexing, I say, "Basically, she's a wife," and wonder if it's horribly sexist or insulting to use that description. Lauren does wash the kids' clothes, make their dinner, help with homework, cuddle after naps. She does not,

however, write notes to the teacher or plan vacations or figure out where we're going to put the hamster Owen desperately wants. And Dean, God bless him, is terrible at those things. I used to think it was lack of training; now I think it's that Y chromosome. Dean is spectacular at spelling Kyrgyzstan and remembering who won the 1976 World Series. Ask him the first name of Hugo's nursery school teacher and he's stumped. Ask him to remember to pick up cat food and it goes in one ear and out the other; on really frustrating days he'll deny ever being told at all (note to self: don't say anything important if the sports section is within ten feet). So there are duties—and they seem to number in the thousands—that fall in the vast gray area that is not-husband-not-nanny, and therefore they are mine.

I come home on an average Tuesday to find the Scholastic book order form submerged in a pile of drawings and Pokémon cards and disemboweled pens on the kitchen counter. I look at the pictures of Clifford paperbacks, boxed sets, games. How many Clifford books do we already have, anyway? Did I order a Clifford cassette the last time, or was I just considering it? Did Dean's sister give Owen a Clifford CD-ROM for Christmas? The questions (unanswerable without a substantial investment of house searching or phone calling) start to jam my circuits, and I think I might burst into tears. I just can't make one more decision. I have a sudden, overwhelming desire to be George Banks, the clueless and routinized father in *Mary Poppins,* when he bursts into the house at six on the dot singing, "I feel a surge of deep satisfaction!" Slippers, sherry, pipe at 6:01. Then: "It's 6:03, and the heirs to my dominion/are scrubbed and tubbed, and adequately fed/And so I'll pat them on the head, and send them off to bed/How lordly is the life I lead!" George at least has a song's length of ignorant bliss before he learns that the children have gone missing. . . .

Unfortunately, the fantasy doesn't quite sustain me as the bathwater sloshes all over the floor and the choice of *Bread and Jam for Frances* over *If You Give a Moose a Muffin* results in fraternal civil war. That's when the exhaustion wins. I call to Dean, who has just arrived home from work, "I can't deal with this anymore!" and he steps in before I really start to yell. I wash my face and brush my teeth and fall into bed the minute I can make a break for it, the millisecond Hugo is finished with his nightly forty-five minutes of getting in and out, in and out of bed. I crawl under the covers like a woman who has walked forty miles through a snowstorm, and remember all over again that—pathetic or not—this really is my favorite moment of the day.

*   *   *

And so there's the guilt. This is one area in which my father and I differ. He has never Wrestled with His Identity as a Parent. He has never, as far as I know, overcompensated for anything. He didn't ever play duck-duck-goose after work, as I did two nights ago, even though it was dark and the grass was wet and I would rather—who are we kidding?—have been inside with a glass of wine. The guilt seems centered on the things I'm missing in my children's lives. I know I miss much, because I feel it: there is a purity to their everyday world that makes my heart ache. When I walk into one of their schools, I feel as if I'm walking into a church; the halls are filled with noble souls who are trying to save the world. I am not of that world in the way that nonworking mothers are—I'm more a frequent visitor—and I suspect that my guilt and sadness about that are part of what makes me so cranky at home.

But my guilt is diminishing as I evolve, and I consider the process of shedding it a significant act of liberation. The older my kids get, the more I'm beginning to realize that they're happy and smart and loving, despite the fact that Mom works. I am trying to eliminate the stubborn fear that children of working mothers grow up to be unhappy adults. I'm making progress, although I'm occasionally derailed by news items like the one I recently saw in the *Wall Street Journal* that described the math scores of children who don't have two parents at home from 6:00 to 9:00 P.M. (Let's just say the chances of Owen and Hugo ever reaching AP calculus are slim.)

35   There's guilt where my marriage is concerned, too, but it's a Mobius strip: guilt and resentment, and more guilt because of the resentment. We are just like many two-career, multiple-child couples I know. I could write a script for one of our arguments and pass it out to half of my suburban neighbors (the 51 percent in my town with working moms); simply change the names and everyone could act out the same neat little domestic drama. Whereas Dean and I used to argue about money and where to live, we now bicker constantly about one thing: who is doing more. Before we had children we were broke but had fun doing effortless activities that didn't cost a dime, like sleeping in. Now we have money but no time together (and, obviously, no sleeping in). We are still partners, but often partners in martyrdom, burning ourselves at the stake on a bonfire of diapers that need to be changed, mittens that need to be found, plumbers who need to be called. We often have a semifight at three in the afternoon to see who is least required at the office and can take the 5:58 train to relieve the nanny. During the week we are rarely, if ever, both home awake with the kids at the same time. Although Dean points out that this is true of most working parents we know, it troubles me that, schedule-wise, we might as well be divorced with joint custody. Because we spend many weekend nights with friends and their children, we eat dinner together as a foursome only about once a week, not five or six times as was the norm in our own childhoods. Is this the worst thing in the world? Is this damaging to my children in the long run? As with everything, it depends on who you ask.

It's these questions without answers that make me insane. Most work questions somehow have ready answers, and when I doubt my abilities as an editor, the moments are fleeting. I doubt my skills as a mother every day. I measure myself against a Platonic motherhood ideal and I'm always coming up short. You could argue that the doubt itself makes me try harder, means I continue to strive. But the doubt is also what makes me irrational, moody, even angry when faced with the chaos that accompanies such fundamental childhood joys as jumping on Mommy and Daddy's newly made bed.

*   *   *

Was my mother ever this angry? It's hard to believe, and scares me when I contemplate it. When I was little, reading a book on the hammock or playing foursquare in the driveway, was my mom actually looking forward to the day when I would go away to college so she could have the house to herself? Didn't she love me more than that?

This, I fear, is how it will be: I will love my children, but my love for them will always be imperfect, damaged by my rigid personality and the demands of my work. I will never be able to share the surprise they feel when they find a cicada in the grass, because stopping to marvel at the cicada means I will miss my morning train. I will never fully love, without qualifiers, the loud, messy place that is the home of two energetic boys. The years will pass, Owen and Hugo will grow, and I will continue to dream about the time I can walk in the front door and feel relaxed.

I will long for a time when I will never yell at my kids just because I am late. Long to be a mother who simply doesn't care that there's Vaseline on my needlepoint rug. To be on my best behavior at home, just as I am at work; to treat my family with the same kindness and respect that I at least pretend to give everyone in my office.

Because before I know it, my boys will be grown. The house will be spotless, and so   40
will I: nice, calm, both at work and at home. Four little feet jumping on the bed will be a distant memory. And things like cicadas will have lost their magic, and my children will be gone for good.

UNDERSTANDING THE TEXT

1. What does van Ogtrop tell us about the kind of person she is? Why is this information important to her main point in this essay? What was your reaction to van Ogtrop as a person, as she presents herself in this essay? How might your sense of her as a person affect your response to her main point in this essay?

2. About half way through her essay (par. 23), van Ogtrop describes a scene in which she breaks down in tears after realizing that she forgot to send something to school with her son. Why is this incident so important to van Ogtrop? What does she mean when she writes at the end of the paragraph, "How did I turn into this?"

3. In what ways does van Ogtrop compare herself to her father? What does this comparison reveal about her as a person? Is the comparison flattering to van Ogtrop? Is it important that it be flattering? Explain.

4. In the third-to-last paragraph of this essay, van Ogtrop writes that she fears her love for her children "will always be imperfect." What does she mean? What solution to this problem does she find, if any? Do you think she is right? Why or why not?

EXPLORING THE TEXT

1. What do the scenes van Ogtrop describes from her family life suggest about her social class and economic status? What might they reflect about her cultural background? Is she a typical American? Would these scenes be familiar to *all* Americans? Explain. What audience do you think van Ogtrop is writing to? What does she assume about her readers' social and cultural background?

2. Do you think van Ogtrop expects readers to sympathize with her when she describes her daily struggles and her sometimes failed efforts to keep her cool at home? Why or why not? Cite specific passages to support your answer.

3. What might this essay reveal about the nature of the kind of love family members have for each other? What might it reveal about love that parents have for their children? About love between two partners in a marriage?

4. In some ways, van Ogtrop's essay might be seen as the price one pays for pursuing a career and trying to raise a family at the same time. What do you think her essay suggests about our society's attitudes regarding the importance of career and family?

ENTERING THE CONVERSATIONS

1. Write an essay in which you describe an experience that you believe reveals some of the challenges of love.

2. In a group of your classmates, share the essays you wrote for Question 1. What kinds of experiences did you and your classmates write about? What similarities and differences can you identify among these essays? How might you explain the differences in these essays? What do you think the essays reveal about our society's attitudes about love and relationships in families?

3. Using van Ogtrop's essay as a primary source and drawing on any other appropriate sources, write an essay for an audience of your classmates in which you define *love*. Alternatively, write an editorial essay for your local newspaper in which you define love in the context of the changing American family.

INFOTRAC

4. Using InfoTrac College Edition and any other appropriate resources, examine the changing role of women in American society and especially the role of women in the workplace. Try to find information about women who pursue careers and raise families at the same time. What challenges do these women and their families face? How typical is van Ogtrop's situation? How typical are the struggles she describes in this essay? What have women done to address these challenges? Try to answer such questions in your research. Then write a report in which you describe the changing role of American women. In your report, present what you learned through your research and discuss implications of the changing role of American women for families, marriage, and the workplace.

5. Review several issues of popular women's magazine such as the ones that van Ogtrop has worked for (e.g. *Glamour*). What do they suggest about the balancing act that van Ogtrop describes in her essay? How do they discuss love and marriage and careers for women? What values regarding family and career do they seem to support? Write a report of your review of these magazines in which you discuss what you found and draw conclusions about how love, marriage, family, and career are discussed in contemporary American society. Alternatively, create a web site in which you present your conclusions.

6. Select a popular television show that you think depicts the balancing act that van Ogtrop describes. Write an essay in which you discuss how this television show presents the balancing act of modern women, and draw your own conclusions about what this show might suggest about the place of women in contemporary society.

In this whimsical, tongue-in-cheek essay, well-known writer Richard Selzer (b.1928) describes love as "an illness" and an "incurable disease." Even if you have never been in love, you will probably understand just what Selzer means. The question is: How? How would you be able to understand love as an illness if you yourself have never experienced lovesickness? One answer is that this idea of love as an illness is a very old one. Literature as far back as the ancient

Love Sick

Greeks contains descriptions of afflicted lovers; indeed, the Greeks gave us the image of Cupid, that pesky little supernatural being who shoots unsuspecting persons with arrows of love. Today, you find the image of the lovesick person not only in literature but also in movies, in popular songs, and even on greeting cards. Selzer gives the image a twist by using medical terms to describe lovesickness. A physician himself, Selzer draws on the language of medicine to paint a picture of his lovesick patient. In doing so, he brings together two kinds of language, the language of popular culture and the language of medical science, to give us a funny, lighthearted way to think about what happens when we are in love.

Richard Selzer is a former professor of surgery and award-winning author of many short stories and essays. Among his books are Rituals of Surgery (1973), Mortal Lessons: Notes on the Art of Surgery (1976), Taking the World in for Repairs (1986), Imagine a Woman (1990), and Confessions of a Knife (1979), in which the following essay first appeared. ◢

RICHARD SELZER

Love is an illness, and has its own set of obsessive thoughts. Behold the poor wretch afflicted with love: one moment strewn upon a sofa, scarcely breathing save for an occasional sigh upsucked from the deep well of his despair; the next, pacing *agitato*, his cheek alternately pale and flushed. Is he pricked? What barb, what gnat stings him thus?

At noon he waves away his plate of food. Unloved, he loathes his own body, and refuses it the smallest nourishment. At half-past twelve, he receives a letter. She loves him! And soon he is snout-deep in his dish, voracious as any wolf at entrails. Greeted by a friend, a brother, he makes no discernible reply, but gazes to and fro, unable to recall who it is that salutes him. Distraught, he picks up a magazine, only to stand wondering what it is he is holding. Was he once clever at the guitar? He can no longer play at all. And so it goes.

Ah, Cupid, thou wanton boy. How cruel thy sport!

See how the man of sorrows leans against a wall, one hand shielding his eyes from vertigo, the other gripping his chest to muffle the palpitations there. Let some stray image of his beloved flit across his mind, her toe perhaps, or scarf, and all at once, his chin and brow gleam with idiotic rapture. But wait! Now some trivial slight is recalled, and once again, his face is a mask of anguish, empurpled and carved with deep lines.

Such, such are the joys of love. May Heaven protect us, one and all, from this happiness. One marvels at the single-celled paramecium, who, without the least utterance of distemper, procreates by splitting in two. One can but envy the paramecium his solitary fission.

Love is an illness and, not unlike its sister maladies, hysteria, hypochondriasis, and melancholia, has its own set of obsessive thoughts. In love, the *idée fixe* that harries the patient every waking hour is not remorse, nor the fear of cancer, nor the dread of death, but that single other *person*. Every disease has its domain, its *locus operandi*. If, in madness, it is the brain, in cirrhosis, the liver, and lumbago, the spine, in love it is that web of knobs and filaments known as the autonomic nervous system. How ironic that here, in this all but invisible network, should lie hidden the ultimate carnal mystery. Mischievous Nature, having arranged to incite copulation by assigning opposite hormones to half the human race, and sculpted the curves of the flesh to accommodate the process, now throws over the primitive rite a magic veil, a web of difficulty that is the autonomic nervous system. It is the malfunction, the deficiency of this system that produces the disease of love. Here it fulminates, driving its luckless victims to madness or suicide. How many the lovers that have taken that final tragic step, and were found swinging from the limb of some lonely tree, airing their pathetic rags? The autonomic nervous system! Why not the massive liver? The solid spleen? Or the skin, from which the poison might be drawn with knife or poultice?

Lying upon the front of each of the vertebrae, from the base of the skull to the tip of the coccyx, is a paired chain of tiny nodes, each of which is connected to the spinal cord and to each other. From these nodes, bundles of nerves extend to meet at relay stations scattered in profusion throughout the body. These ganglia are in anatomical touch with their fellows by a system of circuitry complex and various enough to confound into self-destruction a whole race of computers. Here all is chemical rush and wave-to-wave ripple. Here is fear translated for the flesh, and pride and jealousy. Here dwell zeal and ardor. And love is contracted. By microscopic nervelets, the impulses are carried to all the capillaries, hair follicles and sweat glands of the body. The smooth muscle of the intestine, the lachrymal glands, the bladder, and the genitalia are all subject to the bombardment that issues from this vibrating harp of knobs and strings. Innumerable are the orders delivered: Constrict! Dilate! Secrete! Stand erect! It is all very busy, effervescent.

In defense of the autonomic nervous system, it must be said that it is uncrippled by the intellect or the force of the will. Intuition governs here. Here is one's flesh wholly trustworthy, for it speaks with honesty all the attractions and repulsions of our lives. Consciousness here would be an intruder, justly driven away from the realm of the transcendent. One *feels;* therefore one *is.* No opinion but spontaneous feeling prevails. Is tomorrow's love expected? Yesterday's recalled? Instantly, the thought is captured by the autonomic nervous system. And alchemy turns wish and dream to ruddy reality. The billion capillaries of the face dilate and fill with blood. You blush. You are prettier. Is love spurned? Again the rippling, the dance of energy, and the bed of capillaries constricts, squeezing the blood from the surface to some more central pool. Now you blanch. The pallor of death is upon you. Icy are your own fingertips. It is the flesh responding to the death of love with its own facsimile.

Imagine that you are in the painful state of unrequited love. You are seated at a restaurant table with your beloved. You reach for the salt; at the same moment, she for the pepper goes. Your fingers accidentally touch cellar-side. There is a sudden instantaneous discharge of the autonomic nervous system, and your hand recoils. It is singed by fire. Now, the capillaries of your cheeks are commanded to dilate. They fill with blood. Its color is visible in your skin. You go from salmon pink to fiery red. "Why, you are blushing," she says, and smiles cruelly. Even as she speaks, your sweat glands have opened their gates, and you are coated with wetness. You sop. She sees, and raises one eyebrow. Now the sounds of your intestine, those gurgles and gaseous pops called borborygmi, come distinctly to your ears. You press your abdomen to still them. But, she hears! The people at the neighboring tables do, too. All at once, she turns her face to the door. She rises. Suddenly, it is time for her to go. Unhappy lover, you are in the grip of your autonomic nervous system, and by its betrayal you are thus undone.

Despite that love is an incurable disease, yet is there reason for hope. Should the victim survive the acute stages, he may then expect that love will lose much of its virulence, that it will burn itself out, like other self-limiting maladies. In fact, this is becoming more and more the natural history of love, and a good thing at that. Lucky is he in whom love dies, and lust lives on. For he who is tormented by the protracted fevers of chronic undying love await but a premature and exhausted death. While lust, which engages not the spirit, serves but to restore the vigor and stimulate the circulation.

Still, one dreams of bringing about a cure. For the discoverer of such, a thousand Nobels would be too paltry a reward. Thus I have engaged the initial hypothesis (call it a hunch) that there is somewhere in the body, under the kneecap perhaps, or between the fourth and fifth toes . . . somewhere . . . a single, as yet unnoticed master gland, the removal of which would render the person so operated upon immune to love. Daily, in my surgery, I hunt this *glans amoris,* turning over membranes, reaching into dim tunnels, straining all the warm extrusions of the body for some residue that will point the way.

Perhaps I shall not find it in my lifetime. But never, I vow it, shall I cease from these labors, and shall charge those who come after me to carry on the search. Until then, I would agree with my Uncle Frank, who recommends a cold shower and three laps around the block for the immediate relief of the discomforts of love.

> **STRATEGIES: ADDRESSING THE READER**
> Notice the change in paragraph 9 in the essay to the second person ("you"). Selzer seems to shift from an objective, descriptive point of view to a more personal stance in this paragraph in which he addresses the reader directly as "you." What might he accomplish by doing so?

10

UNDERSTANDING THE TEXT

1. Who is the "poor wretch" that Selzer describes in the opening paragraph of this essay? What exactly is wrong with him?

2. What is the significance of the "paired chain of tiny nodes" that Selzer discusses in paragraph 7? Why does Selzer focus our attention on those tiny nodes? What other term does he use for those tiny nodes?

3. In paragraph 10, Selzer contrasts love with lust. What is the difference between the two, as Selzer sees it? Why is this difference important to his main point in this essay?

EXPLORING THE ISSUES

1. How would you describe Selzer's main purpose in this essay? What central point about love do you think he is making? Cite specific passages to support your answer.

2. What do you think this essay reveals about our culture's attitudes toward love?

3. How do you know that Selzer is poking gentle fun at people in love?

What characteristics of his language choices, his tone, and the details he includes tell you that this is a tongue-in-cheek essay? Cite specific passages in your answer.

4. Examine the medical and scientific language that Selzer uses in this essay. In what ways do you think this language strengthens or weakens the essay? How might this technical language help Selzer accomplish his purposes?

ENTERING THE CONVERSATIONS

1. In an informal essay intended for an audience of your classmates, describe your own experiences with romantic love.

2. In a group of classmates, share the essays you wrote for Question 1, looking for similarities and differences in your descriptions of what it is like to be in love. Discuss what these essays might reveal about our attitudes toward love.

INFOTRAC

3. Is lovesickness an idea that is unique to American or Western culture? Or is it shared among many

different cultures? Using InfoTrac College Edition and any other relevant sources, try to answer these questions in a report intended for an audience of your classmates.

4. Using Selzer's essay as a model, write your own essay describing a person in love. Just as Selzer uses a medical illness as a metaphor for being in love, try to develop your own metaphor on which to base your description of a person in love.

5. Find some descriptions of romantic love in other media. For example, in the 1980s, The J. Geils Band released a song called "Love Stinks" that is a lighthearted complaint about being in love. The popular television series *Sex and the City* examines various kinds of love and the problems inherent in relationships. Identify several such songs, television shows, and/or films and examine the way they portray romantic love. Then write an essay in which you analyze these humorous or lighthearted treatments of romantic love. Refer to Selzer's essay as well. Try to draw conclusions about what these treatments suggest about our society's ways of thinking, talking, and singing about romantic love.

Cheryl, my wife, sometimes tells the story of her grandfather, who died just a few months after his wife died. They were both in their eighties when they died, and they had been married for fifty years. When Cheryl tells the story, she will often say that her grandfather died of a broken heart. He could not go on without the woman he loved so much and spent so much of his life with. I thought about that story when I first read the following passage, in which Mark Doty (b. 1953)

Sweet Chariot

describes the experience of losing his partner, Wally, to AIDS. All of us will experience the death of a loved one at some point in our lives, but the loss of a spouse or partner seems especially wrenching—the more so when it happens as a result of a debilitating disease. Perhaps that's because when two people in love make such a profound commitment to each other, their lives become so deeply entwined that they become almost one. We sometimes hear it put this way: To lose a spouse or partner is to lose a part of yourself. In the following passage, Doty offers a powerful statement about such profound love between two people—in this case, between two gay men. His moving description of the pain that comes with losing such love illustrates the depth of commitment that two people in love can make to one another.

Doty's memoir may challenge our attitudes about same-sex relationships. Its description of the ravages of AIDS may have been what struck many readers when it was first published in 1996, a time when the AIDS epidemic was often front-page news. But years later, AIDS seemed to be less of a focus, and many people in the United States are furiously debating whether same-sex marriage should be legal. As you read, consider how the historical context (continued)

MARK DOTY

I cannot be queer in church, though I've tried, and though I live now in a place where this seems to be perfectly possible for a great many people. Here in Provincetown we have a wonderful Unitarian church, with a congregation largely gay and lesbian, and it pains me a bit to have to admit that when I have gone to services there I have been utterly, hopelessly bored. There's something about the absence of imagery, an oddly flaccid quality of neutrality in the language of worship. I long for a kind of spiritual intensity, a passion, though I can certainly see all the errors and horrors spiritual passions have wrought. I don't know what I want in a church, finally; I think the truth is that I *don't* want a church. My friend Phil has sweetly and politely informed me that it's a spiritual experience for him to be in the company of his fellows, worshipping together at the U.U., and that my resistance to it is really a sort of aesthetic snobbery, a resistance to its public language and marriage of spirituality and social life. I don't want to judge anyone's way of finding a soulful commonality, but nothing puts me less in mind of ultimate things than the friendly

MARK DOTY, "SWEET CHARIOT." FROM *HEAVEN'S COAST* BY MARK DOTY, PP. 17-20. COPYRIGHT © 1996 BY MARK DOTY. REPRINTED BY PERMISSION OF HARPERCOLLINS PUBLISHERS, INC.

(continued) *within which you are reading—as well as your own values and beliefs—might influence your reaction to this passage.*

Mark Doty is an award-winning poet whose collections of poetry include My Alexandria *(1993) and* Sweet Machine *(1998). The following passage is an excerpt from his memoir,* Heaven's Coast *(1996).* ▼

CONVERSATIONS: QUEER
In the first line of this reading (par. 1), Doty refers to himself as "queer." At one time, this term was derogatory and considered an insult to gay persons. But in the 1980s, gay activists began to use the term in a defiant way to proclaim their identity and their right to their sexual preferences. What might Doty's use of the term *queer* suggest about his own sense of identity? Do you think Doty intends the term to be derogatory in this passage?

GLOSS: UNITARIANS
Doty's description of the Unitarian Universalist Church he attended reflects the liberal, open-minded nature of that Christian denomination. The Unitarian Universalist Church was established in 1961 when the Universalists, organized in 1793, merged with the Unitarians, organized in 1825. According to the Unitarian Universalist Association, Unitarian Universalism is a "non-creedal" religion whose members believe that "personal experience, conscience and reason should be the final authorities in religion, and that in the end religious authority lies not in a book or person or institution, but in ourselves."

---

meetings held within my local church's square-boned New England architecture and flourishes of trompe l'oeil.°

Perhaps my discomfort has to do, still, with issues of desire. Wind, glimmering watery horizon and sun, the watchful seals and shimmered flurries of snow seem to me to have far more to do with the life of my spirit. And there is somehow in the grand scale of dune and marsh and sea room for all of human longing, placed firmly in context by the larger world: small, our flames are, though to us raging, essential. There is something so *polite* about these Sunday gatherings of tolerant Unitarians that I feel like longing and need must be set aside. Isn't the part of us that desires, that loves, that longs for encounter and connection—physical and psychic and every other way—also the part of us that knows something about God? The divine, in this world, is all dressed up in mortal clothes, and longing and mortality are so profoundly intertwined as to be, finally, entirely inseparable.

My lover of twelve years died just last month. It astonishes me to write that sentence. It astonishes me that I am writing at all; I have not, till now, and I didn't know when the ability to focus might come back to me. I haven't yet been able to read, and there are many other things I haven't even begun to approach, in the face of this still unbelievable absence. I will be sorting out and naming the things I learned from Wally for years to come, probably for the rest of my life, but here is one thing I know now.

All the last year of Wally's life, he didn't stop wanting. He was unable to walk, since some kind of insidious viral infection which his useless doctors didn't seem to know the first thing about gradually took away his ability to control his body. But he wasn't ever one of those people who let go. Oh, he did, in the sense of accepting what was happening to him, in the sense of not grasping onto what he couldn't have, but he lived firmly in his desires. From the bed where he lived all that year he'd look out onto the street at anything in pants walking by and be fully, appreciatively *interested*. I never for a minute felt hurt by this or left out; it wasn't about me. It was about Wally's way of loving the world. I think in his situation I would have been consumed by frustration and a sense of thwarted desire, but he wasn't. Because his desire wasn't about possession, and his inability to fulfill it wasn't an issue; it was to be in a state of wanting, to be still desiring beauty and grace and sexiness and joy. It was the wanting itself that mattered.

5   A couple of months before Wally died we heard about a couple in the city, one of whom was ill, who needed to give up their little dog, since they felt they couldn't take care of him.

Wally talked and talked about this until it became clear that what

---

°*trompe l'oeil:* French for "trick of the eye," this phrase describes paintings and murals that convey an illusion of structure or space.

he really wanted was for Dino to come to live with us. We already had a dog, Arden, a calm black retriever with a meditative, scholarly disposition, but Wally had his heart set on a new dog who'd sleep next to him and lick his face.

The day that I went to Manhattan to pick up Dino, Jimi and Tony changed their minds; they weren't ready to let him go. Wally was so disappointed that I went to the animal shelter with the intention of finding a small, cuddly dog who'd fit the bill.

What I found was a young golden retriever with enormous energy, a huge tongue, and a phenomenal spirit of pleasure and enjoyment. He didn't just lick Wally's face, he bathed his head, and Wally would scrunch up his face and then grin as though he'd been given the earth's brightest treasure.

Sometimes late at night he'd tell me about other animals he wanted to adopt: lizards, a talking bird, some fish, a little rat.

10 I don't know many men who would want a new dog, a new pact with domestic life, with responsibility, with caring for the abandoned, in the final weeks of their lives. There's a Polaroid I took of Wally with golden Beau curled up and sleeping in our rented hospital bed beside him. He could barely use his hands then—our friend Darren and I would feed him, and give him drinks to sip through a straw—but he's reaching over with his beautiful hardly functional hand to stroke Beau's neck. That is how I will always see my love: reaching toward a world he cannot hold and loving it no less, not a stroke less.

Desire I think has less to do with possession than with participation, the will to involve oneself in the body of the world, in the principle of things expressing itself in splendid specificity, a handful of images: a lover's irreplaceable body, the roil and

CONTEXT: AIDS

Doty's description in paragraph 4 of Wally's physical condition conveys a sense of the effects of AIDS on those suffering from the disease. AIDS, an acronym for acquired immune deficiency syndrome, is caused by HIV, the human immunodeficiency virus. One of the hallmarks of the disease, which was officially identified in 1982, is that it makes patients extremely susceptible to infections by gradually weakening the body's immune system. It is estimated that more than 36 million people worldwide have HIV/AIDS, of whom nearly 1 million are Americans. More than 5 million HIV infections are believed to have occurred since the year 2000.

Scene from *Philadelphia* Starring Tom Hanks

VISUAL CONNECTIONS: *PHILADELPHIA*

In 1993, as the AIDS epidemic was becoming an increasingly important and controversial public health issue, actor Tom Hanks starred in the film *Philadelphia* as a successful lawyer who is fired from his law firm because he is gay. His character, Andrew Beckett, is suffering from AIDS and eventually dies of the disease after suing the law firm for discrimination. The film was nominated for several Academy Awards and generated controversy because of its sympathetic portrayal of a loving relationship between two gay men and its depiction of bigotry against gays. The release of a major film about AIDS and about a gay relationship might be seen as an indication that public discussions of homosexuality had begun to change in the 1990s. Given that Mark Doty's memoir about the loss of his lover to AIDS was published in 1996, it is worth considering the extent to which the historical moment might have shaped Doty's text—and how we might read his text differently today.

shimmer of sea overshot with sunlight, a handful of cherries, the texture and weight of a word. The word that seems most apt is *partake*; it comes from Middle English, literally from the notion of being a part-taker, one who participates. We can say we take a part *of* something, but we may just as accurately say we take part *in* something; we are implicated in another being, which is always the beginning of wisdom, isn't it—that involvement which enlarges us, which engages the heart, which takes us out of the routine limitations of self?

The codes and laws fall away, useless, foolish, finally, hollow little husks of vanity.

The images sustain.

The images allow for desire, allow room for us—even require us—to complete them, to dream our way into them. I believe with all my heart that when the chariot came for Wally, green and gold and rose, a band of angels swung wide out over the great flanks of the sea, bearing him up over the path of light the sun makes on the face of the waters.

15   I believe my love is in the Jordan, which is deep and wide and welcoming, though it scours us oh so deeply. And when he gets to the other side, I know he will be dressed in the robes of comfort and gladness, his forehead anointed with spices, and he will sing—joyful—into the future, and back toward the darkness of this world.

UNDERSTANDING THE TEXT

1. Why does Doty complain about the Unitarian Church he has been attending? How does he explain his uneasiness about the Sunday service at the church? What do his complaints tell us about him and his situation?

2. Why does Doty buy a dog for Wally? What significance does Doty see in how Wally responded to his new dog? Why is this important to his description of his relationship with Wally?

3. Near the end of this passage, Doty discusses "participation," and he explains the origins of the word *partake*. What does this have to do with his description of his love for Wally and his sense of loss at Wally's death? What point is Doty making here about love?

EXPLORING THE TEXT

1. Doty's essay is a statement of his love for his deceased partner, Wally. What do you think his essay reveals about love? Do you think the kind of love Doty describes applies to any couple, whether straight or gay? Explain.

2. In the third-to-last paragraph, Doty writes, "The images sustain." What does he mean by that statement? What does it reveal about the nature of love? And what might it reveal about the role of images—of visual media—in our lives? In answering these questions, consider the many references Doty makes to images in his essay, and examine his descriptions of images, photos, or imagined scenes. What effect do you think these references and descriptions have on this passage?

3. In this passage, Doty clearly identifies himself as a gay man. Certainly, he knew that many people reject homosexuality and that many, if not most, of his readers would not be gay themselves. What effect might that

knowledge have had on Doty's decisions as a writer? Do you think he consciously avoided or included some information because he knew how controversial homosexuality can be? Explain. How did you respond to the knowledge that he is gay? How do you think it affected the way you read this passage? What might your answer to that question reveal about you as a reader?

4. In the final paragraph, Doty refers to the Jordan River, which is located in the Middle East and is mentioned in many stories in the Bible. It is considered a holy river by Christians, Jews, and Muslims alike. What does he mean that Wally is "in the Jordan"? What does he mean that the river is "welcoming" yet "scours us oh so deeply"? Why do you think he ends this passage in this way?

ENTERING THE CONVERSATIONS

1. If you have ever experienced the loss of a loved one—a friend or spouse or family member—then you can certainly empathize with Mark Doty's pain as he describes it in this passage. In an essay intended for an audience of your classmates, write about a time when you have experienced a sense of loss. Try to convey to your readers a sense of the impact that the loss of a loved one had on you.

INFOTRAC

2. Using InfoTrac College Edition and any other relevant resources, examine the current situation with what has been called the AIDS epidemic. What is the extent of AIDS and HIV infection in the United States and elsewhere in the world? Has the situation changed in recent years? What medical advances have occurred recently in AIDS research? What new treatments have been developed? Are the prospects for AIDS

patients better today than they were a decade ago? Try to find answers to these and related questions about AIDS. If possible, interview local healthcare workers or officials who may be involved in AIDS treatment or prevention. Then, on the basis of your research, write a report about AIDS today.

3. Using your research from Question 2, write a letter to the editor of your local newspaper or a regional newsmagazine in which you discuss the situation with AIDS and offer your own perspective on what should be done about AIDS.

4. Write an essay in which you state your position on the issue of same-sex marriage. You may have to do some research to learn more about the current state of the controversy, and you should feel free to draw on Doty's essay and any other relevant sources. In your essay, describe the main issues in the controversy as you understand them and offer support for your own position. Write your essay for an audience of your classmates. Alternatively, write your essay for a wider audience, such as the readers of your local newspaper.

5. *Visual Connections: Philadelphia* on page 241 mentions the film *Philadelphia* (1993). Write an essay examining how this film portrays relationships—not just the relationship between the main character, Andy Beckett (played by actor Tom Hanks), and his partner, but also the relationships among colleagues at the law firm where Hanks's character works and his relationships with his family as well as his relationship with his lawyer, Joe Miller (played by Denzel Washington). In your essay, discuss what this film suggests about such relationships and explain any insights you find in the film about the complexity of human relationships and the many social factors that affect them. Alternatively, write a similar essay about another film of your choice.

One of the most influential Black women scholars in the United States today, bell hooks (b. 1952) is well known for her provocative and unconventional writing about race, gender, education, and culture in well-received books like Talking Back *(1989) and* Teaching to Transgress *(1994). She is perhaps less well known as a prominent student of Buddhism who has written widely on Buddhist ideas about love, relationships, and community. In the fol-*

ON Building A Community OF Love

bell hooks

lowing essay, hooks presents a dialogue with Thich Nhat Hanh, one of the world's foremost teachers of Zen Buddhism, who first gained international attention in the 1960s for his peace activism against the Vietnam War. As hooks tells us in this essay, Thich Nhat Hanh's writings profoundly influenced her own writing, especially her book All about Love *(2001). In this dialogue, she invites Nhat Hanh to explore with her the concepts of love and community from a Buddhist perspective. In doing so, she and Nhat Hanh raise questions about the nature of love among people in a community—questions that go beyond any single religious or cultural perspective. Their examination of Buddhist ideas about love and community can help us think more broadly about what we mean when we talk about love among members of a community.*

This essay can also help us think about how we talk and write about love. The form of the dialogue, which hooks has used in many of her academic books, is as old as Plato's famous dialogues, written more than 2,500 years ago, in which the great philosopher Socrates offers his wisdom by engaging in dialogue with his peers or his students. hooks's dialogues do not follow a strict question-and-answer format but (continued)

As teacher and guide Thich Nhat Hanh has been a presence in my life for more than twenty years. In the last few years I began to doubt the heart connection I felt with him because we had never met or spoken to one another, yet his work was ever-present in my work. I began to feel the need to meet him face to face, even as my intuitive self kept saying that it would happen when the time was right. My work in love has been to trust that intuitive self that kept saying that it would happen when the time was right. My work in love has been to trust that intuition knowledge.

Those who know me intimately know that I have been contemplating the place and meaning of love in our lives and culture for years. They know that when a subject attracts my intellectual and emotional imagination, I am long to observe it from all angles, to know it inside and out.

In keeping with the way my mind works, when I began to think deeply about the metaphysics of love I talked with everyone around me about it. I talked to large audiences and even had wee one-on-one

BELL HOOKS, "ON BUILDING A COMMUNITY OF LOVE: bell hooks MEETS WITH THICH NHAT HAHN TO ASK: HOW DO WE BUILD A COMMUNITY OF LOVE." FROM *SHAMBHALA SUN ONLINE*, JANUARY 2000. FROM THE *SHAMBHALA SUN* MAGAZINE: WWW.SHAMBHALASUN.COM. REPRINTED BY PERMISSION.

(continued) *involve a give-and-take by two people interested in understanding a complicated idea. As you read, consider how this form might help hooks accomplish her goals as a writer. Consider, too, how the non-Western cultural perspective that she and Nhat Hanh take might complicate your own ideas about love and community.*

Born Gloria Watkins, bell hooks is currently distinguished professor of English at City College of the City University of New York. The following dialogue first appeared in 2000 in Shambala Sun Online, *a publication devoted to Buddhism.* ◪

CONVERSATIONS: LOVE
In Chapter 1 of *All about Love* (2001), bell hooks writes, "Imagine how much easier it would be for us to learn how to love if we began with a shared definition. The word 'love' is most often defined as a noun, yet all the more astute theorists of love acknowledge that we would all love better if we used it as a verb." In this dialogue with Thich Nhat Hanh, hooks refers to definitions of love from M. Scott Peck and Erich Fromm, two very popular writers whose work focuses on love and emotional well-being. In doing so, she not only helps her readers better understand her way of defining love, but she also places her essay in the context of a much larger conversation about love and relationships. Consider how that larger conversation, which takes place in books like Peck's and Fromm's as well as in popular media such as television talk shows and films, might influence your reading of this essay.

conversations with children about the way they think about love. I talked about love in every state. Indeed, I encouraged the publishers of my new book *All About Love: New Visions* to launch it with postcards, t-shirts, and maybe even a calendar with the logo "Love in every state." I talked about love everywhere I traveled.

To me, all the work I do is built on a foundation of loving-kindness. Love illuminates matters. And when I write provocative social and cultural criticism that causes readers to stretch their minds, to think beyond set paradigms, I think of that work as love in action. While it may challenge, disturb and at times even frighten or enrage readers, love is always the place where I begin and end.

A central theme of all about love is that from childhood into adulthood we are often taught misguided and false assumptions about the nature of love. Perhaps the most common false assumption about love is that love means we will not be challenged or changed. No doubt this is why people who read writing about racism, sexism, homophobia, religion, etc. that challenges their set assumptions tend to see that work as harsh rather than loving.

Of all the definitions of love that abound in our universe, a special favorite of mine is the one offered in *The Road Less Traveled* by psychoanalyst M. Scott Peck. Defining love as "the will to extend one's self for the purpose of nurturing one's own or another's spiritual growth," he draws on the work of Erich Fromm to emphasize again and again that love is first and foremost exemplified by action—by practice—not solely by feeling.

Fromm's *The Art of Loving* was published when I was four years old. It was the book I turned to in my late teens when I felt confused about the nature of love. His insistence that "love is the active concern for the life and growth of that which we love" made sense to me then and it still does. Peck expands this definition. Knowing that the world would be a paradise of peace and justice if global citizens shared a common definition of love which would guide our thoughts and action, I call for the embrace of such a common understanding in all about love: new visions. That common understanding might be articulated in different words carrying a shared meaning for diverse experiences and cultures.

Throughout the more than twenty years that I have written on the subject of ending domination in whatever form it appears (racism, sexism, homophobia, classism), I have continually sought those paths that would lead to the end of violence and injustice. Since so much of my thinking about love in my late teens revolved around familial and romantic love, it was not until I was in my early twenties writing feminist theory that I began to think deeply about love in relation to domination.

During my first years in college Martin Luther King's message of love as the path to ending racism and healing the wounds of racial

5

hooks is well known for the way she draws on personal experience and adopts a personal voice in her writing, even when she is writing about complicated theoretical topics for an academic audience. In her book *Talking Back,* she argues that "if we are to reach our people and all people . . . we must understand that the telling of one's personal story provides a meaningful example, a way for folks to identify and connect." Here, as she often does in her writing, hooks shares some of her own experiences to introduce her dialogue with Thich Nhat Hanh. Some readers have criticized hooks for this personal writing style. Consider the potential impact of this personal approach on readers. What do you think this approach might help hooks achieve in her writing? What problems do you see with her personal style? What might the difficulties hooks has experienced as an academic writer who wishes to use a more personal writing style tell us about writing in general?

In this section of her essay, hooks explains how two important social and political movements in the United States in the 1960s and 1970s shaped her ways of thinking about love and relationships. She traces a pendulous swing of people involved in the Civil Rights and the women's movements from love to hate and back to love. It might be difficult for us today to understand the intense debates within these movements about how to relate to one's opponents. For example, some Black leaders openly called for violence against Whites to combat the violence of White racism. Some, including Martin Luther King, Jr. disagreed, promoting instead a nonviolent approach based on a belief in equality, justice, and love. Obviously, this experience deeply affected hooks and helped shape her ideas about love and hate. Do you think hooks speaks effectively about these issues to readers who were not alive during the social movements she describes in this passage?

domination had been replaced by a black power movement stressing militant resistance. While King had called for nonviolence and compassion, this new movement called on us to harden our hearts, to wage war against our enemies. Loving our enemies, militant leaders told us, made us weak and easy to subjugate, and many turned their backs on King's message.

Just as the energy of a racially-based civil rights liberation struggle was moving away from a call for love, the women's movement also launched a critique of love, calling on females to forget about love so that we might seize power. When I was nineteen participating in feminist consciousness-raising groups, love was dismissed as irrelevant. It was our "addiction to love" that kept us sleeping with the enemy (men). To be free, our militant feminist leaders told us, we needed to stop making love the center of our imaginations and yearnings. Love could be a good woman's downfall. 10

These two movements for social justice that had captured the hearts and imagination of our nation—movements that began with a love ethic—were changed by leaders who were much more interested in questions of power. By the late seventies it was no longer necessary to silence discussions of love; the topic was no longer on any progressive agenda.

Those of us who still longed to hold on to love looked to religions as the site of redemption. We searched everywhere, all around the world, for the spiritual teachers who could help us return to love. My seeking led me to Buddhism, guided there by the Beat poets, by personal interaction with Gary Snyder. At his mountain home I would meet my first Buddhist nun and walk mindfully with her, all the while wondering if my heart could ever know the sweet peace emanating from her like a perfume mist.

My seeking led me to the work of a Buddhist monk Martin Luther King had met and been touched by—Thich Nhat Hanh. The first work I read by this new teacher in my life was a conversation book between him and Daniel Berrigan, *The Raft Is Not the Shore.*

At last I had found a world where spirituality and politics could meet, where there was no separation. Indeed, in this world all efforts to end domination, to bring peace and justice, were spiritual practice. I was no longer torn between political struggle and spiritual practice. And here was the radical teacher—a Vietnamese monk living in exile—courageously declaring that "if you have to choose between Buddhism and peace, then you must choose peace."

Unlike white friends and comrades who were often contemptuous of me because I had not traveled to the East or studied with important teachers, Thich Nhat Hanh was calmly stating: "Buddhism is in your heart. Even if you don't have any temple or any monks, you can still be a Buddhist in your heart 15 and life." Reading his words I felt an inner rapture and could only repeat, "Be still my heart." Like one wandering in the desert overcome by thirst, I had found water. My thirst was quenched and my spiritual hunger intensified.

For a period of more than ten years since leaving home for college I had felt pulled in all directions by anti-racist struggle, by the feminist movement, sexual liberation, by the fundamentalist Christianity of my upbringing. I wanted to embrace radical politics and still know god. I wanted to resist and be redeemed. *The Raft Is Not the Shore* helped strengthen my spiritual journey. Even though I had not met with Thich Nhat Hanh he was the teacher, along with Chögyam Trungpa Rinpoche, who were my chosen guides. Mixing the two was a fiery combination.

> **GLOSS: THICH NHAT HANH**
> In 1966, Thich Nhat Hanh, a Buddhist monk, was forced to leave his native Vietnam because of his activism against the war then raging in his homeland. He has since become one of the world's foremost Buddhist teachers and peace activists. He established Plum Village in France, a center for the study and practice of what he calls "engaged Buddhism," which has several satellite centers around the world. He is author of dozens of books about Buddhism and about working toward peace.

As all became well with my soul, I began to talk about the work of **Thich Nhat Hanh** in my books, quoting from his work. He helped me bring together theories of political recovery and spiritual recovery. For years I did not want to meet him face to face for fear I would be disappointed. Time and time again I planned to be where he was and the plan would be disrupted. Our paths were crossing but we were never meeting face to face.

Then suddenly, in a marvelous serendipitous way, we were meeting. In his presence at last, I felt overwhelmed with gratitude that not only was I given the blessing of meeting him, but that a pure spirit of love connected us. I felt ecstatic. My heart jumped for joy—such union and reunion to be in the presence of one who has tutored your heart, who has been with you in spirit on your journey.

The journey is also to the teacher and beyond. It is always a path to the heart. And the heart of the matter is always our oneness with divine spirit—our union with all life. As early as 1975, Thich Nhat Hanh was sharing: "The way must be in you; the destination also must be in you and not somewhere else in space or time. If that kind of self-transformation is being realized in you, you will arrive."

Walking on love's path on a sunny day on my way to meet my teacher, I meet Sister [20] Chan Khong. She too has taught me. She felt my heart's readiness. Together we remembered the teacher who is everywhere awakening the heart. As she writes at the end of *Learning True Love,* "I am with you just as you have been with me, and we encourage each other to realize our deepest love, caring and generosity . . . together on the path of love."

* * *

bell hooks: I began writing a book on love because I felt that the United States is moving away from love. The civil rights movement was such a wonderful movement for social justice because the heart of it was love—loving everyone. It was believing, as you taught us yesterday, that we can always start anew; we can always practice forgiveness. I don't have to hate any person because I can always start anew, I can always reconcile. What I'm trying to understand is why are we moving away from this idea of a community of love. What is your thinking about why people are moving away from love, and how we can be part of moving our society towards love?

Thich Nhat Hanh: In our own Buddhist **sangha,** community is the core of everything. The sangha is a community where there should be harmony and peace and understanding. That is something created by our daily life together. If love is there in the community, if we've been nourished by the harmony in the community, then we will never move away from love.

The reason we might lose this is because we are always looking outside of us, thinking that the object or action of love is out there. That is why we allow the love, the harmony, the mature understanding, to slip away from ourselves. This is, I think, the basic thing. That is why we have to go back to our community and renew it. Then love will grow back. Understanding and harmony will grow back. That's the first thing.

The second thing is that we ourselves need love; it's not only society, the world outside, that needs love. But we can't expect that love to come from outside of us. We should ask the question whether we are capable of loving ourselves as well as others. Are we treating our body kindly—by the way we eat, by the way we drink, by the way we work? Are we treating ourselves with enough joy and tenderness and peace? Or are we feeding ourselves with toxins that we get from the market— the spiritual, intellectual, entertainment market?

25   So the question is whether we are practicing loving ourselves? Because loving ourselves means loving our community. When we are capable of loving ourselves, nourishing ourselves properly, not intoxicating ourselves, we are already protecting and nourishing society. Because in the moment when we are able to smile, to look at ourselves with compassion, our world begins to change. We may not have done anything but when we are relaxed, when we are peaceful, when we are able to smile and not to be violent in the way we look at the system, at that moment there is a change already in the world.

So the second help, the second insight, is that between self or no-self there is no real separation. Anything you do for yourself you do for the society at the same time. And anything you do for society you do for yourself also. That insight is very powerfully made in the practice of **no-self.**

bell hooks: I think one of the most wonderful books that Martin Luther King wrote was *Strength to Love.* I always liked it because of the word "strength," which counters the Western notion of love as easy. Instead, Martin Luther King said that you must have courage to love, that you have to have a profound will to do what is right to love, that it does not come easy.

Thich Nhat Hanh: Martin Luther King was among us as a brother, as a friend, as a leader. He was able to maintain that love alive. When you touch him, you touch a **bodhi-sattva,** for his understanding and love was enough to hold everything to him. He tried to transmit his insight and his love to the community, but maybe we have not received it enough. He was trying to transmit the best things to us—his goodness, his love, his nonduality. But because we had clung so much to him as a person, we did not bring the essence of what he was teaching into our community. So now that

GLOSSES

SANGHA

Sangha is a Buddhist term referring to a community or group, such as members of a temple or church. It is also used to refer to larger communities and even to humanity as a whole. Sangha is one of the "three treasures" that Buddhists believe are available to all people; the other two are the Buddha himself and the *dharma,* which refers to the Buddha's teachings.

NO-SELF

When Thich Nhat Hanh writes about "the practice of no-self," he is referring to the Buddhist belief in the fundamental unity of all beings. Buddhist practice is a process of trying to understand the self, through meditation and study, to realize that, ultimately, there is no self but only a unity of all life of which each self is inherently a part. Later, in paragraph 33, Nhat Hanh refers to "interbeing," which is another term for the unity of all beings; in other words, according to Buddhist teachings, each being is inherently a part of every other being.

he's no longer here, we are at a loss. We have to be aware that crucial transmission he was making was not the transmission of power, of authority, of position, but the transmission of the dharma. It means love.

bell hooks: Exactly. It was not a transmission of personality. Part of why I have started writing about love is feeling, as you say, that our culture is forgetting what he taught. We name more and more streets and schools after him but that's almost irrelevant, because what is to be remembered is that strength to love.

That's what we have to draw courage from—the spirit of love, not the image of Martin Luther King. This is so hard in the West because we are such an image and personality driven culture. For instance, because I have learned so much from you for so many years of my life, people kept asking me whether I had met you in person.

Thich Nhat Hanh: (laughs) Yes, I understand.

bell hooks: And I said yes, I have met him, because he has given his love to me through his teachings, through mindfulness practice. I kept trying to share with people that, yes, I would like to meet you some day, but the point is that I am living and learning from his teaching.

Thich Nhat Hanh: Yes, that's right. And that is the essence of interbeing. We had met already in the very non-beginning (laughs). Beginning with longing, beginning with blessings.

bell hooks: Except that you have also taught that to be in the presence of your teacher can also be a moment of transformation. So people say, is it enough that you've learned from books by him, or must you meet him, must there be an encounter?

Thich Nhat Hanh: In fact, the true teacher is within us. A good teacher is someone who can help you to go back and touch the true teacher within, because you already have the insight within you. In Buddhism we call it buddhanature. You don't need someone to transfer buddhanature to you, but maybe you need a friend who can help you touch that nature of awakening and understanding working in you.

So a good teacher is someone who can help you to get back to a teacher within. The teacher can do that in many different ways; she or he does not have to meet you physically. I feel that I have many real students whom I have not met. Many are in cloisters and they never get out. Others are in prison. But in many cases they practice the teachings much better than those who meet me every day. That is true. When they read a book by me or hear a tape and they touch the insight within them, then they have met me in a real way. That is the real meeting.

bell hooks: I want to know your thoughts on how we learn to love a world full of injustice, more than coming together with someone just because they share the same skin or the same language as we do. I ask this question of you because I first learned about you through Martin Luther King's homage to your compassion towards those who had hurt your country.

Thich Nhat Hanh: This is a very interesting topic. It was a very important issue for the Buddha. How we view justice depends on our practice of looking deeply. We may think that justice is everyone being equal, having the same rights, sharing the same kind of advantages, but maybe we have not had the chance to look at the nature

GLOSS: BODHISATTVA
In Buddhism, a *bodhisattva* is a being that, while not yet fully enlightened, is actively striving toward that goal. Conventionally, the term is applied to hypothetical beings with a high degree of enlightenment and power, but as hooks and Nhat Hanh use it in this dialogue, it also refers to people who have made a formal commitment to Buddhist practice and study. Bodhisattva literally means "enlightenment being" in Sanskrit.

of justice in terms of no-self. That kind of justice is based on the idea of self, but it may be very interesting to explore justice in terms of no-self.

bell hooks: I think that's exactly the kind of justice Martin Luther King spoke about—a justice that was for everyone whether they're equal or not. Sometimes in life all things are not equal, so what does it mean to have justice when there is no equality? A parent can be just towards a child, even though they're not equal. I think this is often misunderstood in the West, where people feel that there can be no justice unless everything is the same. This is part of why I feel we have to relearn how we think about love, because we think about love so much in terms of the self.

40   **Thich Nhat Hanh:** Is justice possible without equality?

bell hooks: Justice is possible without equality, I believe, because of compassion and understanding. If I have compassion, then if I have more than you, which is unequal, I will still do the just thing by you.

Thich Nhat Hanh: Right. And who has created inequality?

bell hooks: Well, I think inequality is in our minds. I think this is what we learn through practice. One of the concepts that you and Daniel Berrigan spoke about in *The Raft Is Not the Shore* is that the bridge of illusion must be shattered in order for a real bridge to be constructed. One of the things we learn is that inequality is an illusion.

Thich Nhat Hanh: Makes sense (laughs).

45   **bell hooks:** Before I came here I had been struggling with the question of anger toward my ex-boyfriend. I have taken my vows as a bodhisattva, and so I always feel very depressed when I have anger. I had come to a point of despair because I had so much difficulty with my anger in relation to this man. So yesterday's dharma talk about embracing our anger, and using it, and letting it go, was very essential for me at this moment.

Thich Nhat Hanh: You want to be human. Be angry, it's okay. But not to practice is not okay. To be angry, that is very human. And to learn how to smile at your anger and make peace with your anger is very nice. That is the whole thing—the meaning of the practice, of the learning. By taking a look at your anger it can be transformed into the kind of energy that you need—understanding and compassion. It is with negative energy that you can make the positive energy. A flower, although beautiful, will become compost someday, but if you know how to transform the compost back into the flower, then you don't have to worry. You don't have to worry about your anger because you know how to handle it—to embrace, to recognize, and to transform it. So this is what is possible.

bell hooks: I think this is what people misunderstand about Martin Luther King saying to love your enemies. They think he was just using this silly little phrase, but what he meant was that as Black Americans we need to let our anger go, because holding on to it we hold ourselves down. We oppress ourselves by holding on to anger. My students tell me, we don't want to love! We're tired of being loving! And I say to them, if you're tired of being loving, then you haven't really been loving, because when you are loving you have more strength. As you were telling us yesterday, we grow stronger in the act of loving. This has been, I think, a very hurting thing for Black Americans—to feel that we can't love our enemies. People forget what a great tradition we have as African-Americans in the practice of forgiveness and compassion. And if we neglect that tradition, we suffer.

Thich Nhat Hanh: When we have anger in us, we suffer. When we have discrimination in us, we suffer. When we have the complex of superiority, we suffer. When we have the complex of inferiority, we suffer also. So when we are capable of transforming these negative things in us, we are free and happiness is possible.

50   If the people who hurt us have that kind of energy within them, like anger or desperation, then they suffer. When you see that someone suffers, you might be motivated by a desire to help him not to suffer anymore. That is love also, and love doesn't have any color. Other people may discriminate against us, but what is more important is whether we discriminate against them. If we don't do that, we are a happier person, and as a happier person, we are in a position to help. And anger, this is not a help.

bell hooks: And lastly, what about fear? Because I think that many white people approach black people or Asian people not with hatred or anger but with fear. What can love do for that fear?

Thich Nhat Hanh: Fear is born from ignorance. We think that the other person is trying to take away something from us. But if we look deeply, we see that the desire of the other person is exactly our own desire—to have peace, to be able to have a chance to live. So if you realize that the other person is a human being too, and you have exactly the same kind of spiritual path, and then the two can become good practitioners. This appears to be practical for both.

   The only answer to fear is more understanding. And there is no understanding if there is no effort to look more deeply to see what is there in our heart and in the heart of the other person. The Buddha always reminds us that our afflictions, including our fear and our desiring, are born from our ignorance. That is why in order to dissipate fear, we have to remove wrong perception.

bell hooks: And what if people perceive rightly and still act unjustly?

55 **Thich Nhat Hanh:** They are not able yet to apply their insight in their daily life. They need community to re-

VISUAL CONNECTIONS: ANGER AND ACTIVISM
Throughout this dialogue, Thich Nhat Hanh refers to the importance of love and compassion in dealing with anger and conflict. During the Vietnam War, he preached this same message of love in his activism against the war, even in the face of violence. But other Buddhists took a different path in opposing the war. In 1963, hundreds of newspapers around the world published images like this one depicting a Buddhist monk after he set himself on fire to protest the war. Consider how such a form of protest, which received a great deal of attention at the time, might complicate Thich Nhat Hanh's ideas about the path to peace. How might this historical context have influenced Nhat Hanh's ideas? How might it affect the way you read this essay? Consider, too, the impact of such an image as compared to the written or spoken words of an activist like Thich Nhat Hanh.

© Bettmann/Corbis

Buddhist Monk Committing Ritual Suicide, 1963

GLOSS: SAMADHI
A Sanskrit term for "meditative absorption," *samadhi* refers to a state of mind that Buddhists try to achieve through meditation.

mind them. Sometimes you have a flash of insight, but it's not strong enough to survive. Therefore in the practice of Buddhism, **samadhi** is the power to maintain insight alive in every moment, so that every speech, every word, every act will bear the nature of that insight. It is a question of cleaning. And you clean better if you are surrounded by sangha—those who are practicing exactly the same.

bell hooks: I think that we best realize love in community. This is something I have had to work with myself, because the intellectual tradition of the West is very individualistic. It's not community-based. The intellectual is often thought of as a person who is alone and cut off from the world. So I have had to practice being willing to leave the space of my study to be in community, to work in community, and to be changed by community.

Thich Nhat Hanh: Right, and then we learn to operate as a community and not as individuals. In Plum Village, that is exactly what we try to do. We are brothers and sisters living together. We try to operate like cells in one body.

bell hooks: I think this is the love that we seek in the new millennium, which is the love experienced in community, beyond self.

Thich Nhat Hanh: So please, live that truth and disseminate that truth with your writing, with your speaking. It will be helpful to maintain that kind of view and action.

60 **bell hooks:** Thank you for your open-hearted example.

Thich Nhat Hanh: You're welcome. Thank you.

UNDERSTANDING THE TEXT

1. How does hooks define love? How does her understanding of love play a role in her own writing and in her work as a teacher and a cultural critic? How might your own understanding of love differ from hooks's? In what ways might your understanding of love influence your reaction to this essay?

2. What experiences did hooks have as a young woman that shaped her thinking about love? In what ways did those experiences influence her?

3. Why, according to hooks, was her encounter with the writings of Thich Nhat Hanh, Chögyam Trungpa Rinpoche, and other Buddhist teachers so important in the development of her thinking about social justice and her involvement in the Civil Rights and women's movements?

4. How does Thich Nhat Hanh define *community*? How does he understand the relationship between individuals and communities? What role does love play in that relationship, according to him?

EXPLORING THE ISSUES

1. How would you describe the voices of bell hooks and Thich Nhat Hanh in this dialogue? What role does each voice play? What similarities and differences can you "hear" in their voices? How do you think these similarities or differences might strengthen or weaken this essay?

2. How effective do you think the form of a dialogue is to convey a point or examine an idea? Cite specific passages to support your answer.

3. In paragraph 26, Thich Nhat Hanh refers to "the practice of no-self," which is explained in *Gloss: No-Self* on page 248. Some scholars have pointed out that it is similar to the Christian idea of the Holy Trinity of God the Father, Jesus, and the Holy Spirit. Consider how a reader's

religious beliefs and upbringing might shape his or her response to this dialogue between bell hooks and Thich Nhat Hanh. In what ways do you think Nhat Hanh's references to Buddhist beliefs might help him achieve his goals with readers? What obstacles might his references to Buddhist beliefs present for non-Buddhist readers? How did you react to these references? What might your answer to that question reveal about you as a reader?

4. This essay was originally published in *Shambala Sun,* a Buddhist magazine. Throughout their dialogue, both hooks and Nhat Hanh use many specialized terms from Buddhist teachings, such as *sangha* and *samadhi,* which would be familiar to readers of *Shambala Sun.* Examine the effect of these terms on you as a reader. Do you need to understand these terms if you are to understand the basic points that hooks and Nhat Hanh make about love and community? If you are unfamiliar with these terms, did you find the essay difficult to follow? If hooks and Nhat Hanh had their discussion without using these terms, would the essay have been different in any way? Explain. What might this essay help us understand about the role of specialized language in a piece of writing? What might it suggest about what readers need to know to make sense of any piece of writing?

ENTERING THE CONVERSATIONS

1. In the opening section of this essay, hooks writes about the great influence of the writings of Thich Nhat Hanh and other Buddhist teachers on her. In an essay intended for an audience of your classmates, describe the effect of a book or writer that was especially important to you in some way.

ⓘ INFOTRAC

2. Search InfoTrac College Edition as well as the World Wide Web for

resources on Buddhism and especially on Buddhist ideas about love. Then, drawing on these sources as well as on this essay by bell hooks, write a report in which you examine how love is understood by Buddhism and by Christianity (or another religious tradition of interest to you). What similarities and differences can you identify in how these religious traditions understand love? How does the understanding of love in each tradition seem to affect its religious practices? What conclusions can you draw about religious or cultural differences when it comes to the idea of love?

3. Drawing on this essay and any other relevant sources, write an essay in which you discuss the power of love. Alternatively, create a visual representation (such as a web site or a photo essay) of the power of love.

4. Several films in recent years have focused on the encounter of Westerners with Buddhism. In the film *Beyond Rangoon* (1995), two American women are traveling in Myanmar (formerly Burma), led by internationally famous activist Aung San Suu Kyi, against the military government were violently suppressed. The film examines Buddhist ideas about life and death and is based in part on the notion that a Westerner can learn about life and love by seeing the world as a Buddhist. *Seven Years in Tibet* (1997), based on the famous book of that same title by Heinrich Harrer, tells the story of a German climber trapped in Tibet at the start of World War II. He develops a close relationship to the Dalai Lama and through that relationship comes to understand the world differently. Focusing on these or similar films, write an analysis of how Buddhist ideas are portrayed in contrast to a Western perspective. What do the films suggest about Buddhism? About Western culture? What questions do they raise about culture and community? In your analysis, draw conclusions about how culture affects the way we talk about love.

COMPLICATING
RELATIONSHIPS

R ECENTLY, I WAS SHARING SOME STORIES WITH A COLLEAGUE ABOUT GROWING UP. SHE AND HER HUSBAND HAD JUST MOVED BACK TO HER HOME-TOWN AFTER LIVING IN ANOTHER STATE FOR SEVERAL YEARS, AND THEY WERE LIVING IN A HOUSE OWNED BY HER MOTHER

until they could find a house of their own. She also mentioned that the month before she and her husband moved into the house, her sister and her sister's "partner" had moved out. As we talked further, I learned that my colleague's father lived in a nearby town with *his* partner. Her father, it turns out, is gay—something he revealed when my colleague was only about ten years old. Eventually, I learned, her parents divorced, and her mother raised her and her sister. This all struck me as an unusual family history, very different from my own family's story. But increasingly, what were once unusual and unconventional relationships are be-

> But increasingly, what were once unusual and unconventional relationships are becoming more common.

coming more common. Today, about half of all marriages in the United States end in divorce, which means that there are a great many people who grow up without both parents living in the same home or who grow up in "blended" families—that is, families created when two divorced people with children remarry. You probably know adults who live with their parents—maybe returning home after finishing college. Or maybe you know a single woman raising an adopted child. Or a gay couple raising a family. Indeed, as I am writing this, some states are engaged in intense debates about whether to make same-sex marriages legal.

These developments can challenge our usual ways of thinking about relationships. The debates about same-sex marriage, for example, sometimes call into question our

ideas about *family* and *marriage*. Opponents of same-sex marriage will sometimes argue that these marriages are not natural. Others point out that marriage is a social convention that is as much about economic and legal arrangements as it is about raising families or being in love. Such discussions reveal the complexities of human relationships.

The reading selections in this cluster highlight some of these complexities. David Brooks's essay, for example, is an argument in favor of same-sex marriage, which is likely to remain a controversial issue in the United States for some time. The other readings in this cluster reveal that even the most common and conventional kinds of relationships can be more complicated than we may think. William Jelani Cobb's essay, for instance, explores how marriage among Black slaves in the pre–Civil War American South was tightly controlled and often forbidden, suggesting that the institution of marriage has been used for many different political, social, and economic purposes. Anna Quindlen examines how the complex relationships between a parent and her adolescent children can change over time. And Laura Kipnis asks us to reexamine our society's uneasiness with romantic relationships between college professors and their students. Yet, these four essays barely scratch the surface when it comes to complicating relationships.

As you read these selections, think about the way that we engage in discussions about relationships: What can our language reveal about our values and beliefs? These writers can help us appreciate the fact that when we talk about matters like marriage, we are part of our society's attempts to make sense of the complexities of relationships.

College can be an intense experience, with students and professors often working very closely together. So it isn't really very surprising that students and professors will sometimes find themselves in romantic relationships. But such relationships are usually frowned upon and often expressly prohibited by school policies. Professor Laura Kipnis (b. 1956) asks why. In this provocative essay, she questions policies forbidding faculty members from having romantic rela-

Off Limits: Should Students Be Allowed to Hook Up WITH Professors?

tionships with students, challenging us to reexamine our attitudes about such relationships. As she points out in her essay, colleges are concerned about protecting students from the coercion that can occur if a student feels vulnerable to a faculty member. Professors, after all, have some authority and power over students. But Kipnis thinks the issue is less about protecting students than about regulating behavior. She examines the changing circumstances on university campuses and in our society in general, arguing that our concerns about faculty members romancing their students reflect our general uneasiness about sexuality.

Perhaps just as interesting as her argument is the way Kipnis presents it. As you read, pay attention to Kipnis's writing style and the voice she creates in her essay. In a sense, she is taking part in a conversation about love and sex that people (continued)

LAURA KIPNIS

The burning academic question of the day: Should we professors be permitted to "hook up with" our students, as the kids put it? Or they with us? In the olden days when I was a student (back in the last century) hooking up with professors was more or less part of the curriculum. (OK, I went to art school.) But that was a different era, back when sex—even when not so great or someone got their feelings hurt—fell under the category of experience, rather than injury and trauma. It didn't automatically impede your education; sometimes it even facilitated it.

(continued) *have been having for centuries, but she is doing so in a way that seems very contemporary. Consider whether she is speaking to you.*

Laura Kipnis is a professor in the School of Communication at Northwestern University and a well-known cultural critic. She is the author of Against Love: A Polemic *(2003) and* Bound and Gagged: Pornography and the Politics of Fantasy in America *(1996). This essay was first published in* Slate, *an online magazine, in 2004.* ◪

CONVERSATIONS: FEMINISM AND SEXUALITY

When Kipnis writes that "feminism has taught us to recognize the power dynamics in these kinds of relationships," she is not referring to one specific theory called *feminism;* rather, she is referring to an ongoing set of conversations over the past three decades or so about gender and specifically about the role of women in society. Feminism can thus refer to academic theories about gender, to the women's movement for equal rights, and to a general social perspective on gender roles. Often, feminism refers to a belief that women have been limited in a society defined and controlled by men; sometimes, the term is used more broadly to refer to a critical perspective on power relations among men and women and on the dynamics of gender roles in society. It can be used as both a positive and a negative term. Here, Kipnis calls feminism a "paradigm," which means a broad way of thinking about the world. Consider how her use of the term reflects these many conversations about gender and what it reveals about her own perspective about gender. Consider, too, how those conversations shape the meaning of a term like *feminism* and create a specialized language that a writer like Kipnis can use to make her point.

But such things can't be guaranteed to turn out well—what percentage of romances do?—so colleges around the country are formulating policies to regulate such interactions, to protect against the possibility of romantic adversity. In 2003, the University of California's nine campuses ruled to ban consensual relationships between professors and any students they may "reasonably expect" to have future academic responsibility for; this includes any student known to have an interest in any area within the faculty member's expertise. But while engineering students may still pair-bond with professors of Restoration drama in California, many campuses are moving to prohibit all romance between any professor and any student.

Feminism has taught us to recognize the power dynamics in these kinds of relationships, and this has evolved into a dominant paradigm, the new propriety. But where once the issue was coercion or quid pro quo sex, in institutional neo-feminism the issue is any whiff of sexuality itself—or any situation that causes a student to "experience his or her vulnerability." (Pretty much the definition of sentience, I always thought.) "The unequal institutional power inherent in this relationship heightens the vulnerability of the student and the potential for coercion," the California code warns, as if any relationship is ever absent vulnerability and coercion. But the problem in redressing romantic inequalities with institutional blunt instruments is that it just confers more power on the institutions themselves, vastly increasing their reach into people's lives.

Ironically, the vulnerability of students has hardly decreased under the new paradigm; it's increased. As opportunities for venting injury have expanded, the variety of opportunities to feel injured have correspondingly multiplied. Under the "offensive environment" guidelines, students are encouraged to regard themselves as such exquisitely sensitive creatures that an errant classroom remark impedes their education, such hothouse flowers that an unfunny joke creates a lasting trauma—and will land you, the unfunny prof, on the carpet or in the national news.

My own university is thankfully less prohibitive about student-professor couplings: You may still hook up with students, you just can't harass them into it. (How long before hiring committees at these few remaining enclaves of romantic license begin using this as a recruiting tool? "Yes the winters are bad, but the students are friendly.") But don't think of telling them jokes! Our harassment guidelines warn in two separate places that inappropriate humor violates university policy. (Inappropriateness—pretty much the definition of humor, I always thought.)

Seeking guidance, realizing I was clinging to gainful employment by my fingernails, I signed up for a university sexual-harassment workshop. (Also two e-mail communiqués from the dean advised that nonattendance would be noted.) And what an education I received—though probably not the intended one.

Things kicked off with a "Sexual Harassment Pretest," administered by David, an earnest mid-50ish psychologist, and Beth, an earnest young woman with a masters in social work. It consisted of unanswerable true-false questions like: "If I make sexual comments to someone and that person doesn't ask me to stop, then I guess that my behavior is probably welcome." Everyone seemed grimly determined to play along—probably hoping to get out by cocktail hour—until we were handed a printed list of "guidelines." No. 1: "Do not make unwanted sexual advances."

Someone demanded querulously from the back, "But how do you know they're unwanted until you try?" (OK, it was me.) David seemed oddly flummoxed by the question, and began anxiously jangling the change in his pants pocket. "Do you really want me to answer that?" he asked.

Another person said helpfully, "What about smoldering glances?" Everyone laughed. A theater professor guiltily admitted to complimenting a student on her hairstyle that very afternoon (one of the "Do Nots" on the pretest) but wondered whether as a gay male, not to have complimented her would be grounds for offense. He started mimicking the female student, tossing her mane around in a "notice my hair" manner. People shouted suggestions for other pretest scenarios for him to perform. Rebellion was in the air. Someone who studies street gangs whispered to me, "They've lost control of the room." David was jangling his change so frantically you had to strain to hear what anyone was saying.

My attention glued to David's pocket, I recalled a long-forgotten pop psychology guide to body language that identified change-jangling as an unconscious masturbation substitute. (And isn't **Captain Queeg's** habit of toying with a set of steel marbles in his pants pocket diagnosed by the principal mutineer in Herman Wouk's *Caine Mutiny* as closet masturbation?) If the very leader of our sexual harassment workshop was engaging in potentially offensive public masturbatory-like behavior, what hope for the rest of us!

Let's face it: Other people's sexuality is often just weird and creepy. Sex is leaky and anxiety-ridden; intelligent people can be oblivious about it. Of course the gulf between desire and knowledge has long been a tragicomic staple; these campus codes do seem awfully optimistic about rectifying the condition. For a more pessimistic account, peruse some recent treatments of the student-professor hook-up theme—Coetzee's *Disgrace;* Francine Prose's *Blue Angel;* Mamet's *Oleanna*—in which learning has an inverse relation to self-knowledge, in which professors are emblems of sexual stupidity, and such disasters ensue that it's hard not to read these as cautionary tales, even as they send up the new sexual correctness.

Of course, societies are always reformulating the stories they tell about intergenerational desire and the catastrophes that result, from Oedipus to faculty handbooks. The details vary, also the kinds of catastrophes prophesied—once it was plagues and crop failure, these days it's trauma and injury. Even over the last half-century the nar-

10

STRATEGIES: USING PERSONAL EXPERIENCE
In this section of her essay, Kipnis describes her experience at a workshop on sexual harassment that she attended on her campus. Writers often use their own experiences to help illustrate a point or explore an issue. Compare Kipnis's use of this strategy to the way other writers in this chapter use it (for example, Michael Bérubé on page 278 or Anna Quindlen on page 264).

GLOSS: CAPTAIN QUEEG
Captain Queeg is the main character in *The Caine Mutiny,* a 1952 novel by Herman Wouk about a mutiny aboard an American military ship during World War II. Another character calls attention to Queeg's habit of handling steel marbles that he keeps in his pants pocket.

CONVERSATIONS: NOVELS ABOUT STUDENT–TEACHER RELATIONSHIPS
In paragraph 11, Kipnis mentions three well-known novels that describe relationships between students and their teachers. Notice how Kipnis uses these references to make her point, describing these novels as "cautionary tales." What might these references suggest about how art and literature help shape our ways of understanding issues like relationships between professors and students?

rative has drastically changed. Consider the Freudian account, yesterday's contender as big explanatory story: Children desire their parents, this desire meets up with prohibitions—namely the incest taboo—and is subject to repression. But the desire persists nevertheless, occasionally burbling to the surface in the form of symptoms: that mysterious rash, that obsessional ritual.

Today, intergenerational desire remains the dilemma; what's shifted is the direction of arrows. In the updated version, parents (and parent surrogates) do all the desiring, children are innocent victims. What's excised from the new story is the most controversial part of the previous one: childhood sexuality. Children are returned to innocence, a far less disturbing (if less complex) account of childhood.

Excising student sexuality from campus romance codes just extends the same presumption. But students aren't children. Whether or not it's smart, plenty of professors I know, male and female, have hooked up with students, for shorter and longer durations. (Female professors do it less, and rarely with undergrads.) Some act well, some are assholes, and it would definitely behoove our students to learn the identifying marks of the latter breed early on, because post-collegiate life is full of them too. (Along with all the well-established marriages that started as student-teacher things, of course—another social reality excised from the story.)

15   Let's imagine that knowledge rather than protectionism (or institutional power-enhancement) was the goal of higher education. Then how about workshops for the students too? Here's an idea: "10 Signs That Your Professor Is Sleeping With You To Assuage Mid-Life Depression and Will Dump You Shortly Afterward." Or, "Will Hooking Up With a Prof Really Make You Feel Smarter: Pros and Cons." No doubt we'd all benefit from more self-knowledge about sex, but until the miracle drug arrives that cures the abyss between desire and intelligence, universities might try being educational instead of regulatory on the subject.

UNDERSTANDING THE TEXT

1. What is the main reason that universities adopt policies prohibiting romantic relationships between a student and a faculty member? What is Kipnis's complaint about such policies?

2. What changes does Kipnis see in attitudes toward romantic relationships and toward sexuality as a result of feminism? What problems have these changes brought about, in her view? Do you agree with her? Why or why not?

3. Kipnis writes that she received an education by attending the sexual-harassment workshop at her university, "though probably not the intended one." What did she learn at that workshop? In what sense was what she learned unintended?

4. What is "the new sexual correctness" that Kipnis refers to? In what way does this point support her main argument about university policies prohibiting relationships between professors and students?

5. What does Kipnis mean when she states that university policies governing student–teacher relationships "excise student sexuality from campus romance codes"? In what sense do these policies eliminate sexuality, as Kipnis sees it? Why, in her view, is this a problem?

EXPLORING THE ISSUES

1. How would you characterize Kipnis's writing style? What kind of language does she use? What effect do you think her style is intended to have on readers? What effect did it have on you? Did it make you more or less inclined to take her seriously? Cite specific passages to support your answer.

2. Kipnis briefly discusses humor in this essay, pointing out that jokes with sexual content are considered inappropriate for professors to tell in class. Examine Kipnis's own use of humor. What kinds of humor does she use in making her point? How does this humor contribute to her voice in the essay? How did you respond to her humor? Did you find it effective? Why or why not?

3. Kipnis argues that there is a "new sexual correctness" on college campuses today. Do you agree with her? Why or why not? How might your own experiences and observations of campus life support or complicate her position?

4. In paragraph 3, Kipnis suggests that feminism has influenced our attitudes about gender and sexuality to the degree that an "institutional neo-feminism" has given universities more power to regulate students' sexual behavior. This is a complicated point that requires some understanding of feminism (see *Conversations: Feminism and Sexuality* on page 256). Examine Kipnis's reasoning here. Identify what she sees as positive in feminism as well as what seems problematic to her. Then evaluate her point. Do you find her point a valid one? Do you agree with her? Why or why not?

ENTERING THE CONVERSATIONS

1. Write an editorial for your school newspaper in which you take a position on the issue of romantic relationships between students and their professors.

2. With a group of classmates, examine your college's or university's policies regarding romantic relationships between faculty members and students. Compare its policy to policies at other schools. If possible, interview administrators at your college and perhaps at other colleges for their views about these policies. Try to find out why the policies are in place and the justifications for the specific provisions of the policies. Write a report for an audience of your classmates about these policies, explaining what is allowed and what is prohibited under the policies. Draw conclusions about the appropriateness or effectiveness of such policies.

3. On the basis of your research for Question 2 and working with a group of classmates, rewrite your school's policy regarding romantic relationships between faculty members and students to reflect your views about such relationships.

INFOTRAC

4. In her essay, Kipnis mentions several novels that describe romantic relationships between students and teachers, including *Blue Angel* by Francine Prose and *Disgrace* by J. M. Coetzee. Using InfoTrac College Edition, find reviews of these novels and any other books about relationships between students and teachers. Write an analysis of these reviews. In your analysis, provide an overview of what these reviews say about relationships between faculty members and students, and try to draw conclusions about our culture's attitudes regarding such relationships.

5. In her book *Against Love*, Kipnis writes, "We live in sexually interesting times, meaning a culture which manages to be simultaneously hypersexualized and to retain its Puritan underpinnings, in precisely equal proportions." In paragraph 4 of this essay, Kipnis echoes this statement, offering a critique of what she sees as our society's current attitude toward the treatment of children and young adults. Her critique is consistent with the arguments of some cultural critics who have expressed concern over what they see as a trend toward excessive "political correctness." Consider both sides of this debate and then write an essay in which you offer your perspective. What are the ways in which we, as a society, overprotect our young people? On the other hand, in what ways should we be a little less uptight?

The state of Vermont allowed gay couples to enter into legal "civil unions," which angered opponents of same-sex marriage who believed that civil union *is just another term for marriage. In San Francisco, hundreds of gay couples were married by city officials, igniting a firestorm of protest from opponents of same-sex marriage around the country and resulting in a legal fight that ended with a U.S. court disallowing the marriages. In Massachusetts, the governor*

THE Power OF Marriage

enforced a centuries-old law that seemed to make same-sex marriages illegal in that state, which angered supporters of same-sex marriage. In 2004, some public opinion polls indicated that a majority of Americans were opposed to making same-sex marriages legal, but the same polls often suggested that Americans did not necessarily oppose certain legal rights for same-sex couples. These controversies about same-sex marriage were often portrayed in the media as black-and-white: liberals in favor of same-sex marriage, conservatives opposed to it. But well-known conservative writer David Brooks (b. 1961) argues that supporting same-sex marriage is actually a proper conservative position. His essay seems to complicate the easy, either—or way that the controversy is often presented in popular media.

In considering Brooks's argument, pay attention to how he takes part in the intense conversations in American society about this controversy—and about sexuality in general. Think about how he uses common terms like liberal *or* conservative *and how such terms might convey subtle meanings. Think, too, about how he connects religion and politics. A close look at his essay might reveal why he is such a widely read columnist for the* New York Times, *in which this essay first appeared in 2003.* ▼

DAVID BROOKS

Anybody who has several sexual partners in a year is committing spiritual suicide. He or she is ripping the veil from all that is private and delicate in oneself, and pulverizing it in an assembly line of selfish sensations.

But marriage is the opposite. Marriage joins two people in a sacred bond. It demands that they make an exclusive commitment to each other and thereby takes two discrete individuals and turns them into kin.

Few of us work as hard at the vocation of marriage as we should. But marriage makes us better than we deserve to be. Even in the chores of daily life, married couples find themselves, over the years, coming closer together, fusing into one flesh. Married people who remain committed to each other find that they reorganize and deepen each other's lives. They may eventually come to the point when they can say to each other: "Love you? I am you."

Today marriage is in crisis. Nearly half of all marriages end in divorce. Worse, in some circles, marriage is not even expected. Men and women shack up for a while, produce children and then float off to shack up with someone else.

5 Marriage is in crisis because marriage, which relies on a culture of fidelity, is now asked to survive in a culture of contingency. Today, individual choice is held up as the highest value: choice of lifestyles, choice of identities, choice of cellphone rate plans. Freedom is a wonderful thing, but the culture of contingency means that the marriage bond, which is supposed to be a sacred vow till death do us part, is now more likely to be seen as an easily canceled contract.

Men are more likely to want to trade up, when a younger trophy wife comes along. Men and women are quicker to opt out of marriages, even marriages that are not fatally flawed, when their "needs" don't seem to be met at that moment.

Still, even in this time of crisis, every human being in the United States has the chance to move from the path of contingency to the path of marital fidelity—except homosexuals. Gays and lesbians are banned from marriage and forbidden to enter into this powerful and ennobling institution. A gay or lesbian couple may love each other as deeply as any two people, but when you meet a member of such a couple at a party, he or she then introduces you to a "partner," a word that reeks of contingency.

You would think that faced with this marriage crisis, we conservatives would do everything in our power to move as many people as possible from the path of contingency to the path of fidelity. But instead, many argue that gays must be banished from matrimony because gay marriage would weaken all marriage. A marriage is between a man and a woman, they say. It is women who domesticate men and make marriage work.

Well, if women really domesticated men, heterosexual marriage wouldn't be in crisis. In truth, it's moral commitment, renewed every day through faithfulness, that "domesticates" all people.

10 Some conservatives may have latched onto biological determinism (men are savages who need women to tame them) as a convenient way to oppose gay marriage. But in fact we are not animals whose lives are bounded by our flesh and by our gender. We're moral creatures with souls, endowed with the ability to make covenants, such as the one Ruth made with Naomi: "Where you go I will go, and where you stay I will stay. Your people will be my people and your God my God. Where you die I will die, and there I will be buried."

The conservative course is not to banish gay people from making such commitments. It is to expect that they make such commitments. We shouldn't just allow gay marriage. We should insist on gay marriage. We should regard it as scandalous that two people could claim to love each other and not want to sanctify their love with marriage and fidelity.

CONTEXT: CONTROVERSIES ABOUT SEXUAL PREFERENCE
When I read Brooks's opening paragraph, especially his statement about "spiritual suicide," I could not help think that he was making a subtle reference to the controversial view of some conservative and religious leaders that homosexuality is immoral. Public statements in the 1980s and 1990s by some religious leaders that AIDS, a disease that disproportionately affects gay people, is a punishment for homosexual activity ignited intense reactions in the midst of ongoing debates about sexual orientation. How might these debates influence the way readers will react to Brooks's point here? How do these debates help shape the meaning of a phrase like "spiritual suicide"?

STRATEGIES: ETHOS AND AUDIENCE
In paragraph 8, Brooks clearly identifies himself as a conservative and addresses his readers as "we conservatives." Readers who are familiar with Brooks's writing would not be surprised by such a statement, since he is well known for his conservative views. But this essay appeared on the editorial page of the *New York Times,* a widely circulated newspaper that is generally considered liberal in its viewpoint. As a result, Brooks's address to his readers as "we conservatives" seems somewhat surprising—even intentionally provocative. Maybe Brooks intended it that way, trying to take advantage of his reputation as a conservative. Establishing a reputation among readers is known as *ethos.* It's worth considering how ethos can be influenced by the context of a piece of writing. In this case, how is Brooks's phrase "we conservatives" affected by the fact that he is writing for a newspaper that is generally considered liberal? Would it have the same effect if his essay appeared in a conservative publication?

CONVERSATIONS: RELIGION AND MARRIAGE
In making his argument about same-sex marriage, Brooks makes many religious references. For example, he refers to the biblical account of Ruth and Naomi, women who are thought by many to have been lesbians. He makes it clear that his political stance is conservative, and he closely allies his politics with his religion. The public debates in the United States about same-sex marriage often include religious and moral arguments, and many religious leaders have made public statements condemning laws that allowed same-sex marriage. When the state of Vermont made civil unions legal, some religious leaders called the law immoral. Given the way religion has played a role in debates about same-sex marriage, how does Brooks's use of religious references affect his argument?

When liberals argue for gay marriage, they make it sound like a really good employee benefits plan. Or they frame it as a civil rights issue, like extending the right to vote.

Marriage is not voting. It's going to be up to conservatives to make the important, moral case for marriage, including gay marriage. Not making it means drifting further into the culture of contingency, which, when it comes to intimate and sacred relations, is an abomination.

UNDERSTANDING THE TEXT

1. How does Brooks define marriage in this essay? Do you think his understanding of marriage is widely shared by Americans? Explain.

2. What support does Brooks offer for his assertion that marriage is in crisis? How persuasive do you find this support?

3. What are Brooks's main points in favor of same-sex marriage? What differences does he see in the conservative and liberal positions on this issue?

EXPLORING THE ISSUES

1. Brooks begins this essay with a provocative statement about sexual promiscuity, stating clearly his belief that anyone who has more than one sexual partner in a year is "committing spiritual suicide." Why do you think he begins his essay in this way? What do you think he hopes to accomplish with such a provocative opening? What reaction do you think he expects from readers? How might this opening influence the way readers read the rest of his essay? How did it affect the way you read his essay? What might your reaction reveal about you as a reader?

2. In paragraph 5, Brooks makes a distinction between fidelity in a marriage and what he calls "the culture of contingency," which values individual freedom above all else. In what ways does this culture of contingency weaken marriage, according to Brooks? Do you agree with him? Why or why not? Do you think he fairly and accurately represents the current situation with marriage as a choice between fidelity and freedom? Explain.

3. Notice how Brooks defines the main positions on same-sex marriage as liberal and conservative. Consider whether Brooks's representation of this debate is accurate. Are there really only two positions on this issue—conservative and lib-

eral? What exactly do those two terms—*conservative* and *liberal*—mean here? In what ways might these two terms affect how readers react to Brooks's argument?

ENTERING THE CONVERSATIONS

1. Write an essay for an audience of your classmates in which you state and defend your position on same-sex marriage.

2. Rewrite the essay you wrote for Question 1 for the editorial page of your local newspaper.

INFOTRAC

3. In paragraph 12, Brooks criticizes liberal arguments in favor of same-sex marriage, saying that liberals look at gay marriage primarily as a civil rights issue. Using InfoTrac College Edition and other appropriate resources, find essays by others who promote or oppose gay marriage and consider their reasons for their positions. Try to identify the main arguments for and against same-sex marriage. Then write a report on the state of the controversy, describing the most common positions on the issue and analyzing the arguments

on each side. Try to draw conclusions about how the ongoing public conversations about same-sex marriage are carried on. Alternatively, create a web site on which you present the results of your search and analysis. Be sure to include appropriate links to relevant web sites

4. Consider what this photograph below conveys about marriage and about gay couples. What do you think is being suggested about same-sex marriage in this image? How might this image draw on the ongoing controversies about same-sex marriage to convey its meaning?

5. Write an essay in which you discuss what you believe is the relationship between religious belief and marriage as a legal arrangement. What role does religion play in marriage? To what extent is marriage a legal rather than a religious matter? Try to address such questions in your essay.

6. In a group of classmates, share the essays you wrote for Question 5. Identify the main points of agreement and disagreement among your group members about the relationship between religion and marriage. Try to draw conclusions about the role of religion in marriage in contemporary American society.

First Legally Married Gay Couple in Provincetown, MA, 2004.

© Constantine Manos/Magnum Photos

When I was growing up in the late 1960s
and early 1970s, my mother often gave my
three sisters "permanents," just as Anna
Quindlen (b. 1953) describes her mother
giving her one in the following essay.
Permanents and body waves are usually
done by professionals, but in the 1960s and
1970s drugstores began selling kits for eco-
nomical, do-it-yourself, home permanents.
As Quindlen suggests, getting a "perm"
could be quite a production. I remember my

Say Farewell TO Pin Curls

sisters spending hours in the bathroom, with
towels draped over their shoulders, making
faces because of the nasty smell of the special
chemicals dripping from their wet hair. They
bickered with my mother as she applied the
chemicals and always complained when they
had to get a perm. Perms are not as popular
as they once were, but Quindlen reminds us
that teens and their parents still bicker about
hair and dress styles. What makes her essay
more than just a memory of growing up is
that she explores what these conflicts about
appearance—whether they are over hair
styles or body piercings or clothes—can tell
us about the relationships between parents
and their kids. As a parent, Quindlen now
knows something about those relationships
that she didn't know when her mother was
giving her a perm. She understands how
things like hair styles can play an important
role in one's sense of identity, and in that
regard, I might have included this essay
in Chapter 5 (Identity). As you read
Quindlen's essay, think about how your own
experiences with family and your own sense
of identity might shape the way you respond
to her insights.

Anna Quindlen is an award-winning
writer whose books include the novels
Blessings *(2002) and* One   (continued)

ANNA QUINDLEN

This balmy stretch from Easter until the end of school in June
always reminds me of my mother messing around with my hair. Too
often the kitchen smelled like the wallpaper was being chemically removed because of the fumes from Tonette, the home permanent for
little girls.

Afterward my head looked perpetually surprised. The thick straight
bangs belied the ebullient frizz on either side, so that my face was a
window with a flat shade and ruffled cafe curtains. We all had bangs
then, so that our hair would not be in our faces, a habitual complaint
by the mothers and the nuns. When my hair was in my face my
mother referred to me as Veronica Lake.

Easter, **May Procession,** class pictures, graduation. Pin curls, braids,
ribbons, rollers. There exists not a single photo of significance from
my childhood that shows my head as it was in nature. Occasionally the
day was warm or wet enough to cause the phony curl to release before
the end of the afternoon. This is why I look more or less normal in
first-communion photographs, except for the veil and the hands
prayerfully folded. Sitting here today I can re-create in my mind the

(continued) True Thing *(1996) as well as a number of nonfiction works about issues related to family and gender, such as* Living Out Loud *(1993). She is a regular columnist for* Newsweek *magazine, in which this essay first appeared in 2003.* ◪

STRATEGIES: WORD CHOICE

I love the first line of paragraph 2: "Afterward my head looked perpetually surprised." Here, Quindlen is describing the appearance of her hair after her mother gives her a permanent. We might expect a description of someone's face as "surprised," but not one's hair or head. But Quindlen chooses an adjective—surprised—that we would not usually associate with the appearance of hair. Writing teachers sometimes describe such word choices as "fresh" or "lively."

VISUAL CONNECTIONS: VERONICA LAKE

Veronica Lake was a well-known actress in the 1950s. How is she presented in this photograph? What does this photograph suggest about women? About a woman's appearance, especially her hair? Do you think this is the kind of image Quindlen had in mind when writing this paragraph?

© John Kobal Foundation/Getty Images

Veronica Lake

sensation of bobby pins poking my scalp, the way sleeping on rollers feels like having a shoe box for a pillow. We were groomed then like baby beauty queens.

This is no longer my life, not as a person, not as a parent. I messed with my children's hair only when they were babies, to cut the boys' curls—they cried, I cried—and to secure the weirdly overweening topknot my daughter had for her first year. Still reeling from the counterculture internecine warfare of the late 1960s, I made a deal with myself: no fighting over clothes and hair. (I reserve the right to go ballistic about tats and piercings.) "My hair like Jesus wore it/Hallelujah I adore it/Hallelujah Mary loved her son/Why don't my mother love me?" That was the title song from the first Broadway rock musical, and the question of the time. Fathers threatened to throw sons with ponytails out of the house. What was the point of that?

It is one measure of the **loosey-goosey child rearing** with which our parents sometimes reproach us—"I always let my babies cry themselves to sleep!"—that we have eliminated the barbershop as a battleground. In this way I have acquired a son with a mohawk. I do not like this, although apparently everyone else finds it flattering. Some middle-school boys even wrote a song about it. He has agreed to buzz it back into a more conventional hairstyle in time for the prom.

The prom was the last time I remember letting my mother mess around with my hair. She created a braided bun woven with costume-jewelry pearls and was moved to tears by her skill and my altered appearance. I was luckier than those of my classmates who'd gone to the beauty parlor and came out with immense helmet-hair updos, looking like a cross between the bride and her own grandmother. For graduation my hair hung naturally, long and straight, in my face as I stepped to the podium. I cut it all off three weeks after my mother died, an act not of fashion but of self-abnegation. For a time all my brothers had hair longer than mine. It drove our father nuts.

It occurred to me, looking at mohawk man and his equally unfettered siblings—two atheists, two vegetarians, three writers, three actors, one jock, and all in just three humans!—that there was a sad point to all that sectioning and spraying my mother did. She was trying to ease me, from the head down, into a life of masquerade. A quiet soul who had somehow found herself with a daughter so extroverted that it could be counted as a clinical diagnosis, she must have understood that conformity was my inevitable uncomfortable fate. The conventions of so-called femininity were every bit as rigid, as painful and as false as those manic ringlets that made a brave show until they fell of their own weight. My mother could not have envisioned a future free of girdles and garter belts, deference and duty, perma-nent waves and teasing combs, a future of freedom. But that future was foretold in those boys who let their hair fall to their shoulders, the world according to the Kinks: "Girls will be boys and boys will be girls, it's a mixed up, muddled up, shook up world."

I don't know that it's necessarily easier to take freedom as your birthright, to think if someone looks twice at the cockscomb of hair sprouting above the shaved sides that it's their problem, dude. There are still standards. They are sim-ply looser ones. And there's a tyranny of freedom, too, so that nonconformism becomes the new conformity. But I think this is the better way; a tie, it has always seemed to me, is nothing but a noose with a pleasing pattern. My daughter and her girl-friends all have this trick of making an impromptu bun with their long hair, quick as a wink, and it looks beautiful and un-studied (unsprayed!) and not at all as though they are trying to be miniature adults, which is how I look in so many of those pictures. My boys do their own buzz cuts with clippers they keep in the bathroom. The irony is that I wish they'd let their hair grow longer. But I try to keep my mouth shut. The hair wars, thank God, are over.

GLOSS: MAY PROCESSION
May Procession (par. 3) is a Catholic Church tradition in honor of Mary, mother of Jesus Christ.

CONVERSATIONS: LOOSEY-GOOSEY PARENTING
During the past three or four decades, experts such as Benjamin Spock, Penelope Leach, T. Berry Brazelton, Richard Ferber, and William Sears have sold millions of books with advice to parents about how to raise children "the right way." Sometimes, the advice of-fered by such experts has been controversial and has contradicted traditional attitudes about raising chil-dren. In pagaraph 5 Quindlen offers her own thoughts in the context of this age-old conversation between one generation of parents and the next. In doing so, she reminds us that what we think about child rearing is influenced by historical context, by culture, and by age.

CONTEXT: THE GENERATION GAP
At the end of paragraph 7, when Quindlen writes about a future that was "foretold in those boys who let their hair fall to their shoulders, the world according to the Kinks: 'Girls will be boys and boys will be girls, it's a mixed up, muddled up, shook up world,'" she is referring to the 1960s and early 1970s, when young men began to wear long hair, often in protest against their parents' values and in violation of accepted dress codes. Some observers called this conflict between young people and their parents "the Generation Gap." Today, we sometimes hear about Generation X and how it differs from its parents' generation, which is often called the "Baby Boom" generation, or "the Boomers." These photos re-flect those generational conflicts. Consider what messages can be sent through hair or clothing styles, as in the photos here. The photo on the left shows two contemporary teens. The photo on the right depicts young people at a rock concert in 1969. Consider how the complicated relationships between young people and their parents might be af-fected by historical context and might change—or not—from one generation to the next.

© Margo Silver/Getty Images

© David Hurn/Magnum Photors

UNDERSTANDING THE TEXT

1. Quindlen tells us that she does not like her son's mohawk haircut. Why, then, does she do nothing to get him to change it? What might this suggest about Quindlen as a parent?

2. In paragraph 7, Quindlen describes her mother as "a quiet soul" with an extroverted daughter to whom she tried to teach the conventions of femininity. Why does Quindlen focus attention on her mother in this way? Why does she contrast herself to her mother? How is this contrast important to her main point about growing up and about parenting?

3. Quindlen discusses conformity among teens and what she calls "the tyranny of freedom." What does she mean by that phrase? What point does she make about the social pressures that kids experience as they grow up? Do you think she's right about the "tyranny of conformity"? Why or why not?

EXPLORING THE ISSUES

1. Quindlen draws on memories of her childhood as a girl raised in a Catholic family. How does Quindlen's upbringing as a Catholic shape her sense of her identity? In what ways might this essay differ if she had been raised as a Jew or Muslim or atheist? Do Quindlen's insights about parent-teen relationships depend on her upbringing as a Catholic? Or do you think they apply regardless of one's religious or cultural background? Explain.

2. In paragraph 4, Quindlen writes that she will not fight with her children about clothes and hair. But then she makes the following statement, which she places in parentheses: "I reserve the right to go ballistic about tats and piercings." Why do you think she includes this

statement about tattoos and body piercings? How are those different from hairstyles and clothes? Do you think this statement strengthens or weakens Quindlen's argument? Explain.

3. Quindlen writes about her experiences as a daughter growing up in the 1960s, and she describes some of her experiences with her own son and daughter. How might her experiences have differed from a boy's experiences? Do you think Quindlen adequately accounts for gender in her discussion of the relationships between generations? Explain.

4. As the reading's introduction indicates, this essay was first published in *Newsweek,* a weekly magazine with a large and diverse audience. Who do you think Quindlen believes is in that audience? What kind of readers do you think she is addressing in this essay? Cite specific passages to support your answer.

ENTERING THE CONVERSATIONS

1. Write an essay for an audience of your classmates about an experience in which you have had some kind of conflict with your parents or other important adults in your life who are of an older generation. Tell the story of that conflict in a way that might help your readers gain insight into relationships.

2. In a group of classmates, share the essays you wrote for Question 2. Compare the experiences you each wrote about and try to identify the similarities and differences among those experiences. What might the experiences of your group suggest about relationships between parents and children? Between people of different generations? How might factors such as religious upbringing, racial or ethnic identity, or gender influence these relationships?

INFOTRAC

3. Using InfoTrac College Edition or other appropriate resources, look for contemporary articles or books about raising children today. In particular, try to find articles in newspapers or magazines intended specifically for parents and try to find reviews of books about parenting. Review these materials to get a sense of the main perspectives in American culture today about raising children. What are the important questions and challenges that parents face today? What kinds of advice and support do they receive? Then write a report on the basis of your research, drawing conclusions regarding attitudes about raising children in our culture today. Alternatively, explore differences in attitudes toward child rearing in different cultures. How do views about raising children in American culture differ from views in other cultures? Write a report describing those differences.

4. On the basis of your research for Question 3, create a pamphlet addressed to parents with advice on raising their children today. Alternatively, create a web site with advice for parents. Be sure to pay attention to the design of your site (see Chapter 2 in this book).

5. Write an essay for a general audience (such as readers of your local newspaper) based on your own experience in which you offer your perspective on parent-child relationships, particularly regarding a child's independence from his or her parents.

6. Rewrite Quindlen's essay from the point of view of her child.

Western culture has many stories of forbidden love. In high school, you may have read Shakespeare's Romeo and Juliet, *perhaps the most famous story of forbidden love. Many popular films are based on this same theme. Often, in considering such stories, we focus on the depth of love between the two main characters and on their great efforts to overcome obstacles to their love. In Shakespeare's famous play, for example, Romeo and Juliet risk losing their families*

THE *Other* L-Word

and even their lives to be together. Yet, a closer look at these stories reveals that things may be more complicated than they seem. Romeo and Juliet fall in love against the backdrop of a complex social and political scene. In this sense, Shakespeare's play isn't just about the intensity of romantic love; it is also about how relationships can be deeply influenced by circumstances that can even determine whether two people can be together. In the same way, the following essay by historian William Jelani Cobb explores how historical context can affect love and family. Cobb focuses on Black slaves in the American South before the Civil War. In describing the great legal, cultural, and practical obstacles that slaves had to overcome to be with their loved ones, Cobb reminds us that even something that seems as straightforward as love between two people must be understood in terms of the broader circumstances surrounding a relationship. In this case, forbidden love takes on great political, cultural, and racial significance.

William Jelani Cobb is an assistant professor of history at Spelman College. This essay was first published in 2004 at Africana.com. ▼

WILLIAM JELANI COBB

They have been together for a millennium—or at least look as if they have. They are seated beside each other, arms touching, him shoeless and her head wrapped in cloth and God only knows what they've seen. They are barely past the bitter years of slavery and to tell the truth, it's still hard to tell the difference. The photograph is grainy and slightly out of focus, but you can still make out the weathered lines of years and experience on their faces. And you can still sense the connection forged of those years.

The picture speaks of a quiet fortitude, togetherness in the crucible of slavery, an intimacy that is rarely seen in our discussions of black history.

Sometimes it seems like there's a civil war going on between black men and black women. It's ironic that Valentine's Day takes place during Black History Month, but those two events manage to overlap without ever coinciding—as if there is no love or romance within our collective history in this country. We know of husbands sold away from wives and wives taken from husbands to face the sexual ex-

WILLIAM JELANI COBB, "THE OTHER L-WORD." REPRINTED BY KIND PERMISSION OF THE AUTHOR.

ploitation of white overseers. We know of black men and women who were bred like livestock.

But what we rarely speak of is love in the context of adversity.

The question goes loudly unasked: who needed love more than the enslaved? Beyond the uprisings and the daily resistance, outside of the escapes, arsons and thefts, the most subversive act committed by enslaved black people may have been daring to love each other. The ten-plus generations of black men and women who lived through the ordeal of slavery went to extraordinary lengths to give meaning to their own lives, to construct relationships that might, if only momentarily, dull the pain of forced servitude, to care for others in a society which sought to make black love a contradiction in terms. And that reality is all but lost in our present love deficit.

Filtered through lens of popular media, it seems like there's a **civil war going on between black men and black women.** African Americans are the least likely segment of the population to marry and have a divorce rate that exceeds fifty percent. We are also far less likely to remarry after a divorce than members of other groups. Black radio's airwaves are congested with loveless ballads; rappers boldly declare themselves love-proof—and thereby pain-proof—and disgruntled sirens sing songs of fiscal obligation. In an era where baby-daddies and baby-mamas replace husbands and wives, it's easy to see the destructive legacy of slavery, segregation, incarceration playing itself out. But that's only half of the history— and we've never needed to hear the other side of the story more urgently.

The truth is that marriage and family were extremely important to enslaved black people—despite the obvious difficulties that confronted their relationships. Slave marriages were given no legal recognition, but slaves constructed binding traditions of their own. In addition to **"jumping the broom,"** they also presented each other with blankets whose acceptance indicated that they were now considered married within the community. Others, who could not find a willing clergyman or who had been denied permission to marry, simply married themselves. Still, recognition of their union was important enough that ex-slaves besieged the Freedman's Bureau with requests for marriage ceremonies after emancipation. Three Mississippi counties accounted for 4627 marriages in a single year. The end of slavery also brought with it literally thousands of black people wandering throughout the South in search of husbands and wives who had been sold away from them.

Prior to emancipation, individuals went to great lengths to maintain their relationships. One of the most common causes of slave escapes was to see loved ones on distant plantations. One man set out before sunrise each Sunday morning and walked the entire day to spend a few hours with his wife before having to walk back in time to begin the next day's work. George Sally, enslaved on a sugar plantation in

---

STRATEGIES: VISUAL DESCRIPTION
In the opening paragraph, Cobb describes an old photograph. Initially, he doesn't explicitly tell us that the photo depicts two elderly former slaves who are apparently married or in love, but we can figure that out as we read further. It is not unusual for writers to include vivid descriptions in an essay to help make a point or highlight an event or activity. Here, though, Cobb is describing a photograph as if it were a scene he might be witnessing. Consider what his description might accomplish in his essay. Consider, too, why he might have included this verbal description instead of the photograph itself.

CONVERSATIONS: BLACK MEN VS. BLACK WOMEN
Cobb states at the beginning of paragraph 6, "Filtered through lens of popular media, it seems like there's a civil war going on between black men and black women." Here, he is referring to films, television shows, books, and articles that suggest a strain in relationships between Black men and women in American society. Popular films like *Waiting to Exhale* (1995) depict Black women as dissatisfied with the state of the romantic relationships they have with Black men. Other films, such as *Jungle Fever* (1991) and *Mississippi Masala* (1991), portray the criticism Black men are sometimes subject to when they become romantically involved with women who are not Black. Notice how Cobb uses this larger conversation about Black male-female relationships to introduce his discussion about the importance of romantic love among Black slaves in the United States before the Civil War. Consider, too, how these conversations shape the meaning of Cobb's essay.

VISUAL CONNECTIONS: "JUMPING THE BROOM"

"Jumping the broom" (par. 7) is a ritual that some scholars believe developed because marriages among slaves were not allowed. The slave couple who were marrying stood together next to a broom laid on the ground in front of them and jumped over the broom, which symbolized their new life together and the "sweeping away" of their old ones. This ritual has regained popularity in recent years among Black couples. Consider how this ritual is depicted in these images. What aspects of marriage are portrayed or emphasized in each?

Levon Lewis, *Jumping the Broom*

Modern Day Couple Practicing the Jumping the Broom Ritual

Louisiana, ignored the slaveholder's demands and left to visit his wife—an offense for which he was arrested. (He later stated that he did not mind being arrested for seeing his wife.) Others risked their lives to protect their spouses. While sexual exploitation of married black women by overseers was a constant concern, it was not unheard of for husbands to kill whites who had attacked their wives. One unnamed slave attacked an overseer who had attempted to whip his wife and was himself forced to flee into the woods for eleven months.

William Grose, a slave in Loudon County, Virginia, married a free black woman—against the wishes of the plantation owner, who feared that she might help him escape. William was sold to a widower in New Orleans, who demanded that he take another woman as his wife. He wrote in his autobiography, "I was scared half to death, for I had one wife whom I liked and didn't want another." The couple managed to remain in contact and his wife traveled to New Orleans and found work as a domestic in the family that had bought William. When their relationship was discovered, she was forced to leave New Orleans. Incredibly, William devised a plan to escape and fled to Canada where he and his wife were reunited.

Some black couples managed, despite all odds, to construct long, close-knit   10
unions. In the 1930s, Barbara, a woman who was born into slavery in North Carolina,
told an interviewer the story of how she had met her husband Frank:

> I seen Frank a few times at the Holland's Methodist Church . . . After a while
> Frank becomes a butcher and he was doing pretty good . . . so he comes to
> see me and we courts for a year. We was sitting in the kitchen at the house
> when he asks me to have him. He told me that he knows that he wasn't wor-
> thy, but that he loved me and that he'd do anything he could to please me
> and that he'd always be good to me. When I was fourteen when I got mar-
> ried and when I was fifteen my oldest daughter was born. I had three after
> her and Frank was as proud of them as could be. We was happy. We lived to-
> gether fifty-four years and we was always happy, having only a little bit of ar-
> gument.

Lucy Dunn, who had also been a slave in North Carolina, told a similar tale:

> It was in the little Baptist church where I first seen Jim Dunn and I fell in
> love with him then, I reckons. He said that he loved me then too, but it was
> three Sundays 'fore he asked to see me home. We walked that mile home in
> front of my mother and I was so happy that I ain't thought it was even a half
> mile. We ate cornbread and turnips for dinner and it was night before he
> went home. Mother wouldn't let me walk with him to the gate, so I just sat
> there on the porch and said goodnight.

> He come over every Sunday for a year and finally he proposed. That Sunday
> night I did walk with Jim to the gate and stood under the honeysuckles that
> was smelling so sweet. I heard the big old bullfrogs a-croakin' by the river
> and the whipper-wills a hollerin' in the woods. There was a big yellow moon
> and I reckon Jim did love me. Anyhow, he said so and asked me to marry
> him and he squeezed my hand.

She told her suitor that she would have to think about his proposal. She and her
mother spent the week discussing the seriousness of marriage. Lucy told her mother
that she understood but, "I intends to make a go of it anyhow."

"On Sunday my mother told Jim and you ought to have seen that black boy grin."
They were married a week later. "We lived together fifty-five years and we always loved
each other . . . we had our fusses and our troubles, but we trusted in the lord and we
got through." The old woman wiped away tears as she spoke of her husband. "I loved
him during life and I love him now, though he's been dead for twelve years. I thinks
of him all the time, but it seems like we're young again when I smell honeysuckles or
see a yellow moon."

One hundred and thirty-nine years past slavery, we may have something left to
learn from those enslaved generations. Near the end of her interview, Barbara spoke
a truth that may be more valid now than when she first said it: "My mother died near
twenty years ago and father died four years later. He had not cared to live since
mother left him. I've heard some of the young people laugh about slave love, but
they should envy the love which kept mother and father so close together in life and
even held them in death."

UNDERSTANDING THE TEXT

1. Why does Cobb state that "the most subversive act committed by enslaved black people may have been daring to love each other"? In what ways would love between two slaves have been "subversive"? What do you think this subversiveness suggests about love and marriage?

2. In what specific ways were marriage and family important to slaves, according to Cobb?

3. What do we learn in this essay about the difficulties slaves encountered in trying to maintain loving family relationships? In what ways are these difficulties important to Cobb's main point?

4. What lessons does Cobb draw from the stories he shares about romantic love between slaves? Do you think these lessons are reasonable ones based on the stories he shares? Explain.

EXPLORING THE ISSUES

1. Cobb includes excerpts from narratives by slaves and anecdotes about relationships between slaves. What purposes do these excerpts and anecdotes serve? What does Cobb accomplish by including them? In what ways do you think they strengthen or weaken his essay?

2. In paragraph 6, Cobb refers to popular media portrayals of relationships between Black men and women. (See *Conversations: Black Men vs. Black Women* on page 269.) In the same paragraph, he writes, "We are also far less likely to re-marry after a divorce than members of other groups." Who is the "we" in this sentence? What might it suggest about Cobb's audience? About him? Do you think you are part of Cobb's intended audience? Explain.

3. What do you think Cobb's essay suggests about the nature of love? What might it suggest about the role of race and culture in romantic and family relationships? About the way laws affect such relationships?

ENTERING THE CONVERSATIONS

1. Interview several married couples you know about the circumstances of their relationships. Try to identify any obstacles they may have faced, no matter how small, to their relationship. Then write a report for your classmates in which you tell the stories of the couples you have interviewed and explain the circumstances surrounding their relationships. In your report, try to identify any common problems the couples faced and draw conclusions about some of the factors that can influence a relationship.

INFOTRAC

2. Using InfoTrac College Edition, the Internet, and any other relevant resources, research the laws concerning marriage in the United States or in other nations. Look into the history of such laws. What are the legal restrictions on marriage? What specific aspects of a relationship do laws seem to affect? For example, do they affect a couple's financial status, professional life, or family situations? How might these laws affect different people differently? In other words, do the laws apply differently to people of different races, ages, or ethnic backgrounds? Do they differ for men and women? Do they allow for same-sex relationships? What are the implications of these laws for people in love? Try to answer such questions in your research. Then write a report on the basis of your research.

3. Write an essay analyzing the portrayal of romantic love in one or more popular films that focus on troubled or forbidden relationships (for example, *Mississippi Masala, Jungle Fever, Lolita*). How do these films depict romantic love? What do they reveal about our society's attitudes regarding love and marriage? Try to address such questions, drawing your own conclusions about the nature of the relationships.

4. Select several contemporary songs that address obstacles to romantic relationships. Write a review of these songs in which you discuss what they seem to suggest about the nature of love. Alternatively, write your own song about forbidden love.

RETHINKING RELATIONSHIPS

ONCE HEARD SOMEONE SAY THAT YOU'LL UNDERSTAND YOUR PARENTS BETTER ONCE YOU HAVE CHILDREN OF YOUR OWN. IF THAT'S TRUE, IT'S PROBABLY BECAUSE HAVING CHILDREN PROMPTS PARENTS TO RETHINK THE RELATIONSHIPS BETWEEN PARENTS AND CHILDREN.

The three essays in this cluster ask you to rethink the perspectives on relationships presented in the essays in the two previous clusters in this chapter—just as new parents may rethink their relationships with their own parents. I decided to create this cluster after rereading the essays in the first two clusters and realizing that there was much more to say about relationships. The conversations we are always having in our society about relationships often include perspectives that challenge conventional wisdom. In an important way, that's how attitudes and beliefs can be changed.

> The conversations we are always having in our society about relationships often include perspectives that challenge conventional wisdom.

Judy Syfers Brady's essay, "Why I Want a Wife," is a good example. In that essay, Brady pushes her readers to take a hard look at the roles of husband and wife in a conventional marriage. And it's pretty clear that she doesn't like what she sees. She wants us to reconsider the way we typically think about husbands and wives. You may disagree, but there's no doubt that many Americans see those roles much differently now than they did in the early 1970s when Brady's essay was first published. And it's perspectives like Brady's that helped change our collective minds.

Michael Bérubé's essay is also a kind of reexamination of another essay in this chapter: Laura Kipnis's. He takes up the issue of relationships between college professors and their students, about which Kipnis writes in the second cluster. But unlike Kipnis, Bérubé isn't interested in romantic relationships. Instead, he wants us to look carefully at the teacher-student relationship as it plays out in the classroom. His story of one especially challenging student reveals how complex that teacher-student relationship can be. And in the final essay of this cluster, Peter Sauer directs our attention to a different kind of relationship: our relationship with the natural world and its nonhuman inhabitants. In asking us to look at how we relate to that nonhuman world, he offers some lessons about our relationships with each other.

What I like about this cluster is that the three essays continue the larger conversations about relationships that we are always having, but they do so in ways that won't let us off the hook. Their unusual perspectives don't let us get too comfortable with our own thinking about what relationships are and what they should be. And they help us see why there always seems to be another way to look at our relationships. In this sense, this final cluster is a good example of how writing can be much more than a means of communication; it is also a means of rethinking who we are and reexamining the world around us.

This essay, which was published in the in-augural issue of Ms. *magazine in 1971, is one of the most widely reprinted essays ever written. It shows up in countless college writing textbooks, in books about women's is-sues, on feminist web sites, and in speeches about gender and women's rights. I first came across the essay in the early 1980s, when I was a new writing teacher. When I first assigned it to my students, it sparked the most intense discussion we had all se-*

Why I Want A Wife

mester. Twenty years later, I am still using the essay in some of my classes, and the dis-cussions it provokes are just as intense as that first one. The obvious question is: Why? What is it about this essay that has made it so interesting, engaging, and provocative to readers for so many years? I won't answer that question because I'm sure you'll come up with your own answers. But I will ask you to think about whether this is the same essay today that it was in 1971, when the women's rights movement was just gaining momentum and feminism was a relatively new (and challenging) way of thinking about gender for most Americans. It's rare for an essay to stay relevant for so many years, but this one seems to have remained so. Is that because the essay is just a good piece of writing? Or is it because the issues it addresses and the questions it raises are just as important today as they were in the 1970s? Obviously, readers still find the es-say engaging, but are they reading it the same way today as readers read it in 1971? Keep those questions in mind as you read.

Judy Syfers Brady (b. 1937) continues to write today, focusing much of her atten-tion on cancer and advocating for cancer patients. ▼

JUDY SYFERS BRADY

I belong to that classification of people known as wives. I am A Wife. And, not altogether incidentally, I am a mother.

Not too long ago a male friend of mine appeared on the scene fresh from a recent divorce. He had one child, who is, of course, with his ex-wife. He is looking for another wife. As I thought about him while I was ironing one evening, it suddenly occurred to me that I, too, would like to have a wife. Why do I want a wife?

I would like to go back to school so that I can become economically independent, support myself, and if need be, support those depen-dent upon me. I want a wife who will work and send me to school. And while I am going to school I want a wife to take care of my chil-dren. I want a wife to keep track of the children's doctor and dentist appointments. And to keep track of mine, too. I want a wife to make sure my children eat properly and are kept clean. I want a wife who will wash the children's clothes and keep them mended. I want a wife who is a good nurturing attendant to my children, who arranges for their schooling, makes sure that they have an adequate social life with

JUDY SYFERS BRADY "WHY I WANT A WIFE." FROM "WHY I WANT A WIFE" BY JUDY BRADY (SYFERS). MS. MAGAZINE (1973). REPRINTED BY PERMISSION OF THE AUTHOR.

their peers, takes them to the park, the zoo, etc. I want a wife who takes care of the children when they are sick, a wife who arranges to be around when the children need special care, because, of course, I cannot miss classes at school. My wife must arrange to lose time at work and not lose the job. It may mean a small cut in my wife's income from time to time, but I guess I can tolerate that. Needless to say, my wife will arrange and pay for the care of the children while my wife is working.

I want a wife who will take care of my physical needs. I want a wife who will keep my house clean. A wife who will pick up after my children, a wife who will pick up after me. I want a wife who will keep my clothes clean, ironed, mended, replaced when need be, and who will see to it that my personal things are kept in their proper place so that I can find what I need the minute I need it. I want a wife who cooks the meals, a wife who is a good cook. I want a wife who will plan the menus, do the necessary grocery shopping, prepare the meals, serve them pleasantly, and then do the cleaning up while I do my studying. I want a wife who will care for me when I am sick and sympathize with my pain and loss of time from school. I want a wife to go along when our family takes a vacation so that someone can continue to care for me and my children when I need a rest and change of scene.

5   I want a wife who will not bother me with rambling complaints about a wife's duties. But I want a wife who will listen to me when I feel the need to explain a rather difficult point I have come across in my course of studies. And I want a wife who will type my papers for me when I have written them.

I want a wife who will take care of the details of my social life. When my wife and I are invited out by my friends, I want a wife who takes care of the baby-sitting arrangements. When I meet people at school that I like and want to entertain, I want a wife who will have the house clean, will prepare a special meal, serve it to me and my friends, and not interrupt when I talk about things that interest me and my friends. I want a wife who will have arranged that the children are fed and ready for bed before my guests arrive so that the children do not bother us. I want a wife who takes care of the needs of my guests so that they feel comfortable, who makes sure that they have an ashtray, that they are passed the hors d'oeuvres, that they are offered a second helping of the food, that their wine glasses are replenished when necessary, that their coffee is served to them as they like it. And I want a wife who knows that sometimes I need a night out by myself.

I want a wife who is sensitive to my sexual needs, a wife who makes love passionately and eagerly when I feel like it, a wife who makes sure that I am satisfied. And, of course, I want a wife who will not demand sexual attention when I am not in the mood for it. I want a wife who assumes the complete responsibility for birth control, because I do not want more children. I want a wife who will remain sexually faithful to me so that I do

---

STRATEGIES: DETAILS
Notice that Brady tells us in paragraph 2 that she was ironing clothes one evening when she decided that like her recently divorced friend, she, too, would like a wife. Carefully chosen details can not only help describe a scene but also carry messages that an author wishes to convey to a reader. What do these two details—that she was ironing and that it was in the evening—convey in this context?

CONTEXT: MARRIAGE AND DIVORCE
When Brady wrote this essay in 1971, most Americans lived in traditional households—that is, families made up of a husband, wife, and children. In 1970, more than twice as many Americans lived in traditional families as those living in single or nontraditional households. Today, about the same number of Americans live in traditional families as in single households. Divorce is more common as well, with about half of all marriages today ending in divorce. Consider how these changes in American family lifestyles might affect the way we read this essay.

STRATEGIES: HYPERBOLE
Some critics point out that Brady seems to be creating an unrealistic picture of a typical wife, that she intentionally exaggerates to make her point. Such a strategy, which is often called *hyperbole*, can call readers' attention to common things that they may usually overlook. Would you say that Brady employs hyperbole in this essay? If so, does it work?

These two photos of women in the 1950s seem to depict some of what Brady describes in her essay about a woman's role in the home. What do you think these images convey about women? Consider the extent to which these images reflect not only a particular era but also a particular culture and socioeconomic status.

not have to clutter up my intellectual life with jealousies. And I want a wife who understands that my sexual needs may entail more than strict adherence to monogamy. I must, after all, be able to relate to people as fully as possible.

If, by chance, I find another person more suitable as a wife than the wife I already have, I want the liberty to replace my present wife with another one. Naturally, I will expect a fresh, new life; my wife will take the children and be solely responsible for them so that I am left free.

When I am through with school and have a job, I want my wife to quit working and remain at home so that my wife can more fully and completely take care of a wife's duties.

10   My God, who *wouldn't* want a wife?

UNDERSTANDING THE TEXT

1. Brady tells us that she began wanting a wife while thinking about a recently divorced friend of hers who is looking for a new wife. Why is her friend's situation important in terms of Brady's point in this essay?

2. According to Brady's descriptions of a wife, what are a wife's primary responsibilities? What are a husband's responsibilities? What do these different responsibilities suggest about marriage? About gender?

3. On what grounds would a husband seek to end his marriage to his wife, according to this essay? Are these grounds reasonable, in your view? Does Brady intend them to be? Explain.

EXPLORING THE ISSUES

1. How would you summarize Brady's main point in this essay? Point to specific passages that you think reveal her point. Do you agree with her? Why or why not?

2. What kind of picture of a wife does Brady create? Do you think this picture is accurate, even today? Why or why not? Do you think Brady intended this picture to be accurate? Explain.

3. How would you describe the tone of this essay? Do you find the

tone effective, given Brady's point? Explain, citing specific passages to support your answer.

4. This essay was first published in *Ms.* magazine, which was intended to be a voice for the women's movement in the early 1970s. Who do you think Brady assumed her audience would be? Was she writing to men as well as to women? Explain.

ENTERING THE CONVERSATIONS

1. Write a response to Brady's essay. In a group of classmates, share your responses to Brady's essay. What are the main points of agreement or disagreement about her essay? Is there any relationship between the gender of the members of your group and their responses to this essay? Try to draw conclusions about how gender or other factors you think are important might affect the way readers respond to this essay.

2. Talk to several married couples you know as well as to people who have been divorced. Get their perspectives on marriage and specifically on the roles of husbands and wives in a marriage. Try to learn how they feel about those roles and the challenges facing married couples today. Then write an essay for an audience of your classmates in which you discuss what you learned

about marriage from your conversations. Draw your own conclusions about the roles of husbands and wives in marriage.

3. What do the cartoons below say about marital relationships? About the problems married couples face? About how married couples relate to each other? Where do you think the ideas about marriage portrayed in these cartoons come from? Write an analysis in which you address such questions.

4. Many films depict marital relationships, and sometimes these films spark controversy. In 2004, for example, *The Stepford Wives*, a remake of a 1975 film, was released. Many critics of the film argued that although the new version seemed to portray powerful women (compared to the original version), the real control still rested with the men in the film, who were replacing their wives with compliant robots. According to some of these critics, the film suggested that women's roles have not truly changed since the original movie was released. Examine *The Stepford Wives*, or select several other films that you think reveal important ideas about gender roles, and write an analysis of these films. In your analysis, discuss what you think these films reveal about contemporary attitudes regarding men and women.

"Ah! Here it is!"

"If something is bothering you about our relationship, Lorraine, why don't you just spell it out."

I once had a student very much like John, whom Michael Bérubé (b. 1961) describes in the following essay. My student's name was David, and he challenged me much as John challenged Bérubé. David believed that most professors—and most college students, for that matter—were misguided in their political views and led sinful lives. He was a deeply religious young man who felt it necessary to share his religious views with others. Like Bérubé, I did my best to address David's

Should I Have Asked John TO Cool It?

concerns honestly; I tried to treat him fairly, despite our disagreements. But I was never quite sure how to handle the situations he created in my class. So when I first read this essay, I understood Bérubé's concerns about his student John. But unlike Bérubé, who encountered John after 20 years of teaching, I had David in one of my first classes as a college teacher. The fact that a teacher with Bérubé's long experience would have such difficulty with a student says something about the challenges of teaching and the complexity of the relationships that students and teachers develop with one another.

As a college student, you may have encountered a professor like Bérubé—or like me—with whom you disagreed. Or maybe you've had classes with students like John and David. Such experiences will no doubt influence your reaction to Bérubé's essay— just as my experiences with David influenced my reaction to it. In a sense, in reading Bérubé's essay, you and I will be engaging in different versions of the same conversation about the proper roles and responsibilities of college professors and about the purposes of college education.

Michael Bérubé is the Paterno Family Professor of English at Pennsylvania State University. This essay first appeared in the Chronicle of Higher Education *in 2003.* ▼

MICHAEL BÉRUBÉ

The class started off innocuously enough. We were in our fifth week of an undergraduate honors seminar, reading Ishmael Reed's 1972 novel, *Mumbo Jumbo*, and I was starting to explain how the novel is built on a series of deliberate anachronisms, on the way to asking what these **tropes** from the 1960s were doing in a novel ostensibly set during the Harlem Renaissance. I began in an obvious (though always fun) place, with Abdul Hamid's encounter with PaPa LaBas at a rent party, where Abdul delivers a tirade presaging the rise of the Nation of Islam and protesting U.S. draft policy during the Vietnam War:

> This is the country where something is successful in direct proportion to how it's put over; how it's gamed. Look at the Mormons. . . .The most fundamental book of the Mormon Church, *The Book of Mormon*, is a fraud. If we Blacks came up with something as corny as the Angel of Moroni, something as trite and phony as their story that the book is the record of ancient Americans who came here in 600 BC and perished by AD 400, they would deride us with pejorative adjectival phrases like "so-called" and "would-be." They would refuse to

MICHAEL BÉRUBÉ, "SHOULD I HAVE ASKED JOHN TO COOL IT? STANDARDS OF REASON IN THE CLASSROOM." FROM "SHOULD I HAVE ASKED JOHN TO COOL IT? STANDARDS OF REASON IN THE CLASSROOM." *CHRONICLE OF HIGHER EDUCATION* (2003). REPRINTED BY PERMISSION.

exempt our priests from the draft, a privilege extended to every White hayseed's fruit stand which calls itself a Church. But regardless of the put-on, the hype, the Mormons got Utah, didn't they?

Unfortunately, to most of my students, the passage was just so much mumbo jumbo, so I explained briefly that Muhammad Ali's refusal to fight in Vietnam had been incendiary in the mid-1960s but eventually led the United States to reconsider its criteria for conscientious-objector status; that the comparison between members of the Church of Jesus Christ of Latter-day Saints and members of the Nation of Islam was a fairly common one at the time; and that one nationalist group, the Republic of New Africa, had called for the creation of a separate black nation based in five Southern states, as partial reparation for slavery.

At that point, John, a large white student in the back of the room, snorted loudly and derisively: "That's completely *ridiculous!*" he exclaimed. "It may seem ridiculous to you, yes," I replied, "and, for the record, I don't believe there was any possibility that the Republic of New Africa was going to become a reality. I don't endorse it myself. But it was proposed, and some black nationalists pointedly compared their relation with the U.S. government to that of the Mormons."

But John was just getting started. These people are not Africans, he insisted. They are African-*Americans*. The whole "Africa" thing is a charade; racial separatism and identity politics are tearing this country apart; people have to realize that if they live in this country, no matter how they got here, they are Americans first, and something-Americans second.

Apparently, we had touched a nerve. I pointed out, gently but (I hoped) not patronizingly, that whatever any of us might feel about the various projects of black nationalism, we are, after all, dealing with a character in a novel—a character, I hasten to add, whose reductive brand of nationalism is ultimately undermined in the narrative. It only makes sense to try to understand what he might be ... another example of anachronism in *Mumbo*

... of various colors and genders, ... its, some of them first-generation ... vania, none of them African-... dy to John's outburst. They were ... se of anachronism, and uncertain (as ... en) about whether to take seriously the ... theories about Warren Harding's death, ... Harlem Renaissance, about the role of the ... history, and about the rise of Western culture ... it, the Republic of New Africa had been forgot-... but John simmered throughout the rest of the hour, ... at no one had addressed his comment.

GLOSS: TROPES

Tropes (par. 1) is another term for "figures of speech," which are specialized ways of using language, such as metaphors, analogies, symbols, and so on. Here, Bérubé uses the term to refer to the "deliberate anachronisms" contained in the novel *Mumbo Jumbo*. Anachronisms in this instance are references or events or people in the novel that are intentionally out of place or out of date for the time during which the novel takes place.

STRATEGIES: SUMMARY

In his opening paragraphs, Bérubé summarizes *Mumbo Jumbo,* the novel by Ismael Reed that he had assigned to his students. As a writer, you may often have to summarize another text, as Bérubé does here, and in doing so, you will highlight certain aspects of that text to serve your purposes. Examine how Bérubé summarizes *Mumbo Jumbo.* Consider what he assumes his readers know and do not know, and look at how he uses this summary not only to introduce his essay but also to highlight specific issues that will become important in his discussion of his relationship to his students.

CONTEXT: 2001

Bérubé's reference to the fall of 2001 in paragraph 7 is to the terrorist attacks on the World Trade Center and the Pentagon on September 11, 2001. He calls our attention to how those events affected the atmosphere on his campus and his own approach to teaching during that time. In doing so, he reminds us of the important role that historical context can play in understanding experiences such as the one he is describing in this article. Consider how his experience with John might have been different a year earlier.

Now, I've dealt with students like John before, and I'm sure I'll see them again, no matter what class I'm teaching. But that semester was different; it was the fall of 2001, and students' nerves and political opinions were especially raw. I negotiated any number of delicate exchanges that semester, and for the past two years I've wondered if I've "dealt with" students like John in the best possible way.

After class that day, I talked to John at some length as we wandered through the noon-time campus swarms. He was insistent that membership in the American community requires one to subordinate his or her ethnic-national origin, and that he himself wanted to be understood not as an American of Russian or Polish or German "extraction," but simply as an American among other Americans. And he was just sick and tired of African-Americans refusing to do the same.

I replied by telling John something like this: "Your position has a long and distinguished history in debates over immigration and national identity. It's part of the current critique of multiculturalism, of course, and to a point I have some sympathy with it, because I don't think that social contracts should be based on cultural homogeneity." Deep breath. "That said," I went on, "I have to point out that the terms under which people of African descent might be accepted as Americans, in 1820 or 1920 or whenever, have been radically different from the terms under which your ancestors, whoever they were, could be accepted as Americans. You're right to insist that you shouldn't be defined by one's ancestry, but, unfortunately, most African-Americans—who, by the way, fought and died for integration for many generations—didn't have that option. And it shouldn't be all that surprising that, when African-Americans finally *did* have the option of integrating into the larger national community, some of them were profoundly ambivalent about the prospect."

> **CONVERSATIONS: DEBATES ABOUT NATIONAL IDENTITY**
> Bérubé seems to be telling John that he (John) is part of what Bérubé calls the "long and distinguished history in debates over immigration and national identity." In other words, John's ideas about immigration and national identity don't come from nowhere; they have evolved over many years as a result of ongoing public debates, professional discussions, and related conversations about these issues. And by the same token, Bérubé is also participating in those ongoing discussions, both by addressing these issues in his class and by writing about them in this essay.

10   I didn't press the point that Reed's novel is itself profoundly ambivalent about that profound ambivalence; I thought that we were now on terrain that had little to do with the textual details of *Mumbo Jumbo,* and I was simply trying to come to an understanding with a student who clearly felt very strongly about one of the social issues raised in class. We parted amicably, and I thought that though he wasn't about to agree with me on this one, we had, at least, made our arguments intelligible to each other.

But the dynamic of the class had been changed. From that day forward, John spoke up often, sometimes loudly, sometimes out of turn. He had begun to conceive of himself as the only countervailing conservative voice in a classroom full of liberal-left think-alikes, and he occasionally spoke as if he were entitled to reply to every other student's comment—in a class of 17. He was forceful, intelligent, and articulate. Sometimes he was witty, and he was always knowledgeable about cyberpunk and postmodern science fiction. Often, however, he was obstreperous and out of bounds.

His obstreperousness presented me with not one problem but two. It would have been a relatively simple matter to put the brakes on—to speak to him, in class or afterward, in such a way as to let him know that he was not, in fact, entitled to comment on every other student's comment. But I did not want to contribute to his growing sense of lonely opposition. Meanwhile, his 16 classmates were not, in fact, a unified left-liberal bloc; some of them were recognizably left of center, but not all. Mere weeks after September 11, my students had sounded off on an extraordinary range of questions, including the question of whether that day marked the death of postmodernism, an issue that *New York Times*'s Edward Rothstein had raised. I knew my class contained a handful of people adamantly opposed to military action against the Taliban in Afghanistan (that put them well to the left of me), a handful of people who wanted to redraw the Middle East from scratch in the manner of Paul Wolfowitz, and a handful of people who called themselves libertarians but whose politics didn't go much beyond keep-your-laws-off-my-bong.

Actually, some students agreed with John about one thing or another but were simply annoyed that he was taking up so much class time. They began sending me e-mail messages and speaking to me privately about how they did not want John's remarks to set the parameters for class discussion. One student complained that she was wasting time trying to think of things that John wouldn't reply to; another said that he found anti-porn feminism obnoxious, just as John did, but couldn't stand it when people dismissed feminism so sweepingly as to render suspect other people's more careful critiques (his own, for example). If I asked John to cool it, then, he would undoubtedly feel silenced, and I would be in the position of validating what was perhaps, for him, a stifling liberal hegemony over classroom speech; if I failed to restrain him, I would in effect be allowing him to dominate the class, thereby silencing the other students who'd taken the time to speak to me about the problem.

For the remaining weeks of the semester, I tried to split the difference: John spoke more often than any other student, but I did not recognize him every time he asked; when students criticized his remarks, implicitly or explicitly, I did not validate their criticisms, but I did try to let them speak in rough proportion to their numbers. For a while, order was restored.

15   I've been watching the evolution of campus conservatism for more than 20 years now. I remember vividly the reaction of Accuracy in Academia, Reed Irvine's slightly nutty group that tried to recruit vocal right-wing students to report on and root out "liberal bias" in the classroom. Accuracy in Academia has largely disappeared from public view, but conservative activists have kept up the complaint about liberal campus "bias" all the same, and after September 11 some of their efforts have taken an especially nasty turn. The *National Review*'s culture warrior Stanley Kurtz has recently been instrumental in getting the U.S. House of Representatives to approve a federal "advisory board" to oversee all of the Higher Education Act's Title VI programs in international studies, on the paranoid logic that such programs are spreading anti-Americanism through the works of the late Edward Said; and the at-large culture warrior David Horowitz has begun a dramatic campaign to urge alumni and state legislatures to initiate a "diversity" hiring program to bring more conservative faculty members to the

CONTEXTS: LIBERALISM AND RADICALISM ON CAMPUS
The debate about a "liberal bias" on college campuses in the United States is an old one, but as Bérubé points out here (par. 15), it seems to have heated up in recent years. For example, Bérubé mentions Stanley Kurtz, a research fellow at Stanford University's Hoover Institution, which is known for a conservative political perspective. Kurtz has written about what he believes is a left-wing bias among college faculty members in the United States, and he has called for public vigilance because of the way that various academic disciplines are, in his view, controlled by left-wing thinkers. Perhaps as a result of the criticisms of scholars like Kurtz, a number of self-appointed watchdog groups have appeared in recent years. Bérubé mentions one such group: Accuracy in Academia. Another group that gained national attention was Campus Watch, which claimed to monitor professors on American campuses to identify instances of bias. Bérubé also mentions David Horowitz, a conservative critic whose writing focuses on politics and culture and who has criticized what he describes as the intolerance of left-wing or liberal professors. Consider how this context of debate about political views on campus might shape Bérubé's story about John—and your own response to it. Also consider what these references reveal about Bérubé's perspective.

nation's universities. Horowitz recently received a friendly welcome in Colorado, where he met with Gov. Bill Owens and gave public speeches denouncing, among other things, the liberal-leaning cartoons on the office doors of political-science faculty members.

More interestingly, Horowitz has also circulated an "Academic Bill of Rights" (he recently sent me a copy for comment via e-mail) that draws on statements by the American Association of University Professors about academic freedom that would, if followed closely, prevent precisely the kind of right-wing hiring initiatives Horowitz is touting. By promoting his Bill of Rights, he can then collect leftist denunciations of academic freedom and make the case that the greatest threats to the free exchange of ideas are . . . liberal and leftist faculty members.

Horowitz is exaggerating hysterically when he claims that campuses are one-party states and that 99 percent of all commencement speakers are Democrats, liberals, or Greens. But it's widely understood that English departments are well stocked with liberals, and I've often wished we leftists had less of a presence in literature departments and more of a presence in state legislatures. (Perhaps it's not too late to engineer a straight-up swap.)

Still, I have never seen a conservative student on any of the campuses I've inhabited—Penn State, the Universities of Illinois and Virginia, and Columbia—penalized by a professor for his or her beliefs. I have sometimes seen conservative students made "uncomfortable" by the remarks of their peers, and I can even imagine some particularly hypersensitive conservative undergraduates might be intimidated by the forbidding presence of liberal-leaning cartoons on faculty members' office doors. But I don't believe that universities should be in the business of ensuring their students' comfort in such matters.

I knew that Penn State had weathered an exceptionally unpleasant year in 2000–1, when dozens of students had received anonymous racist letters and e-mail messages, and the leader of the Black Student Caucus had received direct death threats. I knew also that my student John had had some kind of run-in with one of the African-American campus demonstrators that year (in which he told the demonstrator he _____ _____ racist). I took all that into consideration in trying to make John feel as if _____ elcome in my class so long as he respected his peers' _____ nd yet, I couldn't shake the feeling that, although John _____ occasionally feel threatened or uncomfortable in classes _____ n any danger at all. Occasionally the local campus con- _____ the things *they* think the Penn State administration does _____ ecent flier complained that there is now a Paul Robeson _____ nd Robeson was a Communist!), whereas the campus con- _____ a classroom. After I finished shaking my head at the sheer _____ plaint—did these kids really think that the Paul Robeson _____ as the headquarters of a black-activist organization?—I won- _____ of my conservative white students, if given the chance, would _____ Penn State, black in the United States.

_____ we read Richard Powers's 1988 novel, *Prisoner's Dilemma*. Part of _____ ld War II and involves a curious fantasia about how Walt Disney _____ American of Japanese ancestry. Appalled by the 1942 order to intern people of Japanese ancestry living in the United States, Disney manages to get two of his employees out of the camps so that they can help him work on a top-secret project, which will not only win this war but prevent all future wars. I noted that Powers is asking whether it is right to fight a totalitarian enemy by employing totalitarian tactics, and I pointed to passages in which he adduces the internment camps as examples of the game-theory problem known as the prisoner's dilemma, hence the title of the novel. Two prisoners must decide whether to confess or trust each other not to squeal. Almost invariably, prisoners choose to confess, even though mutual trust in the other's steadfastness is clearly the way to go if they want to (a) stay alive and (b) keep their jail time to a minimum. Powers's point, of course, is that a world without mutual trust would be a world of unending world war.

Because it was the fall of 2001, internment camps were hot topics. The two previous times I had taught the novel, in 1995 and 1999, my students had never heard about the imprisonment of Japanese-Americans during World War II, or about the confiscation of their property. But after the debates about the Patriot Act and the detainees in Guantánamo, everyone in the class had heard about the World War II camps, and everyone knew the formerly obscure name of Jeannette Rankin, the Montana representative who had cast the lone vote against the war resolution after Pearl Harbor and who figures in Powers's narrative for that reason. Realizing, then, that everything we said in class about World War II would have sharp resonance for the world after September 11, I mentioned that Powers has been criticized for apparently establishing a kind of moral equivalence between Nazi concentration camps and U.S. internment camps—since the latter, however outrageous and indefensible they were in a putatively democratic nation, were not part of a program of genocide. I asked the class what they thought of that critique.

John wasn't having any of it. There's no moral equivalence here at all; Powers is out of his mind; and even Powers's critics have gone wrong in implicitly agreeing to parse out the different forms of moral wrong at stake—because, and let's get this much straight, the *internment camps were justified.* Far from being "outrageous" and "indefensible," they were a reasonable security precaution in a desperate time and, furthermore, the detainees were treated quite well.

At that point, I have to admit, I was flummoxed. I rarely challenge students directly in the course of class discussion, but I was so stunned that I almost blurted out, "You've got to be kidding." Even if I had, though, I'm not sure John would have heard me: The entire classroom was in a minor uproar, everyone from the pacifists to the drug-law libertarians to the undecideds chiming in at once to criticize; to say, collectively and incoherently, OK, pal, this time you've gone too far. "You know nothing about the Japanese who were imprisoned." "You know nothing about the Constitution." "You're forgetting that the United States actually issued an apology to the internees, as well as financial reparations," students said. For a few seconds, it looked and sounded as if John's classmates wanted to argue him right out of the room.

So, instead of blurting, I whistled. Loud. "All right. Wait a minute." The following silence was punctuated by a few low murmurs. "The object here isn't to pile on," I said over them. "This is, in fact, one of the things the novel wants us to debate."

25   "But John," I added, turning to him, "I do want to remind you that you spoke up quite forcefully, earlier this semester, on behalf of the belief that we're all Americans first, and that our national and ethnic origins shouldn't matter. Didn't the internment camps violate that principle?"

No, he said, because here we were dealing with the possibility of treason during wartime, and some Japanese-Americans had, indeed, been in touch with relatives in Japan in ways that threatened national security. Fine, I said, I believe you're quite mistaken about that, and I will be happy to direct you to sources that will challenge you, but suffice it to say for now that you reject one of the premises of the novel, somewhat more emphatically than Powers's harshest critics on this score. Now, let's take this to the rest of the class. Does the prisoner's dilemma apply to the second world war in the ways Powers suggests? John here says that the camps were justified. If you disagree with him, how can you frame your disagreement by reference to the terms Powers sets out?

We got through the novel, of course—we didn't lose any lives, and no one was injured. It was only literary criticism, after all. But the class had been completely derailed. John was confirmed in his isolation and sense of opposition, his classmates took to eye-rolling and head-shaking at his remarks, and, by the time we got in December to Colson Whitehead's 1999 *The Intuitionist,* a whimsical allegory about racial uplift and the history of elevator inspection, John was complaining that there were no good white characters in the novel. By that point, even I had had enough, and I told him, via e-mail, that his complaint was not only unwarranted on its face but thoroughly beside the point: In this class, I said, we are not in the business of pursuing reductive identity-politics enterprises like looking for "positive images" in literature, regardless of what group images we might be talking about.

GLOSS: DINESH D'SOUZA
Well known for his strident conservative political views and his criticisms of many left-wing academics, Dinesh D'Souza is a fellow at the American Enterprise Institute, an influential conservative Washington, D.C., think tank.

When the semester was over, I wondered whether John's story was the stuff of which right-wing legends are made. Would he remember the seminar as the class in which his right to free speech and debate was trampled by politically correct groupthink (even though he spoke more often than any other single student)? He couldn't possibly contend that I'd graded him on the political content of his remarks, because he'd gotten an A for the course. But there was no question that he felt embattled, that he didn't see any contradictions in his argument about the internment camps, and that he had begun to develop an aggressive/defensive "I'm not a racist, but these people . . ." mode of speaking that would someday get him either in serious trouble with some angry hyphenated-Americans or the job **Dinesh D'Souza** held at the American Enterprise Institute. In the last couple of weeks of the term, I found myself speaking to him almost solicitously, as if to say, "You know, if you understand so little about how some of your remarks might be taken by members of racial minorities, and yet you say so much about them, you could be in for some rough times. You might want to read a manual on tact, perhaps."

But who am I to say such things? For all I know, John might be able to craft a life in which he can deride African-American ambivalence about integration and defend Japanese-American internment camps without ever confronting anyone who disagrees with him.

Reflecting on the course two years later, I've come to see that only a small, intense   30
class can produce the kind of dynamic we dealt with that semester—where I often felt
compelled to restrain students from criticizing someone whose arguments I myself
found obnoxious, and where I had to weigh carefully, seven days a week, what things
I could say to students in the public space of the classroom, and what things I should
reserve for private after-class discussions or follow-up e-mail messages.

And, of course, because of the syllabus, and because of September 11, students
wanted to talk after class, on off days, over the weekend, at midnight on e-mail, with
a professor who would converse with them on all matters local and global. Few critics of academe—and even fewer critics of liberal-left professors—have any idea what
kind of work that entails, which is one reason, surely, why headlines like
"Conservative Student Punished by Stalinist Campus Orthodoxy" strike those of us
who teach as so surreal.

Over my 20 years in teaching, I've had many conservatives in my classes. I think I've
even had a few Stalinists, too. I've had many intelligent, articulate students who behaved as if they had a right to speak more often and at greater length than anyone
else in the room; I've had versions of Reese Witherspoon in *Election* and Hermione
Granger in the *Harry Potter* series, who knew the answers to every question ever asked;
I've had my share of blurters with very little sense of social boundaries, a few of whom
may genuinely have had some degree of Asperger's syndrome, with various autistic
or antisocial symptoms. To all such students—indeed, to all students, those with disabilities and those without—I try to apply the standard of disability law: I make reasonable accommodation for them. The challenge, though, lies in making reasonable
accommodations for students whose standards of "reasonableness" are significantly
different from yours. Few aspects of teaching are so difficult—and, I think, so rarely
acknowledged by people who don't teach for a living.

UNDERSTANDING THE TEXT

1. What issues does Bérubé's initial experiences with John raise for him? Why does he become so preoccupied with John? What specific problems did John cause for him as a teacher?

2. How does Bérubé characterize John's beliefs about race and nationality? How does he respond to those beliefs? Do you think his response to John was reasonable? Why or why not?

3. What is Bérubé's view of the charge that college faculty have a "liberal bias"? Why is this charge an important one, in his view? Do you think he's right? Why or why not?

4. What does Bérubé mean when he states that the challenge for teachers like him "lies in making reasonable accommodations for students whose standards of 'reasonableness' are significantly different from yours"? Do you agree with him? Why or why not?

EXPLORING THE ISSUES

1. In many ways, John is the main character in this essay. How does Bérubé present John to readers? Do you think he tries to describe John fairly? Explain, citing specific passages to illustrate your answer.

2. Bérubé acknowledges that some students might be intimidated by their professors' political views, but he states, "I don't believe that universities should be in the business of ensuring their students' comfort in such matters." What does this statement reveal about Bérubé's view of the purpose of a college education and of the nature of learning in college classrooms? Do you agree with him? Should learning be comfortable for students? Why or why not? How might your own experi-

ences as a college student influence your answer to that question?

3. How does Bérubé portray himself in this essay? What kind of voice does he create through his writing? Do you think his descriptions of his own actions and his views about John are fair and honest? Are they self-serving? How did you respond to his voice and persona as you read the essay? Support your answers with specific passages from the essay.

4. After reading Bérubé's article, how would you answer Bérubé's question: "Should I have asked John to cool it?"

ENTERING THE CONVERSATIONS

1. Write a set of guidelines or a statement of beliefs about how students and teachers should treat one another in a college classroom. Write your statement as if it were to be posted on your school's web site or distributed to students when they are admitted to the school. Be specific and justify your guidelines on the basis of your views about the goals of higher education.

2. Write an essay about an experience you have had in which you were in conflict with a teacher.

3. Bérubé's essay implies a certain kind of relationship between students and teachers. Some of the other essays in this book also deal with student–teacher relationships (for example, Laura Kipnis's essay on page 255, Helen Keller's essay on page 131, and Adrienne Rich's essay on page 197). Drawing on these essays and on your own experiences as a student, write an essay in which you explore the nature of the relationship between teachers and students. Draw conclusions about these relationships and what they can mean to us.

4. Visit some of the web sites devoted to monitoring or critiquing professors or universities (see *Contexts: Liberalism and Radicalism on Campus* on page 281). Try to find sites with different political perspectives. Read their statements about their purposes. Examine the kinds of information and commentary they provide on their sites. (You might see whether there is any information about your own campus or professors you have taken courses from.) Now write an essay in which you analyze these sites. In your essay, describe the sites you visited and what you found there. How accurate or reliable did you find these sites? How useful is the information they provide? What do these sites seem to suggest about the way Americans understand the purposes of higher education? Try to address such questions in your essay. Alternatively, create your own web site in which you offer information and commentary about college or university education.

5. With a group of three or four classmates, hold a mock hearing in which you deliberate about whether or not Michael Bérubé acted appropriately in the situation he describes in his essay. Imagine that John has filed a grievance against Professor Bérubé, and you and your classmates are on the panel that must decide what should be done.

6. Interview several students on your campus about their views of their relationships with professors. Write a report for your classmates in which you discuss what you learned about attitudes on your campus regarding the relationships between students and faculty. Alternatively, write an editorial essay for your school newspaper in which you report on the results of your interviews.

This essay might seem a surprising choice in a cluster of readings about relationships. Writer Peter Sauer (b. 1937) describes a controversy surrounding a sanctioned crow hunt in a small city in upstate New York, which might seem to make this essay more appropriate for the first cluster in Chapter 11: Resources. But as his title suggests, Sauer has more on his mind than the conflict between crow hunters and environmentalists. In a sense, Sauer uses the controversy

THE Crows OF War: U.S. *Foreign* Policy AND THE Relations OF Species

over the crow hunt to explore how humans relate to the nonhuman world. But he is also examining how we relate to one another as human beings. And in that sense, his essay invites us to rethink relationships. It also helps us see that how we think about our relationships with others and with the world around us has a big impact on how we live our lives.

Peter Sauer is a contributing editor to Orion *magazine, in which this essay first appeared in 2003, when the United States had invaded Iraq—a much bigger event than a crow hunt that creates a rich context for his thoughts. Consider how his essay's point is related to that context.* ▼

PETER SAUER

If a society's conviviality with the other-than-human world is a measure of its humanity, a dispute in a small city in upstate New York last winter should have been a warning that this society was losing its grip on both.

The occasion was a weekend crow tournament, in which hunters compete in teams to kill crows. The crows had been debated in the city since they arrived, ten years ago. By 2003, flocks of twenty-five to fifty thousand crows were coming each winter night to roost in the city and departing each day to feed in the surrounding countryside.

PETER SAUER, "THE CROWS OF WAR: U.S. FOREIGN POLICY AND THE RELATIONS OF SPECIES." FROM ORION ONLINE (SEPT.-OCT. 2003). REPRINTED BY PERMISSION OF THE AUTHOR.

As complaints about noise and feces escalated into demands for programs to elim-inate the crows from the business district and around city hall, a group of citizens formed Save the Crows to educate the public about the birds. After a decade of dis-cussing crows and the many methodologies of crow control that other cities had tried and rejected, including sport hunting, the debate was stalemated. When local crow hunters established the annual county crow tournament outside the city in 2002, the citizenry understood that the hunt's effect on the giant flocks of crows would be miniscule. The tournament stirred little controversy in its first two years.

In 2003—no documents found explain why—the hunters decided to open the tournament to hunters from the entire state. In January, they approached the city council for an appropriation to promote the contest as a statewide charitable event, using the slogan "Crow Problem? No Problem!" City council members were favorably impressed. But at their next meeting they found their chamber packed with outraged constituents. The largest citizens' assembly in years condemned the hunt as repug-nant, senseless, disgraceful, redneck, and barbaric, and vowed to boycott and vote against any business or elected official who supported it. The council withdrew its en-dorsements. The mayor followed with a warning to hunters: Anyone discarding dead crows in the dumpster behind the tavern where the annual awards ceremony was held would be in violation of the ordinance that prohibits the transportation of solid waste into the city for disposal and would be arrested. The hunt's leader declared the contest would go on without city support and dared the "old ladies in the city" to stop

5   it. Detailed reports of the brouhaha appeared in local papers.

When people began forwarding stories from the papers to friends on the internet and to listservs, the story became national news. Within forty-eight hours, hunt-ers and hunting organizations, birders, environmentalists, and birding, conserva-tion, and animal rights organizations coast-to-coast were analyzing and elaborating on the tournament's significance. Save the Crow sympathizers expanded the scope and appeal of the debate, and their heated exchanges were probably what convinced CNN and the *New York Times* to cover the tournament. Every pledge of support the group received introduced a new issue, from antihunting and animal rights to wet-lands protection and pesticide use. The majority of the out-of-town protesters who came to the city for the weekend neither understood nor cared about the city's rela-tions with its crows.

The tournament began on the gray, still morning of Saturday, February 1, 2003— one month before the anticipated start of the U.S. invasion of Iraq. Before dawn, the first protesters spread dog and cat food beneath city trees to entice the birds to stay and feed in the city, where discharging firearms is illegal. In the countryside, mean-while, the hunters set up decoys and crow-calling sound systems around their blinds. As the sky lightened, protesters arrived in squads to mob and harass hunters, scare crows with horns, bugles, and flags, rescue wounded birds, and videotape the hunt. One video crew was directed by a paralegal from Washington to collect proof of un-lawful disposals of lead shot, which would be in violation of the federal Resource Conservation and Recovery Act.

It was a windless day, and the crows were flying high, out of range. Only a few shots had been fired before the state police came to umpire the event, which now resem-bled a war game with more than two hundred players scattered over a thirty-mile radius around the city. Officers sped toward infrequent shots and the video teams followed. Reporters roamed about, interviewing protesters and embedding themselves with hunters in blinds. Many participants didn't learn of the Columbia disaster until lunch.

When the hunt ended on Sunday afternoon, 348 crows had been killed, 82 by the winning team. Four protesters had been arrested for interfering with the legal taking of game and jailed when they didn't post bail. The hunters arriving at the tavern to count crowkill and celebrate were greeted by more protesters and a force of city police dispatched to manage the crowds and surveil the dumpster. The dead crows, divvied up in black plastic bags, were carried away to a fox farm and a laboratory at the university. At dusk, the usual scudding clouds of cawing crows returned to settle into and congregate among the lacy winter branches of the city's trees.

STRATEGIES: CHOOSING DETAILS
Notice the last line of paragraph 8, which marks the end of Sauer's narration of the crow hunt. Consider how the selection and placement of the details in this sentence affect the meaning of this passage. Why do you think Sauer ends his narration of the hunt with this sentence? How would his story be different if he had ended the paragraph with the previous sentence (the one beginning, "The dead crows, divvied up in black plastic bags, . . .")?

Before 1972, when the U.S. ratified an international bird treaty with Mexico, crow hunting was legal year-round, and large flocks of crows roosted only in the countryside. By 1999, the treaty's unanticipated effects on the lives of crows, crow hunters, and residents of hundreds of American cities had transformed this society's relations with crows.

10

The treaty required each state to limit crow hunting to 120 days a year. As these rules went into effect, hunters looking for ways to cram a year's worth of satisfying shooting into four months discovered and popularized weekend crow tournaments. No one understands the cause-and-effect relationship, but over the next decade crows began to prefer urban over forest trees for roosting. Ornithologists speculate that lighted city trees may allow the birds to escape from great horned owls. Whatever the reason, by the end of the '80s crows were roosting in small cities from Maine to Ohio, Mississippi to Michigan, and virtually every attempt to drive them away spread them into new neighborhoods and increased their numbers. Though the critical crow-mass varied from city to city, the dilemma it triggered was the same. Humane crow removal programs were expensive and notoriously ineffective while methods that involved killing "innocent" crows were intolerable to many citizens.

VISUAL CONNECTIONS: CROWS
Cartoonists routinely give human characteristics to animals (a strategy that is called *anthropomorphism*). What might this cartoon suggest about the crow hunt described in Sauer's essay? How might the cartoonist's use of anthropomorphism help convey the cartoon's message?

Public sentiment began to turn against the crows in 1999 when the West Nile virus appeared and crows were identified as carriers. The following year, dead crows in upstate New York tested positive for the virus. In 2001, revelations about anthrax raised concerns about weaponized diseases. Two years later, when war preparations had screwed these anxieties tighter, the hunters in the city council chamber called crows "rats with wings," invoking the old rural icon of the crow as sinister surrogate for villainy that has made killing them a cleansing activity for generations of crow haters.

Martin Stanton/The Citizen, Auburn, NY

CONTEXT: WEST NILE VIRUS
West Nile virus (par. 11) is a potentially deadly disease caused by a virus that is believed to be spread by mosquitoes feeding on infected birds. In the late 1990s, public health officials became alarmed by an apparent increase in the number of cases in some parts of the United States, including the northeastern U.S. where the crow hunt Sauer describes took place. One method that health officials used for trying to determine the spread of the disease was to test dead birds for the virus.

But the protesters contributed their share of hating, too. A message on a birding listserv expressed the hope that the "shotgun-toting idiots would stick the dead crows in their pockets with their lunches" and contract West Nile disease. The ability to imagine dead birds as weapons in defense of Nature reflects a zealotry equal to that of the hunters when they evoked the demonic, iconic crow.

By replacing real crows with abstractions, both sides were diminishing their own humanity. But then, this dispute had come to have little to do with crows. This was February 2003, when the abstractions *du jour* were collateral damage and shock and awe. The tournament was a ritual for a human society preparing its flocks for war.

UNDERSTANDING THE TEXT

1. What gave rise to the crow hunt that Sauer describes in this article? What significance does Sauer see in the way the hunt came about?

2. How does the crow hunt become a national news event? What does it suggest to Sauer about how people understand their relationships to nonhuman creatures and to each other?

3. What does Sauer mean when he writes that both sides of this debate "replaced real crows with abstractions"? In what ways is that statement important to his main point?

4. What significance does Sauer see in the timing of this event, which occurred as the United States was preparing to invade Iraq in 2003? Do you think he is right? Why or why not?

EXPLORING THE ISSUES

1. In the opening line of this essay, Sauer refers to the "other-than-human world." What exactly does he mean by that phrase? Why do you think he chose that phrase as opposed to a more common term, such as "natural world" or "nature"? What might his phrase suggest

about his perspective on this issue? What might it suggest about what readers can expect in the rest of his essay?

2. Examine the way Sauer tells the story of the crow hunt (from the beginning of the essay through paragraph 8). How does he portray the various groups involved in the story: the hunters, the protesters, the news media? What messages do you think he conveys in the way he tells this story? How effectively do you think his telling of this story helps reinforce the main point of his essay?

3. What lessons about human nature and human relationships does Sauer take away from the crow hunt? Do you agree with him? Why or why not?

4. What do you think is Sauer's perspective on the relationship between human beings and other living beings? Support your answer with references to specific passages in the essay.

ENTERING THE CONVERSATIONS

1. Write an essay in which you tell a story that reveals something important about human relationships or the relationships between humans and other living beings.

2. Write an essay for your local newspaper or some other appropriate publication in which you present your view of the relationship between humans and other living creatures.

INFOTRAC

3. In his essay, Sauer mentions an international treaty to protect birds, indicating that there has long been conflict over the hunting of birds. Using InfoTrac College Edition and any other relevant resources, investigate this treaty and the current situation with the protection of birds or other animals that are hunted for sport or profit. Then write a report on the basis of your investigation.

4. Write an editorial page essay in which you take a position on hunts such as the crow hunt described in this essay.

5. Create a visual representation (a web site, photo essay, PowerPoint presentation, or some other kind of document) of the sometimes conflicting perspectives of environmentalists, hunters, and others regarding the relationship between humans and the wild.

CREATING THEMES: Extending the Conversations

WITH TEXT

1. Select two or more of the essays in this chapter and examine the way each writer addresses his or her intended audience. Look specifically at the writer's use of language, the organization of the essay, and the kinds of references and information the writer uses. Then write an analysis of the essays you have selected. In your analysis, use specific references to passages in the essays to illustrate your points and draw conclusions about effective strategies for addressing audience in writing.

2. Identify what you consider an important theme that runs through several of the readings in this chapter and write an essay intended for a specific audience about that theme. In your essay, draw on the readings you've selected to support your main point.

3. Select several of the essays in this chapter that you think offer insight into the idea of relationships and write an essay in which you examine what those essays suggest about relationships.

4. In creating this chapter, I identified three main themes having to do with relationships, one for each cluster. Looking over the essays in this chapter, identify a theme that you think is important for a fourth cluster in the chapter. Select the readings that you think would fit best in such a cluster. Then write an essay on that theme, drawing on the four (or more) essays you have selected. Be sure to identify an audience for your essay and a purpose for addressing that audience. For example, you may create a cluster that focuses on marriage and include among the readings the essays by David Brooks and Judy Syfers Brady. Your essay might be intended for young people who are married or planning to get married,

and it might examine some of the challenges to marriage today; you would draw on the essays by Brooks and Brady to help make your points. In creating your theme, feel free to include an essay from another chapter in this book or an essay not included in this book.

5. Drawing on the essays in this chapter and any other relevant resources, create a pamphlet for a specific audience (such as students at your school or people at your workplace) in which you offer advice about relationships.

WITH MEDIA

1. Norman Rockwell is well known for his paintings depicting American life. But he is sometimes criticized for depicting an idealized (and unrealistic) vision that excludes much of American society. Write an analysis of this image in which you discuss what it says about American family life. In your analysis, evaluate this image from a specific perspective.

For example, you might take a feminist perspective. Or you might write in the context of the recent controversies about same-sex marriages. What can be said about this painting from that perspective? Draw conclusions about the values reflected in this image based on the perspective you have adopted. Alternatively, create a visual representation (for example, a photo essay or a web site) of family life as a response to Rockwell's painting.

2. Find several magazine advertisements that have something to do with love—for example, advertisements for diamond engagement rings or for Mother's Day flowers. Examine these advertisements for the way they portray love and try to identify what they suggest about the nature of love. Focus especially on the way they use images to convey their messages. Then write an analysis of these advertisements, describing what you have found and drawing conclusions about the way love is portrayed. Discuss what you

Norman Rockwell, *Family at Dinner Table*

Norman Rockwell Family Agency, Inc.

MAKING THEMES: Extending the Conversations

think these advertisements reveal about popular attitudes regarding love. Alternatively, identify several television commercials that portray love in some way and write a similar analysis of these commercials.

3. Select an issue related to relationships that is addressed by the readings in this chapter (for example, same-sex marriage, parent-teen relationships) and search the World Wide Web for sites that focus on that issue. Identify several such sites and then write an analysis of the sites, examining how they address the issue and how they portray themselves. For example, does a web site for an advocacy group try to convey an image of objectivity or authority about the issue it addresses? Does the site take an overtly slanted view on the issue? What audience does it seem to be addressing? Draw conclusions about how the issue is portrayed on Internet sites and how ideas are conveyed through these sites. Alternatively, create your own web site for the issue you have identified. (Consult Chapter 2 about visual media.)

4. View several popular television talk shows that often focus their programs on relationships (for example, *The Oprah Winfrey Show* or *Dr. Phil*). What kinds of specific topics related to relationships tend to be addressed on these shows? How are relationships presented? What might these shows suggest about relationships in contemporary society? Write an essay in which you try to address such questions. In your essay, describe the shows you viewed and discuss what you think they suggest about attitudes regarding relationships. Alternatively, create a self-help guide (in the form of a pamphlet, a web site, or some other appropriate document) based on the advice about relationships that was presented in these shows.

WITH FILM

1. It is possible that more popular films have been made about romantic love than about any other single topic. Select one or more recent popular films that you think convey a powerful message about love and write an essay in which you discuss that message and how the film conveys it.

2. Many science fiction films portray unusual relationships or seem to call typical relationships into question. Others seem to depict very common human relationships in uncommon circumstances. And there are some that focus on the relationships between humans and machines or technology. A well-known example of such a film is *The Matrix* (1999), which depicts a world controlled by machines, against which humans are rebelling. The film raises many questions about the relationship between humans and the technologies they create as well as about human relationships. Write an essay in which you analyze these questions in *The Matrix* or in another film that addresses the issue of the relationship between humans and technology (such as *2001: A Space Odyssey*).

Chapter **8** Communication

© Underwood & Underwood/Corbis

EVEN BEFORE I GET OUT OF BED IN THE MORNING, I AM COMMUNI-CATING. I USUALLY ASK MY WIFE, CHERYL, IF SHE WANTS TO SHOWER FIRST. WHILE SHE'S IN THE SHOWER, I TURN ON THE RADIO. DURING THE NEXT HOUR, I WILL LISTEN TO NEWS REPORTS AS I MAKE BREAKFAST AND GET READY FOR THE DAY. DURING THAT HOUR, CHERYL AND I WILL TALK

about our plans for the day, the menu for dinner, errands we have to run, items in the news. When my son gets up, he usually turns on the television to get the latest sports news, and sometimes I'll ask him to turn down the volume so I can hear the radio better. Later, after everyone has left for work or school, I'll read the local newspaper as I finish my coffee. Once I sit down at my desk to work, I'll check my e-mail account, reading and responding to various messages I find there. I might also check a web site or two for more news updates or log onto the web-based discussion board that I have set up for one of my classes. There, I'll read the mes-

> As my description of my typical morning suggests, we communicate almost constantly in many different ways.

sages that my students have posted and post my own responses. On some mornings, the phone will ring, and I'll talk to a family member or a colleague. Later, as I'm leaving home for campus, I may write a brief note and stick it on the refrigerator door to remind us of things we need to buy at the grocery store or some other task that needs to be done. On the way to campus, I read road signs or traffic lights, signal to other drivers when I want to turn, place a parking pass on my car windshield, and slow down to signal to pedestrians on campus that they can cross the road. And of course, there's much, much more. You probably do many of the same things every day that I just described. It's amazing, really, how much time we spend communicating.

As my description of my typical morning suggests, we communicate almost constantly in many different ways. Obviously, we talk to one another. But we also read and write in various media, including notes, newspapers and magazines, e-mail, signs, and text messaging. We listen to radio reports and watch television. We talk on telephones. We "read" various kinds of images, from basic symbols like a red traffic light or a rest room sign to more sophisticated visual texts such as music videos or political advertisements. We use body language to let others know that we like or dislike them, that we're interested in what they're saying or doing, that we're uncertain or hesitant, or even that we are angry or threatening. My dog can tell by my facial expression whether or not she should approach me to be petted or stay where she is, and of course, we humans do the same kind of thing with facial expressions all the time. We send messages with our clothes: that we're conventional, hip, practical, conservative, alluring, even knowledgeable. If I am hiking in cold weather in the mountains, the clothes I choose will send a message to my hiking companions that I am prepared (or not) and that I know something about being in the mountains (or not). We might be communicating to others by the kind of car we drive. A gas–electric hybrid car like the Toyota Prius or the Honda Insight, for example, might be a statement about protecting the environment. In church or temple, we bow our heads, and at sporting events, we raise our arms in the air. We fly our nation's flag from our porches, and we wear black to funerals. We drape an American flag over the casket of a military veteran, and we shoot rifles into the air at a veteran's burial. We yawn at meetings, and we kiss our loved ones good night. We never stop using an astonishing array of tools to communicate.

So it's no surprise that scholars, philosophers, scientists, linguists, and psychologists have long been trying to understand communication. More than 2,500 years ago, Aristotle wrote a famous treatise known as the *Rhetoric,* in which he explains the process of persuading an audience through speech (or writing). In a way, Aristotle's book, which is still read today, was one of the first textbooks on using language—similar in many respects to the textbook you're reading right now. Aristotle offered advice to speakers so that they could communicate ideas more effectively to their audiences—advice that is still followed today. In the centuries since then, countless others have tried to understand the complexities of speech, writing, reading, signs, visual art, body language, and every other conceivable kind of communication. Philosophers have devoted their careers to studying human language, and many scientists have done the same. Neurophysiologists use state-of-the-art technologies, such as CAT scans, to map the human brain in their efforts to understand speech and visual communication. Scholars devise new theories, such as semiotics (the study of signs), to explain communication. Linguists describe the thousands of different human languages in their quest to understand speech. Biologists document the many ways in which animals send messages to one another. Yet, even as we continue to communicate with one another about this amazing activity we call communication, we remain daunted by its complexity.

The readings in this chapter expose some of that complexity. Each of the three clusters fo-

cuses on some aspect of communication: the political nature of language, the power of literacy to communicate, and the potential for communication in nonverbal forms. But it wasn't easy to narrow the subject of communication to these three clusters. So despite the variety of these readings, there's much more about communication that I wasn't able to include here. Keep that in mind as you read about the wonder, the power, the challenge, and the limits of the many

> Yet, even as we continue to communicate with one another about this amazing activity we call communication, we remain daunted by its complexity.
>
> Keep that in mind as you read about the wonder, the power, the challenge, and the limits of the many ways we communicate with one another.

ways we communicate with one another. I hope these essays help make you more aware of the crucial role that communication plays in your life and appreciate the subtleties of various forms of communication, such as advertising or music, that affect you every day. I hope, too, that this chapter reinforces a message that I have been trying to send throughout this book: Writing is a wondrous form of communication whose power you can harness in your own life.

THE POLITICS OF LANGUAGE

WHEN I WAS A NEW GRADUATE STUDENT IN THE EARLY 1980S, I UNEXPECTEDLY GOT MY FIRST REAL LESSON IN THE POLITICS OF LANGUAGE. I WAS WALKING DOWN THE HALL TOWARD MY OFFICE ONE AFTERNOON, AND I PASSED THREE WOMEN WHO WERE ALSO NEW GRADUATE STUDENTS. I KNEW THEM WELL FROM CLASSES WE WERE TAKING TOGETHER. AS I PASSED THEM, I SAID, "HI, GIRLS." ALL THREE WOMEN LOOKED

surprised, and one said indignantly, "Girls?!" At the time, I didn't quite understand either their surprise or their indignation. I had grown up in a small, working-class town where women were regularly referred to as "girls." The women who worked in my grandmother's small catering business, all of whom were older than fifty, were known to everyone as "the girls." None of them ever took offense at the term. So what was wrong with calling my three friends, who were in their twenties, "girls"?

To answer that question is to begin to examine the many ways in which even the most ordinary language is political. Words can carry powerful messages that go well beyond dictionary definitions. And those political messages relate to cultural and historical circumstances. In other words, the political meaning of a word depends on context.

My friends helped teach me that lesson by making me aware that the word *girl* is not a neutral term for women, as I had used it. Rather, it is a word that for many people, including my three friends, reflects a sexist view of women. By that time in the early 1980s, the women's movement had helped make people sensitive to the sexism in common expressions, which often emphasize male over female or reflect a negative or even degrading view of women. For example, when I was growing up, it was not only common to refer to all women as girls, but it was also common to hear women referred to as "babes," "foxes," and similar terms that we now considered insulting. The women's movement helped us see that those terms send powerful messages about the status of women— messages that reduce women to physical objects and suggest that the value of a woman is a function of her physical attractiveness to men. Although *girl* didn't necessarily carry such an obviously degrading message in the early 1980s, it

could easily be understood as derogatory when it was used to refer to women because it implied the immaturity of a young girl rather than the maturity of an adult.

But the politics of language does not refer only to the meaning of words. The decision to speak in a certain language or to use a certain dialect can also send powerful messages. During the last few U.S. presidential elections, for example, the candidates often spoke in Spanish to audiences in California, Texas, and Florida, where Spanish-speaking people make up a significant percentage of the population. A candidate's use of Spanish in public speeches is intended to send a message to Spanish-speaking citizens that they matter. It can also send less positive messages, such as the suggestion that citizens are being pandered to during an election campaign.

The writers whose essays are included in this cluster will help you explore these obvious and not-so-obvious ways in which language can be political. They provide you with examples of some of the ways in which we use language to make statements, political and otherwise. Two of them, Amy Tan and Gloria Anzaldúa, share their experiences as bilingual women whose ways of using their different languages reveal how language can be a tool for control as well as a means of empowerment. Deborah Tannen looks at important gender differences in our uses of language. And Gary Sloan focuses our attention on how politicians try to use language for their own purposes. All these writers are concerned with how words can convey different meanings and reflect various political viewpoints. The lessons they can teach may serve you well in a world that is so profoundly shaped by the politics of language.

All of Amy Tan's novels have something to do with China, where her mother was born, and in each one, the Chinese language and cultural heritage are central to the story. The following essay may help explain why. In this essay, Tan (b. 1952) describes her struggles as a student whose mother's "broken" English that wasn't spoken in schools and often caused problems for both Tan and her mother. It quickly becomes clear that despite the difficulties she experienced with her

Mother Tongue

mother, Tan sees something special in her mother's language. It also becomes clear that Tan appreciates the complexities of the different "Englishes" that she learned. She understands, for example, that people can suffer discrimination because they speak in a dialect that is not Standard English. And she knows that a person's language can send different messages to different people, some of which arise from bias and prejudice. Tan's experiences can help us understand why the charged debates about Standard English and bilingual education can have such important consequences for individuals. In a sense, her essay is a vivid personal portrayal of the politics of language. But this essay is also a statement of her own love affair with her language heritage—and with language in general.

Award-winning writer Amy Tan is the author of four novels, including The Joy Luck Club *(1989), which was a New York Times bestseller that was translated into twenty-five languages and made into a movie. The following essay first appeared in the* Threepenny Review *in 1990.* ▾

AMY TAN

I am not a scholar of English or literature. I cannot give you much more than personal opinions on the English language and its variations in this country or others.

I am a writer. And by that definition, I am someone who has always loved language. I am fascinated by language in daily life. I spend a great deal of my time thinking about the power of language—the way it can evoke an emotion, a visual image, a complex idea, or a simple truth. Language is the tool of my trade. And I use them all—all the Englishes I grew up with.

Recently, I was made keenly aware of the different Englishes I do use. I was giving a talk to a large group of people, the same talk I had already given to half a dozen other groups. The nature of the talk was about my writing, my life, and my book, *The Joy Luck Club*. The talk was going along well enough, until I remembered one major difference that made the whole talk sound wrong. My mother was in the room. And it was perhaps the first time she had heard me give a lengthy speech, using the kind of English I have never used with her. I was saying things like, "The intersection of memory upon imagination" and "There is an aspect of my fiction that relates to thus-and-thus"—a speech filled with carefully wrought grammatical phrases, burdened, it suddenly seemed to me, with nominalized forms, past perfect tenses, conditional phrases, all the forms of standard English that I had learned in school and through books, the forms of English I did not use at home with my mother.

Just last week, I was walking down the street with my mother, and I again found myself conscious of the English I was using, the English I do use with her. We were talking about the price of new and used furniture and I heard myself saying this: "Not waste money that way." My husband was with us as well, and he didn't notice any switch in my English. And then I realized why. It's because over the twenty years we've been together I've often used that same kind of English with him, and sometimes he even uses it with me. It has become our language of intimacy, a different sort of English that relates to family talk, the language I grew up with.

5   So you'll have some idea of what this family talk I heard sounds like, I'll quote what my mother said during a recent conversation which I videotaped and then transcribed. During this conversation, my mother was talking about a political gangster in Shanghai who had the same last name as her family's, Du, and how the gangster in his early years wanted to be adopted by her family, which was rich by comparison. Later, the gangster became more powerful, far richer than my mother's family, and one day showed up at my mother's wedding to pay his respects. Here's what she said in part:

STRATEGIES: USING DIALECT
In this paragraph, Tan quotes her mother, whose first language is Chinese, to give us an example of what Tan calls her "family talk." Fiction writers often use dialects like this to help convey a sense of their characters. Such uses of dialect are less common in nonfiction writing, in part because writers often try to avoid embarrassing the people they are quoting, who may feel they sound unintelligent by speaking in dialect. (Tan expresses this view in par. 8 and 9.) In fact, many newspapers and magazines edit quotations so that they do not contain dialects. Consider what messages Tan is sending about dialects by quoting her mother as she does here.

"Du Yusong having business like fruit stand. Like off the street kind. He is Du like Du Zong—but not Tsung-ming Island people. The local people call putong, the river east side, he belong to that side local people. That man want to ask Du Zong father take him in like become own family. Du Zong father wasn't look down on him, but didn't take seriously, until that man big like become a mafia. Now important person, very hard to inviting him. Chinese way, came only to show respect, don't stay for dinner. Respect for making big celebration, he shows up. Mean give lots of respect. Chinese custom. Chinese social life that way. If too important won't have to stay too long. He come to my wedding. I didn't see, I heard it. I gone to boy's side, they have YMCA dinner. Chinese age I was nineteen."

You should know that my mother's expressive command of English belies how much she actually understands. She reads the *Forbes* report, listens to *Wall Street Week,* converses daily with her stockbroker, reads all of Shirley MacLaine's books with ease—all kinds of things I can't begin to understand. Yet some of my friends tell me they understand 50 percent of what my mother says. Some say they understand 80 to 90 percent. Some say they understand none of it, as if she were speaking pure Chinese. But to me, my mother's English is perfectly clear, perfectly natural. It's my mother tongue. Her language, as I hear it, is vivid, direct, full of observation and imagery. That was the language that helped shape the way I saw things, expressed things, made sense of the world.

* * *

Lately, I've been giving more thought to the kind of English my mother speaks. Like others, I have described it to people as "broken" or "fractured" English. But I wince when I say that. It has always bothered me that I can think of no way to describe it other than "broken," as if it were damaged and needed to be fixed, as if it lacked a certain wholeness and soundness. I've heard other terms used, "limited English," for example. But they seem just as bad, as if everything is limited, including people's perceptions of the limited English speaker.

I know this for a fact, because when I was growing up, my mother's "limited" English limited *my* perception of her. I was ashamed of her English. I believed that her English reflected the quality of what she had to say. That is, because she expressed them imperfectly her thoughts were imperfect. And I had plenty of empirical evidence to support me: the fact that people in department stores, at banks, and at restaurants did not take her seriously, did not give her good service, pretended not to understand her, or even acted as if they did not hear her.

My mother has long realized the limitations of her English as well. When I was fifteen, she used to have me call people on the phone to pretend I was she. In this guise, I was forced to ask for information or even to complain and yell at people who had been rude to her. One time it was a call to her stockbroker in New York. She had cashed out her small portfolio and it just happened we were going to go to New York the next week, our very first trip outside California. I had to get on the phone and say in an adolescent voice that was not very convincing, "This is Mrs. Tan."

And my mother was standing in the back whispering loudly, "Why he don't send me check, already two weeks late. So mad he lie to me, losing me money."

And then I said in perfect English, "Yes, I'm getting rather concerned. You had agreed to send the check two weeks ago, but it hasn't arrived."

Then she began to talk more loudly. "What he want, I come to New York tell him front of his boss, you cheating me?" And I was trying to calm her down, make her be quiet, while telling the stockbroker, "I can't tolerate any more excuses. If I don't receive the check immediately, I am going to have to speak to your manager when I'm in New York next week." And sure enough, the following week there we were in front of this astonished stockbroker, and I was sitting there red-faced and quiet, and my mother, the real Mrs. Tan, was shouting at his boss in her impeccable broken English.

We used a similar routine just five days ago, for a situation that was far less humorous. My mother had gone to the hospital for an appointment, to find out about a benign brain tumor a CAT scan had revealed a month ago. She said she had spoken very good English, her best English, no mistakes. Still, she said, the hospital did not apologize when they said they had lost the CAT scan and she had come for nothing. She said they did not seem to have any sympathy when she told them she was anxious to know the exact diagnosis, since her husband and son had both died of brain tumors. She said they would not give her any more information until the next time and she would have to make another appointment for that. So she said she would not leave until the doctor called her daughter. She wouldn't budge. And when the doctor finally called her daughter, me, who spoke in perfect English—lo and behold—we had assurances the CAT scan would be found, promises that a conference call on Monday would be held, and apologies for any suffering my mother had gone through for a most regrettable mistake.

15   I think my mother's English almost had an effect on limiting my possibilities in life as well. Sociologists and linguists probably will tell you that a person's developing language skills are more influenced by peers. But I do think that the language spoken in the family, especially in immigrant families which are more insular, plays a large role in shaping the language of the child. And I believe that it affected my results on achievement tests, IQ tests, and the SAT. While my English skills were never judged as poor, compared to math, English could not be considered my strong suit. In grade school I did moderately well, getting perhaps B's, sometimes B-pluses, in English and scoring perhaps in the sixtieth or seventieth percentile on achievement tests. But those scores were not good enough to override the opinion that my true abilities lay in math and science, because in those areas I achieved A's and scored in the ninetieth percentile or higher.

> **CONTEXT: SECOND-LANGUAGE LEARNERS**
> Like many second-language learners, Tan sometimes struggled with language in school, as she describes in paragraph 15. In the past few decades, educators have paid much more attention to the challenges facing students whose first language is other than English or who live in households where other languages are spoken. Bilingual education programs, in which students are taught in their first language rather than in English, are intended to address the needs of such students, but they have long been controversial and have recently been abandoned by many states. Tan's description in this paragraph provides a vivid example of some of the difficulties facing second-language learners.

This was understandable. Math is precise; there is only one correct answer. Whereas, for me at least, the answers on English tests were always a judgment call, a matter of opinion and personal experience. Those tests were constructed around items like fill-in-the-blank sentence completion, such as, "Even though Tom was _____, Mary thought he was _____." And the correct answer always seemed to be the most bland combinations of thoughts, for example "Even though Tom was shy, Mary thought he was charming," with the grammatical structure "even though" limiting the correct answer to some sort of semantic opposites, so you wouldn't get answers like, "Even though Tom was foolish, Mary thought he was ridiculous." Well, according to my mother, there were very few limitations as to what Tom could have been and what Mary might have thought of him. So I never did well on tests like that.

The same was true with word analogies, pairs of words in which you were supposed to find some sort of logical, semantic relationship—for example, (*Sunset* is to *nightfall* as _____ is to _____." And here you would be presented with a list of four possible pairs, one of which showed the same kind of relationship: *red* is to *spotlight, bus* is to *arrival, chills* is to *fever, yawn* is to *boring.* Well, I could never think that way. I knew what the tests were asking, but I could not block out of my mind the images already created by the first pair, "*sunset* is to *nightfall*"—and I would see a burst of colors against a darkening sky, the moon rising, the lowering of a curtain of stars. And all the other pairs of words—red, bus, spotlight, boring—just threw up a mass of confusing images, making it impossible for me to sort out something as logical as saying: "A sunset precedes nightfall" is the same as "a chill precedes a fever." The only way I would have gotten that answer right would have been to imagine an associative situation, for example, my being disobedient and staying out past sunset, catching a chill at night, which turns into feverish pneumonia as punishment, which indeed did happen to me.

*   *   *

I have been thinking about all this lately, about my mother's English, about achievement tests. Because lately I've been asked, as a writer, why there are not more Asian Americans represented in American literature. Why are there few Asian Americans enrolled in creative writing programs? Why do so many Chinese students go into engineering? Well, these are broad sociological questions I can't begin to answer. But I have noticed in surveys—in fact, just last week—that Asian students, as a whole, always do significantly better on math achievement tests than in English. And this makes me think that there are other Asian American students whose English spoken in the home might also be described as "broken" or "limited." And perhaps they also have teachers who are steering them away from writing and into math and science, which is what happened to me.

Fortunately, I happen to be rebellious in nature and enjoy the challenge of disproving assumptions made about me. I became an English major my first year in college, after being enrolled as pre-med. I started writing nonfiction as a free-lancer the week after I was told by my former boss that writing was my worst skill and I should hone my talents toward account management.

CONVERSATIONS: TESTING ENGLISH

Few educational issues have been more controversial than standardized testing, and in this section of her essay, Tan provides a glimpse into that controversy. The examples of test items that Tan includes in these two paragraphs (16,17) suggest some of the complexities of standardized testing that critics have often cited. When this essay was first published in 1990, standardized testing was becoming more widespread as many states tried to address concerns about low standards in public education. In the late 1990s and the first few years of the twenty-first century, the trend accelerated as federal education policy encouraged states to require standardized testing in core subjects, including English. Consider what Tan's experiences with tests might suggest about the challenges of testing students' language knowledge and skill. This graphic of California standards test scores suggests that more and more students in different income brackets may face the kinds of challenges in math and English that Tan describes in her essay. You might think about how Tan's essay might contribute to the ongoing controversy about standardized testing.

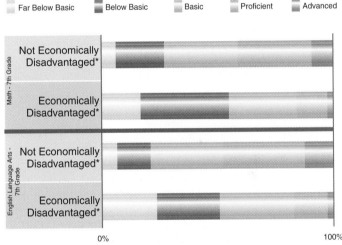

*For the purpose of this chart, "economically disadvantaged" is defined as being eligible for the National School Lunch Program.

Data: EdSource www.edsource.org. Reprinted by permission.

But it wasn't until 1985 that I finally began to write fiction. And at first I wrote using what I thought to be wittily crafted sentences, sentences that would finally prove I had mastery over the English language. Here's an example from the first draft of a story that later made its way into *The Joy Luck Club*, but without this line: "That was my mental quandary in its nascent state." A terrible line, which I can barely pronounce.

Fortunately, for reasons I won't get into today, I later decided I should envision a reader for the stories I would write. And the reader I decided upon was my mother, because these were stories about mothers. So with this reader in mind—and in fact she did read my early drafts—I began to write stories using all the Englishes I grew up with: the English I spoke to my mother, which for lack of a better term might be described as "simple"; the English she used with me, which for lack of a better term

20

might be described as "broken"; my translation of her Chinese, which could certainly be described as "watered down"; and what I imagined to be her translation of her Chinese if she could speak in perfect English, her internal language, and for that I sought to preserve the essence, but neither an English nor a Chinese structure. I wanted to capture what language ability tests can never reveal: her intent, her passion, her imagery, the rhythms of her speech, and the nature of her thoughts.

Apart from what any critic had to say about my writing, I knew I had succeeded where it counted when my mother finished reading my book and gave me her verdict: "So easy to read."

UNDERSTANDING THE TEXT

1. What are "all the Englishes" that Tan grew up with? What exactly does Tan mean by Englishes? What differences are there among the different Englishes she uses? Why are these differences important to her?

2. Tan shares several anecdotes about her mother's use of "broken" or "limited" English in dealing with bankers, doctors, and other professional people. What do these anecdotes reveal about what Tan calls the "limitations" of her mother's English? Why are these limitations important to Tan? What do they suggest about our uses of language? What do they suggest about our attitudes toward language differences?

3. Why is the fact that Asian American students seem to do better in math and science than in other school subjects important to Tan? What does it suggest to her about the role of language in the learning of such students? Do you think she is right? Why or why not?

4. Why does Tan believe that her mother is the best reader for her stories and novels? What might this suggest about a writer's audience?

EXPLORING THE ISSUES

1. In the first two paragraphs, Tan identifies herself as "someone who has always loved language," and not as "a scholar of English or literature." Why do you think Tan begins her essay in this way? How did this beginning affect your view of Tan as the author of this essay? Did it give her more or less credibility, in your view? Explain.

2. In paragraph 3, Tan describes a talk she was giving about her novel *The Joy Luck Club,* and she describes the language she was using in that talk as the "standard English that I had learned in school and through books." Do you think Tan is

criticizing "school English" in her essay? If so, do you think her criticism is valid? Explain, citing specific passages from the text and drawing on your own experience with English to support your answer.

3. Examine Tan's descriptions of her mother. What kind of person is Tan's mother? What characteristics does Tan focus on in her descriptions of her mother? Why do you think Tan emphasizes these characteristics? How might her descriptions of her mother contribute to her main point in this essay?

4. In paragraph 20, Tan shares the following sentence from a draft of one of her stories: "That was my mental quandary in its nascent state." Tan calls this sentence a "terrible line." What do you think she finds terrible about this sentence? Do you agree with her? Why or why not? What might Tan's opinion of this sentence suggest about her views about writing style?

ENTERING THE CONVERSATIONS

1. Write an essay for an audience of your classmates describing an experience in which your use of language was important. The experience can be a time when your use of language was problematic or troubling, a time when your language put you at some kind of advantage or disadvantage, or a time when language played a central role in some event. Describe the experience in a way that helps your readers understand what you might have learned about language through that experience.

2. In a group of classmates, share the essay you wrote for Question 1. Discuss what the experiences you and your classmates described might suggest about language. What was political about the way language was used in your experi-

ences? What conclusions can you draw from your discussion?

INFOTRAC

3. Using InfoTrac College Edition and any other relevant resources, investigate the challenges facing second-language learners in schools today and the programs that educators are developing to address those challenges. Find out what educators have learned about how best to help second-language learners. Write a report on the basis of your research.

4. Try to find someone who is a second-language learner. (See *Context: Second Language-Learners* on page 302.) Interview this person about his or her experiences with language in school as well as outside school. How has that language affected schoolwork or social activities that are done in English? What problems or difficulties has this person experienced. Then write an essay in which you describe the person you interviewed and his or her experiences as a second language-learner. Draw conclusions about the politics of language from your interview.

5. Write an essay in which you present your position on the question of requiring only English in schools, workplaces, government meetings, and elsewhere. (The movement to adopt such requirements is known as the English Only movement. You may want to learn more about it by visiting the web sites of groups that support such requirements.) Explain why you think English should be (or should not be) the exclusive language used in certain circumstances. What are the advantages of requiring (or not requiring) English only? What problems do you see with having different languages in school or the workplace? Try to address such questions in your essay.

Writer and linguist Deborah Tannen (b. 1945) *is perhaps best known for her 1990 book* You Just Don't Understand: Women and Men in Conversation, *which was on* The New York Times *bestseller list for a remarkable four years. In that book, which some critics described as revolutionizing the way we understand communication between men and women, Tannen examines the central role that gender plays in communication. Her work helped popularize the idea of sexual*

Sex, Lies AND Conversation

DEBORAH TANNEN

politics *in the 1990s and emphasized the differences in the way men and women communicate. The following article, which first appeared in* The Washington Post *in 1990, is a shorter version of the analysis that Tannen developed in* You Just Don't Understand. *In this article, Tannen describes the differences in the way men and women communicate and she explains how those differences contribute to problems in male–female relationships. Such problems are often the focus of jokes and popular sitcoms, but Tannen helps us see that the consequences of communication problems in relationships are anything but funny. She also helps us see that the politics of language can play out in the most ordinary interactions between friends and couples, and she reminds us that language, one of the most complex aspects of human life, is further complicated by gender.*

A professor of linguistics at Georgetown University, Deborah Tannen is the author of nineteen books, including books about communication for popular audiences, such as The Argument Culture: Stopping America's War of Words *(1999) and* I Only Say This Because I Love You: Talking to Your Parents, Partner, Sibs, and Kids When You're All Adults *(2002), as well as scholarly works focusing on communication, such as* Gender and Discourse *(1994).* ▼

I was addressing a small gathering in a suburban Virginia living room—a women's group that had invited men to join them. Throughout the evening, one man had been particularly talkative, frequently offering ideas and anecdotes, while his wife sat silently beside him on the couch. Toward the end of the evening, I commented that women frequently complain that their husbands don't talk to them. This man quickly concurred. He gestured toward his wife and said, "She's the talker in our family." The room burst into laughter; the man looked puzzled and hurt. "It's true," he explained. "When I come home from work I have nothing to say. If she didn't keep the conversation going, we'd spend the whole evening in silence."

This episode crystallizes the irony that although American men tend to talk more than women in public situations, they often talk less at home. And this pattern is wreaking havoc with marriage.

The pattern was observed by political scientist Andrew Hacker in the late '70s. Sociologist Catherine Kohler Riessman reports in her book *Divorce Talk* that most of the women she interviewed—but only a few of the men—gave lack of communication as the reason for their divorces. Given the current divorce rate of nearly 50 percent, that amounts to millions of cases in the United States every year—a virtual epidemic of failed conversation.

In my own research, complaints from women about their husbands most often focused not on tangible inequities such as having given up the chance for a career to accompany a husband to his, or doing far more than their share of daily life-support work like cleaning, cooking, social arrangements and errands. Instead, they focused on communication: "He doesn't listen to me," "He doesn't talk to me." I found, as Hacker observed years before, that most wives want their husbands to be, first and foremost, conversational partners, but few husbands share this expectation of their wives.

In short, the image that best represents the current crisis is the stereotypical car- 5 toon scene of a man sitting at the breakfast table with a newspaper held up in front of his face, while a woman glares at the back of it, wanting to talk.

LINGUISTIC BATTLE OF THE SEXES

How can women and men have such different impressions of communication in marriage? Why the widespread imbalance in their interests and expectations?

In the April, 1990 issue of *American Psychologist,* Stanford University's Eleanor Maccoby reports the results of her own and others' research showing that children's development is most influenced by the social structure of peer interactions. Boys and girls tend to play with children of their own gender, and their sex-separate groups have different organizational structures and interactive norms.

I believe these systematic differences in childhood socialization make talk between women and men like cross-cultural communication, heir to all the attraction and pitfalls of that enticing but difficult enterprise. My research on men's and women's conversations uncovered patterns similar to those described for children's groups.

For women, as for girls, intimacy is the fabric of relationships, and talk is the thread from which it is woven. Little girls create and maintain friendships by exchanging secrets; similarly, women regard conversation as the cornerstone of friendship. So a woman expects her husband to be a new and improved version of a best friend. What is important is not the individual subjects that are discussed but the sense of closeness, of a life shared, that emerges when people tell their thoughts, feelings, and impressions.

10 Bonds between boys can be as intense as girls', but they are based less on talking, more on doing things together. Since they don't assume talk is the cement that binds a relationship, men don't know what kind of talk women want, and they don't miss it when it isn't there.

VISUAL CONNECTIONS: CARTOONS AND SOCIAL PROBLEMS

Tannen ends the opening section of this article with a reference to a "stereotypical cartoon scene," such as the one in this cartoon. Tannen's reference to cartoons in this instance suggests the role that cartoons can play in communicating important social and cultural attitudes and trends. The fact that Tannen, an accomplished scholar of linguistics, would make such a reference also suggests the importance of cartoons as a means of communication.

"If I were a car, you could find the words."

STRATEGIES: USING RESEARCH TO SUPPORT A POINT
Notice Tannen's reference in paragraph 7 to Eleanor Maccoby's research on gender differences in children's social interactions. Tannen uses this reference to help build her case for recognizing the importance of gender differences in adult communication. She makes note of the fact that Maccoby is a researcher at Stanford University, one of the most prestigious American universities. Consider how this reference helps Tannen not only support her point about gender differences but also establish her own credibility as an authority on gender and communication.

Boys' groups are larger, more inclusive, and more hierarchical, so boys must struggle to avoid the subordinate position in the group. This may play a role in women's complaints that men don't listen to them. Some men really don't like to listen, because being the listener makes them feel one-down, like a child listening to adults or an employee to a boss.

But often when women tell men, "You aren't listening," and the men protest, "I am," the men are right. The impression of not listening results from misalignments in the mechanics of conversation. The misalignment begins as soon as a man and a woman take physical positions. This became clear when I studied videotapes made by psychologist Bruce Dorval of children and adults talking to their same-sex best friends. I found that at every age, the girls and women faced each other directly, their eyes anchored on each other's faces. At every age, the boys and men sat at angles to each other and looked elsewhere in the room, periodically glancing at each other. They were obviously attuned to each other, often mirroring each other's movements. But the tendency of men to face away can give women the impression they aren't listening even when they are. A young woman in college was frustrated: Whenever she told her boyfriend she wanted to talk to him, he would lie down on the floor, close his eyes, and put his arm over his face. This signaled to her, "He's taking a nap." But he insisted he was listening extra hard. Normally, he looks around the room, so he is easily distracted. Lying down and covering his eyes helped him concentrate on what she was saying.

GLOSS: CROSS-CULTURAL COMMUNICATION
The term *cross-cultural communication* refers to communication between people of different cultures. In paragraph 8, Tannen applies the term to communication between people of different genders within the same culture. She will then use the term in this new sense throughout her article, especially in her conclusion. This is an example of how terms can acquire different meanings as people use them in new ways.

Analogous to the physical alignment that women and men take in conversation is their topical alignment. The girls in my study tended to talk at length about one topic, but the boys tended to jump from topic to topic. The second-grade girls exchanged stories about people they knew. The second-grade boys teased, told jokes, noticed things in the room and talked about finding games to play. The sixth-grade girls talked about problems with a mutual friend. The sixth grade boys talked about 55 different topics, none of which extended over more than a few turns.

LISTENING TO BODY LANGUAGE

Switching topics is another habit that gives women the impression men aren't listening, especially if they switch to a topic about themselves. But the evidence of the 10th-grade boys in my study indicates otherwise. The 10th-grade boys sprawled across their chairs with bodies parallel and eyes straight ahead, rarely looking at each other. They looked as if they were riding in a car, staring out the windshield. But they were talking about their feelings. One boy was upset because a girl had told him he had a drinking problem, and the other was feeling alienated from all his friends.

15   Now, when a girl told a friend about a problem, the friend responded by asking probing questions and expressing agreement and understanding. But the boys dismissed each other's problems. Todd assured Richard that his drinking was "no big problem" because "sometimes you're funny when you're off your butt." And when

Todd said he felt left out, Richard responded, "Why should you? You know more people than me."

Women perceive such responses as belittling and unsupportive. But the boys seemed satisfied with them. Whereas women reassure each other by implying, "You shouldn't feel bad because I've had similar experiences," men do so by implying, "You shouldn't feel bad because your problems aren't so bad."

There are even simpler reasons for women's impression that men don't listen. Linguist Lynette Hirschman found that women make more listener-noise, such as "mhm," "uhuh," and "yeah," to show "I'm with you." Men, she found, more often give silent attention. Women who expect a stream of listener noise interpret silent attention as no attention at all.

Women's conversational habits are as frustrating to men as men's are to women. Men who expect silent attention interpret a stream of listener noise as overreaction or impatience. Also, when women talk to each other in a close, comfortable setting, they often overlap, finish each other's sentences and anticipate what the other is about to say. This practice, which I call "participatory listenership," is often perceived by men as interruption, intrusion and lack of attention.

A parallel difference caused a man to complain about his wife, "She just wants to talk about her own point of view. If I show her another view, she gets mad at me." When most women talk to each other, they assume a conversationalist's job is to express agreement and support. But many men see their conversational duty as pointing out the other side of an argument. This is heard as disloyalty by women, and refusal to offer the requisite support. It is not that women don't want to see other points of view, but that they prefer them phrased as suggestions and inquiries rather than as direct challenges.

In his book *Fighting for Life*, Walter Ong points out that men use "agonistic" or war-like, oppositional formats to do almost anything; thus discussion becomes debate, and conversation a competitive sport. In contrast, women see conversation as a ritual means of establishing rapport. If Jane tells a problem and June says she has a similar one, they walk away feeling closer to each other. But this attempt at establishing rapport can backfire when used with men. Men take too literally women's ritual "troubles talk," just as women mistake men's ritual challenges for real attack.

20

VISUAL CONNECTIONS: BODY LANGUAGE
This image from a popular advertising campaign for the Apple iPod music player might be seen as an example of how body language can communicate feelings or thoughts. The exuberance and joy suggested by the dancing silhouette body in this advertisement would be familiar to most consumers. In paragraphs 12 and 13 Tannen is talking about more subtle forms of body language that send often complex messages in various social situations. Consider how we learn to "read" body language, like dancing, and how that learning is part of communication between men and women.

iPod

Join the digital music revolution.

© Apple Computer, Inc.

THE SOUNDS OF SILENCE

These differences begin to clarify why women and men have such different expectations about communication in marriage. For women, talk creates intimacy. Marriage is an orgy of closeness: you can tell your feelings and thoughts, and still be loved. Their greatest fear is being pushed away. But men live in a hierarchical world, where talk maintains independence and status. They are on guard to protect themselves from being put down and pushed around. This explains the paradox of the talkative man who said of his silent wife, "She's the talker." In the public setting of a guest lecture, he felt challenged to show his intelligence and display his understanding of the lecture. But at home, where he has nothing to prove and no one to defend against, he is free to remain silent. For his wife, being home means she is free from the worry that something she says might offend someone, or spark disagreement, or appear to be showing off; at home she is free to talk.

The communication problems that endanger marriage can't be fixed by mechanical engineering. They require a new conceptual framework about the role of talk in human relationships. Many of the psychological explanations that have become second nature may not be helpful, because they tend to blame either women (for not being assertive enough) or men (for not being in touch with their feelings). A sociolinguistic approach by which male-female conversation is seen as cross-cultural communication allows us to understand the problem and forge solutions without blaming either party.

CONVERSATIONS: SOCIOLINGUISTIC APPROACH

In discussing communication problems in marriages, Tannen advocates a "sociolinguistic approach," which refers to a theoretical perspective on language that emphasizes social and cultural context in communication, rather than understanding language exclusively as a psychological or physiological matter. In fact, Tannen's mention earlier in this paragraph (par. 23) of "psychological explanations" might be seen as a subtle argument in favor of a sociolinguistic instead of a psychological approach to explain communication difficulties between men and women. This is an example of the way that scholars carry on professional conversations about important issues in their academic fields.

Once the problem is understood, improvement comes naturally, as it did to the young woman and her boyfriend who seemed to go to sleep when she wanted to talk. Previously, she had accused him of not listening, and he had refused to change his behavior, since that would be admitting fault. But then she learned about and explained to him the differences in women's and men's habitual ways of aligning themselves in conversation. The next time she told him she wanted to talk, he began, as usual, by lying down and covering his eyes. When the familiar negative reaction bubbled up, she reassured herself that he really was listening. But then he sat up and looked at her. Thrilled, she asked why. He said, "You like me to look at you when we talk, so I'll try to do it." Once he saw their differences as cross-cultural rather than right and wrong, he independently altered his behavior.

Women who feel abandoned and deprived when their husbands won't listen to or report daily news may be happy to discover their husbands trying to adapt once they understand the place of small talk in women's relationships. But if their husbands don't adapt, the women may still be comforted that for men, this is not a failure of intimacy. Accepting the difference, the wives may look to their friends or family for that kind of talk. And husbands who can't provide it shouldn't feel their wives have made unreasonable demands. Some couples will still decide to divorce, but at least their decisions will be based on realistic expectations.

25   In these times of resurgent ethnic conflicts, the world desperately needs cross-cultural understanding. Like charity, successful cross-cultural communication should begin at home.

UNDERSTANDING THE TEXT

1. Why are differences in the ways men and women communicate important, according to Tannen? What are the larger implications of these differences?

2. Examine the major differences in the ways men and women communicate with each other as Tannen describes them in this essay. What do you think they suggest about gender roles in contemporary Western society? Do you think Tannen is suggesting that we reexamine or question these gender roles? Explain, citing specific passages to support your answer.

3. How do "misalignments in the mechanics of conversation" affect the way men and women talk to each other, according to Tannen? How does she account for these misalignments? Do you think she is right, based on your own experiences? Explain.

4. In Tannen's view, how do the main differences in the way men and women communicate contribute to marriage difficulties? How can these problems be remedied, according to Tannen? What do you think her discussion of these problems suggests about language? About gender?

EXPLORING THE ISSUES

1. In a sense, Tannen's solution to the communication problems between men and women comes down to understanding the differences in how men and women communicate. How convincing do you find this solution? Based on your own experiences, do you think this is a feasible solution? Why or why not?

2. Tannen's writing has been described as accessible and readable, even though she writes about complex issues from a scholarly perspective. Evaluate Tannen's writing style. How would you describe it? What are its most noticeable features? Do you find her style accessible and readable? Explain, citing specific examples to support your answer.

3. Throughout this essay, Tannen refers to her own research on social interactions between boys and girls. Keeping in mind that Tannen is a well-known linguistics scholar, what effect did these references to her research have on you as a reader? Do they strengthen or weaken her essay in any way? Did they influence your sense of Tannen as an author? Explain. What might your answers to these questions reveal about you as a reader?

4. This essay was first published in 1990. Yet, the book that is based on the ideas in this article, *You Just Don't Understand: Women and Men in Conversation,* continues to be read today. Do you think Tannen's ideas about gender and communication still apply today? Why or why not? Has anything changed since 1990 that might affect the validity of Tannen's ideas? Explain. What might the continuing popularity of her book say about gender and communication in contemporary society?

ENTERING THE CONVERSATIONS

1. Identify the main characteristics of the way women talk and the way men talk, as Tannen describes them in this essay. Now listen to several conversations among your friends or family members. If possible, tape-record the conversations. (Be sure to ask for the participants' permission first.) Then analyze the conversations using Tannen's ideas. Try to determine whether the conversations fall into the patterns that Tannen describes for men and women. Write a report about your informal study of the conversations you observed. In your report, describe those conversations (where they occurred, who participated) and present your analysis of them, using Tannen's ideas. Draw conclusions about the usefulness of Tannen's ideas for understanding communication between men and women.

2. Based on your work for Question 1 and drawing on Tannen's essay, create a pamphlet for an audience of students at your school (or another audience you wish to address) with advice about how to communicate with members of the opposite sex. Alternatively, create a web site for the same purpose.

3. Write your own analysis of gender differences in communication based on your experiences and your own perspective on how men and women communicate with one another.

4. Select several popular television sitcoms, such as *The King of Queens* or *Everybody Loves Raymond,* and watch several episodes, focusing on how the couples are portrayed in the shows and especially on how they communicate. What characterizes the ways that the male and female characters talk to one another in these shows? Are there similarities and differences in the way the shows portray male–female communication, especially among married couples? What might these shows suggest about cultural attitudes regarding communication between men and women? What might they suggest about the politics of language? Try to address these questions. Then write an essay in which you present your analysis to an audience of your classmates. Alternatively, write a letter to the editor of your local newspaper in which you express your opinion about the portrayal of male–female relationships on popular television shows.

I grew up in a home where my parents and grandparents sometimes used Polish, though only my grandparents really spoke that language. Often, they spoke Polish to refer to specific cultural or religious traditions, such as special holiday rituals. Sometimes, Polish was part of those rituals, such as the Polish Christmas carols that were sung at special holiday church services. And once in a while, Polish words were used when English ones didn't seem quite right, such as when my grandmother referred to a close friend as pani, a term that seemed to have a special meaning that the English word friend didn't quite capture. I never paid much attention to these uses of Polish, maybe because my siblings and I were expected to learn "proper" English. But I think Polish was a way for my grandmother to hold onto a sense of herself as a Pole.

I thought about my grandmother when I first read Gloria Anzaldúa's (1942–2004) provocative essay. Like my grandmother, Anzaldúa uses language—in this case, Chicano Spanish—to maintain her sense of identity. But Anzaldúa goes well beyond my grandmother's efforts to preserve her ethnic heritage. She uses a number of languages, dialects, styles, voices, and textual forms to create an exuberant and defiant statement about herself, her people, and their language. Anzaldúa's essay, which was first published in her book Borderlands/La Frontera (1987), presents a view of language as a way to declare one's autonomy and to resist being silenced. Raised in the borderlands of southwest Texas, she embraced a variety of languages and dialects, including various regional versions of Spanish and Native American languages as well as Standard English. You (continued)

How to Tame a *Wild* Tongue

GLORIA ANZALDÚA

"**We're going to have to control your tongue, "the dentist** says, pulling out all the metal from my mouth. Silver bits plop and tinkle into the basin. My mouth is a motherlode.

The dentist is cleaning out my roots. I get a whiff of the stench when I gasp. "I can't cap that tooth yet, you're still draining," he says.

"We're going to have to do something about your tongue," I hear the anger rising in his voice. My tongue keeps pushing out the wads of cotton, pushing back the drills, the long thin needles. "I've never seen anything as strong or as stubborn," he says. And I think, how do you tame a wild tongue, train it to be quiet, how do you bridle and saddle it? How do you make it lie down?

> Who is to say that robbing a people of
> its language is less violent than war?
> —*Ray Gwyn Smith*[1]

(continued) *may find her unusual approach to writing disconcerting at times. But Anzaldúa would not have wanted it any other way, for she used her writing to challenge our ideas about who we are and how we speak to one another. That provocative approach characterizes all her writing, including* This Bridge Called My Back: Radical Writings by Women of Color *(1981), in which she wrote that she felt compelled to write "because I must keep the spirit of my revolt and myself alive."* ◩

I remember being caught speaking Spanish at recess—that was good for three licks on the knuckles with a sharp ruler. I remember being sent to the corner of the classroom for "talking back" to the Anglo teacher when all I was trying to do was tell her how to pronounce my name. "If you want to be American, speak 'American.' If you don't like it, go back to Mexico where you belong."

"I want you to speak English. *Pa' hallar buen trabajo tienes que saber hablar el inglés bien. Qué; vale toda tu educación si todavía hablas inglés con un 'accent,'*" my mother would say, mortified that I spoke English like a Mexican. At Pan American University, I and all Chicano students were required to take two speech classes. Their purpose: to get rid of our accents.

Attacks on one's form of expression with the intent to censor are a violation of the First Amendment. *El Anglo con cara de inocente nos arrancó la lengua.* Wild tongues can't be tamed, they can only be cut out.

Overcoming the Tradition of Silence

Ahogadas, escupimos el oscuro.
Peleando con nuestra propia sombra
el silencio nos sepulta.

En boca cerrada no entran moscas. "Flies don't enter a closed mouth" is a saying I kept hearing when I was a child. *Ser habladora* was to be a gossip and a liar, to talk too much. *Muchachitas bien criadas,* well-bred girls don't answer back. *Es una falta de respeto* to talk back to one's mother or father. I remember one of the sins I'd recite to the priest in the confession box the few times I went to confession: talking back to my mother, *hablar pa' 'tras, repelar. Hociocona, repelona, chismosa,* having a big mouth, questioning, carrying tales are all signs of being *mal criada.* In my culture they are all words that are derogatory if applied to women—I've never heard them applied to men.

* * *

The first time I heard two women, a Puerto Rican and a Cuban, say the word *"nosotras,"* I was shocked. I had not known the word existed. Chicanas use *nosotros* whether we're male or female. We are robbed of our female being by the masculine plural. Language is a male discourse.

And our tongues have become
dry   the wilderness has
dried out our tongues   and
we have forgotten speech.
            —*Irena Klepfisz[2]*

Even our own people, other Spanish speakers *nos quieren poner candados en la boca.* They would hold us back with their bag of *reglas de academia.*

> *Oyé como ladra:*
> *el lenguaje de la frontera*
> *Quien tiene boca se equivoca.*
> *—Mexican saying*

10   "*Pocho,* cultural traitor, you're speaking the oppressor's language by speaking English, you're ruining the Spanish language," I have been accused by various Latinos and Latinas. Chicano Spanish is considered by the purist and by most Latinos deficient, a mutilation of Spanish.

But Chicano Spanish is a border tongue which developed naturally. Change, *evolución, enriquecimiento de palabras nuevas por invención o adopción* have created variants of Chicano Spanish, *un nuevo lenguaje. Un lenguaje que corresponde a un modo de vivir.* Chicano Spanish is not incorrect, it is a living language.

For a people who are neither Spanish nor live in a country in which Spanish is the first language; for a people who live in a country in which English is the reigning tongue but who are not Anglo; for a people who cannot entirely identify with either standard (formal, Castilian) Spanish nor standard English, what recourse is left to them but to create their own language? A language which they can connect their identity to, one capable of communicating the realities and values true to themselves—a language with terms that are neither *español ni inglés,* but both. We speak a patois, a forked tongue, a variation of two languages.

Chicano Spanish sprang out of the Chicanos' need to identify ourselves as a distinct people. We needed a language with which we could communicate with ourselves, a secret language. For some of us, language is a homeland closer than the Southwest—for many Chicanos today live in the Midwest and the East. And because we are a complex, heterogeneous people, we speak many languages. Some of the languages we speak are

1. Standard English
2. Working class and slang English
3. Standard Spanish
4. Standard Mexican Spanish
5. North Mexican Spanish dialect
6. Chicano Spanish (Texas, New Mexico, Arizona, and California have regional variations)
7. Tex-Mex
8. *Pachuco* (called *caló*)

My "home" tongues are the languages I speak with my sister and brothers, with my friends. They are the last five listed, with 6 and 7 being closest to my heart. From school, the media, and job situations, I've picked up standard and working class English. From Mamagrande Locha and from reading Spanish and Mexican literature, I've picked up Standard Spanish and Standard Mexican Spanish. From *los recién llegados,* Mexican immigrants, and *braceros,* I learned the North Mexican dialect. With Mexicans I'll try to speak either Standard Mexican Spanish or the North Mexican dialect. From my parents and Chicanos living in the Valley, I picked up Chicano Texas Spanish, and I speak it with my mom, younger brother (who married a Mexican and who rarely mixes Spanish with English), aunts, and older relatives.

With Chicanas from *Nuevo México* or *Arizona* I will speak Chicano Spanish a little,   15
but often they don't understand what I'm saying. With most California Chicanas I
speak entirely in English (unless I forget). When I first moved to San Francisco, I'd
rattle off something in Spanish, unintentionally embarrassing them. Often it is only
with another Chicana *tejano* that I can talk freely.

*   *   *

Words distorted by English are known as anglicisms or *pochismos*. The *pocho* is an
anglicized Mexican or American of Mexican origin who speaks Spanish with an accent characteristic of North Americans and who distorts and reconstructs the language according to the influence of English.[3] Tex-Mex, or Spanglish, comes most
naturally to me. I may switch back and forth from English to Spanish in the same sentence or in the same word. With my sister and my brother Nune and with Chicano *tejano* contemporaries I speak in Tex-Mex.

From kids and people my own age I picked up *Pachuco*. Pachuco (the language of
the zoot suiters) is a language of rebellion, both against Standard Spanish and
Standard English. It is a secret language. Adults of the culture and outsiders cannot
understand it. It is made up of slang words from both English and Spanish. *Ruca*
means girl or woman, *vato* means guy or dude, *chale* means no, *simón* means yes,
churro is sure, talk is *periquiar, pigionear* means petting, *que gacho* means how nerdy,
ponte águila means watch out, death is called *la pelona*. Through lack of practice and
not having others who can speak it, I've lost most of the *Pachuco* tongue.

CHICANO SPANISH

Chicanos, after 250 years of Spanish/Anglo colonization, have developed significant
differences in the Spanish we speak. We collapse two adjacent vowels into a single syllable and sometimes shift the stress in certain words such as *maíz/maiz, cohete/cuete*.
We leave out certain consonants when they appear between vowels: *lado/lao, mo-
jado/mojao*. Chicanos from South Texas pronounce *f* as *j* as in *jue (fue)*. Chicanos use
"archaisms," words that are no longer in the Spanish language, words that have been
evolved out. We say *semos, truje, haiga, ansina,* and *naiden*. We retain the "archaic" *j*,
as in *jalar*, that derives from an earlier *h* (the French *halar* or the Germanic *halon*
which was lost to standard Spanish in the sixteenth century), but which is still found
in several regional dialects such as the one spoken in South Texas. (Due to geography, Chicanos from the Valley of South Texas were cut off linguistically from other
Spanish speakers. We tend to use words that the Spaniards brought over from
Medieval Spain. The majority of the Spanish colonizers in Mexico and the Southwest
came from Extremadura—Hernán Cortés was one of them—and Andalucía.
Andalucians pronounce *ll* like a *y*, and their *d*'s tend to be absorbed by adjacent vowels: *tirado* becomes *tirao*. They brought *el lenguaje popular, dialectos y regionalismos*.)[4]

Chicanos and other Spanish speakers also shift *ll* to *y* and *z* to *s*.[5] We leave out initial syllables, saying *tar* for *estar, toy* for *estoy, hora* for *ahora* (*cubanos* and *puertorriqueños*
also leave out initial letters of some words). We also leave out the final syllable such
as *pa* for *para*. The intervocalic *y*, the *ll* as in *tortilla, ella, botella*, gets replaced by *tor-
tia* or *toriya, ea, botea*. We add an additional syllable at the beginning of certain words:

atocar for *tocar, agastar* for *gastar.* Sometimes we'll say *lavaste las vacijas,* other times *lavates* (substituting the *ates* verb endings for the *aste*).

20 We use anglicisms, words borrowed from English: *bola* from ball, *carpeta* from carpet, *máchina de lavar* (instead of *lavadora*) from washing machine. Tex-Mex argot, created by adding a Spanish sound at the beginning or end of an English word such as *cookiar* for cook, *watchar* for watch, *parkiar* for park, and *rapiar* for rape, is the result of the pressures on Spanish speakers to adapt to English.

We don't use the word *vosotros/as* or its accompanying verb form. We don't say *claro* (to mean yes), *imagínate,* or *me emociona,* unless we picked up Spanish from Latinas, out of a book, or in a classroom. Other Spanish-speaking groups are going through the same, or similar, development in their Spanish.

LINGUISTIC TERRORISM

> *Deslenguadas. Somos los del español deficiente.* We are your linguistic nightmare, your linguistic aberration, your linguistic *mestisaje,* the subject of your *burla.* Because we speak with tongues of fire we are culturally crucified. Racially, culturally, and linguistically *somos huérfanos*—we speak an orphan tongue.

Chicanas who grew up speaking Chicano Spanish have internalized the belief that we speak poor Spanish. It is illegitimate, a bastard language. And because we internalize how our language has been used against us by the dominant culture, we use our language differences against each other.

Chicana feminists often skirt around each other with suspicion and hesitation. For the longest time I couldn't figure it out. Then it dawned on me. To be close to another Chicana is like looking into the mirror. We are afraid of what we'll see there. *Pena.* Shame. Low estimation of self. In childhood we are told that our language is wrong. Repeated attacks on our native tongue diminish our sense of self. The attacks continue throughout our lives.

Chicanas feel uncomfortable talking in Spanish to Latinas, afraid of their censure. Their language was not outlawed in their countries. They had a whole lifetime of being immersed in their native tongue; generations, centuries in which Spanish was a first language, taught in school, heard on radio and TV, and read in the newspaper.

25 If a person, Chicana or Latina, has a low estimation of my native tongue, she also has a low estimation of me. Often with *mexicanas y latinas* we'll speak English as a neutral language. Even among Chicanas we tend to speak English at parties or conferences. Yet, at the same time, we're afraid the other will think we're *agringadas* because we don't speak Chicano Spanish. We oppress each other trying to out-Chicano each other, vying to be the "real" Chicanas, to speak like Chicanos. There is no one Chicano language just as there is no one Chicano experience. A monolingual Chicana whose first language is English or Spanish is just as much a Chicana as one who speaks several variants of Spanish. A Chicana from Michigan or Chicago or Detroit is just as much a Chicana as one from the Southwest. Chicano Spanish is as diverse linguistically as it is regionally.

By the end of this century, Spanish speakers will comprise the biggest minority group in the United States, a country where students in high schools and colleges are encouraged to take French classes because French is considered more "cultured."

CONTEXT: THE GROWING SPANISH-SPEAKING MINORITY
Anzaldúa writes in this passage that Spanish-speaking people will constitute the largest minority in the United States by 2000. According to the U.S. Census Bureau, the proportion of the U.S. population described as Hispanic grew from about 9 percent in 1990 to more than 13 percent in 2002, making it the largest minority in the United States by a slight margin. (Blacks represented about 12 percent of the total population, according to the 2000 Census.) This graphic illustrates how many Spanish speakers are widely distributed in the United States. Consider the significance of Anzaldúa's statement about the Spanish-speaking minority in the United States in terms of her argument about language in this essay. Why is this fact important to her? How does it contribute to her argument?

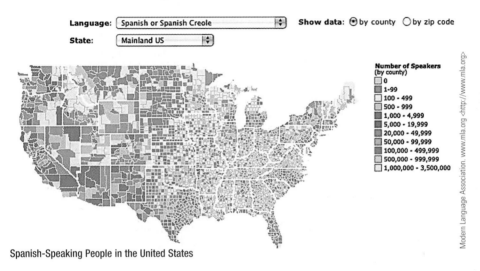

Spanish-Speaking People in the United States

But for a language to remain alive it must be used.[6] By the end of this century English, and not Spanish, will be the mother tongue of most Chicanos and Latinos.

* * *

So, if you want to really hurt me, talk badly about my language. Ethnic identity is twin skin to linguistic identity—I am my language. Until I can take pride in my language, I cannot take pride in myself. Until I can accept as legitimate Chicano Texas Spanish, Tex-Mex, and all the other languages I speak, I cannot accept the legitimacy of myself. Until I am free to write bilingually and to switch codes without having always to translate, while I still have to speak English or Spanish when I would rather speak Spanglish, and as long as I have to accommodate the English speaker rather than having them accommodate me, my tongue will be illegitimate.

I will no longer be made to feel ashamed of existing. I will have my voice: Indian, Spanish, white. I will have my serpent's tongue—my woman's voice, my sexual voice, my poet's voice. I will overcome the tradition of silence.

> My fingers
> move sly against your palm
> Like women everywhere, we speak in code. . . .
>   —*Melanie Kaye/Kantrowitz*[7]

CONVERSATIONS: CHICANO LITERATURE
Anzaldúa describes her struggles to teach and study Chicano literature in the early 1970s. Today, many universities have programs devoted to Chicano literature and related literatures, and works by Chicano writers are assigned in many secondary schools. But Anzaldúa wrote this essay in the late 1980s, when many literary scholars were challenging traditional ideas about which "great" literary works should be assigned in schools and universities. The idea of the "canon" of great literature, which for many years was limited to works by White European writers (mostly male writers), influenced the school curriculum for most of the twentieth century, until scholars began to argue for including works by women and by writers of color who had not previously been represented in English courses and literature programs. Anzaldúa's brief description of her experiences here is a reference to this much larger discussion about what literature should be taught in schools, a discussion that has been occurring for many decades.

"VISTAS," CORRIDOS, Y COMIDA: MY NATIVE TONGUE

In the 1960s, I read my first Chicano novel. It was *City of Night* by John Rechy, a gay Texan, son of a Scottish father and a Mexican mother. For days I walked around in stunned amazement that a Chicano could write and could get published. When I read *I Am Joaquín*[8] I was surprised to see a bilingual book by a Chicano in print. When I saw poetry written in Tex-Mex for the first time, a feeling of pure joy flashed through me. I felt like we really existed as a people. In 1971, when I started teaching High School English to Chicano students, I tried to supplement the required texts with works by Chicanos, only to be reprimanded and forbidden to do so by the principal. He claimed that I was supposed to teach "American" and English literature. At the risk of being fired, I swore my students to secrecy and slipped in Chicano short stories, poems, a play. In graduate school, while working toward a Ph.D., I had to "argue" with one adviser after the other, semester after semester, before I was allowed to make Chicano literature an area of focus.

30   Even before I read books by Chicanos or Mexicans, it was the Mexican movies I saw at the drive-in—the Thursday night special of $1.00 a carload—that gave me a sense of belonging. *"Vámonos a las vistas,"* my mother would call out and we'd all—grandmother, brothers, sister, and cousins—squeeze into the car. We'd wolf down cheese and bologna white bread sandwiches while watching Pedro Infante in melodramatic tearjerkers like *Nosotros los pobres,* the first "real" Mexican movie (that was not an imitation of European movies). I remember seeing *Cuando los hijos se van* and surmising that all Mexican movies played up the love a mother has for her children and what ungrateful sons and daughter suffer when they are not devoted to their mothers. I remember the singing-type "westerns" of Jorge Negrete and Miquel Aceves Mejía. When watching Mexican movies, I felt a sense of homecoming as well as alienation. People who were to amount to something didn't go to Mexican movies, or *bailes,* or tune their radios to *bolero, rancherita,* and *corrido* music.

*   *   *

The whole time I was growing up, there was *norteño* music sometimes called North Mexican border music, or Tex-Mex music, or Chicano music, or *cantina* (bar) music. I grew up listening to *conjuntos,* three- or four-piece bands made up of folk musicians playing guitar, *bajo sexto,* drums, and button accordion, which Chicanos had borrowed from the German immigrants who had come to Central Texas and Mexico to farm and build breweries. In the Rio Grande Valley, Steven Jordan and Little Joe Hernández were popular, and Flaco Jiménez was the accordion king. The rhythms of Tex-Mex music are those of the polka, also adapted from the Germans, who in turn had borrowed the polka from the Czechs and Bohemians.

I remember the hot, sultry evenings when *corridos*—song of love and death on the Texas-Mexican borderlands—reverberated out of cheap amplifiers from the local *cantinas* and wafted in through my bedroom window.

Corridos first became widely used along the south Texas/Mexican border during the early conflict between Chicanos and Anglos. The *corridos* are usually about Mexican heroes who do valiant deeds against the Anglo oppressors. Pancho Villa's song, *"La cucaracha,"* is the most famous one. *Corridos* of John F. Kennedy and his death are still very popular in the Valley. Older Chicanos remember Lydia Mendoza, one of the great border *corrido* singers who was called *la Gloria de Tejas.* Her *"El tango negro,"* sung during the great Depression, made her a singer of the people. The ever-present *corridos* narrated one hundred years of border history, bringing news of events as well as entertaining. These folk musicians and folk songs are our chief cultural mythmakers, and they made our hard lives seem bearable.

I grew up feeling ambivalent about our music. Country-western and rock-and-roll had more status. In the fifties and sixties, for the slightly educated and *agringado* Chicanos, there existed a sense of shame at being caught listening to our music. Yet I couldn't stop my feet from thumping to the music, could not stop humming the words, nor hide from myself the exhilaration I felt when I heard it.

*   *   *

There are more subtle ways that we internalize identification, especially in the forms of images and emotions. For me food and certain smells are tied to my identity, to my homeland. Woodsmoke curling up to an immense blue sky; woodsmoke perfuming my grandmother's clothes, her skin. The stench of cow manure and the yellow patches on the ground; the crack of a .22 rifle and the reek of cordite. Homemade white cheese sizzling in a pan, melting inside a folded *tortilla.* My sister Hilda's hot, spicy *menudo, chile colorado* making it deep red, pieces of *panza* and hominy floating on top. My brother Carito barbequing *fajitas* in the backyard. Even now and 3,000 miles away, I can see my mother spicing the ground beef, pork, and venison with *chile.* My mouth salivates at the thought of the hot steaming *tamales* I would be eating if I were home.

Si le preguntas a mi mamá, "¿Qué eres?"

Identity is the essential core of who
we are as individuals, the conscious
experience of the self inside.
                   —*Gershen Kaufman*[9]

Nosotros los Chicanos straddle the **borderlands.** On one side of us, we are constantly exposed to the Spanish of the Mexicans, on the other side we hear the Anglos' incessant clamoring so that we forget our language. Among ourselves we don't say *nosotros los americanos, o nosotros los españoles, o nosotros los hispanos.* We say *nosotros los*

CONVERSATIONS: LANGUAGE PRACTICES
Notice that many of the words Anzaldúa uses in this essay, such as *tejano, cantina,* and *fajita,* which have become commonly used in English, are italicized throughout the essay. It is a common editorial practice to italicize words from another language when writing in formal English. Perhaps Anzaldúa's editors used italics because it is standard in publishing to do so. But Anzaldúa also insists on writing in a way that does not have "to accommodate the English speaker" (par. 27). You might consider how common editorial practices for Standard English, like italicizing foreign words, might be examples of the "linguistic terrorism" that Anzaldúa criticizes in her essay. Consider, too, how effective her use of untranslated Spanish is as a strategy to combat linguistic terrorism.

STRATEGIES: METAPHOR
Here, as elsewhere in her essay, Anzaldúa refers to the "borderlands," the region where she grew up in southwest Texas along the U.S.-Mexico border. But she uses the term *borderland* to refer to more than that region. Here, it is a metaphor for the way she and her people used language. It is also a metaphor for her very identity as a Chicana. What other meanings does this term have for Anzaldúa?

mexicanos (by *mexicanos* we do not mean citizens of Mexico; we do not mean a national identity, but a racial one). We distinguish between *mexicanos del otro lado* and *mexicanos de este lado.* Deep in our hearts we believe that being Mexican has nothing to do with which country one lives in. Being Mexican is a state of soul–not one of mind, not one of citizenship. Neither eagle nor serpent, but both. And like the ocean, neither animal respects borders.

> *Dime con quien andas y te diré; quien eres.*
> (Tell me who your friends are and I'll tell you who you are.)
> —*Mexican saying*

Si le preguntas a mi mama, "¿Qué eres?" te dirá, "Soy mexicana." My brothers and sister say the same. I sometimes will answer *"soy mexicana"* and at others will say *"soy Chicana" o "soy tejana."* But I identified as *"Raza"* before I ever identified as *"mexicana"* or "Chicana."

As a culture, we call ourselves Spanish when referring to ourselves as a linguistic group and when copping out. It is then that we forget our predominant Indian genes. We are 70–80 percent Indian.[10] We call ourselves Hispanic[11] or Spanish-American or Latin American or Latin when linking ourselves to other Spanish-speaking peoples of the Western hemisphere and when copping out. We call ourselves Mexican-American[12] to signify we are neither Mexican nor American, but more the noun "American" than the adjective "Mexican" (and when copping out).

Chicanos and other people of color suffer economically for not acculturating. This voluntary (yet forced) alienation makes for psychological conflict, a kind of dual identity—we don't identify with the Anglo-American cultural values and we don't totally identify with the Mexican cultural values. We are a synergy of two cultures with various degrees of Mexicanness or Angloness. I have so internalized the borderland conflict that sometimes I feel like one cancels out the other and we are zero, nothing, no one. *A veces no soy nada ni nadie. Pero hasta cuando no lo soy, lo soy.*

40   When not copping out, when we know we are more than nothing, we call ourselves Mexican, referring to race and ancestry; *mestizo* when affirming both our Indian and Spanish (but we hardly ever own our Black) ancestry; Chicano when referring to a politically aware people born and/or raised in the United States; *Raza* when referring to Chicanos; *tejanos* when we are Chicanos from Texas.

GLOSS: CESAR CHAVEZ

In 1962, well-known and sometimes controversial labor activist Cesar Chavez (1927–1993) founded the union that eventually became the United Farm Workers. He worked on behalf of migrant farm workers in the American Southwest and especially in California, most of whom were Spanish-speaking.

Chicanos did not know we were a people until 1965 when **Cesar Chavez** and the farmworkers united and *I Am Joaquín* was published and *la Raza Unida* party was formed in Texas. With that recognition, we became a distinct people. Something momentous happened to the Chicano soul—we became aware of our reality and acquired a name and a language (Chicano Spanish) that reflected that reality. Now that we had a name, some of the fragmented pieces began to fall together—who we were, what we were, how we had evolved. We began to get glimpses of what we might eventually become.

Yet the struggle of identities continues, the struggle of borders is our reality still. One day the inner struggle will cease and a true integration take place. In the meantime, *tenémos que hacer la lucha. ¿Quién está protegiendo los ranchos de mi gente? ¿Quién está tratando de cerrar la fisura entre la India y el blanco en nuestra sangre? El Chicano, si, el Chicano que anida como un ladrón en su propia casa.*

*   *   *

Los Chicanos, how patient we seem, how very patient. There is the quiet of the Indian about us.[13] We know how to survive. When other races have given up their tongue we've kept ours. We know what it is to live under the hammer blow of the dominant *norteamericano* culture. But more than we count the blows, we count the days the weeks the years the centuries the aeons until the white laws and commerce and customs will rot in the deserts they've created, lie bleached. *Humildes* yet proud, *quietos* yet wild, *nosotros los mexicanos-Chicanos* will walk by the crumbling ashes as we go about our business. Stubborn, persevering, impenetrable as stone, yet possessing a malleability that renders us unbreakable, we, the *mestizas* and *mestizos,* will remain.

NOTES

[1]Ray Gwyn Smith, *Moorland Is Cold Country,* unpublished book.

[2]Irena Klepfisz, *"Di rayze aheym/*The Journey Home," in *The Tribe of Dina: A Jewish Women's Anthology,* Melanie Kaye/Kantrowitz and Irena Klepfisz, eds. (Montpelier, VT: Sinister Wisdom Books, 1986), 49.

[3]R. C. Ortega, *Dialectología Del Barrio,* trans. Hortencia S. Alwan (Los Angeles, CA: R. C. Ortega Publisher & Bookseller, 1977), 132.

[4]Eduardo Hernandéz-Chávez, Andrew D. Cohen, and Anthony F. Beltramo, *El Lenguaje de los Chicanos: Regional and Social Characteristics of Language Used by Mexican Americans* (Arlington, VA: Center for Applied Linguistics, 1975), 39.

[5]Hernandéz-Chávez, xvii.

[6]Irena Klepfisz, "Secular Jewish Identity: Yidishkayt in America," in *The Tribe of Dina,* Kaye/Kantrowitz and Klepfisz, eds., 43.

[7]Melanie Kaye/Kantrowitz, "Sign," in *We Speak in Code: Poems and Other Writings* (Pittsburgh, PA: Motheroot Publications, Inc., 1980), 85.

[8]Rodolfo Gonzales, *I Am Joaquín/Yo Soy Joaquín* (New York, NY: Bantam Books, 1972). It was first published in 1967.

[9]Gershen Kaufman, *Shame: The Power of Caring* (Cambridge, MA: Schenkman Books, Inc., 1980), 68.

[10]John R. Chávez, *The Lost Land: The Chicano Images of the Southwest* (Albuquerque, NM: University of New Mexico Press, 1984), 88–90.

[11]"Hispanic" is derived from *Hispanis* (*España,* a name given to the Iberian peninsula in ancient times when it was a part of the Roman Empire) and is a term designated by the U.S. government to make it easier to handle us on paper.

[12]The Treaty of Guadalupe Hidalgo created the Mexican-American in 1848.

[13]Anglos, in order to alleviate their guilt for dispossessing the Chicano, stressed the Spanish part of us and perpetrated the myth of the Spanish Southwest. We have accepted the fiction that we are Hispanic, that is Spanish, in order to accommodate ourselves to the dominant culture and its abhorrence of Indians. Chávez, 88–91.

UNDERSTANDING THE TEXT

1. In what ways is language a male discourse, as Anzaldúa describes it in paragraph 7? Why is this idea important to her? Do you agree with her? Why or why not?

2. What is the importance of Chicano Spanish, according to Anzaldúa? What does her view of this language suggest about language in general?

3. How does Anzaldúa explain the way that Chicano Spanish has developed? What is its relationship to English? Why is this relationship important, in her view? What might it reveal about how languages are viewed and how they are used?

4. Why does Anzaldúa wish "to write bilingually and to switch codes without having always to translate," as she states in paragraph 27? What does this desire suggest about language? Do you think she is right? Why or why not?

5. What is the significance of Mexican film and the various forms of music that Anzaldúa describes from her youth? How do these relate to the Chicano Spanish language that she spoke? How do they contribute to her larger argument about that language?

6. At the end of her essay, Anzaldúa declares that one day "the struggle of identities" for Chicanos will end and "a true integration" will take place. What exactly does she mean by that statement? How would language be part of a true integration?

EXPLORING THE ISSUES

1. What is the effect of including Spanish words and phrases throughout an essay that is mostly written in English, as Anzaldúa does? How might this use of Spanish contribute to her main purpose in this essay? What effect did her using several languages have on you as a reader?

2. Examine how Anzaldúa describes the different languages she speaks. What does she emphasize in these descriptions? What is important to her about each language? What might her descriptions suggest about her view of language? What do you think they might suggest about language as a political tool?

3. In a sense, Anzaldúa's essay is as much about English as it is about Chicano Spanish. What view of English does Anzaldúa present in this essay? How do you think Anzaldúa's view of English—and of language in general—might contribute to larger debates about requiring Standard English in schools?

4. What is the relationship of language to identity, as Anzaldúa understands it? She describes herself variously as Chicana, Spanish, Mexican, *mestiza,* and *tejano,* and she describes a variety of languages and dialects that she uses with various people. How do these different identities and languages relate to one another? What might the complexities of language and dialect that Anzaldúa describes suggest about the role of language in our sense of self?

ENTERING THE CONVERSATIONS

1. In paragraph 27, Anzaldúa writes, "I am my language." Write an essay in which you develop that idea from your own experience and based on your own views about language and identity. Alternatively, write the same essay in an unconventional form, using whatever slang, dialects, or languages you think might help you convey your point—as Anzaldúa does in her essay.

2. Write an essay describing an experience in which you were the victim of what Anzaldúa calls "linguistic terrorism."

3. In a group of classmates, discuss Anzaldúa's approach to writing. How effective do you and your classmates find her writing style, especially her use of different languages and textual forms? What appeals to you and your classmates about her style? What is difficult or ineffective about it? Discuss how your reactions to her writing might reveal your own views—and prejudices—about language.

4. In paragraph 17, Anzaldúa describes some of the slang terms of *Pachuco,* which she describes as a secret slang language of rebellion used by young people. Consider the slang that you or people you know speak or once spoke. What purpose do these dialects serve? Do they matter? How does it make a person feel to speak such a dialect? Then write an essay in which you describe this slang and explain its uses in your life or in the lives of others you know.

5. Using Anzaldúa's essay and any other appropriate essay from this book (or elsewhere), write a letter to the superintendent of your local schools in which you present your views about how language should be taught in schools. Should only Standard English be taught? If so, why? Should other languages and "nonstandard" dialects be part of the school curriculum? Why or why not? How might Anzaldúa's essay serve as a model for the way language should be taught in schools? How might it support an argument for teaching only Standard English? Try to address such questions in your letter. Alternatively, write a letter to the editor of your local newspaper or another publication of your choice in which you express your views about teaching Standard English in schools.

Shortly after the war in Iraq began in March 2003, a number of slogans began appearing on bumper stickers, in newspapers and magazines, on the Internet, and on billboards throughout the United States. Perhaps the most common of these slogans was "Support Our Troops," but other slogans were also popular: "Home of the Brave," "United We Stand," "God Bless America." At the time, these slogans were obviously referring to the war in Iraq and what President George W.

Sleuthing *Patriotic* Slogans

Bush called "the war on terror." They were usually interpreted as expressions of patriotism. But writer Gary Sloan wondered just what these slogans really mean. Writing a few months after the United States and its allies invaded Iraq, Sloan offered a careful, if lighthearted, analysis of some of the most common patriotic slogans at the time. His essay is a good example of the use of irony in political writing. But it has a special twist: Sloan is a retired English professor, and he draws on his expertise as a grammarian to analyze political slogans. His analysis calls attention to the ways in which the larger political meanings of slogans often have little to do with grammar or the technical definitions of words. And he helps us see how language acquires meaning in specific historical and cultural contexts.

As you read this essay, it's worth remembering that it was originally published in Alternet.org, an Internet site that describes itself as a progressive news source. The intended audience for this essay, then, very likely had specific political views about the war in Iraq that Sloan certainly was aware of (and perhaps shared). You might consider how the political views of an audience might shape the meaning of a slogan. Consider, too, how well the irony in Sloan's essay would work with a more conservative audience as compared to a liberal one. ◩

GARY SLOAN

In this best of times and worst of times, the American landscape is dotted with signs, billboards, posters and stickers emblazoned with patriotic slogans. In my hometown, merchants have scrawled on their display windows a smorgasbord of venerable shibboleths: "United We Stand," "Support the Troops," "Pray for the Troops," "Let Freedom Ring," "Home of the Brave," "God Bless America." Taped on many windows is a flyer that reads: "Pro-America Rally in Railroad Park. Bring lawn chairs, flags, and snacks. Dress patriotic."

When I read the flyer, I thought: Shouldn't that be "Dress *patriotically?*"

Because I have spent much of my life studying and teaching language, I respond inappropriately to patriotic slogans: I parse them grammatically and try to explicate them the way I would an obscure fragment in an essay. Like Hamlet, I sometimes become sicklied over with the pale cast of thought when I shouldn't be thinking at all. The slogans are designed to evoke warm feelings of camaraderie and unity, not grimaces and cocked brows.

Yet I persist in my folly. To wit: Many patriotic slogans are in the imperative mood. They issue a command ("Support the Troops," "Pray

GARY SLOAN, "SLEUTHING PATRIOTIC SLOGANS." FROM ALTERNET, APRIL 10, 2003. REPRINTED BY PERMISSION.

VISUAL CONNECTIONS: SLOGANS
In all these photographs, the slogan "Support Our Troops" is used, but consider how the meaning of the slogan might differ in each case. How might Sloan's analysis of such slogans help us understand how their meaning can change depending on the context of their use?

© AP/Wide World Photos

© 2003 David McNew/Getty Images

© Sandy Huffaker/Getty Images

for the Troops"). Commands are risky. They create resistance in natural-born rebels and in patriophobes (those with an excessive fear of patriotism).

5   Are "Let Freedom Ring" and "United We Stand" logically compatible? If everyone exercises freedom of speech and conscience, will we all stand united? Instead of assenting to the war against Iraq, some may opt to ring their dissent. How does one "Support the Troops"? Letters? Pep rallies? Boxes of homemade cookies? Can one support the troops by urging them to obey their consciences even if their consciences conflict with their orders?

"Home of the Brave." Hmm. Brave in what sense? Obviously, many Americans aren't physically brave. Millions are afraid to walk the streets at night or open their doors to strangers. If "brave" refers to moral courage, might the bravest Americans be those who resist the will of the majority? Might it require more bravery to protest Operation Iraqi Freedom than to support it?

"God Bless America" is almost as inscrutable as the utterances of a **Delphi oracle.** Grammatically, the words are in the subjunctive mood. They express a wish or a prayer: "Please, God, bless America," or "May God bless America."

The real conundrum: What do the words mean? In what sense is God to bless America? With good health, bouncing babies, supportive spouses? Good schools? High IQs? Philosophical wisdom? Fat paychecks, sirloin steaks, sport utility vehicles, faster computers, more cable channels, bigger boom boxes? Competitive Superbowls? Better face lifts and liposuction? Speedier cruise missiles, smarter smart bombs, stealthier stealth bombers? Continued monopoly of the planet's natural resources?

And does "America" mean Americans? If so, does it comprise all Americans, including murderers, rapists, thieves, swindlers, embezzlers, muggers, liars, cheats, bullies, pederasts, pornographers, conceited airheads, slobs, slum lords, domestic tyrants, bigots and racists?

10   Or does "America" refer to land, spacious skies and amber waves of grain? Or to some platonic ideal of government embodied in the Declaration of Independence and the Constitution, worthy of being blessed even if some Americans aren't?

Now, if I can just figure out how to dress patriotic.

CONVERSATIONS
CLICHÉS AND QUOTATIONS
In the opening sentence, Sloan recalls a famous line from Charles Dickens's novel *A Tale of Two Cities* (1859): "It was the best of times, it was the worst of times." Many readers will recognize this reference to that famous novel about politics and self-sacrifice that takes place during the French Revolution in the late eighteenth century. In the novel, the main character, Sydney Carton, gives up his life so that the woman he loves can be with her husband, whose life is spared by Carton's sacrifice. But many readers may not recognize this reference to Dickens's novel. Consider how Sloan's use of this reference (which is technically called an *allusion*) might enhance the meaning of this paragraph. What might Sloan wish to suggest with such an allusion? What would his paragraph lose if he had not included this allusion? Will his point be clear to readers who don't recognize the allusion? Sloan makes allusions to other well-known literary works in this essay. Consider the effects of those allusions as well.

GRAMMAR
In this paragraph, Sloan uses a technical grammar term, the *imperative mood,* which refers to statements that are commands. In paragraph 7, he uses another grammar term, the *subjunctive mood,* which is a verb form that describes a possible or desired action or state, not a factual or actual one. (A typical example of subjunctive mood is a statement like this one: "I wish I were home right now.") Sloan is a retired English professor, so he can be expected to be familiar with such technical terms. But he wrote this essay for a much broader audience, not for linguists or grammarians. Consider what purposes his use of these technical terms might serve in this essay. What might they accomplish that less technical terms would not?

GLOSS: THE DELPHI ORACLE
The Oracle at Delphi was Pythia, priestess of the god Apollo in ancient Greek mythology, who resided at the city of Delphi around 1400 B.C. and gave predictions about the future that her listeners often could not make sense of and interpreted in various ways.

UNDERSTANDING THE TEXT

1. What does Sloan mean when he writes that he "responds inappropriately to patriotic slogans"? Why does he describe his responses as "folly"? Do you believe him? Why or why not?

2. In paragraph 8, Sloan asks "What do the words mean?" What do you think his answer is? Do you think he really does not know? Do you agree with him?

3. How would you summarize Sloan's main point about slogans?

EXPLORING THE ISSUES

1. How does Sloan present himself in this essay? What kind of person does he seem to be? What authority does he seem to have for making these kinds of statements about slogans? Do you think he wishes to be taken seriously? Explain, citing specific passages to support your answer.

2. Sloan's essay is a careful analysis of the way language is used in political slogans. His analysis rests on a knowledge of formal grammar and linguistic concepts. How effective do you find his analysis of these common slogans? Does his careful reading of such slogans offer us insights into language use—that we could not otherwise gain? Does Sloan's grammatical analysis lead to a useful understanding of the political uses of language? Does it make us aware of aspects of our language use that we would otherwise miss?

3. How would you describe Sloan's strategy in making his point about political slogans and about political language in general? Does he state his position explicitly? If so, where do you see that statement in his essay? If not, how do you know what his point is? How effective do you think this essay is in conveying Sloan's point? To what extent do you think your answer to that question depends on your own political beliefs? Explain.

ENTERING THE CONVERSATIONS

1. Write a response to Sloan's essay about political slogans.

2. With a group of classmates, write several slogans related to what you believe are the most important current political issues.

3. Listen to a political speech. (You can find transcripts or audiotapes of major speeches from the most recent presidential election on the Internet or in your school library.) Identify any statements that you would describe as political slogans and analyze the way the candidate uses those slogans in his or her speech. What do you think the candidate means by those slogans? Are the slogans being directed to a particular audience?

4. Each of these images shows a vehicle sporting bumper stickers. Consider what overall message each driver might be sending by the selection of specific bumper stickers. What conclusions can you draw about the driver? What purposes do you think each driver might have had in placing these particular bumper stickers on the vehicle? How effective are these bumper stickers in conveying specific messages to others?

© Dave G. Houser/Corbis

© Richard Hamilton Smith/Corbis

WRITING MATTERS

ONCE HAD A STUDENT WHO GOT INTO TROUBLE IN HIGH SCHOOL FOR WRITING AN ESSAY THAT HER TEACHER CONSIDERED INAPPROPRIATE. IN THE ESSAY, THE STUDENT CRITICIZED SCHOOL OFFICIALS FOR POLICIES THAT DID NOT ALLOW STUDENTS TO EXPRESS OPINIONS CRITICAL OF THOSE POLICIES. THE ESSAY DID NOT CONTAIN ANY PROFANE LANGUAGE OR VIOLENT IMAGES, NOR DID IT BELITTLE ANY TEACHERS OR SCHOOL OFFICIALS. BUT THE TEACHER TOOK it to the principal, and the student and her parents were summoned to the principal's office to address "the problem."

What exactly was the problem in this case? Well, I can't speak for the principal, but it seems clear that part of the problem was *writing* itself. Or to put it another way, this student got into trouble because of the power of writing. The school authorities must have feared those written words for some reason. Otherwise, why would they take the essay so seriously? In some important way, that essay mattered. And it mattered because writing matters. You may have heard your English teachers extolling the power of writing as a positive, beneficial thing. And is it. But the power of writing is more complicated than that. So it's no surprise that efforts to control writing through censorship and other means have a long history. Consider the case of acclaimed novelist Salman Rushdie, a British citizen of Indian descent, whose best-selling novel, *The Satanic Verses* (1988), deeply offended many Muslims. In 1989, the Ayatollah Khomeini of Iran, one of the world's great Muslim spiritual leaders at the time, declared the book blasphemous and called for Rushdie's death. Rushdie was forced to live in hiding until the Ayatollah's decree was rescinded in 1998. Rushdie's experience is a frightening reminder of the power of the written word and the consequences writing can sometimes have.

The power of writing can matter in many different, often dramatic ways. For examle, it has been said that when President Abraham Lincoln met Harriet Beecher Stowe, he commented, "So this is the little lady who started the war." Stowe, of course, is the author of *Uncle Tom's Cabin,* a best-selling novel about the lives of Black slaves that was believed to have influenced the view of many Americans about slavery at that time. Lincoln's comment suggests the power of a story like Stowe's to shape opinions and affect public debate about important issues. Or consider Tom Paine's pamphlet *Common Sense,* which was published in 1776 and is estimated to have sold 500,000 copies—at a time when there were only 2.5 million people living in the American colonies. Some historians believe that *Common Sense,* which was Paine's vigorous case for independece from England, was a key factor in generating support for the rebellion against England.

So it's no wonder that there have long been efforts to control what is written and what is read. And don't think that efforts to control writing are limited to governments or religious leaders. If you went to an American elementary or secondary school, chances are your experience there was shaped by censorship. Each year, political organizations, religious groups, parents, and others challenge books used in schools. Sometimes these challenges focus on well-known controversies, such as the debate about teaching creationism along with evolution. But consider this list of the most commonly challenged books in American schools during the 1990s: *The Adventures of Huckleberry Finn* by Mark Twain, *The Catcher in the Rye* by J. D. Salinger, *I Know Why the Caged Bird Sings* by Maya Angelou, *Of Mice and Men* by John Steinbeck, and *Forever* by Judy Blume. *The Diary of Anne Frank* and *Harry Potter and the Goblet of Fire,* a huge international bestseller, have also been favorite targets of censors. These books are considered examples of great writing by many critics, but they must also be examples of the power of writing—a power that is sometimes threatening to many people.

The following essays can help us understand that power. And they remind us that the power of writing can be deeply personal at the same time that it is political and cultural.

I like to read the letters to the editor of my *local newspaper. Most of them have to do with issues that matter only to the people in the region where I live, such as town council decisions on building projects, school budgets, tax increases, problems with local roads, or local political controversies. These may seem like minor issues, but they matter enough to people living in the region to prompt them to express their views in the public forum of the newspaper's editorial*

Nobody Mean *More* to Me Than You AND THE *Future* Life OF Willie Jordan

page. The letters to the editor are one example of how writing matters. Those letters not only provide a forum for opinions, but they also can provoke readers to think about an issue, take up a local cause, or join the conversation about an important local matter. For the students that June Jordan (1936–2002) describes in the following essay, though, writing a letter to the editor of a local newspaper was a much bigger matter. You might even say it was a matter of life and death.

Jordan describes her experience with a college English class she taught at the State University of New York at Stony Brook in 1984. All but a few of the students in the class were Black, and although the course was supposed to focus on literature, it evolved into an examination of Black English. But the lessons the students learned went well beyond the class- (continued)

JUNE JORDAN

Black English is not exactly a linguistic buffalo; as children, most of the thirty-five million Afro-Americans living here depend on this language for our discovery of the world. But then we approach our maturity inside a larger social body that will not support our efforts to become anything other than the clones of those who are neither our mothers nor our fathers. We begin to grow up in a house where every true mirror shows us the face of somebody who does not belong there, whose walk and whose talk will never look or sound "right," because that house was meant to shelter a family that is alien and hostile to us. As we learn our way around this environment, ei-

(continued) *room. The brother of one of Jordan's students was killed in a confrontation with police, which the students in the class interpreted as an example of police violence against Blacks in their city. Ultimately, they decided to combat that violence by writing letters to the editor of a local newspaper to express their outrage about the incident. The difficult debates among Jordan's students about whether to write that letter in Black English or Standard English can tell us a great deal about the politics of language in American society, about the power of writing, and about the limits to that power.*

I have assigned this essay in many of my own classes. My students and I explore its lessons about the connections among race, language, and power. Usually, I ask my students to decide whether they would choose to write the letters to the newspaper as Jordan's students did. I also ask them to justify their decision. It is always a hard decision for them. As you read this essay, think about what decision you might have made in this case—and why.

June Jordan was a poet, essayist, and professor of English at the University of California at Berkeley. Her works include On Call: New Political Essays *(1985) and* June Jordan's Poetry for the People: A Revolutionary Blueprint *(1995). This essay was first published in the* Harvard Educational Review *in 1988.* ◪

STRATEGIES: IDENTIFYING AN AUDIENCE
Notice Jordan's use of the first person in this paragraph. She writes that "Afro-Americans living here depend upon this language for our discovery of the world." Later in the paragraph, she writes that "we should understand its [Black English's] status as an endangered species." Who is the *we* in this sentence? Is it the same *we* as in the previous sentence or is Jordan addressing two different audiences here? It is not unusual for an author to address several different audiences in a piece of writing, but in this case, consider the possibility that Jordan may be sending different messages to different readers.

---

ther we hide our original word habits, or we completely surrender our own voice, hoping to please those who will never respect anyone different from themselves: Black English is not exactly a linguistic buffalo, but we should understand its status as an endangered species, as a perishing, irreplaceable system of community intelligence, or we should expect its extinction, and, along with that, the extinguishing of much that constitutes our own proud, and singular identity.

What we casually call "English," less and less defers to England and its "gentlemen." "English" is no longer a specific matter of geography or an element of class privilege; more than thirty-three countries use this tool as a means of "international communication."[1] Countries as disparate as Zimbabwe and Malaysia, or Israel and Uganda, use it as their non-native currency of convenience. Obviously, this tool, this "English," cannot function inside thirty-three discrete societies on the basis of rules and values absolutely determined somewhere else, in a thirty-fourth other country, for example.

In addition to that staggering congeries of non-native users of English, there are five countries, or 333,746,000 people, for whom this thing called "English" serves as a native tongue.[2] Approximately ten percent of these native speakers of "English" are Afro-American citizens of the U.S.A. I cite these numbers and varieties of human beings dependent on "English" in order, quickly, to suggest how strange and how tenuous is any concept of "Standard English." Obviously, numerous forms of English now operate inside a natural, an uncontrollable, continuum of development. I would suppose "the standard" for English in Malaysia is not the same as "the standard" in Zimbabwe. I know that standard forms of English for Black people in this country do not copy that of whites. And, in fact, the structural differences between these two kinds of English have intensified, becoming more Black, or less white, despite the expected homogenizing effects of television[3] and other mass media.

Nonetheless, white standards of English persist, supreme and unquestioned, in these United States. Despite our multilingual population, and despite the deepening Black and white cleavage within that conglomerate, white standards control our official and popular judgments of verbal proficiency and correct, or incorrect, language skills, including speech. In contrast to India, where at least fourteen languages co-exist as legitimate Indian languages, in contrast to Nicaragua, where all citizens are legally entitled to formal school instruction in their regional or tribal languages, compulsory education

---

[1]*English Is Spreading, but What Is English?* A presentation by Professor S. N. Sridahr, Dept. of Linguistics, S.U.N.Y. at Stony Brook, April 9, 1985; Dean's Conversation among the Disciplines.
[2]Ibid.
[3]*New York Times*, March 15, 1985, Section One, p. 14: Report on study by Linguistics at the University of Pennsylvania.

CONVERSATIONS: BLACK ENGLISH AND STANDARD ENGLISH
For many years, educators, scholars, politicians, and others have debated about how the English language should be taught in schools. In the 1990s, a controversy erupted in Oakland, California, when school officials there declared *Ebonics,* another term for Black English, to be a separate dialect of English and not just slang. They adopted a policy to treat Black English as a foreign language, and they directed schools to teach students who spoke Black English as if Standard English were their second language. The public outcry eventually prompted school officials to drop the policy, but it also provoked a great deal of discussion about Black English, Standard English, and language in general as well as about the responsibilities of schools in teaching English to students of diverse racial, cultural, and linguistic backgrounds. Although Jordan's essay was published several years before the controversy in Oakland, it is part of a debate about English that has been going on for decades in the United States. In particular, in the early part of her essay, Jordan challenges the idea that there is one correct "standard" version of English that should be taught in schools. This debate continues today, and it's worth thinking about how persuasive Jordan's argument is so many years after she wrote it. It's also worth thinking about why this issue of standard English continues to be so controversial. (The essays by Amy Tan and Gloria Anzaldúa earlier in this chapter also address this issue.)

in America compels accommodation to exclusively white forms of "English." White English, in America, is "Standard English."

5 This story begins two years ago, I was teaching a new course, "In Search of the Invisible Black Woman," and my rather large class seemed evenly divided between young Black women and men. Five or six white students also sat in attendance. With unexpected speed and enthusiasm we had moved through historical narratives of the nineteenth century to literature by and about Black women, in the twentieth. I had assigned the first forty pages of Alice Walker's *The Color Purple,* and I came, eagerly, to class that morning:

"So!" I exclaimed, aloud. "What did you think? How did you like it?"

The students studied their hands, or the floor. There was no response. The tense, resistant feeling in the room fairly astounded me.

At last, one student, a young woman still not meeting my eyes, muttered something in my direction:

"What did you say?" I prompted her.

10 "Why she have them talk so funny. It don't sound right."

"You mean the language?"

Another student lifted his head: "It don't look right, neither. I couldn't hardly read it."

At this, several students dumped on the book. Just about unanimously, their criticisms targeted the language. I listened to what they wanted to say and silently marveled at the similarities between their casual speech patterns and Alice Walker's written version of Black English.

But I decided against pointing to these identical traits of syntax; I wanted not to make them self-conscious about their own spoken language—not while they clearly felt it was "wrong." Instead I decided to swallow my astonishment. Here was a negative Black reaction to a prize winning accomplishment of Black literature that white readers across the country had selected as a best seller. Black rejection was aimed at the one irreducibly Black element of Walker's work: the language—Celie's Black English. I wrote the opening lines of *The Color Purple* on the blackboard and asked the students to help me translate these sentences into Standard English:

You better not never tell nobody but God. It'd kill your mammy.
Dear God,

I am fourteen years old. I have always been a good girl. Maybe you can give me a sign letting me know what is happening to me.

Last spring after Little Lucious come I heard them fussing. He was pulling on her arm. She say it too soon, Fonso. I aint well. Finally he leave her alone. A week go by, he pulling on her arm again. She say, Naw, I ain't gonna. Can't you see I'm already half dead, an all of the children.[4]

Our process of translation exploded with hilarity and even hysterical, shocked laugh-   15
ter: The Black writer, Alice Walker, knew what she was doing! If rudimentary criteria
for good fiction includes the manipulation of language so that the syntax and diction
of sentences will tell you the identity of speakers, the probable age and sex and class
of speakers, and even the locale—urban/rural/southern/western—then Walker had
written, perfectly. This is the translation into Standard English that our class produced:

> *Absolutely, one should never confide in anybody besides God. Your secrets could
> prove devastating to your mother.*
>
> Dear God,
>
> I am fourteen years old, I have always been good. But now, could you help
> me to understand what is happening to me?
>
> Last spring, after my little brother, Lucious, was born, I heard my parents
> fighting. My father kept pulling at my mother's arm. But she told him, "It's
> too soon for sex, Alfonso. I am still not feeling well." Finally, my father left
> her alone. A week went by, and he began bothering my mother, again:
> Pulling her arm. She told him, "No, I won't! Can't you see I'm already ex-
> hausted from all of these children?"

(Our favorite line was "It's too soon for sex, Alfonso.")

Once we could stop laughing, once we could stop our exponentially wild improvisations on the theme of Translated Black English, the students pushed me to explain
their own negative first reactions to their spoken language on the printed page. I
thought it was probably akin to the shock of seeing yourself in a photograph for the
first time. Most of the students had never before seen a written facsimile of the way
they talk. None of the students had ever learned how to read and write their own verbal system of communication: Black English. Alternatively, this fact began to baffle or
else bemuse and then infuriate my students. Why not? Was it too late? Could they
learn how to do it, now? And, ultimately, the final test question, the one testing my
sincerity: Could I teach them? Because I had never taught anyone Black English and,
as far as I knew, no one, anywhere in the United States, had ever offered such a
course, the best I could say was "I'll try."

He looked like a wrestler.

He sat dead center in the packed room and, every time our eyes met, he quickly
nodded his head as though anxious to reassure, and encourage, me.

Short, with strikingly broad shoulders and long arms, he spoke with a surprisingly   20
high, soft voice that matched the soft bright movement of his eyes. His name was
Willie Jordan. He would have seemed even more unlikely in the context of
Contemporary Women's Poetry, except that ten or twelve other Black men were taking the course, as well. Still, Willie was conspicuous. His extreme fitness, the muscu-
lar density of his presence underscored the riveted, gentle attention that he gave to
anything anyone said. Generally, he did not join the loud and rowdy dialogue flying
back and forth, but there could be no doubt about his interest in our discussions.

[4]Alice Walker, *The Color Purple*, p. 11, Harcourt Brace, N.Y.

And, when he stood to present an argument he'd prepared, overnight, that nervous smile of his vanished and an irregular stammering replaced it, as he spoke with visceral sincerity, word by word.

That was how I met Willie Jordan. It was in between "In Search of the Invisible Black Woman" and "The Art of Black English." I was waiting for Departmental approval and I supposed that Willie might be, so to speak, killing time until he, too, could study Black English. But Willie really did want to explore Contemporary Women's poetry and, to that end, volunteered for extra research and never missed a class.

Towards the end of that semester, Willie approached me for an independent study project on South Africa. It would commence the next semester. I thought Willie's writing needed the kind of improvement only intense practice will yield. I knew his intelligence was outstanding. But he'd wholeheartedly opted for "Standard English" at a rather late age, and the results were stilted and frequently polysyllabic, simply for the sake of having more syllables. Willie's unnatural formality of language seemed to me consistent with the formality of his research into South African apartheid. As he projected his studies, he would have little time, indeed, for newspapers. Instead, more than 90 percent of his research would mean saturation in strictly historical, if not archival, material. I was certainly interested. It would be tricky to guide him into a more confident and spontaneous relationship both with language and apartheid. It was going to be wonderful to see what happened when he could catch up with himself, entirely, and talk back to the world.

September, 1984: Breezy fall weather and much excitement! My class, "The Art of Black English," was full to the limit of the fire laws. And, in Independent Study, Willie Jordan showed up, weekly, fifteen minutes early for each of our sessions. I was pretty happy to be teaching, altogether!

I remember an early class when a young brother, replete with his ever present pork-pie hat, raised his hand and then told us that most of what he'd heard was "all right" except it was "too clean." "The brothers on the street," he continued, "they mix it up more. Like 'fuck' and 'mother-fuck.' Or like 'shit.'" He waited, I waited. Then all of us laughed a good while, and we got into a brawl about "correct" and "realistic" Black English that led to Rule 1.

25   Rule 1: *Black English is about a whole lot more than mothafuckin.*

As a criterion, we decided, "realistic" could take you anywhere you want to go. Artful places. Angry places. Eloquent and sweetalkin places. Polemical places. Church. And the local Bar & Grill. We were checking out a language, not a mood or a scene or one guy's forgettable mouthing off.

It was hard. For most of the students, learning Black English required a fallback to patterns and rhythms of speech that many of their parents had beaten out of them. I mean *beaten.* And, in a majority of cases, correct Black English could be achieved only by striving for *incorrect* Standard English, something they were still pushing at, quite uncertainly. This state of affairs led to Rule 2.

Rule 2: *If it's wrong in Standard English it's probably right in Black English, or, at least, you're hot.*

It was hard. Roommates and family members ridiculed their studies, or remained incredulous, "You *studying* that shit? At school?" But we were beginning to feel the companionship of pioneers. And we decided that we needed another rule that would establish each one of us as equally important to our success. This was Rule 3.

Rule 3: *If it don't sound like something that come out somebody mouth then it don't sound* ₃₀
right. If it don't sound right then it ain't hardly right. Period.

This rule produced two weeks of compositions in which the students agonizingly tried to spell the sound of the Black English sentence they wanted to convey. But Black English is, preeminently, an oral/spoken means of communication. *And spelling don't talk.* So we needed Rule 4.

Rule 4: *Forget about the spelling. Let the syntax carry you.*

Once we arrived at Rule 4 we started to fly because syntax, the structure of an idea, leads you to the world view of the speaker and reveals her values. The syntax of a sentence equals the structure of your consciousness. If we insisted that the language of Black English adheres to a distinctive Black syntax, then we were postulating a profound difference between white and Black people, *per se*. Was it a difference to prize or to obliterate?

There are three qualities of Black English—the presence of life, voice, and clarity—that testify to a distinctive Black value system that we became excited about and self-consciously tried to maintain.

1. Black English has been produced by a pre-technocratic, if not antitechnological, ₃₅ culture. More, our culture has been constantly threatened by annihilation or, at least, the swallowed blurring of assimilation. Therefore, our language is a system constructed by people constantly needing to insist that we exist, that we are present. Our language devolves from a culture that abhors all abstraction, or anything tending to obscure or delete the fact of the human being who is here and now/the truth of the person who is speaking or listening. Consequently, *there is no passive voice construction possible in Black English.* For example, you cannot say, "Black English is being eliminated." You must say, instead, "White people eliminating Black English." The assumption of the presence of life governs all of Black English. Therefore, overwhelmingly, *all action takes place in the language of the present indicative.* And every sentence assumes the living and active participation of at least two human beings, the speaker and the listener.

2. A primary consequence of the person-centered values of Black English is the delivery of voice. If you speak or write Black English, your ideas will necessarily possess that otherwise elusive attribute, *voice.*

3. One main benefit following from the person-centered values of Black English is that of *clarity.* If your idea, your sentence, assumes the presence of at least two living and active people, you will make it understandable because the motivation behind every sentence is the wish to say something real to somebody real.

*   *   *

As the weeks piled up, translation from standard English into Black English or vice versa occupied a hefty part of our course work.

Standard English (hereafter S.E.): "In considering the idea of studying Black English those questioned suggested—"

(What's the subject? Where's the person? Is anybody alive in there, in that idea?)

Black English (hereafter B.E.): "I been asking people what you think about somebody studying Black English and they answer me like this."

But there were interesting limits. You cannot "translate" instances of Standard English preoccupied with abstraction or with nothing/nobody evidently alive, into Black English. That would warp the language into uses antithetical to the guiding perspective of its community of users. Rather you must first change those Standard English sentences, themselves, into ideas consistent with the person-centered assumptions of Black English.

GUIDELINES FOR BLACK ENGLISH

1. Minimal number of words for every idea: This is the source for the aphoristic and/or poetic force of the language; eliminate every possible word.

2. Clarity: If the sentence is not clear it's not Black English.

3. Eliminate use of the verb *to be* whenever possible. This leads to the deployment of more descriptive and, therefore, more precise verbs.

4. Use *be* or *been* only when you want to describe a chronic, ongoing state of things.

   He *be* at the office, by 9. (He is always at the office by 9.)
   He *been* with her since forever.

5. Zero copula: Always eliminate the verb *to be* whenever it would combine with another verb in Standard English.

   S.E.: She is going out with him.
   B.E.: She going out with him.

6. Eliminate *do* as in:

   S.E.: What do you think? What do you want?
   B.E.: What you think? What you want?

   Rules number 3, 4, 5, and 6 provide for the use of the minimal number of verbs per idea and, therefore, greater accuracy in the choice of verb.

7. In general, if you wish to say something really positive, try to formulate the idea using emphatic negative structure.

   S.E.: He's fabulous.
   B.E.: He bad.

8. Use double or triple negatives for dramatic emphasis.

   S.E.: Tina Turner sings out of this world.
   B.E.: Ain nobody sing like Tina.

9. Never use the *-ed* suffix to indicate the past tense of a verb.

    S.E.: She closed the door.
    B.E.: She close the door. Or, she have close the door.

10. Regardless of international verb time, only use the third person singular, present indicative, for use of the verb *to have,* as an auxiliary.

    S.E.: He had his wallet then he lost it.
    B.E.: He have him wallet then he lose it.
    S.E.: He had seen that movie.
    B.E.: We seen that movie. Or, we have see that movie.

11. Observe a minimal inflection of verbs. Particularly, never change from the first person singular forms to the third person singular.

    S.E.: Present Tense Forms: He goes to the store.
    B.E.: He go to the store.
    S.E.: Past Tense Forms: He went to the store.
    B.E.: He go to the store. Or, he gone to the store. Or, he been to the store.

12. The possessive case scarcely ever appears in Black English. Never use an apostrophe ('s) construction. If you wander into a possessive case component of an idea, then keep logically consistent: *ours, his, theirs, mines.* But, most likely, if you bump into such a component, you have wandered outside the underlying world-view of Black English.

    S.E.: He will take their car tomorrow.
    B.E.: He taking they car tomorrow.

13. Plurality: Logical consistency, continued: If the modifier indicates plurality then the noun remains in the singular case.

    S.E.: He ate twelve doughnuts.
    B.E.: He eat twelve doughnut.
    S.E.: She has many books.
    B.E.: She have many book.

14. Listen for, or invent, special Black English forms of the past tense, such as: "He losted it. That what she felted." If they are clear and readily understood, then use them.

15. Do not hesitate to play with words, sometimes inventing them: e.g. "astropotomous" means huge like a hippo plus astronomical and, therefore, signifies real big.

16. In Black English, unless you keenly want to underscore the past tense nature of an action, stay in the present tense and rely on the overall context of your ideas for the conveyance of time and sequence.

17. Never use the suffix *-ly* form of an adverb in Black English.

    S.E.: The rain came down rather quickly.
    B.E.: The rain come down pretty quick.

18. Never use the indefinite article *an* in Black English.

    S.E.: He wanted to ride an elephant.
    B.E.: He want to ride him a elephant.

19. Invariant syntax: in correct Black English it is possible to formulate an imperative, an interrogative, and a simple declarative idea with the same syntax:

    B.E.: You going to the store?
           You going to the store.
           You going to the store!

Where was Willie Jordan? We'd reached the mid-term of the semester. Students had formulated Black English guidelines, by consensus, and they were now writing with remarkable beauty, purpose, and enjoyment:

> *I ain hardly speakin for everybody but myself so understan that.*—Kim Parks

Samples from student writings:

> Janie have a great big ole hole inside her. Tea Cake the only thing that fit that hole . . .

> That pear tree beautiful to Janie, especial when bees fiddlin with the blossomin pear there growing large and lovely. But personal speakin, the love she get from staring at that tree ain the love what starin back at her in them relationship. (Monica Morris)

> Love is a big theme in, *They Eye Was Watching God.* Love show people new corners inside theyself. It pull out good stuff and stuff back bad stuff . . . Joe worship the doing uh his own hand and need other people to worship him too. But he ain't think about Janie that she a person and ought to live like anybody common do. Queen life not for Janie. (Monica Morris)

> In both life and writin, Black womens have varietous experience of love that be cold like a iceberg or fiery like a inferno. Passion got for the other partner involve, man or woman, seem as shallow, ankle-deep water or the most profoundest abyss. (Constance Evans)

> Family love another bond that ain't never break under no pressure. (Constance Evans)

> You know it really cold / When the friend you / Always get out the fire / Act like they don't know you / When you in the heat. (Constance Evans)

Big classroom discussion bout love at this time. I never take no class where us have any long arguin for and against for two or three day. New to me and great. I find the class time talkin a million time more interestin than detail bout the book. (Kathy Esseks)

As these examples suggest, Black English no longer limited the students, in any   40
way. In fact, one of them, Philip Garfield, would shortly "translate" a pivotal scene from Ibsen's *Doll's House,* as his final term paper.

Nora: I didn't gived no shit. I thinked you a asshole back then, too, you make it so hard for me save mines husband life.

Krogstad: Girl, it clear you ain't any idea what you done. You done exact what I once done, and I losed my reputation over it.

Nora: You asks me believe you once act brave save you wife life?

Krogstad: Law care less why you done it.

Nora: Law must suck.

Krogstad: Suck or no, if I wants, judge screw you wid dis paper.

Nora: No way, man. (Philip Garfield)

But where was Willie? Compulsively punctual, and always thoroughly prepared with neatly typed compositions, he had disappeared. He failed to show up for our regularly scheduled conference, and I received neither a note nor a phone call of explanation. A whole week went by. I wondered if Willie had finally been captured by the extremely current happenings in South Africa: passage of a new constitution that did not enfranchise the Black majority, and militant Black South African reaction to that affront. I wondered if he'd been hurt, somewhere. I wondered if the serious workload of weekly readings and writings had overwhelmed him and changed his mind about independent study. Where was Willie Jordan?

One week after the first conference that Willie missed, he called: "Hello, Professor Jordan? This is Willie. I'm sorry I wasn't there last week. But something has come up and I'm pretty upset. I'm sorry but I really can't deal right now."

I asked Willie to drop by my office and just let me see that he was okay. He agreed to do that. When I saw him I knew something hideous had happened. Something had hurt him and scared him to the marrow. He was all agitated and stammering and terse and incoherent. At last, his sadly jumbled account let me surmise, as follows: Brooklyn police had murdered his unarmed, twenty-five-year-old brother, Reggie Jordan. Neither Willie nor his elderly parents knew what to do about it. Nobody from the press was interested. His folks had no money. Police ran his family around and around, to no point. And Reggie was really dead. And Willie wanted to fight, but he felt helpless.

*   *   *

With Willie's permission I began to try to secure legal counsel for the Jordan family. Unfortunately Black victims of police violence are truly numerous while the resources available to prosecute their killers are truly scarce. A friend of mine at the Center for Constitutional Rights estimated that just the preparatory costs for bringing the cops into court normally approaches $180,000. Unless the execution of

Reggie Jordan became a major community cause for organizing, and protest, his murder would simply become a statistical item.

45   Again, with Willie's permission, I contacted every newspaper and media person I could think of. But the William Bastone feature article in *The Village Voice* was the only result from that canvassing.

Again, with Willie's permission, I presented the case to my class in Black English. We had talked about the politics of language. We had talked about love and sex and child abuse and men and women. But the murder of Reggie Jordan broke like a hurricane across the room.

CONTEXT: POLICE VIOLENCE

Jordan writes in this passage (par. 47) that few issues are "as endemic to Black life as police violence." She wrote that line in 1988, but the issue of police violence against Blacks and other minority populations is a very old one. In the years since her essay was published, there have been several highly publicized instances of such violence, including the beating of Rodney King by Los Angeles police in 1991 and the beating of Abner Louima by New York City police in 1997. In both cases, Black men were severely beaten by White officers, provoking outrage and protest, especially among minority groups. In addition, a number of controversies arose in the late 1990s regarding the police practice of "racial profiling," in which police pay greater attention to people of certain racial or ethnic backgrounds on the assumption that those people are more likely to commit certain crimes. You might consider whether things have changed since Jordan's essay was published and whether readers today might understand the issue of police violence differently than readers in the 1980s.

There are few "issues" as endemic to Black life as police violence. Most of the students knew and respected and liked Jordan. Many of them came from the very neighborhood where the murder had occurred. All of the students had known somebody close to them who had been killed by police, or had known frightening moments of gratuitous confrontation with the cops. They wanted to do everything at once to avenge death. Number One: They decided to compose personal statements of condolence to Willie Jordan and his family written in Black English. Number Two: They decided to compose individual messages to the police, in Black English. These should be prefaced by an explanatory paragraph composed by the entire group. Number Three: These individual messages, with their lead paragraph, should be sent to *Newsday*.

The morning after we agreed on these objectives, one of the young women students appeared with an unidentified visitor, who sat through the class, smiling in a peculiar, comfortable way.

Now we had to make more tactical decisions. Because we wanted the messages published, and because we thought it imperative that our outrage be known by the police, the tactical question was this: Should the opening, group paragraph be written in Black English or Standard English?

50   I have seldom been privy to a discussion with so much heart at the dead heat of it. I will never forget the eloquence, the sudden haltings of speech, the fierce struggle against tears, the furious throwaway, and useless explosions that this question elicited.

That one question contained several others, each of them extraordinarily painful to even contemplate. How best to serve the memory of Reggie Jordan? Should we use the language of the killers—Standard English—in order to make our ideas acceptable to those controlling the killers? But wouldn't what we had to say be rejected, summarily, if we said it in our own language, the language of the victim, Reggie Jordan? But if we sought to express ourselves by abandoning our language wouldn't that mean our suicide on top of Reggie's murder? But if we expressed ourselves in our own language wouldn't that be suicidal to the wish to communicate with those who, evidently, did not give a damn about us/Reggie/police violence in the Black community?

At the end of one of the longest, most difficult hours of my own life, the students voted, unanimously, to preface their individual messages with a paragraph composed in the language of Reggie Jordan. *"At least we don't give up nothing else. At least we stick to the truth: Be who we been. And stay all the way with Reggie."*

It was heartbreaking to proceed, from that point. Everyone in the room realized that our decision in favor of Black English had doomed our writings, even as the distinctive reality of our Black lives always has doomed our efforts to "be who we been" in this country.

I went to the blackboard and took down this paragraph, dictated by the class:

> . . . YOU COPS!
> WE THE BROTHER AND SISTER OF WILLIE JORDAN, A FELLOW STONY BROOK STUDENT WHO THE BROTHER OF THE DEAD REGGIE JORDAN. REGGIE, LIKE MANY BROTHER AND SISTER, HE A VICTIM OF BRUTAL RACIST POLICE, OCTOBER 25, 1984. US APPALL, FED UP, BECAUSE THAT ANOTHER SENSELESS DEATH WHAT OCCUR IN OUR COMMUNITY. THIS WHAT WE FEEL, THIS, FROM OUR HEART, FOR WE AIN'T STAYIN' SILENT NO MORE.

With the completion of this introduction, nobody said anything. I asked for comments. At this invitation, the unidentified visitor, a young Black man, ceaselessly smiling, raised his hand. He was, it so happens, a rookie cop. He had just joined the force in September and, he said he thought he should clarify a few things. So he came forward and sprawled easily into a posture of barroom, or fireside, nostalgia:

"See," Officer Charles enlightened us, "most times when you out on the street and something come down you do one of two things. Over-react or under-react. Now, if you under-react then you can get yourself kilt. And if you over-react then maybe you kill somebody. Fortunately it's about nine times out of ten and you will over-react. So the brother got kilt. And I'm sorry about that, believe me. But what you have to understand is what kilt him: Over-reaction. That's all. Now you talk about Black people and white police but see, now, I'm a cop myself. And (big smile) I'm Black. And just a couple months ago I was on the other side. But see it's the same for me. You a cop, you the ultimate authority: the Ultimate Authority. And you on the street, most of the time you can only do one of two things: over-react or under-react. That's all it is with the brother. Over-reaction. Didn't have nothing to do with race."

That morning Officer Charles had the good fortune to escape without being boiled alive. But barely. And I remember the pride of his smile when I read about the fate of Black policemen and other collaborators, in South Africa. I remember him, and I remember the shock and palpable feeling of shame that filled the room. It was as though that foolish, and deadly, young man had just relieved himself of his foolish, and deadly, explanation, face to face with the grief of Reggie Jordan's father and Reggie Jordan's mother. Class ended quietly. I copied the paragraph from the blackboard, collected the individual messages and left to type them up.

Newsday rejected the piece.

The Village Voice could not find room in their "Letters" section to print the individual messages from the students to the police.

None of the TV news reporters picked up the story.

Nobody raised $180,000 to prosecute the murder of Reggie Jordan.

GLOSS: *NEWSDAY*
One of New York City's most widely read publications, *Newsday* is also one of the largest newspapers in the United States in terms of circulation.

Reggie Jordan is really dead.

I asked Willie Jordan to write an essay pulling together everything important to him from that semester. He was still deeply beside himself with frustration and amazement and loss. This is what he wrote, unedited, and in its entirety:

> Throughout the course of this semester I have been researching the effects of oppression and exploitation along racial lines in South Africa and its neighboring countries. I have become aware of South African police brutalization of native Africans beyond the extent of the law, even though the laws themselves are catalyst affliction upon Black men, women, and children. Many Africans die each year as a result of the deliberate use of police force to protect the white power structure.
>
> Social control agents in South Africa, such as policemen, are also used to force compliance among citizens through both overt and covert tactics. It is not uncommon to find bold-faced coercion and cold-blooded killings of Blacks by South African police for undetermined and/or inadequate reasons. Perhaps the truth is that the only reasons for this heinous treatment of Blacks rests in racial differences. We should also understand that what is conveyed through the media is not always accurate and may sometimes be construed as the tip of the iceberg at best.
>
> I recently received a painful reminder that racism, poverty, and the abuse of power are global problems which are by no means unique to South Africa. On October 25, 1984, at approximately 3:00 P.M. my brother, Mr. Reginald Jordan, was shot and killed by two New York City policemen from the 75th precinct in the East New York section of Brooklyn. His life ended at the age of twenty-five. Even up to this current point in time the Police Department has failed to provide my family, which consists of five brothers, eight sisters, and two parents, with a plausible reason for Reggie's death. Out of the many stories that were given to my family by the Police Department, not one of them seems to hold water. In fact, I honestly believe that the Police Department's assessment of my brother's murder is nothing short of ABSOLUTE BULLSHIT, and thus far no evidence had been produced to alter perception of the situation.
>
> Furthermore, I believe that one of three cases may have occurred in this incident. First, Reggie's death may have been the desired outcome of the police officer's action, in which case the killing was premeditated. Or, it was a case of mistaken identity, which clarifies the fact that the two officers who killed my brother and their commanding parties are all grossly incompetent. Or, both of the above cases are correct, i.e., Reggie's murderers intended to kill him and the Police Department behaved insubordinately.
>
> 90   Part of the argument of the officers who shot Reggie was that he had attacked one of them and took his gun. This was their major claim. They also said that only one of them had actually shot Reggie. The facts, however, speak for themselves. According to the Death Certificate and autopsy report, Reggie was shot eight times from point-blank range. The Doctor who performed the autopsy told me himself that two bullets entered the side of

my brother's head, four bullets were sprayed into his back, and two bullets struck him in the back of his legs. It is obvious that unnecessary force was used by the police and that it is extremely difficult to shoot someone in his back when he is attacking or approaching you.

After experiencing a situation like this and researching South Africa I believe that to a large degree, justice may only exist as rhetoric. I find it difficult to talk of true justice when the oppression of my people both at home and abroad attests to the fact that inequality and injustice are serious problems whereby Blacks and Third World people are perpetually short-changed by society. Something has to be done about the way in which this world is set up. Although it is a difficult task, we do have the power to make a change.

—Willie J. Jordan, Jr.
EGL 487, Section 58, November 14, 1984

It is my privilege to dedicate this book to the future life of Willie J. Jordan, Jr.
August 8, 1985

UNDERSTANDING THE TEXT

1. Why does Jordan believe Black English is an endangered species? What importance do her concerns about Black English have to her overall argument in this essay? Keeping in mind that this essay was first published in 1988, do you think Jordan's concerns about Black English as an endangered species are still valid? Explain.

2. What is the role of Standard English in the story that Jordan tells? What does Jordan's experience with her students suggest about Standard English? Do you think she makes a persuasive case for her own views of Standard English? Why or why not?

3. What is Jordan's purpose in having her students "learn" Black English? What do you think they ultimately learn about Black English and about language in general?

4. In what ways do you think the differences between Black English and Standard English that Jordan's students identified are important? What might these differences suggest about English?

5. Why do Jordan's students ultimately decide to submit their letters to *Newsday* with a note written in Black English? Why does Jordan believe that their decision "doomed" their letters? Do you agree with the students? With Jordan? Why or why not? What might your answers to these questions suggest about your own views regarding Standard English?

EXPLORING THE ISSUES

1. Jordan is telling two stories in this essay: the story of her class and the story of Willie Jordan and his brother. Examine how Jordan tells these two stories and how she weaves them together. How exactly

do they relate to one another? How does Jordan connect them? How effectively do you think Jordan uses these two stories to convey her main ideas about race and language?

2. How does Jordan portray Black English in this essay? What does she emphasize about Black English? How does she compare it to Standard English? What do you think Jordan is trying to suggest about language and race by the way she presents Black English and Standard English in this essay? Do you think she's right? Explain.

3. Jordan tells us that there were five or six White students in her "rather large class." Although she refers repeatedly to her students throughout the essay, she never mentions the White students again. Why do you think she refers to them briefly near the beginning of the essay but nowhere else in the essay? What effect might their presence in her class have had on the discussions about whether to write the letter to *Newsday* in Black English? In what ways might her essay have been different if she had included more description of their role in her class discussions?

4. What do you think Jordan wishes to suggest by ending her essay as she does? Do you think her ending is hopeful in any way? Do you think she intended it to be? Explain, citing specific passages to support your answer.

ENTERING THE CONVERSATIONS

1. With a group of classmates, decide whether Jordan's students were right to submit the letters to *Newsday* with an introductory letter written in Black English. Or should they have written it in Standard English? Try to reach consensus in your group, identifying the main reasons for your group's position. Then

write a statement as a group in which you state and explain your group's position.

2. Write an essay in which you state and defend your own position about the decision made by June Jordan's students.

INFOTRAC

3. Using InfoTrac College Edition, your library, and any other appropriate resources, explore the controversy surrounding Black English, or Ebonics. Try to find sources that present various sides of the controversy about whether or not Black English is a legitimate dialect or simply a slang version of Standard English. If possible, speak to an expert on your campus, such as a professor of English or linguistics. You might also speak to people who use Black English or who grew up or live in areas where many people speak Black English. Then write a report in which you present the findings of your research. In your report, define Black English and provide an overview of what is known or believed about the uses of Black English. Try to present the main arguments for and against defining Black English as a distinct dialect of English (rather than as slang), and draw conclusions about its use in schools or other settings.

4. Examine some examples of contemporary music, such as hip-hop, in which Black English is used. Then write an analysis of the songs you selected using the rules for Black English developed by Jordan and her students. Determine whether the lyrics of songs using Black English conform to the rules described in this essay. Try to draw conclusions about the way musicians use Black English. For example, what can they do with Black English that they could not do with Standard English in their music?

Min Zhan Lu's (b. 1946) remarkable story *about learning to read and write in Chinese Communist schools never fails to provoke vigorous discussion in my classes. Many of my American students are amazed that schooling can be as overtly political as Lu's was. They often comfort themselves by pointing out that such obvious indoctrination does not happen in American schools. Yet, Lu's essay often prompts these same students to look more closely at their experiences in American*

FROM Silence TO Struggle

schools. Often, they are surprised to find some similarities between the way they were taught to write and read and the way Lu was taught. In some ways, the discussion my students and I have about Lu's essay are similar to debates about formal schooling that have been occurring in the United States since modern public schools developed in the nineteenth century. Some scholars trace the rise of public schooling in the United States to the rise of industrialized capitalism, and they make a connection between how writing has been taught in American schools and the needs of the capitalist workplace. Is that connection the same as the obvious political purposes that schooling served in Lu's case? You'll have to answer that question for yourself.

If Lu's essay is about the political nature of writing instruction, it is also about the tensions that can arise when the literacy we learn at home conflicts with the literacy taught in school. Like Lu, many American students learn to read and write at home in different ways and in different languages from what is expected in schools. As you read Lu's compelling story of the challenges she faced, you might consider whether the way you have been taught to write in schools reflects values or beliefs that conflict with your upbringing at home. (continued)

MIN ZHAN LU

Imagine that you enter a parlor. You come late. When you arrive, others have long preceded you, and they are engaged in a heated discussion. . . . You listen for a while, until you decide that you have caught the tenor of the argument; then you put in your oar. Someone answers; you answer him; another comes to your defense; another aligns himself against you, to either the embarrassment or gratification of your opponent, depending upon the quality of your ally's assistance. However, the discussion is interminable. The hour grows late, you must depart. And you do depart, with the discussion still vigorously in progress.

—*Kenneth Burke,* The Philosophy of Literary Form

Men are not built in silence, but in word, in work, in action-reflection.

—*Paulo Freire,* Pedagogy of the Oppressed

My mother withdrew into silence two months before she died. A few nights before she fell silent, she told me she regretted the way she had raised me and my sisters. I knew she was referring to the (continued) *Min Zhan Lu is a professor of English at the University of Wisconsin at Milwaukee. Her many articles and books about writing instruction include* Representing the "Other": Basic Writers and the Teaching of Basic Writing *(1999). She has also written a memoir titled* Shanghai Quartet: The Crossings of Four Women of China *(2001). The following essay first appeared in 1987 in* College English, *a professional journal devoted to issues in the teaching of college English. Because Lu is addressing an audience of academics with expertise in language and literacy, she sometimes uses words in a specialized way. As you read, pay attention to terms that may be unfamiliar to you—terms that Lu's intended audience would understand but that a more general audience may not.* ▼

CONTEXT: THE CULTURAL REVOLUTION
In 1966, Chinese Communist leader Mao Zedong (whose name is written as Mao Tse-tung by Lu) initiated a series of attacks on Communist Party leaders and their supporters that he claimed were intended to rid Chinese society of the influences of capitalism and Western culture. The resulting purge of party leaders, intellectuals, businesspeople, and others led to the persecution of many Chinese people by Mao's followers and especially by the Red Guard, an organization of mostly young people who were loyal to Mao. These purges seriously disrupted China and weakened its economy, and in some cases, armed conflict between factions erupted. People like Lu's family, who were successful businesspeople, spoke English, or had other connections to Western culture, suffered greatly during this "revolution," which lasted in various forms until after Mao's death in 1976.

way we had been brought up in the midst of two conflicting worlds—the world of home, dominated by the ideology of the Western humanistic tradition, and the world of a society dominated by Mao Tse-tung's Marxism. My mother had devoted her life to our education, an education she knew had made us suffer political persecution during the Cultural Revolution. I wanted to find a way to convince her that, in spite of the persecution, I had benefited from the education she had worked so hard to give me. But I was silent. My understanding of my education was so dominated by memories of confusion and frustration that I was unable to reflect on what I could have gained from it.

This paper is my attempt to fill up that silence with words, words I didn't have then, words that I have since come to by reflecting on my earlier experience as a student in China and on my recent experience as a composition teacher in the United States. For in spite of the frustration and confusion I experienced growing up caught between two conflicting worlds, the conflict ultimately helped me to grow as a reader and writer. Constantly having to switch back and forth between the discourse of home and that of school made me sensitive and self-conscious about the struggle I experienced every time I tried to read, write, or think in either discourse. Eventually, it led me to search for constructive uses for such struggle.

From early childhood, I had identified the differences between home and the outside world by the different languages I used in each. My parents had wanted my sisters and me to get the best education they could conceive of—Cambridge. They had hired a live-in tutor, a Scot, to make us bilingual. I learned to speak English with my parents, my tutor, and my sisters. I was allowed to speak Shanghai dialect only with the servants. When I was four (the year after the Communist Revolution of 1949), my parents sent me to a local private school where I learned to speak, read, and write in a new language—Standard Chinese, the official written language of New China.

In those days I moved from home to school, from English to Standard Chinese to Shanghai dialect, with no apparent friction. I spoke each language with those who spoke the language. All seemed quite "natural"—servants spoke only Shanghai dialect because they were servants; teachers spoke Standard Chinese because they were teachers; languages had different words because they were different languages. I thought of English as my family language, comparable to the many strange dialects I didn't speak but had often heard some of my classmates speak with their families. While I was happy to have a special family language, until second grade I didn't feel that my family language was any different than some of my classmates' family dialects.

My second grade homeroom teacher was a young graduate from a missionary school. When she found out I spoke English, she began to practice her English on me. One day she used English when asking me

5

to run an errand for her. As I turned to close the door behind me, I noticed the puzzled faces of my classmates. I had the same sensation I had often experienced when some stranger in a crowd would turn on hearing me speak English. I was more intensely pleased on this occasion, however, because suddenly I felt that my family language had been singled out from the family languages of my classmates. Since we were not allowed to speak any dialect other than Standard Chinese in the classroom, having my teacher speak English to me in class made English an official language of the classroom. I began to take pride in my ability to speak it.

This incident confirmed in my mind what my parents had always told me about the importance of English to one's life. Time and again they had told me of how my paternal grandfather, who was well versed in classic Chinese, kept losing good-paying jobs because he couldn't speak English. My grandmother reminisced constantly about how she had slaved and saved to send my father to a first-rate missionary school. And we were made to understand that it was my father's fluent English that had opened the door to his success. Even though my family had always stressed the importance of English for my future, I used to complain bitterly about the extra English lessons we had to take after school. It was only after my homeroom teacher had "sanctified" English that I began to connect English with my education. I became a much more eager student in my tutorials.

What I learned from my tutorials seemed to enhance and reinforce what I was learning in my classroom. In those days each word had one meaning. One day I would be making a sentence at school: "The national flag of China is red." The next day I would recite at home, "My love is like a red, red rose." There seemed to be an agreement between the Chinese "red" and the English "red," and both corresponded to the patch of color printed next to the word. "Love"

VISUAL CONNECTIONS: THE COLOR RED
Lu discusses the various meanings that the color *red* had for her as a Chinese student. During most of the twentieth century, red was the color associated with communism; to be called a "red" in the United States was to be labeled a Communist or Communist sympathizer. For Chinese Communists, red symbolized the revolution, and it is the dominant color of the Chinese flag (shown here). It is interesting to think about how the meanings associated with the color red have changed since Lu was a young student in the 1950s, especially after the break-up of the former Soviet Union, which, along with China, was the other great Communist power. Many Communist movements continue to use the color to signify revolution, but in the United States, the color no longer is so clearly associated with communism. During the U.S. presidential election of 2004, for example, political observers often spoke of the "red" states, which were considered more conservative, and the "blue" states, considered more liberal. The map shows the states that voted for George W. Bush in red and those voting for John Kerry in blue.

Chinese Flag

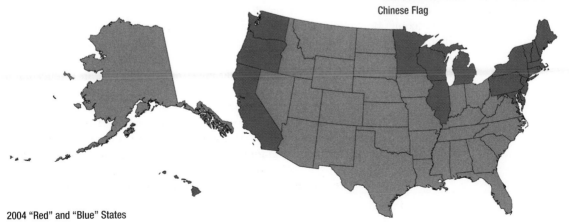

2004 "Red" and "Blue" States

© Jeremy Homer/Corbis

was my love for my mother at home and my love for my "motherland" at school; both "loves" meant how I felt about my mother. Having two loads of homework forced me to develop a quick memory for words and a sensitivity to form and style. What I learned in one language carried over to the other. I made sentences such as, "I saw a red, red rose among the green leaves," with both the English lyric and the classic Chinese lyric—red flower among green leaves—running through my mind, and I was praised by both teacher and tutor for being a good student.

Although my elementary schooling took place during the fifties, I was almost oblivious to the great political and social changes happening around me. Years later, I read in my history and political philosophy textbooks that the fifties were a time when "China was making a transition from a semi-feudal, semi-capitalist, and semi-colonial country into a socialist country," a period in which "the Proletarians were breaking into the educational territory dominated by Bourgeois Intellectuals." While people all over the country were being officially classified into Proletarians, Petty-bourgeois, National-bourgeois, Poor-peasants, and Intellectuals, and were trying to adjust to their new social identities, my parents were allowed to continue the upper middle-class life they had established before the 1949 Revolution because of my father's affiliation with British firms. I had always felt that my family was different from the families of my classmates, but I didn't perceive society's view of my family until the summer vacation before I entered high school.

First, my aunt was caught by her colleagues talking to her husband over the phone in English. Because of it, she was criticized and almost labeled a Rightist. (This was the year of the Anti-Rightist movement in which the Intellectuals became the target of the "socialist class-struggle.") I had heard others telling my mother that she was foolish to teach us English when Russian had replaced English as the "official" foreign language. I had also learned at school that the American and British Imperialists were the arch-enemies of New China. Yet I had made no connection between the arch-enemies and the English our family spoke. What happened to my aunt forced the connection on me. I began to see my parents' choice of a family language as an anti-Revolutionary act and was alarmed that I had participated in such an act. From then on, I took care not to use English outside home and to conceal my knowledge of English from my new classmates.

10   Certain words began to play important roles in my new life at the junior high. On the first day of school, we were handed forms to fill out with our parents' class, job, and income. Being one of the few people not employed by the government, my father had never been officially classified. Since he was a medical doctor, he told me to put him down as an Intellectual. My homeroom teacher called me into the office a couple of days afterwards and told me that my father couldn't be an Intellectual if his income far exceeded that of a Capitalist. He also told me that since my father worked for Foreign Imperialists, my father should be classified as an Imperialist Lackey. The teacher looked nonplussed when I told him that my father couldn't be an Imperialist Lackey because he was a medical doctor. But I could tell from the way he took notes on my form that my father's job had put me in an unfavorable position in his eyes.

The Standard Chinese term **"class"** was not a new word for me. Since first grade, I had been taught sentences such as, "The Working class are the masters of New China." I had always known that it was good to be a worker, but until then, I had never felt threatened for not being one. That fall, "class" began to take on a new meaning for me. I noticed a group of Working-class students and teachers at school. I was made to understand that because of my class background, I was excluded from that group.

Another word that became important was "consciousness." One of the slogans posted in the school building read, "Turn our students into future Proletarians with socialist conscious-ness and education!" For several weeks we studied this slogan in our political philosophy course, a subject I had never had in el-ementary school. I still remember the definition of "socialist consciousness" that we were repeatedly tested on through the years: "Socialist consciousness is a person's political soul. It is the consciousness of the Proletarians represented by Marxist Mao Tse-tung thought. It takes expression in one's action, language, and lifestyle. It is the task of every Chinese student to grow up into a Proletarian with a socialist con-sciousness so that he can serve the people and the motherland." To make the abstract concept accessible to us, our teacher pointed out that the immediate task for stu-dents from Working-class families was to strengthen their socialist consciousnesses. For those of us who were from other class backgrounds, the task was to turn ourselves into Workers with socialist consciousnesses. The teacher never explained exactly how we were supposed to "turn" into Workers. Instead, we were given samples of the rit-ualistic annual plans we had to write at the beginning of each term. In these plans, we performed "self-criticism" on our consciousnesses and made vows to turn our-selves into Workers with socialist consciousnesses. The teacher's division between those who did and those who didn't have a socialist consciousness led me to reify the notion of "consciousness" into a thing one possesses. I equated this intangible "thing" with a concrete way of dressing, speaking, and writing. For instance, I never doubted that my political philosophy teacher had a socialist consciousness because she was from a steelworker's family (she announced this the first day of class) and was a Party member who wore grey cadre suits and talked like a philosophy textbook. I noticed other things about her. She had beautiful eyes and spoke Standard Chinese with such a pure accent that I thought she should be a film star. But I was embar-rassed that I had noticed things that ought not to have been associated with her. I blamed my observation on my Bourgeois consciousness.

At the same time, the way reading and writing were taught through memorization and imitation also encouraged me to reduce concepts and ideas to simple definitions in literature and political philosophy classes, we were taught a large number of quo-tations from Marx, Lenin, and Mao Tse-tung. Each concept that appeared in these quotations came with a definition. We were required to memorize the definitions of

GLOSS: CLASS
The idea of *class* is central to the Marxist political ideology under which Lu grew up in Communist China. Within that ideology, *class* refers to cate-gories that identify people in terms of their rela-tive positions in an economic and political system. In Lu's experience, there were clear delineations among various classes within a Marxist system. But the idea of class in U.S. society isn't so clear-cut. Some people use it to refer to income level; for others, it reflects types of work or working conditions, regardless of income. For example, a worker in an automobile factory might be classi-fied as "working class" even though he or she might earn more money than a teacher or a sales manager, who would be considered "middle class." You might think about the importance of the idea of social class in Lu's experience and how your own experiences might shape the way you react to the stories she tells.

the words along with the quotations. Every time I memorized a definition, I felt I had learned a word: "The national red flag symbolizes the blood shed by Revolutionary ancestors for our socialist cause"; "New China rises like a red sun over the eastern horizon." As I memorized these sentences, I reduced their metaphors to dictionary meanings: "red" meant "Revolution" and "red sun" meant "New China" in the "language" of the Working Class. I learned mechanically but eagerly. I soon became quite fluent in this new language.

As school began to define me as a political subject, my parents tried to build up my resistance to the "communist poisoning" by exposing me to the "great books"— novels by Charles Dickens, Nathaniel Hawthorne, Emily Brontë, Jane Austen, and writers from around the turn of the century. My parents implied that these writers represented how I, their child, should read and write. My parents replaced the word "Bourgeois" with the word "cultured." They reminded me that I was in school only to learn math and science. I needed to pass the other courses to stay in school, but I was not to let the "Red doctrines" corrupt my mind. Gone were the days when I could innocently write. "I saw the red, red rose among the green leaves," collapsing, as I did, English and Chinese cultural traditions. "Red" came to mean Revolution at school, "the Commies" at home, and adultery in *The Scarlet Letter.* Since I took these symbols and metaphors as meanings natural to people of the same class, I abandoned my earlier definitions of English and Standard Chinese as the language of home and the language of school. I now defined English as the language of the Bourgeois and Standard Chinese as the language of the Working class. I thought of the language of the Working class as someone else's language and the language of the Bourgeois as my language. But I also believed that, although the language of the Bourgeois was my real language, I could and would adopt the language of the Working class when I was at school. I began to put on and take off my Working class language in the same way I put on and took off my school clothes to avoid being criticized for wearing Bourgeois clothes.

15   In my literature classes, I learned the Working-class formula for reading. Each work in the textbook had a short "Author's Biography": "X X X, born in 19— in the province of X X, is from a Worker's family. He joined the Revolution in 19—. He is a Revolutionary realist with a passionate love for the Party and Chinese Revolution. His work expresses the thoughts and emotions of the masses and sings praise to the prosperous socialist construction on all fronts of China." The teacher used the "Author's Biography" as a yardstick to measure the texts. We were taught to locate details in the texts that illustrated these summaries, such as words that expressed Workers' thoughts and emotions or events that illustrated the Workers' lives.

I learned a formula for Working-class writing in the composition classes. We were given sample essays and told to imitate them. The theme was always about how the collective taught the individual a lesson. I would write papers about labor-learning experiences or school-cleaning days, depending on the occasion of the collective activity closest to the assignment. To make each paper look different, I dressed it up with details about the date, the weather, the environment, or the appearance of the Master-worker who had taught me "the lesson." But as I became more and more fluent in the generic voice of the Working-class Student, I also became more and more self-conscious about the language we used at home.

For instance, in senior high we began to have English classes ("to study English for the Revolution," as the slogan on the cover of the textbook said), and I was given my first Chinese-English dictionary. There I discovered the English version of the term "class-struggle." (The Chinese characters for a school "class" and for a social "class" are different.) I had often used the English word "class" at home in sentences such as, "So and so has class," but I had not connected this sense of "class" with "class-struggle." Once the connection was made, I heard a second layer of meaning every time someone at home said a person had "class." The expression began to mean the person had the style and sophistication characteristic of the Bourgeoisie. The word lost its innocence. I was uneasy about hearing that second layer of meaning because I was sure my parents did not hear the word that way. I felt that therefore I should not be hearing it that way either. Hearing the second layer of meaning made me wonder if I was losing my English.

My suspicion deepened when I noticed myself unconsciously merging and switching between the "reading" of home and the "reading" of school. Once I had to write a report on *The Revolutionary Family*, a book about an illiterate woman's awakening and growth as a Revolutionary through the deaths of her husband and all her children for the cause of the Revolution. In one scene the woman deliberated over whether or not she should encourage her youngest son to join the Revolution. Her memory of her husband's death made her afraid to encourage her son. Yet she also remembered her earlier married life and the first time her husband tried to explain the meaning of the Revolution to her. These memories made her feel she should encourage her son to continue the cause his father had begun.

I was moved by this scene. "Moved" was a word my mother and sisters used a lot when we discussed books. Our favorite moments in novels were moments of what I would now call internal conflict, moments which we said "moved" us. I remember that we were "moved" by Jane Eyre when she was torn between her sense of ethics, which compelled her to leave the man she loved, and her impulse to stay with the only man who had ever loved her. We were also moved by Agnes in *David Copperfield* because of the way she restrained her love for David so that he could live happily with the woman he loved. My standard method of doing a book report was to model it on the review by the Publishing Bureau and to dress it up with detailed quotations from the book. The review of *The Revolutionary Family* emphasized the woman's Revolutionary spirit. I decided to use the scene that had moved me to illustrate this point. I wrote the report the night before it was due. When I had finished, I realized I couldn't possibly hand it in. Instead of illustrating her Revolutionary spirit, I had dwelled on her internal conflict, which could be seen as a moment of weak sentimentality that I should never have emphasized in a Revolutionary heroine. I wrote another report, taking care to illustrate the grandeur of her Revolutionary spirit by expanding on a quotation in which she decided that if the life of her son could change the lives of millions of sons, she should not begrudge his life for the cause of Revolution. I handed in my second version but kept the first in my desk.

I never showed it to anyone. I could never show it to people outside my family, because it had deviated so much from the reading enacted by the jacket review. Neither could I show it to my mother or sisters, because I was ashamed to have been so moved by such a "Revolutionary" book. My parents would have been shocked to learn that I

20

could like such a book in the same way they liked Dickens. Writing this book report increased my fear that I was losing the command over both the "language of home" and the "language of school" that I had worked so hard to gain. I tried to remind myself that, if I could still tell when my reading or writing sounded incorrect, then I had retained my command over both languages. Yet I could no longer be confident of my command over either language because I had discovered that when I was not careful—or even when I was—my reading and writing often surprised me with its impurity. To prevent such impurity, I became very suspicious of my thoughts when I read or wrote. I was always asking myself why I was using this word, how I was using it, always afraid that I wasn't reading or writing correctly. What confused and frustrated me most was that I could not figure out why I was no longer able to read or write correctly without such painful deliberation.

I continued to read only because reading allowed me to keep my thoughts and confusion private. I hoped that somehow, if I watched myself carefully, I would figure out from the way I read whether I had really mastered the "languages." But writing became a dreadful chore. When I tried to keep a diary, I was so afraid that the voice of school might slip in that I could only list my daily activities. When I wrote for school, I worried that my Bourgeois sensibilities would betray me.

CONVERSATIONS: WRITING AND READING AS SOCIAL ACTS
In this paragraph, Lu is describing the impact of her struggle to write her book report on *The Revolutionary Family*. In doing so, she expresses her fears that she could no longer control her "home language" and her "school language." She writes that "my reading and writing in the 'language' of either home or school could not be free of the interference of the other." This is a compelling example of what scholars sometimes mean when they refer to the social nature of language. It is also an example of what theorists mean when they discuss the "instability" of meaning in writing—in other words, the ways in which the meaning of a text is not completely within the control of the writer but is determined by context. In this case, Lu is influenced by the languages of school and home, and she cannot control those influences completely, even though she is aware of them. In this regard, although she may be writing her own essay, her writing is not completely individual but is always a social act because it is done in the context of the practices and expectations of others. As a scholar of rhetoric and composition, Lu is aware of these issues. In paragraphs 24 and 27, she discusses them directly and uses her own experience to illustrate the social nature of language. Furthermore, in making references to the writing of Kenneth Burke and Raymond Williams, two famous scholars who explored issues in language, she is extending the ongoing scholarly conversations about the nature of writing and the problem of meaning.

The more suspicious I became about the way I read and wrote, the more guilty I felt for losing the spontaneity with which I had learned to "use" these "languages." Writing the book report made me feel that my reading and writing in the "language" of either home or school could not be free of the interference of the other. But I was unable to acknowledge, grasp, or grapple with what I was experiencing, for both my parents and my teachers had suggested that, if I were a good student, such interference would and should not take place. I assumed that once I had "acquired" a discourse, I could simply switch it on and off every time I read and wrote as I would some electronic tool. Furthermore, I expected my readings and writings to come out in their correct forms whenever I switched the proper discourse on. I still regarded the discourse of home as natural and the discourse of school alien, but I never had doubted before that I could acquire both and switch them on and off according to the occasion.

When my experience in writing conflicted with what I thought should happen when I used each discourse, I rejected my experience because it contradicted what my parents and teachers had taught me. I shied away from writing to avoid what I assumed I should not experience. But trying to avoid what should not happen did not keep it from recurring whenever I had to write. Eventually my confusion and frustration over these recurring experiences compelled me to search for an explanation: how and why had I failed to learn what my parents and teachers had worked so hard to teach me?

I now think of the internal scene for my reading and writing about *The Revolutionary Family* as a heated discussion between myself, the voices of home, and those of school. The review on the back of the book, the sample student papers I came across in my composition classes, my philosophy teacher—these I heard as voices of one group. My parents and my home readings were the voices of an opposing group. But the conversation between these opposing voices in the internal scene of my writing was not as polite and respectful as the parlor scene Kenneth Burke has portrayed (see epigraph). Rather, these voices struggled to dominate the discussion, constantly incorporating, dismissing, or suppressing the arguments of each other, like the battles between the hegemonic and counterhegemonic forces described in Raymond Williams' *Marxism and Literature* (108–14).

When I read *The Revolutionary Family* and wrote the first version of my report, I be-   25
gan with a quotation from the review. The voices of both home and school answered, clamoring to be heard. I tried to listen to one group and turn a deaf ear to the other. Both persisted. I negotiated my way through these conflicting voices, now agreeing with one, now agreeing with the other. I formed a reading out of my interaction with both. Yet I was afraid to have done so because both home and school had implied that I should speak in unison with only one of these groups and stand away from the discussion rather than participate in it.

My teachers and parents had persistently called my attention to the intensity of the discussion taking place on the external social scene. The story of my grandfather's failure and my father's success had from my early childhood made me aware of the conflict between Western and traditional Chinese cultures. My political education at school added another dimension to the conflict: the war of Marxist-Maoism against them both. Yet when my parents and teachers called my attention to the conflict, they stressed the anxiety of having to live through China's transformation from a semi-feudal, semi-capitalist, and semi-colonial society to a socialist one. Acquiring the discourse of the dominant group was, to them, a means of seeking alliance with that group and thus of surviving the whirlpool of cultural currents around them. As a result, they modeled their pedagogical practices on this utilitarian view of language. Being the eager student, I adopted this view of language as a tool for survival. It came to dominate my understanding of the discussion on the social and historical scene and to restrict my ability to participate in that discussion.

To begin with, the metaphor of language as a tool for survival led me to be passive in my use of discourse, to be a bystander in the discussion. In Burke's "parlor," everyone is involved in the discussion. As it goes on through history, what we call "communal discourses"—arguments specific to particular political, social, economic, ethnic, sexual, and family groups—form, re-form and transform. To use a discourse in such a scene is to participate in the argument and to contribute to the formation of the discourse. But when I was growing up, I could not take on the burden of such an active role in the discussion. For both home and school presented the existent conventions of the discourse each taught me as absolute laws for my action. They turned verbal action into a tool, a set of conventions produced and shaped prior to and outside of my own verbal acts. Because I saw language as a tool, I separated the process of producing the tool from the process of using it. The tool was made by someone else and was then acquired and used by me. How the others made it before

I acquired it determined and guaranteed what it produced when I used it. I imagined that the more experienced and powerful members of the community were the ones responsible for making the tool. They were the ones who participated in the discussion and fought with opponents. When I used what they made, their labor and accomplishments would ensure the quality of my reading and writing. By using it, I could survive the heated discussion. When my immediate experience in writing the book report suggested that knowing the conventions of school did not guarantee the form and content of my report, when it suggested that I had to write the report with the work and responsibility I had assigned to those who wrote book reviews in the Publishing Bureau, I thought I had lost the tool I had earlier acquired.

Another reason I could not take up an active role in the argument was that my parents and teachers contrived to provide a scene free of conflict for practicing my various languages. It was as if their experience had made them aware of the conflict between their discourse and other discourses and of the struggle involved in reproducing the conventions of any discourse on a scene where more than one discourse exists. They seemed convinced that such conflict and struggle would overwhelm someone still learning the discourse. Home and school each contrived a purified space where only one discourse was spoken and heard. In their choice of textbooks, in the way they spoke, and in the way they required me to speak, each jealously silenced any voice that threatened to break the unison of the scene. The homogeneity of home and of school implied that only one discourse could and should be relevant in each place. It led me to believe I should leave behind, turn a deaf ear to, or forget the discourse of the other when I crossed the boundary dividing them. I expected myself to set down one discourse whenever I took up another just as I would take off or put on a particular set of clothes for school or home.

Despite my parents' and teachers' attempts to keep home and school discrete, the internal conflict between the two discourses continued whenever I read or wrote. Although I tried to suppress the voice of one discourse in the name of the other, having to speak aloud in the voice I had just silenced each time I crossed the boundary kept both voices active in my mind. Every "I think . . ." from the voice of home or school brought forth a "However . . ." or a "But . . ." from the voice of the opponents. To identify with the voice of home or school, I had to negotiate through the conflicting voices of both by restating, taking back, qualifying my thoughts. I was unconsciously doing so when I did my book report. But I could not use the interaction comfortably and constructively. Both my parents and my teachers had implied that my job was to prevent that interaction from happening. My sense of having failed to accomplish what they had taught silenced me.

30   To use the interaction between the discourses of home and school constructively, I would have to have seen reading or writing as a process in which I worked my way towards a stance through a dialectical process of identification and division. To identify with an ally, I would have to have grasped the distance between where he or she stood and where I was positioning myself. In taking a stance against an opponent, I would have to have grasped where my stance identified with the stance of my allies. Teetering along the "wavering line of pressure and counter-pressure" from both allies and opponents, I might have worked my way towards a stance of my own (Burke, *A Rhetoric of Motives* 23). Moreover, I would have to have understood that the voices

in my mind, like the participants in the parlor scene, were in constant flux. As I came into contact with new and different groups of people or read different books, voices entered and left. Each time I read or wrote, the stance I negotiated out of these voices would always be at some distance from the stances I worked out in my previous and my later readings or writings.

I could not conceive such a form of action for myself because I saw reading and writing as an expression of an established stance. In delineating the conventions of a discourse, my parents and teachers had synthesized the stance they saw as typical for a representative member of the community. Burke calls this the stance of a "god" or the "prototype"; Williams calls it the "official" or "possible" stance of the community. Through the metaphor of the survival tool, my parents and teachers had led me to assume I could automatically reproduce the official stance of the discourse I used. Therefore, when I did my book report on *The Revolutionary Family,* I expected my knowledge of the official stance set by the book review to ensure the actual stance of my report. As it happened, I began by trying to take the official stance of the review. Other voices interrupted. I answered back. In the process, I worked out a stance approximate but not identical to the official stance I began with. Yet the experience of having to labor to realize my knowledge of the official stance or to prevent myself from wandering away from it frustrated and confused me. For even though I had been actually reading and writing in a Burkean scene, I was afraid to participate actively in the discussion. I assumed it was my role to survive by staying out of it.

*   *   *

Not long ago, my daughter told me that it bothered her to hear her friend "talk wrong." Having come to the United States from China with little English, my daughter has become sensitive to the way English, as spoken by her teachers, operates. As a result, she has amazed her teachers with her success in picking up the language and in adapting to life at school. Her concern to speak the English taught in the classroom "correctly" makes her uncomfortable when she hears people using "ain't" or double negatives, which her teacher considers "improper." I see in her the me that had eagerly learned and used the discourse of the Working class at school. Yet while I was torn between the two conflicting worlds of school and home, she moves with seeming ease from the conversations she hears over the dinner table to her teacher's words in the classroom. My husband and I are proud of the good work she does at school. We are glad she is spared the kinds of conflict between home and school I experienced at her age. Yet as we watch her becoming more and more fluent in the language of the classroom, we wonder if, by enabling her to "survive" school, her very fluency will silence her when the scene of her reading and writing expands beyond that of the composition classroom.

For when I listen to my daughter, to students, and to some composition teachers talking about the teaching and learning of writing, I am often alarmed by the degree to which the metaphor of a survival tool dominates their understanding of language as it once dominated my own. I am especially concerned with the way some composition classes focus on turning the classroom into a monological scene for the students' reading and writing. Most of our students live in a world similar to my daughter's, somewhere between the purified world of the classroom and the complex world of my adolescence. When composition classes encourage these students to ignore those voices that seem irrelevant to the purified world of the classroom, most students are often able to do so without much struggle. Some of them are so adept at doing it that the whole process has for them become automatic.

However, beyond the classroom and beyond the limited range of these students' immediate lives lies a much more complex and dynamic social and historical scene. To help these students become actors in such a scene, perhaps we need to call their attention to voices that may seem irrelevant to the discourse we teach rather than encourage them to shut them out. For example, we might intentionally complicate the classroom scene by bringing into it discourses that stand at varying distances from the one we teach. We might encourage students to explore ways of practicing the conventions of the discourse they are learning by negotiating through these conflicting voices. We could also encourage them to see themselves as responsible for forming or transforming as well as preserving the discourse they are learning.

35   As I think about what we might do to complicate the external and internal scenes of our students' writing, I hear my parents and teachers saying: "Not now. Keep them from the wrangle of the marketplace until they have acquired the discourse and are skilled at using it." And I answer: "Don't teach them to 'survive' the whirlpool of crosscurrents by avoiding it. Use the classroom to moderate the currents. Moderate the currents, but teach them from the beginning to struggle." When I think of the ways in which the teaching of reading and writing as classroom activities can frustrate the development of students, I am almost grateful for the overwhelming complexity of the circumstances in which I grew up. For it was this complexity that kept me from losing sight of the effort and choice involved in reading or writing with and through a discourse.

Works Cited

Burke, Kenneth. *The Philosophy of Literary Form: Studies in Symbolic Action.* 2nd ed. Baton Rouge: Louisiana State UP, 1967.

——. *A Rhetoric of Motives.* Berkeley: U of California P, 1969.

Freire, Paulo. *Pedagogy of the Oppressed.* Trans. M. B. Ramos. New York: Continuum, 1970.

Williams, Raymond. *Marxism and Literature.* New York: Oxford UP, 1977.

UNDERSTANDING THE TEXT

1. What does Lu mean when she states that this essay is "my attempt to fill up that silence with words" (par. 2)? What silence is she referring to? What led to that silence? In what ways do you think Lu's essay achieves this goal of filling the silence?

2. What were the chief differences between what Lu calls the "discourse of home" and the "discourse of school"? Why were these differences so important to Lu? What might these different discourses suggest about writing?

3. In what ways does school help define Lu as a "political subject"? How do reading and writing contribute to her becoming such a subject? Do you think schooling in the United States defines students as political subjects? Why or why not?

4. Why is writing a book report on *The Revolutionary Family* so difficult and important for Lu? What does she learn through this experience? What does this experience reveal about writing and about language in general?

5. What does Lu mean when she writes about taking an "active role in the argument" (par. 26–28)? What argument is occurring here? How can Lu take an active role in it? What main point do you think she is making about writing in this passage?

6. What is the "metaphor of the survival tool" that Lu uses to refer to language in this article? In what ways was language a survival tool for her? Why does she worry that her daughter and other students see language as a survival tool? Do you

think her concern is valid? Why or why not?

EXPLORING THE ISSUES

1. Lu goes into great detail to describe some of her struggles with reading and writing in school and at home. In paragraphs 15 through 20, she describes specific assignments she completed that were difficult for her because of the different expectations for reading and writing in school and at home. Examine these passages carefully. In what ways were reading and writing really different for Lu at home compared to school? What do you think these scenes reveal about reading and writing?

2. In paragraph 28, Lu writes that in her experiences in China, "Home and school each contrived a purified space where only one discourse was spoken and heard." Explain what Lu means by this statement. Do you think the statement applies to your own experience? Explain.

3. This essay was originally written for *College English,* a specialized academic journal for scholars interested in writing, reading, and teaching. But this is not a typical academic article. Examine the features of Lu's prose and the way she addresses her audience in this essay. What features of her essay do you think indicate that it was intended for an academic audience? What assumptions does she make about her audience? In what ways do you think her essay is appropriate for a more general audience who would not have the same expertise and knowledge about language as readers of *College English*? How effective did you find her writing in the essay? Was it difficult in any way for you? Explain.

4. At the end of her essay, Lu writes that she believes that composition teachers should teach students "from the beginning to struggle." Why does she advocate such an approach to teaching writing? What would that kind of teaching mean for student writers, in your view? Do you agree with her? Why or why not?

ENTERING THE CONVERSATIONS

1. Write an essay describing an experience in which writing or reading was especially difficult or risky for you.

2. Arrange to talk to someone on your campus who was educated in a country other than the United States. (You might visit your campus office for international students or your writing center to find such a person.) If possible, arrange to talk to more than one such person. Find out what their experiences with school were like, especially regarding the way they were taught to write. Get their impressions and opinions about those experiences and how they feel about schooling in the United States. Write a report for your classmates about your interviews. Provide some information about each person you spoke to (where they are from, when they came to the United States and why, and so forth), and describe their experiences with writing instruction in their home country and in the United States. Draw conclusions about how writing is taught and how it might affect individual students. Alternatively, if you are a person who was educated in a country other than the United States, write an essay in which you describe your experiences, comparing how you were taught to read and write there to how writing is taught in the United States.

As I was writing this chapter in 2004, I noticed a news report about video games. The report focused on the concerns of some parents and advocacy groups about the violence of video games, which many people believe are inappropriate for children and teenagers. One of the best-selling video games at the time was Grand Theft Auto: San Andreas. You may have played this game yourself. It is a stunningly violent game, in which players can use powerful weapons to

Solitude AND THE Fortress OF Youth

kill characters on the screen, many of whom are innocent bystanders. The violence is graphic and sustained, and you can easily see why some people would object to it. Often, in discussions about such games on television and radio talk shows, you will hear people describe the violence in these games as "gratuitous"; in other words, it is senseless and serves no legitimate purpose other than to appeal to players' lowest instincts.

Writer Michael Chabon (b. 1963) thinks that such violence does serve a legitimate purpose. He sees it as an important part of an imaginative world that teenagers need to inhabit as they struggle through adolescence and come to terms with the confusing world around them. Their imaginative world also includes books, stories, poems, and other writings that may seem disturbing but that he believes help teenagers cope with their struggles. Whether or not you agree with Chabon, his essay raises complex questions about free expression and the role of art, including literary works, in contemporary society. It also prompts us to think about how writing can serve a variety of purposes in our lives, including helping us cope with the confusions and difficulties of growing up.

Michael Chabon is the author of several novels, including The   (continued)

MICHAEL CHABON

Earlier this month my local paper, *The San Francisco Chronicle*, reported that a college student had been expelled from art school here for submitting a story "rife with gruesome details about sexual torture, dismemberment and bloodlust" to his creative writing class. The instructor, a poet named Jan Richman, subsequently found herself out of a job. The university chose not to explain its failure to renew Ms. Richman's contract, but she intimated that she was being punished for having set the tone for the class by assigning a well-regarded if disturbing short story by the **MacArthur**-winning novelist David Foster Wallace, "Girl with Curious Hair." Ms. Richman had been troubled enough by the student's work to report it to her superiors in the first place, in spite of the fact that it was not, according to the *Chronicle*, "the first serial-killer story she had read in her six semesters on the faculty at the Academy of Art University."

Homicide inspectors were called in; a criminal profiler went to work on the student. The officers found no evidence of wrongdoing. The unnamed student had made no threat; his behavior was not considered suspicious. In the end, no criminal charges were brought.

MICHAEL CHABON, "SOLITUDE AND THE FORTRESS OF YOUTH." FROM *THE NEW YORK TIMES*, APRIL 13, 2004. REPRINTED BY PERMISSION.

(continued) Amazing Adventures of Kavalier & Clay, *which won the Pulitzer Prize for fiction in 2001. This essay first appeared in the* New York Times *in 2004.* ▼

GLOSS: MACARTHUR AWARDS
Sometimes referred to as the "genius awards," the MacArthur Fellowships are given by the John D. and Catherine T. MacArthur Foundation to "talented individuals who have shown extraordinary originality and dedication in their creative pursuits and a marked capacity for self-direction," according to the MacArthur Foundation web site. These prestigious awards are considered a sign of unusual accomplishment and commitment on the part of the artists, activists, scientists, and others who have received them. Think about why Chabon would mention that David Foster Wallace, the author of the short story referred to in this paragraph, won a MacArthur Award.

CONTEXT: THE COLUMBINE SHOOTINGS
Most readers will probably recognize Chabon's reference to the horrible murders at Columbine High School in Colorado in 1999. Dylan Klebold was one of the two students who killed themselves after shooting a teacher and twelve of their classmates. The incident shocked Americans, but Chabon suggests here that it has had broader implications for how Americans think about teenagers in general. Notice how Chabon's argument depends on this incident and the general climate in the United States regarding teens and violence. In other words, think about the extent to which the events at Columbine and their impact on American culture shape Chabon's point. Consider, too, how he uses those events and subsequent incidents, such as the one he discusses in the opening paragraph, to build his argument. This is a good example of how a writer is always working within—and with—a context.

In this regard, the San Francisco case differs from other incidents in California, and around the country, in which students, unlucky enough to have as literary precursor the Columbine mass-murderer Dylan Klebold, have found themselves expelled, even prosecuted and convicted on criminal charges, because of the violence depicted in their stories and poems. The threat posed by these prosecutions to civil liberties, to the **First Amendment** rights of our young people, is grave enough. But as a writer, a parent and a former teenager, I see the workings of something more iniquitous: not merely the denial of teenagers' rights in the name of their own protection, but the denial of their humanity in the name of preserving their innocence.

It is in the nature of a teenager to want to destroy. The destructive impulse is universal among children of all ages, rises to a peak of vividness, ingenuity and fascination in adolescence, and thereafter never entirely goes away. Violence and hatred, and the fear of our own inability to control them in ourselves, are a fundamental part of our birthright, along with altruism, creativity, tenderness, pity and love. It therefore requires an immense act of hypocrisy to stigmatize our young adults and teenagers as agents of deviance and disorder. It requires a policy of dishonesty about and blindness to our own histories, as a species, as a nation, and as individuals who were troubled as teenagers, and who will always be troubled, by the same dark impulses. It also requires that favorite tool of the hypocritical, dishonest and fearful: the suppression of constitutional rights.

We justly celebrate the ideals enshrined in the Bill of Rights, but it is also a profoundly disillusioned document, in the best sense of that adjective. It stipulates all the worst impulses of humanity: toward repression, brutality, intolerance and fear. It couples an unbridled faith in the individual human being, redeemed time and again by his or her singular capacity for tenderness, pity and all the rest, with a profound disenchantment about groups of human beings acting as governments, court systems, armies, state religions and bureaucracies, unchecked by the sting of individual conscience and only belatedly if ever capable of anything resembling redemption.

In this light the Bill of Rights can be read as a classic expression of the teenage spirit: a powerful imagination reacting to a history of overwhelming institutional repression, hypocrisy, chicanery and weakness. It is a document written by men who, like teenagers, knew their enemy intimately, and saw in themselves all the potential they possessed to one day become him. We tend to view idealism and cynicism as opposites, when in fact neither possesses any merit or power unless tempered by, fused with, the other. The Bill of Rights is the fruit of that kind of fusion; so is the teenage imagination.

The imagination of teenagers is often—I'm tempted to say always—the only sure capital they possess apart from the love of their parents, which is a force far beyond their capacity to comprehend or control.

5

GLOSS: FIRST AMENDMENT

The First Amendment in the Bill of Rights to the U.S. Constitution, which Chabon mentions in paragraph 3, guarantees citizens the right to free expression: "Congress shall make no law respecting an establishment of religion, or prohibiting the free exercise thereof; or abridging the freedom of speech, or of the press; or the right of the people peaceably to assemble, and to petition the government for a redress of grievances."

CONVERSATIONS: THE BILL OF RIGHTS

Chabon's point about the U.S. Bill of Rights in paragraphs 5 and 6 is subtle, depending partly on readers having a sense of the debates about the Bill of Rights that have been occurring in the United States since even before it was officially ratified by the states in 1788. Americans often discuss the Bill of Rights and the Constitution as almost sacred documents, and the men who wrote them, the so-called Framers, men like George Washington and Benjamin Franklin, are often referred to in heroic and even saintly terms. But here, Chabon places those documents in historical context, drawing our attention to the complicated political and social circumstances within which the Framers wrote them. From Chabon's point of view, those circumstances, which were characterized by centuries of political repression by monarchs and religious leaders in Europe and by deep social inequalities in European societies, led the men who wrote the U.S. Constitution to have a skeptical view of human nature. As Chabon writes, the Framers had "a profound disenchantment" about the possibility that humans could govern themselves without violence and conflict. This view of the Constitution is not universal, but it is part of the ongoing conversation in the United States about how best to interpret the Constitution. Consider how Chabon's essay, which on the surface seems to be about teen violence and imagination, can also be understood as part of this larger conversation about who we are and how we should govern ourselves. Consider, too, how your own understanding of the U.S. Constitution might affect the way you read this passage and the way you react to Chabon's main argument.

During my own adolescence, my imagination, the kingdom inside my own skull, was my sole source of refuge, my fortress of solitude, at times my prison. But a fortress requires a constant line of supply; those who take refuge in attics and cellars require the unceasing aid of confederates; prisoners need advocates, escape plans, or simply a window that gives onto the sky.

Like all teenagers, I provisioned my garrison with art: books, movies, music, comic books, television, role-playing games. My secret confederates were the works of Monty Python, H. P. Lovecraft, the cartoonist Vaughan Bodé, and the Ramones, among many others; they kept me watered and fed. They baked files into cakes and, on occasion, for a wondrous moment, made the walls of my prison disappear. Given their nature as human creations, as artifacts and devices of human nature, some of the provisions I consumed were bound to be of a dark, violent, even bloody and horrifying nature; otherwise I would not have cared for them. Tales and displays of violence, blood and horror rang true, answered a need, on some deep, angry level that maybe only those with scant power or capital, regardless of their age, can understand.

It was not long before I began to write: stories, poems, snatches of autobiographical jazz. Often I imitated the work of my confederates: stories of human beings in the most extreme situations and states of emotion—horror stories; accounts of madness and despair. In part—let's say in large part, if that's what it takes to entitle the writings of teenagers to unqualified protection under the First Amendment—this was about expression. I was writing what I felt, what I believed, wished for, raged against, hoped and dreaded. But the main reason I wrote stories—and the reason that I keep on writing them today—was not to express myself. I started to write because once it had been nourished, stoked and liberated by those secret confederates, I could not hold back the force of my imagination. I had been freed, and I felt that it was now up to me to do the same for somebody else, somewhere, trapped in his or her own lonely tower.

10 We don't want teenagers to write violent poems, horrifying stories, explicit lyrics and rhymes; they're ugly, in precisely the way that we are ugly, and out of protectiveness and hypocrisy, even out of pity and love and tenderness, we try to force young people to be innocent of everything but the effects of that ugliness. And so we censor the art they consume and produce, and prosecute and suspend and expel them, and when, once in a great while, a teenager reaches for an easy gun and shoots somebody or himself, we tell ourselves that if we had only censored his journals and curtailed his music and video games, that awful burst of final ugliness could surely have been pre-

vented. As if art caused the ugliness, when of course all it can ever do is reflect and, perhaps, attempt to explain it.

10   Let teenagers languish, therefore, in their sense of isolation, without outlet or nourishment, bereft of the only thing that makes it all bearable: knowing that somebody else has felt the way that you feel, has faced it, run from it, rued it, lamented it and transformed it into art; has been there, and returned, and lived, for the only good reason we have: to tell the tale. How confident we shall be, once we have done this, of never encountering the ugliness again! How happy our children will be, and how brave, and how safe!

VISUAL CONNECTIONS: VIOLENT MEDIA
These photos show children playing popular and controversial video games, such as *Grand Theft Auto*. These games allow players to adopt the roles of criminals who engage in often violent criminal activity. Consider what these images might convey about the uses of such games among young people. In what ways do you think the popularity of such games among children and teens might enhance or weaken Chabon's argument in this essay?

UNDERSTANDING THE TEXT

1. How would you summarize Chabon's main argument in this essay? Where does he state his point most clearly? Do you find his argument persuasive? Why or why not? What might your answer to that question suggest about your own views regarding violence and free speech?

2. Chabon writes that "it is in the nature of a teenager to want to destroy." Why is this an important point for his argument? What evidence does he offer to support it? Do you agree with him? Why or why not?

3. What connection does Chabon see between the U.S. Bill of Rights and teenagers? How does this connection help him make his larger point about teenagers?

4. What is the role of imagination in teenagers, according to Chabon? How did his own imagination affect him as a teenager? Do you think he is right about imagination? Explain.

5. What role did art, and especially writing, play in Chabon's teenage life? How can writing serve teens and society in general, in his view? What do you think his view might suggest about writing and the way it is taught in schools?

EXPLORING THE ISSUES

1. Examine how Chabon builds his argument in this essay. What specific points does he make in support of his main argument? What kinds of evidence does he cite? How effectively do you think he supports his argument?

2. Assess the effectiveness of the metaphors Chabon uses to describe the teenage years, especially the metaphor of the prison. How does Chabon develop this metaphor. How

does it advance his main argument about writing and adolescence? In what ways do you think it might strengthen or weaken his essay?

3. In recent years, violent music, games, and videos have become increasingly controversial, and some groups have tried to censor them. Yet, Chabon sees some benefit to such media. What does Chabon's position suggest about his view of human nature and about adolescence? Do you think his view is a common one? Explain. Do you agree with him? Why or why not?

4. How would you describe the tone of Chabon's final paragraph? Is the tone of this paragraph consistent with the rest of his essay? Explain, citing specific passages to support your answer. In what ways do you think his tone here might strengthen or weaken his argument?

ENTERING THE CONVERSATIONS

1. Write an essay describing what it is like to be a teenager based on your own experience and the experiences of your friends and other people you know.

2. In a group of classmates, share the essays you wrote for Question 1. Discuss similarities and differences among your experiences as a teenager and the experiences of your classmates, and try to identify what you and your classmates believe are the main characteristics of the experience of being a teenager. Compare your group's conclusions with Michael Chabon's perspective on teens.

INFOTRAC

3. In recent years, controversies about violence in media such as films, television, music, and especially video games have intensified.

Some groups have made efforts to try to restrict or censor video games, claiming that they have an adverse effect on young people and can actually encourage violent behavior. Using InfoTrac College Edition, the Internet, and any other appropriate resources, investigate these controversies. Identify the main concerns of those who wish to restrict access to violent media images and those who oppose restrictions. Determine whether there is convincing evidence that violent media images and video games do affect young people in certain ways. Write a report on the basis of your research, drawing conclusions about the impact of violent media on young people.

4. On the basis of your research for Question 3, write a letter to the editor of your local newspaper in which you express your view about violence in the media. In your letter, offer your suggestions about what steps, if any, might be taken to address the problem.

5. Create a pamphlet, web site, or some other kind of document that contains advice to parents about how to address the problem of violent video games with their children.

6. Popular movies have long been the focus of concern and protest because of the violence they often contain. The movie rating system was developed to address such concerns; it is intended to restrict children and young teens from seeing certain films and to help parents decide which films are appropriate for their children. However, some people push for greater restrictions and even censorship of popular films. Drawing on Chabon's essay and referring to recent popular films, write an essay in which you state and support your view about whether or not popular films should be restricted or censored in any way.

A few years ago, I had the opportunity to teach a writing class in a prison. My students ranged in age from their teens to their fifties; they were incarcerated for all kinds of crimes, from auto theft and drug trafficking to murder. Many of them could hardly write a correct sentence. But all of them worked hard on their writing, and some of them took advantage of the assignments I gave to tell the stories of their often sad and difficult lives. I often felt that the

Becoming a Poet

power of their writing did not lie so much in what they wrote about but in the fact that for a few hours each week they could escape the dull yet dangerous lives they led in prison and become something other than inmates. Writing gave them a way to feel human again.

Maybe because of that experience I have found this essay by Jimmy Santiago Baca (b. 1952) to be especially powerful. In this essay, which is taken from his autobiography, Working in the Dark: Reflections of a Poet of the Barrio *(1992), Baca describes his own difficult life growing up in the American Southwest, a life characterized by crime and trouble with the law. His descriptions of his horrific experiences while in prison are especially powerful, and they sometimes make me wonder about the men in my prison writing class and what they went through. But Baca's essay is really more about writing than it is about his hard life as a young criminal and an inmate. His essay includes some of the most provocative descriptions of writing that I have ever encountered. Thankfully, few of us have known the degradation and humiliation that Baca suffered in prison, so perhaps we have not experienced the power of writing in the way he has. Yet, I think most (continued)*

JIMMY SANTIAGO BACA

On weekend graveyard shifts at St. Joseph's Hospital I worked the emergency room, mopping up pools of blood and carting plastic bags stuffed with arms, legs, and hands to the outdoor incinerator. I enjoyed the quiet, away from the screams of shotgunned, knifed, and mangled kids writhing on gurneys outside the operating rooms. Ambulance sirens shrieked and squad car lights reddened the cool nights, flashing against the hospital walls: gray—red, gray—red. On slow nights I would lock the door of the administration office, search the reference library for a book on female anatomy and, with my feet propped on the desk, leaf through the illustrations, smoking my cigarette. I was seventeen.

One night my eye was caught by a familiar-looking word on the spine of a book. The title was *450 Years of Chicano History in Pictures.* On the cover were black-and-white photos: Padre Hidalgo exhorting Mexican peasants to revolt against the Spanish dictators; Anglo vigilantes hanging two Mexicans from a tree; a young Mexican woman with rifle and ammunition belts crisscrossing her breast; César Chávez and field workers marching for fair wages; Chicano railroad

JIMMY SANTIAGO BACA, "BECOMING A POET." FROM *WORKING IN THE DARK: REFLECTIONS OF A POET OF THE BARRIO* (1992). PUBLISHER: RED CRANE BOOKS. REPRINTED BY PERMISSION.

(continued) *of us have known moments when we can feel some of that power. And certainly Baca's essay might help us think about what writing can mean in a person's life. I selected this essay for this cluster partly because I hope it will help you gain a sense of what writing might mean in your life.*

In addition to his autobiography, Working in the Dark: Reflections of a Poet of the Barrio *(1992), Jimmy Santiago Baca has written several volumes of poetry, including* Black Mesa Poems *(1987), and has received numerous awards for his writing.* ◢

workers laying creosote ties; Chicanas laboring at machines in textile factories; Chicanas picketing and hoisting boycott signs.

From the time I was seven, teachers had been punishing me for not knowing my lessons by making me stick my nose in a circle chalked on the blackboard. Ashamed of not understanding and fearful of asking questions, I dropped out of school in the ninth grade. At seventeen I still didn't know how to read, but those pictures confirmed my identity. I stole the book that night, stashing it for safety under the slop sink until I got off work. Back at my boardinghouse, I showed the book to friends. All of us were amazed; this book told us we were alive. We, too, had defended ourselves with our fists against hostile Anglos, gasping for breath in fights with the policemen who outnumbered us. The book reflected back to us our struggle in a way that made us proud.

Most of my life I felt like a target in the cross hairs of a hunter's rifle. When strangers and outsiders questioned me I felt the hang-rope tighten around my neck and the trapdoor creak beneath my feet. There was nothing so humiliating as being unable to express myself, and my inarticulateness increased my sense of jeopardy, of being endangered. I felt intimidated and vulnerable, ridiculed and scorned. Behind a mask of humility, I seethed with mute rebellion.

5   Before I was eighteen, I was arrested on suspicion of murder after refusing to explain a deep cut on my forearm. With shocking speed I found myself handcuffed to a chain gang of inmates and bused to a holding facility to await trial. There I met men, prisoners, who read aloud to each other the works of Neruda, Paz, Sabines, Nemerov, and Hemingway. Never had I felt such freedom as in that dormitory. Listening to the words of these writers, I felt that invisible threat from without lessen—my sense of teetering on a rotting plank over swamp water where famished alligators clapped their horny snouts for my blood. While I listened to the words of the poets, the alligators slumbered powerless in their lairs. Their language was the magic that could liberate me from myself, transform me into another person, transport me to other places far away.

And when they closed the books, these Chicanos, and went into their own Chicano language, they made barrio life come alive for me in the fullness of its vitality. I began to learn my own language, the bilingual words and phrases explaining to me my place in the universe. Every day I felt like the paper boy taking delivery of the latest news of the day.

Months later I was released, as I had suspected I would be. I had been guilty of nothing but shattering the windshield of my girlfriend's car in a fit of rage.

Two years passed. I was twenty now, and behind bars again. The federal marshals had failed to provide convincing evidence to extradite me to Arizona on a drug charge, but still I was being held. They had ninety days to prove I was guilty. The only evidence against me was that my girlfriend had been at the scene of the crime with my driver's license in her purse. They had to come up with something else. But there was nothing else. Eventually they negotiated a deal with the actual drug dealer, who took the stand against me. When the judge hit me with a million-dollar bail, I emptied my pockets on his booking desk: twenty-six cents.

One night in my third month in the county jail, I was mopping the floor in front of the booking desk. Some detectives had kneed an old drunk and handcuffed him to the booking bars. His shrill screams raked my nerves like a hacksaw on bone, the desperate protest of his dignity against their inhumanity. But the detectives just laughed as he tried to rise and kicked him to his knees. When they went to the bathroom to pee and the desk attendant walked to the file cabinet to pull the arrest record, I shot my arm through the bars, grabbed one of the attendant's university textbooks, and tucked it in my overalls. It as the only way I had of protesting.

It was late when I returned to my cell. Under my blanket I switched on a pen flashlight and opened the thick book at random, scanning the pages. I could hear the jailer making his rounds on the other tiers. The jangle of his keys and the sharp click of his boot heels intensified my solitude. Slowly I enunciated the words . . . p-o-n-d, ri-pple. It scared me that I had been reduced to this to find comfort. I always had thought reading a waste of time, that nothing could be gained by it. Only by action, by moving out into the world and confronting and challenging the obstacles, could one learn anything worth knowing.   10

Even as I tried to convince myself that I was merely curious, I became so absorbed in how the sounds created music in me and happiness, I forgot where I was. Memories began to quiver in me, glowing with a strange but familiar intimacy in which I found refuge. For a while, a deep sadness overcame me, as if I had chanced on a long-lost friend and mourned the years of separation. But soon the heartache of having missed so much of life, that had numbed me since I was a child, gave way, as if a grave illness lifted itself from me and I was cured, innocently believing in the beauty of life again. I stumblingly repeated the author's name as I fell asleep, saying it over and over in the dark: Words-worth, Words-worth.

Before long my sister came to visit me, and I joked about taking her to a place called Kubla Khan and getting her a blind date with this *vato* named Coleridge who lived on the seacoast and was *malías* on morphine. When I asked her to make a trip into enemy territory to buy me a grammar book, she said she couldn't. Bookstores intimidated her, because she, too, could neither read nor write.

Days later, with a stub pencil I whittled sharp with my teeth, I propped a **Red Chief notebook** on my knees and wrote my first words. From that moment, a hunger for poetry possessed me.

Until then, I had felt as if I had been born into a raging ocean where I swam relentlessly, flailing my arms in hope of rescue, of reaching a shoreline I never sighted. Never solid ground beneath me, never a resting place. I had lived with only the desperate hope to stay afloat; that and nothing more.

15   But when at last I wrote my first words on the page, I felt an island rising beneath my feet like the back of a whale. As more and more

STRATEGIES: USING DETAILS
Throughout this essay, Baca uses physical details to convey a sense of his experiences. But sometimes the details he selects do more than describe the scene. Here, for example, he tells us that the notebook he was writing in was a Red Chief notebook, which was a common brand of notebook often used in schools. Consider what message that detail might convey in this scene and how it might relate to Baca's larger point about literacy and identity. What would he lose in this passage if he had simply mentioned that he had a notebook without specifying that it was a Red Chief notebook?

words emerged, I could finally rest: I had a place to stand for the first time in my life. The island grew, with each page, into a continent inhabited by people I knew and mapped with the life I lived.

I wrote about it all—about people I had loved or hated, about the brutalities and ecstasies of my life. And, for the first time, the child in me who had witnessed and endured unspeakable terrors cried out not just in impotent despair, but with the power of language. Suddenly, through language, through writing, my grief and my joy could be shared with anyone who would listen. And I could do this all alone; I could do it anywhere. I was no longer a captive of demons eating away at me, no longer a victim of other people's mockery and loathing, that had made me clench my fist white with rage and grit my teeth to silence. Words now pleaded back with the bleak lucidity of hurt. They were wrong, those others, and now I could say it.

Through language I was free. I could respond, escape, indulge; embrace or reject earth or the cosmos. I was launched on an endless journey without boundaries or rules, in which I could salvage the floating fragments of my past, or be born anew in the spontaneous ignition of understanding some heretofore concealed aspect of myself. Each word steamed with the hot lava juices of my primordial making, and I crawled out of stanzas dripping with birth-blood, reborn and freed from the chaos of my life. The child in the dark room of my heart, that had never been able to find or reach the light switch, flicked it on now; and I found in the room a stranger, myself, who had waited so many years to speak again. My words struck in me lightning crackles of elation and thunderhead storms of grief.

*   *   *

When I had been in the county jail longer than anyone else, I was made a trustee. One morning, after a fistfight, I went to the unlocked and unoccupied office used for lawyer-client meetings, to think. The bare white room with its fluorescent tube lighting seemed to expose and illuminate my dark and worthless life. And yet, for the first time, I had something to lose—my chance to read, to write; a way to live with dignity and meaning, that had opened for me when I stole that scuffed, secondhand book about the Romantic poets. In prison, the abscess had been lanced.

"I will never do any work in this prison system as long as I am not allowed to get my G.E.D." That's what I told the reclassification panel. The captain flicked off the tape recorder. He looked at me hard and said, "You'll never walk outta here alive. Oh, you'll work, put a copper penny on that, you'll work."

20   After that interview I was confined to deadlock maximum security in a subterranean dungeon, with ground-level chicken-wired windows painted gray. Twenty-three hours a day I was in that cell. I kept sane by borrowing books from the other cons on the tier. Then, just before Christmas, I received a letter from Harry, a charity house samaritan who doled out hot soup to the homeless in Phoenix. He had picked my name from a list of cons who had no one to write to them. I wrote back asking for a grammar book, and a week later received one of Mary Baker Eddy's treatises on salvation and redemption, with Spanish and English on opposing pages. Pacing my cell all day and most of each night, I grappled with grammar until I was able to write a long true-romance confession for a con to send to his pen pal. He paid

me with a pack of smokes. Soon I had a thriving barter business, exchanging my poems and letters for novels, commissary pencils, and writing tablets.

One day I tore two flaps from the cardboard box that held all my belongings and punctured holes along the edge of each flap and along the border of a ream of state-issue paper. After I had aligned them to form a spine, I threaded the holes with a shoestring, and sketched on the cover a hummingbird fluttering above a rose. This was my first journal.

Whole afternoons I wrote, unconscious of passing time or whether it was day or night. Sunbursts exploded from the lead tip of my pencil, words that grafted me into awareness of who I was; peeled back to a burning core of bleak terror, an embryo floating in the image of water, I cracked out of the shell wide-eyed and insane. Trees grew out of the palms of my hands, the threatening otherness of life dissolved, and I became one with the air and sky, the dirt and the iron and concrete. There was no longer any distinction between the other and I. Language made bridges of fire between me and everything I saw. I entered into the blade of grass, the basketball, the con's eye, and child's soul.

> **CONNECTIONS: WRITING AND IMAGINATION**
> In this and the following paragraphs, Baca offers vivid descriptions of how he felt when he was writing. Consider what these images might suggest about writing and about the connections between writing and thinking. Compare Baca's descriptions with the argument that Michael Chabon makes in his essay (page 356) about the importance of imagination in teenagers.

At night I flew. I conversed with floating heads in my cell, and visited strange houses where lonely women brewed tea and rocked in wicker rocking chairs listening to sad Joni Mitchell songs.

Before long I was frayed like a rope carrying too much weight, that suddenly snaps. I quit talking. Bars, walls, steel bunk, and floor bristled with millions of poem-making sparks. My face was no longer familiar to me. The only reality was the swirling cornucopia of images in my mind, the voices in the air. Mid-air a cactus blossom would appear, a snake-flame in blinding dance around it, stunning me like a guard's fist striking my neck from behind.

The prison administrators tried several tactics to get me to work. For six months, after the next monthly prison board review, they sent cons to my cell to hassle me. When the guard would open my cell door to let one of them in, I'd leap out and fight him—and get sent to thirty-day isolation. I did a lot of isolation time. But I honed my image-making talents in that sensory-deprived solitude. Finally they moved me to death row, and after that to "nut-run," the tier that housed the mentally disturbed. 25

As the months passed, I became more and more sluggish. My eyelids were heavy, I could no longer write or read. I slept all the time.

One day a guard took me out to the exercise field. For the first time in years I felt grass and earth under my feet. It was spring. The sun warmed my face as I sat on the bleachers watching the cons box and run, hit the handball, lift weights. Some of them stopped to ask how I was, but I found it impossible to utter a syllable. My tongue would not move, saliva drooled from the corners of my mouth. I had been so heavily medicated I could not summon the slightest gesture. Yet inside me a small voice cried out, I am fine! I am hurt now but I will come back! I am fine!

Back in my cell, for weeks I refused to eat. Styrofoam cups of urine and hot water were hurled at me. Other things happened. There were beatings, shock therapy, intimidation.

Later, I regained some clarity of mind. But there was a place in my heart where I had died. My life had compressed itself into an unbearable dread of being. The strain had been too much. I had stepped over that line where a human being has lost more than he can bear, where the pain is too intense, and he knows he is changed forever. I was now capable of killing, coldly and without feeling. I was empty, as I have never, before or since, known emptiness. I had no connection to this life.

30   But then, the encroaching darkness that began to envelop me forced me to reform and give birth to myself again in the chaos. I withdrew even deeper into the world of language, cleaving the diamonds of verbs and nouns, plunging into the brilliant light of poetry's regenerative mystery. Words gave off rings of white energy, radar signals from powers beyond me that infused me with truth. I believed what I wrote, because I wrote what was true. My words did not come from books or textual formulas, but from a deep faith in the voice of my heart.

I had been steeped in self-loathing and rejected by everyone and everything—society, family, cons, God, and demons. But now I had become as the burning ember floating in darkness that descends on a dry leaf and sets flame to forests. The word was the ember and the forest was my life.

*   *   *

I was born a poet one noon, gazing at weeds and creosoted grass at the base of a telephone pole outside my grilled cell window. The words I wrote then sailed me out of myself, and I was transported and metamorphosed into the images they made. From the dirty brown blades of grass came bolts of electrical light that jolted loose my old self; through the top of my head that self was released and reshaped in the clump of scrawny grass. Through language I became the grass, speaking its language and feeling its green feelings and black root sensations. Earth was my mother and I bathed in sunshine. Minuscule speckles of sunlight passed through my green skin and metabolized in my blood.

Writing bridged my divided life of prisoner and free man. I wrote of the emotional butchery of prisons, and of my acute gratitude for poetry. Where my blind doubt and spontaneous trust in life met, I discovered empathy and compassion. The power to express myself was a welcome storm rasping at tendril roots, flooding my soul's cracked dirt. Writing was water that cleansed the wound and fed the parched root of my heart.

I wrote to sublimate my rage, from a place where all hope is gone, from a madness of having been damaged too much, from a silence of killing rage. I wrote to avenge the betrayals of a lifetime, to purge the bitterness of injustice. I wrote with a deep groan of doom in my blood, bewildered and dumbstruck; from an indestructible love of life, to affirm breath and laughter and the abiding innocence of things. I wrote the way I wept, and danced, and made love.

CONVERSATIONS: THE PRISON WRITER
Baca writes compellingly about how he discovered writing while in prison. His story is not unique. A number of others have earned fame either by discovering writing while in prison or by writing about their experiences while there. Perhaps the most famous is Malcolm X, the controversial Black leader during the Civil Rights Movement whose book *The Autobiography of Malcolm X* (1965) describes how he learned to read and write in prison and then used his language skills to advance his political causes. More recently, a few cases of prison writers have provoked controversy. For example, in his book *Monster: The Autobiography of an L.A. Gang Member* (1993), Sanyika Shakur describes his disturbing, violent life as a gang member and his transformation while in prison, where he educated himself and rejected his former life of crime. Shakur's book was criticized by some who argued that it not only glorified violence but also enabled Shakur to profit from his crimes. Baca's essay might be considered another version of this story of someone who changed his or her life as a result of being imprisoned. It might also be seen as part of a never-ending conversation about the power of writing.

UNDERSTANDING THE TEXT

1. What role do books play in Baca's life? To what extent do you think the impact of books on Baca was related to his circumstances? In other words, would books have meant as much to him if he had not been in prison and suffered abuse there? Explain.

2. What does Baca mean when he writes, "Through language I was free"? In what sense was he free, even when he was in prison? What kind of freedom did his writing give him? What do you think Baca's experiences might suggest about writing in general?

3. Why was Baca subject to such terrible abuse while in prison? Why did his demand about getting a GED result in such harsh treatment? What do you think this experience might suggest about learning? About writing?

4. How does Baca use writing to pull himself out of the terrible state he was in while in prison? What changed in him as a result of his writing? Do you find his descriptions of how he used writing believable? Explain, citing specific passages to support your answer.

EXPLORING THE ISSUES

1. Assess Baca's writing style in this essay. What features of his writing stand out for you? How effective do you find his writing? How might Baca's writing style reflect his own beliefs about writing and its importance in his life?

2. In paragraph 24, Baca describes his mental state in solitary confinement as one in which his "only reality was the swirling cornucopia of images in my mind, the voices in the air." Given his description, his condition could easily be taken as mental illness. However, his earlier descriptions of his writing (for example, in par. 22), which he presents as happy moments, sound very similar to the description in paragraph 24. Examine the way Baca describes his mental state when we was writing and at other times as well. What metaphors and images does he use? What ideas do you think he is trying to convey about writing? What might his experience suggest about language and our sense of self in general? Do you find his descriptions effective? Do you think they accurately convey a sense of the experience of writing?

3. Baca has been acclaimed as a writer who speaks powerfully for Chicanos and for people of color in general. In what ways do you think this essay reflects Baca's desire to speak for his people? Based on this essay, do you think Baca's reputation as a poet of Chicanos and people of color is justified? Why or why not?

4. Baca describes his experiences and his writing as deeply connected to his identity as a Chicano who grew up in a barrio in the southwestern United States. Do you think he imagined his primary audience for this essay to be Chicanos? In what ways might he have been trying to address a wider audience? Do you think you are part of the audience that Baca imagined for this

essay? Explain, citing specific passages to support your answers.

ENTERING THE CONVERSATIONS

1. Write an essay describing an experience in which writing somehow made a difference in your life. Alternatively, write an essay in which you discuss the role that writing has played in your life.

2. In a group of classmates, share the essays you wrote for Question 1. What similarities and differences can you identify among your classmates regarding the role of writing in your lives? What might your essays suggest about writing?

3. In his essay, Baca describes learning about Chicano history through reading and through conversations with other inmates. This passage suggests the importance of telling the story of a people. Write an essay in which you tell your version of the story of your family or some other group or community that you identify with.

4. Write an essay in which you compare Baca's ideas about the connections between writing and identity to the ideas of Gloria Anzaldúa, whose essay begins on page 312.

5. Write an essay that explains how writing can be a means to freedom. Alternatively, create a web site or some other visual document that reflects your sense of how writing can make a person free.

BEYOND WORDS

THE OLD SAYING THAT A PICTURE IS WORTH A THOUSAND WORDS IS ONE WAY TO DESCRIBE THE POWER OF AN IMAGE TO COMMUNICATE. CONSIDER THE PHOTOGRAPHS ON PAGE 53, FOR EXAMPLE. THEY WERE TAKEN FROM A SATELLITE JUST BEFORE AND DURING THE MASSIVE

power outage in the eastern United States and Canada in August 2003. Imagine what you might say about these photographs. There is a lot to say, perhaps about the extent of our electricity usage, about the impact of a blackout on society, about our interconnectedness, about patterns of development in North America. And much more. Or think about it this way: How might you use these photographs to make a statement about, say, energy conservation or the need for changes in the way the power system is managed. A picture can indeed be worth a thousand words.

But it isn't just pictures that are worth a thousand words. All kinds of images can be used to send all kinds of messages. Think about a road sign like this one:

This sign communicates important information to drivers about road conditions—in this case, that there is a downgrade—and indicates specifically to truckers that they will have to shift gears to negotiate the downgrade safely. All this information is communicated without words.

Or think about the American flag. It can be used to communicate patriotism, national pride, ownership (as in the case of a flag painted on the side of a U.S. Army vehicle), remembrance (as when athletes wear flags on their uniforms to honor fallen soldiers), even danger (an upside-down flag is a sign of emergency). When protesters burn American flags, they are making a powerful and often controversial statement. And it's no surprise that many Americans believe that burning the flag should be illegal. Or how about the flag shown on this page. This image changes the familiar symbol of the American flag to make a statement about the role of corporations in American society. How difficult would it be to write an essay that makes such a statement as dramatically and concisely as this image does?

We can communicate just as effectively with sound as well. Think of a siren, for example. Or think of "Taps" played at a funeral. Did you ever notice the music playing in a store at the mall? If you're shopping at a store like The Gap, you're likely to hear hip-hop or other popular music that appeals to young people. But you wouldn't hear that kind of music in a fine jewelry store or a hardware store, where the customers are likely to be much older. Obviously, the music in stores like these is carefully selected to create a certain atmosphere for customers; it tells customers that this is their kind of store. Of course, music can communicate more provocative messages as well, such as the antiwar protest songs of the 1960s and 1970s or the music of a rapper making a statement about racial injustice.

The following three essays explore some of the ways in which we communicate beyond words. These essays ask you to think carefully about how we send and receive messages through various media other than writing. Growing up in today's multimedia world, you are constantly bombarded with messages of all kinds: visual, aural, textual. And your ability to make sense of these messages— and sometimes even to resist them—can profoundly shape your life. These essays can help you appreciate how.

We are surrounded by music: on the radio *and television, in stores, at sporting events, at political or civic celebrations, and in churches, synagogues, mosques, and temples. Much of this music is of course purely entertainment. But music can also communicate ideas, feelings, and beliefs as effectively as any other medium. And in many ways, it may be more effective. As Steve Earle (b. 1955) demonstrates in the following essay, the iconic American folksinger Woody*

IN Praise OF Woodie Guthrie

Guthrie understood the power of music to communicate, and he spent his life using music to make statements about social and political injustices, sometimes at great personal risk. Unlike many of today's successful pop musicians, Guthrie rarely profited from his music, even as his songs were widely distributed and even as some of them became American classics. For Guthrie, music wasn't about money or entertainment; it was a way to speak out and try to change things. As you read Earle's praise of Woody Guthrie, you might think about how Guthrie's view of music compares to—or differs from—your own sense of the purpose of music. And consider how some of the musicians you listen to might use their music much as Guthrie did: to make statements about the world around them.

Earle's essay also helps us see that people themselves can be symbols by virtue of the lives they live. It is as much about what Woody Guthrie means as a cultural figure as it is about the impact of Guthrie's music. In that sense, Earle gives us another example of how we communicate "beyond words."

Earle's essay, which first appeared in the liberal magazine The Nation *in 2003, is also a good example of what rhetorical theorists call* epideictic *discourse—(continued)*

STEVE EARLE

When Bob Dylan took the stage at the 1965 Newport Jazz Festival, all leather and **Ray-Bans** and Beatle boots, and declared emphatically and (heaven forbid) electrically that he wasn't "gonna work on **Maggie's farm** no more," the folk music faithful took it personally. They had come to see the scruffy kid with the dusty suede jacket pictured on the covers of Bob Dylan and Freewheelin'. They wanted to hear topical songs. Political songs. Songs like "The Lonesome Death of Hattie Carroll," "Masters of War" and "Blowin' in the Wind." They wanted the heir apparent. The Dauphin. They wanted Woody Guthrie.

Dylan wasn't goin' for it. He struggled through two electric numbers before he and the Paul Butterfield Blues Band retreated backstage. After a few minutes he returned alone and, armed with only an acoustic guitar, delivered a scathing "It's All Over Now, Baby Blue" and walked.

Woody Guthrie himself had long since been silenced by Huntington's chorea, a hereditary brain-wasting disease, leaving a hole in the heart of American music that would never be filled, and

STEVE EARLE, "IN PRAISE OF WOODIE GUTHRIE." REPRINTED WITH PERMISSION FROM THE JULY 21, 2003 ISSUE OF *THE NATION*. FOR SUBSCRIPTION INFORMATION, CALL 1-800-333-8536. PORTIONS OF EACH WEEK'S NATION MAGAZINE CAN BE ACCESSED AT HTTP://WWW.THENATION.COM

(continued) *that is, a text or speech intended to celebrate someone or something. An accomplished songwriter himself and the author of* Doghouse Roses *(2001), a collection of short stories, Earle is well qualified to celebrate the music of Woody Guthrie and to help us better appreciate the power of music to communicate.* ◗

5

GLOSS: RAY-BANS
Ray-Bans, mentioned in paragraph 1, were a brand of sunglasses popular in the 1960s and 1970s.

CONTEXT: DYLAN, "MAGGIE'S FARM," AND THE NEWPORT JAZZ FESTIVAL
As Earle suggests in the opening paragraphs of this essay, legendary singer-songwriter Bob Dylan's reputation for social and political commentary in his lyrics led to expectations among his fans at the Newport Jazz Festival in 1965. Dylan disappointed them by playing electric music rather than the acoustic folk music they had come to expect. Earle relies on a political interpretation of Dylan's well-known song "Maggie's Farm" to make his point that Dylan's performance at the Newport festival was meant as a statement of his intentions as a musician and an artist. Consider how Earle uses this now-famous incident to help him introduce his main point about the political nature of American folk music.

Dylan may have been the only person present at Newport that day with sense enough to know it.

One does not become Woody Guthrie by design. Dylan knew that because he had tried. We all tried, every one of us who came along later and tried to follow in his footsteps only to find that no amount of study, no apprenticeship, no regimen of self-induced hard travelin' will ever produce another Woody. Not in a million years.

Woody Guthrie was what folks who don't believe in anything would call an anomaly. Admittedly, the intersection of space and time at the corner of July 14, 1912, and Okemah, Oklahoma, was a long shot to produce anything like a national treasure.

Woody was born in one of the most desolate places in America, just in time to come of age in the worst period in our history. Then again, the Dust Bowl itself was no accident either. After the Civil War, the United States government and the railroads, mistakenly believing that the Great Plains would make swell farmland, killed off all the buffalo, effectively neutralizing the indigenous population, and opened up vast expanses of prairie to homesteading. Problem was that the head-high buffalo grass that thrived in the thin topsoil had slowly adapted to its deceptively hostile environment over several thousand years. It took less than seventy years for nonnative water- and mineral-greedy crops to wring every last nutrient from the traumatized earth, creating a vast man-made desert and setting in motion a mass migration of folks from Texas, Arkansas and Oklahoma out west to California, where they hoped against hope for a better life.

Most found only bigotry and exploitation at the hands of wealthy fruit and vegetable growers. Woody found an audience. He sang in the migrant camps and on the picket lines up and down the lush interior valleys. A few well-meaning outsiders were sympathetic to the plight of the migrants, but they were college boys who used a lot of big words like "proletariat" and "bourgeoisie" and unintentionally made the Okies feel small. But Woody was one of their own. He spoke their language and he sang their songs, and every once in a while he'd slip in one of those big words in between a tall tale and an outlaw ballad. As he became more outraged he became more radical, but his songs and his patter always maintained a sense of humor and hope. He said, "I ain't a Communist necessarily, but I been in the red all my life."

Woody arrived at his social conscience organically, over a period of years. Socialism made a lot of sense in the Great Depression. Capitalism had, after all, essentially collapsed and wasn't showing any significant signs of reviving in Pampa, Texas, where Woody spent his late adolescence. The ultimate hillbilly autodidact, he divided his time between teaching himself to play several musical instruments only tolerably well and frequent marathon sessions in the public library, where he clandestinely educated himself. He followed his own haphazard curriculum, one book leading him to another in an endless scavenger hunt for answers that invariably posed even deeper questions. An acute interest in psychology segued into medieval mysticism and from there he stumbled into Eastern philosophy and spiritualism. He went through a poetry period, a Shakespeare period, even a law book period. When, a few years later, he began to travel around the Southwest by thumb and freight train, his mind was wide open when he encountered crusty old radicals who handed out copies of The Little Red Song Book and preached the Gospel of Union. It was only natural that when he began to make up his own songs, he drew on the despair and pain he had witnessed all his life and the lofty ideas that ricocheted around in his head for inspiration. He became the living embodiment of everything a people's revolution is supposed to be about: that working people have dignity, intelligence and value above and beyond the market's demand for their labor.

Not that Woody was a rank-and-file worker. In fact, he managed to avoid manual labor more strenuous than sign-painting his entire life. He was, however, born into the working class and managed to distinguish himself not by "pulling himself up by his bootstraps" and toeing the line but rather by trusting his own talent and vision.

He was no angel, either. Those closest to him sometimes found him hard to love. 10 His family (he had two) sometimes suffered for his convictions, as he constantly sabotaged himself, especially when things were going well financially. In the long run, his political integrity was unassailable, because money and its trappings made him genuinely nervous.

By the time the 1950s **blacklists** got around to folk singers, Woody wasn't affected, as he was already succumbing to the disease that had institutionalized and eventually killed his mother, and he was slowly slipping away. Ramblin' Jack Elliott got there in time to hang out with him out in Coney Island. By the early 1960s Woody was hospital-bound, but he spent weekends at the home of longtime fan Bob Gleason. Bob Dylan and other up-and-coming folkies made the pilgrimage and sang for him there. When Woody finally died, in the fall of 1967, he was eulogized in the *New York Times* and *Rolling Stone*. He left behind an army of imitators and a catalogue of songs that people will be dusting off and singing for as long as they make guitars.

For me personally, Woody is my hero of heroes and the only person on earth that I will go to my grave regretting that I never met. When I invoked his name in "Christmas in Washington," I meant it. Clinton was being re-elected in a landslide and I had voted for him and I wasn't sure why and I needed something to hang on to, someone to say something. I needed, well . . . a hero.

Does all this mean that the world would be a different place if Woody had dodged the genetic bullet and lived? You bet your

CONVERSATIONS: THE DUST BOWL

As Earle indicates in paragraph 6, what has come to be known as the "Dust Bowl" was an environmental and social upheaval in the American Great Plains caused by several years of severe drought in the 1930s. It resulted in a massive loss of farmland and the end of an agricultural livelihood for thousands of American farmers. Many of those farmers, who came to be known as Okies, fled West to California to try to find work in the massive fruit and vegetable farms there. Earle attributes the Dust Bowl to government policies and agricultural practices that grew out of what he calls the "mistaken" belief that the Plains would support farming. Earle's description of the Dust Bowl reveals some of his own social, environmental, and political beliefs. In this regard, this passage can be seen as part of the ongoing debates about how to use the vast landscape and natural resources of the United States.

GLOSS: BLACKLISTS

In the 1950s, many Americans feared that American communist and socialist organizations were being infiltrated or controlled by the Soviet Union, and many people who joined these organizations or sympathized with them were "blacklisted"—that is, they were prevented from working in their professions or excluded from certain professional opportunities. In the case of folk singers who were considered "communist sympathizers," blacklisting meant that their songs would not be played on radio stations, records of their music would not be made or sold by recording companies, and they would not be hired to play in dance halls, at festivals, or in other public settings.

progressive ass! Just imagine what we missed! Woody publishing his second and third books! Woody on the picket lines with Cesar Chavez and the farmworkers singin' "Deportee"! I could go on forever. I have imagined hundreds of similar scenarios, but then at some point it always dawns on me how selfish I am.

Let him go. He did his bit. Besides, as much as we need him right now, I wouldn't wish this post-9/11 world on Woody. He hated Irving Berlin's "God Bless America" more than any other song in the world. He believed that it was jingoistic and exclusive, so he wrote a song of his own. It goes:

> This land is your land
> This land is my land
> From California
> To the New York island
> From the redwood forest
> To the gulf stream waters
> This land was made for you and me.

UNDERSTANDING THE TEXT

1. What was special about Woody Guthrie as a musician, according to Earle? What does Earle's view of Guthrie suggest about his view of music as a popular medium? Do you share his view? Do you think most Americans do? Explain.

2. Earle describes Woody Guthrie as "the living embodiment of everything a people's revolution is supposed to be about: that working people have dignity, intelligence and value above and beyond the market's demand for their labor." In what ways does this description support Earle's larger point about Guthrie and his music? What do you think this description suggests about Earle's own political viewpoint?

3. Why did Guthrie hate the song "God Bless America," according to Earle? What do you think this view of that song suggests about Guthrie? What might Earle's decision to include this information in his essay reveal about Earle's own views?

EXPLORING THE ISSUES

1. Earle describes Woody Guthrie as "working class." What specifically do you think Earle means by that description? Cite specific passages to support your answer. Does Earle's understanding of working class match your own? Explain.

2. In paragraph 13, Earle addresses his readers directly, asking whether Woody Guthrie would have made a difference if he had not died when he did and answering his own question with the statement, "You bet your progressive ass!" What does this line suggest about Earle's intended audi-

ence? This essay was originally published in *The Nation,* a magazine of cultural and political issues that is considered liberal and whose audience is usually assumed to be liberal as well. If Earle had intended this essay for a conservative publication or for a more general audience that included people of many different political perspectives, what revisions would you advise him to make?

3. To what extent does Earle's professional experience as a singer and songwriter affect your reaction to this essay? Do you think Earle's professional identity strengthens or weakens his essay in any way? Does it give him authority to write about Woody Guthrie in a way that someone who is not a musician could not? Explain.

ENTERING THE CONVERSATIONS

1. Write an essay about a person you consider to be a hero of yours. Identify a specific audience for your essay, such as your classmates, the readers of a favorite newspaper or magazine or web site, or some other appropriate audience.

2. Choose one or more contemporary musicians whose music you consider to be about important social or political issues. Write an essay in which you analyze the music of these artists and discuss what you see as their importance.

3. Music videos have become one of the most popular media today. Select one or more music videos that you think send an important social or political message and write an essay in which you discuss how the video (or videos) convey that message.

4. Write a song that expresses your view about an important social or political issue.

5. In the final paragraph, Earle writes that Woody Guthrie hated the song "God Bless America." Here's an excerpt from that song:

While the storm clouds gather far
    across the sea,
Let us swear allegiance to a land
    that's free,
Let us all be grateful for a land so
    fair,
As we raise our voices in a solemn
    prayer:

God Bless America.
Land that I love
Stand beside her, and guide her
Thru the night with a light from
    above.
From the mountains, to the
    prairies,
To the oceans, white with foam
God bless America
My home sweet home.

Write an essay in which you compare this song with Guthrie's "This Land Is Your Land." (You can easily find the complete lyrics for both songs on the Internet.) In your essay, analyze the ideas conveyed by both songs and the way language is used to convey those ideas. How do these two songs differ in the statements they make about America? How do they differ in the way they make those statements? For example, examine the verbs in each song and the way listeners are addressed. Also try to find similarities in the two songs. Draw your own conclusions about the songs—and about the use of music in general to convey a viewpoint.

Television has been called a miracle, a drug, a wasteland, and probably some other more colorful names. In the eighty or so years since it first became a public broadcast medium, television has shaped modern life as much as any other single invention or technological development. For most people today, television is central to their lives for entertainment, information, and socializing. Many people would have trouble even imagining their lives without it. It is esti-

Zapping

BEATRIZ SARLO

mated that the average American watches nearly four hours of television every day. By some estimates, the average American has watched 15,000 hours of TV by the age of eighteen. One study estimates that the average American watches three years worth of television commercials over a lifetime. What other medium has more power to shape our views of the world than TV?

Given that power, it is no surprise that scholars and researchers have been examining the impact of television since it was first available. Cultural critic Beatriz Sarlo (b. 1942) is one of those scholars who wants to understand the place of television in contemporary life. In the following essay, which is taken from her book Scenes from Postmodern Life *(1994), Sarlo, a professor of literature at the University of Buenos Aires, examines the practice of* zapping— *that is, quickly changing television channels with a remote control. She is interested in exploring how this increasingly common practice affects the way we see the world and the way images communicate to us. And she explores how* televisuality, *the nature of television viewing habits, affects other aspects of our lives, such as politics. Her essay can help us appreciate how television communicates in more ways than we might realize.* ▼

The image has lost all intensity. It produces no surprise or intrigue; in the end, it is not especially mysterious or especially transparent. It is there for but a moment, filling up the time it takes to wait for the next image that follows. Likewise this subsequent image fails to surprise or intrigue; it too turns out to lack mystery or even much in the way of transparency. It stays there only a fraction of a second before being replaced by a third image, one that is again unsurprising and unintriguing, as indifferent as the previous two images. This third image lasts an infinitesimal fraction of a second, then dissolves as the screen turns bluish gray. You've intervened by using the remote control. Close your eyes and try to remember the first image: Weren't there people dancing, some white women and black men? Were there also black women and white men? You distinctly remember seeing some long curly hair and a pair of hands tousling and throwing it from the nape of the neck so that it covered a woman's breast, presumably the same woman whose hair it was. Or was that the second image, a closer shot of two or three of the dancers? Was the woman with the curly hair black? She did seem very dark, but perhaps she wasn't black, while the hands playing with the hair were (and so perhaps they were a man's hands). From the third image you remembered other hands, a forearm with bracelets, and the lower part of a woman's face. She was drinking something, from a can. The others carried on dancing behind her. It was hard to tell whether or not the woman drinking was the one with the long, curly hair, but you were sure that it was a woman and that the can was a beer can. Another command from the remote control and the screen lights up again.

One, two, three, four, five, six, seven, eight, nine, fifty-four. There's a close-up of a lion advancing through tropical vegetation; a close-up of an orange oval with black letters against the background of a gas station; a wide shot of a circus ring (though it doesn't seem really to be a circus) full of handwritten placards; a close-up of a woman, three-quarter profile, wearing a lot of makeup, saying "I don't want to listen to you"; two guys leaning on the bonnet of a police car (they're young and they're arguing); a woman's backside, unclothed, moving into the background; a wide shot of a street, in some suburb far from here; Libertad Lamarque about to break into song (though perhaps about to break down in tears rather than into song, because a guy's approaching her and seems to be threatening her); a likable woman making spaghetti for her family while her children and husband are all shouting; one samurai on his knees in front of another, fatter samurai, with Spanish subtitles superimposed on the platform, flush with the screen; another woman heaping up dripping clothes while her mother (you don't know why, but the older woman must be her mother) looks on; Tina Turner in three different poses in three different parts of the screen; then the Mexican singer Alaska, in silhouette (but it's obviously her); a presenter with a squint smiles and shouts; the president of one of those new European republics talking to a reporter in English; two news readers speaking with Spanish accents; Greta Garbo in stockings dancing in a hotel room; Tom Cruise; James Stewart; Alberto Castillo; a close-up of a man turning his head to one side of the screen where you can see part of a woman's face; Fito Páez shaking out his curls; two news readers speaking German; an aerobics class on a beach; a more or less lower-class woman lets out a shout as she looks at the microphone a reporter's pointing toward her; three models sitting in a living room; another couple of models sitting around a coffee table; ten boys surfing; another president; the words *the end* superimposed over a mountainous landscape; a town on fire, with people running carrying bundles of clothes, and some boys strung up by their necks (again, not a scene from around here); Marcello Mastroianni shouts to Sophia Loren, next to a luxury car, on a highway; some children come running into a kitchen and open up the freezer; a symphony orchestra and choir; Orson Welles up on a pulpit, dressed as a priest; Michelle Pfeiffer; an American football game; a game of tennis, women's doubles; two news readers speaking in Spanish but with strange accents; a black person getting punched in the lobby of a bar; two news readers, on the local news, look at each other and laugh; black and white actors in a Brazilian slum speaking Portuguese; Japanese cartoons. A final command from the remote control and the screen returns to bluish gray.

After a while you turn it back on again because it's ten o'clock at night. A very smartly dressed gentleman sitting behind a desk says

STRATEGIES: USING THE SECOND PERSON
This paragraph begins by describing what "you" do with the television remote. This strategy for addressing readers is common in popular writing, but less common in scholarly writing. Consider who "you" might be in this instance. What does Sarlo accomplish in this passage by using the second person ("After a while you turn it back on . . . ") rather than describing this scene in the third person ("After a while *she* turns it back on . . . ")?

good evening and gives a quick overview of what will take place over the course of the next two hours of interviews with politicians and personalities of all kinds. After this, a series of shots shows the set: There are artificial plants simulating natural vegetation, and other spiky floral Japanese-style arrangements; spotlights up above; shots of furniture including sofas, sideboards, tables with little coffee cups, flowerpots, and floral arrangements; a contemporary painting; another painting; overhead lights, and again the gentleman promising to return in a few minutes. Remote control. Now commercials: Again the white women and black men dancing; now it is clear that they are in a Caribbean landscape. Remote control: Two actors make stupid faces, put their heads together, and look at each other. Commercials: A car runs along a highway through a mountainous landscape. A forty-something man opens the door to an apartment, startling a seventeen-year-old boy and a girl of the same age. Remote control. The smartly dressed man returns; on his right and left sit a few well-known politicians along with a woman you don't recognize. You leave the remote control on the arm of the chair and get up. From the kitchen you can hear the beginning of the interview. Five minutes later, the smartly dressed man says he'll see us again after the commercial break. Remote control. Newsflash. Commercials. Situation comedy. Police series. Commercials. A fat man pants while kissing a sleeping woman, who seems to be having a disturbing dream. Commercials.

A young man (who looks as though he could be Richard Gere's identical twin) finishes shaving and throws a gleaming gel-like cologne on his face and bare chest; a remarkably pretty young woman is getting dressed; the man, still shirtless, wanders around his penthouse, goes to the telephone, stops, distracted by something or other, picks up a saxophone and starts to play; the woman is now dressed, in an elegant, formal style; the man carries on playing the sax in his penthouse; the woman makes a gesture of annoyance and goes out onto the street; the man is already on the street with his car and intercepts her; it seems they know each other. A young girl, in a T-shirt and stockings, walks around the apartment she shares with her boyfriend or husband; she makes for the bedroom, looking for something; the bed is unmade and all the while he, while leaning up against the wall, watches her and smiles; all of a sudden the girl lifts up the sheets to find a saxophone; she kneels on the bed and starts to play. The party is at its height, with everyone exchanging meaningful looks and drinking something out of glasses with a lot of ice; a honey-colored liquid that looks like caramel flows from bottles; suddenly everyone turns to look toward one corner of the room because a boy in a white jacket has snatched up his saxophone. In the film, there's a doctor who works in a mental asylum, where he has to deal with all the most enigmatic cases, including that of a madman who, it seems, has come from another planet in order to show us the truth of our own; at home, as a means of distraction from all his worries, the doctor also plays the sax. Tonight's television is like an unanticipated homage to John Coltrane and Charlie Parker. Any moment now the music video channel will turn to Wayne Shorter.

*   *   *

5   The combination of a surfeit of images and a relatively simple gadget, the remote control, has enabled the great advance in interactivity seen over the last few decades.

This advance has not been the product of any technological development originating from the big electronics corporations; rather it has been brought about by ordinary, everyday consumers. It should be obvious enough that we are talking about *zapping*.

A remote control is a syntactic machine, a handheld editing machine with unpredictable and instantaneous results, the basis for a symbolic power exercised according to laws television has taught its viewers. The first law of television is that in any given period of time, the goal should be to produce as great an accumulation of high-impact images as possible; paradoxically, this law implies either that the amount of information per time period is minimal, or that there is a large amount of undifferentiated information (though it is true that the images provide an "information effect"). The second law demands making the most of all the implications of the fact that, except in cases where a program is first recorded and then submitted to operations that are the province of media experts rather than television viewers, it is impossible to read visual or sound discourses retrospectively, because they unfold in real time. Television exploits this feature of real time discourses, treating it as a quality that allows for images to be repeated with no regard for sense. The medium's speed surpasses our capacity to retain its contents. The medium is faster than what it transmits. One effect of this speed is that audio and video tracks may often clash and finally cancel each other out. The third law of television is that there should be no respite from or holding back of the image flow even for a moment, because such pauses conspire against the form of attention most adequate to the mass media aesthetic, and would affect what is considered its greatest value: its varied repetition of the same. The fourth law is that the ideal edit, though not always possible, should bring together a succession of very brief shots; the camera should be in constant motion in order to fill the screen with an array of different images, and to stave off any change in channel.

Television's success resides in its attention to these laws, but they also make for *the structural possibility of zapping*. Alarmed network executives and advertising agencies see zapping as a threat to viewer loyalty. Yet they would be better off accepting that without zapping nobody these days would watch television. What almost half a century ago was an attraction based upon the image has become an attraction sustained by speed. As it has turned from relying on stationary and unhurried wide shots to the dance of the "switcher," television has constantly developed the possibilities its basic three-camera arrangement allows for cutting and montage, without suspecting that there was a point on this road at which it would have to swallow its own medicine. A remote control is much more than a switcher for amateurs.

CONTEXT: THE THREAT OF ZAPPING
A great deal of research has been done by the television advertising industry to determine the effects of zapping on television viewing habits and especially on the impact of commercials on viewers. This research has also explored ways to counteract zapping. If you have been watching television for more than a decade or so, you have probably noticed some of the results of this research. For example, whereas at one time commercials were usually a minute long or even longer, today they are mostly thirty seconds, and many commercials are only fifteen seconds. So there are more commercials during a typical thirty-minute television show than in the past. In addition, commercials have become flashier and more innovative in an effort to persuade viewers to watch them and not to zap to another channel during a commercial.

The switcher is a weapon in the arsenal of the person directing the camera, who can at the press of a button move from one point of view to another, often without apparent rhyme or reason; the remote control belongs to the arsenal of those watching, who can at the press of a button introduce a cut where the camera directors had not thought to cut, effecting a transition from one incomplete image to another incomplete image produced by another camera, on another channel, or on the other side of the planet. Directors use the switcher to set up an anchor in a set (which may be the news-readers' desk or the presenters' living room, a dance floor or staircase in a musical, the garden or chalet in a soap opera). A remote control does not anchor anyone to any particular place; instead it sets up an irreverent and irresponsible dream syntaxis, product of a postmodern unconscious that mixes together images from all over the planet. Optimists may think that we have reached the apotheosis of the "open work," the limit of aleatory art raiding a giant bank of "ready-made" images. But to reach this conclusion requires the cultivation of a cynical indifference to the problem of these images' semantic density.

Zapping raises a series of interesting questions. There is of course the matter of viewer freedom, and the way it is exercised with the speed of an atomic-powered space transporter running around a shopping mall. Every break in the flow requires a supplementary activity. Images are linked together through contiguity rather than superimposed upon each other, and a reading is based upon syntactic subordination rather than coordination (zapping allows us to read as if every image-sentence were potentially connected by the conjunctions "and," "or," or "nor," or simply separated by ellipsis). Zapping abolishes old laws of visual narration that laid down rules about point of view, about transitions from one type of shot to another that might be closer up or pulled farther back, about the relative duration of takes, about superimposition, sequencing, and fades. What we have now is not **Eisenstein's dream** of "sovereign montage," but rather the disappearance of montage, in that montage always presupposes that shots conform to a hierarchical organization. Zapping demonstrates that home montage knows but a single authority, and that is the desire that moves the hand pressing the remote control. Like many other phenomena particular to the culture industry, zapping appears to be a full realization of the democratic ideal. It seems to involve editing self-generated by the consumer, cottage industries of productive television viewers, a liberated crew free to run the media space capsule, family cooperatives of symbolic consumption within which authority is ardently discussed, citizens participating in an electronic public sphere, active viewers who use the remote control to contradict old theories about manipulation, zappers taking on the cultural hegemony of the elites, stubborn saboteurs of ratings measurements, and, should the occasion present itself, masses ready to rebel against the diktats of mass media capitalists.

10   Whatever the validity of these claims, it is true that zapping is television's major innovation. But its newness exaggerates something that has always formed part of the medium's logic. Zapping is simply a more intense version of what commercial television has done from the outset. Zapping was always at the core of televisual discourse, as the mode of production of sequence of images whose point of departure was the presence of more than one camera in the studio. It is a matter of linguistic chance that zapping evokes rapping, musical improvisation on melodic norms or preexisting rhythms, but the idea of televisual zapping does contain something of this improvisation bound by a rigid set of rules. One of these rules would be speed, considered

GLOSS: EISENSTEIN'S DREAM
Russian filmmaker Sergei Michailovich Eisenstein (1898–1948) is credited with developing the technique of *montage,* in which a series of related images appear in quick succession on the screen. "Sovereign montage" refers to Eisenstein's belief that a montage can convey all the necessary information in a film about plot, character, and theme without the need for other conventional film techniques, including sound.

VISUAL CONNECTIONS: THE CROWDED SCREEN

In 2001, CNN's *Headline News* channel changed its on-screen look to include graphical and textual information in addition to the image of the news anchorperson or the news report itself, as the first image shows. This visual approach to reporting the news was soon adopted by other news networks, and the strategy of adding graphics and textual information to the main image on the screen has now become commonplace for other networks as well, including networks like ESPN and the Home Shopping Network. In some ways, these television screens have come to look more like web sites, which have also become more crowded in recent years, as shown in the second image. You might consider how this development complicates Sarlo's analysis in this essay. She wrote the essay in 1994, before television screens became crowded in this way. Does this development strengthen or weaken her analysis?

as medium and goal of a so-called visual rhythm that corresponds to short (and ever shorter) concentration spans. Here attention and duration are two complementary and opposed variables, and conventional wisdom has it that it is only by cutting duration that you will manage to generate attention.

Along the way, what has been lost is silence, which was one of the decisive formal elements of modern art (from Miles Davis to John Cage, from Kasimir Malevich to Paul Klee, or from Carl Dreyer to Michelangelo Antonioni). Television, a near contemporary of the avant-gardes, uses their methods but never their constructive principles. There is no need to attack or defend it for this: Television is none the better nor any the worse for having borrowed some or even many of its methods from the century's "high" art. Its aesthetic is its own. Modern art may have produced works in which silence and emptiness demonstrate the infuriating impossibility of speech and show how we need the unsaid for anything to be said, but this is not why the loss of silence, of emptiness, and of blankness affects television.

This loss of silence, and of visual emptiness, is a problem specific to televisual discourse. Yet it is not the nature of the medium itself that imposes this problem, but rather the way in which the medium has been used, the way in which only some of its technical possibilities have been developed while others have been closed off. Rhythmic acceleration, on the one hand, and the absence of silence or of visual emptiness, on the other, are complementary effects. There are risks television is unable to take, because silence

TV Still from CNN's *Headline News*

Screen Shot of MSNBC.com

or a blank screen (or even concentrating upon a single image) alike go against the culture of perception that television has instituted, a culture echoed and reinforced by its audience through the phenomenon of zapping. Either a single shot that lasts too long or silence on the soundtrack may prompt channel hopping. Market-based television therefore needs what it calls rhythm, although its vertiginous succession of shots constitutes less a rhythmic expression than simply a strategy to avoid zapping. Television puts its trust in the idea that high impact and speed will compensate for the absence of blank spaces and silences, which have to be avoided because they open up the cracks through which zapping slips. We should, however, ask whether in fact things happen exactly the other way around. We should ask whether it is that zapping becomes possible precisely because this overabundant visual discourse has no rhythm; because once all its points are equivalent, the discourse can be cut at any point. It is not television as form, as virtual possibility, that determines that it should be governed by the laws of speed and total temporal satiation; rather it is television as industry, producing commodities at huge cost, that leads it to reduce any risky bets to a minimum.

From all these features of televisual culture arise a specific form of reading and a form of memory. Some image fragments manage to establish themselves in our consciousness with the weight of iconicity, and are recognized, remembered, and cited, while other such fragments are passed by and can be repeated infinitely without boring anybody because, in fact, nobody sees them. These latter images are padding, constituting a gelatinous tide in which other images float and sink, and from which those that have established themselves as recognizable icons then emerge. Icons need this mobile mass of images precisely so they can differentiate themselves from the mass, so they can surprise and circulate at speed. More attractive images require a "contrasting medium." They owe their existence to an army of images that are not remembered, but that pave the way for them. The ever more numerous images that make up this tide of the forgettable are not noticed so long as iconic images exist; when these latter images grow scarce, zapping occurs. All this takes less time to happen than it takes to write about its happening.

The images that make up television's padding are repeated more often than are the "fortunate" images. But these, too, are repeated. Intellectual admirers of the televisual aesthetic recognize that repetition is one of its traits and, with varying degrees of erudition, they trace its origins back to folk culture, to public street spectacles, marionettes, Grand Guignol, nineteenth-century newspaper serials, melodrama, and so on. I am not going to linger on details. It is better that we come to some agreement from the start: Commercial television's serialized repetition *is like* that of other arts and discourses whose prestige has been legitimated by time. Like the newspaper serial, television repeats a structure, a cast of characters, a small ensemble of psychological and moral types, a system of plot devices, and even an arrangement of plot devices.

15   The enjoyment of repeated, familiar structures is pleasurable and pacifying. This pleasure is perfectly legitimate as much for popular cultures as for the educated elite's customary diversions. Repetition is a machine for the production of quiet happiness, in which the world's semantic, ideological, or felt disorder finds eventual realignment or oases in which order is partially restored. The conclusion of a newspa-

per's serialized novel sets things back in their place, and this is appreciated even by postmodernity's fractal, decentered subjects. There is no need to reiterate over and over again what has already been said twenty times over about the newspaper serial, all for the sole purpose of seeking out prestigious antecedents for television, when in truth it neither asks for nor needs them. It would be more of an issue to ask whether the aesthetic effects of televisual repetition evoke the seriality of Alexandre Dumas more than they do that of the justifiably forgotten Paul Feval. In other words, nineteenth-century serial novels ranged from those written by Dumas to those written by Paul Feval. When it comes to television, I am very conscious of who could be its Paul Fevals, but finding its Dumases turns out to be a little trickier. If this comparison brings us to a dead end, we might have to consider that the comparison between television and the nineteenth-century serial novel fails to fit very well. Even Umberto Eco thinks that Balzac is more interesting than the *Dallas* scriptwriters; in fact, only someone who has not seen *Dallas* or has not read Balzac could imagine any possible proof to the contrary.

Given television's novelty, we need to read it using the tools that it itself provides. I started with zapping because that is where televisual discourse's truth lies. Zapping exemplifies a syntactic model (that is to say, the model for a key part of its operation, the way in which one image relates to another) that television set to work long before its viewers invented the "interactive" use of the remote control. Actually existing television in the commercial market has to produce an infinite quantity of broadcast hours per year. So, because its viewers finds themselves obliged to watch too many images, television also has to produce too many. Any *qualitative* relation between two images, from which a third, ideal image would emerge to enable meanings to be built up, is almost an impossibility within the uninterrupted sequence of edits that the market demands of commercial television. It is not, then, that its chance conjunctions of images imply an aesthetic choice that would position television close to aleatory art. Instead, this

CONVERSATIONS: THE DECENTERED POSTMODERN SUBJECT

As the title of the book from which this essay is taken (*Scenes from Postmodern Life*) suggests, Sarlo is analyzing television from a postmodern theoretical perspective. Postmodernism refers loosely to a series of theoretical movements in the latter twentieth century that focused on examining how we know the world around us. Simply put, postmodern theorists question the idea that knowledge can be objective and certain. They also question that idea that each of us has a stable, unique identity; instead, they argue, we each have multiple identities related to our different circumstances and shaped by the different ways of understanding the world that we are subject to (for example, religion, science, philosophy, culture). Here, Sarlo refers to "postmodernity's fractal, decentered subjects," which is common terminology used in theoretical discussions about postmodernism to convey the idea that a person's identity is not singular and stable but always changing. Readers who are familiar with postmodern theory will recognize this phrase, but if you are not familiar with the theory, some of Sarlo's terminology may seem confusing.

Postmodern ideas have been taken up by other fields, including art. In this piece by Faith Ringgold called *Picasso's Studio*, Ringgold combines painting and traditional African quilting to make a statement about the absence of Blacks in Western art. In making such a statement, Ringgold's piece reflects a postmodern perspective on identity.

It's worth thinking about how Sarlo's reference to the postmodern subject contributes to her main idea in this essay. It's also worth thinking about what readers should know about postmodernism to understand the conversations that Sarlo is participating in here.

Faith Ringgold, *Picasso's Studio*, 1991

is a last resort to which television retreats when it has to put hundreds of thousands of images onto the screen each week.

Television's serial repetition is simply a way out of this bottleneck. The hundreds of hours of weekly television (on terrestrial channels and on cable) would be unmanageable were each programming segment to require its own format. This trait of popular literature, of genre cinema, the circus, fairground comedians, folk music, or melodrama (as everybody hastens to remind us, citing still more antecedents whose antiquity is to guarantee prestige) is in fact a response determined by a particular system of production. Seriality guards against any unforeseeable stylistic or structural outlay. In television soaps, the binary system whereby characters are only ever sketched in black and white allows stories to be constructed at the speed demanded by producers who are taping three or four episodes a day. Here, actors know exactly what to expect and scenes repeat a few easily identifiable typologies. Conflicts consist in the confrontation between moral and psychological forces whose predictability is only interrupted by plot complications that, on the one hand, resort to classical topoi and, on the other, actualize these topoi with a set of immediate references that give soaps their themes, taken from the nightly news. The so-called new television of the last few years simply overlays the same decades-old pattern of codified desires with a patchwork of scraps that aim to name reality: political corruption, AIDS, sexual excess, homosexuality, or shady deals in public or private.

A serial aesthetic needs a simple system of traits whose condition is that nuances should be eliminated. Psychological and moral Manichaeism lowers the level of problematization and sutures the cracks opened up by formal and ideological sloppiness. The intellectual fashion that, some years ago now, began as an interest in radio and television soap kitsch and then ended up simply consuming it, fails to reply in any convincing way to indictments of mass culture, even to those judgments that demonized it often without knowing anything about it. It should not be enough to oppose to the elitism of those positions most critical of mass culture, simply their symmetrical inversion under the figure of a neopopulism seduced by the charms of industrial culture.

Variety programs, comedies, children's programs, and music programs make serial repetition into a durable canvas (a kind of phantasmal script outline as rigid as if it were made of iron) that improvisation then adorns with its repetition in variation. This tempered novelty is functional for the whole productive system, from scriptwriters to actors. Moreover, it makes economic sense, because by allowing sets and costumes to be used over and over again, it guarantees that any time investment need only be minimal. Television is loathe to give up on anything that has passed the test of efficiency, and this in no way goes against its interrupted image flow but rather, precisely, is what makes it possible. Very good and very bad programs can be made in serial units: The use of seriality does not in itself guarantee results. It does, though, ensure a mode of production in which repetition makes up for any points at which improvisation (on the part of actors or technicians) breaks down. Yet, and however unpleasant it may seem to bring this up, repetition not only supports but also banalizes the actors' improvisations and becomes no more than a strategy to get out of a jam in dutiful accord with televisual production's greed for time. As in any other art form, improvisation is not so much a substantial quality as it is an ensemble of technical and rhetorical operations. The question of whether it is television comedians or soap opera actors who work most faithfully at improvisation reveals much less about the influence of a theatrical innovation now several decades old than it says about the mode of production in market conditions. Televisual improvisation follows the logic of capitalist serial production more than it corresponds to any aesthetic logic.

Televisual styles very obviously bear the marks of serialized discourse. Comedies, 20 dramas, regionalist programs, and entertainment programs all conform less to a typology of genres (for which psychosocial conflict would be contrasted with an emphasis on the vicissitudes of sentiment, crime mysteries, or the foregrounding of youth, dancing, or music) than they do to a *standard style*: the show. This standard style owes its origins to variety shows, such as comic, music hall, or circus shows. Now the show is the mode of organization for all other stylistic formations: There are news shows, documentary shows, sports highlights shows, political shows at night differentiated from the midday show and the midafternoon show, drama shows, children's shows, comedy shows, and talk shows dealing with the intimacy of people's innermost feelings. The common denominator is miscellaneousness.

This standard style founds *televisuality*. Those who appear on television have to adapt to it, and so politicians, for example, seek to construct their public personae according to its logic and, therefore, to memorize lines of dialogue, gestures, and verbal rhythms. They have to be expert at rapid transitions, changes in speed and direction to stave off audience boredom. The televisual politician's skills are honed in the medium itself, which functions like a school handing out certificates of electronic charisma. It is not just actors, but also anyone who appears on the screen who has to master the condition of televisuality. This mastery has the same importance that being photogenic had in Hollywood's classic period. Televisuality ensures that images belong to the same system of visual representation, by homogenizing them and making them instantly recognizable. It allows for variety because it undergirds the profound unity that sutures the discontinuities between different programs (and advertising collaborates fully in this task). Televisuality is the fluid that give television its consistency and that ensures immediate recognition on the part of its audience. As long as due respect is shown, certain rules can be bent: Some electronic intellectuals retain a certain tone, imported from academia or print journalism, that maintains televisuality's allure without bowing to its commoner forms. This tone makes its difference felt. Standing up to the daily hubbub, it opens up a calm parenthesis challenging the "tyranny of time" and demonstrating that television does not necessarily preclude an hour of reflection from time to time, so long as certain characteristics are maintained. These indispensable features include strong iconic presence, the arbitrary camera movements to which we are all habituated, digitalized images, an attentive ear to what the viewing public has to say, and an appeal to sentiment.

Television shares in what it has already shared out, and what it shares out is in fact what it has picked up in all sorts of places, but always according to the principle that just as the viewing public is television's best interpreter (hence the power of ratings for market-based television), so too television has to know its audience at least as well as its audience knows television. Functioning as a democratic and plebeian mirror, mirroring the totality of viewing publics and starting also to reflect each of its fragments, television constitutes its referents as the viewing public, and its viewers (the public) as referent. How then can we begin to answer the question of whether the public speaks like the star system's celebrities or whether celebrities speak like their viewers?

These traits of televisuality can protect televisual discourses from the discontinuity brought about by zapping. At any point you always know where you are, and can abandon one program to move on to another with the guarantee that what is happening elsewhere will also be intelligible. We vote with the remote. Competition between channels consists of a struggle to occupy the (imaginary) space where zapping might be brought to a halt. All in all, images signify less and less and, paradoxically, are more and more important. From the point of view of form, though television may seem happily victorious over the entire discursive field, in fact it has come to a crossroads.

UNDERSTANDING THE TEXT

1. Sarlo asserts that television images "unfold in real time." Why is this important, in her view? What are the implications of this characteristic of television? Do you think she is right? Why or why not?

2. In what sense is the television remote control a "weapon," according to Sarlo? Why is this idea important to her?

3. In what sense is zapping the "full realization of the democratic ideal," as Sarlo puts it? What does she mean by that statement? In what ways might viewing television without a remote control be "undemocratic"?

4. What are the implications of zapping, according to Sarlo? In what ways does zapping lead to what she calls a "specific form of reading and a form of memory"? What characterizes these forms of reading and memory? How do they change the way we view images?

5. What does Sarlo mean by *televisuality*? What are the main characteristics of televisuality? What are its implications for television networks, for viewers, and for contemporary society in general?

EXPLORING THE ISSUES

1. In the first four paragraphs, Sarlo describes a series of images on a television screen. Sarlo is apparently describing the experiences of a viewer in Brazil, where she lives, but many of those images would be familiar to an American viewer. What do you think these images suggest about television? What might they suggest about television's role in communicating across cultures?

2. Sarlo often uses very specialized terms (such as hegemony, semantic density, montage), some of which you are not likely to find in a common dictionary. Make a list of these terms and try to find the meanings

of the ones you don't know. What might her language suggest about her audience?

3. Sarlo argues that television is shaped more by commercial forces than by aesthetics (par. 19, for example). Evaluate this claim. What evidence does Sarlo present to support this claim? What might this claim suggest about her own theoretical or political viewpoint? Do you think her claim is valid? Why or why not?

4. What do you think Sarlo's essay can tell us about the role of images in contemporary society?

ENTERING THE CONVERSATIONS

1. Observe a friend watching television on several occasions. Pay specific attention to your friend's use of the remote—to zapping. Make some notes about the zapping you observe: how long the person watches before changing channels, what seems to cause the person to watch something for a longer time, and so forth. Try to identify patterns in the person's zapping. After you have finished observing, interview the person to try to find out what he or she was aware of when zapping. Then write a report about your observations. In your report, describe the zapping you observed and discuss any patterns you noticed. Try to draw conclusions about zapping and discuss whether your observations seem to support Sarlo's analysis of zapping.

2. Sarlo asserts that whereas television once relied on "an attraction based on the image," it now relies on speed (par. 7). Test her argument by watching some older television shows, preferably from the 1960s or 1970s, and comparing them to today's shows. In your comparisons, try to select shows that are similar; such as two sitcoms, or two dramas. Watch several episodes of the shows paying attention to how long images remain on the screen, how images are framed on the screen,

and the general visual movement of the shows. Then write a report about your experience, drawing conclusions about whether Sarlo is right about the changing attraction of television. Alternatively, do this kind of analysis with films. For example, in 2004, a remake of the 1970's film *The Stepford Wives* and *The Manchurian Candidate,* were released. Write an essay in which you discuss your analysis, drawing conclusions about how the uses of images have changed in film in the past several decades.

INFOTRAC

3. Zapping has preoccupied the television advertising industry because of concerns that it results in lost revenues for networks. Using InfoTrac College Edition, the Internet, your library, and other appropriate resources, investigate the phenomenon of zapping and examine how the television industry has responded to it. Try to find studies that have been done by advertising or marketing researchers to understand and counteract zapping. Write a report on the basis of your research. Draw conclusions about the importance of zapping and its impact on television business.

4. Write an essay for a general audience (or a specific publication that you read) in which you discuss your own perspective on the impact of television.

5. Create a viewers' guide to television that is intended to educate viewers on how to watch television. Your guide should describe strategies used by television networks and advertisers to address practices like zapping, and it should convey to readers what you think they should know about how television might affect them and how they can view it intelligently. Your guide may take any form you think is appropriate. For example, you can create a pamphlet, a web site, or some other form.

As Bakari Kitwana writes in the following essay, the well-known rapper Chuck D of the rap group Public Enemy declared in 1988 that rap music is "the Black CNN." Chuck D may have been making a point about rap music's role in describing the realities of life facing Black people in contemporary society. But by the turn of the new century, it became clear that rap music had become something even bigger than the Black CNN. Its influence seems to be far-reaching. The sounds of

THE Challenge OF *Rap* Music

rap music blare from everywhere on the radio dial, from hip-hop stations to mainstream top 40 stations. Rappers themselves are no longer exclusively Black but reflect a diversity of racial and ethnic categories. Eminem, who is White, is among the world's most popular rappers, and rappers from Africa, Asia, and South America have found success. Young people of every color and income level now wear hip-hop clothing styles that were once seen only in a few Black neighborhoods in a few big cities. Big mainstream corporations like McDonald's and Coca-Cola use rap music in their television commercials. All of these developments seem to give strength to Kitwana's description of rap music as a cultural movement. Kitwana helps us see that music can communicate and influence in ways that go well beyond the lyrics of songs, such as the antiwar protest music of the 1960s and 1970s or the folk music about which Steve Earle writes in his essay on page 369 in this chapter. Obviously, the angry lyrics of many rap songs express provocative social messages that are similar to protest songs or folk music. But Kitwana shows us that hip-hop as a musical style sends larger messages about race, gender, and social issues as well as about money and success. As a cultural (continued)

BAKARI KITWANA

Mr. Mayor, imagine this was your backyard
Mr. Governor, imagine it's your kids that starve
imagine your kids gotta sling crack to survive,
swing a Mac to be live . . .

—Nas, *"I Want to Talk to You"*

In June 2001, Rush Communications CEO Russell Simmons convened a hip-hop summit in New York City. With the theme "Taking Back Responsibility," the summit focused its agenda on ways to strengthen rap music's growing influence. The 300 participants included major rap artists and industry executives as well as politicians, religious and community leaders, activists, and scholars. Few forces other than rap music, now one of the most powerful forces in American popular culture, could bring together such a diverse gathering of today's African American leaders. In many ways, the summit signaled hip-hop as the definitive cultural movement of our generation.

As the major cultural movement of our time, hip-hop (its music, fashion, attitude, style, and language) is undoubtedly one of the core

BAKARI KITWANA, "THE CHALLENGE OF RAP MUSIC." FROM *HIP HOP GENERATION* BY BAKARI KITWANA. COPYRIGHT (C) 2002 BY BAKARI KITWANA. REPRINTED BY PERMISSION OF BASIC BOOKS, A MEMBER OF PERSEUS BOOKS, L.L.C.

(continued) *movement, hip-hop has also emerged in film, television, and clothing styles, revealing that music can work in connection with other media to communicate effectively to many different audiences. For that reason alone, Kitwana's arguments about hip-hop are worth considering, for they can help us gain insight into the many different ways we can communicate with and beyond words.*

Writer and editor Bakari Kitwana has written about hip-hop culture for a variety of publications, including the Village Voice, The Source, *and the* Progressive. *He is the author of* The Rap on Gansta Rap *(1994),* Why White Kids Love Hip Hop *(2005), and* Hip Hop Generation *(2002), in which this essay first appeared.* ▼

CONVERSATIONS: RAP AS A CULTURAL MOVEMENT
The idea that a form of music can be thought of as a "cultural movement" is not new. In the 1950s and 1960s, many observers saw the rise of rock-'n'-roll music as a youth movement in reaction to some of the values of their parents' generation. Rock-'n'-roll music seemed to express the rebellious views of young people at the same time that it also seemed to influence their views. Certain styles of dress, slang, and social practices (such as popular dances called "sock hops") came to be associated with rock-'n'-roll. This is the sense in which Kitwana describes hip-hop as a cultural movement. In this essay, Kitwana is joining an expanding conversation among scholars, critics, and others about the importance of hip-hop as such a movement. Some of his views about hip-hop have become widely shared among those interested in understanding contemporary culture. Elsewhere in this essay (par. 10, for example), Kitwana refers specifically to books about hip-hop that can be thought of as helping generate this conversation. But this ongoing conversation has often been contentious, too, with some critics offering harsh condemnations of what they believe is the glorification of violence, sexism, and even racism by hip-hop artists.

influences for young African Americans born between 1965 and 1984. To fully appreciate the extent to which this is true, think back for a moment about the period between the mid-1970s and the early 1980s, before rap became a mainstream phenomenon. Before MTV. Before BET's Rap City. Before the Fresh Prince of Bel Air. Before *House Party* I or II. It is difficult now to imagine Black youth as a nearly invisible entity in American popular culture. But in those days, that was the case. When young Blacks were visible, it was mostly during the six o'clock evening news reports of crime in urban America.

In contrast, today it is impossible not to see young Blacks in the twenty-first century's public square—the public space of television, film, and the Internet. Our images now extend far beyond crime reports. For most of our contemporaries, it's difficult to recall when this was not the case. Because of rap, the voices, images, style, attitude, and language of young Blacks have become central in American culture, transcending geographic, social, and economic boundaries.

To be sure, professional athletes, especially basketball players, have for decades been young, Black, highly visible, and extremely popular. Yet, their success just didn't translate into visibility for young Blacks overall. For one thing, the conservative culture of professional sports, central to their identity, was often at odds with the rebellious vein inherent in the new Black youth culture. While household-name ball players towed the generic "don't do drugs and stay in school" party line, rappers, the emissaries of the new Black youth culture, advocated more anti-establishment slogans like "fuck the police." Such slogans were vastly more in synch with the hard realities facing young Blacks—so much so that as time marched on and hip-hop culture further solidified its place in American popular culture, basketball culture would also come to feel its influence.

5   Largely because of rap music, one can tune in to the voices and find the faces of America's Black youth at any point in the day. Having proven themselves as marketable entertainers with successful music careers, rappers star in television sit-coms and film and regularly endorse corporate products (such as Lil'Kim—Candies, Missy Elliot—the Gap, and Common, Fat Joe, and the Goodie Mob—Sprite). In the mid-1980s, a handful of corporations began incorporating hip-hop into their advertisement spots. Most were limited to run-of-the-mill product endorsements. By the late 1990s, however, ads incorporating hip-hop—even those promoting traditionally conservative companies—became increasingly steeped in the subtleties of hip-hop culture. Setting the standard with their extremely hip-hop savvy 1994 Voltron campaign, Sprite broke away from the straight-up celebrity endorsement format. Says Coca-Cola global marketing manager Darryl Cobbin, who was on the cutting edge of this advertising strategy: "I wanted to usher in a real authenticity in terms of hip-hop in advertising. We wanted to pay respect to the music *and* the culture.

What's important is the value of hip-hop culture, not only as an image, but as a method of communication."

By the late 1990s, advertisers like the Gap, Nike, AT&T, and Sony soon followed suit and incorporated hip-hop's nuances into their advertising campaigns. As a result, the new Black youth culture resonates throughout today's media, regardless of what companies are selling (from soft drinks and footwear to electronics and telecommunications).

Of course, none of this happened overnight. In fact, more important than the commercialization of rap was the less visible cultural movement on the ground in anyhood USA. In rap's early days, before it became a thriving commercial entity, dj party culture provided the backdrop for this off-the-radar cultural movement. What in the New York City metropolitan area took the form of dj battles and MC chants emerged in Chicago as the house party scene, and in D.C. it was go-go. In other regions of the country, the local movement owed its genesis to rap acts like Run DMC, who broke through to a national audience in the early 1980s. In any case, by the mid-1980s, this local or underground movement began to emerge in the form of cliques, crews, collectives, or simply kids getting together primarily to party, but in the process rhyming, dj-ing, dancing, and tagging. Some, by the early 1990s, even moved into activism. In large cities like Chicago, San Francisco, Houston, Memphis, New Orleans, Indianapolis, and Cleveland and even in smaller cities and suburban areas like Battle Creek, Michigan, and Champaign, Illinois, as the '80s turned to the '90s, more and more young Blacks were coming together in the name of hip-hop.

In the early 1980s, the "in" hip-hop fashion for New York City Black youth included Gazelles (glasses), sheepskins and leather bombers (coats), Clarks (shoes), nameplates, and name belts. In terms of language, Five Percenter expressions like "word is bond" were commonplace. These hip-hop cultural expressions in those days were considered bizarre by Black kids from other regions of the country. A student at the University of Pennsylvania at the time, Conrad Muhammad, the hip-hop minister, speaks to this in reminiscing on the National Black Students Unity Conference he organized in 1987:

> Jokers were getting off buses with shower caps on, perms and curls. MTV and BET had not yet played a role in standardizing Black youth culture the way they do today. Young people from different cities weren't all dressing the same way. Brothers and sisters were stepping off buses saying "we're from the University of Nebraska, Omaha." "We're from University of Minnesota." "We're from Cal Long Beach."

But by the early to mid-1990s, hip-hop's commercialized element had Black kids on the same page, regardless of geographic region. In this hip-hop friendly national environment, hip-hop designers like Enyce, Mecca, and FUBU were thriving, multi-plat-

VISUAL CONNECTIONS: HIP-HOP FASHION
Images like this one showing young people in hip-hop fashions have become commonplace in recent years, especially in advertisements for clothing. Consider what images like this suggest about hip-hop as a cultural movement. Does this image convey the same kinds of messages about hip-hop that Kitwana argues for in this essay?

© Brand X Pictures/Alamy

inum sales for rap artists were routine (and dwarfed the 1980s mark of success: gold sales), and hip-hop expressions like "blowin' up," "representin'," and "keepin' it real" worked their way into the conversational language of Black youth around the country. Contrast this to the mid-1980s when even those deep into hip-hop didn't see the extent to which a national cultural movement was unfolding.

"Before the Fresh Fest Tour of 1984, few folks were defining hip-hop culture as hip-hop culture," says Hashim Shomari, author of *From the Underground: Hip-Hop as an Agent of Social Change.* "That was a relatively 1990s phenomenon." Practitioners like Africa Bambaataa, Grandmaster Flash, Fab-Five Freddy, Chuck D, and KRS-One were on the frontlines of those who saw the need to flesh out the definitions. Also, it wasn't until the early 1990s that breakthrough books like Joseph Eure and James Spady's *Nation-Conscious Rap* (1991), Michael Gonzales and Havelock Nelson's *Bring the Noise: A Guide to Rap Music and Hip-Hop Culture* (1991), and Tricia Rose's *Black Noise: Rap Music and Black Culture in Contemporary America* (1994) began to discuss hip-hop as an influential culture that went beyond the commercial.

Without question, rap's national exposure played a key role in the uniform way in which the local cultural manifestations evolved. More recently, given rap's commercial success, alongside limited employment options beyond minimum wage-jobs for young Blacks, hip-hop's cultural movement at the local level is increasingly marked by an entrepreneurial element. On the West Coast, East Coast, in southern and northern cities, and in rural and suburban areas in between, young Blacks are pressing their own CDs and selling them "out the trunk" regionally.° many of them are hoping to eventually put their city on the hip-hop map. What all this around the way activity has in common is that kids are tuned in to the same wavelength via hip-hop, some aspiring to be the next Air Jordan of hip-hop, others engaging in what is to them a way of life without commercial popular culture aspirations, and still others tuning in as a basic engagement with the youth culture of our time.

The commercialized element of this cultural movement and the off-the-radar one fuel each other. The underground element provides a steady stream of emerging talent that in turn gets absorbed into commercialization. That new voice and talent again inspires more discussion (about the art form, new styles, trends, language, and larger issues and themes) and more talent at the local level, which later infuses the commercial manifestation of the cultural movement. Case in point: the more recent wave of talent (say, Master P out of New Orleans, Eve from Philly, and Nelly from St. Louis) is similar to the much earlier waves like the Geto Boys out of Houston and Compton's NWA. Those earlier waves of talent (the Geto Boys, NWA, Too Short, E-40, and others) most certainly provided inspiration for the No Limit Soldiers and Ruff Ryders, who came later. Like the earliest waves of artists, each group represents its distinct region, while tapping into the national movement. In turn, Master P, Eve,

°My emphasis here is on Black youth—no disrespect to the countless folks of other racial and ethnic groups down with hip-hop. This is not to say that Latino and to a lesser extent Asian and Native American youth have not been influential in and touched by hip-hop culture. Neither is it meant to ignore the distinctiveness of Caribbean Americans. More recently white kids, a large segment of hip-hop's listening audience, are jumping into the fray. Nevertheless, rap music indisputably remains dominated by Black youth in both its commercial and local manifestations. [Author's note] and Nelly will influence the next wave of talent breaking from the margins into the mainstream.

It's not exactly a chicken-or-egg question, however. Hip-hop as a culture indisputably emerged in the South Bronx in the late 1970s, and in other parts of the northeast shortly thereafter, before branching out around the country in the early 1980s. What's arguable is the extent to which hip-hop would have become the national cultural movement that it is today without commercialization.

In 1988, rapper Chuck D of the rap group Public Enemy described rap music as "the Black CNN." This was certainly true at the grassroots level at the time. However, the decade of the 1990s proved even more profound as rap music became thoroughly accepted and promoted in mainstream American popular culture. As such, rap provided the foundation for a resounding young Black mainstream presence that went far beyond rap music itself.

15   Understanding the degree to which the local and commercial are deeply entrenched and interdependent, one can begin to grasp the far-reaching effects of hip-hop on young Blacks. As the primary vehicle through which young Blacks have achieved a national voice and presence, rap music transmits the new Black youth culture to a national audience. And in the same way as the mainstream media establishes the parameters for national discussion for the nation at large, rap music sets the tone for Black youth. As the national forum for Black youth concerns and often as the impetus for discussion around those issues, rap music has done more than any one entity to help our generation forge a distinct identity.

Another important aspect of what makes rap so substantive in the lives of young Blacks is its multilingual nature. In addition to beaming out hip-hop culture, rap also conveys elements of street culture, prison culture, and the new Black youth culture. Often all of these elements overlap within rap's lyrics and visual images. In the process, images and ideas that define youth culture for this generation—such as designer clothes, like Sean Jean, Phat Farm, and Tommy Hilfiger, ever-changing styles of dress, and local colloquialisms—are beamed out to a captive national audience. Also transmitted are cues of personal style, from cornrows and baby dreads to body piercing and tattoos.

And finally, even more important than fashion, style, and language, the new Black culture is encoded within the images and lyrics of rap and thus help define what it means to be young and Black at the dawn of the millennium. In the process, rap music has become the primary vehicle for transmitting culture and values to this generation, relegating Black families, community centers, churches, and schools to the back burner.

To be sure, rap marked a turning point, a shift from practically no public voice for young Blacks—or at best an extremely marginalized one—to Black youth culture as the rage in mainstream popular culture. And more than just increasing Black youth visibility, rap articulated publicly and on a mass scale many of this generation's beliefs, relatively unfiltered by the corporate structures that carried it. Even when censored with bleeps or radio-friendly "clean" versions, the messages were consistent with the new Black youth culture and more often than not struck a chord with young Blacks, given our generation's unique collective experiences. At the same time, the burgeoning grassroots arts movement was underway. All was essential to rap's movement into the mainstream and its emergence as the paramount cultural movement of our time.

* * *

Although hip-hop has secured its place as a cultural movement, its biggest challenge lies ahead. In the late 1980s when gangsta rap first emerged, community activists and mainstream politicians of the civil rights generation began to challenge rap's content. This criticism forced a dialogue that revealed one of the Black community's best kept secrets, the bitter generational divide between hip-hop generationers and our civil rights/Black power parents.

20   The key concern was Black cultural integrity: how have the very public images of young Blacks in hip-hop music and culture affected the larger Black community? Central to this discussion was the pervasive use of offensive epithets in rap lyrics, such as "nigga," "bitch," and "ho," all of which reinforce negative stereotypes about Blacks. What was the price of this remarkable breakthrough in the visibility of young Blacks in the mainstream culture? Had young rappers simply transferred images of young Black men as criminals from news reports to entertainment? And finally, had the growing visibility of young Black entertainers further marginalized young Black intellectuals and writers, who have remained nearly invisible?

A handful of responses emerged. The response from the rap industry was unanimous: free speech is a constitutional right. The predominant response from rap artists themselves was a proverbial head in the sand. Most reasoned that the older generation was out of touch with the concerns of hip-hop generationers. Just as our parents' generation was unfamiliar with the music, the thinking went, when it came to other matters of our generation, particularly issues involving hip-hop, they, likewise, didn't know what they were talking about. By and large, the question of rap's attack on Black cultural integrity went unaddressed. In fact, the use of incendiary words like "nigga" and "bitch" has become so commonplace in rap's lyrics that today even those in rap's growing white audience routinely use them when referring to each other and often their Black peers (a matter Spike Lee vaguely touched on in the film *Bamboozled*).

Lately, as the theme of the Simmons summit "Taking Back Responsibility" suggests, hip-hop is again undertaking the critical task of questioning its relationship to the community. David Mays, publisher of the hip-hop magazine *The Source*, and Reverend Al Sharpton held a series of summits eight months prior to the Simmons summit, which called for a code of conduct in light of arrests of numerous rappers and the growing association of rappers with criminality. Minister Conrad Muhammad, dubbed the hip-hop minister for the moral voice he's long brought to the hip-hop community, felt the Mays-Sharpton gathering didn't go far enough. Muhammad called for a summit of Black rap artists, rap industry execu-

CONVERSATIONS: OFFENSIVE LYRICS
In this passage, Kitwana refers directly to some of the criticisms of hip-hop music by various critics, including parents groups, religious organizations, and women's groups. As Kitwana suggests, these criticisms have focused on what many people consider offensive lyrics, not only because obscenities are often used but also because rappers sometimes use racial epithets and language that denigrates women. Some advocates for hip-hop have argued that these lyrics reflect the realities of contemporary Black life and call attention to the injustices many Blacks face. In acknowledging these criticisms here, Kitwana might be seen to be offering his response to such criticisms and to encourage advocates for hip-hop to address those criticisms. Consider how your own sense of this debate might influence the way you read this passage and react to Kitwana's view.

tives, and activists to discuss ways of holding the hip-hop industry accountable to the Black community. Appalled by Muhammad's moral challenge to the rap industry, Simmons countered Muhammad with a call for his own summit to be held within a few weeks of the Muhammad one.

Simmons, a major player in the rap industry who earlier began flexing his political muscle by reaching out to Democratic party insiders like Hillary Clinton in her bid for the U.S. Senate, brought together the largest and most media-celebrated summit to date. Joining rap industry insiders were African American notables like minister Louis Farrakhan, NAACP-head Kweisi Mfume, U.S. Representative Cynthia McKinney, and scholars Cornel West and Michael Eric Dyson.

The Simmons event was impressive in terms of sheer numbers and diverse backgrounds. But where it most seriously came up short was in its failure to incorporate the grassroots segment of hip-hop's cultural movement, especially hip-hop generation activists. When hip-hop's true influence as a cultural movement is finally understood, events like these will recognize that the very same synergy at the heart of hip-hop's commercial success has also informed our generation's activists and political theorists. Just as some record executives can give us a blueprint for blowin' up rap acts, the ideas that our generation's activists hold about maximizing rap's potential for social change have been seasoned in their day-to-day work and experience. If our generation's cultural movement is to evolve to have a meaningful political impact, the local segments of hip-hop's cultural movement—from hip-hop generation activists to local entrepreneurs to the everyday hip-hop kids on the block—must not only be brought to the table, but must have a major voice.

*   *   *

25   Furthermore, rather than centering the discussion within our own generation—*and, yes,* including the expertise and insight of our parents' generation—the invitation-only Simmons summit turned to the mostly liberal-integrationist civil rights leadership and music industry executives. The result was predictable: a combination of the traditional music industry call for free speech, which allows for continued blockbuster sales without disrupting the minstrel-esque proven formula for success, and the traditional civil rights activist call for young voters to support Democratic candidates for public office. Neither of these same-game-with-another-name reforms challenge civil righters or industry insiders to do anything different than what they are already doing. Moreover, pushing activists of the civil rights generation to the forefront of this effort is tantamount to casting older-generation R&B singers like Dionne Warwick and Lionel Richie as leads in a 'hood film or featuring them at a concert alongside ODB or Lil' Kim.

Until hip-hop is recognized as a broad cultural movement, rather than simply an influential moneymaker, those who seek to tap into hip-hop's potential to impact social change should not expect substantive progress. A unified front between hip-hop's commercial and grassroots sectors on the issue of sociopolitical action would change the nature of the dialogue. For example, in the same way that the hip-hop community as a cultural movement inherently answered the question, "what is hip-hop culture?" a new inclusive framework inevitably would answer the question, "what do we mean by politicizing the hip-hop generation?" Is our goal to run hip-hop generationers for office, to turn out votes for Democrats and Republicans, to form a third party, or to provide our generation with a more concrete political education?

UNDERSTANDING THE TEXT

1. Why does Kitwana believe that hip-hop is "the definitive cultural movement of our generation," as he puts it? What evidence does he provide to support that statement? Do you agree with him? Why or why not?

2. What factors does Kitwana identify as important in the rise of hip-hop? What do you think these factors and the rise of hip-hop suggest about the role of music in contemporary society?

3. What specific effects has the rise of hip-hop as a national movement had on contemporary society, according to Kitwana? Why are these effects important, in his view? Do you think he's right? Explain.

4. What does Kitwana see as the challenges facing hip-hop music today? What goals does he believe hip-hop should seek to achieve? What does Kitwana's discussion of these challenges and goals suggest about his view of hip-hop and of Black America in general?

EXPLORING THE ISSUES

1. Throughout this essay, Kitwana uses the first person. For example, in paragraph 3 he writes that "it is impossible not to see young Blacks in the twenty-first century's public square," and he then goes on to state that "our images now extend far beyond crime reports." Who is Kitwana referring to here when he mentions "*our* images"? What might his use of the first person suggest about his sense of his intended audience? How did you react to his use of the first person in this essay? What might your answer to that

question suggest about you as a reader?

2. Throughout this essay, Kitwana includes quotations from books and articles as well as from statements by various artists and critics. Examine these quotations. Who are the people that Kitwana quotes? Do they have anything in common? What might his choices of quotations suggest about his sense of his audience? How effective do you think these specific quotations are in helping Kitwana make his argument about hip-hop as a cultural movement?

3. (In paragraphs 22–25), Kitwana criticizes the meeting organized by Russell Simmons (first described in par. 1). Examine these criticisms. What exactly concerns Kitwana about this event? What significance does he see in the event? To whom does Kitwana seem to be addressing his criticisms in this passage? What might this passage suggest about Kitwana's sense of purpose for this essay? How effectively do you think he accomplishes that purpose? Explain.

ENTERING THE CONVERSATIONS

1. Write an essay in which you describe the influence of hip-hop music on contemporary society from your perspective. In your essay, describe the role of hip-hop in your own life and the lives of your friends, family, or others you know. Draw on Kitwana's essay and any other relevant sources to discuss this role and what you see as the impact that hip-hop music has had.

2. Select several popular hip-hop artists that you believe have been influential in the current music

scene. Write an essay in which you analyze their songs for their themes and messages. In your essay, identify what you see as the main themes that these artists address in their music and discuss what those themes might suggest about hip-hop as a musical form and as a cultural movement.

3. Create a photo essay or a web site that defines hip-hop as a cultural movement. Use any images, sounds, and text that you think best reflect your view of hip-hop as a cultural movement and its influence on contemporary society.

4. Write an essay intended for your local newspaper (or another appropriate publication) in which you express your view about the debates over the lyrics of some hip-hop songs. In your essay, discuss your position about lyrics that some people consider offensive and explain why you believe they should or should not be subject to any form of censorship (such as banning songs from some radio stations or preventing the sale of CDs to children or teens).

5. Many colleges now offer courses in hip-hop culture. With a group of classmates, write a proposal for such a course at your school. (If your school already has such a course, you might write a proposal to change it in some way or to add an additional course.) In your proposal, identify the topics or issues your course on hip-hop would address and describe the assignments, readings, activities, and other features of the course. In addition, write a rationale or justification for the course that explains why you believe your school should offer such a course and what benefits it would offer students.

CREATING THEMES: Extending the Conversations

WITH TEXT

1. Identify an issue related to communication that you think is important but that does not appear in this chapter. Write an essay in which you discuss that issue and examine its importance in contemporary society. In your essay, draw on any of the readings in this chapter that you think are relevant to your topic.

2. Several writers in this chapter address issues that have to do with language differences. For example, Gloria Anzaldúa describes her uses of Chicano Spanish and several related languages to make a statement about the connection between those languages and her identity. She also makes a statement about so-called Standard English. Other writers explore similar issues related to Standard English, including June Jordan and Amy Tan. Drawing on several of these essays, write an essay exploring language differences and their impact on contemporary life. In what ways do you think language differences come into play in our lives today? What problems might be associated with language differences? Try to address such questions in your essay and try to draw conclusions about the role of language in our lives.

3. Identify what you think is an important theme that runs through this chapter. Then select several of the readings in which this theme is explored and, drawing from those essays, write an essay discussing that theme.

4. Drawing on the readings in this chapter, write a letter to graduating seniors at your high school in which you offer them advice about communicating in the world after high school. In your letter, share what you have learned about how to communicate effectively in various settings (school, work, and so on), and offer what you think is the advice that they most need to be effective communicators. Draw on any of the readings in this chapter or any other appropriate resources. Alternatively, create a pamphlet, web site, or some other kind of document for the same purpose.

INFOTRAC

5. Write a conventional academic essay in which you discuss what you believe are the implications of recent technological developments (such as the Internet, cell phones, various wireless devices) on the way we communicate in contemporary society. Draw on any of the readings in this chapter and, using InfoTrac College Edition and other appropriate sources, do any additional research that you think would be useful. In your essay, trace the history of the device or technology you have selected and describe its implications for communication today. Discuss what you think its impact will be in the future and draw your own conclusions about its benefits and disadvantages.

6. Write a letter to the editor of your local newspaper or to another appropriate publication in which you express your views and/or concerns about the technology described in Question 5.

WITH MEDIA

1. Write an essay about the power of music as a medium for communication. Draw on any relevant essays in this chapter and use any other appropriate sources. If possible, create a web site or multimedia presentation (using a program like PowerPoint) based on your essay. Incorporate into your web site or presentation clips from songs or music videos, as appropriate.

2. Using PowerPoint or a similar program, create a visual presentation exploring an important theme that you think runs through several of the readings in this chapter. In your presentation, identify that theme and refer to any of the essays in this chapter that develop the theme. Include whatever visual elements you find appropriate.

3. Select several popular television commercials and write an analysis of the messages they send about some idea or issue that is important to you (such as patriotism, race, gender, and so on). In your analysis, focus on how the commercials use certain images, sounds, colors, words, and so forth to convey their messages and draw conclusions about television commercials as a medium for communication. If possible, create a multimedia presentation that focuses on the same analysis (using PowerPoint or some other program or medium).

4. Identify several common visual symbols or images and write an essay analyzing what those symbols mean and how they are used to communicate ideas, beliefs, information, and so forth. Draw on any appropriate essays in this chapter to support your analysis.

5. If you have access to a camera, take several photographs that illustrate an important idea or belief of yours. Use those photographs to create a photo essay or web site that conveys that idea or belief.

6. Choose one of the chapter themes in this book (such as identity, relationships, communication) or some other idea or theme of importance to you and create some kind of nontextual representation of that theme (for example, a photograph or photo essay, a web site, a song, a painting).

CREATING THEMES: Extending the Conversations

WITH FILM

1. Hip-hop has emerged as a film genre in recent years. The best example of the genre is *Eight Mile* (2002), starring rapper Eminem. These films recall other films associated with musical styles, especially rock-'n'-roll films like *Easy Rider* (1969) and *Woodstock* (1970). Select one or more such films and write an essay in which you examine the role music plays in these films. How might music be used to communicate important social messages, and how do these films portray or use music as a medium?

2. Many popular films depict future worlds. Recent films of this kind include *The Matrix* trilogy, the *Star Wars* films, and *1984* (based on George Orwell's novel). Select one or more films that depict our future and examine what those films suggest about communication. Analyze the way the films present communication and especially the technologies they imagine we might use for communicating in the future. Draw conclusions about what these films seem to suggest about human communication.

Chapter **9** Power

© Hulton-Deutsch Collection/Corbis

THE PRESIDENT OF THE UNITED STATES IS SOMETIMES CALLED THE MOST POWERFUL MAN IN THE WORLD. WHAT EXACTLY DOES THAT MEAN? I SUSPECT THAT FOR MANY PEOPLE IT MEANS THAT THE PRESIDENT IS THE COMMANDER IN CHIEF OF THE WORLD'S MOST POWERFUL MILITARY FORCE.

He is the one who decides whether to use that awesome military power, which has an almost unimaginable capacity for destruction. Or maybe it means that the president has the ability to influence government policies that affect the lives of millions of people. For example, in 2003, President George W. Bush proposed an education reform program called No Child Left Behind. Using his substantial influence as president, Bush was able to turn that proposal into new laws and policies affecting what children are taught in schools, how they are evaluated, and how schools are funded. It is no exaggeration to say that No Child Left Behind has

> It seems pretty clear that the men who wrote the U.S. Constitution in 1787 understood the risks of giving one person too much power.

changed schools in important ways and therefore has touched the lives of millions of American schoolchildren. The ability to have such an impact on the lives of others is surely one way to define power.

But the more you think about power, the more you begin to see power in many different aspects of your lives. A police officer has the power to arrest you and take away your physical freedom, if only temporarily. A judge has the power to send you to jail, assuming you have done something to justify incarceration. Your boss may have the power to hire or fire employees. A building inspector has the power to approve or deny your request to build a garage or a deck on your property. A teacher has the power to evaluate your performance in a class by assigning you a grade. A doctor has the power to

prescribe medication. A minister has the power to marry two people—or to influence the spiritual lives of a congregation.

Of course, with such power usually comes responsibility. The president's authority to send troops into war is tempered by the fact that his decision can lead to the deaths of many people. An arrest record can have serious consequences, which is why the law prevents a police officer from arresting someone without just cause. Grades matter to students for a variety of reasons, including remaining eligible for loans, gaining admission to a school, graduating, or finding a job. As a result, a teacher must justify students' grades or face the possibility of having unfair grades changed by a principal or dean. And there are limits to power. It seems pretty clear that the men who wrote the U.S. Constitution in 1787 understood the risks of giving one person too much power, so they placed various limits on a president's power. The three branches of government that you learned about in your social studies classes—legislative, judicial, and executive—are intended to "check" one another so that one branch does not acquire too much power. Because of such careful provisions in the Constitution, even with all his power, the president cannot declare war, for example, without the consent of Congress, and his policy proposals, such as education reform initiatives, must be approved by Congress as well.

When I began thinking about this chapter, I was thinking mostly about this kind of political power, partly because we tend to think of power in either political or physical terms. In fact, I might have called this chapter "Politics" or "Government" because most of the essays have to do with the power of governments, or political power, in some way. It would be useful to read these essays as such because they prompt us to think carefully about the power that government has in our lives. But I also wanted you to think about these essays more broadly. If you read them as investigations into power in general, and not just as essays about political power, how would that change their meaning? For example, Wendell Berry's essay, published shortly after the terrible events of September 11, 2001, indirectly criticizes the U.S. government for many of its economic and social policies. In that sense, we can read this essay as a statement of his political beliefs or as a political criticism of the way the U.S. government wields its power over citizens. But what is Berry saying more broadly about governmental power in our lives? What does his essay suggest about the connection between power and our basic beliefs about how we should live together on the earth? If you approach Berry's essay with those questions in mind, you may read it as something more than a political statement, and it may teach you something more fundamental about the complexities of power in human life.

That's how I'd like you to approach all the essays in this chapter: as essays about specific kinds of power or particular examples of power, but also as essays about power in general—what it is and why we should pay attention to it. As you'll see, not all the essays focus on government. Some deal with more nebulous kinds of power: the power of ideas, of racism and prejudice, of individual acts of resistance, of morality. Writers like Paula Gunn Allen, Henry David Thoreau, bell hooks, and Martin Luther King, Jr. may address governmental power in their essays, but they also ask you to think of power in other complicated ways; they ask you to think about the less obvious ways that various kinds of power

> If you read them as investigations into power in general, and not just as essays about political power, how would that change their meaning?

can affect how we live. And of course, all these writers share one other quality: They have all taken advantage of another kind of power, the power of writing.

THE PROCESS OF POWER

F YOU'VE EVER ATTENDED A SCHOOL BOARD MEETING, OB-
SERVED A TRIAL OR WATCHED CONGRESSIONAL HEARINGS
ON C-SPAN, YOU HAVE WITNESSED THE PROCESS OF GOV-
ERNMENTAL OR POLITICAL POWER. THE MEMBERS OF YOUR
LOCAL SCHOOL BOARD, FOR EXAMPLE, ARE GIVEN AUTHORITY
TO MAKE IMPORTANT DECISIONS ABOUT FUNDING PROGRAMS,
hiring and firing teachers and administrators, establishing
curriculum guidelines, and adopting school policies. While
these decisions may seem minor compared to, say, the decision of the U.S. Congress to approve the appointment of a
secretary of state or a Supreme Court justice, they nevertheless affect the lives of many people in your school district. Such "minor" decisions reflect the power that is entrusted to government officials or school officials by the
residents of a town or state or nation. What is striking is that
even when such decisions are not popular, they are almost
always accepted. In other words, Americans are generally
confident that the process of power in their towns, school
districts, cities, and states is fair and is working, even when
they disagree with a decision or a policy. In fact, it's probably fair to say that most Americans pay little attention to the
thousands of "minor" decisions made each day by officials
in their school districts, towns or cities, and states. The
process of power goes on, and most of us don't even notice
it because we assume it's working the way it should.

That's probably a good thing. It says something important
about the way political or governmental power functions in
American society. But the process of power is often more
subtle and more complicated and sometimes more pernicious than we might realize. And that's what the readings in
this cluster focus on. While we tend to notice the "big" ways
in which power is wielded in the United States, such as the
decision to go to war or the transfer of power after a presidential election, we may not be as aware of the many ways
in which governmental power can directly affect our lives. I
was recently reminded of this in a rather striking way. A few
months after the horrific terrorist attacks of September 11,
2001, the U.S. Border Patrol set up a checkpoint on

Interstate 87 about seventy-five miles south of the Canadian
border in upstate New York. I have been traveling that
stretch of highway for many years, so on my way home from
a hiking trip in early 2002, I was surprised to find myself
stopped at the checkpoint. The Border Patrol agents and
several New York State police officers were questioning drivers, and inspecting some cars. Despite my surprise, I realized that this new checkpoint was the result of new government policies implemented after September 11, 2001, as
part of President George W. Bush's "war on terror." These
policies reflect the power of the government to affect or
even control various aspects of our lives. Drivers like me
have little choice but to stop our cars at a checkpoint like
that one in upstate New York.

Because power can so directly affect our lives, many
writers warn us to be vigilant. Wendell Berry's essay, for example, calls our attention to the ways in which government
can abuse its power even when it seems to be acting on behalf of citizens. In the same way, George Orwell, in what has
become one of the most famous essays ever written in
English, focuses our attention on how governments and
groups can use language to obscure their abuses of power.
And both Lani Guinier and Donna Ladd show us that even
with the many protections included in the U.S. Constitution,
the abuse of power is still possible. These essays remind us
that we should not take for granted the processes of power.

They also remind us that writing itself is one of the most
effective ways to hold governments accountable for the
power that we give them. As you read these essays, think
about how the power of writing can be part of the processes
of power.

Few modern writers have been as influential as George Orwell (1903–1950). Chances are that you have already read some of his writing—perhaps his famous novels 1984 (1949) or Animal Farm (1945). Orwell, born as Eric Blair, reached the height of his career as a writer during and shortly after World War II, which profoundly reshaped the world's political landscape and which gave rise to great fears about government power. Orwell was especially concerned

Politics AND THE *English* Language

about the rise of totalitarian governments after the war, particularly in what came to be known as the "Soviet bloc"—that is, nations like East Germany (which was officially known as the German Democratic Republic) and Poland that were under the influence of the communist government of the Soviet Union. Like many people in Western nations, Orwell considered these governments and their leaders a grave threat to liberty throughout the world, and much of his writing is devoted to exposing the implications of such power. He emerged as one of the twentieth century's most insistent voices regarding issues of political power.

At first glance, the following essay seems to be about writing and about using language carefully, and many English teachers present it that way. But Orwell believed that language was one of the tools of power, and he wished to examine how language can be used to acquire and maintain power. He helps us see that language can be used by those in power to control us without our realizing it. He also helps us see that understanding the complexities of language is one way to resist power. So this essay is not only about political power; it is also about the power of language to shape our understanding of the world.   (continued)

GEORGE ORWELL

Most people who bother with the matter at all would admit that the English language is in a bad way, but it is generally assumed that we cannot by conscious action do anything about it. Our civilization is decadent and our language—so the argument runs — must inevitably share in the general collapse. It follows that any struggle against the abuse of language is a sentimental archaism, like preferring candles to electric light or hansom cabs to aeroplanes. Underneath this lies the half-conscious belief that language is a natural growth and not an instrument which we shape for our own purposes.

Now, it is clear that the decline of a language must ultimately have political and economic causes: it is not due simply to the bad influence of this or that individual writer. But an effect can become a cause, reinforcing the original cause and producing the same effect in an intensified form, and so on indefinitely. A man may take to drink because he feels himself to be a failure, and then fail all the more completely because he drinks. It is rather the same thing that is *(continued) Orwell wrote this essay just after World War II ended, when the world was dividing itself into two opposing camps: the free-market democracies of the West and the socialist or communist nations allied with the Soviet Union and the People's Republic of China. If you think Orwell's concerns about the political uses of language are no longer valid, consider that after the terrorist attacks of September 11, 2001, the U.S. Congress passed the Patriot Act, which expanded the power of some government agencies and which many critics believed undermined the constitutional rights of Americans; the name of the act is an example of the kind of language that Orwell expressed concerns about in this essay.*

This essay was originally published in a journal called Horizon *in 1946.* ▼

CONTEXT: LANGUAGE AND STYLE
Throughout this essay, Orwell uses sophisticated language and includes many words and phrases that were more common in 1946, when this essay was published, than they are today. In paragraph 1, for example, he refers to "archaism," a relatively uncommon word meaning something old or outdated. He also mentions "hansom cabs," which is a kind of horse-drawn carriage. In some cases, Orwell's word choices reflect the style of his time, which may strike you as difficult to read; Orwell also writes in British style, which is somewhat different from American English. You may need to consult your dictionary to help you understand specific passages. This essay reminds us that writing styles and conventions change over time, though we usually don't notice it until we read an essay like this one, which is from a very different historical moment.

happening to the English language. It becomes ugly and inaccurate because our thoughts are foolish, but the slovenliness of our language makes it easier for us to have foolish thoughts. The point is that the process is reversible. Modern English, especially written English, is full of bad habits which spread by imitation and which can be avoided if one is willing to take the necessary trouble. If one gets rid of these habits one can think more clearly, and to think clearly is a necessary first step toward political regeneration: so that the fight against bad English is not frivolous and is not the exclusive concern of professional writers. I will come back to this presently, and I hope that by that time the meaning of what I have said here will have become clearer. Meanwhile, here are five specimens of the English language as it is now habitually written.

These five passages have not been picked out because they are especially bad—I could have quoted far worse if I had chosen—but because they illustrate various of the mental vices from which we now suffer. They are a little below the average, but are fairly representative examples. I number them so that I can refer back to them when necessary:

1. I am not, indeed, sure whether it is not true to say that the Milton who once seemed not unlike a seventeenth-century Shelley had not become, out of an experience ever more bitter in each year, more alien *[sic]* to the founder of that Jesuit sect which nothing could induce him to tolerate.

    Professor Harold Laski (Essay in *Freedom of Expression*)

2. Above all, we cannot play ducks and drakes with a native battery of idioms which prescribes egregious collocations of vocables as the Basic *put up with* for *tolerate* or *put at a loss* for *bewilder*.

    Professor Lancelot Hogben (*Interglossia*)

3. On the one side we have the free personality: by definition it is not neurotic, for it has neither conflict nor dream. Its desires, such as they are, are transparent, for they are just what institutional approval keeps in the forefront of consciousness; another institutional pattern would alter their number and intensity; there is little in them that is natural, irreducible, or culturally dangerous. But *on the other side,* the social bond itself is nothing but the mutual reflection of these self-secure integrities. Recall the definition of love. Is not this the very picture of a small academic? Where is there a place in this hall of mirrors for either personality or fraternity?

    Essay on psychology in *Politics* (New York)

4. All the "best people" from the gentlemen's clubs, and all the frantic fascist captains, united in common hatred of Socialism and bestial horror at the rising tide of the mass revolutionary

movement, have turned to acts of provocation, to foul incendi-
arism, to medieval legends of poisoned wells, to legalize their
own destruction of proletarian organizations, and rouse the agitated petty-bourgeoisie to chauvinistic fervor on behalf of the
fight against the revolutionary way out of the crisis.

Communist pamphlet

5. If a new spirit is to be infused into this old country, there is one
   thorny and contentious reform which must be tackled, and that is
   the humanization and galvanization of the B.B.C. Timidity here
   will bespeak canker and atrophy of the soul. The heart of Britain
   may be sound and of strong beat, for instance, but the British
   lion's roar at present is like that of Bottom in Shakespeare's *A
   Midsummer Night's Dream*—as gentle as any sucking dove. A virile new Britain cannot continue indefinitely to be traduced in the eyes or rather ears, of the world
   by the effete languors of Langham Place, brazenly masquerading as 'standard
   English.' When the Voice of Britain is heard at nine o'clock, better far and infinitely less ludicrous to hear aitches honestly dropped than the present priggish,
   inflated, inhibited, school-ma'amish arch braying of blameless bashful mewing
   maidens!

Letter in *Tribune*

STRATEGIES: EXAMPLES
Here Orwell offers five examples to introduce the specific features of what he considers "bad" writing. He uses a number of
additional examples throughout his essay
to illustrate his points. If you examine
these examples, you'll notice that Orwell
not only uses them to help readers understand his various points, which are
sometimes complex, but he is also
demonstrating through these examples
what he believes are the features of good
writing.

   Each of these passages has faults of its own, but, quite apart from avoidable ugliness, two qualities are common to all of them. The first is staleness of imagery; the
other is lack of precision. The writer either has a meaning and cannot express it, or
he inadvertently says something else, or he is almost indifferent as to whether his
words mean anything or not. This mixture of vagueness and sheer incompetence is
the most marked characteristic of modern English prose, and especially of any kind
of political writing. As soon as certain topics are raised, the concrete melts into the
abstract and no one seems able to think of turns of speech that are not hackneyed:
prose consists less and less of *words* chosen for the sake of their meaning, and more
and more of *phrases* tacked together like the sections of a prefabricated henhouse. I
list below, with notes and examples, various of the tricks by means of which the work
of prose construction is habitually dodged:

DYING METAPHORS

A newly invented metaphor assists thought by evoking a visual image, while on the
other hand a metaphor which is technically "dead" (e.g. *iron resolution*) has in effect
reverted to being an ordinary word and can generally be used without loss of vividness. But in between these two classes there is a huge dump of worn-out metaphors
which have lost all evocative power and are merely used because they save people the
trouble of inventing phrases for themselves. Examples are: *Ring the changes on, take up
the cudgel for, toe the line, ride roughshod over, stand shoulder to shoulder with, play into the
hands of, no axe to grind, grist to the mill, fishing in troubled waters, on the order of the day,
Achilles' heel, swan song, hotbed.* Many of these are used without knowledge of their
meaning (what is a "rift," for instance?), and incompatible metaphors are frequently
mixed, a sure sign that the writer is not interested in what he is saying. Some

Clichés

metaphors now current have been twisted out of their original meaning without those who use them even being aware of the fact. For example, *toe the line* is sometimes written as *tow the line*. Another example is *the hammer and the anvil*, now always used with the implication that the anvil gets the worst of it. In real life it is always the anvil that breaks the hammer, never the other way about: a writer who stopped to think what he was saying would avoid perverting the original phrase.

OPERATORS OR VERBAL FALSE LIMBS

These save the trouble of picking out appropriate verbs and nouns, and at the same time pad each sentence with extra syllables which give it an appearance of symmetry. Characteristic phrases are *render inoperative, militate against, make contact with, be subjected to, give rise to, give grounds for, have the effect of, play a leading part (role) in, make itself felt, take effect, exhibit a tendency to, serve the purpose of, etc., etc.* The keynote is the elimination of simple verbs. Instead of being a single word, such as *break, stop, spoil, mend, kill,* a verb becomes a *phrase,* made up of a noun or adjective tacked on to some general-purpose verb such as *prove, serve, form, play, render.* In addition, the passive voice is wherever possible used in preference to the active, and noun constructions are used instead of gerunds (*by examination of* instead of *by examining*). The range of verbs is further cut down by means of the *-ize* and *de-* formations, and the banal statements are given an appearance of profundity by means of the *not un-* formation. Simple conjunctions and prepositions are replaced by such phrases as *with respect to, having regard to, the fact that, by dint of, in view of, in the interests of, on the hypothesis that;* and the ends of sentences are saved by anticlimax by such resounding commonplaces as *greatly to be desired, cannot be left out of account, a development to be expected in the near future, deserving of serious consideration, brought to a satisfactory conclusion,* and so on and so forth.

PRETENTIOUS DICTION

Words like *phenomenon, element, individual* (as noun), *objective, categorical, effective, virtual, basic, primary, promote, constitute, exhibit, exploit, utilize, eliminate, liquidate,* are used to dress up a simple statement and give an air of scientific impartiality to biased judgments. Adjectives like *epoch-making, epic, historic, unforgettable, triumphant, age-old, inevitable, inexorable, veritable,* are used to dignify the sordid process of international politics, while writing that aims at glorifying war usually takes on an archaic color, its characteristic words being: *realm, throne, chariot, mailed fist, trident, sword, shield, buckler, banner, jackboot, clarion.* Foreign words and expressions such as *cul de sac, ancien régime, deus ex machina, mutatis mutandis, status quo, gleichschaltung, weltanschauung,* are used to give an air of culture and elegance. Except for the useful abbreviations *i.e., e.g.,* and *etc.,* there is no real need for any of the hundreds of foreign phrases now current in the English language. Bad writers, and especially scientific, political, and sociological writers, are nearly always haunted by the notion that Latin or Greek words are grander than Saxon ones, and unnecessary words like *expedite, ameliorate, predict, extraneous, deracinated, clandestine, subaqueous* and hundreds of others

---

[1] An interesting illustration of this is the way in which the English flower names which were in use till very recently are being ousted by Greek ones, *snapdragon* becoming *antirrhinum, forget-me-not* becoming *myosotis,* etc. It is hard to see any practical reason for this change of fashion: it is probably due to an instinctive turning-away from the more homely word and a vague feeling that the Greek word is scientific [Orwell's note].

constantly gain ground from their Anglo-Saxon numbers.[1] The jargon peculiar to Marxist writing (*hyena, hangman, cannibal, petty bourgeois, these gentry, lackey, flunkey, mad dog, White Guard,* etc.) consists largely of words translated from Russian, German, or French; but the normal way of coining a new word is to use Latin or Greek root with the appropriate affix and, where necessary, the size formation. It is often easier to make up words of this kind (*deregionalize, impermissible, extramarital, non-fragmentary* and so forth) than to think up the English words that will cover one's meaning. The result, in general, is an increase in slovenliness and vagueness.

MEANINGLESS WORDS

In certain kinds of writing, particularly in art criticism and literary criticism, it is normal to come across long passages that are almost completely lacking in meaning.[2] Words like *romantic, plastic, values, human, dead, sentimental, natural, vitality,* as used in art criticism, are strictly meaningless, in the sense that they not only do not point to any discoverable object, but are hardly ever expected to do so by the reader. When one critic writes, "The outstanding feature of Mr. X's work is its living quality," while another writes, "The immediately striking thing about Mr. X's work is its peculiar deadness," the reader accepts this as a simple difference of opinion. If words like *black* and *white* were involved, instead of the jargon words *dead* and *living,* he would see at once that language was being used in an improper way. Many political words are similarly abused. The word *Fascism* has now no meaning except in so far as it signifies "something not desirable." The words *democracy, socialism, freedom, patriotic, realistic, justice* have each of them several different meanings which cannot be reconciled with one another. In the case of a word like *democracy,* not only is there no agreed definition, but the attempt to make one is resisted from all sides. It is almost universally felt that when we call a country democratic we are praising it: consequently the defenders of every kind of regime claim that it is a democracy, and fear that they might have to stop using that word if it were tied down to any one meaning. Words of this kind are often used in a consciously dishonest way. That is, the person who uses them has his own private definition, but allows his hearer to think he means something quite different. Statements like *Marshal Pétain was a true patriot, The Soviet Press is the freest in the world, The Catholic Church is opposed to persecution,* are almost always made with intent to deceive. Other words used in variable meanings, in most cases more or less dishonestly, are: *class, totalitarian, science, progressive, reactionary, bourgeois, equality.*

Now that I have made this catalogue of swindles and perversions, let me give another example of the kind of writing that they lead to. This time it must of its nature be an imaginary one. I am going to translate a passage of good English into modern English of the worst sort. Here is a well-known verse from *Ecclesiastes:*

> I returned and saw under the sun, that the race is not to the swift, nor the battle to the strong, neither yet bread to the wise, nor yet riches to men of understanding, nor yet favour to men of skill; but time and chance happeneth to them all.

[2] Example: "Comfort's catholicity of perception and image, strangely Whitmanesque in range, almost the exact opposite in aesthetic compulsion, continues to evoke that trembling atmospheric accumulative hinting at a cruel, an inexorably serene timelessness. . . . Wrey Gardiner scores by aiming at simple bull's-eyes with precision. Only they are not so simple, and through this contended sadness runs more than the surface bittersweet of resignation" (*Poetry Quarterly*) [Orwell's note].

Here it is in modern English:

> Objective considerations of contemporary phenomena compel the conclusion that success or failure in competitive activities exhibits no tendency to be commensurate with innate capacity, but that a considerable element of the unpredictable must invariably be taken into account.

10   This is a parody, but not a very gross one. Exhibit (3) above, for instance, contains several patches of the same kind of English. It will be seen that I have not made a full translation. The beginning and ending of the sentence follow the original meaning fairly closely, but in the middle the concrete illustrations—race, battle, bread— dissolve into the vague phrases "success or failure in competitive activities." This had to be so, because no modern writer of the kind I am discussing—no one capable of using phrases like "objective considerations of contemporary phenomena"—would ever tabulate his thoughts in that precise and detailed way. The whole tendency of modern prose is away from concreteness. Now analyze these two sentences a little more closely. The first contains forty-nine words but only sixty syllables, and all its words are those of everyday life. The second contains thirty-eight words of ninety syllables: eighteen of those words are from Latin roots, and one from Greek. The first sentence contains six vivid images, and only one phrase ("time and chance") that could be called vague. The second contains not a single fresh, arresting phrase, and in spite of its ninety syllables it gives only a shortened version of the meaning contained in the first. Yet without a doubt it is the second kind of sentence that is gaining ground in modern English. I do not want to exaggerate. This kind of writing is not yet universal, and outcrops of simplicity will occur here and there in the worst- written page. Still, if you or I were told to write a few lines on the uncertainty of human fortunes, we should probably come much nearer to my imaginary sentence than to the one from *Ecclesiastes*.

As I have tried to show, modern writing at its worst does not consist in picking out words for the sake of their meaning and inventing images in order to make the meaning clearer. It consists in gumming together long strips of words which have already been set in order by someone else, and making the results presentable by sheer humbug. The attraction of this way of writing is that it is easy. It is easier—even quicker, once you have the habit—to say *In my opinion it is not an unjustifiable assumption that* than to say *I think*. If you use ready-made phrases, you not only don't have to hunt about for the words; you also don't have to bother with the rhythms of your sentences since these phrases are generally so arranged as to be more or less euphonious. When you are composing in a hurry—when you are dictating to a stenographer, for instance, or making a public speech—it is natural to fall into a pretentious, Latinized style. Tags like *a consideration which we should do well to bear in mind* or *a conclusion to which all of us would readily assent* will save many a sentence from coming down with a bump. By using stale metaphors, similes, and idioms, you save much mental effort, at the cost of leaving your meaning vague, not only for your reader but for yourself. This is the significance of mixed metaphors. The sole aim of a metaphor is to call up a visual image. When these images clash—as in *The Fascist octopus has sung its swan song, the jackboot is thrown into the melting pot*—it can be taken as certain that the writer is not seeing a mental image of the objects he is naming; in other words he is not really thinking. Look again at the examples I gave at the beginning of this essay. Professor Laski (1) uses five negatives in fifty-three words. One of these is superfluous, making nonsense of the whole passage, and in addition there is the slip—*alien* for akin—making further nonsense, and several avoidable pieces of clumsiness which increase the general vagueness. Professor Hogben (2) plays ducks and drakes with a battery which is able to write prescriptions, and, while disapproving of the everyday phrase *put up with*, is unwilling to look *egregious* up in the dictionary and see what it means; (3), if one takes an uncharitable attitude towards it, is simply meaningless: probably one could work out its intended meaning by reading the whole of the article in which it occurs. In (4), the writer knows more or less what he wants to say, but an accumulation of stale phrases chokes him like tea leaves blocking a sink. In (5), words and meaning have almost parted company. People who write in this manner usually have a general emotional meaning—they dislike one thing and want to express solidarity with another—but they are not interested in the detail of what they are saying. A scrupulous writer, in every sentence that he writes, will ask himself at least four questions, thus: What am I trying to say? What words will express it? What image or idiom will make it clearer? Is this image fresh enough to have an effect? And he will probably ask himself two more: Could I put it more shortly? Have I said anything that is avoidably ugly? But you are not obliged to go to all this trouble. You can shirk it by simply throwing your mind open and letting the ready-made phrases come crowding in. They will construct your sentences for you—even think your thoughts for you, to a certain extent—and at need they will perform the important service of partially concealing your meaning even from yourself. It is at this point that the special connection between politics and the debasement of language becomes clear.

In our time it is broadly true that political writing is bad writing. Where it is not true, it will generally be found that the writer is some kind of rebel, expressing his private opinions and not a "party line." Orthodoxy, of whatever color, seems to demand a lifeless, imitative style. The political dialects to be found in pamphlets, leading articles, manifestoes, White papers and the speeches of undersecretaries do, of course, vary from party to party, but they are all alike in that one almost never finds in them a fresh, vivid, homemade turn of speech. When one watches some tired hack on the platform mechanically repeating the familiar phrases—*bestial, atrocities, iron heel, bloodstained tyranny, free peoples of the world, stand shoulder to shoulder*—one often has a curious feeling that one is not watching a live human being but some kind of dummy: a feeling which suddenly becomes stronger at moments when the light catches the speaker's spectacles and turns them into blank discs which seem to have no eyes behind them. And this is not altogether fanciful. A speaker who uses that kind of phraseology has gone some distance toward turning himself into a machine. The appropriate noises are coming out of his larynx, but his brain is not involved as it would be if he were choosing his words for himself. If the speech he is making is one that he is accustomed to make over and over again, he may be almost unconscious of what he is saying, as one is when one utters the responses in church. And this reduced state of consciousness, if not indispensable, is at any rate favorable to political conformity.

In our time, political speech and writing are largely the defense of the indefensible. Things like the continuance of British rule in India, the Russian purges and deportations, the dropping of the atom bombs on Japan, can indeed be defended, but only by arguments which are too brutal for most people to face, and which do not square with the professed aims of the political parties. Thus political language has to consist largely of euphemism, question-begging and sheer cloudy vagueness. Defenseless villages are bombarded from the air, the inhabitants driven out into the countryside, the cattle machine-gunned, the huts set on fire with incendiary bullets: this is called *pacification*. Millions of peasants are robbed of their farms and sent trudging along the roads with no more than they can carry: this is called *transfer of population* or *rectification of frontiers*. People are imprisoned for years without trial, or shot in the back of the neck or sent to die of scurvy in Arctic lumber camps: this is called *elimination of unreliable elements*. Such phraseology is needed if one wants to name things without calling up mental pictures of them. Consider for instance some comfortable English professor defending Russian totalitarianism. He cannot say outright, "I believe in killing off your opponents when you can get good results by doing so." Probably, therefore, he will say something like this:

> "While freely conceding that the Soviet regime exhibits certain features which the humanitarian may be inclined to deplore, we must, I think, agree that a certain curtailment of the right to political opposition is an unavoidable concomitant of transitional periods, and that the rigors which the Russian people have been called upon to undergo have been amply justified in the sphere of concrete achievement."

The inflated style itself is a kind of euphemism. A mass of Latin words falls upon the facts like soft snow, blurring the outline and covering up all the details. The great enemy of clear language is insincerity. When there is a gap between one's real and one's declared aims, one turns as it were instinctively to long words and exhausted idioms, like a cuttlefish spurting out ink. In our age there is no such thing as "keeping out of politics." All issues are political issues, and politics itself is a mass of lies, evasions, folly, hatred, and schizophrenia. When the general atmosphere is bad, language must suffer. I should expect to find—this is a guess which I have not sufficient knowledge to verify—that the German, Russian and Italian languages have all deteriorated in the last ten or fifteen years, as a result of dictatorship.

15   But if thought corrupts language, language can also corrupt thought. A bad usage can spread by tradition and imitation even among people who should and do know better. The debased language that I have been discussing is in some ways very convenient. Phrases like *a not unjustifiable assumption, leaves much to be desired, would serve no good purpose, a consideration which we should do well to bear in mind,* are a continuous temptation, a packet of aspirins always at one's elbow. Look back through this essay, and for certain you will find that I have again and again committed the very faults I am protesting against. By this morning's post I have received a pamphlet dealing with conditions in Germany. The author tells me that he "felt impelled" to write it. I open it at random, and here is almost the first sentence I see: "[The Allies] have an opportunity not only of achieving a radical transformation of Germany's social and political structure in such a way as to avoid a nationalistic reaction in Germany itself, but at the same time of laying the foundations of a co-operative and unified Europe." You see, he "feels impelled" to write—feels, presumably, that he has something new

to say—and yet his words, like cavalry horses answering the bugle, group themselves automatically into the familiar dreary pattern. This invasion of one's mind by ready-made phrases (*lay the foundations, achieve a radical transformation*) can only be prevented if one is constantly on guard against them, and every such phrase anaesthetizes a portion of one's brain.

I said earlier that the decadence of our language is probably curable. Those who deny this would argue, if they produced an argument at all, that language merely reflects existing social conditions, and that we cannot influence its development by any direct tinkering with words and constructions. So far as the general tone or spirit of a language goes, this may be true, but it is not true in detail. Silly words and expressions have often disappeared, not through any evolutionary process but owing to the conscious action of a minority. Two recent examples were *explore every avenue* and *leave no stone unturned,* which were killed by the jeers of a few journalists. There is a long list of flyblown metaphors which could similarly be got rid of if enough people would interest themselves in the job; and it should also be possible to laugh the *not un-* formation out of existence,[3] to reduce the amount of Latin and Greek in the average sentence, to drive out foreign phrases and strayed scientific words, and, in general, to make pretentiousness unfashionable. But all these are minor points. The defense of the English language implies more than this, and perhaps it is best to start by saying what it does *not* imply.

To begin with it has nothing to do with archaism, with the salvaging of obsolete words and turns of speech, or with the setting up of a "standard English" which must never be departed from. On the contrary, it is especially concerned with the scrapping of every word or idiom which has outworn its usefulness. It has nothing to do with correct grammar and syntax, which are of no importance so long as one makes one's meaning clear, or with the avoidance of Americanisms, or with having what is called a "good prose style." On the other hand, it is not concerned with fake simplicity and the attempt to make written English colloquial. Nor does it even imply in every case preferring the Saxon word to the Latin one, though it does imply using the fewest and shortest words that will cover one's meaning. What is above all needed is to let the meaning choose the word, and not the other way around. In prose, the worst thing one can do with words is surrender to them. When you think of a concrete object, you think wordlessly, and then, if you want to describe the thing you have been visualizing you probably hunt about until you find the exact words that seem to fit it. When you think of something abstract you are more inclined to use words from the start, and unless you make a conscious effort to prevent it, the existing dialect will come rushing in and do the job for you, at the expense of blurring or even changing your meaning. Probably it is better to put off using words as long as possible and get one's

> **CONVERSATIONS: ADVICE FOR WRITERS**
> In criticizing common writing style and in offering advice for good writing, Orwell is joining an age-old conversation among writers, teachers, grammarians, and other language experts about what is proper language usage. You can trace this conversation back to the ancient Greeks. Aristotle, for example, criticized some of his contemporaries for the way they taught their students to use language in public speaking. If you do a quick search of a website like Amazon.com, you'll find dozens of current books critiquing contemporary writing styles and offering advice for good writing. The specific advice offered in such books varies, but the six rules that Orwell lists in this paragraph routinely show up in various forms in books and articles about writing today, more than sixty years later. It's worth considering why there seems to be a never-ending conversation about how to write well—a conversation that often focuses on how much "bad" writing people produce. What might that say about the nature of writing? And how might Orwell's essay continue to influence our thinking about writing today?

[3] One can cure oneself of the *not un-* formation by memorizing this sentence: *A not unblack dog was chasing a not unsmall rabbit across a not ungreen field* [Orwell's note].

meaning as clear as one can through pictures and sensations. Afterward one can choose—not simply *accept*—the phrases that will best cover the meaning, and then switch round and decide what impressions one's words are likely to make on another person. This last effort of the mind cuts out all stale or mixed images, all prefabricated phrases, needless repetitions, and humbug and vagueness generally. But one can often be in doubt about the effect of a word or a phrase, and one needs rules that one can rely on when instinct fails. I think the following rules will cover most cases:

(i)   Never use a metaphor, simile, or other figure of speech which you are used to seeing in print.

(ii) Never us a long word where a short one will do.

(iii) If it is possible to cut a word out, always cut it out.

(iv) Never use the passive where you can use the active.

(v)   Never use a foreign phrase, a scientific word, or a jargon word if you can think of an everyday English equivalent.

(vi) Break any of these rules sooner than say anything outright barbarous.

These rules sound elementary, and so they are, but they demand a deep change of attitude in anyone who has grown used to writing in the style now fashionable. One could keep all of them and still write bad English, but one could not write the kind of stuff that I quoted in those five specimens at the beginning of this article.

I have not here been considering the literary use of language, but merely language as an instrument for expressing and not for concealing or preventing thought. Stuart Chase and others have come near to claiming that all abstract words are meaningless, and have used this as a pretext for advocating a kind of political quietism. Since you don't know what Fascism is, how can you struggle against Fascism? One need not swallow such absurdities as this, but one ought to recognize that the present political chaos is connected with the decay of language, and that one can probably bring about some improvement by starting at the verbal end. If you simplify your English, you are freed from the worst follies of orthodoxy. You cannot speak any of the necessary dialects, and when you make a stupid remark its stupidity will be obvious, even to yourself. Political language—and with variations this is true of all political parties, from Conservatives to Anarchists—is designed to make lies sound truthful and murder respectable, and to give an appearance of solidity to pure wind. One cannot change this all in a moment, but one can at least change one's own habits, and from time to time one can even, if one jeers loudly enough, send some worn-out and useless phrase—some *jackboot, Achilles' heel, hotbed, melting pot, acid test, veritable inferno,* or other lump of verbal refuse—into the dustbin, where it belongs.

CONTEXT: POLITICAL LANGUAGE THEN AND NOW

Orwell writes that "political language . . . is designed to make lies sound truthful and murder respectable, and to give an appearance of solidity to pure wind." Some critics charged that the "war on terror" declared by President George W. Bush in the aftermath of September 11, 2001, involved the same kind of language that Orwell criticized after World War II. Indeed, many such critics invoked Orwell's work, especially his famous novel *1984,* in which a totalitarian government controls its citizens in large part by controlling language. In that novel, "doublespeak" referred to language that seems to say one thing but means another; it is language that seems clear but isn't—language that makes the good seem bad, and vice versa. Note how the button below, which criticizes the U.S. government's Patriot Act, uses Orwell's ideas about language to convey its criticism.

UNDERSTANDING THE TEXT

1. Why does Orwell assert that there has been a "decline" in the English language at the beginning of his essay? What is the nature of this decline? What causes the decline, in his view? What does this decline have to do with politics, according to him?

2. What are the "mental vices" that Orwell believes are reflected in the examples of bad writing that he provides in this essay? Why are these mental vices important, in his view? Do you think he's right? Why or why not?

3. What is "the special connection between politics and the debasement of language" that Orwell refers to at the end of paragraph 11? Why is this connection important?

4. In what ways does language corrupt thought, according to Orwell? Why does this kind of "corruption" concern him? Do you agree? Explain.

5. What does Orwell mean when he writes that "the worst thing one can do with words is surrender to them" (par. 17)? How can a writer avoid this problem, in his view?

EXPLORING THE ISSUES

1. Examine the examples of "bad" writing that Orwell includes in this essay. What specifically is bad about them, as Orwell sees it? Do you think they are bad in the ways Orwell describes? Explain, referring to specific passages to support your answer. You might also look at your own writing to see whether it has any of the characteristics that Orwell criticizes.

2. Orwell identifies two main problems in writing: "staleness of imagery" and "lack of precision" (par. 4). Examine Orwell's own prose. Does he avoid these two problems? Support your answer with references to specific passages in his essay.

3. Some of the expressions that Orwell criticizes as examples of "bad" writing in this essay are no longer commonly used (for example, *ring the changes on, the hammer and the anvil, jackboot,* and *mailed fist*), but many are. For example, expressions like *Achilles' heel, play into the hands of, status quo, extramarital,* and *utilize,* all of which Orwell criticizes, are common expressions that often appear in popular and academic writing today. Keeping in mind that Orwell wrote this essay more than sixty years ago, how might you explain the fact that so many expressions Orwell criticized are still in wide use today? What might this suggest about the nature of the English language and how it is used?

4. At the end of his essay, Orwell writes that "the present political chaos is connected with the decay of language." He is referring to the complex and tense political situation in Europe after World War II. Do you think this statement is still true today, given the current political situation in the world? Explain.

5. Explain the connection between language use and the process of power, as Orwell understands it. What role does language play in the use or abuse of power, as Orwell sees it? Do you think Orwell's understanding of this connection still applies today? Explain.

ENTERING THE CONVERSATIONS

1. Write an essay responding to Orwell's assertion that we can improve our political situation by using language properly (par. 18). In your essay, explain Orwell's reasoning and offer your own position on whether or not our ways of using language can positively affect our political situation. Include in your essay current examples of political language to support your position.

2. Orwell argues that "political writing is bad writing" and explains some of the specific ways that this is true (par. 12). Examine some contemporary examples of political speeches and writing and analyze them using some of Orwell's criticisms of writing. Then write an essay in which you offer your analysis of contemporary political discourse (speech or writing, including political ads on television, radio, or the Internet). In your essay, discuss what you found when you analyzed current political discourse and offer examples to support your points. Draw conclusions about the nature of contemporary political discourse.

3. Take an essay you have written and edit it using the advice for good writing that Orwell offers in this essay.

4. Create a web site, PowerPoint presentation, or some other kind of document in which you identify current examples of the four "tricks" of bad writing that Orwell describes in this essay (dying metaphors, operators or verbal false limbs, pretentious diction, and meaningless words).

5. In paragraph 9, Orwell rewrites a passage from the Bible in "bad" prose. Following his example and using his analysis of the specific features of bad writing, take a passage from a piece of writing that you consider good and rewrite it in bad style. Once you have finished your rewrite, consider what you have learned about writing by intentionally trying to write bad prose.

6. In today's newspaper or a news web site of your choice, locate an article in which the writer has used one of the following words: *democracy, socialism, freedom, patriotic, realistic,* or *justice.* Examine how the word has been used. Then, drawing on Orwell's essay, write an analysis of the author's use of this word. Has the author made clear what the word means? Is the word used in a way that obscures the author's point? How might Orwell have judged the author's use of the word? Address these questions in your essay.

Most Americans accept majority rule as the *way things should be. In the U.S. political system, for example, the party that wins more seats in the House of Representatives or the Senate controls that body. If more Republicans win seats, then all Senate committees are chaired by Republicans and the Senate is effectively run by Republicans. This winner-take-all approach to political power is a basic principle of the American style of democracy—so basic that many Americans assume*

THE Tyranny OF THE Majority

that democracy is equivalent to majority rule. But some democracies distribute power proportionally, assigning a portion of political power to each party based on the percentage of votes that party received in an election. In parliamentary democracies like Canada or Israel, several parties will compete in elections, and the percentage of the vote that each party receives determines how much power that party will have in the government. Such a system requires that the party with the largest percentage of votes form coalitions with other parties in order for the government to function.

Some political scientists and legal scholars believe that such parliamentary democracies avoid some of the problems associated with the winner-take-all process in the United States. In her carefully reasoned essay, Lani Guinier (b. 1950) explains how American-style majority rule is not always fair and does not necessarily best serve the needs and interests of the minority, especially in a diverse society. Guinier reminds us that some of the Founding Fathers expressed concerns about the possibility that the American political process could result in a "tyranny of the majority," and she suggests some steps to make the American political process fairer. Her essay is part of an ongoing (continued)

LANI GUINIER

I have always wanted to be a civil rights lawyer. This lifelong ambition is based on a deep-seated commitment to democratic fair play—to playing by the rules as long as the rules are fair. When the rules seem unfair, I have worked to change them, not subvert them. When I was eight years old, I was a Brownie. I was especially proud of my uniform, which represented a commitment to good citizenship and good deeds. But one day, when my Brownie group staged a hatmaking contest, I realized that uniforms are only as honorable as the people who wear them. The contest was rigged. The winner was assisted by her milliner mother, who actually made the winning entry in full view of all the participants. At the time, I was too young to be able to change the rules, but I was old enough to resign, which I promptly did.

To me, fair play means that the rules encourage everyone to play. They should reward those who win, but they must be acceptable to those who lose. The central theme of my academic writing is that not all rules lead to elemental fair play. Some even commonplace rules work against it.

(continued) *debate in American society about how to interpret the Constitution and how best to manage the process of power.*

Lani Guinier, a distinguished legal scholar, taught at the University of Pennsylvania before becoming the first black woman tenured professor at Harvard Law School in 1998. She has written extensively about political and legal issues and has published several books, including The Tyranny of the Majority *(1994), in which the following essay first appeared.* ▼

The professional milliner competing with amateur Brownies stands as an example of rules that are patently rigged or patently subverted. Yet, sometimes, even when rules are perfectly fair in form, they serve in practice to exclude particular groups from meaningful participation. When they do not encourage everyone to play, or when, over the long haul, they do not make the losers feel as good about the outcomes as the winners, they can seem as unfair as the milliner who makes the winning hat for her daughter.

Sometimes, too, we construct rules that force us to be divided into winners and losers when we might have otherwise joined together. This idea was cogently expressed by my son, Nikolas, when he was four years old, far exceeding the thoughtfulness of his mother when she was an eight-year-old Brownie. While I was writing one of my law journal articles, Nikolas and I had a conversation about voting prompted by a *Sesame Street Magazine* exercise. The magazine pictured six children: four children had raised their hands because they wanted to play tag; two had their hands down because they wanted to play hide-and-seek. The magazine asked its readers to count the number of children whose hands were raised and then decide what game the children would play.

5   Nikolas quite realistically replied, "They will play both. First they will play tag. Then they will play hide-and-seek." Despite the magazine's "rules," he was right. To children, it is natural to take turns. The winner may get to play first or more often, but even the "loser" gets something. His was a positive-sum solution that many adult rule-makers ignore.

The traditional answer to the magazine's problem would have been a zero-sum solution: "The children—all the children—will play tag, and only tag." As a zero-sum solution, everything is seen in terms of "I win; you lose." The conventional answer relies on winner-take-all majority rule, in which the tag players, as the majority, win the right to decide for all the children what game to play. The hide-and-seek preference becomes irrelevant. The numerically more powerful majority choice simply subsumes minority preferences.

In the conventional case, the majority that rules gains all the power and the minority that loses gets none. For example, two years ago Brother Rice High School in Chicago held two senior proms. It was not planned that way. The prom committee at Brother Rice, a boys' Catholic high school, expected just one prom when it hired a disc jockey, picked a rock band, and selected music for the prom by consulting student preferences. Each senior was asked to list his three favorite songs, and the band would play the songs that appeared most frequently on the lists.

Seems attractively democratic. But Brother Rice is predominantly white, and the prom committee was all white. That's how they got two proms. The black seniors at Brother Rice felt so shut out by the "democratic process" that they organized their own prom. As one black student put it: "for every vote we had, there were eight votes for what they wanted. . . . [W]ith us being in the minority we're always outvoted. It's as if we don't count."

Some embittered white seniors saw things differently. They complained that the black students should have gone along with the majority: "The majority makes a decision. That's the way it works."

10   In a way, both groups were right. From the white students' perspective, this was ordinary decisionmaking. To the black students, majority rule sent the message: "we don't count" is the "way it works" for minorities. In a racially divided society, majority rule may be perceived as majority tyranny.

STRATEGIES: SUMMARY
Notice how Guinier uses her summary of James Madison's political ideas to help explain the problems with majority rule. In these paragraphs and for much of the rest of her essay, she relies on Madison's ideas to lay out her own position on this issue using quotations from his writings. She also relies on Madison's status as one of the Founding Fathers, which gives his words more weight with many American readers than the words of a less revered political figure or scholar.

That is a large claim, and I do not rest my case for it solely on the actions of the prom committee in one Chicago high school. To expand the range of the argument, I first consider the ideal of majority rule itself, particularly as reflected in the writings of James Madison and other founding members of our Republic. These early democrats explored the relationship between majority rule and democracy. James Madison warned, "If a majority be united by a common interest, the rights of the minority will be insecure." The tyranny of the majority, according to Madison, requires safeguards to protect "one part of the society against the injustice of the other part."

For Madison, majority tyranny represented the great danger to our early constitutional democracy. Although the American revolution was fought against the tyranny of the British monarch, it soon became clear that there was another tyranny to be avoided. The accumulations of all powers in the same hands, Madison warned, "whether of one, a few, or many, and whether hereditary, self-appointed, or elective, may justly be pronounced the very definition of tyranny."

CONTEXT: TYRANNY IN HISTORY
The quotation Guinier includes here from a colonist in the late eighteenth century indicates that the historical context within which James Madison and the other Founding Fathers were writing the U.S. Constitution was very different from our own time. This colonist's concerns about tyranny were based on the many examples of powerful monarchs who ruled European nations at the time of the American Revolution. As Americans formed their own government, the world had many tyrannical governments but no examples of the kind of democracy Americans were trying to create. As a result, the idea of the "tyranny of the majority," which may seem odd to many contemporary readers, would have been a very real concern at the time Madison and his colleagues were debating how to form a new government. Today, few Americans have such concerns, which makes Guinier's argument in this essay a little harder to make. Consider how she uses historical information to help her modern readers appreciate the significance of her concerns about majority rule.

As another colonist suggested in papers published in Philadelphia, "We have been so long habituated to a jealousy of tyranny from monarchy and aristocracy, that we have yet to learn the dangers of it from democracy." Despotism had to be opposed "whether it came from Kings, Lords or the people."

The debate about majority tyranny reflected Madison's concern that the majority may not represent the whole. In a homogeneous society, the interest of the majority would likely be that of the minority also. But in a heterogeneous community, the majority may not represent all competing interests. The majority is likely to be self-interested and ignorant or indifferent to the concerns of the minority. In such case, Madison observed, the assumption that the majority represents the minority is "altogether fictitious."

15   Yet even a self-interested majority can govern fairly if it cooperates with the minority. One reason for such cooperation is that the self-interested majority values the principle of reciprocity. The self-interested majority worries that the minority may attract defectors from the majority and become the next

governing majority. The Golden Rule principle of reciprocity functions to check the tendency of a self-interested majority to act tyrannically.

So the argument for the majority principle connects it with the value of reciprocity: You cooperate when you lose in part because members of the current majority will cooperate when they lose. The conventional case for the fairness of majority rule is that it is not really the rule of a fixed group—The Majority—on all issues; instead it is the rule of shifting majorities, as the losers at one time or on one issue join with others and become part of the governing coalition at another time or on another issue. The result will be a fair system of mutually beneficial cooperation. I call a majority that rules but does not dominate a Madisonian Majority.

The problem of majority tyranny arises, however, when the self-interested majority does not need to worry about defections. When the majority is fixed and permanent, there are no checks on its ability to be overbearing. A majority that does not worry about defectors is a majority with total power.

In such a case, Madison's concern about majority tyranny arises. In a heterogeneous community, any faction with total power might subject "the minority to the caprice and arbitrary decisions of the majority, who instead of consulting the interest of the whole community collectively, attend sometimes to partial and local advantages."

"What remedy can be found in a republican Government, where the majority must ultimately decide," argued Madison, but to ensure "that no one common interest or passion will be likely to unite a majority of the whole number in an unjust pursuit." The answer was to disaggregate the majority to ensure checks and balances or fluid, rotating interests. The minority needed protection against an overbearing majority, so that "a common sentiment is less likely to be felt, and the requisite concert less likely to be formed, by a majority of the whole."

Political struggles would not be simply a contest between rulers and people; the political struggles would be among the people themselves. The work of government was not to transcend different interests but to reconcile them. In an ideal democracy, the people would rule, but the minorities would also be protected against the power of majorities. Again, where the rules of decisionmaking protect the minority, the Madisonian Majority rules without dominating. 20

But if a group is unfairly treated, for example, when it forms a racial minority, *and* if the problems of unfairness are not cured by conventional assumptions about majority rule, then what is to be done? The answer is that we may need an *alternative* to winner-take-all majoritarianism. In this book, a collection of my law review articles, I describe the alternative, which, with Nikolas's help, I now call the "principle of taking turns." In a racially divided society, this principle does better than simple majority rule if it accommodates the values

CONVERSATIONS: TURN-TAKING AND THE 2004 U.S. PRESIDENTIAL ELECTION
Ten years after Guinier's essay was published, one of the closest and most controversial presidential elections in U.S. history ended with George W. Bush being reelected by historically slim margins. His party controlled both the U.S. House of Representatives and the U.S. Senate, also by slim margins. In many ways, the 2004 election illustrates some of Guinier's concerns about the winner-take-all approach in American politics: A very small majority effectively gained full power to rule everyone. But circumstances in 2004 were different from 1994, when Guinier's essay was first published. In 2004, many groups who felt that their concerns were being ignored by both the Republican and Democratic Parties began to use alternative ways of voicing their concerns and participating in the political process. One way was the use of alternative media like the Internet to mobilize opposition to the two main political parties, as MoveOn.org, one of the most visible of such groups, did. Consider how the emergence of groups like MoveOn.org might complicate—or lend support to—Guinier's argument for an alternative to simple majority rule in the United States. Consider, too, how the rise of new technologies like the Internet might affect her proposals.

of self-government, fairness, deliberation, compromise, and consensus that lie at the heart of the democratic ideal.

In my legal writing, I follow the caveat of James Madison and other early American democrats. I explore decisionmaking rules that might work in a multi-racial society to ensure that majority rule does not become majority tyranny. I pursue voting systems that might disaggregate The Majority so that it does not exercise power unfairly or tyrannically. I aspire to a more cooperative political style of decisionmaking to enable all of the students at Brother Rice to feel comfortable attending the same prom. In looking to create Madisonian Majorities, I pursue a positive-sum, taking-turns solution.

Structuring decisionmaking to allow the minority "a turn" may be necessary to restore the reciprocity ideal when a fixed majority refuses to cooperate with the minority. If the fixed majority loses its incentive to follow the Golden Rule principle of shifting majorities, the minority never gets to take a turn. Giving the minority a turn does not mean the minority gets to rule; what it does mean is that the minority gets to influence decisionmaking and the majority rules more legitimately.

Instead of automatically rewarding the preferences of the monolithic majority, a taking-turns approach anticipates that the majority rules, but is not overbearing. Because those with 51 percent of the votes are not assured 100 percent of the power, the majority cooperates with, or at least does not tyrannize, the minority.

25   The sports analogy of "I win; you lose" competition within a political hierarchy makes sense when only one team can win; Nikolas's intuition that it is often possible to take turns suggests an alternative approach. Take family decisionmaking, for example. It utilizes a taking-turns approach. When parents sit around the kitchen table deciding on a vacation destination or activities for a rainy day, often they do not simply rely on a show of hands, especially if that means that the older children always prevail or if affinity groups among the children (those who prefer movies to video games, or those who prefer baseball to playing cards) never get to play their activity of choice. Instead of allowing the majority simply to rule, the parents may propose that everyone take turns, going to the movies one night and playing video games the next. Or as Nikolas proposes, they might do both on a given night.

Taking turns attempts to build consensus while recognizing political or social differences, and it encourages everyone to play. The taking-turns approach gives those with the most support more turns, but it also legitimates the outcome from each individual's perspective, including those whose views are shared only by a minority.

In the end, I do not believe that democracy should encourage rule by the powerful—even a powerful majority. Instead, the idea of democracy promises a fair discussion among self-defined equals about how to achieve our common aspirations. To redeem that promise, we need to put the idea of taking turns and disaggregating the majority at the center of our conception of representation. Particularly as we move into the twenty-first century as a more highly diversified citizenry, it is essential that we consider the ways in which voting and representational systems succeed or fail at encouraging Madisonian Majorities.

To use Nikolas's terminology, "it is no fair" if a fixed, tyrannical majority excludes or alienates the minority. It is no fair if a fixed, tyrannical majority monopolizes all the power all the time. It is no fair if we engage in the periodic ritual of elections, but only the permanent majority gets to choose who is elected. Where we have tyranny by The Majority, we do not have genuine democracy.

UNDERSTANDING THE TEXT

1. What specific problems does Guinier see with majority rule in American politics? How serious are these problems, in your view?

2. What is a "Madisonian Majority," according to Guinier? Why are James Madison's ideas about democracy and specifically about majority rule so important, in her view?

3. How would Guinier's alternative "turn-taking" approach to government and political power be fairer to political minorities than the current "winner-take-all majoritarianism" in U.S. politics, in her view? Under what circumstances does Guinier believe that we might need such an alternative? Do you agree with her that these circumstances would require such an alternative? Why or why not?

4. What fundamental values does Guinier hold that shape her view of how government should work? Do you think most Americans share these values? Explain.

EXPLORING THE ISSUES

1. Guinier uses several examples to illustrate the problems with majority rule and to support her argument for changes in the American political process. How effective do you think these examples are in helping her make her case? What might her examples suggest about her sense of her audience?

2. In 1993, when President Bill Clinton nominated Guinier to serve on the U.S. Supreme Court, her nomination was strenuously opposed by many critics who disagreed with her views about affirmative action and "proportional

representation," which is the belief that power should be distributed proportionally according to the percentage of the vote received by each party. Based on this essay, why do you think some Americans would have such severe objections to a person with Guinier's views serving on the U.S. Supreme Court? To what extent do you think this essay might address—or worsen—the concerns of such critics?

3. Guinier includes several anecdotes from her personal life in this essay. How do you think these anecdotes might affect a reader's sense of Guinier as a person and as an authority on the legal issues she is addressing in this essay? Do you think these anecdotes make her essay more or less effective? What might your answer to that question reveal about you as a reader?

4. How would you sum up Guinier's view of democracy? Do you think most Americans share her view? Why or why not?

ENTERING THE CONVERSATIONS

1. Write an essay for an audience of your classmates in which you discuss your basic concerns about the current American political process. In your essay, draw on Guinier's ideas and on any other essays in this cluster to explain or support your position.

2. Visit the web sites of several active political groups, such as MoveOn.org. Try to get a sense of their political views and what their organizations seem to believe about the American political process. Then write a report about what you learned about these groups and their uses of the Internet to participate in the political process.

Alternatively, create a web site on the basis of your research.

INFOTRAC

3. In this essay, Guinier is calling for reforms to the American political process. In recent years, a number of related political reforms have been proposed and debated, including changes to the rules governing campaign funding and even abandoning the electoral college for U.S. presidential elections. Using InfoTrac College Edition and any other relevant resources, investigate current proposals for political reform in the United States, perhaps focusing on one particular reform, such as campaign finance reform or changes in the electoral college system. Try to get a sense of what kinds of reforms are being proposed, by whom, and why. What advantages or disadvantages might the proposed reforms have compared to the current political process? Then write a report for an audience of your classmates in which you discuss what you learned through your research and offer your conclusions about political reform.

4. On the basis of your research for Question 3, write a letter to the editor of your local newspaper (or another appropriate publication) in which you make an argument for or against a specific political reform. In your letter, identify what you believe is the basic problem with the political process today and propose your reform as a way to address that problem.

5. Create a pamphlet (or a web site) whose purpose is to explain what you believe to be the most important aspects of the process of political power in the United States today.

On June 21, 1964, John Chaney, a young *Black man from Mississippi, was traveling with two White companions from New York—Andrew Goodman and Michael Schwerner—when all three were murdered by members of the Ku Klux Klan in Mississippi. The men had been part of an organized effort to register Black voters in Mississippi, which angered the Klan. Their deaths helped galvanize the Civil Rights Movement and bring national pressure on Mississippi and other states to change*

I Hold These Truths
TO Be *Self-Evident*

racist laws. Despite arrests and trials, no one was convicted of the murders.

Like many Americans, writer Donna Ladd (b. 1961) was horrified by those crimes, so much so that she left her native Mississippi, refusing to live in a place where racists could get away with murder. But Ladd returned to Mississippi nearly twenty years later to start a newspaper, the Jackson Free Press. In the following essay, she explains her decision to return to Mississippi and to work for the justice and equality that she once believed could not be achieved there. In explaining her decision, Ladd reveals something important about the process of power in the United States. We tend to associate political power with governments or organized political parties, but Ladd's essay reminds us that power can work in many different ways. Power in a town like Meridian, Mississippi, does not necessarily rest solely with government officials; it can also be wielded by groups like the Klan. The kind of political activism that Chaney, Goodman, and Schwerner engaged in is another way in which power can be wielded—in this case, by people who believed that governments would not correct the injustices that were occurring in places like Meridian. Ladd reminds us that power (continued)

DONNA LADD

"How is everybody?" legendary civil rights activist Bob Moses asked the congregation in his famous whisper. He paused and then added, "Say these words with me."

"I hold these truths to be self-evident . . . "

On Sunday, June 22, I was tucked in a corner at Mt. Zion Methodist Church several miles east of my hometown in the Longdale community of Neshoba County. This was the church that had to be rebuilt after the Ku Klux Klan burned it in 1964. It had risen from the ashes that James Chaney, Andrew Goodman and Mickey Schwerner had poked through on Father's Day, exactly 39 years ago that Sunday. It was the last place they visited before Deputy Sheriff Cecil Price pulled them over, arrested them and hid them in the city jail until the lynch mob could gather and kill them.

The church was overflowing with Longdale residents, legendary civil-rights activists, black and white politicians from Neshoba County and Jackson and beyond, more reporters than last year. We were there to honor the memory of three men who helped pave the way for black Americans to get a piece of the American dream.

DONNA LADD, "I HOLD THESE TRUTHS TO BE SELF-EVIDENT." FROM *JACKSON FREE PRESS,* JULY 8, 2003. HTTP://WWW.JACKSONFREEPRESS.COM/. REPRINTED BY PERMISSION OF THE AUTHOR.

(continued) *is both official and unofficial, both individual and collective. And its workings can be disturbing as well as uplifting.*

The following essay was originally published in July 2003 in the Jackson Free Press.

STRATEGIES: INTERSPERSED QUOTATIONS
One of the most striking features of this essay is the way that Ladd includes quotations from the Declaration of Independence throughout. Most American readers will probably recognize those quotations, which are considered almost sacred in American culture. It is also likely that readers who agree as well as those who disagree with her would all recognize the importance of these quotations. Consider, then, how these quotations affect Ladd's essay. How would her essay differ if she had not included them? What do you think her use of these quotations suggests about Ladd's understanding of her audience? In thinking about those questions, consider that she originally wrote this essay for a local newspaper in Mississippi.

CONVERSATIONS: PATRIOTISM
The question of what it means to be patriotic is an old and often contentious one in the United States, and Ladd offers a point of view about patriotism that is shared by many activists. Several writers whose essays appear in Chapter 5, including Bharati Mukherjee and Oscar Casares, also offer ideas about patriotism, as does Gary Sloan, whose essay appears in Chapter 8. The fact that these different writers address patriotism in various ways might suggest how important this issue is to Americans. It's also worth keeping in mind that many of Ladd's fellow Mississippians also consider themselves patriotic, yet they would disagree with the views she expresses in this essay. Ladd surely knew that when she wrote this essay, which may suggest something important about how discussions of patriotism are carried on in the United States.

"*. . . that all men are created equal . . .*"   5

I've struggled with the idea of patriotism my entire life. As a child growing up in Neshoba County, a place that I then believed sucked more than anywhere on the planet, I openly scorned patriotism, especially in my rebellious, angry high school years. After I learned about the three murders when I was 14—although they'd happened 11 years before; which says something about the ability of a community to clam up—the whole idea of pride in where I was from seemed to be squelched forever. Everyone knew who those murderers were. How could they be free among us, pumping gas, repairing birthstone rings, joining the country club? How could a people, a state, a country that claimed that it believed in justice allow those men their freedom?

I wore this burden of where I was born like a backpack filled with rocks. I wanted out of Neshoba County, out of Mississippi, never to look back. I wanted freedom, and I wanted to live somewhere where I could be proud. I wanted to be where people believed in the "justice for all" part.

So I went in search of my piece of the American puzzle, taking Chaney, Goodman and Schwerner along with me.

"*. . . that they are endowed by their Creator . . . .*"

Indeed, I found a lot. I learned that bigotry could take many different forms, including intense prejudice against the South. I learned that the rest of America had only paid attention to the black Mississippian Chaney because white New Yorkers Goodman and Schwerner died by his side. I also learned much more about Mississippi history than I ever had in Mississippi—including the absolute fact that our institutionalized racism, enforced by every level of our society, was indeed worse than anywhere else. In effect, both the North and the South were right, and wrong, about each other.   10

I learned just enough to be really damned confused about the idea of patriotism. Hoping from afar for nearly 20 years after I left that my state and county would someday criminally prosecute at least one of that lynch mob, I continued to believe passionately in the American constitutional system. As I learned more about the Red Scare, and union-busting, and spying on protesters during the Vietnam era (including the staff of the Kudzu newspaper in Jackson), my belief grew stronger that the ideals that the United States is built on, even if we have not always honored them, can weather any storm.

Along the way, even as I faced squarely the painful honesty of the dark moments of U.S. history that I didn't learn or read about at Neshoba Central, my pride started to grow. And not only my pride in the constitutional principles of the country, but in where I came from, and how far it had come, despite its reticence to convict its own.

I returned two years ago in search of a home I could love. And I found it.

"*. . . with certain unalienable Rights . . .*"

15   The last two years have been interesting. It has felt almost surreal to watch so many of our civil liberties go under the knife, and to hear some frustrated Americans say they'd leave the country if they had somewhere else to go. I used to say that, too. Just as I couldn't wait to leave Mississippi in 1983, I used to romanticize the idea of being an expatriate somewhere like the **Scott Fitzgerald crowd** in Paris during the 1920s. I always thought that if the freedom tide ever turned, and our civil liberties were at stake again, that I'd be outta here in a snap.

GLOSS: THE SCOTT FITZGERALD CROWD
Famous American writer F. Scott Fitzgerald, author of *The Great Gatsby,* was one of several well-known Americans who lived in Europe in the 1920s.

The tide has turned, though, and I'm still here. Not only in the United States, but back home in Mississippi, and loving it, near the place where they've never prosecuted that lynch mob and where state elected officials fear losing votes so much that they won't mothball a symbol of hatred and shame. Since Sept. 11, I've felt no need to publicly display a flag, any flag. Right now, that flag would say to most people that I publicly support military decisions that I believe in my heart are unwise. I can't do that.

But I've been thinking a lot about patriotism lately: It seems that love of your country matters more when other people try to take it away from you.

"*. . . that among these are Life, Liberty and the Pursuit of Happiness.*"

CONTEXT: THE MURDERS OF CHANEY, GOODMAN, AND SCHWERNER
In early 2005, a man named Edgar Ray Killen was arrested and charged with these murders. Killen had been arrested on conspiracy charges in 1964, but his trial ended in a hung jury. He was eventually convicted of the killings in 2005. But even after his trial in 2005, controversy about the 1964 murders continued. Many people who had long called for arrests in the case complained that others who were involved were not arrested along with Killen, who was seventy-nine years old at the time of his arrest. As you read, consider how Killen's arrest, about a year and a half after Ladd wrote this essay, might influence the way you read this essay—and how it might affect Ladd's main point.

Maybe I finally understood my brand of patriotism last Sunday listening to the quiet voice of Bob Moses recite from the Declaration of Independence behind the pulpit at Mount Zion. We live in a country built messily on amazing principles of equality formulated by slaveholders and apologists. It is a country with a foundation of freedom so strong that Mr. Moses, a black man beaten in Mississippi for trying to register blacks to vote, would move his family here to help the next generation, and the next, continue to fight for the freedom and education that our founding fathers promised us, even though they weren't ready to give it to us all. I now believe that the American ideals of equality, justice, pluralism, tolerance, freedom of and from religion and opportunity are worth staying here—in the state and in the United States—and fighting for.

20   Mr. Moses said Sunday, "One of the best things about this country is that you can live a life in struggle." The American dream is just that: a struggle. We must continue to fight to preserve our right to be patriotic, even in dissent, and to ensure that more and more of us, not fewer, can experience what is so special about the American way. That is, after all, the point.

VISUAL CONNECTIONS: THE FLAG

Ladd writes that she will not display the American flag because of her opposition to the war in Iraq that was being waged when she wrote this essay in 2003. At that time, controversy surrounded displays of the flag by both supporters and opponents of the war. In this case, Ladd believes that displaying the flag sends a message of support for the war. But controversy also continued to surround the state flag of Mississippi, which includes the old Confederate flag, which many people, including Ladd, find to be an offensive symbol of racism. Consider what messages these flags might convey—and where these symbols get their meanings.

Mississippi State Flag   Confederate Flag   American Flag

UNDERSTANDING THE TEXT

1. How does Ladd justify her decision to leave her native Mississippi? What do you think this decision reveals about her as a person?

2. What does Ladd learn about "the American puzzle" after living away from Mississippi for almost twenty years? How does what she learned influence her decision to return to Mississippi?

3. In what sense is the American Dream a struggle, in Ladd's view? What might this idea of struggle suggest about American democracy and the process of power in the United States? Do you agree with her? Explain.

EXPLORING THE ISSUES

1. How does Ladd define patriotism? Do you think most Americans share her understanding of patriotism? Do you? Why or why not?

2. Ladd's essay was originally published in her newspaper, the *Jackson Free Press* in Jackson, Mississippi. Obviously, opinions about the murders of Chaney, Goodman, and Schwerner can still cause conflict in Mississippi, even forty years later. What do you think this essay suggests about Ladd's understanding of her readers' view of these murders? Do you think she expects most readers of her newspaper to agree with her about these events? Explain, citing specific passages to support your answer.

3. How would you describe Ladd's voice in this essay? How effective do you think her voice is in helping her make her point? Cite specific passages to support your answer.

4. Ladd states that the more she learned about the dark history of her native state, the more her pride in that state began to grow. How does she explain her pride? Do you think it is justified? Why or why not?

5. What do you think Ladd's decision to return to Mississippi suggests about the process of power in the United States?

ENTERING THE CONVERSATIONS

1. Write an essay in which you offer your own view of what Ladd calls the "struggle" of the American Dream.

2. Write an essay about a time in your life (or in the life of someone you know well) in which you (or the person you know) made a decision based on principle and a desire to make a difference.

3. In a group of classmates, share the essays you wrote for Question 2. What similarities and differences do you see in the experiences that you and your classmates wrote about? What might these essays reveal about how power functions in contemporary society?

INFOTRAC

4. A number of popular films have been made about the Civil Rights Movement in the United States, including *Mississippi Burning* (1988), a controversial film about the 1964 murders of John Chaney, Andrew Goodman, and Michael Schwerner. View this film or other films about the Civil Rights Movement and examine how these films portray the workings of political and legal power in the context of that movement. Then write an essay in which you present your analysis of the film. What might the film reveal about the process of power in the United States? Alternatively, investigate the controversy surrounding *Mississippi Burning*. A number of well-known movie critics harshly criticized the film. Using InfoTrac College Edition, the Internet, and other relevant resources, locate some reviews of the film, examine their criticisms, and write a report about the controversy surrounding the film. In your report, identify the main criticisms of the film and draw conclusions about what this controversy might suggest about how Americans feel about the Civil Rights struggle and the workings of power in American society.

5. Identify one or more symbols that create controversy, such as the state flag of Mississippi (see *Visual Connections: The Flag* on page 421). Examine how these symbols tend to be used and what they mean to various people. Then write an essay discussing the uses of such symbols in political disputes in contemporary American politics. Try to draw conclusions about the role of these symbols in the process of power. Alternatively, create a web site or PowerPoint presentation for the same purpose.

Gay Pride Flag

AIDS   Support Our Troops

AIDS Ribbon and Troop Support Ribbon

© Jeffrey McDonald/istockphoto.com

© Scott Heiner/istockphoto.com

Wendell Berry (b. 1934) has been called *"perhaps the greatest moral essayist of our day"* and *"the unimpeachable Jeffersonian conscience of American public discourse."* He's also been called much less flattering things. When you read the following essay, which Berry wrote shortly after the terrorist attacks of September 11, 2001, you'll begin to see why his writing provokes such strong emotions. Berry is often thought of as a voice for rural values and an advocate for an en-

vironmentally conscious lifestyle, but he sees politics and lifestyle as inseparable; in his view, how we live on the land reflects ethical and moral choices that affect our social, economic, and political lives. So it is no surprise that Berry would see in the terrible events of September 11, 2001, something more than political or ideological conflict between America and its enemies. In this essay, Berry takes direct aim at what he considers the causes of those terrorist attacks. Characteristically, he insists that we not simply condemn those who perpetrated such horrific acts but ask how our consumer-driven lifestyle and our choices as individuals and as a society might have given rise to these acts. In making this argument, Berry risked the anger of Americans. Indeed, you may find yourself angry as you read this unflinching essay. But Berry's thoughts about the events of September 11, 2001, are worth considering for what they might reveal about our beliefs about ourselves and our way of living, and they can help us understand the complexities and consequences of power.

Wendell Berry is the award-winning author of more than forty novels, collections of poetry, and books of essays, and he has written widely for many magazines and newspapers, including Orion, *in which this essay originally appeared in 2001.* ◪

Thoughts IN THE Presence OF Fear

WENDELL BERRY

The time will soon come when we will not be able to remember the horrors of September 11 without remembering also the unquestioning technological and economic optimism that ended on that day.

II. This optimism rested on the proposition that we were living in a "new world order" and a "new economy" that would "grow" on and on, bringing a prosperity of which every new increment would be "unprecedented."

III. The dominant politicians, corporate officers, and investors who believed this proposition did not acknowledge that the prosperity was limited to a tiny percent of the world's people, and to an ever smaller number of people even in the United States; that it was founded upon the oppressive labor of poor people all over the world; and that its ecological costs increasingly threatened all life, including the lives of the supposedly prosperous.

IV. The "developed" nations had given to the "free market" the status of a god, and were sacrificing to it their farmers, farmlands, and communities, their forests, wetlands, and prairies, their ecosystems

CONTEXT: UNQUESTIONING TECHNOLOGICAL AND ECONOMIC OPTIMISM
The optimism Berry discusses in the first few paragraphs of his essay refers to the surging U.S. economy and its influence on the changing global economy in the 1990s and the early years of the twenty-first century. Although the U.S. stock market suffered a serious decline after 2000, the U.S. economy continued to grow, and business leaders and politicians spoke of a "new world order." Obviously, Berry has grave concerns about these developments, concerns shared by others in what he describes in paragraph 5 as "a growing worldwide effort on behalf of economic decentralization, economic justice, and ecological responsibility." Others have called this an antiglobalization movement, and its proponents organized large protests at meetings of international economic organizations like the World Bank. (Vandana Shiva, whose essay on water privatization appears on page 613, is a well-known spokesperson for this movement.) Readers of *Orion,* a magazine focusing on environmental and social issues in which this essay was first published, would recognize Berry's references to this "worldwide movement." You might consider whether you recognized these references. Think about how your understanding of this larger context might influence the way you read Berry's essay.

CONVERSATIONS: TECHNOLOGY AND PROGRESS
When Berry writes that "we had accepted uncritically the belief that technology is only good," he is joining a long-standing conversation about the merits and costs of technology and of technological and scientific progress in general. Along with other well-known critics, including Vandana Shiva and Kirkpatrick Sale (whose essays appear in Chapters 11 and 12, respectively), Berry has questioned the idea that technological and scientific developments represent progress for human society, and he has criticized not only our reliance on technology and science but also our confidence in them. These criticisms are part of an ongoing debate among philosophers, scientists, and others about whether or not science itself is neutral. Berry and others argue that science rests on questionable values and beliefs about humans and their place on the earth. The classic example often cited in these debates is nuclear physics, which has resulted in benefits such as medical treatments for cancer but which has also led to the development of nuclear weapons. Berry would ask whether "pure" scientific inquiry that can lead to such horrible outcomes as nuclear weapons is really neutral and represents genuine progress.

and watersheds. They had accepted universal pollution and global warming as normal costs of doing business.

V. There was, as a consequence, a growing worldwide effort on behalf of economic decentralization, economic justice, and ecological responsibility. We must recognize that the events of September 11 make this effort more necessary than ever. We citizens of the industrial countries must continue the labor of self-criticism and self-correction. We must recognize our mistakes.

VI. The paramount doctrine of the economic and technological euphoria of recent decades has been that everything depends on innovation. It was understood as desirable, and even necessary, that we should go on and on from one technological innovation to the next, which would cause the economy to "grow" and make everything better and better. This of course implied at every point a hatred of the past, of all things inherited and free. All things superseded in our progress of innovations, whatever their value might have been, were discounted as of no value at all.

VII. We did not anticipate anything like what has now happened. We did not foresee that all our sequence of innovations might be at once overridden by a greater one: the invention of a new kind of war that would turn our previous innovations against us, discovering and exploiting the debits and the dangers that we had ignored. We never considered the possibility that we might be trapped in the webwork of communication and transport that was supposed to make us free.

VIII. Nor did we foresee that the weaponry and the war science that we marketed and taught to the world would become available, not just to recognized national governments, which possess so uncannily the power to legitimate large-scale violence, but also to "rogue nations," dissident or fanatical groups and individuals—whose violence, though never worse than that of nations, is judged by the nations to be illegitimate.

IX. We had accepted uncritically the belief that technology is only good; that it cannot serve evil as well as good; that it cannot serve our enemies as well as ourselves; that it cannot be used to destroy what is good, including our homelands and our lives.

X. We had accepted too the corollary belief that an economy (either as a money economy or as a life-support system) that is global in extent, technologically complex, and centralized is invulnerable to terrorism, sabotage, or war, and that it is protectable by "national defense."

XI. We now have a clear, inescapable choice that we must make. We can continue to promote a global economic system of unlimited "free trade" among corporations, held together by long and highly vulnerable lines of communication and supply, but now recognizing that such a system will have to be protected by a hugely expensive police force that will be worldwide, whether maintained by one nation or several or all, and that such a police force will be effective precisely to the extent that it oversways the freedom and privacy of the citizens of every nation.

XII. Or we can promote a decentralized world economy which would have the aim of assuring to every nation and region a local self-sufficiency in life-supporting goods. This would not eliminate international trade, but it would tend toward a trade in surpluses after local needs had been met.

XIII. One of the gravest dangers to us now, second only to further terrorist attacks against our people, is that we will attempt to go on as before with the corporate program of global "free trade," whatever the cost in freedom and civil rights, without self-questioning or self-criticism or public debate.

XIV. This is why the substitution of rhetoric for thought, always a temptation in a national crisis, must be resisted by officials and citizens alike. It is hard for ordinary citizens to know what is actually happening in Washington in a time of such great trouble; for all we know, serious and difficult thought may be taking place there. But the talk that we are hearing from politicians, bureaucrats, and commentators has so far tended to reduce the complex problems now facing us to issues of unity, security, normality, and retaliation.

XV. National self-righteousness, like personal self-righteousness, is a mistake. It is 15 misleading. It is a sign of weakness. Any war that we may make now against terrorism will come as a new installment in a history of war in which we have fully participated. We are not innocent of making war against civilian populations. The modern doctrine of such warfare was set forth and enacted by General William Tecumseh Sherman, who held that a civilian population could be declared guilty and rightly subjected to military punishment. We have never repudiated that doctrine.

XVI. It is a mistake also—as events since September 11 have shown—to suppose that a government can promote and participate in a global economy and at the same time act exclusively in its own interest by abrogating its international treaties and standing apart from international cooperation on moral issues.

XVII. And surely, in our country, under our Constitution, it is a fundamental error to suppose that any crisis or emergency can justify any form of political oppression. Since September 11, far too many public voices have presumed to "speak for us" in saying that Americans will gladly accept a reduction of freedom in exchange for greater "security." Some would, maybe. But some others would accept a reduction in security (and in global trade) far more willingly than they would accept any abridgement of our Constitutional rights.

XVIII. In a time such as this, when we have been seriously and most cruelly hurt by those who hate us, and when we must consider ourselves to be gravely threatened by those same people, it is hard to speak of the ways of peace and to remember that Christ enjoined us to love our enemies, but this is no less necessary for being difficult.

XIX. Even now we dare not forget that since the attack of Pearl Harbor—to which the present attack has been often and not usefully compared—we humans have suffered an almost uninterrupted sequence of wars, none of which has brought peace or made us more peaceable.

20   XX. The aim and result of war necessarily is not peace but victory, and any victory won by violence necessarily justifies the violence that won it and leads to further violence. If we are serious about innovation, must we not conclude that we need something new to replace our perpetual "war to end war"?

XXI. What leads to peace is not violence but peaceableness, which is not passivity, but an alert, informed, practiced, and active state of being. We should recognize that while we have extravagantly subsidized the means of war, we have almost totally neglected the ways of peaceableness. We have, for example, several national military academies, but not one peace academy. We have ignored the teachings and the examples of Christ, Gandhi, Martin Luther King, and other peaceable leaders. And here we have an inescapable duty to notice also that war is profitable, whereas the means of peaceableness, being cheap or free, make no money.

XXII. The key to peaceableness is continuous practice. It is wrong to suppose that we can exploit and impoverish the poorer countries, while arming them and instructing them in the newest means of war, and then reasonably expect them to be peaceable.

CONTEXT: IMAGES OF ARABS AND ISLAM
This paragraph may be the most provocative of the essay because Berry challenges his readers to try to understand America's enemies and to resist ridiculing those enemies, such as in this image. After September 11, 2001, anger toward Arabs intensified in the United States, and reports of anti-Arab bias increased. But some advocacy groups pointed out that negative images of Arabs had been common in the American media for many years. Consider how American attitudes toward Arab peoples and toward Islam after September 11, 2001 might affect readers' responses to this passage. Do you think Berry meant to provoke readers with this passage?

XXIII. We must not again allow public emotion or the public media to caricature our enemies. If our enemies are now to be some nations of Islam, then we should undertake to know those enemies. Our schools should begin to teach the histories, cultures, arts, and language of the Islamic nations. And our leaders should have the humility and the wisdom to ask the reasons some of those people have for hating us.

XXIV. Starting with the economies of food and farming, we should promote at home, and encourage abroad, the ideal of local self-sufficiency. We should recognize that this is the surest, the safest, and the cheapest way for the world to live. We should not countenance the loss or destruction of any local capacity to produce necessary goods.

25   XXV. We should reconsider and renew and extend our efforts to protect the natural foundations of the human economy: soil, water, and air. We should protect every intact ecosystem and watershed that we have left, and begin restoration of those that have been damaged.

XXVI. The complexity of our present trouble suggests as never before that we need to change our present concept of education. Education is not properly an industry, and its proper use is not to serve industries, either by job-training or by industry-subsidized research. Its proper use is to enable citizens to live lives that are economically, politically, socially, and culturally responsible. This cannot be done by gathering or "accessing" what we now call "information"—which is to say facts without context and therefore without priority. A proper education enables young people to put their lives in order, which means knowing what things are more important than other things; it means putting first things first.

XXVII. The first thing we must begin to teach our children (and learn ourselves) is that we cannot spend and consume endlessly. We have got to learn to save and conserve. We do need a "new economy," but one that is founded on thrift and care, on saving and conserving, not on excess and waste. An economy based on waste is inherently and hopelessly violent, and war is its inevitable by-product. We need a peaceable economy.

UNDERSTANDING THE TEXT

1. What was the state of the world before September 11, 2001, in Berry's view? What led to the conditions he describes? Do you agree with his description? Why or why not?

2. What is the "inescapable choice" that Americans must now make, according to Berry? Are these the only two available choices facing us? Explain.

3. Berry writes that "the substitution of rhetoric for thought, always a temptation in a national crisis, must be resisted by officials and citizens alike." What does he mean by that statement? What exactly does he think Americans must resist? Why must they resist it?

4. What is the connection between war and the economic policies that Berry criticizes in this essay? How can peace be achieved, in his view? How feasible do you think Berry's proposals for achieving peace are?

5. What is the role of education in bringing about the changes that Berry advocates? Do you think education can achieve these goals? Explain.

EXPLORING THE ISSUES

1. Based on this essay, how would you describe Berry's political views? What do you think Berry's view of government is? How does he view the power of governments and the power of citizens? Refer to specific passages in your answer.

2. Notice how Berry organizes his essay. Instead of using conventional paragraphs with indentations, he uses Roman numerals for each paragraph. Why do you think he organized his essay in this way? What do you think he accomplishes by organizing the essay as he did rather

than using more conventional means?

3. Berry charges that Americans have an uncritical view of science and technology. Do you agree? Explain. Do you think most Americans would share his criticisms of science and technology? Why or why not?

4. In paragraph 5, Berry asserts that "we citizens of the industrial countries must continue the labor of self-criticism and self-correction. We must recognize our mistakes." Why does Berry believe this labor of self-criticism and self-correction is necessary? To what extent do you think Berry's essay is part of this self-criticism and self-correction? In what ways might the American political process come into play in this labor? Do you think most Americans would agree with Berry about the need for such self-criticism and self-correction? Do you? Why or why not?

5. This essay first appeared in *Orion* magazine, which promotes an environmentalist perspective and reflects a progressive view of social and political issues. It is unlikely that Berry would moderate his voice for a particular audience, but it is also likely that readers of *Orion* would be a sympathetic audience for his essay. How do you think Berry's voice might be received by a more general audience, such as readers of widely circulated publications like *USA Today* or *Newsweek*?

ENTERING THE CONVERSATIONS

1. Write an essay for a general audience, such as readers of your local newspaper or a regional publication, in which you offer your own views about what happened on September 11, 2001. In your essay, try to address the role of government and the workings of power as you discuss those events and their impact.

Alternatively, create a video, web site, PowerPoint presentation, or some other kind of document in which you present your view of the state of the society or the world after September 11, 2001.

2. Berry concludes his essay by describing the steps that he believes we must take to address "the complexity of our present trouble" (paragraphs 24–27). Write an essay in which you offer your own views of what we should do to address the social, political, and environmental problems that Berry describes in this essay.

INFOTRAC

3. In paragraph 23, Berry refers to American attitudes toward Arabs and Islam (see *Context: Images of Arabs and Islam* on page 426). Using InfoTrac College Edition, your library, and any other relevant resources, investigate American attitudes toward Arabs and toward Islam. You might focus your investigation on the popular media or on some other aspect of American society, such as immigration rules or new security measures adopted after September 11, 2001. Look into how Arab people and Islam are portrayed, understood, and treated. You might consider speaking with someone on your campus who might have insight into this issue, such as staff members in your school's office for international students or faculty members who specialize in these issues. Then write a report for your classmates on the basis of your research.

4. Drawing on Berry's essay and any other relevant readings in this book, write an essay in which you discuss what you see as the connections among science, technology, and political power.

THE CONSEQUENCES OF POWER

YOU HAVE PROBABLY HEARD THE SAYING, "POWER CORRUPTS, AND ABSOLUTE POWER CORRUPTS ABSOLUTELY." THAT MAY BE ONE WAY OF DESCRIBING THE CONSEQUENCES OF POWER: THOSE WHO HAVE POWER ARE CORRUPTED BY IT. CERTAINLY, THERE ARE ABUNDANT EXAMPLES OF POLITICAL LEADERS OR RULERS WHO SEEM TO HAVE BEEN CORRUPTED BY THE POWER THEY WIELDED.

The obvious recent example is Saddam Hussein, who ruled Iraq for three decades with often brutal force and whose abuses of power were horrifying. But maybe even more horrifying is the famous Stanford Prison Experiment, conducted in 1971 by psychology professor Philip Zimbardo. In an effort to study the psychology of prison life, Zimbardo recruited twenty-four young male college students as volunteers, half of whom were assigned to be "guards" and half "inmates." The volunteers were to live for two weeks in campus offices that were altered to resemble a prison. But Zimbardo and his research team had to stop the experiment after only six days because the mock prison began to function like a real one. Volunteers who served as guards quickly became authoritarian and abusive, and a few even displayed

> The most frightening aspect of this famous experiment was how quickly average young men adapted to roles in which they exercised power over other people.

sadistic behaviors; many of the inmates suffered severe stress and emotional trauma. The most frightening aspect of this famous experiment was how quickly average young men adapted to roles in which they exercised power over other people. Although none of the volunteers had any experience in law enforcement or corrections, and although they were not given any specific instructions about how to run the "prison," the guards almost immediately began to develop strategies and techniques to gain complete psycho-

logical and physical control over the inmates. They devised methods that are widely used in real prisons: stripping prisoners naked; making them use numbers instead of names; requiring prisoners to wear degrading identical uniforms; taking away the prisoners' ability to make even the most basic decisions, such as going to the bathroom; and confining prisoners to small, isolated rooms. Zimbardo's experiment has been used to explain the behavior of Nazi soldiers and prison guards in World War II and other situations in which ordinary people participated in unspeakable abuses against other human beings. His experiment may be the most compelling evidence that power does indeed corrupt.

Thankfully, few of us ever have to experience the consequences of power in such dramatic and horrible ways. Yet even if the consequences of power are more subtle, they are often no less serious. The readings in this cluster can help us appreciate the subtleties of power. All of these readings address obvious and sometimes disturbing consequences of power. Wole Soyinka, for example, writes about the political oppression by dictators or by other groups, but his real message has to do with the power of the idea of human rights. As these writers reveal, the consequences of power can reach much farther than we might realize.

These readings also help us identify some of the different kinds of power to which we may be subject. Physical force, police authority, military force—these kinds of power can be easy to see. But there are other, less visible kinds of power: the power of fear, the power of identity (or the loss of it), the power of an idea like freedom, the power of hatred. The consequences of these kinds of power may be much more difficult to appreciate, but perhaps they are even more important for us to examine.

A celebrated author of poetry, fiction, essays, and criticism, Paula Gunn Allen (b. 1939), who is of Laguna Pueblo, Sioux, Lebanese, and Scottish descent, has focused much of her writing on what it means to be a Native American, and especially a Native American woman. Often, in composition textbooks like the one you are reading, Allen's writing is included in chapters on identity or culture, and it would have made sense to put the following essay in Chapter 5: Identity, in

Where I Come From Is Like This

which case you might be inclined to read it as an exploration of her identity as a woman and a Native American. But there's another way to read this essay: as an examination of the consequences of power in terms of gender and culture. Allen describes how attitudes about Native Americans in general and Native American women in particular are related to the dominance of White mainstream culture in the United States. As someone who was a "half-breed," as she describes herself, Allen experienced both Native American and mainstream American White culture and was deeply shaped by both. In describing the identity of woman in Native American cultures and in comparing that identity to the way women are understood in mainstream White culture, Allen helps us see that power is assigned to different genders in different ways. She also helps us see that the consequences of power are different from one culture to another. As you read her essay, think about how the ideas we have about men and women can affect the roles that men and women have and therefore help determine the power they can hold. Reading Allen's essay in this way may complicate your own ideas about what it means to be a man or a woman in your culture and community.   (continued)

PAULA GUNN ALLEN

I

Modern American Indian women, like their non-Indian sisters, are deeply engaged in the struggle to redefine themselves. In their struggle they must reconcile traditional tribal definitions of women with industrial and postindustrial non-Indian definitions. Yet while these definitions seem to be more or less mutually exclusive, Indian women must somehow harmonize and integrate both in their own lives.

An American Indian woman is primarily defined by her tribal identity. In her eyes, her destiny is necessarily that of her people, and her sense of herself as a woman is first and foremost prescribed by her tribe. The definitions of woman's roles are as diverse as tribal cultures in the Americas. In some she is devalued, in others she wields considerable power. In some she is a familial/clan adjunct, in some she is as close to autonomous as her economic circumstances and psychological traits permit. But in no tribal definitions is she perceived in the same way as are women in western industrial and postindustrial cultures.

(continued) *Born in New Mexico, Paula Gunn Allen is a distinguished critic who has helped secure an important place for Native American literature in American literary scholarship. She has taught at many universities, including the University of California at Berkeley and the University of California at Los Angeles, before retiring from UCLA in 1999. Among her many novels, books of poetry, and collections of essays are* The Woman Who Owned the Shadows *(1983) and* The Sacred Hoop: Recovering the Feminine in American Indian Traditions *(1986), in which the following essay first appeared.* ◩

In the west, few images of women form part of the cultural mythos, and these are largely sexually charged. Among Christians, the madonna is the female prototype, and she is portrayed as essentially passive: her contribution is simply that of birthing. Little else is attributed to her and she certainly possesses few of the characteristics that are attributed to mythic figures among Indian tribes. This image is countered (rather than balanced) by the witch-goddess/whore characteristics designed to reinforce cultural beliefs about women, as well as western adversarial and dualistic perceptions of reality.

The tribes see women variously, but they do not question the power of femininity. Sometimes they see women as fearful, sometimes peaceful, sometimes omnipotent and omniscient, but they never portray women as mindless, helpless, simple, or oppressed. And while the women in a given tribe, clan, or band may be all these things, the individual woman is provided with a variety of images of women from the interconnected supernatural, natural, and social worlds she lives in.

5   As a half-breed American Indian woman, I cast about in my mind for negative images of Indian women, and I find none that are directed to Indian women alone. The negative images I do have are of Indians in general and in fact are more often of males than of females. All these images come to me from non-Indian sources, and they are always balanced by a positive image. My ideas of womanhood, passed on largely by my mother and grandmothers, Laguna Pueblo women, are about practicality, strength, reasonableness, intelligence, wit, and competence. I also remember vividly the women who came to my father's store, the women who held me and sang to me, the women at Feast Day, at Grab Days, the women in the kitchen of my Cubero home, the women I grew up with; none of them appeared weak or helpless, none of them presented herself tentatively. I remember a certain reserve on those lovely brown faces; I remember the direct gaze of eyes framed by bright-colored shawls draped over their heads and cascading down their backs. I remember the clean cotton dresses and carefully pressed hand-embroidered aprons they always wore; I remember laughter and good food, especially the sweet bread and the oven bread they gave us. Nowhere in my mind is there a foolish woman, a dumb woman, a vain woman, or a plastic woman, though the Indian women I have known have shown a wide range of personal style and demeanor.

My memory includes the Navajo woman who was badly beaten by her Sioux husband; but I also remember that my grandmother abandoned her Sioux husband long ago. I recall the stories about the Laguna woman beaten regularly by her husband in the presence of her children so that the children would not believe in the strength and power of femininity. And I remember the women who drank, who got into fights with other women and with the men, and who often won those battles. I have memories of tired women, partying women, stubborn

VISUAL CONNECTIONS: THE MADONNA
Allen asserts that images of women in Western culture are "sexually charged," and she describes the Madonna in Christian traditions as "essentially passive." This famous image of the Madonna and child was painted in the fifteenth century by Italian artist Raphael. Do you think such an image conveys the messages that Allen suggests? And how does the pop star Madonna draw on attitudes about women in Western culture to make her own statements about women in contemporary society?

Raphael, *Virgin and Child*, ca. 1511

Madonna Performing, 1990

women, sullen women, amicable women, selfish women, shy women, and aggressive women. Most of all I remember the women who laugh and scold and sit uncomplaining in the long sun on feast days and who cook wonderful food on wood stoves, in beehive mud ovens, and over open fires outdoors.

Among the images of women that come to me from various tribes as well as my own are White Buffalo Woman, who came to the Lakota long ago and brought them the religion of the Sacred Pipe which they still practice; Tinotzin the goddess who came to Juan Diego to remind him that she still walked the hills of her people and sent him with her message, her demand, and her proof to the Catholic bishop in the city nearby. And from Laguna I take the images of Yellow Woman, Coyote Woman, Grandmother Spider (Spider Old Woman), who brought the light, who gave us weaving and medicine, who gave us life. Among the Keres she is known as Thought Woman who created us all and who keeps us in creation even now. I remember Iyatiku, Earth Woman, Corn Woman, who guides and counsels the people to peace and who welcomes us home when we cast off this coil of flesh as huskers cast off the leaves that wrap the corn. I remember Iyatiku's sister, Sun Woman, who held metals and cattle, pigs and sheep, highways and engines and so many things in her bundle, who went away to the east saying that one day she would return.

II

Since the coming of the Anglo-Europeans beginning in the fifteenth century, the fragile web of identity that long held tribal people secure has gradually been weakened and torn. But the oral tradition has prevented the complete destruction of the web, the ultimate disruption of tribal ways. The oral tradition is vital; it heals itself and the tribal web by adapting to the flow of the present while never relinquishing its connection to the past. Its adaptability has always been required, as many generations have experienced. Certainly the modern American Indian woman bears slight resemblance to her forebears—at least on superficial examination—but she is still a tribal woman in her deepest being. Her tribal sense of relationship to all that is continues to flourish. And though she is at times beset by her knowledge of the enormous gap between the life she lives and the life she was raised to live, and while she adapts her mind and being to the circumstances of her present life, she does so in tribal ways, mending the tears in the web of being from which she takes her existence as she goes.

My mother told me stories all the time, though I often did not recognize them as that. My mother told me stories about cooking and childbearing; she told me stories about menstruation and pregnancy; she told me stories about gods and heroes, about fairies and elves, about goddesses and spirits; she told me stories about the land and the sky, about cats and dogs, about snakes and spiders; she told me stories about climbing trees and exploring the mesas; she told me stories about going to dances and getting married; she told me stories about dressing and undressing, about sleeping and waking; she told me stories about herself, about her mother, about her grandmother. She told me stories about grieving and laughing, about thinking and doing; she told me stories about school and about people; about darning and mending; she told me stories about turquoise and about gold; she told me European stories and Laguna stories; she told me Catholic stories and Presbyterian stories; she told me city stories and country stories; she told me political stories and religious stories. She told me stories about living and stories about dying. And in all of those stories she told me who I was, who I was supposed to be, whom I came from, and who would follow me. In this way she taught me the meaning of the words she said, that all life is a circle and everything has a place within it. That's what she said and what she showed me in the things she did and the way she lives.

> STRATEGIES: RHYTHM AND REPETITION
> Allen's writing in paragraph 9 is characterized by the repetition of words, phrases, and sentence structure, creating a certain rhythm that differs from other paragraphs in this essay. Writers sometimes use repetition in this way to call attention to an idea or to evoke a certain feeling. What might Allen accomplish through the use of repetition in this paragraph? What do you think she is conveying to her readers through this repetition?

Of course, through my formal, white, Christian education, I discovered that other 10
people had stories of their own—about women, about Indians, about fact, about reality—and I was amazed by a number of startling suppositions that others made about tribal customs and beliefs. According to the un-Indian, non-Indian view, for instance, Indians barred menstruating women from ceremonies and indeed segregated them from the rest of the people, consigning them to some space specially designed for them. This showed that Indians considered menstruating women unclean and not fit to enjoy the company of decent (nonmenstruating) people, that is, men. I was surprised and confused to hear this because my mother had taught me that white people had strange attitudes toward menstruation: they thought something was bad about it, that it meant you were sick, cursed, sinful, and weak and that you had to be very careful during that time. She taught me that menstruation was a normal occurrence, that I could go swimming or hiking or whatever else I wanted to do during my period. She actively scorned women who took to their beds, who were incapacitated by cramps, who "got the blues."

As I struggled to reconcile these very contradictory interpretations of American Indians' traditional beliefs concerning menstruation, I realized that the menstrual taboos were about power, not about sin or filth. My conclusion was later borne out by some tribes' own explanations, which, as you may well imagine, came as quite a relief to me.

The truth of the matter as many Indians see it is that women who are at the peak of their fecundity are believed to possess power that throws male power totally out of kilter. They emit such force that, in their presence, any male-owned or -dominated ritual or sacred object cannot do its usual task. For instance, the Lakota say that a menstruating woman anywhere near a yuwipi man, who is a special sort of psychic, spirit-empowered healer, for a day or so before he is to do his ceremony will effectively disempower him. Conversely, among many if not most tribes, important ceremonies cannot be held without the presence of women. Sometimes the ritual woman who empowers the ceremony must be unmarried and virginal so that the power she channels is unalloyed, unweakend by sexual arousal and penetration by a male. Other ceremonies require tumescent women, others the presence of mature women who have borne children, and still others depend for empowerment on post-menopausal women. Women may be segregated from the company of the whole band or village on certain occasions, but on certain occasions men are also segregated. In short, each ritual depends on a certain balance of power, and the positions of women within the phases of womanhood are used by tribal people to empower certain rites. This does not derive from a male-dominant view; it is not a ritual observance imposed on women by men. It derives from a tribal view of reality that distinguishes tribal people from feudal and industrial people.

CONVERSATIONS: THE WEAKER SEX

In this passage, Allen contrasts the power of Native American women with the characterization of women in White culture as the "weaker sex." Notice that Allen places that phrase in quotation marks. Consider why she did so. It is obvious that attitudes toward women and their roles in mainstream American culture were changing when Allen wrote this essay in 1986, but in much of her other writing, she has criticized the feminist movement in the United States for what she believes is its rejection of tradition, something that Native Americans don't do, according to Allen. In this regard, Allen is part of a much larger conversation in American society about the roles of women in general and about the relationship between mainstream American culture and other cultures, such as Native American cultures, that make up American society. You might read this essay as part of Allen's ongoing effort to challenge the way Americans view Native Americans and women.

Among the tribes, the occult power of women, inextricably bound to our hormonal life, is thought to be very great; many hold that we possess innately the blood-given power to kill—with a glance, with a step, or with a judicious mixing of menstrual blood into somebody's soup. Medicine women among the Pomo of California cannot practice until they are sufficiently mature; when they are immature, their power is diffuse and is likely to interfere with their practice until time and experience have it under control. So women of the tribes are not especially inclined to see themselves as poor helpless victims of male domination. Even in those tribes where something akin to male domination was present, women are perceived as powerful, socially, physically, and metaphysically. In times past, as in times present, women carried enormous burdens with aplomb. We were far indeed from the "weaker sex," the designation that white aristocratic sisters unhappily earned for us all.

I remember my mother moving furniture all over the house when she wanted it changed. She didn't wait for my father to come home and help—she just went ahead and moved the piano, a huge upright from the old days, the couch, the refrigerator. Nobody had told her she was too weak to do such things. In imitation of her, I would delight in loading trucks at my father's store with cases of pop or fifty-pound sacks of flour. Even when I was quite small I could do it, and it gave me a belief in my own physical strength that advancing middle age can't quite erase. My mother used to tell me about the Acoma Pueblo women she had seen as a child carrying huge ollas (water pots) on their heads as they wound their way up the tortuous stairwell carved into the face of the "Sky City" mesa, a feat I tried to imitate with books and tin buckets. ("Sky City" is the term used by the Chamber of Commerce for the mother village of Acoma, which is situated atop a high sandstone table mountain.) I was never very successful, but even the attempt reminded me that I was supposed to be strong and balanced to be a proper girl.

Of course, my mother's Laguna people are Keres Indian, reputed to be the last extreme mother-right people on earth. So it is no wonder that I got notably nonwhite notions about the natural strength and prowess of women. Indeed, it is only when I am trying to get non-Indian approval, recognition, or acknowledgement that my "weak sister" emotional and intellectual ploys get the better of my tribal woman's good sense. At such times I forget that I just moved the piano or just wrote a competent paper or just completed a financial transaction satisfactorily or have supported myself and my children for most of my adult life.

Nor is my contradictory behavior atypical. Most Indian women I know are in the same bicultural bind: we vacillate between being dependent and strong, self-reliant and powerless, strongly motivated and hopelessly insecure. We resolve the dilemma in various ways: some of us party all the time; some of us drink to excess; some of us travel and move around a lot; some of us land good jobs and then quit them; some of us engage in violent exchanges; some of us blow our brains out. We act in these destructive ways because we suffer from the societal conflicts caused by having to identify with two hopelessly opposed cultural definitions of women. Through this destructive dissonance we are unhappy prey to the self-disparagement common to, indeed demanded of, Indians living in the United States today. Our situation is caused by the exigencies of a history of invasion, conquest, and colonization whose searing marks are probably ineradicable. A popular bumper sticker on many Indian cars proclaims: "If You're Indian You're In," to which I always find myself adding under my breath, "Trouble."

III

No Indian can grow to any age without being informed that her people were "savages" who interfered with the march of progress pursued by respectable, loving, civilized white people. We are the villains of the scenario when we are mentioned at all. We are absent from much of white history except when we are calmly, rationally, succinctly, and systematically dehumanized. On the few occasions we are noticed in any way other than as howling, bloodthirsty beings, we are acclaimed for our noble quaintness. In this definition, we are exotic curios. Our ancient arts and customs are used to draw tourist money to state coffers, into the pocketbooks and bank accounts of scholars, and into support of the American-in-Disneyland promoters' dream.

As a Roman Catholic child I was treated to bloody tales of how the savage Indians martyred the hapless priests and missionaries who went among them in an attempt to lead them to the one true path. By the time I was through high school I had the idea that Indians were people who had benefited mightily from the advanced knowledge and superior morality of the Anglo-Europeans. At least I had, perforce, that idea to lay beside the other one that derived from my daily experience of Indian life, an idea less dehumanizing and more accurate because it came from my mother and the other Indian people who raised me. That idea was that Indians are a people who don't tell lies, who care for their children and their old people. You never see an Indian orphan, they said. You always know when you're old that someone will take care of you—one of your children will. Then they'd list the old folks who were being taken care of by this child or that. No child is ever considered illegitimate among the Indians, they said. If a girl gets pregnant, the baby is still part of the family, and the mother is too. That's what they said, and they showed me real people who lived according to those principles.

Of course the ravages of colonization have taken their toll; there are orphans in Indian country now, and abandoned, brutalized old folks; there are even illegitimate children, though the very concept still strikes me as absurd. There are battered children and neglected children, and there are battered wives and women who have been raped by Indian men. Proximity to the "civilizing" effects of white Christians has not improved the moral quality of life in Indian country, though each group, Indian and white, explains the situation differently. Nor is there much yet in the oral tradition that can enable us to adapt to these inhuman changes. But a force is growing in that direction, and it is helping Indian women reclaim their lives. Their power, their sense of direction and of self will soon be visible. It is the force of the women who speak and work and write, and it is formidable.

20   Through all the centuries of war and death and cultural and psychic destruction have endured the women who raise the children and tend the fires, who pass along the tales and the traditions, who weep and bury the dead, who are the dead, and who never forget. There are always the women, who make pots and weave baskets, who fashion clothes and cheer their children on at powwow, who make fry bread and piki bread, and corn soup and chili stew, who dance and sing and remember and hold within their hearts the dream of their ancient peoples—that one day the woman who thinks will speak to us again, and everywhere there will be peace. Meanwhile we tell the stories and write the books and trade tales of anger and woe and stories of fun and scandal and laugh over all manner of things that happen every day. We watch and we wait.

My great-grandmother told my mother: never forget you are Indian. And my mother told me the same thing. This, then, is how I have gone about remembering, so that my children will remember too.

UNDERSTANDING THE TEXT

1. In what ways are women in Native American cultures powerful? What characteristics are associated with women? What might the power of women in Native American cultures suggest about gender roles in those cultures?

2. What role does the oral tradition of Native American cultures play, according to Allen? Why is this tradition important? What do you think this oral tradition suggests about the role of women in Native American cultures and the power they hold?

3. In what sense are the taboos about menstruation that Allen discusses in paragraphs 10–12 about power, as she puts it? What does this example suggest about the power of men and women in Native American and White cultures? What might it suggest about the nature of power in different cultures?

4. Allen describes the "bicultural bind" that Native American women find themselves in (par. 16). What is the nature of this bind? What is the source of this bind, according to Allen? How does it affect the lives of Native American women?

EXPLORING THE ISSUES

1. Allen spends much time in this essay describing Native American women. What do these descriptions communicate about Native American women as a whole? What do they suggest about the relative position of women in Native American cultures? What do they suggest about the power Native American women have within their cultures?

2. Allen has a mixed ancestry that includes Native American, Lebanese, and Scottish blood. She writes of the consequences of this mixed heritage, but she seems to identify herself as Native American. In para-

graph 17, for example, she refers to Native Americans as "we," and throughout her essay, she seems to set herself apart from Whites, or "Anglo-Europeans." Given what you know about Allen and given what she tells you about herself in this essay, why do you think she identifies with her Native American ancestry and not so obviously with any of the other cultures in her ancestry? Does knowing that she is of mixed ancestry affect the way you respond to her arguments in this essay? Explain. What might your answer to that question suggest about your own attitudes regarding ancestry and culture?

3. Near the end of her essay, Allen writes forcefully about the need for Native American women to tell their stories and write their tales. How does Allen understand the role of story and of writing in the power that Native American women possess? To what extent do you think Allen's essay is itself a reflection of that power? How successfully do you think she accomplishes the goal of "remembering" that she refers to in the final paragraph of her essay?

4. How would you describe Allen's voice in this essay? How effectively do you think her voice helps convey her main ideas about Native American women and power? Refer to specific passages to support your answer.

ENTERING THE CONVERSATIONS

1. Write an essay in which you discuss power as it relates to your gender and/or your cultural identity.

2. Allen describes her own contradictory behavior as a woman and explains this behavior as a result of the "bicultural bind" that Native American women find themselves in. Write an essay about a situation or specific event in which you found

yourself facing contradictory expectations or pressures as a result of your gender, race, ethnicity, culture, religion, or national origin. In your essay, explain the specific nature of your bicultural bind and how it has affected you. Also try to convey a sense of how power might have played a role in your situation.

3. Many popular films over the years have focused on Native American culture, sometimes provoking protest from Native Americans who believe that the films misrepresent their culture and insult them. Among these films are *Dances with Wolves* (1990) and *The Missing* (2003). Select one or more of these films or other appropriate films that portray Native American culture and analyze the messages they convey about Native American culture, especially about Native American women. Pay special attention to the power—or lack of it— that Native American women are portrayed to have in these films. Then write an essay discussing your analysis, drawing conclusions about what these films might suggest about mainstream American attitudes toward Native American culture.

4. Interview several women you know about their own views of their power as women. If possible, try to interview women of different ages and life situations, and ask them about their lives so that they might describe experiences that reveal something about their views of themselves as women. Then write a report for your classmates on the basis of your interviews. In your report, try to draw conclusions about power as it relates to women on the basis of what you learned through your interviews.

5. Write a biographical essay about a powerful woman you know.

Wole Soyinka's life can teach us a great deal *about the consequences of power. Born in Nigeria in 1934, Soyinka began his distinguished career as a playwright and novelist shortly after attending University College at Ibadan, Nigeria, from 1952 to 1954 and the University of Leeds in England from 1954 to 1957. His first play,* The Swamp Dwellers, *was produced in 1958, and since then, he has written and produced dozens of plays in addition to writing novels and*

Every Dictator's Nightmare

books of poetry. His plays, which include satiric comedies and explore serious political and philosophical themes, attracted much critical attention. But he also attracted the attention of political leaders. In 1967, during the Nigerian civil war, he was arrested on conspiracy charges and imprisoned for nearly two years. Thirty years later, he was charged with treason by the military dictatorship then ruling Nigeria. There is little question that Soyinka's plays and other writings posed a challenge to those holding power in Nigeria. Dance in the Forest *(1960), for example, criticized the corruption of African rulers in nations, like Nigeria, that had recently won their independence from European colonial powers. His nonfiction book* The Open Sore of a Continent: A Personal Narrative of the Nigerian Crisis *(1996) is a pointed attack on Nigeria's military rulers. Shortly after its publication, the Nigerian government sentenced him to death, though he was living abroad in self-imposed exile at the time. Perhaps his many awards, including the Nobel Prize for Literature, which he won in 1986, make him an even greater threat to those in power because these awards testify that his voice is heard by so many.*
(continued)

WOLE SOYINKA

With the blood-soaked banner of religious fanaticism billowing across the skies as one prominent legacy of this millennium, **Martin Luther's famous theses** against religious absolutism struck me early as a strong candidate for the best idea of the last thousand years. By progressive association, so did the microprocessor and its implications—the liberalization of access to knowledge, and a quantum boost for the transmission of ideas. There is, however, a nobler idea that has spread by its own power in this millennium and that has now begun to flourish: the idea that certain fundamental rights are inherent to all humanity.

Humankind has always struggled to assert certain values in their own right, values that the individual intuitively felt belonged to each person as part of natural existence. It is difficult to imagine a period when such values were not pursued in spasmodic acts of dissent from norms that appeared to govern society even in its most rudimentary form. Even after years of conformity to hallowed precedents, a few dissidents always arise, and they obtain their primary impulse in crucial instances from the individual's seizure of his or her subjective worth.

In the devolution of authority to one individual as the head of a col-

WOLE SOYINKA, "EVERY DICTATOR'S NIGHTMARE." FROM *THE NEW YORK TIMES,* APRIL 18, 1999.

(continued) *In the following essay, which was first published in the* New York Times *in 1999, Soyinka argues that the idea that all human beings have fundamental rights is the greatest challenge to the power of rulers like those who have imprisoned and threatened him. In Soyinka's view, this idea about basic human rights has its own power, a power that can work against the worst consequences of political and military power.* ◥

CONTEXT: THIS MILLENNIUM
This essay was published in 1999, a time when the world was anticipating the end of the second millennium—that is, the second thousand years of recorded human history in Western civilization—and looking toward the beginning of a new one. Soyinka's reference to "this millennium" at the start of his essay suggests that he, too, was taking part in these many conversations related to "Y2K," which provoked both hopefulness and fear among many people. Consider how that historical context influences Soyinka's main argument and whether his argument has less force or validity today.

GLOSS: MARTIN LUTHER'S THESES
In 1517, Martin Luther famously nailed his Ninety-Five Theses to the door of the church in Wittenberg, Germany, an event usually cited as the spark for the religious movement known as the Reformation. Luther's theses criticized the doctrines of the Catholic Church that essentially gave the pope absolute power to determine religious doctrine and practice; the Reformation resulted in the formation of the Protestant churches.

lective, a system of checks on arbitrary authority is prevalent. Take, for instance, monarchical rule among the Yoruba, the people now concentrated in western Nigeria. At the apex is a quasi-deified personage, endowed with supreme authority over his subjects. To preserve the mystic aura of such a ruler, he is never seen to eat or drink. In earlier times, he was not permitted to speak directly to his people but had to employ an intermediary voice, a spokesman. For the highest-ranked kings in the Yoruban world, the *ekeji orisa* (companions to the deities), it was forbidden even to see their faces. Despite the social and psychological distance between the leader and his subjects, the monarch was pledged to rule within a strict contract of authority. Transgression of a taboo, say, or failure to fulfill ceremonial duties on time, resulted in fines, rituals of appeasement or a period of ostracism. The major crime, however, was abuse of power, excessive authoritarianism and a trampling on the rights of the citizenry. For this category of crimes, there was only one response: the king, on being found guilty, was given a covered calabash and invited to retreat to his inner chambers. He understood the sentence: he must never again be seen among the living.

Sometimes, of course, an individual manages to convert collective authority into a personal monopoly. In these instances, society is characterized by tensions, palpable or hidden, between the suppressed rights of the people and the power rapacity of one individual. But where does society ground its claims, its resistant will, in such circumstances? We know that rebellion may be triggered by recollections of more equitable relationships, by material expropriation or by a cultural transgression that affects the spiritual well-being of the community or individual. Such rebellion finds its authority in the belief, in one citizen after another, that the ruler has violated a fundamental condition of human existence.

The *droit du seigneur*, the "right" that confers on the lord the pleasure of deflowering, on her marriage night, the bride of any of his vassals—on what does the ritually cuckolded groom finally ground his rebellion other than a subjective sense of self-worth? What of the Yoruban monarch who, even today in certain parts of my world, tries to exercise his "right" to *gbese le*—that is, to place his royal slipper, symbolically, on any woman who catches his fancy, and thus assign her to his harem? The manor lord's entitlement to compulsory labor from his peasants, the ownership of another being as a slave, the new age of enslavement of womanhood in countries like Afghanistan—the challenges to these and other so-called rights surely commence with the interrogation of self-worth, expanding progressively toward an examination of the common worth of the human entity as a unit of irreducible properties and rights.

It took centuries for societies to influence one another to the critical extent needed to incite the philosophic mind to address the concept of the human race in general, and not simply as members

of a specific race or occupants of a geographical space. In its rudimentary beginnings, each society remained limited by a process that codified its own now-rec-
ognizable collective interests against all others, like the Magna Carta and the Bill
of Rights. Such oaths of fealty by petty chieftains imposed duties on the suzerain
but also entrenched their own equally arbitrary mechanisms of authority and coercion over the next level of society. This sometimes resulted in the bizarre alliance of the monarch with his lowest vassals against his overreaching barons and
chieftains.

Like race and citizenship, religion was not far behind in the exclusionist philosophy of rights, formulating codes to protect the rights of the faithful but denying the
same to others—the Cross against the Crescent, Buddhist versus Hindu the believer
against the infidel. Or simply religion versus secularism. Ground into powder beneath the hooves of the contending behemoths of religion, ideology and race, each
social unit ponders, at least periodically, how he or she differs from cattle or sheep,
from the horses that pull the carriages of majesty, even when such choices are the
mere expressions of the collective will. If order alone ornamentation, social organization, technology, bonding and even productive structures were all that defined the
human species, then what significant properties marked out Homo sapiens as distinct from the rest of the living species?

CONVERSATIONS: CODIFYING THE HUMAN SPECIES
In this paragraph, Soyinka offers an overview of
philosophical and scientific ideas that influenced
how people understood one another and were often
used to justify giving rights to some people while
denying rights to others. He mentions John Hume,
Immanuel Kant, and Georg Hegel, three of the most
important philosophers in Western culture, whose
treatises often focused on morality, thought, and reason. The Encyclopedists, a school of French philosophers that included Voltaire and Jean Rousseau,
advocated a reliance on *reason,* rather than on logic
or religious belief, to solve the great philosophical
and moral problems facing human beings. Reason, or
rational thought, was used by some to justify slavery.
In a sense, Soyinka is joining an age-old conversation about human nature and morality, and by invoking these famous thinkers, he alerts his readers to
that conversation. But he is also offering his perspective on this conversation, which has always
been marked by intense disagreement. After all, this
is really a conversation about good and evil, about
right and wrong, and about the meaning of human
life. The consequences of this conversation are great,
as Soyinka tries to show in this passage.

Polarizations within various micro-worlds—us versus the inferior them—have long been armed with industrious ratio-
nalizations. Christian and Islamic theologians throughout
history have quarried their scriptures for passages that stress
the incontestable primacy of an unseen and unknowable
Supreme Deity who has conferred authority on them. And to
what end? Largely to divide the world into us and the rest.
The great philosophical minds of Europe, like Hume, Hegel
and Kant, bent their prodigious talents to separating the
species into those with rights and those with none, founded
on the convenient theory that some people were human and
others less so. The Encyclopedists of France, products of the
so-called Age of Reason, remain the most prolific codifiers of
the human (and other) species on an ambitiously comprehensive scale, and their scholarly industry conferred a scientific benediction on a purely commercial project that saw
millions of souls dragged across the ocean to serve as beasts
of burden. Religion and commerce—far older professions
than the one that is sometimes granted that distinction, but
of an often-identical temperament—were reinforced by the
authority of new scientific theories to divide humanity into
higher and lower manifestations of the species. The dichotomy of the world was complete.

It took the near triumph of fascism to bring the world to its senses. The horror of
the Holocaust finally took the rulers of the world back to the original question: what
is the true value of humanity? It is to be doubted if the victorious three meeting in
Yalta actually went into any profound philosophical niceties in the discussions that

resulted in the United Nations, that partial attempt to reverse the dichotomizing course of humanity. That course, taken to its ultimate conclusion, had just resulted in an attempted purification of the species, the systematic elimination of millions in gas chambers and a war that mired the potential of Europe in the blood of its youth. After all, the concept of the master race was not new, but it was never before so obsessively articulated and systematically pursued. It was time to rethink the entire fate of humanity. The conversations at Yalta, conversations that led to the birth of the United Nations, were a partial answer to that question.

The first stage was to render the new thinking in concrete terms, to enshrine in a charter of rights the product of the bruising lessons of the immediate past: the United Nations and the Universal Declaration of Human Rights. The informing recognition is that long-suppressed extract of the intuition that humanity had guarded through evolution, one that had been proposed, compromised, amended, vitiated, subverted but never abandoned: that, for all human beings, there do exist certain fundamental rights.

The idea already exists in the Bible, in the Koran, in the Bhagavad-Gita, in the Upanishads, but always in curtailed form, relativist, patriarchal, always subject to the invisible divine realms whose interpreters are mortals with distinct, secular agendas, usually allied to the very arbitrary controls that are a contradiction to such ideas. Quiet, restrained, ignored by but also blissfully indifferent to the so-called world religions, Ifa, the corpus of Yoruban spiritual precepts and secular philosophy, its origins lost in antiquity but preserved and applied till today, annunciates identical ideas through Orunmila, the god of divination:

> *Dandan enia l'ayan ko mu ire lo s'aye . . . Ipo rere naa ni aye-amotan ohung-bogbo, ayo nnigbagbogbo, igbesi laisi ominu tabi iberu ota.*
>
> Certainly, it is the human being that was elected to bring values to the world . . . and his place of good is the knowledge of all things, joy at all times, freedom from anxiety and freedom from fear of the enemy. [Irosu Wori]

Humanity has been straining to seize the fullness of this doctrine, the right to knowledge, the freedom from anxiety, the right to security of existence as inherent to the species. It is only the process of promulgating its pertinence to all mankind that has been long and costly. The kernel of the idea, therefore, is both timeless and new. Its resurrection—the concrete seizure of the idea within this millennium, answering the exigencies of politics, religion and power and securing it within the bedrock of universality—was a **destiny that would first be embraced by France.**

There, alas, the events that gave new life to this idea did not encourage its adoption on a universal scale, indeed not even durably within France itself. The restoration of slavery by Napoleon was surely the most blatant contradiction of the idea, but this did not much trouble the Emperor.

Still, the idea had taken hold, the idea of the rights of man as a universal principle. It certainly motored the passion of the genuine idealists in the abolition of the

GLOSS: THE VICTORIOUS THREE AT YALTA
Soyinka is referring to the famous 1945 meeting at Yalta in the Crimea (now Ukraine) between President Franklin Delano Roosevelt, British Prime Minister Winston Churchill, and Soviet Premier Josef Stalin, at which these leaders made decisions about what would happen to the defeated nations after World War II. (You might think about that momentous meeting in terms of the consequences of power.)

10

GLOSS: FRANCE AND HUMAN RIGHTS
When Soyinka writes that the resurrection of the idea of human rights "was a destiny that would first be embraced by France," he is referring to the French Revolution of 1788, which many intellectuals at the time believed would free European societies from tyranny and result in greater freedoms for all citizens. As Soyinka suggests in the following paragraph, these hopes were never realized. The revolution was followed by a reign of terror and eventually led to the rise of Napoleon, who became ruler of France.

slave trade, who must always be distinguished from those to whom abolition was simply a shrewd commercial calculation. The idea of the American Declaration of Independence—an idea that still lacks full realization—that "all men are created equal, that they are endowed by their Creator with certain unalienable Rights" is an adumbration of that original idea from which the French Revolution obtained its inspiration, one that has continued to convulse the unjust order of the world wherever it has been grasped: the fundamental rights of man.

15   It is an idea whose suppression is the main occupation of dictatorships—be these military or civilian, of the right or the left, secular or theocratic. It is, however, their nightmare, their single province of terror, one that they cannot exorcise, not even through the most unconscionable pogroms, scorched-earth campaigns and crimes against humanity. It is an idea that has transformed the lives of billions and remains poised to liberate billions more, since it is an idea that will not settle for tokenism or for relativism—it implicitly links the liberation of one to the liberation of all. Its gospel of universalism is anchored in the most affective impulse that cynics attribute to the choices made by humanity, self-love, but one that now translates humanity as one's own self.

UNDERSTANDING THE TEXT

1. What is the role of dissent in a society, in Soyinka's view? What motivates dissent? Is this a good thing, as Soyinka sees it? Do you agree with him? Why or why not?

2. Where does the idea of human rights come from, according to Soyinka?

3. According to Soyinka, what are the causes of rebellion? Why are these causes important, in his view? What do they tell us about the nature of human rights and political power?

4. What does Soyinka mean when he writes that the kernel of the idea of fundamental human rights is "both timeless and new" (par. 12)? Do you think he's right? Why or why not?

5. In what sense is the idea of human rights the nightmare of dictatorships?

EXPLORING THE ISSUES

1. When he was awarded the Nobel Prize for Literature in 1986, Soyinka's writing was described by the Nobel Prize Committee as "marked by great scope and richness of words." Do you agree with that description of Soyinka's writing style? Explain, citing specific passages to support your answer. How effective do you find his writing style?

2. In paragraph 11, Soyinka states that the idea of fundamental rights for all human beings already existed in the Bible, the Koran, the Bhagavad-Gita, and the Upanishads, the world's great religious writings before it was written into the United Nations' Universal Declaration of Human Rights in the twentieth century. If so, why did this idea not become more widely accepted? How does Soyinka explain this? Do you think he's right? What might this argument suggest about Soyinka's view of religion?

3. In paragraph 14, Soyinka asserts that the idea of the American Declaration of Independence "still lacks full realization." What do you think he means? Do you agree with him? Explain.

ENTERING THE CONVERSATIONS

1. Write an essay in which you present your view of human rights.

2. Write an essay in which you respond to Soyinka's assertion that the idea of the American Declaration of Independence "still lacks full realization."

3. There are dozens of nongovernmental organizations that advocate and work for human rights, such as Amnesty International and Human Rights Watch, which publish reports about the state of human rights in the world. Visit the web sites of several of these organizations and find out what you can about their efforts. Find out what these organizations are saying about the state of human rights today. Then write an essay in which you report on your findings. Try to draw conclusions about the current status of the idea of human rights, as Soyinka defines it in his essay, and discuss what you think this status suggests about whether this idea is indeed a dictator's nightmare, as Soyinka asserts. Also discuss what your findings might suggest about the consequences of power. Alternatively, create a web site in which you present your findings.

 INFOTRAC

4. Since the Patriot Act was passed by the U.S. Congress following the terrorist attacks of September 11, 2001, many critics have charged that the U.S. government is violating its citizens' civil rights in its efforts to combat terrorism; some critics have even charged that the United States has violated basic human rights. Using InfoTrac College Edition, your library, and any other appropriate resources, investigate the Patriot Act and the debates surrounding it. What are the provisions of the Patriot Act? Why was it enacted? What are the main criticisms of it? How do its supporters answer those criticisms? What have been the implications of the act since it was passed? Try to find answers to such questions through your research. Write a letter to your representative to the U.S. Congress or to your U.S. senator in which you express your support for or your concerns about the Patriot Act and the current state of civil rights in the United States. Alternatively, write a conventional research paper reporting your findings.

If laughter is the best medicine, as the old saying goes, then perhaps it's also one of the inevitable consequences of power. Whenever we look closely at government, we seem to find things to laugh about, and we use humor to criticize the foibles of those in power and those who oppose them. Such political humor has a long tradition in American culture. Some of the most revered writers in American literary history were famous in their day for their political satire, most notably Mark Twain. You

Bill OF Rights Pared Down TO A *Manageable* Six

can get a sense of his brand of political humor in some sections of his best-known novel, The Adventures of Huckleberry Finn, in which minor characters serve as vehicles for Twain's biting criticisms of political officials. Today, the stand-up monologue, in which a comedian pokes fun at current political figures, is a standard part of the acts of popular television comedians like David Letterman and Jay Leno.

The following article, taken from the satiric publication The Onion, is a different kind of humor from the conventional humor of comics like Letterman and Leno. Unlike those comics, The Onion relies on satire and irony of a kind that is less common today. But what lies beneath the barbs and tongue-in-cheek lines are serious ideas about what is wrong with the way power is used in the United States today. Perhaps it takes this kind of off-beat but unflinching humor to make us more aware of the consequences of power.

The following article appeared in The Onion, which has become a well-known publication for political satire, in December 2002. ▼

THE ONION

Washington, DC

Flanked by key members of Congress and his administration, President Bush approved Monday a streamlined version of the Bill of Rights that pares its 10 original amendments down to a "tight, no-nonsense" six.

A Republican initiative that went unopposed by congressional Democrats, the revised Bill of Rights provides citizens with a "more manageable" set of privacy and due-process rights by eliminating four amendments and condensing and/or restructuring five others. The Second Amendment, which protects the right to keep and bear arms, was the only article left unchanged.

Calling the historic reduction "a victory for America," Bush promised that the new document would do away with "bureaucratic impediments to the flourishing of democracy at home and abroad."

"It is high time we reaffirmed our commitment to this enduring symbol of American ideals," Bush said. "By making the Bill of Rights a tool for progress instead of a hindrance to freedom, we honor the true spirit of our nation's forefathers."

The Fourth Amendment, which long protected citizens' homes against unreasonable search and seizure, was among the eliminated amendments. Also stricken was the Ninth Amendment, which stated that the enumeration of certain Constitutional rights does not result in the abrogation of rights not mentioned.

"Quite honestly, I could never get my head around what the Ninth Amendment meant anyway," said

As Supporters Look on, Bush Signs the Bill of Rights Reduction and Consolidation Act

outgoing House Majority Leader Dick Armey (R-TX), one of the leading advocates of the revised Bill of Rights. "So goodbye to that one."

Amendments V through VII, which guaranteed the right to legal counsel in criminal cases, and guarded against double jeopardy, testifying against oneself, biased juries, and drawn-out trials, have been condensed into Super-Amendment V: The One About Trials.

Attorney General John Ashcroft hailed the slimmed-down Bill of Rights as "a positive step."

"Go up to the average citizen and ask them what's in the Bill of Rights," Ashcroft said. "Chances are, they'll have only a vague notion. They just know it's a set of rules put in place to protect their individual freedoms from government intrusion, and they assume that's a good thing."

Ashcroft responded sharply to critics who charge that the Bill of Rights no longer safeguards certain basic, inalienable rights.

"We're not taking away personal rights; we're increasing personal *security*," Ashcroft said. "By allowing for greater government control over the particulars of individual liberties, the Bill of Rights will now offer expanded personal freedoms whenever they are deemed appropriate and unobtrusive to the activities necessary to effective operation of the federal government."

Ashcroft added that, thanks to several key additions, the Bill of Rights now offers protections that

Bush Works on Revisions to the Bill of Rights

Consider how the photograph at the bottom of page 445, which seems to show President Bush "editing" the Bill of Rights, conveys its humor. What specific elements of this image might make it humorous? What knowledge must readers have to understand the humor in the image? You might compare this use of a photograph to other uses of visual elements in political satire, such as television's popular *The Daily Show,* in which comedians satirize current political events by posing as "real" journalists. To what extent might *The Onion* and *The Daily Show* use visual elements in similar ways in their satire? What are the differences in their uses of visual humor?

CONTEXT: THE FOURTH AMENDMENT
The statement attributed to Attorney General John Ashcroft in paragraph 16 relates to a serious point that has been made by supporters of tougher measures to fight terrorism. The original text of the Fourth Amendment reads, "The right of the people to be secure in their persons, houses, papers, and effects, against unreasonable searches and seizures, shall not be violated, and no Warrants shall issue, but upon probable cause, supported by Oath or affirmation, and particularly describing the place to be searched, and the persons or things to be seized." Some law enforcement and antiterrorism experts argue that these restrictions hamper their efforts to protect the nation against terrorism and that the protections guaranteed by the Fourth Amendment must sometimes be limited so that efforts to fight terrorism can be effective. Civil liberties advocates disagree, arguing that limiting these protections opens the door to abuses of power by the police and other law enforcement agencies. You might consider how this context gives force to the humor of this article. Consider, too, the extent to which this kind of satire can actually contribute to serious discussions about government power and individual rights.

were previously lacking, including the right to be protected by soldiers quartered in one's home (Amendment III), the guarantee that activities not specifically delegated to the states and people will be carried out by the federal government (Amendment VI), and freedom of Judeo-Christianity and non-combative speech (Amendment I).

According to U.S. Sen. Larry Craig (R-ID), the original Bill of Rights, though well-intentioned, was "seriously outdated."

"The United States is a different place than it was back in 1791," Craig said. "As visionary as they were, the framers of the Constitution never could have foreseen, for example, that our government would one day need to jail someone indefinitely without judicial review. There was no such thing as suspicious Middle Eastern immigrants back then."

15   Ashcroft noted that recent FBI efforts to conduct investigations into "unusual activities" were severely hampered by the old Fourth Amendment.

"The Bill of Rights was written more than 200 years ago, long before anyone could even fathom the existence of wiretapping technology or surveillance cameras," Ashcroft said. "Yet through a bizarre fluke, it was still somehow worded in such a way as to restrict use of these devices. Clearly, it had to go before it could do more serious damage in the future."

The president agreed.

"Any machine, no matter how well-built, periodically needs a tune-up to keep it in good working order," Bush said. "Now that we have the bugs worked out of the ol' Constitution, she'll be purring like a kitten when Congress reconvenes in January—just in time to work on a new round of counterterrorism legislation."

"Ten was just too much of a handful," Bush added. "Six civil liberties are more than enough."

UNDERSTANDING THE TEXT

1. According to this article, what justification is offered for revising the Bill of Rights? What legitimate criticisms, if any, do you think the authors of this article are making of President Bush and members of the U.S. Congress?

2. In what sense might the Bill of Rights be a "hindrance to freedom"? Do you think there is a serious argument to be made in support of this position? Explain.

3. What do you think this article suggests about the average American and his or her understanding of the U.S. Constitution? Do you think the authors are right about Americans? Why or why not?

4. How does this article portray U.S. political leaders? Do you think this portrait is justified? Explain.

EXPLORING THE ISSUES

1. What must readers know about the Bill of Rights in order to understand the satire in this article? Will the satire "work" for readers who are unfamiliar with the Bill of Rights? Explain.

2. What do you think this article suggests about the consequences of power in U.S. politics?

3. How would you describe the humor of this article? What exactly makes it humorous? Did you find it humorous? Explain, citing specific passages to support your answer. What might your reaction to this article reveal about you as a reader? What might it reveal about your political views?

4. This article is intended to mimic the conventional journalistic style of writing that you would see in regular newspapers. What specific features of the writing in this article characterize that journalistic style? How effectively do you think the authors of this article used journalistic conventions? How much do you think the success of this article as satire depends on that journalistic writing style?

5. How important do you think the photographs included with this article are? How much do they contribute to the effectiveness of the article's satire?

ENTERING THE CONVERSATIONS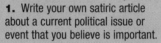

1. Write your own satiric article about a current political issue or event that you believe is important.

2. In a group of classmates, share the articles you wrote for Question 1. Identify any common satiric strategies that you and your classmates used to convey your criticisms in your articles. Discuss those criticisms and how effectively they are conveyed through satire. Try to draw conclusions about the use of satire to convey a serious message about power and politics.

3. Watch several episodes of *The Daily Show* or another television show that includes political satire. (Many television shows that are not necessarily political satires sometimes include political satire, like *The Simpsons*.) Or listen to a radio show that includes political satire. What issues do these shows tend to focus on? How do they convey their points about politics and government? Then write an essay for an audience of your classmates in which you report on what you found. In your essay, describe the shows you watched or listened to and discuss the political messages they send. Draw conclusions about satire as a medium for discussion of serious issues. Alternatively, write a script for your own political satire for television or radio.

4. Find several political cartoons from newspapers or magazines and analyze them for the messages they convey. Then write an essay in which you present your analysis. Include in your essay the cartoons you selected and discuss the messages each cartoon conveys. Try to explain how the cartoonists use satire to convey a serious point. Alternatively, create your own political cartoon that conveys a point about the consequences of power in contemporary American political life.

CHALLENGING POWER

A FEW YEARS AGO, ON A TYPICAL SCHOOL DAY IN DECEMBER, STUDENTS AT MY LOCAL HIGH SCHOOL HAD A KIND OF REBELLION. AT A DESIGNATED TIME DURING A REGULAR MORNING CLASS PERIOD, ABOUT THREE DOZEN STUDENTS GOT UP FROM THEIR SEATS, WALKED OUT OF THEIR CLASSROOMS, AND GATHERED AT THE FRONT OF THE SCHOOL BUILDING. THERE THEY MADE A STATEMENT VOICING

their concerns about a proposal to implement a new "block" schedule, in which the traditional school day would be restructured from seven 45-minute class periods to four 75-minute class periods. This proposal had been brought before the school board several months earlier and had been discussed at various meetings between parents and school officials. The students, however, felt that the decision to adopt the new block schedule had already been made and that the public meetings were held to give the illusion that school officials were accepting input from the community. The students wanted their voices to be heard. So they walked out of class and stood together at the school entrance to declare their protest before school officials appeared, along with local police, to inform them that they were suspended from school for violating school safety policies.

This incident is one small example of a challenge to power. The students had genuine concerns that they believed were ignored by school officials, even though school officials were following standard procedure in implementing a policy change. They believed that those in power had already made up their minds and would do what they wanted regardless of the strong opposition to the proposal. In fact, polls showed that a majority of teachers at the school opposed the proposal, and many parents did, too. So the students decided that they had to step outside the rules to challenge those in power.

Those students were acting in a very American way. In many respects, American history is the story of people who were willing to challenge power. Indeed, the country was founded when the American colonists challenged the greatest military power on earth at the time, Great Britain. Like

the students at my local high school, the colonists believed that their British rulers were not acting in the colonists' best interests, and the only way to change that was to challenge those rulers. I'm not sure that the students who walked out of my local high school thought of themselves as revolutionaries, but in an important way, they were. They were doing what so many Americans and so many people around the world have done for centuries: challenging power to right a wrong or to claim something that is rightfully theirs.

The following essays explore what it means to challenge power. They explore the complexities and consequences of the decision to resist, to break laws that seem unjust, and to challenge ways of thinking about or treating people who are different.

It is an appropriate time to think about challenging power. Recent events, such as the terrorist attacks on September 11, 2001, and the war in Iraq, have led to controversial decisions by the U.S. government that many critics believe amount to abuses of power. During this time, we have seen numerous protests and new strategies for challenging power, such as the use of the Internet and new kinds of grass-roots organizing. But all these developments share something basic with the protest by the students at my high school: They all grow out of a need to change something by challenging those in power. To challenge power in this way may be a very American thing to do, but it is neither easy nor simple. I hope the essays in this cluster will help you appreciate that. I also hope they will help you appreciate the usefulness of writing as a way to challenge power.

When I began working on this section, Amy, my colleague who helped put together this book, confessed that she was having trouble with the following essay by famed American writer Henry David Thoreau (1817–1862). Although she had read the essay before and found its argument provocative, she complained that this time she found herself slogging through the essay. The problem, she said, was that Thoreau's writing is often difficult to follow, which makes his complex argument

Resistance to *Civil* Government

that much harder to understand. She joked that she needed a translator to help her.

My guess is that you may have similar complaints about this famous essay, which was first published in 1849. And it's worth wondering why. This is one of the most widely reprinted and influential essays ever written. Its message still resonates with people today. It shows up in countless textbooks, and it has become part of the canon of American literature as well as of international discussions of human rights. Important figures like Martin Luther King, Jr. and Mahatma Gandhi have acknowledged that it deeply affected their own thinking about power, justice, and change. Why, then, is it so difficult for so many readers today?

I'll let you answer that question for yourself, but keep in mind that any text is a reflection of its time. Some of the features of Thoreau's writing style that you may find difficult were common in his day. Also, every writer makes assumptions about what his or her readers know, and what Thoreau could assume about his readers in 1849 may not apply today. So part of the challenge in reading a text like this one is placing it in historical context so that its references make sense. It may take a bit more effort for readers today to appreciate Thoreau's complex arguments.   (continued)

HENRY DAVID THOREAU

I **HEARTILY ACCEPT the motto,—"That government is best** which governs least"; and I should like to see it acted up to more rapidly and systematically. Carried out, it finally amounts to this, which also I believe,—"That government is best which governs not at all"; and when men are prepared for it, that will be the kind of government which they will have. Government is at best but an expedient; but most governments are usually, and all governments are sometimes, inexpedient. The objections which have been brought against a standing army, and they are many and weighty, and deserve to prevail, may also at last be brought against a standing government. The standing army is only an arm of the standing government. The government itself, which is only the mode which the people have chosen to execute their will, is equally liable to be abused and perverted before the people can act through it. Witness the present Mexican war, the work of comparatively a few individuals using the standing government as their tool; for, in the outset, the people would not have consented to this measure.

This American government—what is it but a tradition, though a recent one, endeavoring to transmit itself unimpaired to posterity, but each instant losing some of its integrity? It has not the vitality and force of a single living man; for a single man can bend it to his will. It

HENRY DAVID THOREAU, "RESISTANCE TO CIVIL GOVERNMENT" (1849).

(continued) *Most important, though, is considering what it is about this essay that has made it such an important piece of writing. Many people believe it to be a fundamental statement about the relationship between government and its citizens, and it is often cited in discussions about resisting unjust uses of power. Thoreau's argument challenges us to examine our individual responsibilities when it comes to government power, and this challenge may be especially important today, an era when the power of some governments, including the United States, extends beyond anything Thoreau could have imagined in 1849. There is little question that Thoreau's message is still relevant today. In that sense, his essay is still part of the important conversations that we are always having about how to live together and how to understand power.* ◤

CONTEXT: A STANDING ARMY AND THE
MEXICAN WAR

For American readers today, the idea of a "standing army"—that is, a military that exists permanently, whether or not there is a war—seems commonsensical. In 1792, a law was passed that gave the U.S. government some authority over local and state militias, but it was not until 1903 that the National Guard was officially formed as an army separate from the state militias. When Thoreau wrote this essay in 1849, a standing army was a controversial idea, partly because there was a long history of European rulers who kept such armies and used them to gain and maintain power rather than to protect citizens. That history made many Americans skeptical about a standing army, which they feared the U.S. government leaders would use for their own purposes. Notice that Thoreau suggests that the United States was doing exactly that by waging war with Mexico at that time, a war that many Americans, including Thoreau, opposed because it was fought to bring Texas into the United States as a slave state. Consider how Thoreau's arguments about government power are shaped by the historical moment when he was writing. Do the political circumstances today make his arguments more or less valid?

is a sort of wooden gun to the people themselves. But it is not the less necessary for this; for the people must have some complicated machinery or other, and hear its din, to satisfy that idea of government which they have. Governments show thus how successfully men can be imposed on, even impose on themselves, for their own advantage. It is excellent, we must all allow. Yet this government never of itself furthered any enterprise, but by the alacrity with which it got out of its way. *It* does not keep the country free. *It* does not settle the West. *It* does not educate. The character inherent in the American people has done all that has been accomplished; and it would have done somewhat more, if the government had not sometimes got in its way. For government is an expedient by which men would fain succeed in letting one another alone; and, as has been said, when it is most expedient, the governed are most let alone by it. Trade and commerce, if they were not made of India rubber, would never manage to bounce over the obstacles which legislators are continually putting in their way; and, if one were to judge these men wholly by the effects of their actions, and not partly by their intentions, they would deserve to be classed and punished with those mischievous persons who put obstructions on the railroads.

But, to speak practically and as a citizen, unlike those who call themselves no-government men, I ask for, not at once no government, but *at once* a better government. Let every man make known what kind of government would command his respect, and that will be one step toward obtaining it.

After all, the practical reason why, when the power is once in the hands of the people, a majority are permitted, and for a long period continue, to rule, is not because they are most likely to be in the right, nor because this seems fairest to the minority, but because they are physically the strongest. But a government in which the **majority rule** in all cases cannot be based on justice, even as far as men understand it. Can there not be a government in which majorities do not virtually decide right and wrong, but conscience?—in which majorities decide only those questions to which the rule of expediency is applicable? Must the citizen ever for a moment, or in the least degree, resign his conscience to the legislator? Why has every man a conscience, then? I think that we should be men first, and subjects afterward. It is not desirable to cultivate a respect for the law, so much as for the right. The only obligation which I have a right to assume is to do at any time what I think right. It is truly enough said that a corporation has no conscience; but a corporation of conscientious men is a corporation *with* a conscience. Law never made men a whit more just; and, by means of their respect for it, even the well-disposed are daily made the agents of injustice. A common and natural result of an undue respect for law is, that you may see a file of soldiers, colonel, captain, corporal, privates, powder-monkeys, and all, marching in admirable order over hill and dale to the wars, against their wills, ay, against their common sense and consciences, which makes it very steep marching indeed, and produces a palpitation of the heart. They have no doubt that it is a damnable business in which they are concerned; they are all peaceably inclined. Now, what are they? Men at all? or small movable forts and magazines, at the service of some unscrupulous man in power? Visit the Navy Yard, and behold a marine, such a man as an American government can make, or such as it can make a man with its black arts—a mere shadow and reminiscence of humanity, a man laid out alive and standing, and already, as one may say, buried under arms with funeral accompaniments, though it may be

> "**Not a drum was heard,** not a funeral note,
> As his corse to the rampart we hurried;
> Not a soldier discharged his farewell shot
> O'er the grave where our hero we buried."

The mass of men serve the state thus, not as men mainly, but as machines, with their bodies. They are the standing army, and the militia, jailers, constables, *posse comitatus,* etc. In most cases there is no free exercise whatever of the judgment or of the moral sense; but they put themselves on a level with wood and earth and stones; and wooden men can perhaps be manufactured that will serve the purpose as well. Such command no more respect than men of straw or a lump of dirt. They have the same sort of worth only as horses and dogs. Yet such as these even are commonly esteemed good citizens. Others, as most legislators, politicians, lawyers, ministers, and office-holders, serve the state chiefly with their heads; and, as they rarely make any moral distinctions, they are as likely to serve the devil, without *intending* it, as God. A very few, as heroes, patriots, martyrs, reformers in the great sense, and *men,* serve the state with their consciences also, and so necessarily resist it for the most part; and they are commonly treated as enemies by it. A wise man will only be useful as a man, and will not submit to be "clay," and "stop a hole to keep the wind away," but leave that office to his dust at least:—

> "**I am too high-born to be propertied,**
> To be a secondary at control,
> Or useful serving-man and instrument
> To any sovereign state throughout the world."

He who gives himself entirely to his fellow-men appears to them useless and selfish; but he who gives himself partially to them is pronounced a benefactor and philanthropist.

How does it become a man to behave toward this American government to-day? I answer, that he cannot without disgrace be associated with it. I cannot for an instant recognize that political organization as *my* government which is the *slave's* government also.

All men recognize the right of revolution; that is, the right to refuse allegiance to, and to resist, the government, when its tyranny or its inefficiency are great and

---

CONVERSATIONS: MAJORITY RULE
In this paragraph (par. 4), Thoreau writes that "a government in which the majority rule in all cases cannot be based on justice." Compare Thoreau's ideas about majority rule and justice to those of Lani Guinier, whose essay appears on page 412 in this chapter. Guinier wrote her essay almost 150 years after Thoreau wrote his, yet the basic issue they address is the same. What might that say about how societies work out problems related to power?

GLOSS: "NOT A DRUM WAS HEARD"
Thoreau is quoting here (par. 4) from "The Burial of Sir John Moore at Corunna," a poem by Charles Wolfe (1791–1823) describing the burial of British General John Moore, who was killed after defeating French forces at Corunna, Spain, in 1809. Consider how Thoreau uses this quotation to make his point about men who serve the state as soldiers.

GLOSS: "I AM TOO HIGH-BORN TO BE PROPERTIED"
This quotation is from Shakespeare's *King John.*

unendurable. But almost all say that such is not the case now. But such was the case, they think, in the Revolution of '75. If one were to tell me that this was a bad government because it taxed certain foreign commodities brought to its ports, it is most probable that I should not make an ado about it, for I can do without them. All machines have their friction; and possibly this does enough good to counterbalance the evil. At any rate, it is a great evil to make a stir about it. But when the friction comes to have its machine, and oppression and robbery are organized, I say, let us not have such a machine any longer. In other words, when a sixth of the population of a nation which has undertaken to be the refuge of liberty are slaves, and **a whole country is unjustly overrun** and conquered by a foreign army, and subjected to military law, I think that it is not too soon for honest men to rebel and revolutionize. What makes this duty the more urgent is the fact that the country so overrun is not our own, but ours is the invading army.

GLOSS: A WHOLE COUNTRY IS UNJUSTLY OVERRUN
The country unjustly overrun is a reference to Mexico, overrun by American military forces.

Paley, a common authority with many on moral questions, in his chapter on the "Duty of Submission to Civil Government," resolves all civil obligation into expediency; and he proceeds to say that "so long as the interest of the whole society requires it, that is, so long as the established government cannot be resisted or changed without public inconveniency, it is the will of God that the established government be obeyed, and no longer"—"This principle being admitted, the justice of every particular case of resistance is reduced to a computation of the quantity of the danger and grievance on the one side, and of the probability and expense of redressing it on the other." Of this, he says, every man shall judge for himself. But Paley appears never to have contemplated those cases to which the rule of expediency does not apply, in which a people, as well as an individual, must do justice, cost what it may. If I have unjustly wrested a plank from a drowning man, I must restore it to him though I drown myself. This, according to Paley, would be inconvenient. But he that would save his life, in such a case, shall lose it. This people must cease to hold slaves, and to make war on Mexico, though it cost them their existence as a people.

10   In their practice, nations agree with Paley; but does any one think that Massachusetts does exactly what is right at the present crisis?

GLOSSES
PALEY
William Paley (1743–1805) was an influential British philosopher and theologian in the eighteenth century. Notice how Thoreau uses ideas from Paley's *Principles of Moral and Political Philosophy* (1785) to justify resistance to government.

"A DRAB OF STATE"
This quotation is taken from a play believed to have been written by Cyril Tourneur (1575–1626) called *The Revenger's Tragedy* (1607). Thoreau seems to use the reference to further his criticism of the laws of Massachusetts regarding slavery.

"A drab of state, a cloth-o'-silver slut,
To have her train borne up, and her soul trail in the dirt."

Practically speaking, the opponents to a reform in Massachusetts are not a hundred thousand politicians at the South, but a hundred thousand merchants and farmers here, who are more interested in commerce and agriculture than they are in humanity, and are not prepared to do justice to the slave and to Mexico, *cost what it may.* I quarrel not with far-off foes, but with those who, near at home, co-operate with, and do the bidding of those far away, and without whom the latter would be harmless. We are accustomed to say, that the mass of men are unprepared; but improvement is slow, because the few are not materially wiser or better than the many. It is not so important that many should be as good as you, as that there be some absolute goodness somewhere; for that will leaven the whole lump. There are thousands who are *in opinion* opposed to slavery and to the war, who yet in effect do nothing to put an end to them; who, esteeming themselves children of Washington and Franklin, sit down with their hands in their pockets, and say that they know not what to do, and do nothing; who even postpone the question of freedom to the question of free-trade, and quietly read the prices-current along with the latest advices from Mexico, after dinner, and, it may be, fall asleep over them both. What is the price-current of an honest man and patriot to-day? They hesitate, and they regret, and sometimes they petition; but they do nothing in earnest and with effect. They will wait, well disposed, for others to remedy the evil, that they may no longer have it to regret. At most, they give only a cheap vote, and a feeble countenance and Godspeed, to the right, as it goes by them. There are nine hundred and ninety-nine patrons of virtue to one virtuous man; but it is easier to deal with the real possessor of a thing than with the temporary guardian of it.

All voting is a sort of gaming, like checkers or backgammon, with a slight moral tinge to it, a playing with right and wrong, with moral questions; and betting naturally accompanies it. The character of the voters is not staked. I cast my vote, perchance, as I think right; but I am not vitally concerned that that right should prevail. I am willing to leave it to the majority. Its obligation, therefore, never exceeds that of expediency. Even voting *for the right* is *doing* nothing for it. It is only expressing to men feebly your desire that it should prevail. A wise man will not leave the right to the mercy of chance, nor wish it to prevail through the power of the majority. There is but little virtue in the action of masses of men. When the majority shall at length vote for the abolition of slavery, it will be because they are indifferent to slavery, or because there is but little slavery left to be abolished by their vote. *They* will then be the only slaves. Only *his* vote can hasten the abolition of slavery who asserts his own freedom by his vote.

I hear of a convention to be held at Baltimore, or elsewhere, for the selection of a candidate for the Presidency, made up chiefly of editors, and men who are politicians by profession; but I think, what is it to any independent, intelligent, and respectable man what decision they may come to? Shall we not have the advantage of his wisdom and honesty, nevertheless? Can we not count upon some independent votes? Are there not many individuals in the country who do not attend conventions? But no: I find that the respectable man, so called, has immediately drifted from his position, and despairs of his country, when his country has more reason to despair of him. He forthwith adopts one of the candidates thus selected as the only *available* one, thus proving that he is himself *available* for any purposes of the demagogue. His vote is of no more worth than that of any unprincipled foreigner or hireling native, who may have been bought. Oh for a man who is a *man*, and, as my neighbor says, has a bone in his back which you cannot pass your hand through! Our statistics are at fault: the population has been returned too large. How many *men* are there to a square thousand miles in this country? Hardly one. Does not America offer any inducement for men to settle here? The American has dwindled into an Odd Fellow—one who may be known by the development of his organ of gregariousness, and a manifest lack of intellect and cheerful self-reliance; whose first and chief concern, on coming into the world, is to see that the almshouses are in good repair; and, before yet he has lawfully donned the virile garb, to collect a fund for the support of the widows and orphans that may be; who, in short ventures to live only by the aid of the Mutual Insurance company, which has promised to bury him decently.

It is not a man's duty, as a matter of course, to devote himself to the eradication of any, even the most enormous wrong; he may still properly have other concerns to engage him; but it is his duty, at least, to wash his hands of it, and, if he gives it no thought longer, not to give it practically his support. If I devote myself to other pursuits and contemplations, I must first see, at least, that I do not pursue them sitting upon another man's shoulders. I must get off him first, that he may pursue his contemplations too. See what gross inconsistency is tolerated. I have heard some of my townsmen say, "I should like to have them order me out to help put down an insurrection of the slaves, or to march to Mexico;—see if I would go"; and yet these very men have each, directly by their allegiance, and so indirectly, at least, by their money, **furnished a substitute.** The soldier is applauded who refuses to serve in an unjust war by those who do not refuse to sustain the unjust government which makes the war; is applauded by those whose own act and authority he disregards and sets at naught; as if the state were penitent to that degree that it hired one to scourge it while it sinned, but not to that degree that it left off sinning for a moment. Thus, under the name of Order and Civil Government, we are all made at last to pay homage to and support our own meanness. After the first blush of sin comes its indifference; and from immoral it becomes, as it were, *un*moral, and not quite unnecessary to that life which we have made.

The broadest and most prevalent error requires the most disinterested virtue to sustain it. The slight reproach to which the virtue of patriotism is commonly liable, the noble are most likely to incur. Those who, while they disapprove of the character and measures of a government, yield to it their allegiance and support are undoubtedly its most conscientious supporters, and so frequently the most serious obstacles to reform. Some are petitioning the State to dissolve the Union, to disregard the requisitions of the President. Why do they not dissolve it themselves—the union between themselves and the State—and refuse to pay their quota into its treasury? Do not they stand in the same relation to the State, that the State does to the Union? And have not the same reasons prevented the State from resisting the Union, which have prevented them from resisting the State?

15   How can a man be satisfied to entertain an opinion merely, and enjoy *it?* Is there any enjoyment in it, if his opinion is that he is aggrieved? If you are cheated out of a single dollar by your neighbor, you do not rest satisfied with knowing that you are cheated, or with saying that you are cheated, or even with petitioning him to pay you your due; but you take effectual steps at once to obtain the full amount, and see that you are never cheated again. Action from principle—the perception and the performance of right—changes things and relations; it is essentially revolutionary, and does

not consist wholly with anything which was. It not only divides states and churches, it divides families; ay, it divides the *individual,* separating the diabolical in him from the divine.

Unjust laws exist; shall we be content to obey them, or shall we endeavor to amend them, and obey them until we have succeeded, or shall we transgress them at once? Men generally, under such a government as this, think that they ought to wait until they have persuaded the majority to alter them. They think that, if they should resist, the remedy would be worse than the evil. But it is the fault of the government itself that the remedy *is* worse than the evil. *It* makes it worse. Why is it not more apt to anticipate and provide for reform? Why does it not cherish its wise minority? Why does it cry and resist before it is hurt? Why does it not encourage its citizens to be on the alert to point out its faults, and *do* better than it would have them? Why does it always crucify Christ, and excommunicate Copernicus and Luther, and pronounce Washington and Franklin rebels?

One would think, that a deliberate and practical denial of its authority was the only offence never contemplated by government; else, why has it not assigned its definite, its suitable and proportionate, penalty? If a man who has no property refuses but once to earn nine shillings for the State, he is put in prison for a period unlimited by any law that I know, and determined only by the discretion of those who placed him there; but if he should steal ninety times nine shillings from the State, he is soon permitted to go at large again.

If the injustice is part of the necessary friction of the machine of government, let it go, let it go; perchance it will wear smooth—certainly the machine will wear out. If the injustice has a spring, or a pulley, or a rope, or a crank, exclusively for itself, then perhaps you may consider whether the remedy will not be worse than the evil; but if it is of such a nature that it requires you to be the agent of injustice to another, then, I say, break the law. Let your life be a counter friction to stop the machine. What I have to do is to see, at any rate, that I do not lend myself to the wrong which I condemn.

As for adopting the ways which the State has provided for remedying the evil, I know not of such ways. They take too much time, and a man's life will be gone. I have other affairs to attend to. I came into this world, not chiefly to make this a good place to live in, but to live in it, be it good or bad. A man has not everything to do, but something; and because he cannot do *everything*, it is not necessary that he should do *something* wrong. It is not my business to be petitioning the Governor or the Legislature any more than it is theirs to petition me; and if they should not hear my petition, what should I do then? But in this case the State has provided no way; its very Constitution is the evil. This may seem to be harsh and stubborn and unconciliatory; but it is to treat with the utmost kindness and consideration the only spirit that can appreciate or deserves it. So is a change for the better, like birth and death which convulse the body.

I do not hesitate to say, that those who call themselves Abolitionists should at once effectually withdraw their support, both in person and property, from the government of Massachusetts, and not wait till they constitute a majority of one, before they suffer the right to prevail through them. I think that it is enough if they have God on

CONTEXT: GOVERNMENT WORKERS
In this passage, Thoreau refers to two government employees that he himself knew: Sam Staples, the tax collector in Thoreau's region; and Sam Hoar, a Massachusetts legislator who traveled to South Carolina to protest that state's policy of imprisoning freed slaves. Thoreau argues that "it is . . . with men and not with parchment that I quarrel." In other words, Thoreau holds government employees responsible for government actions. A similar argument was made by Timothy McVeigh, the man who bombed a federal building in Oklahoma City in 1995, and by the terrorists who attacked the World Trade Center and the Pentagon on September 11, 2001. Consider what Thoreau's position here suggests about individual responsibility. How do you think these recent terrorist events might affect the way readers react to Thoreau's argument today?

their side, without waiting for that other one. Moreover, any man more right than his neighbors constitutes a majority of one already.

I meet this American government, or its representative, the State government, directly, and face to face, once a year—no more—in the person of its tax-gatherer; this is the only mode in which a man situated as I am necessarily meets it; and it then says distinctly, Recognize me; and the simplest, the most effectual, and, in the present posture of affairs, the indispensablest mode of treating with it on this head, of expressing your little satisfaction with and love for it, is to deny it then. My civil neighbor, the tax-gatherer, is the very man I have to deal with—for it is, after all, with men and not with parchment that I quarrel—and he has voluntarily chosen to be an agent of the government. How shall he ever know well what he is and does as an officer of the government, or as a man, until he is obliged to consider whether he shall treat me, his neighbor, for whom he has respect, as a neighbor and well-disposed man, or as a maniac and disturber of the peace, and see if he can get over this obstruction to his neighborliness without a ruder and more impetuous thought or speech corresponding with his action? I know this well, that if one thousand, if one hundred, if ten men whom I could name—if ten *honest* men only—ay, if *one* honest man, in this State of Massachusetts, *ceasing to hold slaves,* were actually to withdraw from this copartnership, and be locked up in the county jail therefor, it would be the abolition of slavery in America. For it matters not how small the beginning may seem to be: what is once well done is done forever. But we love better to talk about it: that we say is our mission. Reform keeps many scores of newspapers in its service, but not one man. If my esteemed neighbor, the State's ambassador, who will devote his days to the settlement of the question of human rights in the Council Chamber, instead of being threatened with the prisons of Carolina, were to sit down the prisoner of Massachusetts, that State which is so anxious to foist the sin of slavery upon her sister—though at present she can discover only an act of inhospitality to be the ground of a quarrel with her—the Legislature would not wholly waive the subject the following winter.

Under a government which imprisons any unjustly, the true place for a just man is also a prison. The proper place to-day, the only place which Massachusetts has provided for her freer and less desponding spirits, is in her prisons, to be put out and locked out of the State by her own act, as they have already put themselves out by their principles. It is there that the fugitive slave, and the Mexican prisoner on parole, and the Indian come to plead the wrongs of his race, should find them; on that separate, but more free and honorable ground, where the State places those who are not *with* her, but *against* her—the only house in a slave State in which a free man can abide with honor. If any think that their influence would be lost there, and their voices no longer afflict the ear of the State, that they would not be as an enemy within its walls, they do not know by how much truth is stronger than error, nor how much more eloquently and effectively he can combat injustice who has experienced a little in his own person. Cast your whole vote, not a strip of paper merely, but your whole influence. A minority is powerless while it conforms to the majority; it is not even a minority then; but it is irresistible when it clogs by its whole weight. If the alternative is to keep all just men in prison, or give up war and slavery, the State will not hesitate which to choose. If a thousand men were not to pay their tax-bills this year, that would not be a violent and bloody measure, as it would be to pay them, and enable the State to commit violence and shed innocent blood. This is, in fact, the definition of a peaceable revolution, if any such is possible. If the tax-gatherer, or any other public officer, asks me, as one has done, "But what shall I do?" my answer is, "If you really wish to do anything, resign your office." When the subject has refused allegiance, and the officer has resigned his office, then the revolution is accomplished. But even suppose blood should flow. Is there not a sort of blood shed when the conscience is wounded? Through this wound a man's real manhood and immortality flow out, and he bleeds to an everlasting death. I see this blood flowing now.

I have contemplated the imprisonment of the offender, rather than the seizure of his goods—though both will serve the same purpose—because they who assert the purest right, and consequently are most dangerous to a corrupt State, commonly have not spent much time in accumulating property. To such the State renders comparatively small service, and a slight tax is wont to appear exorbitant, particularly if they are obliged to earn it by special labor with their hands. If there were one who lived wholly without the use of money, the State itself would hesitate to demand it of him. But the rich man—not to make any invidious comparison—is always sold to the institution which makes him rich. Absolutely speaking, the more money, the less virtue; for money comes between a man and his objects, and obtains them for him; and it was certainly no great virtue to obtain it. It puts to rest many questions which he would otherwise be taxed to answer; while the only new question which it puts is the hard but superfluous one, how to spend it. Thus his moral ground is taken from under his feet. The opportunities of living are diminished in proportion as what are called the "means" are increased. The best thing a man can do for his culture when he is rich is to endeavor to carry out those schemes which he entertained when he was poor. Christ answered the Herodians according to their condition. "Show me the tribute-money," said he;—and one took a penny out of his pocket;—if you use money which has the image of Cæsar on it, and which he has made current and valuable, that is, *if you are men of the State,* and gladly enjoy the advantages of Cæsar's government, then pay him back some of his own when he demands it; "Render therefore to Cæsar that which is Cæsar's, and to God those things which are God's"—leaving them no wiser than before as to which was which; for they did not wish to know.

When I converse with the freest of my neighbors, I perceive that, whatever they may say about the magnitude and seriousness of the question, and their regard for the public tranquility, the long and the short of the matter is, that they cannot spare the protection of the existing government, and they dread the consequences to their property and families of disobedience to it. For my own part, I should not like to think that I ever rely on the protection of the State. But, if I deny the authority of the State when it presents its tax-bill, it will soon take and waste all my property, and so harass me and my children without end. This is hard. This makes it impossible for a man to live honestly, and at the same time comfortably in outward respects. It will not be worth the while to accumulate property; that would be sure to go again. You must hire or squat somewhere, and raise but a small crop, and eat that soon. You must live within yourself, and depend upon yourself always tucked up and ready for a start, and not have many affairs. A man may grow rich in Turkey even, if he will be in all respects a good subject of the Turkish government. Confucius said, "If a state is governed by the principles of reason, poverty and misery are subjects of shame; if a state is not governed by the principles of reason, riches and honors are the subjects of shame." No: until I want the protection of Massachusetts to be extended to me in some distant Southern port, where my liberty is endangered, or until I am bent solely on building up an estate at home by peaceful enterprise, I can afford to refuse allegiance to Massachusetts, and her right to my property and life. It costs me less in every sense to incur the penalty of disobedience to the State than it would to obey. I should feel as if I were worth less in that case.

25   Some years ago, the State met me in behalf of the Church, and commanded me to pay a certain sum toward the support of a clergyman whose preaching my father attended, but never I myself. "Pay," it said, "or be locked up in the jail." I declined to pay. But, unfortunately, another man saw fit to pay it. I did not see why the schoolmaster should be taxed to support the priest, and not the priest the schoolmaster: for I was not the State's schoolmaster, but I supported myself by voluntary subscription. I did not see why the lyceum should not present its tax-bill, and have the State to back its demand, as well as the Church. However, at the request of the selectmen, I condescended to make some such statement as this in writing:—"Know all men by these presents, that I, Henry Thoreau, do not wish to be regarded as a member of any incorporated society which I have not joined." This I gave to the town clerk; and he has it. The State, having thus learned that I did not wish to be regarded as a member of that church, has never made a like demand on me since; though it said that it must adhere to its original presumption that time. If I had known how to name them, I should then have signed off in detail from all the societies which I never signed on to; but I did not know where to find a complete list.

GLOSS: POLL TAX
In Thoreau's day, the government did not collect a general income tax, as it does today; rather, taxes were collected for specific purposes. Poll taxes were essentially voting fees.

I have paid no **poll-tax** for six years. I was put into a jail once on this account, for one night; and, as I stood considering the walls of solid stone, two or three feet thick, the door of wood and iron, a foot thick, and the iron grating which strained the light, I could not help being struck with the foolishness of that institution which treated me as if I were mere flesh and blood and bones, to be locked up. I wondered that it should have concluded at length that this was the best use it could put me to, and had never thought to avail itself of my services in some way. I saw that, if there was a wall of stone between me and my townsmen, there was a still more difficult one to climb or break through, before they could get to be as free as I was. I did not for a moment feel confined, and the walls seemed a great waste of stone and mortar. I felt as if I alone of all my townsmen had paid my tax. They plainly did not know how to treat me, but behaved like persons who are underbred. In every threat and in every compliment there was a blunder; for they thought that my chief desire was to stand the other side of that stone wall. I could not but smile to see how industriously they locked the door on my meditations, which followed them out again without let or hindrance, and they were really all that was dangerous. As they could not reach me, they had resolved to punish my body; just as boys, if they cannot come at some person against whom they have a spite, will abuse his dog. I saw that the State was half-witted, that it was timid as a lone woman with her silver spoons, and that it did not know its friends from its foes, and I lost all my remaining respect for it, and pitied it.

Thus the State never intentionally confronts a man's sense, intellectual or moral, but only his body, his senses. It is not armed with superior wit or honesty, but with superior physical strength. I was not born to be forced. I will breathe after my own fashion. Let us see who is the strongest. What force has a multitude? They only can force me who obey a higher law than I. They force me to become like themselves. I do not hear of *men* being *forced* to have this way or that by masses of men. What sort of life were that to live? When I meet a government which says to me, "Your money or your life," why should I be in haste to give it my money? It may be in a great strait, and not know what to do: I cannot help that. It must help itself; do as I do. It is not worth the while to snivel about it. I am not responsible for the successful working of the machinery of society. I am not the son of the engineer. I perceive that, when an acorn and a chestnut fall side by side, the one does not remain inert to make way for the other, but both obey their own laws, and spring and grow and flourish as best they can, till one, perchance, overshadows and destroys the other. If a plant cannot live according to its nature, it dies; and so a man.

The night in prison was novel and interesting enough. The prisoners in their shirt-sleeves were enjoying a chat and the evening air in the doorway, when I entered. But the jailer said, "Come, boys, it is time to lock up"; and so they dispersed, and I heard the sound of their steps returning into the hollow apartments. My room-mate was introduced to me by the jailer as "a first-rate fellow and a clever man." When the door was locked, he showed me where to hang my hat, and how he managed matters there. The rooms were whitewashed once a month; and this one, at least, was the whitest, most simply furnished, and probably the neatest apartment in the town. He naturally wanted to know where I came from, and what brought me there; and, when I had told him, I asked him in my turn how he came there, presuming him to be an honest man, of course; and, as the world goes, I believe he was. "Why," said he, "they accuse me of burning a barn; but I never did it." As near as I could discover, he had probably gone to bed in a barn when drunk, and smoked his pipe there; and so a barn was burnt. He had the reputation of being a clever man, had been there some three months waiting for his trial to come on, and would have to wait as much longer; but he was quite domesticated and contented, since he got his board for nothing, and thought that he was well treated.

He occupied one window, and I the other; and I saw that if one stayed there long, his principal business would be to look out the window. I had soon read all the tracts that were left there, and examined where former prisoners had broken out, and where a grate had been sawed off, and heard the history of the various occupants of that room; for I found that even here there was a history and a gossip which never circulated beyond the walls of the jail. Probably this is the only house in the town where verses are composed, which are afterward printed in a circular form, but not published. I was shown quite a long list of verses which were composed by some young men who had been detected in an attempt to escape, who avenged themselves by singing them.

I pumped my fellow-prisoner as dry as I could, for fear I should never see him again; but at length he showed me which was my bed, and left me to blow out the lamp.

30

It was like travelling into a far country, such as I had never expected to behold, to lie there for one night. It seemed to me that I never had heard the town-clock strike before, nor the evening sounds of the village; for we slept with the windows open, which were inside the grating. It was to see my native village in the light of the Middle Ages, and our Concord was turned into a Rhine stream, and visions of knights and castles passed before me. They were the voices of old burghers that I heard in the streets. I was an involuntary spectator and auditor of whatever was done and said in the kitchen of the adjacent village-inn—a wholly new and rare experience to me. It was a closer view of my native town. I was fairly inside of it. I never had seen its institutions before. This is one of its peculiar institutions; for it is a shire town. I began to comprehend what its inhabitants were about.

STRATEGIES: USING NARRATIVE TO MAKE A POINT
Thoreau devotes several paragraphs to his experiences in jail after he refused to pay a poll tax. If you read this passage carefully, you'll see that Thoreau is doing more than just telling the story of his famous night in jail. Writers sometimes use narrative to help convey their ideas in essays, like this one, that are argumentative or analytical. Consider what Thoreau accomplishes with this brief narrative. What ideas does he convey? How does this narrative support main points that he makes elsewhere in his essay? Notice, too, how Thoreau draws lessons from his experience, which he sums up in paragraph 33.

In the morning, our breakfasts were put through the hole in the door, in small oblong-square tin pans, made to fit, and holding a pint of chocolate, with brown bread, and an iron spoon. When they called for the vessels again, I was green enough to return what bread I had left; but my comrade seized it, and said that I should lay that up for lunch or dinner. Soon after he was let out to work at haying in a neighboring field, whither he went every day, and would not be back till noon; so he bade me good-day, saying that he doubted if he should see me again.

When I came out of prison—for some one interfered, and paid that tax—I did not perceive that great changes had taken place on the common, such as he observed who went in a youth and emerged a tottering and gray-headed man; and yet a change had to my eyes come over the scene—the town, and State, and country—greater than any that mere time could effect. I saw yet more distinctly the State in which I lived. I saw to what extent the people among whom I lived could be trusted as good neighbors and friends; that their friendship was for summer weather only; that they did not greatly propose to do right; that they were a distinct race from me by their prejudices and superstitions, as the Chinamen and Malays are; that in their sacrifices to humanity, they ran no risks, not even to their property; that after all they were not so noble but they treated the thief as he had treated them, and hoped, by a certain outward observance and a few prayers, and by walking in a particular straight though useless path from time to time, to save their souls. This may be to judge my neighbors harshly; for I believe that many of them are not aware that they have such an institution as the jail in their village.

It was formerly the custom in our village, when a poor debtor came out of jail, for his acquaintances to salute him, looking through their fingers, which were crossed to represent the grating of a jail window, "How do ye do?" My neighbors did not thus salute me, but first looked at me, and then at one another, as if I had returned from a long journey. I was put into jail as I was going to the shoemaker's to get a shoe which was mended. When I was let out the next morning, I proceeded to finish my errand, and, having put on my mended shoe, joined a huckleberry party, who were impatient to put themselves under my conduct; and in half an hour—for the horse was soon tackled—was in the midst of a huckleberry field, on one of our highest hills, two miles off, and then the State was nowhere to be seen.

35   This is the whole history of **"My Prisons."**

I have never declined paying the highway tax, because I am as de-
sirous of being a good neighbor as I am of being a bad subject; and
as for supporting schools, I am doing my part to educate my fellow-
countrymen now. It is for no particular item in the tax-bill that I refuse
to pay it. I simply wish to refuse allegiance to the State, to withdraw and stand aloof
from it effectually. I do not care to trace the course of my dollar, if I could, till it buys
a man or a musket to shoot one with—the dollar is innocent—but I am concerned
to trace the effects of my allegiance. In fact, I quietly declare war with the State, after
my fashion, though I will still make what use and get what advantage of her I can, as
is usual in such cases.

If others pay the tax which is demanded of me, from a sympathy with the State,
they do but what they have already done in their own case, or rather they abet injustice to a greater extent than the State requires. If they pay the tax from a mistaken
interest in the individual taxed, to save his property, or prevent his going to jail, it is
because they have not considered wisely how far they let their private feelings interfere with the public good.

This, then, is my position at present. But one cannot be too much on his guard in
such a case, lest his action be biased by obstinacy or an undue regard for the opinions of men. Let him see that he does only what belongs to himself and to the hour.

I think sometimes, Why, this people mean well; they are only ignorant; they would
do better if they knew how: why give your neighbors this pain to treat you as they are
not inclined to? But I think, again, This is no reason why I should do as they do, or
permit others to suffer much greater pain of a different kind. Again, I sometimes say
to myself, When many millions of men, without heat, without ill-will, without personal feeling of any kind, demand of you a few shillings only, without the possibility,
such is their constitution, of retracting or altering their present demand, and without the possibility, on your side, of appeal to any other millions, why expose yourself
to this overwhelming brute force? You do not resist cold and hunger, the winds and
the waves, thus obstinately; you quietly submit to a thousand similar necessities. You
do not put your head into the fire. But just in proportion as I regard this as not
wholly a brute force, but partly a human force, and consider that I have relations to
those millions as to so many millions of men, and not of mere brute or inanimate
things, I see that appeal is possible, first and instantaneously, from them to the Maker
of them, and, secondly, from them to themselves. But, if I put my head deliberately
into the fire, there is no appeal to fire or to the Maker of fire, and I have only myself
to blame. If I could convince myself that I have any right to be satisfied with men as
they are, and to treat them accordingly, and not according, in some respects, to my
requisitions and expectations of what they and I ought to be, then, like a good
Mussulman and fatalist, I should endeavor to be satisfied with things as they are, and
say it is the will of God. And, above all, there is this difference between resisting this
and a purely brute or natural force, that I can resist this with some effect; but I cannot expect, like Orpheus, to change the nature of the rocks and trees and beasts.

40   I do not wish to quarrel with any man or nation. I do not wish to split hairs, to make
fine distinctions, or set myself up as better than my neighbors. I seek rather, I may
say, even an excuse for conforming to the laws of the land. I am but too ready to con-

GLOSS: "MY PRISONS"
**Thoreau is referring to *Le Mie Prigioni* by
Silvio Pellico (1789–1854), an Italian
imprisoned for eight years by his
government.**

GLOSS: "WE MUST AFFECT OUR COUNTRY AS OUR PARENTS"
This quotation is from *Battle of Alcazar* by George Peele, a sixteenth century writer.

form to them. Indeed, I have reason to suspect myself on this head; and each year, as the tax-gatherer comes round, I find myself disposed to review the acts and position of the general and State governments, and the spirit of the people, to discover a pretext for conformity.

> "**We must affect our country as our parents,**
> And if at any time we alienate
> Our love or industry from doing it honor,
> We must respect effects and teach the soul
> Matter of conscience and religion,
> And not desire of rule or benefit."

I believe that the State will soon be able to take all my work of this sort out of my hands, and then I shall be no better a patriot than my fellow-countrymen. Seen from a lower point of view, the Constitution, with all its faults, is very good; the law and the courts are very respectable; even this State and this American government are, in many respects, very admirable and rare things, to be thankful for, such as a great many have described them; but seen from a point of view a little higher, they are what I have described them; seen from a higher still, and the highest, who shall say what they are, or that they are worth looking at or thinking of at all?

However, the government does not concern me much, and I shall bestow the fewest possible thoughts on it. It is not many moments that I live under a government, even in this world. If a man is thought-free, fancy-free, imagination-free, that which is *not* never for a long time appearing *to be* to him, unwise rulers or reformers cannot fatally interrupt him.

I know that most men think differently from myself; but those whose lives are by profession devoted to the study of these or kindred subjects, content me as little as any. Statesmen and legislators, standing so completely within the institution, never distinctly and nakedly behold it. They speak of moving society, but have no resting-place without it. They may be men of a certain experience and discrimination, and have no doubt invented ingenious and even useful systems, for which we sincerely thank them; but all their wit and usefulness lie within certain not very wide limits. They are wont to forget that the world is not governed by policy and expediency. **Webster** never goes behind government, and so cannot speak with authority about it. His words are wisdom to those legislators who contemplate no essential reform in the existing government; but for thinkers, and those who legislate for all time, he never once glances at the subject. I know of those whose serene and wise speculations on this theme would soon reveal the limits of his mind's range and hospitality. Yet, compared with the cheap professions of most reformers, and the still cheaper wisdom and eloquence of politicians in general, his are almost the only sensible and valuable words, and we thank Heaven for him. Comparatively, he is always strong, original, and, above all, practical. Still, his quality is not wisdom, but prudence. The lawyer's truth is not truth, but consistency or a consistent expediency. Truth is always in harmony with herself, and is not concerned chiefly to reveal the justice that may consist with wrong-doing. He well deserves to be called, as he has been called, the Defender of the Constitution. There are really no blows to be given by him but defen-

GLOSS: WEBSTER
A reference to Daniel Webster (1782–1852), a U.S. senator at the time. The quotations in this paragraph are taken from a speech about slavery that Webster gave to the Senate.

sive ones. He is not a leader, but a follower. His leaders are the **men of '87.** "I have never made an effort," he says, "and never propose to make an effort; I have never countenanced an effort, and never mean to countenance an effort, to disturb the arrangement as originally made, by which the various States came into the Union." Still thinking of the sanction which the Constitution gives to slavery, he says, "Because it was a part of the original compact—let it stand." Notwithstanding his special acuteness and ability, he is unable to take a fact out of its merely political relations, and behold it as it lies absolutely to be disposed of by the intellect—what, for instance, it behooves a man to do here in America to-day with regard to slavery, but ventures, or is driven, to make some such desperate answer as the following, while professing to speak absolutely, and as a private man—from which what new and singular code of social duties might be inferred? "The manner," says he, "in which the governments of those States where slavery exists are to regulate it is for their own consideration, under their responsibility to their constituents, to the general laws of propriety, humanity, and justice, and to God. Associations formed elsewhere, springing from a feeling of humanity, or any other cause, have nothing whatever to do with it. They have never received any encouragement from me, and they never will."

They who know of no purer sources of truth, who have traced up its stream no higher, stand, and wisely stand, by the Bible and the Constitution, and drink at it there with reverence and humility; but they who behold where it comes trickling into this lake or that pool, gird up their loins once more, and continue their pilgrimage toward its fountain-head.

45   No man with a genius for legislation has appeared in America. They are rare in the history of the world. There are orators, politicians, and eloquent men, by the thousand; but the speaker has not yet opened his mouth to speak who is capable of settling the much-vexed questions of the day. We love eloquence for its own sake, and not for any truth which it may utter, or any heroism it may inspire. Our legislators have not yet learned the comparative value of free-trade and of freedom, of union, and of rectitude, to a nation. They have no genius or talent for comparatively humble questions of taxation and finance, commerce and manufacturers and agriculture. If we were left solely to the wordy wit of legislators in Congress for our guidance, uncorrected by the seasonable experience and the effectual complaints of the people, America would not long retain her rank among the nations. For eighteen hundred years, though perchance I have no right to say it, the New Testament has been written; yet where is the legislator who has wisdom and practical talent enough to avail himself of the light which it sheds on the science of legislation?

The authority of government, even such as I am willing to submit to—for I will cheerfully obey those who know and can do better than I, and in many things even those who neither know nor can do so well—is still an impure one: to be strictly just, it must have the sanction and consent of the governed. It can have no pure right over my person and property

VISUAL CONNECTIONS: RESISTANCE TO GOVERNMENT
Thoreau advocates individual resistance on the basis of individual conscience, and he himself refused to pay taxes as a protest against U.S. government actions. But there can be many forms of resistance, including individual expressions of protest like this poster, which was created in 2004 to criticize U.S. security policies. Consider the effectiveness of these visual expressions of resistance. To what extent do you think such a visual expression is consistent with Thoreau's argument?

but what I concede to it. The progress from an absolute to a limited monarchy, from a limited monarchy to a democracy, is a progress toward a true respect for the individual. Even the Chinese philosopher was wise enough to regard the individual as the basis of the empire. Is a democracy, such as we know it, the last improvement possible in government? Is it not possible to take a step further towards recognizing and organizing the rights of man? There will never be a really free and enlightened State until the State comes to recognize the individual as a higher and independent power, from which all its own power and authority are derived, and treats him accordingly. I please myself with imagining a State at least which can afford to be just to all men, and to treat the individual with respect as a neighbor; which even would not think it inconsistent with its own repose if a few were to live aloof from it, not meddling with it, nor embraced by it, who fulfilled all the duties of neighbors and fellow-men. A State which bore this kind of fruit, and suffered it to drop off as fast as it ripened, would prepare the way for a still more perfect and glorious State, which also I have imagined, but not yet anywhere seen.

UNDERSTANDING THE TEXT

1. Early in his essay, Thoreau claims that government itself has not accomplished any of the things we often give it credit for, such as educating people or keeping the nation free. These things, he asserts, are the result of "the character inherent in the American people." If so, what *has* government done, according to Thoreau? What purpose does it serve? Why is it necessary, in his view?

2. Thoreau spends a great deal of time discussing slavery, which was still legal and widespread in the United States when he wrote this essay. Why is the issue of slavery important to his larger point about civil disobedience?

3. What is Thoreau's view of patriotism? How does patriotism figure into his argument about resistance to government?

4. Under what circumstances does Thoreau believe it is acceptable or even necessary for a person to break the law? On what principles does Thoreau base his arguments for breaking the law?

5. How does Thoreau define freedom? How does his definition of freedom inform his arguments about resisting government? Do you think most Americans would agree with his definition of freedom today? Why or why not?

6. What is the ideal state, in Thoreau's view? Do you think most Americans today would agree with Thoreau about the ideal government? Do you? Why or why not?

EXPLORING THE ISSUES

1. How would you describe Thoreau's tone in this essay? How effectively do you think his tone helps him convey his arguments? How do you think Thoreau's tone compares to the tone of political debate in the United States today, especially in view of the increase in television and radio political talk shows as well as Internet blogs?

2. In paragraph 20, Thoreau argues that Abolitionists—that is, people who wanted to abolish slavery—were justified in withdrawing their support for the government because "they have God on their side." Today, there are a number of controversies, like those surrounding capital punishment and abortion, in which one side or another claims to have God on its side. In some cases, people concerned about these issues advocate violence, as in the case of some radical antiabortion groups that have bombed abortion clinics. What do you think Thoreau would say about such situations, if he were alive today? In what ways do you think his argument for civil disobedience might intensify these controversies? In what ways might his essay help us address such controversies?

3. Thoreau himself did many of the things that he argues honest people should do. For example, he lived a relatively independent life with few possessions, which he says people of conscience may have to do (par. 24); he refused to pay certain taxes to support a government that he believed was unjust, for which he was jailed (par. 26). Because his writing had made him famous, Thoreau's readers would likely have known these things about him. How might that knowledge have affected the strength of his arguments? Do you think Thoreau intentionally included references to his own life to make his essay more persuasive to readers of his day? Explain. In what ways does this knowledge about Thoreau affect your response to his arguments?

ENTERING THE CONVERSATIONS

1. Write an essay in which you discuss what you believe is the relevance (or irrelevance) of Thoreau's argument about civil disobedience today.

2. Write an essay describing an experience in which you resisted authority. In your essay, explain the circumstances you were in and why you decided to resist authority. Try to tell your story in a way that conveys your view of authority and individual responsibility.

 INFOTRAC

3. American history includes famous examples of civil disobedience. But there are many other less famous examples of civil disobedience today. Select one or more instances of civil disobedience that you know about and investigate those events. What issues were involved? What laws or policies were those who engaged in civil disobedience resisting? What did they hope to accomplish? What led to their actions? How did the authorities respond? What was the outcome of the actions? Try to answer these questions through your research, using InfoTrac College Edition, your library, and other appropriate resources. Then write a report about the events. In your report, describe the situations and issues, and explain the outcomes of the acts of civil disobedience that occurred. Try to draw conclusions on the basis of these events about resisting power. Alternatively, create a web site based on your research.

4. Using Thoreau's main argument in this essay, write a letter to the editor of your local newspaper or some other appropriate publication explaining why you think civil disobedience is (or is not) justified in the case of an important current controversy (such as capital punishment, abortion, or a war involving U.S. troops).

"Pair w/ "Tyranny of the Majority"

If you consider the fact that only two other *Americans have a national holiday celebrating their lives (Presidents' Day honors George Washington and Abraham Lincoln), then it's clear that Martin Luther King, Jr. (1929–1968) occupies a very special place in American history. King was not an elected official or a military leader. In fact, his fame arose from his resistance to government. His leadership during the Civil Rights Movement helped change discrimina-*

Letter FROM Birmingham Jail

tory laws and racist attitudes in the United States, and he is honored for those efforts. But as the following letter reveals, King's views were not limited to racial issues and the desire for racial equality, for which he is most remembered; he was also a political leader of a kind. This letter, which he wrote from a jail cell after being arrested during demonstrations he led against segregation in Alabama in 1963, presents a philosophy of nonviolent resistance to government when that government has unjust policies or laws. King's philosophy of nonviolent resistance, which cuts across racial lines, has been invoked by people facing oppression throughout the world.

It's worth noting that the Martin Luther King, Jr. holiday was controversial from its beginnings. President Ronald Reagan signed it into law in 1983 in the midst of intense debate, but some states refused to recognize it. Arizona did not approve the holiday until 1992, and New Hampshire officially called the holiday Civil Rights Day, finally changing the name to Martin Luther King, Jr. Day in 1999. Many people believe that racism explains this opposition to the holiday, but it may also be that many Americans remain uncomfortable with the idea of honoring someone (continued)

MARTIN LUTHER KING, JR.

My Dear Fellow Clergymen: April 16, 1963

While confined here in the Birmingham city jail, I came across your recent statement calling my present activities "unwise and untimely." Seldom do I pause to answer criticism of my work and ideas. If I sought to answer all the criticisms that cross my desk, my secretaries would have little time for anything other than such correspondence in the course of the day, and I would have no time for constructive work. But since I feel that you are men of genuine good will and that your criticisms are sincerely put forth, I want to try to answer your statement in what I hope will be patient and reasonable terms.

I think I should indicate why I am here in Birmingham, since you have been influenced by the view which argues against "outsiders coming in." I have the honor of serving as president of the Southern Christian Leadership Conference, an organization operating in every southern state, with headquarters in Atlanta, Georgia. We have some eighty-five affiliated organizations across the South, and one of them (continued) *who resisted government. Indeed, in his letter, King criticizes people he describes as "moderates" for not resisting unjust laws, even when they agreed that those laws were unjust. King argues that these moderates, like all people, have a moral responsibility to resist such laws, and he charged that their complacency amounted to support for injustice. As you read, you might reflect on your own views about your responsibilities as a citizen and as a person with certain moral and ethical beliefs. How would you respond to King's call for resistance to injustice?*

Martin Luther King, Jr.'s efforts in Birmingham, Alabama, and elsewhere during the Civil Rights Movement helped secure the passage of the Civil Rights Bill in 1963. He was honored for his work with the Nobel Prize for Peace in 1964. An assassin's bullet ended his life in 1968. ▼

STRATEGIES: RESPONDING TO CRITICISM
King's letter was a response to a statement released by eight White Alabama clergymen who objected to the demonstrations King led against segregation in Alabama; they called for both Whites and Blacks to "observe the principles of law and order and common sense." It may be that King originally intended this letter to be read only by those clergy, but given King's stature as a national leader of the Civil Rights Movement, it is likely that he knew his letter would be read by many others. In that sense, his use of the second person *you* may have several meanings. Consider how the apparent rhetorical situation—a letter from one clergyman to others—enables King to accomplish certain goals with this letter that another situation—for example, a letter to the editor of a newspaper or to the governor of Alabama—might not. You might also consider that many of the Christian gospels were written in the form of letters from one of the apostles to specific groups of people (for example, to the Corinthians). Consider, too, how differently we might read this letter today compared to 1963 at the height of the Civil Rights Movement, a time of great social and political conflict in the United States.

is the Alabama Christian Movement for Human Rights. Frequently we share staff, educational, and financial resources with our affiliates. Several months ago the affiliate here in Birmingham asked us to be on call to engage in a nonviolent direct-action program if such were deemed necessary. We readily consented, and when the hour came we lived up to our promise. So I, along with several members of my staff, am here because I was invited here. I am here because I have organizational ties here.

But more basically, I am in Birmingham because injustice is here. Just as the prophets of the eighth century B.C. left their villages and carried their "thus saith the Lord" far beyond the boundaries of their home towns, and just as the Apostle Paul left his village of Tarsus and carried the gospel of Jesus Christ to the far corners of the Greco-Roman world, so am I compelled to carry the gospel of freedom beyond my own home town. Like Paul, I must constantly respond to the Macedonian call for aid.

Moreover, I am cognizant of the interrelatedness of all communities and states. I cannot sit idly by in Atlanta and not be concerned about what happens in Birmingham. Injustice anywhere is a threat to justice everywhere. We are caught in an inescapable network of mutuality, tied in a single garment of destiny. Whatever affects one directly, affects all indirectly. Never again can we afford to live with the narrow, provincial, "outside agitator" idea. Anyone who lives inside the United States can never be considered an outsider anywhere within its bounds.

5   You deplore the demonstrations taking place in Birmingham. But your statement, I am sorry to say, fails to express a similar concern for the conditions that brought about the demonstrations. I am sure that none of you would want to rest content with the superficial kind of social analysis that deals merely with effects and does not grapple with underlying causes. It is unfortunate that demonstrations are taking place in Birmingham, but it is even more unfortunate that the city's white power structure left the Negro community with no alternative.

In any nonviolent campaign there are four basic steps: collection of the facts to determine whether injustices exist; negotiation; self-purification; and direct action. We have gone through all these steps in Birmingham. There can be no gainsaying the fact that racial injustice engulfs this community. Birmingham is probably the most thoroughly segregated city in the United States. Its ugly record of brutality is widely known. Negroes have experienced grossly unjust treatment in courts. There have been more unsolved bombings of Negro homes and churches in Birmingham than in any other city in the nation. These are the hard, brutal facts of the case. On the basis of these conditions, Negro leaders sought to negotiate with the city fathers. But the latter consistently refused to engage in good-faith negotiation.

CONVERSATIONS: "OUTSIDE AGITATOR"
During the Civil Rights Movement and the movement against the Vietnam War in the 1960s and 1970s, this phrase—"outside agitator", which King mentions in paragraph 4—was often used by law enforcement and government officials to describe protesters. Some people considered the phrase an implicit insult intended to suggest that protesters were actually connected to communist organizations and other groups hostile to the United States. Notice in paragraph 4 how King subtly shifts the focus of the phrase from "agitator" to "outsider." He then undermines the phrase by arguing that since we are all interrelated, no one can be considered an "outsider." Although this term is rarely used today, it is a good example of how words or phrases acquire meanings in certain contexts. King relies on his readers' understanding of the meanings of this phrase to make his point here.

Then, last September, came the opportunity to talk with leaders of Birmingham's economic community. In the course of the negotiations, certain promises were made by the merchants—for example, to remove the stores' humiliating racial signs. On the basis of these promises, the Reverend Fred Shuttlesworth and the leaders of the Alabama Christian Movement for Human Rights agreed to a moratorium on all demonstrations. As the weeks and months went by, we realized that we were the victims of a broken promise. A few signs, briefly removed, returned; the others remained.

As in so many past experiences, our hopes had been blasted, and the shadow of deep disappointment settled upon us. We had no alternative except to prepare for direct action, whereby we would present our very bodies as means of laying our case before the conscience of the local and the national community. Mindful of the difficulties involved, we decided to undertake a process of self-purification. We began a series of workshops on nonviolence, and we repeatedly asked ourselves: "Are you able to accept blows without retaliating?" "Are you able to endure the ordeal of jail?" We decided to schedule our direct-action program for the Easter season, realizing that except for Christmas, this is the main shopping period of the year. Knowing that a strong economic-withdrawal program would be the byproduct of direct action, we felt that this would be the best time to bring pressure to bear on the merchants for the needed change.

Then it occurred to us that Birmingham's mayoral election was coming up in March, and we speedily decided to postpone action until after election day. When we discovered that the Commissioner of Public Safety, Eugene "Bull" Connor, had piled up enough votes to be in the run-off, we decided again to postpone action until the day after the run-off so that the demonstrations could not be used to cloud the issues. Like many others, we waited to see Mr. Connor defeated, and to this end we endured postponement after postponement. Having aided in this community need, we felt that our direct-action program could be delayed no longer.

10   You may well ask, "Why direct action? Why sit-ins, marches, and so forth? Isn't negotiation a better path?" You are quite right in calling for negotiation. Indeed, this is the very purpose of direct action. Nonviolent direct action seeks to create such a crisis and foster such a tension that a community which has constantly refused to negotiate is forced to confront the issue. It seeks so to dramatize the issue that it can no longer be ignored. My citing the creation of tension as part of the work of the nonviolent resister may sound rather shocking. But I must confess that I am not afraid of the word "tension." I have earnestly opposed violent tension, but there is a type of constructive, nonviolent tension which is necessary for growth. Just as Socrates felt that it was necessary to create a tension in the mind so that individuals could rise from the bondage of myths and half-truths to the unfettered realm of creative analysis and objective appraisal, so must we see the need for nonviolent gadflies to create the kind of tension in society that will help men rise from the dark depths of prejudice and racism to the majestic heights of understanding and brotherhood.

The purpose of our direct-action program is to create a situation so crisis-packed that it will inevitably open the door to negotiation. I therefore concur with you in your call for negotiation. Too long has our beloved Southland been bogged down in a tragic effort to live in monologue rather than dialogue.

One of the basic points in your statement is that the action that I and my associates have taken in Birmingham is untimely. Some have asked: "Why didn't you give the new city administration time to act?" The only answer that I can give to this query is that the new Birmingham administration must be prodded about as much as the outgoing one, before it will act. We are sadly mistaken if we feel that the election of Albert Boutwell as mayor will bring the millennium to Birmingham. While Mr. Boutwell is a much more gentle person than Mr. Connor, they are both segregationists, dedicated to maintenance of the status quo. I have hoped that Mr. Boutwell will be reasonable enough to see the futility of massive resistance to desegregation. But he will not see this without pressure from devotees of civil rights. My friends, I must say to you that we have not made a single gain in civil rights without determined legal and nonviolent pressure. Lamentably, it is an historical fact that privileged groups seldom give up their privileges voluntarily. Individuals may see the moral light and voluntarily give up their unjust posture; but, as **Reinhold Niebuhr** has reminded us, groups tend to be more immoral than individuals. *True?*

GLOSS: REINHOLD NIEBUHR
Protestant theologian Reinhold Niebuhr (1892–1971) examined the relationship between Christianity and modern politics.

We know through painful experience that freedom is never voluntarily given by the oppressor; it must be demanded by the oppressed. Frankly, I have yet to engage in a direct-action campaign that was "well timed" in the view of those who have not suffered unduly from the disease of segregation. For years now I have heard the word "Wait!" It rings in the ear of every Negro with piercing familiarity. This "Wait" has almost always meant "Never." We must come to see, with one of our distinguished jurists, that "justice too long delayed is justice denied."

We have waited for more than 340 years for our constitutional and God-given rights. The nations of Asia and Africa are moving with jetlike speed toward gaining political independence, but we still creep at horse-and-buggy pace toward gaining a cup of coffee at a lunch counter. Perhaps it is easy for those who have never felt the stinging darts of segregation to say, "Wait." But when you have seen vicious mobs lynch your mothers and fathers at will and drown your sisters and brothers at whim; when you have seen hate-filled policemen curse, kick, and even kill your black brothers and sisters; when you see the vast majority of your twenty million Negro brothers smothering in an airtight cage of poverty in the midst of an affluent society; when you suddenly find your tongue twisted and your speech stammering as you seek to explain to your six-year-old daughter why she can't go to the public amusement park that has just been advertised on television, and see tears welling up in her eyes when she is told that Funtown is closed to colored children, and see ominous clouds of inferiority beginning to form in her little mental sky, and see her beginning to distort her personality by developing an unconscious bitterness toward white people; when you have to concoct an answer for a five-year-old son who is asking,

STRATEGIES: A HUMAN FACE
Notice how King moves from abstract principles to concrete details describing the impact of racism and the laws he considers unjust. He includes a series of vivid images to put a human face on the abstract arguments that he makes. Consider how this strategy helps King make his appeal to his fellow clergy, who all work with members of their own congregations and who could appreciate the human misery that King describes in this passage.

"Daddy, why do white people treat colored people so mean?"; when you take a cross-country drive and find it necessary to sleep night after night in the uncomfortable corners of your automobile because no motel will accept you; when you are humiliated day in and day out by nagging signs reading "white" and "colored"; when your first name becomes "nigger," your middle name becomes "boy" (however old you are) and your last name becomes "John," and your wife and mother are never given the respected title "Mrs."; when you are harried by day and haunted by night by the fact that you are a Negro, living constantly at tiptoe stance, never quite knowing what to expect next, and are plagued with inner fears and outer resentments; when you are forever fighting a degenerating sense of "nobodiness"—then you will understand why we find it difficult to wait. There comes a time when the cup of endurance runs over, and men are no longer willing to be plunged into the abyss of despair. I hope, sirs, you can understand our legitimate and unavoidable impatience.

15   You express a great deal of anxiety over our willingness to break laws. This is certainly a legitimate concern. Since we so diligently urge people to obey **the Supreme Court's decision of 1954** outlawing segregation in the public schools, at first glance it may seem rather paradoxical for us consciously to break laws. One may well ask: "How can you advocate breaking some laws and obeying others?" The answer lies in the fact that there are two types of laws; just and unjust. I would be the first to advocate obeying just laws. One has not only a legal but a moral responsibility to obey just laws. Conversely, one has a moral responsibility to disobey unjust laws. I would agree with St. Augustine that "an unjust law is no law at all."

Now, what is the difference between the two? How does one determine whether a law is just or unjust? A just law is a man-made code that squares with the moral law or the law of God. An unjust law is a code that is out of harmony with the moral law. To put it in the terms of St. Thomas Aquinas: An unjust law is a human law that is not rooted in eternal law and natural law. Any law that uplifts human personality is just. Any law that degrades human personality is unjust. All segregation statutes are unjust because segregation distorts the soul and damages the personality. It gives the segregator a false sense of superiority and the segregated a false sense of inferiority. Segregation, to use the terminology of the Jewish philosopher Martin Buber, substitutes an "I–it" relationship for an "I–thou" relationship and ends up relegating persons to the status of things. Hence segregation is not only politically, economically, and sociologically unsound, it is morally wrong and sinful. **Paul Tillich** has said that sin is segregation. Is not segregation an existential expression of man's tragic separation, his awful estrangement, his terrible sinfulness? Thus it is that I can urge men to obey the 1954 decision of the Supreme Court, for it is morally right; and I can urge them to disobey segregation ordinances, for they are morally wrong.

Let us consider a more concrete example of just and unjust laws. An unjust law is a code that a numerical or power majority group compels a minority group to obey but does not make binding on itself. This is *difference* made legal. By the same token, a just law is a code that a majority compels a minority to follow and that it is willing to follow itself. This is *sameness* made legal.

GLOSSES

THE SUPREME COURT'S DECISION OF 1954
King refers here to the famous decision by the U.S. Supreme Court in the case of *Brown* v. *Board of Education of Topeka* in which the Court overturned the policy of providing "separate but equal" education for Black children.

PAUL TILLICH
Paul Tillich (1885–1965) was a Christian theologian who addressed basic philosophical questions of human existence.

[handwritten margin note: Examples of unjust laws?]

Let me give another explanation. A law is unjust if it is inflicted on a minority that, as a result of being denied the right to vote, had no part in enacting or devising the law. Who can say that the legislature of Alabama which set up that state's segregation laws was democratically elected? Throughout Alabama all sorts of devious methods are used to prevent Negroes from becoming registered voters, and there are some counties in which, even though Negroes constitute a majority of the population, not a single Negro is registered. Can any law enacted under such circumstances be considered democratically structured?

Sometimes a law is just on its face and unjust in its application. For instance, I have been arrested on a charge of parading without a permit. Now, there is nothing wrong in having an ordinance which requires a permit for a parade. But such an ordinance becomes unjust when it is used to maintain segregation and to deny citizens the First-Amendment privilege of peaceful assembly and protest.

Protest

I hope you are able to see the distinction I am trying to point out. In no sense do I advocate evading or defying the law, as would the rabid segregationist. That would lead to anarchy. One who breaks an unjust law must do so openly, lovingly, and with a willingness to accept the penalty. I submit that an individual who breaks a law that conscience tells him is unjust, and who willingly accepts the penalty of imprisonment in order to arouse the conscience of the community over its injustice, is in reality expressing the highest respect for law.

20

Of course, there is nothing new about this kind of civil disobedience. It was evidenced sublimely in the refusal of Shadrach, Meshach, and Abednego to obey the laws of **Nebuchadnezzar,** on the ground that a higher moral law was at stake. It was practiced superbly by the early Christians, who were willing to face hungry lions and the excruciating pain of chopping blocks rather than submit to certain unjust laws of the Roman Empire. To a degree, academic freedom is a reality today because Socrates practiced civil disobedience. In our own nation, the Boston Tea Party represented a massive act of civil disobedience.

examples of civil disobedience

We should never forget that everything Adolf Hitler did in Germany was "legal" and everything the **Hungarian freedom fighters** did in Hungary was "illegal." It was "illegal" to aid and comfort a Jew in Hitler's Germany. Even so, I am sure that, had I lived in Germany at the time, I would have aided and comforted my Jewish brothers. If today I lived in a Communist country where certain principles dear to the Christian faith are suppressed, I would openly advocate disobeying that country's anti-religious laws.

I must make two honest confessions to you, my Christian and Jewish brothers. First, I must confess that over the past few years I have been gravely disappointed with the white moderate. I have almost reached the regrettable conclusion that the Negro's great stumbling block in his stride toward freedom is not the White Citizen's Councilor or the Ku Klux Klanner, but the white moderate, who is more devoted to "order" than to justice; who prefers a negative peace which is the absence of tension to a positive peace which is the presence of justice; who constantly says, "I agree with you in the goal you seek, but I cannot agree with your methods of direct ac-

GLOSSES

NEBUCHADNEZZAR

Nebuchadnezzar was the King of Babylon, described in the Book of Daniel of the Bible, who forced the Jewish people to worship a gold image of himself. He ordered Shadrach, Meshach, and Abednego, who refused his command, thrown into a furnace, but according to the biblical account, they were unharmed.

HUNGARIAN FREEDOM FIGHTERS

In 1956, Hungarian citizens temporarily overthrew the communist dictatorship in their country. Unwilling to confront the Soviet Union, Western democracies stood by as the Red Army suppressed the revolt by force.

Moderates more harmful

tion"; who paternalistically believes he can set the timetable for another man's free-dom; who lives by a mythical concept of time and who constantly advises the Negro to wait for a "more convenient season." Shallow understanding from people of good will is more frustrating than absolute misunderstanding from people of ill will. Lukewarm acceptance is much more bewildering than outright rejection.

I had hoped that the white moderate would understand that law and order exist for the purpose of establishing justice and that when they fail in this purpose they be-come the dangerously structured dams that block the flow of social progress. I had hoped that the white moderate would understand that the present tension in the South is a necessary phase of the transition from an obnoxious negative peace, in which the Negro passively accepted his unjust plight, to a substantive and positive peace, in which all men will respect the dignity and worth of human personality. Actually, we who engage in nonviolent direct action are not the creators of tension. We merely bring to the surface the hidden tension that is already alive. We bring it out in the open, where it can be seen and dealt with. Like a boil that can never be cured so long as it is covered up but must be opened with all its ugliness to the nat-ural medicines of air and light, injustice must be exposed, with all the tension its ex-posure creates, to the light of human conscience and the air of national opinion, before it can be cured.

analogies

25   In your statement you assert that our actions, even though peaceful, must be con-demned because they precipitate violence. But is this a logical assertion? Isn't this like condemning a robbed man because his possession of money precipitated the evil act of robbery? Isn't this like condemning Socrates because his unswerving commit-ment to truth and his philosophical inquiries precipitated the act by the misguided populace in which they made him drink hemlock? Isn't this like condemning Jesus because his unique God-consciousness and never-ceasing devotion to God's will pre-cipitated the evil act of crucifixion? We must come to see that, as the federal courts have consistently affirmed, it is wrong to urge an individual to cease his efforts to gain his basic constitutional rights because the quest may precipitate violence. Society must protect the robbed and punish the robber.

I had also hoped that the white moderate would reject the myth concerning time in relation to the struggle for freedom. I have just received a letter from a white brother in Texas. He writes: "All Christians know that the colored people will receive equal rights eventually, but it is possible that you are in too great a religious hurry. It has taken Christianity almost two thousand years to accomplish what it has. The teachings of Christ take time to come to earth." Such an attitude stems from a tragic misconception of time, from the strangely irrational notion that there is something in the very flow of time that will inevitably cure all ills. Actually, time itself is neutral; it can be used either destructively or constructively. More and more I feel that the people of ill will have used time much more effectively than have the people of good will. We will have to repent in this generation not merely for the hateful words and actions of the bad people, but for the appalling silence of the good people. Human progress never rolls in on wheels of inevitability; it comes through the tireless efforts of men willing to be coworkers with God, and without this hard work, time itself be-comes an ally of the forces of social stagnation. We must use time creatively, in the knowledge that the time is always ripe to do right. Now is the time to make real the promise of democracy and transform our pending national elegy into a creative psalm of brotherhood. Now is the time to lift our national policy from the quicksand of racial injustice to the solid rock of human dignity.

You speak of our activity in Birmingham as extreme. At first I was rather disappointed that fellow clergymen would see my nonviolent efforts as those of an extremist. I began thinking about the fact that I stand in the middle of two opposing forces in the Negro community. One is a force of complacency, made up in part of Negroes who, as a result of long years of oppression, are so drained of self-respect and a sense of "somebodiness" that they have adjusted to segregation; and in part of a few middle-class Negroes who, because of a degree of academic and economic security and because in some ways they profit by segregation, have become insensitive to the problems of the masses. The other force is one of bitterness and hatred, and it comes perilously close to advocating violence. It is expressed in the various black nationalist groups that are springing up across the nation, the largest and best-known being Elijah Muhammad's Muslim movement. Nourished by the Negro's frustration over the continued existence of racial discrimination, this movement is made up of people who have lost faith in America, who have absolutely repudiated Christianity, and who have concluded that the white man is an incorrigible "devil."

I have tried to stand between these two forces, saying that we need emulate neither the "do-nothingism" of the complacent nor the hatred and despair of the black nationalist. For there is the more excellent way of love and nonviolent protest. I am grateful to God that, through the influence of the Negro church, the way of nonviolence became an integral part of our struggle.

If this philosophy had not emerged, by now many streets of the South would, I am convinced, be flowing with blood. And I am further convinced that if our white brothers dismiss as "rabble-rousers" and "outside agitators" those of us who employ nonviolent direct action, and if they refuse to support our nonviolent efforts, millions of Negroes will, out of frustration and despair, seek solace and security in black-nationalist ideologies—a development that would inevitably lead to a frightening racial nightmare.

Oppressed people cannot remain oppressed forever. The yearning for freedom eventually manifests itself, and that is what has happened to the American Negro. Something within has reminded him of his birthright of freedom, and something without has reminded him that it can be gained. Consciously or unconsciously, he has been caught up by the *Zeitgeist*, and with his black brothers of Africa and his brown and yellow brothers of Asia, South America, and the Caribbean, the United States Negro is moving with a sense of great urgency toward the promised land of racial justice. If one recognizes this vital urge that has engulfed the Negro community, one should readily understand why public demonstrations are taking place. The Negro has many pent-up resentments and latent frustrations, and he must release them. So let him march; let him make prayer pilgrimages to the city hall; let him go on freedom rides—and try to understand why he must do so. If his repressed emotions are not released in nonviolent ways, they will seek expression through violence; this is not a threat but a fact of history. So I have not said to my people, "Get rid of your discontent." Rather, I have tried to say that this normal and healthy discontent can be channeled into the creative outlet of nonviolent direct action. And now this approach is being termed extremist.

But though I was initially disappointed at being categorized as an extremist, as I continued to think about the matter I gradually gained a measure of satisfaction from the label. Was not Jesus an extremist for love: "Love your enemies, bless them that curse you, do good to them that hate you, and pray for them which despitefully use you, and persecute you." Was not Amos an extremist for justice: "Let justice roll down like waters and righteousness like an everflowing stream." Was not Paul an extremist for the Christian gospel: "I bear in my body the marks of the Lord Jesus." Was not Martin Luther an extremist: "Here I stand; I cannot do otherwise, so help me God." And John Bunyan: "I will stay in jail to the end of my days before I make a butchery of my conscience." And Abraham Lincoln: "This nation cannot survive half slave and half free." And Thomas Jefferson: "We hold these truths to be selfevident, that all men are created equal. . . ." So the question is not whether we will be extremists, but what kind of extremists we will be. Will we be extremists for hate or for love? Will we be extremists for the preservation of injustice or for the extension of justice? In that dramatic scene on Calvary's hill three men were crucified. We must never forget that all three were crucified for the same crime—the crime of extremism. Two were extremists for immorality, and thus fell below their environment. The other, Jesus Christ, was an extremist for love, truth, and goodness, and thereby rose above his environment. Perhaps the South, the nation, and the world are in dire need of creative extremists.

I had hoped that the white moderate would see this need. Perhaps I was too optimistic; perhaps I expected too much. I suppose I should have realized that few members of the oppressor race can understand the deep groans and passionate yearnings of the oppressed race, and still fewer have the vision to see that injustice must be rooted out by strong, persistent, and determined action. I am thankful, however, that some of our white brothers in the South have grasped the meaning of this social revolution and committed themselves to it. They are still all too few in quantity, but they are big in quality. Some—such as Ralph McGill, Lillian Smith, Harry Golden, James McBride Dabbs, Ann Braden, and Sarah Patton Boyle—have written about our struggle in eloquent and prophetic terms. Others have marched with us down nameless streets of the South. They have languished in filthy, roach-infested jails, suffering the abuse and brutality of policemen who view them as "dirty nigger-lovers." Unlike so many of their moderate brothers and sisters, they have recognized the urgency of the moment and sensed the need for powerful "action" antidotes to combat the disease of segregation.

Let me take note of my other major disappointment. I have been so greatly disappointed with the white church and its leadership. Of course, there are some notable exceptions. I am not unmindful of the fact that each of you has taken some significant stands on this issue. I commend you, Reverend Stallings, for your Christian stand on this past Sunday, in welcoming Negroes to your worship service on a non-segregated basis. I commend the Catholic leaders of this state for integrating Spring Hill College several years ago.

But despite these notable exceptions, I must honestly reiterate that I have been disappointed with the church. I do not say this as one of those negative critics who can always find something wrong with the church. I say this as a minister of the gospel, who loves the church; who was nurtured in its bosom; who has been sustained by its spiritual blessings and who will remain true to it as long as the cord of life shall lengthen.

When I was suddenly catapulted into the leadership of the bus protest in Montgomery, Alabama, a few years ago, I felt we would be supported by the white church. I felt that the white ministers, priests, and rabbis of the South would be among our strongest allies. Instead, some have been outright opponents, refusing to understand the freedom movement and misrepresenting its leaders; all too many others have been more cautious than courageous and have remained silent behind the anesthetizing security of stained-glass windows.

In spite of my shattered dreams, I came to Birmingham with the hope that the white religious leadership of this community would see the justice of our cause and, with deep moral concern, would serve as the channel through which our just grievances could reach the power structure. I had hoped that each of you would understand. But again I have been disappointed.

There was a time when the church was very powerful—in the time when the early Christians rejoiced at being deemed worthy to suffer for what they believed. In those days the church was not merely a thermometer that recorded the ideas and principles of popular opinion; it was a thermostat that transformed the mores of society. Whenever the early Christians entered a town, the people in power became disturbed and immediately sought to convict the Christians for being "disturbers of the peace" and "outside agitators." But the Christians pressed on, in the conviction that they were "a colony of heaven," called to obey God rather than man. Small in number, they were big in commitment. They were too God-intoxicated to be "astronomically intimidated." By their effort and example they brought an end to such ancient evils as infanticide and gladiatorial contests.

Things are different now. So often the contemporary church is a weak, ineffectual voice with an uncertain sound. So often it is an archdefender of the status quo. Far from being disturbed by the presence of the church, the power structure of the average community is consoled by the church's silent—and often even vocal—sanction of things as they are.

But the judgment of God is upon the church as never before. If today's church does not recapture the sacrificial spirit of the early church, it will lose its authenticity, forfeit the loyalty of millions, and be dismissed as an irrelevant social club with no meaning for the twentieth century. Every day I meet young people whose disappointment with the church has turned into outright disgust.

Perhaps I have once again been too optimistic. Is organized religion too inextricably bound to the status quo to save our nation and the world? Perhaps I must turn my faith to the inner spiritual church, the church within the church, as the true *ekklesia* and the hope of the world. But again I am thankful to God that some noble souls from the ranks of organized religion have broken loose from the paralyzing chains of conformity and joined us as active partners in the struggle for freedom. They have left their secure congregations and walked the streets of Albany, Georgia, with us. They have gone down the highways of the South on torturous rides for freedom. Yes, they have gone to jail with us. Some have been dismissed from their churches, have lost the support of

GLOSS: *EKKLESIA*
Ekklesia is a Greek word meaning assembly, congregation, or church.

© AP Photo/Bill Hudson

VISUAL CONNECTIONS: POLICE BRUTALITY
During the Civil Rights Movement, photographs like the one on the left, taken during King's march on Birmingham, were commonly published in U.S. newspapers, and they helped galvanize national support for the movement. Consider how such images can communicate some of the same messages that King is conveying in his written letter. Consider, too, the effects that images, conveyed through both print and television, can have in movements such as King's or in more recent events, such as the beating of Rodney King by Los Angeles police in 1991 (shown in the photo on the right).

MAR. 3 1991

© 2002 Getty Images

their bishops and fellow ministers. But they have acted in the faith that right defeated is stronger than evil triumphant. Their witness has been the spiritual salt that has preserved the true meaning of the gospel in these troubled times. They have carved a tunnel of hope through the dark mountain of disappointment.

I hope the church as a whole will meet the challenge of this decisive hour. But even if the church does not come to the aid of justice, I have no despair about the future. I have no fear about the outcome of our struggle in Birmingham, even if our motives are at present misunderstood. We will reach the goal of freedom in Birmingham and all over the nation, because the goal of America is freedom. Abused and scorned though we may be, our destiny is tied up with America's destiny. Before the pilgrims landed at Plymouth, we were here. Before the pen of Jefferson etched the majestic words of the Declaration of Independence across the pages of history, we were here. For more than two centuries our forebears labored in this country without wages; they made cotton king; they built the homes of their masters while suffering gross injustice and shameful humiliation—and yet out of a bottomless vitality they continued to thrive and develop. If the inexpressible cruelties of slavery could not stop us, the opposition we now face will surely fail. We will win our freedom because the sacred heritage of our nation and the eternal will of God are embodied in our echoing demands.

Before closing I feel impelled to mention one other point in your statement that has troubled me profoundly. You warmly commended the Birmingham police force for keeping "order" and "preventing violence." I doubt that you would have so warmly commended the police force if you had seen its dogs sinking their teeth into unarmed, nonviolent Negroes. I doubt that you would so quickly commend the policemen if you were to observe their ugly and inhumane treatment of Negroes here in the city jail; if you were to watch them push and curse old Negro women and young Negro girls; if you were to see them slap and kick old Negro men and young boys; if you were to observe them, as they did on two occasions, refuse to give us food because we wanted to sing our grace together. I cannot join you in your praise of the Birmingham police department.

It is true that the police have exercised a degree of discipline in handling the demonstrators. In this sense they have conducted themselves rather "nonviolently" in public. But for what purpose? To preserve the evil system of segregation. Over the past few years I have consistently preached that nonviolence demands that the means we use must be as pure as the ends we seek. I have tried to make clear that it is wrong to use immoral means to attain moral ends. But now I must affirm that it is just as wrong, or perhaps even more so, to use moral means to preserve immoral ends. Perhaps Mr. Connor and his policemen have been rather nonviolent in public, as was Chief Pritchett in Albany, Georgia, but they have used the moral means of nonviolence to maintain the immoral end of racial injustice. As T. S. Eliot has said, "The last temptation is the greatest treason: To do the right deed for the wrong reason."

I wish you had commended the Negro sit-inners and demonstrators of Birmingham for their sublime courage, their willingness to suffer, and their amazing discipline in the midst of great provocation. One day the South will recognize its real heroes. They will be the James Merediths, with the noble sense of purpose that enables them to face jeering and hostile mobs, and with the agonizing loneliness that characterizes the life of the pioneer. They will be old, oppressed, battered Negro women, symbolized in a seventy-two-year-old woman in Montgomery, Alabama, who rose up with a sense of dignity and with her people decided not to ride segregated buses, and who responded with ungrammatical profundity to one who inquired about her weariness: "My feets is tired, but my soul is at rest." They will be the young high school and college students, the young ministers of the gospel and a host of their elders, courageously and nonviolently sitting in at lunch counters and willingly going to jail for conscience's sake. One day the South will know that when these disinherited children of God sat down at lunch counters, they were in reality standing up for what is best in the American dream and for the most sacred values in our Judeo-Christian heritage, thereby bringing our nation back to those great wells of democracy which were dug deep by the founding fathers in their formulation of the Constitution and the Declaration of Independence.

> **GLOSS: JAMES MEREDITH**
> In the fall of 1962, James Meredith was the first Black student to attend the University of Mississippi. When he enrolled in the university, riots broke out on campus.

Never before have I written so long a letter. I'm afraid it is much too long to take your precious time. I can assure you that it would have been much shorter if I had been writing from a comfortable desk, but what else can one do when he is alone in a narrow jail cell, other than write long letters, think long thoughts, and pray long prayers?

If I have said anything in this letter that overstates the truth and indicates an unreasonable impatience, I beg you to forgive me. If I have said anything that understates the truth and indicates my having a patience that allows me to settle for anything less than brotherhood, I beg God to forgive me.

I hope this letter finds you strong in the faith. I also hope that circumstances will soon make it possible for me to meet each of you, not as an integrationist or a civil-rights leader but as a fellow clergyman and a Christian brother. Let us all hope that the dark clouds of racial prejudice will soon pass away and the deep fog of misunderstanding will be lifted from our fear-drenched communities, and in some not too distant tomorrow the radiant stars of love and brotherhood will shine over our great nation with all their scintillating beauty.

Yours for the cause of Peace and Brotherhood,
Martin Luther King, Jr.

UNDERSTANDING THE TEXT

1. How does King explain his presence in Birmingham, Alabama? Why is it important for him to do so?

2. In his letter, King explains that there are four steps to a nonviolent campaign (par. 6), the last of which is "direct action." Why is it important for him to explain these steps? What is he able to reveal to his readers about the situation in Birmingham and about his movement by explaining in detail the need for direct action?

3. How does King justify breaking the law? How does he distinguish between a just law and an unjust law? What is the fundamental basis on which to judge laws, in King's view? Do you find his justification for breaking unjust laws persuasive? Why or why not?

4. Why does King criticize "the white moderate"? In what sense are White moderates, who agree with King's demands for civil rights for Blacks, an obstacle to change, in King's view? Why do you think King spends so much time discussing White moderates?

5. What are the advantages of nonviolent resistance for trying to change unjust laws, according to King?

6. Why does King not object to being labeled an "extremist"? How does King's discussion of this term compare to the way the term tends to be used today? Do you think Americans would find his acceptance of the term *extremist* convincing today? Explain.

EXPLORING THE ISSUES

1. How would you describe King's voice in this letter? To what extent do you think his voice contributes to the persuasiveness (or the lack of persuasiveness) of his arguments? How does his voice in this letter fit in with your own sense of Martin Luther King, Jr. from what you have read or heard?

2. Throughout his essay, King makes references to many writers, thinkers, and well-known texts, including the Bible and works of philosophy. How do these references contribute to King's argument? What do they reveal about King as a writer and a person? What do they suggest about his sense of his audience? Do you think these references are effective? Why or why not?

3. In this letter, King is responding to a written statement by eight White ministers who criticized his efforts to fight segregation in Birmingham, Alabama. As a reader, you do not have that statement in front of you, but King refers to it several times in this letter. What effect do you think these references to the statement have on King's overall argument? Does it make any difference that you do not have the White ministers' statement? Explain.

4. Americans have always been concerned about mixing religion and politics. The U.S. Constitution has several provisions that prohibit the government either from adopting an official religion or from preventing citizens from worshipping as they choose. Yet King bases his arguments for resisting unjust laws largely on his own Christian beliefs. What do you think King's use of religious beliefs might suggest about the role of religion in American society? How do you think Americans today might react to King's views about the relationship between religion and politics?

ENTERING THE CONVERSATIONS

1. Write an essay describing an experience you've had when you resisted authority as a result of your beliefs or principles.

2. The national holiday honoring Martin Luther King, Jr. was controversial from the time it was first proposed by President Ronald Reagan in 1983. Some Americans still oppose the holiday. Write a letter to the editor of your local newspaper or to one of your state or local elected officials expressing your views about the Martin Luther King, Jr. holiday. In your letter, draw on King's "Letter from a Birmingham Jail" to support your position about the holiday.

INFOTRAC

3. Martin Luther King, Jr. was a controversial figure during his life, and he remains so even many years after his death in 1968. Using InfoTrac College Edition, your library, and other appropriate resources, investigate King's life and his work as a civil rights leader. Try to identify the reasons he was disliked, opposed, and even hated by some people but revered by so many others, and try to understand the opposition to the national holiday that was established in his honor. Then write a report in which you present what you learned about King and the controversy surrounding him. Try to draw conclusions about the consequences of challenging power.

4. Working with a group of classmates, create a website in which you present your view of Martin Luther King, Jr.'s efforts as a civil rights activist and especially of his views about nonviolent resistance to government. Design your site for a general audience and emphasize what you think are the most important or problematic of King's ideas about nonviolent resistance.

5. Write an essay in which you analyze King's views about nonviolent resistance in terms of controversies that are occurring today. Select one or more controversies in which citizens object to and oppose their government's policies or laws (such as the war in Iraq, abortion, or environmental policies), and use those situations to discuss what you see as the importance of King's ideas. Discuss as well concerns you might have about his views.

In the following essay, well-known scholar *and cultural critic bell hooks writes that she has long had "the craving to speak, to have a voice, and not just any voice but one that could be identified as belonging to me." That statement might serve as a good summary of the main theme of hooks's impressive body of work: the importance of being heard. And being heard is one way to challenge power. For hooks, power is fundamentally about ideas and attitudes, which must be*

Talking Back

challenged when they lead to oppression and injustice. She grew up poor in the rural American South, where ideas about race and gender were as powerful in shaping her life and the lives of those around her as laws or government policies. To challenge power, then, sometimes means to challenge ways of thinking; it means questioning conventional attitudes and beliefs. And most of all, it means not remaining silent. As she does in this essay, hooks has written relentlessly about speaking out and claiming one's voice. At the heart of her message is the idea that what makes us human, what gives us dignity, is not language itself but the willingness to use it to give voice to our concerns, especially in the face of injustice and inequality.

Although she is an academic, part of hooks's appeal is that her messages about race, gender, and culture reach beyond academic audiences. If she doesn't sound like an academic to you, it may be because she tries not to so that you can enter the conversations that matter to her. She is always concerned that some people are excluded from important conversations because of how language is used in those conversations. So she avoids academic jargon, even when she is writing about complicated or (continued)

bell hooks

In the world of the southern black community I grew up in, "back talk" and "talking back" meant speaking as an equal to an authority figure. It meant daring to disagree and sometimes it just meant having an opinion. In the "old school," children were meant to be seen and not heard. My great-grandparents, grandparents, and parents were all from the old school. To make yourself heard if you were a child was to invite punishment, the back-hand lick, the slap across the face that would catch you unaware, or the feel of switches stinging your arms and legs.

To speak then when one was not spoken to was a courageous act—an act of risk and daring. And yet it was hard not to speak in warm rooms where heated discussions began at the crack of dawn, women's voices filling the air, giving orders, making threats, fussing. Black men may have excelled in the art of poetic preaching in the male-dominated church, but in the church of the home, where the everyday rules of how to live and how to act were established, it was black women who preached. There, black women spoke in a language so (continued) *theoretical issues, and she draws on her own experiences in her essays and books in a way that is rare in academic writing. In this way, she uses writing as a powerful way to speak out and to challenge power.*

For more information on bell hooks, see the introduction for "On Building a Community of Love" on page 244. ▼

CONVERSATIONS: SILENCE

Here and throughout this essay, hooks refers to silence or to being silent. But those terms mean something more than just being quiet. *Silence* in this context has a more complicated set of meanings related to culture and power; it refers to the matter of who is allowed (or not allowed) to speak on the basis of cultural beliefs and social status. Cultural attitudes about race, gender, and related matters influence who can speak, who cannot, and who will listen. For example, White men may have more opportunity or authority to speak out in American culture than, for example, an Arab immigrant woman. So for hooks and other scholars concerned about racism, sexism, and other kinds of social injustice, to speak out is not just a matter of expressing your individual opinion; it is also a challenge to cultural attitudes, and it is a way to take responsibility for changing those attitudes. Silence, then, is accepting things as they are and acquiescing to unjust cultural attitudes (similar to Martin Luther King, Jr.'s criticisms of "white moderates" on page 472 in his essay). This more specialized meaning of silence emerges from many academic and cultural discussions about race, gender, and related issues. Writers like hooks have helped give this term its special meanings.

rich, so poetic, that it felt to me like being shut off from life, smothered to death if one were not allowed to participate.

It was in that world of woman talk (the men were often silent, often absent) that was born in me the craving to speak, to have a voice, and not just any voice but one that could be identified as belonging to me. To make my voice, I had to speak, to hear myself talk—and talk I did—darting in and out of grown folks' conversations and dialogues, answering questions that were not directed at me, endlessly asking questions, making speeches. Needless to say, the punishments for these acts of speech seemed endless. They were intended to silence me—the child—and more particularly the girl child. Had I been a boy, they might have encouraged me to speak believing that I might someday be called to preach. There was no "calling" for talking girls, no legitimized rewarded speech. The punishments I received for "talking back" were intended to suppress all possibility that I would create my own speech. That speech was to be suppressed so that the "right speech of womanhood" would emerge.

Within feminist circles, silence is often seen as the sexist "right speech of womanhood"—the sign of woman's submission to patriarchal authority. This emphasis on woman's silence may be an accurate remembering of what has taken place in the households of women from WASP backgrounds in the United States, but in black communities (and diverse ethnic communities), women have not been silent. Their voices can be heard. Certainly for black women, our struggle has not been to emerge from silence into speech but to change the nature and direction of our speech, to make a speech that compels listeners, one that is heard.

5   Our speech, "the right speech of womanhood," was often the soliloquy, the talking into thin air, the talking to ears that do not hear you—the talk that is simply not listened to. Unlike the black male preacher whose speech was to be heard, who was to be listened to, whose words were to be remembered, the voices of black women—giving orders, making threats, fussing—could be tuned out, could become a kind of background music, audible but not acknowledged as significant speech. Dialogue—the sharing of speech and recognition—took place not between mother and child or mother and male authority figure but among black women. I can remember watching fascinated as our mother talked with her mother, sisters, and women friends. The intimacy and intensity of their speech—the satisfaction they received from talking to one another, the pleasure, the joy. It was in this world of woman speech, loud talk, angry words, women with tongues quick and sharp, tender sweet tongues, touching our world with their words, that I made speech my birthright—and the right to voice, to authorship, a privilege I would not be denied. It was in that world and because of it that I came to dream of writing, to write.

Writing was a way to capture speech, to hold onto it, keep it close. And so I wrote down bits and pieces of conversations, confessing in cheap diaries that soon fell apart from too much handling, expressing the intensity of my sorrow, the anguish of speech—for I was always saying the wrong thing, asking the wrong questions. I could not confine my speech to the necessary corners and concerns of life. I hid these writings under my bed, in pillow stuffings, among faded underwear. When my sisters found and read them, they ridiculed and mocked me—poking fun. I felt violated, ashamed, as if the secret parts of my self had been exposed, brought into the open, and hung like newly clean laundry, out in the air for everyone to see. The fear of exposure, the fear that one's deepest emotions and innermost thoughts will be dismissed as mere nonsense, felt by so many young girls keeping diaries, holding and hiding speech, seems to me now one of the barriers that women have always needed and still need to destroy so that we are no longer pushed into secrecy or silence.

Despite my feelings of violation, of exposure, I continued to speak and write, choosing my hiding places well, learning to destroy work when no safe place could be found. I was never taught absolute silence, I was taught that it was important to speak but to talk a talk that was in itself a silence. Taught to speak and yet beware of the betrayal of too much heard speech, I experienced intense confusion and deep anxiety in my efforts to speak and write. Reciting poems at Sunday afternoon church service might be rewarded. Writing a poem (when one's time could be "better" spent sweeping, ironing, learning to cook) was luxurious activity, indulged in at the expense of others. Questioning authority, raising issues that were not deemed appropriate subjects brought pain, punishments—like telling mama I wanted to die before her because I could not live without her—that was crazy talk, crazy speech, the kind that would lead you to end up in a mental institution. "Little girl," I would be told, "if you don't stop all this crazy talk and crazy acting you are going to end up right out there at Western State."

CONTEXT: MADNESS

When hooks mentions "madness" here, she is referring to cultural attitudes that expected women to defer to men and to keep their ideas and opinions to themselves. Women who did not do so, like hooks herself, were often believed to suffer from mental disorders. In fact, in the nineteenth and early twentieth centuries, women who were outspoken were often "treated" by doctors for mental illness. In recent decades, of course, such attitudes have been challenged, and many theorists have examined how medicine and other disciplines used science to justify sexist or racist beliefs. Understanding this historical context makes this passage in hooks's essay even more disturbing. It can help us see how frightening and risky it was for her to speak out.

Madness, not just physical abuse, was the punishment for too much talk if you were female. Yet even as this fear of madness haunted me, hanging over my writing like a monstrous shadow, I could not stop the words, making thought, writing speech. For this terrible madness which I feared, which I was sure was the destiny of daring women born to intense speech (after all, the authorities emphasized this point daily), was not as threatening as imposed silence, as suppressed speech.

Safety and sanity were to be sacrificed if I was to experience defiant speech. Though I risked them both, deep-seated fears and anxieties characterized my childhood days. I would speak but I would not ride a bike, play hardball, or hold the gray kitten. Writing about the ways we are traumatized in our growing-up years, psychoanalyst Alice Miller makes the point in *For Your Own Good* that it is not clear why childhood wounds become for some folk an opportunity to grow, to move forward rather than backward in the process of self-realization. Certainly, when I reflect on the trials of my growing-up years, the many punishments, I can see now that in resistance

I learned to be vigilant in the nourishment of my spirit, to be tough, to courageously protect that spirit from forces that would break it.

While punishing me, my parents often spoke about the necessity of breaking my spirit. Now when I ponder the silences, the voices that are not heard, the voices of those wounded and/or oppressed individuals who do not speak or write, I contemplate the acts of persecution, torture—the terrorism that breaks spirits, that makes creativity impossible. I write these words to bear witness to the primacy of resistance struggle in any situation of domination (even within family life); to the strength and power that emerges from sustained resistance and the profound conviction that these forces can be healing, can protect us from dehumanization and despair.

These early trials, wherein I learned to stand my ground, to keep my spirit intact, came vividly to mind after I published *Ain't I A Woman* and the book was sharply and harshly criticized. While I had expected a climate of critical dialogue, I was not expecting a critical avalanche that had the power in its intensity to crush the spirit, to push one into silence. Since that time, I have heard stories about black women, about women of color, who write and publish (even when the work is quite successful) having nervous breakdowns, being made mad because they cannot bear the harsh responses of family, friends, and unknown critics, or becoming silent, unproductive. Surely, the absence of a humane critical response has tremendous impact on the writer from any oppressed, colonized group who endeavors to speak. For us, true speaking is not solely an expression of creative power; it is an act of resistance, a political gesture that challenges politics of domination that would render us nameless and voiceless. As such, it is a courageous act—as such, it represents a threat. To those who wield oppressive power, that which is threatening must necessarily be wiped out, annihilated, silenced.

Recently, efforts by black women writers to call attention to our work serve to highlight both our presence and absence. Whenever I peruse women's bookstores, I am struck not by the rapidly growing body of feminist writing by black women, but by the paucity of available published material. Those of us who write and are published remain few in number. The context of silence is varied and multi-dimensional. Most obvious are the ways racism, sexism, and class exploitation act to suppress and silence. Less obvious are the inner struggles, the efforts made to gain the necessary confidence to write, to re-write, to fully develop craft and skill—and the extent to which such efforts fail.

Although I have wanted writing to be my life-work since childhood, it has been difficult for me to claim "writer" as part of that which identifies and shapes my everyday reality. Even after publishing books, I would often speak of wanting to be a writer as though these works did not exist. And though I would be told, "you are a writer," I was not yet ready to fully affirm this truth. Part of myself was still held captive by domineering forces of history, of familial life that had charted a map of silence, of right speech. I had not completely let go of the fear of saying the wrong thing, of being punished. Somewhere in the deep recesses of my mind, I believed I could avoid both responsibility and punishment if I did not declare myself a writer.

One of the many reasons I chose to write using the pseudonym bell hooks, a family name (mother to Sarah Oldham, grandmother to Rosa Bell Oldham, great-grandmother to me), was to construct a writer-identity that would challenge and subdue all impulses leading me away from speech into silence. I was a young girl buying bubble gum at the corner store when I first really heard the full name bell hooks. I had just "talked back" to a grown person. Even now I can recall the surprised look, the mocking tones that informed me I must be kin to bell hooks—a sharp-tongued woman, a woman who spoke her mind, a woman who was not afraid to talk back. I claimed this legacy of defiance, of will, of courage, affirming my link to female ancestors who were bold and daring in their speech. Unlike my bold and daring mother and grandmother, who were not supportive of talking back, even though they were assertive and powerful in their speech, bell hooks as I discovered, claimed, and invented her was my ally, my support.

15   That initial act of talking back outside the home was empowering. It was the first of many acts of defiant speech that would make it possible for me to emerge as an independent thinker and writer. In retrospect, "talking back" became for me a rite of initiation, testing my courage, strengthening my commitment, preparing me for the days ahead—the days when writing, rejection notices, periods of silence, publication, ongoing development seem impossible but necessary.

Moving from silence into speech is for the oppressed, the colonized, the exploited, and those who stand and struggle side by side a gesture of defiance that heals, that makes new life and new growth possible. It is that act of speech, of "talking back," that is no mere gesture of empty words, that is the expression of our movement from object to subject—the liberated voice.

UNDERSTANDING THE TEXT

1. What role did hooks's upbringing as a Black girl have on her beliefs about speaking out? In what ways have her race and gender influenced her thinking about herself and the need to speak out?

2. How did hooks come to writing as a young girl? In what way is her writing related to her upbringing among Black women? What purpose did writing serve for her?

3. What was hooks's reaction to the intense criticisms of her first book, *Ain't I A Woman?* What lessons did she learn from those criticisms? In what ways is this learning on her part important to her larger point about speaking out?

4. Why did hooks feel as though she was not a writer, even after publishing several articles and books? What connection does this feeling have to her upbringing? What might it suggest about writing and the risks associated with it?

5. In paragraph 14, hooks explains why she chose to write under her pseudonym bell hooks. What do you think her choice might reveal about the risks associated with challenging power through writing?

EXPLORING THE TEXT

1. hooks refers to Black women who write as "us." What does that way of referring to herself suggest about how hooks imagines her audience for this essay? Do you think she is writing exclusively for other Black women? Why or why not? If so, do you think her essay can still speak to other kinds of readers? Explain, citing specific passages to support your answer.

2. At one point in her essay, hooks states that she writes "to bear witness to the primacy of resistance struggle in any situation of domination (even within family life)." In what way do you think her essay does (or does not) bear witness? Do you agree with her about the importance of doing so? Why or why not? Do you think your own racial background and gender have anything to do with your answer to that question? Explain. How does "bearing witness" challenge power?

3. hooks claims that she endured intense criticism after her first book, *Ain't I A Woman?*, was published. Based on what you know about her and on your reading of this essay, why do you think she was criticized? What might such criticisms suggest about her message?

4. What do you think hooks's essay suggests about writing as a way to speak out and challenge power?

5. hooks tries hard to write in a way that is accessible to the widest possible audience and not to write in a way that only scholars can understand. Based on her writing in this essay, do you think she succeeds? Explain, citing specific passages to support your answer.

ENTERING THE CONVERSATIONS

1. Write an essay for an audience of your classmates in which you tell the story of an experience in which you were silenced in the way that hooks describes being silenced in this essay.

2. In a group of classmates, share the stories you wrote for Question 1. Examine the different situations in which each of you felt silenced or unable to speak out. Can you iden-

tify any similarities in those situations? Are there differences based on race, ethnicity, gender, class, or similar factors? What do these stories reveal about the risks and benefits of speaking out in certain situations? Now, drawing on this discussion and the essays written by you and your classmates, write an editorial for your local newspaper (or your school newspaper) about what it means to speak out.

3. Think about social or political issues that matter most to you. Have you ever felt silenced on those issues—unable to voice your opinion about them in certain circumstances (such as in the experience you might have written about for Question 1)? Now consider ways in which you might speak out on those issues. Using whatever medium or means seems appropriate to you, and considering how your voice might affect your intended audience, make a statement about an issue of concern to you. You might consider writing a letter to the editor of your local newspaper or using some other medium to express your view, such as a flyer or pamphlet that might be posted on your campus, a website, or even a video (assuming you have access to the appropriate technology).

4. With a group of classmates, review the documents or materials you created for Question 3. Examine them not only for the messages they convey but also for the impact that those messages might have on a specific audience, intended or not. Consider how ethical each effort to speak out is (or isn't). Try to draw conclusions about the consequences of speaking out on complex and important social or political issues.

Growing up in the 1960s and 1970s, I watched television news reports of the protests against the Vietnam War and of the civil rights marches and demonstrations. Sometimes during these news reports, my parents would complain about the protesters. Like most adults I knew then, my parents did not participate in demonstrations or protests, and they criticized others for doing so. I can remember them arguing vigorously with a cousin who joined civil rights marches in

American Splendor

Washington, D.C. All my relatives are patriotic and believe deeply in American democracy. My father served in the Air Force during the Korean War, and he sometimes talked about how he and his fellow servicemen and servicewomen helped keep the United States free. Yet he and most of my other relatives criticized protesters who voiced their views by demonstrating and marching.

I wonder what my relatives might think about the following essay by Chisun Lee, in which Lee writes "nothing is more American than protest." Lee believes that "protest is the essence of American democracy." Writing during the U.S. presidential election in 2004, Lee questions the government's efforts to control or prevent demonstrations, especially those against the war in Iraq. By raising questions about these efforts to control protest, Lee raises larger questions about the importance of challenging power. These are important questions, especially since new forms of political protest and dissent, such as the use of the Internet, have emerged in recent years. Lee's essay reminds us that democracy can be messy, and even when Americans agree that democracy is good, they can disagree about how it should be done.

Chisun Lee is a staff writer for the Village Voice, in which this essay first appeared in 2004. ▼

CHISUN LEE

Nothing is more American than protest. Protest is what enables this nation, in its angriest moments, to progress, not self-destruct. It converts the despair of minorities into demands, turning the rage against oppression into an impetus for transformation. It makes a nation of individualists come together in struggle against exploitation and injustice. It keeps presidents from becoming monarchs and people from becoming subjects. Protest is the essence of American democracy.

Next month, when the Republican convention comes to New York City, protest will get put to the test. The sitting president will accept his party's nomination to run for re-election to the highest office in the nation. Hundreds of thousands of ordinary people will join their voices in a united, public cry: Get George W. Bush out.

Democracy doesn't get bigger than this.

Not that anyone would know it at the moment. Somehow the debate over protest at the convention has dwindled to squabbles over lawn upkeep and police efficiency. Officials have masterfully reduced the discussion to the bureaucracy-speak of "negotiation," trapping

CHISUN LEE, "AMERICAN SPLENDOR." FROM *VILLAGE VOICE*, JULY 20, 2004.
HTTP://WWW.VILLAGEVOICE.COM/PRINT/ISSUES/0429/LEE.PHP

protest organizers, who are trying to secure people enough space to avoid mass arrests, into the same prosaic terms. Many otherwise politically active New Yorkers are even plotting to skip town, and a whole segment of the population seems to have grown accustomed to e-dissenting from the comfort of home.

5   Which would be a tragedy: Not in a generation has the need for protest been so great.

Since the last presidential election, the U.S. has lost nearly a thousand young lives in a deeply controversial war with no certain end. Civil rights and civil liberties—won through some of the most pitched protests in the nation's history—are being revised in the name of security. Problems of poverty, education, and health care remain dangerously acute.

The nation is emerging from a period of post-9-11 crisis, ready to declare affirmatively, not just reactively, what it wants to be. The key question is: How much say will ordinary people have in setting the nation's course?

The power of protest is a funny thing to try to describe. You know it when you see it. You only really get it if you've done it. Once you taste it, you never forget it. And you tend to remember your first.

You might have shown up full of fury, ready to defy the police. You might have been nervous, afraid one of those crazy anarchists you'd heard about would set off a pipe bomb. You might have known it would be huge, since it was for a popular cause, but still you were stunned once you got there, awed by the incomparable feeling you never could have imagined that comes from standing together with thousands of strangers in a single rally for a better world.

10   Or you might have shown up to discover you were just one of a few. You might have felt silly at first, thinking you should never have come. But then you saw the grief in the eyes of the mother whose son was killed by a cop, or the fatigue of the immigrant worker who just couldn't be pushed anymore, or the quiet dignity of a blue-collar crew handing out flyers to save their jobs. And a few people shook your hand and were happy to meet you. And then you were glad you showed up, because you knew for the first time how solidarity feels.

The power of protest is its incredible optimism. Authoritarian types like to paint protesters as outsiders, as antisocial troublemakers who can't live within the lines. But protest is really an almost miraculous expression of faith in the human spirit and in democracy. It is proof that people still believe, despite an abundance of signs to the contrary, that if they just keep trying, the system eventually will work.

It is a miracle of optimism that people protest when a man becomes president without a majority of their votes, rather than storming the halls of government in revolution. It is a miracle of optimism that people

---

CONTEXT: THE 2004 REPUBLICAN NATIONAL CONVENTION
When the Republican Party held its national convention in 2004 to nominate President George W. Bush for reelection, the United States was engaged in a controversial war in Iraq that caused deep disagreements among many Americans. As preparations for the convention were made, authorities and convention organizers were planning to implement some of the most extensive security measures ever used for a political convention, which was being held in New York City, just a short distance away from the site of the terrorist attacks on the World Trade Center on September 11, 2001. At the same time, groups opposed to the war and to the reelection of George W. Bush were planning large demonstrations. As Lee notes in paragraph 4, convention organizers, city officials, and representatives from groups planning to protest negotiated for weeks before the convention, which added to the already widespread concerns about security at the convention. Consider how that context helps shape the way readers might have responded to Lee's essay when it was first published a few weeks before the Republican convention in 2004. To what extent might readers respond differently to her arguments today?

STRATEGIES: REPETITION
In paragraph 12 and the next, Lee uses the same sentence structure for four consecutive sentences, repeating the same clause at the beginning of each sentence ("It is a miracle of optimism that . . ."). What effect does this use of repetition have on you as a reader? Why might Lee have chosen to use repetition at this point in her essay?

CONVERSATIONS: E-DISSENTING

When Lee writes that "a whole segment of the population seems to have grown accustomed to e-dissenting from the comfort of home," she is referring in part to the emergence of dozens of advocacy groups that primarily use the Internet to promote their causes. One such group is MoveOn.org, which became influential during the 2004 U.S. presidential election. This image shows a page from the MoveOn.org website in early 2005, when the group was opposing President George W. Bush's proposal to reform Social Security. Many observers have hailed the emergence of groups like MoveOn.org, considering them an effective way to involve more citizens in political action. Lee seems to suggest here that "e-dissenting" isn't as powerful as traditional marches or demonstrations. In making this suggestion, she is joining an ongoing debate about how to participate in democracy.

© 2005 MoveOn.org

protest when they lose loved ones in a war they believe was corruptly conceived, rather than taking up arms themselves. It is a miracle of optimism that people protest when innocent people keep getting killed by the police, or when the friends of the leaders keep getting richer but everyone else stays poor.

It is the miracle of protest that, despite the undemocratic advantages that wealth and connections bestow in this country, the people sometimes win.

If the dispute over the convention demonstrations goes through the courts, it is unlikely that protest will be discussed as the democratic miracle that it is. Judges are not typically populists, and precedents concerning the right to protest are conservative if not outright hostile. The law generally says that, if the authorities offer some kind of arguable Plan B and utter the words "public safety," they win.

That's what happened when United for Peace and Justice—the huge umbrella organization of protest groups currently making news in its negotiations with city officials—sued over the denial of a permit to march against the invasion of Iraq on February 15, 2003. The court opinions spoke of parade formations and contact people and advance notice of numbers of attendees—all areas where organizers evidently fell short. It was impossible to tell that a desperately urgent question of national policy hung in the balance, and that people were bursting to convey a tremendous message of opposition to the commanders in power.

But the wonder of that moment was, the protesters lived by the rules. Instead of marching, hundreds of thousands dutifully jammed into metal pens and dodged police horses in the stationary rally that officials allowed—one that stretched practically the length of Manhattan. These were democrats, not rebels.

The war still happened. President Bush gave the protests on that day, which numbered 6 million participants worldwide, as much consideration as he might have a postcard sent to the White House by a fourth-grader.

That kind of disdain only adds to the fire. Such is the miracle of protest and democracy: Ignored, the people keep coming. They never give up.

UNDERSTANDING THE TEXT

1. Why does Lee believe that the need for protest was so great during the U.S. presidential election in 2004? What do you think this need for protest suggests about American democracy? What might it suggest about power in U.S. politics?

2. What is the power of protest, according to Lee? Why is it important to democracy? How does this power relate to the power of government?

3. Why is it important that protesters "lived by the rules," as Lee writes in paragraph 16, even when they deeply disagreed with the authorities who set those rules? What does this suggest about power and protest in American society? Do you think Lee is right about this point? Why or why not?

4. What is the difference between "democrats" and "rebels," in Lee's view? Why is this difference important?

EXPLORING THE ISSUES

1. Lee refers to *democracy* several times in her essay. How do you think Lee defines democracy? Do you share her definition? Do you think most Americans do? Explain, citing specific passages to support your answer.

2. In paragraphs 8–10, Lee uses the second person ("you") to describe the power of protest. Why do you think she does so? What is gained by using the second person in this situation? To what extent do you think Lee's use of the second person in this instance contributes to or detracts from the effectiveness of her argument?

3. Lee asserts "the power of protest is its incredible optimism." What exactly does she mean by that statement? What might this statement suggest about her view of people in general? What might it suggest about her view of government? Do you think she's right about protest's optimism? Why or why not?

ENTERING THE CONVERSATIONS

1. In the first paragraph, Lee writes, "Protest is the essence of American democracy." Write an essay in which you discuss and/or respond to this statement.

2. In paragraph 4, Lee mentions "e-dissenting," or using the Internet to engage in political advocacy (see *Conversations: E-Dissenting* on page 488). Search the Internet for the websites of political advocacy groups that have become important participants in political action. Try to find several such sites representing various political viewpoints. Investigate the websites of these groups. Read the explanations of who they are and what they hope to accomplish. Try to find out how they use the Internet to promote their causes. Then write a report on the basis of your research about e-dissenting. Describe the websites you visited. Try to draw conclusions about the role of e-dissenting in political protest and in challenging power. Alternatively, with a group of classmates, create a website for your own advocacy group, applying to your site the lessons you learned by researching the sites of other advocacy groups.

3. Create a flyer containing advice for people who plan to attend a political demonstration or protest march. In your flyer, convey your sense of the role protest plays in American democracy and offer suggestions to protesters for how to engage in protest as you believe they should.

INFOTRAC

4. As political protests have increased in recent years, debates about the appropriateness of protest have also intensified. Using InfoTrac College Edition, the Internet, and any other appropriate resources, find editorials, articles, and essays about political protest in contemporary American society. Try to identify the main arguments for and against protest. Then write a report on the basis of your research. Draw on Lee's essay or any other essays in this chapter as well as on the resources you found through your research. Try to draw your own conclusions about protest in American democracy.

CREATING THEMES: Extending the Conversations

WITH TEXT

1. Drawing on several of the essays in this chapter, write an essay in which you define *power* and discuss how power affects our lives.

2. Write your own statement about an individual's responsibility to the government.

3. Write a conventional academic essay in which you compare the views of Henry David Thoreau, Martin Luther King, Jr., bell hooks, and any other appropriate writers in this chapter regarding resistance to authority. In your essay, identify any major similarities among the writers you chose and discuss the fundamental beliefs that they have about individual rights and government authority. On the basis of your comparison, draw conclusions about resisting government or power.

4. Identify an issue related to power that you think is important but that does not appear in this chapter. Write an essay in which you discuss that issue and examine its importance in contemporary society. In your essay, draw on any of the readings in this chapter that you think are relevant to your topic.

5. Select three or four authors whose essays appear in this chapter and write a dialogue in which these authors discuss power. In your dialogue, try to draw from the essays written by the authors you've selected and focus your dialogue on what you believe are key issues related to power.

WITH MEDIA

1. Many popular television shows depict government or law enforcement. For example, *The West Wing* focuses on presidential power; *Law and Order* tells stories involving law enforcement and legal professionals. Select several such television shows and watch several episodes. Then write an essay in which you discuss how political or legal power—or other kinds of power—is portrayed in these shows. What conclusions can you draw about cultural attitudes regarding power?

2. Using PowerPoint or a similar program, create a visual presentation exploring an important theme that you think runs through several of the readings in this chapter. In your presentation, identify this theme and refer to any of the essays in this chapter that develop the theme. Include whatever visual elements you find appropriate.

3. Artists and others often use images to voice protests or to resist or challenge power. Consider these images as efforts to resist or challenge power. What messages do they convey? How do the images use common images or symbols to make their points? How effective do you think these images are as a way to challenge power? Select several of these images (or other images you can find) and write an essay in which you try to answer these questions. In your essay, discuss what the images you have chosen say about power and examine the strategies used to convey their messages.

Erika Rothenberg, *Freedom of Expression National Monument*, Foley Square, New York, 2004

CREATING THEMES: Extending the Conversations

Draw conclusions about the use of images as a tool for resisting power.

4. Photographs often convey powerful messages about power and protest. Select one or more of the following photographs, or find other appropriate photographs, and examine them for the messages they convey. Analyze the way the images convey their messages. Then write an essay presenting your analysis. Alternatively, take a photograph of your own in which you convey a message about power or protest.

WITH FILM

1. It is not uncommon for popular films to portray government power as sinister and oppressive. For example, *The X-Files* (1998) depicted a vast government conspiracy involv-ing experiments to create a race of human-alien hybrids. Films like *Enemy of the State* (1998) depict ordinary citizens caught up in a web of government secrecy and clandestine power, and some films about historical events suggest the existence of similar conspiracies—for example *JFK* (1991). Even classic films, such as *Mr. Smith Goes to Washington* (1939), portray government as somehow less honest than the ordinary citizen. Select several such films and analyze those films for what they suggest about government and its power. Then write an essay presenting your analysis. Draw conclusions about what these films might reveal about American attitudes regarding government power.

2. Many films have been made about famous leaders or resistance movements. Among such films are *Gandhi* (1982) and the more recent film about Cuban revolutionary Che Guevera, *The Motorcycle Diaries* (2004). Select one of these films, or a similar film about a historical figure or resistance movement, and examine how that film portrays the workings of power and especially the challenges to power. Then write an essay in which you discuss what the film suggests about power and resistance to power. In your essay, you might draw on the essays by Henry David Thoreau (page 449) and Martin Luther King, Jr. (page 466) or other essays from this chapter.

© Suzanne Kreiter/The Boston Globe

© Tom Hood/AP Photo

© Photodisc Blue

Chapter 10 Spaces

WHILE I WAS WORKING ON THIS CHAPTER IN 2005, I LEARNED THAT THE BRILLIANT AMERICAN PLAYWRIGHT ARTHUR MILLER DIED AT HIS HOME IN CONNECTICUT. MILLER WAS THE AUTHOR OF THE CLASSIC PLAYS *DEATH OF A SALESMAN* AND *THE CRUCIBLE,* WHICH YOU MAY HAVE BEEN ASKED TO READ IN SCHOOL. GIVEN MILLER'S STATURE

a writer, his passing was an important event, and news organizations reported extensively on it. But one radio report I heard stood out for me: an interview with Tom Cole, a friend of Miller's who was in the house that Miller lived in when he wrote *Death of a Salesman.* Cole described the small, cabinlike studio that Miller built near the main house on his land. According to Cole, Miller had the idea for his famous play before he began building the studio, but it wasn't until the studio was completed that he could actually write the play. Cole told the interviewer that as soon as Miller finished building his studio, he put down his tools and began writing, stopping

> I have asked my students to de-scribe how they write, and most of them confide a need to write in a certain place with certain features.

only when he had finished the first act of the play—forty-eight hours later.

I was struck by this report because it sounded so familiar. There are many stories of famous writers working in a special room or place. I re-member visiting Nathaniel Hawthorne's home in Salem, Massachusetts, which he called "the Old Manse," and being shown the room where Hawthorne wrote some of his most famous sto-ries. Scott Russell Sanders, whose essay appears in this chapter, has a small cabin on his land in rural Indiana that he built specifically for writ-ing. My guess is that when you write, you like to do so in a certain place: at your desk, perhaps with a special kind of music playing, or maybe sitting on a favorite chair with a yellow legal pad or a laptop computer. Over the years, I have

asked my students to describe how they write, and most of them confide a need to write in a certain place with certain features. Recently, I was surprised to learn that I, too, have this need. When my family and I moved to a new home, I gave up a room that had been my study for nine years. It had certain features that seemed to make it especially appropriate for writing: built-in bookshelves, a built-in desk, two large windows, and a cozy, quiet atmosphere. Our new home had no extra room for me to use as a study, so I put my desk and some bookshelves in our partially finished basement. But I soon found that I was uncomfortable writing there. Each morning, I would start working there, but after a time, I would take my books, notes, and computer upstairs and work at the kitchen table, which had a view of the backyard through a large back door. For some reason, like Arthur Miller and like most of my students, I needed a certain kind of physical space where I could feel comfortable writing.

This need for creating a special place is not limited to writers, of course. Human beings in general seem to have a natural desire to create special places for themselves where they can

> Human beings in general seem to have a natural desire to create special places for themselves.

work, find privacy or solitude, worship, remem-ber, commemorate certain people or events, or just live out their daily routines. Drive through any city or town and you will see parks, monu-ments, and special buildings—spaces that people have created for special purposes. If you have visited any national parks, such as Yellowstone National Park in Wyoming, the first national park ever created, then you have been to natural or wild places that have been set aside as special. And if you have visited the great monuments in Washington, D.C., or a famous battlefield, such as Gettysburg in Pennsylvania or the Little Bighorn in Montana, you have seen a different kind of space, set aside to memorialize historical figures or events. These are sacred spaces, just as a church or temple or mosque is sacred. And they matter deeply in our lives. If you think about a place like Jerusalem in the Middle East and the often bloody conflicts that have been fought there for centuries, you get a sense of how important these spaces can be.

This chapter examines the significance of such spaces. The three clusters in the chapter focus on three ways of thinking about the spaces we create and use and value. The writers whose essays are included in this chapter describe many different kinds of spaces, and they offer different ways of thinking about our relationship to the physical and imagined spaces that are important to us, from wilderness to cities, from wide open spaces to the cozy rooms where writers write to the virtual world of the Internet. I hope these essays help you better understand the important spaces in your own life—including your own writing spaces.

CREATING SPACES

MOVE-IN DAY ON COLLEGE CAMPUSES IS A KIND OF CLINIC ON CREATING SPACES. IF YOU'VE EVER BEEN ON A CAMPUS WHEN STUDENTS ARE MOVING IN FOR THE NEW SCHOOL YEAR, YOU KNOW THAT THE ACTIVITY ISN'T OVER ONCE ALL THE CARS AND VANS ARE UNLOADED. FOR THE NEXT SEVERAL DAYS, STUDENTS WILL ORGANIZE AND DECORATE THEIR DORM ROOMS, AND THEIR CREATIVITY IN DOING SO IS BOUNDLESS.

They will rearrange furniture, hang posters and photos on the walls, set up stereos, computers, televisions, and video games, and stow their clothes and other belongings in every available space. Most dorm rooms that I've seen are small, but their size never seems to limit what students can do in making the rooms comfortable, useful, and unique. If you've ever moved into a dorm, an apartment, or another living space, then you know something about what it means to create a personal space that you will use for living and working. But most of us never think about how complex and interesting this process really is.

What kinds of spaces are these? How do you help create them? And how do they affect your life?

The readings in this cluster invite you to think about just that. They explore some of the many ways in which human beings create the spaces they inhabit and the spaces they use for all kinds of important purposes. In one sense, each of these readings examines a different kind of space that we create. Environmentalist Jack Turner's essay explores the wilderness not so much as a natural space but as an economic space. In other words, he shows how the natural landscape is redefined as an economic space, which affects how we understand and use that landscape. Rhonda Lokeman's essay describes a different kind of space: one that memorializes or commemorates. In this case, Lokeman discusses what should be done at "Ground Zero," the site of the terrorist attacks on the World Trade Center in New York City on September 11, 2001. Like other sites where terrible but important events have occurred, Ground Zero has become a sacred space, one that Americans view and use much differently than other spaces. Will Yandik's essay looks at a much more mundane space: the American lawn. He helps us see that even seemingly ordinary spaces can have more complicated meanings than we might realize. Together, these essays remind us that the spaces we create are as much in our minds as in the physical world around us.

Of course, these essays describe only three of the many different kinds of spaces we imagine, create, and use. As you read these essays, you might also consider some of the other spaces in your life: the classroom space you may be in right now, for example, or the room where you're reading this text, or even the "community space" that is created by participating in the writing and reading activities that this book—and your composition course—invite you to do. What kinds of spaces are these? How do you help create them? And how do they affect your life? These are some of the questions that the essays in this cluster might help you answer.

If you live in the American West or if you have ever visited there, you have a sense of what people mean when they talk about wide-open spaces. It can seem that the prairies and mountains and valleys go on forever. But whenever I have visited the more remote regions of the West, I have always been struck by something else about those wide-open spaces: No matter where you go, you see evidence that people have been there before. And usually, people have been there for something

Economic Nature

other than sightseeing. They have been there for farming or ranching, for mining and logging, for hunting and trapping. Usually, such activities are what we mean when we talk about the vast resources of the West.

That kind of talk concerns writer Jack Turner (b. 1942). As an environmentalist, he is worried about the abuse of the land that is evident everywhere in the West. And he helps us see that the way we talk about the land is a big part of what is wrong with the way we use it. We describe the land as something that is "valuable" in economic terms, as a "resource" that has monetary value, as something to be used rather than cared for. In the following essay, Turner explains why this way of describing the land is at the heart of the environmental problems facing the American West. As he writes, "language is power," and the language we use to describe the land has the power to shape how we think about it and what we do with it. His provocative essay helps us see that the physical spaces around us are shaped by the way we think about them, that our ideas help determine what we see and what we do. That's an important point to keep in mind at a time when some of the environmental problems that Turner refers to in his essay are becoming ever more difficult to solve. (continued)

JACK TURNER

The conservation movement is, at the very least, an assertion that these interactions between man and land are too important to be left to chance, even that sacred variety of chance known as economic law.

—Aldo Leopold

We live surrounded by scars and loss. Each of us carries around a list of particular offenses against our place: a clear-cut, an overgrazed meadow, a road, a dam. Some we grudgingly accept as necessary, others we judge mistakes. The mistakes haunt us like demons, the demons spawn avenging spirits, and the presence of demons and spirits helps make a place our home. It is not accidental that "home" and "haunt" share deep roots in Old English, that we speak of the home of an animal as its haunt, or that "haunt" can mean both a place of regular habitation and a place marked by the presence of spirits. Like scars, the spirits are reminders—traces by which a past remains present.

JACK TURNER, "THE SETTLING OF THE AMERICAN WEST." FROM *THE ABSTRACT WILD*, BY JACK TURNER. © 1996 JOHN S. TURNER. REPRINTED BY PERMISSION OF THE UNIVERSITY OF ARIZONA PRESS.

(continued) *Jack Turner is a mountain guide and former philosophy professor who has written widely on environmental issues. The following essay first appeared in his book* The Abstract Wild *(1996).* ▼

GLOSS: CUTTHROATS AND BROWNS
Turner is referring to a species of trout known as cutthroat that inhabits many rivers and lakes in the American West. Later in this paragraph, he refers to another species of trout, brown trout.

Forty years ago **big cutthroats** cruised the Gros Ventre River of Jackson Hole, Wyoming. Now, in late summer, dust blows up the river bed. It's as dry as an arroyo in Death Valley, a dead river drained by ranchers. Each autumn much of Jackson Lake, the jewel of Grand Teton National Park, is a mud flat baking in the sun, its waters drained to irrigate potatoes. Without good snowfalls each winter the lake could disappear and with it **the big browns,** and with those browns, Gerard Manley Hopkins' "rose moles all in stipple upon trout that swim."[1] The western border of Yellowstone National Park can be seen from outer space, a straight line cut through a once fine forest by decades of clearcutting. From the summits of the Tetons, I see to the west a mosaic of farms scaring the rounded hills and valleys, as though someone had taken a razor to the face of a beautiful woman. Farther west, the sockeye salmon no longer come home from the sea. The rivers are wounded by their absence.

These wounds and scars are not random. We attribute the damage to particular people or corporations or to generalities like industrialization, technology, and Christianity, but we tend to ignore the specific unity that made *these* particular wounds possible. This unity lies in the resource economies of the West: forestry, grazing, mineral extraction, and the vast hydrological systems that support agriculture. Healing those wounds requires altering these economies, their theories, practices, and most deeply and importantly, their descriptions of the world, for at the most fundamental level the West has been wounded by particular uses of language.

Modern economics began in postfeudal Europe with the social forces and intellectual traditions we call the **Enlightenment.** On one level, its roots are a collection of texts. Men in England, France, and Germany wrote books; our Founders read the books and in turn wrote letters, memoranda, legislation, and the Constitution, thus creating a modern civil order of public and private sectors. Most of the problems facing my home today stem from that duality: water rights, the private use of public resources, public access through private lands, the reintroduction of wolves into Yellowstone National Park, wilderness legislation, the private cost of grazing permits on public lands, military overflights, nuclear testing, the disposal of toxic waste, county zoning ordinances—the list is long. We are so absorbed by these tensions, and the means to resolve them, that we fail to notice that our maladies share a common thread—the use of the world conceived of as a collection of resources.

5   Almost everyone agrees the use of public and private resources is out of kilter, but here agreement ends. This absence of agreement is the key to our difficulties, not, for instance, the cost of grazing fees.

1. From Gerard Manley Hopkins' poem "Pied Beauty."

A civil society is marked by a barely conscious consensus of beliefs, values, and ideals—of what constitutes legitimate authority, on what symbols are important, on what problems need resolution, and on limits to the permissible. I think of this consensus as a shared vision of the good. Historically, our shared vision of the good derived from shared experience and interests in a shared place. In the West, these "sharings" have vanished—assuming, of course, they ever existed. We share no vision of the good, especially concerning economic practices. One of many reasons for this is the growing realization that our current economic practices are creating an unlivable planet.

The decline in consensus also erodes trust. Trust is like glue—it holds things together. When trust erodes, personal relations, the family, communities, and nations delaminate. To live with this erosion is to experience modernity.[2] The modern heirs of the Enlightenment believe material progress is worth the loss of shared experience, place, community, and trust. Others are less sanguine. But in the absence of alternatives the feeling of dilemma becomes paramount: most of us in the West feel stuck.

Daniel Kemmis's fine book *Community and the Politics of Place* traces some of the West's current dilemmas to the often conflicting visions of Jefferson and Madison, and no doubt some of our dilemmas can be discussed productively in this context. But I think the problems lie deeper. After all, Jefferson and Madison derived their ideas from the works of Enlightenment figures, especially John Locke and Adam Smith, men whose thought was a mixture of classical science, instrumental reason, and Christian revelation.

The heirs of Locke and Smith are the members of the so-called **Wise Use Movement.** Its vigor derives from an accurate assessment: the social order they believe in *requires* Christian revelation, pre-Darwinian science, pre-particle physics, and a model of reason as the maximization of utility. The accuracy of this assessment, in turn, disturbs both liberals and conservatives who wish to preserve Enlightenment ideals while jettisoning the Christian foundations upon which those ideals rest. Unfortunately, that reduces social theory to economics. As John Dunn concluded twenty-five years ago in *The Political Thought of John Locke,* " 'Lockean' liberals of the contemporary United States are more intimately than they realize the heirs of the egalitarian promise of

2. See Anthony Giddens, *The Consequences of Modernity.* Trust doesn't disappear, but its focus moves from kin and community to abstract systems, especially money and a culture of experts.

CONVERSATIONS: THE ENLIGHTENMENT

When Turner writes that modern economics grows out of "the social forces and intellectual traditions we call the Enlightenment," he is joining a longstanding philosophical debate about how we understand the world and our relationship to it. The Enlightenment is generally considered to encompass a number of intellectual developments during the eighteenth century and later—developments based on the idea that *reason*, as opposed to *belief* or *faith*, is the most important human intellectual trait and can lead not only to a better understanding of the world but also to better societies. (The arguments made in the Declaration of Independence are based on ideas associated with the Enlightenment; James Madison and Thomas Jefferson, whom Turner mentions in paragraph 8, were influenced by Enlightenment ideas.) The "social forces and intellectual traditions" Turner mentions include the rise of modern science, which is based on the idea that the physical world can be described accurately through rigorous observation and experimentation. Some contemporary critics believe that modern science assumes a separation between humans and the world they inhabit, and they argue that this separation is part of the cause of many problems now facing human beings, including serious environmental problems. The separation of the public and private that Turner discusses in this paragraph is also an idea that grew out of the Enlightenment. Later, in paragraph 7, Turner refers to "modernity," which is another way to describe the ideas associated with the Enlightenment. One of those ideas is *progress*, which Turner criticizes in paragraph 7.

Consider how Turner's main arguments are part of these much larger conversations about how we understand ourselves as human beings. Does knowing something about those conversations affect how you might read Turner's essay? Do you need to know about them in order to appreciate Turner's point?

GLOSS: THE WISE USE MOVEMENT

The Wise Use Movement refers to an effort, mostly in the American West, to oppose the preservation of wilderness; the movement advocates using wilderness areas "wisely" for various purposes, including development, logging, farming, and mining in addition to recreation. Notice how Turner bases his criticisms of this movement on his analysis of Enlightenment ideas in the preceding paragraphs.

Calvinism. If the religious purpose and sanction of the calling were to be removed from Locke's theory, the purpose of individual human life and of social life would both be exhaustively defined by the goal of the maximization of utility" (250). That's where we are now. Instead of a shared vision of the good, we have a collection of property rights and utility calculations.

10   Since I am a Buddhist, I do not restrict equality to human beings, nor do I justify it by Christian revelation. Nor do I see any reason to restrict "common" (as in "the common good") or "community" to groups of human beings. Other citizens of the West have different understandings and justifications of these key political terms, so part of the solution to the West's differences involves language.

Between Newton and the present, the language of physical theory changed and our conception of reality has changed with it. Unfortunately, the languages of our social, political, and economic theories have endured despite achieving mature formulation before widespread industrialization, the rise of technology, severe overpopulation, the explosion of scientific knowledge, and globalization of economies. These events altered our social life without altering theories *about* our social life. Since a theory is merely a description of the world, a new set of agreements about the West requires some new descriptions of the world and our proper place in it.

Against this background, environmentalism, in the broadest sense, is a new description of the world. The first imaginings of the movement have led to what *Newsweek* has called "the war for the West." Attorney Karen Budd, who often supports Wise Use agendas, says, "The war is about philosophy," and she's right.[3] The fight is over intellectual, not physical, resources. Environmentalists fight to reduce the authority of certain descriptions—e.g., "private property"— and to extend the authority of other descriptions—e.g., "ecosystem." It is the language of pilgrims who entered the wilderness and found not Him, but the Wild.

These new forces have occupied the border of our minds—strange figures claiming high moral ground, like Sioux along the ridges of the Missouri. It's unsettling. Folks employed in traditional economies are circling the wagons of old values

---

VISUAL CONNECTIONS: GRIDS

Turner discusses the impact of the grid-based survey system that was adopted in the United States in the eighteenth century. He claims the squares on such a grid have no relation to "the biological order of life." Nevertheless, the grid became a powerful way for White settlers to understand the American West and thus to make decisions about how to use the land. It remains so today. Grid maps are used for a variety of purposes, including designing commercial and housing developments, identifying municipal "zones" for specific uses, planning water supply systems, and identifying locations for wells. The image below shows a portion of a typical grid map of part of the Mississippi River Valley. What view of the land might this image reflect? How might it influence the way we "see" the land and its physical features? What assumptions about the land and our relationship to it does this image reflect?

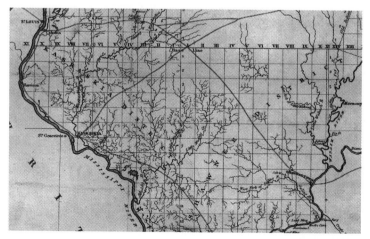

3. Bill Turque, "The War for the West," *Newsweek* 118, no. 14 (Setember 30, 1991): 18; Florence Williams, "Sagebrush Rebellion."

and beliefs. Their tone and posture is defensive, as it must be for those who, hurled into the future, adamantly cling to the past.

II

The pioneers who settled the West imposed their descriptions on a place they called wilderness and on people they called savages. Neither were, by definition, a source of moral value. The great debates of Jefferson, Madison, Hamilton, and Adams were filled with Enlightenment ethics, revelation, science, political theory, and economic theory. The pioneers brought these ideas west to create a moral and rational order in a new land. Their ideas of what was moral and rational were connected by economics.

The government's great surveys redescribed the western landscape. In 1784 the federal government adopted a **system of rectangular surveying** first used by the French for their national survey. The result was a mathematical grid: six-mile squares, one-mile squares.[4] Unfold your topo map and there they are, little squares everywhere. Fly over a town or city and you will see people living in a matrix resembling a computer chip. The grid also produced rectangular farms, national parks, counties, Indian reservations, and states, none of which have any relation to the biological order of life.

The grid delighted the pioneers though; they believed a rationalized landscape was a good landscape. It was a physical expression of order and control—the aim of their morality. The idea, of course, was to sell the grid for cash. Indeed, the selling of the grid was the primary reason for its existence. This shifted the locus of the sacred from place to private property. As John Adams said, "Property must be sacred or liberty cannot exist." So the grid was sold to farmers, ranchers, and businessmen, and the places long sacred to the indigenous population simply vanished behind the grid, behind lines arrogantly drawn on paper. With the places gone, the sense of place vanished too—just disappeared.

The sale didn't work out quite as planned. Some land was sold, but often for as little as $1.25 an acre. Other land passed "free" to those who worked it. What was not sold became public land or was reserved to imprison the remnants of the indigenous population. Much of it was simply given to commercial interests.

The railroads alone received 233 million acres. For comparison, consider that Yellowstone National Park's boundaries encompass 2.3 million acres, and that in 1993 our entire national park system—including parks, national monuments, historic sites, historic parks, memorials, military parks, battlefields, cemeteries, recreational areas, lake shores, seashores, parkways, scenic trails, and rivers, in the lower forty-eight *and* Alaska—totals 79 million acres. Consider also that 59 percent of our wilderness areas (which, combined, total 91 million acres) are smaller than Disney World.

Agricultural practices forever destroyed the autonomy of the land sold to farmers and ranchers. Jefferson wrote that "those who labor in the earth are the chosen people of God, if ever He had a chosen people, whose breasts He has made His peculiar deposit for substantial and genuine virtue. It is the focus in which he keeps alive that sacred fire, which otherwise might escape from the face of the earth"[5] God's chosen

4. Paul Shepard describes this process in "Varieties of Nature Hating," chapter 7 of *Man in the Landscape.*

5. Quoted in Kemmis in *Community and Politics of Place,* 20.

perceive it good to move water around with irrigation systems; they perceive it good to introduce foreign species of plants and animals; they perceive it good to destroy all that is injurious to their flocks and gardens. In short, they perceive as good that which is good for farmers and ranchers.

20   Federalists were less convinced of the inherent goodness of farmers, and in retrospect, of course, they were correct. (After all, farmers had burned women at the stake in New England, and, in other parts of the world still boiled and ate their enemies.) Their solution was a federal system of checks and balances. Just as the free market would transform the pursuit of economic self-interest into the common good, so a federal government would transform the pursuit of political self-interest into the common good. Unfortunately, the pursuit of self-interest merely produced more self-interest, an endless spiral that we now recognize as simple greed.

In short, the social order of the American West was a mishmash of splendid ideals and pervasive blindness—a rationalized landscape settled by Christians holding private property as sacred and practicing agriculture and commerce under the paternal eye of the federal government. Eventually, of course, these forces proved unequal in power and effect.

STRATEGIES: REPETITION
Notice that this and the following four paragraphs all begin with the same sentence: "Things change." Consider why Turner might begin five consecutive paragraphs with the same brief sentence. What might this repetition accomplish at this point in his essay? How does the repetition of this brief sentence relate to the ideas expressed in these paragraphs?

Things change. Governmental regulations, commercial greed, and the expanding urban population gobbled up family farms, ranches, and communities, and left in their place industrial agriculture, large tracts of empty land held by banks, subdivisions, and malls. In Wyoming, for instance, only 2 percent to 4 percent of jobs now depend on agriculture.

Things change. The little squares got smaller and smaller as the scale of the social order changed. First there was the section, then the acre, then the hundred-foot lot, then wall-to-wall town houses, then condos. Last year the town of Jackson, Wyoming, contemplated building three-hundred-square-foot housing—about the size of a zoo cage. Most people live in tiny rented squares and the ownership of sacred property is an aging dream. The moral force of private property, derived from owning land, usually large amounts of land, has dropped accordingly. For most people, the problems connected with large holdings of private land are inconsequential. Asking citizens to lament the government's incursion into private-property rights increasingly obliges them to feel sorry for the rich, an obligation that insults their sense of justice.

25   Things change. The federal system of checks and balances consistently stalls and sabotages federal legislation, making hash of federalism. Every time Congress meets, it is pressured to gut the Clean Air Act and the EPA. Despite widespread regional and national support, twenty years elapsed between the passage of the Endangered Species Act and the reintroduction of wolves in Yellowstone.

Things change. Even the mathematical grid is under attack. The idea that our social units should be defined by mathematical squares projected upon Earth from arbitrary points in space appears increasingly silly. One result is the interest in bioregionalism, the view that drainage, flora, fauna, land forms, and the spirit of a place should influence culture and social structure, define its boundaries, and ensure that evolutionary processes and biological diversity persist.

Things change. A new generation of historians has redescribed our past, deflating the West's myths with rigorous analysis of our imperialism, genocide, exploitation, and abuse; our vast hierarchies of wealth and poverty; the collusion of the rich and the government, especially over water; the biological and ecological ignorance of many farmers, ranchers, and capitalists; and, finally, how our old histories veiled the whole mess with nods to Republican and Jeffersonian ideals. Anyone who bothers to read the works of Donald Worster, Dee Brown, Patricia Nelson Limerick, and Richard White will be stripped forever of the comfortable myths of pioneer and cowboy.[6]

Few, I believe, would deny these changes, and yet in our public discourse of hearings and meetings and newspaper editorials we continue to trade in ideas appropriate to a small homogeneous population of Christian agriculturists occupying large units of land. We continue to believe that politicians represent people, that private property assures liberty, and that agriculture, commerce, and federal balances confer dignity and respect on the West and its people. Since this is largely illusion, it is not surprising that we face problems.

Only one widely shared value remains—money—and this explains our propensity to use business and economics rather than moral debate and legislation to settle our differences. When "the world" shrinks into a rationalized grid stuffed with resources, greed goes pandemic.

Many conservation and preservation groups now disdain moral persuasion, and many have simply given up on government regulation. Instead, they purchase what they can afford or argue that the market should be used to preserve everything from the ozone layer to biodiversity. They offer rewards to ranchers who allow wolves to den on their property, they buy trout streams, they pay blackmail so the rich will not violate undeveloped lands. They defend endangered species and rain forests on economic grounds. Instead of seeing modern economics as the problem, they see it as the solution.

This rejection of persuasion creates a social order wherein economic language (and its extensions in law) exhaustively describes our world and, hence, *becomes* our world. Moral, aesthetic, cultural, and spiritual orders are then merely subjective tastes of no social importance. It is thus no wonder that civility has declined. For me this new economic conservation "ethic" reeks of cynicism—as though having failed to persuade and woo your love, you suddenly switched to cash. The new economic conservationists think they are being rational; I think they treat Mother Nature like a whorehouse.

Ironically, the Enlightenment and civil society were designed to rescue us from such moral vacuums. The Enlightenment taught that human beings need not bow to a force beyond themselves, neither church nor king. Now we are asked to bow to markets and incentives.

Shall we bow to the new king? Can the moral concerns of the West be resolved by economics? Can new incentives for

6. See Worster, *Under Western Skies;* Brown, *Bury My Heart at Wounded Knee;* Limerick, *The Legacy of Conquest;* and White, *It's Your Misfortune and None of My Own.*

30

CONTEXT: GREEN CAPITALISM
In this paragraph and paragraph 29, Turner criticizes the idea that market forces can be used to preserve the environment. One example of this "green capitalism" is the buying and selling of "pollution rights" by large industrial concerns whose operations pollute the air or water. Using this approach, which the U.S. government recently began to implement, companies are given the rights to cause a specified amount of pollution. They are not allowed to exceed that specified amount, but they can purchase the rights to cause additional pollution from other companies, which can profit from selling all or part of their pollution rights. In this way, advocates of this approach say, total pollution limits can be set, and the market will then force companies to stay within those limits or pay for the rights to exceed the limits. New Resource Economics, an organization Turner describes in the following paragraph, is one group that supports this green capitalist approach to environmental protection.

recycling, waste disposal, and more efficient resource use end the environmental crisis? Can market mechanisms restore the quality of public lands? Does victory lie in pollution permits, tax incentives, and new mufflers? Will **green capitalism** preserve biodiversity? Will money heal the wounds of the West?

One group that answers these questions in the affirmative is New Resource Economics. It welcomes the moral vacuum and fills it with markets and incentives. As economic theory it deserves scrutiny by economists. I am not an economist but a mountaineer and desert rat. Nonetheless, I shall have my say even though the word "economics" makes me hiss like Golem in Tolkien's *The Hobbit:* "I hates it, I hates it, I hates it *forever.*" For I believe classical economic theory, and all the theories it presupposes, is destroying the magic ring of life.

III

In the winter of 1992 I flew to Seattle at the generous invitation of the Foundation for Research on Economics and the Environment to attend a conference designed to acquaint environmental writers with the ideas of New Resource Economics. The conference was held amidst a mise-en-scène of assurance and power—tasteful, isolated accommodations, lovely meals, good wine. I felt like a barbarian called to Rome to applaud its splendor.

35   The best presentations were careful, devastating analyses of the inefficiency and incompetence of the U.S. Forest Service. In sharp contrast were other presentations with vague waves at the preferred vocabulary of self-interest: incentives, market, liberty. They exuded an attitude of *"You see!"* as though the realm of sylvan possibilities was limited to two choices: socialism or New Resource Economics. They were Eric Hoffer's true believers, folks who had seen the light and are frustrated and angry that others fail to see economics as the solution to our environmental plight.

I not only failed to see the light, I failed to understand what was new about New Resource Economics. The theory applies ideas about markets that are now more than two hundred years old. After a while I had the feeling of watching the morally challenged tinker with notions rapidly disappearing over the horizon of history as they attempted to upgrade one antiquated idea into another. And yet I have little doubt they will succeed.

Having just flown over the devastated forests east of Seattle, I wanted to scream, "See the fate of the Earth, the rape of the land!"—but I knew they would respond calmly with talk of incentives and benefits and inefficiency.

Finally I understood. The conference's hidden agenda was to persuade environmental writers to describe nature with an economic vocabulary. They had a theory, and like everyone with a theory, they were attempting to colonize with their theoretical vocabulary, thus eliminating other ways of describing the world.

The conference literature reeked of colonization. Vernon L. Smith's paper, *Economic Principles in the Emergence of Humankind,* describes magic, ritual, and foraging patterns in hunter-gatherer cultures with terms like "opportunity cost," "effort prices," and "accumulated human capital."[7] Michael Rothchild, in *Bionomics: Economy as Ecosystem,* extends economic vocabulary to ecosystems and animal behavior; a

---

7. Opening address at the 1991 Mont Pelerin Society Meeting, Big Sky, Montana.

niche becomes an organism's "profession," its habitat and food "basic resources," its relations to habitat simply a part of the "economy of nature."

In *Reforming the Forest Service,* Randal O'Toole claims that "although the language 40 used by ecologists differs from that of economists, it frequently translates into identical concepts. Where economists discuss efficiency, decentralization, and incentives, ecologists discuss the maximum power principle, diversity, and feedback loops." O'Toole also maintains that "these very different terms have identical meanings," and he concludes that "ecological systems are really economic systems, and economic systems are really ecological systems" (193).

The redescription of everything with economic language is characteristic of those who sit in the shade of the Chicago school of economics. Thus Richard Posner, in *The Economic Aspects of Law,* colonizes legal issues with economic vocabulary. Regarding children, Posner thinks "the baby shortage and black market are the result of legal restrictions that prevent the market from operating as freely in the sale of babies as of other goods. This suggests as a possible reform simply eliminating the restriction."[8] Bunker, Barnes, and Mosteller's *Costs, Risks, and Benefits of Surgery* does the same for medical treatment.

Indeed, all areas of our social life have been redescribed in economic language. If you like the theory in one area, you will probably like it everywhere. Nor is economic redescription limited to social issues. For example, Robert Nozick, in *The Examined Life,* applies economic language to the question of why we might love our spouses.

> Repeated trading with a fixed partner with special resources might make it rational to develop in yourself specialized assets for trading with that partner (and similarly on the partner's part toward you); and this specialization gives some assurance that you will continue to trade *with that party* (since the invested resources would be worth much less in exchanges with any third party). Moreover, to shape yourself and specialize so as to better fit and trade with that partner, and therefore to do so less well with others, you will want some commitment and guarantee that the party will continue to trade with you, a guarantee that goes beyond the party's own specialization to fit you. (77–78)

In a footnote, Nozick says, "This paragraph was suggested by the mode of economic analysis found in Oliver Williamson, *The Economic Institutions of Capitalism.*"

Why stop with love? In *The New World of Economics* by McKenzie and Tullock, sex becomes a calculated rational exchange.

> [I]t follows that the quantity of sex demanded is an inverse function of price. . . . The reason for this relationship is simply that the rational individual will consume sex up to the point that the marginal benefits equal the marginal costs. . . . If the price of sex rises relative to other goods, the consumer will "rationally" choose to consume more of the other goods and less sex. (Ice cream, as well as many other goods, can substitute for sex if the relative price requires it.)[9]

8. Quoted in Kenneth Lux, *Adam Smith's Mistake,* 202.

9. Quoted in Lux, 203.

So, many men are bores, and what to do? Why bother with arguments, why not just giggle? Unfortunately, too much is at stake.

If we are to preserve a semblance of democracy in the West, we must become crystal clear about how economists colonize with their language.

45 To start, look at an example of redescription by a theory I disapprove of. Consider, for instance, psycho-babble.

"What did you do today?"

"I cleaned my desk."

"Ah yes, being *anal compulsive* again."

"No, it was just a mess."

50 "No need to be *defensive*."

"I'm not being *defensive*, I'm just disagreeing with you."

"Yes, but you disagree with me because you have an *unresolved conflict* with your father."

"No, I always got along well with Dad."

"Of course you believe that, but the conflict was *unconscious*."

55 "There was no conflict!"

"I am not your father! Please don't *cathect* your speech with *projected aggression*."

Ad infinitum. Ad nauseam.

Resource, market, benefits, rational, property, self-interest function the same way as *conflict, unconscious, cathect,* and *projected aggression.* They are simply the terms a particular theory uses to describe the world. By accepting those descriptions, you support and extend the theory. You could decide to ignore the theory, or conclude that the theory is fine in its limited context but shouldn't be extended into others. But if we don't want the fate of our forests decided by bar graphs, we need to cease talking about forests as measurable resources. That does not require you to stop talking to your investment banker about the bar graphs in her analysis of your portfolio.

Economists and scientists have conned us into speaking of trees as "resources," wilderness as a "management unit," and picas gathering grass for the winter because of "incentives." In accepting their descriptions, we allow a set of experts to define our concerns in economic terms and predetermine the range of possible responses. Often we cannot even raise the issues important to us because the economic language of others excludes our issues from the discussion. To accept this con emasculates not only radical alternatives, but all alternatives. Every vocabulary shapes the world to fit a paradigm. If you don't want nature reduced to economics, then *refuse to use its language.*

60 This process of theoretical redescription has been termed "colonization" because it privileges one description of the world and excludes others. The Sioux say the Black Hills are "sacred land," but they have found that "sacred land" does not appear in the language of property law. There is no office in which to file a claim for sacred land. If they filed suit, they'd discover that the Supreme Court tends to protect religious belief but not religious practices in a particular place—a very Protestant view of religion.

Language is power. Control people's language and you won't need an army to win the war for the West. There will be nothing to debate. If we are conned into describing the life of the Earth and our home in terms of benefits, resources, self-interest, models, and budgets, then democracy will be dead.

What to do? I have five suggestions.

First, refuse to talk that way. It's like smoking, or eating lard. Just say no, and point out that your concerns cannot be expressed in that language.

Second, develop a talent for light-hearted humor using economic language. Here again, Thoreau was a prophet. Henry knew a great deal about economics. He read Locke and his followers in both his junior and senior years at Harvard; he was acquainted with the ideas of Smith, Ricardo, Say, and Franklin; and he helped run his family's pencil business when the industry was becoming increasingly competitive and undergoing rapid change. But Thoreau flips economic language on its head. (Remember, the first chapter of *Walden* is titled "Economy.") His "trade" turns out to be with the Celestial Empire; his "enterprises" are inspecting snow storms and sunrises; he "sinks his capital" into hearing the wind; he "keeps his accounts" by writing in his journal; and he gleefully carries the cost of rye meal out to four decimal places: $1.0475. Nothing is fixed, all is metaphor, even economics.

Third, become so intimate with the process of economic description, you *experience* what's wrong with it. Since economics is a world of resources—physical resources, cultural resources, recreational resources, visual resources, human resources—our wonderfully diverse, joyful world must be reduced to measurable resources. This involves abstraction, translation, and a value. Just as time is abstracted from experience and rendered mechanical (the clock) so it can be measured, space is abstracted from place and becomes property: measurable land. In the same way, trees are abstracted into board-feet, wild rivers are abstracted into acre-feet, and beauty is abstracted into a scene whose value is measured by polls.

Economics reduces everything to a unit of measurement because it requires that everything be commensurate—"capable of being measured by a common standard"—its standard. The variety of these calculable units may be great—board-feet, time, tons, hours—but all of these units can be translated into a common value similar to the way different languages can be translated. Both types of translation require something common. In linguistic translation, it is meaning; in economic translations, it is money—not the change in your pocket, but the stuff that blips on computer screens and bounces off satellite dishes from Germany to Japan in less than a second. An hour's labor is worth a certain amount of money; so is three hundred board-feet of redwood.

Once everything is abstracted into commensurate units and common value, economic theory is useful. If the value of one kind of unit (computer chips) grows in value faster than another kind of unit (board-feet), economic theory says translate board-feet into money into computer chips. In ordinary English: Clear-cut the last redwoods for cash and buy Intel stock. If you don't like deciding the fate of redwoods by weighing the future of Intel, then you probably won't like economics.

Refuse these three moves—the abstraction of things into resources, their commensurability in translatable units, and the choice of money as the value of the units—and economic theory is useless.

Once you understand the process, it's easy to recognize examples. For instance, in *Reforming the Forest Service,* Randal O'Toole describes walking in the mountains as a wilderness experience using a recreational resource that generates benefits: cash and jobs (206). These benefits are compared to other possible uses of the resource, say, grazing and logging, that generate other benefits. The benefits can then be compared. This provides a rational basis for budget maximization. Your walk in the Tetons becomes, by redescription, an economic event.

70   A fourth way to subvert economic language is to realize that nothing of great value is either abstract or commensurate. Start with your hand. The workman's compensation office can tell you the value of your hand in dollars. Consider your daughter. An insurance company or litigation lawyer can tell you her value in dollars. What is your home place worth? Your lover's hair? A stream? A species? Wolves in Yellowstone? Carefully imagine each beloved person, place, animal, or thing redescribed in economic language. Then apply cost-benefit analysis. What results is a feeling of sickness familiar from any forest sale or predator-control proposal. It is the sickness of being forced to use a language that ignores what matters in your heart.

Finally, realize that describing life—the completely individual, unique here-now alive *this*—with abstractions is especially dissonant. Consider the "resources" used in a biology class. The founder of experimental physiology, Claude Bernard, said that the man of science "no longer hears the cry of animals, he no longer sees the blood that flows, he sees only his idea and perceives only organisms concealing problems which he intends to solve."[10] He sees only the idea that will give him something to do in the world. Meanwhile the screams of animals in laboratory experiments are redescribed as "high-pitched vocalizations."

In an extraordinary essay, "Pictures at a Scientific Exhibition," William Jordon, an entomologist, describes his graduate education and the ghastly (his word) treatment of animals it required.

> Fifteen years ago I saw several of my peers close down their laboratory for the evening, and as they cleaned up after the day's experimentation they found that three or four mice were left over. The next experiments were not scheduled for several weeks, and *it wasn't worth the cost and effort to keep the mice alive until then.* My friends simply threw the extras into a blender, ground them up, and washed them down the sink. This was called the Bloody Mary solution. Several days ago I talked with another old peer from my university days, and she informs me that the new, humane method for discarding extra mice in her lab is to seal them in a plastic bag and put it in the freezer.
>
> I repeat: the attitude toward nonhuman life has not changed among experimental biologists. Attitude is merely a projection of one's values, and their values have not changed; they do not respect life that is not human. (199, my emphasis)

Science, including economics, tends to reduce nonhuman life to trash. The screaming animals, the dead coyotes, the Bloody Mary mice, the stumps, the dead rivers—all are connected by these processes of abstraction, commensurability, and financial value. There is no logical necessity for us to describe the world this way. The Apaches didn't do it, and we need to reach a point where we don't do it either.

10. Quoted in Evernden, *The Natural Alien,* 16.

We need to find another way of describing the world and our experience in it. Leave this pernicious, mean-spirited way of talking behind. One of my heroes said he could imagine no finer life than to arise each morning and walk all day toward an unknown goal forever. **Basho** said this *is* our life. So go for a walk and clear the mind of this junk. Climb right up a ridge, over the talus and through the whitebark pine, through all those charming little grouse wortleberries, and right on into the blue sky of Gary Snyder's *Mountains and Rivers Without End:*

> *the blue sky*
> *the blue sky*
>
> *The Blue Sky*
> is the land of
>
> OLD MAN MEDICINE BUDDHA
>
> where the eagle
> that flies out of sight,
>
> *flies.*[11]

GLOSS: BASHO
Seventeenth century Japanese poet Matsuo Basho is considered a master of haiku, a specialized form of poetry.

Works Cited

Brown, Dee. *Bury My Heart at Wounded Knee.* New York: Henry Holt, 1970.

Dunn, John. *The Political Thought of John Locke.* New York: Cambridge University Press, 1969.

Evernden, Neil. *The Natural Alien.* Toronto: University of Toronto Press, 1993.

Giddens, Anthony. *The Consequences of Modernity.* Stanford, CA: Stanford University Press, 1990.

Jordan, William. "Pictures at a Scientific Exhibition." In *Divorce Among Gulls: An Uncommon Look at Human Nature.* San Francisco: North Point Press, 1991.

Kemmis, Daniel. *Community and the Politics of Place.* Norman, OK: University of Oklahoma Press, 1990.

Limerick, Patricia Nelson. *The Legacy of Conquest: The Unbroken Past of the American West.* New York: W. W. Norton, 1987.

Lux, Kenneth. *Adam Smith's Mistake.* Boston: Shambhala, 1990.

Nozick, Robert. *The Examined Life.* New York: Simon and Schuster, 1990.

O'Toole, Randal. *Reforming the Forest Service.* Washington, D.C: Island Press, 1988.

Rothchild, Michael. *Bioeconomics: Economy as Ecosystem.* New York: Henry Holt: 1992.

Shepard, Paul. *Man in the Landscape: A Historic View of the Esthetics of Nature.* College Station, TX: Texas A&M University Press, 1991.

11. Snyder, *No Nature,* 80.

White, Richard. *It's Your Misfortune and None of My Own.* Norman, OK: University of Oklahoma Press, 1993.

Williams, Florence, "Sagebrush Rebellion 2." *High Country News* 24(3) (Feb. 24, 1992).

Worster, Donald. *Under Western Skies: Nature, and History in the American West.* New York: Oxford University Press, 1992.

UNDERSTANDING THE TEXT

1. What is the "common thread" that Turner sees in the various environmental problems we face today? Why is it important to understand this common thread, in Turner's view?

2. In what sense are the controversies about the environment really fights about "intellectual resources" rather than physical resources, according to Turner? Why is language an important part of these fights? What does Turner mean when he states that addressing these controversies will require "new descriptions of the world and our proper place in it" (par. 11)?

3. Why does Turner call economics "the new king" (par. 32)? What problems does he see with relying on economics to solve environmental problems? Do you agree with him? Why or why not?

4. What are Turner's chief complaints about the conference that he attended on economics and the environment (par. 34)? How do his complaints about this conference relate to his larger argument about protecting the environment?

5. Turner offers five suggestions for resisting the use of economic language to describe the land (par. 62–71). Why does he insist on resisting economic language in this way? What do his five suggestions reveal about his own values regarding the land and our relationship to it?

EXPLORING THE ISSUES

1. Turner refers to himself as a resident of the American West, and he draws from his experiences living in the West to help make his arguments. To what extent do you think his identifying himself as a "Westerner" influences your response to his argument? Do you think Turner expects readers who

are not from the West to react differently to his argument than readers who live in the West? Explain, citing specific passages to support your answer.

2. Notice the epigraph by Aldo Leopold at the beginning of this essay. Why do you think Turner included this quotation? What basic ideas or beliefs does it introduce that are relevant to Turner's main argument? Does it make a difference that the quotation is from Aldo Leopold, a famous environmentalist? Explain.

3. Turner uses many quotations from books, poems, and other kinds of texts in his essay, and he refers to many historical events, philosophical ideas, and important political figures. Examine these references. What do you think they contribute to Turner's argument? Do they make his essay more or less effective, in your view? What do these references suggest about Turner as a writer, a thinker, and a person? What might they suggest about his sense of his audience?

4. What criticisms does Turner make of the idea of private property? How does private property contribute to the environmental problems that concern him? Do you think he is right about private property? Why or why not?

ENTERING THE CONVERSATIONS

1. Write an essay in response to Turner's essay. In your essay, draw on your own experiences and on any relevant examples or events that you think are appropriate to address Turner's main argument about defining nature in economic terms.

INFOTRAC

2. Turner bases his argument on his criticisms of Enlightenment ideas and values. Although the Enlighten-

ment was a complicated set of social and intellectual developments and there is much disagreement among scholars about what the Enlightenment means, there is general agreement on some of the main ideas associated with the Enlightenment. Using InfoTrac College Edition, your library, and other appropriate resources (including perhaps faculty members in philosophy or history at your school), investigate the Enlightenment. Try to find out what main ideas are associated with that movement and how those ideas have affected the way we think and act even today. Try also to identify some of the current controversies regarding the Enlightenment—controversies that Turner himself has contributed to. Then write a report about the Enlightenment. In your report, describe this important movement as clearly as you can and discuss the main ideas associated with it. Discuss as well how those ideas still affect us today.

4. Using the Internet or your library, find several newspaper or magazine articles or even television reports about current environmental controversies. If possible, find articles about an environmental controversy in the region where you live. Examine the way the land is described in these articles. What ideas or beliefs about the land are conveyed in these articles? What kind of language is used to describe the land or natural spaces? Then write an essay in which you address such questions. Discuss how language is used to describe the land or the natural environment in popular press reports. On the basis of your analysis, draw conclusions about Turner's argument regarding land as an "economic space."

5. Create a visual representation of Turner's idea of "economic nature." Use any appropriate technology available: a web page, PowerPoint, photography, or similar technology.

"Ground Zero"

Surely, you have heard the old saying, "less
is more." But what exactly does it mean? In
the following essay, journalist Rhonda
Chriss Lokeman offers one answer. In this
case, Lokeman suggests that the less we do
with sacred places, the more we honor what
happened there. Lokeman is writing specifically about Ground Zero in New York City,
the site of the World Trade Center that were
destroyed in the terrorist attacks of September
11, 2001. When she wrote this essay in

Minimalist Memorial Can Do Justice TO 9/11

2004, intense public debate was occurring
about what would be done with that special
place. Because of the scale of the tragedy that
occurred there, the question of what should
be done with the site had great significance
not only for New Yorkers but for Americans
in general. Shortly after the attacks, a special commission was formed to make recommendations about the site, and a number of
proposals were submitted for review. Some
people felt that the best way to honor the people who died at Ground Zero was to rebuild
businesses and residences there so that the
site would become a lively, busy neighborhood again. Others believed that the only
way to honor the dead was to construct some
kind of special memorial there. But what
kind of memorial? Because the spot had become so sacred, that question was difficult to
answer. Lokeman offers her answer: Less is
more. It is an answer that not only prompts
us to think about what a truly sacred space
should look and feel like, but it also raises
larger questions about why we need such
spaces and how we should use (continued)

RHONDA CHRISS LOKEMAN

Sometimes less is more.

Sometimes the austere defies pure definition by introducing a prosperity that, while not currently realized, becomes a richness of raw
emotion that trickles onto the solitude of grief and despair.

Sometimes a cry, once open-mouthed and speechless, becomes audible to all as a primal scream. It comes without warning. There you
stand, visibly vulnerable, reliving the painful past and stunned by your
own humanity in a public space.

We must not forget that sometimes the quiet speaks volumes. We see
it, we hear it, in **the flame that burns "eternal"** at a president's grave.

This has happened with visitors to the Vietnam Veterans Memorial in   5
Washington, D.C. It has happened at the Oklahoma City National
Memorial. It likely will happen years from now in New York City where

(continued) *them. If you have been to Ground Zero, you may have felt some of the emotions that Lokeman describes in this poignant essay. But even if you haven't, you will certainly appreciate her thoughts, for all of us create and visit sacred spaces.*

Rhonda Chriss Lokeman is a writer and editor for Kansas City Star, *in which this essay was first published in 2004.* ◪

STRATEGIES: USING CONTEXT

In these first four paragraphs, despite the vivid physical details that Lokeman includes (such as an "open-mouthed and speechless" cry), she does not refer to a specific place but to a general "public space." Yet as a reader, you probably knew that she was describing a special kind of place like Ground Zero or a war monument. The title is one way that you might have known that. But if you had been reading this when it was first published in early 2004, you would probably have known what Lokeman was referring to even without the reference to 9/11 in the title. That's because at that time there was much discussion about what kind of memorial would be constructed at the site of the terrorist attacks of September 11, 2001. Many well-known architects competed to have their designs used for the site, and there were public hearings in New York to discuss proposals for rebuilding the site. All this was covered in the national press because the events of September 11, 2001, remained so important in American political life. Consider how Lokeman can rely on that context as she decides what information to include—and what to leave out—so that her readers understand her point. This is a good example of how a writer can use the historical context that at the same time inevitably shapes her writing.

GLOSS: THE ETERNAL FLAME

This reference (par. 4) is to the flame that burns on the grave of President John F. Kennedy in Arlington National Cemetery in Virginia. The flame has been burning since Kennedy's burial after he was assassinated in 1963.

last week city officials announced the winning design for the memorial to those slain in the 9/11 attacks at the World Trade Center twin towers.

A wall, just a wall, people said of the Vietnam Veterans Memorial. Many insisted that such seemingly simplistic architecture could not fully interpret the sense of loss during the Southeast Asian conflict.

They pointed to the architect, the twentysomething Maya Lin. Barely old enough to order her first cosmopolitan, her age was seen as proof of her inexperience at the drawing board.

She couldn't be expected to present an authentic representation of a conflict that divided the nation into thirds: those for the war, those against it, and those against the Americans in uniform who returned home.

A nation whose citizens were used to memorializing its war dead with marble, with obelisks, with granite generals on horseback was not ready to try something new. That's what they said at the time.

Then they went to see it. Then they saw Lin's vision. They ran their fingers over the names of the known and the strangers. They took their children there. They wept. Then they were touched deeply in places they had kept locked inside themselves for years.

Something similar happened after the Oklahoma City National Memorial was announced. It called for a row of 168 chairs, one for each victim, and a reflecting pool between two "time gates," one marked 9:01 and the other marked 9:03. These would stand on the site where domestic terrorists detonated a truck bomb at 9:02 a.m. on April 19, 1995. Some saw the design as insufficient for such hallowed ground as the former Alfred P. Murrah Federal Building.

The design team of husband-wife architects Hans Ekkehard Butzer and Torrey Butzer and associate Sven Berg was criticized as unimaginative. Even though the memorial selection jury included eight family members and survivors, some in the public still didn't fully embrace the design. The minimalist style was misconstrued at first as a minimalization of the tragedy.

But when the memorial was open to the public in October 1998, people flocked to it. They saw how at night the 168 chairs, each bearing the name of a victim, were lit from underneath. It was shockingly beautiful for its simplicity.

People saw how the sun reflected on the pool between the twin gates of time. They saw well-behaved little children dip flowers into the water in silence, as if they knew.

Visitors found that the remembrance was actually in three components: the outdoor memorial, a museum and a terrorism institute.

Once again, less was more.

Now, New York City architect Michael Arad's design, "Reflecting Absence," has drawn howls as a lightweight memorial to those slain on Sept. 11, 2001. Its minimalist aesthetic has been declared unsuitable by some survivors and relatives.

VISUAL CONNECTIONS: MINIMALIST MEMORIALS

As Lokeman notes, the designs of the Vietnam Veterans Memorial and Oklahoma City National Memorial were controversial. Some critics complained that they were too simple. The images below show these two memorials. What ideas or feelings do you think are conveyed by the way space is used in each design?

Vietnam Veterans Memorial in Washington, D.C.

Oklahoma City Bombing Memorial

The jury, which consisted of 13 members, including a widow of a victim, has come under fire. What's absent from "Reflecting Absence," some have said, is an image of the brave men and women who sacrificed their lives to save others. The design cannot fully reflect a horror of this magnitude, some have said. Where have we heard this before?

Chosen from among 5,200 entries from 63 countries, Arad's minimalist design is said to belie a tragedy that took nearly 3,000 victims. As originally unveiled, his design features two pools in the towers' footprints. The pools are surrounded by a ribbon featuring the names of those slain on Sept. 11 in New York and the Pentagon as well as those slain after the first tower bombing in 1993. It features an alcove, a place where people can light candles and a cascading water curtain.

This week a revised design will be unveiled. It is hoped that there won't be much tampering with the original concept and that the modifications will be better received.

Arad's design, like other contemporary memorials, reveals a certain psychology necessary in architecture. This ghost in the machinery must help the design appeal not merely to the individual but to the grieving nation as well.

This is no simple task, and it has fallen on 31-year-old shoulders. But, as witnessed before, it can over time and in the right hands be done.

UNDERSTANDING THE TEXT

1. What does Lokeman mean that "sometimes the quiet speaks volumes" (par. 4)? How does this point relate to her larger argument about Ground Zero in New York City?

2. What arguments does Lokeman present in favor of a minimalist approach to memorials? What support does she offer for these arguments? How convincing do you find her arguments? Explain.

3. What is the challenge facing the designer of the memorial to be built at the site of the September 11, 2001, terrorist attacks in New York City, according to Lokeman? What does this challenge suggest about how we understand special places like Ground Zero? What might it suggest about how we create spaces at such locations?

EXPLORING THE ISSUES

1. How would you summarize Lokeman's main point in this essay? Is her main point only about the design of the memorial for Ground Zero in New York City? Or does she have something to say about how we create and use such special places in general?

2. At several points in her essay, Lokeman describes the reactions of people to the special places created as memorials to those who died in war or in events like the attacks of September 11, 2001. What do you think Lokeman's descriptions of these reactions suggest about the importance of such spaces? What

do they suggest about how we create and use these spaces?

3. In writing this essay, Lokeman was joining a national conversation about what should be done at the sites of the terrorist attacks of September 11, 2001. She offers her opinion about the kind of memorial that should be built at Ground Zero, yet she was writing from Kansas City. What do you think her essay suggests about how decisions about special places like Ground Zero are made in the United States? What might it suggest about the role of writing in these larger conversations in U.S. society?

4. In paragraph 20, Lokeman refers to the decision about the memorial at Ground Zero that was to be revealed in January 2004. She writes, "It is hoped that there won't be much tampering with the original concept and that the modifications will be better received." Notice that she does not say, "*I* hope . . ." Instead she uses the passive voice ("It is hoped . . ."). Why do you think she does so? What might be gained or lost by using the passive voice in this situation?

ENTERING THE CONVERSATIONS

1. Using the information in this book and additional information you gather about the memorial to be built at Ground Zero in New York City, write an essay expressing your view of the design of that memorial.

2. Submit a proposal for your own design of a memorial at Ground Zero

in New York City, or some other place, or a memorial commemorating an event you consider important. Use PowerPoint, desktop publishing software, a web page, or any other appropriate medium to present or illustrate your design and explain the features of your design.

3. In a group of classmates, share the proposals you wrote for Question 2. Examine the proposals for what they seem to suggest about how members of your group understand special places and what should be done with them. Discuss each proposal and how it conveys its ideas through the proposed design of the memorial. What might your discussion suggest about how we view the spaces we create at special locations like Ground Zero?

4. Find a memorial or similar sacred space near your school or home and examine the design of that space. What ideas, perspectives, beliefs, or feelings does that space convey? How do specific features of the design convey its ideas or feelings? Write an essay in which you discuss this space and try to answer these questions. If possible, include a photo or some other graphic to illustrate the space you are writing about.

5. On the basis of your work for Question 4, write a letter to your town council or other official body that is responsible for the public spaces in your area in which you express your support for or complaints about the space you described in the essay you wrote for Question 4.

I have come to dislike lawns. When they're taken care of, they look nice. But after years of mowing lawns (first, my father's lawn when I was growing up and then my own lawn) and toiling for hours in the summer sun to eliminate weeds, grow grass in shady spots where it doesn't want to grow, and fertilize the grass that does grow, I have come to see lawn care as a burden and a waste of time. Most Americans seem to disagree with me. In most places, when the weather per-

Ridding THE *American* Landscape OF Lawn

WILL YANDIK

mits, American homeowners spend hours toiling in their lawns. And lawn care is a multibillion-dollar business that keeps growing. Whenever I see someone mowing a lawn or loading bags of fertilizer into the trunk of a car, I can't help but think of all the time Americans spend on this endless task of keeping lawns neat and tidy. So I was pleased when I first read the following essay by Will Yandik. Yandik shares my dislike of lawns. But his reasons are perhaps more complicated than mine. In criticizing the traditional American lawn, Yandik reveals that there's more to the way we think about lawns than it might seem. Although lawns may seem natural to most Americans, Yandik shows that they are in fact artificial in a number of ways and that they reflect certain beliefs about how to use the land; they also contribute to serious environmental and social problems. You may disagree with him (especially if you enjoy doing yard work!), but his analysis helps us see that the spaces we create say a lot about us and our relationship to the land we live on. (continued)

One landscape remains unchallenged in our built environment, a vernacular Virgin Mary, worshiped seasonally by millions—the lawn. Anyone who doubts that Americans are willing to place form ahead of function need only observe an August suburb and its throngs sweating their way to a perfect carpet of green. We cultivate more grass than wheat, corn, or tobacco, with almost 50,000 square miles of grass in the U.S. alone—an area roughly the size of New York State. The lawn's adverse effects on the environment are well documented: chemical pollution and runoff, a voracious appetite for water, mowers that belch hydrocarbons. Yet I suggest another reason, an aesthetic one, to rethink the concept of the lawn. It is an outdated pastoral fantasy, a bland backdrop that hinders the imaginative use of landscape. Much of what we dislike about sprawl is simply lawn. It is time for a change, and architects must be part of that change. After (continued) *Will Yandik (b. 1977) is a freelance writer who has written about landscaping and architecture for numerous publications, including* Preservation *and* Architectural Record, *in which this essay first appeared in 2001.* ▼

CONVERSATIONS: SPRAWL

Yandik writes (par. 1) "much of what we dislike about sprawl is simply lawn." In making that statement, he is joining a much larger conversation about what has come to be called *sprawl*. In the 1990s, the rapid development of rural and wilderness areas into suburbs, corporate office parks, strip malls, so-called big box retailers (such as Wal-Mart), and industrial parks created a variety of environmental concerns, including the loss of wilderness and farmland, water and air pollution, and lifestyle problems, such as the increasing reliance on cars to get to and from the places people need to be every day. Some environmental groups began to identify this problem as "suburban sprawl" and called for initiatives to reduce sprawl. Some states and towns implemented "smart growth" ordinances to limit development or require developers to keep "open spaces" available in their developments. Although Yandik's essay does not address the problem of sprawl directly, his complaints about the typical American lawn are similar to the complaints voiced by opponents of sprawl and advocates of "smart growth." You might consider how much you know about the debates about sprawl and how your knowledge (or lack of it) might affect the way you read his essay.

---

all, the lawn is more architecture than landscape, more design than nature. It is no more natural than the concrete that often forms its border; in fact, we exterminate any real nature (moles, grubs, dandelions) that violates our green. The lawn is the imposition of designed interior space onto an exterior frame (thus the ubiquitous description of a healthy lawn as a "carpet"), and this kind of design may have outgrown its purpose. As new architectural designs break free from strict, boxlike intersections of 90-degree angles, it is less important to provide a horizontal, neutral surface to complement those axes.

The origins of the lawn are in Western Europe, likely in the British Isles, where the Atlantic climate keeps native grasses naturally green and short. What began as practical, enclosed grazing fields evolved into the estate lawn, cultivated by an upper class that was drunk on classical pastoral literature. Wealthy colonial families in North America slavishly imitated the English landscape until the middle class caught on in the 19th century, encouraged by fashion leaders such as A. J. Downing, who urged others to adopt "the unrivaled beauty of [England's] velvet lawns." The lawn flourished in the new suburbs, reaching its icon status after World War II, when Madison Avenue challenged returning soldiers to fight crabgrass instead of an evil empire.

QUEST FOR PERFECTION

The lawn has become a quest for perfection, a singular standard of color, shape, and texture. A flip through a grass seed catalog is initially inspiring and expansive—Bermuda grass, buffalo grass, centipede grass, St. Augustine, zoysia—but the poetry ends with the nomenclature. The seeds are used to produce the same uniform shapes. The aesthetic problem with the lawn is that it allows no room for innovation, growth, or art. The lawn is a front door, a symbolic façade constructed to communicate conformity. It advertises that the owner honors such values as dependability and hygiene. In essence, I shave, therefore I mow. The idea of the lawn has become so universally sacred that in the arid Southwest even gravel and hardscaping have been painted green and arranged in squares.

Must the lawn always be the green canvas, the neutral background for an architectural event—something that unifies brighter, bolder colors and textures? Mark Wigley, author of *The Electric Lawn*, describes architects' renderings: "It is assumed that wherever there is nothing specified in the drawing there is grass. The lawn is treated like the paper on which the projects are drawn, a tabula rasa without any inherent interest, a background that merely clears the way for the main event." A problem arises when we fail to recognize that the periphery in architectural renderings constitutes most of our built environment. As the boundaries of our cities fade into suburbs, we realize that the lawn surrounds more than the single-family bungalow.

In paragraph 1, Yandik states that "the lawn is more architecture than landscape, more design than nature." To what extent might these photographs support his statement—or not? One shows a typical suburban lawn and the other a golf course, which is a different kind of lawn. What do lawns suggest about how we create spaces and our relationship to the land?

© Tony Roberts/Corbis

© Richard Berenholtz/Corbis

Our schools, hospitals, libraries, museums, and corporate headquarters have become isolated in lawn.

5   Some successful lawn alternatives already exist. **Xeriscaping** with varied, drought-resistant grasses and cacti has become popular in the West, and some landscapers use native wildflowers and indigenous shrubs creatively in the East. But there must be a stronger relationship between architect and landscaper or, better yet, architects willing to design whole landscapes. Architects rely too heavily on the lawn to sew buildings together. The result is often a predictable composition that triggers our knee-jerk reactions against nonurban environments. The lawn prevents the suburb from achieving a balance of harmonious differences—the juxtaposition of different architectural styles and textures described and admired by critics like **Ada Louise Huxtable.** By replacing the lawn with an architectural landscape that integrates geometry within existing regional and natural geographic variation, we could advance suburbs beyond the predictable and prosaic.

FUSING STRUCTURE AND LAND

The 1994 Japanese Soft and Hairy House by Ushida-Findlay Partnership illustrates a more ambitious lawn replacement. A simple motif that could be expanded, the design fuses structure and natural topography. An unfussy tangle of native vegetation coils around the roof of the smooth, sculptural frame; the composition cannot be teased apart. Viewed from ground level, the green elements provide a hairy texture against the sky, softening the concrete and stucco and pulling the piece together. A similar example is the 1987 Brunsell Residence by Obie Bowman, AIA, in Sea Ranch, Calif. The house appears to have been raised from the surrounding California grasses. Natural elements are not sacrificed through the introduction of geometry to the landscape, but rather assimilated into the composition. The architectural design expands beyond the four walls and bleeds into its environment. More recently, the

Diamond Ranch High School by Morphosis in Diamond Bar, Calif., integrated classrooms into the natural topography of low hill barrens and scrub oak of a Los Angeles suburb. No dirt was removed or added. By cantilevering buildings off a hillside slope and choreographing the irregular rooflines with the natural contour of the landscape, the school campus eliminates the lawn.

If lawn-alternative designs exist, why then have they had such limited impact? One obstacle is zoning ordinances. In many municipalities, homeowners must specifically devote a certain percentage of their property to lawn, and citizens have the right to sue if their neighbor's grass grows a few inches above regulated standards. Another obstacle is simply consumer resistance. Americans have been taught for more than a century that the lawn is a safe, responsible statement of taste. Therefore, this time-tested standard will not vanish overnight. And despite the lawn's negative qualities, the lawn and garden industry successfully markets a familiar, accessible product. It's a reality that is unmistakable, but not immutable. Architects, like all artists, should pride themselves on pushing, rather than following, consumer tastes. Our landscape begs for an alternative to the sea of green.

GLOSSES

XERISCAPING

Xeriscaping (par. 5) is the practice of landscaping with slow-growing, drought tolerant plants to conserve water and reduce yard waste.

ADA LOUISE HUXTABLE

A Pulitzer Prize–winning architecture critic for the *Wall Street Journal,* Ada Louise Huxtable (par. 5) has written books and many articles about architectural issues.

CONTEXT: AUDIENCE

Yandik wrote this essay for *Architectural Record,* a specialized kind of magazine sometimes called a trade publication. The readers of that magazine are mostly professionals involved with architecture, planning, and design. But most of the readers of *Architectural Record* are also Americans, and many of them are homeowners as well. To what extent do you think Yandik addresses his audience as professionals? To what extent does he address them as part of this larger audience of American homeowners? And how might readers who are not homeowners and who have no lawn (for example, city dwellers who rent an apartment) react to his discussion about the importance of lawns in American culture? This is a good example of an essay in which a writer might address several different audiences at once.

UNDERSTANDING THE TEXT

1. Yandik claims that when it comes to their lawns, Americans "place form ahead of function." What does he mean by that statement? What evidence does he offer to support it? Why is this statement important to his larger point about lawns in this essay? Do you agree with him? Why or why not?

2. What are Yandik's primary complaints about American lawns? What do you think these complaints suggest about Yandik's values regarding lifestyle and the way we use the land?

3. How did lawns gain their "icon status" in the United States, according to Yandik? What do you think this status of lawns suggests about the relationship between social class and the spaces people create in American culture?

EXPLORING THE TEXT

1. How would you describe Yandik's writing style in this essay? What specific features of his writing (for example, his word choice or use of images) contribute to his style? How effective do you think his style is? Does it help make his argument more persuasive? Explain, citing specific passages in your answer.

2. Yandik presents a lot of information in this essay, including facts and figures, historical background, quotations, and examples of special architectural projects. In that sense, you might think of this essay as a kind of research paper, in which Yandik uses research to help him make his argument about lawns. Examine the information he includes. How effectively do you think he uses this information to help illustrate and support his arguments?

3. Yandik argues that we need to achieve "a balance of harmonious differences" in the lawns and buildings we create. Explain what he means by this concept of "harmonious differences." What does this concept reveal about his own values regarding the spaces we create and the lifestyles we have? To what extent do you think Americans would agree with Yandik? Do you? Explain.

4. In paragraph 6, Yandik discusses a number of architectural designs that he thinks provide good alternatives to the typical American lawn. What do these descriptions suggest about Yandik's sense of his audience? How do you think knowledge of the projects mentioned in this passage might affect the way readers read this passage? To what extent is Yandik's essay part of a specialized conversation that doesn't include "general" readers?

ENTERING THE CONVERSATIONS

1. Write an essay in response to Yandik's essay. In your essay, explain why you agree with his complaints about lawns, or offer a rebuttal to his argument. Discuss your own beliefs about how we should create the spaces we inhabit.

INFOTRAC

2. In the past decade or so, the problem of suburban sprawl has become an important social and environmental issue in the United States (see *Conversations: Sprawl* on page 517). In recent years, many towns and states have attempted to address the problems associated with sprawl through various regulations and land-use measures. Such efforts are sometimes called "smart growth." Using InfoTrac College Edition, the Internet, and any other appropriate resources, find out what you can about the problem of sprawl and the so-called smart growth movement. Write a report on the ba-

sis of your research. Describe what sprawl is and the problems it causes, and discuss what efforts have been made to address it. Draw conclusions about what these efforts seem to suggest about how we create and use spaces in U.S. society.

3. On the basis of your research for Question 4, write a letter to the editor of your local newspaper or some other appropriate publication in which you express your views about efforts to control sprawl.

4. The images in *Visual Connections: Lawn Landscaping* on page 518 and the image below show a golf course and some typical American suburban homes. In these instances, the lawns are carefully created. Consider what these created spaces suggest about our attitudes toward the land? What do they suggest about how we imagine and use spaces? To what extent are these elaborate spaces necessary or practical? Can these spaces be made differently and still be useful? Write an essay in which you try to answer such questions. Use these photographs or other appropriate photographs you may have of lawns or similar spaces.

© Lester Lefkowitz/Corbis

USING SPACES

Cuyahoga Falls

THE TOWN WHERE I GREW UP IN NORTHEASTERN PENNSYLVANIA WAS ORIGINALLY A COMPANY TOWN, BUILT BY A MINING COMPANY FOR ITS EMPLOYEES. IN THE MID-NINETEENTH CENTURY, THE COMPANY CONSTRUCTED A NUMBER OF IDENTICAL HOUSES IN SMALL NEIGHBORHOODS NEAR THE COAL MINES IT OWNED, AND THEN IT RENTED OR SOLD THE HOMES TO THE MINERS WHO WORKED FOR IT.

After World War II, the coal mines closed, and the company sold off its holdings, including the homes it originally built there. Today, the town looks like just about any other town, with its own neighborhoods, public parks, roads, and municipal buildings. But if you look carefully as you walk or drive through some of the older neighborhoods, you'll notice that all the houses are the same. They're the same size, the same design, and built of the same materials. Over the years, though, the new owners of the homes remodeled them by painting them, adding rooms, changing doors and windows, putting up awnings, building porches or patios, and generally making each home distinctive.

> Although all of those houses are basically identical, each is unique.

And that's what strikes me whenever I visit those neighborhoods today: Although all of those houses are basically identical, each is unique. The owners took those identical houses and made them their own spaces. You've seen a similar phenomenon if you've ever walked through a large corporate office building. Usually, each office or cubicle in such a building is identical: the same size and shape, with the same office furniture. Yet each employee will decorate that space differently, with photos, paperweights, calendars, and other items that make it his or her own space. All the workers in that office building are using the space available to them in a similar way: They are doing the work they were hired to do. Yet they also use that space differently to express their own sense of ownership and individuality. I wonder: What do the old neighborhoods in my hometown or the offices in a typical corporate building say about how we use the spaces available to us?

The essays in this cluster may give us a way to answer that question. Each essay examines a slightly different example of how people use the spaces around them—spaces they themselves create, such as a cabin, and natural spaces, such as a prairie or a forest. In many ways, these four essays address the same kinds of questions about spaces that the essays in the first cluster in this chapter ("Creating Spaces") address. I could have mixed and matched the four essays in this cluster with the four in the first cluster. But I wanted to divide them up in this way to help you think about the differences between how we create spaces that are integral to our lives and how we *use* those spaces once we create them. I also wanted you to see that how we create and use spaces has as much to do with our *ideas* about spaces as it does with more practical matters, such as the size of a space or its location. In other words, how we *think about* the spaces around us influences what we do with those spaces. I hope these essays will encourage you to think carefully about the spaces in your own life. And I hope they'll help you appreciate how writing is also a way to create and use spaces.

*New developments
Apartments*

Recently, I was talking to my brother about
*his habit of falling asleep each night with
the television on. My brother is a busy guy.
He's a high school guidance counselor, a
football and golf coach, and the father of two
active boys. Every night, he has to have the
television on to fall asleep. Otherwise, he
says, his mind just races and he becomes too
restless to sleep.*

*Maybe my brother should read the follow-
ing essay by well-known writer Scott Russell*

Stillness

*Sanders (b. 1945). Sanders describes a prob-
lem similar to my brother's: a busy life that
leaves him with too much on his mind. He
confides to us that what is on his mind is
more than just his many professional and
family commitments; he is also worried
about the many problems in the world beyond his own small place in Indiana, where
he makes his home. How, he asks, can we be
expected to deal with the frantic pace of our
own lives and attend to the pain and suffering in the wider world, too?*

*One answer is to find stillness, which for
Sanders means a small hut that he built on
his property. In describing that hut and
what he does there, Sanders is also describing the importance of certain spaces that we
create for ourselves. He is offering us a way
to think about how we use space in general
and about our relationship to the spaces we
inhabit. My guess is that you have some
place like Sanders's hut—a space where you
can take a break from the regular pace of
your life. Maybe it's a room in your home or
a spot on your campus; maybe it's a favorite
booth in a coffee shop or diner near your
home, or perhaps a favorite bench in the city
park. Whatever that space, Sanders's essay
may help you better understand your need
for it.*   (continued)

SCOTT RUSSELL SANDERS

Through the aisle of waving woodland sunflowers and purple
ironweed, I approach a cedar hut where I plan to sit quietly for a few
hours, gathering the scattered pieces of myself. Resting at the foot of
a hill between a meadow and a forest, surrounded by a deck and railing, the tiny cabin seems to float on the earth like a gabled houseboat
the color of whole wheat bread. Grasshoppers lurch aside with a clat-
ter as I move along the path, but hummingbirds and butterflies continue blithely feeding. Here in southern Indiana the tall grasses have
bent down under the weight of their seeds, the maples and sycamores
have begun to release a few crisp leaves, and the creeks have sunk into
their stony troughs.

I climb the stairs and leave my sandals on the deck. The boards feel
warm against the soles of my feet. The pressure of sunlight draws the
fruity smell of cedar from the clapboard siding. I turn a key in the
lock, swing the door inward, then hesitate on the threshold, gazing
into this room where I hope to recover my balance. The two carpenters, friends of mine, who built this hut for me to use as a studio have
removed the last of their tools and swept the place clean. The vacancy

(continued) *Scott Russell Sanders, who teaches creative writing at Indiana University, has written numerous essays, novels, and short stories for which he has been widely acclaimed. The following essay was published in* Orion *magazine in 2001.*
▾

both attracts and daunts me. The pine floor, still unmarked, is fragrant and shiny with varnish, like a bare stage the moment before a play begins. The walls seem watchful, for they, too, are covered with planks of yellow pine, and the knots burn like a constellation of eyes.

Overcoming my wariness, I go inside, carrying with me only a pen, a journal, the clothes on my back, and the buzz in my head. I have come here in hopes of calming that buzz, the better to hear voices aside from my own. I open the windows and sit cross-legged on the floor with my back against a wall and my face to the east, where the meadow brightens with morning. I draw in a deep breath, let it go, and try to shed a feeling of decadence for sitting here alone, idle, on a Sunday morning.

My wife knows I am here, but she is the only one, and she urged me to come. As of one o'clock this afternoon, Ruth and I will have been married thirty-three years, and in that time our lives have been braided together so tightly, so richly, that I cannot imagine myself apart from her. And yet we both recognize my periodic need for solitude and stillness, a need that has grown more acute over the years.

We arranged for the building of this hut on some land we own at the edge of a state forest a few miles from our house in town, so that I would have a place to withdraw. I realize what a privilege it is to have such a refuge, what a luxury to claim a second roof when so many people lack any shelter at all, and I do not know how long I can bear to keep it. "Don't spoil your studio by feeling guilty," says Ruth, who has come to know my guilt all too well since the day of our wedding. She drove me out here this morning to inaugurate this quiet space, dropped me off at the end of the gravel path with a kiss and a blessing, then went on about her errands. We'll rendezvous this evening to celebrate our anniversary by sharing a meal with friends.

Although I must eventually return to house and work and a host of obligations, for a few hours, at least, nobody will disturb me. There is no telephone in this room, no television, no radio, no computer, no electrical device at all except for a light and a fan overhead. I do not switch them on, because the sun gives me all the light I need and a breeze through the windows keeps me cool. Although cars rumble past now and then on a road that skirts the far side of the meadow, they disrupt the stillness only briefly. Otherwise, I hear the churr of cicadas and crickets, the rattle and purl of birdsong, the drumming of a woodpecker, and the trickle of these words as they run from my mind through my fingers onto the page.

Sunlight pouring through a southern window forms a bright rhomboid on the wooden floor. Even without a watch, by tracking this brilliant shape as it changes through the day I could mark noon as the moment when the corners are square. If I stayed longer, if I devoted myself to recording the dance of light over the gleaming boards, I could trace out sunrise and sunset, equinox and solstice, all the cycles

STRATEGIES: EXTENDED METAPHOR
Sanders writes that he once learned in a physics class that a frog will not jump out of a pot of water before the water boils. In the next few paragraphs, he continually refers back to this image of the frog in the pot. Writers sometimes use this strategy, called *extended metaphor,* to convey certain ideas or make a specific point. What ideas or points does Sanders convey through this metaphor of the frog in the pot?

CONVERSATIONS: SLOWING DOWN
In this passage (par. 9), Sanders offers his description of the fast pace of modern life, and he tells us in the next paragraph that he intended to slow down the pace of his own life. His description may sound familiar to you because the idea that our lives today are too fast-paced has become a common one. Many popular books and articles offer advice for slowing down and regaining control of our lives, and some popular television personalities, such as talk show host Oprah Winfrey, regularly share their ideas for living more deliberately. In the 1980s, a movement called "voluntary simplicity" emerged in reaction to the fast pace of modern life; its proponents argued that our lives were so cluttered with possessions and responsibilities that we were missing the real joy of living. In the 1990s, the "slow food movement" reflected similar concerns, proposing that people slow down to enjoy their meals with one another rather than grabbing quick meals by themselves at fast-food restaurants. At the same time, yoga, meditation, and similar practices became popular with many people who felt that their lives were too busy. These and similar developments in modern American culture might be seen as part of an ongoing conversation about how best to live our lives. If we think of Sanders's essay as part of that conversation, how might that affect the way we read it?

of the turning year. But I will not do so, for I wish to shrug off time for a spell, to dwell in the present. I drift so often into past and future, jerked around by memory and expectation, that I lose the savor of the moment. I have come to this empty room to break free of tasks and deadlines, to cast off worry and grief.

Dust motes float lazily before me in a shaft of light, twitching as they collide with one another. I learned in freshman physics class that this perpetual shimmy is called Brownian motion, and the higher the temperature, the faster the particles move. In that same class I was also told that if you put a frog in a pot of cold water on a stove and then gradually raise the heat, the poor benighted creature will boil before it has the sense to jump out of the pot. I never tested this claim on a frog, but I have come to believe that a version of it holds true for many people, including myself.

As the demands on our time and attention multiply, we move faster and faster to keep up with them, crowding our calendars, shuttling from place to place and deadline to deadline, strapping phones to our belts, carrying chores everywhere in satchels and laptops, working through lunch and supper and weekends and holidays, getting and spending twenty-four hours a day. Many of us take pills to lull us to sleep, pills to wake us up, and pills to soothe our nerves. Many of us hire strangers to raise our children, to buy presents for our loved ones, to clean our houses and cook our food. Instead of slowing down when the pace becomes frantic, we enlarge our highways and pipelines and cables, we buy gadgets and software guaranteed to help us do everything more quickly, we push down on our accelerators. Instead of deciding there's something wrong with this pot as the water roils about us, we flail our arms and thrash our legs to keep from drowning.

I have decided to climb out of the pot, which is why I've come to this empty hut on a Sunday morning. The room is four paces wide by five paces long, about twelve feet by fifteen, and open to the steep rafters overhead. All the surfaces are wood, a reminder that this place is a gift of trees. There are windows in each wall and two skylights in the ceiling. Looking east I see the meadow, a sweep of grasses polished by sun. To the south I see a grove of sycamores, a thicket of blackberries, and a field grown up in goldenrod and ragweed and saplings. The forest begins just beyond the railing of the deck to the west, mainly oak and maple and hickory and beech, rank after rank of big trees rising up a slope into deepening shade and continuing on for several miles before yielding to the next road. Through windows in the north wall I see a welter of blowzy flowers and weeds, and a path leading to the gravel drive where Ruth dropped me off.

On a Sunday morning in town I could have worshiped with any of several dozen congregations, from staid Episcopalians to Holy Rollers, but they are all too noisy for my taste, too intent on scriptures and formulas, too eager to lasso the great mystery with words. I could have sat in silence with Buddhists or Quakers, waiting for insight, and yet even they often quarrel about the truth as soon as they rise from meditation, and over the years their arguments have led to schisms and feuds. The world is manifestly one, and each of us is part and parcel of that unity, so our quarrels about religious doctrine can only estrange us from the reality we seek.

Although I can't let go of language entirely, as witness these lines stretching across the pages of my journal, I do manage to sit for long spells in a wakeful hush. I keep my eyes open because I wish through stillness to enter the world, not escape from it. I wish to bear in mind all the creatures that breathe, which is why I've chosen to make my retreat here within the embrace of meadow and woods. The panorama I see through the windows is hardly wilderness, and yet every blade of grass, every grasshopper, every sparrow and twig courses with a wild energy. The same energy pours through me. Although my body grows calm from sitting still, I rock slightly with the slow pulse of my heart. My ears fill with the pulse of crickets and cicadas proclaiming their desires. My breath and the clouds ride the same wind.

In his *Pensées*, **Pascal** remarks: "When all are moving precipitously toward excesses, none seems to be so moving. He who stops makes the mad rush of the others perceptible, as would a fixed point." Those others may decide for themselves whether their lives have sped out of control. The mad rush that concerns me is my own. By sitting still, I can measure the crazed motion of my customary days.

GLOSS: PASCAL'S *PENSÉES*
The *Pensées* is a collection of notes written by French philosopher Blaise Pascal (1623–1662) in which he explored his ideas about human nature. These notes, which were published after Pascal's death, were apparently intended to be part of a treatise defending Christianity.

In those customary days, I work almost every waking hour. Even during the rare pauses—while shaving, taking a shower, waiting for the teakettle to boil, pedaling my bicycle to and from the office—I find myself compiling lists and scheduling tasks. I read as I dash from appointment to appointment, jot notes on a clipboard in the car, lug everywhere a backpack stuffed with chores. When I lie down in exhaustion at night, sleep seems like an interruption in the round of toil. So far I haven't swallowed any pills to soothe my frazzled nerves. I've resisted the sales pitches for tools designed to speed up my life. I carry neither beeper nor cell phone nor palm pilot, feeling already too thoroughly connected to other people's demands. And yet, so long as I'm awake I feel driven to accomplish things, to redeem the time.

Why do I keep such a frantic pace? Not to rake in more money, because my wife and I could live quite well on half of what we earn. Nor to win fame, because I recognize how small and brief my life is. Nor to secure happiness, because I realize that happiness comes to me only in the moments when I slow down. Nor to meet the expectations of a boss, because I am my own boss. Then why the endless toil? Maybe I'm still trying to satisfy the insatiable needs of my parents as I sensed those needs in childhood. Maybe I'm still trying to ease the ache that drove my father to drink, even though he is long since dead, and I'm struggling to relieve the dismay and anger my mother felt because of his drinking. Or it could be that I'm trying to placate the Protestant God I learned about as a boy, the stern judge who watches us every moment, recording how we use our days, a God I've tried to banish from my thoughts but who keeps burrowing back in through the mind's basement. Or perhaps, like anyone who can't help seeing damage and pain in every direction, I'm only trying to avoid the bite of conscience.

I've been spared the turmoil of war, the pain of exile, the cramp of hunger. As far as I know, I'm free of disease. No one treats me with spite or scorn. I lead a blessed life, a rarity on this suffering planet, and yet much of the time I feel torn asunder by the needs I see around me, needs that outstrip my power to respond. From the circle of my family and friends, on out through the ever-larger circles of my students, my neighbors, the members of my community, the people in this country and in distant lands, and the earth itself with all its imperiled creatures, there are far more claims on my thought and compassion than I can meet.

I would not speak of this dilemma if it were only mine, but I watch many others race again and again through the cycle of widening concern, frenzied effort, and exhaustion. Whatever the source of conscience—parents, God, solemn books, earnest friends, the dictates of biology—it is adapted to a narrower space than the one we inhabit. Limited to a small tribe or a community of a few hundred people, conscience may prompt us to serve others in a balanced and wholesome way. But when television and newspapers and the Internet bring us word of dangers by the thousands and miseries by the millions and needful creatures by the billions; when pleas for help reach us around the clock; when aching faces greet us on every street—then conscience either goes numb or punishes us with a sense of failure.

I often lie awake at night, rehearsing the names of those I've disappointed by failing to give them all they asked. I don't say this to make myself out as a generous soul. I am hardly that; I feel defenseless rather than virtuous. The truth is that I've come to fear the claims that other beings make on me, because their numbers grow relentlessly. I wish to love my neighbor, but the neighborhood has expanded so far, and the neighbors have become so many, that my love is stretched to the breaking point. I'm tempted to run away, beyond reach of the needy voices. So I make of this hut a hiding place.

Sitting cross-legged, eyes open to this room filled with light, I ride my breath in and out as if it were the swells and troughs of a mild sea, and soon the strings of duty that bind me to the world begin to fall slack. Thoughts of the sea remind me of kayaking in Glacier Bay twelve months ago with my son and his fiancée and an Alaskan friend. Some days the water was choppy and we had hard going, especially into the wind. Other days the water lay as smooth and glossy as the pine floor in this room, and we glided over the surface with ease. My breath now feels like that effortless paddling.

20   I remember the way otters floated on their backs among the kelp beds, the way seals bobbed to the surface beside our kayaks and studied us with their dark eyes, the way humpback whales breached with a snort from their blowholes and a wave of their flukes, and I remember how the water erased all sign of their passage moments after they dove again. Even a storm tousled the sea only so long as the wind blew, leaving no mark after the sky cleared. Gradually I breathed in the equanimity of this imperturbable sea. By the end of our week in Glacier Bay, after camping each night on shore in the neighborhood of bears and eating fresh salmon cooked over driftwood fires and talking under the stars with people I love, I felt as serene as those waters on the calmest days.

We began our trip home from Alaska by taking a sauna and bathing in a creek at my friend's house on an island near Juneau, a house almost as simple and not much bigger than the hut where I record these memories. He had built the cabin and its furniture with timber salvaged from the beaches of Glacier Bay. We ate food from his garden and root cellar, drank water from his cistern, relieved ourselves in his privy with a view into the dripping forest of hemlock and spruce. His place was so close in spirit to the wilderness that it left my newfound tranquility unruffled.

My son and his fiancée and I parted from my friend and flew in a shuddering single-engine plane through rain to Juneau. Already in that small airport I felt dizzy from the onslaught of noise, the blabbing televisions, the clutter of machines, the milling, fretful travelers. From there we flew to Seattle, where the crowds and racket and hard surfaces and bustling carts and droning conveyor belts seemed like the stage props of nightmare. Then we stopped over at the airport in Las Vegas around midnight, and a two-hour delay forced us to leave the plane and make our way into the pandemonium of grunting loudspeakers, maundering drinkers, clanking slot machines, and wailing sirens. I felt I had descended into bedlam. I could not fathom how this midnight delirium and the serenity of Glacier Bay belonged on the same planet. Here was a frenzy beyond anything I had ever seen, and I knew with absolute certainty that it pointed the way to madness.

> **CONNECTIONS: OUR CROWDED LIVES**
> In many ways, Sanders's description of returning to the fast pace of modern American life after spending time in the Alaskan backcountry is similar to critic Beatriz Sarlo's description of the practice of "zapping" through television channels and to related developments in popular media (see *Visual Connections: The Crowded Screen* on page 379). Sarlo's focus in her essay is very different from Sanders's, but what they observe about modern life is similar. You might consider how the different conversations Sarlo and Sanders are part of shape the way they observe modern life.

But was my life back home so different? Was my crowded calendar, my backpack stuffed with chores, my head crammed with duties, any less crazed? What jackpot was I after? Measured against the serenity I had felt in the wilderness, my usual life seemed as hectic and frazzled as this delirium in the casino. The twin images of Las Vegas and Glacier Bay have stayed with me ever since, like the opposite poles in a force field.

The hut creaks as the boards expand in the sun, like an animal stretching as it wakes. Tonight, after the sun goes down, the joints of cedar and pine will creak again as they cool. The hummingbirds will keep darting from blossom to blossom until the cold drives them south for winter. The crickets will keep on singing day and night until the first heavy frost, and then they will carry their song with them into the ground. Even in the depths of winter, beneath soil frozen as hard as iron, hearts will beat in burrows, and the creek will run beneath a skin of ice. There is no absolute stillness in nature. In the nails that hold this building together, electrons whirl. Even the dead yield their substance in a ferment of decay.

As I write these words in my journal, I'm forced to acknowledge a deeper source   25
for the frantic pace of my ordinary days. I suspect I'm trying to stave off death. If I work without ceasing, maybe death will think I'm a good boy, useful and industrious, too valuable for extinction. If I serve others all my waking hours, maybe death will pass by the ones I love. If I write books, teach classes, give speeches, donate money, lobby politicians, and march in the streets, maybe death will spare the millions of species endangered by our prodigal ways.

When I was growing up in the country, a neighbor boy warned me never to lie still for long in an open field, because the turkey vultures would spiral overhead, waiting to feast on me. Especially if you're lying down, he told me, keep fidgeting, so they know you're alive. Except for rare passages of calm, I have kept fidgeting ever since.

On our drive out here this morning, Ruth and I passed a vulture that was tearing bright red strands from a possum flattened on the road. At the sound of our engine, the bird hunched protectively over its meal and thrust its beak into the bloody mess for another scrap. I found nothing gruesome in the sight, for the vulture was doing necessary work, obeying an appetite as clean and simple as gravity. This gawky black bird with its featherless head the color of blood was not death itself but only one of death's janitors. Without all the dutiful scavengers, from bacteria to wolves, our planet would be layered in corpses. Instead, the living dismantle the dead, and out of the debris new life rises.

Over the past few years, Ruth and I watched Alzheimer's disease whittle her mother to a thin reed, which finally snapped. Month by month, each of our surviving parents has lost certain blessings of body and mind—a range of hearing and sight, fine control of the fingers, strength of legs, precision of memory, the names of familiar things. Ruth and I have ached over this paring down, even as we know our own turn will come if we live long enough. Age strips away our powers as well as our possessions. By giving myself to this empty room, perhaps like the monk who sleeps in his coffin I am only preparing myself for an emptiness over which I will have no choice.

The Hebrew root of sabbath means "to rest." In anticipation of this Sunday morning's retreat, I copied into my notebook the fourth commandment delivered by Moses to the people of Israel:

> Remember the sabbath day, and keep it holy. Six days you shall labor and do all your work. But the seventh day is a sabbath to the Lord your God; you shall not do any work—you, your son or your daughter, your male or female slave, your livestock, or the alien resident in your towns.

So keeping the sabbath holy means not only that we should rest from our own labors but also that we should grant rest to all those beings—both human and nonhuman—whose labor serves us.

30   According to Moses, God went further in demanding restraint from this wandering tribe once they entered the promised land. Every seventh year the land was to be left fallow; the fields were not to be plowed and the grapevines not to be pruned; and whatever grew of itself on the land was to be left alone. Every fiftieth year, slaves were to be set free, leased property was to be restored to its original owners, and the earth was to be granted a solemn rest. Why? Because, God proclaims through Moses, "the land is mine; with me you are but aliens and tenants."

These ancient rules are instructions in humility. For six days we make the Creation serve our needs, but on the seventh day we must leave the Creation alone. We may hold title to the land, but we may not claim it for our own, as if it were ours to do with as we choose. Whatever our religious views, we might do well to recover the idea of the sabbath, not only because we could use a solemn day of rest once a week, but also because the earth could use a respite from our demands. Whether or not we accept the idea of a Creator, we should admit we're not the makers of this bountiful and beautiful earth, we're only guests here, just passing through, and we have no right to devour the promised land.

A spider lowers itself by a thread from a rafter, settling a few inches from my outstretched feet. It's only a smidgen of life, no bigger than a grain of rice, with a bright red dot for a body and legs so fine they're all but invisible. Even in so small a creature—and in ones much smaller, as I know from gazing through microscopes—

there is room for hunger and purpose. The spider sets off across the floor, slowing up at the joints between boards like a skier straddling crevasses. Against the caramel grain in the pine, the bright spark of a body glows like a burning coal. It crawls over the carcass of a ladybug, stops to examine a dead wasp, eventually trundles into a dark corner where it begins laying out the warp for a web.

The spider does not rest every seventh day, nor do the warblers singing now from the branches of a sumac just outside the window, nor do the crickets sawing away at their lovelorn tune in the grass. They pursue their passions as long as their breath holds out. They needn't be reminded to restrain themselves, for nature curbs their appetites soon enough with frost or drought or some other calamity. Among all the menagerie, it seems, we alone must be taught to curb our own appetites. We alone need reminding that the condition of our lease on the promised land is that we restrain ourselves.

The industry of the spider makes me notice the stiffness in my legs. How long have I sat here? Two hours? Three? Whenever she finishes her errands, Ruth will be coming to pick me up. I rise and stretch. The gleaming floor, so smooth, tempts my feet. I wonder for a moment if the holy sabbath allows for dancing, then I dance anyway, a slow and clumsy shuffle, the way a bear might dance. My feet brushing the wood make the whispery sound of a broom. Since nobody is around to hear how badly I sing, I go ahead and sing. It's a love ballad that I'll repeat for Ruth tonight when we celebrate our anniversary. At the sound of my voice, the crickets and cicadas and warblers surrounding the hut cease their chorus, but in a little while they resume, overcome by desire, and we sing together our amorous tunes.

Before long the dancing covers me in sweat. I lie on the floor where a breeze from the windows cools me. This room is a haven. Eventually I'll put a table, a chair, a lamp, and a meditation cushion in here, but for now I prefer to leave it bare. The two skylights in the ceiling open onto rectangles of blue. Clouds drift across those openings, coiling and merging like foam at the confluence of rivers. Every few seconds, barn swallows wheel across, there a moment and then gone, like thoughts. Suddenly, through my framed patch of sky, two red-tailed hawks glide past. I leap to my feet and throw open the door and step onto the deck to watch them sail away beyond the rim of trees.

And so, without planning to leave my hermitage, I'm drawn outside by a pair of birds. Standing in the open air, I realize I'm hungry, I'm thirsty, and I'm eager for company. I want to see Ruth, my bride of thirty-three years. I want to walk with her through our neighborhood in the evening as lights come on in the houses. I long to hold my children and catch up on their lives. I want to share food with friends. I want to sit with my students and talk over the ancient questions. I want to walk among crowds at the farmers' market and run my hands over the melons and apples and squash. I want to do good work—not every waking hour, and not for every worthy cause, but enough work to ease some pain and bring some hope and free some beauty in a few lives. I want to carry back into my ordinary days a sense of the stillness that gathers into the shape of a life, scatters into fragments, and then gathers again.

Waiting in the sunshine, I listen to the rumble of cars approaching the hut along the blacktop road, for one of those cars will bring Ruth, who will find a husband more peaceful and joyful and grateful than the one she left here this morning.

UNDERSTANDING THE TEXT

1. Why did Sanders arrange to have his hut built? What needs does the hut fulfill? What do you think his hut might suggest about the role of special places in our lives?

2. What does Sanders mean when he uses the term *stillness*? Why does he seek this stillness? What does stillness have to do with his hut? Why must he go there in search of stillness? Do you think stillness, as he defines it, can only be found in a specific place? Explain.

3. Why does Sanders wish to "let go of language" (par. 12)? What would it mean to do so? Why is he not able to let go of language?

4. What dilemma does Sanders describe in this essay? What is the source of this dilemma? What does it have to do with Sanders's hut? What do you think this dilemma suggests about Sanders as a person?

5. Sanders writes that the first day he spent in his hut was also his wedding anniversary. What connection does Sanders make between that important event and his need for stillness?

EXPLORING THE ISSUES

1. What do you think this essay suggests about the relationship between specific places and the emotional life of human beings? What might it suggest about how people use certain kinds of spaces? Cite specific passages to support your answer.

2. Sanders's writing is often praised for its vividness and the effectiveness of his descriptions. Select one or more passages from this essay that you think are particularly descriptive and analyze them. What words or phrases does Sanders use in his descriptions? How does he use sound or imagery to depict the scenes he describes? What ideas about his subject matter does he use his descriptions to convey? How effective do you think his descriptive writing is?

3. Sanders makes a number of references to religion in this essay, and at one point, he muses that he may be "trying to placate the Protestant God I learned about as a boy." He also discusses *conscience* throughout the essay. Based on this essay, what do you think Sanders's view of religion is? What do his views of religion have to do with his desire for stillness? What might religion have to do with Sanders's relationship to his hut?

4. At several points in his essay, Sanders writes about death. For example, in paragraphs 27 and 28, he offers images of death in the natural world and of his own inevitable death. Why does Sanders include these images? What do they have to do with his hut? What do they have to do with his desire for stillness? What do you think Sanders's discussions of death suggest about the role of certain spaces in our lives?

ENTERING THE CONVERSATIONS

1. Write an essay describing a special place of your own. In your essay, describe that place in a way that conveys its significance for you.

2. Write a conventional academic essay in which you discuss where you think the need for special places, such as Sanders's hut, comes from? Why do people need such spaces? What is it about these spaces that we need to make us feel comfortable? What does this need suggest about humans—or about our cultures? Discuss such questions in your essay. Refer where appropriate to Sanders's essay and to your own experience with special places in your life.

3. In paragraph 17, Sanders writes, "But when television and newspapers and the Internet bring us word of dangers by the thousands and miseries by the millions and needful creatures by the billions; when pleas for help reach us around the clock; when aching faces greet us on every street—then conscience either goes numb or punishes us with a sense of failure." Write an essay in which you respond to this statement. In your essay, discuss your own view of this problem of conscience that Sanders describes, and try to address the question of what this problem might suggest about modern life. If appropriate, discuss also whether our use of space has anything to do with this problem.

4. Using whatever appropriate technology you have available (such as computer graphics programs, web authoring software, or video or still photography), create a document that represents an important space in your life. Try to create your document in a way that conveys its importance to you.

5. Find a place where you might have a moment of stillness, such as Sanders describes in his essay. Occupy that place for a time. Then write a brief essay in which you describe what happened when you sought stillness in that place. In your essay, draw conclusions about stillness and how we might use particular spaces to achieve it. Discuss whether you agree with Sanders's view of stillness and place, based on your own experience.

I remember the first time I drove across what we often call America's "heartland." Following Interstate 80 across Indiana, Illinois, Iowa, Nebraska, and into Wyoming, I was struck by the vastness of the landscape and by the seemingly endless fields of corn and soybeans. In the part of Pennsylvania where I grew up, farms were usually collections of a few old barns surrounded by modest fields that were separated by stone and barbed wire fences or by stands of trees.

Keeping A *Lost* World Alive

Those Pennsylvania farms were nothing like the huge agricultural operations in Illinois and Iowa. As I drove past these farms, I remember thinking that I was in the nation's "breadbasket" that I had learned about in school. We studied the history of Europeans who settled the West, and we were taught to be proud of what American farmers had accomplished by turning those prairies into productive farmland. You might say that we learned to appreciate the hard work of those who put the land to good use.

Writer Verlyn Klinkenborg (b. 1953) asks us to look again at those farms. He reminds us that the way we have used those prairies has had consequences that we might not fully appreciate. It is easy to see the long rows of corn and the huge silos where corn is stored before being processed for our tables. More difficult to see is the impact that agriculture has had on the land. In the following essay, Klinkenborg directs our attention to what we can't easily see when we drive past those huge farms. And he focuses our attention on what those farms replaced: the rich, diverse ecosystem of the prairie, which offered many benefits that we are only now learning to appreciate. His essay is a kind of lesson in how we use the spaces around us— a lesson that may encourage (continued)

VERLYN KLINKENBORG

Look deep enough into the history of almost any Iowa town and you come to the primordial 19th-century tale of breaking the prairie as if it were a herd of wild horses. It took special plows and large teams of draft animals. The first step was skinning the earth, turning over the sod, exposing unimaginably fertile soil. But what really broke the prairie was ending the cycle of wildfires and then draining the land, ditching the sloughs and laying tile to carry away water that was good for wildlife and thick stands of native vegetation but not so good for alien row crops. In a modern Iowa soybean field in midsummer, it's easy to see that fire isn't much of a threat anymore. What's hard to see is the drainage network that underlies much of the arable land in the state. Farmers are still adding to that network even now.

The Iowa prairie was well and truly broken. The conventional figure is that 80 percent of the state was once prairie and that 99.9 percent of it is now gone, replaced by what used to be mixed farms and are now almost exclusively corn and soybean fields. A couple of weeks ago, on a beautiful windswept day, I turned off the blacktop in (continued) *us to exercise caution when we are deciding how to use natural spaces.*

Verlyn Klinkenborg grew up on an Iowa farm and has written widely about rural life for many publications, including The New Yorker, Esquire, National Geographic, Mother Jones, *and the* New York Times, *in which this essay first appeared in 2003.* ▼

Cherokee County, in northwest Iowa, onto a gravel road not far from the tiny town of Larabee. Down that road, two small pieces of land totaling 200 acres—a little more than half the average size of an Iowa farm last year—interrupted the symmetry of soybeans and corn. There was a sign identifying this as the Steele Prairie Preserve, another that said "Do Not Spray" and a wide spot in the road with room for one car. That was it, except for the wind and what that small prairie remnant implied.

Standing at the edge of that swath of unmowed, unsprayed, untilled vegetation was like visiting a small body of water preserved to commemorate what an ocean looked like before it was drained. Two hundred acres barely permits the word "prairie," which, in the American experience, implies a horizonwide stretch of grassland. And yet for all its meagerness, the Steele Prairie Preserve suggests the grandeur to which it had once belonged. It had been kept alive by a family that cut wild prairie hay from it well after their neighbors were planting hybrid corn and alfalfa.

Biological complexity and diversity sound like abstractions, until you see a patch of prairie beside the monotony of a soybean field, a whole county of soybean fields. Though these acres could only hint at the way real prairie would reflect the wind—catching its oceanic sweep—the wind was different here. Instead of a sound like rustling newsprint from corn and soybeans, there was a sibilance that seemed to merge with the birdsong rising from the community of tall-grass plants. It was a richer note than anything you hear in a pasture or a hayfield, if only because no one ever lets a pasture or hayfield grow so tall.

There are tiny stands of native prairie all across the Midwest, in graveyards, along rail lines, in parks and flood plains. There is even a "Prairie Directory of North America," by Charlotte Adelman and Bernard Schwartz, that will guide you to the sites. Most are only a few acres, and it takes work to keep them from being invaded by non-native plants. In states where the prairies were richest, like Iowa, those last stands serve as much to remind people of oxen shoulder-

VISUAL CONNECTIONS: FARMING THE PRAIRIE

As Klinkenborg indicates, millions of acres of wild prairie in the United States have been converted to farmland. For the most part, Americans seem to take for granted the vast agricultural operations that now grow much of our food or feed for livestock on land that was once open prairie. Farming, after all, seems to hold a special place in American culture, and images of farm life abound in American culture. The image below shows a mural that was painted in the 1930s and now hangs in a library at Iowa State University. Consider what messages about farming and the land are conveyed in this mural. How do those messages relate to Klinkenborg's point about the prairie and our use of it?

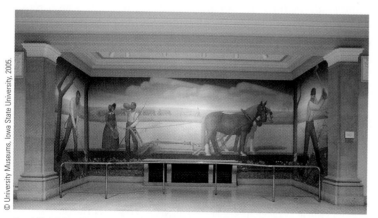

Grant Wood, Breaking the Prairie Sod, 1936–37.

ing the plows forward as to preserve the species that once made up the great sweeps of grasses and forbs. It has always been easier to see the wealth of the black soil that lay under the prairie than the wealth of the prairie itself. Last month, I saw that soil freshly turned by a moldboard plow at a threshing bee in Granite, Iowa, and its blackness was still exhilarating.

There's no getting back to the prairies, of course. The time for preserving a larger share of them slipped away even as modern agriculture was coming into its stride. The great figure in preserving Iowa's prairies was **Ada Hayden,** and she died in 1950, after canvassing the state for remnants worth setting aside. And though the prairie restoration movement has gathered force over the past decade, restoring a prairie is a little like restoring an ocean. It takes more than the right collection of species and the best of intentions. It means regenerating the elemental forces of nature, unleashing a biological synergy that dwarfs what we usually mean when we use that word. To this day the Steele Prairie Preserve is maintained by fire. As beautiful as it is in full bloom, I wished I could be there to see it burn.

GLOSS: ADA HAYDEN
Ada Hayden (1884–1950) was the first woman to earn a doctorate from Iowa State University, where she taught botany. She campaigned to preserve the prairies of the American Great Plains.

VISUAL CONNECTIONS: PRAIRIE BURNING
When Klinkenborg writes that he wishes he could see the prairie burn, he expresses a view of fire that is probably not shared by most Americans. Indeed, controversies have arisen because of policies that allow natural fires to burn in forests. Consider how common attitudes about fire might reflect our views or beliefs about natural spaces. What reaction do you have to this photograph of a prairie fire, for example? What might your reaction reveal about your view of natural spaces?

Prairie Burning

UNDERSTANDING THE TEXT

1. What were the consequences of farming for the prairies of Iowa? Why are these consequences important, in Klinkenborg's view?

2. Klinkenborg writes "it has always been easier to see the wealth of the black soil that lay under the prairie than the wealth of the prairie itself." What is "the wealth of the black soil" that he refers to here? How is that different from "the wealth of the prairie itself"? How does the difference in these two ways of calculating wealth relate to Klinkenborg's main idea in this essay?

3. Why is fire so important to prairies? What does fire suggest to Klinkenborg about natural spaces like prairies and how humans use them?

EXPLORING THE ISSUES

1. Klinkenborg grew up on a farm, yet he seems to criticize farming. Based on this essay, what do you think his view of farming is? What is his view of our relationship to the land and how we should use it? Do you think most Americans would share his view? Explain, citing specific passages to support your answer.

2. Klinkenborg ends his essay with a reference to fire, stating that he wishes he could watch the prairie at the Steele Prairie Preserve burn. It is clear from this essay that he appreciates the prairie and supports the efforts to preserve it at places like Steele Prairie Preserve. Why, then, do you think he ends his essay in

this way? What point does his ending emphasize or reinforce? Do you think this ending is effective? Why or why not?

3. This essay was originally published in the *New York Times,* and it is likely that many of its readers would never have seen a prairie, except perhaps in photographs. Klinkenborg describes the prairie in his essay, and it is worth asking whether his descriptions might be effective for readers who may never have seen a prairie. Examine his descriptions of the prairie. How effective do you think they are? Do you think they would be more or less effective for someone who may never have seen a prairie? Do you think Klinkenborg was aware of such readers as he was writing these descriptions? Explain.

ENTERING THE CONVERSATIONS

1. Write an essay in which you describe a place, such as the prairie that Klinkenborg describes in his essay, that has been transformed in some way by human activity. In your essay, try to convey your own perspective about how that place has been used and what its transformation might suggest about how people use the spaces that are part of their lives.

🔦 INFOTRAC

2. Klinkenborg's essay is partly about the unintended consequences of farming on the prairie. Using InfoTrac College Edition, your library, and any other appropriate resources, investigate farming on U.S.

prairies (or in another location of interest to you). Learn about the history of farming there and about some of its social, economic, political, and environmental consequences. If possible, talk to someone who may be knowledgeable about the subject, such as a professor of agriculture or a local farmer. Also keep in mind that many organizations have an interest in these issues, including environmental organizations and farming organizations. Their web sites may be good resources to consult. Write a report on what you learned through your research.

3. On the basis of your research for Question 2, write a letter to the editor of your local paper or another appropriate publication in which you express your view about the way we have used places like the prairie.

4. Create a web site, PowerPoint presentation, or similar kind of document in which you present an important space in your life. Your document should convey a sense of what that space is and how it is used; it should also convey a sense of the significance of that space in your life.

5. Write a proposal to the appropriate dean or committee at your school about a space on your campus that you believe is important in some way and should be preserved. In your proposal, describe the place and explain why you believe it is important. Propose how you think it should be preserved and/or used. Include photos or other visual elements, if appropriate.

Why would anyone want to live here? I have
wondered about that as I have driven
through the vast open stretches of prairie in
Great Plains states like Nebraska and
Kansas. Having grown up in a part of the
United States that is well populated, I have
found it hard to imagine what it might be like
to live in a region with so few people. In the
following essay, writer Diane Dufva Quantic
(b. 1941) helps us appreciate the appeal of
living in such places. Unlike many observers,

Uncommon Buffalo AND THE *Buffalo* Commons

who lament the loss of population in the more
remote regions of the American Great Plains,
Quantic sees value in such sparsely populated areas. As a result, she supports a controversial idea that emerged in the 1980s
amid concerns about population loss in those
regions: the idea of a Buffalo Commons, a
vast area of the United States stretching from
the Canadian border to the Mexican border
that would preserve much of the prairie where
buffalo once roamed freely in great numbers.
Quantic imagines that establishing such a
commons would help preserve what is best
about living in the wide-open spaces of the
Great Plains. In making her case for the proposal to create a Buffalo Commons, Quantic
invites us to reflect on where we live. As you
read, you might consider why the idea of a
Buffalo Commons would be opposed by some.
What values regarding our use of the spaces
around us might opponents and supporters
of this proposal share—or not share?

Diane Dufva Quantic is associate profes-
sor of English at Wichita State University
and author of The Nature of the Place: A
Study of Great Plains Fiction (1995).
This essay was published in the Prairie
Writers Circle in 2004. ▼

DIANE DUFVA QUANTIC

Most Americans know that the American bison, commonly
called the buffalo, was almost extinct by 1900, the victim of slaughter
and expanding white settlement. In the past 20 years or so, the term
"Buffalo Commons" has become a popular catchphrase that usually
refers to another disaster: the death of the small towns of the High
Plains, a result of an exodus of young people, a lack of economic
growth and an aging population.

Frank and Deborah Popper, two East Coast professors, proposed
the term when their study of High Plains, geographical statistics spot-
lighted sparse and declining population. Why not, they suggested,
turn the most distressed areas of the region into a vast common pasture for its natives, the American bison?

At first, the term Buffalo Commons was a lightning rod, attracting
doomsday prophets and defenders of civilized life in small towns and
rural areas across the Great Plains. But in the past few years, the term
has garnered a more optimistic connotation.

I've followed this debate with interest as I travel to lead book

DIANE DUFVA QUANTIC, "UNCOMMON BUFFALO AND THE BUFFALO COMMONS." FROM
PRAIRIE WRITERS CIRCLE, AUGUST 4, 2004. REPRINTED BY PERMISSION.

CONTEXT: BUFFALO COMMONS

As Quantic explains in these first few paragraphs, the idea of the Buffalo Commons emerged from a 1987 study of population decline by two researchers, Frank and Deborah Popper. Since that study was published, the controversial idea of creating a great "common" space across the U.S. Great Plains states has gained supporters. Essentially, the Buffalo Commons would be a kind of natural zone where buffalo, other wildlife, and human beings would coexist in greater harmony with the natural landscape of the prairie. It would restore and protect large portions of the original prairie and remove political boundaries that create obstacles for preserving the prairie. Advocacy groups such as the Great Plains Restoration Council have endorsed the idea and worked to implement it. These supporters point out that in many parts of the Great Plains, population density is actually lower today than it was in 1893, when Frederick Jackson Turner famously declared that the American frontier was closed. As a result, they argue, in many places the Buffalo Commons is already becoming a reality. This map shows the area where the Buffalo Commons would be created. Quantic states in paragraph 3 that this idea has "garnered a more optimistic connotation" in recent years. You might consider how current political, economic, and environmental developments, including growing concerns about global warming, might influence the way people react to the Buffalo Commons proposal today compared to the late 1980s, when the idea was first proposed.

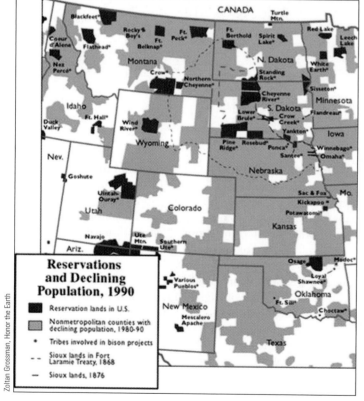

Zoltan Grossman, Honor the Earth

discussions for the Kansas Humanities Council. Often our reading leads us into conversations about the future of the Great Plains, particularly about the future of the place we happen to be sitting.

These occasions lead me to believe that the original Buffalo Commons model, which suggests an either/or face-off between civilization and emptiness, is really a false dilemma. Rather, the term can suggest a way of living already common on the Plains. When I ask people why they live in a place so unforgiving, I get straight, immediate answers: wide-open spaces, inconstant weather, even isolation, traits that would discourage many.

Bison know how to survive these harsh conditions, and the people who live in these places have proved equally adaptable. The decision to live among a scattered population requires careful attention to the way life is lived, for both animals and people.

When I spent some months in Chadron, Neb., I was reminded of distances daily. Even in January, a grocery clerk asked if I needed dry ice to preserve my frozen items. I was invited to join years-old Chadron dinner clubs. These examples reflect a commons concept: looking out for shoppers who might have long drives home and creating occasions to soothe isolation by coming together for good food and conversation.

For many people of the region, Buffalo Commons reflects affection for the place itself. I met young people who intended to leave, tired of living where people and opportunities are so sparse. But I also met people who moved back, unable to live for long anyplace else. The lack of physical barriers and the immense sky that intimidate some people invigorate those who choose to live here. Like the buffalo, Plains people know how to survive on their own in blizzards and drought—and economic downturns.

Recently I was back in Chadron at the annual meeting of the Mari Sandoz Heritage Society discussing Sandoz's book, *The Buffalo Hunters*. Historians, bison ranchers and the instructor of "buffalo management" on the Pine Ridge Indian Reservation told of their experiences with animals they have come to admire for their endurance and intelligence.

Today, almost 300,000 bison roam America's grasslands, most owned by private ranchers and Indian tribes who raise them for profit. Ranchers and researchers have observed their bison herds for decades and know their animals intimately. These people tell of family groups, the communal care of the calves and the animals, ability to survive any kind of weather without human intervention. No wonder the American bison is the iconic animal of the Great Plains. Their intelligence and adaptation embody the commons ideal.

The Buffalo Commons seems to be developing unguided by any grand scheme, and it may well be the future of the Great Plains. I imagine it not as a desolation of abandoned home places and empty pastures, but rather a region where people find rich reward in the face of challenge and adversity.

STRATEGIES: BUILDING A CASE FOR THE BUFFALO COMMONS

In paragraph 6 and elsewhere in the essay, Quantic describes the people who live in the Great Plains as "adaptable." Consider the image of the residents of this region that she presents and how she uses that image to help build her case in favor of the proposal for the Buffalo Commons. Would her argument be less effective without these images of hardy, community-oriented people who reside in the Great Plains? What do these images suggest about Quantic's sense of her audience and their values regarding lifestyle?

UNDERSTANDING THE TEXT

1. Why has the idea of the Buffalo Commons been controversial? What do you think this controversy suggests about how Americans think about the land and the way it should be used?

2. In what ways is the controversy about the Buffalo Commons a false dilemma, according to Quantic?

3. What advantages does Quantic see to living in sparsely populated regions of the Great Plains? What do these advantages suggest about Quantic's values regarding lifestyle?

4. Quantic describes the American bison as "the iconic animal of the Great Plains." What qualities of the bison does she value? What do these qualities suggest about her own views regarding the spaces we use in our lives?

EXPLORING THE ISSUES

1. In many ways, this essay is as much about *community* as it is about using spaces. Based on Quantic's statements about the communities of the Great Plains, what do you think is the relationship between community and space, as she understands it? Do you think her understanding of this relationship applies only to remote places like small towns in the Great Plains, or does it apply to any location? Explain.

2. Quantic grew up in Kansas and has focused her professional work as an English professor on the writ-ing of authors from the American West. To what extent does her background give her credibility as a writer speaking out on the issue of establishing a Buffalo Commons? Do you think her argument would be less effective if she did not have this background? Explain.

3. In paragraph 10, Quantic refers to "the commons ideal." What exactly does she mean by that term? In what ways is this ideal important to the proposal to establish a Buffalo Commons? Do you think most Americans would agree with this ideal? Explain.

ENTERING THE CONVERSATIONS

1. Write an essay in which you describe an important common space in your own life or in the region where you live. In your essay try to convey a sense of the importance of this space to you and the other people living near there.

2. In a group of classmates, share the essays you wrote for Question 1. What kinds of common spaces did the members of your group describe in their essays? What similarities and differences can you identify in these spaces? What might your essays suggest about the idea of common spaces? What do they suggest about using spaces in general?

INFOTRAC

3. Using InfoTrac College Edition, your library, the Internet, and other relevant resources, investigate the idea of the Buffalo Commons. Try to learn about the study by Frank and Deborah Popper that originally gave rise to the idea, and look into groups like the Great Plains Restoration Council that support the idea. If possible, talk to someone who is knowledgeable about this issue (such as a person representing a group like the Great Plains Restoration Council or a professor at your school who might have expertise in this subject). Then write a report about the history and current status of the proposal to create a Buffalo Commons. In your report, try to draw conclusions about what this proposal suggests about how we use the important spaces in our lives. Alternatively, research the general idea of "the commons" and write a report on the idea of the commons in American society.

4. Visit a common space at your school or in the area where you live (such as a student center, a park, or a municipal building) and spend some time observing how that space is used. Then write an essay based on what you observed. In your essay, describe how people tend to use the space you visited and draw conclusions about common spaces in our lives. Alternatively, create a visual representation of that space (for example, a web site, PowerPoint presentation, or photo essay) that conveys your sense of how that space is used.

A few years ago, I was on a backcountry trip *in the White Mountains in northern New Hampshire. I stayed for a few nights in a rustic log cabin without electricity or plumbing located a few miles from the nearest road and accessible only by a vigorous hike. On the front door of the cabin was a sign: "No cell phones." Apparently, the caretaker of the cabin prohibited cell phones because he wanted to preserve the wilderness atmosphere of the cabin. I was glad he did.*

Disconnected Urbanism

Today, cell phones are everywhere, and the traditional telephone, which has been an important means of communication for nearly a century, is being replaced by wireless communications devices. Complaints about cell phone use in public places are almost as common as cell phones themselves, so you probably won't be surprised to read Paul Goldberger's (b. 1950) criticisms of the use of cell phones on city streets. But there's more to Goldberger's essay than complaints about the annoyance of having to listen to someone's private telephone conversation in a public place or hearing a cell phone ring in a place you don't expect it. Goldberger is concerned about something more: how we use public spaces like city streets. He argues that cell phones are changing our relationship to those spaces, which he believes may be a sign that we ourselves are changing in ways we may not realize. Given the rapid increase in cell phone use and the expansion of wireless communications networks in recent years, Goldberger's concerns are worth considering. And I couldn't help noticing that when I returned to that cabin in New Hampshire's White Mountains in 2005, the sign about cell phones was no longer there.

Pulitzer Prize–winning author Paul Goldberger is the architecture (continued)

PAUL GOLDBERGER

There is a connection between the idea of place and the reality of cellular telephones. It is not encouraging. Places are unique—or at least we like to believe they are—and we strive to experience them as a kind of engagement with particulars. Cell phones are precisely the opposite. When a piece of geography is doing what it is supposed to do, it encourages you to feel a connection to it that, as in marriage, forsakes all others. When you are in Paris you expect to wallow in its Parisness, to feel that everyone walking up the Boulevard Montparnasse is as totally and completely there as the lampposts, the kiosks, the facade of the Brasserie Lipp—and that they could be no place else. So we want it to be in every city, in every kind of place. When you are in a forest, you want to experience its woodsiness; when you are on the beach, you want to feel connected to sand and surf.

This is getting harder to do, not because these special places don't exist or because urban places have come to look increasingly alike. They have, but this is not another rant about the monoculture and sameness of cities and the suburban landscape. Even when you are in (continued) *critic at* The New Yorker. *He has written many books and articles on urban design, preservation, and architecture. This essay first appeared in* Metropolis *magazine in 2003.* ◪

CONTEXT: CELL PHONE USE
According to the U.S. Census Bureau, cell phone subscribers increased from 34 million in 1995 to approximately 159 million in 2003. With this increase in cell phone use has come various concerns, such as the potential dangers of using cell phones while driving or the lack of courtesy by cell phone users in certain public places, such as churches or concert halls.

GLOSS: FLANEUR
A *flaneur* is a person who strolls along idly.

a place that retains its intensity, its specialness, and its ability to confer a defining context on your life, it doesn't have the all-consuming effect these places used to. You no longer feel that being in one place cuts you off from other places. Technology has been doing this for a long time, of course—remember when people communicated with Europe by letter and it took a couple of weeks to get a reply? Now we're upset if we have to send a fax because it takes so much longer than e-mail.

But the cell phone has changed our sense of place more than faxes and computers and e-mail because of its ability to intrude into every moment in every possible place. When you walk along the street and talk on a cell phone, you are not on the street sharing the communal experience of urban life. You are in some other place—someplace at the other end of your phone conversation. You are there, but you are not there. It reminds me of the title of Lillian Ross's memoir of her life with William Shawn, *Here But Not Here.* Now that is increasingly true of almost every person on almost every street in almost every city. You are either on the phone or carrying one, and the moment it rings you will be transported out of real space into a virtual realm.

This matters because the street is the ultimate public space and walking along it is the defining urban experience. It is all of us—different people who lead different lives—coming together in the urban mixing chamber. But what if half of them are elsewhere, there in body but not in any other way? You are not on Madison Avenue if you are holding a little object to your ear that pulls you toward a person in Omaha.

The great offense of the cell phone in public is not the intrusion of its ring, although that can be infuriating when it interrupts a tranquil moment. It is the fact that even when the phone does not ring at all, and is being used quietly and discreetly, it renders a public place less public. It turns the boulevardier into a sequestered individual, the **flaneur** into a figure of privacy. And suddenly the meaning of the street as a public place has been hugely diminished.

I don't know which is worse—the loss of the sense that walking along a great urban street is a glorious shared experience or the blurring of distinctions between different kinds of places. But these cultural losses are related, and the cell phone has played a major role in both. The other day I returned a phone call from a friend who lives in Hartford. He had left a voice-mail message saying he was visiting his son in New Orleans, and when I called him back on his cell phone—area code 860, Hartford—he picked up the call in Tallahassee. Once the area code actually meant something in terms of geography: it outlined a clearly defined piece of the earth; it became a form of identity. Your telephone number was a badge of place. Now the area code is really not much more than three digits; and if it has any connection to a place, it's just the telephone's home base. An area code today is more like a car's license plate. The downward spiral that began with the end of the old telephone exchanges that truly did connect to a place—RHinelander 4 and BUtterfield 8 for the Upper East Side, or CHelsea 3 downtown, or UNiversity 4 in Morningside Heights—surely culminates in the placeless area codes such as 917 and 347 that could be anywhere in New York—or anywhere at all.

VISUAL CONNECTIONS: CELL PHONES
Goldberger describes cell phones as "infuriating" intrusions in public places, but today, cell phones are commonly portrayed as a convenient and useful technology. Consider what these images, commonly used in advertisements, say about the use of cell phones.

It's increasingly common for cell-phone conversations to begin with the question, "Where are you?" and for the answer to be anything from "out by the pool" to "Madagascar." I don't miss the age when phone charges were based on distance, but that did have the beneficial effect of reinforcing a sense that places were distinguishable from one another. Now calling across the street and calling from New York to California or even Europe are precisely the same thing. They cost the same because to the phone they are the same. Every place is exactly the same as every other place. They are all just nodes on a network—and so, increasingly, are we.

UNDERSTANDING THE TEXT

1. Why is it important to Goldberger that a specific city or place is unique? What might that suggest about his sense of place and our relationship to places like cities?

2. Goldberger writes that "the great offense of the cell phone . . . is the fact that even when the phone does not ring at all, and is being used quietly and discreetly, it renders a public place less public." In what sense does the cell phone render a public place less public? Why is that a problem, in Goldberger's view? Do you agree with him? Why or why not?

3. In what sense does the cell phone help make every place like every other place? Why does this concern Goldberger? Do you think it should concern him? Explain.

EXPLORING THE ISSUES

1. In a sense, Goldberger is writing about two spaces in this essay: the public space of the city street and the "virtual" space of the cell phone. What basic distinction does Goldberger make between these two spaces? Why is that distinction important? What might it suggest about Goldberger's values regarding lifestyle and the spaces we live in?

2. Goldberger describes walking along a city street as "a glorious shared experience" (par. 6). What is glorious about walking along a city street, in Goldberger's view? What does this statement reveal about Goldberger's lifestyle preferences? What does it reveal about his view of cities? Do you think most people would agree with him that walking along a city street is a glorious shared experience? Why or why not?

3. How would you describe Goldberger's voice in this essay? What features of his voice stand out for you? Do you think his voice is effective? Explain, citing specific passages to illustrate your answer.

ENTERING THE CONVERSATIONS

1. Write an essay in which you express your own views about cell phones and their use today.

INFOTRAC

2. Communications technologies like the cell phone and the Internet have developed rapidly in the past decade or so, and as Goldberger's essay suggests, these technologies can affect our lives in a variety of ways—intended or not. Select one

such technology and, using InfoTrac College Edition, the library, and any other appropriate resources, investigate its development and its effects on modern life. Then write a report on the basis of your research. Try to draw conclusions about the impact of the technology you have researched on the important places in our lives.

3. On the basis of your research for Question 2, write a letter to the editor of your local newspaper or another appropriate publication in which you express your own concerns about an important new communications technology and how it tends to be used today.

4. Write an essay in which you explore the connection between technology and how we use the spaces around us. Draw on Goldberger's essay and any other essay in this chapter (or on other readings that are not in this book) to help support your points.

5. Create a web site intended to educate people on using their cell phones appropriately in public places. On your site, identify several important common places that people frequent and offer advice for using (or not using) cell phones in those places.

VALUING PLACE

FOR A TIME, I LIVED IN THE MIDWESTERN UNITED STATES, AND ALTHOUGH I ENJOYED LIVING THERE, I SOMETIMES FELT OUT OF PLACE. I MISSED THE MOUNTAINS AND FORESTS AND EVEN THE WEATHER OF THE NORTHEASTERN UNITED STATES WHERE I GREW UP. THE LANDSCAPE OF THE MIDWEST SEEMED TO LACK THE FEA-tures or characteristics that I needed to feel at home. sometimes i would talk about this sense of being out of place with friends who grew up in the Midwest but lived in the East, and they would confide that they had similar feelings. They felt out of place in the eastern states where I grew up. One colleague of mine, who grew up in the Northwest but has now lived in upstate New York for many years, clearly still feels out of place and often talks about Washington State as "home."

> **Whatever the specific connection, somehow these places are part of who we are; they shape our sense of identity and purpose.**

I was thinking about these feelings as I compiled the readings for this cluster. And the more I thought about them, the more I realized how important a sense of place can be in our lives. Paradoxically, American culture seems to value mobility. As soon as the nation was established, Americans were pushing into the frontier of the West and didn't stop until much of the land between the Atlantic and Pacific Oceans had been settled. American history is marked by large migrations of people: waves of immigrants in the nineteenth and early twentieth centuries from European nations and more recent immigrations from Asian and Latin American countries; the movement of millions of Blacks from the American South to northern industrial cities like Chicago and Cleveland after the Civil War; more recently, the shifting of the U.S. population from the Northeast to the Southwest and Southeast, seen in the dramatic growth of cities like Denver, Las Vegas, and Atlanta.

Yet for all this movement, people still seem to need a connection to a place. The essays in this cluster explore that need. They examine the many different ways in which we come to value certain places, as individuals and as members of larger communities or cultures. Sometimes that place is a town or region or even a kind of landscape—like a desert or a lake—that holds emotional importance for us. Sometimes it is a place, like a battlefield or Ground Zero in New York City, where something momentous happened and where we feel a need to remember. Whatever the specific connection, somehow these places are part of who we are; they shape our sense of identity and purpose. We value these places because they help us find value in our lives. These essays are about that kind of value in our lives.

Few Americans remain in the same place *their entire lives, and even those who remain in the same town usually move from one house to another during their lifetime. Of course, many Americans move much farther than that. You probably know someone who has moved to another city or state to attend school, to work, or to start a new life in some way. You may have done so yourself. Americans take this kind of mobility for granted. Indeed, this mobility is often*

THE Sense OF Place

thought of as a good thing, a mark of the special individuality of Americans. But award-winning writer Wallace Stegner (1909–1993) questions whether this aspect of the American character really is a good thing. In the following essay, Stegner discusses the wanderlust of Americans and examines what it means for their sense of themselves as individuals and as a culture. He asserts that the classic American individualist who exhibits the pioneer spirit that is most often praised in books and stories and histories "is not a full human being." That's because for Stegner, one's identity and wholeness are intimately tied to a place, whether that place be your birthplace or a place you came to later in life and eventually settled into. A deep connection to such a place, Stegner believes, is essential if Americans are to be healthy as a people. Stegner's viewpoint might feel disconcerting because American culture values mobility and individualism and considers both a part of what it means to be successful. But his essay may help you think in new ways about your own connection to place.

Pulitzer Prize–winning writer Wallace Stegner was the author of thirty books, including novels, histories, and works of nonfiction. He taught writing at (continued)

WALLACE STEGNER

If you don't know where you are, says Wendell Berry, you don't know *who* you are. Berry is a writer, one of our best, who after some circling has settled on the bank of the Kentucky River, where he grew up and where his family has lived for many generations. He conducts his literary explorations inward, toward the core of what supports him physically and spiritually. He belongs to an honorable tradition, one that even in America includes some great names: Thoreau, Burroughs, Frost, Faulkner, Steinbeck—lovers of known earth, known weathers, and known neighbors both human and nonhuman. He calls himself a "placed" person.

But if every American is several people, and one of them is or would like to be a placed person, another is the opposite, the displaced person, cousin not to Thoreau but to Daniel Boone, dreamer not of Walden Pond but of far horizons, traveler not in Concord but in wild unsettled places, explorer not inward but outward. Adventurous, restless, seeking, asocial or antisocial, the displaced American persists by the million long after the frontier has vanished.

WALLACE STEGNER, "THE SENSE OF PLACE." FROM *WHERE THE BLUEBIRD SINGS TO THE LEMONADE SPRINGS* BY WALLACE STEGNER. PUB MODERN LIBRARY ISBN: 0375759328 PAGE 199-206. ORIGINALLY PUBLISHED AS A PAMPHLET BY THE WISCONSIN HUMANITIES COUNCIL HTTP://WWW.WISCONSINHUMANITIES.ORG/

(continued) *Stanford, where he started the creative writing program, and at the University of Utah, the University of Wisconsin, and Harvard University. The following essay is from* Where the Bluebird Sings to the Lemonade Springs *(1992).* ◪

VISUAL CONNECTIONS: THAT ROMANTIC ATAVIST
In this passage (par. 4), Stegner describes the figure of the classic American individualist, a figure deeply embedded in American culture. (His use of the term *atavist,* which refers to someone with the characteristic of a remote ancestor that is lost in more recent generations, suggests that he believes the class individualist has disappeared in recent generations.) Yet this figure shows up regularly in American film, literature, and other popular cultural media, such as advertising. This image depicts one of the most famous figures in American advertising, the cowboy in advertisements for Marlboro cigarettes. The Marlboro man, as this figure came to be known, eventually became controversial, as antismoking activists tried to remove ads such as these from media that target children and teens. Consider what this image conveys about the idea of the individual.

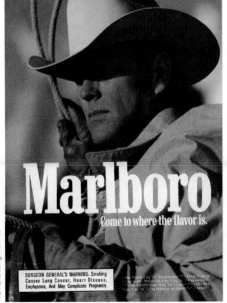

The Advertising Archives

He exists to some extent in all of us, the inevitable by-product of our history: the New World transient. He is commoner in the newer parts of America—the West, Alaska—than in the older parts, but he occurs everywhere, always in motion.

To the placed person he seems hasty, shallow, and restless. He has a current like the Platte, a mile wide and inch deep. As a species, he is non-territorial, he lacks a stamping ground. Acquainted with many places, he is rooted in none. Culturally he is a discarder or transplanter, not a builder or conserver. He even seems to like and value his rootlessness, though to the placed person he shows the symptoms of nutritional deficiency, as if he suffered from some obscure scurvy or pellagra of the soul.

Migratoriness has its dangers, unless it is the traditional, seasonal, social migratoriness of shepherd tribes, or of the academic tribes who every June leave Cambridge or New Haven for summer places in Vermont, and every September return to their winter range. Complete independence, absolute freedom of movement, are exhilarating for a time but may not wear well. **That romantic atavist** we sometimes dream of being, who lives alone in a western or arctic wilderness, playing **Natty Bumppo** and listening to the loons and living on moose meat and moving on if people come within a hundred miles, is a very American figure but he is not a full human being. He is a wild man of the woods, a Sasquatch.

He has many relatives who are organized as families— 5 migrant families that would once have followed the frontier but that now follow construction booms from Rock Springs to Prudhoe Bay, or pursue the hope of better times from Michigan to Texas, or retire from the Midwestern farm to St. Petersburg or Sunshine City, or still hunt the hippie heaven from Sedona to Telluride to Sand Point. These migrants drag their exposed roots and have trouble putting them down in new places. Some don't *want* to put them down, but at retirement climb into their RVs and move with the seasons from national park to national park, creating a roadside society out of perpetual motion. The American home is often a mobile home.

I know about this. I was born on wheels, among just such a family. I know about the excitement of newness and possibility, but also know the dissatisfaction and hunger that result from placelessness. Some towns that we lived in were never real to me. They were only the raw material of places, as I was the raw material of a person. Neither place nor I had a chance of being anything unless we could live together for a while. I spent my youth envying people who had lived all their lives in the houses they were born in, and had attics full of proof that they *had* lived.

GLOSS: NATTY BUMPPO
Natty Bumppo (par. 4) is a character who appeared in several novels by James Fenimore Cooper, including *Last of the Mohicans* (1826). A pioneer who explored unsettled wilderness, Bumppo personified rugged American individualism.

The **deep ecologists** warn us not to be anthropocentric, but I know no way to look at the world, settled or wild, except through my own human eyes. I know that it wasn't created especially for my use, and I share the guilt for what the members of my species, especially the migratory ones, have done to it. But I am the only instrument that I have access to by which I can enjoy the world and try to understand it. So I must believe that, at least to human perception, a place is not a place until people have been born in it, have grown up in it, lived in it, known it, died in it—have both experienced and shaped it, as individuals, families, neighborhoods, and communities, over more than one generation. Some are born in their place, some find it, some realize after long searching that the place they left is the one they have been searching for. But whatever their relation to it, it is made a place only by slow accrual, like a coral reef.

CONVERSATIONS: DEEP ECOLOGISTS
"Deep ecology" (par. 7) is a philosophy that is based on the principle of the inter-relatedness of all life on Earth. Based on the thinking of Norwegian philosopher Arn Naess, deep ecology promotes the idea that human beings are part of an inter-connected web of life and therefore do not have special status. Instead of an *anthro-pocentric* perspective—that is, viewing the world from a perspective that places human beings at the center of interest and value—deep ecologists advocate an *ecocentric* view that understands all life as equally valuable. Here Stegner refers to this view and rejects it. In doing so, he is joining an ongoing conversation about the relationship between human beings and the natural world.

Once, as George Stewart reminded us in *Names on the Land,* the continent stretched away westward without names. It had no places in it until people had named them, and worn the names smooth with use. The fact that Daniel Boone killed a bear at a certain spot in Kentucky did not make it a place. It began to be one, though, when he remembered the spot as Bear Run, and other people picked up the name and called their settlement by it, and when the settlement became a landmark or destination for travelers, and when the children had worn paths through its woods to the schoolhouse or swimming hole. The very fact that people remembered Boone's bear-killing, and told about it, added something of placeness.

No place is a place until things that have happened in it are remembered in history, ballads, yarns, legends, or monuments. Fictions serve as well as facts. Rip Van Winkle, though a fiction, enriches the Catskills. Real-life Mississippi spreads across unmarked boundaries into Yoknapatawpha County. Every one of the six hundred rocks from which the Indian maiden jumped to escape her pursuers grows by the legend, and people's lives get lived around and into it. It attracts family picnics and lovers' trysts. There are names carved in the trees there. Just as surely as do the quiet meadows and stone walls of Gettysburg, or the grassy hillside above the Little Big Horn where the Seventh Cavalry died, even a "phony" place like the Indian maiden's rock grows by human association.

10   In America the process of cumulative association has gone a good way by now in stable, settled, and especially rural areas—New England, the Midwest, the South—but hardly any way at all in the raw, migrant west. For one thing, the West has been raided more often than settled, and raiders move on when they have got what they came for. Many western towns never lasted a single human lifetime. Many others have changed so fast that memory cannot cling to them; they are unrecognizable to anyone who knew them twenty years ago. And as they change, they may fall into the hands of planners and corporations, so that they tend to become more and more alike. Change too often means stereotype. Try Gillette, Wyoming, not too long ago a sleepy cowtown on the verge of becoming a real place, now a coal boomtown that will never be a place.

Changing everywhere, America changes fastest west of the 100th meridian. Mining booms, oil booms, irrigation booms, tourist booms, culture booms as at Aspen and Sun Valley, crowd out older populations and bring in new ones. Communities lose their memory along with their character. For some, the memory can over time be reinstated. For many, the memory too will be a transient, for irrigation agribusinesses from California and Arizona to Idaho has by now created a whole permanent underclass of the migrant and dispossessed, totally placeless people who will never have a chance to settle down anywhere, who will know a place briefly during the potato or cantaloupe or grape harvest, and then they move on.

As with life, so with literature. Except in northern California, the West has never had a real literary outpouring, a flowering of the sort that marked New England, the Midwest, and the South. As I have noted elsewhere, a lot of what has been written is a literature of motion, not of a place. There is a whole tradition of it, from Mark Twain's *Roughing It* to Kerouac's *On the Road.* Occasionally we get loving place-oriented books such as Ivan Doig's *This House of Sky* and Norman Maclean's *A River Runs Through It,* but even while we applaud them we note that they are only memorials to places that used to be, not celebrations of ongoing places. They are nostalgic before history has taken its second step, as much a looking-back as *Huckleberry Finn* was for Mark Twain.

And that is a curious phenomenon, that nostalgia that has marked American writing ever since Irving and Cooper. From our very beginnings, and in the midst of our perpetual motion, we have been homesick for the old folks at home and the old oaken bucket. We have been forever bidding farewell to the last of the Mohicans, or the last of the old-time cattlemen, or the last of the pioneers with the bark on, or the vanishing wilderness. Just at random, read Willa Cather's *A Lost Lady* or Conrad Richter's *The Sea of Grass* or Larry McMurtry's *Horseman, Pass By,* or even William Dean Howells's *The Rise of Silas Lapham,* with its portrait of a businessman possessed of an antique and doomed integrity. We have made a tradition out of mourning the passing of things we never had time really to know, just as we have made a culture out of the open road, out of movement without place.

Freedom, especially free land, has been largely responsible. Nothing in our history has bound us to a plot of ground as feudalism once bound Europeans. In older, smaller, more homogeneous and traditional countries, life was always more centripetal, held in tight upon its center. In Ireland, for example, Yeats tells us, "there is no river or mountain that is not associated in the memory with some event or legend. . . . I would have our writers and craftsmen of many kinds master this history and these legends, and fix upon their memory the appearance of mountains and rivers and make it all visible again in their arts, so that Irishmen, even though they had gone thousands of miles away, would still be in their own country."

America is both too large and too new for that sort of universal recognition. It was 15 just the lack of such recognitions and acceptance, the lack of a complex American society rooted in richly remembered places, that led Washington Irving to transplant European legends to the Catskills, and Hawthorne to labor at creating what he called a usable past. The same lacks drove Henry James, later, to exploit his countrymen not as dwellers in their own country but more often as pilgrims and tourists abroad, hunting what their own country did not provide. When native themes, characters, and places did emerge, they were likely to be local-colorish, exploiting the local picturesque and probably mourning its passing, or expressions of our national restlessness, part of the literature of the road.

GLOSS: CARL JUNG
Acclaimed psychologist Carl Jung (1875–1961) was a student of Sigmund Freud who eventually developed his own influential theories of the human psyche.

Indifferent to, or contemptuous of, or afraid to commit ourselves to, our physical and social surroundings, always hopeful of something better, hooked on change, a lot of us have never stayed in one place long enough to learn it, or have learned it only to leave it. In our displaced condition we are not unlike the mythless man that **Carl Jung** wrote about, who lives "like one uprooted, having no true link either with the past, or with the ancestral life which continues within him, or yet with contemporary human society. He . . . lives a life of his own, sunk in a subjective mania of his own devising, which he believes to be the newly discovered truth."

Back to Wendell Berry, and his belief that if you don't know where you are you don't know who you are. He is not talking about the kind of location that can be determined by looking at a map or a street sign. He is talking about the kind of knowing that involves the senses, the memory, the history of a family or a tribe. He is talking about the knowledge of place that comes from working in it in all weathers, making a living from it, suffering from its catastrophes, loving its mornings or evenings or hot noons, valuing it for the profound investment of labor and feeling that you, your parents and grandparents, your all-but-unknown ancestors have put into it. He is talking about the knowing that poets specialize in.

It is only a step from his pronouncement to another: that no place is a place until it has had a poet. And that is about what Yeats was saying only a moment ago.

No place, not even a wild place, is a place until it has had that human attention that at its highest reach we will call poetry. What Frost did for New Hampshire and Vermont, what Faulkner did for Mississippi and Steinbeck for the Salinas Valley, Wendell Berry is doing for his family corner of Kentucky, and hundreds of other place-loving people, gifted or not, are doing for places they were born in, or reared in, or have adopted and made their own.

CONTEXT: THE ANNIVERSARY OF THE ARRIVAL OF COLUMBUS
Stegner writes in this paragraph that "in a few months it will be half a millennium since Europeans first laid eyes on this continent." He is referring here to the 500-year anniversary of the arrival of Christopher Columbus in "the New World," which was marked in 1992, when this essay was first published. Although Stegner makes only a passing reference to this anniversary, which sparked controversy at the time, it provides a special context for his essay, especially since Columbus's arrival began a migration from Europe to the Americas that is still occurring today. You might consider how this event helps give significance to Stegner's essay—and how it might have shaped the response of readers when it was first published in 1992.

I doubt that we will ever get the motion out of the Americans, for everything in his culture of opportunity and abundance has, up to now, urged motion on him as a form of virtue. Our tradition of restlessness will not be outgrown in a generation or two, even if the motives for restlessness are withdrawn. But after all, in a few months it will be half a millennium since Europeans first laid eyes on this continent. At least in geographical terms, the frontiers have been explored and crossed. It is probably time we settled down. It is probably time we looked around us instead of looking ahead. We have no business, any longer, in being impatient with history. We need to know our history in much greater depth, even back to geology, which, as Henry Adams said, is only history projected a little way back from Mr. Jefferson.

History was part of the baggage we threw overboard when we launched ourselves into the New World. We threw it away because it recalled old tyrannies, old limitations, galling obligations, bloody memories. Plunging into the future through a landscape that had no history, we did both the country and ourselves some harm along with some good. Neither the country nor the society we built out of it can be healthy until we stop raiding and running, and learn to be quiet part of the time, and acquire the sense not of ownership but of belonging.

"The land was ours before we were the land's," says Robert Frost's poem. Only in the act of submission is the sense of place realized and a sustainable relationship between people and earth established.

CONVERSATIONS: A LANDSCAPE WITH NO HISTORY

When Stegner writes in this paragraph that people from the Old World plunged "into the future through a landscape that had no history," he is apparently referring to the fact that the Native peoples who inhabited the New World when the Europeans arrived had no written language and therefore no written history. However, many critics would dispute this view, since the cultures that existed in the Americas at the time of Christopher Columbus's arrival had rich oral traditions and passed their histories down from one generation to the next through stories and songs. Stegner seems to suggest here (and earlier in his essay) that without a written literature and written history, a place or a culture can have no history, which is a view that many scholars have criticized as being "Euro-centric"—that is, a view emphasizing a European perspective on the world.

UNDERSTANDING THE TEXT

1. Who are the "placed" person and the "displaced" person, according to Stegner? What are the major distinctions between them? Why are these distinctions important?

2. What is "the process of cumulative association" that Stegner describes in this essay (par. 10–11)? Why is this process important in understanding a sense of place? Do you think Stegner is right about this process? Explain.

3. What is the importance of history and story, including literature, in providing a sense of place?

4. What unique characteristics have enabled Americans to make "a culture out of the open road," as Stegner puts it (par. 13)? How do these characteristics affect Americans' relationship to place? What problems does Stegner see with this relationship? Do you agree with him? Why or why not?

5. In what ways can we really know a place, according to Stegner? What kind of knowledge about a place does he value? What does such knowledge suggest about our relationship to a place?

EXPLORING THE ISSUES

1. Stegner criticizes the mobility of Americans and asserts that "it is probably time we settled down." Based on this essay, how would you characterize Stegner's views regarding lifestyle and place? What does he value most? What do you think would be the consequences of a lifestyle based on his values? Do you think most Americans would agree with him? Do you? Why or why not?

2. Stegner makes many references to well-known authors, literary

works, and historical figures in this essay. What do these references reveal about Stegner's sense of his audience? In what ways do you think they contribute to or detract from the effectiveness of his essay? Do you think a reader must recognize these references to appreciate Stegner's point? Explain. To what extent do you think these references helped or hindered you as you read this essay?

3. Throughout his essay, Stegner refers to Americans collectively as "we," and he makes many generalizations about Americans. For example, in paragraph 16, he writes, "Indifferent to, or contemptuous of, or afraid to commit ourselves to, our physical and social surroundings, always hopeful of something better, hooked on change, a lot of us have never stayed in one place long enough to learn it, or have learned it only to leave it." What assumptions does Stegner make about Americans that enable him to make such generalizations? Do you think these generalizations are accurate or valid and apply to all Americans? Or are there differences among different groups of Americans that Stegner is ignoring? Explain, citing specific passages to support your answer.

4. In paragraph 18, Stegner writes that "no place is a place until it has had a poet." What do you think he means by that statement? What does this statement reveal about Stegner's view of poetry or literature in general? What does it suggest about how humans understand their relationship to place? Do you agree with this statement? Why or why not?

ENTERING THE CONVERSATIONS

1. Write an essay about a place that conveys your sense of connection to that place.

2. In a group of classmates, share the essays you wrote for Question 1. What kinds of places did you and your classmates describe? What similarities and differences can you identify in those places and the connection people feel to them? What might these essays suggest about the importance of place in our lives?

3. Stegner writes that "a place is not a place until people have been born in it, have grown up in it, lived in it, known it, died in it—have both experienced and shaped it, as individuals, families, neighborhoods, and communities, over more than one generation" (par. 7). Write an essay in which you develop this idea. Draw on your own experience, Stegner's essay, and any other appropriate essays or resources to help you develop this idea and support your perspective on it.

4. Interview several people you know about important places in their lives. Try to interview people in different kinds of circumstances—for example, a retired person, a college student, someone you know who has lived in different places, perhaps an international student. In your interviews, ask these people to describe important places in their lives and try to get a sense of why those places are important to them. Then write an essay in which you report on your interviews. In your essay, describe the people you interviewed and the places they described to you. Try to draw conclusions from these interviews about what a "sense of place" means.

5. Create a webpage, photo essay, or similar kind of document that illustrates your interpretation of Stegner's phrase *a sense of place.*

E. B. White (1899–1985) is considered by many to be America's preeminent essayist. He is probably better known by most Americans for his children's books, Charlotte's Web *(1952) and* Stuart Little *(1945), which are still enjoyed by millions of readers today. But if you attended school in the United States, it's possible that you were also assigned to read the following essay. A study published in 2000 revealed that this essay was the most frequently reprinted essay*

Once More TO THE Lake

in composition textbooks (such as the one you're reading right now) during the previous fifty years. It's worth examining why.

White, who also coauthored one of the best-selling writing handbooks ever published, The Elements of Style, *is usually praised for his simple but elegant writing style and for his carefully crafted descriptions. This essay, which was first published in* Harper's *magazine in 1941, may give you some sense of how White earned his reputation as a superb stylist. But certainly, this essay has more to offer a reader than an effective writing style. Something about the way White explores his subject continues to resonate with readers even more than a half century after he wrote this essay. I first read the essay when I was a new graduate student in my early twenties, and it immediately reminded me of the lake in Pennsylvania where I spent summers during my teenage years. White's descriptions of being on the lake felt familiar to me, almost as if he were describing my own experiences. That sense of familiarity may be one reason that readers connect with this essay. But as I've become older and raised my own family, my response to White's essay has changed. Now I read it as a father who shares some of White's joys and fears as a* (continued)

E. B. WHITE

One summer, along about 1904, my father rented a camp on a lake in Maine and took us all there for the month of August. We all got ringworm from some kittens and had to rub Pond's Extract on our arms and legs night and morning, and my father rolled over in a canoe with all his clothes on; but outside of that the vacation was a success and from then on none of us ever thought there was any place in the world like that lake in Maine. We returned summer after summer—always on August 1st for one month. I have since become a salt-water man, but sometimes in summer there are days when the restlessness of the tides and the fearful cold of the sea water and the incessant wind which blows across the afternoon and into the evening make me wish for the placidity of a lake in the woods. A few weeks ago this feeling got so strong I bought myself a couple of bass hooks and a spinner and returned to the lake where we used to go, for a week's fishing and to revisit old haunts.

I took along my son, who had never had any fresh water up his nose and who had seen lily pads only from train windows. On the journey over to the lake I began to wonder what it would be like. I wondered (continued) *parent. And the ending of the essay, which has generated so much discussion over the years, means something different to me now than it did when I was younger. Maybe what makes an essay great is its richness, the way it can prompt us to explore complex ideas or issues that change but remain important over a lifetime.*

But this essay is also about a place: a lake that was special to White. And whatever else we might think about this essay, it may help us appreciate the value of special places in our lives and the complexity of our connection to those places. For surely, this lake was a more complicated place to White than just a place to take a walk down memory lane.

Elwyn Brooks White was a columnist for The New Yorker *for many years. His columns were collected in two volumes,* One Man's Meat *(1942) and* The Points of My Compass *(1962). He also published other essay collections in addition to his children's books and* The Elements of Style, *which he coauthored with William Strunk Jr.* ✇

CONTEXT: WILD LAKES

White describes the lake where he and his family vacationed not as a "wild lake" but one that was "undisturbed" and "seemed infinitely remote and primeval." Such places are increasingly hard to find as regions like the area in Maine where White took his family have become developed for resorts and vacation homes. Real estate values in such places have increased dramatically in the past few decades so that visiting them is not affordable for many people. It's worth considering whether the experience that White describes in this essay requires a remote and undisturbed place like this lake. Or does the nature of the place itself not matter? In other words, can this kind of experience happen in any place? If not, will some readers be unable to appreciate the value of this place to White?

5

how time would have marred this unique, this holy spot—the coves and streams, the hills that the sun set behind, the camps and the paths behind the camps. I was sure that the tarred road would have found it out and I wondered in what other ways it would be desolated. It is strange how much you can remember about places like that once you allow your mind to return into the grooves which lead back. You remember one thing, and that suddenly reminds you of another thing. I guess I remembered clearest of all the early mornings, when the lake was cool and motionless, remembered how the bedroom smelled of the lumber it was made of and the wet woods whose scent entered through the screen. The partitions in the camp were thin and did not extend clear to the top of the rooms, and as I was always the first up I would dress softly so as not to wake the others, and sneak out into the sweet outdoors and start out in the canoe, keeping close along the shore in the long shadows of the pines. I remembered being very careful never to rub my paddle against the gunwale for fear of disturbing the stillness of the cathedral.

The lake had never been what you would call a wild lake. There were cottages sprinkled around the shores, and it was in farming country although the shores of the lake were quite heavily wooded. Some of the cottages were owned by nearby farmers, and you would live at the shore and eat your meals at the farmhouse. That's what our family did. But although it wasn't wild, it was a fairly large and undisturbed lake and there were places in it which, to a child at least, seemed infinitely remote and primeval.

I was right about the tar: it led to within half a mile of the shore. But when I got back there, with my boy, and we settled into a camp near a farmhouse and into the kind of summertime I had known, I could tell that it was going to be pretty much the same as it had been before—I knew it, lying in bed the first morning, smelling the bedroom, and hearing the boy sneak quietly out and go off along the shore in a boat. I began to sustain the illusion that he was I, and therefore, by simple transposition, that I was my father. This sensation persisted, kept cropping up all the time we were there. It was not an entirely new feeling, but in this setting it grew much stronger. I seemed to be living a dual existence. I would be in the middle of some simple act, I would be picking up a bait box or laying down a table fork, or I would be saying something, and suddenly it would be not I but my father who was saying the words or making the gesture. It gave me a creepy sensation.

We went fishing the first morning. I felt the same damp moss covering the worms in the bait can, and saw the dragonfly alight on the tip of my rod as it hovered a few inches from the surface of the water. It was the arrival of this fly that convinced me beyond any doubt that everything was as it always had been, that the years were a mirage and there had been no years. The small waves were the same, chucking the rowboat under the chin as we fished at anchor, and the boat was the same boat, the same color green and the ribs broken in the same places, and under the floor-boards the same freshwater leavings and débris—the dead helgramite, the wisps of moss, the rusty discarded fishhook, the dried blood from yesterday's catch. We stared silently at the tips of our rods, at the dragonflies that came and went. I lowered the tip of mine into the water, tentatively, pensively dislodging the fly, which darted two feet away, poised, darted two feet back, and came to rest again a little farther up the rod. There had been no years between the ducking of this dragonfly and the other one—the one that was part of memory. I looked at the boy, who was silently watching his fly, and it was my hands that held his rod, my eyes watching. I felt dizzy and didn't know which rod I was at the end of.

We caught two bass, hauling them in briskly as though they were mackerel, pulling them over the side of the boat in a businesslike manner without any landing net, and stunning them with a blow on the back of the head. When we got back for a swim before lunch, the lake was exactly where we had left it, the same number of inches from the dock, and there was only the merest suggestion of a breeze. This seemed an utterly enchanted sea, this lake you could leave to its own devices for a few hours and come back to, and find that it had not stirred, this constant and trustworthy body of water. In the shallows, the dark, water-soaked sticks and twigs, smooth and old, were undulating in clusters on the bottom against the clean ribbed sand, and the track of the mussel was plain. A school of minnows swam by, each minnow with its small individual shadow, doubling the attendance, so clear and sharp in the sunlight. Some of the other campers were in swimming, along the shore, one of them with a cake of soap, and the water felt thin and clear and unsubstantial. Over the years there had been this person with the cake of soap, this cultist, and here he was. There had been no years.

Up to the farmhouse to dinner through the teeming, dusty field, the road under our sneakers was only a two-track road. The middle track was missing, the one with the marks of the hooves and the splotches of dried, flaky manure. There had always been three tracks to choose from in choosing which track to walk in; now the choice was narrowed down to two. For a moment I missed terribly the middle alternative. But the way led past the tennis court, and something about the way it lay there in the sun reassured me; the tape had loosened along the backline, the alleys were green with plantains and other weeds, and the net (installed in June and removed in September) sagged in the dry noon, and the whole place steamed with midday heat and hunger and emptiness. There was a choice of pie for dessert, and one was blueberry and one was apple, and the waitresses were the same country girls, there having been no passage of time, only the illusion of it as in a dropped curtain—the waitresses were still fifteen; their hair had been washed, that was the only difference—they had been to the movies and seen the pretty girls with the clean hair.

Summertime, oh summertime, pattern of life indelible, the fade-proof lake, the woods unshatterable, the pasture with the sweetfern and the juniper forever and ever, summer without end; this was the background, and the life along the shore was the design, the cottages with their innocent and tranquil design, their tiny docks with

---

STRATEGIES: METAPHOR

This paragraph (par. 5) is one of the most famous passages in American nonfiction writing. Notice how White describes this seemingly simple scene of him and his son fishing from a rowboat. Consider how White uses the images of the lake surface and the dragonfly as metaphors to convey his ideas in this essay. What ideas do you think he is conveying with these metaphors?

CONVERSATIONS: AMERICAN FAMILY LIFE

In paragraph 8, White offers a description of "the American family at play." It is possible that at the time he wrote this essay, the scene he describes in this passage was common. In other words, perhaps he was describing the typical American family on vacation in the middle of the twentieth century. Many readers might therefore find this scene familiar. But many readers might not. Consider whether White's descriptions focus on a certain kind of American family or a certain segment of American society. And consider how this description might apply today: Is this scene typical of American families today? Such questions may help us see that in describing such scenes, White was participating in a larger conversation about the American family. Some critics would see his descriptions as based on an ideal view of the family, one that is associated with a certain social class and cultural background, and they might charge that such descriptions contribute to false myths about the family in American society. As you read, you might consider whether such criticisms are valid. Consider, too, what White's essay might contribute to this ongoing conversation about the American family.

the flagpole and the American flag floating against the white clouds in the blue sky, the little paths over the roots of the trees leading from camp to camp and the paths leading back to the outhouses and the can of lime for sprinkling, and at the souvenir counters at the store the miniature birch-bark canoes and the post cards that showed things looking a little better than they looked. This was the **American family at play,** escaping the city heat, wondering whether the newcomers in the camp at the head of the cove were "common" or "nice," wondering whether it was true that the people who drove up for Sunday dinner at the farmhouse were turned away because there wasn't enough chicken.

It seemed to me, as I kept remembering all this, that those times and those summers had been infinitely precious and worth saving. There had been jollity and peace and goodness. The arriving (at the beginning of August) had been so big a business in itself, at the railway station the farm wagon drawn up, the first smell of the pineladen air, the first glimpse of the smiling farmer, and the great importance of the trunks and your father's enormous authority in such matters, and the feel of the wagon under you for the long ten-mile haul, and at the top of the last long hill catching the first view of the lake after eleven months of not seeing this cherished body of water. The shouts and cries of the other campers when they saw you, and the trunks to be unpacked, to give up their rich burden. (Arriving was less exciting nowadays, when you sneaked up in your car and parked it under a tree near the camp and took out the bags and in five minutes it was all over, no fuss, no loud wonderful fuss about trunks.)

10   Peace and goodness and jollity. The only thing that was wrong now, really, was the sound of the place, an unfamiliar nervous sound of the outboard motors. This was the note that jarred, the one thing that would sometimes break the illusion and set the years moving. In those other summertimes all motors were inboard; and when they were at a little distance, the noise they made was a sedative, an ingredient of summer sleep. They were one-cylinder and two-cylinder engines, and some were make-and-break and some were jump-spark, but they all made a sleepy sound across the lake. The one-lungers throbbed and fluttered, and the twin-cylinder ones purred and purred, and that was a quiet sound too. But now the campers all had outboards. In the daytime, in the hot mornings, these motors made a petulant, irritable sound; at night, in the still evening when the afterglow lit the water, they whined about one's ears like mosquitoes. My boy loved our rented outboard, and his great desire was to achieve single-handed mastery over it, and authority, and he soon learned the trick of choking it a little (but not too much), and the adjustment of the needle valve. Watching him I would remember the things you could do with the old one-cylinder engine with the heavy fly-wheel, how you could have it eating out of your hand if you got really close to it spiritually. Motor boats in those days didn't have clutches, and

you would make a landing by shutting off the motor at the proper time and coasting in with a dead rudder. But there was a way of reversing them, if you learned the trick, by cutting the switch and putting it on again exactly on the final dying revolution of the flywheel, so that it would kick back against compression and begin reversing. Approaching a dock in a strong following breeze, it was difficult to slow up sufficiently by the ordinary coasting method, and if a boy felt he had complete mastery over his motor, he was tempted to keep it running beyond its time and then reverse it a few feet from the dock. It took a cool nerve, because if you threw the switch a twentieth of a second too soon you could catch the flywheel when it still had speed enough to go up past center, and the boat would leap ahead, charging bull-fashion at the dock.

We had a good week at the camp. The bass were biting well and the sun shone endlessly, day after day. We would be tired at night and lie down in the accumulated heat of the little bedrooms after the long hot day and the breeze would stir almost imperceptibly outside and the smell of the swamp drift in through the rusty screens. Sleep would come easily and in the morning the red squirrel would be on the roof, tapping out his gay routine. I kept remembering everything, lying in bed in the mornings—the small steamboat that had a long rounded stern like the lip of a Ubangi, how quietly she ran on the moonlight sails, when the older boys played their mandolins and the girls sang and we ate doughnuts dipped in sugar, and how sweet the music was on the water in the shining night, and what it had felt like to think about girls then. After breakfast we would go up to the store and the things were in the same place—the minnows in a bottle, the plugs and spinners disarranged and pawed over by the youngsters from the boys' camp, the fig newtons and the Beeman's gum. Outside, the road was tarred and cars stood in front of the store. Inside, all was just as it had always been, except there was more Coca-Cola and not so much Moxie and root beer and birch beer and sarsaparilla. We would walk out with a bottle of pop apiece and sometimes the pop would backfire up our noses and hurt. We explored the streams, quietly, where the turtles slid off the sunny logs and dug their way into the soft bottom; and we lay on the town wharf and fed worms to the tame bass. Everywhere we went I had trouble making out which was I, the one walking at my side, the one walking in my pants.

One afternoon while we were there at that lake a thunderstorm came up. It was like the revival of an old melodrama that I had seen long ago with childish awe. The second-act climax of the drama of the electrical disturbance over a lake in America had not changed in any important respect. This was the big scene, still the big scene. The whole thing was so familiar, the first feeling of oppression and heat and a general air around camp of not wanting to go very far away. In midafternoon (it was all the same) a curious darkening of the sky, and a lull in everything that had made life tick; and then the way the boats suddenly swung the other way at their moorings with the coming of a breeze out of the new quarter, and the premonitory rumble. Then the kettle drum, then the snare, then the bass drum and cymbals, then crackling light against the dark, and the gods grinning and licking their chops in the hills. Afterward the calm, the rain steadily rustling in the calm lake, the return of light and hope and spirits, and the campers running out in joy and relief to go swimming in the rain, their bright cries perpetuating the deathless joke about how they were getting simply drenched, and the children screaming with delight at the new sensation of bathing in the rain, and the joke about getting drenched linking the generations in a strong indestructible chain. And the comedian who waded in carrying an umbrella.

When the others went swimming my son said he was going in too. He pulled his dripping trunks from the line where they had hung all through the shower, and wrung them out. Languidly, and with no thought of going in, I watched him, his hard little body, skinny and bare, saw him wince slightly as he pulled up around his vitals the small, soggy, icy garment. As he buckled the swollen belt suddenly my groin felt the chill of death.

UNDERSTANDING THE TEXT

1. What exactly made the lake in Maine that White and his family visited so special? Why does White describe it as "this holy spot"? Was there anything special about that particular lake that made it different from other lakes White might have visited? What might the connection White felt to this particular lake suggest about how and why we value specific places?

2. What is the "illusion" that White begins to experience once he has arrived with his family at the lake where he vacationed as a child? What is the "dual existence" he begins to feel? Why is this dual existence important to White? What does it suggest about the value of special places in our lives?

3. In what ways had the sounds of the lake changed for White? What do you think these changes suggest about that place? What might they suggest about our sense of place in general?

4. Why does White feel "the chill of death" as he watches his son pull on a wet pair of shorts? What do you think White is emphasizing about the experience of returning to the lake by ending his essay with this line?

EXPLORING THE ISSUES

1. What do you think this essay suggests about relationships, especially the relationship between parent and child? What role does place play in such relationships?

2. In many ways, this essay is about memory. What do you think the essay suggests about our memories and their role in our lives? What does it suggest about the role of memory in the way we under-

stand and value certain places in our lives?

3. A great deal has changed since White wrote this essay more than sixty years ago, including the technologies we now use in our lives and the way Americans spend their leisure time. Many places like the lake White describes have been transformed by rising real estate prices and increasing populations (see *Context: Wild Lakes* on page 552). How might these kinds of changes influence the way readers today respond to White's essay? Do you think these changes affect the main ideas White explores? Explain.

4. White has earned much acclaim for his writing style. How would you describe White's writing style? What characteristics of his prose do you think contribute to his style? Do you think his writing deserves its reputation? Explain, citing specific passages to support your answer.

ENTERING THE CONVERSATIONS

1. Write an essay about a place that was special to you or your family when you were growing up. In your essay, try to convey a sense of why that place was special and what role it seemed to play in your life.

2. This essay has been discussed as an essay about time, memory, place, change, and relationships. Identify the idea or issue in this essay that seems most important or striking to you and write an essay in which you discuss that idea. In your essay, examine how White explores this idea or issue in his descriptions of the lake and the events that took place there.

3. In a group of classmates, share the essays you wrote for Question 2. Identify any similarities and differ-

ences in the ideas that each of you took away from White's essay. Draw conclusions about what your group's essays might suggest about how we make sense of essays like White's "Once More to the Lake."

INFOTRAC

4. Like White, many people vacation at a special place that has some meaning for them or their families. But vacationing has changed in many ways since White's essay was published in 1941. Using InfoTrac College Edition, the Internet, your library, and other relevant resources (such as travel organizations like the American Automobile Association), investigate how Americans tend to spend their vacations today. How have vacations changed in the years since White wrote this essay? What kinds of vacations are most popular today? Why do Americans vacation as they do? Try to answer such questions in your research. Then write a report based on your research. In your report, draw conclusions about the role of place in the way people spend vacations.

5. Find several flyers, Internet sites, magazine advertisements, or similar promotional materials that advertise specific vacation spots. Examine how these materials present the places they are promoting. What do they emphasize about these places? What ideas or feelings do they try to convey? What audiences do they seem to target? Then write a report in which you discuss what you found in examining these materials. Try to draw conclusions about the role of place in the way we think about vacations.

6. Create a flyer, web site, or other appropriate kind of document in which you advertise a place that is special to you for some reason.

The next time you draw some water from the *tap, think about where that water came from. If you live in the Northeast, it may have come from a lake or reservoir or river. In the Midwest, water is often supplied by huge underground aquifers as well as by rivers and the Great Lakes. In these cases, your water probably came from somewhere not too far away. But if you live in the West, it is quite likely that the water from your faucet traveled a great distance. Residents of*

Remembering Water

some of Arizona's cities, for example, receive their water from the Colorado River hundreds of miles away. If you're in Los Angeles, your water probably came from the Owens Valley, some 250 miles away.

But although we know that water is essential for life, we may take it for granted. Karen Piper doesn't. In the following essay, Piper tells a story of her relationship to her father and to a special place in the desert where water is precious. Piper grew up in the Owens Valley in California. As she makes clear in her essay, she and other residents of the Owens Valley are still angry about the aqueduct, built in the early 1900s, that carries water from their valley to the distant city of Los Angeles. But Piper's essay isn't so much about the controversy over water as it is about the importance of water to the valley where she grew up and especially about her relationship with her father. In exploring that relationship and the role water plays in it, Piper helps us appreciate the special value of certain places in our relationships with important people in our lives.

Karen Piper teaches literature at the University of Missouri–Columbia. She is the author of Cartographic Fictions: Maps, Race, and Identity *(2001). The following essay was published in* Sierra *magazine in 1996.* ▼

KAREN PIPER

In the desert, you can see it coming. Time sits on the horizon like rain clouds, holding out. In the cities, you carry it around in your pocket. Time is organized around where you have to be. You dash blindly around busy corners, always racing against it. But in the desert, the world sits on the horizon, refusing to move. Before I moved to the city, I used to know what that meant. Now I found myself trying to remember, waking up every morning to look at the mountains and see what they held. If there were clouds there, you knew there might be rain. It could pour down like a dropped bucket minutes from your house, or evaporate right over your head before you could lick it on your lips. But you knew there was something to wait for. You could watch time coming.

I came back home because my father was still waiting for the clouds over the hills; I thought he needed me. He was losing his memory, as the city had made me lose mine. So I came back for both of us. My father said he would look down at his feet, which would look the same, but the ground was different. I don't know if he was forgetting things, or remembering them too well. He remembered the names of World War II bombers, the orange groves in L.A., the way Morocco looked

KAREN PIPER, "REMEMBERING WATER" FROM *SIERRA* (JULY-AUGUST, 1996). REPRINTED BY PERMISSION OF THE AUTHOR.

in the rain. He could tell you what the valley looked like in 1945—he remembered who lived down the street during the war, but it was as if his memory didn't have room for anything else: his kids' names, where he lived now.

The doctors said it was transient amnesia, but I think they said this to protect us from the word we were all dreading: **Alzheimer's.** My father carried his disease around in his shirt pocket, so he wouldn't forget. When people asked about his health, he would bring it out and laugh. He was proud to own this name. My sister and I needed our father to hold together our memories, to hold together the world before we were born. When he got sick, this stopped happening and I began to realize for the first time that I was mortal—as if, when I faded away in his mind, I would fade away in the world.

My dad remembered a lake in the Mojave, just outside our hometown. He would point at an empty lake bed, filled with alkali salts, and see steamships crossing. He said that in "the days before Los Angeles" there had been a lake that was more than a hundred miles around. He saw things like that, that sounded like unicorns to me. I would try to picture steamships in a Mark Twain fashion, but was confronted by the reality of miles and miles of white sand, dust devils racing across the surface.

So when I came home, I brought my dad to the lake, looking for a cure. Anyone   5
who lives long enough in the desert begins to be infected by a search for water. You look for it everywhere because it is life. After a while, you can feel it in the groundwater beneath your feet, the springs in the back canyons, the clouds over the hills that may never come by. You know that water is always coming down somewhere, even if not on you, or else you would not be alive. Papago Indian children insist that "the desert smells like rain"—scientists tried to explain that this is because the creosote bushes exude an aromatic oil that fills the air when it rains. But I do not think that this is what the children mean.

When I left for college, I let that place evaporate; embarrassed, I gave it up. I didn't believe in water yet. I thought the desert was a drying-up old woman; I thought she had betrayed me by making me different. It would take the blank look on my father's face to bring me back home, to make me start looking in the cracks of the desert, at the places he was pointing to with his memory. We would walk the surface of that empty lake, walk to the aqueduct which was carrying his life away to Los Angeles. I would face it, this time, with him. I would return to the truth of the stolen water.

I used to drive around at night, in the days when I was desperate to leave. I wanted L.A.—I wanted to dress like them, taste their food, be in their manicured green back yards. Where I lived, there were only smashed snakes on the road and skittish coyotes, reminding me of the desolation of the place. But every now and then, a white owl would make a wild dash past my windshield like God. And I knew the white owl was bringing me home. White owls aren't supposed to exist out there, you see. The

---

STRATEGIES: METAPHORS AND SIMILES FOR TIME
Time is not an easy thing to describe or understand, and writers often use figures of speech such as metaphors or similes to convey ideas about time. Here Piper writes that in the desert "time sits on the horizon like rain clouds"; she uses a different metaphor to describe time in the city: "In the cities, you carry it around in your pocket." These are strong images that not only convey certain ideas about time but also help us "see" the desert and the city as physical spaces. So Piper is using these figures of speech to do more than just say something clever about time. And she will refer back to them later in the essay to help her develop her ideas further. Consider how these images help Piper convey the larger ideas she is exploring in this essay.

GLOSS: ALZHEIMER'S
This terrible disease afflicts mostly older people, and among its symptoms are not just loss of memory but often confusion as a person's memories become jumbled. Alzheimer's disease distorts time for those who have the disease, but Piper seems to be saying something about time for people without Alzheimer's, too. (Judith Levine, whose essay appears in Chapter 12, also writes about Alzheimer's disease.)

Indian children write about them, but only as a myth. When I left for college, this one bird was implanted in my mind, making me late for work, making me remember my father.

I came home, more for myself than for him. I came home to learn the names of things, to remember places I'd tried to forget, to look for the springs. I knew that if you waited, they would come, trickling over your shoes at night, tugging at your hair. The fingers of rain and owls and moonlight would wrap themselves around you.

Water is the religion of the desert. It insinuates itself into the cracks of consciousness and allows the mind to move. The doctor said that, in aging, the fluids of the brain begin to dissolve, making brain cells shrink slightly. This is why, when my father's brain began to dry up, I wanted to search for the water again. We used to go to the lake when I was young and thought that desert oases only existed on television. Los Angeles had sucked the water away and put it on TV, took it away for the pulse of the city. I feel now that they took my father's blood, eliminated his history, his memories, to support the city's life. My father's blood and brain fluid is flowing through the streets of Los Angeles, watering their lawns and filling their glasses. It's hard to say what it is to be forgotten.

10   My dad and I returned to the lake, and walked across it to the aqueduct that intercepted its water, to the captured rain that made its way past our feet encased in concrete. To us it was a vial of precious liquid, and our mouths watered at the sight. The lake was behind us, a strange moonscape of salt formations in a valley that seems to end only at the snow peaks of the Sierra. After it was drained in 1912 by the Los Angeles Department of Water and Power, the lake started producing dust storms, an eerie reminder of something gone wrong. Before Los Angeles, the valley sustained deep saltgrass meadows and marshes filled with everything from willows to brine shrimp to tule elk. Now Los Angeles looms always over the horizon, like a hallucination. My father knew what Los Angeles meant and tried to teach me. The city was everywhere, he said—the city was coming to get us. When you stand in the center of Owens Lake, history declares you dead.

The lake didn't go without a fight—the Owens Valley residents bombed the L.A. aqueduct over and over, trying to stop construction. If you walk out onto the lake now, you will not hear the explosions, you will not see the tourists, you will not feel the shadows of waterfowl overhead. The lake is silent, silent as the aqueduct waters that run down smoothly cemented passageways, diverting the river away from the lake toward its new destination. The desert becomes the haunting of Los Angeles, though the citizens of Los Angeles have not been told to listen. They will pour it out of their faucets into their blood, pour the desert as life into their veins.

We used to go there to walk the surface, play with the rocks that looked like they were from the moon, imagine the Star Trek episodes that were shot there. The Department of Water and Power passes out booklets at the Owens Lake visitor center claiming that this is a "prehistoric" lake, whose salt waters were completely useless even before its disappearance. "Prehistoric," in this case, obviously means "before Los Angeles." Anyone in the valley will tell you when the lake really disappeared, that history was diverted down aqueduct channels toward L.A. Scientists are proposing that the only solution to the dust storms created by the lake may be to set up a sprinkler system to stabilize the surface. The dust is a health hazard of unknown proportions. My sister has lupus—like so many others in my town—and my father is losing his mind. They have not yet defined the dimensions of this hazard. Sometimes we would pick up rocks and suck on them.

So I brought him here again, looking for the cure. Nearly 80 years after the water had gone, my father and I stood on the banks of that stolen river and tried to remember, dreaming of the forgotten lake as if our mere reverie would make Los Angeles sink back into the ground. I had lived in L.A. for four years, but I came home because to him, water didn't come from the faucet. I went back to its source, to my memories. My father knew we could have life again if the water stopped going to L.A. I couldn't stay there, betraying that dream. I had to start imagining, like him—to look at the ground and see something different. We looked across the lake and saw heat waves, dousing the lake bed in imaginary water. My father tried to fill in the blank spaces in his mind, while I tried to fill the lake with water. I tried to remember a lake I had never seen. I knew that it had existed, and I knew that the remembering was sweet, and tasted warm like water.

The lake stands forgotten but will not go away. I dream of a time when the water will spill over its banks again, bringing back life. I dream of a time when the relationships that were destroyed through its disappearance will feel that first drop of fluid binding them together, steadily, like flowing blood. And then my father will not have to work so hard to hold us together, to keep us alive in the desert. The first green grass will sprout from the banks, and the first tule elk will creep down to the marshes, and the first shrimp egg will open back to life. The desert is not dead, is not brown, is not desolate. It is only that it has temporarily forgotten itself, forgotten where the water is hiding. The birds have stopped coming here on their long migrations because the desert has lost its watering hole. These things are still there, just waiting to be remembered. My father and I once stood on the banks and stared that forgetting in the face, trying to remember the scent of where we lived.

Our trek to the aqueduct had been a long one, and we were greeted with a sign 15 that warned: "These waters are the municipal water supply of the City of Los Angeles. Trespassing-Loitering Forbidden by Law." The sign was filled with bullet holes. I glanced around in the falling darkness and saw no one. Stepping over the dusty, concrete banks of the aqueduct, I took my father's hand, and led him in. The water was cool as ice in the night and the shock of life was waiting for us there. Watching the clouds over the horizon, we knew the rain was coming. We knew the mud and dust would be washed away with time. And I led him down to the source, like his first baptism. He smiled, white as an owl, and drank.

UNDERSTANDING THE TEXT

1. What "cure" is Piper looking for when she brings her father to the lake in the desert? What does this cure have to do with the desert?

2. In paragraph 6, Piper writes that she didn't "believe in water yet" when she left home for college. What does she mean? How might you believe in water? And why is this so important for her?

3. How do Piper's views of the desert and her feelings about the desert change over time? What causes these changes? What do you think these changes suggest about our relationship to certain special places in our lives?

4. Piper describes the water of the desert lake as "stolen," and she criticizes the authorities, including the Los Angeles Department of Water and Power, for taking it (par. 9–10). What was lost when the water was diverted from the desert to the city, in Piper's view? What do you think her view suggests about the importance of water in our lives?

5. What, ultimately, do Piper and her father find when they return to the desert? Do they find what Piper hoped to find? Explain.

EXPLORING THE ISSUES

1. Piper's writing is rich in figures of speech, such as metaphor and simile (see *Strategies: Metaphors and Similes for Time* on page 559). Identify some of the other figures of speech that Piper uses in this essay, especially those referring to water and to the desert. How effective do you find these figures of speech? Do you notice any patterns to them? Explain. What ideas does Piper seem to convey through her uses of these figures of speech?

2. This essay is as much about memory as it is about the special places in the desert that she visits with her father. What is the connection between memory and place for Piper? What might her essay suggest about the importance of memory when it comes to special places?

3. In the final paragraph, Piper describes taking her father to the water flowing in the aqueduct "like his first baptism." This reference reminds us that water has great cultural and religious significance and symbolism. Examine the way Piper describes water in this essay. What do her references to water convey about the significance she sees in water? Do you think Piper's view of water is consistent with the way water tends to be viewed in American culture? Explain.

4. Throughout her essay, Piper refers to the conflicts about water in California. These conflicts involve questions about who owns the land and the water that is on it. What questions do you think Piper's essay raises about the ownership of important places? What questions does it raise about the connection between individuals and the land?

ENTERING THE CONVERSATIONS

1. Write an essay about an experience you had in which water—or a place where water is somehow important—played a significant role.

2. Write an essay examining the role of a special place in an important relationship in your life.

3. The 1974 classic film *Chinatown* tells a story about the struggle over water rights in California. If you can access this film, watch it and pay attention to the ideas about water and water rights that the film seems to convey. Then write a brief review

of the film focusing on what it seems to say about our uses of water. Draw conclusions about what this film suggests about the way we understand water and our relationship to places where water is scarce.

INFOTRAC

4. In her essay, Piper refers to the controversy surrounding the diversion of water from the Owens Valley in California. This vast project has had significant social, political, environmental, and economic effects on the region (see *Context: Owens Lake* on page 560). But this is just one example of controversies involving water and water rights throughout the United States, especially in places like the West, where water tends to be scarce. Using InfoTrac College Edition, the Internet, and any other relevant resources, identify one such controversy and investigate it. If there is such a controversy in the region where you live, you may wish to investigate that situation. If possible, talk to people involved in the controversy or who have knowledge of it. Find out what the focus of the controversy is. Try to understand the various points of view of those involved and learn something about how the controversy came to be. Then write a report on the controversy. Draw conclusions about what this controversy suggests about water and our relationship to it today.

5. Create a photo essay, video, web site, or some other appropriate kind of document in which you present your view of the role water plays in your life. Try to examine not only the practical importance of water as a physical need but also other less obvious ways in which water is important in your life.

In the months following the terrorist attacks *of September 11, 2001, many people I know visited the site of the Word Trade Center in New York City, the place now known as Ground Zero. In every case, those people had few words to say about what it was like to see the place where so many people died in such a horrific way. The words they did use—"amazing," "unbelievable," "horrible," "incredible"—seemed inadequate to convey their feelings about that now-sacred*

Where Nothing Says Everything

place and the magnitude of what happened there. There's just no way to describe it, a few of them said.

Writer Suzanne Berne (b. 1961) would probably agree with that, but the following essay, which she wrote just a few months after September 11, 2001, comes as close as anything I have read to conveying the sense of horror, reverence, and awe that people feel when they visit Ground Zero. In her essay, Berne tells the story of her own visit to that place, and she provides a picture of the impact of the site on those who visit it. Her essay is a powerful statement about the value of such places. As you read, consider not only what Berne seems to be saying about what makes these places special—aside from the events that took place there—but also how Berne conveys a sense of what it's like to be there. Her essay can tell us something about the power of writing to evoke the places we value.

Novelist Suzanne Berne's books include A Crime in the Neighborhood *(1997) and* A Perfect Arrangement *(2001). This essay first appeared in the* New York Times *in 2002.*

SUZANNE BERNE

On a cold, damp March morning, I visited Manhattan's financial district, a place I'd never been, to pay my respects at what used to be the World Trade Center. Many other people had chosen to do the same that day, despite the raw wind and spits of rain, and so the first thing I noticed when I arrived on the corner of Vesey and Church Streets was a crowd.

Standing on the sidewalk, pressed against aluminum police barricades, wearing scarves that flapped into their faces and woolen hats pulled over their ears, were people apparently from everywhere. Germans, Italians, Japanese. An elegant-looking Norwegian family in matching shearling coats. People from Ohio and California and Maine. Children, middle-age couples, older people. Many of them were clutching cameras and video recorders, and they were all craning to see across the street, where there was nothing to see.

At least, nothing is what it first looked like, the space that is now ground zero. But once your eyes adjust to what you are looking at, "nothing" becomes something much more potent, which is absence.

STRATEGIES: POINT OF VIEW
In paragraph 3, Berne shifts from the third person point of view ("he" or "she" or "they") to the second person ("you"). For the rest of the essay, Berne refers to "you." Consider the effect of this shift on you as a reader. In what ways might the essay be different if Berne had remained with a third-person point of view? What do you think Berne accomplishes by using the second person?

VISUAL CONNECTIONS: A GREAT BOWL OF LIGHT
Berne describes the site of the attacks on the World Trade Center in New York City as "a great bowl of light." Some people have proposed that the memorial to be built on that site use light to memorialize the towers that once stood there. The photograph shown here was taken on September 11, 2003, at a ceremony to commemorate the victims of the attacks. Consider how such uses of light can convey messages that perhaps are difficult to convey in words. To what extent does this photograph coincide with Berne's perspective on Ground Zero?

But to the out-of-towner, ground zero looks at first simply like a construction site. All the familiar details are there: the wooden scaffolding; the cranes, the bulldozers and forklifts; the trailers and construction workers in hard hats; even the dust. There is the pound of jackhammers, the steady beep-beep-beep of trucks backing up, the roar of heavy machinery.

5   So much busyness is reassuring, and it is possible to stand looking at the cranes and trucks and feel that mild curiosity and hopefulness so often inspired by construction sites.

Then gradually your eyes do adjust, exactly as if you have stepped from a dark theater into a bright afternoon, because what becomes most striking about this scene is the light itself.

Ground zero is a great bowl of light, an emptiness that seems weirdly spacious and grand, like a vast plaza amid the dense tangle of streets in lower Manhattan. Light reflecting off the Hudson River vaults into the site, soaking everything—especially on an overcast morning—with a watery glow. This is the moment when absence begins to assume a material form, when what is not there becomes visible.

Suddenly you notice the periphery, the skyscraper shrouded in black plastic, the boarded windows, the steel skeleton of the shattered Winter Garden. Suddenly there are the broken steps and cracked masonry in front of Brooks Brothers. Suddenly there are the firefighters, the waiting ambulance on the other side of the pit, the police on every corner. Suddenly there is the enormous cross made of two rusted girders.

And suddenly, very suddenly, there is the little cemetery attached to St. Paul's Chapel, with tulips coming up, the chapel and grounds miraculously undamaged except for a few plastic-sheathed gravestones. The iron fence is almost invisible beneath a welter of dried pine wreaths, banners, ribbons, laminated poems and prayers and photographs, swags of paper cranes, withered flowers, baseball hats, rosary beads, teddy bears. And flags, flags everywhere, little American flags fluttering in the breeze, flags on posters drawn by Brownie troops, flags on T-shirts, flags on hats, flags streaming by, tied to the handles of baby strollers.

It takes quite a while to see all of this; it takes even longer to come up with something to say about it.

An elderly man standing next to me had been staring fixedly across the street for some time. Finally he touched his son's elbow and said: "I watched those towers being built. I saw this place when they weren't there." Then he stopped, clearly struggling with, what for him, was a double negative, recalling an absence before there was an absence. His son, waiting patiently, took a few photographs. "Let's get out of here," the man said at last.

Again and again I heard people say, "It's unbelievable." And then they would turn to each other, dissatisfied. They wanted to say something more expressive, more meaningful. But it is unbelievable, to stare at so much devastation, and know it for devastation, and yet recognize that it does not look like the devastation one has imagined.

Like me, perhaps, the people around me had in mind images from television and newspaper pictures: the collapsing buildings, the running office workers, the black plume of smoke against a bright blue sky. Like me, they were probably trying to superimpose those terrible images onto the industrious emptiness right in front of them. The difficulty of this kind of mental revision is measured, I believe, by the brisk trade in World Trade Center photograph booklets at tables set up on street corners.

Determined to understand better what I was looking at, I decided to get a ticket for the viewing platform beside St. Paul's. This proved no easy task, as no one seemed to be able to direct me to South Street Seaport, where the tickets are distributed. Various police officers whom I asked for directions, waved me vaguely toward the East River, differing degrees of boredom and resignation on their faces. Or perhaps it was a kind of incredulousness. Somewhere around the American Stock Exchange, I asked a security guard for help and he frowned at me, saying, "You want tickets to the disaster?"

Finally I found myself in line at a cheerfully painted kiosk, watching a young juggler try to entertain the crowd. He kept dropping the four red balls he was attempting to juggle, and having to chase after them. It was noon; the next available viewing was at 4 P.M.

Back I walked, up Fulton Street, the smell of fish in the air, to wander again around St. Paul's. A deli on Vesey Street advertised a view of the World Trade Center from its second-floor dining area. I went in and ordered a pastrami sandwich, uncomfortably aware that many people before me had come to that same deli for pastrami sandwiches who would never come there again. But I was here to see what I could, so I carried my sandwich upstairs and sat down beside one of the big plate-glass windows.

And there, at last, I got my ticket to the disaster.

I could see not just into the pit now, but also its access ramp, which trucks had been traveling up and down since I had arrived that morning. Gathered along the ramp were firefighters in their black helmets and black coats. Slowly they lined up, and it became clear that this was an honor guard, and that someone's remains were being carried up the ramp toward the open door of an ambulance.

Everyone in the dining room stopped eating. Several people stood up, whether out of respect or to see better, I don't know. For a moment, everything paused.

15

CONTEXT: CREATING A PROPER MEMORIAL
Sawyer's description in this passage (par. 12) of the dissatisfaction that visitors to Ground Zero felt may help explain some of the controversy that continued to swirl around the proposals for the memorial to be built there. As Rhonda Chriss Lokeman's essay (which appears on page 512 in this chapter) indicates, disagreements about what kind of memorial should be built at Ground Zero were intense from the very moment that government officials decided to build a memorial. At the time Sawyer's essay was published in 2002, proposals for such a memorial were being submitted and ideas about what should be done with the site were being debated. But even after a design was accepted in 2004, controversy continued. In May, 2005, for example, well-known businessman Donald Trump publicly criticized the revised plans for the site and proposed rebuilding the towers that once stood there. Consider how Sawyer's perspective on the site might fit into this controversy. Consider, too, how the ongoing controversy about what to do with the site might shape how readers respond to this essay.

20   Then the day flowed back into itself. Soon I was outside once more, joining the tide of people washing around the site. Later, as I huddled with a little crowd on the viewing platform, watching people scrawl their names or write "God Bless America" on the plywood walls, it occurred to me that a form of repopulation was taking effect, with so many visitors to this place, thousands of visitors, all of us coming to see the wide emptiness where so many were lost. And by the act of our visiting—whether we are motivated by curiosity or horror or reverence or grief, or by something confusing that combines them all—that space fills up again.

UNDERSTANDING THE TEXT

1. What does Berne mean when she refers to *absence* in this essay? Why is this absence important in reference to Ground Zero in New York City?

2. What activities does Berne describe as taking place around the site of the World Trade Centers? What is the significance of these activities? What do they say about places like the site of the attacks on the World Trade Center?

3. In what sense is the space where the World Trade Center once stood filling up again? What do you think this "filling up" suggests about special places like Ground Zero?

EXPLORING THE ISSUES

1. Examine the way Berne tells the story of her visit to Ground Zero. What information about her visit does she include? What does she seem to leave out? How does she organize her essay? What is the effect of this way of organizing her essay on you as a reader?

2. At several points in her essay, Berne describes the reactions and words of people around her who also came to see the site of the attacks on the World Trade Center. What do these reactions suggest about the impact of that place on those who visit it? What ideas about the value or meaning of a place does Berne convey through these descriptions?

3. In paragraph 14, Sawyer writes that a security guard asked her whether she wanted "tickets to the disaster." In paragraph 17 Sawyer tells us that she finally got her "ticket to the disaster." What do you think she means by this phrase? Does it mean the same thing to her and the security guard? Explain.

4. Throughout this essay, Berne includes much description of what she sees during her visit to the World Trade Center site. What kinds of details does she tend to include in her descriptions? What does she emphasize in these descriptions? What ideas or feelings do you think she conveys through these descriptions? How effective did you find these descriptions in conveying a sense of what it is like to visit that place?

ENTERING THE CONVERSATIONS

1. Attempting to describe the magnitude of the impact of the death of thousands of people can be overwhelming. If you have never been to the site of the World Trade Center in New York City, you may have visited another place that has great importance, such as a war memorial or a battlefield or cemetery for those who died in battle or some other kind of tragic event. Or maybe you've seen a place of great natural beauty, such as the Grand Canyon. Write an essay about such a place that you have visited. In your essay, try to describe this place in a way that conveys its magnitude and significance.

2. Using photographs, video, web authoring software, PowerPoint, or any other appropriate technology, create a visual representation of a place that you consider sacred or special in some way. In your representation, try to convey a sense of the significance of the place.

3. Write a letter to the editor of the *New York Times* in which you express your views about what should be done with the site of the World Trade Center. (For this assignment, you might refer to the essay by Rhonda Chriss Lokeman on page 512 of this chapter.)

4. In a conventional academic essay, discuss differences and similarities in the way Suzanne Berne and Rhonda Chriss Lokeman (whose essay appears on page 512 of this chapter) understand the value of the site of the terrorist attacks on the World Trade Center in New York City.

CREATING THEMES: Extending the Conversations

WITH TEXT

1. Identify an important issue related to the idea of spaces that is explored in several readings in this chapter. Then, drawing on those readings, write an essay in which you discuss that issue and examine its importance in contemporary society.

2. Rearrange the essays in this chapter according to two or three themes related to the idea of spaces that you think are important—themes that you think are related to important issues today. Then write a brief essay explaining why you arranged the essays in this way. In your essay, discuss what larger conversations your themes might be part of today.

3. Many of the writers whose essays appear in this chapter explore their relationships to specific places. For example, Karen Piper and E. B. White describe their visits as adults to places that were important to them as children; Rhonda Chriss Lokeman and Suzanne Berne discuss the importance of Ground Zero. Select one or more of these essays, and in a conventional academic essay, discuss the way these writers explore their relationships to a place. Examine how these writers portray that relationship and discuss what these relationships reveal about the value of certain places in our lives.

4. Several of the essays in this chapter describe a return to a place that they left when they were younger. For example, Karen Piper left the desert region where she was raised to live in a city and then returned years later when her father was old and ill. E. B. White describes

taking his family to a lake where his father took him as a young child. Drawing on these essays, any other appropriate essays in this book, and your own experience, write an essay about returning to a significant place in your life.

5. Write a letter to the editor of your local paper in which you express your views about preserving a place of importance in the region where you live. In your letter, explain the importance of this place and discuss your ideas for what should be done to preserve that place.

INFOTRAC

6. In the past few decades, the idea of *open space* has gained supporters as many regions of the United States continue to develop rapidly. Commercial and residential development often changes the regional landscape in ways that concern many residents. For example, farms are sometimes sold to developers as suburbs grow out from cities into surrounding rural areas, dramatically changing the character of the area and often resulting in a variety of social, economic, and environmental problems. In response to these developments, many towns have implemented controversial policies that limit or prohibit development in certain areas. Using InfoTrac College Edition, the Internet, your library, and any other relevant resources, investigate the loss of open space and what is being done about it. You might focus your investigation on your own region, if these problems concern people where you live. Then write a report on the basis of your research. Try to draw conclu-

sions about the value of open spaces in our lives.

WITH MEDIA

1. Using appropriate technologies available to you (such as PowerPoint, desktop publishing software, or web authoring software), create a visual representation of a special place or places in your life that conveys the value of that place.

2. Find several magazine or Internet advertisements that depict a specific place or kind of place. For example, advertisements for vacation spots, such as beach resorts and ski areas, usually include photographs or other images of those places. Public service announcements about fire prevention or proper disposal of waste will often include images of natural places. And many product advertisements include such images as well; for example, ads for pickup trucks will often include images of off-road locations. Select several such documents and analyze the way they portray certain places through the use of images. What messages do these images send about those places and our relationships to them? What ideas or values do these image seem to convey. Address such questions in an essay in which you discuss what you learned about how images are used in these documents and what they suggest about our beliefs about certain kinds of places.

3. Identify a theme in this chapter related to spaces that you think is important and create a visual representation of that theme (for example, a photograph or photo essay, a web site, a painting).

CREATING THEMES: Extending the Conversations

WITH FILM

1. Many popular films focus on a specific place or are set in a location that is central to the story told in the film. For example, many of Woody Allen's films focus on New York City as a special place. By contrast, many films take place in wilderness or frontier areas that are depicted as special; for example, films such as *Dances with Wolves* (1990) and *Jeremiah Johnson* (1972) are set in the American West, a location that is important to the stories told in the films. Select one or more films in which a certain place plays an important role and examine how that place is portrayed. What ideas or attitudes about that place does the film convey? What values about place seem to be conveyed by the film? Then write an essay in which you discuss place as it is treated in these films.

2. If you have access to a video camera, create a film about an important place in your life or the region where you live. Working with a group of classmates, write a script for this film and use appropriate software (such as *iMovie* or *Windows Movie Maker*) to edit your film. Create your film in a way that conveys a sense of the importance of the place you are depicting.

3. Science Fiction films such as *The Matrix* (1999) series often depict the earth in the future. Select one or more such films and examine how they present the earth of the future as a living space. What ideas do these films convey about spaces in our lives? What messages might these films be sending about the spaces we create and inhabit? Write an essay in which you try to address such questions.

Chapter **11** **Resources**

Renee Lynn/Stone/Getty Images

RECENTLY, MY WIFE AND I BEGAN LOOKING INTO SOLAR ENERGY. WE HAD BECOME CONCERNED ABOUT THE WORSENING ENVIRONMEN- TAL PROBLEMS WE WERE READING ABOUT IN THE MEDIA, ESPE- CIALLY GLOBAL CLIMATE CHANGE, AND WE WANTED TO MAKE CHANGES IN OUR LIFESTYLE TO REDUCE OUR IMPACT ON THE EARTH. PART OF OUR

motivation came from learning that while the United States has only about 5 percent of the world's population, it consumes 20 to 25 per- cent of the world's resources. That means Americans contribute disproportionately to pol- lution and to global climate change. Such fig- ures reveal that the American lifestyle is in many ways wasteful and potentially causes serious en- vironmental damage. We wanted to see what we could do in our own lives to try to change that.

As we talked with experts, we learned that it is relatively easy to incorporate solar electricity, which produces no pollution, into a home. We also learned about how much energy we waste

> Such figures reveal that the American lifestyle is in many ways wasteful and potentially causes serious environmental damage.

every day. Many appliances that we rely on, like our washer and dryer, microwave oven, televi- sion, and dishwasher, use electricity inefficiently. The typical light bulbs that illuminate our home also waste electricity. We learned that even when many appliances are turned off, they continue to use power. The more we learned, the more we began to realize that just by living our lives in a typical American way, we are wasting resources needlessly. Alternatives to our wasteful use of re- sources exist. Solar electricity is one such alter- native. Newer, more energy-efficient appliances and compact fluorescent light bulbs use far less electricity than older appliances and conven- tional light bulbs. Washing dishes by hand rather than in a dishwasher wastes less water and uses less electricity. The new gas-electric hybrid cars use less fuel and cause far less pollution

than conventional cars and trucks. More impor- tant, small changes in our lifestyle can reduce our use of resources. For example, buying lo- cally grown vegetables and fruits rather than produce that is trucked from hundreds or thou- sands of miles away, as most groceries sold in the United States are, also reduces pollution.

All this seems straightforward enough. But as we learned about these easy ways to reduce our use of resources and reduce our impact on the earth, we also came to realize that most Americans are unaware of how wasteful their lifestyles are, and many don't care. Many of our family members and friends considered our ef- forts to change our wasteful lifestyle silly, too ex- pensive, or inconvenient. They agreed that Americans live wastefully, but few were willing to consider small changes in their lifestyles, such as car pooling or using energy-efficient light bulbs. Ultimately, what we learned is that how we Americans use resources is so deeply woven into our way of life that we can't always *see* the impact we have.

The readings in this chapter aren't necessarily about changing your lifestyle, but they may help

> Just by living and using the resources we need every day, we affect the land and other people in ways we may never see.

you begin to appreciate the many ways in which we take basic resources for granted. The food we eat, the water we drink, the land we occupy for our homes, the gas we burn in our cars, the elec- tricity we use for so many purposes—all these uses of resources have consequences, many of which we may be unaware of. Several essays in this chapter also show that many of the resources we take for granted are limited. For example, in some places in the world, including parts of the United States, water is scarce and has become the focus of controversy and conflict, as Vandana Shiva describes in her essay. Similarly, as Michael Pollan reveals, land used to grow feed corn for cattle can be damaged by environmentally unsound agricultural practices. So even the simple decision to eat one kind of food rather than another may actually harm the environment.

And that may be the real lesson to be learned from the readings in this chapter: that we are interconnected in a multitude of ways to each other and to everything around us. Just by living and using the resources we need every day, we affect the land and other people in ways we may never see.

NECESSITIES

WHAT DO YOU REALLY NEED TO LIVE? THE OB-VIOUS ANSWERS ARE FOOD, WATER, SHELTER, AND AIR. CERTAINLY, THOSE ARE NECESSITIES. WITHOUT THEM, YOU COULD NOT SURVIVE. BUT THE ISSUE IS MORE COMPLICATED THAN THAT. THINK FOR A MOMENT ABOUT FOOD. IF YOU'RE TALKING ABOUT SURVIVAL, THEN YOUR NEEDS ARE PRETTY BASIC. YOU NEED ENOUGH CALORIES TO SUSTAIN YOUR BODY, AND YOU NEED A CERTAIN

combination of proteins, fats, carbohydrates, minerals, and vitamins to stay healthy. Beyond that, you don't actually *need* any specific kind of food to survive. You don't *need* meat, for example. You can get the proteins and vitamins contained in meat from other food sources. And of course, there are big differences in the nutritional value of different kinds of meat. You may have heard, for example, that white meat from chicken is healthier in some ways than beef. Or maybe you've heard that buffalo meat, which has become

> Beyond that, you don't actually *need* any specific kind of food to survive.

more commonly available in some parts of the United States, is healthier than beef. And some kinds of beef are better than others, depending on how the cattle were raised and processed and which cut of beef you select. The more you look into food, the more there is to see. And the more questions you might have about the foods we consider necessities.

I selected the readings for this cluster to highlight some of these complexities of something we tend to take for granted as a necessity: food. These readings focus our attention on different aspects of food, and each selection raises different questions about what we eat, why we choose the foods we eat, and how we produce our food. For example, Brenda Peterson describes some of the odd experiences she has had as someone who grew up eating wild game. Her essay raises interesting questions about our attitudes regarding certain kinds of food. Richard Corliss raises different questions about the foods we eat, such as whether or not it makes sense to give up eating meat altogether. And well-known writer Barbara Kingsolver tells us about her efforts to change her family's eating habits. Her essay helps us see that there is so much more that goes into producing and consuming the food we eat than we usually realize. Together, these essays encourage us to look a little more closely at a necessity that is central to our lives and around which we have built many beliefs, attitudes, habits, and traditions. But we can look just as closely at other necessities in our lives, including shelter and water. Keep that in mind as you read.

I grew up in a region where hunting is an important pastime, and sometimes we ate wild game at our family meals—usually venison (deer meat), rabbit, and some kinds of wild fowl. Even though such meals were common in the region of Pennsylvania where I lived, most people I knew, including many members of my family, didn't much care to eat wild game. They preferred beef or chicken, animals raised on farms and processed for sale in local markets rather

Growing Up Game

than killed and prepared by the hunters in our family. Why?

Novelist Brenda Peterson (b. 1950) addresses that question in the following essay. She describes growing up in a family where wild game was a staple. That made her unusual, something she realized only when she moved from her family's remote mountain home in Oregon to a large city to attend college. In telling us about her experiences with wild game, Peterson examines the attitudes Americans have about food. Why, she asks, does it matter to some people that the meat they eat was killed by a hunter rather than raised on a farm and slaughtered at a food processing plant? She considers her own mixed feelings about the game she grew up eating. Her thoughts about her experiences may help us think more carefully about our own beliefs and attitudes regarding food.

Brenda Peterson is the author of several novels and collections of essays, including Animal Heart *(2004) and* Singing to the Sound: Visions of Nature, Animals, and Spirit *(2000). The following essay was first published in* Seattle Weekly *in 1990 and reprinted in* Living by the Water: True Stories of Nature and Spirit *(1991).* ▼

BRENDA PETERSON

When I went off to college, my father gave me, as part of my tuition, fifty pounds of moose meat. In 1969, eating moose meat at the University of California was a contradiction in terms. Hippies didn't hunt. I lived in a rambling Victorian house that boasted sweeping circular staircases, built-in lofts, and a landlady who dreamed of opening her own health food restaurant. I told my housemates that my moose meat in its nondescript white butcher paper was from a side of beef my father had bought. The carnivores in the house helped me finish off such suppers as sweet-and-sour moose meatballs, mooseburgers (garnished with the obligatory avocado and sprouts), and mooseghetti. The same dinner guests who remarked upon the lean sweetness of the meat would have recoiled if I'd told them the not-so-simple truth: that I grew up on game, and the moose they were eating had been brought down, with one shot through his magnificent heart, by my father—a man who had hunted all his life and all of mine.

One of my earliest memories is of crawling across the vast continent of crinkled linoleum in our Forest Service cabin kitchen down

STRATEGIES: SELECTING DETAILS
In paragraph 1 Peterson describes the source of the moose meat her father gave her when she went to college: the moose her father killed "with one shot through his magnificent heart." Consider what ideas Peterson is conveying here through her choice of details. For example, how would this passage be different if she had not used the adjective "magnificent" to describe the moose's heart?

splintered back steps, through wildflowers growing wheat-high. I was eye-level with grasshoppers who scolded me on my first solo trip outside. I made it to the shed, a cool and comfortingly square shelter that held phantasmagoric metal parts; they smelled good, like dirt and grease. I had played a long time in this shed before some maternal shriek made me lift up on my haunches to listen to those urgent, possessive sounds that were my name. Rearing up, my head bumped into something hanging in the dark; gleaming white, it felt sleek and cold against my cheek. Its smell was dense and musty and not unlike the slabs of my grandmother's great arms after her cool, evening sponge baths. In that shed I looked up and saw the flensed body of a doe; it swung gently, slapping my face. I felt then as I do even now when eating game: horror and awe and kinship.

Growing up those first years on a Plumas National Forest station high in the Sierra Nevada near Oregon was somewhat like belonging to a white tribe. The men hiked off every day into their forest and the women stayed behind in the circle of official cabins, breeding. So far away from a store, we ate venison and squirrel, rattlesnake and duck. My first rattle, in fact, was from a diamondback rattler my father killed as we watched, by snatching it up with a stick and winding it, whiplike, around a redwood sapling. Rattlesnake tastes just like chicken, but has many fragile bones to slither one's way through. We also ate rainbow trout, rabbit, and geese galore. The game was accompanied by such daily garden dainties as fried okra, mustard greens, corn fritters, wilted lettuce (our favorite because of that rare, blackened bacon), new potatoes and peas, stewed tomatoes, barbecued butter beans.

I was four before I ever had a beef hamburger, and I remember being disappointed by its fatty, nothing taste and the way it fell apart at the seams whenever my teeth sank into it. Smoked pork shoulder came much later, in the South; and I was twenty-one, living in New York City, before I ever tasted leg of lamb. I approached that glazed rack of meat with a certain guilty self-consciousness, as if I unfairly stalked those sweet-tempered white creatures myself. But how would I explain my squeamishness to those urban sophisticates? How explain that I was shy with mutton when I had been bred on wild things?

5   Part of it, I suspect, had to do with the belief I'd also been bred on: we become the spirit and body of animals we eat. As a child eating venison, I liked to think of myself as lean and lovely just like the deer. I would never be caught dead just grazing while some man who wasn't even a skillful hunter crept up and conked me over the head. If someone wanted to hunt me, he must be wily and outwitting. He must earn me.

CONTEXT: PRAYER
The quotation in this paragraph is a reference to a common Christian prayer said upon taking a meal. Often, this prayer is understood as gratitude to God for the meal, but here Peterson explains that for her family, which depended on hunting wild game for their food, the prayer had a different meaning. Her use of this quotation is a good example of how the meaning of a word or phrase can change depending on the context within which it is used.

My father had also taught us as children that animals were our brothers and sisters under their skin. They died so that we might live. And of this sacrifice we must be mindful. "God make us grateful for what we are about to receive," took on new meaning when we imagined the animal's surrender to our own appetites. We also used all the animal, so that an elk became elk steaks, stew, salami, and sausage. His head and horns went on the wall to watch us more earnestly than any

baby-sitter, and every Christmas Eve we had a ceremony of making our own moc-
casins for the new year out of whatever Father had tanned. "Nothing wasted," my father would always say, or, as we munched on sausage cookies made from moosemeat
or venison, "Think about who you're eating." We thought of ourselves as intricately
linked to the food chain. We knew, for example, that a forest fire meant, at the end
of the line, we'd suffer too. We'd have buck stew instead of venison steak, and the
meat would be stringy, withered-tasting, because in the animal kingdom, as it seemed
with humans, only the meanest and leanest and orneriest survived losing their
forests.

Once when I was in my early teens, I went along on a hunting trip as the "main
cook and bottle-washer," though I don't remember any bottles; none of these hunters
drank alcohol. There was something else coursing through their veins as they rose
long before dawn and disappeared, returning to my little camp most often dragging

---

VISUAL CONNECTIONS: HUNTING
Hunting has always been part of American culture and is associated with certain values, which may differ from the values that
Peterson associates with hunting in this essay. For example, consider what messages these two images convey about hunting. The
first shows the cover of a popular hunting magazine; the second is an advertisement for an ammunition company. What values do you
think these images suggest are associated with hunting?

Sports Afield Magazine Cover

Winchester Gun Advertisement

a doe or pheasant or rabbit. We ate innumerable cornmeal-fried fish, had rabbit stew seasoned only with blood and black pepper.

This hunting trip was the first time I remember eating game as a conscious act. My father and Buddy Earl shot a big doe and she lay with me in the back of the tarp-draped station wagon all the way home. It was not the smell I minded, it was the glazed great, dark eyes and the way that head flopped around crazily on what I knew was once a graceful neck. I found myself petting this doe, murmuring all those graces we'd been taught long ago as children. Thank you for the sacrifice, thank you for letting us be like you so that we can grow up strong as game. But there was an uneasiness in me that night as I bounced along in the back of the car with the deer.

What was uneasy is still uneasy—perhaps it always will be. It's not easy when one really starts thinking about all this: the eating game, the food chain, the sacrifice of one for the other. It's never easy when one begins to think about one's most basic actions, like eating. Like becoming what one eats: lean and lovely and mortal.

10   Why should it be that the purchase of meat at a butcher shop is somehow more righteous than eating something wild? Perhaps it has to do with our collective unconscious that sees the animal bred for slaughter as doomed. But that wild doe or moose might make it without the hunter. Perhaps on this primitive level of archetype and unconscious knowing we even believe that what's wild lives forever.

My father once told this story around a hunting campfire. His own father, who raised cattle during the Great Depression on a dirt farm in the Ozarks, once fell on such hard times that he had to butcher the pet lamb for supper. My father, bred on game or their own hogs all his life, took one look at the family pet on that meat platter and pushed his plate away. His siblings followed suit. To hear my grandfather tell it, it was the funniest thing he'd ever seen. "They just couldn't eat Bo-Peep," Grandfather said. And to hear my father tell it years later around that campfire, it was funny, but I saw for the first time his sadness. And I realized that eating had become a conscious act for him that day at the dinner table when Bo-Peep offered herself up.

Now when someone offers me game, I will eat it with all the qualms and memories and reverence with which I grew up eating it. And I think I will always have this feeling of horror and awe and kinship. And something else—full knowledge of what I do, what I become.

UNDERSTANDING THE TEXT

1. Early in her essay, Peterson writes that she feels "horror and awe and kinship" when she eats game. What does she mean? Why does she have these different feelings about eating game? What do these different feelings suggest about her attitudes regarding the food she eats?

2. What is the source of Peterson's uneasiness about eating wild game? What do you think her uneasiness reveals about her values regarding the way she lives and the way she uses resources?

3. What does Peterson mean when she writes that eating was a "conscious act" for her and her father? Do you think most people share this sense of eating? Explain.

EXPLORING THE ISSUES

1. Peterson sets up a contrast between the eating habits of her family and the more conventional eating habits of other Americans that she met. What does this contrast suggest about attitudes regarding food in American culture? What do you think it suggests about the role of food in society in general?

2. Most of this essay is devoted to anecdotes from Peterson's past and to descriptions of experiences she had with food. But the essay is not really a narrative; that is, she is not telling a story in the conventional sense. Her anecdotes and descriptions are not in chronological order. Examine how she organizes this es-

say. How does she relate one anecdote or experience to the others? How effective do you think her organization of this passage is?

3. Many controversies about food have developed in the years since this essay was first published in 1991. For example, some animal rights activists have led campaigns against the treatment of animals raised for food, such as chickens or veal calves. Controversy has also surrounded the growing of genetically modified foods, which are varieties of plants such as corn that are genetically changed to produce higher yields or to resist disease. In addition, environmental groups have made people more aware of how environmentally destructive the raising of some animals for food can be, especially cattle. Consider whether these controversies and related developments since 1991 might influence the way readers respond to Peterson's essay. To what extent do you think her essay would provoke different responses in 1991 compared to today?

ENTERING THE CONVERSATIONS

1. Write an essay in which you discuss your own views about food. Like Peterson, consider the sources of the foods you typically eat and whether the sources of your food make any difference to you—and why.

2. In a group of classmates, share the essays you wrote for Question 1. What similarities or differences can you identify among your group members regarding their attitudes

toward food, especially the sources of the foods they eat? What do you think your group discussion might reveal about our attitudes regarding important resources like food?

3. Write an essay for a specific audience (such as readers of your local newspaper or students at your school) in which you present and explain your views about hunting.

INFOTRAC

4. Producing the food we eat has various kinds of environmental impacts, including land and water pollution and the use of other resources, such as fuel to transport foods over great distances or electricity to process and store foods. Using InfoTrac College Edition, the Internet, your library, and other relevant resources, examine the environmental impact of the foods you eat. Identify one or more of the most common or important foods in your diet (for example, hamburger or milk or bread) and investigate how those foods are produced and transported. Try to determine what specific environmental consequences the production of those foods has. Then write a report on the basis of your research. In your report, draw conclusions about the impact of your eating habits on the environment.

5. On the basis of your research for Question 4, create a flyer intended to educate a general audience about the environmental impact of the consumption of common foods. Alternatively, create a web site for the same purpose.

I have a friend who grows apples as a hobby. *He owns several acres of land, on which he has dozens of apple trees. Each fall, he harvests the apples to sell at local markets. Although it isn't his main source of income, growing and selling apples require an enormous effort and a great deal of his time. He does it mostly because he loves it. He enjoys tending the trees, the feeling of being outdoors, and the satisfaction of using the land productively. More than most of us, I sus-*

A *Good* Farmer

pect, he appreciates what goes into growing the foods we eat, something we tend to take for granted. In some ways, the following essay is about how much we take for granted when it comes to food. In this essay, award-winning writer Barbara Kingsolver (b. 1955) describes her family's attempt to change their lives so that they would live less wastefully and more in line with the agrarian values that she was raised by on her own family's farm. This lifestyle change had a lot to do with food, and Kingsolver describes some of the changes her family made in what they ate, how they ate, and their awareness of food in general. In sharing her experience with us, Kingsolver perhaps raises our awareness about the impact of the choices we make when it comes to the foods we eat. She also helps us see that these choices are not only about convenience or habit but also about basic values that we may not often think about. For Kingsolver and her family, moving to a family farm was an effort to live by their values. Unlike my friend, Kingsolver states bluntly that farming is not a hobby for her. It is an effort to reject what she believes is the wasteful American lifestyle in favor of a more ethical way of life. As you read, consider whether your own lifestyle reflects your values. (continued)

BARBARA KINGSOLVER

Sometime around my fortieth birthday I began an earnest study of agriculture. I worked quietly on this project, speaking of my new interest to almost no one because of what they might think. Specifically, they might think I was out of my mind. Why? Because at this moment in history it's considered smart to get out of agriculture. And because I already embarked on a career as a writer, doing work that many people might consider intellectual and therefore superior to anything involving the risk of dirty fingernails. Also, as a woman in my early 40s, I conformed to no right-minded picture of an apprentice farmer. And finally, with some chagrin I'll admit that I grew up among farmers and spent the first decades of my life plotting my escape from a place that seemed to offer me almost no potential for economic, intellectual or spiritual satisfaction.

It took nigh onto half a lifetime before the valuables I'd casually left behind turned up in the lost and found.

The truth, though, is that I'd kept some of that treasure jingling in my pockets all along: I'd maintained an interest in gardening, always,

BARBARA KINGSOLVER, "A GOOD FARMER." FROM *THE NATION*, NOVEMBER 2003. REPRINTED BY PERMISSION OF THE FRANCES GOLDIN LITERARY AGENCY.

(continued) *Barbara Kingsolver is the author of eleven books, including the award-winning* The Poisonwood Bible *(1998) and* Last Stand: America's Virgin Lands *(2002). The following essay, which first appeared in* The Nation *magazine in 2003, was adapted from an essay that appeared in* The Essential Agrarian Reader: The Future of Culture, Community, and the Land *(2003).* ▾

CONVERSATIONS: THE FAMILY FARM
In paragraph 7, Kingsolver describes some of the scenes she associates with growing up on a family farm, which has long been an important part of American culture but has been slowly disappearing as agriculture has become an increasingly large-scale, corporate business. According to the Economic Policy Institute, for example, more than 72,000 family farms disappeared between 1993 and 1999, a decline of 8 percent. The U.S. Department of Agriculture reports that in 1978, 87 percent of farms were "sole proprietorships"—that is, owned by one person or family; in 1997, that figure had declined to 52 percent. During the same period, "nonfamily" ownership of farms increased from 0.3 percent to 5.6 percent. These figures reflect the growth of "agribusiness," but they also suggest that agriculture is changing to meet the demands of expanding food markets. Some people believe that the traditional family farm is an outdated lifestyle that can't keep up with a changing agricultural marketplace, a view that Kingsolver alludes to in the following paragraph. But many people share Kingsolver's concern about the disappearance of the family farm, and the images she includes in this paragraph suggest some of the reasons for that concern. Consider what ideas these images convey about the family farm and how Kingsolver depicts the family farmer. Consider, too, what Kingsolver's picture of the family farm might leave out. How might her essay fit into the ongoing conversations about the importance of the family farm in American culture?

dragging it with me wherever I went, even into a city backyard where a neighbor who worked the night shift insisted that her numerous nocturnal cats had every right to use my raised vegetable beds for their litter box. (I retaliated, in my way, by getting a rooster, who indulged his right to use the hour of 6 AM for his personal compunctions.) In graduate school I studied ecology and evolutionary biology, but the complex mathematical models of predator-prey cycles only made sense to me when I converted them in my mind to farmstead analogies—even though, in those days, the ecology department and the college of agriculture weren't on speaking terms. In my 20s, when I was trying hard to reinvent myself as a person without a Kentucky accent, I often found myself nevertheless the lone argumentative voice in social circles where "farmers" were lumped with political troglodytes and devotees of all-star wrestling.

Once in the early 1980s, when cigarette smoking had newly and drastically fallen from fashion, I stood in someone's kitchen at a party and listened to something like a Greek chorus chanting out the reasons why tobacco should be eliminated from the face of the earth, like smallpox. Some wild tug on my heart made me blurt out, "But what about the tobacco farmers?"

5 "Why," someone asked, glaring, "should I care about tobacco farmers?"

I was dumbstruck. I couldn't form the words to answer: Yes, it is carcinogenic, and generally grown with too many inputs, but tobacco is the last big commodity in America that's still mostly grown on family farms, in an economy that won't let these farmers shift to another crop. If it goes extinct, so do they.

I couldn't speak because my mind was flooded with memory, pictures, scents, secret thrills. Childhood afternoons spent reading Louisa May Alcott in a barn loft suffused with the sweet scent of aged burley. The bright, warm days in late spring and early fall when school was functionally closed because whole extended families were drafted to the cooperative work of setting, cutting, stripping or hanging tobacco. The incalculable fellowship measured out in funerals, family reunions, even bad storms or late-night calvings. The hard-muscled pride of showing I could finally throw a bale of hay onto the truckbed myself. (The year before, when I was 11, I'd had the less honorable job of driving the truck.) The satisfaction of walking across the stage at high school graduation in a county where my name and my relationship to the land were both common knowledge.

But when pressed, that evening in the kitchen, I didn't try to defend the poor tobacco farmer. As if the deck were not already stacked against his little family enterprise, he was now tarred with the brush of evil along with the companies that bought his product, amplified its toxicity and attempted to sell it to children. In most cases it's just the more ordinary difficulty of the small family enterprise failing to measure up to the requisite standards of profitability and efficiency. And in every case, the rational arguments I might frame in its favor will carry no weight without the attendant silk purse full of memories and sighs and songs of what family farming is worth. Those values are an old currency now, accepted as legal tender almost nowhere.

I found myself that day in the jaws of an impossible argument, and I find I am there still. In my professional life I've learned that as long as I write novels and nonfiction books about strictly human conventions and constructions, I'm taken seriously. But when my writing strays into that muddy territory where humans are forced to own up to our dependency on the land, I'm apt to be declared quaintly irrelevant by the small, acutely urban clique that decides in this country what will be called worthy literature. (That clique does not, fortunately, hold much sway over what people actually read.) I understand their purview, I think. I realize I'm beholden to people working in urban centers for many things I love: They publish books, invent theater, produce films and music. But if I had not been raised such a polite Southern girl, I'd offer these critics a blunt proposition: I'll go a week without attending a movie or concert, you go a week without eating food, and at the end of it we'll sit down together and renegotiate "quaintly irrelevant."

10   This is a conversation that needs to happen. Increasingly I feel sure of it; I just don't know how to go about it when so many have completely forgotten the genuine terms of human survival. Many adults, I'm convinced, believe that food comes from grocery stores. In **Wendell Berry's** novel *Jayber Crow,* a farmer coming to the failing end of his long economic struggle despaired aloud, "I've wished sometimes that the sons of bitches would starve. And now I'm getting afraid they actually will."

Like that farmer, I am frustrated with the imposed acrimony between producers and consumers of food, as if this were a conflict in which one could possibly choose sides. I'm tired of the presumption of a nation divided between rural and urban populations whose interests are permanently at odds, whose votes will always be cast different ways, whose hearts and minds share no common ground. This is as wrong as blight, a useless way of thinking, similar to the propaganda warning us that any environmentalist program will necessarily be antihuman. Recently a national magazine asked me to write a commentary on the great divide between "the red and the blue"—imagery taken from election-night coverage that colored a map according to the party each state elected, suggesting a clear political difference between the rural heartland and urban coasts. Sorry, I replied to the magazine editors, but I'm the wrong person to ask: I live in red, tend to think blue and mostly vote green. If you're looking for oversimplification, skip the likes of me.

Better yet, skip the whole idea. Recall that in many of those red states, just a razor's edge under half the voters likely pulled the blue lever, and vice versa—not to mention the greater numbers everywhere who didn't even show up at the polls, so far did they feel from affectionate toward any of the available options. Recall that farmers and hunters, historically, are more active environmentalists than many progressive, city-dwelling vegetarians. (And conversely, that

GLOSS: WENDELL BERRY
Wendell Berry is a well-known writer who advocates a simple, environmentally sound lifestyle and who often writes about rural values. His essay, "Thoughts in the Presence of Fear," appears in Chapter 9.

CONVERSATIONS: RED AND BLUE STATES
During the 2004 U.S. presidential election, "red" and "blue" became a common way to refer to more conservative and more liberal states, respectively. Consider how Kingsolver assumes that her readers understand what red and blue mean in this context; that is, she assumes her readers are familiar with current conversations about the political and cultural divisions in American society. (See *Visual Connections: The Color Red* on page 345 in Chapter 8 for an image of a map of the red and blue states during the 2004 U.S. presidential election.)

some of the strongest land-conservation movements on the planet were born in the midst of cities.) Recall that we all have the same requirements for oxygen and drinking water, and that we all like them clean but relentlessly pollute them. Recall that whatever lofty things you might accomplish today, you will do them only because you first ate something that grew out of dirt.

We don't much care to think of ourselves that way—as creatures whose cleanest aspirations depend ultimately on the health of our dirt. But our survival as a species depends on our coming to grips with that, along with some other corollary notions, and when I entered a comfortable midlife I began to see that my kids would get to do the same someday, or not, depending on how well our species could start owning up to its habitat and its food chain. As we faced one environmental crisis after another, did our species seem to be making this connection? As we say back home, Not so's you'd notice.

If a middle-aged woman studying agriculture seems strange, try this on for bizarre: Most of our populace and all our leaders are participating in a mass hallucinatory fantasy in which the megatons of waste we dump in our rivers and bays are not poisoning the water, the hydrocarbons we pump into the air are not changing the climate, overfishing is not depleting the oceans, fossil fuels will never run out, wars that kill masses of civilians are an appropriate way to keep our hands on what's left, we are not desperately overdrawn at the environmental bank and, really, the kids are all right.

OK, if nobody else wanted to talk about this, I could think about it myself and try to pay for my part of the damage, or at least start to tally up the bill. This requires a good deal of humility and a ruthless eye toward an average household's confusion between need and want. I reckoned I might get somewhere if I organized my life in a way that brought me face to face with what I am made of. The values I longed to give my children—honesty, cooperativeness, thrift, mental curiosity, physical competence— were intrinsic to my agrarian childhood, where the community organized itself around a sustained effort of meeting people's needs. These values, I knew, would not flow naturally from an aggressive consumer culture devoted to the sustained effort of inventing and engorging people's wants. And I could not, as any parent knows, prohibit one thing without offering others. So we would start with the simple and obvious: eschewing fast food for slow food, with the resulting time spent together in the garden and kitchen regarded as a plus, not a minus. We would skip TV in favor of interesting family work. We would participate as much as possible in the production of things our family consumes and the disposal of the things we no longer need. It's too easy to ignore damage you don't see and to undervalue things you haven't made yourself. Starting with food.

Meal preparations at our house, then, would not begin with products, like chicken tenders and frozen juice concentrate, but with whole things, like a chicken or an apple. A chicken or apple, what's more, with a background we could check up on. Our younger daughter was only a toddler when we first undertook this enterprise, but she seemed to grasp the idea. On a family trip once when we ate in a Chinese restaurant, she asked skeptically, "What was this duck's last name?"

What began as a kind of exercise soon turned into a kind of life, which we liked surprisingly well. It's enough to turn your stomach, anyway, to add up the fuel, money

CONTEXT: "OUR GUSTATORY INDUSTRIES"
In this paragraph (par. 17), Kingsolver offers her perspective on the food processing and distribution industry in the United States today. Specifically, she complains about the highly processed nature of common foods in the American diet and about the resources used to transport, store, and preserve food. Her complaints are based on increasing evidence that this food system may be both environmentally destructive and unhealthy. In early 2005, for example, a study was released that indicated that the high sodium content of the American diet was contributing to thousands of deaths each year; most of the sodium in the typical American's diet is contained in processed foods. Similarly, the shipping of common foods over long distances uses up resources and contributes to air and water pollution. One study indicated that the average food product in the United States is transported 1,500 miles from where it is produced to where it is consumed.

and gunk that can go into food that isn't even about food. Our gustatory industries treat food items like spoiled little celebrities, zipping them around the globe in luxurious air-conditioned cabins, dressing them up in gaudy outfits, spritzing them with makeup and breaking the bank on advertising, for heaven's sake. My farm-girl heritage makes me blush and turn down tickets to that particular circus. I'd rather wed my fortunes to the sturdy gal-next-door kind of food, growing what I need or getting it from local "you pick" orchards and our farmers' market.

In making the effort to get acquainted with my food chain, I found country lanes and kind people and assets I had not known existed in my community. To my amazement, I found a Community Shared Agriculture grower sequestered at the end of a dirt road within walking distance of my house, and he helped me fix an irrigation problem that had stumped me for months. I found others who would help me introduce a gardening program into my children's elementary school. I befriended the lone dairyman in my county who refuses to give hormones to his cows, not because he's paid more for the milk he sells to the cooperative (he isn't) but because he won't countenance treating his animals that way. I learned about heritage breeds, and that one of the rarest and tastiest of all turkeys, the Bourbon Red, was first bred a stone's throw from my hometown in Kentucky. I've come to know this bird inside and out, and intend to have my own breeding flock of them. I've become part of a loose-knit collective of poultrywomen who share tools and recipes and, at the end of the day, know how to make a real party out of harvest time. All in the house that good food built.

There is more to the story. It has come to pass that my husband and I, in what we hope is the middle of our lives, are in possession of a farm. It's not a hobby homestead, it is a farm, somewhat derelict but with good potential. It came to us with some twenty acres of good, tillable bottomland, plus timbered slopes and all the pasture we can ever use, if we're willing to claim it back from the brambles. A similar arrangement is available with the seventy-five-year-old apple orchard. The rest of the inventory includes a hundred-year-old clapboard house, a fine old barn that smells of aged burley, a granary, poultry coops, a root cellar and a century's store of family legends. No poisons have been applied to this land for years and, we vow, none ever will be.

I've never loved any earthly thing so much. It seems to my husband and me that this farm is something we need to work hard to deserve. As a former tobacco farm, it had a past without a future. But now that its future is in our hands, we recognize that it ought to feed people—more than just our family and those who come to our table. Precisely because of tobacco's changing fortunes, we're now situated in a community of farmers who are moving with courage and good cheer into the production of a regionally distributed line of organic produce. This economic project may be small in the eyes of global capitalism, but it concerns us greatly, for its success or failure will be felt large in our schools, churches and neighborhood businesses, not to mention our soil and streams, as these farmers make choices and, I hope, remain among us on their land. My family hopes to contribute to the endeavor as best we can, as producers as well as consumers, though with regard to the former we acknowledge our novice status. For several years now we've received from each other as gifts, on nearly all occasions, such books as are written by Gene Logsdon, Michael Phillips, Elliot Coleman, Carol Ekarius, Vandana Shiva, Wendell Berry. Some other wife might wish for diamond earrings, but my sweetheart knew I wanted *Basic Butchering*.

STRATEGIES: REFERENCES
Notice the specific authors that Kingsolver mentions in her list of the kinds of books she and her family give each other as gifts. Selecting references carefully in the way Kingsolver does in paragraph 20 is a strategy by which writers can convey messages to readers. What messages is Kingsolver conveying through this list of authors? Essays by Vandana Shiva and Wendell Berry appear in this book, so you can learn something about these two authors by reading the introductions to their essays. You might want to do a quick Internet search to learn about the other authors. Consider what assumptions about her readers Kingsolver is making here.

Our agrarian education has come in as a slow undercurrent beneath our workaday lives and the rearing of our children. Only our closest friends, probably, have taken real notice of the changes in our household: that nearly all the food we put on our table, in every season, was grown in our garden or very nearby. That the animals we eat took no more from the land than they gave back to it, and led sunlit, contentedly grassy lives. Our children know how to bake bread, stretch mozzarella cheese, ride a horse, keep a flock of hens laying, help a neighbor, pack a healthy lunch and politely decline the world's less wholesome offerings. They know the first fresh garden tomato tastes as good as it does partly because you've waited for it since last Thanksgiving, and that the awful ones you could have bought at the grocery in between would only subtract from this equation. This rule applies to many things beyond tomatoes. I have noticed that the very politicians who support purely market-driven economics, which favors immediate corporate gratification over long-term responsibility, also express loud concern about the morals of our nation's children and their poor capacity for self-restraint. I wonder what kind of tomatoes those men feed their kids.

I have heard people of this same political ilk declare that it is perhaps sad but surely inevitable that our farms are being cut up and sold to make nice-sized lawns for suburban folks to mow, because the most immediately profitable land use must prevail in a free country. And yet I have visited countries where people are perfectly free, such as the Netherlands, where this sort of disregard for farmland is both illegal and unthinkable. Plenty of people in this country, too, seem to share a respect for land that gives us food; why else did so many friends of my youth continue farming even while the economic prospects grew doubtful? And why is it that more of them each year are following sustainable practices that defer some immediate profits in favor of the long-term health of their fields, crops, animals and watercourses? Who are the legions of Americans who now allocate more of their household budgets to food that is organically, sustainably and locally grown, rather than buying the cheapest products they can find? My husband and I, bearing these trends in mind, did not contemplate the profitable option of subdividing our farm and changing its use. Frankly, that seemed wrong.

It's an interesting question, how to navigate this tangled path between money and morality: not a new question by any means, but one that has taken strange turns in modern times. In our nation's prevailing culture, there exists right now a considerable confusion between prosperity and success—so much so that avarice is frequently confused with a work ethic. One's patriotism and good sense may be called into

doubt if one elects to earn less money or own fewer possessions than is humanly possible. The notable exception is that a person may do so for religious reasons:
Christians are asked by conscience to tithe or assist the poor; Muslims do not collect
interest; Catholics may respectably choose a monastic life of communal poverty; and
any of us may opt out of a scheme that we feel to be discomforting to our faith. It is
in this spirit that we, like you perhaps and so many others before us, have worked to
rein in the free market's tyranny over our family's tiny portion of America and install
values that override the profit motive. Upon doing so, we receive a greater confidence in our children's future safety and happiness. I believe we are also happier
souls in the present, for what that is worth. In the darkest months I look for solace in
seed catalogues and articles on pasture rotation. I sleep better at night, feeling safely
connected to the things that help make a person whole. It is fair to say this has been,
in some sense, a spiritual conversion.

Modern American culture is fairly empty of any suggestion that one's relationship
to the land, to consumption and food, is a religious matter. But it's true; the decision
to attend to the health of one's habitat and food chain is a spiritual choice. It's also
a political choice, a scientific one, a personal and a convivial one. It's not a choice between living in the country or the town; it is about understanding that every one of
us, at the level of our cells and respiration, lives in the country and is thus obliged to
be mindful of the distance between ourselves and our sustenance. I have worlds to
learn about being a good farmer. Last spring when a hard frost fell upon our orchards on May 21, I felt despair at ever getting there at all. But in any weather, I may
hope to carry a good agrarian frame of mind into my orchards and fields, my
kitchen, my children's schools, my writing life, my friendships, my grocery shopping
and the county landfill. That's the point: It goes everywhere. It may or may not be a
movement—I'll leave that to others to say. But it does move, and it works for us.

UNDERSTANDING THE TEXT

1. In paragraphs 2 and 3, Kingsolver mentions "valuables" and "treasure." What is she referring to? What does her use of these terms suggest about her beliefs when it comes to farming and living in general?

2. Why does Kingsolver believe that we must have a conversation about where our food comes from? Do you agree with her? Why or why not?

3. What is the "mass hallucinatory fantasy" that Kingsolver claims most Americans are participating in (par. 14)? What does this claim reveal about Kingsolver's values and her political perspective?

4. In what ways do Americans confuse their needs and their wants, according to Kingsolver? What are the consequences of this confusion? What can be done about it, in her view? Do you agree with her? Why or why not?

5. What are the benefits of living on a family farm, according to Kingsolver? Why are these benefits important not just to her family but to the society in general?

EXPLORING THE ISSUES

1. Kingsolver discusses an opposition between farmers and city dwellers, between rural and urban populations. In paragraph 9, for example, she complains about "the small, acutely urban clique that decides in this country what will be called worthy literature" and refers to "people working in urban centers." In paragraph 11, she refers to "the presumption of a nation divided between rural and urban populations." Examine how Kingsolver uses this opposition between farmer (or rural dweller) and city dweller. What characteristics does she associate with each group? In what ways does

she favor one over the other? What values of her own does she reveal in the way she presents these two groups? Do you think her characterization of farmers and city dwellers is accurate or fair? Explain.

2. How would you describe Kingsolver's tone in this essay? What features of her writing contribute to her tone? In what ways do you think her tone reinforces her main point? Do you think her tone strengthens or weakens her essay? Explain, citing specific passages to support your answer.

3. What do you think Kingsolver's title, "A Good Farmer," means? In what sense is a farmer "good," in her view? What does her title suggest about her own values?

4. Kingsolver bases much of her argument about how we think about and consume food on her own experience and her family's experience. How effectively do you think Kingsolver uses these experiences to support her main argument in this essay? Do you think that the kinds of experiences she and her family had would appeal to most people? Would such experiences be possible for most Americans? Explain.

ENTERING THE CONVERSATIONS

1. Write an essay in which you describe an experience you have had that was somehow related to farming or gardening or the production of food (such as working at a food processing plant, a restaurant, an orchard, or a food market). Describe your experience in a way that conveys an important idea or point about our attitudes toward food.

INFOTRAC

2. In this essay, Kingsolver writes passionately about the experience of

living on a family farm in the United States. However, the family farm may be declining (see *Conversations: The Family Farm* on page 581). Using InfoTrac College Edition, your library, and other relevant resources, investigate the state of the American family farm today. Try to find out whether the family farm is in fact declining. Also, try to get a sense of the role or status of the family farm in American culture. If possible, talk to someone at your school who may have expertise on this subject or talk to local farmers or farming experts. You may wish to focus your research on the situation with family farming in your region or state. Then write a report on the basis of your research. In your report, draw your own conclusions about the status of the family farm and its role in American society.

4. Write a standard academic essay in which you analyze Kingsolver's representation of the family farm. Discuss how Kingsolver presents the experience of living on a family farm, and discuss the basic values and beliefs she holds that shape her view of the family farm. Identify any problems you see in her depiction of the family farm, and offer your own conclusions about attitudes toward farming in American culture.

5. Kingsolver suggests that the choices each person makes affect the larger world to some degree. Write an essay in which you consider the choices you have made as you participate in the consumer culture, focusing specifically on the foods you eat. What are the choices you typically make about food? Why do you think you make these specific choices? What impact do you think your choices have? What would you like to do differently? Why? Try to address such questions in your essay.

A few years ago, a student of mine wrote an essay in which she made a very persuasive argument against eating meat. In her essay, she cited many statistics to support her claim that eating meat was not only less healthy than a vegetarian diet but also that it contributed to environmental damage because of the way cattle, chickens, and pigs are raised and processed. She concluded that becoming a vegetarian was therefore an ethical matter as well as a matter of health. Her essay was one

Should We *All* Be Vegetarians?

RICHARD CORLISS

F**IVE REASONS TO EAT MEAT:**

1) It tastes good

2) It makes you feel good

3) It's a great American tradition

4) It supports the nation's farmers

5) Your parents did it

of the most compelling pieces of writing I had read regarding the decision to avoid eating meat. Not long ago, that student, who is now a high school English teacher, contacted me, and we met at a local restaurant to talk about teaching and to catch up with each other. For her dinner, she ordered a large hamburger.

You might call my former student a hypocrite, but I think the matter is more complicated. I have no doubt that she believed what she wrote in her essay, but I also think she learned how challenging it can be to give up eating meat if you live in the United States. The following article helps explain why. As writer Richard Corliss (b. 1944) points out in this article, meat is not only a major part of the American diet, but it is also part of American culture. Think hamburgers on the Fourth of July and hot dogs at the baseball park. Moreover, despite health risks associated with eating meat, becoming a vegetarian has risks of its own. Corliss's article explores these complexities and helps us see that a basic necessity like food is not always as basic as it might seem.

Richard Corliss writes about popular culture for Time *magazine, in which the following article appeared in 2002. (Corliss was assisted in writing this article by reporters Melissa August, Matthew Cooper, David Bjerklie, Lisa McLaughlin, Wendy Cole, and Jeffrey Ressner.)* ▼

Oh, sorry . . . those are five reasons to smoke cigarettes. Meat is more complicated. It's a food most Americans eat virtually every day: at the dinner table; in the cafeteria; on the barbecue patio; with mustard at a ballpark; or, a billion times a year, with special sauce, lettuce, cheese, pickles, onions on a sesame-seed bun. Beef is, the TV commercials say, "America's food"—the Stars and Stripes served up medium rare—and as entwined with the nation's notion of its robust frontier heritage as, well, the Marlboro Man.

But these days America's cowboys seem a bit small in the saddle. Those cattle they round up have become politically incorrect: for many, meat is an obscene cuisine. It's not just the additives and ailments connected with the consumption of beef, though a dish of hormones, E. coli bacteria or the scary specter of mad-cow disease might be effective enough as an appetite suppressant. It's that more and more Americans, particularly young Americans, have started engaging in a practice that would once have shocked their parents. They are eating their vegetables. Also their grains and sprouts. Some 10 million Americans today consider themselves to be practicing vegetarians, according to a *Time* poll of 10,000 adults; an additional 20 million have flirted with vegetarianism sometime in their past.

To get a taste of the cowboy's ancient pride, and current defensiveness, just click on South Dakota cattleman Jody Brown's web site, www.ranchers.net, and read the new meat mantras: "Vegetarians don't live longer, they just look older"; and "If animals weren't meant to be eaten, then why are they made out of meat?" (One might ask the same of humans.) For Brown and his generation of unquestioning meat eaters, dinner is something the parents put on the table and the kids put in their bodies. Of his own kids, he says, "We expect them to eat a little of everything." So beef is served nearly every night at the Brown homestead, with nary a squawk from Jeff, 17, Luke, 13, and Hannah, 11. But Jody admits to at least one liberal sympathy. "If a vegetarian got a flat tire in my community," he says, "I'd come out and help him."

For the rancher who makes his living with meat or the vegetarian whose diet could someday drive all those breeder-slaughterers to bankruptcy, nothing is simple any more. Gone is the age of American innocence, or naiveté when such items as haircuts and handshakes, family names and school uniforms, farms and zoos, cowboys and ranchers, had no particular political meaning. Now everything is up for rancorous debate. And no aspect of our daily lives—our lives as food consumers—gets more heat than meat.

For millions of vegetarians, beef is a four-letter word; veal summons charnel visions of infanticide. Many children, raised on hit films like *Babe* and *Chicken Run,* recoil from eating their movie heroes and switch to what the meat defeaters like to call a "nonviolent diet." Vegetarianism resolves a conscientious person's inner turf war by providing an edible complex of good-deed-doing: to go veggie is to be more humane. Give up meat, and save lives! 5

Of course, one of the lives you could save or at least prolong is your own. For vegetarianism should be about more than not eating; it's also about smart eating. You needn't be a born-again foodist to think this. The American Dietetic Association, a pretty centrist group, has proclaimed that "appropriately planned vegetarian diets are healthful, are nutritionally adequate and provide health benefits in the prevention and treatment of certain diseases."

So, how about it? Should we all become vegetarians? Not just teens but also infants, oldsters, athletes—everyone? Will it help us live longer, healthier lives? Does it work for people of every age and level of work activity? Can we find the right vegetarian diet and stick to it? And if we can do it, will we?

CONVERSATIONS: POPULAR CULTURE AND OUR FRONTIER HERITAGE
Corliss makes several references (par. 1) that are probably familiar to most Americans. For example, the phrase "special sauce, lettuce, cheese, pickles, onions on a sesame-seed bun" is a reference to a popular advertisement for McDonald's restaurants from several years ago; similarly, the phrase "America's food" is a reference to an advertising campaign by U.S. producers of beef. These references suggest that writers like Corliss rely on their readers' familiarity with various aspects of popular culture, such as well-known advertisements. They also assume that readers are familiar with certain ideas that are part of the culture. For example, later in this paragraph (par. 1), Corliss associates meat with what he calls "the nation's notion of its robust frontier heritage," which is reflected in the image of the famous Marlboro Man in cigarette advertisements. (For an image of the Marlboro Man, see *Visual Connections: That Romantic Atavist* on page 545 in Chapter 10.) Here Corliss assumes his readers understand the idea of the frontier, which is well established in American culture. This brief paragraph provides a good example of how much knowledge readers and writers bring to a text; it also shows how that knowledge helps shape the meaning that readers and writers make in a piece of writing.

There are as many reasons to try vegetarianism as there are soft-eyed cows and soft-hearted kids. To impressionable young minds, vegetarianism can sound sensible, ethical and—as nearly 25% of adolescents polled by Teenage Research Unlimited said—"cool." College students think so too. A study conducted by Arizona State University psychology professors Richard Stein and Carol Nemeroff reported that, sight unseen, salad eaters were rated more moral, virtuous and considerate than steak eaters. "A century ago, a high-meat diet was thought to be health-favorable," says Paul Rozin of the University of Pennsylvania. "Kids today are the first generation to live in a culture where vegetarianism is common, where it is publicly promoted on health and ecological grounds." And kids, as any parent can tell you, spur the consumer economy; that explains in part the burgeoning sales of veggie burgers (soy, bulgur wheat, cooked rice, mushrooms, onions and flavorings in Big Mac drag) in supermarkets and fast-food chains.

Children, who are signing on to vegetarianism much faster than adults, may be educating their parents. Vegetarian food sales are savoring double-digit growth. Top restaurants have added more meatless dishes. Trendy "living foods" or "raw" restaurants are sprouting up, like Roxanne's in Larkspur, Calif., where no meat, fish, poultry or dairy items are served, and nothing is cooked to temperatures in excess of 118°F. "Going to my restaurant," says Roxanne Klein, "is like going to a really cool new country you haven't experienced before."

10   Like any country, vegetarianism has its hidden complexities. For one thing, vegetarians come in more than half a dozen flavors, from sproutarians to pesco-pollo-vegetarians. The most notorious are the vegan (rhymes with intriguin' or fatiguin') vegetarians. The Green Party of the movement, vegans decline to consume, use or wear any animal products. They also avoid honey, since its production demands the oppression of worker bees. TV's favorite vegetarian, the cartoon 8-year-old **Lisa Simpson,** once had a crush on a fellow who described himself as "a Level Five vegan—I don't eat anything that casts a shadow." Among vegan celebrities: the rock star Moby and Ohio Congressman Dennis Kucinich, who swore off steak for breakfast and insists he feels much better starting his day with miso soup, brown rice or oat groats.

CONTEXT: LISA SIMPSON
The author describes Lisa Simpson, a character on the animated television sitcom *The Simpsons,* as "TV's favorite vegetarian." This mention of the character of Lisa Simpson not only suggests how well known this television show was at the time this article was published, but it also indicates how important television can be as a cultural medium. In this case, *The Simpsons,* which is intended to be entertainment, also becomes part of the ongoing conversations in American society about such matters as diet and lifestyle.

To true believers—who refrain from meat as an A.A. member does from drink and do a spit-take if told that there's gelatin in their soup—a semivegetarian is no vegetarian at all. A phrase like pesco-pollo-vegetarian, to them, is an oxymoron, like "lapsed Catholic" or "semivirgin." *Vegetarian Times,* the bible of this particular congregation, lays down the dogma: "For many people who are working to become vegetarians, chicken and fish may be transitional foods, but they are not vegetarian foods . . . the word 'vegetarian' means someone who eats no meat, fish or chicken."

Clear enough? Not to many Americans. In a survey of 11,000 individuals, 37% of those who responded "Yes, I am a vegetarian" also reported that in the previous 24 hours they had eaten red meat; 60% had eaten meat, poultry or seafood. Perhaps those surveyed thought a vegetarian is someone who, from time to time, eats vegetables as a side dish—say, alongside a prime rib. If more than one-third of people in a large sample don't know the broadest definition of vegetarian, one wonders how they can be trusted with something much more difficult: the full-time care and picky-picky feeding of their bodies, whatever their dietary preferences.

We know that fruits, vegetables, grains, legumes and nuts are healthy. There are any number of studies that show that consuming more of these plant-based foods reduces the risk for a long list of chronic maladies (including coronary artery disease, obesity, diabetes and many cancers) and is a probable factor in increased longevity in the industrialized world. We know that on average we eat too few fruits and vegetables and too much saturated fat, of which meat and dairy are prime contributors. We also know that in the real world, real diets—vegetarian and nonvegetarian—as consumed by real people range from primly virtuous to pig-out voracious. There are meat eaters who eat more and better vegetables than vegetarians, and vegetarians who eat more artery-clogging fats than meat eaters.

The International Congress on Vegetarian Nutrition, a major conference on the subject, was held this spring at Loma Linda (Calif.) University. The research papers presented there included some encouraging if

VISUAL CONNECTIONS: CHARTING VEGETARIANS
This graphic accompanied Corliss's article when it was first published in *Time* magazine. Such charts are commonly used in news magazines and newspapers to illustrate the article or to add information related to the article. Consider what this graphic might contribute to Corliss's article. Does it add anything that cannot be conveyed through writing in the article itself?

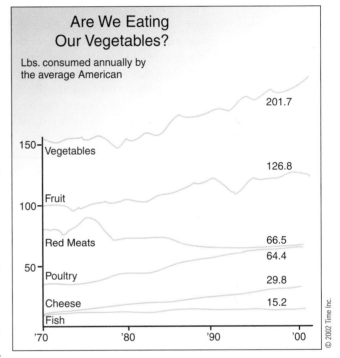

Are We Eating Our Vegetables?

Lbs. consumed annually by the average American

© 2002 Time Inc.

tentative findings: that a predominantly vegetarian diet may have beneficial effects for kidney and nerve function in diabetics, as well as for weight loss; that eating more fruits and vegetables can slow, and perhaps reverse, age-related declines in brain function and in cognitive and motor performance—at least in rats; that vegetarian seniors have a lower death rate and use less medication than meat-eating seniors; that vegetarians have a healthier total intake of fats and cholesterol but a less healthy intake of fatty acids (such as the heart-protecting omega-3 fatty acids found in fish oil).

15　　But one paper suggested that low-protein diets (associated with vegetarians) reduce calcium absorption and may have a negative impact on skeletal health. And although several studies on Seventh-Day Adventists (typically vegetarians) indicated that they have a longer-than-average life expectancy, other studies found that prostate-cancer rates were high in Adventists, and one study found that Adventists were more likely to suffer hip fractures.

Can it be that vegetarianism is bad for your health? That's a complex issue. There's a big, beautiful plant kingdom out there; you ought to be able to dine healthily on this botanical bounty. With perfect knowledge, you can indeed eat like a king from the vegetable world. But ordinary people are not nutrition professionals. While some vegetarians have the full skinny on how to watch their riboflavin and vitamins D and B12, many more haven't a clue. This is one reason that vegetarians, in a study of overall nutrition, scored significantly lower than nonvegetarians on the USDA's Healthy Eating Index, which compares actual diet with USDA guidelines.

Another reason is that vegans skew the stats, because their strict avoidance of meat, eggs and dairy products can lead to deficiencies in iron, calcium and vitamin B12. "These nutrients are the problem," says Johanna Dwyer, a professor of nutrition and medicine at Tufts University. "At least among the vegans who are also philosophically opposed to fortified foods and/or vitamin and mineral supplements."

Debates about the efficacy of vegetarianism follow us from cradle to wheelchair. In 1998 child-care expert Dr. Benjamin Spock, who became a vegetarian late in life, stoked a stir by recommending that children over the age of 2 be raised as vegans, rejecting even milk and eggs. The American Dietetic Association says it is possible to raise kids as vegans but cautions that special care must be taken with nursing infants (who don't develop properly without the nutrients in mother's milk or fortified formula). Other researchers warn that infants breast-fed by vegans have lower levels of vitamin B12 and DHA (an omega-3 fatty acid), important to vision and growth.

And there is always the chance of vegetarian theory gone madly wrong in practice. A Queens, N.Y., couple were indicted last May for first-degree assault, charged with nearly starving their toddler to death on a strict diet of juices, ground nuts, herbal tea, beans, flaxseed and cod-liver oils. At 16 months, the girl weighed 10 lbs., less than half the normal weight of a child her age. Their lawyer's defense: "They felt that they have their own lifestyle. They're vegetarians." The couple declined to plea-bargain, and are still in jail awaiting trial.

20   Many children decide on their own to become vegetarians and are declaring their preference at ever more precocious ages; it's often their first act of domestic rebellion. But a youngster is at a disadvantage insisting on a rigorous cuisine before he or she can cook food—or buy it or even read—and when the one whose menu is challenged is the parent: nurturer, disciplinarian and executive chef. Alicia Hurtado of Oak Park, Ill., has been a vegetarian half her life—she's 8 now—and mother Cheryle mostly indulges her daughter's diet. Still, Mom occasionally sneaks a little chicken broth into Alicia's pasta dishes. "When she can read labels," Cheryle says, "I'll be out of luck."

By adolescence, kids can read the labels but often ignore the ingredients. Research shows that calcium intake is often insufficient in American teens. By contrast, lacto-ovo teens usually have abundant calcium intake. For vegans, however, consuming adequate amounts of calcium without the use of fortified foods or supplements is difficult without careful dietary planning. Among vegan youth who do not take supplements, there is reason for concern with respect to iron, calcium, vitamins D and B12, and perhaps also selenium and iodine.

For four years Christina Economos has run the Tufts longitudinal health study on young adults, a comprehensive survey of lifestyle habits among undergraduates. In general, she finds that "kids who were most influenced by family diet and health values are eating healthy vegetarian or low-meat diets. But there is a whole group of students who decide to become vegetarians and do it in a poor way. The ones who do it badly don't know how to navigate in the vegetarian world. They eat more bread, cheese and pastry products and load up on salad dressing. Their saturated-fat intake is no lower than red-meat eaters, and they are more likely to consume inadequate amounts of vitamin B12 and protein. They may think they are healthier because they are some sort of vegetarian and they don't eat red meat, but in fact they may be less healthy."

Jenny Woodson, 20, now a junior at Duke, has been a vegetarian from way back. At 6, on a trip to McDonald's, she ordered a tossed salad. When Jenny lived in a dorm at high school, she quickly realized that teens do not live on French fries and broccoli alone. "We ended up making vegetarian sandwiches with bagels and ingredients from the salad bar, cheese fries and stuffed baked potatoes with cottage cheese." Jenny and her friends were careful to avoid high-fat, calorie-laden fare at the salad bar, but for those who don't exercise restraint, salad-bar fixings can become vegetarian junk food.

STRATEGIES: EXAMPLES
Notice the examples of two young people who are vegetarians described in these paragraphs 23 and 24. Both are women. One attended Duke, a prestigious university; the other lives in a suburb of St. Louis. Consider how the author uses these examples to convey specific ideas about being a vegetarian. Consider, too, whether these two people are in any way typical of Americans.

Maggie Ellinger-Locke, 19, of the St. Louis, Mo., suburb of University City, has been a vegetarian for eight years and went vegan at 15. Since then she has not worn leather or wool products or slept under a down comforter. She has not used cups or utensils that have touched meat. "It felt like we were keeping kosher," says Maggie's mother Linda, who isn't Jewish. At high school Maggie was ridiculed, even shoved to the ground, by teen boys who apparently found her eating habits threatening. She found a happy ending, of sorts, enrolling at Antioch College, where she majors in ecofeminism. "Here," she says, "the people on the defensive are the ones who eat meat."

Maggie hit a few potholes on the road to perfection. Until recently, she smoked up to two packs of cigarettes a day (cigarettes, after all, are plants fortified with nicotine), quitting only because she didn't want to support the tobacco business. And she freely admits to an eating disorder: for the past year she has been bulimic, bingeing and vomiting sometimes as much as once a day to cope with stress. But she insists she is true to her beliefs: even when bingeing, she remains dedicated to vegan consumption.

25

The American Dietetic Association found that vegetarian diets are slightly more common among adolescents with eating problems but that "recent data suggest that adopting a vegetarian diet does not lead to eating disorders." It can be argued that most American teens already have an eating disorder—fast food, soft drinks and candy are a blueprint for obesity and heart trouble. Why should teens be expected to purge their bad habits just because they have gone veggie? Still, claims Simon Chaitowitz of the pro-vegetarian and animal-rights group Physicians Committee for Responsible Medicine, "Kids are better off being junk-food vegetarians than junk-food meat eaters."

Maybe. According to Dr. Joan Sabate, chairman of the Loma Linda nutrition conference, there are still concerns over vegetarian diets for growing kids or lactating women. When you are in what he calls "a state of high metabolic demand," any diet that excludes foods makes it harder to meet nutrient requirements. But he is quick to add that "for the average sedentary adult living in a Western society, a vegetarian diet meets dietary needs and prevents chronic diseases better than an omnivore diet."

Like kids and nursing moms, athletes need to be especially smart eaters. Their success depends on bursts of energy, sustained strength and muscle mass, factors that require nutrients more easily obtained from meat. For this reason, relatively few top athletes are vegetarians. Besides, says sports nutritionist Suzanne Girard Eberle, the author of *Endurance Sports Nutrition,* "lots of athletes have no idea how their bodies work. That's why fad diets and supplements are so attractive to them."

Eberle notes that vegetarian diets done correctly are high in fiber and low in fat. "But where are the calories?" she asks. "World-class endurance athletes need in excess of 5,000 or 6,000 calories a day. Competition can easily consume 10,000. You need to eat a lot of plant-based food to get those calories. Being a vegetarian athlete is hard, really hard to do right."

30   It's not that easy for the rest of America, either. Middle-aged to elderly adults can also develop deficiencies in a vegetarian diet (as they can, of course, with a poor diet that includes meat). Deficiencies in vitamins D and B12 and in iodine, which can lead to goiter, are common. The elderly tend to compensate by taking supplements, but that approach carries risks. Researchers have found cases in which vegetarian oldsters, who are susceptible to iodine deficiency, had dangerously high and potentially toxic levels of iodine in their bodies because they overdid the supplements.

Meat producers acknowledge that vegetarian diets can be healthy. They also have responded to the call for leaner food; the National Pork Board says that, compared with 20 years ago, pork is on average 31% lower in fat and 29% lower in saturated fat, and has 14% fewer calories and 10% less cholesterol. But the defenders of meat and dairy can also go on the offensive. They mention the need for B12. And then they ratchet up the fear factor. Kurt Graetzer, CEO of the Milk Processor Education Program, scans the drop in milk consumption (not only by vegans but by kids who prefer soda, Snapple and Fruitopia) and declares, "We are virtually developing a generation of osteoporotic children."

Dr. Michelle Warren, a professor of medicine at New York Presbyterian Medical Center in New York City—and a member of the Council for Women's Nutrition Solutions, which is sponsored by the National Cattlemen's Beef Association—expresses concern about calcium deficiency connected with a vegan diet: "The most serious consequences are low bone mass and osteoporosis. That is a permanent condition." Warren says that in her practice, she has seen young vegetarians with irregular periods and loss of hair. "And there's a peculiar color, a yellow tinge to the skin," that occurs in people who eat a lot of vegetables rich in beta carotene in combination with a low-calorie diet. "I think it's very unattractive." She also is troubled by the reasons some young vegetarians give for their choice of diet. One female patient, Warren says, wouldn't eat meat because she was told it was the reason her father had a heart attack.

Michael Jacobson, executive director of the Center for Science in the Public Interest in Washington, sees most of the meat and dairy lobby's arguments as desperate, disingenuous scare stories. "It unmasks the industry's self-interest," he says, "when it voices concern about B12 while hundreds of thousands of people are dying prematurely because of too much saturated fat from meat and dairy products." Indeed, according to David Pimentel, a Cornell ecologist, the average American consumes 112 grams of protein a day, twice the amount recommended by the National

Academy of Sciences. "This has implications for cancer risks and stress on the urinary system," says Pimentel. "And with this protein comes a lot of fat. Fully 40% of our calories—and heavy cardiovascular risks—come from fat."

Pimentel argues that vegetarianism is much more environment-friendly than diets revolving around meat. "In terms of caloric content, the grain consumed by American livestock could feed 800 million people—and, if exported, would boost the U.S. trade balance by $80 billion a year." Grain-fed livestock consume 100,000 liters of water for every kilogram of food they produce, compared with 2,000 liters for soybeans. Animal protein also demands tremendous expenditures of fossil-fuel energy—eight times as much as for a comparable amount of plant protein. Put another way, says Pimentel, the average omnivore diet burns the equivalent of a gallon of gas per day—twice what it takes to produce a vegan diet. And the U.S. livestock population—cattle, chickens, turkeys, lambs, pigs and the rest—consumes five times as much grain as the U.S. human population. But then there are 7 billion of them; they outnumber us 25 to 1.

In the spirit of fair play to cowboy Jody Brown and his endangered breed, let's entertain two arguments in favor of eating meat. One is that it made us human. "We would never have evolved as large, socially active hominids if we hadn't turned to meat," says Katharine Milton, an anthropologist at the University of California, Berkeley. The vegetarian primates (orangutans and gorillas) are less social than the more omnivorous chimpanzees, possibly because collecting and consuming all that forage takes so darned much time. The early hominids took a bold leap: 2.5 million years ago, they were cracking animal bones to eat the marrow. They ate the protein-rich muscle tissue, says Milton, "but also the rest of the animal—liver, marrow, brains—with their high concentrations of other nutrients. Evolving humans ate it all."

Just as important, they knew why they were eating it. In Milton's elegant phrase, "Solving dietary problems with your head is the trajectory of the primate order." Hominids grew big on meat, and smart on that lovely brain-feeder, glucose, which they got from fruit, roots and tubers. This diet of meat and glucose gave early man energy to burn—or rather, energy to play house, to sing and socialize, to make culture, art, war. And finally, about 10,000 years ago, to master agriculture and trade—which provided the sophisticated system that modern humans can use to go vegetarian.

The other reason for beef eating is, hold on, ethical—a matter of animal rights. The familiar argument for vegetarianism, articulated by Tom Regan, a philosophical founder of the modern animal-rights movement, is that it would save Babe the pig and *Chicken Run*'s Ginger from execution. But what about Bugs Bunny and Mickey Mouse? asks Steven Davis, professor of animal science at Oregon State University, pointing to the number of field animals inadvertently killed during crop production and harvest. One study showed that simply mowing an alfalfa field caused a 50% reduction in the gray-tailed vole population. Mortality rates increase with each pass of the tractor to plow, plant and harvest. Rabbits, mice and pheasants, he says, are the indiscriminate "collateral damage" of row crops and the grain industry.

By contrast, grazing (not grain-fed) ruminants such as cattle produce food and require fewer entries into the fields with tractors and other equipment. Applying (and upending) Regan's least-harm theory, Davis proposes a ruminant-pasture model of food production, which would replace poultry and pork production with beef, lamb and dairy products. According to his calculations, such a model would result in the deaths of 300 million fewer animals annually (counting both field animals and cattle) than would a completely vegan model. When asked about Davis' arguments, Regan, however, still sees a distinction: "The real question is whether to support production systems whose very reason for existence is to kill animals. Meat eaters do. Ethical vegetarians do not."

The moral: there is no free lunch, not even if it's vegetarian. For now, man is perched at the top of the food chain and must live with his choice to feed on the living things further down. But even to raise the question of a harvester Hiroshima is to show how far we have come in considering the humane treatment of that which is not human. And we still have a way to go. "It may take a while," says actress and vegetarian Mary Tyler Moore, "but there will probably come a time when we look back and say, 'Good Lord, do you believe that in the 20th century and early part of the 21st, people were still eating animals?'"

40   It may take a very long while. For most people, meat still does taste good. And can "America's food" ever be tofu?

UNDERSTANDING THE TEXT

1. Why is the matter of eating meat or being a vegetarian no longer simple, according to Corliss? Do you think it ever was? Explain.

2. What are the main reasons for becoming a vegetarian, according to this article? What do you think these reasons suggest about Americans' eating habits and attitudes toward food?

3. What are some of the challenges of having a true vegetarian diet? Why are these challenges important, according to the author? What do you think these challenges reveal about our habits and attitudes relating to food?

4. What are the reasons for eating meat, according to this article? Do you think these reasons are persuasive? Why or why not? What might your answer to that question suggest about your own values regarding food and lifestyle?

EXPLORING THE ISSUES

1. How would you characterize the writing style in this article? What specific features of the writing style—such as word choice, figures of speech, sentence structure, or rhythm—are most distinctive, in your view? Do you find this writing style effective? Explain.

2. Corliss cites many statistics, refers to scientific studies of nutri-

tion, provides examples, and quotes food researchers. Examine his use of information and evidence in this article. What kinds of information seem to be emphasized? How effectively do you think the specific points raised in the article are supported by information and evidence?

3. This article originally appeared in *Time* magazine, a large-circulation weekly news magazine that reaches a general audience. *Time* is known for informative articles that present an in-depth discussion of timely issues or events. This was intended to be such an article rather than an editorial that presents an opinion about an issue or event. To what extent do you think this article succeeds in presenting its subject fairly and objectively? Do you think the author favors one side or another in the debates about whether or not to eat meat? Explain, citing specific passages to support your answer.

4. Corliss depicts representatives of various groups in this article, including cattle ranchers and beef producers, nutritionists and scientists, and vegetarians. Examine the picture he paints of these groups. What does he seem to emphasize about each? Do you think his picture of these groups is accurate and fair? Why or why not?

ENTERING THE CONVERSATIONS

1. Write an essay in which you make a case for or against becom-

ing a vegetarian. Base your argument on your own principles for living and for using resources.

2. In a group of classmates, share the essays you wrote for Question 1. Identify the main arguments for and against becoming a vegetarian. Try to draw conclusions about what these arguments might reveal about your attitudes regarding food.

3. Create a web site, PowerPoint presentation, flyer, or some other appropriate kind of document in which you educate a general audience about the pros and cons of eating meat or becoming a vegetarian. Draw on this article and other appropriate resources in creating your document.

4. Write a letter to the editor of your local newspaper indicating why you believe people who live in your region should or should not eat meat.

5. Watch television to find advertisements about food—for example, advertisements for fast-food restaurants, certain snack foods or other food products, or food stores. (Or look for similar advertisements in newspapers, magazines, or on the Internet.) Select several common ads for popular products or restaurants and analyze them for the messages they seem to convey about food in general. Then write a report on the basis of your analysis. Try to draw conclusions about American attitudes regarding food.

THE POLITICS OF CONSUMPTION

walmart

I N THE 1990S, SEVERAL HUMAN RIGHTS ORGANIZATIONS AND OTHER ADVOCACY GROUPS BEGAN A CAMPAIGN AGAINST LABOR EXPLOITATION BY WESTERN CORPORA- TIONS WITH FACTORIES IN DEVELOPING NATIONS. THESE GROUPS TRIED TO PUBLICIZE THE POOR WORKING CONDITIONS AND LOW WAGES OF WORKERS IN COUNTRIES LIKE INDONESIA, MEXICO, AND THAILAND, WHERE

many different kinds of consumer products, including popular brands of clothing and shoes, were made for large Western companies. On the university campus where I work, this campaign energized some student groups, who organized a local campaign to stop the university from selling clothing that is manufactured under such conditions. That campaign was successful, and today, all the clothing with the university's logo is manufactured by companies that have tried to address the problem of exploited workers. In other words, if you buy a T-shirt with my university's logo on it, you should be confident that it was manufactured by a worker who was paid a decent wage and enjoys decent working conditions.

But how would you know for sure? The terrible conditions and the abuse of workers in some factories in developing

> But our choices as consumers are not only about price or the quality of the product; those choices are also political.

nations came to light only because some human rights organizations documented the cases through interviews with workers, secret videos and photographs taken at the factories, and other kinds of evidence that was not always easy to obtain. Some of the nations where these factories are located have few laws or regulations to protect workers or the environment, which is one reason that Western corporations build the factories there in the first place. So if a corporation that makes, say, athletic shoes announces that it will make sure workers are treated and paid well, you may simply have to take their word for it.

You may also have to pay more for those athletic shoes. In some cases, companies that manufacture such items close down their factories in the United States and move them to developing nations to lower their costs. If they pay workers less and have lower production costs, they can charge less for their products. Of course, this means that some American workers will be out of jobs. So if you saved some money on a pair of athletic shoes or a popular brand of clothing, you may have done so because someone else is out of a job. And you may have helped maintain a system that exploits workers in other nations and pollutes their land as well.

These circumstances reveal how complicated the matter of consumption can be. Often, you buy something because you need it or want it. You try to get it at the lowest price. That makes sense. But our choices as consumers are not only about price or the quality of the product; those choices are also political. They have consequences that we often cannot see or don't know about. Even if you choose to buy a product—or refuse to buy a product—because of how or where it was made, you may still be doing social, economic, or environmental harm without realizing it. And change often comes only through hard-fought campaigns like the one on my campus.

The readings in this chapter explore some of these complexities of being a consumer. They examine different situations in which the production and consumption of the resources we need—food, water, clothing—have consequences that are sometimes disturbing. They may help you better understand the politics of the choices you make about those resources. I chose these readings because they focus on important matters that affect all of us. But I also chose them because they are part of ongoing and important conversations around the world about how we should live. I hope they'll prompt you to think about your own participation in those conversations.

No doubt you have heard the term globaliza- *tion. But what exactly does it mean? The fol- lowing essay by Helena Norberg-Hodge pro- vides some answers. In fact, you might think of this essay as an extended definition of glob- alization. Globalization is often defined as the expansion of markets and the increase in so- cial and economic exchanges among people, communities, and nations throughout the world. And certainly, globalization is that. But Norberg-Hodge explores the social, cul-*

THE March OF THE Monoculture

tural, economic, political, and environmental impacts of globalization. In doing so, she helps us see how complex globalization really is. She is especially concerned about the costs of globalization that may not be obvious as consumerism expands into regions of the world where it previously did not exist. Although she acknowledges that the global consumer culture that is replacing many local cultures may bring more material goods for people, she points out that it may also cause lo- cal cultures to disappear. More important, it may not result in greater well-being for indi- viduals. In other words, making more con- sumer goods available to people in remote places like Ladakh, a mountainous region of northern India that Norberg-Hodge describes in her essay, may not ultimately improve their lives. In sharing these concerns, Norberg- Hodge helps us see how interconnected we all are, which makes the political aspects of con- sumerism even more complicated.

Helena Norberg-Hodge is the founder and director of The International Society for Ecology and Culture, a nonprofit organiza- tion promoting biodiversity and local cul- ture. She has written extensively about globalization and its impact on local cultures and the environment. This essay first ap- peared in Ecologist *magazine in 1999.* ▼

HELENA NORBERG-HODGE

Around the world, the pressure to conform to the expecta- tions of the spreading, consumer monoculture is destroying cultural identity, eliminating local economies and erasing regional differ- ences. As a consequence the global economy is leading to uncer- tainty, ethnic friction, and collapse, where previously there had been relative security and stability.

For many, the rise of the global economy marks the final fulfillment of the great dream of a "Global Village." Almost everywhere you travel today you will find multi-lane highways, concrete cities and a cultural landscape featuring grey business suits, fast-food chains, Hollywood films and cellular phones. In the remotest corners of the planet, Barbie, Madonna and the Marlboro Man are familiar icons. From Cleveland to Cairo to Caracas, *Baywatch* is entertainment and *CNN* news.

The world, we are told, is being united by virtue of the fact that everyone will soon be able to indulge their innate human desire for a Westernised, urbanised consumer lifestyle. West is best, and joining the bandwagon brings closer a harmonious union of peaceable, ra- tional, democratic consumers "like us."

HELENA NORBERG-HODGE, "THE MARCH OF THE MONOCULTURE." THIS ARTICLE FIRST APPEARED IN THE MAY-JUNE 1999 ISSUE OF *THE ECOLOGIST*, VOL. 29, NO. 3, WWW. THEECOLOGIST.ORG. REPRINTED BY PERMISSION.

This world-view assumes that it was the chaotic diversity of cultures, values and beliefs that lay behind the chaos and conflicts of the past: that as these differences are removed, so the differences between us will be resolved. As a result, all around the world, villages, rural communities and their cultural traditions, are being destroyed on an unprecedented scale by the impact of globalising market forces. Communities that have sustained themselves for hundreds of years are simply disintegrating. The spread of the consumer culture seems virtually unstoppable.

CONSUMERS R US: THE DEVELOPMENT OF THE GLOBAL MONOCULTURE

5   Historically, the erosion of cultural integrity was a conscious goal of colonial developers. As applied anthropologist Goodenough explained: "The problem is one of creating in another a sufficient dissatisfaction with his present condition of self so that he wants to change it. This calls for some kind of experience that leads him to reappraise his self-image and re-evaluate his self-esteem."[1] Towards this end, colonial officers were advised that they should:

1. Involve traditional leaders in their programmes.

2. Work through bilingual, acculturated individuals who have some knowledge of both the dominant and the target culture.

3. Modify circumstances or deliberately tamper with the equilibrium of the traditional culture so that change will become imperative.

4. Attempt to change underlying core values before attacking superficial customs."[2]

It is instructive to consider the actual effect of these strategies on the well-being of individual peoples in the South. For example, the Toradja tribes of the Poso district in central Celebes (now Sulawesi, Indonesia) were initially deemed completely incapable of 'development' without drastic intervention. Writing in 1929, A.C. Kruyt reported that the happiness and stability of Toradja society was such that "development and progress were impossible" and that they were "bound to remain at the same level".[3]

Toradja society was cashless and there was neither a desire for money nor the extra goods that might be purchased with it. In the face of such contentment, mission work proved an abject failure as the Toradjas had no interest in converting to a new religion, sending their children to school or growing cash crops. So, in 1905 the Dutch East Indies government decided to bring the Poso region under firm control, using armed force to crush all resistance. As a result of relocation and continual government harassment, mortality rates soared among the Toradjas. Turning to the missionaries for help, they were "converted" and began sending their children to school. Eventually they began cultivating coconut and coffee plantations and began to acquire new needs for oil lamps, sewing machines, and 'better' clothes. The self-sufficient tribal economy had been superseded, as a result of deliberate government action.

In many countries, schooling was the prime coercive instrument for changing "underlying core values" and proved to be a highly effective means of destroying self-esteem, fostering new 'needs,' creating dissatisfactions, and generally disrupting traditional cultures. An excerpt from a French reader designed in 1919 for use by French West African school-children gives a flavour of the kinds of pressure that were imposed on children:

"It is . . . an advantage for a native to work for a white man, because the Whites are better educated, more advanced in civilisation than the natives . . . You who are intelligent and industrious, my children, always help the Whites in their task. That is a duty."[4]

THE SITUATION TODAY: CULTURAL EROSION

Today, as wealth is transferred away from nation states into the rootless casino of the   10
money markets, the destruction of cultural integrity is far subtler than before. Corporate and government executives no longer consciously plan the destruction they wreak—indeed they are often unaware of the consequences of their decisions on real people on the other side of the world. This lack of awareness is fostered by the cult of specialisation and speed that pervades our society—the job of a public relations executive is confined to producing business-friendly soundbites—time pressures and a narrow focus prevent a questioning of the overall impact of corporate activity. The tendency to undermine cultural diversity proceeds, as it were, on "automatic pilot" as an inevitable consequence of the spreading global economy.

But although the methods employed by the masters of the "Global Village" are less brutal than in colonial times, the scale and effects are often even more devastating. The computer and telecommunications revolutions have helped to speed up and strengthen the forces behind the march of a global monoculture, which is now able to disrupt traditional cultures with a shocking speed and finality which surpasses anything the world has witnessed before.

PREYING ON THE YOUNG

Today, the Western consumer conformity is descending on the less industrialised parts of the world like an avalanche. "Development" brings tourism, Western films and products and, more recently, satellite television to the remotest corners of the Earth. All provide overwhelming images of luxury and power. Adverts and action films give the impression that everyone in the West is rich, beautiful and brave, and leads a life filled with excitement and glamour.

In the commercial mass culture which fuels this illusion, advertisers make it clear that Westernised fashion accessories equal sophistication and "cool." In diverse "developing" nations around the world, people are induced to meet their needs not through their community or local economy, but by trying to 'buy in' to the global market. People are made to believe that, in the words of one U.S. advertising executive in China, "imported equals good, local equals crap."

Even more alarmingly, people end up rejecting their own ethnic and racial characteristics—to feel shame at being who they are. Around the world, blonde-haired blue-eyed Barbie dolls and thin-as-a-rake "cover girls" set the standard for women. Already now, seven-year-old girls in Singapore are suffering from eating disorders. It is not unusual to find east Asian women with eyes surgically altered to look more European, dark-haired southern European women dying their hair blonde, and Africans with blue- or green-coloured contact lenses aimed at "correcting" dark eyes.

15   The one-dimensional, fantasy view of modern life promoted by the Western media, television and business becomes a slap in the face for young people in the "Third World." Teenagers, in particular, come to feel stupid and ashamed of their traditions and their origins. The people they learn to admire and respect on television are all "sophisticated" city dwellers with fast cars, designer clothes, spotlessly clean hands and shiny white teeth. Yet they find their parents asking them to choose a way of life that involves working in the fields and getting their hands dirty for little or no money, and certainly no glamour. It is hardly surprising, then, that many choose to abandon the old ways of their parents for the siren song of a Western material paradise.

For millions of young people in rural areas of the world, modern Western culture appears vastly superior to their own. They see incoming tourists spending as much as $1,000 a day—the equivalent of a visitor to the U.S. spending about $50,000 a day. Besides promoting the illusion that all Westerners are multi-millionaires, tourism and media images also give the impression that we never work—since for many people in "developing" countries, sitting at a desk or behind the wheel of a car does not constitute work.

People are not aware of the negative social or psychological aspects of Western life so familiar to us: the stress, the loneliness and isolation, the fear of growing old alone, the rise in clinical depression and other "industrial diseases" like cancer, stroke, diabetes and heart problems. Nor do they see the environmental decay, rising crime, poverty, homelessness and unemployment. While they know their own culture inside out, including all of its limitations and imperfections, they only see a glossy, exaggerated side of life in the West.

LADAKH: THE PRESSURE TO CONSUME

My own experience among the people of Ladakh or "Little Tibet," in the trans-Himalayan region of Kashmir, is a clear, if painful, example of this destruction of traditional cultures by the faceless consumer monoculture. When I first arrived in the area 23 years ago, the vast majority of Ladakhis were self-supporting farmers, living in small scattered settlements in the high desert. Though natural resources were scarce and hard to obtain, the Ladakhis had a remarkably high standard of living—with beautiful art, architecture and jewellery. Life moved at a gentle pace and people enjoyed a degree of leisure unknown to most of us in the West. Most Ladakhis only really worked for four months of the year, and poverty, pollution and unemployment were alien concepts. In 1975, I remember being shown around the remote village of Hemis Shukpachan by a young Ladakhi called Tsewang. It seemed to me, a newcomer, that all the houses I saw were especially large and beautiful, and I asked Tsewang to show me the houses where the poor lived. He looked perplexed for a moment, then replied, "We don't have any poor people here."

STRATEGIES: THE EXAMPLE OF LADAKH
Norberg-Hodge describes at length her experiences in the mountainous region of northern India called Ladakh. In doing so, she is employing two common strategies for supporting a position or making an argument: the use of example and the use of personal experience. In this case, she uses Ladakh as an extended example to illustrate what she sees as the damage that Western consumer culture can do to local cultures. But she also discusses Ladakh as someone who has had long experience there. In this way, she speaks as an authority who has greater knowledge of the situation than her readers or others who may be experts on globalization. You might consider how effective you found Norberg-Hodge's use of Ladakh as an example of the impact of globalization and consider as well whether her experience there gives her credibility to write about these issues.

In recent years external forces have caused massive and rapid disruption in Ladakh. Contact with the modern world has debilitated and demoralised a once-proud and self-sufficient people, who today are suffering from what can best be described as a cultural inferiority complex. When tourism descended on Ladakh some years ago, I began to realise how, looked at from a Ladakhi perspective, our modern, Western culture appears much more successful, fulfilled and sophisticated than we find it to be from the inside.

In traditional Ladakhi culture, virtually all basic needs—food, clothing and shelter, [20] were provided without money. Labour was free of charge, part of an intricate and long-established web of human relationships. Because Ladakhis had no need for money, they had little or none. So when they saw outsiders—tourists and visitors—coming in, spending what was to them vast amounts of cash on inessential luxuries, they suddenly felt poor. Not realising that money was essential in the West—that without it, people often go homeless or even starve—they didn't realise its true value. They began to feel inadequate and backward. Eight years after Tsewang had told me that Ladakhis had no poverty, I overheard him talking to some tourists. "If you could only help us Ladakhis," he was saying, "we're so poor."

Tourism is part of the overall development which the Indian government is promoting in Ladakh. The area is being integrated into the Indian, and hence the global, economy. Subsidised food is imported from the outside, while local farmers who had previously grown a variety of crops and kept a few animals to provide for themselves have been encouraged to grow cash crops. In this way they are becoming dependent on forces beyond their control—huge transportation networks, oil prices, and the fluctuations of international finance. Over the course of time, financial inflation obliges them to produce more and more, so as to secure the income that they now need in order to buy what they used to grow themselves. In political terms, each Ladakhi is now one individual in a national economy of 800 million, and, as part of a global economy, one of about six billion.

As a result of external investments, the local economy is crumbling. For generation after generation Ladakhis grew up learning how to provide themselves with clothing and shelter; how to make shoes out of yak skin and robes from the wool of sheep; how to build houses out of mud and stone. As these building traditions give way to "modern" methods, the plentiful local materials are left unused, while competition for a narrow range of modern materials—concrete, steel and plastic—skyrockets. The same thing happens when people begin eating identical staple foods, wearing the same clothes and relying on the same finite energy sources. Making everyone dependent on the same resources creates efficiency for global cor-

VISUAL CONNECTIONS: CONSUMER CULTURE
Norberg-Hodge argues that consumer culture changes the ideas about lifestyle and "the good life" that people in various cultures may have. Consider, for example, what this advertisement for clothing might suggest about the good life. To what extent do you think advertisements like this one for common consumer goods might support or complicate Norberg-Hodge's argument?

The Advertising Archives

porations, but it also creates an artificial scarcity for consumers, which heightens competitive pressures.

As they lose the sense of security and identity that springs from deep, long-lasting connections to people and place, the Ladakhis are starting to develop doubts about who they are. The images they get from outside tell them to be different, to own more, to buy more and to thus be "better" than they are. The previously strong, outgoing women of Ladakh have been replaced by a new generation—unsure of themselves and desperately concerned with their appearance. And as their desire to be "modern" grows, Ladakhis are turning their backs on their traditional culture. I have seen Ladakhis wearing wristwatches they cannot read, and heard them apologising for the lack of electric lighting in their homes—electric lighting which, in 1975, when it first appeared, most villagers laughed at as an unnecessary gimmick. Even traditional foods are no longer a source of pride; now, when I'm a guest in a Ladakhi village, people apologise if they serve the traditional roasted barley, ngamphe, instead of instant noodles.

Ironically, then, modernisation—so often associated with the triumph of individualism—has produced a loss of individuality and a growing sense of personal insecurity. As people become self-conscious and insecure, they feel pressured to conform, and to live up to an idealised image. By contrast, in the traditional village, where everyone wore essentially the same clothes and looked the same to the casual observer, there was more freedom to relax. As part of a close-knit community, people felt secure enough to be themselves.

25   In Ladakh, as elsewhere, the breaking of local cultural, economic and political ties isolates people from their locality and from each other. At the same time, life speeds up and mobility increases—making even familiar relationships more superficial and brief. Competition for scarce jobs and political representation within the new centralised structures increasingly divides people. Ethnic and religious differences began to take on a political dimension, causing bitterness and enmity on a scale hitherto unknown. With a desperate irony, the monoculture—instead of bringing people together, creates divisions that previously did not exist.

As the fabric of local interdependence fragments, so do traditional levels of tolerance and co-operation. In villages near the capital, Leh, disputes and acrimony within previously close-knit communities, and even within families, are increasing. I have even seen heated arguments over the allocation of irrigation water, a procedure that had previously been managed smoothly within a co-operative framework. The rise in this kind of new rivalry is one of the most painful divisions that I have seen in Ladakh. Within a few years, growing competition has actually culminated in violence—and this in a place where, previously, there had been no group conflict in living memory.

DEADLY DIVISIONS

The rise of divisions, violence and civil disorder around the world are the consequence of attempts to incorporate diverse cultures and peoples into the global monoculture. These divisions often deepen enough to result in fundamentalist reaction and ethnic conflict. Ladakh is by no means an isolated example.

In Bhutan, where different ethnic groups had also lived peaceably together for hundreds of years, two decades of economic development have resulted in the widespread destruction of decentralised livelihoods and communities—unemployment, once completely unknown, has reached crisis levels. Just like in Ladakh, these pressures have created intense competition between individuals and groups for places in schools, for jobs, for resources. As a result, tensions between Buddhists and Bhutanese Hindus of Nepalese origin have led to an eruption of violence and even a type of "ethnic cleansing."

Elsewhere, Nicholas Hildyard has written of how, when confronted with the horrors of ethnic cleansing in Yugoslavia or Rwanda, it is often taken for granted that the cause must lie in ingrained and ancient antagonisms. The reality, however, as Hildyard notes, is different:

> **CONTEXT: DEADLY DIVISIONS**
> In this section, Norberg-Hodge refers to several regions of the world where conflicts have intensified in recent years, including Bhutan, a tiny Himalayan nation to the north of India; the former Yugoslavia, which is now often referred to as the Baltic region and where bloody ethnic and religious conflicts erupted in the 1990s (Kosovo, which Norberg-Hodge mentions in paragraph 31, is in this region); and Rwanda, an African nation where thousands of people were killed in ethnic conflicts in the 1990s. As Norberg-Hodge suggests in this passage, experts have debated the causes of these conflicts, which have occurred in regions where religious and ethnic diversity has existed for hundreds of years. Notice how Norberg-Hodge uses this global political context to help make her argument against globalization. Consider, too, how this context might influence the way readers respond to her argument. You might think about how your own knowledge of these events affects your reaction to her argument.

"Scratch below the surface of inter-ethnic civil conflict, and the shallowness and deceptiveness of 'blood' or 'culture' explanations are soon revealed. 'Tribal hatred' (though a real and genuine emotion for some) emerges as the product not of 'nature' or of a primordial 'culture,' but of a complex web of politics, economics, history, psychology and a struggle for identity."[5]

In a similar vein, Michel Chossudovsky, Professor of Economics at the University of Ottawa, argues that the current Kosovo crisis has its roots at least partly in the macroeconomic reforms imposed by Belgrade's external creditors such as the International Monetary Fund (IMF). Multi-ethnic Yugoslavia was a regional industrial power with relative economic success. But after a decade of Western economic ministrations and five years of disintegration, war, boycott, and embargo, the economies of the former Yugoslavia are in ruins. Chossudovsky writes:

"In Kosovo, the economic reforms were conducive to the concurrent impoverishment of both the Albanian and Serbian populations contributing to fuelling ethnic tensions. The deliberate manipulation of market forces destroyed economic activity and people's livelihood creating a situation of despair."[6]

It is sometimes assumed that ethnic and religious strife is increasing because modern democracy liberates people, allowing old, previously suppressed, prejudices and hatreds to be expressed. If there was peace earlier, it is thought it was the result of oppression. But after more than twenty years of first-hand experience on the Indian subcontinent, I am convinced that economic 'development' not only exacerbates existing tensions but in many cases actually creates them. It breaks down human-scale structures, it destroys bonds of reciprocity and mutual dependence, while encouraging people to substitute their own culture and values with those of the media. In effect this means rejecting one's own identity—rejecting one's self.

Ultimately, while the myth makers of the "Global Village" celebrate values of togetherness, the disparity in wealth between the world's upper income brackets and the 90 percent of people in the poor countries represents a polarisation far more extreme than existed in the 19th century. Use of the word "village"—intended to suggest relative equality, belonging and harmony—obscures a reality of high-tech islands of privilege and wealth towering above oceans of impoverished humanity struggling to survive. The global monoculture is a dealer in illusions—while it destroys traditions, local economies and sustainable ways of living, it can never provide the majority with the glittering, wealthy lifestyle it promised them. For what it destroys, it provides no replacement but a fractured, isolated, competitive and unhappy society.

References

1. Quoted, John Bodley, *Victims of Progress*, Mayfield Publishing, 1982, pp. 111–112.

2. Ibid., p.112.

3. Ibid., p.129.

4. Ibid., p.11.

5. N. Hildyard, *Briefing 11—Blood and Culture: Ethnic Conflict and the Authoritarian Right*, The Cornerhouse, 1999.

6. M. Chossudovsky, *Dismantling Yugoslavia, Colonising Bosnia*, Ottawa, 1996, p. 1.

UNDERSTANDING THE TEXT

1. Norberg-Hodge describes some of the effects of colonialism on local cultures throughout the world. What lessons does she see in these examples of the impact of colonialism? What are the differences between the destruction of local cultures as a result of globalization and the destruction caused by colonizing in previous eras? Why is this difference important, according to Norberg-Hodge?

2. Why, according to Norberg-Hodge, do people in developing regions of the world often reject their local cultures and ethnic backgrounds? What might this rejection suggest about the power of consumer culture?

3. What are the most obvious characteristics of Western consumer culture, as Norberg-Hodge sees it? Do you think her description of Western culture is fair and/or accurate? Why or why not?

4. How does monoculture lead to division and conflict, according to Norberg-Hodge? Do you think her analysis of this process is correct? Why or why not?

EXPLORING THE ISSUES

1. One way to read this essay is as an argument against globalization. To support her argument, Norberg-Hodge cites various kinds of evidence, including examples of situations in which local cultures were affected by Western nations; she also quotes from experts and draws on her own experiences working in Ladakh. Examine the way Norberg-Hodge supports her argument with such evidence. How effectively do you think she supports her claims? What do you think her use of evidence suggests about her assumptions about her readers?

2. Norberg-Hodge describes globalization and consumerism in negative terms, often using figures of speech

and colorful phrases to do so. In paragraph 12, she describes the movement of consumerism into less industrialized parts of the world as "an avalanche"; in paragraph 3, she refers to the spread of consumerism as a "bandwagon." Examine Norberg-Hodge's use of figurative language in this essay. What ideas or impressions do you think she conveys through the language she uses to describe globalization? How effective do you think her use of language in this essay is?

3. Early in her essay, Norberg-Hodge writes "we are told" that the world is being united in a global consumer culture. Who is the "we" she refers to here? Is this "we" the same as the "myth makers" that she refers to in her final paragraph? Examine how Norberg-Hodge represents those whom she might consider to be supporters of globalization. Do you think she represents such people fairly? Explain, citing specific passages to support your answer.

4. One of Norberg-Hodge's chief complaints against globalization is that consumer culture reflects certain values that many local cultures do not share. She rejects the idea that a Western-style consumer culture is good for all people, and she describes some of the benefits of non-Western cultures, such as Ladakh. Based on your reading of this essay, what values regarding lifestyle and community do you think Norberg-Hodge holds? Do you think most Western readers share these values?

ENTERING THE CONVERSATIONS

1. Write an essay in which you respond to Norberg-Hodge's essay. Focus your response on her view of Western consumer culture and explain why you agree or disagree with her concerns about consumerism.

INFOTRAC

2. Norberg-Hodge refers to *globalization* without explicitly defining what it is. Although you can get a sense of how she defines globalization, it is also true that the term refers to a complicated set of developments and that different people may have different definitions of it. Using InfoTrac College Edition, your library, and other appropriate resources, investigate the idea of globalization. Find out how it tends to be defined, and try to determine how different interest groups (for example, environmental groups, free trade organizations) tend to define and use the term. Visit the web sites of such groups to get a sense of their view of globalization. Write a report on the basis of your research. Discuss the different ways globalization is defined and describe the different views of it you found. Offer your own definition of the term.

3. Write an essay in which you describe what you see as the benefits and/or drawbacks of a modern consumer-oriented lifestyle. Then, in a group of classmates, share your essays. Identify the main benefits and drawbacks that members of your group believe a modern consumer lifestyle has. Draw conclusions about the values that you and your classmates seem to have regarding lifestyle, and discuss the extent to which these values are influenced by consumer culture. Alternatively, create a web page intended to educate people about the impact of a modern consumer lifestyle.

4. Collect several television, print, or Internet advertisements that you believe convey important ideas about modern consumer culture. Analyze the advertisements you collect to identify the ideas they convey about being a consumer. Create a PowerPoint presentation, a web site, or some other appropriate document in which you present the results of your analysis.

In 2004, a film called Super Size Me was released. The film documented the experiences of Morgan Spurlock, who decided to see how a diet of fast food might affect his weight and health. He spent a month traveling around the United States, interviewing nutrition experts about the problem of obesity and eating only in fast-food restaurants. Spurlock's experiment resulted in his gaining twenty-five pounds and receiving a warning from his doctors that he should

Fat AND Politics: Suing *Fast Food* Companies

abandon the diet because it was causing serious health problems.

Interestingly, Spurlock conceived the idea for his film after he heard a news report about two women who sued McDonald's Corporation, claiming that McDonald's food caused their weight problems. They lost the lawsuit, but writer Michael Stephens would probably support their decision to sue. In the following essay, Stephens argues that lawsuits may be the best way to force fast-food corporations to address what he believes is their role in the unhealthy American diet. But as he shows in this essay, the issue is a much more complicated matter than just weight gain from a poor diet. Stephens believes that the modern American diet arises from fundamental changes over the past few centuries in the way Americans get their food and the way they think about food. You may disagree with him about the usefulness of suing companies like McDonald's, but his essay raises important questions about the relationship among food, culture, and politics.   (continued)

MICHAEL STEPHENS

Anti-tobacco lawyer John Banzhaf is presently building more solid test cases against food corporations for knowingly selling products that are injurious to consumers' health. Banzhaf will send a letter to McDonald's, Wendy's, Burger King, Pizza Hut, Taco Bell and Kentucky Fried Chicken this month, demanding that they label their food as containing substances that may be as addictive as nicotine.

At the same time, there is talk of imposing a "fat tax" and/or forcing manufacturers to put health warnings on certain foods, similar to the warnings on tobacco products. McDonalds is apparently feeling the pressure. They have recently issued a request to their meat suppliers to reduce the quantity of antibiotics in their meat, perhaps a pre-emptive measure, intended to demonstrate concern about the health impact of their products in case of future lawsuits.

MICHAEL STEPHENS, "FAT AND POLITICS: SUING FAST FOOD COMPANIES." FROM *POPMATTERS* (JULY 2, 2003). HTTP://WWW.POPMATTERS.COM/ REPRINTED BY PERMISSION.

(continued) *Michael Stephens is an editor of* Popmatters.com, *an online magazine about culture and politics, in which this essay first appeared in 2003.* ▼

CONTEXT: SUING CORPORATIONS
In these opening paragraphs, Stephens describes an atmosphere in which large fast-food corporations like McDonald's and Burger King have made adjustments to their products in response to lawsuits or the fear of lawsuits. Since this essay was published in 2003, however, the federal government has moved to make it harder for citizens to sue large corporations. During the 2004 U.S. presidential election, incumbent President George W. Bush campaigned against what he called "frivolous lawsuits" against corporations, arguing that lawsuits increase prices and ultimately hurt consumers. After the election, he urged Congress to pass legislation that would restrict the kind of lawsuits that Stephens refers to in this essay. In addition, some states have adopted similar legislation. For example, in 2004, the Missouri state legislature passed a bill called the "Common Sense Consumption Act," which would prevent people from suing fast-food restaurants for obesity-related health problems. Consider how these recent developments might affect the way you read Stephens's essay.

Many issues are bundled in the politics of fat: government responsibility versus individual responsibility; free enterprise versus government regulation; industrial profit versus public health. A fair debate is made more difficult because the media, influenced by the enormous revenue from fast food corporations, typically treat the issue in a derisory fashion: It's all about greedy lawyers, a sue-happy culture and irresponsible consumers. Yet there is more to the fat issue than is suggested by these pre-digested media reductions.

Because it affects people on so many levels, fat is moving to the center-stage of American politics. First there is the issue of health. 36% of Americans are overweight and about two thirds of these are obese. Obesity greatly increases the individual's risk of developing diabetes, heart disease, cancer, and other chronic diseases. Diet is so important to health that 80% of heart disease and cancer could be eliminated by simple changes in our eating habits, such as reducing meat consumption and increasing fresh fruit and vegetable consumption. Yet, despite these known facts, in 1996 only 22.7% of American adults ate the recommended five servings a day of fruit and vegetables.

5   The economic consequences of fat in the American diet are equally dramatic. The medical costs of obesity were conservatively estimated at $51.6 billion in 1994. By now this figure would at least have doubled. More recent studies show that obesity is associated with higher costs for chronic health problems than either smoking or drinking. Only aging is associated with higher medical costs. Heart disease, the number one killer in America, is closely linked to diet, and cost over $300 billion in medical care in 2002. The medical cost of diabetes, also directly linked to obesity, rose from $44 billion in 1997 to $91.8 billion in 2002. These figures do not include the hundreds of billions lost in American productivity every year to fat-related health problems.

But food preferences are so personal and so emotionally charged that they are highly resistant to rational arguments about change. Dietary choices are developed from early childhood through cultural, regional, ethnic, familial and commercial influences. To challenge these habits is, in many ways, to challenge our very identity. Hot dogs and mustard at baseball games, turkey and gravy at Thanksgiving, hamburgers and steaks on the grill in summertime: Our national foods and the cultural contexts in which they are eaten are indivisible.

Indeed, they are more than just "choices"—they are a part of the American identity. Shrimp and grits and collard greens and fatback are distinct, traditional elements in southern African American culture. Individual variations on recipes and cooking styles are still passed down through families and are important to our familial and personal history. We are what we eat on so many interwoven levels that woe betide the politician who wants to regulate the contents of our refrigerators.

Yet the balance of influences on our dietary choices has changed dramatically over the last two centuries. Two hundred years ago,

STRATEGIES: FACTS AND FIGURES

In paragraphs 4 and 5 and elsewhere in this essay, Stephens includes many statistics and related information to describe the health crisis related to obesity and to support his own view of that crisis. Because such factual information is generally considered important in modern society, these statistics can be an effective way for a writer to make and support a point. You might think about how these statistics affect the way you read this passage. It's worth noting that if you were writing a research paper for one of your classes, you would probably be expected to cite the sources of statistical information; however, in popular newspapers and magazines, sources are not always identified. In this and the following paragraph, for example, Stephens includes figures without citing the sources of those figures. You might consider why sources are often unidentified in newspapers and magazines, yet citations are required in most academic writing. What difference do you think it would have made if Stephens had cited his sources?

people tended to stay in one small region for most of their lives and had little or no access to the world outside. The influences on their diet were predominantly regional and familial. They ate the foods that were home grown, hand reared, or caught in their locale. Fresh meat, seafood, vegetables and fruits could not be transported thousands of miles in a few hours, so people tended only to eat locally grown, seasonal produce and locally butchered meat. All the crops, vegetables and fruits were organic, because chemical fertilizers and pesticides had not been invented. All the eggs and chickens were "free range," and growth hormones, antibiotics and steroids were not fed to livestock, so all meat and dairy produced was chemical free. Supermarkets, mass media, and industrial food production techniques did not exist. Even eating in restaurants was a rare experience for most, since the majority population lived in rural areas and the few restaurants that existed were in cities.

In the 20th century, however, the forces that influenced the 18th and 19th century American diet were radically transformed by industry, corporate franchising, and the media. The invention of the automobile, the development of superhighways and urbanization helped to spread fast food franchises, supermarkets, and convenience foods. Regional, cultural, ethnic and familial influences on diet faded as all regional and ethnic preferences were homogenized by the universal presence of fast food franchises. Modern children's food preferences are more powerfully influenced by television advertising than by familial or regional influences. Moreover, modern parents, who were raised on television, supermarket shopping, and convenience foods pass on to their children the food preferences that they developed under these commercial influences. Eating cereal for breakfast, for example, is a manufactured food tradition created by industry and the media.

CONVERSATIONS: FAST FOOD, HEALTH, AND LEGAL RIGHTS

Stephens argues that the presence of trans fat in fast foods and convenience foods is a serious health risk, a claim that some recent medical studies have supported. In making this claim, Stephens is joining an ongoing conversation about health and food consumption that involves not just nutrition science and medicine but also popular culture. Books about diet and lifestyle continue to be among the best-selling books available, and health foods represent a growing segment of the food industry. But as Stephens suggests in the first sentence of paragraph 12, he is also joining a debate about the role of government in our lives. Laws are one way that government can protect citizens from abuses by powerful corporations. But the questions of whether individuals should be responsible for their own health and whether they need government to protect them from things like the dangers of fast food are complicated. By joining this debate, Stephens's essay is part of the process by which such questions are addressed in the public arena.

10   Breakfast cereals like Froot Loops, Cap'n Krunch, Cocoa Puffs, and Lucky Charms, and many other children's foods such as Oreo Cookies, Eggo Waffles, Jif Peanut Butter, frozen pizza, frozen french fries, and hundreds of breads and baked goods, contain trans fats. Trans fats, or partially hydrogenated oils, increase shelf life and are cheap, so their use is advantageous to manufacturers. However, epidemiological evidence suggests that trans fats account for about 100,000 premature deaths from cardiological disease in the United States each year. Some health care professionals consider trans fat consumption as serious a health risk as smoking, and it has been argued that eating a McDonald's Happy Meal is as damaging as smoking three cigarettes.

The opponents of lawsuits against the fast food industry argue that "everyone knows" that McDonald's and Burger King sell high-fat foods and that those who eat these foods do so by their own free choice. Yet, knowledge alone is not enough to combat the power of life-long exposure to the media and to the omnipresence of fast food franchises and convenience foods. Partially hydrogenated oils have been used in American food manufacture since the 1920s—time for several generations of Americans to incorporate trans fats into their everyday diet and to normalize the consumption of hundreds of foods containing trans fats. Precisely because food preferences are formed over time and are deeply ingrained in our lifestyle, it is difficult for people to change their dietary habits, even when it is revealed that some ingredients in these foods are unhealthy or dangerous.

What is really at stake in the politics of fat is the extent to which government should restrict corporate and media influences on the American diet. There is no choice for consumers when every street corner and highway is crowded with fast food franchises and no healthy alternatives are available. There is no possibility of informed consumer decisions, when saturation advertising entirely overwhelms the cautionary messages of doctors and health professionals.

VISUAL CONNECTIONS: CHALLENGING FOOD HABITS
Stephens's essay is one means for making an argument against fast food as a contributor to an unhealthy lifestyle. Artists and filmmakers use other media to make similar arguments. This image by Ron English and the recent film *Super Size Me* are two examples. Consider the differences in how an artist or a filmmaker might make an argument compared to a writer like Stephens.

Ron English, Phat Food Billboard

© Ron English/Popaganda

Still from *Super Size Me*

Capital Pictures

Only the food manufacturers have the resources and the media access to balance their own marketing and distribution power with cautionary labels and informational campaigns. Only economic pressure can force food manufacturers to eliminate their use of trans fats and other dangerous ingredients, especially in foods that are aggressively marketed to children.

As John Banzhaf constructs his case, instead of pursuing the unproven notion that fast foods contain addictive ingredients, he should consider the more insidious and pervasive power of the media and commerce to create unhealthy dietary preferences and to eliminate real consumer freedom of choice.

UNDERSTANDING THE TEXT

1. In paragraph 6, Stephens writes, "Our national foods and the cultural contexts in which they are eaten are indivisible." What does he mean by this statement? Why is this connection between food and culture important when it comes to health problems like obesity? What do you think that connection suggests about the politics of food consumption?

2. In paragraphs 8 and 9, Stephens reviews some of the history of food production and consumption in the United States. What are the implications of this history? What lessons does Stephens see in that history? How can that history help us better understand current health-related problems such as obesity?

3. Why isn't knowing that fast food is unhealthy enough to persuade some people, especially those with health problems, to avoid eating it, according to Stephens? Why is it so difficult for people to change their eating habits, even when they know those habits may be unhealthy? What might that situation suggest about the political and cultural aspects of food in American society?

4. What is Stephens's main reason for supporting lawsuits against fast-food companies? Do you agree with him that such lawsuits are necessary? Why or why not?

EXPLORING THE ISSUES

1. Stephens argues that consumers have no real freedom of choice in their diets because no healthy alternatives to fast foods exist. He also argues that advertising for fast foods "overwhelms the cautionary messages of doctors and health professionals" (par. 12). Therefore, either government steps in to protect consumers or consumers must file lawsuits to force companies to offer healthier alternatives. Consider what Stephens's argument suggests about the role of the government in how we distribute and consume food. What exactly should the role of government be when it comes to matters like our diet? Do you think Stephens is right that government is responsible for ensuring that citizens have healthy diets? Why or why not? If not, what can be done about the problems Stephens describes in this essay?

2. In paragraphs 8 and 9, Stephens reviews some of the history of food production and consumption in the United States. What points does he use this history to make? How effective do you think this passage is in helping him make his larger argument about fast food in the American diet?

3. Some researchers have examined class differences in the American diet, suggesting that people from lower socioeconomic groups often have less healthy diets than wealthier people; some research also suggests that poorer people tend to eat more fast food because it is so inexpensive. This research would seem to support Stephens's argument, yet he does not mention it. Do you think Stephens's argument applies to *all* Americans? Why or why not? Do you think one's income level or social class has an important influence on diet? If so, would that strengthen or weaken Stephens's argument? Explain.

ENTERING THE CONVERSATIONS

1. Write an essay in which you offer your own view about the American diet. In your essay, draw on Stephens's essay, your own experiences, and any other appropriate readings from this book to support or explain your position.

2. Stephens claims that the media are largely to blame for the food choices available to Americans and for Americans' eating habits. Test his claim by analyzing a number of television, print, Internet, or other advertisements about food. Try to select ads for popular food products or fast-food restaurants, and examine these ads for the ideas about food and health that they convey. Then write a report on what you found. In your report, describe the ads you selected and explain why you selected them. Discuss what you learned about the messages they convey about food and diet. Draw conclusions about whether or not you think your analysis supports Stephens's claims.

3. Create a web site, PowerPoint presentation, pamphlet, or some other appropriate document intended to educate consumers about the influence of the media on their eating habits. (You might use your analysis for Question 2 as a basis for your document.)

4. Write a letter to the editor of your local newspaper or another appropriate publication in which you express your views about the use of lawsuits to force fast-food companies to offer healthier food choices to consumers.

5. For one week, record everything you eat. Then determine how much of your diet includes fast food or popular processed foods that are widely advertised on television or other media. Then, drawing on this experience, write a brief essay in which you respond to Stephens's argument about fast food.

6. Visit your library or a local bookstore to find some recent bestselling books on diet, such as books describing the Atkins diet or the South Beach diet. Select one or more such diets and examine what they seem to suggest about the American diet and about American attitudes toward food. Write an essay in which you discuss these diets and the messages they send about food and diet.

Not long ago, I moved from a city where my water came from a city-operated water supply system to a rural area where my water comes from a well on my property. I learned how much I took water for granted. Previously, I didn't worry much about the quality of my water or about whether my water supply was trustworthy. I just paid my water bill every month, and the water flowed whenever I turned on a faucet in my home. But having a well means that I need to have

Privatising Water Will Lead TO War

my water tested for safety, keep the well system in good working order, and avoid wasting water. I also learned that the town and state I live in have many laws and regulations to protect water. There are restrictions regarding how close to a stream or lake you can put a building. I never thought much about this before, but now I have become aware of how political water can be.

The following essay by internationally known women's rights and environmental activist Vandana Shiva (b. 1952) can teach us even more about the politics of water. Shiva's focus is on the growing worldwide trend to privatize water supplies. In recent years, private companies have been buying, building, or operating what were once public water systems, and in some cases, companies have purchased lakes and other major sources of water. As Shiva points out, there are profound consequences to this privatization of water. She worries that the people who will be most affected by privatization are the poor and those with the least political power. She makes her vigorous argument against privatization with those people in mind and with the health of the earth as a whole in mind as well. Whether you agree with her argument or not, her essay may get you thinking differently about water as a political issue.   (continued)

VANDANA SHIVA

The **right to water is common to all beings and is a gift of** creation; it is a natural right, a birthright. Common rights go hand in hand with common responsibility: a common responsibility to conserve water, use it sustainably, and share it equitably. The culture of conservation of these "common" rights has supported human life and all life on Earth for millennia.

Poorly conceived "development," which increased commerce but decreased life's renewable potential and created huge social and environmental devastation, has left us with polluted rivers, depleted groundwater, desertified soils and thirsty people. The solution being offered to the water scarcity created by non-sustainable development is privatisation, or private-public partnerships. Unfortunately, privatisation leads to an acceleration in the non-sustainable use of water and a deepening of the hydrological divide, with corporations owning and controlling water. This will lead to those with wealth buying more than their fair share, and those without purchasing power being denied their water rights, and hence their right to life. Privatisation of water is the ultimate human rights violation, the ultimate human wrong.

VANDANA SHIVA, "CAPTIVE WATER: PRIVATISING WATER WILL LEAD TO WAR." FROM *RESURGENCE* ISSUE 219 (JULY/AUGUST 2003). REPRINTED BY PERMISSION FROM *RESURGENCE* MAGAZINE, A JOURNAL OF ECOLOGY, SPIRITUALITY AND THE ARTS. WWW.RESURGENCE.ORG.

(continued) A physicist by training, Vandana Shiva founded the Research Foundation for Science, Ecology, and Technology, which supports biodiversity and advocates the protection of indigenous foods and local cultures. She is also director of Bija Vidyapeeth, the International College for Sustainable Living, in India. The following essay was first published in Resurgence *magazine in 2003.* ◪

In India, the Shivnath river in the Chattisgarh region has already been privatised and sold to the RWL company, which uses police force to prevent local communities from accessing the river. The villages of Rasmara, Mohlai, Siloda, Mahmara and Peepal Chhedi have lost their rights to fish, bathe and wash in the river. Wells within a radius of one kilometre from the river have been forcibly shut down by the company.

Even the Sacred Ganges is not safe from privatisation. Suez, the world's largest water corporation, is setting up a plant in Delhi at Sonia Vihar to sell Ganges water to the rich people of Delhi. Ondeo Degremont, a subsidiary of Suez Lyonnaise des Eaux, has been awarded a two-billion rupee contract for the design, building and operation of a plant to produce 635 million litres of drinking water a day.

5   A common response is that this water-production plant in Delhi does not imply privatising the Ganga. However, in order for water to be diverted from the Ganga to the Yamuna basin to be sold by Suez, the traditional rights and access to drinking water and irrigation for local communities in the Ganga basin are denied. Urban areas get increased commercial supplies by denying rural areas access to their needs for sustenance.

The water for the Suez-Degremont plant in Delhi will come from the Tehri dam through the Upper Ganga Canal and then through a giant pipeline to Delhi. The Upper Ganga Canal, which starts at Haridwar and carries the holy water of Ganga, is the main source of irrigation for this region.

The Ganges is not just a giver of peace after death: she is a source of prosperity in life. The Gangetic plain is one of the most fertile regions of the world. At the beginning of the ploughing season in Bihar, prior to planting their seeds, farmers put Ganges water in a pot and set it aside in a special place in the field to ensure a good harvest.

The Ganges waters, the lifeline of northern India and India's food security, are being handed over to Suez to quench the thirst of Delhi's elite even as a hundred thousand people are being forceably and violently removed from their homes in Tehri for the

VISUAL CONNECTIONS: BATHING IN THE GANGES
This photograph accompanied Shiva's essay when it was first published. What messages do you think it conveys about water and our relationship to it?

© Bruno Barbey/Magnum Photos

Tehri dam. Tehri, the capital of the ancient kingdom of Garhwal on the banks of the Ganga in the Himalayas, is in the process of being submerged.

The Tehri dam project is located in the outer Himalaya in the Tehri-Garhwal district of Uttaranchal. It is planned to be the fifth highest dam in the world—260.5 meters high and spread over an area of forty-five square kilometers. The dam will submerge 4,200 hectares of the most fertile flat land in the Bhagirathi and Bhilangana valleys without really benefiting the region in any way.

The huge Tehri dam is located in a seismic fault zone. This area is earthquake-prone. Between 1816 and 1991, the Garhwal region has witnessed seventeen earthquakes, the most recent ones being the Uttarkashi earthquake of October 1991 and the Chamoli earthquake of 1998. The International Commission on Large Dams has declared the site "extremely hazardous."

In the event of this dam collapsing due to an earthquake or any other fault, the devastation would be unimaginable. This huge reservoir built at such a height would be emptied in twenty-two minutes. Within sixty minutes Rishikesh would be under 260 metres of water. Soon after, Haridwar would be totally submerged. Bijnor, Meerut, Hapur and Bulandshahar would be under water within twelve hours. Thus the dam is potentially dangerous for large parts of northwestern India, and large areas in the Gangetic plains would be devastated in the event of such a mishap. It is also estimated that the life of the dam would not be more than thirty years because of heavy sedimentation.

Privatisation of water is justified on the ground that full costs must be paid when water giants eventually get their water markets. However, as the case of the Suez plant in Delhi shows, the corporations get the water for free without paying for the full social and environmental costs to those rural communities from whom the water is taken.

India has got into huge debt for the loans taken from the World Bank for the Ganga Canal. At the same time, the giant pipeline is being built through public finances. In effect the public pays the price while transnational companies make the profit.

In August, 2002, more than 5,000 farmers gathered to protest the laying of the giant pipeline to supply the water from the river Ganga to the Sonia Vihar Water Plant for Delhi. The rally was launched from Haridwar—one of the oldest and holiest cities of India built on the banks of Ganga—where the farmers, together with priests, citizens and worshippers of Ganga, announced that "Ganga is not for Sale," and vowed to defend the freedom of this holy river. The sacred waters of the Ganga cannot be the property of any one individual or a company.

In March this year, Ganga Yatra undertook a journey from Tehri to Delhi. With us on the march were Sunderlal Bahuguna, who has been sitting at the Tehri dam site as a witness to both the destruction and the perennial spiritual values related to the Ganga; Oscar Oliviera of Bolivia, who with fellow citizens drove out **Bechtel** and regained social control over Cochabamba's water; and Magasasay award winner

---

CONTEXT: GEOGRAPHY

In paragraphs 3–5, Shiva discusses several rivers in India. Most readers outside India would probably recognize the Ganges River, which is considered a sacred river by Hindus, who make up a large proportion of India's population, and which is one of the best-known rivers in the world. But the other rivers mentioned here are very likely unfamiliar to most readers who are not from that region. Consider whether you think readers need to be familiar with the geography of the region Shiva is describing to understand and appreciate her point. Also, what might her references to these Indian rivers, villages, and cities suggest about her sense of her audience?

GLOSS: BECHTEL

The Bechtel Corporation is one of the world's largest companies. It is best known as a construction company that builds large and complex structures, such as dams and nuclear power plants.

Rajender Singh of Tarun Bharat Sangh. People from all over the world are making known their opposition to water privatisation.

Sadly, more than a hundred women have committed suicide as a result of water scarcity in the Tehri region over the last few years. Women who came from 250 villages to meet us say that their sacred mother, the river Ganga, has been reduced to receiving them in death and no longer gives them life. Women are still sitting in protest in the ruins of the ancient city of Tehri, refusing to give up their struggle. They say they will commit collective suicide if forced to move.

Throughout 2003, the Year of Fresh Water, a Jal Yatra—water journey—is being undertaken across India to recover waters and rivers as commons, to conserve water by shifting to water-prudent crops and farming methods, and to resist privatisation.

Among the mega-projects we have to address is the proposal to link all of India's rivers through super-dams and super-canals at a cost of $200 billion, which is 200 times what India spends on education, three times what the government collects in taxes, twenty-five per cent of our GDP, and U.S. $72 billion more than India's total external debt. This mega-project offers new opportunities for privatisation, but creates heavy costs for our rivers and our people. More than five million people will be displaced; our living rivers will be killed. Ecosystems, people and communities will be deprived of water as it is imprisoned by giant dams and giant canals of cement. Free-flowing rivers supporting life will be transformed into captive waters. Free people with free access to their bathing ghats, their wells, their tanks and ponds will become bonded to giant water companies and water bureaucracies. This is a nightmare of slavery and a recipe for extinction of species and cultures.

CONVERSATIONS: MOVEMENTS AND NATIONS

Shiva, an internationally known activist for human rights, has been especially active in advocating for people in developing nations like her native India whom she believes are exploited by large Western corporations and governments. When she refers to "our movement" in this paragraph, she identifies herself with certain groups of people, and she openly opposes those from Western nations who she believes do not share the values she describes in this paragraph. In some ways, Shiva's essay is part of a worldwide conversation that has intensified in recent years as globalization has accelerated (see Helena Norberg-Hodge's essay beginning on page 599 for a discussion of globalization). This complicated set of conversations has to do in part with how we use resources and who decides. It's worth thinking about how widely the values that Shiva describes in this paragraph might be shared by people in countries outside her native India.

Our movement to protect water and defend the water freedom and water rights of all people and all species is called Jal Swaraj Abhiyan—the Water Democracy, Water Sovereignty movement. It is part of our movement for Earth Democracy, Living Democracy. It is a movement in the defence of life, of the integrity and sanctity of the rivers of our cultures, and of our capacities to be conservers and custodians of our precious common water heritage. For us, water democracy is necessary for peace because centralised, commodified systems are creating water wars. We want to create water peace: peace with the Earth and all her species, and peace between all peoples.

UNDERSTANDING THE TEXT

1. Why does Shiva believe that the privatization of water is "the ultimate human rights violation, the ultimate wrong"? Do you agree with her? Why or why not?

2. What concerns does Shiva have about the Tehri Dam? How are those concerns related to her larger argument against the privatization of water?

3. In what ways have people resisted the privatization of water? What significance does Shiva see in these examples of resistance? What might her discussion of these examples suggest about her own values?

EXPLORING THE ISSUES

1. How would you describe the tone of this essay? What features of the writing help create this tone? Do you think Shiva's tone strengthens or weakens this essay? Explain, citing specific passages to support your answer.

2. One way to read Shiva's essay is as an argument against the privatization of water or an argument in favor of preserving water rights for all people. But in several respects, Shiva's essay is not a conventional argument—at least not according to the conventions of academic writing in Western culture. Examine how Shiva constructs her argument. How does she organize it? How does she move from one main point to the next? What kinds of evidence does she offer to support her argument?

How might her way of making her argument differ from the way you have been taught to write an argument? How persuasive do you find her argument? What might your answer to that question suggest about your expectations as a reader?

3. Throughout her essay, Shiva refers specifically to corporations, governments, and residents of particular regions. What do you think her descriptions of or references to these various groups suggest about her own political views?

ENTERING THE CONVERSATIONS

1. In her opening paragraph, Shiva writes, "Common rights go hand in hand with common responsibility: a common responsibility to conserve water, use it sustainably, and share it equitably." Write an essay in which you discuss this statement and offer your own views about the matter of "common rights."

INFOTRAC

2. Shiva mentions many different situations in India in which there is conflict about water rights. But conflict over water rights is occurring throughout the world. Using InfoTrac College Edition, your library, the Internet, and other relevant resources, investigate such conflicts. If possible, focus your investigation on a conflict or controversy involving water in the region where you live. Try to identify the issues involved and the positions taken by those in-

volved in the conflicts. Also try to get a sense of how widespread or common such conflicts are and where in the world they tend to be happening. Then write a report on the basis of your research. In your report, draw conclusions about the politics of water—and of other important resources.

3. On the basis of your research for Question 2, write a letter to the editor of your local newspaper or some other appropriate publication in which you express your views about conflicts over water rights, either in the region where you live or elsewhere.

4. Write an essay in which you discuss what you believe are good reasons for privatizing water.

5. Shiva refers to a number of water-related projects in her native India to illustrate her concerns about the trend to privatize water supplies. But this trend is not limited to India. Using InfoTrac College Edition, your library, and other relevant resources, investigate this trend. Find out why water supplies and systems are being privatized. What are the pros and cons of this trend? Who benefits and who is disadvantaged by it? What impact has it had? What steps have been taken to oppose it? Try to answer these questions in your research. Then write a report about what you learned. Draw your own conclusions about whether privatizing water is a good idea or not.

USE AND CONSEQUENCES

IF YOU ARE AT ALL CONSCIOUS OF YOUR HEALTH, YOU PROBABLY PAY ATTENTION TO WHAT YOU EAT. SO WHEN YOU GO TO THE SUPERMARKET, YOU'RE LIKELY TO BUY FRESH FRUITS AND VEGETABLES. YOU MIGHT CHOOSE CHICKEN INSTEAD OF BEEF. AND MAYBE YOU BUY A LOAF of whole wheat bread instead of white. Today, most supermarkets in the United States offer all these foods and more all year round. There really isn't any season for fresh foods any longer. In the past, you couldn't buy, say, peaches in February because February is not part of the growing season for peaches in the United States. But these days, you can buy peaches any time of year. In the summer, those peaches were probably grown in Georgia or Maryland; if you buy peaches in February, they probably came from Chile or Brazil. The same is true of grapes, plums, and many other kinds of fruits and vegetables. And of course, in addition to these common foods, supermarkets often sell many different specialty foods from all over the world.

At first glance, the availability of these foods seems like a good thing. It means that you have a lot of choices when you shop and that you can buy a variety of fresh, healthy foods all year long. But there are costs to this convenience. For one thing, most of the food Americans buy is grown far from where they live, which means that it must be transported over long distances. Typically, foods grown in the United States are trucked from where they are produced to where they are consumed; those trucks not only consume gas or diesel fuel, but they also contribute to air pollution and greenhouse gases. Foods grown outside the United States may be flown from farm to market, which uses enormous amounts of fuel and also contributes to pollution. Even if foods are transported by ship, the process contributes to the degradation of sea and coastal ecosystems.

Of course, foods must also be stored, and many foods have to be kept cool. Storage, especially cold storage, uses electricity, which adds to the destruction of the environment because most electricity is generated by coal- or oil-fired plants, which causes air pollution. The packaging used for even the freshest food is often made of plastic, which is

manufactured from oil that must be pumped from underground oil wells and transported to manufacturing plants; packaging made of cardboard may be manufactured from recycled materials, but much of it is made from trees. And many foods, especially fresh produce, must be picked by hand, often by poorly paid migrant workers whose working conditions are often bad.

Had enough? All this—and more—goes into your simple choice to buy a peach or a bunch of grapes at your local market. And I haven't even begun to discuss clothing, or the energy you use to keep your home or apartment or dorm room lit and warm, or the impact of the car you drive or the bus you ride.

The point is that everything you consume, every resource you use to stay alive and healthy, has social, economic, and environmental consequences. Living your life in a typical American way causes environmental harm and may do social and economic harm as well—usually to people and places far from where you live. When you buy a shirt or a bunch of grapes, or when you drive your car to school or work, you are part of the problem.

The readings in this cluster explore some of the consequences of our uses of resources. They examine some hidden costs of common foods like corn or of leisure activities like skiing. They help us see that the choices we make every day affect people and the environment throughout the world. And perhaps they will help us be more mindful of the impact we each have on the earth. These readings also illustrate how writing about these issues can contribute to our collective efforts to reduce our impact and live together more responsibly.

When I first read this essay, I couldn't help *remembering long, lazy summers I spent as a boy. Those summers always included picnics and cookouts, and there was always watermelon on the picnic table. I suspect writer David Margolick (b. 1958) would be pleased that his essay evoked such memories in one of his readers because, in many ways, his essay is about memories: memories of a past that he recalls with happiness. It is also about change: the progress that is repre-*

THE Seeds OF A *Summer* Revolt

sented by new kinds of food products, such as the seedless watermelon. You might think that someone like Margolick would have better things to do than complain about seedless watermelons. But his essay is really about the consequences of the decisions we make about seemingly trivial things like the seeds in watermelons. As Margolick argues in the following essay, the disappearance of the traditional watermelon says something about who we are as a modern people. It also says something about what we value and how we use the resources available to us. I never really thought about those little black seeds as important, but the next time I have a slice of watermelon, I think I'll remember Margolick's complaints.

David Margolick is a contributing editor at Vanity Fair. *This essay was first published in the* New York Times *in 2003.* ◪

DAVID MARGOLICK

Maybe it ran on the obituary page and I just missed it. But a notable death has apparently occurred, and has thus far gone unrecorded. The venerable watermelon—the one with seeds—has died, of entirely unnatural causes. It was at least 5,000 years old, and lived, well, fondly in our memories.

For a long time, watermelon as we have known and loved it has been an endangered species. Everywhere you look these days, whether in state-of-the-art supermarkets or those quaint "farm stands" whose fruit often comes out of the same crates from the same California conglomerates, all you see is the newfangled "seedless" variety. Where I live, only one store held out, and there I'd always go.

But the other day I learned, much to my horror, that it, too, had succumbed. On the shelf were nothing but those anemic, emaciated slices of pseudo-watermelon, with no black seeds in sight. No one wanted real watermelons anymore, the woman there told me matter-of-factly. Seeds, it seems, are inconvenient. What had already befallen oranges and grapefruit, with predictably disastrous, deflavorizing results, had spread.

STRATEGIES: INTRODUCTIONS

Notice how Margolick jumps right into his subject with his opening sentence. As a reader, you aren't sure what "it" is in this opening sentence, so you have to read more. This is one strategy writers sometimes use to draw readers into an essay. Sometimes student writers introduce their subjects with broad statements intended to provide background, but often such introductions drag and fail to draw readers into the essay. Here Margolick offers a different—and very effective—model for beginning an essay.

CONVERSATIONS: GENETICALLY MODIFIED FOODS

When Margolick writes in paragraph 7 that this essay is not another "screed" (a long monotonous speech or piece of writing) about genetically modified foods, he is joining ongoing and intense conversations in the United States and throughout the world about the use of certain food crops that have been genetically altered to grow better or to resist certain pests or diseases. As these foods have been developed, they have become increasingly controversial, in part because of concerns that they can lead to unintended consequences, including environmental damage or health problems among humans as well as livestock or wildlife. Margolick's statement here suggests that he wants his readers to know that his essay is not an argument for or against such foods. Consider how his reference to these larger conversations about genetically modified foods helps establish his focus and cues his readers on how to read his essay.

GLOSS: OMAHA STEAKS AND MACKINAW FUDGE

Omaha Steaks and Mackinaw Fudge are specialty foods available through mail order. They have gained reputations for being high quality as well as high priced. What messages might Margolick's references to these food items convey about food and about his own views of food?

And spread not to just any old fruit. Watermelon, at least as nature meant it to be, is one of those foods like raisins or olive oil or maple syrup that is very nearly perfect as is. It is tasty, sweet, crunchy, nutritious, and fun—cotton candy without the calories or cavities—which is why it has always been a summertime staple.

5   They were harvesting them 5,000 years ago in Egypt. The word has been in English dictionaries at least since 1615.

But watermelon had seeds, and until recently that never posed a problem. Suddenly, however, we have grown impatient with them. Seeds are a nuisance. They're messy. So you do away with them, and if the essence goes with it, who will care? Or even notice?

This is not yet another screed about genetically engineered food, but a matter of aesthetics. The new watermelons taste tasteless. They lack the texture and tang of the real thing. Even the crystallized inner core, whose whitened chunks break off so deliciously, is only a simulacrum. These newfangled strains have but one advantage: they can be consumed more quickly and easily.

It is also a matter of tradition, and history. What is summer without spitting out watermelon seeds, either on a plate, or on the ground—by August, some of them would inevitably sprout, even those spat out on sand—or at your brother, or an inch farther than anyone else? Or chewing on, or swallowing a few, by mistake, and worrying whether they'd take root in your stomach? The wimpy white seeds they've not yet managed to eliminate entirely—give them a few more years, and they surely will—have no throw weight at all.

Americans love not only to eat a lot, but to eat easily. And prettily. They would rather buy something that looks perfect than tastes perfect. Someday soon, I suppose, there will be apples without cores and peaches without pits. Eat up the old kind while the going's good.

10   Conventional watermelon will not disappear entirely, of course. A few farmers will still grow them, catering to the carriage trade. You will still be able to find them abroad. Perhaps Restoration Hardware will carry them, alongside the likes of Ovaltine and Ipana toothpaste. Or they will be featured in those tiny advertisements in the backs of glossy magazines, like **Omaha steaks or Mackinaw fudge,** available for overnight delivery.

But who among us will be able to afford the postage?

UNDERSTANDING THE TEXT

1. What makes the watermelon such a distinctive food, in Margolick's view? What might Margolick's views about the watermelon suggest about our attitudes toward food? What might his views suggest about the connection between food and culture?

2. What are Margolick's complaints about the seedless watermelons? Do you think his complaints are valid? Why or why not?

3. In what sense is the watermelon a matter of tradition and history, according to Margolick? Do you think most Americans share this view? Do you share it? Explain.

EXPLORING THE ISSUES

1. Margolick asserts that his concern about the disappearance of the traditional watermelon is "a matter of aesthetics" (par. 7). What does he mean by that statement? What do aesthetics have to do with food? What might Margolick's statement suggest about his attitudes regarding food and his values for lifestyle? Do you agree with him? Why or why not?

2. Margolick ends his essay with a question. What idea or point do you think he is trying to convey with this conclusion? How effective do you think this conclusion is?

3. How would you describe the tone of this essay? What features of the writing help create its tone? To what extent do you think the tone contributes to Margolick's main point in this essay? Cite specific passages to support your answer.

4. Margolick's essay is nostalgic, and he shares some of his memories involving watermelons. What ideas do his memories convey about food? What does his nostalgia reveal about his own values regarding lifestyle? What do they reveal about him as a person?

ENTERING THE CONVERSATIONS

1. Write an essay about a food that has special significance for you or your family, as the watermelon seems to have for Margolick.

2. In a group of classmates, share the essays you wrote for Question 1. As a group, discuss this question: What do these essays reveal about the role of food in American culture—or any culture?

3. Write an essay in support of the seedless watermelon. Draw on Margolick's essay, if appropriate.

 INFOTRAC

4. In paragraph 7, Margolick refers to genetically modified foods, a topic that has become increasingly controversial in recent years. Many individuals and advocacy groups have concerns about the possible consequences of the growing use of genetically modified foods, and some groups have launched campaigns to oppose these foods. In some cases, people are concerned that crops, such as corn or certain fruits, that are genetically modified to resist certain pests or diseases may create "super-species" of other plants that will damage local ecosystems. Proponents of genetically modified foods sometimes argue that such crops reduce the need for farmers to use pesticides and herbicides, thereby helping protect the environment. Using InfoTrac College Edition, the Internet, your library, and other appropriate resources, investigate the issue of genetically modified foods. Find out what kinds of foods have been genetically modified and why. Examine the possible consequences of such modifications. Try to find out what steps have been taken by companies or governments to address the concerns about these foods. Get a sense of the arguments on all sides of the issue. Then write a report about what you learned. In your report, explain what genetically modified foods are and how they are used and discuss the concerns about them. Draw conclusions about whether the use of these foods is a good idea and discuss what you think they suggest about our use of resources in general.

5. On the basis of your research for Question 4, write a letter to your state or federal representative (such as your senator) or to the secretary of agriculture in your state in which you express your views about genetically modified foods and offer your suggestions about what steps the government should take to address your concerns.

6. Select an important or distinctive food and create a web site, PowerPoint presentation, or another appropriate kind of document in which you present your perspective on the importance of this food in your culture or community.

The other readings in this cluster all have something to do with the environmental or social consequences of our uses of various resources, such as food or the land. This essay is different, and included it in this cluster because I think it's important to consider the less obvious consequences of the way we use the land. In this essay, acclaimed novelist Jamaica Kincaid (b. 1949) takes a careful look at the flower garden to reveal so much more than we normally see there. In

Sowers AND Reapers: THE *Unquiet* World OF A *Flower* Bed

Kincaid's view, gardens are not the quiet, orderly, pleasant retreats that we usually assume them to be. As she once said in an interview, "Everything has all sorts of sides. . . . The garden has a peculiar side to it, a qualifying side. For instance, most of the nations that have serious gardening cultures also have, or had, empires. You can't have this luxury of pleasure without somebody paying for it." In focusing her gaze so closely on something so common, Kincaid teaches us how to see consequences, both large and small, in how we use the land around us. She finds meaning in gardens that may be hidden from our view, and that meaning is not always pleasant or uplifting. For Kincaid, that's as it should be. As she said in the same interview, "We enjoy things far too much, and it leads to incredible pain and suffering." Much of her writing is devoted to exposing that pain and suffering, as this provocative essay demonstrates.

Kincaid is the author of several critically acclaimed novels, including Lucy *(1990) and* Mr. Potter *(2002), as* (continued)

JAMAICA KINCAID

Why must people insist that the garden is a place of rest and repose, a place to forget the cares of the world, a place in which to distance yourself from the painful responsibility that comes with being a human being?

The day after I spoke to a group of people at the **Garden Conservancy's** tenth-anniversary celebration, in Charleston, South Carolina, an American man named Frank Cabot, the chairman and founder of the organization and a very rich man, who has spent some of his money creating a spectacular garden in the surprisingly hospitable climate of eastern Canada, told me that he was sorry I had been invited, that he was utterly offended by what I had said and the occasion I had used to say it, for I had done something unforgivable— I had introduced race and politics into the garden.

(continued) *well as works of nonfiction, including* My Brother *(1997), about her brother's losing battle with AIDS, and several books about gardening. She also wrote for* The New Yorker, *in which the following essay first appeared in 2001.* ◪

GLOSS: THE GARDEN CONSERVANCY
Founded in 1989, the Garden Conservancy (par. 2) is a nonprofit organization dedicated to the preservation of famous gardens throughout the United States.

There were three of us on a panel, and our topic was "My Favorite Garden." One of the speakers said that his favorite was Hidcote Manor, in England, created by an American Anglophile named Lawrence Johnston. (A very nice climbing yellow rose, which is sometimes available through the Wayside Gardens catalogue, is named after him.) There are at least a thousand gardens in every corner of the world, but especially in England, that should come before Hidcote as a choice for favorite garden. The garden of the film-maker Derek Jarman, who succumbed to AIDS in 1994, is a particularly good example. Dramatically set in the shadow of a nuclear-power station in Dungeness, Kent, surrounding a one-story house that has been painted black, this garden, when I saw it, was abloom with poppies in brilliant shades and with Crambe maritima (sea kale) and pathways lined with pebbles, the kind found at the seashore, and all sorts of worn-down objects that looked as if they were the remains of a long-ago shipwreck just found. When you see it for the first time, it so defies what you expect that this thought really will occur to you: Now, what is a garden? And, at the same time, you will be filled with pleasure and inspiration.

Another man spoke of a garden he was designing in Chicago which would include a re-creation of a quadripartite garden made by prisoners in Auschwitz. (This way of organizing a garden is quite common, and it has a history that begins with Genesis 2:10—"A river issues from Eden to water the garden, and it then divides and becomes four branches.") The garden in Auschwitz was created over many years and by many people, all of whom were facing death, and it gave me a sharp pang to realize that, while waiting to be brutally murdered, some people had made a garden.

5   I had prepared a talk in which I was going to say that my favorite garden is the Garden of Eden, because every time I see a garden that I love it becomes my favorite garden until I see another garden that I love and completely forget the garden that so dominated my affections a short time before; and also because this garden, Eden, is described in the fewest words I have ever seen used to describe a garden, and yet how unforgettable and vivid the description remains: "And from the ground the Lord God caused to grow every tree that was pleasing to the sight and good for food, with the tree of life in the middle of the garden, and the tree of knowledge of good and bad."

But after that man spoke of the Holocaust garden, a nice speech on Eden was no longer possible.

I heard myself telling my audience that I had been surprised to see, on the way into my hotel, in the little park across the way, a statue of John Caldwell Calhoun, that inventor of the rhetoric of states' rights and the evil encoded in it, who was elected Vice-President of the United States twice. I remarked on how hard it must be for the black citizens of Charleston to pass each day by the statue of a man who hated them, cast in a heroic pose. And then I wondered if anyone in

GLOSS: QUADRIPARTITE GARDEN

As Kincaid notes in paragraph 4, the quadripartite garden is a very old form of garden in which the garden is laid out in four major quadrants. The aerial photograph of the Middleton Plantation reveals its quadripartite structure. The four quadrants in such gardens can be further divided, as in the schematic image below. Kincaid mentions that there is a reference to the quadripartite garden in the Bible. The Koran also mentions the quadripartite garden.

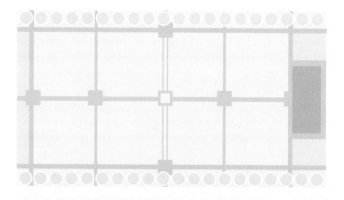

© Bob Krist/Corbis

Middleton Plantation, Charleston, SC

the audience had seen the Holocaust memorial right next to the statue of John Caldwell Calhoun: a strange cryptlike, crib-like structure, another commemoration of some of the people who were murdered by the Germans. Then I said that John Caldwell Calhoun was not altogether so far removed from Adolf Hitler; that these two men seem to be more in the same universe than not.

It was all this and more that I said that made Frank Cabot angry at me, but not long after his outburst I joined a group of attendees to the conference who were going off to tour and have dinner at Middleton Place, the famous plantation. Middleton is a popular destination for Americans who are interested in gardens, garden history, or a whiff of the sweet stench that makes up so much of American history. It is, on the one hand, a series of beautiful rooms in the garden sense: there is a part for roses only, there is a part for azaleas, there is a part for camellias, and so on and so on. The most spectacular part of the garden is a grassy terrace made by human hands, and on the slope of the terrace are small and perfectly regular risings, so that when seen from below they look like stiff pleats in a skirt that has just been disturbed by a faint breeze. At the foot of the terrace are two small lakes that have been fashioned to look like a butterfly stilled by chloroform. It is all very beautiful, even slightly awesome; and then there is the awfulness, for those gardens and that terrace and those lakes were made by slaves. The water from the river adjacent to the plantation was channelled to floor the rice fields, and this was done by slaves, who had brought their rice-cultivation skills with them from Africa. For, as far as I know, there are no rice fields in England, Scotland, Ireland, or Wales. I was feeling quite sad about all this when I came upon a big rubble of bricks. It was all that remained of the main house on the plantation in the wake of the strategy, conceived by that ingenious pyromaniac and great general from the North, William Tecumseh Sherman, which had helped to bring the traitorous South to its knees. As I walked toward a tent to have a dinner of black-eyed peas and rice, ribs and chicken and sweet potatoes, a dinner that I think of as the cuisine of black people from the American South, and where I would hear the Lester Lanin orchestra accompany a white man imitating the voice of Louis Armstrong as he sang songs made famous by Louis Armstrong, I ran into Mr. Frank Cabot, and I kept from him a fact that I happen to know: Arthur Middleton, of Middleton plantation, was one of the signers of the Declaration of Independence.

Nowhere is the relationship between the world and the garden better documented than in Thomas Jefferson's "Garden and Farm Books," and obsessively detailed account of his domestic life. People like to say that Jefferson is an enigma, that he was a man of contradictions, as if those things could not be said of just about anybody. But you have only to read anything he wrote, and you will find the true man, Thomas Jefferson, who is always so unwittingly transparent, always most revealing when confident that he has covered his tracks. He tried to write an autobiography, but he stopped before he had written a hundred pages. In it he states that he was born, that his father's name was Peter, that he wrote the Declaration of Independence, that he went to France and witnessed the French Revolution. The whole thing reads as if it were composed by one of the many marble busts of him which decorate the vestibules of government buildings. The Jefferson to be found in the autobiography is the unwittingly transparent Jefferson. The Jefferson who is confident that he has covered his tracks is to be found in the "Garden and Farm Books." The first entry in the "Garden" book is so beautiful, and so simple a statement: "1766. Shadwell. Mar. 30. Purple hyacinth begins to bloom." It goes on: "Apr. 6. Narcissus and Puckoon open. [Apr.] 13. Puckoon flowers fallen. [Apr.] 16. a bluish colored, funnel-formed flower in low-grounds in bloom." (This must have been Mertensia virginica.) The entries continue in this way for years, until 1824: the peas are sown, the asparagus planted, the fruit trees planted, the vegetables reaped. Each entry reads as if it were a single line removed from a poem: something should come before, and something should come after. And what should come before and after is to be found in the "Farm" book, and it comes in the form of a list of names: Ursula, George, Jupiter, Davy, Minerva, Caesar, and Jamy; and the Hemings, Beverly, Betty, Peter, John, and Sally. (Why is it that people who readily agree that Jefferson owned Sally Hemings cannot believe that he slept with her?) It is they who sowed the peas, dug the trenches, and filled them with manure. It is they who planted and harvested the corn. And when Jefferson makes this entry in his "Garden" book, on April 8, 1794—"our first dish of Asparagus"—it is they who have made it possible for him to enjoy asparagus. None of these names appear in the "Garden" book; the garden is free of their presence, but they turn up in the "Farm" book, and in painful, but valuable-to-know, detail. Little Beverly Hemings, Jefferson's son by Sally, must have been a very small boy the year that he was allotted one and a half yards of wool. One year, John Hemings, Sally's uncle, received, along with Sally's mother, seven yards of linen, five yards of blue wool, and a pair of shoes. On and on it goes: the garden emerging from the farm, the garden unable to exist without the farm, the garden kept apart from the farm, race and politics kept out of the garden.

But, you know, the garden Jefferson made at Monticello is not really very good. You don't see it and think, Now, there is something I would like to do. It is not beautiful in the way that the garden George Washington's slaves made at Mount Vernon is beautiful. (I owe this new appreciation of Mount Vernon to Mac Griswold and her excellent book *Washington's Gardens at Mount Vernon: Landscape of the Inner Man.*) There is hardly anything featured in the garden at Monticello that makes you want to rush home, subdue a few people, and re-create it. And the reason might be that Jefferson was less interested in the garden than in the marvellous things grown there. Each year, I order packets of something he grew, Dolichos lablab, purple hyacinth beans, something no garden should be without. What is beautiful about Monticello is the views, whether you are looking out from the house or looking at it from far away. Jefferson did not so much make a garden as a landscape. The explanation for this may be very simple: his father was a surveyor. This might also explain why he is responsible for some of the great vistas we know—the American West.

Not long after I returned from Charleston, a small amount of money that I had not expected came my way. In my ongoing conversation with my garden, I had for a very long time wanted to build a wall to add to its shape and character. So I immediately called Ron Pembroke, the maker of the most excellent landscapes in the area where I live. My house is situated on a little rise, a knoll, and I find the way it looks from many angles in the general landscape to be very pleasing, and so I had firmly in mind just the kind of wall I wanted. But Ron Pembroke, after walking me up and down and back and forth with a measuring tape in his hand, and taking me in his truck to see the other walls he had built, convinced me that my design was really quite ugly and that his was beautiful and superior.

And so began the building of two hundred-foot-long walls, one above the other, separated by a terrace eight feet wide. One day, four men arrived in the yard, and they were accompanied by big pieces of machinery, including, of course, an earth-mover. The men began to rearrange the slope that fell away from the house, and by the end of the day my nice house looked as if it were the only thing left standing after a particularly disastrous natural event. The construction of the walls went on. Day after day, four men, whose names were Jared Clawson, Dan, Tony, and John, came and dug trenches and pounded stakes into the ground after they had looked through a surveyor's instrument many times. One day, truckloads of coarsely pummelled gray stone were deposited in the driveway and carefully laid at the bottom of the trenches. Another day, truckloads of a beautiful gray, blue, yellowish, and glistening stone were delivered and left on the lawn. This stone came from a quarry in Goshen, Massachusetts, Ron Pembroke told me. It is the stone he prefers to use when he builds walls, and it is more expensive than other kinds of stone, but it does display his work to best advantage. My two walls, he said, would most likely require a hundred tons of stone.

The walls started to take shape, at first almost mysteriously. The four men began by placing stones atop one another, in a staggered arrangement, so that always one stone was resting on top of two. In the beginning, each stone they picked up seemed to be just the perfect one needed. But then things began to get more difficult. Sometimes a stone would be carried to the wall with great effort and, after being pounded into place, it would not look quite right to Tony and Dan and John and Jared Clawson.

And did I say that all this was being done in the autumn? I do not know if that is the ideal time to build a wall, but I was so happy to see my walls being made that I became very possessive of the time spent on them and wanted the four men to be building only my walls. I didn't begrudge them lunchtime or time taken to smoke a cigarette, but why did they have to stop working when the day was at an end, and why did the day have to come to an end, for that matter? How I loved to watch those men work, especially the man named Jared Clawson. It was he who built the stairs that made it possible to walk from the lower wall to the eight-foot-wide terrace, and then up to the level ground of a patio, which was made flush with the top of the upper wall. And the stairs were difficult to make, or so it seemed to me, for it took Jared Clawson ten days to make them.

One day, it was finished. The walls were built, and they looked fantastic. My friend   15
Paige had given me twelve bottles of champagne, a present for my twentieth wedding anniversary. I loved the taste of this champagne so much that I gave a bottle to each of the men who had helped build my walls. How glad was my spirit when, at the end of all this, Ron Pembroke presented me with a bill, and I in turn gave him a check for the complete amount, and there was nothing between us but complete respect and admiration and no feeling of the injustice of it all, no disgust directed toward me and my nice house, beautifully set off by those dramatic walls, for he had his own house and his own wall and his own spouse and his own anniversary.

At the foot of the lower wall, I have planted five hundred daffodils, ranging in shade from bright yellow to creamy white. In the terrace separating the lower and the upper walls, I have planted two hundred Tulipa "Mrs. J. T. Scheepers," which is perhaps my favorite tulip in the world. In the four beds on either side of the patio, I have planted two hundred Tulipa "Blue Diamond," a hundred Tulipa "Angelique," and only fifty of Tulipa "Black Hero" because they were so expensive. Towering above these hundreds of bulbs, I planted the magnolias "Woodsman" and "Elizabeth" and "Miss Honeybee"; and then Magnolia zenii and Magnolia denudata. At the beginning of the woodland, which I can see from a certain angle if I am standing on the upper wall, I planted a hundred Fritillaria meleagris and fifty each of Galanthus elwesii and Galanthus nivalis.

Ron Pembroke refilled the trenches with a rich topsoil, a mixture of composted organic material and riverbank soil, but I did not see one earthworm wriggling around in it, and this made me worry, for I have such a reverence for earthworms, whose presence signifies that the soil is good. Their anxious, iridescent, wriggly form, when confronted with broad daylight, is very reassuring. We may be made from dust (the dust of the garden, I presume), but it is not to dust that we immediately return; first, we join the worms.

The garden is not a place to lose your cares; the garden is not a place of rest and repose. Even God did not find it so.

UNDERSTANDING THE TEXT

1. What significance does Kincaid see in the gardens she visited while attending the Garden Conservancy's celebration in South Carolina? What do her remarks about these gardens reveal about her values in general and her views about gardens in particular? What does the reaction of some of her audience reveal about their values?

2. Why do you think Kincaid does not share with Mr. Cabot her knowledge that Arthur Middleton, the original owner of the plantation they were visiting, was one of the signers of the Declaration of Independence (par. 8)?

3. What does Thomas Jefferson reveal about himself in his "Garden and Farm Books," according to Kincaid? Why is this important to her? What does it suggest about her own values and viewpoint?

4. What does Kincaid mean when she writes that there was "no feeling of injustice" between her and the man who built her garden wall when the wall was completed? How does that statement relate to her earlier descriptions of famous gardens, such as Thomas Jefferson's gardens at Monticello?

EXPLORING THE ISSUES

1. How would you describe the tone of this essay? Do you think the tone is appropriate for the main point Kincaid is making? Explain, citing specific passages to support your answer.

2. Why do you think Kincaid ends her essay as she does? Why did she include a reference to the Garden of Eden, even after describing her own joy at having her garden wall completed? What idea or point do you think she tries to emphasize with her ending? Do you think her ending is effective? Why or why not? What might your answer to that question suggest about your own expectations as a reader?

3. This essay is largely devoted to two experiences of Kincaid's: her visit to the Garden Conservancy celebration in Charleston, South Carolina, and her hiring a landscape architect to build a garden wall at her home in Vermont. Consider how Kincaid uses these two experiences to make her point about gardens. In what ways do you think the similarities and contrasts between these two experiences help her convey her ideas about gardens?

4. This essay first appeared in *The New Yorker*, a venerable magazine that is generally considered to reflect a sophisticated, cosmopolitan perspective and is often read for its literary writing. What assumptions do you think Kincaid makes about her audience for this essay? What does she expect her readers to know? Do you think you are a member of her intended audience? Why or why not?

ENTERING THE CONVERSATIONS

1. Visit a public garden in your town or region or on your campus, and examine it for the kinds of ideas and messages that Kincaid finds in the gardens that she describes in this essay. In effect, ask questions of the garden you visit in the way that Kincaid asks questions of the gardens she visits. For example, who or what does the garden commemo-rate? Who created the garden? Who maintains it? What does it suggest about your community? About nature? Try to answer these and other questions as you visit the garden. Then write an essay in which you describe the garden you visited and discuss what kinds of messages or ideas are conveyed by that garden. Draw conclusions about what this garden might say about how we use land.

2. On the basis of your analysis for Question 1, write a letter to the authority responsible for the public garden you visited in which you propose changes to the garden to address concerns you may have about the messages the garden sends.

3. Using appropriate computer software (such as a standard drawing or graphics program) or using conventional pencil and paper, design a garden that conveys an important idea or principle or a garden that commemorates a person or event that you believe deserves notice. Write a brief essay explaining the specific characteristics of your design.

4. If possible, visit several gardens in the area where you live and take photographs of them. Then create a web page, PowerPoint presentation, or another appropriate kind of document in which you present an analysis of the statements these gardens might be making.

5. As I noted in the introduction to this reading (page 622), Kincaid believes that "we enjoy things far too much, and it leads to incredible pain and suffering." Write an essay in which you respond to this statement.

You are probably aware that whenever you turn on a light in your home or start up a car, you are using resources in a way that causes pollution and may contribute to larger environmental problems like global warming. But have you ever considered the possibility that eating a nacho chip or having an ear of corn at a summer picnic may add to serious social, environmental, and health problems? Writer Michael Pollan believes you should. In the following essay,

When A Crop Becomes King

Pollan examines the extensive role of corn in the American diet and food production system. Corn, he shows us, is a key ingredient in many of the foods we commonly eat; it is also the primary feed for livestock. It may be the most successful plant we cultivate. But Pollan documents the damage that our uses of corn have caused—to our environment as well as to our own health. It is a sobering essay, one that reveals the complexity of the systems we have created to produce, distribute, and consume important resources like food. Pollan's essay reminds us that everything we use has consequences; it also reminds us that understanding these consequences can be a challenge. His essay is an example of the way that writing can be an important part of the process by which we identify and address that challenge.

Pollan is the author of The Botany of Desire: A Plant's-Eye View of the World *(2001) and* Second Nature: A Gardener's Education *(1991). This article was first published in the* New York Times *in 2002.* ▼

MICHAEL POLLAN

Here in southern New England the corn is already waist high and growing so avidly you can almost hear the creak of stalk and leaf as the plants stretch toward the sun. The ears of sweet corn are just starting to show up on local farm stands, inaugurating one of the ceremonies of an American summer. These days the nation's nearly 80 million-acre field of corn rolls across the countryside like a second great lawn, but this wholesome, all-American image obscures a decidedly more dubious reality.

Like the tulip, the apple and the potato, *Zea mays* (the botanical name for both sweet and feed corn) has evolved with humans over the past 10,000 years or so in the great dance of species we call domestication. The plant gratifies human needs, in exchange for which humans expand the plant's habitat, moving its genes all over the world and remaking the land (clearing trees, plowing the ground, protecting it from its enemies) so it might thrive.

Corn, by making itself tasty and nutritious, got itself noticed by Christopher Columbus, who helped expand its range from the New

MICHAEL POLLAN, "WHEN A CROP BECOMES KING." FROM *THE NEW YORK TIMES* JULY 19, 2002. REPRINTED BY PERMISSION OF THE AUTHOR.

World to Europe and beyond. Today corn is the world's most widely planted cereal crop. But nowhere have humans done quite as much to advance the interests of this plant as in North America, where *Zea mays* has insinuated itself into our landscape, our food system—and our federal budget.

One need look no further than the $190 billion **farm bill** President Bush signed last month to wonder whose interests are really being served here. Under the 10-year program, taxpayers will pay farmers $4 billion a year to grow ever more corn, this despite the fact that we struggle to get rid of the surplus the plant already produces. The average bushel of corn (56 pounds) sells for about $2 today; it costs farmers more than $3 to grow it. But rather than design a program that would encourage farmers to plant less corn—which would have the benefit of lifting the price farmers receive for it—Congress has decided instead to subsidize corn by the bushel, thereby insuring *Zea mays* dominion over its 125,000-square mile American habitat will go unchallenged.

At first blush this subsidy might look like a handout for farmers, but really it's a 5 form of welfare for the plant itself—and for all those economic interests that profit from its overproduction: the processors, factory farms, and the soft drink and snack makers that rely on cheap corn. For *Zea mays* has triumphed by making itself indispensable not to farmers (whom it is swiftly and surely bankrupting) but to the Archer Daniels Midlands, Tysons and Coca-Colas of the world.

Our entire food supply has undergone a process of "cornification" in recent years, without our even noticing it. That's because, unlike in Mexico, where a corn-based diet has been the norm for centuries, in the United States most of the corn we consume is invisible, having been heavily processed or passed through food animals before it reaches us. Most of the animals we eat (chickens, pigs and cows) today subsist on a diet of corn, regardless of whether it is good for them. In the case of beef cattle, which evolved to eat grass, a corn diet wreaks havoc on their digestive system, making it necessary to feed them antibiotics to stave off illness and infection. Even farm-raised salmon are being bred to tolerate corn—not a food their evolution has prepared them for. Why feed fish corn? Because it's the cheapest thing you can feed any animal, thanks to federal subsidies. But even with more than half of the 10 billion bushels of corn produced annually being fed to animals, there is plenty left over. So companies like A.D.M., Cargill and ConAgra have figured ingenious new ways to dispose of it, turning it into everything from ethanol to Vitamin C and biodegradable plastics.

By far the best strategy for keeping *Zea mays* in business has been the development of high-fructose corn syrup, which has all but pushed sugar aside. Since the 1980's, most soft drink manufacturers have switched from sugar to corn sweeteners, as have most snack makers. Nearly 10 percent of the calories Americans consume now come from corn sweeteners; the figure is 20 percent for many children. Add to that all the corn-based animal protein (corn-fed beef, chicken and pork) and the corn qua corn (chips, muffins, sweet corn) and you have a plant that has become one of nature's greatest success stories, by turning us (along with several other equally unwitting species) into an expanding race of corn eaters.

So why begrudge corn its phenomenal success? Isn't this the way domestication is supposed to work?

The problem in corn's case is that we're sacrificing the health of both our bodies and the environment by growing and eating so much of it. Though we're only beginning to understand what our cornified food system is doing to our health, there's cause for concern. It's probably no coincidence that the wholesale switch to corn sweeteners in the 1980's marks the beginning of the epidemic of obesity and Type 2 diabetes in this country. Sweetness became so cheap that soft drink makers, rather than lower their prices, super-sized their serving portions and marketing budgets. Thousands of new sweetened snack foods hit the market, and the amount of fructose in our diets soared.

10   This would be bad enough for the American waistline, but there's also preliminary research suggesting that high-fructose corn syrup is metabolized differently than other sugars, making it potentially more harmful. A recent study at the University of Minnesota found that a diet high in fructose (as compared to glucose) elevates triglyceride levels in men shortly after eating, a phenomenon that has been linked to an increased risk of obesity and heart disease. Little is known about the health effects of eating animals that have themselves eaten so much corn, but in the case of cattle, researchers have found that corn-fed beef is higher in saturated fats than grass-fed beef.

We know a lot more about what 80 million acres of corn is doing to the health of our environment: serious and lasting damage. Modern corn hybrids are the greediest of plants, demanding more nitrogen fertilizer than any other crop. Corn requires more pesticide than any other food crop. Runoff from these chemicals finds its way into the groundwater and, in the Midwestern corn belt, into the Mississippi River, which carries it to the Gulf of Mexico, where it has already killed off marine life in a 12,000 square mile area.

To produce the chemicals we apply to our cornfields takes vast amounts of oil and natural gas. (Nitrogen fertilizer is made from natural gas, pesticides from oil.) America's corn crop might look like a sustainable, solar-powered system for producing food, but it is actually a huge, inefficient, polluting machine that guzzles fossil fuel—a half a gallon of it for every bushel.

So it seems corn has indeed become king. We have given it more of our land than any other plant, an area more than twice the size of New York State. To keep it well fed and safe from predators we douse it with chemicals that poison our water and deepen our dependence on foreign oil. And then in order to dispose of all the corn this cracked system has produced, we eat it as fast as we can in as many ways as we can—turning the fat of the land into, well, fat. One has to wonder whether corn hasn't at last succeeded in domesticating us.

UNDERSTANDING THE TEXT

1. What is it about corn that has made it such a successful plant, according to Pollan? What does the success of corn suggest about the relationship between humans and the plants they use?

2. In what sense is corn "invisible" in the American diet? What are the consequences of our uses of corn? What might these consequences suggest about our food production and distribution system?

3. What does Pollan mean when he writes that corn may have "domesticated" humans? Do you think he's right? Why or why not?

EXPLORING THE ISSUES

1. Throughout this essay, Pollan describes corn as if it is conscious. For example, in paragraph 3, he writes that corn "got itself noticed" by "making itself tasty and nutritious," and it "insinuated itself" into our food system—as if corn has intentions and purpose. Why do you think Pollan refers to corn in this way? What does he accomplish by doing so? What ideas about corn, plants, and the relationship between plants and humans does he convey by describing corn in this way?

2. Pollan is clearly not a fan of the ways in which corn has become so central to the American diet, and he offers facts, figures, and other evidence to support his claim that corn is detrimental to the health of humans, animals, and the environment. Examine this evidence. What kinds of information does Pollan use to support his claim? What other kinds of information does he exclude? What do you think Pollan's choice of evidence suggests about his sense of his readers' expectations? How effectively do you think his evidence supports his position

about the cultivation and consumption of corn?

3. Pollan criticizes the role of corn in the American food production system, but he offers no specific alternative or solution to the problems he describes. Based on what he does include in this essay, what kinds of solutions or steps do you think Pollan would advocate for addressing these problems?

4. Given Pollan's arguments about corn in this essay, what do you think are his values regarding food and lifestyle? Do you think most Americans would share his values? Explain, citing specific passages to support your answer.

ENTERING THE CONVERSATIONS

1. Identify an important resource, such as a food like corn or a fuel like gasoline, and write an essay in which you discuss its role in your life and the consequences of its use.

INFOTRAC

2. In paragraph 4, Pollan refers to some of the federal agricultural subsidies that support the cultivation of corn. He suggests that these subsidies are largely responsible for the widespread uses of corn in processed foods and as animal feed. Using InfoTrac College Edition, your library, and other appropriate resources, investigate federal agricultural subsidies, especially those related to corn. If possible, speak to farmers or other agricultural experts in your area about the cultivation of corn and/or about agricultural subsidies. Try to find out how these subsidies work and what effect they have on farming and on food markets. Then write a report on the basis of your research. In your report, try to evaluate Pollan's claims based

on what you learned through your research.

3. In paragraph 6, Pollan notes that a typical Mexican diet contains corn, but he does not see that diet as a cause for concern. Find out about the differences in the ways Americans use corn and the ways corn is used in Mexican culture or other cultures in which corn is a staple. Then write an essay in which you discuss what you learned about the role of corn in other cultures and how it compares to the uses of corn in American culture.

4. Select a food item that is a main part of your diet and investigate the source, production, and distribution of that food. Try to find out where and how the food item is grown or produced, how it is distributed, and how it tends to be consumed. If possible, identify the consequences of its production and distribution—for example, the energy used to grow, produce, or harvest it, the people who do the work, the use of fuel to transport and store it, and so on. Then write a report in which you describe the "journey" of this food item to your plate. Draw conclusions about the consequences of our dietary choices. Alternatively, do the same kind of investigation for some other important resource in your life, such as water or clothing.

5. On the basis of your research for Question 4, create a pamphlet, web site, or some other kind of document in which you present the "journey" of the item you investigated.

6. Write a letter to the person in charge of food services on your school campus in which you express your concerns about the impact of our uses of certain foods, such as corn, and propose changes in food policy on your campus to address your concerns.

In early 2005, I visited Whiteface Mountain in upstate New York. Whiteface is well known as the site of the alpine ski events in the 1980 Winter Olympic Games, during which American skier Phil Mahre won a silver medal and the U.S. hockey team defeated the formidable Soviet hockey team on its way to a gold medal. But the operators of Whiteface Mountain also want to be known for something else: being environmentally responsible. While I was there, I learned that Whiteface is

THE *Ski* Store AND THE *Real* Cost OF Fun

a charter member of Sustainable Slopes, an initiative by ski areas to reduce their significant impact on their local and regional environments. This initiative includes reducing the use of water for making snow, employing efficient technologies to reduce electricity use, and educating skiers about how they can reduce their own impact on the environment. I was pleased to learn about Sustainable Slopes because recreation like skiing causes great environmental damage. But as internationally acclaimed environmentalist Donella Meadows (1941–2001) points out in the following essay, the impact of recreational activities goes well beyond the obvious environmental damage that we can see when we visit a ski area. Her essay offers a lesson in how much we can affect the environment and other people by the simple choices we make, even choices to engage in seemingly wholesome activities like skiing.

Donella Meadows was a professor of biophysics at Dartmouth College and founder of the Sustainability Institute, which promotes environmentally sustainable lifestyles. She authored many books about environmental issues, including The Limits to Growth *(1972) and* Beyond the Limits *(1992), and wrote a column distributed by the Sustainability Institute called* The Global Citizen, *in which this essay was first published in 1998.* ◪

DONELLA MEADOWS

A 17-year-old friend convinced me to take her to a ski store on a Saturday afternoon right before the supposed start of the supposed ski season. I guess it's been 20 years since I was last in a ski store.

This one was a happy place, full of torchy colors and young, energetic people. It was packed, but my companion was blonde and tall and slim and beautiful, so three young, energetic salesmen buzzed right up to us.

During the next hour, as she questioned and pondered and tried on and rejected and enthused and racked up many bucks on her papa's credit card, I absorbed the modern world of skiing.

"Are you an aggressive skier?" they asked, and when she said she liked to go really fast, they led her off to the aggressive skis, the aggressive boots, the aggressive bindings. These are made of supermetals and superplastics and superfabrics, bonded in layers with superglues. "Imagine all the toxics," I thought. "And that layered stuff can never be recycled. And it will last in a landfill for a million years."

I must have been the only person in the store with such thoughts. My companion had long conversations with the salesmen about 5 shaped skis, cutting edges on sharp turns and what an extra quarter-inch of height in the bindings does for maneuverability. She picked out equipment of steel gray and flaming red.

I pondered, "What if all this care and design, this cleverness, these exotic materials, this money went to ending hunger? Or solar collectors? What if these great young people poured their boundless energy into reforestation or insulating the houses of the poor or at least the kind of skiing where you have to haul yourself to the top of the hill?"

I shared none of these dark thoughts with my bright friend. But all the next week, a week in December during which the temperature in New England hovered between 40 and 60 and the ski areas couldn't even make artificial snow, all through that strangely balmy week I was in a bah! humbug! mood. "They load their pricey skis into their gas-guzzling vans," I harrumphed to myself. "They drive to mountains covered with effluent from diesel-belching, stream-destroying snow guns. They use still more fossil fuel to pull themselves uphill so they can slide down. Then they're surprised when global warming comes along."

Finally I turned to some wise 23-year-olds for enlightenment. "Why is this high-tech, high-expense, high-emission kind of skiing fun?" I asked them. "Or, no, cancel that, I can see why it's fun. But why isn't cross-country skiing just as much fun? Or snowball fights or skating or snowshoeing or any of the less destructive ways to play outside in the winter?"

"Because they're not IN," my friends explained patiently. "Because you can't compare your flashy equipment with your friends' flashy equipment. Because the good parties are on the ski slopes. Because no one sells designer clothes for snowshoeing. Because it's fun to go really fast."

I listened, and then I dug out my copy of *Brave New World* (written in 1932 by Aldous Huxley) and found the place where the Director of Hatcheries describes why his society programs children to hate nature.

" 'Primroses and landscapes,' he pointed out, 'have one grave defect: they are gratuitous. A love of nature keeps no factories busy. It was decided to abolish the love of nature . . . but not the tendency to consume transport. For of course it was essential

10

CONVERSATIONS: DYSTOPIAS AND UTOPIAS
In this passage (par. 10), Meadows quotes from
the well-known novel *Brave New World* by
Aldous Huxley, which describes a frightening
future in which everything is controlled through
technology, even the characteristics of human
beings, who are developed in test tubes. The
world described in Huxley's novel is an example of a *dystopia,* a carefully controlled world
or community in which the quality of life is undesirable. Dystopias can be thought of as the
opposite of *utopias*—that is, ideal worlds in
which the most difficult problems of our societies are solved. In referring to Huxley's novel
in this way, Meadows is using an ongoing conversation about how to improve our world to
help make her point about our current lifestyle.
Obviously, she sees in Huxley's terrible imaginary world some similarities to the world we
have created. Novels like *Brave New World* are
thus an important part of the way ideas about
how we should live are examined and discussed. Essays like this one by Meadows are
part of that process, too.

that they should keep on going to the country, even though they
hated it. The problem was to find an economically sounder reason
for consuming transport than a mere affection for primroses and
landscapes. It was duly found.'"

" 'We condition the masses to hate the country,' concluded the
Director. 'But, simultaneously we condition them to love all country sports. At the same time we see to it that all country sports shall
entail the use of elaborate apparatus. So that they consume manufactured articles as well as transport. . . .'"

Old Aldous got our number 66 years ago, didn't he? But he did
not foresee the possibility of environmental backlash.

It's easy to label environmentalists as anti-fun grinches. It would
be easy to label my young friend as shallow or gullible. Neither she
nor I deserve those labels. There is nothing I want more for her
than that she should have fun. And she would never deliberately
hurt other people or the earth. She is just doing what I did
when I was 17, going out with friends, having fun. In my day we
had lots of fun without much in the way of fossil fuel, fancy equipment, or credit cards. But the economy had not yet perfected
the art of conditioning us to buy elaborate apparatus and consume transport.

15   She's not to blame. If blame is useful here, it should be directed toward an amor-
phous system that charges her papa a high price, but gives neither him nor her any
sense of real, full costs.

And I'm not a killjoy. I've just been educated to see the whole system, to see how
those real, full costs fall upon the air and the waters and the land and the climate in
ways that will ruin the very fun that is causing the damage in the first place. And I'm
old enough to know that there are far less costly, far more sustainable kinds of joy
and fun.

UNDERSTANDING THE TEXT

1. What characterizes "the modern world of skiing," in Meadows's view? What do you think modern skiing reveals about how we spend our leisure time?

2. What is the appeal of a sport like skiing, as Meadows describes it? Do you think this is a fair or accurate depiction of this kind of leisure activity? Explain.

3. Who or what is to blame for the destructive ways that we tend to have fun today, according to Meadows? Do you think she's right? Why or why not?

EXPLORING THE ISSUES

1. Throughout this essay, Meadows comments on the activities around her in the ski store. What do her comments reveal about her values or her perspective? How do you think her comments affect her credibility? Explain. To what extent do her comments affect the way you respond to her essay?

2. In the final paragraph of this essay, Meadows writes that she has been "educated to see the whole system, to see how those real, full costs fall upon the air and the waters and the land and the climate in ways that will ruin the very fun that is causing the damage in the first place." What exactly does she mean by that statement? How might she have been "educated" in this way, while her seventeen-year-old friend and her friend's father and others have not been? What does this statement suggest about Meadows? What do you think it suggests about how we come to understand the world around us and our impact on it?

3. Meadows bases this essay on one experience with a young friend, with whom she visited a ski store. Examine how Meadows uses this experience in her essay. What ideas or arguments does she convey through telling about this experience? How effective do you think her use of this experience is to convey her point?

4. Some readers might reject Meadows's analysis of skiing as too extreme. If we accept her main premise about the consequences of our leisure activities, it is possible to conclude that *anything* we do for recreation is environmentally destructive and therefore should be avoided. Do you think Meadows's argument is too extreme? Why or why not? If it is, how might we reasonably address her concerns about the impact of our activities?

ENTERING THE CONVERSATIONS

1. Write a response to Meadows's essay, especially to her point that "there are far less costly, far more sustainable kinds of joy and fun" than skiing (par. 16). If you ski or snowboard, you might draw on your own experience in your response to Meadows. If you don't ski or snowboard, you might draw on your experience with other leisure activities.

2. In paragraph 6, Meadows asks, "What if all this care and design, this cleverness, these exotic materials, this money went to ending hunger? Or solar collectors? What if these great young people poured their boundless energy into reforestation or insulating the houses of the poor or at least the kind of skiing where you have to haul yourself to the top of the hill?" Write an essay in which you respond to her questions.

3. Create a photo essay, web site, PowerPoint presentation, or some other appropriate document that presents your view of the impact of your favorite leisure activity.

4. Write an essay in which you describe a utopian community where the kinds of problems Meadows describes in her essay don't exist.

CREATING THEMES: Extending the Conversations

WITH TEXT

1. Select a resource, such as food, energy, or water. Drawing on several of the readings in this chapter as well as your own experience, write an essay in which you carefully examine the way that resource is used in contemporary society. Discuss some of the social, economic, political, or environmental issues associated with that resource. Try to examine recent developments that might affect how that resource is used.

2. Identify what you consider an important theme that runs through several of the readings in this chapter and write an essay intended for a specific audience about that theme. Draw on the readings you've selected to support your main point.

3. Select several essays in this chapter and examine them from the perspective of race, class, gender, culture, or some other important factor. Write an essay in which you present your analysis. For example, you might select three or four essays that address issues related to food and examine those essays in terms of gender. In what ways might gender be an issue for these writers? How might gender figure into the argument or analysis in the essay? To what extent do the essays seem to reflect biases or problematic attitudes about gender? If the author does not seem to consider gender, how should the author have addressed gender as part of the issue he or she wrote about? In your essay, try to address such questions.

4. Identify an issue in this chapter about which you feel strongly and about which you disagree with one or more of the authors whose essays are included here. Write an essay in which you present your view of your selected issue, drawing from any appropriate essays in the chapter.

WITH MEDIA

1. Visit the web sites of organizations devoted to issues somehow related to our use of resources. For example, you might visit the sites of environmental groups concerned about the loss of the rain forest or the damage to water resources. Examine how the sites you've selected present the issue. Examine the messages they try to convey and the way they present their own position and the positions of others on that issue. Look at the strategies they seem to use to persuade visitors about the validity of their position. Write an essay in which you present your analysis. Discuss the ideas and messages conveyed by the sites you visited about the resource-related issue you have selected. Draw your own conclusions about what these sites might suggest about current attitudes regarding our uses of resources.

2. Using appropriate computer software or conventional pencil and paper, design a home that reflects your beliefs about how we should use resources. Include some explanation of the specific features of your design and how they reflect your beliefs about how to live responsibly.

3. Drawing on several of the essays in this chapter and any other relevant resources, create a pamphlet, web site, PowerPoint presentation, video, or another appropriate kind of document for a specific audience intended to educate that audience about our uses of specific resources and concerns you may have about those uses of resources.

4. Alexis Rockman, the artist who created the image below, writes that her artworks are "information-rich depictions of how our culture perceives and interacts with plants and animals, and the role culture plays in influencing the direction of natural history." What messages do you think this work conveys about how American culture perceives plants

Alexis Rockman, *The Farm*, 2000

CREATING THEMES: Extending the Conversations

and animals? Write an essay in which you answer that question. Draw on any appropriate readings in this chapter to develop your ideas about this piece of art. Alternatively, find another work of art that carries messages about our relationship to important resources and write an essay in which you discuss those messages.

5. The following images all have something to do with resources. Some of them send obvious messages about how we use resources; in others, the messages are more subtle. Select several of these images (or others you may have found) and write an essay in which you discuss the messages they convey about using resources. Alternatively, create an image of your own (for example, a photo, a sketch, a painting) that conveys a message about using resources.

WITH FILM

1. In the popular film *The Matrix* (1999), the main character Neo (played by actor Keanu Reeves) learns that the world was dramati-

cally altered by a war between human beings and machines. One result of that war was the destruction of Earth's atmosphere. In a sense, this film can be interpreted as conveying certain messages about how humans use resources.

Select one or more popular films that you think make some kind of statement about our uses of resources and our responsibility (or

lack of) for using resources. Write an essay in which you discuss the messages those films convey.

2. Popular films often depict characters who lead very conventional lives. Select a film in which the main characters are ordinary people, and examine how the film portrays the characters' use of resources. Address such questions and present your analysis of the film you have selected.

How can you help protect **the prairie and the penguin?**

Simple. Visit www.earthshare.org and learn how the world's leading environmental groups are working together under one name. And how easy it is for you to help protect the prairies and the penguins and the planet.

www.earthshare.org

One environment. One simple way to care for it.

Earth Share

© Earth Share

This is a nuclear powered toaster.

Notice its uncanny resemblance to an ordinary one.

The Advertising Archives

Less cars, more world. **Drivers wanted.**

www.adbusters.org

A FEW YEARS AGO, A LARGE INVESTMENT COMPANY RAN A TELEVISION ADVERTISING CAMPAIGN TO PROMOTE ITS RETIREMENT PLANNING SERVICES. THE POINT WAS TO ENCOURAGE POTENTIAL CUSTOMERS TO HIRE THE COMPANY TO HELP PLAN FOR RETIREMENT. THE MESSAGE WAS THAT YOU HAVE TO BE READY FOR ANYTHING BECAUSE YOU

never know what might happen. The tag line was, "In life, the only constant is change." As a writer, I enjoyed the paradoxical idea that change is a constant (this kind of paradoxical expression is called an *oxymoron*). But that tag line expresses a profound idea that has been explored for centuries by philosophers, theologians, poets, and even scientists: the idea of change over time.

At first glance, this idea of inevitable change seems simple and commonsensical. Of course things change. Everything changes. Even seemingly permanent things like mountains or oceans change over time. And our efforts to de-

> Everything changes. Even seemingly permanent things like mountains or oceans change over time.

feat time, to create permanence or to seek immortality, are futile. That's the message of the famous poem "Ozymandias" (1818) by the great British poet Percy Bysshe Shelley (1792–1822):

I met a traveller from an antique land,
Who said—"Two vast and trunkless legs of
    stone
Stand in the desert. . . . Near them, on the
    sand,
Half sunk a shattered visage lies, whose
    frown,
And wrinkled lip, and sneer of cold command,
Tell that its sculptor well those passions
    read
Which yet survive, stamped on this lifeless
    things,

The hand that mocked them, and the
    heart that fed;
And on the pedestal, these words appear:
My name is Ozymandias, King of Kings,
Look on my Works, ye Mighty, and despair!
Nothing beside remains. Round the decay
Of that colossal Wreck, boundless and bare
The lone and level sands stretch far away."

Shelley's poem is about the futility and foolishness of our efforts to resist time and the inevitable changes its passage brings; it is also about the deep human desire not only to be recognized and even honored, as reflected in the monument of himself that King Ozymandias had sculpted, but also to feel that our lives have some permanent meaning that transcends time. Shelley's poem gives voice to this need and perhaps reflects how much humans struggle to deal with change.

There was a more recent and humorous television commercial in early 2005 that speaks to this same struggle—an ad for a special promotion by a national pizza restaurant chain by which customers could order three different kinds of pizza for the same price. In the commercial, a pizza deliveryman brings three pizzas to the home of a customer, who announces triumphantly that the special promotion allows him to order any kind of pizzas he wants. When his wife reminds him that despite all the choices he has, he ordered three pepperoni pizzas, the man says dejectedly, "I fear change." Obviously, the commercial is poking fun at a person who, given many different choices, chooses the same old pepperoni pizza. But the fear of change seems to be widely shared. You can see it in the way people follow the same daily routines for years, maybe even for their entire lives. You see it in the way various kinds of reform efforts, such as school reform or Social Security reform, make many people nervous. You see it in the nostalgia that many people feel for the past. And perhaps you see it in rituals that focus on change—rituals like graduation or wedding ceremonies, in which hope and happiness mix with some sadness and anxiety about the uncertainties that lie ahead.

Even science has tried to understand the phenomenon of change. The last three lines of Shelley's poem "Ozymandias" depict an image of the desert as all that remains of Ozymandias' kingdom, suggesting that only Nature itself survives change. Astronomers and physicists have learned how the universe itself is always changing; indeed, Albert Einstein's theory of relativity, one of the most important scientific developments in history, explains that time itself is not constant but can change in relationship to space.

If all this seems abstract, the readings in this chapter may make it more concrete. These readings explore some of the many ways in which we confront change in our lives. From technological developments, such as cell phones and computers, that have dramatically changed the way we communicate and live together, to the loss of a loved one, which is perhaps the most difficult kind of change we face, to medical discoveries that may change our lives in the face of disease or environmental damage—these readings highlight the kinds of changes that can shape our lives. They also illuminate the challenges that

> When his wife reminds him that despite all the choices he has, he ordered three pepperoni pizzas, the man says dejectedly, "I fear change."

change presents. How we face those challenges is perhaps one of the most important questions we must answer, individually and together. The varied readings in this chapter may help you appreciate how writers have explored these challenges—and how writing itself is one of the most important ways that humans have tried to meet those challenges.

LIVING WITH CHANGE

WHEN I WAS GROWING UP, I LOVED HEARING STORIES OF THE PAST TOLD BY THE OLDER MEMBERS OF MY FAMILY. AT FAMILY GATHERINGS, THE ELDERS WOULD OFTEN SIT AT THE TABLE LONG AFTER DINNER, TALKING ABOUT ISSUES OF THE DAY AND RECENT FAMILY HAPPENINGS. EVENTUALLY, THEY WOULD GET AROUND TO TELLING STORIES OF YEARS PAST. MY GRANDMOTHER IN PARTICULAR LIKED TO TELL STORIES

about what it was like to grow up in the early decades of the nineteenth century, a time when automobiles were new, telephones were rare, and television was not yet invented. She would talk about how momentous an event it was when her family finally had a telephone installed in their home. And she would describe evenings when she would gather with others at a neighbor's home to watch the only television in the neighborhood. I vividly recall her telling us about her own grandmother, who insisted before she died in the

> To listen to my grandmother's stories about these changes was to get a sense of how she and her family lived with changes that often impacted their lives in dramatic ways.

1920s that her body be taken to the cemetery in a horse-drawn hearse because she never trusted automobiles, which could move without being pulled by a horse. The development of the automobile was a change that was too dramatic for her to deal with.

I enjoyed hearing these stories because I was always fascinated by how different life was for my grandmother when she was growing up compared to the life I knew as a child. I could not imagine living at a time when telephones and cars and televisions were not common. And I was amazed by the many changes that my grandmother, who died in 1994, witnessed in her lifetime. Not only did she see important technological developments, such as television and automobiles, that profoundly changed how we live, but she also saw dramatic political, scientific, and social developments that reshaped the world, including World Wars I and II, the moon landings, the Civil Rights Movement, and other developments that I studied about in my history classes. To listen to my grandmother's stories about these changes was to get a sense of how she and her family lived with changes that often impacted their lives in dramatic ways.

The readings in this cluster are about living with change—sometimes dramatic, sometimes not. These essays offer insight into how human beings adjust to changes, big and small. From Deborah Tannen's look at how the way she communicates with loved ones has changed to Judith Levine's heartfelt description of the difficulties she faced in learning to live with a father suffering from Alzheimer's disease, these essays help us see that we are always living with change.

In the past decade or so, e-mail has become *one of the most common and important means of communication. Although messages have been sent electronically over computer networks since the 1970s, it wasn't until the early 1990s that e-mail became widely available commercially through large service providers like AOL. Since then, its use has increased dramatically to the point that it is now essential for many people in school, at work, and in their personal lives.*

Connections

If you use e-mail, you probably use it every day to communicate about mundane matters like the weather as well as important issues related to work or school. But because e-mail has become so common, you probably don't think much about how modern life has been changing as a result of this form of communication. Deborah Tannen (b. 1945), an internationally known expert in interpersonal communication, does think about it. In the following essay, Tannen describes some of her experiences using e-mail to communicate with important people in her life. At first glance, these experiences are rather typical. But Tannen carefully considers how this new medium might affect our relationships with each other, including relationships that are shaped by difficult challenges—in this case, a terminal illness. She explores the role that e-mail played in such a relationship that she had, and she compares that experience to her experiences using older forms of communication, such as telephones or letters. In doing so, Tannen reveals how complex these changes in how we communicate really are, especially when we look at them in human terms. I remember being struck by this heartfelt essay when I first read it shortly after it was published in 1998. I think it's even more (continued)

DEBORAH TANNEN

My father never knew his father. Until he was seven, he lived with his mother and sister in his grandparents' home: a Hasidic household in Warsaw. His grandfather was the closest he ever came to having a father.

In 1920, when my father was twelve, he left Poland to emigrate with his mother and sister to the United States, and he saw his grandfather for the last time. As my father tells it, his grandfather took him on his knee to say good-bye. Tears ran down the old man's face and into his long white beard. He knew he would never see his grandchild again. Even if the Holocaust had not taken his grandfather's life, my father would not have been able to return to Poland for a visit during his grandfather's lifetime. He wouldn't have been able to take the time off work to sail across the ocean, and he wouldn't have been able to afford the trip.

In 1966, I graduated from college, worked for six months, saved all the money I earned, and flew to Europe on a one-way ticket through Luxembourg on Icelandic Airlines. I ended up in Greece, where I (continued) *important today because it helps us understand how we are dealing with changes that are so common that we may no longer see them.*

Deborah Tannen is Professor of Linguistics at Georgetown University and has written numerous books about communication. The following essay was first published in How We Want to Live *(1998), edited by Susan and Porter Shreve. For more information on Deborah Tannen, see page 306.*

CONTEXT: THE USE OF E-MAIL
A 2005 study by the Pew Internet and American Life Project found that 58 percent of Americans use e-mail daily compared to 45 percent just four years earlier. This increase in the use of e-mail is related to the rapidly expanding use of online communication in general. The same study found that in 2005 81 percent of all teenagers were going online regularly. On a typical day in 2004, 70 million Americans logged onto the Internet, a 37 percent increase from 2000. The Pew study also found that Americans regularly use e-mail for a variety of purposes, including for religious or spiritual discussions and to communicate with their political representatives. These dramatic changes have occurred after Tannen wrote this essay, and it's worth considering whether these changes strengthen or weaken her main point.

lived for nearly two years, teaching English. I communicated with my parents by mail—but from time to time I would telephone them: I'd go to the main post office in downtown Athens, fill out a form, and wait until someone called my name and indicated in which booth my parents' voices would materialize. Sometimes I waited hours for the call to be put through—until the planned evening surprise had become a terrifying, sleep-destroying, wee-hours-of-the-morning alarm. "Do me a favor," my mother once said. "If it's after midnight, don't call." "But I've been waiting to put the call through for four hours," I said. "I didn't plan it to be after midnight." And there were not only telephones, but airplanes. During that year, my parents celebrated their thirty-fifth wedding anniversary, and they gave each of their children $1000. I used a portion of mine to fly home to New York City for their anniversary party.

In 1996, my oldest sister went to Israel for a year. Within a few weeks, she subscribed to Compuserve and hooked up her laptop computer to e-mail—and my other sister and my nieces all got on e-mail, too. Within a month, my sister was in daily communication with us all—much more frequent contact than our weekly (or biweekly or monthly) telephone calls had been when my sister was home in upstate New York.

5   And another surprise: my other sister, who generally is not eager to talk about her feelings, opened up on e-mail. One time I called her and we spoke on the phone; after we hung up, I checked my e-mail and found a message she had sent before we spoke, in which she revealed personal information that she hadn't mentioned on the phone. I asked her about this (on e-mail), and she explained, "The telephone is so impersonal." At first this seemed absurd: How could the actual voice of a person in conversation be more impersonal than on-screen little letters detached from the writer? But when I thought about it, it made sense: Writing e-mail is like writing in a journal; you're alone with your thoughts and your words, safe from the intrusive presence of another person.

I was the second person in my university department to get a computer. The first was my colleague Ralph. The year was 1980. Ralph got a Radio Shack TRS 80; I got a used Apple 2-Plus. He helped me get started, and before long helped me get on Bitnet, the precursor to the Internet. Though his office was next to mine, we rarely had extended conversations except about department business. Shy and soft-spoken, Ralph mumbled, so I could barely tell he was speaking. But when we were using e-mail, we started communicating daily in this (then) leisurely medium. We could send each other messages without fear of imposing, since the receiver determines when to log on and read and respond. Soon I was getting long self-revealing messages from Ralph. We moved effortlessly among discussions of department business, our work, and our lives. Through e-mail Ralph and I became friends.

Ralph recently forwarded to me a message he had received from his niece, a college freshman. "How nice," I commented, "that you have such a close relationship with your niece. Do you think you'd be in touch with her if it weren't for e-mail?" "No," he replied. "I can't imagine we'd write each other letters regularly or call on the phone. No way." E-mail makes possible connections with relatives, acquaintances, or strangers, that wouldn't otherwise exist. And it enables more frequent and different communication with people you're already close to. Parents are in daily contact with their children at college; people discover and reunite with long lost friends. One woman discovered that e-mail brought her closer to her father. He would never talk much on the phone (as her mother would), but they have become close since they both got on-line.

The Internet and the World Wide Web are creating networks of human connection unthinkable even a few years ago. But at the same time that technologically enhanced communication enables previously impossible loving contact, it also enhances hostile and distressing communication. Along with the voices of family members and friends, telephones bring into our homes the annoying voices of solicitors who want to sell something—at dinnertime. (My father-in-law startles a telephone solicitor by saying, "We're eating dinner, but I'll call you back. What's your home phone number?" To the nonplussed caller he explains, "Well, you're calling me at home; I thought I'd call you at home, too.") Even more unnerving, in the middle of the night come frightening obscene calls and stalkers.

The Internet ratchets up anonymity by homogenizing all messages into identical-appearing print and making it almost impossible to trace messages back to the computer that sent them. As the ease of using the Internet has resulted in more and more people logging on and sending messages to more and more others with whom they have a connection, it has also led to more communication with strangers, and this has led to "flaming": vituperative messages that verbally attack. Flaming results from the anonymity not only of the sender but also of the receiver. It is easier to feel and express hostility against someone far removed whom you do not know, like the rage that some drivers feel toward an anonymous car that cuts them off. If the driver to whom you've flipped the finger turns out to be someone you know, the rush of shame you feel is evidence that anonymity was essential for your expression—and experience—of rage.

10   Less and less of our communication is face to face, and more often with people we don't know. Technology that brings people closer also isolates us in a bubble. When

CONVERSATIONS: COMMUNICATION AND TECHNOLOGY
Tannen writes in paragraph 10, that "less and less of our communication is face to face, and more often with people we don't know." She is referring here primarily to communication through the Internet but also to electronic communications technologies like television and radio. In expressing these concerns, Tannen is taking part in several related conversations about technology and communication that seem to have intensified in recent decades as new communications technologies and especially the Internet have become ever more common. In the 1990s, when this essay was first published, many experts examined not only how the rapid development of these technologies might affect the way individuals communicate but also how these technologies might be shaping important social and cultural practices and traditions. For example, much attention was paid during the 2004 U.S. presidential election to how the political candidates used the Internet for fund-raising, communicating their messages to the public, and soliciting volunteers. Some experts argued that these uses of the Internet were changing how Americans participated in political activities. You might consider whether Tannen's concerns about the impersonal nature of much communication are as valid today as when she wrote this essay in 1998. Also, consider how she uses her own experiences as a person—rather than her expertise as a scholar—to contribute to ongoing discussions about human communication. What might that tell us about how writers contribute to our understanding of important issues?

Agree?

GLOSS: *HOWDY DOODY*
Howdy Doody (par. 10) was a popular children's
television show in the 1950s.

I was a child, my family got the first television on our block, and the neighborhood children gathered in our dining room to watch *Howdy Doody*. Before long, every family had their own TV—just one, so that in order to watch it, families came together. Now many families have more than one television, so each family member can watch what they like—alone. The spread of radio has followed the same pattern. Early radios were like a piece of furniture around which a family had to gather in order to listen. Now radio listeners may have a radio in every room, one in the car, and another—equipped with headphones—for jogging. These technologies now exert a centrifugal force, pulling people apart—and increasing the likelihood that their encounters with each other will be anonymous and hostile.

Electronic communication is progress; it makes human relationships different. But it also makes human relationships more the same—there's more of what's good and more of what's bad. In the end, we graft the new possibilities onto what has always been there.

E-mail gave me the chance to be in touch with someone who was dying far away. College friends, Larry and I were not so close that we would make special trips to visit each other on opposite coasts, but we kept in touch through occasional notes, and we got together whenever we found ourselves in the same town. I learned from another college friend—on e-mail—that Larry was diagnosed with lung cancer. I didn't want to call Larry on the phone; that seemed too intrusive. I didn't know if he wanted to talk about his cancer with people like me; maybe he wanted to curl into his family. So I sent him an e-mail message, and he sent one in reply. Soon we were exchanging messages regularly. E-mail gave me a little path I could walk along. For two years, Larry kept me informed of how he was doing, and what the chemotherapy was doing to him—and asked me how my book was coming and whether I had managed to put up pictures in my new house yet. In April 1996 he was back to work and gaining weight. But then e-mail brought the bad news: new lesions were found, and the doctors held out no more hope.

On December 24, 1996, Larry wrote, "I will miss our e-mails, Deb. It was great being your friend, and I will always remain so." On December 27 I got messages—both on e-mail and on my telephone answering machine—telling me Larry had died the night before. I could not just sit at my desk that day and work. And e-mail was not immediate enough for the connection I wanted. I called friends who had been closer to Larry than I, to learn as much as I could about his last days. And I called friends who had been less close, to tell them. I spent much of that day talking with friends from our college circle. We told each other our memories of Larry's life, creating our own memorial to observe his passing from our lives.

My father never knew exactly when his grandfather died. When my friend Larry died, how much it meant that the telephone made it possible to spend the day talking to others who knew him. How much it meant that Larry said good-bye. This is a gift he gave me, and technology made it possible. That is progress. But the way we used technology—the telephone and e-mail—that was human emotion and experience as old as time.

Back to her father from the intro.

UNDERSTANDING THE TEXT

1. According to Tannen, how have e-mail and the Internet affected human communication in general? Does she see these changes as beneficial? Do you agree with her? Why or why not?

2. In paragraph 10, Tannen writes, "Technology that brings people closer also isolates us in a bubble." What does she mean by that statement? How does she account for this apparent paradox that technology can bring us closer and isolate us at the same time? What might this characteristic of technology suggest about how we deal with change?

3. What does Tannen's experience with Larry reveal about how e-mail can affect human relationships? How was Tannen's experience with Larry different from her father's experience with his father? Why is that difference important, in Tannen's view? What role did technology play in each case? What do you think these situations suggest about the role of technological change in human life?

EXPLORING THE ISSUES

1. In paragraph 5, Tannen writes that "writing e-mail is like writing in a journal." Do you think she's right? Explain. She also describes e-mail as very different from talking on a telephone. In what ways do you think these two means of communicating with another person are similar or different?

2. Tannen includes numerous personal anecdotes throughout this essay. Evaluate her use of anecdotes. What kinds of anecdotes does she include? What points does she make through these anecdotes? Do you think her use of anecdotes is effective? Explain, citing specific passages to support your answer.

3. Tannen describes her use of several technologies in this essay, including the telephone, airplanes, ships, television, e-mail. What purpose do these technologies serve in her life? How do they affect her relationships with the important people in her life? Do you think Tannen sees these technologies generally as positive? Explain.

4. Tannen mentions *progress* only twice in this essay: first, when she writes that "electronic communication is progress," and again in the final paragraph, where she writes that technology made it possible for Larry to say good-bye before he died. What do you think she means by progress in these instances? Is progress the same as change, in Tannen's view? Explain. What do you think are Tannen's attitudes about technology and progress in general? Cite specific passages to support your answer.

5. Tannen is an accomplished scholar who has written for specialized academic audiences, and as the introductions to this essay and to her essay in Chapter 8 indicate (page 306), she has also written best-selling books for a general audience. What kind of audience do you think Tannen imagined for this essay? What assumptions does she make about her audience? Do you think you are part of her intended audience? Explain.

ENTERING THE CONVERSATIONS

1. Write an essay about an important experience you had that somehow involved e-mail.

2. At one point in her essay, Tannen writes that "E-mail makes possible connections with relatives, acquaintances, or strangers, that wouldn't otherwise exist." Based on your own experiences with e-mail and the Internet, write an essay for an audience of your classmates in which

you examine this statement and assess its validity. Do you agree or disagree? Why? Describe some of your own experiences with e-mail and other communications technologies to help support your position.

INFOTRAC

3. In the years since Tannen's essay was first published, e-mail has become an increasingly important medium for communication. Investigate the impact of e-mail using InfoTrac College Edition, the Internet, your library, and other appropriate resources. Find out about the development of e-mail and its increasing use in contemporary society. Investigate its influence on important matters, such as education, business, and government. You might also interview people you know about their uses of e-mail. You might participate in online conversations (such as a web-based discussion group or a blog) to learn more about how others view this issue and how they conduct discussions online. Write a report about what you learned. Assess the impact of e-mail and draw conclusions about the changes it seems to have caused or influenced.

4. Create a web page, PowerPoint presentation, or other appropriate kind of document in which you present your view of the role of e-mail in contemporary society. Include in your document your conclusions about changes that e-mail seems to have created.

5. Test some of Tannen's claims about e-mail as a medium for communication by analyzing several e-mail messages that you or other people you know have written. For example, examine the messages to see what role e-mail seems to play in the relationships between the senders and recipients. Write a report on the basis of your analysis.

I have some friends from England who lived *and worked in the United States for several years. They were both successful professionals who enjoyed their work, but they were sometimes amused by American attitudes about work. Americans take work much too seriously, they would sometimes say. This statement might surprise many Americans, but for someone who grew up in Western Europe, it would make perfect sense. In Western European nations, the average*

IN America, It's Work *First* AND Play Never

worker has four or more weeks of vacation time compared to the standard two weeks in the United States. A study released in 2004 showed that the average American worker uses only eight days of vacation, so even the two weeks that most American workers receive is misleading. The same study showed that most Americans are also working longer hours than they did a decade ago. Often, when such studies are released, economists and politicians focus on what these studies can tell us about the health of the U.S. economy. But well-known writer Ellen Goodman (b. 1941) thinks that these figures tell us something troubling about the well-being of American workers. In the following essay, Goodman examines American attitudes toward work, and she expresses concern about what she sees as the loss of separation between work and our personal lives. She is concerned as well about the decrease in time off from work. These trends worry Goodman because of what they suggest about the lack of balance in our lives. Her essay may prompt you to reexamine your own attitudes about work. I included it in this chapter because I hope it will also get you thinking about how we live with changes that we may not notice—such as the increase in time at work and the decrease in (continued)

ELLEN GOODMAN

Back in the days when the word e-mail was a typo, the "working vacation" was nothing more than an **oxymoron.** After all, you were either vacationing or working. On the job or off.

Now it's become an emblem of the American economy and George W. Bush, its current CEO, is spending this month as a role model on his 1,600-acre Prairie Chapel Ranch in Crawford, Texas.

This has raised the ire of the likes of Sen. **Robert Byrd,** who thundered, "Who's watching the White House?" But it's also raised the dismay of others who watch the vacationer-in-chief conducting business and attending fund-raisers and ask, "Is he having any fun yet?"

Well, are we?

Do you remember those wonderful yesteryears when an earlier 5 Republican president under the spell of the Maine ocean breezes came out in favor of two or three months worth of vacation? William Howard Taft said it was "necessary in order to enable one to continue his work the next year with that energy and effectiveness which it ought to have." Admittedly, the rotund Taft was a bit of a hedonist in (continued) *leisure time. How do such changes affect the way we live? Think about that question as you read.*

Ellen Goodman is a Pulitzer Prize–winning columnist for the Boston Globe. *Her biweekly column appears in hundreds of newspapers. The following essay appeared in her column in 2003.*

GLOSSES

OXYMORON
An *oxymoron* is an apparent paradox or contradiction.

SENATOR BYRD
Robert Byrd is a U.S. senator from West Virginia.

CONTEXT: GEORGE W. BUSH'S VACATIONS
In this passage (par. 2), Goodman refers to the habit of President George W. Bush to spend an extended period of time working at his ranch in Texas rather than at the White House. As Goodman notes here, unlike many former presidents, who would take a short vacation at a family home or resort and then return to work in Washington, D.C., George W. Bush would work for several weeks at his ranch, calling it a "working vacation." Note how Goodman relies on her readers' knowledge of Bush's habits to make her point about work and vacation time. Note, too, how she uses the current political context to introduce her main topic.

STRATEGIES: ASIDES
Notice the parenthetical comment—"trust me on this"—that Goodman includes in this paragraph 17. Writers sometimes use such asides as stylistic devices—that is, to help create a certain tone or voice in their writing. But they can also use asides to help reinforce or make a point. What point might Goodman be making with this aside?

the food department, but it shows how far we've drifted on a summer tide from real vacation.

Americans have always been a touch suspicious of leisure. Our Puritan patriarchs not only famously regarded idle hands as the devil's workshop, they believed the grindstone cleared the path to salvation. We've long been wary of both the idle rich and the idle poor as threats to our democracy.

In the early 20th century, a few hard-working researchers declared that a little time off was a good thing. Not surprisingly, they decided that "brain workers" needed a rest from days spent laboring in the minds, while physical workers could do without it. The idea of vacations finally caught on in the middle and working classes, but it was never codified into the law.

Now we arrive at the summer of the incredible shrinking American vacation. It's predicted that we'll take 10 percent less time off than last year, and last year was no week at the beach.

Americans have notoriously fewer vacation days than workers in any other industrialized country. While Europeans get four or five weeks paid leave by law and even the Chinese get three weeks, we average eight days after a year with one company and 10 days after three years. Thirteen percent of American companies offer no paid vacation at all.

10 Even more remarkable than how few days we get is how few we take. We essentially give back $21 million in time owed but not taken. And in an Expedia poll, one out of five workers said they feel guilty taking vacations.

So, which came first in the great vacation deprivation: the economy or the culture? Insecurity or guilt? The work ethic or the whip?

There's no doubt that a shaky economy breeds fear that any vacation could be permanent. Labor economist Barry Bluestone at Northeastern University points to a changing and insecure economy as the biggest factor. After all, he says, "We always had the Protestant work ethic. Are we more Protestant than last year? I don't think so." But then the tenured Bluestone confessed to being on a working vacation himself.

Joe Robinson, founder of a grass-roots campaign (http://www.worktolive.info) to get a minimum three weeks of paid leave, also acknowledges the role of cultural attitudes that teach "our esteem and self-worth can only come from producing and doing tasks all day."

Americans do have a stunning capacity for turning everything into work. If you don't believe that, think about the waiters everywhere who approach your table with the inevitable question: "Are you still working on that?" They make it sound as if chewing pasta was an onerous job to complete.

15 We not only workout, we play hard, instead of playfully. It's the spirit that turns vacations into work.

VISUAL CONNECTIONS: TAKING A VACATION

In early 2005, Universal Studios theme park in Orlando, Florida, began an advertising campaign based on the kind of information about work and leisure that Goodman cites in this paragraph 10. As Goodman notes, studies show that Americans have less vacation time than workers in other nations and that most Americans don't use their allotted vacation time. Universal Studio's television advertisements included one showing an undertaker who thanks Americans for working themselves to their graves and another advertisement showing a corporate CEO who smugly notes that the American workers who don't take their vacations are turning their time into money for the company. This image from the Universal Studios theme park web site shows statistics indicating that American workers who do not take vacations are at risk for a host of health problems. Consider how effectively Universal Studios theme park presents this information as a way to persuade people to visit the popular theme park. Consider, too, what such an advertisement campaign might suggest about American attitudes regarding work and vacations.

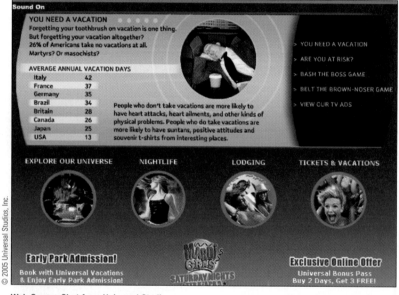

Web Screen Shot from Universal Studios

The irony is that "working vacation" came into the lingo with a wink and a nod. Now the ruse has become a reality. Fully equipped with the toys of e-mail, voice mail, cell-phones, labor trumps leisure. It's the reason why 83 percent of vacationers, tethered by technology and anxiety and expectations, check in at the office.

So here we are. A working vacation means wearing boots while you carry the weight of the world on your shoulders. It means standing on the beach talking to your clients. And it means—trust me on this—sitting at a laptop looking at words on a screen instead of an ocean view.

The blessing is that we can now have a vacation without the guilt. And of course without the vacation.

As for rest, recreation, and time off? Well, fellow Americans, we're still working on that.

UNDERSTANDING THE TEXT

1. Why is Goodman concerned about the lack of vacation time among American workers? Do you think her concerns are justified? Why or why not?

2. What explains the fact that American workers take little vacation time, in Goodman's view? What do you think this explanation suggests about American attitudes toward work and leisure?

3. Why does Goodman call working vacations a "ruse" (par. 16)? What does this suggest about her own attitudes regarding work and leisure? Do you think most Americans would agree with her? Explain.

EXPLORING THE ISSUES

1. Goodman argues that there is a trend in the United States toward more time at work and less time on vacation. Examine how she establishes this point and how she supports her argument.

2. How would you describe Goodman's voice in this essay? What characteristics of her writing contribute to her voice? How effective do you think her voice is for the argument she is making?

3. Goodman suggests that vacations serve an important purpose and that these trends toward more work and less vacation time are troubling. In what ways do you think these trends might be seen as positive? Do you think most Americans would agree with Goodman that these trends are worrisome? Explain.

ENTERING THE CONVERSATIONS

1. Write a letter to your boss (or to an imaginary boss, if you are not currently employed) in which you propose a policy regarding vacation time. In your letter, justify your pro-posed policy on the basis of your ideas about work and leisure and on the basis of how you think the policy will benefit the company or business you work for.

2. Create a web site to advocate for more leisure time and less time at work. Design your site so that it not only presents your viewpoint about work and leisure but also provides information about such matters as how much time Americans and workers in other nations spend working and on vacation. Alternatively, write a letter to the editor of your local newspaper or another appropriate publication in which you express your view about work and leisure.

INFOTRAC

3. Using InfoTrac College Edition, your library, and other relevant resources, investigate work and leisure practices and attitudes of Americans and people in other nations. Consider talking to a professor of business, sociology, or economics who may have expertise on this topic; you might also talk to students from other countries about attitudes toward work in their cultures. Then write a report on the basis of your research. Draw conclusions about the role of work and leisure in our lives and how our attitudes about these issues may be influenced by culture.

4. Using these cartoons (or others you might find), write an essay in which you examine how the cartoons might rely on American attitudes about work for their humor. Discuss also what messages about work these cartoons might convey.

"I'm looking for a workaholic who feels the great job he does is compensation enough."

www.CartoonStock.com

"I've got an assistant now, dear. I should be able to spend more time with you and the kids ...how many is it we've got now?"

www.CartoonStock.com

"Now will you take back everything you said when I insisted on bringing my desk on the cruise?"

www.CartoonStock.com

You've probably heard the expression, "People change." Usually, this expression refers to someone changing his or her beliefs, opinions, preferences, or personality traits, and often it means change for the better. Sometimes people change in ways that are not for the better, and those changes can create great difficulties for them and their loved ones. The following essay by writer Judith Levine (b. 1952) is about such a change. In this essay, Levine describes her experiences

Anger

with her father, who suffers from Alzheimer's disease, a debilitating condition in which the afflicted person progressively loses mental function and sinks into dementia. Usually, this memory loss worsens over time, and as the disease progresses, the person's ability to function at even the most basic tasks, such as eating or bathing, slowly deteriorates. The memory loss becomes so acute that the person may have little sense of time, and memories of experiences in the past become confused with happenings in the present. Ultimately, the person's very personality begins to change as he or she loses touch with daily reality. It's a horrible condition that takes a heavy toll on both those afflicted with the disease and those who care for them, as Levine vividly describes in her essay. But Levine isn't just dealing with the effects of this terrible disease; she is also struggling to come to terms with her complicated and difficult relationship with her father. In that sense, Levine tells the story of that relationship as she witnesses the progress of her father's disease. As she learns to live with the changes the disease causes, she is also learning about herself—and perhaps changing as a result.

Judith Levine is author of several books, including the award-winning (continued)

JUDITH LEVINE

"**I** don't have any more," says Dad, his whole body a shrug of resignation.

We are eating supper on a small white round Melamite table shoved into the corner of Mom and Dad's blue and white, barely "eat-in" kitchen. Mom and I occupy two straight-backed white Melamite chairs, a punitive imitation of modernism, on either side of the table. Dad sits between us on an antique pine ladderback, carried in from the living room.

At **Walden Pond,** Thoreau had three chairs: one for solitude, two for company, three for society. Tonight, here on West Twenty-fourth Street in Manhattan, it's one for loneliness, two for conspiracy, three for exclusion.

The pine chair is Dad's last repair job, monument to his Alzheimer's disease. A few years ago, when he refitted a loose rung in its back, he glued the shaped wood upside down with its garlanded edge drooping toward the floor like a fruited vine. Mom couldn't bear to correct him, he'd wanted so badly to be useful. Now, the chair (continued) Harmful to Minors: The Perils of Protecting Children from Sex (2002), and numerous articles in Harper's, The Village Voice, and Salon, among other publications. The following essay first appeared in her book Do You Remember Me? A Father, a Daughter, and a Search for Self (2004). ▼

GLOSS: WALDEN POND
In his famous book *Walden,* nineteenth century writer Henry David Thoreau described his experiences living a self-sufficient life in a small cabin he built on Walden Pond in Massachusetts. (Thoreau's essay "Resistance to Civil Government" appears on page 449.) Consider what messages Levine's reference to Thoreau's spare cabin might convey in paragraph 3.

and its formerly identical twin flank the upright piano. Among the first purchases of their marriage, the chairs are a pair like them: one "normal," straight, sturdy, and modestly festooned, the other a clownish imitation of normalcy, permanently out of whack.

Alone in the kitchen, the chair seems forlorn, though not so much as its occupant. "I have no boat. I don't have any money!" Dad rummages in his shirt pocket. "I don't have."

Mom answers: "You don't need money, dear."

"My boat, do you remember, Jude? I had in that, that—" He waves his arm outward and upward, compassing what I understand to be the coast of Maine. "A beautiful piece, handsome." The landlocked sailor smiles distantly.

"It was handsome," I say.

"But we had, we had to—we had to."

A familiar lament, the lost boat. Twenty-five years ago it was Dad who tired of sailing, biking, and blueberry-picking and instigated the sale of the steep-roofed little house on the ocean that Mom and I still mourn like a deceased member of the family. These points are no longer debated. "Maine" has become symbolic, its truth bigger than the details.

That truth resides in every photograph of Dad on the boat, face tilted back to gauge the luff of the sail, pipe in teeth, wind in hair, forearm relaxed on the tiller. The boat was pleasure, status, mastery, masculinity. "No boat," he mutters, pushing rice onto his spoon with his index finger. He glowers at Mom. "You have money." Turns to me with a disgusted sigh. "She's always making money."

"Dad, she doesn't make any money either," I say, insisting futilely on reason. "She's retired, like you."

"You have money!" he snaps at me. I don't reply. He heckles.

"Don't you have money? Don't you have money?"

I confess. "Yes, I have money."

A nod of finality—*I rest my case.*

"Not much," I appeal.

He has returned to mashing hacked chicken flesh into the heap of rice soaking in the slick of salad oil he has poured over the whole mess. "She always has money," he says to his plate.

We sit in silence for a long minute.

"You have your things, too," I say, hearing condescension in my voice as I enumerate the items he carries each time he leaves the house. "You have your Metrocard, your senior citizen card, your keys." I leave out the plastic forks, magazine subscription cards, combs, and pencils and pens in a white pocket protector he also totes, a few of which he loses each week. "Everything you need."

"Myuh-myuh-myuh-myuh-myuh-MYA," he mimics the cadence of my sentence and chuckles mordantly. "I need, I need." His hand goes out for yet another chicken breast.

Mom and I lean forward, like two flanks of a defensive army, thwarting him. "Dad, you already—" "Stan, look at—"

With a dangerously large gesture, Dad shoos us both away but forgoes the second helping. Returning to work on his meal, he anchors a half-eaten piece of chicken with a spoon and forefinger and saws at it with an upside-down butter knife. I reach to flip the knife over.

"You!" he barks, pushing my hand away. "I'll!!"

25   Unfettered, Dad would eat the whole chicken. Assurances that he's already had a meal, as little as ten minutes earlier, are met with skepticism, sometimes outrage. Even hunger, it seems, is a function of memory.

"I am aware that I am no longer able to do the things I used to do," he pronounces after a while, almost calmly. It is 2001 and my father was diagnosed with Alzheimer's six years ago. He is most cogent when expressing his disintegration.

*   *   *

We eat in near silence, Mom and I exchanging a few words while Dad maneuvers chicken on spoon or knife or (once in a while) fork to his mouth, dripping juice onto his chin, which is wrinkled in disgruntlement.

Mom appears to be mentally thumbing through tactics: blandish, distract, ignore, commiserate. Sympathize, as in, *Yes, you are right. You are not what you used to be. That must be hard for you.* This last comes rarely. Sympathy stripped of judgment or advice is not big in our family's repertoire. Perhaps she thinks it will only reaffirm his despair. Or her own. "I can't save him," she has told me more than once, "but I am determined not to go down with him." She feels him like a drowning swimmer with his arms locked round her neck.

> **STRATEGIES: CONVEYING UNSPOKEN THOUGHTS**
> In this and the following three paragraphs, Levine uses italics to convey the unspoken thoughts of her mother. Of course, the words are Levine's assumptions or guesses about what her mother is thinking at that moment, but she uses this strategy to try to convey some of the complex and difficult emotions her mother is experiencing as she deals with her husband's disease. Consider what these italicized comments suggest about Levine's view of her mother—and herself.

Tonight, she chooses commiseration. *Co-miseration:* a few comradely yards' swim alongside him in the drowning pool. "You know, Stanley, you're not the only one," she says. "We're all getting older. Every day. I'm getting older too. None of our friends are what they used to be." She ticks off the casualty list: Ruth's eyes, Sonje's paralyzed left side, Helen's cancer. "We're all losing something. We're all in the same boat."

30   "*You're* losing?" Dad snorts. Meaning, I infer, *You're not losing your mind.* And to what boat is she referring? Didn't he just point out that he doesn't *have* a goddamn boat.

"I've lost too," Mom says. *I have lost my husband.* A thin shell of anger closes around the pain in her voice. In our battle-ready family, the wounded are wary of resting undefended.

Dad reaches back and perches a water glass on the edge of the cabinet behind him. Mom and I simultaneously lunge at it. Amusement animates his face as he watches the hysterical pair he can so easily provoke. In this moment of disorder, he makes a final point: "I don't have." And then, "I don't want to talk about it anymore."

"Okay," I say.

"I don't want to talk about it anymore!"

35   "I said okay."

"Okay," says Mom, whether in relief or surrender I cannot tell.

*   *   *

Daddy is too big. I am small. His head is huge, his hair so thick it has muscles of its own. He loves to tickle me, but refuses to stop when my pleasure turns to desperation. He calls me "Little Jood," rhymes with "good." But his voice is loud, as if he were addressing a large audience, not one little girl.

His power is always poised to explode through his large body. Fear robs him of grace; he lugs his temper around like a tank of volatile gas, its incendiary potential seeming to scare him almost as much as it does the rest of us. Our tiny Queens apartment compresses him. We kids are told to be quiet, Dad is in his room with "a splitting headache." I imagine his head breaking in half with a loud crack, like a huge walnut. Once, in a rage, he slams a fist through the wall.

Dad is jubilantly silly. A summer camp director, he dances before all the campers with a fake plastic knife on a headband that looks as if it's stabbed through his head. "Hotchky potky!" he shouts with joy, usually in public places and always to his children's mortification. He surges through the waves at Jones Beach with me on his salty-slick back. I feel both secure and unsafe, wondering if he just might (jokingly) flip his passenger off into the bottomless ocean.

He has funny names for things. A fart is a "poopel," and poopels are funny. "Poopel" is also pseudo-Yiddish, because it is related to a gastrointestinal function, and all things gastrointestinal are Jewish. Jewish is funny. Our family adopts a dog from friends. His name is Lox, his sister's name is Bagels. People find this cute. The Jewish things that are funniest are those that are in some way distasteful or painful, or at least inspire ambivalence—organ meats, poopels, mothers. Dad tells James and me the endless, directionless saga of Seymour Lipschitz, a runny-nosed, violin-playing skinny melink from the East Bronx, and Herman Schullenklopper, the strapping, daring diver from railway bridges and stealer of nickel pickles who is Seymour's idol and tormentor. In this more or less autobiographical story, Seymour is (of course) Jewish, Herman is probably German. One of Dad's remaining "jokes," since Alzheimer's, is to call out playfully and plaintively, for no particular reason, "Sey-mour! Sey-mour!," a "Jewish" name. He laughs, mystifying everyone with his painfully unfunny humor.

*   *   *

As I grow up I learn to joke with, or at, Dad. I become cockier, but I'm still scared of him. When I am nine, shortly after we move to the suburbs, I leave my bike unlocked at school and it is stolen. Fearing punishment, I run away. Two hours later, when I return, Mom is weeping, Dad apoplectic.

"How many times have I told you not to leave the bike?" he bellows. "How many times have I told you to chain it up?" His rage ratchets up and up, he can't seem to stop. *How many times, how many times, how many times!*

I duck past him, run to the bathroom, and lock myself in. He is yelling from the other side of the door. "I TOLD YOU NOT TO LEAVE IT! I'm not buying you another bike!"

STRATEGIES: CHARACTERIZATION
Although this essay is not fictional, Levine employs some of the techniques that fiction writers use to convey their characters to readers. In this paragraph and the following ones, Levine shares some childhood memories of her father. In the process, she not only conveys a sense of what he was like when he was much younger, but she also sets up a contrast to what he is like today. In addition, she tells us a great deal about her own relationship with her father. As you read this section, note the scenes from her childhood that Levine includes here and the information and ideas they convey about her and her father.

40

"Okay, don't. I'll buy another one with my allowance."

"*How many times have I told you?* You're not getting another bike!"

45   "I said I'd buy my own."

GLOSS: CROHN'S DISEASE
Levine is referring here to Crohn's disease, a serious digestive tract disorder that can afflict a person over a long period of time.

As usual when Dad and I fight, Mom interjects only occasional pleas for us both to stop. Now, though, she needs to use the bathroom. Her **Crohn's** is exacerbated by stress. I agree to come out if Dad won't hit me.

"All right, I promise! I *said,* I promise!" he shouts the second time I insist he promise. But when I push the door and peer around it like I've seen the cops do on TV, it is suddenly yanked open. From my left side I see a hand swoop in like the wing of a landing bird. It thuds flat and thick from my forehead to my jawbone.

I duck past him and around the corner to my room, where I slam the door and push a chair against it. I lie back on my orange corduroy bedspread, nursing the betrayal, which stings more than the blow. After a while, though, my dizziness and tears subside into a sort of epiphany. Striking me, Dad has displayed not authority but weakness in the face of his own impulses, not control but frustration at the limits of his authority. His palm is huge, but using it makes him puny. My hurt turns to dispassion. My eyes dry.

50   I address my threadbare Teddy bear: *Do I love Dad?* In my family, this is a legitimate question. Mom and Dad both felt they had been forced to love undeserving parents, and they did not want to burden their own children with what they saw as an emotionally confusing hypocrisy. To them, a child's unconditional love is compulsory love, so it was not required of James and me. For their part, my parents may have loved us, but we did not assume they did.

Do I love Dad? Beary stares in solemn witness, one button eye hanging by a black thread. The answer is no.

*   *   *

When I am a teenager, Dad and I fight over the usual things: chores, my clothes, the music I like, and because it is the sixties, sex and drugs. We make a misery of what ought to be fun. He takes me to the tennis court but instructs me so sternly that I throw the racket to the ground in tears. He takes me sailing, but corrects me so relentlessly that we are not speaking by the time we pick up the mooring. I don't learn either to play tennis or to sail. When I am an adult, I watch him avidly trounce my six-year-old niece, Jessie, at checkers, picking the red disks off the board as a brave tear rolls down her cheek.

It almost seems that we fight *for* fun. We fight about things that concern or interest neither of us, like cars or opera, or arcane subjects, like the temperature inside caves, about which neither of us knows anything. We goad each other, skirmish over politics, even when we agree. For instance, we fight about feminism. I know he supports women's rights; his marriage has been remarkably egalitarian. But I also think he can't stand it that I know more than he does about the subject. This may or may not be because I am a woman.

We know each other through our fights. I believe this means I know him well. Anger limits him; besides depression, it is his chief emotion. This makes him efficiently knowable. At the same time, he is large in his anger, a maestro of anger. He can be artfully angry, sensuously angry, wittily angry, coolly and warmly angry; he even can seem contentedly angry.

I begin to chart our relationship as a series of jagged spikes connected by flat lines: 55 arguments interspersed with absences. I ask myself again and again in different situations whether I love him. The answer is always the same: *No, I do not love my father.*

* * *

Toward James, three and a half years my senior, Dad is dismissive at best, violent at worst. If you have to deserve the love you get at the Levines, James keeps coming up short. Dad takes his son to Washington for his thirteenth birthday. At the Lincoln Memorial, he suggests they "race" to read the Gettysburg Address. Although the reading is silent, Dad claims victory. In high school, every report card brings a conflagration. A German tutor is enlisted, whom James resists with aloof humor and persistently low grades. Dad seems to pay no attention to James's competence in all things mechanical, his charm and wit and good looks. He flirts with James's girlfriend, Leila. When she does not respond, he takes another tack. "We were in Jamie's room making out," Leila recalls. "Your father just barged in without knocking. He looked at us, half-dressed on the bed, and he just laughed. This supercilious laugh, as if we were cute."

All Dad's friends tell me he boasted about James and me.

James leaves home at eighteen without a word. Dad is shocked. "He was totally devastated by it. I think he was looking for reasons," says a colleague of Dad's at the school where he worked as a psychologist. "Such a bright man, with so much compassion for and perception of others that he met or counseled. It's a shame he couldn't use any of that for himself and his son." To me, Dad's surprise that his son ran off is evidence of the reason his son ran off.

During this time, James becomes a carpenter. Some years later, Dad and Mom visit him and his wife and first child in Montana.

My brother takes my parents to see a house he is building. He does not remember 60 a single positive remark from Dad. But when Dad returns to New York he tells a friend that his son is "the Michelangelo of carpentry."

* * *

Home from college at Christmas freshman year, girded by feminism and my first round of psychotherapy, I decide to tell Dad what a terrible father he was. I march into his bedroom, where he is reading. He puts down his book and looks up. I launch into my *J'accuse*. He was self-involved, volatile, unjust, overbearing, cruel to James, and negligent of me. He was not there to protect me; he was hardly there at all. "All you ever did," I tell him with nineteen-year-old certitude, "was criticize." I add that he's an asshole if he doesn't know why James left. I look not at him, but at his mother's Mexican hand-blown cobalt-blue glass jar, my favorite heirloom, spilling dim blue light onto the battered pine dresser.

I expect a fight, so I am thrown off when instead of roaring, he grovels. He did not have a father, he explains, so he didn't know how to father. He pleads for

Contradictions

understanding. It is the first and last time I see him in tears. I remain impassive, un-forgiving. But when I leave my parents' bedroom, I feel hurt, unheard and—though no voices were raised—fought with.

The next day, Mom comes into my room and sits on the bed. She asks me to go easy on Dad. "He's always been threatened by strong women, like his mother," she says. "And like you." I'm flattered but also disgusted. Why does Mom, a strong woman herself, play Dad's toady?

"He's fifty-two years old. He can grow up already," I mutter. I am like that blue glass jar: fire-made, a container of cold light.

*   *   *

65   "Water?" Mom asks, taking a carafe from the refrigerator and carrying it to the table.

"No thanks." The water is a little beige and tastes a little sweet. Dad sometimes pours undrunk soda back into it.

"I don't want to go there," Dad says. Mom and I look at each other. We surmise he's talking about his "program," the day care for adults with memory loss that is held in a community room of their apartment complex.

"You need to go," Mom replies. "Everyone depends on you. They miss you when you're not there."

It's another old discussion, a script Dad has memorized. He knows Mom's part too: a monologue of affirmation that he can reliably prompt. For Mom, who no longer has the energy to make him feel virile, it's a vehicle of unambiguous praise.

70   Usually her cheerleading works. And in fact, he likes the program. But lately, her exhortations are less honest, and he seems to know it. For the first few years the staff pretended Dad was the program's consulting psychologist. He attended meetings, took "notes." He even adopted a fractured version of the workplace plaint—too many clients, short funds, disorganized administration, etc. In the apartment, he erected a version of a busy home office on the radiator cover under the south-facing window in their bedroom, collecting, sorting, stacking, and restacking the postcards and circulars, magazines, and envelopes he finds around the house.

But as his dementia advances, his temper and rambling monologues make him unwelcome at the staff meetings; his anxiety about moving from one activity to an-other turns him from a help to a hindrance in organizing meals or cleanup. The workers have ceased to "consult" him. Superfluous in the last place he felt crucial, Dad is frustrated and angry, and expressing these feelings has only pushed him fur-ther to the margin. Without articulate language, he resorts to a more direct means of expression. Once, when the music instructor declines to take one of his sugges-tions, Dad slugs him.

"I can't go to that now," he says between spoonfuls of chicken-rice porridge. "It's anymore."

"They miss you when you aren't there," Mom repeats.

"You're not me!"

75   Mom, who has learned to let most things drop, is not dropping this. She reprises the earlier theme of loss. Because of his program, she seems to be telling Dad, he is

actually better off than she. She volunteers at a public garden and a pacifist organization, yes. But volunteers are a dime a dozen. She comes and goes at these places; they could live without her, she says. Whereas Dad's daily connection with the people in the group gives him continuity and purpose. She reminds him of the praise and affection he gets there. "You are really needed," she says. "At this point in our lives, that is a very lucky thing."

Dad's lucky? When his slack face arranges itself into an approximation of understanding, he also looks incredulous. I share the sentiment. I am beginning to feel as I often do in their altercations, exasperated by both of them.

Why is she persevering? Maybe it's nostalgia. This exchange, rare for its length and relative coherence, almost resembles a normal dinner table conversation. Or maybe she has seized this occasion to tell him, with me as witness, how she feels about her life. No longer running a large nonprofit agency, she is bereft of worldly responsibility and recognition, which is now supplanted by the private drudgery of responsibility for home and husband. The fate she escaped, uncommonly, in the prefeminist 1950s and '60s has finally caught up with her. She is needed, but only by Dad. And rather than recognize her for the competence with which she looks after all his needs, he resents her for the competence he's lost. Rather than show gratitude for the minor independence she arranges for him, he blames her for his dependence. Rather than loving her for caring, he hates her for taking care of him.

CONVERSATIONS: THE PREFEMINIST 1950s AND 1960s

Levine's reference to the "prefeminist 1950s and '60s" in this passage can be seen as part of a larger conversation about the role of women in American society and the changes in women's roles since World War II. Levine describes her mother as a woman who was unusual in the professional success she enjoyed earlier in her life, at a time when most women would not have enjoyed success outside the home. She obviously admires her mother for living that successful life, but she also reveals her own views about women in expressing her dismay about her mother's present situation. Consider how Levine's discussion of her mother depends to some extent on the ongoing debates about gender in American culture.

A lull in food consumption cues Mom to clear the table. It's all the same to Dad, just another arbitrary change of activity, though he has only half finished the vast quantity before him. He gets up to "help," moving the dirty dishes from the table straight to the cupboard. I tensely hold my tongue.

Back in his seat, Dad sets about tidying the environs within his reach. He picks up the spoon, turning and contemplating it, waiting for its message to rise to the shiny surface, wipes the spoon with the paper napkin, folds the napkin into a small square, lays the spoon on the napkin. Then, moving the spoon neatly to the right of the napkin, he fashions a scraper of the tiny paper square and proceeds to steer each crumb on his place mat toward a central pile, transfers the crumbs to a larger pile near the table's edge, and finally negotiates a swift drop of collected crumbs over the side and into his hand, dropping about half onto the floor. Looking around for a place to empty his palm, he shakes the crumbs out beside the mat, then scrapes that pile again into his left hand. Holding the crumbs in his half-cupped hand, he licks the napkin and rubs at each grease spot on the mat. Then he smacks his hands briskly together, scattering the crumbs onto the floor.

Mom, readying dessert, ignores him. When she sits down with a bundt cake and coffee, he grasps her arm, repeats her name, and repeats it again and again—"Lil, Lil, Lil"—until she doles out acknowledgment for his housekeeping, a coin in his palm. His eyes turn to me, asking for more.

But I look away, silent. After just an afternoon and evening with him, I am emptied of affirmation, and what spills into its place is my reflexive resistance to his lifelong

80

demand for it. More than the extra chores he has created, what is irritating me is the unspoken requirement that I collaborate in the charade that he's taking care of everything. It is the same illusion my mother has perpetuated all her married life, and now the day care staff has joined in too. The first time it was farce. Now, it's tragedy.

At the moment, for Mom's sake, it seems easiest to collaborate. "It's true, Dad. You're a leader at your program." That's not saying much, considering the competition, but I am not exactly lying either. Despite the staff's efforts at industry and jollity, the esprit in that cinderblock room is vegetal at best. Dad is the life of the party. When he's not pissed off at someone, he is a singer and dancer, lady's man, and all-around happy camper. I tell him now, "You're definitely the most fun guy in that room."

He looks skeptically from Mom to me and back. Are we ganging up? Although he angles for flattery outside, in this kitchen nothing inflames him more than phony compliments. And more often than not, he wagers that Mom's and my compliments are phony. If he doesn't want to go to his program, why are we insisting? He knows why: because it lets Mom *get rid of him.* He tries expressing this complicated idea. "She's always going," he says to me, his hands fluttering up and out like quails flushed from a forest floor. "There here and there and there and there." Mom and I look at one another—conspiratorially?

"Dad, why can't you hear what Mom and I are saying? People like you in the group. That's all."

85   His face darkens. "Like me?"

"They like you."

He laughs, the parody of a villain—**Boris Badenov.** "They like me."

"Yes, the people in your group like you."

A pause, while he regroups. "What are you talking about?"

90   "You understand," I say. "We're saying people need you."

"What?"

"People need you."

Angrier: "I need you?"

He's a man who can't take yes for an answer, Mom always says. But his refusal is more selective than that. He pulls desperately for yeses most anywhere he can get them, but when one comes from a person close to him, like Mom or me, he can't stop himself from rebuffing it. "Dad," I hiss. "Listen. To. What. We. Are. Saying."

95   "They need me?" His voice rises, then steadies. "You need me?" Upheaval, his most familiar emotion, seems to stabilize him.

"Mom and I are saying that people like you and need you."

"You need me?"

*   *   *

Our last fair fight, just before Alzheimer's, is about the fact that we fight. It takes place in another blue and white room, this one in upstate New York, a few country houses after the sale of the house in Maine. It is sometime in the 1980s, and we are talking about **the Chinese student dissidents,** one of whom has been imprisoned. Dad, a barely reconstructed Stalinist, is calling the students "counterrevolutionaries." The Chinese have it a lot better than they had before the Revolution, he says. They have food, they have housing. There is too little to go around in China as it is. Why do they need consumer goods? As for democracy, economic rights must come first. I'm saying that people are willing to sacrifice a lot while a revolution is going on, but once it is won, they expect the goods they were promised. They want democracy. They also want blue jeans.

> **CONTEXT: THE CHINESE DISSIDENTS**
> In this passage, Levine is referring to the prodemocracy protests, led by students, that occurred in China in 1989. Thousands of protesters filled the vast Tiananmen Square in Beijing, where they remained for several weeks, demanding greater political freedoms. The protests ended violently when the Chinese army entered the square, arresting thousands of dissidents and wounding and killing thousands more. Estimates of the dead range from several hundred to more than 7,000.

The argument is fueled by what Freud called the narcissism of small differences. In the big picture, we are on the same side. But we will disagree over the details, and struggle over that last half inch of disputed territory, until one of us is bleeding.

Later, I think, this is a debate about scarcity—about how much a person can expect when resources are few, when everyone feels deprived. In his life, Dad has learned to expect little. Neglected child, adolescent of the Depression, husband whose wife loves him but cannot provide the bottomless affection he longs for, he tries for contentment. Yet his need spills over. I, postwar Baby Boomer, entitled child of peace, plenty, and psychotherapy, want more. Like the young Chinese, my expectations are high, and so are my disappointments.

After about an hour, I yield on one point. Immediately, Dad runs around to the opposite corner, the one I'd just stepped away from, to keep the punches flying. I raise my fists for the next round, then drop them. Suddenly, I am exhausted.

"I can't stand this anymore," I scream, tearful. "You won't even let me agree with you. If all you want to do is argue, I can't talk to you." I add: "I don't want to talk to you. Ever again." And, like a tragic hero in the last act, I fall upon my sword. (Actually, I go upstairs to read.)

When he recounts the event to my brother on the phone a few days later, Dad says, "You know Judy. She wants everybody to agree with her, but she'll never agree with anyone else." Of course, he's right. I am my father's daughter, a girl who won't take yes for an answer.

* * *

Dad cuts the slice of bundt cake Mom has served him in half and half again. He stirs four packets of Nutrasweet into his black coffee, powdering the area around the cup as he tears into the little pink envelopes. "I don't want to talk about it anymore," he says.

"Okay," says Mom. "So we won't talk about it."

"Okay," I say.

"Okay!" says Dad.

He bisects the cake until there is no piece big enough to pick up with a fork and gathers the remnants into his spoon. Then he turns his body fully toward me. "So. What do *you* think?"

I work at gathering the remnants of the subject, if there was one, back into cogency. Dad may no longer be a master of repartee, but now that he's demented he's gotten good at driving other people out of their minds. "Ye-es," he prompts. "Go on . . ."

110   "You're right," I say, coolly. "You aren't what you used to be."

It takes him a minute. That comment was way too long ago for him to remember. "THAT's what you think!?"

"Dad, I'm agreeing with you."

He chuckles sarcastically. I go back to my cake. He waits, alert. "Ye-es?"

"What I think," I say finally, "is that you *do* want to talk about it." For my nimbleness in debate, I credit a lifetime of paternal tutelage.

115   Cornered, he strikes. "Do you need me?"

I pause, unwilling to reassure him. "You're my father—"

"Do you need me?"

"Well, I can take care of myself, if that's what you mean."

"You're not me! You don't know me!" He spits cake crumbs.

120   I parry. "Well, I know you better than I did as a child. I mean, we spend much more time together now than we did then."

"You did that," he grumbles.

"Oh," I retort, constructing an argument far more logical than the one he's flailing around in. "It was my fault you were never there." My sarcastic chuckle is almost identical to his.

Dad is drifting. Rage is his only raft.

"Judy, don't—" says Mom quietly.

125   "We spend an afternoon almost every week together," I say. Then I taint goodwill with ill: "I can't remember ever spending an afternoon with you in my childhood." Feeling slightly guilty, I cast around for an antidote. "And—" I hesitate, unwilling to say our time together feels good, "and I think we're closer than we were."

He slams his big hands flat on the table, flipping his fork onto the floor and rattling the cake plates. He rises from the table. "I don't need you!"

The kitchen shrinks. Dad fills one end with his fulminating, Mom clutters the other, tossing little scraps of diplomacy: "Jude, he's just trying to—" "Stan, take it easy. Judy doesn't mean—"

I stand in my tight corner, shoulder Dad out of my way, clump through the door into the living room, and wildly start to collect my jacket and bag. "Okay, Dad," I shout back toward the kitchen. "Have it your way. Nobody needs you. You don't need anybody."

But he is hard behind me. I feel his heat and noise like a furnace opening at my back. He muscles around to face me, forces his face into mine, close enough to kiss. Fierce gibberish and spittle hit my cheek. "You *need* me?" That old grimace of sarcasm, now twisted crazy.

130   "All right," I shout. "Fuck you! People hate you. That what you want to hear?"

We are inches from each other's bodies, our torsos leaning in, then pulling away, hands drawing backward, afraid of striking—a boxing video run in reverse. "DON'T MAKE ME STUPID!" he shouts.

He grabs at my bag and jacket—to harass me or hold me? We are almost equal in size now, he stooped and shrunken, I tall in my heeled sandals. *Now we're close,* I think. *Now we are connecting. This is what we need each other for.* I am shaking, but not crying.

My eyes follow the creases beside his mouth down to the wattles of his neck. A perverse energy shivers through me. When **Jane Eyre's** beloved, the mesmerizingly potent Mr. Rochester, is blinded, "his power dropped and my Soul grew straight," she says. I am stronger and nimbler than my father. My hands could easily collar that neck. *I could hurt him.*

I push past him, slam the front door behind me, and make for the stairwell, my shoes clapping like sparse applause—for what?—on the six flights' descent. In the subway to Brooklyn I scribble what I can remember on a pad of tiny yellow Post-its. The pages flutter into my straw bag, sticking to each other and everything else. They are the beginnings of the book I hope will help me know my father. But knowing him may be no easier than fighting with him.

> **GLOSS: JANE EYRE**
> Here Levine is referring to the classic nineteenth century novel *Jane Eyre* by Charlotte Bronte. In the novel, Mr. Rochester is the strong, wealthy man who falls in love with Jane Eyre.

The teaching or revelation any power of writing.

* * *

When I reach home, I can barely lift my legs up the three flights of stairs to my apartment. I peel the Post-its from my bag and spread them on my desk, quickly typing some sequence of the events at Mom and Dad's apartment into the journal in my computer. My reconstruction is probably more logical than reality. I often do this with Dad's sentences too: in retrospect I rearrange the syntax, insert missing subjects, verbs, and transitions. It's almost involuntary, the same way retelling a dream constructs a narrative of scattered images and feelings.

I call Mom, worried that Dad's rage might have spilled onto her. She says no; he turned contrite the instant I left. "I'm all alone. You're the only one I have," he told her. "I love you," he said, followed by his twin declaration, "I need you." This she recounts with weary dread in her voice. She tells me, "When you were kids, I used to ask myself, in the midst of the screaming and crying and hitting, 'How can I stay with a man who cares so little about his children?'"

"So how could you?" I ask. As I teenager, when I had absolute opinions about what was acceptable in a relationship (that is, before I'd actually been in one), I used to exhort her to leave him. Now her tone changes. She talks about how supportive he was of her work, how patient with her illness, how funny. She doesn't mention my outburst this evening. But I know that my temper, my messing with Dad's emotions, has only left her more to clean up. She says Dad floated to lucidity, as often happens. "He looked at me that way, with his same old plaintiveness," Mom says, "and he asked me, 'What did I do to my children?'" The funny part, she says, is that he always wanted more children, four or five. "He loved fatherhood." 135

I hang up the phone, flip through my mail, wash the dishes in the sink. I'm happy to be in my own lemon-lime-colored kitchen with its shelves of bright, mismatched fifties dishes and a clutch of apricot-colored tulips wilting in a vase on the table. It's late, but I call Paul, who lives in Vermont. He answers groggily but is happy to talk. We chat about the tax sale of his neighbor's property, about the emu chicks at the organic farm further down the hill. We arrange Paul's next trip to New York, the exchange of cars and cat. Paul's house is in Vermont, my apartment is in Brooklyn, we both have offices and phones in each other's houses. I live in Vermont in the summer; during the year we go back and forth, sometimes together, sometimes apart.

Usually the logistics of our peripatetic relationship irritate, but tonight they seem simple; they center me. As always I ask how our cat, Julius, is. "He's fine," answers Paul cheerfully, as always.

"I had a huge fight with my father tonight," I say after a while.

"How'd you manage that?" Paul asks, laughing gently.

"He's still . . . himself. You know."

140   "And you're yourself."

"Yeah," I say, feeling sheepish. "I'm myself." We're both silent for a minute. "Well," I say, "I've gotta figure out a better way to deal with it."

Paul laughs again, patient with the obvious. "That would be a good idea, Judith."

UNDERSTANDING THE TEXT

1. What does the opening scene (par. 1–36) of this passage reveal about Alzheimer's disease? What does it reveal about Levine and her family? What does it suggest about the changes in her life that she has been confronting as her father's disease worsens?

2. What reactions do Levine and her mother have to her father's disease? What do these reactions reveal about them as individuals? What do they reveal about their family?

3. What is the nature of Levine's relationship with her father? How does her relationship with him affect her ways of dealing with his disease?

4. What effects does Levine's father's disease have on her mother? How does it affect her parents' marriage? What do you think the impact of the disease on her parents' relationship suggests about the kind of marriage they have had? What might it suggest about the challenges of confronting change in *any* relationship?

5. What is the charade that Levine believes her mother and the day care staff are carrying on with her father? What does this situation suggest about the efforts of her family to deal with the changes brought on by her father's Alzheimer's disease?

6. What does Levine learn through the experience of dealing with her father's Alzheimer's disease?

EXPLORING THE ISSUES

1. This essay is as much about family relationships as it is about dealing with Alzheimer's disease and the changes it brings. What do you think this essay suggests about family relationships? What does it

say about the love between parents and children?

2. Levine's Jewish identity and culture are an important part of this story. What role does her family's Jewish heritage play in their relationships to one another? What role does it play in their efforts to deal with her father's disease? What do you think this story suggests about cultural heritage and its role in how we confront difficult changes in our lives?

3. This story is obviously told from Levine's perspective. It is her version of her family's past and of their efforts to deal with the present, which is so profoundly shaped by Alzheimer's disease. How credible do you think Levine is as the teller of this story? Do you trust her as the writer? Why or why not? How trustworthy do you think her descriptions of her family members are? Of herself? Explain, citing specific passages to support your answer.

4. Throughout this passage, Levine uses dialogue to convey what is happening in the scenes she is describing and to relate the conversations that occurred in those scenes. How effective do you think her use of dialogue is? What goals do you think the dialogue enables Levine to accomplish as the writer telling this story?

5. In paragraph 133, Levine refers to her notes for the book from which this passage is taken. Why do you think she makes such a reference to her own book? What does she mean when she says that this is the book she hopes will help her know her father? Based on this passage, do you think she succeeds in knowing her father through writing this book? Explain.

ENTERING THE CONVERSATIONS

1. Write an essay in which you describe an experience you have had

dealing with a challenging or trying change in your own family life.

2. This essay could easily have been placed in Chapter 7 (Relationships). Write an essay in which you discuss what Levine's story might suggest about relationships, especially parent–child relationships, and change within relationships. In your essay, draw on your own experiences and any other essays in this book to help support your analysis of Levine's essay.

INFOTRAC

3. Alzheimer's disease typically afflicts the elderly, and it is increasing among Americans as the population ages. It is an ironic result of the fact that Americans are living longer than ever before. The disease is also poorly understood, very difficult to treat, and without a cure. Use InfoTrac College Edition, the Internet, and other relevant resources to research Alzheimer's disease. Visit the web sites of organizations devoted to understanding the disease and supporting those afflicted with it and their families. If possible, talk to your doctor or other medical professionals in your area about the disease. Then write a report on the basis of your research. In your report, be sure to discuss the impact of the disease not only on the person suffering from it but also on his or her family and loved ones, and draw conclusions about the changes this disease may cause in individual lives as well as in American society in general.

4. On the basis of your research for Question 3, create a pamphlet, web site, or similar kind of document whose purpose is to provide information about Alzheimer's disease and offer advice to people who may be dealing with the changes it can cause in their lives.

PROGRESS

I N THE PAST DECADE OR SO, MEDICAL RESEARCHERS HAVE BECOME INCREASINGLY ALARMED BY THE EMERGENCE OF SO-CALLED "SUPERBUGS," NEW AND ESPECIALLY VIRULENT STRAINS OF BACTERIA THAT ARE RESISTANT TO ANTIBIOTICS. SCIENTISTS BELIEVE THEY KNOW HOW THESE SUPERBUGS DEVELOP: THROUGH THEIR NATURAL REPRODUCTION CYCLES, THEY MUTATE SO THAT

subsequent generations of the bacteria develop immunity to drugs that killed previous generations. It's a classic example of natural selection. Since the development of antibiotics, which were hailed as "miracle drugs" in the early twentieth century, common infections that once killed millions of people could be defeated. And as new bacteria emerged, new drugs were developed to combat them. If you were ever given medication for an ear infection or bronchitis, then you have benefited from these drugs, like millions of other people. For most of the past century, antibiotics have been considered one of medical science's great success stories, an example of the march of modern civilization. Like other im-

> We tend to believe that we can always find a scientific or technological fix to any problem

portant scientific and technological breakthroughs, such as electricity or anesthetics, antibiotics improved our lives. That's progress.

But the appearance of drug-resistant bacteria is one sign that progress may be a more complicated matter than we usually think. The overuse of antibiotics to defeat dangerous bacteria has ironically helped give rise to even more dangerous bacteria. In the same way, our astonishing technological developments and industrial growth, which have given us the comforts of warm homes, bright lights, and fast cars, have also caused a host of environmental and social problems and seem to be contributing to global warming, which may be a looming catastrophe. Our technological prowess has enabled us to devise increasingly sophisticated

devices for communicating with each other throughout the world, but it has also enabled us to create ever deadlier weapons of awesome power. In short, human progress on so many different fronts is undeniable, but it may also be a mixed bag.

You may reject the idea that progress can be a mixed bag. Most of us seem to believe that progress is a good thing, despite the kinds of problems just described. Indeed, our collective belief in progress often seems unshakeable. We tend to believe that we can always find a scientific or technological fix to any problem. After all, we have often done so in the past.

A few years ago at a family gathering, I was talking to a cousin of mine who is a doctor. I told him about a newspaper article I had recently read describing the drug-resistant bacteria, and I expressed my concern that these new strains of bacteria could create a widespread health crisis in the coming decades. I mentioned that some scientists have begun to lobby the medical community to drastically reduce their use of antibiotics so that they do not contribute to the development of other strains of drug-resistant bacteria. My cousin, a smart and caring man who has been a family physician for more than twenty years, dismissed my concerns. The drug companies will eventually come up with new drugs to kill these new bacteria, he said. He had absolute confidence in modern science to meet this challenge.

The readings in this cluster may temper that confidence. They complicate our ideas about progress and they raise questions about our collective belief in progress as a good thing. They also help us see some of the consequences of the amazing scientific and technological developments that we usually consider signs of progress.

As a child, I was terrified of the dentist. Not only was it often painful to have my teeth worked on with scary-sounding drills and other strange-looking metal instruments, but I also hated needles, which dentists sometimes use. Today, I still don't like going to the dentist, but I'm no longer so fearful of it. That's mostly because modern technology and new dental techniques have made most dental procedures almost painless. Procedures like filling a cavity are much easier

THE Myth OF Progress

and more effective than they once were. Even the needles are better, and a good dentist can give you an injection that you don't even feel. Clearly, when it comes to dentistry, things are much better than they were twenty or thirty years ago. Similar improvements have occurred in medicine, communications, transportation, and other important areas of our lives. No wonder that for most of us the very idea of progress is a positive one.

Writer Kirkpatrick Sale (b. 1937) would agree that dentistry might be better today than in the past, but he has serious doubts about whether progress, as we usually understand that term, has benefited humanity in general. In the following essay, Sale examines what progress has meant for the world's people today, and the picture he paints is not a happy one. Where others may see improvement as a result of scientific or technological progress, Sale sees a more complicated picture. He focuses attention on the consequences of progress, not just for those who may benefit from it but for those whose lives are no better and maybe even worse as a result of progress. His argument will strike many readers as pessimistic, but his essay may also prompt you to look again at the world that progress has given us.   (continued)

KIRKPATRICK SALE

I can remember vividly sitting at the dinner table arguing with my father about progress, using upon him all the experience and wisdom I had gathered at the age of fifteen. Of course we live in an era of progress, I said, just look at cars—how clumsy and unreliable and slow they were in the old days, how sleek and efficient and speedy they are now.

He raised an eyebrow, just a little. And what has been the result of having all these wonderful new sleek and efficient and speedy cars, he asked. I was taken aback. I searched for a way to answer. He went on.

How many people die each year as a result of these speedy cars, how many are maimed and crippled? What is life like for the people who produce them, on those famous assembly lines, the same routinized job hour after hour, day after day, like **Chaplin's film?** How many fields and forests and even towns and villages have been paved over so that these cars can get to all the places they want to get to— and park there? Where does all the gasoline come from, and at what cost, and what happens when we burn it and exhaust it?

KIRKPATRICK SALE, "THE MYTH OF PROGRESS." FROM *EARTH CRASH EARTH SPIRIT*, JULY 22, 2003 HTTP://ECES.ORG/.

(continued) *Kirkpatrick Sale has written many articles and books on technology and environmental issues, including* Rebels against the Future: The Luddites and Their War on the Industrial Revolution *(1995) and* The Green Revolution: The American Environmental Movement, 1962–1992 *(1993). He is also a contributing editor of* The Nation *magazine. The following essay was published in* Earth Crash Earth Spirit *in 2003.* ☑

GLOSSES
CHAPLIN'S FILM
Sale is referring to *Modern Times* (1936), a famous silent film directed by Charlie Chaplin, seen as his protest against the industrial age, in which the Tramp, a character played by Chaplin, works at one point on a factory assembly line.

CARL BECKER
American historian Carl Becker (1873–1945) studied intellectual history and especially the Enlightenment (see *Conversations: The Enlightenment* on page 498). The essay Sale refers to was titled "Progress" and appeared in the *Encyclopedia of Social Sciences* in 1934.

E. E. CUMMINGS
Sale is referring in paragraph 7 to "pity this busy monster, manunkind," a poem by e. e. cummings (1894–1962):

pity this busy monster, manunkind,

not. Progress is a comfortable disease:
your victim (death and life safely beyond)

plays with the bigness of his littleness
- electrons deify one razorblade
into a mountainrange; lenses extend
unwish through curving wherewhen till unwish
returns on its unself.

A world of made
is not a world of born—pity poor flesh

and trees, poor stars and stones, but never this
fine specimen of hypermagical

ultraomnipotence. We doctors know

a hopeless case if—listen: there's a hell
of a good universe next door; let's go

Consider how poetry might be part of the ongoing conversations in modern society about issues like progress. Consider, too, how Sale uses this reference to participate in those conversations.

Before I could stammer out a response—thankfully—he went on to tell me about an article written on the subject of progress, a concept I had never really thought of, by one of his Cornell colleagues, the historian **Carl Becker,** a man I had never heard of, in the *Encyclopedia of Social Sciences,* a resource I had never come across. Read it, he said.

I'm afraid it was another fifteen years before I did, though in the meantime I came to learn the wisdom of my father's skepticism as the modern world repeatedly threw up other examples of invention and advancement—television, electric carving knife, microwave oven, nuclear power—that showed the same problematic nature of progress, taken in the round and negatives factored in, as did the automobile. When I finally got to Becker's masterful essay, in the course of a wholesale re-examination of modernity, it took no scholarly armament of his to convince me of the peculiar historical provenance of the concept of progress and its status not as an inevitability, a force as given as gravity as my youthful self imagined, but as a cultural construct invented for all practical purposes in the Renaissance and advancing the propaganda of capitalism. It was nothing more than a serviceable myth, a deeply held unexamined construct—like all useful cultural myths—that promoted the idea of regular and eternal improvement of the human condition, largely through the exploitation of nature and the acquisition of material goods.

Of course by now it is no longer such an arcane perception. Many fifteen-year-olds today, seeing clearly the perils with which modern technology has accompanied its progress, some of which threaten the very continuance of the human species, have already worked out for themselves what's wrong with the myth. It is hard to learn that forests are being cut down at the rate of 56 million acres a year, that desertification threatens 8 billion acres of land worldwide, that all of the world's seventeen major fisheries are in decline and stand a decade away from virtual exhaustion, that 26 million tons of topsoil is lost to erosion and pollution every year, and believe that this world's economic system, whose functioning exacts this price, is headed in the right direction and that direction should be labeled "progress."

E. E. Cummings once called progress a "comfortable disease" of modern "manunkind," and so it has been for some. But at any time since the triumph of capitalism only a minority of the world's population could be said to be really living in comfort, and that comfort, continuously threatened, is achieved at considerable expense.

Today of the approximately 6 billion people in the world, it is estimated that at least a billion live in abject poverty, lives cruel, empty, and mercifully short. Another 2 billion eke out life on a bare subsistence level, usually sustained only by one or another starch, the majority without potable drinking water or sanitary toilets. More than 2 million more live at the bottom edges of the money economy but with incomes less than $5,000 a year and no property or savings, no net worth to pass on to their children.

That leaves less than a billion people who even come close to struggling for lives of comfort, with jobs and salaries of some regularity, and a quite small minority at the top of that scale who could really be said to have achieved comfortable lives; in the world, some 350 people can be considered (U.S. dollar) billionaires (with slightly more than 3 million millionaires), and their total net worth is estimated to exceed that of 45 per cent of the world's population.

10   This is progress? A disease such a small number can catch? And with such inequity, such imbalance?

In the U.S., the most materially advanced nation in the world and long the most ardent champion of the notion of progress, some 40 million people live below the official poverty line and another 20 million or so below the line adjusted for real costs; 6 million or so are unemployed, more than 30 million said to be too discouraged to look for work, and 45 million are in "disposable" jobs, temporary and part-time, without benefits or security. The top 5 percent of the population owns about two-thirds of the total wealth; 60 percent own no tangible assets or are in debt; in terms of income, the top 20 percent earn half the total income, the bottom 20 percent less than 4 percent of it.

Poster from Cincinnati Industrial Exposition

All this hardly suggests the sort of material comfort progress is assumed to have provided. Certainly many in the U.S. and throughout the industrial world live at levels of wealth undreamed of in ages past, able to call forth hundreds of servant-equivalents at the flip of a switch or turn of a key, and probably a third of this "first world" population could be said to have lives of a certain amount of ease and convenience. Yet it is a statistical fact that it is just this segment that most acutely suffers from the true "comfortable disease," what I would call affluenza: heart disease, stress, over-

Consider the following two images, which show automobile assembly lines. The first shows an assembly line from the mid-twentieth century, when each job along the line was performed by a worker. The second shows a current assembly line, on which almost every job is performed by a machine. Such technological change is often presented as progress. What is the nature of such progress? What are its consequences? To what extent do such images support or complicate Sale's point?

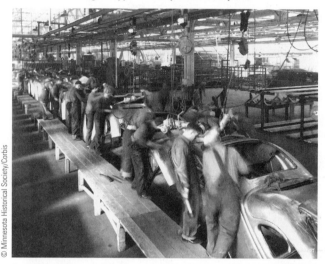

Ford Automobile Assembly Line, 1935

Computerized Auto Assembly Line, 1995

work, family dysfunction, alcoholism, insecurity, anomie, psychosis, loneliness, impotence, alienation, consumerism, and coldness of heart.

Leopold Kohr, the Austrian economist whose seminal work, *The Breakdown of Nations,* is an essential tool for understanding the failures of political progress in the last half-millennium, often used to close his lectures with this analogy.

Suppose we are on a progress-train, he said, running full speed ahead in the approved manner, fueled by the rapacious growth and resource depletion and cheered on by highly rewarded economists. What if we then discover that we are headed for a precipitous fall to a certain disaster just a few miles ahead when the tracks end at an uncrossable gulf? Do we take advice of the economists to put more fuel into the engines so that we go at an ever-faster rate, presumably hoping that we build up a head of steam so powerful that it can land us safely on the other side of the gulf; or do we reach for the brakes and come to a screeching if somewhat tumble-around halt as quickly as possible?

Progress is the myth that assures us that full-speed-ahead is never wrong. Ecology is the discipline that teaches us that it is disaster.   15

Before the altar of progress, attended by its dutiful acolytes of science and technology, modern industrial society has presented an increasing abundance of sacrifices from the natural world, imitating on a much grander and more devastating scale the religious rites of earlier empires built upon similar conceits about the domination of nature. Now, it seems, we are prepared to offer up even the very biosphere itself.

No one knows how resilient the biosphere, how much damage it is able to absorb before it stops functioning—or at least functioning well enough to keep the human species alive. But in recent years some very respectable and authoritative voices have suggested that, if we continue the relentless rush of progress that is so stressing the earth on which it depends, we will reach that point in the quite near future. The Worldwatch Institute, which issues annual accountings of such things, has warned that there is not one life-support system on which the biosphere depends for its existence—healthy air, water, soil, temperature, and the like—that is not now severely threatened and in fact getting worse, decade by decade.

Not long ago a gathering of elite environmental scientists and activists in Morelia, Mexico, published a declaration warning of "environmental destruction" and expressing unanimous concern "that life on our planet is in grave danger." And recently the U.S. Union of Concerned Scientists, in a statement endorsed by more than a hundred Nobel laureates and 1,600 members of national academies of science all over the world, proclaimed a "World Scientists' Warning to Humanity" stating that the present rates of environmental assault and population increase cannot continue without "vast human misery" and a planet so "irretrievably mutilated" that "it will be unable to sustain life in the manner that we know."

The high-tech global economy will not listen; cannot listen. It continues apace its expansion and exploitation. Thanks to it, human beings annually use up some 40% of all the net photosynthetic energy available to the planet Earth, though we are but a single species of comparatively insignificant numbers. Thanks to it, the world economy has grown by more than five times over in the last 50 years and is continuing at a dizzying pace to use up the world's resources, create unabating pollution and waste, and increase the enormous inequalities within and between all nations of the world.

Suppose an Objective Observer were to measure the success of Progress—that is to say, the capital-P myth that ever since the **Enlightenment** has nurtured and guided and presided over that happy marriage of science and capitalism that has produced modern industrial civilization.

Has it been, on the whole, better or worse for the human species? Other species? Has it brought humans more happiness than there was before? More justice? More equality? More efficiency? And if its ends have proven to be more benign than not, what of its means? At what price have its benefits been won? And are they sustainable?

The Objective Observer would have to conclude that the record is mixed, at best. On the plus side, there is no denying that material prosperity has increased for about a sixth of the world's humans, for some beyond the most avaricious dreams of kings and potentates of the past. The world has developed systems of transportation and communication that allow people, goods, and information to be exchanged on a scale and at a swiftness never before possible. And for maybe a third of these humans longevity has been increased, along with a general improvement in health and sanitation that has allowed the expansion of human numbers by about tenfold in the last three centuries.

STRATEGIES: PLACING NUMBERS IN CONTEXT
In paragraph 8, Sale is citing figures to support his claim, which he states in the previous paragraph, that those who live comfortably under capitalism do so "at considerable expense." Notice how the first figure he provides is 6 billion, the approximate total world population. This figure provides a context for the figures he provides later in this paragraph and elsewhere in the essay. Consider how the impact of those latter figures might be changed if Sale had not included the figure of 6 billion here.

On the minus side, the costs have been considerable. The impact upon the earth's species and systems to provide prosperity for a billion people has been, as we have seen, devastatingly destructive—only one additional measure of which is the fact that it has meant the permanent extinction of perhaps 500,000 species this century alone. The impact upon the remaining five-sixths of the human species has been likewise destructive, as most of them have seen their societies colonized or displaced, their economies wrenched and shattered, and their environments transformed for the worse in the course of it, driving them into an existence of deprivation and misery that is almost certainly worse than they ever knew, however difficult their times past, before the advent of industrial society.

And even the billion whose living standards use up what is effectively 100 percent of the world's available resources each year to maintain, and who might be therefore assumed to be happy as a result, do not in fact seem to be so. No social indices in any advanced society suggest that people are more content than they were a generation ago, various surveys indicate that the "misery quotient" in most countries has increased, and considerable real-world evidence (such as rising rates of mental illness, drugs, crime, divorce, and depression) argues that the results of material enrichment have not included much individual happiness.

25   Indeed, on a larger scale, almost all that Progress was supposed to achieve has failed to come about, despite the immense amount of money and technology devoted to its cause. Virtually all of the dreams that have adorned it over the years, particularly in its most robust stages in the late 19th century and in the past twenty years of computerdom, have dissipated as utopian fancies—those that have not, like nuclear power, chemical agriculture, manifest destiny, and the welfare state, turned into nightmares. Progress has not, even in this most progressive nation, eliminated poverty (numbers of poor have increased and real income has declined for 25 years), or drudgery (hours of employment have increased, as has work within the home, for both sexes), or ignorance (literacy rates have declined for fifty years, test scores have declined), or disease (hospitalization, illness, and death rates have all increased since 1980).

It seems quite simple: beyond prosperity and longevity, and those limited to a minority, and each with seriously damaging environmental consequences, progress does not have a great deal going for it. For its adherents, of course, it is probably true that it doesn't have to; because it is sufficient that wealth is meritorious and affluence desirable and longer life positive. The terms of the game for them are simple: material betterment for as many as possible, as fast as possible, and nothing else, certainly not considerations of personal morality or social cohesion or spiritual depth or participatory government, seems much to matter.

But the Objective Observer is not so narrow, and is able to see how deep and deadly are the shortcomings of such a view. The Objective Observer could only conclude that since the fruits of Progress are so meager, the price by which they have been won is far too high, in social, economic, political, and environmental terms, and that neither societies nor ecosystems of the world will be able to bear the cost for more than a few decades longer, if they have not already been damaged beyond redemption.

Herbert Read, the British philosopher and critic, once wrote that "only a people serving an apprenticeship to nature can be trusted with machines." It is a profound insight, and he underscored it by adding that "only such people will so contrive and control those machines that their products are an enhancement of biological needs, and not a denial of them."

An apprenticeship to nature—now there's a myth a stable and durable society could live by.

CONVERSATIONS: HERBERT READ AND CONTROLLING MACHINES
Many popular films have explored the relationship between humans and the machines they create. In recent years, among the best-known of such films have been *The Matrix, The Matrix Reloaded,* and *The Matrix Revolutions,* a trilogy that tells the story of a future generation of humans fighting to regain control of the world from a race of sophisticated machines. These films can be seen as part of longstanding conversations in modern society about the nature of progress and the role of technology in human life. British philosopher and art critic Herbert Read (1893–1968), whom Sale mentions here (par. 28), was also well known as an anarchist who was deeply skeptical of government and technological progress. Thinkers like Read have been part of these conversations for centuries, and it is worth considering how their writing, as well as essays like this one by Sale, relates to visual art, such as film, in these conversations. In what ways do films like *The Matrix* carry on these conversations?

UNDERSTANDING THE TEXT

1. In what sense is progress a "cultural construct," in Sale's view? In what sense is it a useful myth? What's wrong with this myth, as Sale sees it? Do you agree with him? Why or why not?

2. In paragraph 5, Sale writes that "the modern world repeatedly threw up other examples of invention and advancement—television, electric carving knife, microwave oven, nuclear power—that showed the same problematic nature of progress." What do these examples of invention and advancement have in common? What does Sale believe they indicate about the problematic nature of progress? Do you think most people would agree with him about these examples? Explain.

3. What is "comfortable disease," according to Sale? What might this idea suggest about Sale's own values regarding lifestyle and progress?

4. In what sense is the record of progress "mixed," according to Sale? Do you think he's right? Why or why not?

5. Who is the "Objective Observer" to which Sale refers in paragraph 20 and later in his essay? How does this Objective Observer fit into Sale's main argument about progress?

EXPLORING THE ISSUES

1. How would you characterize Sale's tone in this essay? What specific features of his writing help create this tone? Do you think his tone is appropriate for the main point he makes in this essay? Explain, citing specific passages to support your answer.

2. At the end of his essay, Sale refers to a "stable and durable society." What do you think he means by that phrase? Based on this essay, what do you think he believes such a society might look like? Do you think most people would share his view of such a society? Explain.

3. What do you learn about Sale and his own background in this essay? How does this information about Sale influence the way you read his essay? Does it affect your response to his argument in any way? Explain.

4. Throughout this essay, Sale supports his claims with many statistics and related factual information. Examine this information. What kinds of information does he tend to use as evidence to support his claims? How effectively do you think this information supports his claims? To what extent does it make his argument more or less persuasive, in your view?

ENTERING THE CONVERSATIONS

1. Write an essay in which you define *progress*. Draw on Sale's essay and any other relevant resources to support your definition.

2. In paragraph 21, Sale poses a series of questions about the results of progress in modern industrial society: "Has it been, on the whole, better or worse for the human species? Other species? Has it brought humans more happiness than there was before? More justice? More equality? More efficiency? And if its ends have proven

to be more benign than not, what of its means? At what price have its benefits been won? And are they sustainable?" Write an essay in which you offer your answer to these questions. In your essay, draw on Sale's essay and any other relevant readings to help support your position on these issues.

3. Write a response to Sale's essay in which you explain why you agree with his viewpoint on progress or offer your perspective on why progress, as you understand it, has been beneficial to humanity.

4. Create a visual representation of progress. Use PowerPoint, web authoring software, camera or video technology, or any other appropriate medium for your representation.

INFOTRAC

5. Throughout his essay, Sale refers to a number of problems that he associates with progress in modern industrial society. For example, he refers to environmental destruction, poverty among a majority of the world's population, and great inequities in the way the world's wealth and resources are distributed. Select one of the problems Sale identifies in his essay and use InfoTrac College Edition, the Internet, your library, and other appropriate resources to investigate that problem. Try to determine the extent of the problem as well as its apparent causes. Examine the current state of the problem. Then write a report on the basis of your research. Draw conclusions about whether Sale's concerns about and representation of the problem are valid.

In August 2003, the largest power outage in U.S. history occurred, leaving a vast region of the northeastern United States without electricity for most of a day and, in some areas, for more than a week. When the power went out, I was in my kitchen preparing dinner for some friends who were at that moment driving from Ohio to my home in upstate New York. Not long after the power went out, they called me from a gas station about an hour away from my home. They

A Shock to the System

were nearly out of gas and afraid they wouldn't make it to my home. But they couldn't fill their tank because the gas pumps at the station weren't working. The pumps needed electricity to pump gas.

When I first read the following essay by Anna Quindlen (b. 1953), which was published a week after that power outage, I thought about my friends' situation: They needed one form of energy (electricity) to get another form of energy (gasoline) to get to my home; without electricity, they were stranded, even though their car did not use electricity to run. Their situation illustrated the energy dependence that has become part of the American lifestyle. As Quindlen notes in her essay, we have become so accustomed to using energy to do just about anything—getting from one place to another, ordering a pizza, keeping warm or cool, entertaining ourselves—that we think of energy as our "birthright," as Quindlen calls it. We expect it to be always available; rarely do we think about the larger impact of how we use energy. Quindlen believes that we should be thinking about that impact because it is our lifestyle, which we tend to think of as a sign of progress, that has created problems lead-ing to events like the power outage of 2003. Her provocative essay is a call (continued)

ANNA QUINDLEN

Whenever you run into a bear out here in the country, some-one will invariably ask if it was big. I never really know how to answer. All bears appear large to me, even the cubs. Something about the slope of the forehead, the glint of the eyes, the teeth and the claws. I don't take the time to assess relative size because I am so agog at the sheer bearness of the thing. Unlike Harrison Ford, a bear is not a creature you peer at in passing, thinking, 'Is that really . . . ?' It has a certain unmistakability.

The bear have become yet another species on the list of inconve-nient animals in this part of America, right up there with the trash-picker possums and, of course, those loathsome shrubbery eaters, the deer. My favorite bear anecdote was the animal accused of getting physical after a man had proffered a bagel to get the bear to stick around for a photograph. The bear wanted more. What I want is an answer to this question: who gives a 250-pound wild animal baked goods?

The way in which modern people interact with their animal coun-terparts is one of those things that make us look as though our *(continued) for us to reexamine our ideas about progress—and part of a longstanding debate in Western culture about progress.*

Anna Quindlen is a best-selling author and Pulitzer Prize–winning columnist for Newsweek, *in which the following essay appeared in 2003. For more information on Anna Quindlen, see page 264.* ▼

CONTEXT: THIS PART OF AMERICA
Quindlen is referring to New Jersey (par. 2) when she mentions "this part of America." Specifically, she is referring to a landscape of expanding towns and suburbs that have crept into the remaining forested areas of this populous state—areas that are still home to many kinds of wildlife, including bears. In the summer 2003, when this essay was first published, several New Jersey towns were trying to address problems with deer and bear, as Quindlen notes in this paragraph. But these problems are not unique to New Jersey. In many parts of the United States where residential and commercial development is encroaching on wilderness areas, similar problems have arisen. In Colorado, for example, residential development into the foothills of the Rocky Mountains outside Denver has resulted in increasing encounters between people and mountain lions, some of which have ended in serious injury and even death. So although Quindlen is writing specifically about "this part of America," she is addressing a problem that is occurring in many other places a well. This is an example of how a writer can draw on a local context to make a larger point about an important issue. (See Peter Sauer's essay on page 287 for another perspective on this "problem" of wildlife.)

STRATEGIES: FORMATTING FOR EMPHASIS
One way writers can emphasize a point or an idea is to use formatting, as Quindlen does here (par. 4). By setting off this sentence as a separate paragraph, Quindlen makes it more noticeable than it would be as part of the preceding paragraph, thereby focusing her readers' attention on her point.

---

evolution took place on a bell curve and it's currently on the downside. Most of us now act toward native creatures the way our ancestors once acted toward Native Americans: we know that they were here first so we're willing to tolerate them as long as they don't demand to share when we build unattractive structures atop their former homes. If they don't cooperate, we slaughter them.

5   Ultimately the deer **abattoirs** along the highway, or the pest-control experts pulling bats out of attics, are, as one town official in New Jersey said of the bears not long ago, signs of a 'people problem.' Beneath it all is a cosmic question: how do Americans plan to live over the long haul? This was reinforced last week when, all over the Northeast, the power went out and millions found themselves suddenly humbled by their sheer reliance on electricity. What was remarkable was that the reaction was much the same as it is, on a smaller scale, to the animals. No talk of changing behavior, of finding a balance. Once the biggest power outage in history had begun, the only concern was for getting the juice back as quickly as possible. There was a faint undercurrent of revoked privilege. Where was the air conditioning, the pizza delivery, the ballgame on TV, all the things once seen as gifts and now assumed as birthrights?

What you saw time and time again was hubris brought low, people accustomed to instant communication without phone service, people accustomed to flying anywhere and at any time grounded at the airport. It was also hubris writ large. Office buildings, designed with windows that will not open, turning into saunas in the August sun. Office systems utterly dependent on computers turning into ghost towns in ghost cities.

Americans have been careless and casual with our natural resources for a long time. Can an accounting be long delayed? You could look at middle-class travelers sleeping like the homeless on the steps of public buildings during the blackout and see a vision of future unnatural disasters. The delivery grid is poorly conceived.

The fail-safe systems must be improved. But not a word about a world so profligate with its power that it uses as much to fuel the advertising glitz of Times Square as it once used to sustain an entire town.

Watch great cities fade to black, look at the unchecked and unsightly over development all around them, and it is hard to imagine this will be a livable country a hundred years from now. The battle between human and animal is merely a reflection of that. Public officials are notoriously leery of the long view, but ordinary people are no better. The great contradiction: all those alleged nature lovers who fall for a forested range, then bring in the bulldozers. According to the National Association of Home Builders, the average American home has doubled in size in the past century. (Its report calls this a Century of Progress. Guess it depends on your definition.) This is not because families are larger. Quite the contrary. The three-car-garage-and-great-room trend—a great room being a living room on steroids—reflects family life that has devolved into individual isolation, everyone with his own TV and computer, centrally cooled to a frosty edge or heedlessly heated.

Irony of ironies, New York City may soon have a greater unbroken stretch of green (Happy 150th Birthday, Central Park!) than the suburbs that once lured its people with the promises of grass and trees. The animals thus become more and more of a nuisance: get out of our way! Occasionally, we are forcibly reminded that human beings have created an environment in which, in some ways, we have less control than ever before; after all, the lack of power is, by definition, powerlessness. Meanwhile New Jersey, the most densely populated state (in case you hadn't noticed), wants very much to allow the hunting of bears. No one seems to have considered the obvious alternative: instead of issuing hunting permits, call a moratorium on building permits. Permanently.

GLOSS: ABATTOIR
Abattoir (par. 5) is another term for slaughterhouse.

CONVERSATIONS: PROGRESS
Quindlen's brief parenthetical (par. 9) reference to a report titled a "Century of Progress" suggests that she is joining a much larger and longstanding conversation about the nature of progress and the relationship between humans and the earth. Earlier, in paragraph 5, she poses what she calls a "cosmic" question that is part of this conversation: "How do Americans plan to live over the long haul?" In one way or another, all the essays in this cluster are part of this conversation about progress, and it is worth thinking about how Quindlen uses the term here in comparison to how other writers use it. How does she define progress here? In what ways does her essay contribute to our collective effort to answer the question she has posed about how we will live over the long haul?

VISUAL CONNECTIONS: THE PRICE OF COMFORT
Quindlen's complaints about the wasteful American lifestyle are part of an ongoing debate in the United States about how we should live and about our responsibilities as consumers. Consider how these cartoons contribute to that debate.

UNDERSTANDING THE TEXT

1. Why does Quindlen describe the bear as an "inconvenient" animal? What do you think this term suggests about the relationship between humans and wildlife? How does this idea of inconvenient animals fit into Quindlen's main argument?

2. What was the main reaction to the power outage in 2003, as Quindlen sees it? What does that reaction suggest about our attitudes toward natural resources, wildlife, and lifestyle, in her view? Do you think she's right? Why or why not?

3. What is the main lesson Quindlen sees in the power outage that occurred in 2003? Do you think her views about this situation are common views? Explain.

4. What would be gained by adopting a moratorium on building permits, as Quindlen proposes in her final paragraph? What does such a proposal suggest about Quindlen's own values?

EXPLORING THE ISSUES

1. Summarize Quindlen's main point in this essay, citing specific passages to support your answer. Do you agree with her? Why or why not?

2. How would you characterize Quindlen's writing style in this essay? What features of her prose contribute to her style? How effective do you find her writing style? Explain, citing specific passages to support your answer.

3. In paragraph 9, Quindlen writes that "public officials are notoriously leery of the long view, but ordinary people are no better." In fact, she seems to criticize Americans in general in this essay. What is the basis of her criticisms? Do you think her criticisms are valid? Why or why not? What might your answer to that question suggest about your own views regarding lifestyle?

ENTERING THE CONVERSATIONS

1. Write a response to Quindlen's essay in which you offer your own view of the American lifestyle and the progress it represents.

2. Visit the web sites of several advocacy groups or organizations concerned about issues of lifestyle, environmental protection, or the use of resources. For example, you might visit sites for groups advocating "smart growth" to control suburban sprawl or the sites of organizations advocating more responsible uses of resources. In searching for sites, consider using the following terms: *smart growth, sustainability, lifestyle, environmental impact.* Try to visit sites representing different viewpoints on these issues. Examine these sites for the messages they send about lifestyle and its impact on the environment. Examine, too, *how* they convey their messages. Consider whether they promote change, or progress, or not. Then create your own web site in which you offer a guide to these various sites. On your site, explain the purpose of your site and include links to the sites you have reviewed. Convey your own viewpoint about the impact of the American lifestyle. Alternatively, write an essay in which you present your review of the web sites you visited.

INFOTRAC

3. In paragraph 9, Quindlen mentions that the size of the average American home has doubled in the past century. (It is now about 2,400 square feet.) This fact is sometimes cited by advocates of "smart growth," who are concerned about reducing the environmental impact of the American lifestyle; these advocates argue that typical American homes are wasteful and use space in environmentally unsound ways. Quindlen refers in this paragraph to some other ways that the American is wasteful—for example, the excessive use of air conditioning or heating or an unnecessary number of inefficient electric appliances, such as televisions. Use InfoTrac College Edition, the Internet, and other appropriate resources to investigate Quindlen's claims. Try to find out the environmental impact of common components of the American lifestyle, such as housing, transportation, and entertainment. How do these components affect the environment? How are resources typically used in the American lifestyle? What common activities or practices are wasteful? You might focus your research on one component of the American lifestyle, such as housing, food, entertainment, or transportation. Try to find out what impact people have by engaging in typical American activities, such as driving a car or living in a typical home. Then write a report on the basis of your research. In your report, present what you learned about the impact of the American lifestyle and draw conclusions about whether or not Quindlen's claims are valid.

4. Write a letter to the editor of your local newspaper or another appropriate publication in which you express your viewpoint about the impact of the American lifestyle (or the lifestyle in another country where you may live); propose solutions to the problems you see with that lifestyle.

Not long ago, my wife and I looked into *"community-based agriculture."* That term refers to small, locally owned farms that produce fruits, vegetables, meats, and other products for sale in local markets. Usually, these products are raised organically, so community-based agriculture does less damage to the local environment than conventional farming methods. In addition, because the products are sold locally, they do not require much energy (such as gasoline) to trans-

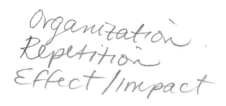

Organization
Repetition
Effect/Impact

Ecological Destruction AND A *Vermont* Farm IN May

port them. Many community-based farms operate on the basis of *"memberships."* If you become a member, you not only can buy the farm's products, but you can also volunteer to work on the farm, which enables the farmers to keep their costs lower by not having to hire many workers or use large machines to grow and harvest their crops. Several of our friends have joined such farms, and we have considered doing so as well. We thought it might be a way to support local farmers and reduce our own impact on the environment.

Such small-scale farms are often considered *"alternative"* or *"back-to-the-land"* operations. They are not usually thought of as progress. The following essay by internationally known environmentalist Donella Meadows might convince you that such operations are indeed progress—just the kind of progress we need in the face of the global destruction of the ecosystems on which we depend. In her essay, Meadows discusses a discouraging report on the state of the world's ecosystems, but she also describes some of the efforts she has made on her own farm to reduce the impact on the   (continued)

DONELLA MEADOWS

The timing is unbearable. Here on my desk in the middle of the blooming, buzzing month of May is the best report yet on the state of the world's ecosystems. Best not because it contains good news—it doesn't—but because it's short and clear and blunt.

The report evaluates the health of our life support system with a simple grid of colored squares. Five columns across the top list the five kinds of ecosystems from which we live—agricultural land, coastal waters, forests, freshwater, grazing land. Four rows down rank each of these systems according to their ability to produce what we need from them: food and fiber, water (both quality and quantity), and biodiversity (the support of other species). The colors of the squares cover a range from "excellent" to "bad."

One glance reveals that there's no "excellent." There's one "bad" (freshwater biodiversity) and four "poors" (ag land water quality, ag

DONELLA MEADOWS, "ECOLOGICAL DESTRUCTION AND A VERMONT FARM IN MAY." COPYRIGHT © 2000 SUSTAINABILITY INSTITUTE DONELLA MEADOWS ARCHIVE, HTTP://WWW.STSTAINER.ORG/DHM_ARCHIVE (ACCESSED 02-11-05).

(continued) *environment. Her essay offers an uplifting note at a time when most of the news about our earth is not encouraging. It may be that the small, positive steps Meadows describes in her essay represent a new way of thinking about progress.*

Donella Meadows (1941–2001) wrote widely about environmental issues. The following essay first appeared in 2000 in her column, Global Citizen, *which was distributed by the Sustainability Institute. For more information on Donella Meadows, see page 634.* ▼

land biodiversity, forest biodiversity, freshwater quality). Eight "fairs," only three "goods" (ag land production, forest production, freshwater production). Three squares are blank, meaning not relevant or not assessed.

That's all I can take in one dose. I sigh and wander outside, where our farm is twittering. Warblers migrate through in waves, barn swallows swoop for black flies, an oriole pours forth joy from a blooming apple tree. Wow! The song of an oriole is liquid gold, and then to see its brilliant orange and black against white blossoms! The colors on that grid may be gloomy, but the colors in this little spot in Vermont are amazing.

VISUAL CONNECTIONS: THE BEST REPORT YET

The report Meadows refers to here and throughout her essay is *World Resources 2000–2001: People and Ecosystems: The Fraying Web of Life,* released jointly by the United Nations Development Programme, United Nations Environment Programme, the World Bank, and the World Resources Institute. Here is the graphic from the report that Meadows describes. Consider not only the information conveyed in this graphic (which, as Meadows notes, is not good news) but *how* the information is conveyed: In what ways might this visual representation present information more effectively than a verbal description? This graphic was not included in Meadows's original essay. Consider how effectively she describes this graphic in paragraph 2—and whether or not her description captures the visual impact of the graphic.

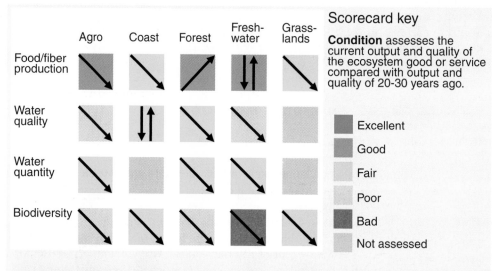

Changing capacity asses the underlying biological ability of the ecosystem to continue to provide the good or service.

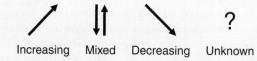

Increasing   Mixed   Decreasing   Unknown

Scores are expert judgements about each ecosystem good or service over time, without regard to changes in other ecosystems. Scores estimate the predominant global condition or capacity by balancing the relative strength and reliability of the various indicators described in the notes on data quality. When regional findings diverge, in the absence of global quality, weight is given to better-quality data, larger geographic coverage, and longer time series. Pronounced differences in global trends are scored as "mixed" if a net value cannot be determined. Serious inadequacy of current data is scored as "unknown."

The story isn't over yet. The planet is still full of magnificent things worth saving.   5

That oriole fortifies me to study the chart more carefully. The colors of the boxes show the present state of each ecosystem. Within each box is an arrow showing its direction of change. The arrow slopes up if the ecosystem's capacity is increasing, down if it is decreasing, both up and down if the trend is mixed. Of the seventeen squares two are mixed (coastal water quality, freshwater production). One is improving (forest production—the legend says that forest plantations and natural forest cutting are increasing and there's no fiber scarcity in sight.) Fourteen, including forest biodiversity and water quality and quantity, are pointing down.

That's on a global scale. These are the systems that sustain human life. Whew! Time to go outside again.

There's some nice bottomland on this farm, one of the main reasons we came here. For one year we left in it alfalfa and grass, then we plowed under seven acres, sowed a cover crop, plowed that down, picked out the big rocks, spread manure and lime, harrowed. Stephen and Kerry, our vegetable farmers, are planting it now to supply 50 subscribing families with fresh-picked produce from June through October. Next year we'll be able to certify the land as organic. I'd call it "good"; we're aiming to get it up to "excellent."

The story isn't over. At least in small places people are actively building resources instead of tearing them down.

The report was put out by a page-long list of scientists and advisors convened by   10
the UN Development Program, the UN Environmental Program, the World Bank, and the World Resources Institute. Just in case their grid doesn't convey the point, these august bodies conclude in italics, "The current rate of decline in the long-term productive capacity of ecosystems could have devastating implications for human development and the welfare of all species."

Dozens of groups have come to a similar conclusion over the past decade, but somehow it hasn't sunk in. Listen to the chatter of the media, the pronouncements of politicians, the forecasts of economists, and you don't hear any recognition of what must be the most important fact of the present world. We are undermining the systems that support all people and all production. Why don't we even TALK about this? Why can't we FOCUS on it?

The pastures sloping up from the bottomland are that intense May green, spangled with yellow dandelions. Our three horses and ten cows are in heaven up there. We're keeping the stock count low; we'll do rotational grazing to help build fertility.

High up on the ridge the forest is light-green lace. We worry about that forest. Acid rain falls on it. Climate change encourages the spread of pests like the woolly adelgid, which kills hemlocks and is moving north toward us. The chestnuts, elms, butternuts are already gone. Though we hope to make our forest more productive, it's not possible to move a small place toward "excellent," if systems all around are crashing down from "fair" to "poor" to "bad."

The story is far from over. Life is bursting forth, pushing, throbbing, aiming toward fertility, productivity, purity and the most astonishing beauty. It's an awesome force working in our direction, if we would let it do so.

STRATEGIES: REPETITION
The first line of paragraph 14 is a statement that Meadows repeated, in slightly different versions, three times in this essay (see also par. 5 and 9). Often, writers will use repetition to emphasize a point or call attention to an idea. Consider what Meadows accomplishes by repeating this statement.

UNDERSTANDING THE TEXT

1. Why is the timing of the report on the state of the world's ecosystems "unbearable," according to Meadows? What do you think her use of that term suggests about her own perspective? What might it suggest about her as a person?

2. What does Meadows's own farm have to do with the report on the world's ecosystems? What does that connection suggest about the relationship between local and global environments?

3. What are Meadows's concerns about the report on the state of the world's ecosystems? Do you think her concerns are valid? Why or why not?

EXPLORING THE ISSUES

1. In a sense, in this essay Meadows is telling the "story" of her experience of reading the report on the state of the world's ecosystems. Examine how she tells that story. How does she organize the essay? What information, images, or events does she include? How does she present the information, images, or events to her readers? How does she use this "story" to make her main point? How effective do you find this way of presenting her point? Explain.

2. Throughout this essay, Meadows discusses and described colors. Examine her references to color. What colors does she refer to and why? What ideas or messages does she convey through her repeated references to color. What do you think she accomplishes through these references?

3. In her final paragraph, Meadows repeats the statement, "The story is far from over." She then discusses the "awesome force" of life. What message do you think she emphasizes in this concluding paragraph? Do you find her message valid? Explain, citing specific passages to support your answer.

ENTERING THE CONVERSATIONS

1. In paragraph 9, Meadows writes, "At least in small places people are actively building resources instead of tearing them down." Her own Vermont farm is one such place. Write an essay about another such "small place" that you know about. The place you write about may be a place you have direct experience with, a place you have read about, or a project that someone you know is involved in. In your essay, describe that place and how it is "building resources." Draw conclusions about what this place might suggest about progress.

2. Write a proposal for a project that would make your school campus the kind of "small place" that Meadows describes in paragraph 9. Address your proposal to the appropriate officer on your campus (such as the dean of campus life or the director of buildings and grounds). Include any appropriate visual components, such as graphs or photos, to support your proposal.

INFOTRAC

3. In paragraph 11, Meadows states that the issue of the destruction of the ecosystems is not being talked about. Examine this claim. Is she right that this issue is not on the public agenda? Using InfoTrac College Edition, the Internet, your library, and other appropriate resources, try to determine whether and how the issue of the destruction of ecosystems is addressed in various media and by various groups and/or governments. Find out if states or the U.S. government has tried to address these problems with any recent programs or laws. Find out as well whether any international treaties or efforts have been undertaken to address these problems (for example, international agreements such as the Kyoto Protocol regarding global climate change). Talk to faculty members at your school who may have expertise in these areas (for example, environmental studies, biology, business, public policy, or political science). You might also talk to representatives of appropriate government agencies (such as your state department of environmental conservation) or advocacy groups (such as the Environmental Defense Fund or the Sierra Club). Then write a report on the basis of your research. In your report, describe your research and present your findings. Draw conclusions about the extent to which the destruction of the world's ecosystems is being addressed.

4. On the basis of your research for Question 3, write a letter to the editor of a widely circulated publication, such as *USA Today,* expressing your views about the state of the world's ecosystems today.

5. Drawing on Meadows's essay and any other appropriate essays in this book, write an essay discussing progress. In your essay, define progress and offer your own viewpoint about it.

WHERE ARE WE NOW?

I F YOU PAY ANY ATTENTION TO AMERICAN POLITICS, THEN YOU KNOW THAT THE PRESIDENT'S ANNUAL STATE OF THE UNION ADDRESS IS A BIG EVENT. IN THE WEEKS LEADING UP TO THE ADDRESS, THE PRESS IS FULL OF RE-PORTS ABOUT WHAT THE SPEECH WILL CONTAIN, AND PUNDITS DISCUSS THE PROS AND CONS OF VARIOUS RHETORICAL STRATEGIES THAT THEY BELIEVE THE PRESIDENT SHOULD ADOPT. THE SPEECH ITSELF, WHICH IS DELIVERED TO A

joint session of the U.S. Congress with many guest digni-taries in the audience, is televised throughout the world. After the address, journalists and experts of all stripes ana-lyze its message and look for clues to the president's strate-gies and policies in the coming year, and critics assess its quality as a speech. The president of the United States is of-ten thought of as the world's most powerful person, so it is no surprise that the State of the Union address receives so much attention.

> For various reasons, these mo-ments cause us to stop and reflect, to think about where we are and where we might want to go.

But it's worth thinking about the very idea of a State of the Union address. For all its political complexity, the funda-mental purpose of the speech is to examine the state of the nation at a specific moment in time—to take stock of where we are now. In various ways and forms, we all do the same kind of thing from time to time. Often, we do so at important milestones in our lives—for example, at our graduation from high school or college or at a wedding. Annual celebrations of important historical events, such as Veterans Day or the

Fourth of July, are also occasions for taking stock. We also take stock individually at important moments in our lives, such as when we accept a new job or move to a new home. And sometimes we take stock of our lives when faced with a sudden sad event, such as the death of a loved one or a serious illness. For various reasons, these moments cause us to stop and reflect, to think about where we are and where we might want to go. This kind of "stock-taking" seems to be an important human impulse.

The essays in this cluster can be thought of as a kind of stock-taking—as reflections, from various perspectives, on where we are as individuals and as a society. At first glance, these three readings may seem to have little in common. Each addresses a very different subject. But all of them re-flect on a moment or an event in a way that is almost like a personal state of the union address. They offer insights and pose questions that can help us think about where we are and where we might be headed. I selected these essays not because they explicitly take stock of a situation or moment, the way a graduation speech or a State of the Union address does; rather, I think these essays show that as writers we often engage in this kind of reflecting and wondering and taking stock. In this way, these three very different essays are very much alike, and they reveal the power of writing to help us understand our current situations and explore pos-sibilities for the future.

As he tells us in his opening sentence, John Leland (b. 1959) wrote this essay when Americans were getting ready to celebrate the Fourth of July, an annual event of family picnics, community celebrations, and fireworks. For Leland, the holiday is cause to think about the state of American culture more than two centuries after the event that the Fourth of July commemorates: the signing of the Declaration of Independence. Specifically, he uses the occasion to reflect on that famous

Pursuing Happiness in Our Time

phrase from the Declaration, "the pursuit of happiness." In pondering that phrase, Leland focuses our attention on the state of America as a society. And he poses some thorny questions. Leland asks us to think about how we understand happiness, arguing that many Americans seem to define happiness as superficial and selfish. He also believes that our current ideas about happiness, which he thinks are shaped by consumerism, are very different from what the authors of the Declaration of Independence had in mind. Ironically enough, this is not a very happy essay, but I chose it for this cluster because I think it encourages us to do something that we don't often do: define just what happiness is. As Leland tries to show in this essay, defining happiness is not only an intellectual exercise. Our ideas about happiness influence the way we live our lives. And writers like Leland can influence our ideas about happiness—which may say something about the power of writing to help us take stock of our lives.

A reporter for the New York Times, John Leland is author of Hip: The History (2004) and many articles about popular culture for Spin, Newsday, The Village Voice, and Newsweek, among others. The following essay appeared in the New York Times in 2003. ▼

JOHN LELAND

This week, as Americans celebrate the 227th anniversary of the Declaration of Independence, smokers in New York will huddle outside once smoky bars, prevented by a **new law** from lighting up inside, and lovers in Texas will go home disencumbered of the state's anti-sodomy law, which the Supreme Court overturned on Thursday. The smokers and lovers can trace their new status to Thomas Jefferson's manifesto, in particular the four-word phrase that rounded out his list of inalienable rights. As participants in what we have come to call the culture wars, they are the losers and winners of the pursuit of happiness.

For more than two centuries, Jefferson's phrase has hovered over this fractious churning, drawing in as many combatants as there are notions of happiness. While most Americans can agree on definitions of life and liberty, the Declaration's first two inalienable rights, happiness is another matter. In a nation of immigrants and strivers, dropouts and resisters, sectarians and self-help gurus, Jefferson left behind an endlessly mutating set of fighting words. What he left vague, generations have vied to spell out, by force of law or just by force.

With all due respect to life and liberty, it is this third battleground—characterized not as a fixed goal but a constant chase—that both animates Americans' daily lives and ties them in knots.

Among its other tangles, the pursuit underlies two enduring strains of American unhappiness: the culture wars and the ravenous consumer culture.

This contradiction is essential to the national identity. Happiness "doesn't have any legal meaning," said Richard A. Posner, a federal appeals court judge who has written about rights and society. "Happiness is not a word on which you can found a lawsuit." Yet it shapes American life in both broader and more paradoxical ways: the pursuit of happiness is the defining passion of a country whose signature voice is the blues.

This holiday, you can see this pursuit everywhere: in the booty-centric videos of MTV, the balloon-filled shopathons at appliance dealers, the expanses of the cultural landscape devoted to cooking or yoga.

It is at the mall and in the dull machinations of local government, where last week a Manhattan woman, protesting restrictions on dancing in most city nightspots, offered her own spin on Jefferson: "I have a right to life, liberty and the pursuit of happiness," said Jen Miller, who belongs to a group called Dance Liberation Front. "And what is the pursuit of happiness if not dancing?"

When Jennifer Lopez sings, "Don't be fooled by the rocks that I got, I'm still Jenny on the block," she means that she still shares her fans' pursuit of happiness, even if she has personal shoppers to score many of the essential accessories.

To Jefferson and his contemporaries, the meaning of happiness was clear and relatively circumscribed, said Pauline Maier, professor of American history at the Massachusetts Institute of Technology and author of *American Scripture: Making the Declaration of Independence.*

"I don't think it meant pleasure in our sense of carnal pleasures or material   10
wealth," she said. "Happiness demanded a good government. That seems so crazy to us. But when they spoke of the ideal, they used biblical language: 'to be at peace under your vine and fig tree with none to make you afraid.'"

For the founders, children of the Enlightenment, the pursuit of happiness replaced older imperatives like religious or filial duty, an upheaval to which Jefferson wisely did not call attention.

Yet happiness is not a fixed quantity, and pursuit by its nature keeps keeping on, as they say in the rap game. As definitions of happiness multiplied over time, the pursuit doubled back on itself. Though happiness seems a non-zero-sum game, meaning one person's joy should not prevent another from being happy, in practice the multiplicity of happiness has led to conflict. In a diverse society, the pursuit of happiness inevitably becomes a threat.

"At some level it's the beginning of the culture wars," said Roger Pilon, director of the center for constitutional studies at the Cato Institute, a libertarian research group. "People understand the First Amendment protection of free speech, but we have a hard time going beyond that to understanding the protections to action generally, like the pursuit of happiness."

CONTEXT: ANTI-SMOKING LAWS
The "new law" Leland mentions in paragraph 1 (and discusses in par. 16) refers to a law banning smoking in restaurants and bars that the New York State legislature passed in 2003. A few other states have passed similar laws. Notice how Leland uses this context to help him make his argument about the pursuit of happiness. Consider whether readers need to know about these laws to understand Leland's point.

CONVERSATIONS: THE ENLIGHTENMENT
For a discussion of the great eighteenth century movement known as the Enlightenment, which emphasized reason as the highest value, see *Conversations: The Enlightenment* on page 499.

CONVERSATIONS: THE CULTURE WARS

Since the 1980s, the idea of "the culture wars" has become a common one in public discussions about American political and cultural life. Often, this idea is associated with controversial issues, such as abortion, the teaching of evolution and sex education in schools, and women's rights. The controversies surrounding such issues are said to arise from a more fundamental conflict of values. But this is just one version of what the culture wars are. Various critics and scholars have different ways of defining these "wars." In paragraph 15, Leland quotes scholar Stanley Fish, who defines the culture wars as "an abiding struggle . . . between those who embrace the libertarian ethic of complete freedom, pursuing whatever happiness you want as long as it doesn't harm anyone else, and others who say that what is required is a society that rewards virtue, that actively discourages unhealthy activity, in order to allow the most happiness for the most people." Notice that Leland himself does not define the term. Nor does he discuss disagreements about what the term means. He simply uses the term in a way that assumes there is such a thing as the culture wars. The fact that he does so may be an indication of how powerful our larger conversations as a society can be, since the idea of culture wars seems to have arisen from conversations about specific controversies rather than from a single event or series of events that might be described as "wars."

The culture wars—which have escalated since the 1960's, when even Hubert H. Humphrey called for a "politics of happiness"—arise from competing claims to happiness, the individual and the collective, said Stanley Fish, dean of the college of liberal arts and sciences at the University of Illinois at Chicago.

15   "There's an abiding struggle," he said, "between those who embrace the libertarian ethic of complete freedom, pursuing whatever happiness you want as long as it doesn't harm anyone else, and others who say that what is required is a society that rewards virtue, that actively discourages unhealthy activity, in order to allow the most happiness for the most people."

In the case of the smokers in New York, Mayor Michael R. Bloomberg held the public health of bar employees—one measure of collective happiness—above the desires of those seeking nicotine pleasures. Public happiness won out over individual happiness. Conversely, in the Texas case the Supreme Court recognized individuals' right to private happiness above any competing claim that sexual diversity diminished anyone else's happiness. In each case, the pursuit of happiness has left somebody unhappy.

As befits the agility of Jefferson's phrase, though, the lines of the culture wars can grow blurry. Most people pursue happiness from several camps at once, conquering in one as they are thwarted in another. The frustrated smokers in New York may be packing prescription doses of Viagra, paid for by Medicaid. The lovers in Texas may be happy that their children's schools ban certain clothing. The pursuit of happiness now can mean the pursuit of limits on happiness.

This logistic snarl, which turns the pursuit against itself, is only one piece of a broader legacy of disappointment, said Darrin M. McMahon, an associate professor of history at Florida State University who is writing a book on the history of happiness. "We're constantly being told that we've failed if we feel unhappy," Mr. McMahon said. "Happiness is not just a right but a duty. Now we're taught to believe if we're not happy all the time we need S.S.R.I.'s," he said, referring to the antidepressant drugs known as selective serotonin reuptake inhibitors. By charging each American to pursue happiness, and making the pursuit a civic duty, Jefferson burdened his descendants with a condition Mr. McMahon called "the unhappiness of not being happy."

This condition reflects not the failed pursuit of happiness but the successes. **Alexis de Tocqueville and Ralph Waldo Emerson,** in the next century, saw that happiness was being pursued apace, if to unintended effect. "Our people are surrounded with greater external prosperity and general well-being than the Indians or Saxons," Emerson wrote, "yet we are sad but they are not."

The remedy, of course, is the pursuit of still more happiness, preferably through   20 *(handwritten: "We shop, Therefore, We are?")*
shopping. There is little cultural conflict in the pursuit of a washer/dryer or a nice
set of clubs. This American acquisitiveness, which drives the economy, is an extension
of Jefferson's ideal, said Jackson Lears, a history professor at Rutgers University and
author of *Fables of Abundance: A Cultural History of Advertising in America.* In claiming
the pursuit of happiness as an inalienable right, Mr. Lears said, Jefferson mirrored
the overarching logic of the free market: "each individual pursuing his own happiness will contribute to the general welfare."

Mr. Lears added that as market
definitions of happiness began to
grow with the economy in the 19th
century, they brought their own
doses of unhappiness.

"The consumer culture," he
said, "is about keeping us dissatisfied and unhappy, until we get the
next thing. For Jefferson and his generation of thinkers, the whole notion of happiness was more sustainable, embedded in social and community responsibility."

> **GLOSS: ALEXIS DE TOCQUEVILLE AND RALPH WALDO EMERSON**
> A French aristocrat, Alexis de Tocqueville (1805–1859) is known for his book
> *Democracy in America* (1835), in which he offered his observations about the special
> characteristics of the American people and their attempts to create a democratic soci-
> ety. Ralph Waldo Emerson (1803–1882) was one of the most influential American
> philosophers. He was a leader in the intellectual movement known as transcendental-
> ism, which espoused a view of truth as residing in the individual soul.

Even this pursuit of happiness has never been for everyone. In an early draft of the
Declaration, the slave-owning Jefferson excoriated King George III for violating "the
sacred rights of life and liberty" of American slaves, but said nothing about their pur-
suit of happiness. And lately, there has been no talk of the role of happiness in the *(handwritten: ← good point)*
rebuilding of Iraq. After so much social conflict, perhaps Americans have learned
their lesson.

But more likely they are responding to another Jeffersonian paradox: that the pursuit of happiness, an ideal to which any people might aspire, bundles the arrogance,
entitlement and loose morality that so much of the world hates about America. The
happiness wars, as the culture wars might be called, only get more intense when the
rest of the world is asked to play too.

So here's to life, liberty and the pursuit of inhibited selective serotonin reuptake.   25
To say nothing of prices so low they're practically giving it away.

UNDERSTANDING THE TEXT

1. What does consumerism have to do with happiness and the problems associated with the pursuit of happiness that Leland describes in this essay?

2. In what sense does the pursuit of happiness lead to conflict? Why is it important to understand that, in Leland's view? Do you think he's right? Why or why not?

3. What different definitions of happiness have emerged in American culture over the years since the Declaration of Independence identified "the pursuit of happiness" as an inalienable right? How does the current way of defining happiness differ from the idea of happiness in the Declaration, according to this essay? What do you think these different definitions suggest about the nature of happiness and its role in our lives?

4. In paragraph 24, Leland writes that the culture wars might be called "the happiness wars." What does he mean? What does happiness have to do with the culture wars, as Leland sees it? Do you agree with him? Explain.

EXPLORING THE ISSUES

1. In this essay, Leland makes many references to pop culture, in- cluding music, to past and recent political events, and to various experts. He also quotes from various books and articles by scholars and other experts. Examine these references. What do you think they suggest about Leland as a writer and thinker? What do they suggest about Leland's assumptions about his audience? Who do you think he believes his audience is? Are you part of that audience? Explain.

2. In paragraph 20, Leland writes, "There is little cultural conflict in the pursuit of a washer/dryer or a nice set of clubs." Do you think he's right? Explain. (You might wish to draw on other readings in this book in answering that question.)

3. How would you summarize Leland's main point in this essay? Do you think most Americans share his views about the pursuit of happiness? Explain, citing specific passages to support your answer.

4. Based on this essay, what do you think is Leland's general view of American culture? Cite specific passages to support your answer.

ENTERING THE CONVERSATIONS

1. Write a response to Leland in which you present your own views about the pursuit of happiness in contemporary American society. In your essay, attempt to define happi- ness, drawing on your own experience, Leland's essay, and any other appropriate readings from this book.

2. Much of Leland's essay is devoted to criticism of consumerism. Create a visual representation of what you believe to be the relationship between consumerism and happiness. Your representation can be a photo essay, a web site, a video, a PowerPoint presentation, or any other appropriate medium.

3. Interview several people about their views of the pursuit of happiness in modern society. Try to interview people who have different lifestyles and backgrounds. For example, interview one or more of your classmates, an elderly relative, a faculty member at your school, or maybe your doctor or dentist. Ask the people you interview about their ideas regarding happiness and how they seek happiness in their own lives. Then write an essay in which you discuss your findings. In your essay, describe the people you interviewed and discuss any similarities in their views about the pursuit of happiness. Draw conclusions about the pursuit of happiness in contemporary society.

4. Create a web site or pamphlet whose purpose is to offer advice about the pursuit of happiness in modern society.

In the following essay, well-known environmental writer Bill McKibben (b. 1960) describes his experience hiking in the forest: "Mostly I float along in a self-contained bubble of my own thoughts, plans, and hopes." When I first read that line, I immediately understood what McKibben was describing because I have had that very same experience. I have spent much of my adult life hiking the forest and mountain trails of the northeastern United States—some of the

A Shirt *Full* OF Bees

same trails that McKibben refers to in this essay—and only in recent years have I realized how often my experience on those trails was just as McKibben describes it; like him, I have been there physically but not mentally or emotionally. I was missing what was around me, without realizing it. I think I was always focused on my destination—a mountaintop or the other end of the trail—and not on the hike itself or my immediate surroundings during the hike. It took a rather frightening experience with a nest of angry bees to help McKibben see how much he wasn't seeing on the trail. In the following essay, McKibben is really looking more deeply at how we experience the world around us—something philosophers and writers have been doing for centuries. In that sense, McKibben's essay is really part of a longstanding tradition in Western culture that includes such iconic writers as Henry David Thoreau. Like those writers, McKibben interprets his own experience to offer insight into our collective experience as human beings. I hope you find his essay as thought provoking as I did. Or maybe you already see the world around you more clearly than McKibben and I did.

Bill McKibben is the author of The End of Nature *(1990) and* (continued)

BILL MCKIBBEN

I remember once hiking with my friend the naturalist and writer Terry Tempest Williams. We were near my home in the Adirondack Mountains of upstate New York, working our way up a steep, piny trail, when all of a sudden she came to a halt and dropped to her knees. There in front of her was a newt in its red eft phase—maybe three inches long, neon orange.

Now these newts are, at various seasons and in various places, nearly ubiquitous—I've counted them by the hundreds on mile-long portages to small ponds; I've shamelessly used them as enticements to keep my daughter going on trails; I've even stopped and admired their bulbous architecture and articulated gait. So it was fun to sit with Terry for a moment and show off my measly store of natural history lore.

For a moment. Even five moments. But right about then I started to get a little bored. And started to realize, not for the first time, what a miserable excuse for a nature lover I was. Terry could—and did—crouch there on her haunches for a good half hour, lost in the world of the newt. It was enough to fill her imagination—a world in a grain

BILL MCKIBBEN, "A SHIRT FULL OF BEES." FROM *YOGA INTERNATIONAL* (AUG/SEPT 2004). REPRINTED BY PERMISSION OF THE AUTHOR.

(continued) Enough: Staying Human in an Engineered Age *(2003) as well as numerous articles on environmental issues for* The New Yorker, Orion, *and other publications. The following essay appeared in* Yoga International *in 2004.* ◩

STRATEGIES: USING ANECDOTE
McKibben opens this essay with an anecdote about an experience he had while hiking with a friend. This anecdote not only introduces McKibben's subject but it can also draw readers into the essay by focusing attention on an event rather than an idea or argument. After relating the anecdote, McKibben interprets it for us in a way that introduces the idea of connection—or lack of connection—to the world around us, an idea that becomes the focus of his essay. This is an effective way of using anecdote to frame an essay.

Tone

or two of orange amphibian. Some people—and surely once upon a time most people—just connect to the world around them, easily and profoundly.

But I—well, I was bored. I wanted to push on to the top. That was our goal, after all. Motion. This incident reminded me how little I really was in contact with the outdoors despite all the thousands of hours I spend there each year. Mostly I float along in a self-contained bubble of my own thoughts, plans, and hopes, my mind firing away like a pinball machine, each new thought a flashing light or ringing bell to distract me from the reality at hand. I can walk a mile or two at a speedy clip and realize that I've hardly seen anything, that I'm in almost as deep a glaze as when I'm driving. I'll stop for a moment when I get to the top of a hill or a mountain—the big picture will move me—but then it's on and on. I'm outside but I'm inside.

5   The moments when that sac is punctured and the world comes flooding in are sweet—they linger in my memory, the moments I will savor someday when I'm down to my last few hours. Some of them are dramatic—full moon rising while I'm on a glacier high on Mount Rainier, the light revealing the curve of the earth. Some are subtle— three or four days into a solo backpacking trip, when I suddenly realize that the little newscaster who lives in my head has temporarily run short of things to say and has simply shut up. But none was more profound than the day when they almost got me.

"They," in this case, does not mean grizzly bears or mountain lions or tiger sharks. The Adirondacks, for all the millions of acres of big wilderness, are a pretty tame place. No poisonous snakes, save for one colony of timber rattlers along Lake George. No nasty carnivores. Wolves exist only in hopeful rumor; the panther was extirpated. There's hardly even any poison ivy. You can get giardiasis, but that's about it.

Or so I thought until, walking in the woods behind my house, I stepped on a yellow jacket nest. I was hiking off trail, a couple of miles from home, dog at my side. As usual, I was deep in some extremely important line of thought, probably having to do with an enormously wise piece of writing I was about to undertake. And then, all of a sudden, there was the most unbelievable pain washing up my stomach toward my neck. It came so fast, as pure a splash of feeling as if someone had tossed a pot of boiling water in my direction. And it hurt so much, a purity of pain I've never experienced before or since. In my memory it expresses itself almost as a flash of white light.

At first I had no idea what was going on. I was climbing a very steep slope, which is why the yellow jackets were at waist level when they boiled out of the hill. I couldn't see them—I just turned and ran, which is hard on a 40-degree incline. I hadn't gone five steps before I cracked into a tree branch, cutting my forehead and closing one eye. But the pain was still there, and with nothing to fight, my flight reflex kept pumping. Finally, after a quarter mile of nearly blind flight, just a few insects were still clinging to me and I was able to pull off my shirt and flick them off.

The pain subsided from a shriek to a roar. I collected enough of my wits to get started home (thankful for all the thousands of hours I'd spent wandering that forest so that the landmarks were obvious even to my frazzled mind). But I hadn't gone very far before hives started to appear across my torso—big, swelling cones. I am cursed with an overactive imagination, and I instantly began to recall stories I'd heard of people dying from bee stings—how their throats swelled shut and they choked to death, unless there was someone standing by with a scout knife ready to perform an emergency tracheotomy. My dog was the best dog I've ever had, but I doubted she was up to surgery. Statistics started flashing in my brain: How often had people downplayed some danger (avalanche, lightning, shark attack) by saying, "More people die each year of bee stings"? It's a very comforting thought, until you step on a yellow jacket nest.

STRATEGIES: DESCRIPTION
In this passage (par. 6-12), McKibben provides an extended description of his experience with the nest of yellow jackets. In fact, he devotes nearly half his essay to a description of this experience. In doing so, McKibben focuses attention not only on the physical event—getting stung by bees and being taken to the hospital—but also on his state of mind (especially in par. 10). Notice how McKibben uses details to convey the scene and to describe his state of mind. Consider what purposes his careful descriptions serve in this essay. This is a good example of how description can be used to convey an idea or make a point in addition to painting a picture of a specific scene or event.

*   *   *

That panic gave way, though, to the most remarkable set of emotions I can recall. Suddenly I found myself praying, and it was not the prayer you might expect. Instead it was a psalm of thanks: Thank you, God, for this hemlock stand, in all its drooping hemlockness. Thank you, God, for that old yellow birch snag, rotting where it leans, ventilated with sapsucker holes. Thank you for that crow, for those wintergreen shrubs, for that living, sparkling creek, for the humidity, the damp, hanging air. Thank you for gravity, which I seemed to feel as a force for the first time. I stopped a second to stroke the bark of a red pine, all jigsaw rough. I didn't see a red eft, but there was a small pile of deer droppings, a drift of blue feathers where a bird had met its end, a vein of quartz in a gray rock. Any such sight could have occupied me for hours—it was as if I were part of all this, not some observer or, worse yet, some astronaut wandering through it sustained by the oxygen of his chattering thoughts. The boundaries had blurred.

10

The high didn't last, of course. Within half an hour I was home, and my wife was screaming at the blood pouring down my face, and I was screaming at her to forget about the goddamn blood and get me to the hospital. Which is a long way away from where we live—by the time we arrived, the hives were so spectacular that the doctor stretched me out on a gurney and started sticking IVs into my wrists. Before long there were steroids and antihistamines and all manner of stuff flowing in, and some hours later I was back home and had the radio on and the newspaper in my face, and all was back to normal.

But not completely back to normal. It was as if the tears of pain had irrigated my eyes, and for weeks afterward the world seemed in sharper focus whenever I stepped outside. Have you ever had a brand-new car, with a perfectly clean windshield? Or cleaned a pair of really grimy eyeglasses? It was like that, except emotionally. Everything seemed dear and noble and complete. I seemed to move in the world, not

VISUAL CONNECTIONS: A SHARPER FOCUS

Visual artists often try to focus attention on things around us that we might not normally notice, in the way that McKibben seems to see those things on his hike. In these two photographs of a forest in winter, for example, our attention is directed to common sights in a way that may prompt us to see those sights differently—to notice a pattern or to see a relationship we might not have noticed before. Consider how such visual media might convey the kind of experience McKibben describes in his essay.

© Robert Yagelski

© Robert Yagelski

through it. The layers of insulation between me and the real world had been removed, and now the breeze was whistling through. You could say this new state had a dreamlike quality, but it would have been more accurate to say just the opposite—that it felt as if I had woken up from a dream.

Slowly, of course, I've fallen back asleep. The newscast inside my head has returned to full volume, or nearly so. As maybe it has to—I'd go crazy, or write poetry, if I were that open to the world all the time. The flood of sensation, and of a kind of love, was very nearly unbearable in its beauty. And yet I desperately want it back too—and wonder if it really takes an experience of finding yourself lower down on the food chain for it to kick in. Is it human nature that abstracts us from the world, or is it some effect of consumer culture? Can we be creatures too, and find some of our satisfaction there—or are we condemned to keep the world forever at arm's length? That's a deeper question than I'm qualified to answer—the best stab at it I've ever read is in David Abram's book *The Spell of the Sensuous*—but it seems to me one of the key questions we face.

And here is how I'd like to pose it. We speak often, and sentimentally, of being "enchanted" by the natural world. But what if it's the other way around? What if we are enchanted, literally, by the human world we live in? That seems entirely more likely—that the consumer world amounts to a kind of lulling spell, chanted tunefully and eternally by the TV, the billboard, the suburb. A spell that convinces us that the things we want most from the world are comfort, convenience, security. A spell that by now we sing to each other. A spell that, should it start to weaken, we try to strengthen with medication, with consumption, with noise. A slightly frantic enchantment, one that has to get louder all the time to block out the troubling question constantly forming in the back of our minds: "Is this all there is?"

15   If so, then for us as individuals and as a society the deep question becomes how to break that spell. A kiss offers the traditional antidote, of course, but a kiss is what the culture keeps giving us. A nice, soft kiss, day after day. Sometimes a shirt full of bees

seems more effective. "Turn off the air conditioner," the great desert writer Ed Abbey would tell tourists when he was a ranger at Arches National Monument in southwest Utah. "Take off your sunglasses. Get out of the car." Feel the heat, feel the cold, feel something. All those senses—all those emotions—work outside the narrow range in which we normally set our personal thermostats.

It is a sorry thing to admit that you're so thick it takes 76 yellow jacket bites to pierce you. I hope I never get a booster shot; I want to learn how to do it with newts too. But the lesson was well worth the price—that desperate clarity was one of the greatest gifts the world ever gave me. When I try to imagine the holy spirit, I hear buzzing.

CONVERSATIONS: ASKING DEEPER QUESTIONS
In paragraph 13, McKibben poses a question—"Are we condemned to keep the world forever at arm's length?"—that he claims he is "qualified to answer." The "deeper" question he is posing here is one that philosophers and others have been trying to answer for centuries: What is the nature of our being? Thus, McKibben is joining a longstanding discussion about who we are and about our relationship to the world we live in. You might see his reference to David Abram's *The Spell of the Sensuous* (1996), in which Abram explores the relationship between humans and the physical environment, as a reference to this discussion. And you might consider how this larger discussion helps give meaning to his experience of getting stung by bees.

UNDERSTANDING THE TEXT

1. McKibben writes that "some people—and surely once upon a time most people—just connect to the world around them, easily and profoundly" (par. 3). What does he mean by "connect to the world" in this passage? Why is this kind of connection important to him? Do you think he's right that most people at one time were able to make this kind of connection? Explain.

2. What was the nature of the "high" that McKibben experienced after his encounter with the bees' nest? What did he realize as a result of this experience? What do you think McKibben's reaction to this experience reveals about him as a person? What does it suggest about his sense of his relationship to the world around him?

3. In what sense are we "enchanted" by the human world, in McKibben's view? Do you think he's right? Why or why not?

EXPLORING THE ISSUES

1. McKibben tells us a lot about himself in this essay. What do we learn about him as a person? What kind of image of himself does he present to his readers? Do you think this image is flattering or positive? What response do you have to the way he presents himself in this essay? Do you think your sense of him as a person makes the essay more or less effective for you as a reader? Explain.

2. In paragraph 13, McKibben asks, "Is it human nature that abstracts us from the world, or is it some effect of consumer culture?" Based on this essay, how do you think McKibben answers this question? How would you answer this question?

3. McKibben ends his essay by stating, "When I try to imagine the holy spirit, I hear buzzing." What do you think he means by that statement? Why does he use religious imagery in this statement? What does that imagery suggest about his interpretation of his experience with the bees? What does it suggest about his view of the relationship between humans and the natural world?

ENTERING THE CONVERSATIONS

1. Write an essay in which you describe an experience that opened your eyes in some way or prompted a realization of some kind in you.

2. Create a visual representation (such as a PowerPoint presentation or photo essay) of the experience you wrote about for Question 1. Try to convey a sense of the realization you came to as a result of that experience.

3. McKibben writes in paragraph 14 that consumer culture is a kind of spell that blocks out the question, "Is this all there is?" Write an essay in which you discuss this idea of consumer culture as a "spell." In your essay, define consumer culture as you understand it and discuss what you see as its effects on people. Draw your own conclusions

about whether McKibben is right or not about consumer culture.

4. Go to a place you see or visit regularly—such as the student center on your campus, a coffee shop or restaurant, a riverfront or beach, or a park where you play basketball, jog, or walk your dog—and observe that place for a time. Focus your attention on aspects of that place that you don't usually notice. Try to "see" the place as if you are visiting it for the first time. Then write a brief essay for an audience of your classmates in which you describe what you saw and discuss any insights or realization you might have had as a result of your observations. Alternatively, write the same essay for a wider audience who has never visited the place you are describing.

5. Many popular books and articles offer advice about slowing down and experiencing the world more fully. Popular radio and television shows also take up this subject; television talk shows such as *Oprah*, for example, often have guests who discuss this topic. Find several articles or books that offer such advice for living, watch several TV shows devoted to this subject, or listen to a radio show in which the subject is discussed. Get a sense of the advice for living that is offered, and try to determine how the writers or guests understand the problems they see with the conventional modern lifestyle. Then write an essay in which you discuss what these books or programs seem to suggest about modern life and about the connection between humans and the world around them.

If you look at the The New York Times best-seller lists in any given week, you will find memoirs and autobiographies among the listed titles. Sometimes such books are written by people of a relatively young age about some important and timely experience—for example, the memoir of a famous athlete who retires at age thirty-five or forty or a political memoir by a former government official who witnessed a momentous event. But often, the best-selling memoirs or autobiographies are

Ironies

written by authors who neither are famous nor have had extraordinary experiences. But readers are engaged by the efforts of these authors to reflect on their lives and draw lessons from their experiences.

The following essay by Harriet Epstein (b. 1922) fits into that tradition of reflection. Epstein was part of the American women's movement in the 1960s and 1970s, a movement that in many ways transformed American society. As someone who has witnessed that transformation and is now older, Epstein can look back and assess not only where her own life has taken her but also where the women's movement has taken other women. The ironies she sees as she takes stock of her life and of the women's movement may reflect her own sensibilities as a person, but they may also reflect insights into the complexities of modern life that apply to all of us. And maybe that's why memoirs like this are so popular with many readers: They offer models to help us make sense of our own lives.

Harriet Epstein is a freelance writer. This essay appeared in Humanist *magazine in 1999.* ▼

HARRIET EPSTEIN

Thomas à Kempis, a German ecclesiastic and writer who lived from 1380 to 1471, certainly understood life and its absurdities when he pronounced those prophetic words, "Man proposes, but God disposes." Case in point.

There were three of us, back in 1972, in the heady days of the National Organization for Women—the bra-burning era of women's evolvement. We were all working on a consumer magazine, trying to write and unravel the changes that were coming fast and furious for women, men, and everyone. It was an exciting, energizing time for us—upper-income, suburbanite matrons. We were eagerly searching to expand ourselves and fulfill our potential. Living near each other in a tree-lined, gracious, suburban community, we were typical of women everywhere—stepping out of our insulated cocoons, ready to break free, after **Betty Friedan's** *Feminine Mystique* had shaken us up.

I had made a speech at a meeting of the Brandeis National Women's Committee, long before the magazine days, surprising even myself, as I tried to joke, with New Yorker-like whimsy, about our seemingly perfect life-styles. We awoke each morning, jumped into

HARRIET EPSTEIN, "IRONIES." FROM *THE HUMANIST*, MARCH 1999, VOL. 59, NO. 2, PAGE 46. REPRINTED BY PERMISSION OF THE AUTHOR.

In 1963, author Betty Friedan published *The Feminine Mystique,* a book that many scholars believe sparked the modern women's movement. As Epstein suggests in paragraph 2, Friedan's book inspired many women, provoking them to rethink their roles in American society. Friedan's book may have helped start the modern women's movement, but it might also be seen as part of a much older debate in American society about the role of women, a debate that stretches back to the women's suffrage movement in the nineteenth century. Friedan's book has come to symbolize feminism, and the very mention of it signals that Epstein is part of this ongoing debate. Epstein's experience with the feminist movement is also an example of how these larger debates in a society can shape a person's sense of self and even influence her life choices.

our Calvins, raced off for tennis or golf, showered and lunched at our clubs, only to return home to our scruffy, dungareed daughters, who scoffed at our mundane, prosaic lives.

"What were we missing?" I asked, as I introduced the two attractive women from NOW who had come to answer the question. "We were lacking involvement in the transformation of women," they said. "It was time to share in the events of the world, to lend our energies and abilities to help create change."

5   Yes, those were heady days for us, and how lucky we three were. Lucky to have the magazine—a vehicle to help us embark on the path to self-discovery, to enable us to unleash all our unused talents.

Though we were excited and challenged by the thought of self-actualization, we were each somewhat different in our views of the movement. Two were strong feminists, bemoaning the inadequacy of men. Though their men always appeared to be upstanding and responsible, doing everything men were expected to do, it was clearly a time for women generally to be dissatisfied and yearning for much, much more.

I, on the other hand, had some reservations about all those provocative new ideas. Hadn't men also been conflicted, I pondered, as they faced the pressure to achieve success as husbands, fathers, and breadwinners? Weren't they also locked into the culture that had formed them as much as it did women? So, while I thoroughly appreciated the need for the women's goals, I couldn't stop wondering and feeling apprehensive about where it would all lead.

GLOSS: CONSCIOUSNESS-RAISING GROUPS
During the early women's movement in the 1960s and 1970s, women—and eventually men—who supported the movement often formed discussion groups, known as "consciousness-raising groups," intended to help them become more aware of the sexism and gender discrimination they were subject to in American culture.

Some time later, I was invited to sit in on an early men's **consciousness-raising group,** where a number of searching men had gathered to try to understand the changes in their wives and see if they themselves could evolve. It was a revelation to see these sensitive guys sharing ideas. But as I sat, taking notes for the article I would write, disquieting thoughts hit me again. Would women really be happy if men gave up their once strong, leadership personas and became softer, gentler, like this group?

Confusion soon erupted, accelerating rapidly. Women moved on to begin the job of self-fulfillment, and divorce increased to an incredible rate. Everyone was becoming more preoccupied with him- or herself. Books began flooding the market, giving permission to do just about anything that brought total happiness. And, almost simultaneously, the sexual revolution was granting greater permission to do whatever supplied instantaneous pleasures. Remember **Plato's Retreat?** And what about **Essalen** and the supposedly healing sexual weekends that experts were promoting, all in the name of feeling and experiencing?

But no one seemed too disturbed about the consequences. No one, I thought, but   10
me. I continued to be anxious, while most everyone, including my two buddies, remained more gung ho than concerned.

The ironies progressed as we each moved on in our lives, dealing with what I believe were actually three revolutions: the "women's," the "sexual," and the "me too."
Here's what happened.

The strongest feminist, a photographer, quickly aligned herself with
women's groups, traveling all over with them, educating herself, and
taking photos at their meetings. She soon left home and family so she
would be more available to concentrate on her work. When she moved
to New York City, she created a bit of a stir among her friends and
neighbors, who were saddened and puzzled by her behavior, for she
had left two children. She'd always been a devoted wife and mother.

Finally, after she was mugged and robbed several times, self-fulfillment
didn't look so tantalizing. Luckily, she was able to return home in just
enough time to salvage everything before it was too late. I questioned
her, one day, as we sat on the lawn of that beautiful home she had run
from, asking her why she had come back. "Could I support all this?"
she asked, as we both sadly acknowledged the grim realities. Today, she
once again enjoys a comfortable, upscale life, continues her career,
and is probably very glad she returned in time. For her, the destruction of a still-functioning family was fortunately avoided.

GLOSS: PLATO'S RETREAT AND ESSALEN
Plato's Retreat was a club in New York
City that became well known in the 1980s
as a place for singles to meet. It was associated with a "liberated" lifestyle and
became synonymous with sexual freedom. As Epstein suggests in paragraph 9,
Essalen was a lifestyle movement characterized by retreats that included various
activities, such as massage, intended to
heal mind and body. Its retreats also came
to be associated with sexual freedom. It's
worth considering what Epstein's references to Plato's Retreat and Essalen suggest about her and her sense of her audience.

The second feminist, an accomplished writer, continued growing and improving in
her work, gradually achieving notable success as a columnist, earning the recognition
she had so eagerly sought. And, oh, the grand irony! The husband she had always de-
rided became the key to and star in all her articles. With wit and humor, she learned
to use him to great advantage, as she cleverly joked about all his once-irritating idio-
syncrasies. She was now artfully helping people laugh and identify with human frail-
ties and life's realities. Yes, she, too, had salvaged her marriage, without serious
trauma, and furthered her career much more.

15   And what was the fate of she who had persisted in her empathy for men? How did
life treat me, the lady who had always suffered with trepidation about the repercus-
sions of those three revolutions? Perhaps you've already guessed. This poor, trusting,
searching soul was divorced from a thirty-four-year marriage by the man for whom
she had made excuses, wanted to understand and stay with forever. Irony of ironies,
I alone was the one who became totally liberated and free.

So, how have things been for me, the liberated, free lady who fate had befuddled?
I'll tell you. It's been tough and adventurous, difficult, challenging, and interesting.
This formerly one-man woman and supporter of men changed radically and became
an adventurous single. It was painful at first, but I gave myself total permission to
bury guilts and jumped right into the contemporary society. Soon, all the misadven-
tures I had once cautioned my young daughter about became an accepted life-style
for this aging single.

Now, let's review the situation. My friends thirsted for independence; I had it
foisted upon me. They sustained stability and security; I wound up with adventure,
many varied experiences, and freedom. To my amazement, I soon discovered it was

possible to care for more than one man. Fate had offered me a bonus and, suddenly, I found that it was possible to enjoy sex with someone other than my former husband. All the years of anger and frustration at my inability to avoid a divorce I didn't want were canceled out by a host of new possibilities.

And about those three revolutions—did they make any of us wiser, more satisfied, better able to deal with life's vagaries? Did we three succeed in fulfilling all our potential? For my two friends, who can say? One thing is fairly certain: each of us may have questioning moments. Perhaps they sometimes think they envy my new life; I certainly have moments when I miss theirs. Surely no one is happy all the time.

But happily, we can all remember the delicious wisdom of that all-knowing philosopher Auntie Marne, who cautioned: "Life's a banquet, but most of the poor SOBs are starving to death."

UNDERSTANDING THE TEXT

1. Why did Epstein have reservations about some of the criticisms of men made by feminists? How do her reservations relate to her main point in this essay? What do you think her reservations suggest about her values as a woman?

2. In paragraph 11, Epstein states that she witnessed three "revolutions" during these years of the women's movement: the "women's," the "sexual," and the "me too." What were each of these revolutions? How did they relate to each other? What lessons can be learned from each of these revolutions?

3. Epstein writes that her divorce from her husband of thirty-four years left her "totally liberated and free" (par. 15). What does she mean? In what sense is her "liberation" one of the ironies she writes about in this essay? What lessons does she derive from this "liberation"? Do you think those lessons apply to other women? Why or why not?

EXPLORING THE ISSUES

1. In a sense, this essay is the story of three women who were involved in the American feminist movement of the 1970s and later. Examine how Epstein tells this story. What information does she include? What events does she focus on? What information is left out? Obviously, Epstein is telling her story and the stories of her two friends from her own point of view, but do you think she presents a fair and believable picture of her friends? In other words, do you trust her story? Why or why not?

2. Epstein chose to title this essay "Ironies." What ironies does she write about in this essay? What

lessons does she derive from these ironies? What do you think these ironies suggest about gender in American culture? Do you find Epstein's title an appropriate one? Explain.

3. Epstein ends her essay with this quotation: "Life's a banquet, but most of the poor SOBs are starving to death." What idea is she conveying with this quotation? What ironies, if any, does this quote refer to? How effective do you find her conclusion?

4. This essay is Epstein's reflection on her life. How appropriate do you think her voice is for such a reflection? Is there anything "reflective" about her voice in this essay? Explain, citing specific passages to support your answer.

ENTERING THE CONVERSATIONS

1. Write an essay in which you look back on some aspect of your own life and reflect on it. How have things changed? How has your perspective changed? Forecast how you think it might change again in the future.

🔍 **INFOTRAC**

2. The women's movement of the 1960s and 1970s can be seen as a major social development in American culture in the twentieth century. Epstein's essay is an indication of how deeply this movement affected the lives of some women. Using InfoTrac College Edition, your library, and any other appropriate resources, investigate the women's movement and its impact on women in American society. Focus your investigation on some aspect of women's lives that you consider important: their roles as family care-

givers, women in the professional world or the workplace, women in politics, or some similar aspect of women in society. Try to determine the impact of the women's movement on this aspect of women's lives. Then write a report about what you learned. In your report, draw conclusions about the roles of women in American society today and the prospects for changes in those roles in the future.

3. Interview several women you know about their experiences *as women* in contemporary American culture. Try to interview women of different ages and life situations (for example, professional women, full-time mothers, college students, and so forth). Ask them about how they believe women are perceived in American society today and whether or not they feel limited in any way as women. Try to get a sense of whether they believe the women's movement has benefited them. Then write an essay in which you discuss what you learned from your interviews. Draw conclusions about the role of women in contemporary American society.

4. Create a web site, PowerPoint presentation, or similar document in which you present your view of the status and roles of women in contemporary American society.

5. Read *The Feminine Mystique* (1963) by Betty Friedan and write a review of it from your perspective as a reader today. In your review, assess the extent to which Friedan's ideas remain valid today.

6. Write a public service announcement for radio, television, or the Internet in which you convey a sense of the possibilities open to young women in American society today.

CREATING THEMES: Extending the Conversations

WITH TEXT

1. Write an essay about an important change you have experienced in your life. Tell the story of that change in a way the reveals its importance in your life and how you dealt with it.

2. Identify what you consider to be an important theme that runs through several of the readings in this chapter and write an essay intended for a specific audience about that theme. In your essay, draw on the readings you've selected to support your main point.

3. Identify an important current controversy that you believe arises from some kind of important change. For example, in 2005, the U.S. Congress debated a controversial bill that would open the Arctic National Wildlife Refuge to oil drilling, which would be a change in a longstanding policy to protect that wilderness environment; the bill was introduced in part because of the changing situation with the world's oil supplies, and some critics argued that this situation required changes in our lifestyle rather than more oil drilling. Select such a controversy that you believe is important and write an essay examining that controversy. In your essay, discuss the changes that have created the controversy, and draw your own conclusions about what these changes might ultimately mean for those involved in the issue and for American society or the world in general.

4. Write a proposal for a change that you believe should happen in your school or community. Address the proposal to the appropriate audience (such as your school president, your local town council or school board, or some other government official). In your proposal, describe the situation that you believe needs to be changed and explain why you

think change is needed. Justify the change you are proposing and explain how it will address the problems you have described in your proposal.

5. Interview several older people you know who have witnessed momentous events in their lifetime. Ask them about the changes they have seen over the course of their lives and get a sense of how they believe these changes have affected them and their communities. Then write an essay discussing what you learned from your interviews.

WITH MEDIA

1. Create a web site that reflects your view of an important change you have witnessed in your community. For example, your hometown may have experienced significant economic development in recent years or the loss of an important employer; perhaps there was a controversy about the construction of a large retail store that has created new problems for your town. Identify such a change that concerns you and construct your web site in a

way that conveys your perspective on that change.

2. Write a script for a television or radio documentary that focuses on the most important changes you have witnessed in your lifetime. Draw on several of the readings in this chapter to help explore the issues you address in your documentary.

3. Create a flyer or brochure presenting your perspective about a change that you believe is affecting your local community. For example, you might live in a place that is experiencing controversy about building a new school, allowing the construction of a new shopping mall, or changing a law that affects where local teens can ride their skateboards. Select such an issue that is affecting your community and focus your flyer or brochure on that issue.

4. Drawing on any appropriate essays in this chapter and on other relevant resources, create a PowerPoint presentation, video, or another appropriate kind of presentation for a specific audience (for example, students at your school or

Four years ago it was John McCain
This year, they're smearing John Kerry
George Bush
Denounce the smear
Get back to the issues
APPROVED BY JOHN KERRY AND PAID FOR BY KERRY-EDWARDS 2004, INC.

Greg Campbell/AP Photo

CREATING THEMES: Extending the Conversations

© AP Photo/John Kerry for President, 2004

© Rich Pedroncelli/AP Photo

people at your workplace) intended to educate that audience about an important change that is occurring in your community.

5. Political campaigns often focus on the need for change. Using the following images or other images (or political advertisements from television or the Internet) that you have found, examine how political campaigns communicate their ideas about change. Evaluate the effectiveness of such efforts to convey a need for change.

WITH FILM

1. Many popular films tell stories about how people have dealt with difficult changes in their lives. For example, *About Schmidt* (2002), starring Jack Nicholson, describes the challenges facing a nondescript actuary from Omaha whose wife dies soon after he retires; the film explores his struggle to deal with

such momentous life changes as retirement and the death of a loved one. Similarly, *One True Thing* (1998) tells the story of a young professional woman (played by Renee Zellweger) who returns to her small hometown to care for her terminally ill mother; she is dealing with several difficult changes that force her to reevaluate her own life and her relationships to those around her. Select one or more such films that examine change and analyze what these films seem to suggest about change in human life. Then write an essay in which you present your analysis of these films. Draw conclusions about what these films might suggest about prevailing attitudes in American culture regarding change in our lives.

2. The idea of progress implies change that is positive. However, as several of the readings in this chapter (especially in Cluster 2) indicate,

the idea of progress is complex. Not everyone agrees that progress means change for the better. That complexity has sometimes been explored in film. For example, science-fiction films such as *The Matrix* (1999) present a more pessimistic view of technological change. Films like *The Mosquito Coast* (1986) explore some of the harmful effects of technological progress—in this case, the effects of technological progress on an indigenous community in Central America. Select several films that you believe explore the ideas of progress or change associated with technology, and examine the messages that these films convey about technology, society, and progress. Write an essay in which you discuss some of the insights you believe these films might offer.

▣ COMP21

The *Comp21: Composition in the 21st Century* CD-ROM includes additional clusters of material for the thematic chapters of *The Thomson Reader*. The CD-ROM clusters contain readings, images, audio clips, and video clips for each of the eight chapter themes—helping students see how critical writing and reading go beyond the standard essay. Below is a list of all the media assets included on the *Comp21: Composition in the 21st Century* CD-ROM.

Text Library

Samuel Adams, On American Independence
Spiro Agnew, Television News Coverage
Maya Angelou, Champion of the World
Brett Aronowitz, Can You Write Computerese?
St. Augustine, Book 5 of *Confessions*
Bill Berkeley, Is America An Empire?
William Jennings Bryan, Imperialism
Thomas Bulfinch, Prometheus and Pandora
Edmund Burke, from *Beauty and the Sublime*
John Carey, Global Warming
Andrew Carnegie, The Gospel of Wealth
Russell Conwell, Acres of Diamonds
Joan Didion, from *Los Angeles Notebook*
John Dryden, Preface to *Fables, Ancient, and Modern*
W. E. B. DuBois, from *The Souls of Black Folk*
Dwight D. Eisenhower, Farewell Address
T. S. Eliot, Tradition and the Individual Talent
Ralph Waldo Emerson, Nature
Michael Farrady, The Force of Gravitation
Chris Fordney, Water Woes
Benjamin Franklin, Ephemera
John J. Fraser, Jr., Dealing with The Parent Whose Judgment Is Impaired by Alcohol Or Drugs
Erik L. Goldman, *Roe v. Wade* at 30 Years
Vincent Marie Hugo, In Defense of His Son
Samuel P. Huntington, The Hispanic Challenge
Thomas Jefferson, Declaration of Independence
Lyndon Baines Johnson, The Great Society
Lyndon Baines Johnson, Let Us Continue

Barbara Jordan, Who Them Will Speak for the Common Good?
John F. Kennedy, Inaugural Speech
John F. Kennedy, Ich bin ein Berliner
Maya Lin, Between Art and Architecture
Abraham Lincoln, Emancipation Proclamation
Abraham Lincoln, The House Divided Against Itself
Richard Lowry, Profiles in Cowardice
William Lutz, Doublespeak
General Douglas MacArthur, Farewell Address to Congress
Niccolo Machiavelli, from *The Prince*
George C. Marshall, The Marshall Plan
H. L. Mencken, The Diverging Streams of English
Horace Miner, Body Ritual Among Nacirema
John Henry Newman, The Idea of a University
Richard Nixon, The Great Silent Majority
Richard Nixon, Resignation Speech
Blaise Pascal, from *Thoughts*, Sections 339-348
Emily Post, Pronunciation
Ronald Reagan, First Inaugural Address
Franklin Delano Roosevelt, The Great Arsenal of Democracy
Franklin Delano Roosevelt, Pearl Harbor Address to the Nation
Theodore Roosevelt, A Trip After Mountain Sheep
Theodore Roosevelt, On American Motherhood
Mike Rose, I Just Wanna Be Average
Margaret Sanger, Two Classes of Women
Adam Smith, The Division of Labour
Goldwin Smith, The Secret Beyond Science
Jonathan Swift, A Modest Proposal
Henry David Thoreau, Where I Lived and What I Lived For
Harry S. Truman, The Truman Doctrine
Dave Wann, Build Better Neighborhoods
Booker T. Washington, A Slave Among Slaves
H. G. Wells, from *A Short History of the World: The Development of Modern Political & Social Ideas*
Walt Whitman, from *Specimen Days*

Mary Wollstonecraft, A Vindication of the Rights
of Woman
The *Economist* (US), Islam in the West
How to Share the Earth
Imagining a Cleaner, Greener Tomorrow
Women's Lives and Post-Abortion Syndrome, 30
Years Later: A Long, Cold Journey to the Truth

Audio Library
Spiro Agnew, Television News Coverage
Andrew Carnegie, The Gospel of Wealth
Russell Conwell, Acres of Diamonds
Dwight D. Eisenhower, Farewell Address
Lyndon Baines Johnson, The Great Society
Lyndon Baines Johnson, Let Us Continue
Barbara Jordan, Who Them Will Speak for the
Common Good?
John F. Kennedy, Ich bin ein Berliner
John F. Kennedy, Inaugural Speech
General Douglas MacArthur, Farewell Address to
Congress
George C. Marshall, The Marshall Plan
Richard Nixon, The Great Silent Majority
Richard Nixon, Resignation Speech
Ronald Reagan, First Inaugural Address
Franklin Delano Roosevelt, The Great Arsenal of
Democracy
Franklin Delano Roosevelt, Pearl Harbor Address
to the Nation
Harry S. Truman, The Truman Doctrine

Image Library
1960s college classroom
A Chinese garden
Adolf Hitler & Benito Mussolini
Adolf Hitler addressing a crowd
Aerial view of island
Antiwar protestors, 1967
Assorted squash
Basketball
Bas-Relief of a battle
Big Red Spot on planet Jupiter
Birthday party
Body styles on General Motors
Boxing
Brother and sister

Buzz Aldrin landing on the moon
Buzzards in trees
Camel at Great Wall in Western China
Cathedral at Milan, Italy
Ceiling paintings in the Strahov Library
Changing of the Guard at Buckingham Palace
Child holding adult's hand
Christmas tree farm
Civil Rights March on Washington
Clouds
Compactor burying trash at landfill site
Comparison of 1924 Model T Touring Car
Contrast of mosque and skyscraper
Cougar
Cowboys on horse
Dance with Death cartoon
Dental exam
Department store model TV Room
Diablo Dam, Washington
Diagram of human eyesight
Dog and cat
Dog herding sheep
Dolphin
Driver's speed monitored by radar display
Earth from space
Earth from the moon
Eggs for sale
Eiffel Tower from below, Paris, France
Embossed book cover illustration
Eruption of Mount Saint Helens
Faculty Council of Tuskegee Institute
Fall tress reflected
Father holding baby
Female judge
Fence over hill
Fireworks
First successful powered Wright Brothers flight
Five presidents at dedication of the Reagan
Library
Flag Raising at Iwo Jima
Flight Information Monitor at Frankfurt
Ford Motor Company assembly line
Ford Motor Company show room
Fruit in baskets
Gateway Arch in St. Louis, Missouri
George Armstrong Custer

Golden Gate Bridge
Gorbachev and Bush signing START
Grand Masters of the Teutonic Knights
Grapefruit
Great Sphinx and the Pyramid of Khafre
Group of Children going to school
Group portrait of Elvis impersonators
Harvesting equipment
Harvesting tea in terraced fields
Holy Family Cathedral, Barcelona, Spain
I Want You poster
International coins
International flags
International money
Io, one of Jupiter's moons
Irrigation system
Keep Abortion Legal
Lambs
Landfill for hospital waste
Leaning Tower of Pisa
Lemon
Lemon pie
Library in Vienna
Louis Armstrong
Man on campus
Manhattan Bridge
Mayan Pyramid
Meerkats
Members of the 396th Infantry, WWI
Model of the Endocrine, Nervous, and Skeletal
    Systems
Mothers Against Drunk Driving sign
Mount Rushmore
Mountain biking
National Recovery Administration poster
Nebraska family in front of their sod house
New citizens saying the pledge of allegiance
New Jobs for Women poster
New York City street scene
New York Stock Exchange
Nursery
Ocean Drive
Old and new building in Mexico City
Palace of Versailles
Paul Klee, *Senecio*
People with drinks

Plant detail
Pouring silver
President Bush had Thanksgiving with Desert
    Storm troops
Presidents Bush, Reagan, Carter, Ford, Nixon
Pro-Gay Marriage Rally in Boston
Prohibition Party poster
Protests against school segregation
Prototype of Taj Mahal, India
Raccoon
Red Tomato among green tomatoes
Rio Grande and the Chisos Mountains
Route 66 road sign
Runners at starting block
Saint Basil's Cathedral, Moscow, Russia
Sand Dunes in Central China
Save Sugar poster
Saving for education
Silver Falls
Singapore Banking sign
Sitting Bull
Skaters racing
Skull Smoking a Cigarette
Skyscrapers and Hong Kong Harbor
Snowboarding
Space Shuttle blastoff
St. Patrick's Cathedral
Statue of Liberty
Statue of Liberty 2
Stonehenge
Suffragist marching, 1912
Swimmers diving
Teacher and boy with globe
The Alamo in San Antonio, TX
The Capitol building at night
The Colosseum
The Empire State Building
The Great Sphinx, Egypt
The Parthenon in Athens, Greece
The Pentagon
The White House at night
Theraveda monks in a Khmer Community
Times Square in NY
Tower Bridge, London
Trevi Fountain, Rome, Italy
US Navy poster

Vegetable and fruit display
Vineyard
Vote Here sign beside American flag
Washington Monument
Wave
Wedding cake
Wedding carriage ride
Wheat farm
Woman and a cat
Woman at checkout line

Video Library
English: Who Needs It?
For Better or For Worse
From *Salvation* by Langston Hughes
Homeland Security at Any Cost
IQ and Race
Suburban Sprawl
Terror Watch: Is Profiling Too Much?

TEXT CREDITS

This page constitutes an extension of the copyright page. We have made every effort to trace the ownership of all copyrighted material and to secure permission from copyright holders. In the event of any question arising as to the use of any material, we will be pleased to make the necessary corrections in future printings. Thanks are due to the following authors, publishers, and agents for permission to use the material indicated.

Chapter 5. 67: Sojourner Truth, "Ain't I a Woman?" (1851). **70:** N. Scott Momaday, "The Way to Rainy Mountain" From *The Reporter* (1967). Reprinted by permission of University of New Mexico Press. **77:** Bobbie Ann Mason, "Being Country." From *Clear Springs* by Bobbie Ann Mason. Copyright © 1999 by Bobbie Ann Mason. Used by permission of Random House, Inc. **83:** Maxine Hong Kingston, "No Name Woman." From *The Woman Warrior* by Maxine Hong Kingston, copyright © 1975, 1976 by Maxine Hong Kingston. Used by permission of Alfred A. Knopf, a division of Random House. Inc. **93:** Dagoberto Gilb, "You Know Him By His Labors, But Not His Face." Reprinted by kind permission of the author. **96:** Gregory Jay, "Who Invented White People" From speech given by Gregory Jay, http://www.uwm .edu/%7Egjay/Whiteness/Whitenesstalk.htm- Reprinted by permission. **105:** Erin Aubry Kaplan, "Black Like I Thought I Was" LA Weekly, October 3, 2003 http://www.laweekly.com/. Reprinted by permission. **110:** Oscar Casares, "Crossing the Border Without Losing Your Past." Copyright © 2003 by *The New York Times* Company. Reprinted with permission. **114:** Bharati Mukherjee, "American Dreamer." Copyright © 1997 by Bharati Mukherjee. Originally published in *Mother Jones*. Reprinted by permission of the author. **121:** Ranjani Nellore, "The Girl with the Red Dot" From AlterNet.org, May 12, 2004. Reprinted by permission.

Chapter 6. 130: Alanis Morissette, "You Learn" From *Jagged Little Pill*. **130:** Helen Keller, "The Day Language Came Into My Life." Copyright © 1903, Helen Keller, used with the permission of the American Foundation for the Blind. **135:** Richard Wright, "The Library Card." From *Black Boy* by Richard Wright. Copyright © 1937, 1942, 1944, 1945 by Richard Wright; renewed © 1973 by Ellen Wright. Reprinted by permission of HarperCollins Publishers, Inc. **143:** Annie Dillard, "Living Like Weasels" from *Teaching A Stone To Talk: Expeditions And En-*

counters by Annie Dillard. Copyright © 1982 by Annie Dillard. Reprinted by permission of HarperCollins Publishers, Inc. **148:** Sawyer, Susan. "On Being Proved Wrong." From *Meanjin* (Dec. 2002). Vol 61, no. 4, 2002. Reprinted by permission. **156:** Maya Angelou, "Graduation", copyright © 1969 and renewed 1997 by Maya Angelou, from *I Know Why the Caged Bird Sings* by Maya Angelou. Used by permission of Random House, Inc. of the author. **166:** Paulo Freire, "Banking Concept of Education." From *Pedagogy of the Oppressed*, copyright © 1970, 1993 Continuum International Publishing Group. Reprinted by permission of The Continuum International. **179:** Richard Rodriguez, "The Desire of Achievement". From *Hunger of Memory* by Richard Rodriguez. Reprinted by permission of David R. Godine, Publisher, Inc. Copyright © 1982 by Richard Rodriguez. **197:** Adrienne Rich, "Taking Women Students Seriously." From *On Lies, Secrets, and Silence: Selected Prose 1966-1978* by Adrienne Rich. Copyright © 1979 by W. W. Norton & Company, Inc. Used by permission of the author and W. W. Norton & Company, Inc. **206:** Thomas Moore, "Eternal Water: Satisfying the Thirst of the Soul and the Needs of the Body" From *Resurgence,* No. 217 (March/April 2003) Reprinted with permission from Resurgence Magazine. www.resurgence.org. **210:** Langston Hughes, "Salvation" from *The Big Sea* by Langston Hughes. Copyright © 1940 by Langston Hughes. Copyright renewed 1968 by Arna Bontemps and George Houston Bass. Reprinted by permission of Hill and Wang, a division of Farrar, Straus and Giroux, LLC. **214:** Shunryu Suzuki, "Waterfall." From *Zen Mind, Beginner's Mind* by Shunryu Suzuki. © 1970 by Weatherhill Inc. Reprinted by permission of Shambhala Publications, Inc.

Chapter 7. 225: Kristin van Ogtrop, "Attila the Honey I'm Home." From *The Bitch in the House* (2002) by Cathi Hanauer. Reprinted by permission of the author. **235:** Richard Selzer, "Lovesick." From *Confessions of a Knife* by Richard Selzer. Copyright © 1987. Reprinted by permission of Georges Borchardt, Inc., for the author. **239:** Mark Doty, "Sweet Chariot." From *Heaven's Coast* by Mark Doty, pp. 17-20. Copyright © 1996 by Mark Doty. Reprinted by permission of HarperCollins Publishers, Inc. **244:** bell hooks, "On Building a Community of Love: bell hooks Meets with Thich Nhat Hanh to Ask: How Do We Build a Community of Love." From

PHOTO AND CARTOON CREDITS

AUTHOR AND TITLE INDEX